3ds Max® 2008 Bible

Kelly L. Murdock

BICENTENNIAL
1807
WILEY
2007
BICENTENNIAL

Wiley Publishing, Inc.

3ds Max® 2008 Bible

Published by
Wiley Publishing, Inc.
10475 Crosspoint Boulevard
Indianapolis, IN 46256
www.wiley.com

Copyright © 2008 by Wiley Publishing, Inc., Indianapolis, Indiana

Published simultaneously in Canada

ISBN: 978-0-470-18760-9

Manufactured in the United States of America

10 9 8 7 6 5 4 3 2 1

For general information on our other products and services or to obtain technical support, please contact our Customer Care Department within the U.S. at (800) 762-2974, outside the U.S. at (317) 572-3993 or fax (317) 572-4002.

Library of Congress Cataloging-in-Publication Data available from the publisher.

About the Author

Kelly Murdock has been authoring computer books for many years now and still gets immense enjoyment from the completed work. His book credits include various 3D, graphics, multimedia, and Web titles, including seven previous editions of this book, *3ds Max Bible*. Other major accomplishments include *Edgeloop Character Modeling for 3D Professionals Only*, *Maya 6 and 7 Revealed*, *LightWave 3D 8 Revealed*, *Poser 6 and 7 Revealed*, *3D Game Animation For Dummies*, *gmax Bible*, *Adobe Atmosphere Bible*, *Master VISUALLY HTML and XHTML*, *JavaScript Visual Blueprint*, and co-authoring duties on two editions of the *Illustrator Bible* (for versions 9 and 10) and three editions of the *Adobe Creative Suite Bible*.

With a background in engineering and computer graphics, Kelly has been all over the 3D industry and still finds it fascinating. He's used high-level CAD workstations for product design and analysis, completed several large-scale visualization projects, created 3D models for feature films and games, worked as a freelance 3D artist, and even done some 3D programming. Kelly's been using 3D Studio since version 3 for DOS. Kelly has also branched into training others in 3D technologies. He teaches at the local university and is a frequent speaker at various conferences.

In his spare time, Kelly enjoys the outdoors while rock climbing, mountain biking, or skiing.

The siege at Castle Grim was long and hard,
Yet nothing could penetrate its icy guard,
Until an innocent smile made a simple plea
That broke down the walls and set everyone free.

Depression was a tower that reached to the sky,
Looming over the country and all who passed by,
No one could ascend to its powerful stand,
Until a simple laugh reduced it to sand.

Solemn and serious the dark fortress stood alone
With a moat of despair causing all within to groan,
A delightful joke made the prisoners grin,
And a brilliant light started to shine from within.

When the wheels of the world grind you down
And your fleeting happiness begins to drown,
Turn to a smile, laugh, or grin,
And you'll soon find a way to win.

To my wonderful Aunt Sue, who knows the power of a smile
and a laugh. 2007

Credits

Senior Acquisitions Editor
Stephanie McComb

Project Editor
Martin V. Minner

Technical Editor
Kevin Davenport

Copy Editor
Gwenette Gaddis Goshert

Editorial Manager
Robyn Siesky

Business Manager
Amy Knies

Sr. Marketing Manager
Sandy Smith

Vice President and Executive Group Publisher
Richard Swadley

Vice President and Publisher
Barry Pruett

Project Coordinator
Lynsey Osborn

Graphics and Production Specialists
Stacie Brooks
Joyce Haughey
Jennifer Mayberry
Barbara Moore
Ronald Terry

Quality Control Technicians
David Faust
John Greenough

Media Development Project Supervisor
Laura Moss

Media Development Specialist
Kit Malone

Proofreading
Nancy Rapoport

Indexing
Broccoli Information Mgt.

Cover Design
Michael Trent

Cover Illustration
Joyce Haughey

Anniversary Logo
Richard Pacifico

Contents

Contents

Contents

Contents

Part III: Modeling Basics   239

Chapter 10: Learning Modeling Basics and Working with Subobjects and Helpers 241

Chapter 11: Drawing and Editing 2D Splines and Shapes 253

Contents

Contents

Part V: Animation and Rendering Basics   489

Chapter 20: Understanding Animation and Keyframe Basics 491

Contents

Part VIII: Advanced Animation Techniques 771

Chapter 32: Using Animation Modifiers 773

Chapter 33: Animating with the Expression Controller and Wiring Parameters 787

Contents

Part IX: Dynamic Animation

Chapter 36: Creating Particles and Particle Flow. 863

Contents

Contents

Part XI: Advanced Lighting and Rendering   1021

Chapter 44: Working with Advanced Lighting, Light Tracing, and Radiosity 1023

Chapter 45: Using Atmospheric and Render Effects 1039

Chapter 48: Compositing with Render Elements and the Video Post Interface 1113

Contents

Every time I enter the computer room (which my wife calls the dungeon), my wife still says that I am off to my "fun and games." I, as always, flatly deny this accusation, saying that it is serious work that I am involved in. But later, when I emerge with a twinkle in my eye and excitedly ask her to take a look at my latest rendering, I know that she is right. Working with 3D graphics is pure "fun and games."

My goal in writing this book was to take all my fun years of playing and working in 3D and boil them down into something that's worthwhile for you, the reader. This goal was compounded by the fact that all you Max-heads out there are at different levels. Luckily, this book is thick enough to include a little something for everyone.

The audience level for the book ranges from beginning to intermediate, with a smattering of advanced topics for the seasoned user. If you're new to Max, then you'll want to start at the beginning and move methodically through the book. If you're relatively comfortable making your way around Max, then review the Table of Contents for sections that can enhance your fundamental base. If you're a seasoned pro, then you'll want to watch for coverage of the features new to Release 2008.

Another goal of this book is to make it a complete reference for Max. To achieve this goal, I've gone into painstaking detail to cover almost every feature in Max, including coverage of every primitive, material and map type, modifier, and controller.

As this book has come together, I've tried to write the type of book that I'd like to read. I've tried to include a variety of scenes that are infused with creativity. It is my hope that these examples will not only teach you how to use the software, but also provide a creative springboard for you in your own projects. After all, that's what turns 3D graphics from work into "fun and games."

Who Is Max?

Max has made a major leap in its version number with this release, jumping from version 9 to version 2008. That is 1,999 version releases since the last edition. Actually, aligning the version number to the year helps users identify when each release was made available, a lesson learned from Microsoft.

Before we go any further, I should explain my naming convention. The official name of the product in this release is 3ds Max 2008, but I simply refer to it as Max. This reference is a nickname given to a piece of software that has become more familiar to me than the family pets (whose names are Fuzzy, Curious, Zoot, Snickers, and Lexi). Note: I have not been successful in training Max to come when I call or to sit on command, but it will on occasion play dead.

One way we humans develop our personalities is to incorporate desirable personality traits from those around us. Max's personality is developing as well: Every new release has incorporated a plethora of desirable new features. Many of these features come from the many additional plug-ins being developed to enhance Max. With each new release, Max has adopted many features that were available as plug-ins for previous releases. Several new features have been magically assimilated into the core product, such as the Character Studio or the Hair and Fur system. These additions make Max's personality much more likable, like a human developing a sense of humor.

Other personality traits are gained by stretching in new directions. Max and its developers have accomplished this feat as well. Many of the new features are completely new, not only to Max, but also to the industry. As Max grows up, it will continue to mature by adopting new features and inventing others. I just hope Max doesn't experience a mid-life crisis in the next version.

Along with adopted features and new developments, the development teams at Autodesk have also sought the feedback from Max users. This feedback has resulted in many small tweaks to the package that enable scenes to be created quicker and easier.

Some additional factors have appeared in Max's house that certainly have an impact on Max's development. First is the appearance of Max's adopted brother, Maya. There are other siblings in the Autodesk household (including MotionBuilder and AutoCAD), but Maya is closest in age to Max and its personality likely will rub off in different ways.

The second big factor is that Max has developed an alter ego that imagines it is a superhero. The 3ds Max installation discs ship with both 32-bit and 64-bit versions. The 64-bit version overcomes the 2GB hardware restriction and lets users work with huge datasets. This represents a huge leap forward in the scale of models that we can work with. In time, I see Max assuming this superhero persona permanently.

About This Book

Let me paint a picture of the writing process. It starts with years of experience, which are followed by months of painstaking research. There were system crashes and personal catastrophes and the always-present, ever-looming deadlines. I wrote into the early hours of the morning and during the late hours of the night—burning the candle at both ends and in the middle all at the same time. It was grueling and difficult, and spending all this time staring at the Max interface made me feel like . . . well . . . like an animator.

Sound familiar? This process actually isn't much different from what 3D artists, modelers, and animators do on a daily basis and, like you, I find satisfaction in the finished product.

Tutorials aplenty

I've always been a very visual learner—the easiest way for me to gain knowledge is by doing things for myself while exploring at the same time. Other people learn by reading and comprehending ideas. In this book, I've tried to present information in a number of ways to make the information usable for all types of learners. That is why you see detailed discussions of the various features along with tutorials that show these concepts in action.

The tutorials appear throughout the book and are clearly marked with the "Tutorial" label in front of the title. They always include a series of logical steps, typically ending with a figure for you to study and compare. These tutorial examples are provided on the book's DVD to give you a firsthand look and a chance to get some hands-on experience.

I've attempted to "laser focus" all the tutorials down to one or two key concepts. All tutorials are designed to be completed in 10 steps or less. This means that you probably will not want to place the results in your portfolio. For example, many of the early tutorials don't have any materials applied because I felt that using materials before they've been explained would only confuse you.

I've attempted to think of and use examples that are diverse, unique, and interesting, while striving to make them simple, light, and easy to follow. I'm happy to report that every example in the book is included on the DVD along with the models and textures required to complete the tutorial.

The tutorials often don't start from scratch, but instead give you a starting point. This approach lets me "laser focus" the tutorials even more; and with fewer, more relevant steps, you can learn and experience the concepts without the complexity. On the book's DVD, you will find the Max files that are referenced in Step 1 of most tutorials.

In addition to the starting point files, every tutorial has been saved at the completion of the tutorial steps. These files are marked with the word *final* at the end of the filename. If you get stuck in a tutorial, simply open the final example and compare the settings.

I've put lots of effort into this book, and I hope it helps you in your efforts. I present this book as a starting point. In each tutorial, I've purposely left out most of the creative spice, leaving room for you to put it in— you're the one with the vision.

Eighth time around

This book is now in its eighth edition and, like aged cheese, is getting better with time. This edition is packed with the maximum number of pages that can be bound into a paperback book, so if you're planning on taking a book to read on a subway ride, take this book and leave all the others behind. I'd hate to think that I caused some loyal readers back pain.

Several changes have been made in this edition. First of all, many of the older tutorials have been retired to make room for the new features. I've also included a new Quick Start. I've also made room for new sections throughout the book covering the new features.

Although I've strived to make the book comprehensive, there are some features that have fallen by the wayside and only remain in the software for backward compatibility. The Dynamics utility, for instance, has been replaced with the much more agile reactor system. These deprecated features are mentioned, but not covered in depth. If you need to learn about these features, I suggest you look for a previous edition of the *3ds Max Bible* where these older features were covered.

Designed for educators

Since the last edition, I've begun teaching at a couple of different colleges and universities, and the experience has made me rethink how the book is organized. Previous editions presented all the information on specific topics like animation together. This is a fine approach for experienced users who are getting up to speed with Max, but for students just starting out, this comprehensive approach easily overloads beginners before they even get out of the starting gate.

The new approach splits the book into beginning level topics that cover modeling, animation, and rendering before moving on to the advanced features in each topic. This allows the first half of the book to be used for beginning students as an introduction to the software without digging too deep into the advanced, trickier features.

How this book is organized

Many different aspects of 3D graphics exist, and in some larger production houses, you might be focused on only one specific area. However, for smaller organizations or the general hobbyist, you end up wearing all the hats—from modeler and lighting director to animator and post-production compositor. This book is organized to cover all the various aspects of 3D graphics, regardless of the hat on your head.

If you're so excited to be working with Max that you can't decide where to start, then head straight for the Quick Start. The Quick Start is a single chapter-long tutorial that takes you through the creation and animation of an entire scene. This Quick Start was included in response to some feedback from readers of the first edition who complained that they didn't know where to start. For those of you who were too anxious to wade through a mountain of material before you could create something, this Quick Start is for you.

The book is divided into the following parts:

- **Quick Start**—This single chapter (which is actually a chapter in Part I) is an entire animation project presented in several focused tutorials. It is designed to whet your appetite and get you up to speed and producing animations immediately.

- **Part I: Getting Started with 3ds Max**—Whether it's understanding the interface, working with the viewports, dealing with files, or customizing the interface, the chapters in this part get you comfortable with the interface so you won't get lost moving about this mammoth package.

- **Part II: Working with Objects**—Max objects can include meshes, cameras, lights, Space Warps, and anything that can be viewed in a viewport. This part starts by introducing the various primitive objects and also includes chapters on how to reference, select, clone, group, link, transform, and modify these various objects.

- **Part III: Modeling Basics**—Max includes several different ways to model objects. This part includes chapters covering the basic modeling methods and constructs including working with spline shapes, meshes, and polys. It also introduces modifiers and the Modifier Stack.

- **Part IV: Materials, Cameras, and Lighting Basics**—This part shows how to apply basic materials to objects including maps. It then delves into using cameras and lights, but it focuses on the basics of these topics while avoiding the advanced features.

- **Part V: Animation and Rendering Basics**—The simplest animation features include keyframing, constraints, and controllers. With these topics, you'll be able to animate scenes. This part also covers the basics of rendering scenes.

- **Part VI: Advanced Modeling**—This part continues the modeling features with coverage of XRefs, the Schematic View, mesh modifiers, compound objects, NURBS, patches, hair, fur, and cloth.

- **Part VII: Advanced Materials**—The Advanced Materials part include coverage of unwrapping, UV coordinates, pelt mapping, the Render to Texture interface, and Normal maps.

- **Part VIII: Advanced Animation Techniques**—After users are comfortable with the basics of animation, they can move on to advanced techniques, including animation modifiers, the expression controller, wiring parameters, the Track View, and the Motion Mixer.

- **Part IX: Dynamic Animation**—This part covers creating animation sequences using physics calculations. It includes coverage of particles, Space Warps, the cool features of reactor, and using forces to animate hair and cloth.

- **Part X: Working with Characters**—I cover creating and working with bipeds, bone systems, rigging, skinning, and character crowds. I also provide coverage of the various inverse kinematics methods.

■ **Part XI: Advanced Lighting and Rendering**—Advanced lighting concepts include using the Light Tracer and Radiosity, and the advanced rendering topics include Atmospheric and Render Effects, network rendering, raytracing, and mental ray. This part also describes the compositing process using the Video Post interface.

■ **Part XII: MAXScript and Plug-Ins**—This part provides details on using Max's scripting language, MAXScript, and on using plug-ins.

■ **Appendixes**—At the very end of this book, you'll find four appendixes that cover the new features of Max 2008, installation and system configuration, Max keyboard shortcuts, and the contents of the book's DVD.

Using the book's icons

The following margin icons are used to help you get the most out of this book:

NOTE   Notes highlight useful information that you should take into consideration.

TIP   Tips provide additional bits of advice that make particular features quicker or easier to use.

CAUTION   Cautions warn you of potential problems before you make a mistake.

NEW FEATURE   The New Feature icon highlights features that are new to the 2008 release.

CROSS-REF   Watch for the Cross-Ref icon to learn where in another chapter you can go to find more information on a particular feature.

ON the DVD   This icon points you toward related material on the book's DVD.

The book's DVD

Computer-book CD-ROMs are sometimes just an afterthought that include a handful of examples and product demos. This book's DVD, however, includes a diverse selection of 3D models that you can use in your projects if you choose. Many of these models are used in the tutorials. The DVD also includes the Max files for every tutorial.

If you haven't noticed yet, most of this book is printed in black and white. This can make seeing the details (and colors) of the figures difficult. The DVD includes a complete searchable version of the book along with all the figures in color.

Color insert pages

The possibilities of Max are endless, but many individuals and groups have pushed the software a long way. As a sampling of the finished work that can be created, I've included a set of color insert pages that showcase some amazing work done with Max. The 3D artists represented in these pages give you some idea of what is possible.

Acknowledgments

I have a host of people to thank for their involvement in this major work. The order in which they are mentioned doesn't necessarily represent the amount of work they did.

Thanks as always to my dear wife, Angela, and my sons, Eric and Thomas, without whose support I wouldn't get very far. They are my QA team and my brainstorming team who always provide honest feedback on my latest example. We have had many family sessions to think of good tutorial examples, and I'm always amazed with what they come up with. One of my favorites that hasn't been implemented yet is a tutorial of a group of bicycles chasing an ice cream truck.

In the first edition, the task at hand was too big for just me, so I shared the pain with two co-authors—Dave Brueck and Sanford Kennedy (both of whom have gone on to write books of their own). I still thank them for their work, which, although overhauled, retains their spirits. In a later edition, I again asked for help, a request that was answered by Sue Blackman. Sue provided several excellent examples that show off the power of the Track View interface. Thanks for your help, Sue.

Major thanks to the editors and personnel at Wiley. I'd like to specifically thank Stephanie McComb, who has stepped into an established team and done a great job. Her encouragement, dedication and positive attitude have made a big difference as I've faced some tough deadlines. Huge thanks to Marty Minner (the double M), who has once again managed the entire editing process, and to Gwenette Gaddis Goshert (the triple G) for her excellent copy editing input. Their comments during the review cycle always crack me up. Maybe someday I'll understand Marty's and Gwenette's love of doughnuts.

I'd also like to thank Kevin Davenport for taking on the technical editing in a crunched schedule. Additional thanks go out to Laura Moss and her co-workers in the Media Development department for chasing down the required permissions and for compiling the resources for the DVD, and finally, to the entire staff at Wiley who helped me on this journey. Of particular note are the cover designers who have been delightfully stuck on reptiles and amphibians for the covers to the last several editions. I'm starting to refer to the titles by their cover creature, i.e., "hand me the frog book next to the lizard book."

The various people who work in the graphics industry are amazing in their willingness to help and support. I'd like to thank first of all Rob Hoffman, Fenella Basilio, and the entire Autodesk team for their timely support and help. I'd also like to thank the talented people at Zygote Media, Curious Labs, and Viewpoint Digital Media for many of their models, which make the examples much more interesting (you can only do so much with the teapot after all). Thanks to Michael Valentine at Zygote Media and Tom Avikigos at Digimation for help in securing a new set of Viewpoint models. Additional thanks go out to David Mathis, Sue Blackman, and Chris Murdock for completing models used in some of the tutorials.

Finally, I'd like to thank the many artists who contributed images for the color insert pages for sharing their talent, knowledge, and vision with us. They are an inspiration to me.

Part I

Getting Started with 3ds Max

Quick Start

Creating and Flying Through a Greek Temple

When you first got your hands on 3ds Max, you were probably focused on one goal — creating cool 3D images and animations. I know that many of you bought Max to make money, claim a tax write-off, earn a way to Hollywood, or impress your girlfriend or boyfriend, but I'll just ignore those reasons for now. The goal is to create something cool.

If you've perused this book's Table of Contents or thumbed through its many pages, you've seen sections on modeling, materials, dynamics, and other topics. But if you're like me, you don't want to wade through tons of material before you have something to show off to Mom. (Actually, if you're like me, then you've opened straight to the special effects section, in which case you won't be reading this.)

The purpose of this Quick Start is to give you a taste of what Max can do. This soaring view of the software from 20,000 feet is intended to show you the big picture before you delve into the details. It exposes you to some of the most common features and hopefully whets your appetite for the more in-depth chapters to follow.

This part of the book is intended for those new to the software. If you're an experienced user, then your mom no doubt is already impressed with your work, so you can happily advance to whichever chapter appeals to you. (Forgive me for catering to the "newbie," but we were all beginners once.)

Greek Temples — Planning the Production

For this Quick Start, let's focus on something historical. And what could be more historical than recreating a Greek temple like the Parthenon or the Temple of Apollo. Although many of these ancient buildings are ornate, if you break down the building into pieces, you'll find that the majority of the building is simple primitive objects.

Max works very well with primitive objects and includes lots of tools for quickly creating multiples of such objects. The foundation of many Greek temples is the column. Greek columns come in three different styles — Doric, Ionic, and Corinthian. Of these, the Doric column is the simplest, so we'll create our temple using this style.

If you search online, you can find plenty of reference images that can aid you as you begin to build both the columns and the temple structure.

NOTE   Most images you find in books and magazines or on the Web are copyrighted, so be aware of the licensing before deciding to use a sketch you find.

After doing a bunch of research, you should have a good idea of what a Doric style column looks like and how many columns you need to create the temple structure. The Doric column is fluted and tapered and has a circular piece at the top. On top of the columns are two box layers called the Architrave and the Frieze. The Frieze layer usually has some ornate carvings in it. Beneath the temple is a set of stepped platforms that form stairs leading to the temple. The roof of the structure is a triangular prism.

Within the center of the columns is a central building with solid walls and some additional columns. The columns are positioned in a rectangular shape with six columns at each end and twelve along each side.

The goal of the project is not only to build a Greek temple, but to animate a walk through the temple, so we complete the project by drawing a path through the temple that a camera can take. With a definite plan, we're ready to begin. This Quick Start is divided into separate tutorials, with each tutorial containing a series of easy-to-follow steps. These steps are intended to show you the results of performing certain Max operations, but feel free to deviate from these steps to create your own results. Being creative and exploring the software is the best way to learn.

ON the DVD   After each of the following tutorials, I saved the scene file. You can find these files in the Quick Start directory on the book's DVD.

Modeling the Greek Temple

The modeling process is divided into several simple tutorials. The first step in the production is to model a single Doric column. This column can then be cloned and placed throughout the scene as needed. After the framework of columns is in place, you can add the other needed pieces including the roof and stepped platforms. The following tutorials show one modeling technique, but many others exist. As you explore the various modeling techniques, find and develop methods that work well for you.

Tutorial: Building a Doric column

Our first step begins with the task of modeling a single Doric column. We first start by creating a shape that we can extrude to form the column, then we'll use a modifier to taper the column and finish by adding the top of the column.

To create a single Doric column, follow these steps:

1. Start by resetting the interface with the File ⇨ Reset menu command. Answer Yes in the warning box that appears.

2. Before modeling the column, turn on the Snaps Toggle in the main toolbar so that all created points will snap to the grid points. Configure the Snaps figure by right-clicking the Snaps Toggle button. This opens the Grid and Snap Settings dialog box. Make sure the Grid Points option is selected, and close the dialog box.

3. Select Create ⇨ Shapes ⇨ Star, and drag in the Top viewport to create a star shape. In the Parameters rollout, set the Radius1 and Radius2 values to 95 and 80, the Points value to 16, and both the Fillet Radius1 and Fillet Radius2 values to 10. This creates a cross-section shape of the column.

NOTE This chapter uses Generic Units. You can change the units using the Units Setup dialog box, which is opened using the Customize ⇨ Units Setup menu command.

4. Open the Modify panel, and choose the Extrude modifier from the Modifiers List at the top of the Command Panel. In the Parameters rollout, set the Amount value to 1200 and the Segments value to 10. Click the Zoom Extents All button in the lower-right corner to fit the column in all viewports.

5. With the column selected, choose the Modifiers ⇨ Parametric Deformers ⇨ Taper menu command. In the Parameters rollout, set the Amount value to –0.2. This tapers the column to the top.

6. Select the Create ⇨ Standard Primitives ⇨ Cone menu command, and drag in the Top viewport to create a new inverted cone object that extends from the top of the column upward. The Parameters for this object are Radius1, 75, Radius2, 105, Height, 100, and Sides, 24. Then select and move the cone upward until it sits on top of the column. You can zoom in on the Left viewport to see the top of the column up close. You need to disable the Snaps Toggle in order to align the two top pieces.

7. Select the Create ⇨ Standard Primitives ⇨ Cylinder menu command, and drag in the Top viewport to create a new cylinder object that is the same size as the previous cone object. The Parameters for this object are Radius, 105, Height, 60, and Sides, 24. Then select and move the cylinder upward until it sits on top of the cone on the column.

8. Select the column, choose the Tools ⇨ Align command, and then click the cone object to align it to the column. This causes the Align Selection dialog box to open. Select the X Position and Z Position option and the Center options for the Current and Target objects, and click the OK button. This aligns the centers of the cone and column objects. Then repeat this step for the cylinder object.

9. Select all three objects, and choose the Group ⇨ Group menu command to group the three objects into a single group. In the Group dialog box that appears, name the group **Column**.

The Doric column is now complete, as shown in Figure QS.1, and ready to be placed.

FIGURE QS.1

The column object is complete and grouped together.

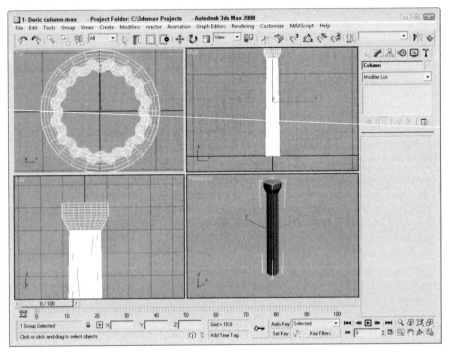

Tutorial: Cloning and positioning the Doric columns

With the Doric column finished and grouped, we can quickly place several columns around a defined path using the Spacing Tool. To plan the layout correctly, we need to do some counting. If we create a rectangle with the right ratios, then the columns easily fall into place. Because there are six columns on the end with 5 lengths between them and twelve on each side with 11 lengths between, we need to create a rectangle that has a ratio of 5:11 in order to get the layout right.

To clone and position all the columns, follow these steps:

1. Zoom out of the Top viewport, and select the Create ➪ Standard Primitives ➪ Rectangle menu command. Then drag in the Top viewport to create a rectangle. In the Parameters rollouts, set the Length value to 2000 and the Width value to 4400. This creates a rectangle with the proper ratio.

2. Select the column object, and choose the Tools ➪ Spacing Tool menu command. This opens the Spacing Tool dialog box. From the drop-down list, choose the Centered, Specify Spacing option and enter the Spacing value of 400. Then click the Pick Path button, and click the rectangle in the Top viewport. This automatically clones the selected column and spaces them at equal intervals around the rectangle. Then close the Spacing Tool dialog box.

3. Click the Zoom Extents All button in the lower-right corner to see the laid out columns in all viewports.

The laid out columns are positioned around a rectangular path, as shown in Figure QS.2.

FIGURE QS.2

The Spacing Tool quickly positions all the columns about a rectangular path.

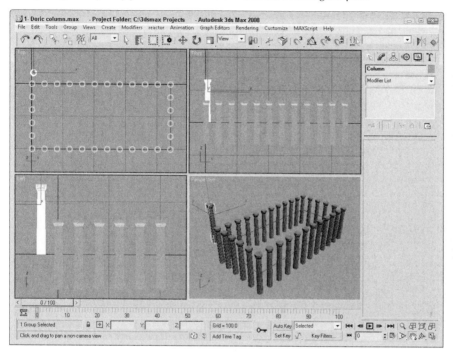

Tutorial: Finishing the Greek Temple

With all the columns in place, we simply need to add the roof and the stairs, and the modeling part of the project is done.

To finish the Greek temple, follow these steps:

1. Using the Top viewport, select the Create ➪ Standard Primitives ➪ Box menu command and drag to create a box object. Set its parameters to 2400 for the Length, 4840 for the Width, and –100 for the Height. This creates a box object that surrounds all the columns.

2. In the Left viewport, select all the columns and drag them upward using the Select and Move tool by dragging the green Y-axis to constrain the movement to a single axis.

3. Select the foundation box object, and choose the Tools ➪ Array menu command. This opens the Array dialog box. Within the Incremental Y-axis for the Move row, enter a value of -100, and set the Incremental X and Z-axes for the Scale row to 105. Then set the 1D Count value to 6, and click OK. This creates the stairs leading to the castle.

> **NOTE** If you click the Preview button in the Array dialog box, then you can see the results before you close the dialog box.

4. Select the top stair box object, and while holding down the Shift key, drag the selected box object to the top of the columns in the Left viewport. When you release the mouse button, the Clone

Options dialog box appears. Select the Copy option, name the cloned box **Architrave**, and click OK. Open the Modify panel, and change the Height value to –160. Then move the box upward again to be on top of the columns.

5. Select the Architrave object, and while holding down the Shift key, drag the selected box object upward using the Y-axis in the Left viewport. In the Clone Options dialog box, name the cloned box **Frieze**, and click the OK button. Open the Modify panel, and change the Height value to –200, the Length Segments to 12, and the Width Segments to 24. Then move the box upward again to be on top of the Architrave object.

6. With the Frieze object selected, right-click in the viewport and choose the Convert To ⇨ Convert to Editable Poly menu command from the pop-up quadmenu. This changes the box from a simple box to a poly object where you can edit its subobjects.

7. Open the Modify panel, click the Polygon subobject mode, press and hold the Ctrl key, and then select every other square on the Frieze object all the way around the temple using the Left and Front viewports. Then right-click the viewport title for the Left viewport, select Views ⇨ Right to change the Left viewport to the Right viewport, press and hold the Ctrl key, and continue to select squares around the Frieze box object. Then change the Front view to the Back view, and finish the selection.

NOTE The polygons will turn red when selected in Polygon subobject mode.

8. With every other polygon subobject selected all the way around the Frieze level, click the options box icon to the right of the Extrude button in the Edit Polygons rollout. In the Extrude Polygons dialog box that appears, select the Group option, set the Extrusion Height to 20, and click OK. This makes the selected squares stick out from the unselected squares. Then click the Polygon subobject option in the top of the Modifier Stack to exit Polygon subobject mode.

9. Select the Create ⇨ Extended Primitives ⇨ Prism menu command, and drag in the Right viewport to create a triangular-shaped prism object to be the roof to the temple. In the Parameters rollout, set the Side1, 2, and 3 Lengths to 2500, 1400, and 1300 and the Height to 4900. Then position the roof in the Top viewport to cover the columns.

10. In the Right viewport, select and right-click the extra column that isn't under the roof and select the Hide Selection menu command from the pop-up quadmenu.

The temple is now complete, as shown in Figure QS.3, and ready for the next steps of applying materials.

Tutorial: Adding Architectural & Design materials

After the modeling is complete, you can add materials to the objects to improve their look. Materials are added using the Material Editor, which is opened using the Rendering ⇨ Material Editor menu command or by pressing the M keyboard shortcut.

Max includes a special set of materials that are used to dress up buildings and architectural designs, but they require that the mental ray render engine be enabled. After the mental ray render engine is enabled using the Render Scene dialog box, you can access the Architectural & Design materials in the Material Editor.

Although the Architectural & Design materials can create a variety of realistic materials, we apply some unique materials that weren't readily available in ancient Greece to give our temple a unique look.

FIGURE QS.3

With a little more work, the model is completed and ready for materials.

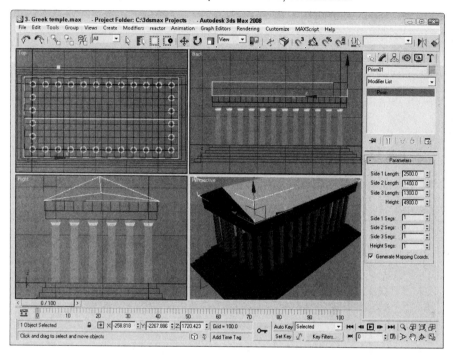

To add Architectural & Design materials to the Greek temple, follow these steps:

1. Select the Render ➪ Render menu command (or press the F10 key) to open the Render Scene dialog box. At the very bottom of the Common panel is the Assign Renderer rollout. Within this rollout, click the button to the right of the Production renderer and then double-click the mental ray Renderer option in the Choose Renderer dialog box that opens. Then close the Render Scene dialog box.

2. Select the Rendering ➪ Material Editor menu command (or press the M key) to open the Material Editor. Click the Standard material button, select the Arch & Design material from the Material/Map Browser, and click OK. Select to Discard the old material, and click OK.

3. In the Templates rollout at the top of the Material Editor, select the Brushed Metal template. Then drag the Brushed Metal material from its sample slot in the Material Editor, and drop it on the roof object.

4. Select the second sample slot, and repeat the preceding step to choose the Arch & Design material with the Brushed Copper template. Then drop this material on the steps of the temple. Finally, repeat this step again, and choose the Glass (Solid Geometry) template and apply it to the columns. The Material Editor holds each of the selected materials, as shown in Figure QS.4.

TIP A quicker way to apply a material to multiple objects is to select all the objects in the viewport, select the material sample slot in the Material Editor and click the Assign Material to Selection button.

9

The Material Editor lets you configure and apply materials to scene objects.

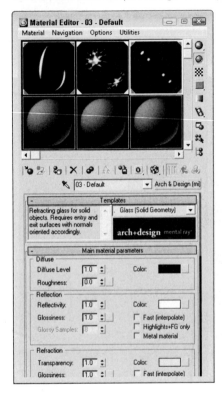

With materials applied to the Greek temple, the objects in the viewport will look different, but we can't see a rendered view until we add some lights to the scene.

Tutorial: Adding a Sun & Sky system

Another benefit of having the mental ray renderer enabled is that you also can use the Sun & Sky system. This system simulates outdoor lighting from a distant source like the sun and generates a sky for the background and a ground plane also.

To add a Sun & Sky system to the scene, follow these steps:

1. Because the Sun & Sky system adds a ground plane to the scene, we need to reposition the temple so it is located above the default grid plane. Use the Edit ⇨ Select All menu command (or press the Ctrl+A shortcut) to select all objects, and then move them in the Right viewport above the default grid.

2. Select the Create ⇨ Lights ⇨ Daylight System menu command, and drag in the Top viewport to add a compass helper to the scene. Then click and drag to position the Sun light icon above the temple. This also automatically adds the mr Physical Sky map to the Environment panel.

3. With the Daylight system added to the scene, you can view the sky background within the viewport. To do so, select the Rendering ➪ Environment menu command (or press the 8 key) to open the Environment panel. Then enable the Use Map option, and close the Environment dialog box. Next, choose the Views ➪ Viewport Background menu command to open the Viewport Background dialog box, enable the Use Environment Background and the Display Background options, and close the dialog box.

4. Then click the Maximize Viewport button in the lower-right corner of the interface to make the Perspective viewport full sized.

The viewport now shows the temple with a background sky and a ground plane, as shown in Figure QS.5.

FIGURE QS.5

The Sky background is visible within the viewport.

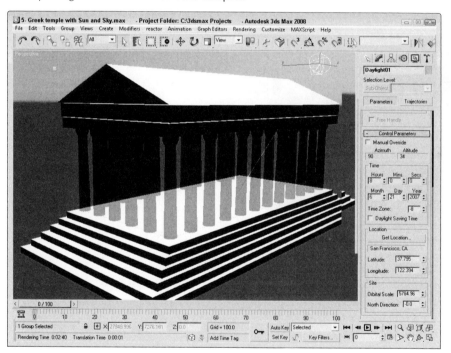

Tutorial: Rendering the temple

Before moving to animation, we can render the scene now that lights have been added. Rendering is configured using the Render Scene dialog box.

To render the temple scene, follow these steps:

1. Use the viewport navigation controls, located in the lower-right corner of the interface, to position the temple view just the way you like it. You also can position the location of the Sun in the sky using the Control Parameters rollout that is available when the Sun light object is selected.

2. Select the Rendering ⇨ Render menu command (or press the F10 key), and open the Indirect Illumination panel. Turn on the Enable Final Gather option, and set the Preset to Medium. This computes a global illumination model by determining how light rays bounce about the scene.

3. Back in the Common panel of the Render Scene dialog box, select the image size in the Common Parameters rollout and click the Render button. The active viewport automatically is rendered and displayed in the Render Frame Window.

The rendered temple image, as shown in Figure QS.6, includes all the materials, lighting effects, reflections, and refractions caused by the glass columns.

FIGURE QS.6

The rendered image of the temple includes the lighting effects.

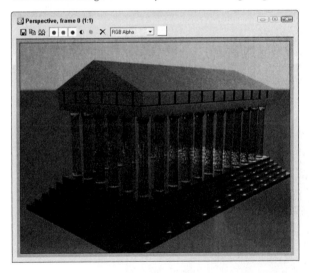

Tutorial: Animating a camera flying through the scene

After the scene is looking good, we can work on creating an animated fly through. To do this, we create a custom camera and attach that camera to a path that moves through the scene. We can then switch the viewport to see what the camera sees.

To animate a camera flying through the scene, follow these steps:

1. Click the Maximize Viewport toggle button in the lower-right corner of the interface to toggle back to four viewports. Then zoom out of the Top viewport so you can see space on either side of the temple.

2. Select the Create ⇨ Cameras ⇨ Free Camera menu command, and click to the left of the temple to add a free camera to the scene in the Top viewport. By default, the camera is pointing down, but this will be fixed when we attach it to a path.

3. Select the Create ⇨ Shapes ⇨ Line menu command, and click in the Top viewport to create a path that starts at the left and moves through the temple to the right before circling back around and returning on the outside of the temple back to the left. Right-click to exit point creation mode.

4. Zoom out of both the Left and Front viewports, open the Modify panel, and select the Vertex sub-object mode. Then select and modify the path points in the Left and Front views so the path moves through the temple by raising some of the points. Click the Vertex subobject button to exit subobject mode.

5. Select the camera object, and choose the Animation ⇨ Constraints ⇨ Path Constraint menu command. Then click the path moving through the temple. The camera is automatically moved to the beginning of the path, and keyframes are added to the Track Bar so the camera moves along the path. The use the Select and Rotate tool to align the camera so it points down the path. Scroll down in the Command Panel until you find the Path Parameters rollout, and enable the Follow option.

6. Select the Perspective viewport, right-click the viewport title, and select Views ⇨ Camera01 to switch the viewport to the camera view. Then enable the Auto Key button at the bottom of the interface, and scrub the Time Slider to see the animated camera in the viewport. At different places along the path, rotate the camera so the temple is in view. With the Auto Key button enabled, rotation keys are automatically created.

7. Maximize the camera view, and click the Play button to see the resulting animation.

Figure QS.7 shows one frame of the final animation. Using the Render Scene dialog box, you can render the entire animation, or you can use the Animation ⇨ Make Preview menu command to create a preview of the animation.

FIGURE QS.7

One frame of the final fly-through animation

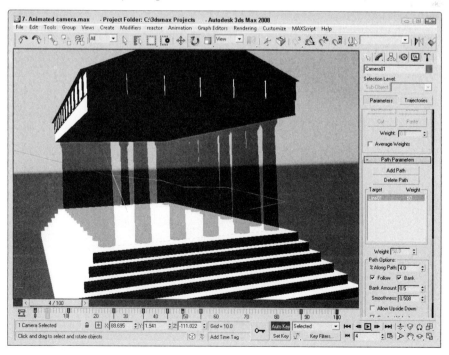

13

Summary

I hope you're happy with your first footsteps into Max. This chapter exposed you to a number of important aspects of Max, including the following:

- An approach to modeling using primitives
- Applying Architectural & Design materials to different scene objects
- Using the Sun & Sky system
- Animating the camera using a Path constraint

But hold onto your seats, because so much of the software lies ahead. In Chapter 1, you start easily with an in-depth look at the Max interface. If you feel ready for more advanced challenges, review the Table of Contents and dive into any topic that looks good.

Chapter 1

Exploring the Max Interface

W ell, here we are again with a new version of Max, and the first question on the minds of existing users is "Did the interface change?" The answer is a happy "very little." Most serious users would rather go through root canal surgery than have their user interface (UI) change, and Autodesk has learned and respected this valued opinion by keeping the interface changes to a minimum.

As you look around the new interface, you'll see that everything is still there but that Max has a few new additions. You may find yourself saying, as you navigate the interface, "where did that come from?" But, just like encountering a new house in your neighborhood, over time you'll become accustomed to the addition and may even meet some new friends.

Why is the software interface so important? Well, consider this: The interface is the set of controls that enable you to access the program's features. Without a good interface, you may never use many of the best features of the software or spend a frustrating bit of time locating those features. A piece of software can have all the greatest features, but if the user can't find or access them, then the software won't be used to its full potential. Max is a powerful piece of software with some amazing features, and luckily the interface makes these amazing features easy to find and use.

The interface's purpose is to make the software features accessible, and in Max you have many different ways to access the features. Some of these access methods are faster than others. This design is intentional because it gives beginning users an intuitive command and advanced users direct access. For example, to undo a command, you can choose Edit ⇨ Undo (requiring two mouse clicks), but as you gain more experience, you can simply click the Undo icon on the toolbar (only one click); an expert with his hands on the keyboard can press Ctrl+Z without having to reach for the mouse at all. All three of these methods have the same result, but you can use the one that is easiest for you.

IN THIS CHAPTER

Learning the interface elements

Previewing the menu commands

Becoming familiar with the toolbars

Using the Command Panel

Examining the Lower Interface Bar

Interacting with the interface

Getting help

Has the Max interface succeeded? Yes, to a degree, but like most interfaces, it always has room for improvement, and we hope that each new version takes us closer to the perfect interface (but I'm still looking for the "read my thoughts" feature). Autodesk has built a loophole into the program to cover anyone who complains about the interface — customization. If you don't like the current interface, you can change it to be exactly what you want.

CROSS-REF   Customizing the Max interface is covered in Chapter 4, "Customizing the Max Interface and Setting Preferences."

This chapter examines the latest incarnation of the Max interface and presents some tips that make the interface feel comfortable, not cumbersome.

The Interface Elements

If you're new to the Max interface, the first order of business is to take a stroll around the block and meet the neighbors. The Max interface has a number of interface elements that neatly group all the similar commands together. For example, all the commands for controlling the viewports are grouped together in the Viewport Navigation Controls found in the lower-right corner of the interface.

NOTE   If all the details of every interface command were covered in this chapter, it would be an awfully long chapter. So for those commands that are covered in more detail elsewhere, I include a cross-reference to the chapter where you can find their coverage.

The entire interface can be divided into five easy elements. Each of these interface elements, in turn, has groupings of sub-elements. The five main interface elements are listed here and shown separated in Figure 1.1:

- **Menus:** This is the default source for most commands, but also one of the most time-consuming interface methods. The menus are found along the top edge of the Max window.
- **Toolbars:** Max includes several toolbars of icon buttons that provide single-click access to features. These toolbars can float independently or can be docked to an interface edge. The main toolbar is the only toolbar that is visible by default.
- **Viewports:** Four separate views into the scene show the Top, Front, Left, and Perspective viewpoints.
- **Command Panel:** The major control panel located to the right of the four viewports, it has six tabbed icons at its top that you can click to open the various panels. Each panel includes rollouts containing parameters and settings. These rollouts change depending on the object and tab that is selected.
- **Lower Interface Bar:** Along the bottom edge of the interface window is a collection of miscellaneous controls.

In addition to these default elements are several additional interface elements that aren't initially visible when Max is first loaded. These additional interface elements include the following:

- **Floating toolbars:** Several additional toolbars are available as floating toolbars. You access them by choosing Customize ⇨ Show UI ⇨ Show Floating Toolbars or by selecting them from the toolbar's right-click pop-up menu.

- **Quadmenus:** Right-clicking on the active viewport reveals a pop-up menu with up to four panes, referred to as a quadmenu. *Quadmenus* offer context-sensitive commands based on the object or location being clicked and provide one of the quickest ways to access commands.

- **Dialog boxes and editors:** Some commands open a separate window of controls. These dialog boxes may contain their own menus, toolbars, and interface elements. A good example of this interface element type is the Material Editor, which has enough controls to keep you busy for a while.

FIGURE 1.1

Max includes five main interface elements.

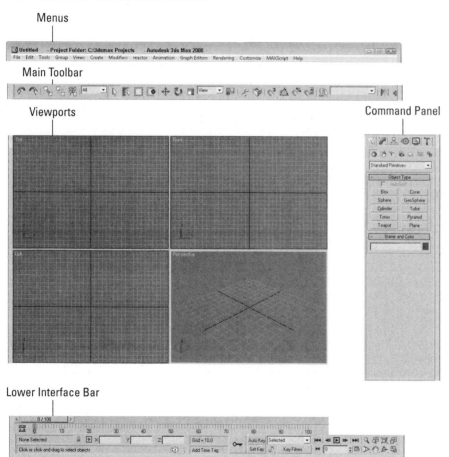

Menus

Main Toolbar

Viewports

Command Panel

Lower Interface Bar

Using the Menus

The pull-down menus at the top of the Max interface include most of the features available in Max and are a great place for beginners to start. Several of the menu commands have corresponding toolbar buttons and keyboard shortcuts. To execute a menu command, you can choose it from the menu with the mouse cursor, click its corresponding toolbar button if it has one, or press its keyboard shortcut. You can also select commands using the keyboard arrows and press the Enter key to execute them.

The main menu includes the following options: File, Edit, Tools, Group, Views, Create, Modifiers, reactor, Animation, Graph Editors, Rendering, Customize, MAXScript, and Help. Unlike some other programs, these menu options do not disappear if not needed. The list is set, and they are always there when you need them.

If a keyboard command is available for a menu command, it is shown to the right of the menu item. If an ellipsis (three dots) appears after a menu item, that menu command causes a separate dialog box to open. A small black arrow to the right of a menu item indicates that a submenu exists. Clicking the menu item or holding the mouse over the top of a menu item makes the submenu appear. Toggle menu options (such as Views ⇨ Show Ghosting) change state each time they are selected. If a toggle menu option is enabled, a small check mark appears to its left; if disabled, no check mark appears.

CROSS-REF   A complete list of keyboard shortcuts can be found in Appendix C, "Max Keyboard Shortcuts."

You can also navigate the menus using the keyboard by pressing the Alt key by itself. Doing so selects the File menu, and then you can use the arrow keys to move up and down and between menus. With a menu selected, you can press the keyboard letter that is underlined to select and execute a menu command. For example, pressing Alt and then F (for File) and N (for New) executes the File ⇨ New command; or you can press Alt, use the down arrow to select the New command, and press the Enter key.

TIP   By learning the underlined letters in the menu, you can use the keyboard to quickly access menu commands, even if the menu command doesn't have an assigned keyboard shortcut. And because you don't need to stretch for the Y key while holding down the Ctrl key, underlined menu letters can be faster. For example, by pressing Alt, G, and U successively, you can access the Group ⇨ Ungroup menu command. The keyboard buffer remembers the order of the letters you type regardless of how fast they are keyed, making it possible to quickly access menu commands using the keyboard. Over time, you can learn patterns to help you remember how to access certain menu commands, such as Alt, C, H, E for creating an ellipse.

Not all menu commands are available at all times. If a menu command is unavailable, then it is grayed out, as shown in Figure 1.2, and you cannot select it. For example, the Clone command is available only when an object is selected, so if no objects are selected, the Clone command is grayed out and unavailable. After you select an object, this command becomes available.

FIGURE 1.2

All menus feature visual clues.

Disabled command   Keyboard shortcut

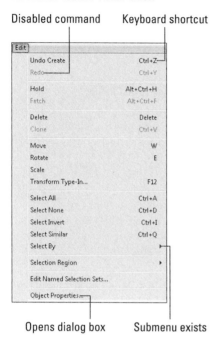

Opens dialog box   Submenu exists

Using the Toolbars

Now that you've learned the menu two-step, it is time for the toolbar one-step. The main toolbar appears by default directly under the menus at the top of the Max window. Using toolbars is one of the most convenient ways to execute commands because most commands require only a single click.

Docking and floating toolbars

By default the main toolbar is docked along the top edge of the interface above the viewport, but you can make any docked toolbar (including the main toolbar), a floating toolbar by clicking and dragging the two vertical lines on the left (or top) end of the toolbar away from the interface edge. After you separate it from the window, you can resize the floating toolbar by dragging on its edges or corners. You can then drag and dock it to any of the window edges or double-click on the toolbar title bar to automatically dock the toolbar to its latest location. Figure 1.3 shows the main toolbar as a floating panel.

If you right-click on any floating toolbar away from the buttons, you can access a pop-up menu that includes options to dock or float the current toolbar, access the Customize UI window, or show or hide any of the toolbars or the Command Panel. The main toolbar can be hidden with the Alt+6 keyboard shortcut.

FIGURE 1.3

The main toolbar includes buttons and drop-down lists for controlling many of the most popular Max functions.

CROSS-REF You can customize the buttons that appear on any of the toolbars. See Chapter 4, "Customizing the Max Interface and Setting Preferences."

If you select the Customize ➪ Show UI ➪ Show Floating Toolbars menu command, several additional tool-bars appear. These are floating toolbars. You also can make them appear by selecting them individually from the toolbar right-click pop-up menu. These floating toolbars include Axis Constraints, Layers, reactor, Extras, Render Shortcuts, Snaps, Animation Layers, and Brush Presets.

Using tooltips and flyouts

All icon buttons (including those found in toolbars, the Command Panel, and other dialog boxes and windows) include tooltips, which are identifying text labels. If you hold the mouse cursor over an icon button, the tooltip label appears. This feature is useful for identifying buttons. If you can't remember what a specific button does, hold the cursor over the top of it and the tooltip gives you its name.

All toolbar buttons with a small triangle in the lower-right corner are flyouts. A *flyout* is a single toolbar button that expands to reveal additional buttons. Click and hold on the flyout to reveal the additional icons, and drag to select one. Figure 1.4 shows the flyout for the Align button on the main toolbar.

FIGURE 1.4

Flyout menus bundle several toolbar buttons together.

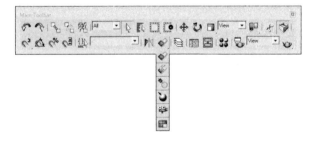

NOTE The General panel of the Preference Settings dialog box contains an option for setting the number of milliseconds to wait before the flyout appears.

Learning the main toolbar

On smaller resolution screens, the main toolbar is too long to be entirely visible. To see the entire main tool-bar, you need to set your monitor resolution to be at least 1280 pixels wide. To scroll the toolbar to see the end, position the cursor on the toolbar away from the buttons, such as below one of the drop-down lists (the cursor changes to a hand); then click and drag the toolbar in either direction. Using the hand cursor to scroll also works in the Command Panel, Material Editor, and any other place where the panel exceeds the given space.

TIP   **The easiest way to scroll the main toolbar is to drag with the middle mouse button.**

Toolbar buttons that open dialog boxes such as the Layer Manager, Material Editor, and Render Scene buttons are toggle buttons. When the dialog box is open, the button is highlighted yellow, indicating that the dialog box is open. Clicking on a highlighted toggle button closes the dialog box. Corresponding menus (and keyboard shortcuts) work the same way, with a small check mark appearing to the left of the menu command when a dialog box is opened.

Table 1.1 lists the controls found in the main toolbar. Buttons with flyouts are separated with commas.

TABLE 1.1

Main Toolbar Buttons

Toolbar Button	Name	Description
	Undo (Ctrl+Z)	Removes the last performed command. You can set the levels of Undo in the Preferences dialog box.
	Redo (Ctrl+Y)	Brings back the last command that was undone.
	Select and Link	Establishes links between objects.
	Unlink Selection	Breaks links between objects.
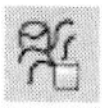	Bind to Space Warp	Assigns objects to be modified by a space warp.
 All	Selection Filter drop-down list	Limits the type of objects that can be selected.
	Select Object (Q)	Chooses an object.
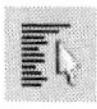	Select by Name (H)	Opens a dialog box for selecting objects by name.
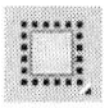 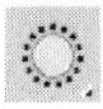 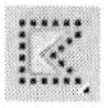 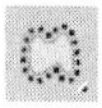 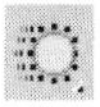	Rectangular Selection Region, Circular Selection Region, Fence Selection Region, Lasso Selection Region, Paint Selection Region (Ctrl+F to cycle)	Determines the shape used for selecting objects with the mouse.
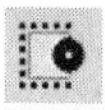	Window/Crossing Toggle	Specifies whether an object must be crossed or windowed to be selected.

continued

TABLE 1.1 (continued)

Toolbar Button	Name	Description
	Select and Move (W)	Selects an object and allows positional translations.
	Select and Rotate (E)	Selects an object and allows rotational transforms.
	Select and Uniform Scale, Select and Non-Uniform Scale, Select and Squash (R to cycle)	Selects an object and allows scaling transforms using different methods.
View	Reference Coordinate System drop-down list	Specifies the coordinate system used for transforms.
	Use Pivot Point Center, Use Selection Center, Use Transform Coordinate Center	Specifies the center about which rotations are completed.
	Select and Manipulate	Selects an object and allows parameter manipulation via a manipulator.
	Keyboard Shortcut Override Toggle	Allows keyboard shortcuts for the main interface and the active dialog box or feature set to be used when enabled. Only main interface shortcuts are available when disabled.
	Snap Toggle 2D, Snap Toggle 2.5D, Snap Toggle 3D (S)	Specifies the snap mode. 2D snaps only to the active construction grid, 2.5D snaps to the construction grid or to geometry projected from the grid, and 3D snaps to anywhere in 3D space.
	Angle Snap Toggle (A)	Causes rotations to snap to specified angles.
	Percent Snap (Shift+Ctrl+P)	Causes scaling to snap to specified percentages.
	Spinner Snap Toggle	Determines the amount a spinner value changes with each click.
	Edit Named Selection Sets	Opens a dialog box for creating and managing selection sets.
New Set	Named Selection Sets drop-down list	Lists and allows you to select a set of named objects.
	Mirror Selected Objects	Creates a mirrored copy of the selected object.

Toolbar Button	Name	Description
	Align (Alt+A),	Opens the alignment dialog box for positioning objects, allows objects to be aligned by their normals, determines the location of highlights, and aligns objects to a camera or view.
	Quick Align,	
	Normal Align (Alt+N),	
	Place Highlight (Ctrl+H),	
	Align to Camera,	
	Align to View	
	Layer Manager	Opens the Layer Manager interface where you can work with layers.
	Open Curve Editor	Opens the Function Curves Editor.
	Open Schematic View	Opens the Schematic View window.
	Material Editor (M)	Opens the Material Editor window.
	Render Scene Dialog (F10)	Opens the Render Scene dialog box for setting rendering options.
View	Render Type drop-down list	Selects the area or objects to render.
	Quick Render (Production),	Produces a quick test rendering of the current viewport without opening the Render Scene dialog box.
	Quick Render (ActiveShade)	

Using the Viewports

The four viewports make up the largest area of the entire interface and provide a way of viewing the objects within the scene. Each of the viewports is configurable and can be unique from the others.

CROSS-REF Understanding how to work with the viewports is vital to accomplishing tasks with Max, so viewports have an entire chapter dedicated just to them — Chapter 2, "Controlling and Configuring the Viewports."

Using the Command Panel

If there is one place in Max, besides the viewports, where you'll spend all your time, it's the Command Panel (at least until you're comfortable enough with the quadmenus). The Command Panel is located to the right of the viewports along the right edge of the interface. This is where all the specific parameters, settings, and controls are located. The Command Panel is split into six panels, each accessed via a tab icon located at its top. These six tabs are Create, Modify, Hierarchy, Motion, Display, and Utilities.

You can pull away the Command Panel from the right window edge as a floating dialog box, as shown in Figure 1.5, by clicking on the open space to the right of the tabbed icons at the top of the Command Panel and dragging away from the interface edge. You can also dock it to the left window edge, which is really handy if you're left-handed. While it's a floating panel, you can resize the Command Panel by dragging on its edges or corners (but its width remains constant).

After you've pulled the Command Panel or any of the toolbars away from the interface, you can re-dock them to their last position by double-clicking on their title bar. You can also right-click on the title bar to access the pop-up menu of floating toolbars, but the pop-up menu also includes options to Dock (either Left or Right for the Command Panel or Left, Right, Top or Bottom for toolbars) and Float.

FIGURE 1.5
_____

The Command Panel includes six separate panels accessed via tab icons.

Working with rollouts

Most of the controls, buttons, and parameters in the Command Panel are contained within sections called rollouts. A *rollout* is a grouping of controls positioned under a gray, boxed title, as shown in Figure 1.6. Each rollout title bar includes a plus or minus sign (a minus sign indicates that the rollout is open; a plus sign shows closed rollouts). Clicking the rollout title opens or closes the rollout. You can also reposition the order of the rollouts by dragging the rollout title and dropping it above or below the other rollouts.

 **You cannot reposition some of the rollouts, such as the Object Type and the Name and Color rollouts found in the Create panel.**

FIGURE 1.6

Open and close rollouts by clicking on the rollout title.

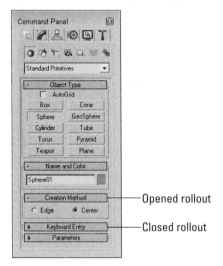

————Opened rollout

————Closed rollout

Right-clicking away from the buttons in a rollout presents a pop-up menu where you can select to close the rollout you've clicked in, Close All, Open All, or Reset Rollout Order. The pop-up menu also lists all available rollouts within the current panel with a check mark next to the ones that are open.

Expanding all the rollouts often exceeds the screen space allotted to the Command Panel. If the rollouts exceed the given space, then a small vertical scroll bar appears at the right edge of the Command Panel. You can drag this scroll bar to access the rollouts at the bottom of the Command Panel, or you can click away from the controls when a hand cursor appears. With the hand cursor, click and drag in either direction to scroll the Command Panel. You can also scroll the Command Panel with the scroll wheel on the mouse.

CROSS-REF You can customize the Command Panel like the other toolbars. Customizing the Command Panel is covered in Chapter 4, "Customizing the Max Interface and Setting Preferences."

Increasing the Command Panel's width

The Command Panel can also be doubled or tripled (or any multiple as long as you have room) in width by dragging its left edge toward the center of the interface. The width of the Command Panel is increased at the expense of the viewports. Figure 1.7 shows the Command Panel double its normal size.

Tutorial: Rearranging the interface for lefties

I used to work for a company that required that all computers have the mouse to the left of the keyboard. We swapped computers often, and the boss hated having to move the mouse to the other side of the keyboard (and you thought your work environment was weird). The reality is that some people like it on the left and others prefer it on the right, and Max can accommodate both.

With the Command Panel on the right side of the interface, the default Max interface obviously favors right-handers, but with the docking panels, you can quickly change it to be friendly to lefties.

FIGURE 1.7

Increase the width of the Command Panel by dragging its left edge.

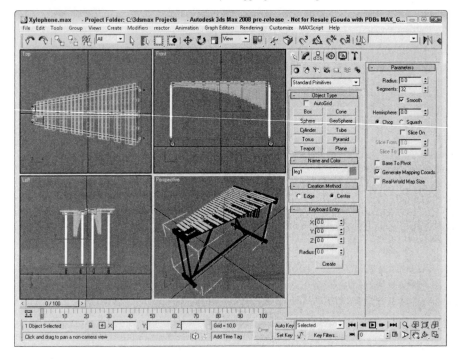

To rearrange the interface for lefties, follow these steps:

1. Click the Command Panel on the empty space to the right of the Utilities tab, and drag toward the center of the interface. As you drag the Command Panel away from the right edge, the cursor changes.

2. Continue to drag the Command Panel to the left edge, and the cursor changes again to indicate that it will be docked when released. Release the mouse button, and the Command Panel docks to the left side.

3. For an even easier method, you can right-click on the Command Panel's title bar and select Dock ⇨ Left from the pop-up menu.

Figure 1.8 shows the rearranged interface ready for all you southpaws.

TIP   To save the interface changes, use the Customize ⇨ Save Custom UI Scheme menu. The maxstart.cui file is loaded by default when Max is started.

FIGURE 1.8

Left-handed users can move the Command Panel to the left side.

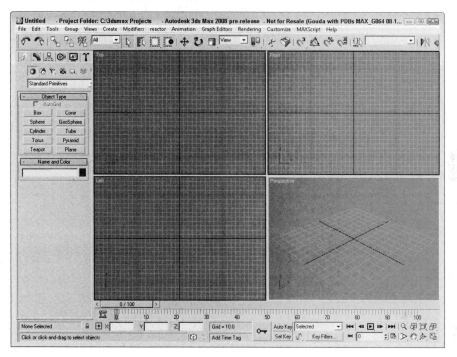

Using the Lower Interface Bar Controls

The last major interface element isn't really an interface element but just a collection of several sets of controls located along the bottom edge of the interface window. These controls cannot be pulled away from the interface like the main toolbar, but you can hide them using Expert Mode (Ctrl+X). These controls, shown in Figure 1.9, include the following from left to right:

- **Time Slider:** The Time Slider, located under the viewports, enables you to quickly locate a specific frame. It spans the number of frames included in the current animation. Dragging the Time Slider can move you quickly between frames. Clicking the arrow buttons on either side of the Time Slider moves to the previous or next frame (or key).

- **Track Bar:** The Track Bar displays animation keys as color-coded rectangles with red for positional keys, green for rotational keys, and blue for scale keys. Parameter change keys are denoted by gray rectangles. Using the Track Bar, you can select, move, and delete keys. The button at the left end of the Track Bar is the Open Mini Curve Editor button. It provides access to the animation function curves.

- **Status Bar:** The Status Bar is below the Track Bar. It provides valuable information, such as the number and type of objects selected, transformation values, and grid size. It also includes the Selection Lock Toggle, Transform Type-In fields, and the value of the current Grid size.

- **Prompt Line:** The Prompt Line is text located at the bottom of the window. If you're stuck as to what to do next, look at the Prompt Line for information on what Max expects. To the right of the Prompt Line is the Communication Center button for setting how often Max looks for updates. The Prompt Line also includes buttons for enabling Adaptive Degradation, accessing Communication Center, and adding and editing Time Tags, which are used to name specific animation frames.

- **Key Controls:** These controls are for creating animation keys and include two different modes — Auto Key (keyboard shortcut, N) and Set Key (keyboard shortcut, '). Auto Key mode sets keys for any changes made to the scene objects. Set Key mode gives you more precise control and sets keys for the selected filters only when you click the Set Keys button (keyboard shortcut, K).

- **Time Controls:** Resembling the controls on an audio or video device, the Time Controls offer an easy way to move through the various animation frames and keys. Based on the selected mode (keys or frames), the Time Controls can move among the first, previous, next, and last frames or keys.

- **Viewport Navigation Controls:** In the lower-right corner of the interface are the controls for manipulating the viewports. They enable you to zoom, pan, and rotate the active viewport's view.

NEW FEATURE   The Adaptive Degradation button on the Prompt Line is new to 3ds Max 2008. Right-clicking this button opens the Adaptive Degradation settings panel in the Viewport Configuration dialog box.

FIGURE 1.9

The Lower Interface Bar includes several sets of controls.

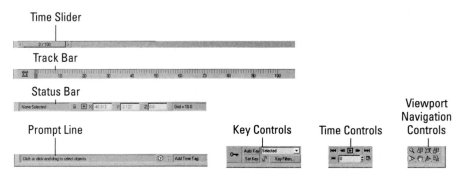

Interacting with the Interface

Knowing where all the interface elements are located is only the start. Max includes several interactive features that make the interface work. Learning these features makes the difference between an interface that works for you and one that doesn't.

Gaining quick access with the right-click quadmenus

Quadmenus are pop-up menus with up to four separate sections that surround the cursor, as shown in Figure 1.10. Right-clicking in the active viewport opens these quadmenus. The contents of the menus depend on the object selected.

TIP   Many of the real pros use quadmenus extensively. One reason is that they can access the commands from the mouse's current location using a couple of clicks without having to go all the way to the Command Panel to click a button.

FIGURE 1.10

Quadmenus contain a host of commands in an easily accessible location.

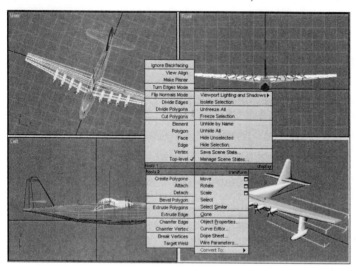

Clicking with the left mouse button away from the quadmenu closes it. For each menu, the last menu item selected is displayed in blue. To quickly access the blue menu item again, simply click the gray-shaded bar for the quadrant that contains the blue menu item. Using Customize ➪ Customize User Interface, you can specify which commands appear on the quadmenus, but the default options have just about everything you need.

If you press and hold the Alt, Ctrl, and Shift keys while right-clicking in the active viewport, you can access specific sets of commands; Shift+right-click opens the Snap options, Alt+right-click opens Animation commands, Ctrl+right-click opens a menu of primitives, Shift+Alt+right-click opens a menu of reactor commands, and Ctrl+Alt+right-click opens a menu of rendering commands.

Understanding the button color cues

Max's interface uses color cues to help remind you of the current mode. When a button is yellow, it warns that it has control of the interface. For example, if one of the select buttons on the main toolbar is selected, it turns yellow and any dragging in the viewport affects the object; however, if one of the Viewport Navigation Control buttons is selected, it turns yellow and dragging the viewport changes the view. Knowing what the current mode is at all times can keep you out of trouble.

TIP   Right-clicking in the active viewport exits any Viewport Navigation mode that has control and returns control to the most recent transform tool. Right-clicking in one of the inactive viewports keeps the focus where it is and makes that clicked viewport active.

Another common button color is red. When either the Auto Key or Set Key buttons are depressed, they turn red. The edge of the active viewport being animated along with the Time Slider also turns red. This reminds you that any modifications will be saved as a key.

Toggle buttons are buttons that can be turned on and off. Example toggle buttons include the Snap buttons. When a toggle button is enabled, it also turns yellow. Toggle buttons highlighted in blue are non-exclusive, but they notify you of a mode that is enabled, such as the Key Mode Toggle or the Affect Pivot Only button.

CROSS-REF   All interface colors can be customized using the Customize User Interface dialog box, which is discussed in Chapter 4, "Customizing the Max Interface and Setting Preferences."

Using drag-and-drop features

Dialog boxes that work with files benefit greatly from Max's drag-and-drop features. The Material Editor, Background Image, View File, and Environmental Settings dialog boxes all use drag and drop. These dialog boxes let you select a file or a material and drag it on top of where you want to apply it. For example, with the Maps rollout in the Material Editor open, you can drag a texture image filename from Windows Explorer or the Asset Manager and drop it on the Map button. You can even drag and drop Max files from Windows Explorer into the Max interface to open them.

Controlling spinners

Spinners are those little controls throughout the interface with a value field and two small arrows to its right. As you would expect, clicking the up arrow increases the value and clicking the down arrow decreases the value. The amount of the increase or decrease depends on the setting in the General tab of the Preference Settings dialog box. Right-clicking on the spinner resets the value to its lowest acceptable value. Another way to control the spinner value is to click the arrows and drag with the mouse. Dragging up increases the value, and dragging down decreases it.

The effect of the spinner drag is shown in the viewport if the Update During Spinner Drag menu option is enabled in the Views menu. If the cursor is located within a spinner, you can press Ctrl+N to open the Numeric Expression Evaluator, which lets you set the value using an expression. For example, you can set a spinner value by adding numbers together as you would using a calculator. An expression of 30+40+35 sets the value to 105.

CROSS-REF   Chapter 33, "Animating with the Expression Controller and Wiring Parameters," covers the Numeric Expression Evaluator in more detail.

Understanding modeless and persistent dialog boxes

Many dialog boxes in Max are *modeless*, which means that the dialog box doesn't need to be closed before you can work with objects in the background viewports. The Material Editor is an example of a modeless dialog box. With the Material Editor open, you can create, select, and transform objects in the background. Other modeless dialog boxes include the Material/Map Browser, the Render Scene dialog box, the Video Post dialog box, the Transform Type-In dialog box, the Display and Selection Floaters, and the various graph editors. Pressing the Ctrl+~ keyboard shortcut closes all open dialog boxes. Pressing the same keyboard shortcut again reopens the dialog boxes that were previously closed.

Another feature of many, but not all, dialog boxes is *persistence,* which means that values added to a dialog box remain set when the dialog box is reopened. This feature applies only within a given Max session. Choosing the File ➪ Reset command button or exiting and restarting Max resets all the dialog boxes.

Getting Help

If you get stuck, Max won't leave you stranded. You can turn to several places in Max to get help. The Help menu is a valuable resource that provides access to references and tutorials. The User Reference and MAXScript Reference are comprehensive help systems that work like a Web browser. The Tutorial command loads the tutorials, which offer a chance to gain valuable experience.

When Max first loads, users are greeted with a Welcome Screen, shown in Figure 1.11, that includes seven Essential Skills Movies. These simple movies explain the basics of working with Max. The Welcome Screen includes a link to Area, which is the Autodesk community site. The Area Web site is another excellent resource for help. After viewing the videos, you can disable the Show this dialog at startup option to prevent the Welcome Screen from appearing next time you start Max. You can access the Welcome Screen at any time using the Help menu.

CROSS-REF The Welcome Screen with its helpful video clips is new to 3ds Max 2008.

FIGURE 1.11

The Welcome Screen includes video clips that show the basic skills for working with Max.

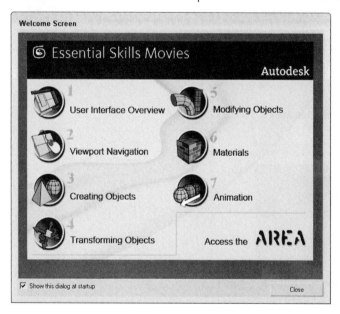

The Help ⇨ Data Exchange Solutions menu opens a Web page that explains how to use the FBX format to exchange files with other software packages. The next set of help menu commands applies to users with 3ds Max subscriptions. They let you access various e-Learning lessons, submit and view support requests, and edit your subscription profiles. All of these commands require that you enter your subscription contract number.

The Hotkey Map displays an interactive interface for learning all the keyboard shortcuts. Additional Help presents help systems for any external plug-ins that are loaded. The 3ds max on the Web options (Online Support, Updates, Resources, Partners, and Training) automatically open a Web browser and load the Autodesk Support Web pages or look for updates.

The Activate 3ds Max command lets you enter an activation number to authorize the software. The License Borrowing option lets you borrow and return the current Max license for use on another computer. The About 3ds Max command opens the About dialog box. This dialog box displays the serial number and current display driver.

Browser-based reference guides

The New Features Guide, User Reference, MAXScript Reference, and Tutorials are Web browser–based help interfaces. An organized list of topics is available in the left navigation pane, as shown in Figure 1.12, and the right includes a pane where the details on the selected topic are displayed. Across the top are five toolbar buttons used to control the interface. The Hide button hides the left navigation pane, the Back and Forward buttons move between visited pages, the Print button prints the information in the right pane, and the Options button displays a pop-up menu of options.

FIGURE 1.12

The User Reference includes panels for viewing the index of commands and searching the reference.

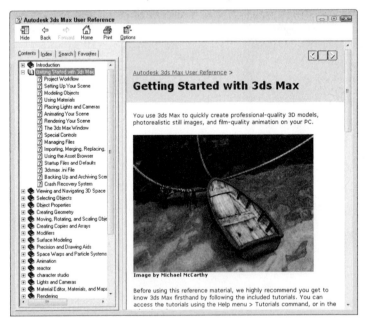

Above the left navigation pane are five tabs that open separate panels when selected. The Contents panel displays a list of topics; the Index panel lists all topics alphabetically; the Search panel includes a text field where you can search for specific keywords; the Favorites panel keeps a list of bookmarks to topics you add to the list; and the Query panel lets you type a question and query for answers.

Throughout the textual descriptions, keywords linked to other related topics are highlighted in blue and underlined.

Online help

The Web offers many sites that can also help, and Max links to the Online Support, Updates, Resources, Partners, and Training pages on the Autodesk site from the Help ➪ 3ds max on the Web menu. Selecting either of these menu commands automatically opens a Web browser and loads the Autodesk Web pages.

Summary

You should now be familiar with the interface elements for Max. Understanding the interface is one of the keys to success in using 3ds Max. Max includes a variety of different interface elements. Among the menus, toolbars, and keyboard shortcuts, several ways to perform the same command exist. Discover the method that works best for you.

This chapter covered the following topics:

- The interface elements
- Viewing and using the pull-down menus
- Working with toolbars
- Accessing the Command Panel
- Learning the lower interface controls
- Interacting with the Max interface
- Getting additional help

In this chapter, we've skirted about the viewports covering all the other interface elements, but in the next chapter, we're going to hit the viewports head-on.

Chapter 2

Controlling and Configuring the Viewports

Although Max consists of many different interface elements, such as panels, dialog boxes, and menus, the viewports are the main areas that will catch your attention. The four main viewports make up the bulk of the interface. You can think of the viewports as looking at the television screen instead of the remote. Learning to control and use the viewports can make a huge difference in your comfort level with Max. Nothing is more frustrating than not being able to rotate, pan, and zoom the view.

The viewports have numerous settings that you can use to provide thousands of different ways to look at your scene, and beginners can feel frustrated at not being able to control what they see. This chapter includes all the details you need to make the viewports reveal their secrets.

IN THIS CHAPTER

Understanding 3D space

Using the Viewport Navigation Control buttons

Controlling the viewport settings with the Viewport Configuration dialog box

Loading a viewport background image

Understanding 3D Space

It seems silly to be talking about 3D space because we live and move in 3D space. If we stop and think about it, 3D space is natural to us. For example, consider trying to locate your kids at the swimming pool. If you're standing poolside, the kids could be to your left or right, in front of you or behind you, or in the water below you or on the high dive above you. Each of these sets of directions represents a dimension in 3D space.

Now imagine that you're drawing a map that pinpoints the kid's location at the swimming pool. Using the drawing (which is 2D), you can describe the kid's position on the map as left, right, top, or bottom, but the descriptions of above and below have been lost. By moving from a 3D reference to a 2D one, the number of dimensions has decreased.

The conundrum that 3D computer artists face is how do you represent 3D objects on a 2D device such as a computer screen? The answer that 3ds Max provides is to present several views, called *viewports*, of the scene. A viewport is a small window that displays the scene from one perspective. These viewports are the windows into Max's 3D world. Each viewport has numerous settings and viewing options.

Axonometric versus Perspective

When it comes to views in the 3D world, two different types exist—Axonometric and Perspective. Axonometric views are common in the CAD world where the viewer is set at an infinite distance from the object such that all parallel lines remain parallel. A Perspective view simulates how our eyes actually work and converges all points to a single location off in the distance.

You can see the difference between these two types of views clearly if you look at a long line of objects. For example, if you were to look down a long row of trees lining a road, the trees would eventually merge on the horizon. In Axonometric views, lines stay parallel as they recede into the distance. Figure 2.1 shows this example with the Axonometric view on the left and the Perspective view on the right.

FIGURE 2.1

Axonometric and Perspective views

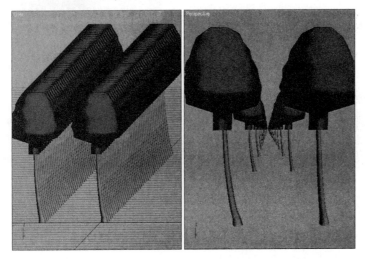

Orthographic and Isometric views

If you dig a little deeper into Axonometric views, you find two different types—Orthographic and Isometric. Orthographic views are displayed from the perspective of looking straight down an axis at an object. This reveals a view in only one plane. Because orthographic viewports are constrained to one plane, they show the actual height and width of the object, which is why the CAD world uses orthographic views extensively. Isometric views are not constrained to a single axis and can view the scene from any location, but all dimensions are still maintained.

Learning viewports in Max

Available orthographic viewports in Max include Front, Back, Top, Bottom, Left, and Right. Max starts up with the Top, Front, and Left orthographic viewports visible. The top-left corner of the viewport displays the viewport name. The fourth default viewport is a Perspective view.

Figure 2.2 shows the viewports with Viewpoint model of a PT-328 U.S. Torpedo boat. You can see the model from a different direction in each viewport. If you want to measure the boat's length from aft to stern, you could get an accurate measurement using the Top or Left viewport, whereas you can use the Front and Left viewports to measure its precise height. So, using these different viewports, you can accurately work with all object dimensions.

FIGURE 2.2

The Max interface includes four viewports, each with a different view.

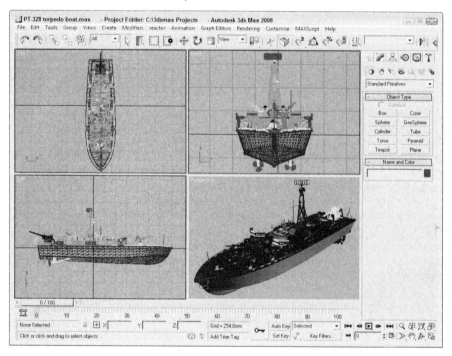

Isometric views in Max are called User viewports. You can create a User viewport by rotating any of the Orthographic views.

TIP   Max includes several keyboard shortcuts for quickly changing the view in the active viewport including T (Top View), B (Bottom View), F (Front View), L (Left View), C (Camera View), $ (Spotlight View), P (Perspective View), and U (Isometric User View). Pressing the V key opens a quadmenu that lets you select a new view.

Using the Viewport Navigation Controls

The standard viewports show you several different views of your current project, but within each viewport you can zoom in on certain objects, pan the view, or rotate about the center of the viewport. To zoom, pan, and rotate the default views, you need to use the Viewport Navigation Control buttons. These eight buttons are located at the bottom-right corner of the window. In Table 2.1, the keyboard shortcut for each button is listed in parentheses next to its name.

 The active viewport is always marked with a yellow border.

TABLE 2.1

Viewport Navigation Controls

Toolbar Button	Name	Description
Q	Zoom (Alt+Z or [or])	Moves closer to or farther from the objects in the active viewport by dragging the mouse or zooming by steps with the bracket keys.
⊞	Zoom All	Zooms in to or out of all the viewports simultaneously by dragging the mouse.
◻	Zoom Extents (Ctrl+Alt+Z), Zoom Extents Selected	Zooms in on all objects or just the selected object until it fills the active viewport.
⊞	Zoom Extents All (Ctrl+Shift+Z), Zoom Extents All Selected (Z)	Zooms in on all objects or just the selected object until it fills all the viewports.
▷ ⊡	Field of View, Region Zoom (Ctrl+W)	The Field of View button (available only in the Perspective view) controls the width of the view. The Region Zoom button zooms in to the region selected by dragging the mouse.
✋ 👣	Pan (Ctrl+P or I), Walk Through	Moves the view to the left, to the right, up, or down by dragging the mouse or by moving the mouse while holding down the I key. The Walk Through feature moves through the scene using the arrow keys or a mouse like a first-person video game.
⟳	Arc Rotate (Ctrl+R), Arc Rotate Selected, Arc Rotate SubObject	Rotates the view around the global axis, selected object, or subobject by dragging the mouse.
⧉	Min/Max Toggle (Alt+W)	Makes the active viewport fill the screen replacing the four separate viewports. Clicking this button a second time shows all four viewports again.

CAUTION When one of the Viewport Navigation buttons is selected, it is highlighted yellow. You cannot select, create, or transform objects while one of these buttons is highlighted. Right-clicking in the active viewpoint reverts to select object mode.

Zooming a view

You can zoom in to and out of the scene in several ways. Clicking the Zoom (Alt+Z) button enters zoom mode where you can zoom in to and out of a viewport by dragging the mouse. This works in whichever viewport you drag in. To the right of the Zoom button is the Zoom All button, which does the same thing as the Zoom button, only to all four viewports at once. If you hold down the Ctrl key while dragging in Zoom mode, the zoom action happens more quickly, requiring only a small mouse movement to get a large zoom amount. Holding down the Alt key while dragging in Zoom mode has the opposite effect — the zoom happens much more slowly and a large mouse move is required for a small zoom amount. This is helpful for fine tuning the zoom.

The Zoom Extents (Ctrl+Alt+Z) button zooms the active viewport so that all objects (or the selected objects with the Zoom Extents Selected button) are visible in the viewport. A Zoom Extents All (Ctrl+Shift+Z) button is available for zooming in all viewports to all objects' extents; the most popular zoom command is Zoom Extents All Selected (Z), which is for zooming in to the extents of the selected objects in all viewports.

You can use the brackets keys to zoom in ([) and out (]) by steps. Each key press zooms in (or out) another step. The Region Zoom (Ctrl+W) button lets you drag over the region that you want to zoom in on. If you select a non-orthogonal view, such as the Perspective view, the Region Zoom button has a flyout called the Field of View. Using this button, you can control how wide or narrow the view is. This is like using a wide angle or telephoto lens on your camera. This feature is different from zoom in that the perspective is distorted as the Field of View is increased.

 **Field of View is covered in more detail in Chapter 18, "Configuring and Aiming Cameras."**

Panning a view

The Viewport Navigation Controls also offer two ways to pan in a viewport. In Pan mode (Ctrl+P), dragging in a viewport pans the view. Note that this doesn't move the objects, only the view. The second way to pan is to hold down the I key while moving the mouse. This is known as an *interactive* pan. In addition, the Ctrl and Alt keys can be held down to speed or slow the panning motions.

Walking through a view

The Walk Through button, found as a flyout button under the Pan button, allows you to move through the scene in the Perspective or Camera viewport using the arrow keys or the mouse just as you would if you were playing a first-person computer game. When this button is active, the cursor changes to a small circle with an arrow inside it that points in the direction you are moving.

CAUTION **The Pan button is a flyout only if the Perspective view or a Camera view is selected.**

The Walk Through feature includes several keystrokes for controlling the camera's movement. The arrow keys move the camera forward, left, back, and right (or you can use the W, A, S, and D keys). You can change the speed of the motion with the Q (accelerate) and Z (decelerate) keys or with the [(decrease step size) and] (increase step size) keys. The E and C keys (or the Shift+up or Shift+down arrows) are used to move up and down in the scene. The Shift+spacebar key causes the camera to be set level. Dragging the mouse while the camera is moving changes the direction in which the camera points.

Rotating a view

Rotating the view can be the most revealing of all the view changes. When the Arc Rotate (Ctrl+R) button is selected, a rotation guide appears in the active viewport, as shown in Figure 2.3. This rotation guide is a circle with a square located at each quadrant. Clicking and dragging the left or right squares rotates the view side to side; the same action with the top and bottom squares rotates the view up and down. Clicking within the circle and dragging rotates within a single plane, and clicking and dragging outside of the circle rotates the view about the circle's center either clockwise or counterclockwise. If you get confused, look at the cursor, which changes depending on the type of rotation. The Ctrl and Alt keys also can speed and slow the rotating view. Figure 2.3 also shows a viewport that has been maximized using the Min/Max Toggle button.

FIGURE 2.3

The rotation guide appears whenever the Arc Rotate button is selected.

Rotation guide

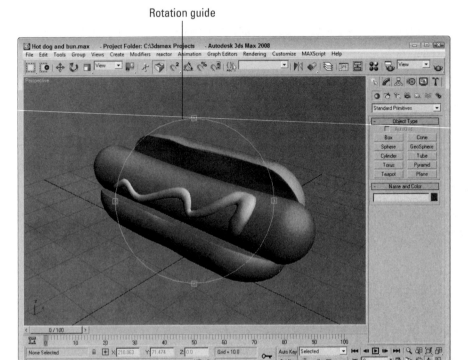

 If you rotate an orthogonal view, it automatically becomes a User view.

Controlling viewports with a scroll wheel

Now that I've explained the Viewport Navigation Control buttons and listed their keyboard shortcuts, I'll explain the easiest way to control the viewports — and clicking on the buttons isn't it. Often, the quickest way to control the viewports is with the mouse. To really get the benefit of the mouse, you need to use a mouse with a scroll wheel (which also acts as a middle mouse button).

Rolling the scroll wheel in the active viewport zooms in to and out of the viewport by steps just like the bracket keys ([and]). You can zoom precisely by holding down the Ctrl and Alt keys while dragging the scroll wheel. Clicking and dragging the scroll wheel button pans the active viewport. Clicking and dragging with the Alt button held down rotates the active viewport. If the scroll wheel isn't working, check the Viewports panel in the Preference Settings dialog box. You can select to use the scroll wheel control to pan and zoom in the viewports or to define and use Strokes.

CAUTION Be careful when zooming in with the scroll wheel. If you zoom in too far, the internal field of width approaches its minimum value and zooming becomes unstable. If this happens, you can select the Views ⇨ Undo View Change (Shift+Z) menu command to undo the zoom or use the Zoom Extents button.

CROSS-REF Strokes are covered in Chapter 4, "Customizing the Max Interface and Setting Preferences."

Controlling camera and spotlight views

You can set any viewport to be a camera view (C) or a spotlight view ($) if a camera or a spotlight exists in the scene. When either of these views is active, the Viewport Navigation Control buttons change. In camera view, controls for dolly, roll, truck, pan, orbit, and field of view become active. A light view includes controls for falloff and hotspots.

CROSS-REF Chapter 18, "Configuring and Aiming Cameras," and Chapter 19, "Using Lights and Basic Lighting Techniques," cover these changes in more detail.

Tutorial: Navigating the active viewport

Over time, working with the Viewport Navigation Controls becomes second nature to you, but you need to practice to get to that point. In this tutorial, you get a chance to take the viewports for a spin — literally.

To practice navigating a viewport, follow these steps:

1. Open the Bruce the dog.max file from the Chap 02 directory on the DVD.

    This file includes a model of a dog (affectionately named Bruce) created by Viewpoint. It provides a reference as we navigate the viewport. The active viewport is the Perspective viewport.

2. Click the Min/Max Toggle button (or press Alt+W) to make the Perspective viewport fill the space of all four viewports.

3. Click the Pan button (or press Ctrl+P), and drag the window until Bruce's head is centered in the viewport. Then click the Zoom button (or press Alt+Z), and drag in the Perspective viewport until Bruce's head fills the viewport, as shown in Figure 2.4. Right-click in the viewport to exit the selected navigation tool.

4. Choose Views ⇨ Save Active Perspective View to save the current view of the dog's head.

5. Click the Zoom Extents button (or press Ctrl+Alt+Z) to size the entire dog body in the current viewport.

6. Click the Arc Rotate button (or press Ctrl+R), and drag from the left square on the rotation guide to the right. This rotates Bruce to make his front side more visible, as shown in Figure 2.5. Good boy, Bruce.

FIGURE 2.4

The Perspective viewport is zoomed in on the dog's head using the Zoom and Pan controls.

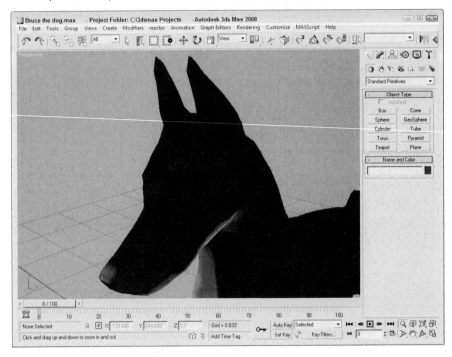

If you tried this tutorial as outlined, try it again using the mouse's scroll wheel.

Undoing and saving Viewport changes

If you get lost in your view, you can undo and redo viewport changes with Views ⇨ Undo View Change (Shift+Z) and Views ⇨ Redo View Change (Shift+Y). These commands are different from the Edit ⇨ Undo and Edit ⇨ Redo commands, which can undo or redo geometry changes.

You can save changes made to a viewport by using the Views ⇨ Save Active Viewport menu command. This command saves the Viewport Navigation settings for recall. To restore these settings, use Views ⇨ Restore Active Viewport.

NOTE   The Save and Restore Active Viewport commands do not save any viewport configuration settings, just the navigated view. Saving an active view uses a buffer, so it remembers only one view for each viewport.

Disabling and refreshing viewports

If your scene gets too complicated, you can experience some slow-down waiting for each viewport to be updated with changes, but fear not, because several options will come to your rescue. The first option to try is to disable a viewport.

FIGURE 2.5

The Perspective viewport after a slight rotation shows Bruce's good side.

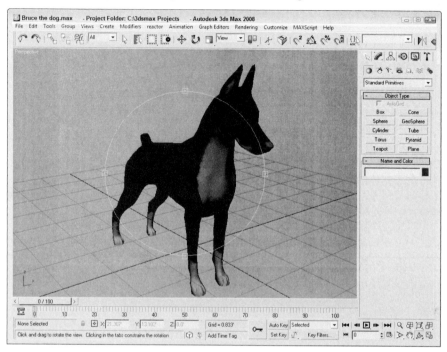

You can disable a viewport by right-clicking on the viewport's name and selecting the Disable View menu command from the pop-up menu, or you can press the keyboard shortcut, D. When a disabled viewport is active, it is updated as normal; when it is inactive, the viewport is not updated at all until it becomes active again. Disabled viewports are identified by the word "Disabled," which appears next to the viewport's name in the upper-left corner.

Another trick to increase the viewport update speed is to disable the View ⇨ Update During Spinner Drag menu option. Changing parameter spinners can cause a slowdown by requiring every viewport to update as the spinner changes. If the spinner is changing rapidly, it can really slow even a powerful system. Disabling this option causes the viewport to wait for the spinner to stop changing before updating.

Sometimes when changes are made, the viewports aren't completely refreshed. This typically happens when dialog boxes from other programs are moved in front of the viewports. If this happens, you can force Max to refresh all the viewports with the Views ⇨ Redraw All Views (keyboard shortcut, `) menu command.

The Redraw All Views (keyboard shortcut, `) command refreshes each viewport and makes everything visible again. (As objects get moved around, they often mask one another and lines disappear.) Activate All Maps turns on all maps, and Deactivate All Maps turns off all maps. Material maps can take up lots of memory and can slow the viewport rendering.

The Adaptive Degradation Toggle (O) is an option that enables the viewport display to degrade the image resolution (by downgrading the rendering method) in order to maintain a consistent frame rate. This can help when you're trying to navigate a complex scene that is taking a while to redraw.

 **More on Adaptive Degradation is covered later in this chapter.**

Maximizing the active viewport

Sooner or later, the viewports will feel too small. When this happens, you have several ways to increase the size of your viewports. The first trick to try is to change the viewport sizes by clicking and dragging any of the viewport borders. Dragging on the intersection of the viewports resizes all the viewports. Figure 2.6 shows the viewports after being dynamically resized.

TIP You can return to the original layout by right-clicking on any of the viewport borders and selecting Reset Layout from the pop-up menu.

The second trick to try is to use the Min/Max Toggle (Alt+W) to expand the active viewport to fill the space reserved for all four viewports, as shown previously in Figure 2.3. Clicking the Min/Max Toggle (or pressing Alt+W) a second time returns to the defined layout.

FIGURE 2.6

You can dynamically resize viewports by dragging their borders.

Maximizing the viewport helps temporarily, but you can take another step before convincing your boss that you need a larger monitor. You can enter Expert Mode by choosing Views ➪ Expert Mode (Ctrl+X). It maximizes the viewport space by removing the main toolbar, the Command Panel, and most of the Lower Interface Bar.

With most of the interface elements gone, you'll need to rely on the menus, keyboard shortcuts, and quad-menus to execute commands. To re-enable the default interface, click the Cancel Expert Mode button in the lower right of the Max window (or press Ctrl+X again). Figure 2.7 shows the interface in Expert Mode.

FIGURE 2.7

Expert Mode maximizes the viewports by eliminating most of the interface elements.

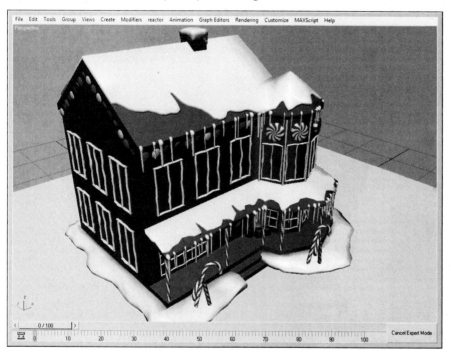

Configuring the Viewports

If the Viewport Navigation Controls help define what you see, then the Viewport Configuration dialog box helps define how you see objects in the viewports. You can configure each viewport using this dialog box. To open this dialog box, choose the Customize ➪ Viewport Configuration menu command. You can also open this dialog box by right-clicking the viewport's name located in the upper-left corner of each viewport and choosing Configure from the pop-up menu. The pop-up menu itself includes many of the settings found in the Viewport Configuration dialog box, but the dialog box lets you alter several settings at once. You can also make this dialog box appear for the active viewport by right-clicking any of the Viewport Navigation Control buttons in the lower-right corner.

The Viewport Configuration dialog box contains several panels, including Rendering Method, Layout, Safe Frames, Adaptive Degradation, Regions, Statistics, and Lighting and Shadows. The Preference Settings dialog box also includes many settings for controlling the behavior and look of the viewports.

 See Chapter 4, "Customizing the Max Interface and Setting Preferences," for more on the Preference Settings dialog box and all its options.

Setting the viewport rendering method

Complex scenes take longer to display and render. The renderer used for the viewports is highly optimized to be very quick, but if you're working on a huge model with lots of complex textures and every viewport is set to display the highest quality view, then updating each viewport can slow the program to a crawl. The Viewport Configuration dialog box's Rendering Method panel, shown in Figure 2.8, lets you set the rendering settings for the Active Viewport, All Viewports, or All but Active viewport.

TIP If you ever get stuck waiting for Max to complete a task, such as redrawing the viewports, you can always press the Escape key to suspend any task immediately and return control to the interface.

FIGURE 2.8

The Rendering Method panel holds controls for specifying the Rendering Level and several other viewport rendering options.

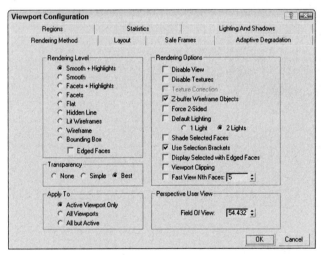

NOTE These settings have no effect on the final rendering specified using the Rendering menu. They affect only the display in the viewport.

Rendering levels

The Rendering Level options, from slowest to fastest, include the following:

■ **Smooth+Highlights:** Shows smooth surfaces with lighting highlights.

■ **Smooth:** Shows smooth surfaces without any lighting effects.

■ **Facets+Highlights:** Shows individual polygon faces and lighting highlights.

- **Facets:** Shows individual polygon faces without any lighting effects.
- **Flat:** Shows the entire object using a single color.
- **Hidden Line:** Shows only polygon edges facing the camera.
- **Lit Wireframes:** Shows all polygon edges with lighting effects.
- **Wireframe:** Shows all polygon edges only.
- **Bounding Box:** Shows a box that would enclose the object.

Although it really isn't a rendering method, the Edged Faces option shows the edges for each face when a shaded rendering method is selected. You can enable and disable this option with the F4 keyboard shortcut. Figure 2.9 shows, side by side, all the various viewport rendering methods applied to a simple sphere.

FIGURE 2.9

The viewport rendering methods are shown from left to right. First Row: Smooth+Highlights, Smooth, Facets+Highlights, Facets, and Flat. Second Row: Hidden Line, Lit Wireframes, Wireframe, Bounding Box, and Edged Faces applied to Smooth+Highlights.

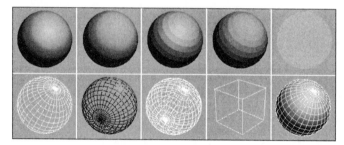

The most common rendering setting is Wireframe. It gives a good representation of the object while redrawing very quickly. By default the Top, Front, and Left viewports are set to Wireframe, and the Perspective viewport is set to Smooth+Highlights. Faceted rendering displays every face as a flat plane, but it shows the object as a solid model and is good for checking whether objects overlap. The Smooth rendering level shows a rough approximation of the final rendering. Setting the rendering level to include highlights shows the effect of the lights in the scene.

 Many effects, such as bump maps, transparent maps, and shadows, cannot be seen in the viewport and show up only in the final render.

Viewing transparency

In addition to these shading types, you also can set the viewport to display objects that contain transparency (which is set in the Object Properties dialog box). The three Transparency options are None, which doesn't display any transparency; Simple, which cross-hatches the transparent object; and Best, which includes a transparency effect for a smooth look. Figure 2.10 shows these three transparency options with the help of a hungry little animated creature and his ghostly rival.

Rendering options

The Rendering Options section within the Rendering Method panel includes several other options, such as Disable View (D) and Disable Textures. These options can help speed up viewport updates or increase the visual detail of the objects in the viewport.

FIGURE 2.10

The viewport transparency options include None, Simple, and Best.

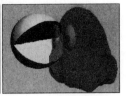

> **TIP** At any time during a viewport update, you can click the mouse or press a key to cancel the redraw. Max doesn't make you wait for a screen redraw to be able to execute commands with the mouse or keyboard shortcuts.

The Disable Textures option turns off texture rendering for quick viewport updates. The Texture Correction option speeds rendering updates by interpolating the current texture rather than re-rendering. Texture Correction (along with Disable View and Viewport Clipping) is one of the options available in the pop-up menu by right-clicking the viewport name.

A z-buffer is an area of memory used to keep track of each object's distance from the camera. Enabling Z-Buffer Wireframe Objects causes the wireframe objects to be drawn from back to front. If your wireframe lines seem to be disappearing, it could be that the viewport is drawing the lines in whatever order and some lines that should appear in the back are being drawn on top of the ones in the front. Enabling this option helps prevent that.

Force 2-Sided makes both sides of all faces visible. For example, suppose you have a sphere with a hole in it. This setting enables you to see the interior surface of the sphere through the hole. Figure 2.11 shows a sphere with a star-shape cutout of its surface. The left image has the Force 2-Sided option disabled, and the image on the right has it enabled.

FIGURE 2.11

The Force 2-Sided option makes the interior of objects visible.

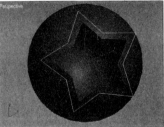

The Default Lighting toggle deactivates your current lights and uses the default lights. This option can be helpful when you're trying to view objects in a dark setting because the default lighting illuminates the entire scene without requiring you to remove or turn off lights. You can also specify whether default lighting uses one light or two. The one-light option creates a single light positioned behind the viewer and at an angle to the scene. Scenes with one light update quicker than scenes with two lights.

Making selected objects visible

You use Shade Selected Faces (F2) to shade selected subobject faces in red, making them easy to see.

NOTE The Shade Selected Faces (F2) option, which shades selected subobject faces, is different from the Views ⇨ Shade Selected menu command, which turns on shading for the selected object in all viewports.

The Use Selection Brackets option displays white corners around the current selection. Selection brackets are useful for helping you see the entire size of a grouped object but can be annoying if left on with many objects selected. Uncheck this option (or press the J key) to make these brackets disappear.

The option to Display Selected with Edged Faces helps to highlight the selected object. If this option is enabled, then the edges of the current selection are displayed regardless of whether the Edged Faces check box is enabled. Figure 2.12 shows the grips of an M-203 rifle that was created by Viewpoint Datalabs selected with the Display Selected with Edged Faces and the Use Selection Brackets options enabled. These options make the current selection easy to see.

FIGURE 2.12

The Display Selected with Edged Faces and Use Selection Brackets options make identifying the current selection easy.

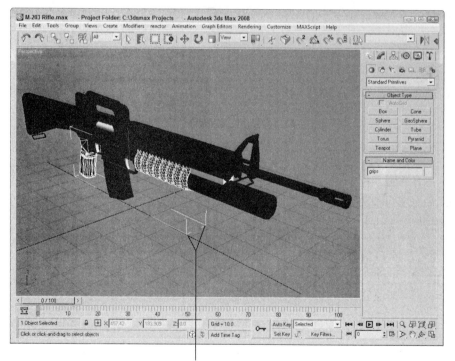

Selection brackets

Using clipping planes

Clipping planes define an invisible barrier beyond which all objects are invisible. For example, if you have a scene with many detailed mountain objects in the background, working with an object in the front of the scene can be difficult. By setting the clipping plane between the two, you can work on the front objects without having to redraw the mountain objects every time you update the scene. This affects only the viewport, not the rendered output.

Enabling the Viewport Clipping option places a yellow line with two arrows on the right side of the viewport, as shown in Figure 2.13. The top arrow represents the back clipping plane, and the bottom arrow is the front clipping plane. Drag the arrows to set the clipping planes. You can quickly turn Viewport Clipping on or off by right-clicking the viewport name and choosing Viewport Clipping from the pop-up menu.

FIGURE 2.13

The clipping planes can be used to show the interior of this car model.

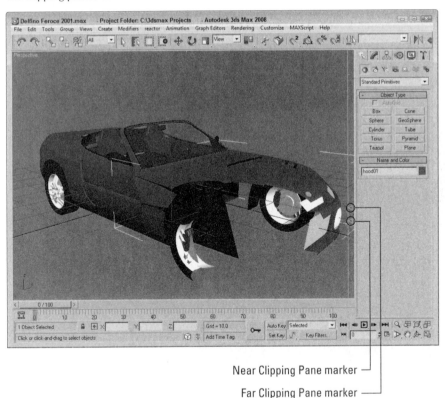

Near Clipping Pane marker

Far Clipping Pane marker

Enabling Fast View

The Fast View option speeds viewport updates by drawing only a limited number of faces. The spinner value determines how often faces are drawn. For example, a setting of 5 would draw only every fifth face. This option renders viewport updates much quicker and gives you an idea of the objects without displaying the entire object.

Tutorial: Viewing the interior of a heart with Clipping Planes

You can use the Clipping Planes setting in the Viewport Configuration dialog box to view the interior of a model such as this heart model created by Viewpoint.

To view the interior of a heart model, follow these steps:

1. Open the Heart interior.max file from the Chap 02 directory on the DVD.

2. Choose Customize ⇨ Viewport Configuration to open the Viewport Configuration dialog box. Enable the Viewport Clipping option and the Force 2-Sided option, and then close the dialog box.

3. The Clipping Plane markers appear to the right of the viewport. The top marker controls the back clipping plane, and the bottom marker controls the front clipping plane. Drag the bottom clipping plane marker upward to slice through the heart model to reveal its interior, as shown in Figure 2.14.

FIGURE 2.14

By using Clipping Planes, you can reveal the interior of a model.

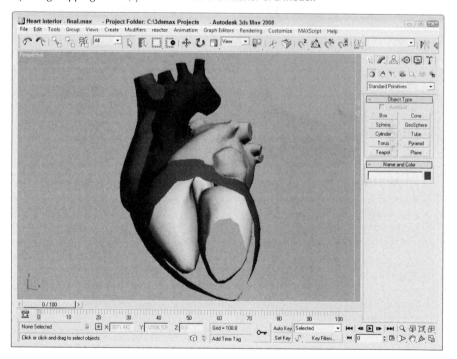

Setting the Field of View

You can also alter the Field of View (FOV) for the Perspective view in the Viewport Configuration dialog box. To create a fish-eye view, increase the FOV setting to 10 or less. The maximum FOV value is 180, and the default value is 45. You can also change the Field of View using the Field of View button in the Viewport Navigation Controls. The Viewport Configuration dialog box, however, lets you enter precise values.

CROSS-REF See Chapter 18, "Configuring and Aiming Cameras," for more coverage on Field of View.

Grabbing a viewport image

It's not rendering, but you can grab an image of the active viewport using the Tools ➪ Grab Viewport. Before grabbing the image, a simple dialog box appears asking you to add a label to the grabbed image. The image is loaded into the Rendered Frame Window, and its label appears in the lower-right corner of the image, as shown in Figure 2.15.

FIGURE 2.15

A viewport image can be grabbed using a menu command found in the Tools menu.

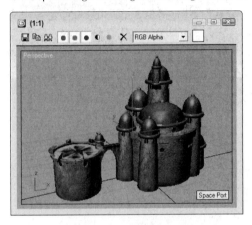

Altering the Viewport layout

Now that you've started to figure out the viewports, you may want to change the number and size of viewports displayed. The Layout panel, shown in Figure 2.16, in the Viewpoint Configuration dialog box, offers several layouts as alternatives to the default layout (not that there is anything wrong with the default and its four equally sized viewports).

After selecting a layout from the options at the top of the panel, you can assign each individual viewport a different view by clicking on each viewport in the Layout panel and choosing a view from the pop-up menu. The view options include Perspective, User, Front, Back, Top, Bottom, Left, Right, ActiveShade, Track, Schematic, Grid (Front, Back, Top, Bottom, Left, Right, Display Planes), Extended (Asset Browser, Motion Mixer, Biped Animation WorkBench, MAXScript Listener), and Shape. All of these view options are also available by right-clicking on the viewport title in the upper-left corner of the viewport. Figure 2.17 shows a viewport layout with the Track view, Schematic view, Asset Browser, and Perspective views open.

Views can also be set to Camera and Spotlight if they exist in the scene. Each camera and light that exists is listed by name at the top of the pop-up menu.

FIGURE 2.16

The Layout panel offers many layout options.

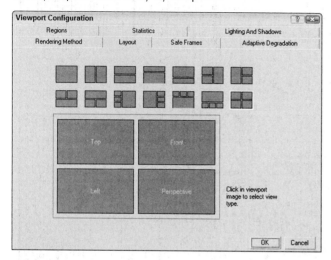

FIGURE 2.17

Other interfaces such as the Track view, Schematic view, and Asset Browser can be opened within a viewport.

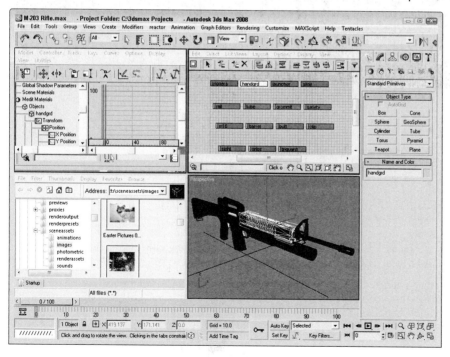

Using Safe Frames

Completing an animation and converting it to some broadcast medium, only to see that the whole left side of the animation is being cut off in the final screening, can be discouraging. If you rely on the size of the active viewport to show the edges of the final output, you could be way off. Using the Safe Frames feature, you can display some guides within the viewport that show where these clipping edges are.

The Safe Frames panel of the Viewport Configuration dialog box lets you define several safe frame options, as shown in Figure 2.18, including the following:

- **Live Area:** Marks the area that will be rendered, shown as yellow lines. If a background image is added to the viewport and the Match Rendering Output option is selected, then the background image will fit within the Live Area.

- **Action Safe:** The area ensured to be visible in the final rendered file, marked with light blue lines; objects outside this area will be at the edge of the monitor and could be distorted.

- **Title Safe:** The area where the title can safely appear without distortion or bleeding, marked with orange lines.

- **User Safe:** The output area defined by the user, marked with magenta lines.

- **12-Field Grid:** Displays a grid in the viewport, marked with a pink grid.

FIGURE 2.18

The Safe Frames panel lets you specify areas to render.

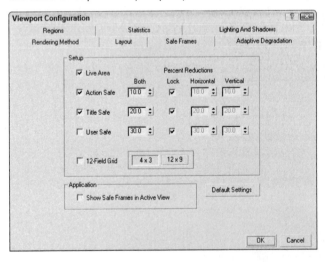

For each type of safe frame, you can set the percent reduction by entering values in the Horizontal, Vertical, or Both fields. The 12-Field Grid option offers 4 × 3 and 12 × 9 aspect ratios.

The Show Safe Frames in Active View option displays the Safe Frame borders in the active viewport. You can quickly enable or disable Safe Frames by right-clicking the viewport name and choosing Show Safe Frame in the pop-up menu (or you can use the Shift+F keyboard shortcut).

Figure 2.19 shows an elongated Perspective viewport with all the safe frame guides enabled. The Safe Frames show that the top and bottom of my dinosaur will be cut off when rendered.

FIGURE 2.19

Safe frames provide guides that help you see when the scene objects are out of bounds.

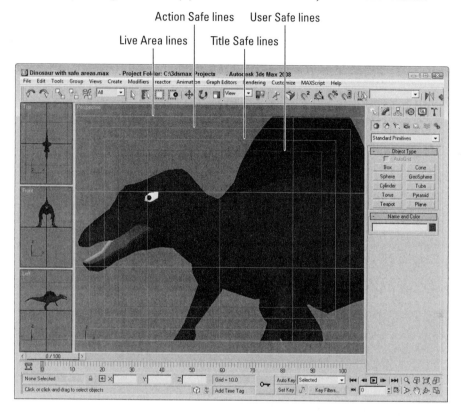

Understanding Adaptive Degradation

When you are previewing a complex scene with hundreds of objects in a viewport, updating the viewport can slow to a crawl. This can make viewing your work difficult and slow. The feature in Max that addresses this issue is called Adaptive Degradation, and although it sounds like a weapon that some alien might use to disarm you, it enables you to force a viewport to display at a pre-specified number of frames per second. If the display update takes too long to maintain the goal frames per second rate, then it automatically degrades the rendering level in order to maintain the frame rate. This option is very helpful because when you're testing an animation, you are not as concerned about the model details or textures.

NEW FEATURE Adaptive Degradation has been improved in 3ds Max 2008 with an option to hide objects, a priority setting based on how close objects are to the screen, and an option to never degrade the selected object.

The Adaptive Degradation panel is available in the Viewport Configuration dialog box, as shown in Figure 2.20.

FIGURE 2.20

The Adaptive Degradation panel maintains a defined frame rate by degrading the rendering level.

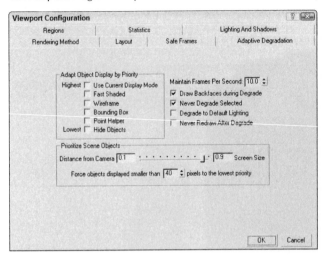

 You can enable Adaptive Degradation by using the Views ⇨ Adaptive Degradation menu command (or by pressing the O key). You also can turn Adaptive Degradation on and off with a button located at the bottom of the interface between the Prompt Bar and the Communication Center button. The Adaptive Degradation button looks like a simple cube. Adaptive Degradation, when enabled, is used when needed to keep the display updates fast. When the Adaptive Degradation button is enabled, it is highlighted yellow. When the viewport is being degraded, the button turns cyan.

 Right-clicking on the Adaptive Degradation button opens the Adaptive Degradation panel in the Viewport Configuration dialog box.

The Adapt Object Display by Priority section contains several display options listed in order from the most difficult to render (Use Current Display Mode) to the easiest (Hide Objects). Every display option that is selected can be used during the degrade process. For example, if the Fast Shaded, Wireframe, and Bounding Box options are enabled, and if the viewport is having trouble updating, then the prioritized objects are displayed using the Bounding Box rendering method and other objects are displayed using the Wireframe or Fast Shaded methods. If the display is still below the target frames per second, then more prioritized objects are degraded to the Bounding Box method.

Different scene objects can degrade to different levels based on their priority. Object priority is set using a slider, which can be based on the object's distance from the camera, and Screen Size, which equates to the object's size in the viewport. If the slider is all the way to the left, then objects farther from the front of the scene are degraded first. If the slider is all the way to the right, then smaller objects are degraded first. Another option can force all objects smaller than a designated size to the lowest enabled display setting.

In the Maintain Frames Per Second field, you enter the frame rate that you want to maintain.

> **NOTE** Remember that film generally runs at 24 fps, television at 30 fps, Web animations at 12 fps, and high-res games at 60 fps.

The FPS setting includes several options. The Draw Backfaces during Degrade option causes all object backfaces to appear. The Never Degrade Selected option keeps the selected object from changing its display and is a helpful option if you want a main character to remain displayed in its current display mode.

> **TIP** If you have another unselected object in the scene that you want to keep visible, you can enable the Never Degrade option in the Object Properties dialog box. This option prevents the object from being degraded.

The Degrade to Default Lighting option turns off all lighting effects, which can be a display bottleneck and uses only default lighting. The Never Redraw After Degrade option prevents the viewports from being refreshed when the mouse button is released while Adaptive Degradation is enabled.

> **TIP** Another way to speed the frame rate in the active viewport is to disable (D) the inactive viewports.

To enable Adaptive Degradation in the viewports, follow these steps:

1. Open the Delfino Feroce 2001.max file from the Chap 02 directory on the DVD.

   This file includes a realistic car model created by Viewpoint Datalabs.

2. Select the Edit ⇨ Select All (Ctrl+A) menu command to select all the car's objects.

3. Hold down the Shift key and drag the car with the Select and Move tool. In the Clone Options dialog box that opens, enter a value of **5** for the Number of Copies. If your computer is fast enough to display all copies of the car without any trouble, try increasing the number of copies.

   This creates five more copies of the selected car.

4. Right-click on the Adaptive Degradation button at the bottom of the interface. In the Adaptive Degradation panel of the Viewport Configuration dialog box, set the Maintain Frames Per Second value to **25**, enable the Use Current Display Mode, Wireframe, and Bounding Box options, and drag the slider to the left to the Distance from Camera side. Then click the OK button. Click on the Adaptive Degradation button to enable it.

   The Adaptive Degradation button turns yellow when enabled.

5. Click on the Arc Rotate button in the Viewport Navigation Controls and drag in the viewport.

   Notice how the cars farthest from the camera are degraded to bounding boxes.

6. Right-click on the Adaptive Degradation button again and drag the slider all the way to the right so that Screen Size affects what is degraded. Then close the Viewport Configuration dialog box and drag in the viewport again.

   Notice this time how the smaller objects are degraded, as shown in Figure 2.21.

> **TIP** Pressing the 7 key enables statistics mode in the viewport so you can see in real time the frames per second.

FIGURE 2.21

Smaller objects are degraded to wireframe and bounding boxes based on their size in the current viewport.

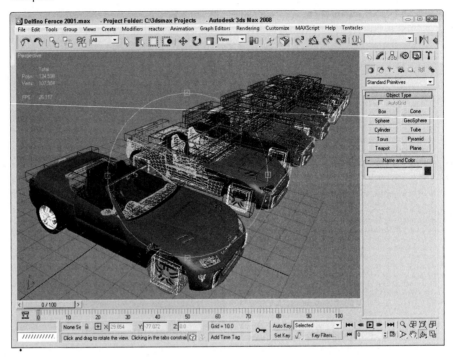

Defining regions

The Regions panel enables you to define regions and focus your rendering energies on a smaller area. Complex scenes can take considerable time and machine power to render. Sometimes, you want to test render only a portion of a viewport to check material assignment, texture map placement, or lighting.

You can define the size of the various Regions in the Regions panel of the Viewport Configuration dialog box, shown in Figure 2.22.

After you've specified a Blowup Region or a Sub Region, you can select to render using these regions by selecting Region or Blowup from the Render Type drop-down list on the far-right end of the main toolbar and clicking the Quick Render button. After clicking the Quick Render button, the specified region is displayed as an outline in the viewport and an OK button appears in the lower-right corner of the viewport. You can move this outline to reposition it or drag its edge or corner handles to resize the region. The new position and dimension values are updated in the Regions panel for next time. Click the OK button to begin the rendering process.

The difference between these two regions is that the Sub Region displays the Rendered Frame Window in black, except for the specified sub-region. The Blowup Region fills the entire Rendered Frame Window, as shown in Figure 2.23.

FIGURE 2.22

The Regions panel enables you to work with smaller regions within your scene.

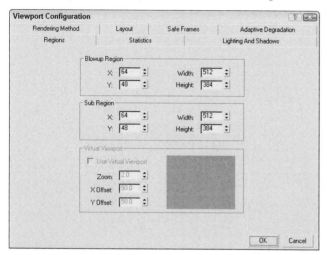

FIGURE 2.23

The image on the left was rendered using the Sub Region option; the right image used the Blowup Region.

 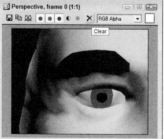

CROSS-REF You can learn more about Render Types and the Rendered Frame Window in Chapter 22, "Learning to Render a Scene."

The Virtual Viewport is a feature that lets you zoom in and pan within the viewport image using the numeric keypad. This feature is available only if you are using the OpenGL display driver. You can check to see which display driver you are using by selecting Help ➪ About 3ds Max. This command opens a credits screen that lists the current driver. You can change the current display driver in the Viewport panel of the Preference Settings dialog box.

If you have OpenGL set as the current display driver, then you can select Use Virtual Viewport to display the viewport in the area to the right. Using the Zoom, X, and Y Offset values, you can specify where the virtual viewport looks or you can drag the rectangular outline in the visible screen to the right.

Once the Virtual Viewport feature is enabled, you can use the divide key (/) on the numeric keypad to turn the virtual viewport on and off. Use the plus (+) and minus (–) numeric keypad keys to zoom in and out, and use the 2, 4, 6, and 8 keys on the numeric keypad to pan within the virtual viewport.

 The Virtual Viewport feature is available only if you are using the OpenGL driver. If you've specified either the Software Z-Buffer or the Direct X driver, then this option isn't available.

Viewing statistics

The Statistics panel, shown in Figure 2.24, lets you display valuable statistics in the viewport window. These statistics can include Polygon Count, Triangle Count, Edge Count, Vertex Count, and Frames Per Second. You can also select to view these statistics for all the objects in the scene (Total), for just the selected object, or for both. Statistics can be toggled on and off for the active viewport using the 7 key.

FIGURE 2.24

The Statistics panel lets you display polygon count and frames per second in the viewport.

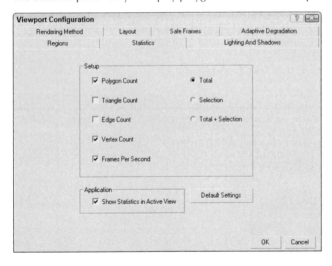

By enabling the Show Statistics in Active View option, the selected statistics are overlaid on the active viewport, as shown in Figure 2.25.

Displaying Lights and Shadows

The final Viewport Configuration panel is the Lighting and Shadows panel, shown in Figure 2.26. This panel sets the default Viewport Shading method, which is used to show lights and shadows interactively in the viewport.

NEW FEATURE The ability to interactively view lights and shadows in the viewport is new to 3ds Max 2008.

FIGURE 2.25

The active viewport can be set to display the selected statistics.

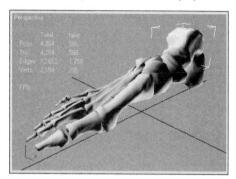

FIGURE 2.26

The Lighting and Shadows panel includes default settings for displaying interactive lights and shadows in the viewport.

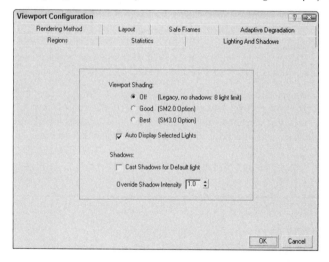

The options available in the Lighting and Shadows panel are Off, which shows no shadows and limits the lights to 8; Good, which allows interactive lights and fast shadowing; and Best, which allows high-quality per pixel shadowing with up to 64 concurrent lights.

Previewing shadows in the viewport requires the Direct3D driver to be used and your video card must support Shader Model 2.0 (for the Good display option) or Shader Model 3.0 (for the Best display option). You can check to see which viewport shading method you can use by selecting the Views ⇨ Diagnose Video Hardware menu command. This runs a script that reports its findings in the MAXScript Listener window, as shown in Figure 2.27.

FIGURE 2.27

The Views ➪ Diagnose Video Hardware menu runs a script in the Listener window that shows which shading method is supported by your video card.

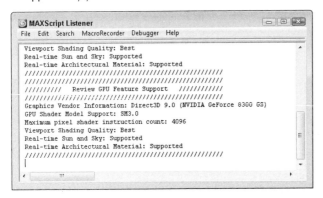

Another option, Auto Display Selected Lights, is helpful when you're working on placing and aiming lights in the scene. It causes the selected light to automatically be displayed in the shaded viewport. This option also can be enabled using the right-click quadmenu.

For the Shadows options, you can enable a setting to Cast Shadows for Default Light, which is a good idea if you're placing objects. It allows you to see if they are positioned where the shadows are cast on them. You also can override the Shadow Intensity to dim the shadows if they are too dark.

Regardless of the option selected in the Lighting and Shadows panel, you can change the Viewport Shading mode and settings at any time by right-clicking in the active viewport and selecting the Viewport Lighting and Shadows ➪ Viewport Shading menu in the quadmenu. The quadmenu also includes options for locking lights and enabling shadows. Figure 2-28 shows the results in the viewport for the Off, Good, and Best options.

FIGURE 2.28

Viewport Shading can be set to Off, Good, or Best.

To enable lighting and shadows in the viewports, follow these steps:

1. Open the Foot bones.max file from the Chap 02 directory on the DVD.

   This file includes a set of foot bones created by Viewpoint Datalabs. There is also an Omni light added to the scene.

2. Right-click in the viewport and select Viewport Lighting and Shadows ⇨ Viewport Shading ⇨ Best from the pop-up quadmenu.

   If shadows are enabled for the light, then you'll see them in the viewport. If you don't see any shadows, then select the light object and choose the Viewport Lighting and Shadows ⇨ Enable Viewport Shadows Selected option from the pop-up quadmenu.

3. Click on the Select and Move toolbar button and drag the light object about the scene.

   The shadows under the foot bones are automatically updated as the light is moved, as shown in Figure 2.29.

FIGURE 2.29

Lights and shadows are updated in real time when the light is moved about the scene.

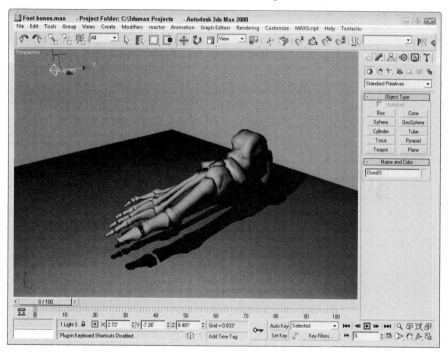

Working with Viewport Backgrounds

Remember in grade school when you realized that you could immediately draw really well using tracing paper (where all you needed to do was follow the lines)? Well, it's not quite tracing paper, but you can load background images into a viewport that can help as you create and position your objects.

Loading viewport background images

The Views ⇨ Viewport Background menu command (Alt+B) opens a dialog box, shown in Figure 2.30, in which you can select an image or animation to appear behind a viewport. Each viewport can have a different background image. The displayed background image is helpful for aligning objects in a scene, but it is for display purposes only and will not be rendered. To create a background image to be rendered, you need to specify the background in the Environment dialog box, opened using the Rendering ⇨ Environment (keyboard shortcut, 8) menu command.

FIGURE 2.30

The Viewport Background dialog box lets you select a background source image or animation.

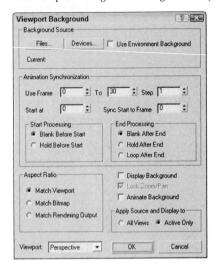

If the background image changes, you can update the viewport using the Views ⇨ Update Background Image menu command (Alt+Shift+Ctrl+B). This is helpful if you have the background image opened in Photoshop at the same time. You can update the background image, save it, and then immediately update the image in Max. The Views ⇨ Reset Background Transform menu command automatically rescales and re-centers the background image to fit the viewport. You should use this if you've changed the viewport size or changed the background's size.

The Files button opens the Select Background Image dialog box, where you can select the image to load. The Devices button lets you obtain a background from a device such as a Video Recorder. If an environment map is already loaded into the Environment dialog box, you can simply click the Use Environment Background option. Keep in mind that the background image will not be rendered unless it is made into an Environment map.

CROSS-REF Environment maps are covered in Chapter 22, "Learning to Render a Scene."

Loading viewport background animations

The Animation Synchronization section of the Viewport Background dialog box lets you set which frames of a background animation sequence are displayed. The Use Frame and To values determine which frames of the loaded animation are used. The Step value trims the number of frames that are to be used by selecting every Nth frame. For example, a Step value of 4 would use every fourth frame.

TIP Loading an animation sequence as a viewport background can really help as you begin to animate complex motions, like a running horse. By stepping through the frames of the animation, you can line up your model with the background image for realistic animations.

The Start At value is the frame in the current scene where this background animation would first appear. The Sync Start to Frame value is the frame of the background animation that should appear first. The Start and End Processing options let you determine what appears before the Start and End frames. Options include displaying a blank, holding the current frame, and looping.

If you select an animation as the background, make sure that the Animate Background option is selected. Also note that the viewport background is not visible if the Display Background option is not selected.

The Aspect Ratio section offers options for setting the size of the background image. You can select to Match Viewport, Match Bitmap, or Match Rendering Output.

The Lock Zoom/Pan option is available if either the Match Bitmap option or the Match Rendering Output option is selected. This option locks the background image to the geometry so that when the objects in the scene are zoomed or panned, the background image follows. If the background gets out of line, you can reset its position with the Views ⇨ Reset Background Transform command.

CAUTION When the Lock Zoom/Pan option is selected, the background image is resized when you zoom in on an object. Resizing the background image fills the virtual memory, and if you zoom in too far, the background image could exceed your virtual memory. If this happens, a dialog box appears to inform you of the problem and gives you the option of not displaying the background image.

You can set the Apply Source and Display to option to display the background in All Views or in the active viewport only.

Tutorial: Loading reference images for modeling

When modeling a physical object, you can get a jump on the project by taking pictures with a digital camera of the front, top, and left views of the object and then load them as background images in the respective viewports. The background images can then be a reference for your work. This is especially helpful with models that need to be precise. You can even work from CAD drawings.

To load the background images of a brass swan, follow these steps:

1. Choose File ⇨ New (or press Ctrl+N) to open a blank scene file.
2. Right-click on the Front viewport to make it the active viewport, and choose Views ⇨ Viewport Background (or press Alt+B).

   The Viewport Background dialog box opens.
3. Click on the Files button, and in the File dialog box that opens, select the Brass swan-front view.jpg image from the Chap 02 directory on the DVD.
4. Select the Match Bitmap, Display Background, Lock Zoom/Pan, and Active Only options, and click OK to close the dialog box.

   The image now appears in the background of the Front viewport.
5. Repeat Steps 2 through 4 for the Top and Left viewports.

Figure 2.31 shows the Max interface with background images loaded in the Front, Top, and Left viewports.

FIGURE 2.31

Adding a background image to a viewport can help as you begin to model objects.

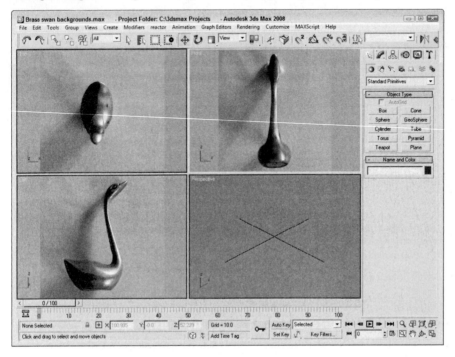

Summary

Viewports are the window into the Max world. Remember that if you can't see it, you can't work with it, so you need to learn to use the viewports. You can also configure viewports to display just the way you desire.

This chapter covered the following topics:

- 3D space and the various viewport types
- The various Viewport Navigation Control buttons
- The Rendering Level and Display options in the Viewport Configuration dialog box
- The other panels of the Viewport Configuration dialog box that allow you to change the layout, safe frames, regions, statistics, and viewport shading options.
- How to use Adaptive Degradation to maintain a constant frame rate for viewports
- A viewport background image

In the next chapter, you find out all the details about working with files, including loading, saving, and merging scene files. The next chapter also covers import and export options for interfacing with other software packages.

Chapter 3

Working with Files, Importing, and Exporting

IN THIS CHAPTER

Saving, opening, merging, and archiving files

Importing and exporting objects and scenes

Importing objects from external packages such as Illustrator

Working with file utilities such as the Asset Browser

Accessing scene files' information

Complex scenes can end up being a collection of hundreds of files, and misplacing any of them will affect the final output, so learning to work with files is critical. This chapter focuses on working with files, whether they are object files, texture images, or background images. Files enable you to move scene pieces into and out of Max. You can also export and import files to and from other packages.

Working with Max Scene Files

Of all the different file types and formats, there is one file type that you probably will work with more than any other — the max format. Max has its own proprietary format for its scene files. These files have the .max extension and allow you to save your work as a file and return to it at a later time. Max also supports files saved with the .chr extension used for character files.

When Max starts, a new scene opens. You can start a new scene at any time with the File ⇨ New (Ctrl+N) command. Although each instance of Max can have only one scene open at a time, under Windows XP, you can open multiple copies of Max, each with its own scene instance.

Starting a new scene deletes the current scene, but Max asks you whether you want to keep the objects and hierarchy, keep the objects, or make everything new, as shown in Figure 3.1. Starting a new scene with the File ⇨ New menu command maintains all the current interface settings, including the viewport configurations, any interface changes, viewport backgrounds, and any changes to the Command Panel. To reset the interface, choose File ⇨ Reset. When reset, all interface settings return to their default states, but interface changes aren't affected.

FIGURE 3.1

When creating a new scene, you can keep the current objects or select New All.

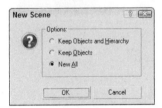

Saving files

After you start up Max, the first thing you should learn is how to save your work. After a scene has changed, you can save it as a file. Before a file is saved, the word "Untitled" appears in the title bar; after you save the file, its name appears in the title bar. Choose File ➪ Save (Ctrl+S) to save the scene. If the scene hasn't been saved yet, then a Save File As dialog box appears, as shown in Figure 3.2. You can also make this dialog box appear using the File ➪ Save As command. After a file has been saved, using the File ➪ Save command saves the file without opening the File dialog box. Pretty simple — just don't forget to do it often.

FIGURE 3.2

Use the Save File As dialog box to save a scene as a file.

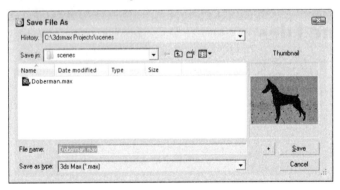

The Save File As dialog box keeps a history list of the last five directories that you've opened. You can select these directories from the History drop-down list at the top of the dialog box. The buttons in this dialog box are the standard Windows file dialog box buttons used to go to the last folder visited, go up one directory, create a new folder, and to view a pop-up menu of file view options. The options include Thumbnails, Tiles, Icons, List, and Details. The thumbnail option displays an image of the active viewport, which is useful when you open files, but when you save files for the first time, the thumbnail is blank.

NOTE   If you try to save a scene over the top of an existing scene, Max presents a dialog box confirming this action.

 Clicking the button with a plus sign to the right of the Save button automatically appends a number onto the end of the current filename and saves the file. For example, if you select the myScene.max file and click the plus button, a file named myScene01.max is saved.

TIP Use the auto increment file number and Save button to save progressive versions of a scene. This is an easy version control system. If you need to backtrack to an earlier version, you can.

The File menu also includes an option to Save Selected. This option saves the current selected objects to a separate scene file. If you create a single object that you might use again, select the object and use the Save Selected option to save it to a directory of models. A File ⇨ Save Copy As menu command also is available that lets you save the current scene to a different name without changing its current name.

Another useful feature for saving files is to enable the Auto Backup feature in the Files panel of the Preference Settings dialog box. This dialog box can be accessed with the Customize ⇨ Preferences menu command, which is covered later in this chapter.

Opening files

When you want to open a file you've saved, you may do so by choosing File ⇨ Open (Ctrl+O), which opens a file dialog box that is the same as the one used to save files, as shown in Figure 3.2. Max can open files saved with the .max and .chr extensions. Max also can open VIZ Render files that have the .drf extension. Selecting a file and clicking the plus button opens a copy of the selected file with a new version number appended to its name.

If Max cannot locate resources used within a scene (such as maps) when you open a Max file, then the Missing External Files dialog box, shown in Figure 3.3, appears, enabling you to Continue without the file or to Browse for the missing files. If you click the Browse button, the Configure External File Paths dialog box opens, where you can add a path to the missing files.

FIGURE 3.3

The Missing External Files dialog box identifies files for the current scene that are missing.

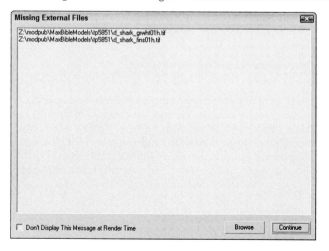

If you open a file that includes features that have changed since the previous version, then Max presents an obsolete data format warning statement. Resaving the file can fix this problem. However, if you save a file created with a previous version of Max as a Max 2008 scene file, then you won't be able to open the file again in the previous versions of Max.

 **You can disable the Obsolete File Message in the Files panel of the Preference Settings dialog box.**

The most recently opened scenes are listed in the File ➪ Open Recent submenu. Selecting these scenes from the list opens the scene file.

You can also open files from the command line by placing the filename after the executable name, i.e., 3dsmax.exe myFile.max. You can also use the –L switch after the executable name to open the last file that was opened.

Setting a Project Folder

By default, Max opens to the Scenes directory where Max is installed, but you can set a Project Folder that may be located anywhere on your local hard drive or on the network. All file dialog boxes will then open to the new project folder automatically. The File ➪ Set Project Folder menu opens a dialog box where you can select a project folder. After a project folder is selected, the folder is automatically populated with a series of resource folders.

Within the project folder's root is a file with the .mxp extension named the same as the project folder. This file is a simple text file that can be opened within a text editor. Editing this file lets you define which sub-folders are created within the project folder. The defined project folder also is visible within the title bar.

Merging and replacing objects

If you happen to create the perfect prop in one scene and want to integrate the prop into another scene, you can use the Merge menu command. Choose File ➪ Merge to load objects from another scene into the current scene. Using this menu command opens a file dialog box that is exactly like the Save As dialog box, but after you select a scene and click the Open button, the Merge dialog box, shown in Figure 3.4, appears. This dialog box displays all the objects found in the selected scene file. It also has options for sorting the objects and filtering certain types of objects. Selecting an object and clicking the OK button loads the object into the current scene.

 **The Merge dialog box is very similar to the Select Objects dialog box.**

If you ever get involved in a modeling duel, then you'll probably be using the File ➪ Replace menu command at some time. A modeling duel is when two modelers work on the same rough model of named objects and the animator (or boss) gets to choose which object to use. With the File ➪ Replace menu command, you can replace a named object with an object of the same name in a different scene. The objects are selected using the same dialog box shown in Figure 3.4, but only the objects with identical names in both scene files display. If no objects with the same name appear in both scene files, a warning box is displayed.

FIGURE 3.4

The Merge dialog box lists all the objects from a merging scene.

Archiving files

By archiving a Max scene along with its reference bitmaps, you can ensure that the file includes all the necessary files. This is especially useful if you need to send the project to your cousin to show off or to your boss and you don't want to miss any ancillary files. Choose File ➪ Archive to save all scene files as a compressed archive. The default archive format is .zip (but you can change it in the Files panel of the Preference Settings dialog box to use whatever archive format you want). The Archive System lets you specify which archive program Max uses to archive your files. Maxzip is the default, but you can change it to whichever program you want to use.

Saving an archive as a .zip file compiles all external files, such as bitmaps, into a single compressed file. The File Type drop-down list of the File Archive dialog box also includes an option to create a List of Files. When you select this file type, a text file is created that lists all relevant files and their paths.

Getting out

As you can probably guess, you use the File ➪ Exit command to exit the program, but only after it gives you a chance to save your work. Clicking on the window icon with an X on it in the upper right has the same effect (but I'm sure you knew that).

Setting File Preferences

The Files panel of the Preference Settings dialog box holds the controls for backing up, archiving, and logging Max files. You can open this dialog box using the Customize ➪ Preferences menu command. Figure 3.5 shows this panel.

FIGURE 3.5

The Files panel includes an Auto Backup feature.

Handling files

The Files panel includes several options that define how to handle files. The first option is to Convert File Paths to UNC (Universal Naming Convention). This option displays file paths using the Universal Naming Convention for any files accessed over a mapped drive. The Convert Local File Paths to Relative option causes all paths to be saved internally as relative paths to the project folder. This is useful if all files you access are in the same folder, but if you use files such as bitmaps from a different folder, then be sure to disable this option.

The next option is Backup on Save. When you save a file using the File ⇨ Save (Ctrl+S) menu command, the existing file is overwritten. The Backup on Save option causes the current scene file to be saved as a backup (with the name MaxBack.bak in the 3dsmax\autobak directory) before saving the new file. If the changes you made were a mistake, you can recover the file before the last changes by renaming the MaxBack.bak file to MaxBack.max and reopening it in Max.

Another option to prevent overwriting your changes is the Increment on Save option. This option adds an incremented number to the end of the existing filename every time it is saved. This retains multiple copies of the file and is an easy version-control method for your scene files. This way, you can always go back to an earlier file when the client changes his mind. With this option enabled, the MaxBack.bak file isn't used.

The Compress on Save option compresses the file automatically when it is saved. Compressed files require less file space but take longer to load. If you're running low on hard drive space, then you'll want to enable this option.

 **Another reason to enable the Compress on Save option is that large files (100MB or greater) load into the Network Queue Manager much more quickly when compressed for network rendering.**

The Save Viewport Thumbnail Image option saves a 64 × 64-pixel thumbnail of the active viewport along with the file. This thumbnail is displayed in the Open dialog box and can also be seen from Windows Explorer on Windows XP, as shown in Figure 3.6. Saving a thumbnail with a scene adds about 9K to the file size.

 **TIP** The Save Viewport Thumbnail Image option is another good option to keep enabled. Thumbnails help you to find scene files later, and nothing is more frustrating than seeing a scene's filename without a thumbnail.

FIGURE 3.6

Max files with thumbnails show up in Windows Explorer on Windows XP.

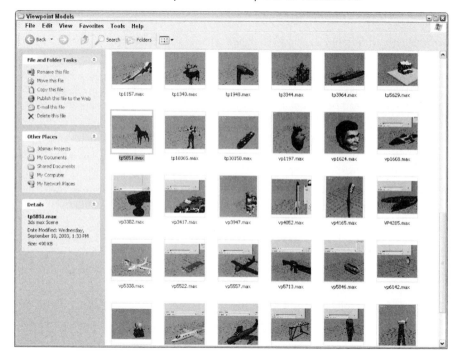

NOTE Windows Vista doesn't currently support displaying Max thumbnails.

In addition to a thumbnail, Max also offers an option to save the Schematic View with the file. Although Max can generate a new Schematic View from an existing file, saving the Schematic View with the file is quicker if you work with this view often. Saving File Properties with the file is also helpful, but be warned that saving this extra info with the file increases its file size slightly. Still, doing so is worth the effort because you can easily locate and understand the scene file later on.

When a Max file created in a previous version of Max is opened, a warning dialog box appears that says, "Obsolete data format found — Please resave file." To eliminate this warning, disable the Display Obsolete File Message option. The warning dialog box also includes an option to Don't Display Again that enables this option when selected.

When textures are updated, the Reload Textures on Change option forces the textures to be reloaded when they are altered. This slows your system while Max waits for the textures to reload, but offers the latest look immediately.

The Recent Files in File Menu option determines the number of recently opened files that appear in the File ⇨ Open Recent menu. The maximum value is 50.

Backing up files

The Auto Backup feature in Max can save you from the nightmare of losing all your work because of a system crash. With Auto Backup enabled, you can select the number of Autobak files to keep around and how often the files are backed up. The backup files are saved to the directory specified by the Configure Paths dialog box. The default is to save these backups to the 3dsmax\autoback directory. You can also select a name for the backup files.

NOTE   **Even if you have this feature enabled, you should still save your file often.**

This is how it works: If you've set the number of backup files to 2, the interval to 5 minutes, and the backup name to MyBackup, then after five minutes the current file is saved as MyBackup1.max. After another five minutes, another file named MyBackup2.max is saved, and then after another five minutes, the MyBackup1.max file is overwritten with the latest changes.

If you lose your work as a result of a power failure or by having your toddler accidentally pull out the plug, you can recover your work by locating the Autobak file with the latest date and reloading it into Max. This file won't include all the latest changes — only updates up to the last backup save.

TIP   **I highly recommend that you keep the Auto Backup option enabled. This feature has saved my bacon more than once. Also, if you enter a different autoback name for different projects, then you won't accidentally overwrite a backed-up project.**

Tutorial: Setting Auto Backup

Now that I have stressed that setting up Auto Backup is an important step to do, let's run through exactly how to set it up.

To set up the Auto Backup feature, follow these steps:

1. Open the Preference Settings dialog box by choosing Customize ⇨ Preferences, and click the Files panel.
2. Turn on Auto Backup by selecting the Enable option in the Auto Backup section.
3. Set the number of Autobak files to **5**.

NOTE   **To maintain version control of your Max scenes, use the Increment on Save feature instead of increasing the Number of Autobak Files.**

4. Set the Backup Interval to the amount of time to wait between backups.

   The Backup Interval should be set to the maximum amount of work that you are willing to redo. (I keep my settings at 15 minutes.) You can also give the Auto Backup file a name.

5. Auto Backup saves the files in the directory specified by the Auto Backup path. To view where this path is located, choose Customize ⇨ Configure Paths.

Maintaining log files

You can also use the Files panel to control log files. Log files keep track of any errors and warnings, general command info, and any debugging information. You can set log files to never be deleted, expire after so many days, or keep a specified file size with the latest information. If your system is having trouble, checking the error log gives you some idea as to what the problem is. Logs are essential if you plan on developing any custom scripts or plug-ins. You can select that the log contain all Errors, Warnings, Info, and Debug statements.

Each entry in the log file includes a date-time stamp and a three-letter designation of the type of message with DBG for debug, INF for info, WRN for warning, and ERR for error messages followed by the message. The name of the log file is Max.log. It is saved in the 3dsmax\network subdirectory.

Importing and Exporting

If you haven't noticed, Max isn't the only game in town. A number of different 3D packages exist, and exchanging files between them is where the importing and exporting menu commands come in. You can find both of these commands in the File menu.

Importing supported formats

Choose File ➪ Import to open the Import dialog box. This dialog box looks like a typical Windows file dialog box. The real power comes with the various Import Settings dialog boxes that are available for each format. The settings in the Import Settings dialog box are different for the various format types.

Another common import dialog box offers options to merge the imported objects with the current scene or to completely replace the current scene. For many formats, you can also convert units on the imported file. For example, importing a 3D Studio file opens a simple dialog box, shown in Figure 3.7. With the Convert Units option selected, Max assumes that the 3DS file is based in inches and converts it to the currently defined units.

FIGURE 3.7

The 3DS Import dialog box enables you to merge objects into or completely replace the current scene.

If any of the object names in the imported scene match those in the current scene, an Import Name Conflict dialog box opens, allowing you to rename the imported objects, or you can Skip or Cancel the import.

Max can import several different formats, including the following:

- Autodesk (FBX, DAE)
- 3D Studio Mesh, Projects, and Shapes (3DS, PRJ, SHP)

- Adobe Illustrator (AI)
- LandXML/DEM/DDF
- AutoCAD (DWG, DXF)
- Motion Analysis (HTR, TRC)
- Initial Graphics Exchange Standard (IGE, IGS, IGES)
- Autodesk Inventor (IPT, IAM)
- Lightscape (LS, VW, LP)
- StereoLithography (STL)
- Wavefront Material and Object (MTL, OBJ)
- VRML (WRL, WRZ)
- VIZ Material XML Import (XML)

NEW FEATURE The AutoCAD DWG import has been improved in 3ds Max 2008. The improvements include the ability to import mapping type and UVs. It also includes support for Daylight systems.

Import preference

The Files panel of the Preference Settings dialog box has a single option dealing with importing — Zoom Extents on Import. When this option is enabled, it automatically zooms all viewports to the extent of the imported objects. Imported objects can often be scaled so small that they aren't even visible. This option helps you to locate an object when imported.

Exporting supported formats

In addition to importing, you'll sometimes want to export Max objects for use in other programs. You access the Export command by choosing File ⇨ Export. You also have the option to Export Selected (available only if an object is selected).

Max can export to several different formats, including the following:

- Autodesk (FBX)
- 3D Studio (3DS)
- Adobe Illustrator (AI)
- ASCII Scene Export (ASE)
- AutoCAD (DWG, DXF)
- Initial Graphics Exchange Standard (IGS)
- JSR-184 (M3G)
- Lightscape Material, Blocks, Parameters, Layers, Preparations, and Views (ATR, BLK, DF, LAY, LP, VW)
- Motion Analysis (HTR)
- Publish to DWF (DWF)
- Wavefront Material and Object (MTL, OBJ)
- StereoLithography (STL)
- Shockwave 3D Scene Export (W3D)
- VRML97 (WRL)

Moving files to and from Maya and MotionBuilder

Autodesk has a host of other products that deal with 3D including Maya and MotionBuilder, so you may find yourself having to move scene files between Max and Maya at some time. The best format to transport files among Max, Maya, and MotionBuilder is the FBX format. Autodesk controls this format and has endowed it with the ability to seamlessly transport files among these packages.

 The FBX format also is the format to choose when transferring files back and forth with Softimage XSI.

The FBX format includes support for all the scene constructs, including animation, bone systems, morph targets, and animation cache files. It has an option to embed textures with the export file or to convert them to the TIF format. Other import and export settings deal with the system units and world coordinate orientation. You also have the ability to filter specific objects. The FBX Import and FBX Export dialog boxes are shown in Figure 3.8.

 The FBX import/export option supports the Collada (DAE) file format, which is a group working to establish a universal format for exchanging 3D data.

FIGURE 3.8

The FBX Import and Export dialog boxes provide the best way of transferring among Max, Maya, and MotionBuilder.

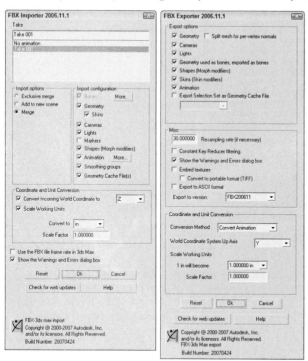

Exporting to the JSR-184 (M3G) format

The JSR-184 export option lets you save a scene to a format that can be viewed on mobile devices that support the Java 2 Micro Edition standard interface, such as mobile phones and PDA devices.

Because wireless devices have such a limited bandwidth, the JSR-184 Exporter dialog box, shown in Figure 3.9, includes several options for optimizing the exported scene. This dialog box lists the Max scene hierarchy, the JSR-184 scene hierarchy, and the parameters for the selected scene object. Using the toolbar buttons at the top of the dialog box, you can change the hierarchy that is to be exported.

FIGURE 3.9

The JSR-184 Export dialog box lets you choose which resources to export.

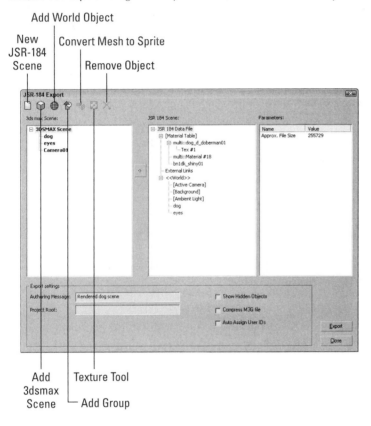

Before a scene can be exported, the Max scene must include a camera and you must specify an Active Camera in the JSR-184 Exported dialog box. When a material map is selected from the JSR-184 hierarchy list, the Texture Tool icon on the toolbar becomes active. Clicking this button opens the Texture Tool dialog box, shown in Figure 3.10, where you can precisely control the size and format of the exported maps.

To view the exported M3G files, the default installation of Max includes an M3G Player, which can be found along with the other Max programs in Start ➪ Programs ➪ Autodesk ➪ 3ds Max 2008 ➪ JSR Viewer. To use this player, the Java Runtime Environment needs to be installed. You can install it from the Max setup disc.

NOTE The JSR Viewer application is built using Java. If you're having trouble with the viewer, try installing the latest Java version from the installation DVD.

FIGURE 3.10

The Texture Tool lets you specify the exact size of texture maps to be exported for mobile devices.

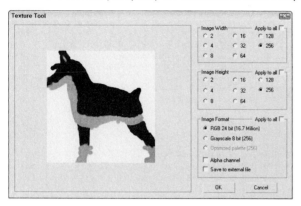

Exporting to the DWF format

The Design Web Format (DWF) is an ideal format for displaying your textured models to others via the Web. It creates relatively small files that can be attached easily to an email. You can use the File ➪ Publish to DWF menu command to export the current scene to this format. This command opens a dialog box of options that specify to Group by Object or Group by Layer. You also can choose to publish the Object Properties, Materials, Selected Objects Only, or Hidden Objects. Another option is to Rescale Bitmaps to a size entered in pixels.

Saved files can be viewed in the Autodesk DWF Viewer, shown in Figure 3.11. The Autodesk DWF Viewer can be downloaded for free from the Autodesk Web site. This provides a way for users without Max installed to view models.

The Autodesk DWF Viewer is automatically installed along with 3ds Max. If you want to view the exported files in the viewer, simply enable the Show DWF in Viewer option in the DWF Publish Options dialog box. The viewer includes controls for transforming the model, changing its shading and view, and printing the current view.

Exporting utilities

In addition to the menu commands found in the File menu, Max includes a couple of utilities that export specific information: the Lighting Data Export Utility and the Material XML Exporter Utility. You can access these utilities from the Utilities panel in the Command Panel by clicking the More button and selecting them from the pop-up list that appears.

Lighting Data Export Utility

The Lighting Data Export Utility exports exposure control data for a scene's Illuminance and Luminance values. These files can be saved as PIC or TIF files, which you can select in the 2D Lighting Data Exporter rollout. You also can set an image's Width and Height dimensions.

FIGURE 3.11

The Autodesk DWF Viewer is used to view files exported using the DWF format.

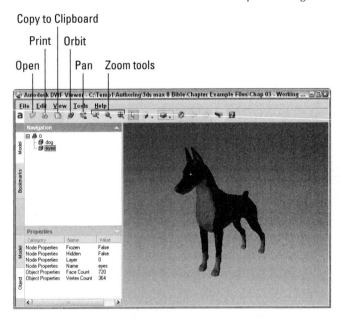

CAUTION Exposure Control must be enabled for this utility to be enabled. You can learn about exposure control in Chapter 45, "Using Atmospheric and Render Effects."

Material XML Exporter Utility

The Material XML Exporter Utility exports a selected material to an XML file format, where it can be easily shared with other users. After you select this utility, the Parameters rollout offers four options for selecting the material to export: the Material/Map Browser, the Object List, Pick Object in Scene, and All Objects in Scene.

The utility also offers several export options including Native XML, export to an Autodesk Tool Catalog, and using an XSLT template. You also can select to export the material with a thumbnail and along with its mapping modifiers.

Tutorial: Importing vector drawings from Illustrator

In most companies, a professional creative team uses an advanced vector drawing tool such as Illustrator to design the company logo. If you need to work with such a logo, learning how to import the externally created file gives you a jumpstart on your project.

NOTE When importing vector-based files into Max, only the lines are imported. Max cannot import fills, blends, or other specialized vector effects. All imported lines are automatically converted to Bézier splines in Max.

Although Max can draw and work with splines, this feature takes a backseat to the vector functions available in Adobe Illustrator. If you have an Illustrator (AI) file, you can import it directly into Max.

To import Adobe Illustrator files into Max, follow these steps:

1. Within Illustrator, save your file as "Box It Up Co logo" using the .AI file format by choosing File ⇨ Save As.

 When saving the Illustrator file, don't use the latest file format. For this example, I've saved the file using the Illustrator 8 format instead of the latest Illustrator CS, CS2, or CS3 formats.

Figure 3.12 shows a logo created using Illustrator.

FIGURE 3.12

A company logo created in Illustrator and ready to save and import into Max

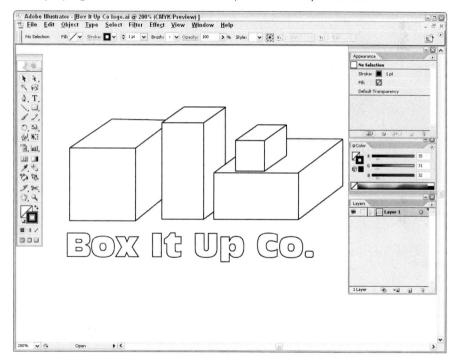

2. Open Max, and choose File ⇨ Import.

   A file dialog box opens.

3. Select Adobe Illustrator (AI) as the File Type. Locate the file to import, and click OK.

   The AI Import dialog box asks whether you want to merge the objects with the current scene or replace the current scene.

4. For our purposes, select the replace the current scene option and click OK.

5. The Shape Import dialog box asks whether you want to import the shapes as single or multiple objects. Select multiple, and click OK.

Figure 3.13 shows the logo after it has been imported into Max. Notice that all the fills are missing.

FIGURE 3.13

A company logo created in Illustrator and imported into Max

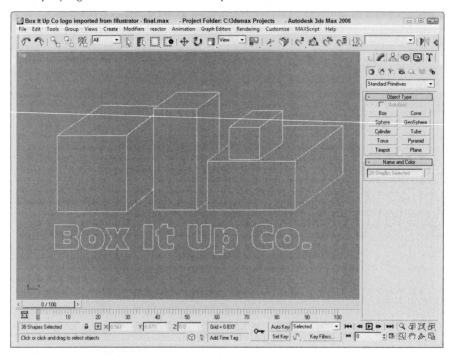

CROSS-REF Spline objects that are imported from Illustrator appear in Max as Editable Spline objects. You can learn more about Editable Splines in Chapter 11, "Drawing and Editing 2D Splines and Shapes."

Using the File Utilities

With all these various files floating around, Max has included several utilities that make working with them easier. The Utilities panel of the Command Panel includes several useful utilities for working with files. You can access these utilities by opening the Utilities panel and clicking the More button to see a list of available utilities.

Using the Asset Browser utility

The Asset Browser utility is the first default button in the Utility panel. Clicking this button opens the Asset Browser window. The Asset Browser resembles Windows Explorer, except that it displays thumbnail images of all the supported formats contained within the current directory. Using this window, shown in Figure 3.14, you can browse through directory files and see thumbnails of images and scenes.

FIGURE 3.14

The Asset Browser window displays thumbnails of the files in the current directory.

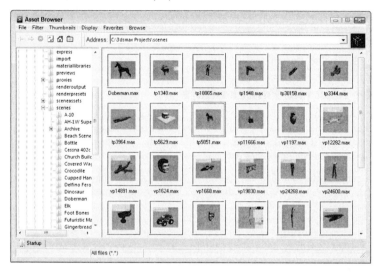

The supported file types include AVI, BMP, CIN, CEL, DDS, GIF, HDRI, IFL, IPP, JPEG, MPEG, PNG, PSD, MOV, RGB, RLA, RPF, VST, TIF, and YUV. These types are the same ones that the File ➪ View File command can open. All files with these extensions are viewable within the Asset Browser. You can select to view only a certain type of file using the Filter menu. You also can view and filter MAXScript and AutoCAD DWG files.

TIP Open and display the Asset Manager within a viewport by right-clicking the viewport title and choosing Views ➪ Extended ➪ Asset Manager from the pop-up menu.

You also can drag and drop files from the Asset Browser window to Max. Drag a scene file, and drop it on Max's title bar to open the scene file within Max. You can drop image files onto the map buttons in the Material Editor window or drop an image file onto a viewport to make a dialog box appear, which lets you apply the image as an Environment Map or as a Viewport Background, respectively.

The Asset Browser window is modeless, so you can work with the Max interface while the Asset Browser window is open. Double-clicking an image opens it full size in the Rendered Frame window.

The Asset Browser also can act as a Web browser to look at content online. When the Asset Browser first opens, a dialog box reminds you that online content may be copyrighted and cannot be used without consent from the owner.

The Display menu includes three panes that you can select. The Thumbnail pane shows the files as thumbnails. You can change the size of these thumbnails using the Thumbnails menu. The Explorer pane displays the files as icons the same as you would see in Windows Explorer. The Web pane displays the Web page for the site listed in the Address field.

To view Web sites, you need to be connected to the Internet. The Asset Browser can remember your favorite Web sites using the Favorites menu. The Asset Browser window also includes the standard Web browser navigation buttons, such as Back, Forward, Home, Refresh, and Stop. You also can find these commands in the Browse menu.

Max keeps thumbnails of all the images you access in its cache. The cache is a directory that holds thumbnails of all the recently accessed images. Each thumbnail image points to the actual directory where the image is located. Choose File ⇨ Preferences to open the Preferences dialog box, in which you can specify where you want the cache directory to be located. To view the cached files, choose Filter ⇨ All in Cache. The Preferences dialog box also includes options to define how to handle dropped files. The options include Always Merge or Import, Always XRef, or Ask Each Time.

Choose File ⇨ Print to print the file view or Web window.

Finding files with the Max File Finder utility

Another useful utility for locating files is the Max File Finder utility, which you get to by using the More button in the Utilities panel. When you select this utility, a rollout with a Start button appears in the Utility panel. Clicking this button opens the MAXFinder dialog box. Using MAXFinder, you can search for scene files by any of the information listed in the File Properties dialog box.

You can use the Browse button to specify the root directory to search. You can select to have the search also examine any subfolders. Figure 3.15 shows the MAXFinder dialog box locating all the scene files that include the word *blue*.

FIGURE 3.15

You can use the MAXFinder utility to search for scene files by property.

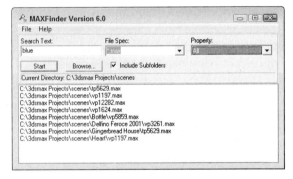

Collecting files with the Resource Collector utility

When a scene is created, image and object files can be pulled from several different locations. The Resource Collector utility helps you consolidate all these files into one location. The settings for this utility appear in the Parameters rollout in the Utility panel of the Command Panel, as shown in Figure 3.16. The Output Path is the location where the files are collected. You can change this location using the Browse button.

The utility includes options to Collect Bitmaps, to include the Max scene file, and to compress the files into a compressed WinZip file. The Copy option makes copies of the files, and the Move option moves the actual file into the directory specified in the Output Path field. The Update Materials option updates all material paths in the Material Editor. When you're comfortable with the settings, click the Begin button to start the collecting.

FIGURE 3.16

The Resource Collector utility can compile all referenced files into a single location.

Using the File Link Manager utility

The File Link Manager utility (which also can be accessed using the File ➪ File Link Manager menu) lets you use external AutoCAD files in the same way that you use Max's XRef features. By creating links between the current Max scene and an external AutoCAD file, you can reload the linked file when the external AutoCAD file has been updated and see the updates within Max.

This utility is divided into three panels — Attach, Files, and Presets. The Attach panel includes a File button to select and open a DWG or DXF file. The Attach panel also includes options to rescale the file units, a button to select which layers to include, and a button to attach the file. The Files panel displays each linked AutoCAD file along with icons to show if the linked file has changed. A Reload button allows you to click to reload the linked file within Max. The Preset panel lets you define file linking presets.

Using i-drop

To make accessing needed files from the Web even easier, Autodesk has created a technology known as i-drop that lets you drag files from i-drop–supported Web pages and drop them directly into Max. With i-drop, you can drag and drop Max-created light fixture models, textures, or any other Max-supported file from a light manufacturer's Web site into your scene without importing and positioning a file. This format allows you to add geometry, photometric data, and materials.

Accessing File Information

As you work with files, several dialog boxes in Max supply you with extra information about your scene. You can use this information to keep track of files and record valuable statistics about a scene.

Displaying scene information

If you like to keep statistics on your files (to see whether you've broken the company record for the model with the greatest number of faces), you'll find the Summary Info dialog box useful. Use the File ➪ Summary Info menu command to open a dialog box that displays all the relevant details about the current scene, such as the number of objects, lights, and cameras; the total number of vertices and faces; and various model settings, as well as a Description field where you can describe the scene. Figure 3.17 shows the Summary Info dialog box.

The Summary Info dialog box shows all the basic information about the current scene.

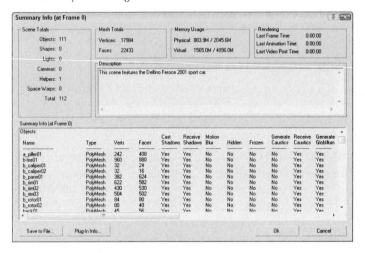

The Plug-In Info button on the Summary Info dialog box displays a list of all the plug-ins currently installed on your system. Even without any external plug-ins installed, the list is fairly long because many of the core features in Max are implemented as plug-ins. The Summary Info dialog box also includes a Save to File button for saving the scene summary information as a text file.

Viewing file properties

As the number of files on your system increases, you'll be wishing you had a card catalog to keep track of them all. Max has an interface that you can use to attach keywords and other descriptive information about the scene to the file. The File ⇨ File Properties menu command opens the File Properties dialog box. This dialog box, shown in Figure 3.18, includes three panels: Summary, Contents, and Custom. The Summary panel holds information such as the Title, Subject, and Author of the Max file and can be useful for managing a collaborative project. The Contents panel holds information about the scene such as the total number of objects and much more. Much of this information also is found in the Summary Info dialog box. The Custom panel, also shown in Figure 3.18, includes a way to enter a custom list of properties such as client information, language, and so on.

NOTE   You also can view the File Properties dialog box information while working in Windows Explorer by right-clicking the file and selecting Properties. Three unique tabs are visible: Summary, Contents, and Custom. The Summary tab holds the file identification information, including the Title, Subject, Author, Category, Keywords, and Comments.

FIGURE 3.18

The File Properties dialog box contains workflow information such as the scene author, comments, and revision dates.

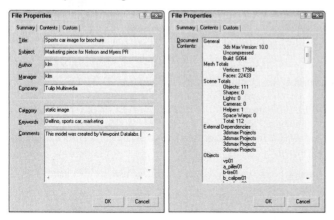

Viewing files

Sometimes, looking at the thumbnail of an image isn't enough to help you decide whether you have the right image. For these cases, you can quickly load the image in question into a viewer to look at it closely. The File ➪ View Image File menu command opens the View File dialog box shown in Figure 3.19. This dialog box lets you load and view graphic and animation files using the Rendered Frame Window or the default Media Player for your system.

FIGURE 3.19

The View File dialog box can open an assortment of image and animation formats.

CROSS-REF The Rendered Frame Window is discussed in more detail in Chapter 22, "Learning to Render a Scene."

The View File dialog box includes several controls for viewing files. The Devices and Setup buttons let you set up and view a file using external devices such as video recorders. The Info button lets you view detailed information about the selected file. The View button opens the file for viewing while leaving the View File dialog box open. The Open button opens the selected file and closes the dialog box. At the bottom of the View File dialog box, the statistics and path of the current file are displayed.

The View File dialog box can open many types of files, including Microsoft videos (AVI), MPEG files, bitmap images (BMP), Kodak Cineon (CIN), Combustion (CWS), Graphics Image Format (GIF), Radiance HDRI image files (HDR), Image File List (IFL), JPEG images (JPG), OpenEXR image files (EXR), Portable Network Graphics (PNG), Adobe Photoshop images (PSD), QuickTime movies (MOV), SGI images (RGB), RLA images, RPF images, Targa images (TGA, VST), Tagged Image File Format images (TIF), Abekas Digital Disk (YUV), and DirectDraw Surface (DDS) images.

You use the Gamma area on the View File dialog box to specify whether an image uses its own gamma settings or the system's default setting, or whether an override value should be used.

Summary

Working with files lets you save your work, share it with others, and reload it for more work. This chapter covered the following topics:

- Creating, saving, opening, merging, and archiving files
- Understanding the various import and export types
- Importing models from other programs, such as Illustrator and Poser
- Working with the file utilities, such as the Asset Browser
- Using the Summary Info and File Properties dialog boxes to keep track of scene files

By now, you should be feeling more comfortable with the user interface, but if you want to make some changes to the interface, the next chapter covers how to customize it.

Chapter 4

Customizing the Max Interface and Setting Preferences

W hen you get into a new car, one of the first things you do is to rearrange the seat and mirrors. You do this to make yourself comfortable. The same principle can apply to software packages: Arranging or customizing an interface makes it more comfortable to work with.

Early versions of Max allowed only minimal changes to the interface, but later versions enable significant customization. The Max interface can be customized to show only the icons and tools that you want to see. Max also has a rather bulky set of preferences that you can use to set almost every aspect of the program. This chapter covers various ways to make the Max interface more comfortable for you.

Using the Customize User Interface Window

The Customize menu provides commands for customizing and setting up the Max interface. The first menu item is the Customize User Interface menu command. This command opens the Customize User Interface dialog box. This dialog box includes five panels: Keyboard, Toolbars, Quads, Menus, and Colors. You can also access this dialog box by right-clicking any toolbar away from the buttons and selecting Customize from the pop-up menu.

Customizing keyboard shortcuts

If used properly, keyboard shortcuts can increase your efficiency dramatically. Figure 4.1 shows the Keyboard panel of the Customize User Interface dialog box. In this panel, you can assign shortcuts to any command and define sets of shortcuts. You can assign keyboard shortcuts for any of the interfaces listed in the Group drop-down list. When an interface is selected from the Group drop-down list, all its commands are listed below, along with their current keyboard shortcuts. You can

IN THIS CHAPTER

Using the Customize User Interface dialog box

Creating custom keyboard shortcuts, toolbars, quadmenus, menus, and colors

Customizing the Command Panel buttons

Loading and saving custom interfaces

Configuring paths

Setting system units

Setting preferences

disable the keyboard shortcuts for any of these interfaces using the Active option located next to the drop-down list.

> **NOTE** To access the defined keyboard shortcuts for the various interfaces, the Keyboard Shortcut Override Toggle button on the main toolbar must be enabled. If this button is disabled, then only the keyboard shortcuts for the Main UI are active.

FIGURE 4.1

The Keyboard panel enables you to create keyboard shortcuts for any command.

Groups that have a large number of commands are split into categories. You can use the Category drop-down list to filter only select types of commands. This helps you to quickly locate a specific type of command such as controllers, modifiers, or Space Warps. Entering a keyboard shortcut into the Hotkey field shows in the Assigned to field whether that key is currently assigned to a command. You can Assign the hotkey to the selected command or Remove the hotkey from its current assignment.

If the Overrides Active option is enabled, then the Editable Poly commands that are marked in bold text can be activated by pressing and holding a keyboard shortcut. When you release the keyboard shortcut, the original mode is restored. For example, if you are working in Extrude mode, you can press and hold the Shift+Ctrl+B keyboard shortcut to access the Bevel command. When you release the keyboard shortcut, the Extrude mode is active again. The amount of time that passes before the press-and-hold keyboard shortcut becomes active is set by the Delay to Override value.

> **NEW FEATURE** The Overrides Active and the Delay to Override options in the Keyboard panel of the Customize User Interface dialog box are new to 3ds Max 2008.

You can use the Write Keyboard Chart button to output all the keyboard commands to a text file. Using this feature, you can print and post a chart of keyboard shortcuts next to your computer monitor. You can also Load, Save, and Reset selected keyboard shortcut sets. Keyboard shortcut sets are saved as .kbd files in the UI directory where Max is installed.

CROSS-REF You can find a reference of the available default keyboard shortcuts in Appendix C, "3ds Max 2008 Keyboard Shortcuts."

Tutorial: Assigning keyboard shortcuts

Do you use both hands to control the mouse? If not, one hand is idle most of the time. If you can train this hand to control features using the keyboard, then you can be much more efficient.

To assign a new keyboard shortcut to create a Sphere object, follow these steps:

1. Open the Customize User Interface dialog box by choosing Customize ➪ Customize User Interface.

2. Open the Keyboard panel, and select Main UI in the Group drop-down list. Scroll through the list, and select the Sphere command.

TIP With a list of objects available, you can quickly jump close to a desired item by typing the first letter of the item. For example, pressing the S key jumps to the first item that begins with an *S*.

3. Place the cursor in the Hotkey field, and press Alt+Shift+Ctrl+S keys together. This enters the hotkey into the field. In the default interface, this key isn't assigned to any command. Click the Assign button to assign the hotkey to the command.

4. Click the Save button to save the keyboard shortcut set as myShortcuts.kbd. You can load the resulting set from the Chap 04 directory on the DVD.

5. The final step is to try out the shortcut. Close the Customize User Interface dialog box, press the new keyboard shortcut, Alt+Shift+Ctrl+S, and drag in a viewport to create a sphere.

Customizing toolbars

You can use the Customize User Interface dialog box's Toolbar panel to create custom toolbars. Figure 4.2 shows this panel.

The Toolbars panel of the Customize User Interface dialog box includes the same Group and Category drop-down lists and command list as the Keyboard panel. Clicking the New button opens a simple dialog box where you can name the new toolbar. The Delete button lets you delete toolbars. You can delete only toolbars that you've created. The Rename button lets you rename the current toolbar. The Hide option makes the selected toolbar hidden.

Use the Load and Save buttons to load and save your newly created interface, including the new toolbar, to a custom interface file. Saved toolbars have the .cui extension.

After you create a new toolbar, you can drag the commands in the Action list to either a new blank toolbar created with the New button or to an existing toolbar. By holding down the Alt key, you can drag a button from another toolbar and move it to your new toolbar. Holding down the Ctrl key and dragging a button retains a copy of the button on the first toolbar.

If you drag a command that has an icon associated with it, the icon appears on the new toolbar. If the command doesn't have an icon, then the text for the command appears on the new toolbar.

FIGURE 4.2

The Toolbars panel in the Customize User Interface dialog box enables you to create new toolbars.

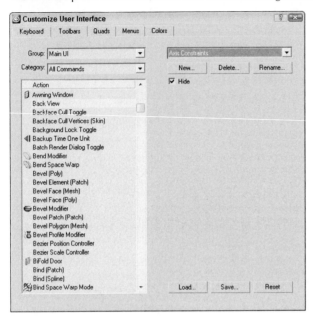

Tutorial: Creating a custom toolbar

If you've been using Max for a while, you probably have several favorite commands that you use extensively. You can create a custom toolbar of all your favorite commands. To show you how to do this, we create a custom toolbar for the compound objects.

To create a custom toolbar for creating compound objects, follow these steps:

1. Open the Customize User Interface dialog box by choosing Customize ⇨ Custom User Interface.

2. Open the Toolbars panel, and click the New button. In the New Toolbar dialog box that appears, name the toolbar Compound Objects. After you click OK, a new blank toolbar appears.

3. Select the Main UI group and the Objects Compounds category from the drop-down lists on the left. Then drag each command in the Action list to the new blank toolbar.

4. Click the Save button to save the changes to the customized interface file. You can load the resulting toolbar from the Chap 04 directory on the DVD. It is named Compound Objects toolbar.cui.

NOTE Don't be alarmed if the toolbar icons show up gray. Gray icons are simply disabled. When the tool is enabled, they are shown in color.

Figure 4.3 shows the new toolbar. With the new toolbar created, you can float, dock, or edit this toolbar just like the other toolbars. Notice that some of the tools have icons and others have text names.

FIGURE 4.3

A new toolbar of compound objects created using the Customize User Interface dialog box

You can right-click any of the buttons on any of the existing toolbars, except for the main toolbar, to access a pop-up menu. This pop-up menu enables you to change the button's appearance, delete the button, edit the button's macro script, or open the Customize User Interface dialog box.

CROSS-REF To learn more about editing macro scripts, see Chapter 49, "Automating with MAXScript."

Changing a button's appearance

Selecting the Edit Button Appearance command from the right-click pop-up menu opens the Edit Macro Button dialog box, shown in Figure 4.4. This dialog box enables you to quickly change the button's icon, tooltip, or text label. Each icon group shows both the standard icon and the grayed-out disabled version of the icon. Default buttons can also be changed. The Odd Only check box shows only the standard icons.

FIGURE 4.4

The Edit Macro Button dialog box provides a quick way to change an icon, tooltip, or text label.

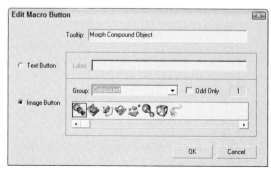

NOTE If a text label doesn't fit within the toolbar button, you can increase the button width using the Fixed Width Text Buttons spinner in the General panel of the Preference Settings dialog box.

Tutorial: Adding custom icons

The Max interface uses two different sizes of icons. Large icons are 24 × 24 pixels, and small icons are 16 × 15 pixels. Large icons can be 24-bit color, and small ones must be only 16-bit. Multiple icons can be placed side by side in a single file. The easiest way to create some custom toolbars is to copy an existing set of icons into an image-editing program, make the modifications, and save them under a different name. You can find all the icons saved as BMPs and used by Max in the 3dsmax\UI\Icons directory.

To create a new group of icons, follow these steps:

1. Select a group of current icons to edit from the UI directory, and open them in Photoshop. I selected the Patches group, which includes all the files that start with the word *Patches*. This group includes only two icons. To edit icons used for both large and small icon settings and both active and inactive states, open the following four files: Patches_16a.bmp, Patches_16i.bmp, Patches_24a.bmp, and Patches_24i.bmp.

2. In each file, the icons are all included side by side in the same file, so the first two files are 32 × 15 and the second two are 48 × 24. Edit the files, being sure to keep each icon within its required dimensions.

3. When you finish editing or creating the icons, save each file with the name of the icon group in front of the underscore character. My files were saved as Kels_16a.bmp, Kels_16i.bmp, Kels_24a.bmp, and Kels_24i.bmp, so they show up in Kels group in the Edit Macro Button dialog box. Copy these four edited files from the Chap 04 directory on the DVD to the 3dsmax\UI\Icons directory.

4. After the files are saved, you need to restart Max. The icon group is then available within the Customize User Interface dialog box when assigned to a command.

Figure 4.5 shows the Edit Macro Button dialog box with my custom icon group named Kels open.

FIGURE 4.5

The Edit Macro Button dialog box with a custom icon group selected

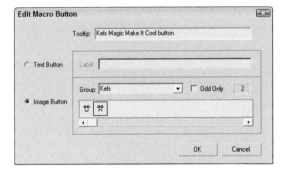

Customizing quadmenus

The third panel in the Customize User Interface dialog box allows you to customize the quadmenus. You can open quadmenus by right-clicking on the active viewport or in certain interfaces. Figure 4.6 shows this panel.

To the left of the panel are the Group and Category drop-down lists and a list of actions that are the same as the Keyboard and Toolbars panels, but the Quads panel also includes a Separator and a list of Menu commands. Quadmenus can include separators to divide the commands into different sections and menus that appear at the top of the standard interface.

The drop-down list at the top right of the Quads panel includes many different quadmenu sets. These quadmenus appear in different locations, such as within the ActiveShade window. Not only can you customize the default viewport quadmenus, but you also can create your own named custom quadmenus with the New button or you can rename an existing quadmenu. The Quad Shortcut field lets you assign a keyboard shortcut to a custom quadmenu.

FIGURE 4.6

The Quads panel of the Customize User Interface dialog box lets you modify pop-up quadmenus.

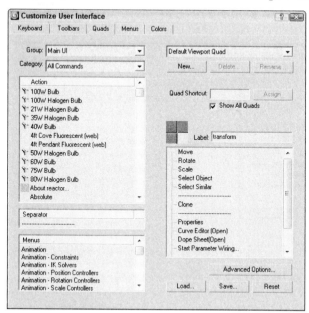

> **TIP** Several quadmenus have keyboard shortcuts applied to them. Right-clicking with the Shift key held down opens the Snap quadmenu. Other shortcuts include Alt+right-click for the Animation quadmenu, Ctrl+right-click for the Modeling quadmenu, Shift+Alt+right-click for the reactor quadmenu, and Ctrl+Alt+right-click for the Lighting/Rendering quadmenu.

If the Show All Quads option is disabled, it causes only a single quadmenu to be shown at a time when unchecked. Although only one quadmenu is shown at a time, the corner of each menu is shown, and you can switch between the different menus by moving the mouse over the corner of the menu. This is useful if you want to limit the size of the quadmenu.

The four quadrants of the current quadmenu are shown as four boxes. The currently selected quadmenu is highlighted yellow, and its label and commands are shown in the adjacent fields. Click the gray boxes to select one of the different quadmenus.

To add a command to the selected quadmenu, drag an action, separator, or menu from the panes on the left to the quadmenu commands pane on the right. You can reorder the commands in the quadmenu commands pane by dragging the commands and dropping them in their new location. To delete a command, just select it and press the Delete key or select Delete Menu Item from the right-click pop-up menu.

If you right-click on the commands in the right pane, a pop-up menu appears with options to delete or rename the command. Another command allows you to flatten a submenu, which displays all submenu commands on the top level with the other commands.

Custom quadmenus can be loaded and saved as menu files (with the .mnu extension).

The Quads panel also includes an Advanced Options button. Clicking this button opens the Advanced Quad Menu Options dialog box, shown in Figure 4.7. Using this dialog box, you can set options such as the colors used in the quadmenus.

FIGURE 4.7

The Advanced Quad Menu Options dialog box lets you change quadmenu fonts and colors.

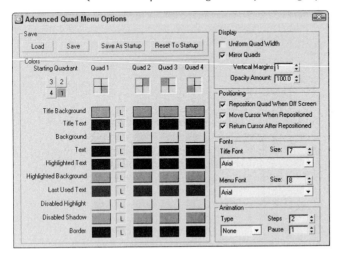

Changes to the Advanced Quad Menu Options dialog box affect all quadmenus. You can load and save these settings to files (with the .qop extension). The Starting Quadrant determines which quadrant is first to appear when the quadmenu is accessed. You can select to change the colors for each quadmenu independent of the others. The column with the L locks the colors so they are consistent for all quadmenus if enabled.

The remainder of the Advanced Quad Menu Options dialog box includes settings for controlling how the quadmenus are displayed and positioned, as well as the fonts that are used.

The Animation section lets you define the animation style that is used when the quadmenus appear. The animation types include None, Stretch, and Fade. The Stretch style slowly stretches the quadmenus until they are full size over the designated number of steps, and the Fade style slowly makes the quadmenus appear.

 I personally don't like to wait for the quadmenus to appear, so I keep the Animation setting set to None.

Customizing menus

The Menus panel of the Customize User Interface dialog box allows you to customize the menus used at the top of the Max window. Figure 4.8 shows this panel.

This panel includes the same Group and Category drop-down lists and the Action, Separator, and Menus panes found in the Quads panel. You can drag and drop these commands to the menu pane on the right. Menus can be saved as files (with the .mnu extension). In the menu pane on the right, you can delete menu items with the Delete key or by right-clicking and selecting Delete Item from the pop-up menu.

FIGURE 4.8

You can use the Menus panel of the Customize User Interface dialog box to modify menus.

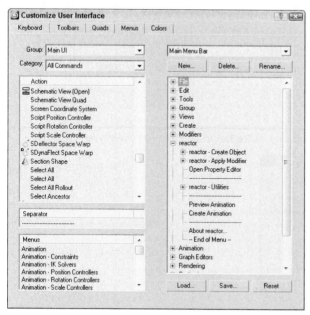

 If you place an ampersand (&) character in front of a custom menu name letter, that letter is underlined and can be accessed using the Alt key; for example, Alt+F opens the File menu.

Tutorial: Adding a new menu

Adding a new menu is easy to do with the Customize User Interface dialog box. For this example, you tack another menu to the end of the Tools menu.

To add another menu item to the Tools menu, follow these steps:

1. Choose Customize ➪ Customize User Interface to open the Customize User Interface dialog box.
2. Click the Menus tab to open the Menus panel.
3. In the top-left drop-down list, select Main UI from the Group drop-down list and Tools from the Category drop-down list.

    Expand the Tools menu in the right pane by clicking on the plus sign to its left.
4. Locate the Cross Hair Cursor Toggle menu item in the Action list, drag it to the right, and drop it right after the Channel Info Editor menu item.

    As you drag, a blue line indicates where the menu will be located.
5. Click the Save button to save the menu as a file. You can find the customized menu from this example in the Chap 04 directory on the DVD.

After you save the new menu file, you need to restart Max before you can see the changes. You can reset the default UI by choosing Customize ➪ Revert to Startup Layout.

Customizing colors

Within Max, the colors often indicate the mode in which you're working. For example, red marks animation mode. Using the Colors panel of the Customize User Interface dialog box, you can set custom colors for all Max interface elements. This panel, shown in Figure 4.9, includes two panes. The upper pane displays the available items for the interface selected in the Elements drop-down list. Selecting an item in the list displays its color in the color swatch to the right.

NEW FEATURE   The ability to change the subobject selection color is new to 3ds Max 2008.

FIGURE 4.9

You can use the Colors panel of the Customize User Interface dialog box to set the colors used in the interface.

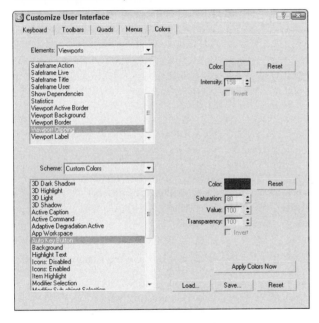

The lower pane displays a list of the custom colors that can be changed to affect the appearance of the interface. For example, Highlight Text isn't an element; it's an interface appearance. The Scheme drop-down list can alter the color scheme between custom colors and the Windows Default Colors.

You can save custom color settings as files with the .clr extension. You can use the Apply Colors Now button to immediately update the interface colors.

Customizing Modify and Utility Panel Buttons

 The Modify panel and the Utilities panel in the Command Panel both include a button called Configure Button Sets that allows you to configure how the modifiers are grouped and which utility buttons appear in the Utilities panel.

In the Modify panel, the Configure Modifier Sets button is the right-most button directly under the Modifier Stack. This button opens a pop-up menu that lists all the modifier categories. The top pop-up menu command is Configure Modifier Sets, which opens a dialog box, shown in Figure 4.10, when selected. Using this dialog box, you can control which modifiers are grouped with which sets.

FIGURE 4.10

The Configure Modifier Sets dialog box lets you group the modifiers as you want.

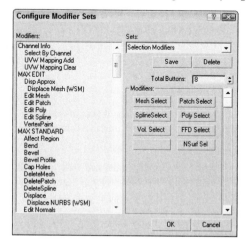

To add a modifier to a set, select the set from the Sets drop-down list and drag the modifier from the list of Modifiers on the left to the button set on the right. To create a new set, simply type a new name into the Sets field. After a set has changed, you need to save it with the Save button.

You can find the same Configure Button Sets button on the Utilities panel. Clicking this button opens a similar dialog box where you can drag from a list of Utilities to a list of buttons on the right. These buttons are then displayed in the Utilities panel.

Working with Custom Interfaces

If you've changed your interface, you'll be happy to know that the Customize menu includes a way for you to save and then reload your custom setup. This feature is especially helpful for users who share a copy of Max.

 Any custom .ui file can be loaded as the default interface from the command line by adding a –c and the .ui filename after the 3dsmax.exe file (for example, 3dsmax.exe –c my_interface.ui).

Saving and loading a custom interface

Custom interface schemes are saved with the .ui extension using the Customize ➪ Save Custom UI Scheme menu command. When you save a custom scheme, Max opens a file dialog box where you can name the .ui file, and then the Custom Scheme dialog box, shown in Figure 4.11. This dialog box lets you choose which customizations to include in the custom scheme. It also lets you select the icon type to use. The options are Classic and 2D Black and White.

FIGURE 4.11

The Custom Scheme dialog box appears when you're saving a custom interface and lets you select which items to include.

You can load saved user interface schemes with Customize ➪ Load Custom UI. The default Max install includes several predefined interface setups located in the UI directory. These standard interfaces are available:

- **DefaultUI:** Default interface that opens when Max is first installed.
- **Ame-dark:** Displays the standard interface with black windows, backgrounds, and viewports. All the icons and menus are light gray, and many of the icons are different, as shown in Figure 4.12.
- **Ame-light:** Same as the Ame-dark layout, except the icons and menus are black and the backgrounds are all light gray. Many icons are different here, too.
- **ModularToolbarsUI:** An interface that breaks the main toolbar into many smaller toolbars that are easier to move and arrange.

You also can use both the Load Custom UI and Save Custom UI menu commands to save and load any of the custom user interface files types, including these:

- Interface Scheme files (.ui)
- UI files (.cui)
- Menu files (.mnu)
- Color files (.clr)
- Keyboard Shortcut files (.kbd)
- Quadmenu Options files (.qop)

Tutorial: Saving a custom interface

You can save personalized interfaces for later recall in the 3dsmax\UI directory where Max is installed. If you save a custom UI Scheme as the MaxStart.ui file, then your custom interface is loaded automatically when Max starts.

 **NOTE** If you want to return the default UI setup, you can use the Customize ➪ Revert to Startup Layout command, which uses the "_startup.ui" file.

FIGURE 4.12

If you prefer a darker interface, then try loading the Ame-dark scheme.

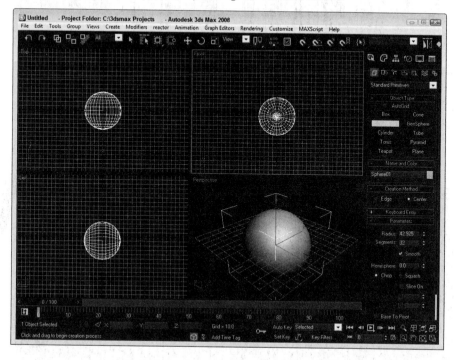

To have Max start with your custom interface, follow these steps:

1. Customize your interface by making any desired changes.
2. Choose Customize ⇨ Save Custom UI Scheme.

    The Save Custom UI Scheme dialog box opens.
3. Open the UI subdirectory (if you are not already there), select the MaxStart.ui file, and click OK.
4. Click OK to replace the existing file.

 You can set Max to automatically save your interface changes when exiting. Select the Save UI Configuration on Exit option in the General tab of the Preference Settings dialog box.

Locking the interface

After you're comfortable with your interface changes, locking the interface to prevent accidental changes is a good idea. To lock the current interface, choose Customize ⇨ Lock UI Layout (or press the Alt+0 keyboard shortcut). Locking the interface prevents changes by dragging interface elements, but you can still make interface changes using the pop-up menus.

Reverting to the startup interface

When you're first playing around with Max's customization features, really messing things up can be easy. If you get in a bind, you can reload the default startup interface (MaxStart.ui) with the Customize ⇨ Revert to Startup UI Layout command. Using the File ⇨ Reset menu command does not reset changes to the layout.

NOTE   If your MaxStart.ui file gets messed up, you can reinstate the original default interface setup by deleting the MaxStart.ui file before starting Max. However, do not overwrite the default UI file because this file is needed to reinstate the default UI.

Switching between default and custom interfaces

The Customize ⇨ Custom UI and Defaults Switcher menu command opens an interactive window that presents several options for selecting initial settings and interface schemes, as shown in Figure 4.13. At the top of the window, you can select an option, and then details about the selected option are displayed.

FIGURE 4.13

This window explains the benefits of the different initial settings and scheme choices.

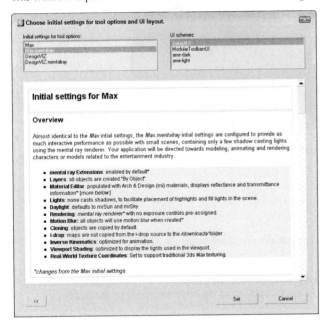

The initial settings for the tool options list include Max, Max.mentalray, DesignVIZ, and DesignVIZ.mentalray. These different selections cause the default settings for the various controls to change. For example, the default renderer for Max is the Scanline renderer, but for the Max.mentalray option, mental ray is the default renderer.

The schemes list includes the same custom interfaces listed earlier, along with any custom interfaces that have been saved.

After selecting the initial settings and scheme to use, click the Set button to commit the selections to the interface. The button with arrows on it in the lower left displays the initial information page again.

Tutorial: Creating custom initial settings

You can add your own custom set of initial settings to the Defaults Switcher, which lets you quickly set a large number of custom settings.

To add a custom set of initial settings to the Default Switcher, follow these steps:

1. Locate the Defaults folder where Max is installed. Copy and rename one of the folders. The folder can contain three different settings files: CurrentDefaults.ini, Medit.mat, and MaxStart.max.

2. Open the CurrentDefaults.ini file within a text editor, and carefully edit this file to include the settings you want to use. You can find details on each of these settings in the User Reference.

3. Save the default materials to appear in the Material Editor as Medit.mat and the Max file to initially open as MaxStart.max.

> **NOTE** If any of the settings within the CurrentDefaults.ini file or if the other files are missing from the new settings folder, then the settings and files within the default Max directory are used.

4. Select the Customize ⇨ Custom UI and Defaults Switcher menu command. The new folder's name appears in the list. Select the new name to load the defined settings.

Configuring Paths

When strolling through a park, chances are good that you'll see several different paths. One might take you to the lake and another to the playground. Knowing where the various paths lead can help you as you navigate around the park. Paths in Max lead, or point, to various resources, either locally or across the network.

All paths can be configured using two distinct Configure Paths dialog boxes found in the Customize menu: Configure User Paths and Configure System Paths. The Configure User Paths dialog box is used to specify where to look for scene resource files like scenes, animations, and textures. The Configure System Paths dialog box is used to specify where the system looks to load files that Max uses like fonts, scripts, and plug-ins.

Configuring user paths

The Configure User Paths dialog box, shown in Figure 4.14, holds the path definitions to all the various resource folders. The dialog box includes three panels: File I/O, External Files, and XRefs.

The main panel in the Configure User Paths dialog box is the File I/O panel. The Project Folder is listed at the top of the dialog box and can be changed in this dialog box or with the File ⇨ Set Project Folder menu. This panel includes entries for Animations, Archives, Auto Backup, Bitmap Proxies, Downloads, Export, Expressions, Images, Import, Materials, Max Start, Photometric, Previews, Render Assets, Render Output, Render Presets, Scenes, Sounds, and Video Post. If you select any of these entries, you can click the Modify button to change its path. All paths are set by default to folders contained within the designated Project Folder, but you can change them to whatever you want. The Make Relative and Make Absolute buttons cause the selected entry to be displayed as a relative path based on the Project Folder or an absolute path.

> **TIP** Personally, I like to keep all my content in a separate directory from where the application is installed. That way, new installs or upgrades don't risk overwriting my files. To do this, simply change the Project Folder to a location separate from the 3ds Max installation directory.

FIGURE 4.14

The Configure User Paths dialog box specifies where to look for various resources.

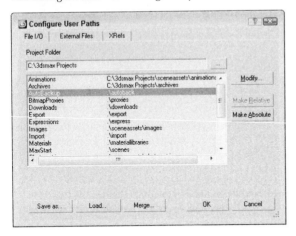

Under the External Files and XRefs panels, you can add and delete paths that specify where Max looks to find specific files. All paths specified in both these panels are searched in the order they are listed when you're looking for resources such as plug-ins, but file dialog boxes open only to the first path. Use the Move Up and Move Down buttons to realign path entries.

 **Using the Customize ⬦ Revert to Startup UI Layout command does not reset path configuration changes.**

At the bottom of the Configure User Paths dialog box are buttons for saving, loading, and merging the defined configuration paths into a separate file. These files are saved using the .mxp format. This file can be found in the root of the Project Folder.

 **Setting up a Project Folder on the network gives every team member access to all the project files and synchronizes all the paths for a project.**

Configuring system paths

Max default paths are listed in the Configure System Paths dialog box, shown in Figure 4.15. When Max is installed, all the paths are set to point to the default subdirectories where Max was installed. To modify a path, select the path and click the Modify button. A file dialog box lets you locate the new directory.

The Configure System Paths dialog box also includes the 3rd Party Plug-Ins panel where you can add directories for Max to search when looking for plug-ins.

FIGURE 4.15

FIGURE 4.15

The Configure System Paths dialog box specifies additional paths.

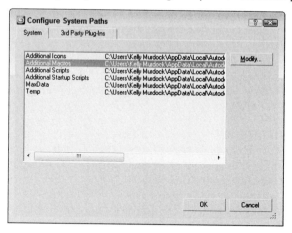

Selecting System Units

One of the first tasks you need to complete before you can begin modeling is to set the system units. The system units have a direct impact on modeling and define the units that are represented by the coordinate values. Units directly relate to parameters entered with the keyboard. For example, with the units set to meters, a sphere created with the radius parameter of 2 would be 4 meters across.

Max supports several different measurement systems, including Metric and U.S. Standard units. You can also define a Custom units system. (I suggest parsecs if you're working on a space scene.) Working with a units system enables you to work with precision and accuracy using realistic values.

 **Most game engines work with meters, so if you're building assets for a game, set the units to meters.**

To specify a units system, choose Customize ➪ Units Setup to display the Units Setup dialog box, shown in Figure 4.16. For the Metric system, options include Millimeters, Centimeters, Meters, and Kilometers. The U.S. Standard units system can be set to the default units of Feet or Inches displayed as decimals or fractional units. You can also select to display feet with fractional inches or feet with decimal inches. Fractional values can be divided from 1/1 to 1/100 increments.

Using Custom and Generic units

To define a Custom units system, modify the fields under the Custom option, including a units label and its equivalence to known units. The final option is to use the default Generic units. Generic units relate distances to each other, but the numbers themselves are irrelevant. You can also set lighting units to use American or International standards. Lighting units are used to define Photometric lights.

FIGURE 4.16

The Units Setup dialog box lets you choose which units system to use. Options include Metric, U.S. Standard, Custom, and Generic.

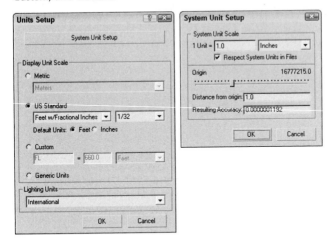

At the top of the Units Setup dialog box is the System Unit Setup button. This button opens the System Unit Scale dialog box, also shown in Figure 4.15. This dialog box enables you to define the measurement system used by Max. Options include Inches, Feet, Miles, Millimeters, Centimeters, Meters, and Kilometers.

For example, when using Max to create models that are to be used in the Unreal game editor, you can use the Custom option to define a unit called the Unreal Foot unit that sets 1 Uft equal to 16 units, which matches the units in the Unreal editor just fine.

A multiplier field allows you to alter the value of each unit. The Respect System Units in Files toggle presents a dialog box whenever a file with a different system units setting is encountered. If this option is disabled, all new objects are automatically converted to the current units system.

The Origin control helps you determine the accuracy of an object as it is moved away from the scene origin. If you know how far objects will be located from the origin, then entering that value tells you the Resulting Accuracy. You can use this feature to determine the accuracy of your parameters. Objects farther from the origin have a lower accuracy.

CAUTION Be cautious when working with objects that are positioned a long way from the scene origin. The farther an object is from the origin, the lower its accuracy and the less precisely you can move it. If you are having trouble precisely positioning an object (in particular, an object that has been imported from an external file), check the object's distance from the origin. Moving it closer to the origin should help resolve the problem.

Handling mismatched units

Imagine designing a new ski resort layout. For such a project, you'd want to probably use kilometers as the file units. If your next project is to design a custom body design on a racecar, then you'll want to use meters as the new units. If you need to reopen the ski resort project while your units are set to meters, then you'll get a File Load: Units Mismatch dialog box, shown in Figure 4.17.

This dialog box reminds you that the units specified in the file that you are opening don't match the current units setting. This also can happen when trying to merge in an object with a different units setting. The dialog box lists the units used in both the file and the system and offers two options. The Rescale the File Objects to the System Unit Scale option changes the units in the file to match the current system units setting. The second option changes the system units to match the file unit settings.

TIP If you rescale the file object to match the system file units setting, then the objects will either appear tiny or huge in the current scene. Use the Zoom Extents All button to see the rescaled objects in the viewport.

FIGURE 4.17

The Units Mismatch dialog box lets you sync up units between the current file and the system settings.

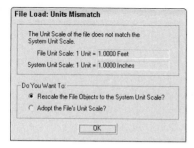

Rescaling world units

If you discover halfway through your scene that you're working with the wrong units, you can use the Rescale World Units utility to scale up the entire scene or just selected objects. To access this utility, click the Utilities panel and then the More button. In the utilities list, select the Rescale World Units utility and click OK.

The Rescale World Units dialog box has a Scale Factor value, which is the value by which the scene or objects are increased or decreased. If your world was created using millimeter units and you need to work in meters, then increasing by a Scale Factor of 1000 will set the world right.

Setting Preferences

The Preference Settings dialog box lets you configure Max so it works in a way that is most comfortable for you. You open it by choosing Customize ⇨ Preferences. The dialog box includes eleven panels: General, Files, Viewports, Gamma and LUT, Rendering, Animation, Inverse Kinematics, Gizmos, MAXScript, Radiosity, and mental ray.

General preferences

The first panel in the Preference Settings dialog box is for General settings, as shown in Figure 4.18. The General panel includes many global settings that affect the entire interface.

FIGURE 4.18

The General panel lets you to change many UI settings.

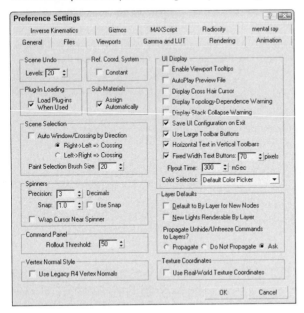

TIP The quickest way I've found to open the Preference Settings dialog box is to right-click the Spinner Snap Toggle button.

Undo Levels and the Reference Coordinate System

The Scene Undo spinner sets the number of commands that can be kept in a buffer for undoing. A smaller number frees up memory, but does not let you backtrack through your work. The default Undo Levels is 20.

The Reference Coordinate System setting makes all transform tools use the same coordinate system and transform center when the Constant option is enabled. If disabled, each transform uses the coordinate system last selected.

Loading Plug-Ins and Sub-Material settings

The Load Plug-Ins When Used option keeps plug-ins out of memory until they are accessed. This saves valuable memory and still makes the plug-ins accessible.

The Automatic Sub-Material Assignment option, when checked, enables materials to be dragged and dropped directly onto a subobject selection. This applies the Multi/Sub-Object material to the object with the dropped material corresponding with the subobject selection's Material ID.

Scene Selection settings

The Auto Window/Crossing by Direction option lets you select scene objects using the windowing method (the entire object must be within the selected windowed area to be selected) and the crossing method (which selects objects if their borders are crossed with the mouse) at the same time, depending on the direction that the mouse is dragged. If you select the first option, then the Crossing method is used when the mouse is dragged from right to left and the Window method is used when the mouse is dragged from left to right.

 I like to keep the Auto Window/Crossing by Direction option disabled. I use the Crossing selection method and find that I don't always start my selection from the same side.

The Paint Selection Brush Size value sets the default size of the Paint Selection Brush. In the default interface, this size is set to 20. If you find yourself changing the brush size every time you use this tool, then you can alter its default size with this setting.

Spinner, Rollout, and Vertex Normal settings

Spinners are interface controls that enable you to enter values or interactively increase or decrease the value by clicking the arrows on the right. The Preference Settings dialog box includes settings for changing the number of decimals displayed in spinners and the increment or decrement value for clicking an arrow. The Use Spinner Snap option enables the snap mode.

 You also can enable the snap mode using the Spinner Snap button on the main toolbar.

 Right-click on a spinner to automatically set its value to 0 or its lowest threshold.

You can also change the values in the spinner by clicking the spinner and dragging up to increase the value or down to decrease it. The Wrap Cursor Near Spinner option keeps the cursor close to the spinner when you change values by dragging with the mouse, so you can drag the mouse continuously without worrying about hitting the top or bottom of the screen.

The Rollout Threshold value sets how many pixels can be scrolled before the rollup shifts to another column. This is used only if you've made the Command Panel wider or floating.

The Use Legacy R4 Vertex Normals option computes vertex normals based on the Max version 4 instead of the newer method. The newer method is more accurate but may affect smoothing groups. Enable this setting only if you plan on using any models created using Max R4 or earlier.

Interface Display settings

The options in the UI Display section control additional aspects of the interface. The Enable Viewport Tooltips option can toggle tooltips on or off. Tooltips are helpful when you're first learning the Max interface, but they quickly become annoying and you'll want to turn them off.

The AutoPlay Preview File setting automatically plays Preview Files in the default media player when they are finished rendering. If this option is disabled, you need to play the previews with the Animation ⇨ View Preview menu command. The Display Cross Hair Cursor option changes the cursor from the Windows default arrow to a crosshair cursor similar to the one used in AutoCAD.

For some actions, such as non-uniform scaling, Max displays a warning dialog box asking whether you are sure of the action. To disable these warnings, uncheck this option (or you could check the Disable this Warning box in the dialog box). Actions with warnings include topology-dependence and collapsing the Modifier Stack.

The Save UI Configuration on Exit switch automatically saves any interface configuration changes when you exit Max. You can deselect the Use Large Toolbar Buttons option, enabling the use of smaller toolbar buttons and icons, which reclaims valuable screen real estate.

The Horizontal Text in Vertical Toolbars option fixes the problem of text buttons that take up too much space, especially when printed horizontally on a vertical toolbar. You can also specify a width for text buttons. Any text larger than this value is clipped off at the edges of the button.

The Flyout Time spinner adjusts the time the system waits before displaying flyout buttons. The Color Selection drop-down list lets you choose which color selector interface Max uses.

Layer settings

If you select an object and open its Properties dialog box, the Display Properties, Rendering Control, and Motion Blur sections each have a button that can toggle between ByLayer and ByObject. If ByObject is selected, then the options are enabled and you can set them for the object in the Properties dialog box, but if the ByLayer option is selected, then the settings are determined by the setting defined for all objects in the layer in the Layer Manager.

The settings in the Preference Settings dialog box set the ByLayer option as the default for new objects and new lights. You also have an option to propagate all unhide and unfreeze commands to the layer. You can select Propagate, Do Not Propagate, or Ask.

Real-World Texture Coordinates setting

The Use Real-World Texture Coordinates setting causes the Real-World Scale or the Real-World Map Size option in the Coordinates rollout to be enabled. This setting is off by default, but it can be enabled to be the default by using this setting.

> **CROSS-REF** Real-World Texture Coordinates is a mapping method explained in more detail in Chapter 17, "Adding Material Details with Maps."

Files panel preferences

The Files panel holds the controls for backing up, archiving, and logging Max files. You can set files to be backed up, saved incrementally, or compressed when saved.

> **CROSS-REF** The Files panel is covered in Chapter 3, "Working with Files, Importing, and Exporting."

Viewport preferences

The viewports are your window into the scene. The Viewports panel, shown in Figure 4.19, contains many options for controlling these viewports.

> **CROSS-REF** Although the viewports were the major topic in Chapter 2, "Controlling and Configuring the Viewports," the viewport preference settings are covered here.

Viewport Parameter options

The Use Dual Planes option enables a method designed to speed up viewport redraws. Objects close to the scene are included in a front plane, and objects farther back are included in a back plane. When this option is enabled, only the objects on the front plane are redrawn.

In subobject mode, the default is to display vertices as small plus signs. The Show Vertices as Dots option displays vertices as either Small or Large dots. The Draw Links as Lines option shows all displayed links as lines that connect the two linked objects.

> **CAUTION** I've found that keeping the Draw Links as Lines option turned on can make it confusing to see objects clearly, so I tend to keep it turned off.

FIGURE 4.19

The Viewports panel contains several viewport parameter settings.

When the Backface Cull on Object Creation option is enabled, the backside of an object in wireframe mode is not displayed. If disabled, you can see the wireframe lines that make up the backside of the object. The Backface Cull option setting is determined when the object is created, so some objects in your scene may be backface culled and others may not be. Figure 4.20 includes a sphere and a cube on the left that are backface culled and a sphere and cube on the right that are not.

 The Object Properties dialog box also contains a Backface Cull option.

FIGURE 4.20

Backface culling simplifies objects by hiding their backsides.

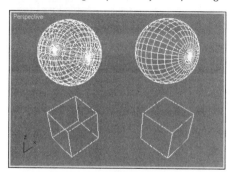

The Attenuate Lights option causes objects farther back in a viewport to appear darker. Attenuation is the property that causes lights to diminish over distance.

In the Viewport Configuration dialog box, you can set Safe Regions, which are borders that the renderer includes. The Mask Viewport to Safe Region option causes the objects beyond the Safe Region border to be invisible.

The Update Background While Playing option causes viewport background bitmaps to be updated while an animation sequence plays. Viewport backgrounds can be filtered if the Filter Environment Background option is enabled, but this slows the update time. If this option is disabled, the background image appears aliased and pixelated.

NOTE The Low-Res Environment Background option didn't improve viewport performance that much, so the option has been removed in 3ds Max 2008.

The Display World Axis option displays the axes in the lower-left corner of each viewport. The Grid Nudge Distance is the distance that an object moves when Grid Nudge (+ and – on the numeric keypad) keys are used. Objects without scale, such as lights and cameras, appear in the scene according to the Non-Scaling Object Size value. Making this value large makes lights and camera objects very obvious.

Enabling ghosting

Ghosting is similar to the use of "onion-skins" in traditional animation, causing an object's prior position and next position to be displayed. When producing animation, knowing where you're going and where you've come from is helpful.

Max offers several ghosting options. You can set whether a ghost appears before the current frame, after the current frame, or both before and after the current frame. You can set the total number of ghosting frames and how often they should appear. You can also set an option to show the frame numbers.

CROSS-REF For a more detailed discussion of ghosting, see Chapter 20, "Understanding Animation and Keyframe Basics."

Using the middle mouse button

If you're using a mouse that includes a middle button (this includes a mouse with a scrolling wheel), then you can define how the middle button is used. The two options are Pan/Zoom and Stroke.

Panning, rotating, and zooming with the middle mouse button

The Pan/Zoom option pans the active viewport if the middle button is held down, zooms in and out by steps if you move the scrolling wheel, rotates the view if you hold down the Alt key while dragging, and zooms smoothly if you drag the middle mouse button with the Ctrl and Alt keys held down. You can also zoom in quickly using the scroll wheel with the Ctrl button held down, or more slowly with the Alt key held down. You can select options to zoom about the mouse point in the Orthographic and Perspective viewports. If disabled, you'll zoom about the center of the viewport. The Right Click Menu Over Selected Only option causes the quadmenus to appear only if you right-click on top of the selected object. This is a bad idea if you use the quadmenus frequently.

TIP I've found that using the middle mouse button along with the Alt key for rotating is the simplest and easiest way to navigate the viewport, so although Strokes is a clever idea, I always set the middle mouse button to Pan/Zoom.

Using Strokes

The Stroke option lets you execute commands by dragging a pre-defined stroke in a viewport. With the Stroke option selected, close the Preference Settings dialog box and drag with the middle mouse button held down in one of the viewports. A simple dialog box identifies the stroke and executes the command associated with it. If no command is associated, then a simple dialog box appears that lets you Continue (do nothing) or Define the stroke.

Another way to work with strokes is to enable the Strokes Utility. This is done by selecting the Utility panel, clicking the More button, and selecting Strokes from the pop-up list of utilities. This utility makes a Draw Strokes button active. When the button is enabled, it turns yellow and you can draw strokes with the left mouse button and access defined strokes with the middle mouse button.

If you select to define the stroke, the Define Stroke dialog box, shown in Figure 4.21, is opened. You can also open this dialog box directly by holding down the Ctrl key while dragging a stroke with the middle mouse button. In the upper-left corner of this dialog box is a grid. Strokes are identified by the lines they cross on this grid as they are drawn. For example, an "HK" stroke would be a vertical line dragged from the top of the viewport straight down to the bottom.

FIGURE 4.21

The Define Stroke dialog box lets you define specific command strokes that are executed by drawing the stroke with the middle mouse button.

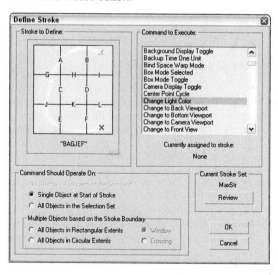

With a stroke identified, you can select a command in the upper-right pane. This is the command that executes when you drag the stroke with the middle mouse button in the viewport. For each command, you can set the options found below the stroke grid. These options define what the command is executed on.

All defined strokes are saved in a set, and you can review the current set of defined strokes with the Review button. Clicking this button opens the Review Strokes dialog box where all defined strokes and their commands are displayed, as shown in Figure 4.22.

FIGURE 4.22

The Review Strokes and Stroke Preferences dialog boxes list all defined strokes and their respective commands.

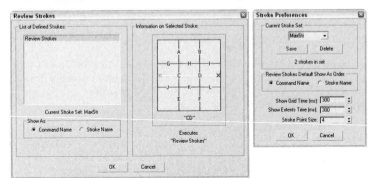

One of the commands available in the list of commands is Stroke Preferences. Using this command opens the Stroke Preferences dialog box, also shown in Figure 4.21, where you can save and delete different stroke sets, specify to list commands or strokes in the Review Strokes dialog box, set how long the stroke grid and extents appear, and set the Stroke Point Size.

Choosing and configuring display drivers

If you look closely at the right end of the title bar, you notice that the Display driver is displayed and set to Direct X. When Max is installed, it loads the latest Direct X drivers and sets the display to use those drivers, but you can change the display driver to OpenGL or to Software if your video card doesn't support the needed drivers.

The Display Drivers section in the Viewports panel of the Preference Settings dialog box lists the currently installed driver. Clicking the Configure Driver button opens a dialog box of settings for the current driver. Clicking the Choose Driver button opens the Direct3D Driver Setup dialog box, shown in Figure 4.22. This dialog box lets you change the Direct3D version, but unless you have a reason to change it, keep it set to DirectX 10.0 or you'll disable some features. The Software (RefRast) and Debug Use Flags options are enabled only if you have a debug version of Direct3D installed on your system.

If you click the Revert from Direct3D button, the Graphics Driver Setup dialog box, also shown in Figure 4.23, opens. This dialog box lets you change the display driver. The options include Software, OpenGL, Direct3D (which is recommended because the Max installation includes the latest drivers), and Custom. If you change the display driver, you need to restart Max.

CAUTION   The Graphics Driver Setup dialog box displays the options only for the drivers that it finds on your system, but just because an option exists doesn't mean it works correctly. If a driver hangs your system, you can restart it from a command line with the –h flag after 3dsmax.exe to force Max to present the Graphics Driver Setup dialog box again or use the Start ⇨ Programs ⇨ Autodesk ⇨ 3ds Max 2008 ⇨ Change Graphics Mode program icon to restart the program.

The Configure Driver option opens a dialog box of configurations for the driver that is currently installed. The various configuration dialog boxes include options such as specifying the Texture Size, which is the size of the bitmap used to texture map an object. Larger maps have better image quality but can slow down your display.

FIGURE 4.23

You use the Direct3D Driver Setup and the Graphics Driver Setup dialog boxes to select a different display driver.

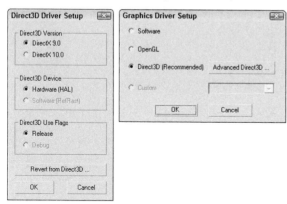

All the display driver configuration settings present tradeoffs between image quality and speed of display. By tweaking the configuration settings, you can optimize these settings to suit your needs. In general, the more memory available on your video card, the better the results.

 You can learn more about the various display drivers in Appendix B, "Installing and Configuring 3ds Max 2008."

Gamma preferences

The Gamma and LUT panel, shown in Figure 4.24, controls the gamma correction for the display and for bitmap files. It also includes a Browse button for loading an Autodesk Look-up Table (LUT) file. A Look-up Table is a file that holds all the color calibration settings that can be shared across different types of software and hardware within a studio to maintain consistency.

Setting screen gamma

Have you ever noticed in an electronics store that television-screen displays vary in color? Colors on monitor screens may be fairly consistent for related models, but may vary across brands. *Gamma settings* are a means by which colors can be consistently represented regardless of the monitor that is being used.

Gamma value regulates the contrast of an image. It is a numerical offset required by an individual monitor in order to be consistent with a standard. To enable gamma correction for Max, open the Gamma panel in the Preference Settings dialog box and click the Enable Gamma Correction option. To determine the gamma value, use the spinner or adjust the Gamma value until the gray square blends in unnoticeably with the background.

LUT files can be loaded from other software to ensure consistency across several calibrated monitors in a studio.

 3ds Max cannot create LUT files, but it can use existing LUT files created in other software packages, such as Combustion.

FIGURE 4.24

Enabling gamma correction makes colors consistent regardless of the monitor.

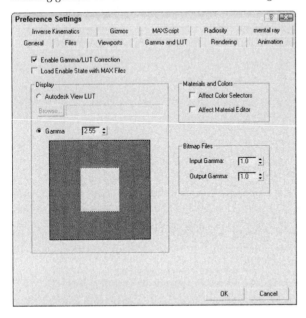

Propagating gamma settings

Although gamma settings have a direct impact on the viewports, they do not affect the colors found in the Color Selector or in the Material Editor. Using the Affect Color Selectors and Affect Material Editor options, you can propagate the gamma settings to these other interfaces also.

Setting bitmap gamma

Many bitmap formats, such as TGA, contain their own gamma settings. The Input Gamma setting for Bitmap files sets the gamma for bitmaps that don't have a gamma setting. The Output Gamma setting is the value set for bitmaps being output from Max.

 Match the Input Gamma value to the Display Gamma value so that bitmaps loaded for textures are displayed correctly.

Other preference panels

The remaining preference panels including Rendering, Animation, Inverse Kinematics, Gizmos, MAXScript, Radiosity, and mental ray are covered in the related chapter.

CROSS-REF   The details of the Rendering Preferences panel are covered in Chapter 22, "Learning to Render a Scene." The Animation Preferences panel is covered in Chapter 20, "Understanding Animation and Keyframe Basics." To learn more about Applied IK and Interactive IK, see Chapter 41, "Working with Inverse Kinematics." See Chapter 7, "Transforming Objects, Pivoting, Aligning, and Snapping" for more detail on Gizmo preferences. Check out Chapter 49, "Automating with MAXScript" for more on MAXScript commands and preferences. Swing over to Chapter 44, "Working with Advanced Lighting, Light Tracing, and Radiosity," for greater detail on Radiosity preferences. Look to Chapter 46, "Raytracing and mental ray," for more detail on the mental ray renderer.

Summary

You can customize the Max interface in many ways. Most of these customization options are included under the Customize menu. In this chapter, you learned how to use this menu and its commands to customize many aspects of the interface. Customizing makes the Max interface more efficient and comfortable for you.

Specifically, this chapter covered the following topics:

- Using the Customize User Interface dialog box to customize keyboard shortcuts, toolbars, quad-menus, menus, and colors
- Customizing buttons on the Modify and Utility panels
- Saving and loading custom interfaces
- Configuring paths
- Setting system units
- Setting preferences

Part II, "Working with Objects," is next. The first chapter covers the primitive objects and gets some objects into a scene for you to work with.

Part II

Working with Objects

Chapter 5

Creating and Editing Primitive Objects

S o what exactly did the Romans use to build their civilization? The answer is lots and lots of basic blocks. The basic building blocks in Max are called *primitives*. You can use these primitives to start any modeling job. After you create a primitive, you can then bend it, stretch it, smash it, or cut it to create new objects, but for now, we focus on using primitives in their default shape.

This chapter covers the basics of primitive object types and introduces the various primitive objects, including how to accurately create and control them. You also use these base objects in the coming chapters to learn about selecting, cloning, grouping, and transforming.

Modeling is covered in depth in Part III, but first you need to learn how to create some basic blocks and move them around. Later, you can work on building a civilization. I'm sure workers in Rome would be jealous.

Creating Primitive Objects

Max is all about creating objects and scenes, so it's appropriate that one of the first things to learn is how to create objects. Although you can create complex models and objects, Max includes many simple, default geometric objects called primitives that you can use as a starting point. Creating these primitive objects can be as easy as clicking and dragging in a viewport.

Using the Create menu

The Create menu offers quick access to the buttons in the Create panel. All the objects that you can create using the Create panel you can access using the Create menu. Selecting an object from the Create menu automatically opens the Create panel and selects the correct category, subcategory, and button needed to create the object. After selecting the menu option, you simply need to click in one of the viewports to create the object.

Using the Create panel

The creation of all default Max objects, such as primitive spheres, shapes, lights, and cameras, starts with the Create panel (or the Create menu, which leads to the Create panel). This panel is the first in the Command Panel, indicated by an icon of an arrow pointing to a star.

Of all the panels in the Command Panel, only the Create panel (shown in Figure 5.1) includes both categories and subcategories. After you click the Create tab, seven category icons are displayed. From left to right, they are Geometry, Shapes, Lights, Cameras, Helpers, Space Warps, and Systems.

The Create panel is the place you go to create objects for the scene. These objects could be geometric objects like spheres, cones, and boxes or other objects like lights, cameras, or Space Warps. The Create panel contains a huge variety of objects. To create an object, you simply need to find the button for the object that you want to create, click it, click in one of the viewports, and *voilà* — instant object.

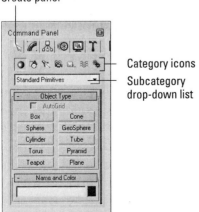 After you select the Geometry button (which has an icon of a sphere on it), a drop-down list with several subcategories appears directly below the category icons. The first available subcategory is Standard Primitives. After you select this subcategory, several text buttons appear that enable you to create some simple primitive objects.

NOTE The second subcategory is called Extended Primitives. It also includes primitive objects. The Extended Primitives are more specialized and aren't used as often.

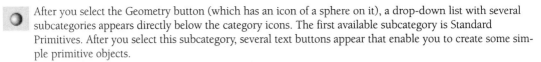

FIGURE 5.1

The Create panel includes categories and subcategories.

Create panel

Command Panel

Category icons
Subcategory
drop-down list

Standard Primitives

Object Type
AutoGrid
Box   Cone
Sphere GeoSphere
Cylinder Tube
Torus   Pyramid
Teapot Plane

Name and Color

As an example, click the button labeled Sphere (not to be confused with the Geometry category, which has a sphere icon). Several rollouts appear at the bottom of the Command Panel: These rollouts for the Sphere primitive object include Name and Color, Creation Method, Keyboard Entry, and Parameters. The rollouts for each primitive are slightly different, as well as the parameters within each rollout.

If you want to ignore these rollouts and just create a sphere, simply click and drag within one of the viewports, and a sphere object appears. The size of the sphere is determined by how you drag the mouse before releasing the mouse button. Figure 5.2 shows the new sphere and its parameters.

You can create primitive spheres easily by dragging in a viewport.

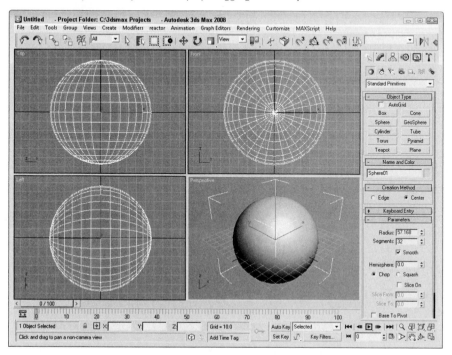

When an object button, such as the Sphere button, is selected, it turns dark yellow. This color change reminds you that you are in creation mode. Clicking and dragging within any viewport creates an additional sphere. While in creation mode, you can create many spheres by clicking and dragging several times in one of the viewports. To get out of creation mode, right-click in the active viewport or click the Select Object button or one of the transform buttons on the main toolbar.

After you select a primitive button, several additional rollouts magically appear. These new rollouts hold the parameters for the selected object and are displayed in the Create panel below the Name and Color rollout. Altering these parameters changes the object. The button remains selected, allowing you to create more objects until you select a different button, click on a toolbar button, or right-click in the active viewport.

Naming and renaming objects

Every object in the scene can have both a name and a color assigned to it. Each object is given a default name and random color when first created. The default name is the type of object followed by a number. For example, when you create a sphere object, Max labels it "Sphere01." These default names aren't very exciting and can be confusing if you have many objects. You can change the object's name at any time by modifying the Name field in the Name and Color rollout of the Command Panel.

NOTE Each object in Max has a unique name. Max is smart enough to give each new object a different name by adding a sequential number to the end of the name. This helps prevent the confusion of naming two objects the same way.

CROSS-REF Names and colors are useful for locating and selecting objects, as you find out in Chapter 6, "Selecting Objects, Setting Object Properties, and Using Layers and the Scene Explorer."

The Tools ⇨ Rename Objects menu command opens a dialog box that lets you change the object name of several objects at once. The Rename Objects dialog box, shown in Figure 5.3, lets you set the Base Name along with a Prefix, a Suffix, or a number. These new names can be applied to the selected objects or to the specific objects that you pick from the Select Objects dialog box.

FIGURE 5.3

The Rename Objects dialog box can rename several objects at once.

Assigning colors

The object color is shown in the color swatch to the right of the object name. This color is the color that is used to display the object within the viewports and to render the object if a material isn't applied. To change an object's color, just click the color swatch next to the Name field to make the Object Color dialog box appear. This dialog box, shown in Figure 5.4, lets you select a different color or pick a custom color.

FIGURE 5.4

You use the Object Color dialog box to define the color of objects displayed in the viewports.

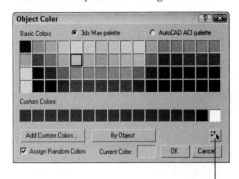

Select by Color button

The Object Color dialog box includes the standard 3ds Max palette and the AutoCAD ACI palette. The AutoCAD palette has many more colors than the Max palette, but the Max palette allows a row of custom colors. Above the Cancel button is the Select by Color button. Click this button to open the Select Objects dialog box where you can select all the objects that have a certain color.

With the Object Color dialog box, if the Assign Random Colors option is selected, then a random color from the palette is chosen every time a new object is created. If this option is not selected, the color of all new objects is the same until you choose a different object color. Making objects different colors allows you to more easily distinguish between two objects for selection and transformation.

The Object Color dialog box also includes a button that toggles between By Layer and By Objects, which appears only when an object is selected. Using this button, you can cause objects to accept color according to their object definition or based on the layer of which they are a part.

You can select custom colors by clicking the Add Custom Colors button. This button opens a Color Selector dialog box, shown in Figure 5.5. Selecting a color and clicking the Add Color button adds the selected color to the row of Custom Colors in the Object Color palette. You can also open the Color Selector by clicking on the Current Color swatch. The current color can then be dragged to the row of Custom Colors.

 **You can fill the entire row of Custom Colors by clicking repeatedly on the Add Color button.**

FIGURE 5.5

The Color Selector dialog box lets you choose new custom colors.

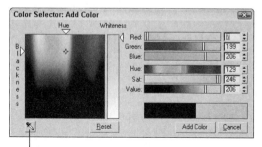

Sample screen color

The Color Selector dialog box defines colors using the RGB (red, green, and blue) and HSV (hue, saturation, and value) color systems. Another way to select colors is to drag the cursor around the rainbow palette on the left. After you find the perfect custom color to add to the Object Color dialog box, click the Add Color button. This custom color is then available wherever the Object Color dialog box is opened.

Object colors are also important because you can use them to select and filter objects. For example, the Selection Floater (which you can open by choosing Tools ⇨ Selection Floater) includes a Sort by Color setting. You can also choose Edit ⇨ Select by ⇨ Color menu (or click the Select by Color button) to select only objects that match a selected color.

NOTE **You can set objects to display an object's default color or its Material Color. These options are in the Display Color rollout under the Display panel (the fifth tab from the left in the Command Panel with an icon of a monitor). You can set them differently for Wireframe and Shaded views.**

The Sample Screen Color tool lets you select colors from any open Max window, including the Rendered Scene window. This gives you the ability to sample colors directly from a rendered image. To use this tool, simply click it and drag around the screen. The cursor changes to an eyedropper. If you click and drag around the window, the color is instantly updated in the Color Selector dialog box. If you hold down the Shift key while dragging, then the selected colors are blended together to create a summed color.

 The Sample Screen Color tool works only within Max windows.

NEW FEATURE The Sample Screen Color tool is new to 3ds Max 2008.

Using the Color Clipboard

The object color is one of the first places where colors are encountered, but it certainly won't be the last. If you find a specific color that you like and want to use elsewhere, you can use the Color Clipboard utility to carry colors to other interfaces. You can access this utility using the Tools ⇨ Color Clipboard menu command, which opens the Utilities panel, as shown in Figure 5.6.

FIGURE 5.6

The Color Clipboard utility offers a way to transport colors.

When selected, the Color Clipboard appears as a rollout in the Utilities panel and includes four color swatches. These color swatches can be dragged to other interfaces like the Material Editor. Clicking on any of these swatches launches the Color Selector. The New Floater button opens a floatable Color Clipboard that holds 12 colors, shown in Figure 5.7. Right-clicking the color swatches opens a pop-up menu with Copy and Paste options. Using this clipboard, you can open and save color configurations. The files are saved as Color Clipboard files with the .ccb extension.

FIGURE 5.7

The Color Clipboard floating palette can hold 12 colors.

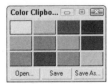

Using different creation methods

You actually have a couple of ways to create primitive objects by dragging in a viewport. With the first method, the first place you click sets the object's initial position. You then need to drag the mouse to define the object's first dimension and then click again to set each additional dimension, if needed. Primitive objects with a different number of dimensions require a different number of clicks and drags.

For example, a sphere is one of the simplest objects to create. To create a sphere, click in a viewport to set the location of the sphere's center, drag the mouse to the desired radius, and release the mouse button to complete. A Box object, on the other hand, requires a click-and-drag move to define the base (width and depth), and another drag-and-click move to set the height. If you ever get lost when defining these dimensions, check the Prompt Line to see what dimension the interface expects next.

When you click a primitive object button, the Creation Method rollout appears and offers different methods for creating the primitives. For example, click the Sphere button, and the Creation Method rollout displays two options: Edge and Center. When you choose the Edge method, the first viewport click sets one edge of the sphere, and dragging and clicking again sets the diameter of the sphere. The default Center creation method defines the sphere's center location; dragging sets the sphere's radius. The creation method for each primitive can be different. For example, the Box primitive object has a creation method for creating perfect cubes. Table 5.1 shows the number of clicks required to create an object and the creation methods for each primitive object.

 **TIP** If you're dragging to create a primitive object and halfway through its creation you change your mind, you can right-click to eliminate the creation of the object.

TABLE 5.1

Primitive Object Creation Methods

Primitive Object	Number of Viewport Clicks to Create	Default Creation Method	Other Creation Method
Box	2	Box	Cube
Cone	3	Center	Edge
Sphere	1	Center	Edge
GeoSphere	1	Center	Diameter
Cylinder	2	Center	Edge

continued

127

TABLE 5.1   *(continued)*

Primitive Object	Number of Viewport Clicks to Create	Default Creation Method	Other Creation Method
Tube	3	Center	Edge
Torus	2	Center	Edge
Pyramid	2	Base/Apex	Center
Teapot	1	Center	Edge
Plane	1	Rectangular	Square
Hedra	1	-	-
Torus Knot	2	Radius	Diameter
ChamferBox	3	Box	Cube
ChamferCyl	3	Center	Edge
OilTank	3	Center	Edge
Capsule	2	Center	Edge
Spindle	3	Center	Edge
L-Ext	3	Corners	Center
Gengon	3	Center	Edge

Primitive Object	Number of Viewport Clicks to Create	Default Creation Method	Other Creation Method
 C-Ext	3	Corners	Center
RingWave	2	-	-
Hose	2	-	-
Prism	3	Base/Apex	Isosceles

NOTE Some primitive objects, such as the Hedra, RingWave, and Hose, don't have any creation methods.

Using the Keyboard Entry rollout for precise dimensions

When creating a primitive object, you can define its location and dimensions by clicking in a viewport and dragging, or you can enter precise values in the Keyboard Entry rollout, located in the Create panel. Within this rollout, you can enter the offset XYZ values for positioning the origin of the primitive and the dimensions of the object. The offset values are defined relative to the active construction plane that is usually the Home Grid.

When all the dimension fields are set, click the Create button to create the actual primitive. You can create multiple objects by clicking the Create button several times. After a primitive is created, altering the fields in the Keyboard Entry rollout has no effect on the current object, but you can always use the Undo feature to try again.

Altering object parameters

The final rollout for all primitive objects is the Parameters rollout. This rollout holds all the various settings for the object. Compared to the Keyboard Entry rollout, which you can use only when creating the primitive, you can use the Parameters rollout to alter the primitive's parameters before or after the creation of the object. For example, increasing the Radius value after creating an object makes an existing sphere larger. This works only while the primitive mode is still enabled.

The parameters are different for each primitive object, but you can generally use them to control the dimensions, the number of segments that make up the object, and whether the object is sliced into sections. You can also select the Generate Mapping Coordinates option (which automatically creates material mapping coordinates that are used to position texture maps) and the Real-World Map Size option (which lets you define a texture's dimensions that are maintained regardless of the object size).

NOTE After you deselect an object, the Parameters rollout disappears from the Create tab and moves to the Modify tab. You can make future parameter adjustments by selecting an object and clicking the Modify tab.

Recovering from mistakes and deleting objects

Before going any further, you need to be reminded how to undo the last action with the Undo menu command. The Undo (Ctrl+Z) menu command will undo the last action, whether it's creating an object or changing a parameter. The Redo (Ctrl+Y) menu command lets you redo an action that was undone.

NOTE A separate undo feature for undoing a view change is available in the Views menu. The Views ⇨ Undo View Change (Shift+Z) applies to any viewport changes like zooming, panning, and rotating the view.

You can set the levels of undo in the Preference Settings dialog box. If you right-click on either the Undo button or the Redo button on the main toolbar, a list of recent actions is displayed. You can select any action from this list to be undone.

TIP Another way to experiment with objects is with the Hold (Alt+Ctrl+H) and Fetch (Alt+Ctrl+F) features, also found in the Edit menu. The Hold command holds the entire scene, including any viewport configurations, in a temporary buffer. You can recall a held scene at any time using the Fetch command. This is a quick alternative to saving a file.

The Edit ⇨ Delete menu command removes the selected object (or objects) from the scene. (The keyboard shortcut for this command is, luckily, the Delete key, because anything else would be confusing.)

Tutorial: Exploring the Platonic solids

Among the many discoveries of Plato, an ancient Greek mathematician and philosopher, were the mathematical formulas that defined perfect geometric solids. A perfect geometric solid is one that is made up of polygon faces that are consistent throughout the object. The five solids that meet these criteria have come to be known as the Platonic solids.

Using Max, you can create and explore these interesting geometric shapes. Each of these shapes is available as a primitive object using the Hedra primitive object. The Hedra primitive object is one of the Extended Primitives.

To create the five Platonic solids as primitive objects, follow these steps:

1. Open the Create panel, click the Geometry category button, and select Extended Primitives from the subcategory drop-down list. Click the Hedra button to enter Hedra creation mode, or select the Create ⇨ Extended Primitives ⇨ Hedra menu command.

2. Click in the Top viewport, and drag to the left to create a simple Tetrahedron object.

   After the object is created, you can adjust its settings by altering the settings in the Parameters rollout.

CAUTION Primitive parameters are available in the Create panel only while the new object is selected. If you deselect the new object, then the parameters are no longer visible in the Create panel, but you can access the object's parameters in the Modify panel.

3. Select the Tetra option in the Parameters rollout, set the P value in the Family Parameters section to **1.0**, and enter a value of **50** for the Radius. Be sure to press the Enter key after entering a value to update the object. Enter the name **Tetrahedron** in the Object Name field.

4. Click and drag again in the Top viewport to create another Hedra object. In the Parameters rollout, select the Cube/Octa option, and enter a value of **1.0** in the Family Parameter's P field and a value of **50** in the Radius field. Name this object **Octagon**.

5. Drag in the Top viewport to create another object. The Cube/Octa option is still selected. Enter a value of **1.0** in the Family Parameter's Q field this time, and set the Radius to **50**. Name this object **Cube**.

6. Drag in the Top viewport again to create the fourth Hedra object. In the Parameters rollout, select the Dodec/Icos option, enter a value of **1.0** in the P field, and set the Radius value to **50**. Name the object **Icosahedron**.

7. Drag in the Top viewport to create the final object. With the Dodec/Icos option set, enter **1.0** for the Q value, and set the Radius to **50**. Name this object **Dodecahedron**.

8. To get a good look at the objects, click the Perspective viewport, press the Zoom Extents button, and maximize the viewport by clicking the Min/Max Toggle (or press Alt+W) in the lower-right corner of the window.

Figure 5.8 shows the five perfect solid primitive objects. Using the Modify panel, you can return to these objects and change their parameters to learn the relationships between them. Later in this chapter, you can read about the Hedra primitive in greater detail.

FIGURE 5.8

The octagon, cube, tetrahedron, icosahedron, and dodecahedron objects; Plato would be amazed.

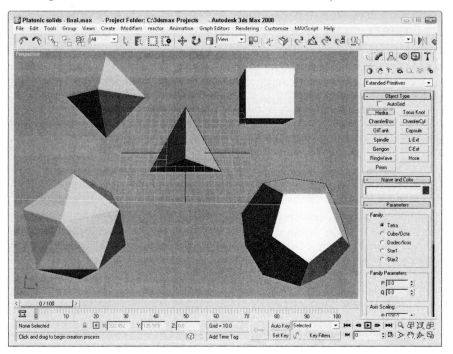

Exploring the Primitive Object Types

In the Create panel are actually two different subcategories of geometric primitives: Standard Primitives and Extended Primitives. These primitives include a diverse range of objects from simple boxes and spheres to complex torus knots. You can create all these primitives from the Create panel.

Standard Primitives

The Standard Primitives include many of the most basic and most used objects, including boxes, spheres, and cylinders. Figure 5.9 shows all the Standard Primitives.

The Standard Primitives: Box, Sphere, Cylinder, Torus, Teapot, Cone, GeoSphere, Tube, Pyramid, and Plane

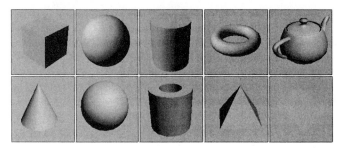

Box

You can use the Box primitive to create regular cubes and boxes of any width, length, and height. Holding down the Ctrl key while dragging the box base creates a perfect square for the base. To create a cube, select the Cube option in the Creation Method rollout. A single click and drag completes the cube.

The Length, Width, and Height Segment values indicate how many polygons make up each dimension. The default is only one segment.

Sphere

Spheres appear everywhere from sports balls to planets in space. Spheres are also among the easiest primitives to create. After clicking the Sphere button, simply click and drag in a viewport.

In the Parameters rollout, the Segments value specifies the number of polygons that make up the sphere. The higher the number of segments, the smoother the sphere is. The default value of 32 produces a smooth sphere, and a value of 4 actually produces a diamond-shaped object. The Smooth option lets you make the sphere smooth or faceted. Faceted spheres are useful for identifying faces for modifications. Figure 5.10 shows five spheres. The one on the left has 32 Segments and the Smooth option turned on. The remaining spheres have the Smooth option disabled with Segment values of 32, 16, 8, and 4.

Sphere primitives of various Segment values with the Smooth option turned on and off

The Parameters rollout also lets you create hemispheres. The hemisphere shape is set by the Hemisphere value, which can range from 0.0 to 1.0, with 0 being a full sphere and 1 being nothing at all. (A value of 0.5 would be a perfect hemisphere.) With the Hemisphere value specified, you now have two options with which to deal with the unused polygons that make up the originating sphere: the Chop option, which removes the unused polygons, and the Squash option, which retains the polygons but "squashes" them to fit in the hemisphere shape.

Figure 5.11 shows two hemispheres with Hemisphere values of 0.5. The Edged Faces option was enabled in the Viewport Configuration dialog box so you could see the polygon faces. The left hemisphere was created using the Chop option, and the right hemisphere was created with the Squash option. Notice how many extra polygons are included in the right hemisphere.

FIGURE 5.11

Creating hemispheres with the Chop and Squash options

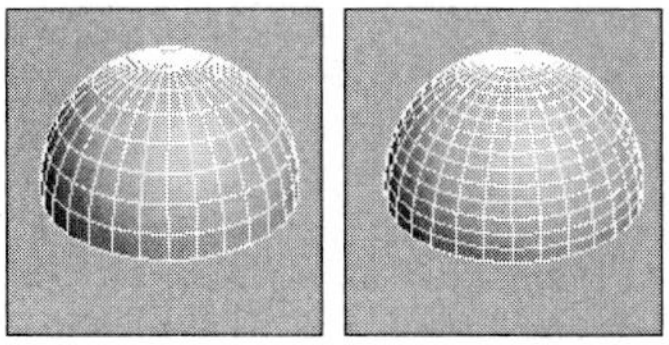

The Slice option enables you to dissect the sphere into slices (like segmenting an orange). The Slice From and Slice To fields accept values ranging from 0 to 360 degrees. Figure 5.12 shows three spheres that have been sliced. Notice that, because the Segments value hasn't changed, all slices have the same number of faces.

 **NOTE** You can use the Slice feature on several primitives, including the sphere, cylinder, torus, cone, tube, oiltank, spindle, chamfercyl, and capsule.

FIGURE 5.12

Using the Slice option to create sphere slices

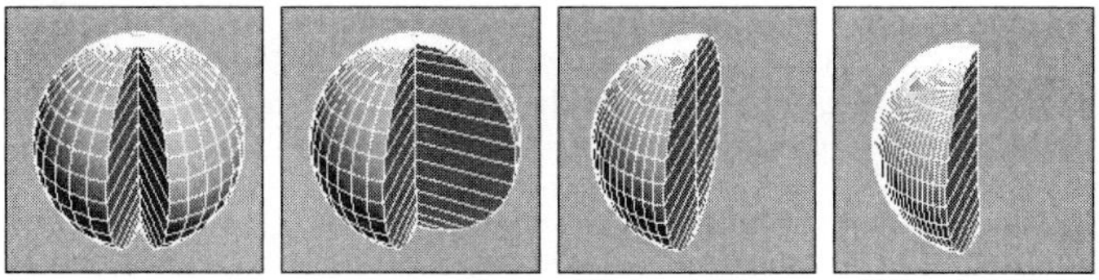

The Base to Pivot parameter determines whether the position of the pivot point is at the bottom of the sphere or at the center. The default (with the Base to Pivot setting not enabled) sets the pivot point for the sphere at the center of the sphere.

Cylinder

You can use a cylinder in many places — for example, as a pillar in front of a home or as a car driveshaft. To create one, first specify a base circle and then a height. The default number of sides is 18, which produces a smooth cylinder. Height and Cap Segments values define the number of polygons that make up the cylinder sides and caps. The Smooth and Slice options work the same as they do with a sphere (see the preceding section).

> **TIP** If you don't plan on modifying the ends of the cylinder, make the Cap Segments equal to 1 to keep the model complexity down.

Torus

A *Torus* (which is the mathematical name for a "doughnut") is a ring with a circular cross section. To create a Torus, you need to specify two radii values. The first is the value from the center of the Torus to the center of the ring; the second is the radius of the circular cross section. The default settings create a Torus with 24 segments and 12 sides. The Rotation and Twist options cause the sides to twist a specified value as the ring is circumnavigated.

Figure 5.13 shows some sample Toruses with a Smooth setting of None. The first three have Segments values of 24, 12, and 6. The last two have Twist values of 90 and 360. The higher the number of segments, the rounder the Torus looks when viewed from above. The default of 24 is sufficient to create a smooth Torus. The number of sides defines the circular smoothness of the cross section.

FIGURE 5.13

Using the Segments and Twist options on a Torus

The Parameters rollout includes settings for four different Smooth options. The All option smoothes all edges, and the None option displays all polygons as faceted. The Sides option smoothes edges between sides, resulting in a Torus with banded sides. The Segment option smoothes between segment edges, resulting in separate smooth sections around the Torus.

The Slice options work with a Torus the same way as they do with the sphere and cylinder objects (see the section "Sphere" earlier in this chapter).

Teapot

Okay, let's all sing together, "I'm a little teapot, short and stout. . . ." The teapot is another object that, like the sphere, is easy to create. Within the Parameters rollout, you can specify the number of Segments, whether the surface is smooth or faceted, and which parts to display, including Body, Handle, Spout, and Lid.

> **NOTE** You may recognize most of these primitives as standard shapes, with the exception of the teapot. The teapot has a special place in computer graphics. In early computer graphics development labs, the teapot was chosen as the test model for many early algorithms. It is still included as a valuable benchmark for computer graphics programmers.

Cone

The Cone object, whether used to create ice cream cones or megaphones, is created exactly like the cylinder object except that the second cap can have a radius different from that of the first. You create it by clicking and dragging to specify the base circle, dragging to specify the cone's height, and then dragging again for the second cap to create a Cone.

In addition to the two cap radii and the Height, parameter options include the number of Height and Cap Segments, the number of Sides, and the Smooth and Slice options.

GeoSphere

The GeoSphere object is a sphere created by using fewer polygon faces than the standard Sphere object. This type of sphere spreads the polygon faces, which are all equal in size, around the object, instead of concentrating them on either end like the normal Sphere object. This makes the GeoSphere a better choice for surface modeling because its polygon resolution is consistent. Geospheres also render more quickly and have faster transformation times than normal spheres. One reason for this is that a GeoSphere uses triangle faces instead of square faces.

In the Parameters rollout are several Geodesic Base Type options, including Tetra, Octa, and Icosa. The Tetra type is based on a four-sided tetrahedron, the Octa type is based on an eight-sided Octahedron, and the Icosa type is based on the 20-sided Icosahedron. Setting the Segment value to 1 produces each of these Hedron shapes. Each type aligns the triangle faces differently.

GeoSpheres also have the same Smooth, Hemisphere, and Base to Pivot options as the Sphere primitive. Selecting the Hemisphere option changes the GeoSphere into a hemisphere, but you have no additional options like Chop and Squash. GeoSphere primitives do not include an option to be sliced.

Tutorial: Comparing Spheres and GeoSpheres

To prove that GeoSpheres are more efficient than Sphere objects, follow these steps:

1. Create a normal Sphere, and set its Segment value to **4**.
2. Next to the Sphere object, create a GeoSphere object with a Tetra Base Type and the number of Segments set to **4**.
3. Create another GeoSphere object with the Octa Base Type and **4** Segments.
4. Finally, create a GeoSphere with the Icosa Base Type and **4** Segments.

Figure 5.14 shows these spheres as a comparison. The normal sphere, shown to the left, looks like a diamond, but the GeoSpheres still resemble spheres. Notice that the Icosa type GeoSphere, shown in the lower right, produces the smoothest sphere.

FIGURE 5.14

Even with a similar number of segments, GeoSpheres are much more spherical.

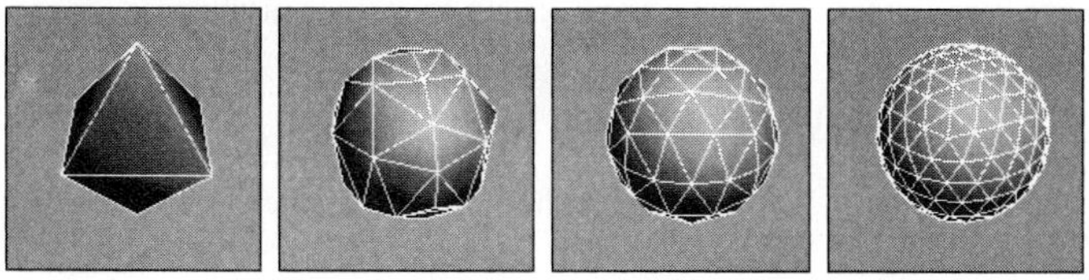

Tube

The Tube primitive is useful any time you need a pipe object. You can also use it to create ring-shaped objects that have rectangular cross sections. Creating a Tube object is very similar to the Cylinder and Cone objects. Tube parameters include two radii for the inner and outer tube walls. Tubes also have the Smooth and Slice options.

Pyramid

Pyramid primitives are constructed with a rectangular base and triangles at each edge that rise to meet at the top, just like the ones in Egypt, only easier to build. Two different creation methods are used to create the base rectangle. With the Base/Apex method, you create the base by dragging corner to corner, and with the Center method, you drag from the base center to a corner.

The Width and Depth parameters define the base dimensions, and the Height value determines how tall the pyramid is. You can also specify the number of segments for each dimension.

Plane

The Plane object enables you to model the Great Plains (good pun, eh?). The Plane primitive creates a simple plane that looks like a rectangle, but it includes Multiplier parameters that let you specify the size of the plane at render time. This feature makes working in a viewport convenient because you don't have to worry about creating a huge plane object representing the ground plane that makes all other scene objects really small in comparison.

 **TIP**   Dense plane objects can be made into a terrain by randomly altering the height of each interior vertex with a Noise modifier.

The Plane primitive includes two creation methods: Rectangle and Square. The Square method creates a perfect square in the viewport when dragged. You can also define the Length and Width Segments, but the real benefits of the Plane object are derived from the use of the Render Multipliers.

The Scale Multiplier value determines how many times larger the plane should be at render time. Both Length and Width are multiplied by equal values. The Density Multiplier specifies the number of segments to produce at render time. The Total Faces value lets you know how many polygons are added to the scene using the specified Density Multiplier value.

Using these multipliers, you can create a small Plane object in the scene that automatically increases to the size and density it needs to be when rendered. This allows you to use the Zoom Extents button to see all objects without having a huge Plane object define the extents.

Extended Primitives

Access the Extended Primitives by selecting Extended Primitives in the subcategory drop-down list in the Create panel. These primitives aren't as generic as the Standard Primitives but are equally useful (see Figure 5.15).

Hedra

Hedras, or Polyhedra, form the basis for a class of geometry defined by fundamental mathematical principles. In addition to Plato, Johannes Kepler used these Polyhedra as the basis for his famous "Harmony of the Spheres" theory. The Hedra primitives available in Max are Tetrahedron, Cube/Octahedron, Dodecahedron/Icosahedron, and two Star types called Star1 and Star2. From these basic Polyhedra, you can create many different variations.

The Family section options determine the shape of the Hedra. Each member of a Hedra pair is mathematically related to the other member. The Family Parameters include P and Q values. These values change the Hedra between the two shapes that make up the pair. For example, if the Family option is set to Cube/Octa, then a P value of 1 displays an Octagon, and a Q value of 1 displays a Cube. When both P and Q values are set to 0, the shape becomes an intermediate shape somewhere between a Cube and an Octagon. Because the values are interrelated, only one shape of the pair can have a value of 1 at any given time. Both P and Q cannot be set to 1 at the same time.

FIGURE 5.15

The Extended Primitives: Hedra, ChamferBox, OilTank, Spindle, Gengon, RingWave, Hose, Torus Knot, ChamferCyl, Capsule, L-Ext, C-Ext, and Prism

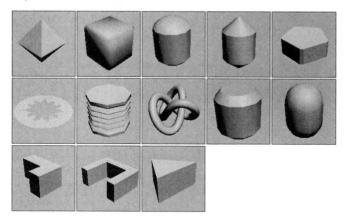

Figure 5.16 shows each of the basic Hedra Families in columns from left to right: Tetra, Cube/Octa, Dodec/Icos, Star1, and Star2. The top row has a P value of 1 and a Q value of 0, the middle row has both P and Q set to 0, and the bottom row sets P to 0 and Q to 1. Notice that the middle row shapes are a combination of the top and bottom rows.

FIGURE 5.16

The Hedra Families with the standard shapes in the top and bottom rows and the intermediate shapes in the middle row

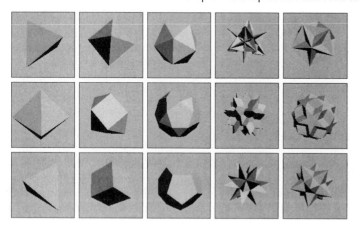

The relationship between P and Q can be described in this manner: When the P value is set to 1 and the Q value is set to 0, one shape of the pair is displayed. As the P value decreases, each vertex becomes a separate face. The edges of these new faces increase as the value is decreased down to 0. The same holds true for the Q value.

TIP Altering the P and Q parameters can create many unique shapes. For each Hedra, try the following combinations: P = 0, Q = 0; P = 1, Q = 0; P = 0, Q = 1; P = 0.5, Q = 0.5; P = 0.5, Q = 0; P = 0, Q = 0.5. These represent the main intermediate objects.

As the geometry of the objects changes, the Hedra can have as many as three different types of polygons making up the faces. These polygons are represented by the P, Q, and R Axis Scaling values. Each type of face can be scaled, creating sharp points extending from each face. If only one unique polygon is used for the faces, then only one Axis Scaling parameter is active. The Reset button simply returns the Axis Scaling value to its default at 100. For example, using the R Axis Scaling value, pyramid shapes can be extended from each face of a cube.

Figure 5.17 shows some results of using the Axis Scaling options. One of each family type has been created and displayed in the top row for reference. The bottom row has had an axis scaled to a value of 170. This setting causes one type of polygon face to be extended, thereby producing a new shape.

FIGURE 5.17

Hedras with extended faces, compliments of the Axis Scaling option

The Vertices parameter options add more vertices and edges to the center of each extended polygon. The three options are Basic, which is the default and doesn't add any new information to the Hedra; Center, which adds vertices to the center of each extended polygon; and Center and Sides, which add both center vertices and connecting edges for each face that is extended using the Axis Scaling options. With these options set, you can extend the polygon faces at your own discretion.

Way at the bottom of the Parameters rollout is the Radius value.

ChamferBox

A *chamfered* object is one whose edges have been smoothed out, so a ChamferBox primitive is a box with beveled edges. The parameter that determines the amount of roundness applied to an edge is *Fillet*. In many ways, this object is just a simple extension of the Box primitive.

The only additions in the Parameters rollout are two fields for controlling the Fillet dimension and the Fillet Segments. Figure 5.18 shows a ChamferBox with Fillet values of 0, 5, 10, 20, and 30 and the Smooth option turned on.

Cylindrical extended primitives

The Extended Primitives include several objects based on the Cylinder primitive that are very similar. The only real difference is the shape of the caps at either end. These four similar objects include the OilTank, Spindle, ChamferCyl, and Capsule. Figure 5.19 shows these similar objects side by side.

FIGURE 5.18

A ChamferBox with progressively increasing Fillet values

FIGURE 5.19

Several different cylindrical extended primitive objects exist, including Oil Tank, Spindle, ChamferCyl, and Capsule.

OilTank

OilTank seems like a strange name for a primitive. This object is essentially the Cylinder primitive with dome caps like you would see on a diesel truck transporting oil. The Parameters rollout includes an additional option for specifying the Cap Height. The Height value can be set to indicate the entire height of the object with the Overall option or the height to the edge of the domes using the Centers option. The only other new option is Blend, which smoothes the edges between the cylinder and the caps. All cylindrical primitives can also be sliced just like the sphere object.

Spindle

The Spindle primitive is the same as the OilTank primitive, except that the dome caps are replaced with conical caps. All other options in the Parameters rollout are identical to the OilTank primitive.

ChamferCyl

The ChamferCyl primitive is very similar to the ChamferBox primitive, but applied to a cylinder instead of a box. The Parameters rollout includes some additional fields for handling the Fillet values.

Capsule

The Capsule primitive is a yet another primitive based on the cylinder, but this time with hemispherical caps. This object resembles the OilTank primitive very closely. The only noticeable difference is in the border between the cylinder and caps.

Gengon

The Gengon primitive creates and extrudes regular polygons such as triangles, squares, and pentagons. There is even an option to Fillet (or smooth) the edges. To specify which polygon to use, enter a value in the Sides field.

Figure 5.20 shows five simple Gengons with different numbers of edges.

FIGURE 5.20

Gengon primitives are actually just extruded regular polygons.

RingWave

The RingWave primitive is a specialized primitive that you can use to create a simple gear or a sparkling sun. It consists of two circles that make up a ring. You can set the circle edges to be wavy and even fluctuate over time. You can also use RingWaves to simulate rapidly expanding gases that would result from a planetary explosion. If you're considering a Shockwave effect, then you should look into using a RingWave primitive.

The Radius setting defines the outer edge of the RingWave, and the Ring Width defines the inner edge. This ring can also have a Height. The Radial and Height Segments and the number of Sides determine the complexity of the object.

The RingWave Timing controls set the expansion values. The Start Time is the frame where the ring begins at zero, the Grow Time is the number of frames required to reach its full size, and the End Time is the frame where the RingWave object stops expanding. The No Growth option prevents the object from expanding, and it remains the same size from the Start frame to the End frame. The Grow and Stay option causes the RingWave to expand from the Start Time until the Grow Time frame is reached and remain full grown until the End Time. The Cyclic Growth begins expanding the objects until the Grow Time is reached. It then starts again from zero and expands repeatedly until the End Time is reached.

The last two sections of the Parameters rollout define how the inner and outer edges look and are animated. If the Edge Breakup option is on, then the rest of the settings are enabled. These additional settings control the number of Major and Minor Cycles, the Width Flux for these cycles, and the Crawl Time, which is the number of frames to animate.

The Surface Parameters section includes an option for creating Texture Coordinates, which are the same as mapping coordinates for applying textures. There is also an option to Smooth the surface of the object.

Figure 5.21 shows five animated frames of a RingWave object with both Inner and Outer Edge Breakup settings. Notice that the edges change over the different frames.

FIGURE 5.21

Five frames of a rapidly expanding and turbulent RingWave object

Tutorial: Creating a pie

This tutorial provides a very different recipe for creating a pie using a RingWave object. Although the RingWave object can be animated, you also can use it to create static objects such as this pie, or moving objects such as a set of gears.

To create a pie using the RingWave object, follow these steps:

1. Select Create ➪ Extended Primitives ➪ RingWave, and drag in the Top viewport to create a RingWave object.

2. In the Parameters rollout, set the Radius to **115**, the Ring Width to **90**, and the Height to **30**.

3. In the RingWave Timing section, select the No Growth option. Then enable the Outer Edge Breakup option, set the Major Cycles to **25**, the Width Flux to **4.0**, and the Minor Cycles to **0**.

4. Enable the Inner Edge Breakup option. Set the Major Cycles to **6**, the Width Flux to **15**, and the Minor Cycles to **25** with a Width Flux of **10**.

Figure 5.22 shows a nice pie object as good as Grandmother made. You can take this pie one step further by selecting Modifiers ➪ Parametric Deformers ➪ Taper to apply the Taper modifier and set the Amount to 0.1.

FIGURE 5.22

This pie object was created using the RingWave object.

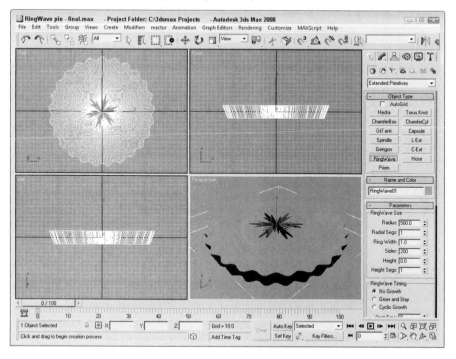

Torus Knot

A Torus Knot is similar to the Torus covered earlier, except that the circular cross section follows a 3D curve instead of a simple circle. The method for creating the Torus Knot primitive is the same as that for creating the Torus. The Parameters rollout even lets you specify the base curve to be a circle instead of a knot. A knot is a standard, mathematically defined 3D curve.

Below the Radius and Segment parameters are the P and Q values. These values can be used to create wildly variant Torus Knots. The P value is a mathematical factor for computing how the knot winds about its vertical axis. The maximum value is 25, which makes the knot resemble a tightly wound spool. The Q value causes the knot to wind horizontally. It also has a maximum value of 25. Setting both values to the same number results in a simple circular ring.

Figure 5.23 shows some of the beautiful shapes that are possible by altering the P and Q values of a Torus Knot. These Torus Knots have these values: the first has P = 3, Q = 2; the second has P = 1, Q = 3; the third has P = 10, Q = 15; the fourth has P = 15, Q = 20; and the fifth has P = 25, Q = 25.

FIGURE 5.23

Various Torus Knots display the beauty of mathematics.

When the Base Curve is set to Circle, like those in Figure 5.23, the P and Q values become disabled, and the Warp Count and Warp Height fields become active. These fields control the number of ripples in the ring and their height. Figure 5.24 shows several possibilities. From left to right, the settings are Warp Count = 5, Warp Height = 0.5; Warp Count = 10, Warp Height = 0.5; Warp Count = 20, Warp Height = 0.5; Warp Count = 50, Warp Height = 0.5; and Warp Count = 100, Warp Height = 0.75.

FIGURE 5.24

Torus Knots with a Circle Base Curve are useful for creating impressive rings.

In addition to the Base Curve settings, you can also control several settings for the Cross Section. The Radius and Sides values determine the size of the circular cross section and the number of segments used to create the cross section. The Eccentricity value makes the circular cross section elliptical by stretching it along one of its axes. The Twist value rotates each successive cross section relative to the previous one creating a twisting look along the object. The Lumps value sets the number of lumps that appear in the Torus Knot, and the Lump Height and Offset values set the height and starting point of these lumps.

The Smooth options work just like those for the Torus object by smoothing the entire object, just the sides, or none. You can also set the U and V axis Offset and Tiling values for the mapping coordinates.

L-Ext

The L-Ext primitive stands for L-Extension. You can think of it as two rectangular boxes connected at right angles to each other. To create an L-Ext object, you need to first drag to create a rectangle that defines the overall area of the object. Next, you drag to define the Height of the object, and finally, you drag to define the width of each leg.

The Parameters rollout includes dimensions for Side and Front Lengths, Side and Front Widths, and the Height. You can also define the number of Segments for each dimension.

C-Ext

The C-Ext primitive is the same as the L-Ext primitive with an extra rectangular box. The C shape connects three rectangular boxes at right angles to each other.

The Parameters rollout includes dimensions for Side, Front, and Back Lengths and Widths, and the Height. You can also define the number of Segments for each dimension. These primitives are great if your name is Clive Logan or Carrie Lincoln. No, actually, these primitives are used to create architectural beams.

Prism

The Prism primitive is essentially an extruded triangle. If you select the Base/Apex creation method, then each of the sides of the base triangle can have a different length. With this creation method, the first click in the viewport sets one edge of the base triangle, the second click sets the opposite corner of the triangle that affects the other two edges, and the final click sets the height of the object.

The other creation method is Isosceles, which doesn't let you skew the triangle before setting the height.

Hose

The Hose primitive is a flexible connector that can be positioned between two other objects. It acts much like a spring but has no dynamic properties. In the Hose Parameters rollout, you can specify the Hose as a Free Hose or Bound to Object Pivots. If the Free Hose option is selected, you can set the Hose Height. If the Bound to Object Pivots option is selected, then two Pick Object buttons appear for the Top and Bottom objects. Once bound to two objects, the hose stretches between the two objects when either is moved. You can also set the Tension for each bound object.

For either the Bound Hose or Free Hose, you can set the number of Segments that make up the hose; whether the flexible section is enabled; to smooth along the Sides, Segments, neither, or all; whether the hose is Renderable; and to Generate Mapping Coordinates for applying texture maps. If the flexible section is enabled, then you can set where the flexible section Starts and Ends, the number of Cycles, and its Diameter.

You can also set the Hose Shape to Round, Rectangular, or D-Section. Figure 5.25 shows a flexible hose object bound to two sphere objects.

Tutorial: Creating a bendable straw

If you've ever found yourself modeling a juice box (or drinking from a juice box and wondering, "How would I model this bendable straw?"), then this tutorial is for you. The nice part about the Hose primitive is that once you've created the model, you can reposition the straw and the bend changes as needed, just like a real straw.

FIGURE 5.25

The Hose object flexes between its two bound objects.

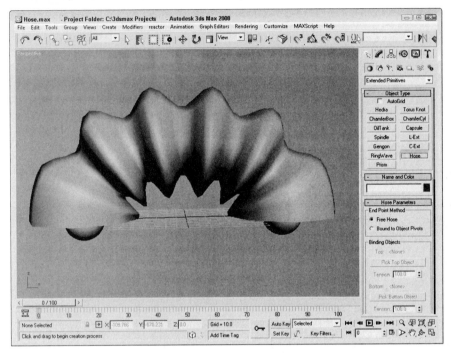

To create a bendable straw, follow these steps:

1. Open the Bendable straw.max file from the Chap 05 directory on the DVD.

   This file includes two Tube primitives to represent the top and bottom portions of a straw. I've oriented their pivot points so the Z-axis points toward where the Hose primitive will go.

2. Select Create ⇨ Extended Primitives ⇨ Hose, and drag in the Top viewport close to where the two straws meet. Select the Bound to Object Pivots option, click on the Pick Top Object button, and select the top Tube object. Then click on the Pick Bottom Object button, and select the bottom Tube object. This step positions the Hose object between the two Tube pieces.

3. In the Hose Parameters rollout, set the Tension for the Top object to 35, the Tension for the bottom object to **10.0**. Set the Segments to **40**, the Starts value to **0**, the Ends value to **100**, the Cycles to **10**, and the Diameter to **24**. Make sure that the Renderable option is enabled, and enable the Round Hose option with a Diameter of **20.0**.

Figure 5.26 shows the completed bendable straw created using a Hose primitive.

Modifying object parameters

Primitive objects provide a good starting point for many of the other modeling types. They also provide a good way to show off parameter-based modeling.

FIGURE 5.26

Use the Hose primitive to connect two objects.

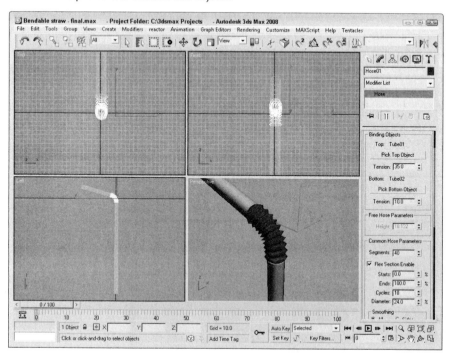

All objects have parameters. These parameters help define how the object looks. For example, consider the primitive objects. The primitive objects contained in Max are parametric. Parametric objects are mathematically defined, and you can change them by modifying their parameters. The easiest object modifications to make are simply changing these parameters. For example, a sphere with a radius of 4 can be made into a sphere with a radius of 10 by simply typing a 10 in the Radius field. The viewports display these changes automatically when you press the Enter key.

NOTE When an object is first created, its parameters are displayed in the Parameters rollout of the Create panel. As long as the object remains the current object, you can modify its parameters using this rollout. After you select a different tool or object, the Parameters rollout is no longer accessible from the Create panel, but if you select the object and open the Modify panel, all the parameters can be changed for the selected object.

Tutorial: Filling a treasure chest with gems

I haven't found many treasure chests lately, but if I remember correctly, they are normally filled with bright, sparkling gems. In this tutorial, we fill the chest with a number of Hedra primitives and alter the object properties in the Modify panel to create a diverse offering of gems.

To create a treasure chest with many unique gems, follow these steps:

1. Open the Treasure chest of gems.max file from the Chap 05 directory on the DVD.

   This file includes a simple treasure chest model.

145

2. Select Create ⇨ Extended Primitives ⇨ Hedra to open the Extended Primitives subcategory in the Create panel. At the top of the Object Type rollout, enable the AutoGrid option and select the Hedra button.

   The AutoGrid option causes creates all new objects on the surface of other objects.

3. Create several Hedra objects.

   The size of the objects doesn't matter at this time.

4. Open the Modify panel, and select one of the Hedra objects.

5. Alter the values in the Parameters rollout to produce a nice gem.

6. Repeat Step 5 for all Hedra objects in the chest.

Figure 5.27 shows the resulting chest with a variety of gems.

FIGURE 5.27

A treasure chest full of gems quickly created by altering object parameters

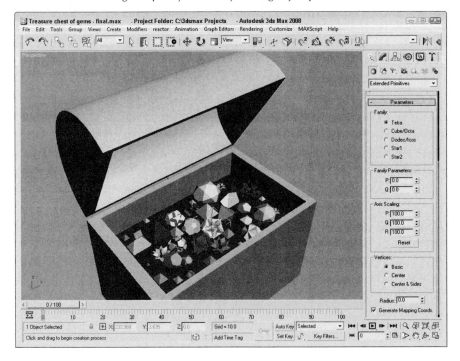

Architecture Primitives

If you wander about the various departments at Autodesk, you run into several groups that deal with products for visualizing architecture, including the well-known product AutoCAD. This product is used by a vast number of engineers and architects to design the layouts for building physical structures.

Along with AutoCAD is VIZ, another very popular package that would be considered a close sibling to Max. AutoCAD VIZ is used to create visualizations of AutoCAD data and, like Max, deals with modeling, rendering, and shading 3D objects. In fact, many of the new features found in Max were originally developed for VIZ.

Using AEC Objects

Included in the features that have migrated over from VIZ are all the various architectural objects commonly found in buildings. These objects can all be found in the Create ⇨ AEC Objects menu. The AEC Objects menu includes many different architecture primitives: Foliage, Railings, Walls, Doors, Stairs, and Windows.

Foliage

The Foliage category includes several different plants all listed in the Favorite Plants rollout, shown in Figure 5.28. The available plants include a Banyan tree, Generic Palm, Scotch Pine, Yucca, Blue Spruce, American Elm, Weeping Willow, Euphorbia, Society Garlic, Big Yucca, Japanese Flowering Cherry, and Generic Oak.

CAUTION The various foliage objects are large models that can quickly slow down the scene if multiple copies are added to a scene. For example, a single Banyan tree has more than 50,000 polygons. Adding several such trees to your scene can make it quite slow.

FIGURE 5.28

The Favorite Plants rollout shows thumbnails of the various plants.

At the bottom of the Favorite Plants rollout is a button called Plant Library that opens a dialog box where you can see the details of all the plants, including the total number of faces. The winner is the Banyan tree with 100,000 faces. Using the Parameters rollout, you can set the Height, Density, and Pruning values for each of these plants. Also, depending on the tree type, you can select to show the Leaves, Trunk, Fruit, Branches, Flowers, and Roots, and you can set the Level of Detail to Low, Medium, or High.

Railings

The Railings option lets you pick a path that the railing will follow. You can then select the number of Segments to use to create the railing. For the Top Rail, you can select to use No Railing or a Round or Square Profile and set its Depth, Width, and Height. You can also set parameters for the Lower Rails, Posts (which appear at either end), and Fencing (which are the vertical slats that support the railing).

The Lower Rails, Posts, and Fencing sections feature an icon that can be used to set the Spacing of these elements. The Spacing dialog box that opens looks like the same dialog box that is used for the Spacing Tool, where you can specify a Count, Spacing value, and Offsets.

Walls

Walls are simple, with parameters for Width and Height. You can also set the Justification to Left, Center, or Right. The nice part about creating wall objects is that you can connect several walls together just like the Line tool. For example, creating a single wall in the Top viewport extends a connected wall from the last point where you clicked that is connected to the previous wall. Right-click to exit wall creation mode. Figure 5.29 shows a room of walls created simply by clicking at the intersection points in the Top view.

FIGURE 5.29
_____

Rooms of walls can be created simply by clicking where the corners are located.

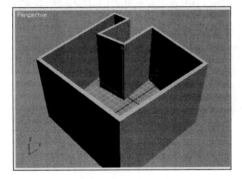

Doors

The Doors category includes three types of doors: Pivot, Sliding, and BiFold. Each of these types has its own parameters that you can set, but for each of these door types, you can set its Height, Width, and Depth dimensions and the amount the door is Open.

Be aware when creating doors that Doors have two different Creation Methods — Width/Depth/Height and Width/Height/Depth. The first is the default, and it requires that the first click sets the Width, the second click sets the Depth, and the third click sets the Height. The Parameters rollout includes options to flip the direction in which the door opens. This is very handy if you position your door incorrectly.

Stairs

The Stairs category includes four types of stairs: LType, Spiral, Straight, and UType. For each type, you can select Open (single slats with no vertical backing behind the stairs), Closed (each stair includes a horizontal and vertical portion), or Box (the entire staircase is one solid object). For each type, you also can control the parameters for the Carriage (the center support that holds the stairs together), Stringers (the base boards that run along the sides of the stairs), and Railings.

The Rise section determines the overall height of the staircase. It can be set by an Overall height value, a Riser Height value (the height of each individual stair), or by a Riser Count (the total number of stairs). You also can specify the Thickness and Depth of the stairs.

Windows

The Windows category includes six types of windows: Awning, Casement, Fixed, Pivoted, Projected, and Sliding. As with doors, you can choose from two different Creation Methods. The default Creation Method creates windows with Width, then Depth, and then Height. Parameters include the Window and Frame dimensions, the Thickness of the Glazing, and Rails and Panels. You can also open all windows, except for the Fixed Window type.

Tutorial: Add stairs to a clock tower building

I'll leave the architectural design to the architects, but for this example, we create a simple staircase and add it to the front of a clock tower building.

To add stairs to a building, follow these steps.

1. Open the Clock tower building.max file from the Chap 05 directory on the DVD. This file includes a building with a clock tower extending from its center, but the main entrance is empty.

2. Select Create ➪ AEC Objects ➪ Straight Stair. Click and drag in the Top viewport from the location where the lower-left corner of the stair is located and drag to the upper-left corner of the stairs where the stairs meet the entryway into the building to set the stair's length. Then drag across to set the stairs' width and click at the opposite side of the entryway. Then drag downward in the Left viewport to set the stairs' height and click. Then right-click in the Top viewport to exit Stairs creation mode.

3. With the stairs selected, click the Select and Move (W) button in the main toolbar and drag the stairs in the Front viewport until they align with the front of one side of the entryway.

4. Open the Modify panel, and select the Box option in the Parameters rollout. Then adjust the Overall Rise value so it matches the entryway.

5. Select Tools ➪ Mirror, and select the Copy option with an Offset of around −140 about the X-Axis. Click OK.

Figure 5.30 shows the clock tower building with stairs.

FIGURE 5.30

The AEC Objects category makes adding structural objects like stairs easy.

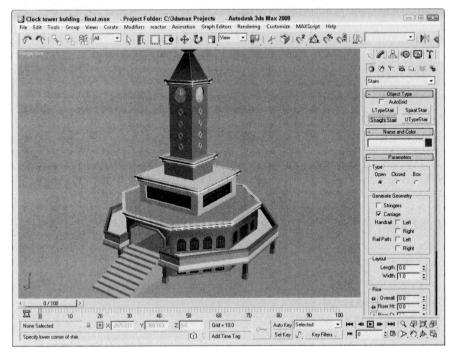

Summary

Primitives are the most basic shapes and often provide a starting point for more ambitious modeling projects. The two classes of primitives — Standard and Extended — provide a host of possible objects. This chapter covered the following topics:

- The basics of creating primitives by both dragging and entering keyboard values
- How to name objects and set and change the object color
- The various creation methods for all the primitive objects
- The various primitives in both the Standard and Extended subcategories
- The possible parameters for each of the primitive objects
- Creating AEC Objects, including plants, railings, doors, and windows

Now that you know how to create objects, you can focus on selecting them after they're created, which is what the next chapter covers. You can select objects in numerous ways. Layers and setting object properties are also discussed.

Chapter 6

Selecting Objects, Setting Object Properties, and Using Layers and the Scene Explorer

Now that you've learned how to create objects and had some practice, you've probably created more than you really need. To eliminate, move, or change the look of any objects, you first have to know how to select the object. Doing so can be tricky if the viewports are all full of objects lying on top of one another. Luckily, Max offers several selection features that make looking for a needle in a haystack easier.

Max offers many different ways to select objects. You can select by name, color, type, and even material. You can also use selection filters to make only certain types of objects selectable. And after you've found all the objects you need, you can make a selection set, which will allow you to quickly select a set of objects by name. Now where is that needle?

All objects have properties that define their physical characteristics, such as shape, radius, and smoothness, but objects also have properties that control where they are located in the scene, how they are displayed and rendered, and what their parent objects are. These properties have a major impact on how you work with objects; understanding them can make objects in a scene easier to work with.

IN THIS CHAPTER

Selecting objects using toolbars and menus

Using named selection sets

Setting object properties

Hiding and freezing objects

Working with layers

Exploring the Scene Explorer

Selecting Objects

Max includes several methods for selecting objects — the easiest being simply clicking on the object in one of the viewports. Selected objects turn white and are enclosed in brackets called *selection brackets*.

In addition to turning white and displaying selection brackets, several options allow you to mark selected objects. You can find these options in the Viewport Configuration dialog box (which you access with the Customize ➪ Viewport Configuration menu command); they include selection brackets (keyboard shortcut, J) and edged faces (F4). Either or both of these options can be enabled, as shown in Figure 6.1. Another way to detect the selected object is that the object's axes appear at the object's pivot point. The Views ⇨ Shade Selected command turns on shading for the selected object in all viewports.

CAUTION
The Viewport Configuration dialog box also includes an option to Shade Selected Faces (F2), but this option shades only selected subobject faces.

FIGURE 6.1

Selected objects can be highlighted with selection brackets (left), edged faces (middle), or both (right).

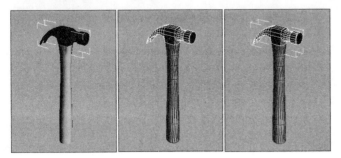

With many objects in a scene, clicking directly on a single object, free from the others, can be difficult, but persistence can pay off. If you continue to click an object that is already selected, then the object directly behind the object you clicked on is selected. For example, if you have a row of spheres lined up, you can select the third sphere by clicking three times on the first object.

TIP
In complicated scenes, finding an object is often much easier if it has a relevant name. Be sure to name your new objects using the Name and Color rollout. If a single object is selected, its name appears in the Name and Color rollout.

Selection filters

Before examining the selection commands in the Edit menu, I need to tell you about Selection Filters. With a complex scene that includes geometry, lights, cameras, shapes, and so on, selecting the exact object that you want can be difficult. Selection filters can simplify this task.

A selection filter specifies which types of objects can be selected. The Selection Filter drop-down list is located on the main toolbar. Selecting Shapes, for example, makes only shape objects available for selection. Clicking a geometry object with the Shape Selection Filter enabled does nothing.

The available filters include All, Geometry, Shapes, Lights, Cameras, Helpers, and Space Warps. If you're using Inverse Kinematics, you can also filter by Bone, IK Chain Object, and Point.

The Combos option opens the Filter Combinations dialog box, shown in Figure 6.2. From this dialog box, you can select combinations of objects to filter. These new filter combinations are added to the drop-down list. For example, to create a filter combination for lights and cameras, open the Filter Combinations dialog box, select Lights and Cameras, and click Add. The combination is listed as LC in the Current Combinations section, and the LC option is added to the drop-down list.

The Filter Combinations dialog box also includes a list of additional objects. Using this list, you can filter very specific object types, such as a Boolean object or a Box primitive. In fact, the Bone, IK Chain Object, and Point filters that appear in the default main toolbar drop-down list all come from this additional list.

FIGURE 6.2

The Filter Combinations dialog box enables you to create a custom selection filter.

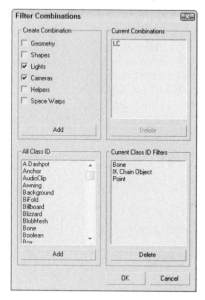

Select buttons

On the main toolbar are several buttons used to select objects, shown in Table 6.1. The Select Object button looks like the arrow cursor. The other three buttons select and transform objects. They are Select and Move (W), Select and Rotate (E), and Select and Scale (R). These commands also are available on the quadmenu. The final selection button is the Select and Manipulate button. With this button, you can select and use special helpers such as sliders.

TABLE 6.1

Select Buttons

Button	Description
	Select Object (Q)
	Select and Move (W)
	Select and Rotate (E)
	Select and Scale (R)
	Select and Manipulate

CROSS-REF See Chapter 7, "Transforming Objects, Pivoting, Aligning, and Snapping" for more details on the Select and Transform buttons.

Selecting with the Edit menu

The Edit menu includes several convenient selection commands. The Edit ➪ Select All (Ctrl+A) menu command does just what you would think it does: It selects all unfrozen and unhidden objects in the current scene of the type defined by the selection filter. The Edit ➪ Select None (Ctrl+D) menu command deselects all objects. You can also simulate this command by clicking in any viewport away from all objects. The Edit ➪ Select Invert (Ctrl+I) menu command selects all objects defined by the selection filter that are currently not selected and deselects all currently selected objects.

The Edit ➪ Select Similar (Ctrl+Q) command selects all objects that are similar to the current selection. If multiple objects are selected, the Select Similar command selects the objects that meet the criteria for being similar to each of the selected objects. Objects are similar if they meet one of the following criteria:

- Same object type such as lights, helpers, or Space Warps
- Same primitive object such as Sphere, Box, or Hedra
- Same modeling type such as Editable Spline, Editable Poly, or Editable Patch
- Imported objects from an AutoCAD DWG file that have the same style applied
- Same applied material
- Objects existing on the same layer

NEW FEATURE The Edit ➪ Select Similar command is new to 3ds Max 2008.

Figure 6.3 shows a treasure chest of Hedra gems created in Chapter 5. With a single object selected, choosing Edit ➪ Select Similar (Ctrl+Q) causes all Hedra primitive objects to be selected.

Choosing Edit ➪ Select by ➪ Color lets you click a single object in any of the viewports. All objects with the same color as the one you selected are selected. Even if you already have an object of that color selected, you still must select an object of the desired color. Be aware that this is the object color, not the applied material color. This command, of course, does not work on any objects without an associated color, such as Space Warps.

Select by Name

Choosing Edit ➪ Select by ➪ Name opens the Select From Scene dialog box, which is a version of the Scene Explorer dialog box, except that you can't change any parameters. Clicking the Select by Name button on the main toolbar, positioned to the right of the Select Object button, or pressing the keyboard shortcut, H, can also open this dialog box.

CROSS-REF The Scene Explorer dialog box is covered in detail later in this chapter.

You select objects by clicking their names in the list and then clicking the OK button, or by simply double-clicking a single item. To pick and choose several objects, hold down the Ctrl key while selecting. Holding down the Shift key selects a range of objects.

FIGURE 6.3

The Select Similar command selects all Hedra objects.

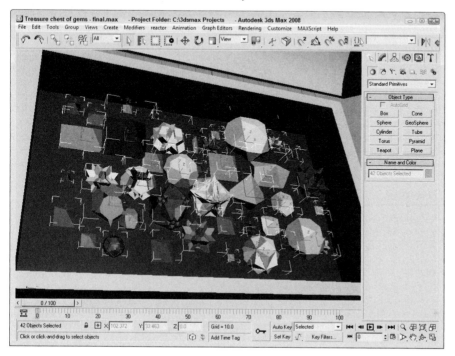

Select by Region

The Edit ➪ Region command lets you select from one of two different methods for selecting objects in the viewport using the mouse. First, make sure that you're in select mode, and then click away from any of the objects and drag over the objects to select. The first method for selecting objects is Window Selection. This method selects all objects that are contained completely within the dragged outline. The Crossing Selection method selects any objects that are inside or overlapping the dragged outline. You can also access these two selection methods via the Window Selection buttons on the main toolbar — Window and Crossing, shown in Table 6.2.

> **TIP** If you can't decide whether to use the Crossing or Window selection method, you can select to use both. The General panel of the Preference Settings dialog box provides an option to enable Auto Window/Crossing by Direction. When this option is enabled, you can select a direction and the Crossing selection method is used for all selections that move from that direction. The Window selection method is used for all selections that move from the opposite direction. For example, if you select Left to Right for the Crossing selection method, then moving from Left to Right uses the Crossing selection method and selecting from Right to Left uses the Window selection method.

You can also change the shape of the selection outline. The Selection Region button on the main toolbar to the left of the Selection Filter drop-down list includes flyout buttons for Rectangular, Circular, Fence, Lasso, and Paint Selection Regions, shown in Table 6.3.

TABLE 6.2

Window Selection Buttons

Button	Description
	Window
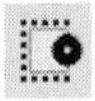	Crossing

TABLE 6.3

Shape-Shifting Selection Region Buttons

Button	Description
	Rectangular
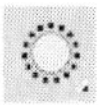	Circular
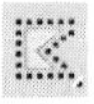	Fence
	Lasso
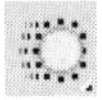	Paint

The Rectangular selection method lets you select objects by dragging a rectangular section (from corner to corner) over a viewport. The Circular selection method selects objects within a circle that grows from the center outward. The Fence method lets you draw a polygon-shaped selection area by clicking at each corner. Simply double-click to finish the fenced selection. The Lasso method lets you draw by freehand the selection area. The Paint method lets you choose objects by painting an area. All objects covered by the paint brush area are selected.

Pressing the Q keyboard shortcut selects the Select Object mode in the main toolbar, but repeated pressing of the Q keyboard shortcut cycles through the selection methods. Figure 6.4 shows each of the selection methods.

Selecting multiple objects

As you work with objects in Max, you'll sometimes want to apply a modification or transform to several objects at once. You can select multiple objects in several ways. With the Select by Name dialog box open, you can choose several objects from the list using the standard Ctrl and Shift keys. Holding down the Ctrl key selects or deselects multiple list items, but holding down the Shift key selects all consecutive list items between the first selected and the second selected items.

FIGURE 6.4

The drill's front is selected using the Rectangular, Circular, Fence, and Lasso selection methods.

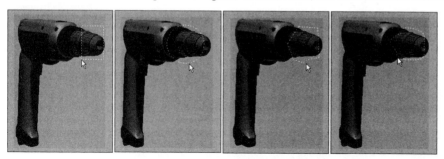

The Ctrl key also works when selecting objects in the viewport using one of the main toolbar Select buttons. You can tell whether you're in select mode by looking for a button that's highlighted yellow. If you hold down the Ctrl key and click an object, then the object is added to the current selection set. If you click an item that is already selected, then it is deselected. If you drag over multiple objects while holding down the Ctrl key, then all items in the dragged selection are added to the current selection set.

The Alt key deselects objects from the current selection set, which is opposite of what the Ctrl key does.

If you drag over several objects while holding down the Shift key, then the selection set is inverted. Each item that was selected is deselected, and vice versa.

Object hierarchies are established using the Link button on the main toolbar. You can select an entire hierarchy of objects by double-clicking on its parent object. You can also select multiple objects within the hierarchy. When you double-click an object, any children of that object are also selected. When an object with a hierarchy is selected, the Page Up and Page Down keys select the next object up or down the hierarchy.

Another way to select multiple objects is by dragging within the viewport using the Window and Crossing Selection methods discussed previously in the "Select by Region" section.

Using the Paint Selection Region tool

The Paint Selection Region tool is the last flyout button under the Rectangle Selection Region button. Using this tool, you can drag a circular paint brush area over the viewports, and all objects or subobjects underneath the brush are selected.

The size of the Selection Paint brush is shown as a circle when the tool is selected and may be changed using the Paint Selection Brush Size field in the General panel of the Preference Settings dialog box. Right-clicking on the Paint Selection Region button on the main toolbar automatically opens the Preference Settings dialog box. Figure 6.5 shows how the Paint Selection Region may be used to select several spheres by dragging over them.

Tutorial: Selecting objects

To practice selecting objects, we work with a simple model of the lion toy. When you're finished, you can throw this model to your dog for a chew toy.

157

FIGURE 6.5

The Paint Selection Region tool makes it easy to select spheres by dragging.

Paint Selection brush

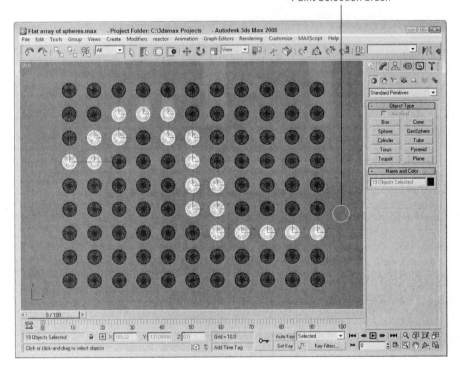

To select objects, follow these steps:

1. Open the Lion toy.max scene, which you can find in the Chap 06 directory on the DVD.

2. Click the Select Object button (or press the Q key), and click the lion's body in one of the viewports.

    In the Command Panel, the name for this object, lion, is displayed in the Name and Color rollout.

3. Click the Select and Move button (or press the W key), click the lion's body, and drag in the Perspective viewport to the right.

    As you can see, the lion's head and body form an object independent of the other parts of the lion object. Moving it separates it from the rest of the model's parts.

4. Choose Edit ➪ Undo Move (or press Ctrl+Z) to piece the lion back together.

5. With the Select and Move tool still selected, drag an outline around the entire lion in the Top view to select all the lion parts, and then click and drag the entire lion again.

    This time, the entire lion moves as one entity, and the name field displays Multiple Selected.

6. Open the Select Objects dialog box by clicking the Select by Name button on the main toolbar (or by pressing the H key).

    All the individual parts that make up this model are listed.

7. Double-click the nose object listed in the dialog box.

The Select Objects dialog box automatically closes, and the nose object becomes selected in the viewports.

Figure 6.6 shows our lion friend with just its nose object selected. Notice that the name of the selected object in the Name and Color rollout says "nose."

FIGURE 6.6

A lion cartoon character with its white selected nose.

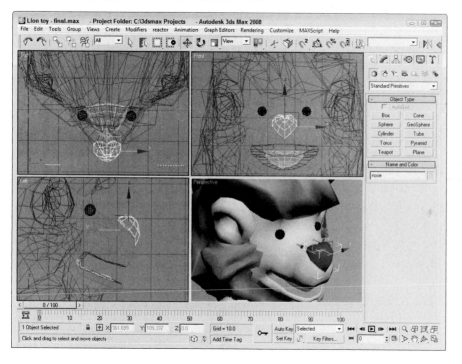

Locking selection sets

If you've finally selected the exact objects that you want to work with, you can disable any other selections using the Selection Lock toggle button on the Status Bar (it looks like a lock). When this button is enabled, it is colored yellow, and clicking objects in the viewports won't have any effect on the current selection. The keyboard shortcut toggle for this command is the spacebar.

CAUTION   In Photoshop and Illustrator, the spacebar is the keyboard shortcut to pan, but in Max it locks the current selection. If you accidentally lock the current selection, then you can't select any other objects until the lock is removed.

Using named selection sets

With a group of selected objects, you can establish a selection set. Once established as a selection set, you can recall this group of selected objects at any time by selecting its name from the Named Selection Set drop-down list on the main toolbar, or by opening the Named Selection Sets dialog box, shown in Figure 6.7.

You can access this dialog box using the Edit Named Selection Sets button on the main toolbar or by selecting the Edit ➪ Named Selection Sets menu command. To establish a selection set, type a name in the Named Selection Set drop-down list toward the right end of the main toolbar or use the dialog box.

FIGURE 6.7

The Edit Named Selections dialog box lets you view and manage selection sets.

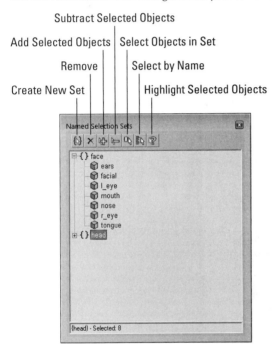

You can also create named selection sets for subobject selections. Be aware that these subobject selection sets are available only when you're in subobject edit mode and only for the currently selected object.

Editing named selections

After you've created several named selection sets, you can use the Named Selections Sets dialog box to manage the selection sets. The buttons at the top let you create and delete sets, add or remove objects from a set, and select and highlight set objects. You can also move an object between sets by dragging its name to the set name to which you want to add it. Dragging one set name onto another set name combines all the objects from both sets under the second set name. Double-clicking on a set name selects all the objects in the set.

Isolating the current selection

The Tools ➪ Isolate Selection (Alt+Q) menu command hides all objects except for the selected object. It also zooms to extents on the object in the active viewport. And it opens a simple dialog box with an Exit Isolation button in it. Clicking this button or selecting the Isolate command again exits isolation mode and displays all the objects again.

Isolate Selection mode is very convenient for working on a certain area. Figure 6.8 shows the Isolate Selection mode for a selection set that includes all elements of the lion toy's face.

FIGURE 6.8

Isolated Selection mode lets you focus on the details of the selected object.

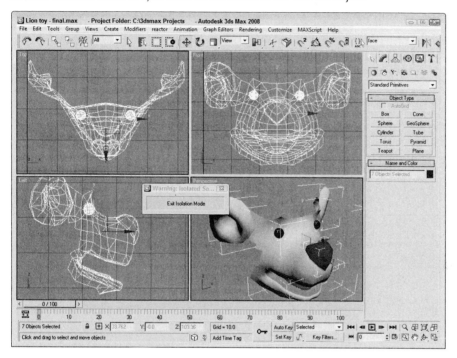

Selecting objects in other interfaces

In addition to selecting objects in the viewports, you can use many of the other interfaces and dialog boxes to select objects. For example, the Material Editor includes a button that selects all objects in a scene with the same material applied.

 The Select by Material button opens the Select Object dialog box with all objects that use the selected material highlighted.

Another way to select objects is in the Track View, which can be opened using the Graph Editors ➪ New Track View menu command. To view all the objects, click the + sign that precedes the Objects track. You can identify the Objects track by a small yellow cube. A hierarchy of all the objects in a scene is displayed. At the bottom left of the Track View window is the Select by Name text field. Typing an object name in this field automatically selects the object's track in the editor's window, but not in the viewport. Clicking the yellow cube icon selects the object in the viewport.

A third interface that you can use to select objects is the Schematic View, which is opened using the Graph Editors ➪ New Schematic View menu command. It offers a hierarchical look at your scene and displays all links and relationships between objects. Each object in the Schematic View is displayed as a rectangular node.

To select an object in the viewport, find its rectangular representation in the Schematic View and simply click it. To select multiple objects in the Schematic View, you need to enable Sync Selection mode with the Select ⇨ Sync Selection command in the Schematic View menu and then drag an outline over all the rectangular nodes that you want to select.

The Schematic View also includes the Select by Name text field, just like the Curve Editor, for selecting an object by typing its name.

CROSS-REF The Material Editor is covered in detail in Chapter 14, "Exploring the Material Editor," the Track View is covered in Chapter 34, "Working with Function Curves in the Track View," and the Schematic View interface is covered in Chapter 24, "Working with the Schematic View."

Setting Object Properties

After you select an object or multiple objects, you can view their object properties by choosing Edit ⇨ Object Properties. Alternatively, you can right-click the object and select Properties from the pop-up menu. Figure 6.9 shows the Object Properties dialog box. This dialog box includes four panels — General, Advanced Lighting, mental ray, and User Defined.

FIGURE 6.9

The Object Properties dialog box displays valuable information about a selected object.

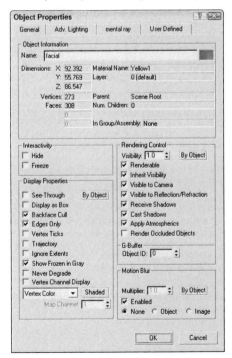

162

Viewing object information

For a single object, the General panel of the Object Properties dialog box lists details about the object in the Object Information section. These details include the object's name; color; extent distances from the origin along the X-, Y-, and Z-axes; number of vertices and faces; the object's parent; the object's Material Name; the number of children attached to the object; the object's group name if it's part of a group; and the layer on which the object can be found. All this information (except for its name and color) is for display only and cannot be changed.

 The two fields under the Vertices and Faces are used only when the properties for a Shape are being displayed. These fields show the number of Shape Vertices and Shape Curves.

If the properties for multiple objects are to be displayed, the Object Properties dialog box places the text "Multiple Selected" in the Name field. The properties that are in common between all these objects are displayed. With multiple objects selected, you can set their display and rendering properties all at once.

The Object Properties dialog box can be displayed for all geometric objects and shapes, as well as for lights, cameras, helpers, and Space Warps. Not all properties are available for all objects.

 The Hide and Freeze options included in the Interactivity section are covered later in this chapter in the "Hiding and Freezing Objects" section.

Setting display properties

Display properties don't affect how an object is rendered, only how it is displayed in the viewports. In this section, along with the Rendering Control and Motion Blur sections, are three By Object/By Layer toggle buttons. If the By Object button is displayed, then options can be set for the selected object, but if the By Layer option is enabled, then all options become disabled and the object gets its display properties from the layer settings found in the Layer Manager.

NOTE You can also find and set the same Display Properties that are listed in the Object Properties dialog box in the Display Properties rollout of the Display panel in the Command Panel and in the Display Floater.

The See-Through option causes shaded objects to appear transparent. This option is similar to the Visibility setting in the Rendering Control section, except that it doesn't affect the rendered image. It is only for displaying objects in the viewports. This option really doesn't help in wireframe viewports. Figure 6.10 shows the lion toy model with spheres behind it with and without this option selected.

FIGURE 6.10

The See-Through display property can make objects transparent in the viewports.

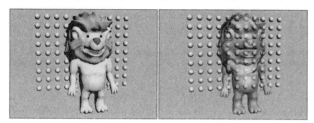

Many of these display properties can speed up or slow down the viewport refresh rates. For example, Display as Box increases the viewport update rate dramatically for complex scenes, but at the expense of any detail. This setting can be useful to see how the objects generally fit in comparison to one another. This option can also be accessed from the Viewport Configuration dialog box or from the Viewport name right-click pop-up menu, but the Object Properties dialog box lets you set this option for a single object instead of for the entire viewport.

When the Backface Cull option is enabled, it causes the faces on the backside of the object to not be displayed. Max considers the direction that each normal is pointing and doesn't display a face if its normal points away from the view. A normal is a vector that extends perpendicular to the face and is used to determine the orientation of individual faces. This option produces the same result of the Force 2-Sided option in the Viewport Configuration dialog box, except that it can be applied to a single object and not the entire viewport. This display option works only in wireframe viewports.

The Edges Only option displays only the edges of each object when the viewport is set to Wireframe mode. When Edges Only is not selected, a dashed line indicates the junction of individual faces.

When the Vertex subobject mode is selected for an object, all vertices for the selected object appear as blue + signs. The Vertex Ticks option displays all object vertices in this same way without requiring the Vertex subobject mode. Figure 6.11 shows the lion toy mesh with this option enabled. The Trajectory option displays the animation path that the object follows. You can also make the trajectory of the selected object appear without enabling the Trajectory option by selecting the Trajectories button in the Motion panel.

FIGURE 6.11

The Vertex Ticks option displays all vertices as small blue tick marks.

The Trajectory option displays any animated motions as a spline path.

CROSS-REF   To learn more about using animated motion paths, see Chapter 20, "Understanding Animation and Keyframe Basics."

The Ignore Extents option causes an object to be ignored when you are using the Zoom Extents button in the Viewport Navigation controls. For example, if you have a camera or light positioned at a distance from the objects in the scene, then anytime you use the Zoom Extents All button, the center objects are so small that you cannot see them because the Zoom Extents needs to include the distance light. If you set the Ignore Extent option for the camera or light, then the Zoom Extents All button zooms in on just the geometry objects.

When objects are frozen, they appear dark gray, but if the Show Frozen in Gray option is disabled, then the object appears as it normally does in the viewport. The Never Degrade option causes the object to be removed from the Adaptive Degradation settings used to maintain a given frame rate to get the animation timing right.

NEW FEATURE The Never Degrade option is new to 3ds Max 2008.

The Vertex Channel Display option displays the colors of any object vertices that have been assigned colors. You can select to use Vertex Color, Vertex Illumination, Vertex Alpha, Map Channel Color, or Soft Selection Color. The Shaded button causes the meshes to be shaded by the vertex colors. If the Shaded button is disabled, the object is unshaded. You can assign vertex colors only to editable meshes, editable polys, and editable patches. If the Map Channel Color option is selected, you can specify the Map Channel.

CROSS-REF For more information about vertex colors, check out Chapter 31, "Creating Baked Textures and Normal Maps."

Setting rendering controls

In the Object Properties dialog box, the Rendering Controls section includes options that affect how an object is rendered.

The Visibility spinner defines a value for how opaque (non-transparent) an object is. A value of 1 makes the object completely visible. A setting of 0.1 makes the object almost transparent. The Inherit Visibility option causes an object to adopt the same visibility setting as its parent.

TIP The Visibility option can also be animated for making objects slowly disappear.

The Renderable option determines whether the object is rendered. If this option isn't selected, then the rest of the options are disabled because they don't have any effect if the object isn't rendered. The Renderable option is useful if you have a complex object that takes a while to render. You can disable the renderability of the single object to quickly render the other objects in the scene.

You can use the Visible to Camera and Visible to Reflection/Refraction options to make objects invisible to the camera or to any reflections or refractions. This feature can be useful when you are test-rendering scene elements and raytraced objects.

TIP If an object has the Visible to Camera option disabled and the Cast Shadows option enabled, then the object isn't rendered, but its shadows are.

The Receive Shadows and Cast Shadows options control how shadows are rendered for the selected object. The Apply Atmospherics options enable or disable rendering atmospherics. Atmospheric effects can increase the rendering time by a factor of 10, in some cases.

CROSS-REF Atmospheric and render effects are covered in Chapter 45, "Using Atmospheric and Render Effects."

The Render Occluded Objects option causes the rendering engine to render all objects that are hidden behind the selected object. The hidden or occluded objects can have glows or other effects applied to them that would show up if rendered.

You use the G-Buffer Object Channel value to apply Render or Video Post effects to an object. By matching the Object Channel value to an effect ID, you can make an object receive an effect. A g-buffer is a temporary bit of memory used to process an image that isn't interrupted by transferring the data to the hard disk.

CROSS-REF The Video Post interface is covered in Chapter 48, "Compositing with Render Elements and the Video Post Interface."

Enabling Motion Blur

You can also set Motion Blur from within the Object Properties dialog box. The Motion Blur effect causes objects that move fast (such as the Road Runner) to be blurred (which is useful in portraying speed). The render engine accomplishes this effect by rendering multiple copies of the object or image.

CROSS-REF More information on these blur options is in Chapter 22, "Learning to Render a Scene."

The Object Properties dialog box can set two different types of Motion Blur: Object and Image. Object motion blur affects only the object and is not affected by the camera movement. Image motion blur applies the effect to the entire image and is applied after rendering.

CROSS-REF A third type of Motion Blur is called Scene Motion Blur and is available in the Video Post interface. See Chapter 48, "Compositing with Render Elements and the Video Post Interface," for information on using Scene Motion Blur.

You can turn the Enabled option on and off as an animation progresses, allowing you to motion blur select sections of your animation sequence. The Multiplier value is enabled only for the Image Motion Blur type. It is used to set the length of the blur effect. The higher the Multiplier value, the longer the blurring streaks. The Motion Blur settings found in the Object Properties dialog box can be overridden by the settings in the Render Scene dialog box.

CAUTION If the Motion Blur option in the Object Properties dialog box is enabled but the Motion Blur option in the Renderer panel of the Render Scene dialog box is disabled, then motion blur will not be included in the final rendered image.

Using the Advanced Lighting and mental ray panels

The second and third panels in the Object Properties dialog box contain object settings for working with Advanced Lighting and the mental ray renderer. Using the settings in the Advanced Lighting panel, you can exclude an object from any Advanced Lighting calculations, set an object to cast shadows and receive illumination, and set the number of refine iterations to complete.

The mental ray panel includes options for making an object generate and/or receive caustics and global illumination.

CROSS-REF Advanced Lighting is covered in Chapter 44, "Working with Advanced Lighting, Light Tracing, and Radiosity," and the mental ray renderer is covered in Chapter 46, "Raytracing and mental ray."

Using the User-Defined panel

The User-Defined panel contains a simple text window. In this window, you can type any sort of information. This information is saved with the scene and can be referred to as notes about an object.

Hiding and Freezing Objects

Hidden and frozen objects cannot be selected, and as such they cannot be moved from their existing positions. This becomes convenient when you move objects around in the scene. If you have an object in a correct position, you can freeze it to prevent it from being moved accidentally or you can hide it from the viewports completely. A key difference between these modes is that frozen objects are still rendered, but hidden objects are not.

You can hide and freeze objects in several ways. You can hide or freeze objects in a scene by selecting the Hide or Freeze options in the Object Properties dialog box. You can also hide and freeze objects using the Display Floater dialog box, which you access by choosing Tools ➪ Display Floater.

TIP   Several keyboard shortcuts can be used to hide specific objects. These shortcuts are toggles, so one press makes the objects disappear and another press makes them reappear. Object types that can be hidden with these shortcuts include cameras (Shift+C), geometry (Shift+G), grids (G), helpers (Shift+H), lights (Shift+L), particle systems (Shift+P), shapes (Shift+S), and Space Warps (Shift+W).

The Hide option makes the selected object in the scene invisible, and the Freeze option turns the selected object dark gray (if the Show Frozen in Gray option in the Object Properties dialog box is enabled) and doesn't allow it to be transformed or selected. You cannot select hidden objects by clicking in the viewport.

NOTE   When you use the Zoom Extents button to resize the viewports around the current objects, hidden objects aren't included.

Using the Display Floater dialog box

The Display Floater dialog box includes two tabs: Hide/Freeze and Object Level. The Hide/Freeze tab splits the dialog box into two columns, one for Hide and one for Freeze. Both columns have similar buttons that let you hide or freeze Selected or Unselected objects, By Name or By Hit. The By Name button opens the Select Objects dialog box (which is labeled Hide or Freeze Objects). The By Hit option lets you click in one of the viewports to select an object to hide or freeze. Each column also has additional buttons to unhide or unfreeze All objects, By Name, or in the case of Freeze, By Hit. You can also select an option to Hide Frozen Objects.

NOTE   Other places to find the same buttons found in the Display Floater are the Hide and Freeze rollouts of the Display panel of the Command Panel and in the right-click quadmenu.

The Object Level panel of the Display Floater lets you hide objects by category such as All Lights or Cameras. You can also view and change many of the Display Properties that are listed in the Object Properties dialog box.

Figure 6.12 shows the Hide/Freeze and Object Level panels of the Display Floater dialog box.

Using the Display panel

If you took many of the features of the Display Floater and the Object Properties dialog box and mixed them together with some new features, the result would be the Display panel. You access this panel by clicking the fifth icon from the left in the Command Panel (the icon that looks like a monitor screen).

The first rollout in the Display panel, shown in Figure 6.13, is the Display Color rollout. This rollout includes options for setting whether Wireframe and Shaded objects in the viewports are displayed using the Object Color or the Material Color.

FIGURE 6.12

The Display Floater dialog box includes two panels: Hide/Freeze and Object Level.

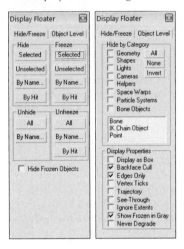

FIGURE 6.13

The Display panel includes many of the same features as the Display Floater and the Object Properties dialog box.

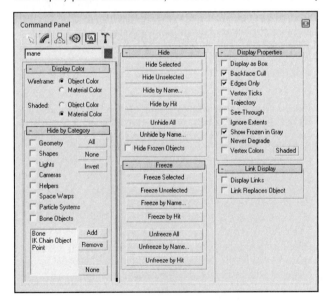

The panel also includes a Hide by Category rollout. Using this rollout, you can add new categories that will appear in the Object Level panel of the Display Floater. To add a new category, click the Add button of the Hide by Category rollout. The Add Display Filter list appears, as shown in Figure 6.14. From this list, you can choose specific object categories to add to the Hide by Category list.

FIGURE 6.14

From this dialog box, you can add new categories to the Hide by Category list.

The Display panel also includes Hide and Freeze rollouts that include the same buttons and features as the Hide/Freeze panel of the Display Floater. You also find a Display Properties rollout that is the same as the list found in the Display Floater's Object Level panel and the Object Properties dialog box.

The Link Display rollout at the bottom of the Display panel includes options for displaying links in the viewports. Links are displayed as lines that extend from the child to its parent object. Using the Link Replaces Object option, you can hide the objects in the viewport and see only the links.

Tutorial: Hidden toothbrushes

In this example, I've hidden several toothbrushes in the scene, and your task is to find them. To find the hidden objects, follow these steps:

1. Open the Toothbrushes.max scene file.

    This file appears to contain only a single toothbrush, but it really contains more. Can you find them? The toothbrush model was created by Viewpoint Datalabs. You can find it in the Chap 06 directory on the DVD.

2. Locate the hidden object in the scene by opening the Display Floater (choose Tools ➪ Display Floater).

3. In the Display Floater, select the Hide/Freeze tab. In the Unhide section, click the Name button.

    The Unhide Objects dialog box appears, which lists all the hidden objects in the scene.

4. Select the green toothbrush object from the list, and click the Unhide button.

    The Unhide Objects dialog box closes, and the hidden objects become visible again.

> **NOTE** Notice that the Display Floater is still open. That's because it's modeless. You don't need to close it to keep working.

5. To see all the remaining objects, click the Unhide All button in the Display Floater.

Figure 6.15 shows the finished scene with all toothbrushes visible.

FIGURE 6.15

Here are toothbrushes for the whole family; just remember which color is yours.

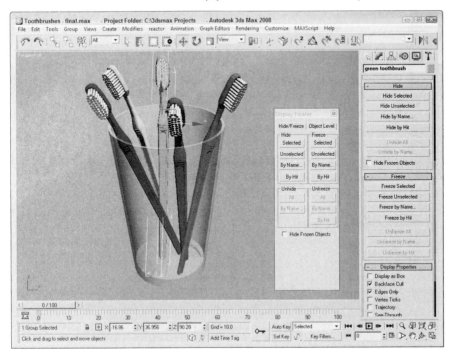

Using Layers

So what does 3ds Max have in common with a wedding cake? The answer is layers. Layers provide a way to separate scene objects into easy-to-select and easy-to-work-with groupings. These individual layers have properties that can then be turned on and off.

CROSS-REF Animation sequences also can be split into layers using the Animation Layers. You can learn more about these layers in Chapter 35, "Using Animation Layers and the Motion Mixer."

Using the Layer Manager

You create, access, and manage layers through the Layer Manager dialog box, shown in Figure 6.16. This dialog box is a floater that can remain open as you work with objects in the viewports. You can access the Layer Manager using the Tools ➪ Layer Manager menu command, by clicking the Layer Manager button on the main toolbar, or by clicking on the same button in the Layers toolbar.

CROSS-REF These layers are different from Animation Layers that are used to break an animation sequence into several different parts that can be blended together. Animation Layers are covered in Chapter 35, "Using Animation Layers and the Motion Mixer."

FIGURE 6.16

The Layer Manager lists all the layers and the objects contained within each layer.

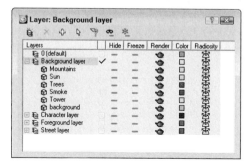

After you've set up your layers, you can control them using the Layers toolbar, shown in Figure 6.17, rather than having the Layer Manager open. You can access the Layers toolbar by right-clicking the main toolbar away from the buttons and selecting the Layers toolbar from the pop-up menu or by selecting the Customize ➪ Show UI ➪ Floating Toolbars menu command.

FIGURE 6.17

Use the Layers toolbar to set the active layer.

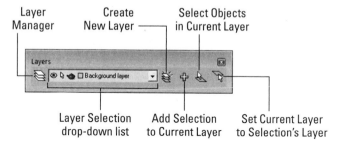

Table 6.4 lists the buttons found in the Layer Manager.

TABLE 6.4

Layer Manager Buttons

Button Icon	Name	Description
	Create New Layer	Creates a new layer that includes the selected objects.
	Delete Highlighted Empty Layers	Deletes a layer if the layer is highlighted and empty.

continued

Button Icon	**Name**	**Description**
✚	Add Selected Objects to Highlighted Layer	Adds any selected objects to the current highlighted layer.
▷	Select Highlighted Objects and Layers	Selects in the viewports any highlighted layers or objects.
◁	Highlight Selected Object's Layers	Highlights the layer of the viewport's selected object in the Layer Manager.
👓	Hide/Unhide All Layers	Toggles between hiding and unhiding all layers.
✳	Freeze/Unfreeze All Layers	Toggles between freezing and unfreezing all layers.

TABLE 6.4 *(continued)*

With the Layer Manager open, you can create new layers by clicking the Create New Layer button. This adds a new layer to the manager, names it "Layer01," and includes any selected objects as part of the layer. If you click the layer's name, you can rename it. Layer 0 is the default layer to which all objects are added, if other layers don't exist. Layer 0 cannot be renamed.

NOTE   Although you can rename layers in the Layer Manager, you cannot use the Layer Manager to rename objects. To rename an object from the Layer Manager, simply click on the object's icon to open the Object Properties dialog box where you can change the object's name.

Creating a new layer automatically makes the new layer the current layer as denoted by the check mark in the first column of the Layer Manager. All new objects that are created are automatically added to the current layer. Only one layer can be current at a time, but several layers or objects can be highlighted. To highlight a layer, click it in the Layer Manager. Highlighted layers are highlighted in yellow.

A highlighted layer can be deleted with the Delete Highlighted Empty Layer button, but only if it is not the current layer and it doesn't contain any objects.

Newly created objects are added to the current layer (the one marked with a check mark in the first column of the Layer Manager). If you forget to select the correct layer for the new objects, you can select the objects in the viewports, highlight the correct layer, and use the Add Selected Objects to Highlighted Layer button to add the objects to the correct layer.

NOTE   Every object can be added only to a single layer. You cannot add the same object to multiple layers.

The Select Highlighted Objects and Layers button selects the highlighted layers (and objects) in the viewports. This provides a way to select all the objects on a given layer. If an object in the viewports is selected, you can quickly see which layer it belongs to with the Highlight Selected Object's Layers button.

If you expand the layer name in the Layer Manager, you see a list of all the objects contained within the layer. If you click the Layer icon (to the left of the layer's name), the Layer Properties dialog box, shown in Figure 6.18, opens. Clicking the Object icon opens the Object Properties dialog box.

FIGURE 6.18

The Layer Properties dialog box is similar to the Object Properties dialog box, but it applies to the entire layer.

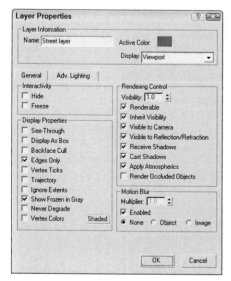

Using the Layer List

The main section of the Layer Manager (and repeated in the Layers toolbar) is the layer list and its columns, which allow you to turn certain properties on and off. The properties in the columns include Hide, Freeze, Render, Color, and Radiosity. If a property is enabled, a simple icon is displayed; if disabled, a dash is displayed. If an object is set to get its property from the layer (by clicking the ByLayer button in the Object Properties dialog box), then a dot icon is displayed. Individual objects within a layer can have different properties. You can sort the column properties by clicking on the column head.

You can toggle these properties on and off by clicking on them. You can also set these properties in the Layers toolbar. The Hide toggle determines whether the layer's objects are visible in the viewports. The Freeze toggle makes objects on a layer unselectable. The Render toggle enables the layer's objects to be rendered. The Color toggle sets the layer color. Layer 0 is set to assign random colors and cannot be changed. The Radiosity toggle includes the layer's objects in the radiosity calculations.

The Layer Manager also includes a right-click pop-up menu that includes many of the same commands found as buttons, but a unique set of commands found in the right-click pop-up menu are the Cut and Paste commands. With these commands, you can select objects in one layer to cut and paste into another layer.

CAUTION   If multiple objects are selected within the Layer Manager, then right-clicking on an object's name deselects all the selected objects. To maintain the current selection, right-click within the Layer Manager, away from the Layers column.

Tutorial: Dividing a scene into layers

As a scene begins to come together, you'll start to find that it is difficult to keep track of all the different pieces. This is where the layers interface can really help. In this example, we take a simple scene and divide it into several layers.

To divide a scene into layers, follow these steps:

1. Open the Elk on hill layers.max scene file.

   You can find it in the Chap 06 directory on the DVD. This file includes an Elk model created by Viewpoint Datalabs.

2. Select Tools ⇨ Layer Manager to open the Layer Manager.

3. With no objects selected, click the Create New Layer button and name the layer **Hill and trees**. Click the Create New Layer button again, and name this layer **Elk**. Click the Create New Layer button again, and create a layer named **Background and light**. The Layer Manager now includes four layers, including layer 0.

4. In the Layer Manager, click on the first column for the Elk layer to make it the current layer. With the Edit ⇨ Select All (Ctrl+A) menu command, select all objects in the scene and click the Add Selected Objects to Highlighted Layer button in the Layer Manager.

5. Expand the Elk layer by clicking the + icon to the left of its name.

   This displays all the objects within this layer.

6. Select all the trees and the hill objects by holding down the Ctrl key and clicking each object's name in the Layer Manager. Then right-click away from the names, and select Cut from the pop-up menu. Then select the Hill and trees layer, and select Paste from the right-click pop-up menu.

7. Select the background and light objects from within the Elk layer, and click the Select Highlighted Objects and Layers button. Then select the Background and light layer, and click the Add Selected Objects to Highlighted Layer button to move the background and light objects to the correct layer.

You can now switch between the layers, depending on which one you want to add objects to or work on, and you can change properties as needed. For example, to focus on the deer object, you can quickly hide the other layers using the Layer Manager. Figure 6.19 shows the various layers and the objects in each layer.

FIGURE 6.19

All objects assigned to a layer can be viewed in the Layer Properties dialog box.

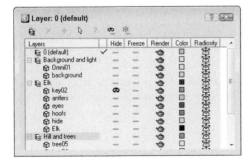

Using the Scene Explorer

The Scene Explorer is a one-stop shop for all scene objects and display properties. It displays all the objects in the scene in a hierarchical list along with various display properties. It allows you to filter the display so you can see just what you want and customize the display so only those properties you want to see are visible. The Scene Explorer also lets you select, rename, hide, sort, freeze, link, and delete objects and to change the object color.

 **The Scene Explorer interface is new to 3ds Max 2008.**

A new Scene Explorer dialog box, shown in Figure 6.20, is opened using the Tools ⇨ Open Explorer: Scene Explorer menu command (Alt+Ctrl+O). Using the Tools ⇨ New Scene Explorer menu command, you can open a new view. Each subsequent Scene Explorer view is numbered, but these individual views also can be named using the View field at the top of each Scene Explorer window. Each new or named view can be recalled with the Tools ⇨ Saved Scene Explorers menu, and the Tools ⇨ Manage Scene Explorers opens a simple dialog box where you can Load, Save, Delete, and Rename the saved views.

NOTE   **Scene Explorer views are automatically saved and reloaded with the Max file.**

FIGURE 6.20

The Scene Explorer dialog box displays all scene objects and their display properties.

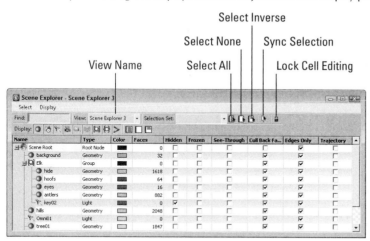

All scene objects in the Scene Explorer are listed in hierarchical order with children objects indented under their parent objects and all scene objects indented under the Scene Root object. You can expand or contract children objects by clicking the plus (+) or minus (-) icon to the left of the parent object.

Selecting and filtering objects

If you click an object in the Scene Explorer dialog box, the object row is highlighted. Holding down the Ctrl key lets you click to select multiple objects, or you can use the Shift key to select a range of adjacent objects. Selected objects also can be removed from the current selection with the Ctrl key held down.

The Select menu also includes options for selecting objects. The All (Ctrl+A), None (Ctrl+D), and Invert (Ctrl+I) menu commands work like expected, selecting all objects, deselecting all objects, and selecting the inverse of the current selection.

The Select Children (Ctrl+C) option causes all children objects to automatically be selected when the parent is selected. The Select Influences option selects all influence objects that are attached to the selected objects. An influence object is an object that controls or shapes another object. For example, when a sphere is constrained to follow an animation path, the path is an influence object to the sphere. Another example is a skin mesh being influenced by a biped rig. The Select Dependencies option selects any objects that are dependent on the selected object, such as an instance and reference.

When the Select ⇨ Sync Selection option is enabled, any objects selected in the Scene Explorer dialog box are automatically selected in the viewports also. This also works in reverse causing any objects selected in the viewport to be selected in the Scene Explorer dialog box.

The Scene Explorer recognizes any defined Selection Sets and lets you select these sets from the drop-down list at the top of the interface.

The Display toolbar includes several object type icons. The yellow icons are selected and allowed to be viewed in the Scene Explorer. To filter out a specific object type, disable its icon, and then all objects of that type are no longer displayed in the list. To the right end of the Display toolbar are buttons to Select All categories, Display None, and Display Invert. These same commands are available in the Display ⇨ Object Types menu along with an option to Hide the Display Toolbar. The available object types are listed in Figure 6.21.

FIGURE 6.21

The Display toolbar in the Scene Explorer dialog box lets you filter the object types that are displayed.

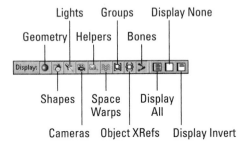

Finding objects

You also can use the Find field to search the hierarchy for a specific object by name. All objects that match the typed characters are selected. If you enable the Select ⇨ Find Case Sensitive option, uppercase characters are distinguished from lowercase characters.

If the Select ⇨ Use Wildcards option is selected, you can use wildcards to locate objects. Acceptable wildcards include an asterisk (*) for multiple characters in a row and a question mark (?) for single characters. For example, an entry of **hedra*** selects all objects beginning with "hedra," regardless of the ending and **hedra?1** finds "hedra01" and "hedra11" but not "hedra02" or "hedra0001".

The Select ⇨ Use Regular Expressions option provides yet another way to search for specific objects. Regular expressions are commonly used in various scripting languages and require specific syntax in order to locate objects. Table 6.5 lists some common regular expression characters.

TABLE 6.5

Common Regular Expression Syntax

Character	Description	Example
[htk]	Used to define a group of search characters	Matches all objects beginning with the letters *h*, *t*, and *k*
Eye|light|key	Used to separate words to search for	Matches all objects beginning with eye, light, or key
\w	Used to identify any letter or number, just like the ? wildcard	Matches any number or letter
\s	Used to identify any white space	Matches any space between words, no matter the length
\d	Used to identify any single digit number	Matches any single-digit number, 0 through 9
[^geft]	Used to match all objects except for the ones inside the brackets	Matches all objects except for those that begin with *g*, *e*, *f*, or *t*
t.*1	Used to match multiple letters in between two specified characters	Matches all objects that begin with the letter *t* and end with the number 1

If regular expressions seem confusing, you also can search using the Advanced Search dialog box, shown in Figure 6.22. This dialog box is opened using the Select ⇨ Search. In the Property field, you can search by Name, Type, Color, Faces, or any of the other available columns. In the Condition, the options include Starts With, Does Not Start With, Contains String, Does Not Contain String, Regular Expression Matches, and Inverse Regular Expression Matches. Multiple criteria can be added to the search list.

FIGURE 6.22

The Advanced Search dialog box lets you select search criteria using drop-down lists.

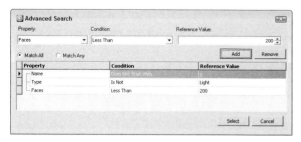

Editing in the Scene Explorer

Any of the display properties listed in the Scene Explorer can be enabled by simply clicking the check box to enable the property. If multiple objects are selected when a property is enabled or disabled, the same property is enabled or disabled for all the selected objects at the same time.

NOTE   If the Lock Cell Editing button is enabled, none of the properties can be changed.

If you click the column name, you can sort all the listed objects either in descending or ascending order. Click the column name once to sort in ascending order and again to sort in descending order. You also can right-click and select the sorting order from the pop-up menu. For example, if you click the Faces column, all the objects are sorted so the objects with the smallest number of faces are listed at the top of the interface and the objects with the most faces are listed at the bottom.

You also can rearrange the columns by dragging and dropping them to a new location. Selecting the Display ➪ Column Chooser menu opens the Column Chooser dialog box, shown in Figure 6.23. This dialog box lists all the available remaining display property columns. To add one to the Scene Explorer, simply select it from the Column Chooser and drop it where you want it.

 The width of each column can be altered by dragging on either side. To reset all column widths, right-click a column name and choose Best Fit (all columns) from the pop-up menu.

FIGURE 6.23

The Column Chooser dialog box holds all the display properties not currently available in the Scene Explorer.

Summary

Selecting objects enables you to work with them, and Max includes many different ways to select objects. In this chapter, you've done the following:

- Learned how to use selection filters
- Selected objects with the Edit menu by Name, Color, and Region
- Selected multiple objects and used a named selection set to find the set easily
- Selected objects using other interfaces
- Accessed the Object Properties dialog box to set Display and Rendering settings for an object
- Learned how to hide and freeze objects
- Separated objects using layers
- Used the Scene Explorer dialog box

Now that you've learned how to select objects, you're ready to move them about using the transform tools, which are covered in the next chapter.

Chapter 7

Transforming Objects, Pivoting, Aligning, and Snapping

IN THIS CHAPTER

Transforming objects

Controlling transformations with the Transform Gizmos, the Transform Type-Ins, and the Transform Managers

Working with pivot points and axis constraints

Aligning objects with the align tools

Using grids and snapping objects to common points

lthough a *transformation* sounds like something that would happen during the climax of a superhero film, transformation is simply the process of "repositioning" or changing an object's position, rotation, or scale. So moving an object from here to there is a transformation. Superman would be so jealous.

Max includes several tools to help in the transformation of objects, including the Transform Gizmos, the Transform Type-In dialog box, and the Transform Managers.

This chapter covers each of these tools and several others that make transformations more automatic, such as the alignment, grid, and snap features.

Translating, Rotating, and Scaling Objects

So you have an object created, and it's just sitting there — sitting and waiting. Waiting for what? Waiting to be transformed. To be moved a little to the left or rotated around to show its good side or scaled down a little smaller. These actions are called transformations because they transform the object to a different state. Transformations are different from modifications. Modifications change the object's geometry, but transformations do not affect the object's geometry at all.

The three different types of transformations are translation (which is a fancy word for moving objects), rotation, and scaling.

Translating objects

The first transformation type is *translation* or moving objects. This is identified in the various transform interfaces as the object's Position. You can move objects

179

along any of the three axes or within the three planes. You can move objects to an absolute coordinate location or move them to a certain offset distance from their current location.

 To move objects, click the Select and Move button on the main toolbar (or press the W key), select the object to move, and drag the object in the viewport to the desired location. Translations are measured in the defined system units for the scene, which may be inches, centimeters, meters, and so on.

Rotating objects

 Rotation is the process of spinning the object about its Transform Center point. To rotate objects, click the Select and Rotate button on the main toolbar (or press the E key), select an object to rotate, and drag it in a viewport. Rotations are measured in degrees, where 360 degrees is a full rotation.

Scaling objects

Scaling increases or decreases the overall size of an object. Most scaling operations are uniform, or equal in all directions. All Scaling is done about the Transform Center point.

 To scale objects uniformly, click the Select and Uniform Scale button on the main toolbar (or press the R key), select an object to scale, and drag it in a viewport. Scalings are measured as a percentage of the original. For example, a cube scaled to a value of 200 percent is twice as big as the original.

Non-uniform scaling

 The Select and Scale button includes two flyout buttons for scaling objects non-uniformly, allowing objects to be scaled unequally in different dimensions. The two additional tools are Select and Non-Uniform Scale, and Select and Squash, shown in Table 7.1. Resizing a basketball with the Select and Non-Uniform Scale tool could result in a ball that is oblong and taller than it is wide. Scaling is done about whatever axes have been constrained (or limited) using the Restrict Axes buttons on the Axis Constraints toolbar.

Squashing objects

 The Squash option is a specialized type of non-uniform scaling. This scaling causes the constrained axis to be scaled at the same time that the opposite axes are scaled in the opposite direction. For example, if you push down on the top of a basketball by scaling the Z-axis, the sides, or the X- and Y-axes, it bulges outward. This simulates the actual results of such materials as rubber and plastic.

 You can cycle through the different Scaling tools by repeatedly pressing the R key.

Figure 7.1 shows a basketball that has been scaled using uniform scaling, non-uniform scaling, and squash modes.

FIGURE 7.1

These basketballs have been scaled using uniform, non-uniform, and squash modes.

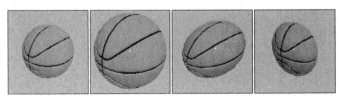

> **NOTE** It is also important to be aware of the order of things. Transformations typically happen at the top of the stack after all object properties and modifiers are applied. More on the stack is covered in Chapter 13, "Introducing Modifiers and Using the Modifier Stack."

Using the transform buttons

The three transform buttons located on the main toolbar are Select and Move, Select and Rotate, and Select and Uniform Scale, as shown in Table 7.1. Using these buttons, you can select objects and transform them by dragging in one of the viewports with the mouse. You can access these buttons using three of the big four keyboard shortcuts — Q for Select Objects, W for Select and Move, E for Select and Rotate, and R for Select and Scale.

TABLE 7.1

Transform Buttons

Toolbar Button	Name	Description
 ✛	Select and Move (W)	Enters move mode where clicking and dragging an object moves it.
 ↻	Select and Rotate (E)	Enters rotate mode where clicking and dragging an object rotates it.
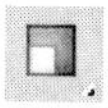  ▯ ◪ ▤	Select and Uniform Scale (R), Select and Non-Uniform Scale, Select and Squash	Enters scale mode where clicking and dragging an object scales it.

Working with the Transformation Tools

To help you in your transformations, you can use several tools to transform objects (and you don't even need a phone booth). These tools include the Transform Gizmos, the Transform Type-In dialog box (F12), Status Bar transform fields, and the Transform Managers.

Working with the Transform Gizmos

The Transform Gizmos appear at the center of the selected object (actually at the object's pivot point) when you click one of the transform buttons. The type of gizmo that appears depends on the transformation mode that is selected. You can choose from three different gizmos, one for each transformation type. Each gizmo includes three color-coded arrows, circles, and lines representing the X-, Y-, and Z-axes. The X-axis is colored red, the Y-axis is colored green, and the Z-axis is colored blue. Figure 7.2 shows the gizmos for each of the transformation types — move, rotate, and scale.

If the Transform Gizmo is not visible, you can enable it by choosing Views ⇨ Show Transform Gizmo or by pressing the X key to toggle it on and off. You can use the – (minus) and = (equal) keys to decrease or increase the gizmo's size.

The Transform Gizmos let you constrain a transformation to a single axis or a plane.

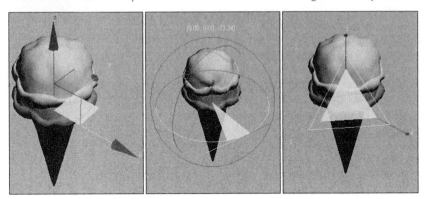

Using the interactive gizmos

Moving the cursor over the top of one of the Transform Gizmo's axes in the active viewport selects the axis, which changes to yellow. Dragging the selected axis restricts the transformation to that axis only. For example, selecting the red X-axis on the Move Gizmo and dragging moves the selected object along only the X-axis.

 **The transformation gizmos provide an alternate (and visual) method for constraining transformations along an axis or plane. This reduces the need for the Axis Constraint buttons, which have been removed to a separate floating toolbar. Learning to use these gizmos is well worth the time.**

The Move Gizmo

In addition to the arrows for each axis, in each corner of the Move Gizmo are two perpendicular lines for each plane. These lines let you transform along two axes simultaneously. The colors of these lines match the various colors used for the axes. For example, in the Perspective view, dragging on a red and blue corner would constrain the movement to the XZ plane. Selecting one of these lines highlights it. At the center of the Move Gizmo is a Center Box that marks the pivot point's origin.

The Rotate Gizmo

The Rotate Gizmo surrounds the selected object in a sphere. A colored line for each axis circles the surrounding sphere. As you select an axis and drag, an arc is highlighted that shows the distance of the rotation along that axis and the offset value is displayed in text above the object. Clicking on the sphere away from the axes lets you rotate the selected object in all directions. Dragging on the outer gray circle causes the selected object to spin about its center.

The Scale Gizmo

The Scale Gizmo consists of two triangles and a line for each axis. Selecting and dragging the center triangle uniformly scales the entire object. Selecting a slice of the outer triangle scales the object along the adjacent two axes, and dragging on the axis lines scales the object in a non-uniform manner along a single axis.

TIP **To keep the various gizmo colors straight, simply remember that RGB = XYZ.**

Setting gizmo preferences

For each of these gizmos, you can set the preferences using the Gizmos panel in the Preference Settings dialog box, shown in Figure 7.3. In this panel for all gizmos, you can turn the gizmos on or off, set to Show Axis Labels, Allow Multiple Gizmos, and set the Size of the gizmo's axes. The Allow Multiple Gizmos option enables a separate gizmo for each selection set object. The Labels option labels each axis with an X, Y, or Z.

FIGURE 7.3

The Gizmos panel in the Preference Settings dialog box lets you control how the Transform Gizmos look.

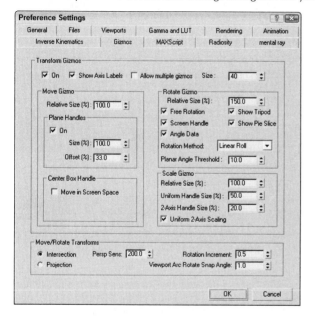

For the Move Gizmo section, you can set the Relative Size of the gizmo, which is relative to the top Size value, so a setting of 100% makes the size of the gizmo a full 30 and a setting a 50% makes it 15, or half the full Size value. You can also select to turn the plane handles on or off and set their Size and Offset values, which determine how large the highlighted planes are and where they are located relative to the center of the gizmo. A Size value of 100% extends the plane handles to be as long as the axis handles. You can also enable the Center Box Handle for moving in all three axes.

The Rotate Gizmo preferences also include a Relative Size value. The Free Rotation option enables you to click and drag between the axes to rotate the object freely along all axes. The Show Tripod option displays the axes tripod at the center of the object. The Screen Handle option displays an additional gray circle that surrounds all the axes. Dragging on this handle spins the object about the viewport's center. The Show Pie Slice highlights a slice along the selected axis that is as big as the offset distance. The Angle Data option displays the rotation values above the gizmo as it's being rotated.

The Gizmos panel offers three Rotation Methods: Linear Roll, Circular Crank, and Legacy R4. The Linear Roll method displays a tangent line at the source point where the rotation starts. The Circular Crank method rotates using the gizmo axes that surround the object. The Legacy R4 method uses a gizmo that looks just like the Move Gizmo that was available in the previous Max version. The Planar Angle Threshold value determines the minimum value to rotate within a plane.

The Scale Gizmo section can also set a Relative Size of the gizmo. The Uniform Handle Size value sets the size of the inner triangle, and the 2-Axis Handle Size value sets the size of the outer triangle. The Uniform 2-Axis Scaling option makes scaling with the outer triangle uniform along both axes.

The Move/Rotate Transforms section has some additional settings that control how objects move in the Perspective viewport. The Intersection and Projection options are for two different modes. The Intersection mode moves objects faster the farther they get from the center. In Projection mode, the Perspective Sensitivity value is used to set the mouse movements to the distance of the transformation. Small values result in small transformations for large mouse drags. The Rotation Increment value sets the amount of rotation that occurs for a given mouse drag distance, and the Viewport Arc Rotate Snap Angle sets where the arc snaps to.

Using the Transform Type-In dialog box

The Transform Type-In dialog box (F12) lets you input precise values for moving, rotating, and scaling objects. This command provides more exact control over the placement of objects than dragging with the mouse.

The Transform Type-In dialog box allows you to enter numerical coordinates or offsets that can be used for precise transformations. Open this dialog box by choosing Tools ➪ Transform Type-In or by pressing the F12 key.

> **TIP** Right-clicking any of the transform buttons opens the Transform Type-In dialog box, but the dialog box opens for whichever button is enabled, regardless of which button you right-click.

The Transform Type-In dialog box is modeless and allows you to select new objects as needed or to switch between the various transforms. When the dialog box appears, it displays the coordinate locations for the pivot point of the current selection in the Absolute: World column.

Within the Transform Type-In dialog box are two columns. The first column displays the current Absolute coordinates. Updating these coordinates transforms the selected object in the viewport. The second column displays the Offset values. These values are all set to 0.0 when the dialog box is first opened, but changing these values transforms the object along the designated axis by the entered value. Figure 7.4 shows the Transform Type-In dialog box for the Move Transform.

> **NOTE** The name of this dialog box changes depending on the type of transformation taking place and the coordinate system. If the Select and Move button is selected along with the world coordinate system, the Transform Type-In dialog box is labeled Move Transform Type-In and the column titles indicate the coordinate system.

FIGURE 7.4

The Transform Type-In dialog box displays the current Absolute coordinates and Offset values.

Using the status bar Type-In fields

The status bar includes three fields labeled X, Y, and Z for displaying transformation coordinates. When you move, rotate, or scale an object, the X, Y, and Z offset values appear in these fields. The values depend on the type of transformation taking place. Translation shows the unit distances, rotation displays the angle in degrees, and scaling shows a percentage value of the original size.

When you click the Select Objects button, these fields show the absolute position of the cursor in world coordinates based on the active viewport.

You can also use these fields to enter values, as with the Transform Type-In dialog box. The type of transform depends on which transform button you select. The values that you enter can be either absolute coordinates or offset values, depending on the setting of the Transform Type-In toggle button that appears to the left of the transform fields. This toggle button lets you switch between Absolute and Offset modes, shown in Table 7.2.

> **TIP** If you right-click any of these fields, a pop-up menu appears where you can cut, copy, or paste the current value.

TABLE 7.2

Absolute/Offset Buttons

Button	Description
	Absolute
	Offset

Understanding the Transform Managers

To keep track of the position of every object in a scene, internally Max records the position of the object's vertices in reference to a Universal Coordinate System (UCS). This coordinate system defines vertex position using the X, Y, and Z coordinates from the scene's origin.

However, even though Max uses the UCS to internally keep track of all the points, this isn't always the easiest way to reference the position of an object. Imagine a train with several cars. For each individual train car, it is often easier to describe its position as an offset from the car in front of it.

The Transform Managers are three types of controls that help you define the system about which objects are transformed. These controls, found on the main toolbar and on the Axis Constraints toolbar, directly affect your transformations. They include the following:

- **Reference Coordinate System:** Defines the coordinate system about which the transformations take place.
- **Transform Center settings:** The Pivot Point Center, the Selection Center, and the Transform Coordinate Center. These settings specify the center about which the transformations take place.
- **Axis Constraint settings:** Allow the transformation to happen using only one axis or plane. These buttons are on the Axis Constraints toolbar.

Understanding reference coordinate systems

Max supports several reference coordinate systems based on the Universal Coordinate System, and knowing which reference coordinate system you are working with as you transform an object is important. Using the wrong reference coordinate system can produce unexpected transformations.

Within the viewports, the UCS coordinates are displayed as a set of coordinates in the lower-left corner of the viewport and the transform gizmo is oriented with respect to the reference coordinate system.

To understand the concept of reference coordinate systems, imagine that you're visiting the Grand Canyon and are standing precariously on the edge of a lookout. To nervous onlookers calling the park rangers, the description of your position varies from viewpoint to viewpoint. A person standing by you would say you are next to him. A person on the other side of the canyon would say that you're across from her. A person at the floor of the canyon would say you're above him. And a person in an airplane would describe you as being on the east side of the canyon. Each person has a different viewpoint of you (the object), even though you have not moved.

Max recognizes the following reference coordinate systems:

■ **View Coordinate System:** A reference coordinate system based on the viewports; X points right, Y points up, and Z points out of the screen (toward you). The views are fixed, making this perhaps the most intuitive coordinate system to work with.

■ **Screen Coordinate System:** Identical to the View Coordinate System, except the active viewport determines the coordinate system axes, whereas the inactive viewports show the axes as defined by the active viewport.

■ **World Coordinate System:** Specifies X pointing to the right, Z pointing up, and Y pointing into the screen (away from you). The coordinate axes remain fixed regardless of any transformations applied to an object. For Max, this system matches the UCS.

■ **Parent Coordinate System:** Uses the reference coordinate system applied to a linked object's parent and maintains consistency between hierarchical transformations. If an object doesn't have a parent, then the world is its parent and the system works the same as the World Coordinate System.

■ **Local Coordinate System:** Sets the coordinate system based on the selected object. The axes are located at the pivot point for the object. You can reorient and move the pivot point using the Pivot button in the Hierarchy panel.

■ **Gimbal Coordinate System:** Provides interactive feedback for objects using the Euler XYZ controller. If the object doesn't use the Euler XYZ controller, then this coordinate system works just like the World Coordinate System.

■ **Grid Coordinate System:** Uses the coordinate system for the active grid.

■ **Working Coordinate System:** Lets you transform the selected object about the scene's Working Pivot as defined in the Hierarchy panel.

■ **Pick Coordinate System:** Lets you select an object about which to transform. The Coordinate System list keeps the last four picked objects as coordinate system options.

All transforms occur relative to the current reference coordinate system as selected in the Referenced Coordinate System drop-down list found on the main toolbar.

Each of the three basic transforms can have a different coordinate system specified, or you can set it to change uniformly when a new coordinate system is selected. To do this, open the General panel in the Preference Settings dialog box and select the Constant option in the Reference Coordinate System section.

Using a transform center

All transforms are done about a center point. When transforming an object, you must understand what the object's current center point is, as well as the coordinate system in which you're working.

The Transform Center flyout consists of three buttons: Use Pivot Point Center, Use Selection Center, and Use Transform Coordinate Center, which are shown in Table 7.3. Each of these buttons alters how the transformations are done. The origin of the Transform Gizmo is always positioned at the center point specified by these buttons.

TABLE 7.3

Transform Center Buttons

Button	Description
	Use Pivot Point Center
	Use Selection Center
	Use Transform Coordinate Center

Pivot Point Center

Pivot points are typically set to the center of an object when the object is first created, but they can be relocated anywhere within the scene including outside of the object. Relocating the pivot point allows you to change the point about which objects are rotated. For example, if you have a car model that you want to position along an incline, moving the pivot point to the bottom of one of the tires allows you to easily line up the car with the incline.

CROSS-REF Pivot points are discussed in detail in the next section.

Selection Center

The Use Selection Center button sets the transform center to the center of the selected object or objects regardless of the individual object's pivot point. If multiple objects are selected, then the center is computed to be in the middle of a bounding box that surrounds all the objects.

Transform Coordinate Center

The Transform Coordinate Center button uses the center of the Local Coordinate System. If the View Coordinate System is selected, then all objects are transformed about the center of the viewport. If an object is selected as the coordinate system using the Pick option, then all transformations are transformed about that object's center.

When you select the Local Coordinate System, the Use Transform Center button is ignored and objects are transformed about their local axes. If you select multiple objects, then they all transform individually about their local axes. Grouped objects transform about the group axes.

Figure 7.5 shows the ice cream cone and firecracker object using the different transform center modes. The left image shows the Pivot Point Center mode, the middle image shows the Selection Center mode with both objects selected, and the right image shows the Transform Coordinate Center mode. For each mode, notice that the Move Gizmo is in a different location.

FIGURE 7.5

The Move Gizmo is located in different places, depending on the selected Transform Center mode.

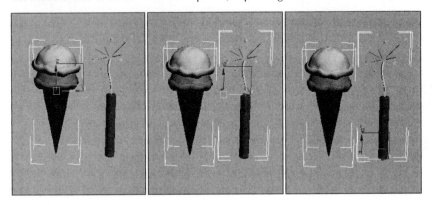

Selecting Axis Constraints

Three-dimensional space consists of three basic directions defined by three axes: X, Y, and Z. If you were to stand on each axis and look at a scene, you would see three separate planes: the XY plane, the YZ plane, and the ZX plane. These planes show only two dimensions at a time and restrict any transformations to the two axes. These planes are visible from the Top, Left, and Front viewports.

By default, the Top, Left, and Front viewports show only a single plane and thereby restrict transformations to that single plane. The Top view constrains movement to the XY plane, the Left or Right side view constrains movement to the YZ plane, and the Front view constrains movement to the ZX plane. This setting is adequate for most modeling purposes, but sometimes you might need to limit the transformations in all the viewports to a single plane. In Max, you can restrict movement to specific transform axes using the Restrict Axes buttons in the Axis Constraints toolbar. You access this toolbar, shown in Figure 7.6, by right-clicking on the main toolbar (away from the buttons) and selecting Axis Constraints options from the pop-up menu.

FIGURE 7.6

The Axis Constraints toolbar includes buttons for restricting transformations to a single axis or plane.

The first four buttons on this toolbar are Restrict axes buttons: Restrict to X (F5), Restrict to Y (F6), Restrict to Z (F7), and the flyout buttons, Restrict to XY, YZ, and ZX Plane (F8). The last button is the Snaps Use

Axis Constraints toggle button. The effect of selecting one of the Restrict axes buttons is based on the selected coordinate system. For example, if you click the Restrict to X button and the reference coordinate system is set to View, then the object always transforms to the right because, in the View Coordinate System, the X-axis is always to the right. If you click the Restrict to X button and the coordinate system is set to Local, the axes are attached to the object, so transformations along the X-axis are consistent in all viewports (with this setting, the object does not move in the Left view because it shows only the YZ plane).

> **CAUTION** If the axis constraints don't seem to be working, check the Preference Settings dialog box and look at the General panel to make sure that the Reference Coordinate System option is set to Constant.

Additionally, you can restrict movement to a single plane with the Restrict to Plane flyouts consisting of Restrict to XY, Restrict to YZ, and Restrict to ZX. (Use the F8 key to cycle quickly through the various planes.)

> **NOTE** If the Transform Gizmo is enabled, then the axis or plane that is selected in the Axis Constraints toolbar initially is displayed in yellow. If you transform an object using a Transform Gizmo, then the respective Axis Constraints toolbar button is selected after you complete the transform.

Locking axes transformations

To lock an object's transformation axes on a more permanent basis, go to the Command Panel and select the Hierarchy tab. Click the Link Info button to open the Locks rollout, shown in Figure 7.7. The rollout displays each axis for the three types of transformations: Move, Rotate, and Scale. Make sure that the object is selected, and then click the transformation axes that you want to lock. Be aware that if all Move axes are selected, you won't be able to move the object until you deselect the axes.

> **NOTE** Another option is to use the Display floater to freeze the object.

Locking axes is helpful if you want to prevent accidental scaling of an object or restrict a vehicle's movement to a plane that makes up a road.

FIGURE 7.7

The Locks rollout can prevent any transforms along an axis.

The Locks rollout displays unselected X, Y, and Z check boxes for the Move, Rotate, and Scale transformations. By selecting the check boxes, you limit the axes about which the object can be transformed. For example, if you check the X and Y boxes under the Move transformation, the object can move only in the Z direction of the Local Coordinate System.

 These locks work regardless of the axis constraint settings.

Tutorial: Landing a spaceship in port

Transformations are the most basic object manipulation that you will do and probably the most common. This tutorial includes a spaceship object and a spaceport. The goal is to position the spaceship on the landing pad of the spaceport, but it is too big and in the wrong spot. With a few clever transformations, we'll be set.

To transform a spaceship to land in a spaceport, follow these steps:

1. Open the Transforming spaceship.max file from the Chap 07 directory on the DVD.

2. To prevent any extraneous movements of the spaceport, select the spaceport by clicking it. Open the Hierarchy panel, and click the Link Info button. Then in the Locks rollout, select all nine boxes to restrict all transformations so that that spaceport won't be accidentally moved.

3. To position the spaceship over the landing platform, select the spaceship object and click on the Select and Move button in the main toolbar (or press the W key). The Move Gizmo appears in the center of the spaceship object. If you don't see the Move Gizmo, press the X key. Make sure that the Reference Coordinate System is set to View and that the Use Selection Center option is enabled. Right-click on the Left viewport to make it active, select the red X-axis line of the gizmo, and drag to the right until the center of the spaceship is over the landing pad.

4. Right-click on the Front viewport, and drag the red X-axis gizmo line to the left to line up the spaceship with the center of the landing pad.

5. Click the Select and Uniform Scale button (or press the R key). Place the cursor over the center gizmo triangle, and drag downward until the spaceship fits within the landing pad.

6. Click the Select and Move button again (or press the W key), and drag the green Y-axis gizmo line downward in the Front viewport to move the spaceship toward the landing pad.

7. Click the Select and Rotate button (or press the E key). Right-click on the Top viewport, and drag the blue Z-axis gizmo circle downward to rotate the spaceship clockwise so that its front end points away from the buildings.

Figure 7.8 shows the spaceship correctly positioned.

FIGURE 7.8

Transformation buttons and the Transform Gizmos were used to position this spaceship.

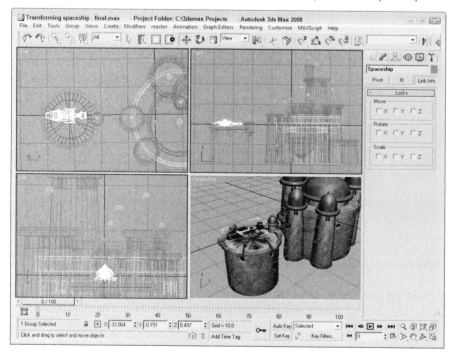

Using Pivot Points

An object's pivot point is the center about which the object is rotated and scaled and about which most modifiers are applied. Pivot points are created by default when an object is created and are usually created at the center or base of an object. You can move and orient a pivot point in any direction, but repositioning the pivot cannot be animated. Pivot points exist for all objects, whether or not they are part of a hierarchy.

CAUTION   Try to set your pivot points before animating any objects in your scene. If you relocate the pivot point after animation keys have been placed, all transformations are modified to use the new pivot point.

Positioning pivot points

To move and orient a pivot point, open the Hierarchy panel in the Command Panel and click the Pivot button. At the top of the Adjust Pivot rollout are three buttons; each button represents a different mode. The Affect Pivot Only mode makes the transformation buttons affect only the pivot point of the current selection. The object does not move. The Affect Object Only mode causes the object to be transformed, but not the pivot point. The Affect Hierarchy Only mode allows an object's links to be moved.

The pivot point is easily identified as the place where the Transform Gizmo is located when the object is selected, as shown in Figure 7.9.

FIGURE 7.9

The Transform Gizmo is located at the object's pivot point.

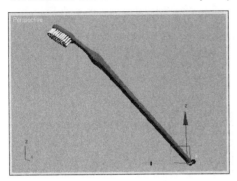

NOTE Using the Scale transformation while one of these modes is selected alters the selected object but has no effect on the pivot point or the link.

Aligning pivot points

Below the mode buttons are three more buttons that are used to align the pivot points. These buttons are active only when a mode is selected. These buttons are Center to Object/Pivot, Align to Object/Pivot, and Align to World. The first two buttons switch between Object and Pivot, depending on the mode selected. You may select only one mode at a time. The button turns light blue when selected.

The Center to Object button moves the pivot point so that it is aligned with the object center, and the Center to Pivot button moves the object so it is centered on its own pivot point. The Align to Object/Pivot button rotates the object or pivot point until the object's Local Coordinate System and the pivot point are aligned. The Align to World button rotates either the object or the pivot to the World Coordinate System. For example, if the Affect Object Only mode is selected and the object is separated from the pivot point, clicking the Center to Pivot button moves the object so that its center is on the pivot point.

Under these three alignment buttons is another button labeled Reset Pivot, which you use to reset the pivot point to its original location.

Using the Working Pivot

Underneath the Adjust Pivot rollout is the Working Pivot rollout. Working Pivots are handy if you want to position an object using a temporary pivot without having to change the default object pivot. To position a Working Pivot, click the Edit Working Pivot button. This enters a mode just like the Affect Pivot Only button described above, except it works with the working pivot.

NEW FEATURE The Working Pivot feature is new to 3ds Max 2008.

After the Working Pivot is in place, you can select to use it instead of the object pivot by clicking the Use Working Pivot button. The Working Pivot stays active until you disable it in the Hierarchy panel. The

Working Pivot works for all objects in the scene. When the Working Pivot is active, reminder text, "USE WP" appears in all the viewports under the viewport name; when the Edit Working Pivot mode is enabled, this text reads, "EDIT WP."

 You can quickly enable the Working Pivot by selecting the Working option from the Reference Coordinate System drop-down list in the main toolbar.

The Working Pivot rollout includes several buttons to help position the Working Pivot. The Align to View button reorients the Working Pivot to the current view. The Reset button moves the Working Pivot to the object pivot location of the selected object or to the view center if no object is selected.

NOTE **There is only one working pivot that you can use, but it can be used by any selected object.**

The Place Pivot to View button enters a mode identified by "PLACE WP VIEW" in the viewports that lets you place the Working Pivot anywhere in the current viewport by simply clicking where it should be. This is great for visually eyeballing the Working Pivots location. The Place Pivot to Surface button (PLACE WP SURFACE) enters a mode where you can position the Working Pivot on the surface of an object by interactively dragging the cursor over the object surface. The cursor automatically reorients itself to be aligned with the surface normal. If the Align to View option is selected, then the Working Pivot is automatically aligned to the current view when the View mode is used.

Transform adjustments

The Hierarchy panel of the Command Panel includes another useful rollout labeled Adjust Transform. This rollout includes another mode that you can use with hierarchies of objects. Clicking the Don't Affect Children button places you in a mode where any transformations of a linked hierarchy don't affect the children. Typically, transformations are applied to all linked children of a hierarchy, but this mode disables that.

The Adjust Transform rollout also includes two buttons that allow you to reset the Local Coordinate System and scale percentage. These buttons set the current orientation of an object as the World coordinate or as the 100 percent standard. For example, if you select an object, move it 30 units to the left, and scale it to 200 percent, these values are displayed in the coordinate fields on the status bar. Clicking the Reset Transform and Reset Scale buttons resets these values to 0 and 100 percent.

You use the Reset Scale button to reset the scale values for an object that has been scaled using non-uniform scaling. Non-uniform scaling can cause problems for child objects that inherit this type of scaling, such as shortening the links. The Reset Scale button can remedy these problems by resetting the parent's scaling values. When the scale is reset, you won't see a visible change to the object, but if you open the Scale Transform Type-In dialog box while the scale is being reset, you see the absolute local values being set back to 100 each.

 **If you are using an object that has been non-uniformly scaled, using Reset Scale before the item is linked saves you some headaches if you plan on using modifiers.**

Using the Reset XForm utility

You can also reset transform values using the Reset XForm utility. To use this utility, open the Utility panel and click the Reset XForm button, which is one of the default buttons. The benefit of this utility is that you can reset the transform values for multiple objects simultaneously. This happens by applying the XForm modifier to the objects. The rollout for this utility includes only a single button labeled Reset Selected.

Tutorial: A bee buzzing about a flower

By adjusting an object's pivot point, you can control how the object is transformed about the scene. In this example, you animate a bee's flapping wings by repositioning the wings' pivot points. You then reposition the pivot point for the entire bee so it can rotate about the flower object.

To control how a bee rotates about a flower, follow these steps:

1. Open the Buzzing bee.max file from the Chap 07 directory on the DVD.

    This file includes a bee created from primitives and a flower model created by Zygote Media.

2. Click the bee object to select it, and press Z to zoom in on it in all viewports. Click on the right wing, open the Hierarchy panel, and click on the Affect Pivot Only button. This displays the pivot point in the center of the wing oriented to the wing surface. Select the Local coordinate system from the list in the main toolbar. This orients the transform gizmo to match the pivot's orientation. Drag the wing's pivot point along its X-axis to the place where the wing contacts the body object. Then select the left wing, and move its pivot to the position where it contacts the body object.

3. Click the Auto Key button (or press N) to enable animate mode, and drag the Time Slider to frame 1. Then, with the Select and Rotate button (E), rotate the wing about its Z-axis until it is almost vertical in the Front viewport. Notice how the wing rotates about its new pivot point. Then drag the Time Slider to frame 2, and rotate the wing back to its original position. Click the Auto Key button again (N) to disable key mode.

4. If you want to make these rotations repeat throughout the animation using the Track View, right-click on the wing object and select Curve Editor in the pop-up quadmenu that appears. This opens a Track View with the Rotation tracks selected. In the Track View, select Controller ➪ Out-of-Range Types to open the Param Out-of-Range Types dialog box, select the Loop option, and click OK. Then close the Track View.

 Working with the Track View is beyond the scope of this chapter, but you can find more information on the Track View in Chapter 34, "Working with Function Curves in the Track View."

5. Repeat Steps 3 and 4 for the second wing object. Press the Play Animation button to see both wings flap for the entire animation.

6. Select all parts that make up the bee in the Top viewport, select Group ➪ Group, and name the object **bee**. Then select the bee and the flower in the Left viewport, and press Z to zoom in on them.

7. With the bee group selected, click the Affect Pivot Only button in the Hierarchy panel and move the pivot point to the center of the flower in the Front viewport. Click the Affect Pivot Only button again to disable it.

NOTE If you don't want to move the object pivot in Step 7, you can use the Working Pivot to rotate the bee around the flower or you could select the Pick coordinate system and select the flower.

8. Enable the Auto Key button (N) again, and drag to frame 35. With the Select and Rotate button (E), rotate the bee in the Top viewport a third of the way around the flower. Drag the Time Slider to frame 70, and rotate the bee another third of the way. With the Time Slider at frame 100, complete the rotation. Click the Auto Key button again to display key mode.

9. Click the Play button (/) to see the final rotating bee.

Figure 7.10 shows the bee as it moves around the flower where its pivot point is located.

FIGURE 7.10

By moving the pivot point of the bee, you can control how it spins about the flower.

Using the Align Commands

The Align commands are an easy way to automatically transform objects. You can use these commands to line up object centers or edges, align normals and highlights, align to views and grids, and even line up cameras.

Aligning objects

Any object that you can transform, you can align, including lights, cameras, and Space Warps. After selecting the object to be aligned, click the Align flyout button on the main toolbar or choose Tools ⇨ Align (or press Alt+A). The cursor changes to the Align icon. Now, click a target object with which you want to align all the selected objects. Clicking the target object opens the Align Selection dialog box with the target object's name displayed in the dialog box's title, as shown in Figure 7.11.

The Align Selection dialog box includes settings for the X, Y, and Z positions to line up the Minimum, Center, Pivot Point, or Maximum dimensions for the selected or target object's bounding box. As you change the settings in the dialog box, the objects reposition themselves, but the actual transformations don't take place until you click the Apply button or the OK button.

CROSS-REF   Another way to align objects is with the Clone and Align tool, which is covered in Chapter 8, "Cloning Objects and Creating Object Arrays."

FIGURE 7.11

The Align Selection dialog box can align objects along any axes by their Minimum, Center, Pivot, or Maximum points.

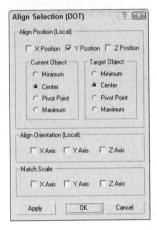

Using the Quick Align tool

 The first flyout tool under the Align tool in the main toolbar (and in the Tools menu) is the Quick Align tool (Shift+A). This tool aligns the pivot points of the selected object with the object that you click on without opening a separate dialog box.

Aligning normals

You can use the Normal Align command to line up points of the surface of two objects. A Normal vector is a projected line that extends from the center of a polygon face exactly perpendicular to the surface. When two Normal vectors are aligned, the objects are perfectly adjacent to one another. If the two objects are spheres, then they touch at only one point.

 To align normals, you need to first select the object to move (this is the source object). Then choose Tools ➪ Normal Align or click the Normal Align flyout button under the Align button on the main toolbar (or press Alt+N). The cursor changes to the Normal Align icon. Drag the cursor across the surface of the source object, and a blue arrow pointing out from the face center appears. Release the mouse when you've correctly pinpointed the position to align.

Next, click the target object, and drag the mouse to locate the target object's align point. This is displayed as a green arrow. When you release the mouse, the source object moves to align the two points and the Normal Align dialog box appears, as shown in Figure 7.12.

When the objects are aligned, the two points match up exactly. The Normal Align dialog box lets you specify offset values that you can use to keep a distance between the two objects. You can also specify an Angle Offset, which is used to deviate the parallelism of the normals. The Flip Normal option aligns the objects so that their selected normals point in the same direction.

Objects without any faces, like Point Helper objects and Space Warps, use a vector between the origin and the Z-axis for normal alignment.

FIGURE 7.12

The Normal Align dialog box allows you to define offset values when aligning normals.

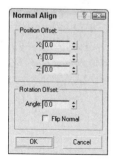

Tutorial: Aligning a kissing couple

Aligning normals positions two faces directly opposite one another, so what better way to practice this tool than to align two faces?

To connect the kissing couple using the Normal Align command, follow these steps:

1. Open the Kissing couple.max file from the Chap 07 directory on the DVD.

    This file includes two extruded shapes of a boy and a girl. The extruded shapes give us flat faces that are easy to align.

2. Select the girl shape, and choose the Tools ⇨ Normal Align menu command (or press Alt+N). Then click and drag the cursor over the extruded shape until the blue vector points out from the front of the lips, as shown in Figure 7.13.

3. Then click and drag the cursor over the boy shape until the green vector points out from the front of the lips. This vector pointing out from the face is the surface normal. Then click and release the mouse, and the Normal Align dialog box appears. Enter a value of **5** in the Z-Axis Offset field, and click OK.

Figure 7.13 shows the resulting couple with normal aligned faces.

FIGURE 7.13

Using the Normal Align feature, you can align object faces.

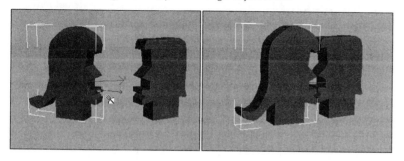

In the Align button flyout are two other common ways to align objects: Align Camera and Place Highlight (Ctrl+H). To learn about these features, see Chapter 18, "Configuring and Aiming Cameras," and Chapter 19, "Using Lights and Basic Lighting Techniques," respectively.

Aligning to a view

The Align to View command provides an easy and quick way to reposition objects to one of the axes. To use this command, select an object and choose Tools ➪ Align to View. The Align to View dialog box appears, as shown in Figure 7.14. Changing the settings in this dialog box displays the results in the viewports. You can use the Flip command for altering the direction of the object points. If no object is selected, then the Align to View command cannot be used.

FIGURE 7.14

The Align to View dialog box is a quick way to line up objects with the axes.

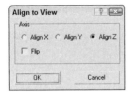

The Align to View command is especially useful for fixing the orientation of objects when you create them in the wrong view. All alignments are completed relative to the object's Local Coordinate System. If several objects are selected, each object is reoriented according to its Local Coordinate System.

 Using the Align to View command on symmetrical objects like spheres doesn't produce any noticeable difference in the viewports.

Using Grids

When Max is started, the one element that is visible is the Home Grid. This grid is there to give you a reference point for creating objects in 3D space. At the center of each grid are two darker lines. These lines meet at the origin point for the World Coordinate System where the coordinates for X, Y, and Z are all 0.0. This point is where all objects are placed by default.

In addition to the Home Grid, you can create and place new grids in the scene. These grids are not rendered, but you can use them to help you locate and align objects in 3D space.

The Home Grid

You can turn the Home Grid on and off by choosing Views ➪ Grid ➪ Show Home Grid (you can also turn the Home Grid on and off for the active viewport using the G key). If the Home Grid is the only grid in the scene, then by default it is also the construction grid where new objects are positioned when created.

You can access the Home Grid parameters (shown in Figure 7.15) by choosing Customize ⇨ Grid and Snap Settings. You can also access this dialog box by right-clicking the Snap, Angle Snap, or Percent Snap toggle buttons located on the main toolbar.

In the Home Grid panel of the Grid and Snap Settings dialog box, you can set how often Major Lines appear, as well as Grid Spacing. (The Spacing value for the active grid is displayed on the status bar.) You can also specify to dynamically update the grid view in all viewports or just in the active one.

The User Grids panel lets you activate any new grids when created.

FIGURE 7.15

The Home Grid and User Grids panels of the Grid and Snap Settings dialog box let you define the grid spacing.

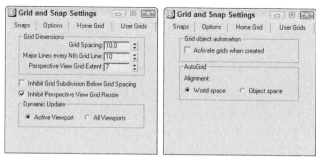

Creating and activating new grids

In addition to the Home Grid, you can create new grids. To create a new Grid object, select the Create ⇨ Helpers ⇨ Grid menu command, or open the Create panel, select the Helpers category, and click the Grid button. In the Parameters rollout are settings for specifying the new grid object's dimensions, spacing, and color, as well as which coordinate plane to display (XY, YZ, or ZX).

You can designate any newly created grid as the default active grid. To activate a grid, make sure that it is selected and choose Views ⇨ Grids ⇨ Activate Grid Object. Keep in mind that only one grid may be active at a time, and the default Home Grid cannot be selected. You can also activate a grid by right-clicking the grid object and selecting Activate Grid from the pop-up menu. To deactivate the new grid and reactivate the Home Grid, choose Views ⇨ Grids ⇨ Activate Home Grid, or right-click the grid object and choose Activate Grid ⇨ Home Grid from the pop-up quadmenu.

You can find further grid settings for new grids in the Grid and Snap Settings dialog box on the User Grids panel. The settings include automatically activating the grid when created and an option for aligning an AutoGrid using World space or Object space coordinates.

Using AutoGrid

You can use the AutoGrid feature to create a new construction plane perpendicular to a face normal. This feature provides an easy way to create and align objects directly next to one another without manually lining them up or using the Align features.

The AutoGrid feature shows up as a check box at the top of the Object Type rollout for every category in the Create panel. It becomes active only when you're in Create Object mode.

To use AutoGrid, click the AutoGrid option after selecting an object type to create. If no objects are in the scene, then the object is created as usual. If an object is in the scene, then the cursor moves around on the surface of the object with its coordinate axes perpendicular to the surface that the cursor is over. Clicking and dragging creates the new object based on the precise location of the object under the mouse.

The AutoGrid option stays active for all new objects that you create until you turn it off by unchecking the box.

TIP Holding down the Alt key before creating the object makes the new construction grid visible, disables the AutoGrid option, and causes all new objects to use the new active construction grid. You can disable this active construction grid by enabling the AutoGrid option again.

Tutorial: Creating a spyglass

As you begin to build objects for an existing scene, you find that working away from the scene origin is much easier if you enable the AutoGrid feature for the new objects you create. This feature enables you to position the new objects on (or close to) the surfaces of the nearby objects. It works best with objects that have pivot points located at their edges, such as Box and Cylinder objects.

In this example, you quickly create a spyglass object using the AutoGrid without needing to perform additional moves.

To create a spyglass using the AutoGrid and Snap features, follow these steps:

1. Before starting, click the Left viewport and zoom way out so you can see the height of the spyglass pieces.
2. Select Create ⇨ Standard Primitives ⇨ Cylinder, and drag from the origin in the Top viewport to create a Cylinder object. Set the Radius value to **40** and the Height value to **200**. Then enable the AutoGrid option in the Object Type rollout.
3. Drag from the origin again in the Top viewport to create another Cylinder object. Set its Radius to **35** and its Height to **200**. Repeat this step three times, reducing the Radius by 5 each time.

Figure 7.16 shows the resulting spyglass object.

FIGURE 7.16

This spyglass object was created quickly and easily using the AutoGrid option.

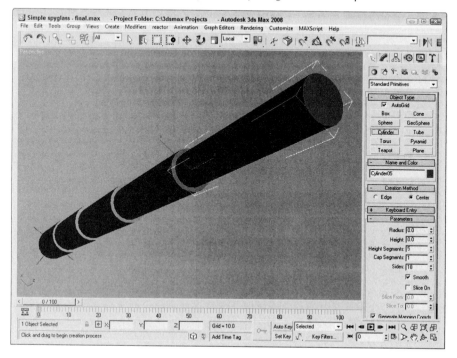

Using Snap Options

Often, when an object is being transformed, you know exactly where you want to put it. The Snap feature can be the means whereby objects get to the precise place they should be. For example, if you are constructing a set of stairs from box primitives, you can enable the Edge Snap feature to make each adjacent step be aligned precisely along the edge of the previous step. With the Snap feature enabled, an object automatically moves (or snaps) to the specified snap position when you place it close enough. If you enable the Snap features, they affect any transformations that you make in a scene.

Snap points are defined in the Grid and Snap Settings dialog box that you can open by choosing Customize ⇨ Grid and Snap Settings or by right-clicking any of the first three Snap buttons on the main toolbar (these Snap buttons have a small magnet icon in them). Figure 7.17 shows the Snaps panel of the Grid and Snap Settings dialog box for Standard and NURBS objects. NURBS stands for Non-Uniform Rational B-Splines. They are a special type of object created from spline curves.

CROSS-REF In addition to the snap points for standard objects, the Snaps panel also includes a list of snap points for NURBS objects. For more information on NURBS, see Chapter 27, "Modeling with Patches and NURBS."

FIGURE 7.17

The Snaps panel includes many different points to snap to depending on the object type.

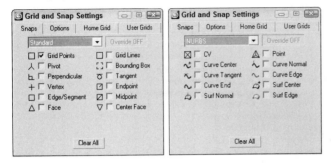

After snap points have been defined, the Snap buttons on the main toolbar activate the Snaps feature. The first Snaps button consists of a flyout with three buttons: 3D Snap toggle, 2.5D Snap toggle, and 2D Snap toggle. The 2D Snap toggle button limits all snaps to the active construction grid. The 2.5D Snap toggle button snaps to points on the construction grid as well as projected points from objects in the scene. The 3D Snap toggle button can snap to any points in 3D space.

Tutorial: Creating a 2D outline of an object

The 2.5D snap can be confusing. It limits snapping to the active construction grid, but within the active grid, it can snap to 3D points that are projected onto the active grid. You can create a 2D representation of a 3D object by snapping to the vertices of the suspended object.

To create a 2D outline of a cylinder object, follow these steps:

1. Select the Create ➪ Standard Primitives ➪ Cylinder menu to create a simple cylinder object.
2. Select and rotate the cylinder so it is suspended and rotated at an angle above the construction grid.
3. Click and hold the Snap toggle button, and select the 2.5D Snap flyout option. Then right-click on the Snap toggle and select only the Vertex option in the Snaps panel. Then close the Grid and Snap Settings dialog box.
4. Choose the Create ➪ Shapes ➪ Line menu and create a line in the Top viewport by snapping to the points that make the outline of the cylinder.

Figure 7.18 shows the finished methane molecule.

 Right-clicking the snap toggles opens the Grid and Snap Settings dialog box, except for the Spinner Snap toggle, which opens the Preference Settings dialog box.

These Snap buttons control the snapping for translations. To the right are two other buttons: Angle Snap toggle and Percent Snap. These buttons control the snapping of rotations and scalings.

 The keyboard shortcut for turning the Snaps feature on and off is the S key.

With the Snaps feature enabled, the cursor becomes blue crosshairs wherever a snap point is located.

FIGURE 7.18

FIGURE 7.18

The 2.5D snap feature snaps to vertices of 3D objects projected onto the active grid.

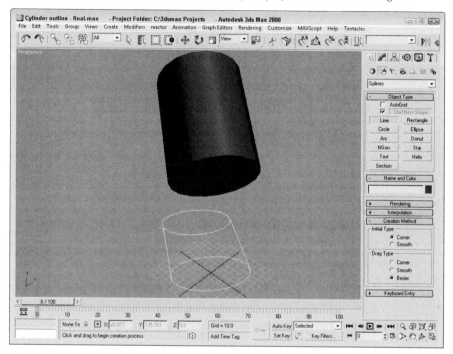

Setting snap points

The Snap tab in the Grid and Snap Settings dialog box has many points that can be snapped to in two categories: Standard and NURBS. The Standard snap points (previously shown in Figure 7.17) include the following:

- **Grid Points:** Snaps to the Grid intersection points
- **Grid Lines:** Snaps only to positions located on the Grid lines
- **Pivot:** Snaps to an object's pivot point
- **Bounding Box:** Snaps to one of the corners of a bounding box
- **Perpendicular:** Snaps to a spline's next perpendicular point
- **Tangent:** Snaps to a spline's next tangent point
- **Vertex:** Snaps to polygon vertices
- **Endpoint:** Snaps to a spline's end point or the end of a polygon edge
- **Edge/Segment:** Snaps to positions only on an edge
- **Midpoint:** Snaps to a spline's midpoint or the middle of a polygon edge
- **Face:** Snaps to any point on the surface of a face
- **Center Face:** Snaps to the center of a face

Several snap points specific to NURBS objects, such as NURBS points and curves, are also shown in Figure 7.17. These points include:

- **CV:** Snaps to any NURBS Control Vertex subobject
- **Point:** Snaps to a NURBS point
- **Curve Center:** Snaps to the center of the NURBS curve
- **Curve Normal:** Snaps to a point that is normal to a NURBS curve
- **Curve Tangent:** Snaps to a point that is tangent to a NURBS curve
- **Curve Edge:** Snaps to the edge of a NURBS curve
- **Curve End:** Snaps to the end of a NURBS curve
- **Surf Center:** Snaps to the center of a NURBS surface
- **Surf Normal:** Snaps to a point that is normal to a NURBS surface
- **Surf Edge:** Snaps to the edge of a NURBS surface

Setting snap options

The Grid and Snap Settings dialog box holds a panel of Options, shown in Figure 7.19, in which you can set whether markers display, the size of the markers, and their color. If you click the color swatch, a Color Selector dialog box opens and enables you to select a new color. The Snap Preview Radius defines the radial distance from the snap point required before the object that is being moved is displayed at the target snap point as a preview. This value can be larger than the actual Snap Radius and is meant to provide visual feedback on the snap operation. The Snap Radius setting determines how close the cursor must be to a snap point before it snaps to it.

The Angle and Percent values are the strengths for any rotate and scale transformations, respectively. The Snap to Frozen Objects lets you control whether frozen items can be snapped to. You can also cause translations to be affected by the designated axis constraints with the Use Axis Constraints option. The Display Rubber Band option draws a line from the object's starting location to its snapping location. The Use Axis Center as Start Snap Point automatically positions the initial snap point at the center of the transform axis. This provides a good first guess on where you want the snapping to start.

FIGURE 7.19

The Options panel includes settings for marker size and color and the Snap Strength value.

Within any viewpoint, holding down the Shift key and right-clicking in the viewport can access a pop-up menu of grid points and options. This pop-up quadmenu lets you quickly add or reset all the current snap points and change snap options, such as Transformed Constraints and Snap to Frozen.

Using the Snaps toolbar

As a shortcut to enabling the various snapping categories, you can access the Snaps toolbar by right-clicking on the main toolbar away from the buttons and selecting Snaps from the popup menu. The Snaps toolbar, shown in Figure 7.20, can have several toggle buttons enabled at a time. Each enabled button is highlighted in yellow.

FIGURE 7.20

The Snaps toolbar provides a quick way to access several snap settings

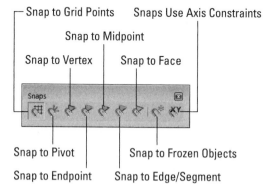

Tutorial: Creating a lattice for a methane molecule

Many molecules are represented by a lattice of spheres. Trying to line up the exact positions of the spheres by hand could be extremely frustrating, but using the Snap feature makes this challenge . . . well . . . a snap.

One of the simpler molecules is methane, which is composed of one carbon atom surrounded by four smaller hydrogen atoms. To reproduce this molecule as a lattice, we first need to create a tetrahedron primitive and snap spheres to each of its corners.

To create a lattice of the methane molecule, follow these steps:

1. Right-click the Snap toggle button in the main toolbar to open the Grid and Snap Settings, and enable the Grid Points and Vertex options. Then click the Snap toggle button (or press the S key) to enable 3D Snap mode.

2. Select the Create ➪ Extended Primitives ➪ Hedra menu command, set the P Family Parameter to **1.0**, and drag in the Top viewport from the center of the Home Grid to the first grid point to the right to create a Tetrahedron shape.

3. Click and hold the Snap toggle button, and select the 3D Snap flyout option. Select the Create ➪ Standard Primitives ➪ Sphere menu command. Right-click in the Left viewport, and drag from the top left vertex to create a sphere. Set the sphere's Radius to **25**.

4. Create three more sphere objects with Radius values of 25 that are snapped to the vertices of the Tetrahedron object.

5. Finally, create a sphere in the Top viewport using the same snap point as the initial tetrahedron. Set its Radius to **80**.

Figure 7.21 shows the finished methane molecule.

FIGURE 7.21

A methane molecule lattice drawn with the help of the Snap feature

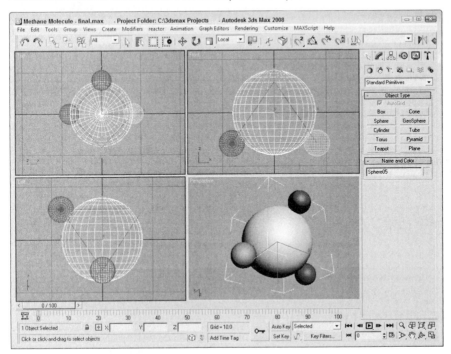

Summary

Transforming objects in Max is one of the fundamental actions you can perform. The three basic ways to transform objects are moving, rotating, and scaling. Max includes many helpful features to enable these transformations to take place quickly and easily. In this chapter, we covered these features:

- Using the Move, Rotate, and Scale buttons and the Transform Gizmos
- Transforming objects precisely with the Transform Type-In dialog box and status bar fields
- Using Transform Managers to change coordinate systems and lock axes
- Aligning objects with the align tool, aligning normals, and aligning to views
- Manipulating pivot points and using a Working Pivot
- Working with grids
- Setting up snap points
- Snapping objects to snap points

In the next chapter, you work more with multiple objects by learning how to clone objects. Using these techniques, you could very quickly have too many objects (and you were worried that there weren't enough objects).

Chapter 8

Cloning Objects and Creating Object Arrays

The only thing better than one perfect object is two perfect objects. Cloning objects is the process of creating copies of objects. These copies can maintain an internal connection (called an instance or a reference) to the original object that allows them to be modified along with the original object. For example, if you create a school desk and clone it multiple times as an instance to fill a room, then changing the parameter of one of the desks automatically changes it for all the other desks also.

An *array* is a discrete set of regularly ordered objects. So creating an array of objects involves cloning several copies of an object in a pattern, such as in rows and columns or in a circle.

I'm sure you have the concept for that perfect object in your little bag of tricks, and this chapter lets you copy it over and over after you get it out.

Cloning Objects

You can clone objects in Max in a couple of ways (and cloning luckily has nothing to do with DNA or gene splices). One method is to use the Edit ➪ Clone (Ctrl+V) menu command, and another method is to transform an object while holding down the Shift key. You won't need to worry about these clones attacking anyone (unlike *Star Wars: Episode II*).

Using the Clone command

You can create a duplicate object by choosing the Edit ➪ Clone (Ctrl+V) menu command. You must select an object before the Clone command becomes active, and you must not be in a Create mode. Selecting this command opens the Clone Options dialog box, shown in Figure 8.1, where you can give the clone a name and specify it as a Copy, Instance, or Reference. You can also copy any controllers associated with the object as a Copy or an Instance.

CAUTION   The Edit menu doesn't include the common Windows cut, copy, and paste commands because many objects and subobjects cannot be easily pasted into a different place. However, you will find a Clone (Ctrl+V) command, which can duplicate a selected object.

FIGURE 8.1

The Clone Options dialog box defines the new object as a Copy, Instance, or Reference.

CROSS-REF   The difference between Copy, Instance, and Reference is discussed in the "Understanding Cloning Options" section in this chapter.

When a clone is created with the Clone menu, it is positioned directly on top of the original, which makes distinguishing it from the original difficult. To verify that a clone has been created, open the Select by Name dialog box by pressing H and look for the cloned object (it has the same name, but an incremented number has been added). To see both objects, click the Select and Move button on the main toolbar and move one of the objects away from the other.

Using the Shift-clone method

An easier way to create clones is with the Shift key. You can use the Shift key when objects are transformed using the Select and Move, Select and Rotate, and Select and Scale commands. Holding down the Shift key while you use any of these commands on an object clones the object and opens the Clone Options dialog box. This Clone Options dialog box is identical to the dialog box previously shown, except it includes a spinner to specify the number of copies.

Performing a transformation with the Shift key held down defines an offset that is applied repeatedly to each copy. For example, holding down the Shift key while moving an object five units to the left (with the Number of Copies set to 5) places the first cloned object five units away from the original, the second cloned object ten units away from the original object, and so on.

Tutorial: Cloning dinosaurs

The story behind *Jurassic Park* is pretty exciting, but in Max we can clone dinosaurs without their DNA.

To investigate cloning objects, follow these steps:

1. Open the Cloning dinosaurs.max file found in the Chap 08 directory of the DVD.
2. Select the dinosaur object by clicking it in one of the viewports.
3. With the dinosaur model selected, choose Edit ⇨ Clone (or press Ctrl+V).
   The Clone Options dialog box appears.
4. Name the clone **First clone**, select the Copy option, and click OK.

5. Click the Select and Move button (or press the W key) on the main toolbar. Then in the Top viewport, click and drag the dinosaur model to the right.

As you move the model, the original model beneath it is revealed.

6. Select each model in turn, and notice the name change in the Create panel's Name field. Notice that the clone is even the same object color as the original.

7. With the Select and Move button still active, hold down the Shift key, click the cloned dinosaur in the Top viewport, and move it to the right again. In the Clone Options dialog box that appears, select the Copy option, set the Number of Copies to **3**, and click OK.

8. Click the Zoom Extents All button (or press Shift+Ctrl+Z) in the lower-right corner to view all the new dinosaurs.

Three additional dinosaurs have appeared, equally spaced from each other. The spacing was determined by the distance that you moved the second clone before releasing the mouse. Figure 8.2 shows the results of our dinosaur cloning experiment. (Now you'll need to build a really strong fence.)

FIGURE 8.2

Cloning multiple objects is easy with the Shift-clone feature.

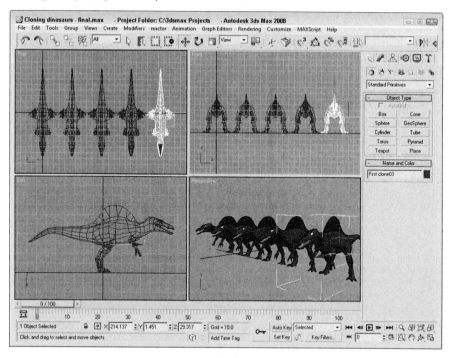

Understanding Cloning Options

When cloning in Max, you're offered the option to create the clone as a copy, an instance, or a reference. This is true not only for objects, but for materials, modifiers, and controllers as well.

209

Working with copies, instances, and references

When an object is cloned, the Clone Options dialog box appears. This dialog box enables you to select to make a copy, an instance, or a reference of the original object. Each of these clone types is unique and offers different capabilities.

A copy is just what it sounds like — an exact replica of the original object. The new copy maintains no ties to the original object and is a unique object in its own right. Any changes to the copy do not affect the original object, and vice versa.

Instances are different from copies in that they maintain strong ties to the original object. All instances of an object are interconnected, so that any geometry modifications (done with modifiers or object parameters) to any single instance changes all instances. For example, if you create several instances of a mailbox and then use a modifier on one of them, all instances are also modified.

> **NOTE**   **Instances and references can have different object colors, materials, transformations (moving, rotating, or scaling), and object properties.**

References are objects that inherit modifier changes from their parent objects, but do not affect the parent when modified. Referenced objects get all the modifiers applied to the parent and can have their own modifiers as well. For example, suppose that you have an apple object and a whole bunch of references to that apple. Applying a modifier to the base apple changes all the remaining apples, but you can also apply a modifier to any of the references without affecting the rest of the bunch.

> **CROSS-REF**   **Instances and references are tied to the applied object modifiers, which are covered in more detail in Chapter 13, "Introducing Modifiers and Using the Modifier Stack."**

 At any time, you can break the tie between objects with the Make Unique button in the Modifier Stack. The Views ⇨ Show Dependencies command shows in magenta any objects that are instanced or referenced when the Modify panel is opened. This means that you can easily see which objects are instanced or referenced from the current selection.

Tutorial: Creating instanced doughnuts

Learning how the different clone options work will save you lots of future modifications. To investigate these options, let's take a quick trip to the local doughnut shop.

To clone some doughnuts, follow these steps:

1. Create a doughnut using the Torus primitive by selecting Create ⇨ Standard Primitives ⇨ Torus, and then dragging and clicking twice in the Top viewport to create a torus object.

2. Click the torus object in the Top viewport to select it.

3. With the doughnut model selected, click the Select and Move button (or press the W key). Hold down the Shift key, and in the Top viewport, move the doughnut upward. In the Clone Options dialog box, select the Instance option, set the Number of Copies to **5**, and click OK. Click the Zoom Extents All (or press the Shift+Ctrl+Z key) button to widen your view.

4. Select all objects with the Edit ⇨ Select All (Ctrl+A) command, and then Shift+drag the doughnuts in the Top viewport to the right. In the Clone Options dialog box, select the Instance option again and **3** for the Number of Copies and click OK. This creates a nice array of two dozen doughnuts. Click the Zoom Extents All button (or press the Z key) to see all the doughnuts.

5. Select a single doughnut, and in the Parameters rollout of the Modify panel, set Radius1 to **20** and Radius2 to **10**.

   This makes a nice doughnut and changes all doughnuts at once.

6. Select the Modifiers ⇨ Parametric Deformers ⇨ Bend command. Then in the Parameters rollout of the Command Panel, enter **25** in the Angle field and select the X Bend Axis.

This adds a slight bend to the doughnuts.

CROSS-REF   You can use modifiers to alter geometry. You can learn about using modifiers in Chapter 13, "Introducing Modifiers and Using the Modifier Stack."

Figure 8.3 shows the doughnuts all changed exactly the same. You can imagine the amount of time it would take to change each doughnut individually. Using instances made these changes easy.

FIGURE 8.3

Two dozen doughnut instances ready for glaze

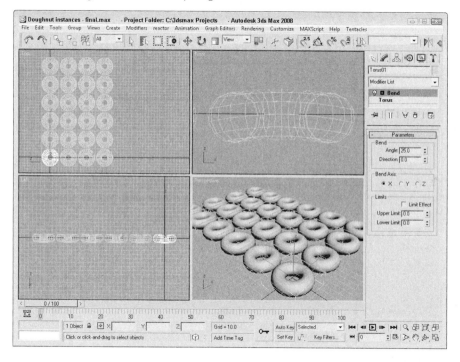

Tutorial: Working with referenced apples

Now that we have filled our bellies with doughnuts, we need some healthful food for balance. What better way to add balance than to have an apple or two to keep the doctor away?

To create some apples using referenced clones, follow these steps:

1. Open the Referenced Apples.max file from the Chap 08 directory on the DVD.
2. Select the apple, and Shift+drag with the Select and Move (W) tool in the Top viewport to create a cloned reference. Select the Reference option in the Clone Options dialog box. Then close the Clone Options dialog box.

3. Select the original apple again, and repeat Step 2 until several referenced apples surround the original apple.

4. Select the original apple in the middle again, and choose the Modifiers ⇨ Subdivision Surfaces ⇨ MeshSmooth command. In the Subdivision Amount rollout, set the number of Iterations to **2**.

   This smoothes all the apples.

5. Select one of the surrounding apples, and apply the Modifiers ⇨ Parametric Deformers ⇨ Taper command. Set the Amount value to **0.5** about the Z-axis.

6. Select another of the surrounding apples, and apply the Modifiers ⇨ Parametric Deformers ⇨ Squeeze command. Set the Axial Bulge Amount value to **0.3**.

7. Select another of the surrounding apples, and apply the Modifiers ⇨ Parametric Deformers ⇨ Squeeze command. Set the Radial Squeeze Amount value to **0.2**.

8. Select another of the surrounding apples, and apply the Modifiers ⇨ Parametric Deformers ⇨ Bend command. Set the Angle value to **20** about the Z axis.

> **NOTE** As you apply modifiers to a referenced object, notice the thick gray bar in the Modifier Stack. This bar, called the Derived Object Line, separates which modifiers get applied to all referenced objects (below the line) and which modifiers get applied to only the selected object (above the line). If you drag a modifier from above the gray bar to below the gray bar, then that modifier is applied to all references.

Using referenced objects, you can apply the major changes to similar objects, but still make minor changes to objects to make them a little different. Figure 8.4 shows the apples. Notice that they are not all exactly the same.

FIGURE 8.4

Even apples from the same tree should be slightly different.

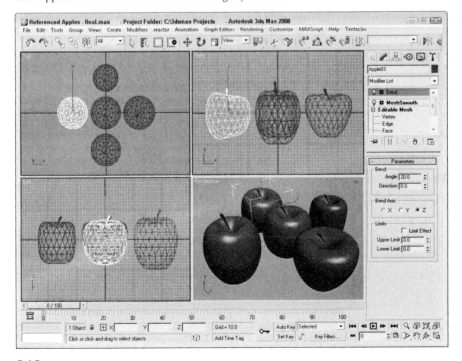

Mirroring Objects

Have you ever held the edge of a mirror up to your face to see half of your head in the mirror? Many objects have a natural symmetry that you can exploit to require that only half an object be modeled. The human face is a good example. You can clone symmetrical parts using the Mirror command.

Using the Mirror command

The Mirror command creates a clone (or No Clone if you so choose) of the selected object about the current coordinate system. To open the Mirror dialog box, shown in Figure 8.5, choose Tools ⇨ Mirror, or click the Mirror button located on the main toolbar. You can access the Mirror dialog box only if an object is selected.

FIGURE 8.5

FIGURE 8.5

The Mirror dialog box can create an inverted clone of an object.

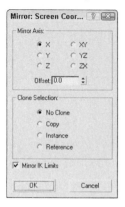

Within the Mirror dialog box, you can specify an axis or plane about which to mirror the selected object. You can also define an Offset value. As with the other clone commands, you can specify whether the clone is to be a Copy, an Instance, or a Reference, or you can choose No Clone, which flips the object around the axis you specify. The dialog box also lets you mirror Inverse Kinematics Limits, which reduces the number of IK parameters that need to be set.

 **Learn more about inverse kinematics in Chapter 41, "Working with Inverse Kinematics."**

Tutorial: Mirroring a robot's leg

Many characters have symmetry that you can use to your advantage, but to use symmetry, you can't just clone one half. Consider the position of a character's right ear relative to its right eye. If you clone the ear, then the position of each ear will be identical, with the ear to the right of the eye, which would make for a strange looking creature. What you need to use is the Mirror command, which clones the object and rotates it about a selected axis.

In this example, we have a complex mechanical robot with one of its legs created. Using Mirror, you can quickly clone and position its second leg.

To mirror a robot's leg, follow these steps:

1. Open the Robot mech.max file from the Chap 08 directory on the DVD.

   This file includes a robot with one of its legs deleted.

2. Select all objects that make up the robot's leg in the Left viewport, and open the Mirror dialog box with the Tools ⇨ Mirror menu command.

3. In the Mirror dialog box, select X as the Mirror Axis and Instance as the Clone Selection. Change the Offset value until the cloned leg is in position, which should be at around **–2.55**.

NOTE   The mirror axis depends on the viewport, so make sure that the Left viewport is selected.

   Any changes made to the dialog box are immediately shown in the viewports.

4. Click OK to close the dialog box.

NOTE   By making the clone selection an instance, you can ensure that any future modifications to the right half of the figure are automatically applied to the left half.

Figure 8.6 shows the resulting robot — which won't be falling over now.

FIGURE 8.6

A perfectly symmetrical robot, compliments of the Mirror tool

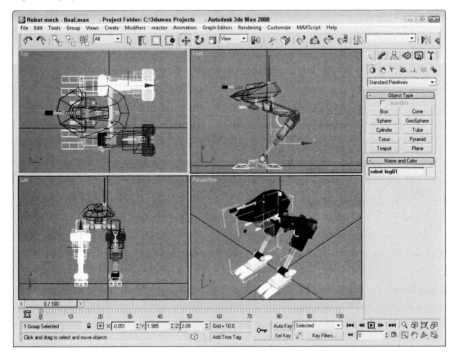

Cloning over Time

Another useful way to create multiple copies of an object is to have an object be created based on its position during a specific frame of an animation. This cloning at specific times is accomplished with the Snapshot feature.

Using the Snapshot command

The Snapshot command creates a static copies, instances, references, or even meshes of a selected object as it moves along an animation path. For example, you could create a series of footprints by animating a set of footprints moving across the screen from frame 1 to frame 100, and then choose Tools ➪ Snapshot and enter the number of steps to appear over this range of frames in the Snapshot dialog box. The designated number of steps are created at regular intervals for the animation range. Be aware that the Snapshot command works only with objects that have an animation path defined.

 You can open the Snapshot dialog box by choosing Tools ➪ Snapshot or by clicking the Snapshot button (under the Array flyout on the Extras toolbar). Snapshot is the second button in the flyout. In the Snapshot dialog box, shown in Figure 8.7, you can choose to produce a single clone or a range of clones over a given number of frames. Selecting Single creates a single clone at the current frame.

NOTE When you enter the number of Copies in the Snapshot dialog box, a copy is placed at both the beginning and end of the specified range, so if your animation path is a closed path, two objects are stacked on top of each other. For example, if you have a square animation path and you want to place a copy at each corner, you need to enter a value of 5.

FIGURE 8.7

The Snapshot dialog box lets you clone a Copy, Instance, Reference, or Mesh.

TIP The Snapshot tool can also be used with particle systems.

Tutorial: Create a path through a maze

The Snapshot tool can be used to create objects as a model is moved along an animated path. In this example, we create a series of footsteps through a maze.

To create a set of footprints through a maze with the Snapshot tool, follow these steps:

1. Open the Path through a maze.max file from the Chap 08 directory on the DVD. This file includes a set of animated footprints that travel to the exit of a maze.

2. Select both footprint objects at the entrance to the maze.

3. Choose the Tools ➪ Snapshot menu to open the Snapshot dialog box. Select the Range option, set the number of Copies to **20**, and select the Instance option. Then click the OK button.

Figure 8.8 shows the path of footsteps leading the way through the maze, which are easier to follow than breadcrumbs.

FIGURE 8.8

The Snapshot tool helps to build a set of footprints through a maze.

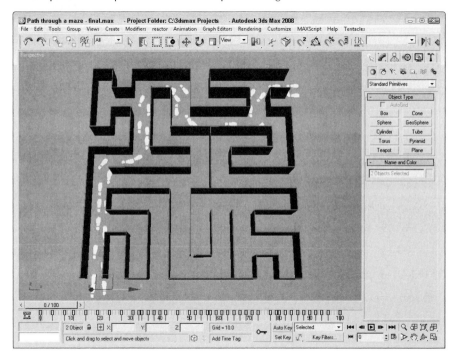

Spacing Cloned Objects

The Snapshot tool offers a convenient way to clone objects along an animation path, but what if you want to clone objects along a path that isn't animated? The answer is the Spacing tool. The Spacing tool can position clones at regular intervals along a path by either selecting a path and the number of cloned objects or by picking two points in the viewport.

Using the Spacing tool

You access the Spacing tool by clicking the last button in the flyout under the Array button on the Extras toolbar (the Extras toolbar can be made visible by right-clicking on the main toolbar away from the buttons).

You can also access it using the Tools ➪ Spacing Tool (Shift+I) menu command. When accessed, it opens the Spacing Tool dialog box, shown in Figure 8.9. At the top of this dialog box are two buttons: Pick Path and Pick Points. If a path is selected, its name appears on the Pick Path button.

FIGURE 8.9

The Spacing Tool dialog box lets you select how to position clones along a path.

You can also specify Count, Spacing, Start Offset, and End Offset values. The drop-down list offers several preset options, including Divide Evenly, Free Center, End Offset, and more. These values and preset options are used to define the number and spacing of the objects. The spacing and position of the objects depend on the values that are included. For example, if you include only a Count value, then the objects are evenly spaced along the path including an object at each end. If an offset value is included, then the first or last item is moved away from the end by the offset value. If a Spacing value is included, then the number of objects required to meet this value is included automatically.

The Lock icons next to the Start and End Offset values force the Start or End Offset values to be the same as the Spacing value. This has the effect of pushing the objects away from their end points.

Before you can use either the Pick Path or Pick Points buttons, you must select the object to be cloned. Using the Pick Path button, you can select a spline path in the scene, and cloned objects are regularly spaced according to the values you selected. The Pick Points method lets you click to select the Start point and click again to select an end point. The cloned objects are spaced in a straight line between the two points.

The two options for determining the spacing width are Edges and Centers. The Edges option spaces objects from the edge of its bounding box to the edge of the adjacent bounding box, and the Centers option spaces objects based on their centers. The Follow option aligns the object with the path if the path is selected. Each object can be a copy, instance, or reference of the original. The text field at the bottom of the dialog box displays for your information the number of objects and the spacing value between each.

TIP Lining up objects to correctly follow the path can be tricky. If the objects are misaligned, you can change the object's pivot point so it matches the viewport coordinates. This makes the object follow the path with correct position.

You can continue to modify the Spacing Tool dialog box's values while the dialog box is open, but the objects are not added to the scene until you click the Apply button. The Cancel button closes the dialog box.

Tutorial: Stacking a row of dominoes

A good example of using the Spacing tool to accomplish something that is difficult in real life is to stack a row of dominoes. It is really a snap in Max regardless of the path.

To stack a row of dominoes using the Spacing tool, follow these steps:

1. Open the Row of dominoes.max file from the Chap 08 directory on the DVD.

   This file includes a single domino and a wavy spline path.

2. Select the domino object, and open the Spacing tool by selecting the flyout button under the Array button on the Extras toolbar (or by pressing Shift+I).

3. In the Spacing Tool dialog box, click the Pick Path button and select the wavy path.

   The path name appears on the Pick Path button.

4. From the drop-down list in the Parameters section of the Spacing Tool dialog box, select the Count option with a value of **35**.

   This is the same as the Divide Evenly, Objects at Ends option in the drop-down list.

5. Select the Edges context option, check the Follow check box, and make all clones Instances. Click Apply when the result looks right, and close the Spacing Tool dialog box.

Figure 8.10 shows the simple results. The Spacing Tool dialog box remains open until you click the Cancel button.

FIGURE 8.10

These dominoes were much easier to stack than the set in my living room.

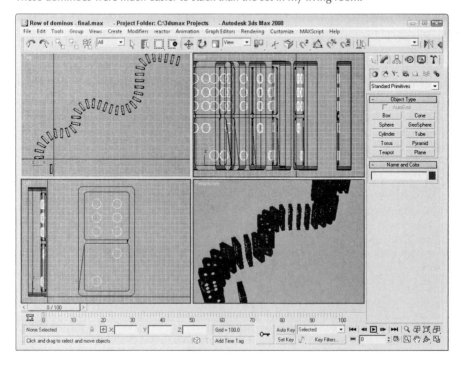

Using the Clone and Align Tool

Imagine you're working on a production team and the modeler assigned to the project says he needs some more time to make the building columns "something special." Just as you prepare to give him the "deadlines don't die" speech, you remember the Clone and Align tool. Using this tool, you can place proxy objects where the detailed ones are supposed to go. Then, when the detailed object is ready, the Clone and Align tool lets you clone the detailed object and place it where all the proxies are positioned. This, of course, makes the modeler happy and doesn't disrupt your workflow. Another production team victory.

Aligning source objects to destination objects

Before selecting the Tools ➪ Clone and Align tool, you need to select the detailed object that you want to place. This object is referred to as the *source object*. Selecting the Clone and Align tool opens a dialog box, shown in Figure 8.11. From this dialog box, you can pick the proxy objects that are positioned where the source objects are supposed to go. These proxy objects are referred to as *destination objects*. The dialog box shows the number of source and destination objects that are selected.

 The Align tool is covered in Chapter 7, "Transforming Objects, Pivoting, Aligning, and Snapping."

FIGURE 8.11

The Clone and Align dialog box lets you choose which objects mark the place where the source object should go.

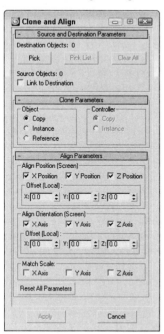

The Clone and Align dialog box also lets you select whether source objects are cloned as copies, instances, or references. In the Align Parameters rollout, you can specify the object's position and orientation using the same controls that are used to align objects, including any Offset values.

As you make changes in the Clone and Align dialog box, the objects are updated in the viewports, but these changes don't become permanent until you click the Apply button. The Clone and Align dialog box is *persistent*, meaning that, after being applied, the settings remain until they are changed.

Tutorial: Cloning and aligning objects

To practice using the Clone and Align tool, you'll open a beach scene with a single set of grouped trees. Several other box objects have been positioned and rotated about the scene. The trees will be the source object and the box objects will be the destinations.

To position and orient several high-res trees using the Clone and Align tool, follow these steps:

1. Open the Trees on beach.max file from the Chap 08 directory on the DVD.

   This file includes a beach scene created by Viewpoint Datalabs.

2. Select the tree objects that have been grouped together, and open the Clone and Align dialog box by selecting the Tools ⇨ Clone and Align menu command.

3. In the Clone and Align dialog box, click the Pick button and select each of the box objects in the scene.

4. In the Align Parameters rollout, enable the X and Y axes for the Positions and the X, Y, and Z axes for the Orientation. Then click the Apply button.

Figure 8.12 shows the simple results. Notice that the destination objects have not been replaced and are still there.

FIGURE 8.12

Using the Clone and Align dialog box, you can place these trees to match the stand-in objects' position and orientation.

Creating Arrays of Objects

Now that you've probably figured out how to create arrays of objects by hand with the Shift-clone method, the Array command multiplies the fun by making it easy to create many copies instantaneously. The Array dialog box lets you specify the array dimensions, offsets, and transformation values. These parameters enable you to create an array of objects easily.

 Access the Array dialog box by selecting an object and choosing Tools ➪ Array or by clicking the Array button on the Extras toolbar. Figure 8.13 shows the Array dialog box. The top of the Array dialog box displays the coordinate system and the center about which the transformations are performed.

The Array dialog box is also *persistent*. You can reset all the values at once by clicking the Reset All Parameters button. You can also preview the current array settings without actually creating an array of objects using the Preview button. The Display as Box option lets you see the array as a bounding box to give you an idea of how large the array will be.

FIGURE 8.13

The Array dialog box defines the number of elements and transformation offsets in an array.

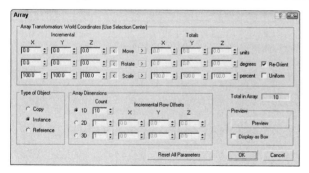

Linear arrays

Linear arrays are arrays in which the objects form straight lines, such as rows and columns. Using the Array dialog box, you can specify an offset along the X-, Y-, and Z-axes at the top of the dialog box and define this offset as an incremental amount or as a total amount. To change between incremental values and total values, click the arrows to the left and right of the Move, Rotate, and Scale labels. For example, an array with 10 elements and an incremental value of 5 will position each successive object a distance of 5 units from the previous one. An array with 10 elements and a total value of 100 will position each element a distance of 10 units apart by dividing the total value by the number of clones.

The Move row values represent units as specified in the Units Setup dialog box. The Rotate row values represent degrees, and the Scale row values are a percentage of the selected object. All values can be either positive or negative values.

Clicking the Re-Orient check box causes the coordinate system to be reoriented after each rotation is made. If this check box isn't enabled, then the objects in the array do not successively rotate. Clicking the Uniform check box to the right of the Scale row values disables the Y and Z Scale value columns and forces the scaling transformations to be uniform. To perform non-uniform scaling, simply deselect the Uniform check box.

The Type of Object section lets you define whether the new objects are copies, instances, or references, but unlike the other cloning tools, the Array tool defaults to Instance. If you plan on modeling all the objects in a similar manner, then you will want to select the Instance or Reference options.

In the Array Dimensions section, you can specify the number of objects to copy along three different dimensions. You can also define incremental offsets for each individual row.

CAUTION You can use the Array dialog box to create a large number of objects. If your array of objects is too large, your system may crash.

Tutorial: Building a white picket fence

To start with a simple example, we create a white picket fence. Because a fence repeats, we need only to create a single slat; then we use the Array command to duplicate it consistently.

To create a picket fence, follow these steps:

1. Open the White picket fence.max file from the Chap 08 directory on the DVD.

2. With the single fence board selected, choose Tools ➪ Array or click on the Array button on the Extras toolbar to open the Array dialog box.

3. In the Array dialog box, click the Reset All Parameters button to start with a clean slate. Then enter a value of **50** in the X column's Move row under the Incremental section. (This is the incremental value for spacing each successive picket.) Next, enter **20** in the Array Dimensions section next to the 1D radio button. (This is the number of objects to include in the array.) Click OK to create the objects.

TIP The Preview button lets you see the resulting array before it is created. Don't worry if you don't get the values right the first time. The most recent values you entered into the Array dialog box stay around until you exit Max.

4. Click the Zoom Extents All button (or press Shift+Ctrl+Z) in the lower-right corner of the Max window to see the entire fence in the viewports.

Figure 8.14 shows the completed fence.

Circular arrays

 You can use the Array dialog box for creating more than just linear arrays. All transformations are done relative to a center point. You can change the center point about which transformations are performed using the Use Selection Center button on the main toolbar. The three flyout options are Use Pivot Point Center, Use Selection Center, and Use Transform Coordinate Center.

CROSS-REF For more about how these settings affect transformations, see Chapter 7, "Transforming Objects, Pivoting, Aligning, and Snapping."

Tutorial: Building a Ferris wheel

Ferris wheels, like most of the rides at the fair, entertain by going around and around, with the riders seated in chairs spaced around the Ferris wheel's central point. The Array dialog box can also create objects around a central point.

 In this example, you use the Rotate transformation along with the Use Transform Coordinate Center button to create a circular array.

FIGURE 8.14

Tom Sawyer would be pleased to see this white picket fence, created easily with the Array dialog box.

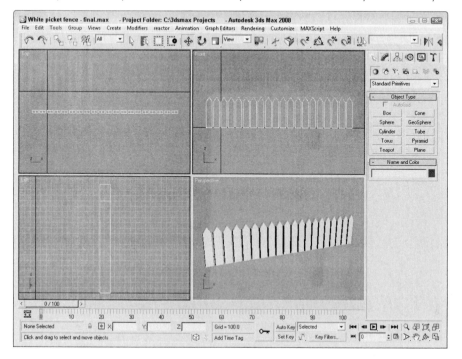

To create a circular array, follow these steps:

1. Open the Ferris wheel.max file from the Chap 08 directory on the DVD.

   This file has the Front viewport maximized to show the profile of the Ferris wheel.

2. Click the Use Pivot Point Center button on the main toolbar, and drag down to the last icon, which is the Use Transform Coordinate Center button.

   The Use Transform Coordinate Center button becomes active. This button causes all transformations to take place about the axis in the center of the screen.

3. Select the light blue chair object, and open the Array dialog box by choosing Tools ⇨ Array or by clicking the Array button on the Extras toolbar. Before entering any values into the Array dialog box, click the Reset All Parameters button.

4. Between the Incremental and Totals sections are the labels Move, Rotate, and Scale. Click the arrow button to the right of the Rotate label. Set the Z column value of the Rotate row to **360** degrees, and make sure that the Re-Orient option is disabled.

   A value of 360 degrees defines one complete revolution. Disabling the Re-Orient option keeps each chair object from gradually turning upside down.

5. In the Array Dimensions section, set the 1D spinner Count value to **8** and click the OK button to create the array.

6. Next select the green strut, and open the Array dialog box again with the Tools ⇨ Array command. Select the Re-Orient option, and leave the rest of the settings as they are. Click the OK button to create the array.

223

Figure 8.15 shows the resulting Ferris wheel. You can click the Min/Max toggle in the lower-right corner to view all four viewports again.

FIGURE 8.15

A circular array created by rotating objects about the Transform Coordinate Center

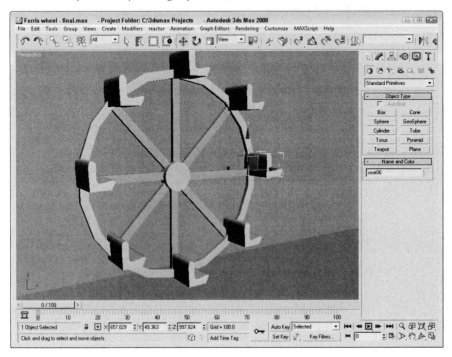

Working with a ring array

You can find the Ring Array system by opening the Create panel and selecting the Systems category. Clicking the Ring Array button opens a Parameters rollout. In this rollout are parameters for the ring's Radius, Amplitude, Cycles, Phase, and the Number of elements to include.

You create the actual array by clicking and dragging in one of the viewports. Initially, all elements are simple box objects surrounding a green dummy object.

The Amplitude, Cycles, and Phase values define the sinusoidal nature of the circle. The Amplitude is the maximum distance that you can position the objects from the horizontal plane. If the Amplitude is set to 0, then all objects lie in the same horizontal plane. The Cycles value is the number of waves that occur around the entire circle. The Phase determines which position along the circle starts in the up position.

Tutorial: Using Ring Array to create a carousel

Continuing with the theme park attractions motif, this example creates a carousel. The horse model comes from Poser but was simplified using the MultiRes modifier.

To use a Ring Array system to create a carousel, follow these steps:

1. Open the Carousel.max file from the Chap 08 directory on the DVD.

    This file includes a carousel structure made from primitives along with a carousel horse.

2. Open the Create panel, select the Systems category, and click the Ring Array button. Drag in the Top viewport from the center of the carousel to create a ring array. Then enter a Radius value of **250**, an Amplitude of **20**, a Cycles value of **3**, and a Number value of **6**.

NOTE If the Ring Array object gets deselected, you can access its parameters in the Motion panel, not in the Modify panel.

3. Select the Ring Array's Dummy object in the Left viewport, select the Tools ⇨ Align menu command, and then click on the center cylinder. The Align Selection dialog box opens. Enable the X, Y, and Z Position options and choose the Center options for both the Current and Target objects and click the Apply button. This aligns the ring array to the center of the carousel.

4. Select the horse object, and choose the Tools ⇨ Clone and Align menu command. In the Clone and Align dialog box that opens, select the Instance options along with the X, Y, and Z Position and Orientation options. Then click the Pick button and click on each of the boxes in the ring array. Set the Offset values for the X and Y Orientation values to **90** to fix the orientation of the placed horses. Then click the Apply button and close the Clone and Align dialog box.

Figure 8.16 shows the finished carousel. Notice that each horse is at a different height. Once the horses are placed, you can delete or hide the ring array object.

FIGURE 8.16

The horses in the carousel were created using a Ring Array system.

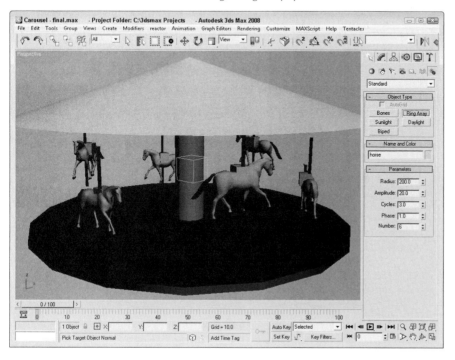

Summary

Many ways to clone an object are available. You can use the Clone command under the Edit menu or the Shift-clone feature for quickly creating numerous clones. Clones can be copies, instances, or references. Each differs in how it retains links to the original object. You can also clone using the Mirror, Snapshot, and Spacing tools.

Arrays are another means of cloning. You can use the Array dialog box to produce clones in three different dimensions, and you can specify the offset transformations.

This chapter covered the following cloning topics:

- Cloning objects and Shift-cloning
- Understanding copies, instances, and references
- Using the Mirror, Snapshot, Spacing, and Clone and Align tools
- Building linear, circular, and spiral arrays of objects
- Using the Ring Array system

In the next chapter, you learn to group objects and link them into hierarchies. Then you'll be able to organize into structures all the objects that you've learned to create.

Chapter 9

Grouping, Linking, and Parenting Objects

N ow that you've learned how to select and clone objects, you'll want to learn how to group objects in an easily accessible form, especially as a scene becomes more complex. Max's grouping features enable you to organize all the objects that you're dealing with, thereby making your workflow more efficient.

Another way of organizing objects is to build a linked hierarchy. A linked hierarchy attaches, or links, one object to another and makes it possible to transform the attached object by moving the object to which it is linked. The arm is a classic example of a linked hierarchy: When the shoulder rotates, so do the elbow, wrist, and fingers. Establishing linked hierarchies can make moving, positioning, and animating many objects easy.

IN THIS CHAPTER

Grouping objects

Building assemblies

Understanding root, parent, and child relationships

Linking and unlinking objects

Working with Groups

Grouping objects organizes them and makes them easier to select and transform. Groups are different from selection sets in that groups exist like one object. Selecting any object in the group selects the entire group, whereas selecting an object in a selection set selects only that object and not the selection set. You can open groups to add, delete, or reposition objects within the group. Groups can also contain other groups. This is called *nesting groups*.

Creating groups

The Group command enables you to create a group. To do so, simply select the desired objects and choose Group ⇨ Group. A simple Name Group dialog box opens and enables you to give the group a name. The newly created group displays a new bounding box that encompasses all the objects in the group.

TIP You can easily identify groups in the Select from Scene dialog box by using the Groups display toggle. Groups appear in bold in the Name and Color rollout of the Command Panel.

Ungrouping objects

The Ungroup command enables you to break up a group (kind of like a poor music album). To do so, simply select the desired group and choose Group ➪ Ungroup. This menu command dissolves the group, and all the objects within the group revert to separate objects. The Ungroup command breaks up only the currently selected group. All nested groups within a group stay intact.

The easiest way to dissolve an entire group, including any nested groups, is with the Explode command. This command eliminates the group and the groups within the group and makes each object separate.

Opening and closing groups

The Open command enables you to access the objects within a group. Grouped objects move, scale, and rotate as a unit when transformed, but individual objects within a group can be transformed independently after you open a group with the Open command.

To move an individual object in a group, select the group and choose Group ➪ Open. The white bounding box changes to a pink box. Then select an object within the group, and move it with the Select and Move button (keyboard shortcut, W). Choose Group ➪ Close to reinstate the group.

Attaching and detaching objects

The Attach and Detach commands enable you to insert or remove objects from an opened group without dissolving the group. To attach objects to an existing group, you select an object, select the Attach menu command, and then click on the group to which you want to add the object. To detach an object from a group, you need to open the group and select the Detach menu command. Remember to close the group when finished.

CROSS-REF Editable objects, like the Editable Poly, also can make use of an Attach feature, but attaching objects to an editable object permanently combines the objects together. You can learn more about the Editable Poly objects in Chapter 12, "Modeling with Polygons."

Tutorial: Grouping a plane's parts together

Positioning objects relative to one another takes careful and precise work. After spending the time to place the wings, tail, and prop on a plane exactly where they need to be, transforming each object by itself can misalign all the parts. By grouping all the objects together, you can move all the objects at once.

For this tutorial, you can get some practice grouping all the parts of an airplane together. Follow these steps:

1. Open the T-28 Trojan plane.max file from the Chap 09 directory on the DVD. This file includes a model created by Viewpoint Datalabs.

2. Click the Select by Name button on the main toolbar (or press the H key) to open the Select from Scene dialog box. In this dialog box, notice all the different plane parts. Click the Select All button to select all the separate objects, and click the OK button to close the dialog box.

3. With all the objects selected, choose Group ➪ Group to open the Group dialog box. Give the group the name **Plane**, and click OK.

4. Click the Select and Move button (or press W), and click and drag the plane.

    The entire group now moves together.

Figure 9.1 shows the plane grouped as one unit. Notice how only one set of brackets surrounds the plane in the Perspective viewport. The group name is displayed in the Name field of the Command Panel instead of listing the number of objects selected.

FIGURE 9.1

The plane moves as one unit after its objects are grouped.

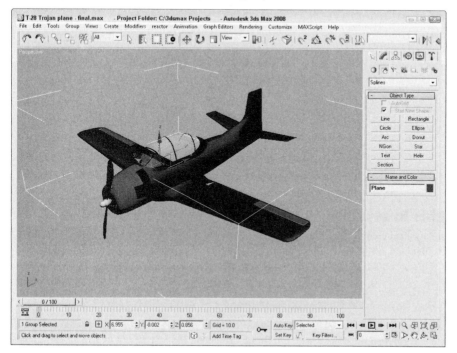

Building Assemblies

At the bottom of the Group menu is a menu item called Assembly with a submenu that looks frightfully similar to the Group menu. The difference between a group and an assembly is that an assembly can include a light object with a Luminaire helper object as its head. This enables you to build light fixtures where the light is actually grouped (or assembled) with the light stand objects. Once built, you can control the light by selecting and moving the light assembly.

After you've created the geometry for a light assembly, you can create an assembly with the Group ➪ Assembly ➪ Assemble menu command. This opens the Create Assembly dialog box, shown in Figure 9.2, where you can name the assembly and add a Luminaire object as the head object.

Because the Luminaire object is the head object, you can see its parameters in the Modify panel whenever the assembly is selected. Its parameters include a Dimmer value and a Filter Color. These parameters are used only if they are wired to an actual light object included in the assembly.

> **NOTE** If you apply a modifier to an assembly, it affects only the Luminaire head object, so Parametric Deformation modifiers like Twist have no effect. If you open the assembly, you can select and apply a modifier to an individual assembly object.

FIGURE 9.2

The Create Assembly dialog box lets you choose a light head object.

Adding lights to assemblies

If you know that your light characteristics aren't going to change, then set up the parameters for your light object before you build the assembly and the light object will provide constant light. If you ever need to change a light setting, just open the assembly with the Group ➪ Assembly ➪ Open menu command. Then select the light object, and its parameters appear in the Modify panel, or you can access the light parameters using the Tools ➪ Light Lister dialog box. After you've changed the light parameters, close the assembly again with the Group ➪ Assembly ➪ Close menu command.

NOTE   Adding a light object to an assembly without wiring it to the Luminaire object works the same as if you grouped the objects with the Group command. The real benefit of an assembly comes from wiring the light parameters.

All other commands in the Assembly submenu work just like their counterparts in the Group menu.

Wiring Luminaire helper objects to light objects

Luminaire objects can be confusing because they don't actually add light to an assembly. If you're curious about the Luminaire objects, you can find them in the Assembly Heads subcategory of the Helper category.

The benefit of the Luminaire helper object is that it can add to an assembly some simple parameters that are accessible whenever the assembly is selected. These parameters work only if you wire them to the parameters of the light object included in the assembly.

CROSS-REF   You can learn more about wiring parameters in Chapter 20, "Understanding Animation and Keyframe Basics."

To wire Luminaire parameters to the light object's parameters, select the assembly and open the Parameter Wiring dialog box with the Animation ➪ Wire Parameters ➪ Parameter Wiring Dialog menu command (or press the Alt+5 shortcut). In the left pane, locate and select the Dimmer parameter under the Object (Luminaire) track. Locate and select the Multiplier parameter under the Object (Light) track, which is under the Assembly01 track in the right pane. Click the one-way connection button in the center of the dialog box that links the Dimmer to the Multiplier parameters, and click the Connect button. Next, wire the FilterColor parameter to the light's Color parameter. Figure 9.3 shows the Parameter Wiring dialog box for this simple assembly.

FIGURE 9.3

The Parameter Wiring dialog box can make the light object's Multiple parameter into a Dimmer switch.

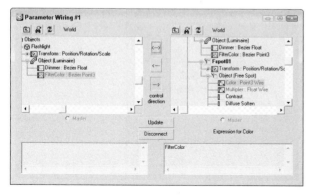

After the assembly light is wired to the Luminaire parameters, you can use the Dimmer and Filter Color parameters in the Modify panel whenever the assembly is selected.

Tutorial: Creating a flashlight assembly

One of the most portable of lights is the ubiquitous flashlight. In this tutorial, we create an assembly and wire the light parameters to the Luminaire head object's parameters.

To create a flashlight assembly, follow these steps:

1. Open the Flashlight assembly.max file from the Chap 09 directory on the DVD.

   This file includes a flashlight model with a single free spotlight.

2. Select all objects within the scene with the Edit ➪ Select All (Ctrl+A) menu command. Then select the Group ➪ Assembly ➪ Assemble menu command. In the Create Assembly dialog box, name the assembly **Flashlight** and click OK.

3. To wire the Luminaire head object's parameters to the light object, select Animation ➪ Wire Parameters ➪ Parameter Wire Dialog (Alt+5). This opens the Parameter Wiring dialog box with the Object (Luminaire) track selected in the left pane. Expand the Object (Luminaire) track, and select the Dimmer parameter.

4. In the right pane of the Parameter Wiring dialog box, expand the Flashlight track, locate and expand the Fspot01 light object, and select the Multiplier track under the Object (Free Spot) track. Then click the Control Direction arrow in the center of the dialog box that points to the right, and click Connect.

5. With the Parameter Wiring dialog box still open, select the FilterColor track in the left pane and the Color track in the right pane, and connect these two parameters with the Connect button. Click the Close button in the upper-right corner of the dialog box.

6. In the Luminaire Parameters rollout of the Modify panel, drag the Dimmer parameter down to 1.0 and watch light in the flashlight dim.

Figure 9.4 shows the resulting flashlight assembly. This light fixture can now be positioned and used in the scene.

FIGURE 9.4

This flashlight assembly can be controlled using the simple Luminaire parameters.

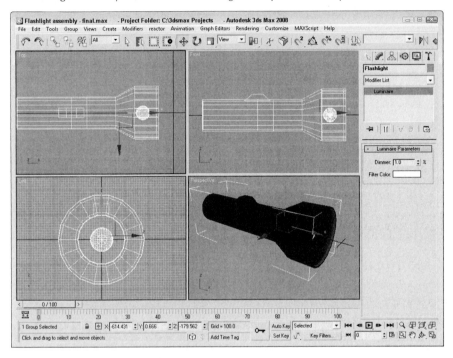

Understanding Parent, Child, and Root Relationships

Max uses several terms to describe the relationships between objects. A *parent object* is an object that controls any secondary, or child, objects linked to it. A *child object* is an object that is linked to and controlled by a parent. A parent object can have many children, but a child can have only one parent. Additionally, an object can be both a parent and a child at the same time. Another way to say this is:

- Child objects are linked to parent objects.
- Moving a parent object moves its children with it.
- Child objects can move independently of their parents.

A hierarchy is the complete set of linked objects that includes these types of relationships. Ancestors are all the parents above a child object. Descendants are all the children below a parent object. The root object is the top parent object that has no parent and controls the entire hierarchy.

Each hierarchy can have several branches or subtrees. Any parent with two or more children represents the start of a new branch.

CROSS-REF The default hierarchies established using the Link tool are referred to as forward-kinematics systems, in which control moves forward down the hierarchy from parent to child. In forward-kinematics systems, the child has no control over the parent. An inverse-kinematics system (covered in Chapter 41, "Working with Inverse Kinematics") enables child objects to control their parents.

All objects in a scene, whether linked or not, belong to a hierarchy. Objects that aren't linked to any other objects are, by default, children of the *world object,* which is an imaginary object that holds all objects.

NOTE You can view the world object, labeled Objects, in the Track View. Individual objects are listed under the Objects track by their object name.

You have several ways to establish hierarchies using Max. The simplest method is to use the Link and Unlink buttons found on the main toolbar. You can also find these buttons in the Schematic View window. The Hierarchy panel in the Command Panel provides access to valuable controls and information about established hierarchies. When creating complex hierarchies, a bones system can help.

CROSS-REF The Schematic View window is covered in Chapter 24, "Working with the Schematic View," and bone systems are covered in Chapter 40, "Understanding Rigging and Working with Bones."

Building Links between Objects

The main toolbar includes two buttons that you can use to build a hierarchy: Link and Unlink. The order of selection defines which object becomes the parent and which becomes the child.

Linking objects

The Link button always links children to the parents. To remind you of this order, remember that a parent can have many children, but a child can have only one parent.

To link two objects, click the Link button. This places you in Link mode, which continues until you turn it off by selecting another button, such as the Select button or one of the Transform buttons. When you're in Link mode, the Link button is highlighted dark yellow.

With the Link button highlighted, click an object, which will be the child, and drag a line to the target parent object. The cursor arrow changes to the link icon when it is over a potential parent. When you release the mouse button, the parent object flashes once and the link is established. If you drag the same child object to a different parent, the link to the previous parent is replaced by the link to the new parent.

Once linked, all transformations applied to the parent are applied equally to its children about the parent's pivot point. A *pivot point* is the center about which the object rotates.

Unlinking objects

The Unlink button is used to destroy links, but only to the parent. For example, if a selected object has both children and a parent, clicking the Unlink button destroys the link to the parent of the selected object, but not the links to its children.

To eliminate all links for an entire hierarchy, double-click an object to select its entire hierarchy and click the Unlink button.

Tutorial: Linking a family of ducks

What better way to show off parent-child relationships than with a family? I could have modeled my own family, but for some reason, my little ducks don't always like to follow me around.

To create a linked family of ducks, follow these steps:

1. Open the Linked duck family.max file from the Chap 09 directory on the DVD. This file includes several simple ducks lined up in a row.

2. Click the Select and Link button in the main toolbar, and drag a line from the last duck to the one just in front of it.

> **TIP** You can link several objects at once by highlighting all the objects you want to link and dragging the selected objects to the parent object. This procedure creates a link between the parent object and each selected object.

3. Continue to connect each duck to the one in front of it.

4. Click the Select and Move button (or press the W key), and move the Mommy duck. Notice how all the children move with her.

Figure 9.5 shows the duck family as they move forward in a line. The Link button made it possible to move all the ducks simply by moving the parent duck.

FIGURE 9.5

Linked child ducks inherit transformations from their parent duck.

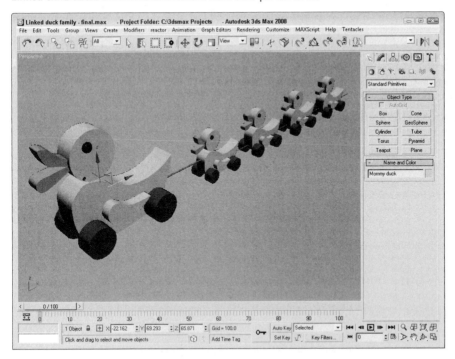

Displaying Links and Hierarchies

The Display panel includes a rollout that lets you display all the links in the viewports. After links have been established, you can see linked objects listed as a hierarchy in several places. The Select Objects dialog box, opened with the Select by Name button (or with the H key), can display objects in this manner, as well as the Schematic and Track Views.

Displaying links in the viewport

You can choose to see the links between the selected objects in the viewports by selecting the Display Links option in the Link Display rollout of the Display panel. The Display Links option shows links as lines that run between the pivot points of the objects with a diamond-shaped marker at the end of each line; these lines and markers are the same color as the object.

NOTE The Display Links option can be enabled or disabled for each object in the scene. To display the links for all objects, use the Edit ⇨ Select All (Ctrl+A) command and then enable the Display Links option.

The Link Display rollout also offers the Link Replaces Object option, which removes the objects and displays only the link structure. This feature removes the complexity of the objects from the viewports and lets you work with the links directly. Although the objects disappear, you can still transform the objects using the link markers.

Viewing hierarchies

The Select From Scene dialog box (also called the Scene Explorer) and the Schematic and Track Views can display the hierarchy of objects in a scene as an ordered list, with child objects indented under parent objects.

Clicking the Select by Name button (H) on the main toolbar opens the Scene Explorer dialog box; select the Display ⇨ Children menu to see all the children under the selected object. Figure 9.6 shows the Select From Scene dialog box with the Display Children menu enabled.

CROSS-REF You can learn more about the Scene Explorer in Chapter 6, "Selecting Objects, Setting Object Properties, and Using Layers and the Scene Explorer."

FIGURE 9.6

The Select From Scene dialog box indents all child objects under their parent.

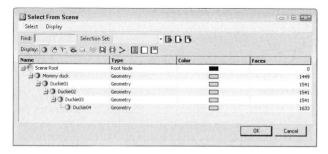

The Schematic View (opened with the Graph Editors ⇨ New Schematic View menu command) presents a graph in which objects are represented by rectangle nodes with their hierarchical links drawn as lines running between them.

CROSS-REF For more information on using the Schematic View, see Chapter 24, "Working with the Schematic View."

The Track View (opened with the Graph Editors ⇨ New Track View menu command) displays lots of scene details in addition to the object hierarchy. In the Track View, you can easily expand and contract the hierarchy to focus on just the section you want to see or select.

CROSS-REF For more information on using the Track View, see Chapter 34, "Working with Function Curves in the Track View."

Working with Linked Objects

If you link some objects together and set some animation keys, and the magical Play button starts sending objects hurtling off into space, chances are good that you have a linked object that you didn't know about. Understanding object hierarchies and being able to transform those hierarchies are the keys to efficient animation sequences.

All transformations are done about an object's pivot point. You can move and reorient these pivot points as needed by clicking the Pivot button under the Hierarchy panel.

Several additional settings for controlling links are available under the Hierarchy panel of the Command Panel (the Hierarchy panel tab looks like a mini-organizational chart). Just click the Link Info button. This button opens two rollouts if a linked object is selected. You can use the Locks and Inherit rollouts to limit an object's transformations and specify the transformations that it inherits.

CROSS-REF I present more information on object transformations in Chapter 7, "Transforming Objects, Pivoting, Aligning, and Snapping."

Locking inheriting transformations

The Inherit rollout, like the Locks rollout, includes check boxes for each axis and each transformation, except that here, all the transformations are selected by default. By deselecting a check box, you specify which transformations an object does not inherit from its parent. The Inherit rollout appears only if the selected object is part of a hierarchy.

For example, suppose that a child object is created and linked to a parent and the X Move Inherit check box is deselected. As the parent is moved in the Y or Z directions, the child follows, but if the parent is moved in the X direction, the child does not follow. If a parent doesn't inherit a transformation, then its children don't either.

Using the Link Inheritance utility

The Link Inheritance utility works in the same way as the Inherit rollout of the Hierarchy panel, except that you can apply it to multiple objects at the same time. To use this utility, open the Utility panel and click the More button. In the Utilities dialog box, select the Link Inheritance utility and click OK. The rollout for this utility is identical to the Inherit rollout discussed in the previous section.

Selecting hierarchies

You need to select a hierarchy before you can transform it, and you have several ways to do so. The easiest method is to simply double-click an object. Double-clicking the root object selects the entire hierarchy, and double-clicking an object within the hierarchy selects it and all of its children.

After you select an object in a hierarchy, pressing the Page Up or Page Down keyboard shortcut selects its parent or child objects. For example, if you select the Mommy duck object and press Page Down, the first baby duck object is selected and the Mommy duck object is deselected. Selecting any of the baby duck objects and pressing Page Up selects the duck object in front of it.

Linking to dummies

Dummy objects are useful as root objects for controlling the motion of hierarchies. By linking the parent object of a hierarchy to a dummy object, you can control all the objects by moving the dummy.

To create a dummy object, select Create ➪ Helpers ➪ Dummy, or open the Create panel, click the Helpers category button (this button looks like a small tape measure), and select the Standard category. Within the Object Type rollout is the Dummy button; click it, and then click in the viewport where you want the dummy object to be positioned. Dummy objects look like wireframe box objects in the viewports, but dummy objects are not rendered.

Tutorial: Circling the globe

When you work with complex models with lots of parts, you can control the object more easily if you link it to a Dummy object and then animate the dummy object instead of the entire model. To practice doing this, we create a simple animation of an airplane flying around the globe. To perform this feat, we create a dummy object in the center of a sphere, link the airplane model to it, and rotate the dummy object. This tutorial involves transforming and animating objects, which are covered in other chapters.

CROSS-REF Rotating objects is covered in Chapter 7, "Transforming Objects, Pivoting, Aligning, and Snapping," and the basics of animation are covered in Chapter 20, "Understanding Animation and Keyframe Basics."

To link and rotate objects using a dummy object, follow these steps:

1. Open the Circling the globe.max file found in the Chap 09 directory on the DVD.

   This file includes a texture mapped sphere with an airplane model positioned above it. The airplane model was created by Viewpoint Datalabs.

2. Select Create ➪ Helpers ➪ Dummy, and then drag in the center of the Sphere to create a Dummy object. With the Dummy object selected, choose the Tools ➪ Align menu command (or press the Alt+A shortcut) and click on the globe. In the Align Selection dialog box, enable the X, Y and Z Position options along with the Center options and click the Ok button to align the centers of the dummy and globe objects.

3. Because the dummy object is inside the sphere, creating the link between the airplane and the dummy object can be difficult. To simplify this process, select and right-click the sphere object, and then select Hide Selection from the pop-up menu.

   This hides the sphere so that you can create a link between the airplane and the dummy object.

4. Click the Select and Link button on the main toolbar, and drag a line from the airplane to the dummy object.

5. Click the Auto Key button (or press N) to enable animation key mode, and drag the Time Slider to frame 100. Then click the Select and Rotate button on the main toolbar (or press E), and select the dummy object. Then rotate the dummy object about its X-axis, and notice how the linked airplane also rotates over the surface of the sphere.

6. Select the dummy object, and right-click to access the pop-up quadmenu. Then select the Unhide All menu command to make the sphere visible again.

By linking the airplane to a dummy object, you don't have to worry about moving the airplane's pivot point to get the correct motion. Figure 9.7 shows a frame from the final scene.

FIGURE 9.7

With a link to a dummy object, making the airplane circle the globe is easy.

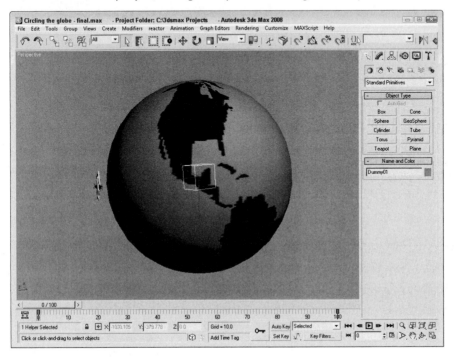

Summary

As scenes become more complex, the name of the game is organization. You can organize objects within the scene in several ways, including grouping, linking, and building hierarchies.

In this chapter, you've done the following:

- Grouped objects using the Group menu and learned to work with groups
- Learned about parent, child, and root relationships
- Created a hierarchy of objects using the Link and Unlink features
- Viewed links in the viewport
- Learned how to create and use dummy objects

In the next chapter, we jump headfirst into modeling by covering the basics of modeling and working with subobjects and helper objects.

Part III

Modeling Basics

Chapter 10

Learning Modeling Basics and Working with Subobjects and Helpers

Modeling is the process of pure creation. Whether it is sculpting, building with blocks, construction work, carving, architecture, or advanced injection molding, many different ways exist for creating objects. Max includes many different model types and even more ways to work with these model types.

This chapter introduces the various modeling methods in Max. It also explains the common modeling components, including normals and subobjects. The chapter also covers many utilities and helpers that, well, help as you begin to model objects. The purpose of this chapter is to whet your whistle for modeling and to cover some of the general concepts that apply to all models. More specific details on the various modeling types are presented in the subsequent chapters, so onward into the realm of creation.

Exploring the Model Types

You can climb a mountain in many ways, and you can model one in many ways. You can make a mountain model out of primitive objects like blocks, cubes, and spheres, or you can create one as a polygon mesh. As your experience grows, you discover that some objects are easier to model using one method and some are easier using another. Max offers several different modeling types to handle various modeling situations.

Parametric objects versus editable objects

All geometric objects in Max can be divided into two general categories — parametric objects and editable objects. *Parametric* means that the geometry of the object is controlled by variables called parameters. Modifying these parameters modifies the geometry of the object. This powerful concept gives parametric objects lots of flexibility. For example, the sphere object has a parameter called

Radius. Changing this parameter changes the size of the sphere. Parametric objects in Max include all the objects found in the Create menu.

Editable objects do not have this flexibility of parameters, but they deal with subobjects and editing functions. The editable objects include Editable Spline, Mesh, Poly, Patch, and NURBS. Editable objects are listed in the Modifier Stack with the word *Editable* in front of their base object (except for NURBS objects, which are simply called NURBS Surfaces). For example, an editable mesh object is listed as Editable Mesh in the Modifier Stack.

> **NOTE**   Actually, NURBS objects are a different beast altogether. When created using the Create menu, they are parametric objects, but after you select the Modify panel, they are editable objects with a host of subobject modes and editing functions.

Editable objects aren't created; instead, they are converted or modified from another object. When a primitive object is converted to a different object type like an Editable Mesh or a NURBS object, it loses its parametric nature and can no longer be changed by altering its base parameters. Editable objects do have their advantages, though. You can edit subobjects such as vertices, edges, and faces of meshes — all things that you cannot edit for a parametric object. Each editable object type has a host of functions that are specific to its type. These functions are discussed in the coming chapters.

> **NOTE**   Several modifiers enable you to edit subobjects while maintaining the parametric nature of an object. These include Edit Patch, Edit Mesh, Edit Poly, and Edit Spline.

Max includes the following model types:

- **Primitives:** Basic parametric objects such as cubes, spheres, and pyramids. The primitives are divided into two groups consisting of Standard and Extended Primitives. The AEC Objects are also considered primitive objects. A complete list of primitives is covered in Chapter 5, "Creating and Editing Primitive Objects."

- **Shapes and splines:** Simple vector shapes such as circles, stars, arcs, and text, and splines such as the Helix. These objects are fully renderable. The Create menu includes many parametric shapes and splines. These parametric objects can be converted to Editable Spline objects for more editing. These are covered in Chapter 11, "Drawing and Editing 2D Splines and Shapes."

- **Meshes:** Complex models created from many polygon faces that are smoothed together when the object is rendered. These objects are available only as Editable Mesh objects. Meshes are also covered in Chapter 12.

- **Polys:** Objects composed of polygon faces, similar to mesh objects, but with unique features. These objects are also available only as Editable Poly objects. Poly objects are covered together in Chapter 12, "Modeling with Polygons."

- **Patches:** Based on spline curves; patches can be modified using control points. The Create menu includes two parametric Patch objects, but most objects can also be converted to Editable Patch objects. Chapter 27, "Modeling with Patches and NURBS," covers patches in detail.

- **NURBS:** Stands for Non-Uniform Rational B-Splines. NURBS are similar to patches in that they also have control points. These control points define how a surface spreads over curves. NURBS are covered in Chapter 27, "Modeling with Patches and NURBS."

- **Compound objects:** A miscellaneous group of model types, including Booleans, loft objects, and scatter objects. Other compound objects are good at modeling one specialized type of object such as Terrain or BlobMesh objects. All the Compound objects are covered in Chapter 26, "Working with Compound Objects."

- **Particle systems:** Systems of small objects that work together as a single group. They are useful for creating effects such as rain, snow, and sparks. Particles are covered along with the Particle Flow interface in Chapter 36, "Creating Particles and Particle Flow."

■ **Hair and fur:** Modeling hundreds of thousands of cylinder objects to create believable hair would quickly bog down any system, so hair is modeled using a separate system that represents each hair as a spline. The Hair and Fur modifiers are covered in Chapter 28, "Adding and Styling Hair, Fur, and Cloth."

■ **Cloth systems:** Cloth — with its waving, free-flowing nature — behaves like water in some cases and like a solid in others. Max includes a specialized set of modifiers for handling cloth systems. Creating and using a cloth system is discussed in Chapter 28, "Adding and Styling Hair, Fur, and Cloth."

> **NOTE** Hair, fur, and cloth are often considered effects or dynamic simulations instead of modeling constructs, so their inclusion on this list should be considered a stretch.

With all these options, modeling in Max can be intimidating, but you learn how to use each of these types the more you work with Max. For starters, begin with primitive or imported objects and then branch out by converting to editable objects. A single Max scene can include multiple object types.

Converting to editable objects

Of all the commands found in the Create menu and in the Create panel, you won't find any menus or sub-categories for creating editable objects.

To create an editable object, you need to import it or convert it from another object type. You can convert objects by right-clicking on the object in the viewport and selecting the Convert To submenu from the pop-up quadmenu, or by right-clicking on the base object in the Modifier Stack and selecting the object type to convert to in the pop-up menu.

Once converted, all the editing features of the selected type are available in the Modify panel, but the object is no longer parametric and loses access to its common parameters such as Radius and Segments. However, Max also includes specialized modifiers such as the Edit Poly modifier that maintain the parametric nature of primitive objects while giving you access to the editing features of the Editable object. More on these modifiers is presented in the later modeling chapters.

> **CAUTION** If a modifier has been applied to an object, the Convert To menu option in the Modifier Stack pop-up menu is not available until you use the Collapse All command.

The pop-up menu includes options to convert to editable mesh, editable poly, editable patch, and NURBS. If a shape or spline object is selected, then the object can also be converted to an editable spline. Using any of the Convert To menu options collapses the Modifier Stack.

> **NOTE** Objects can be converted between the different types several times, but each conversion may subdivide the object. Therefore, multiple conversions are not recommended.

Converting between object types is done automatically using Max's best guess, but if you apply one of the Conversion modifiers to an object, several parameters are displayed that let you define how the object is converted. For example, the Turn to Mesh modifier includes an option to Use Invisible Edges, which divides polygons using invisible edges. If this option is disabled, then the entire object is triangulated. The Turn to Patch modifier includes an option to make quads into quad patches. If this option is disabled, all quads are triangulated.

The Turn to Poly modifier includes options to Keep Polygons Convex, Limit Polygon Size, Require Planar Polygons, and Remove Mid-Edge Vertices. The Keep Polygons Convex option divides any polygon that is concave, if enabled. The Limit Polygon Size option lets you specify the maximum allowable polygon size. This can be used to eliminate any pentagons and hexagons from the mesh. The Require Planar Polygons option keeps adjacent polygons as triangles if the angle between them is greater than the specified

Threshold value. The Remove Mid-Edge Vertices option removes any vertices caused by intersections with invisible edges.

All Conversion modifiers also include options to preserve the current subobject selection (including any soft selection) and to specify the Selection Level. The From Pipeline option uses the current subobject selection that is selected on the given object. After a Conversion modifier is applied to an object, you must collapse the Modifier Stack in order to complete the conversion.

Understanding Normals

Before moving on to the various subobjects, you need to understand what a normal is and how it is used to tell which way the surface is facing. Normals are vectors that extend outward perpendicular to the surface of an object. These vectors aren't rendered and are used only to tell which way the surface face is pointing. If the normal vector points toward the camera, then the polygon is visible, but if it is points away from the camera, then you are looking at its backside, which is visible only if the Backface Cull option in the Object Properties dialog box is disabled.

Several other properties also use the normal vector to determine how the polygon face is shaded, smoothed, and lighted. Normals are also used in dynamic simulations to determine collisions between objects.

Viewing normals

In all mesh subobject modes except for Edge, you can select the Show Normals option to see any objects normals and set a Scale value. Figure 10.1 shows a Plane, a Box, and a Sphere object. Each object has been converted to an Editable Mesh with all faces selected in Face subobject mode and with the Show Normals option selected.

FIGURE 10.1

The Show Normals option shows the normal vectors for each face in a plane, a cube, and a sphere.

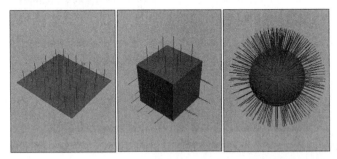

Tutorial: Cleaning up imported meshes

Many 3D formats are mesh-based, and importing mesh objects sometimes can create problems. By collapsing an imported model to an Editable Mesh, you can take advantage of several of the editable mesh features to clean up these problems.

CROSS-REF The Modifier menu includes two modifiers that you can use to work with normals. The Normals and Edit Normals modifiers are covered in Chapter 25, "Deforming Surfaces and Using the Mesh Modifiers."

Figure 10.2 shows a model that was exported from Poser using the 3ds format. Notice that the model's waist is black. It appears this way because I've turned off the Backface Cull option in the Object Properties dialog box. If it were turned on, his waist would be invisible. The problem here is that the normals for this object are pointing in the wrong direction. This problem is common for imported meshes, and we fix it in this tutorial.

To fix the normals on an imported mesh model, follow these steps:

1. Open the Hailing taxi man with incorrect normals.max file from the Chap 10 directory on the DVD.
2. Select the problem object — the waist on the right mesh. Open the object hierarchy by clicking the plus sign to the left of the Editable Mesh object in the Modifier Stack, and then select Element subobject mode.
3. In the Selection rollout, select the Show Normals option and set the Scale value to a small number such as **0.1**.

   The normals are now visible. Notice that some of them point outward and some of them point inward.
4. With the element subobject still selected, click the Unify button in the Surface Properties rollout and then click the Flip button until all normals are pointing outward.

This problem is fixed, and the waist object is now a visible part of the mesh. The fixed mesh on the right looks just like the original mesh on the left without the ugly black shorts, as shown in Figure 10.2.

FIGURE 10.2

This mesh suffers from objects with flipped normals, which makes them invisible.

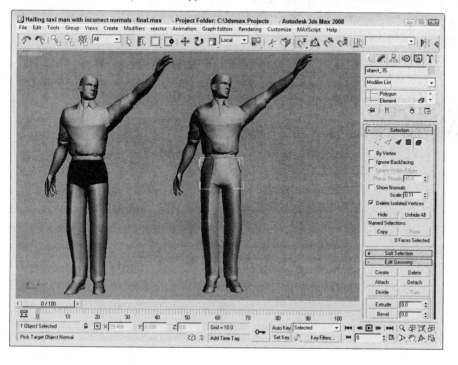

Working with Subobjects

All the editable modeling types offer the ability to work with subobjects. Subobjects are the elements that make up the model and can include vertices, edges, faces, polygons, and elements. These individual subobjects can be selected and transformed just like normal objects using the transformation tools located on the main toolbar. But, before you can transform these subobjects, you need to select them. You can select subobjects only when you're in a particular subobject mode. Each editable object type has a different set of subobjects.

If you expand the object's hierarchy in the Modifier Stack (by clicking the small plus sign to the left of the object's name), all subobjects for an object are displayed, as shown in Figure 10.3. Selecting a subobject in the Modifier Stack places you in subobject mode for that subobject type. You can also enter subobject mode by clicking on the subobject icons located at the top of the Selection rollout or by pressing the 1 through 5 keys on the keyboard. When you're in subobject mode, the subobject title and the icon in the Selection rollout are highlighted yellow. You can work with the selected subobjects only while in subobject mode. To transform the entire object again, you need to exit subobject mode, which you can do by clicking either the subobject title or the subobject icon, or by pressing one of the keyboard shortcuts, 1–5.

 **TIP** You can also access the subobject modes using the right-click quadmenu. To exit a subobject mode, select Top Level in the quadmenu.

FIGURE 10.3

Expanding an editable object in the Modifier Stack reveals its subobjects.

Subobjects

Subobjects icons

Subobject selections can be locked with the Selection Lock Toggle (spacebar) and be made into a Selection Set by typing a name into the Named Selection Set drop-down list on the main toolbar. After a Selection Set is created, you can recall it anytime you are in that same subobject mode. Named Selection Sets can then be copied and pasted between objects using the Copy and Paste buttons found in the Selection rollout for most editable objects.

Using Soft Selection

When working with editable mesh, poly, patches, or splines, the Soft Selection rollout, shown in Figure 10.4, becomes available in subobject mode. Soft Selection selects all the subobjects surrounding the current selection and applies transformations to them to a lesser extent. For example, if a face is selected and moved a distance of 2, then with linear Soft Selection, the neighboring faces within the soft selection range move a distance of 1. The overall effect is a smoother transition.

> **NOTE** The Soft Selection options are different for the various modeling types. For example, the Editable Mesh includes a standard set of options like those in Figure 10.4, but the Editable Poly object has more options, including a Paint Soft Selection mode.

FIGURE 10.4

The Soft Selection rollout is available only in subobject mode.

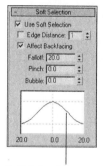

Soft Selection curve

The Use Soft Selection parameter enables or disables the Soft Selection feature. The Edge Distance option sets the range (the number of edges from the current selection) that the Soft Selection will affect. If disabled, the distance is determined by the Falloff amount. The Affect Backfacing option applies the Soft Selection to selected subobjects on the backside of an object. For example, if you are selecting vertices on the front of a sphere object and the Affect Backfacing option is enabled, then vertices on the opposite side of the sphere are also selected.

The Soft Selection curve shows a graphical representation of how the Soft Selection is applied. The Falloff value defines the spherical region where the Soft Selection has an effect. The Pinch button sharpens the point at the top of the curve. The Bubble button has an opposite effect and widens the curve. Figure 10.5 shows several sample values and the resulting curve.

> **CROSS-REF** For Editable Poly objects, the bottom of the Soft Selection rollout includes a Paint Soft Selection section. You can use these controls to paint the soft selection weights that subobjects receive. For more information on the paint interface and these controls, see Chapter 25, "Deforming Surfaces and Using the Mesh Modifiers."

Tutorial: Soft selecting a heart shape from a plane

Soft Selection enables a smooth transition between subobjects, but sometimes you want the abrupt edge. This tutorial looks at moving some subobject vertices in a plane object with and without Soft Selection enabled.

FIGURE 10.5

The Soft Selection curve is affected by the Falloff, Pinch, and Bubble values.

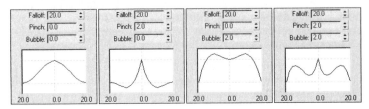

To move subobject vertices with and without Soft Selection, follow these steps:

1. Open the Soft selection heart.max file from the Chap 10 directory on the DVD.

   This file contains two simple plane objects that have been converted to Editable Mesh objects. Several vertices in the shape of a heart are selected.

2. The vertices on the first plane object are already selected; in Vertex subobject mode, click the Select and Move button (or press the W key), move the cursor over the selected vertices, and drag upward in the Left viewport away from the plane.

3. Exit subobject mode, select the second plane object, and enter Vertex subobject mode. The same vertices are again selected. Open the Soft Selection rollout, enable the Use Soft Selection option, and set the Falloff value to **40**.

4. Click the Select and Move button (or press the W key), and move the selected vertices upward. Notice the difference that Soft Selection makes.

Figure 10.6 shows the two resulting plane objects with the heart selections.

FIGURE 10.6

Soft Selection makes a smooth transition between the subobjects that are moved and those that are not.

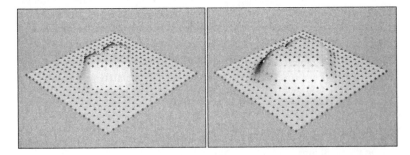

When you select subobjects, they turn red. Non-selected subobjects are blue, and soft selected subobjects are a gradient from orange to yellow, depending on their distance from the selected subobjects. This visual clue provides valuable feedback on how the Soft Selection affects the subobjects. Figure 10.7 shows the selected vertices from the preceding tutorial with Falloff values of 0, 20, 40, 60, and 80.

For the Editable Poly and Editable Patch objects, the Soft Selection rollout includes a Shaded Face Toggle button below its curve. This button shades the surface using the soft selection gradient colors, as shown in

Figure 10.8. This shaded surface is displayed in any shaded viewports. The cooler colors have less of an impact over the transform.

FIGURE 10.7

A gradient of colors shows the transition zone for soft selected subobjects.

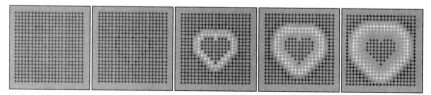

FIGURE 10.8

The Shaded Face Toggle shades the surface using the soft selection gradient colors.

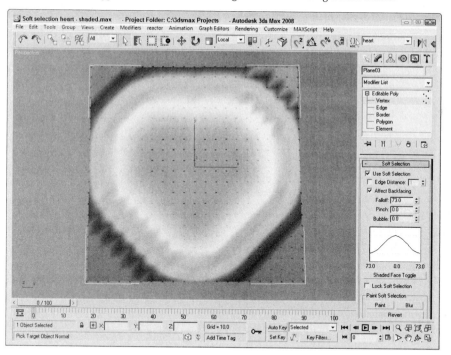

Applying modifiers to subobject selections

The preceding chapter introduced modifiers and showed how they can be applied to entire objects. But you can also apply modifiers to subobjects. If the modifier isn't available for subobjects, it is excluded from the Modifier List or disabled in the Modifiers menu.

If your object isn't an editable object with available subobjects, you can still apply a modifier using one of the specialized Select modifiers. These modifiers let you select a subobject and apply a modifier to it without having to convert it to a non-parametric object. These Select modifiers include Mesh Select, Poly Select, Patch Select, Spline Select, Volume Select, FFD Select, and NURBS Surface Select. You can find all these modifiers in the Modifiers ⇨ Selection Modifiers submenu.

After you apply a Select modifier to an object, you can select subobjects in the normal manner using the hierarchy in the Modifier Stack or the subobject icons in the Parameters rollout. Any modifiers that you apply after the Select modifier (they appear above the Select modifier in the Modifier Stack) affect only the subobject selection.

Modeling Helpers

In the Create panel (and the Create menu) is a category of miscellaneous objects called helpers (the icon looks like a tape measure). These objects are useful in positioning objects and measuring dimensions. The buttons in the Helper category include Dummy, Crowd, Delegate, ExposeTM, Grid, Point, Tape, Protractor, and Compass.

CROSS-REF The Crowd and Delegate helpers are discussed in Chapter 42, "Creating and Animating Bipeds and Crowds," and the Expose Transform helper object is covered in Chapter 32, "Using Animation Modifiers."

Using Dummy and Point objects

The Dummy object is a useful object for controlling complex object hierarchies. A Dummy object appears in the viewports as a simple cube with a pivot point at its center, but the object will not be rendered and has no parameters. It is used only as an object about which to transform objects. For example, you could create a Dummy object that the camera could follow through an animation sequence. Dummy objects are used in many examples throughout the remainder of the book.

The Point object is very similar to the Dummy object in that it also is not rendered and has minimal parameters. A Point object defines a point in space and is identified as an X, an Axis Tripod, or a simple Box. The Center Marker option places an X at the center of the Point object (so X really does mark the spot). The Axis Tripod option displays the X-, Y-, and Z-axes, the Cross option extends the length of the marker along each axis, and the Box option displays the Point object as a Box. The Size value determines how big the Point object is.

 The Size parameter actually makes Point helpers preferred over Dummy helpers because you can parametrically change their size.

The Constant Screen Size option keeps the size of the Point object constant, regardless of how much you zoom in or out of the scene. The Draw on Top option draws the Point object above all other scene objects, making it easy to locate. The main purpose for the Point object is to mark positions within the scene.

 Point objects are difficult to see and easy to lose. If you use a point object, be sure to name it so you can find it easily in the Select from Scene dialog box.

Measuring coordinate distances

The Helpers category also includes several handy utilities for measuring dimensions and directions. These are the Tape, Protractor, and Compass objects. The units are all based on the current selected system units.

Using the Measure Distance tool

In the Tools menu is a command to Measure Distance. This tool is easy to use. Just select it, and click at the starting point and again at the ending point; the distance between the two clicks is shown in the Status Bar at the bottom of the interface. Measure Distance also reports the Delta values in the X, Y, and Z directions. You can use this tool with the Snap feature enabled for accurate measurements.

Using the Tape helper

You use the Tape object to measure distances. To use it, simply drag the distance that you would like to measure and view the resulting dimension in the Parameters rollout. You can also set the length of the Tape object using the Specify Length option. You can move and reposition the endpoints of the Tape object with the Select and Move button, but the Rotate and Scale buttons have no effect.

Using the Protractor helper

The Protractor object works in a manner similar to the Tape object, but it measures the angle between two objects. To use the Protractor object, click in a viewport to position the Protractor object. (The Protractor object looks like two pyramids aligned point to point and represents the origin of the angle.) Then click the Pick Object 1 button, and select an object in the scene. A line is drawn from the Protractor object to the selected object. Next, click the Pick Object 2 button. The angle-formed objects and the Protractor object are displayed in the Parameters rollout. The value changes when either of the selected objects or the Protractor is moved.

 **NOTE**   All measurement values are presented in gray fields within the Parameters rollout. This gray field indicates that the value cannot be modified.

Using the Compass helper

The Compass object identifies North, East, West, and South positions on a planar star-shaped object. You can drag the Compass object to increase its size.

CROSS-REF   The Grid helper object is discussed along with grids in Chapter 7, "Transforming Objects, Pivoting, Aligning, and Snapping." The Compass object is mainly used in conjunction with the Sunlight System, which you can learn about in Chapter 19, "Using Lights and Basic Lighting Techniques."

Using the Measure utility

In the Utilities panel is another useful tool for getting the scoop on the current selected object: the Measure utility. You can open the Measure utility as a floater dialog box, shown in Figure 10.9. This dialog box displays the object's name along with its Surface Area, Volume, Center of Mass, Length (for shapes), and Dimensions. It also includes an option to lock the current selection.

FIGURE 10.9

The Measure utility dialog box displays some useful information.

Using the Level of Detail utility

As a scene is animated, some objects are close to the camera and others are far from it. Rendering a complex object that is far from the camera doesn't make much sense. Using the Level of Detail (LOD) utility, you can have Max render a simpler version of a model when it is farther from the camera and a more complex version when it is close to the camera.

CROSS-REF   **The MultiRes modifier can also create real-time level of detail updates. It is covered in Chapter 25, "Deforming Surfaces and Using the Mesh Modifiers."**

To open the utility, click the More button in the Utility panel and select the Level of Detail utility. A single rollout is loaded into the Utility panel, as shown in Figure 10.10. To use this utility, you need to create several versions of an object and group them together. The Create New Set button lets you pick an object group from the viewports. The objects within the group are individually listed in the rollout pane.

If you select a listed object, you can specify the Threshold Units in pixels or as a percentage of the target image. For each listed item, you can specify minimum and maximum thresholds. The Image Output Size values are used to specify the size of the output image, and the different models used are based on the size of the object in the final image. The Display in Viewports check box causes the appropriate LOD model to appear in the viewport.

FIGURE 10.10

The Level of Detail utility (split into two parts) can specify how objects are viewed, based on given thresholds.

Summary

Understanding the basics of modeling helps you as you build scenes. In this chapter, you've seen several different object types that are available in Max. Many of these types have similar features such as Soft Selection. Several helper objects can assist as well. This chapter covered the following topics:

- Understanding parametric objects and the various modeling types
- Viewing normals
- Using subobjects and soft selections
- Using helper objects and utilities

Now that you have the basics covered, you're ready to dive into the various modeling types. The first modeling type on the list is splines and shapes, which is covered in the next chapter.

Chapter 11

Drawing and Editing 2D Splines and Shapes

IN THIS CHAPTER

Working with shape primitives

Editing splines and shapes

Working with spline subobjects

Using spline modifiers

Many modeling projects start from the ground up, and you can't get much lower to the ground than 2D. But this book is on 3D, you say? What place is there for 2D shapes? Within the 3D world, you frequently encounter flat surfaces — the side of a building, the top of a table, a billboard, and so on. All these objects have flat 2D surfaces. Understanding how objects are composed of 2D surfaces will help as you start to build objects in 3D. This chapter examines the 2D elements of 3D objects and covers the tools needed to work with them.

Working in 2D in Max, you use two general objects: splines and shapes. A *spline* is a special type of line that curves according to mathematical principles. In Max, splines are used to create all sorts of shapes such as circles, ellipses, and rectangles.

You can create splines and shapes using the Create ⇨ Shapes menu, which opens the Shapes category on the Create panel. Just as with the other categories, several spline-based shape primitives are available. Spline shapes can be rendered, but they are normally used to create more advanced 3D geometric objects by extruding or lathing the spline. You can even find a whole group of modifiers that apply to splines. You can use splines to create animation paths as well as Loft and NURBS objects, and you will find that splines and shapes, although they are only 2D, are used frequently in Max.

Drawing in 2D

Shapes in Max are unique from other objects because they are drawn in 2D, which confines them to a single plane. That plane is defined by the viewport used to create the shape. For example, drawing a shape in the Top view constrains the shape to the XY plane, whereas drawing the shape in the Front view constrains it to the ZX plane. Even shapes drawn in the Perspective view are constrained to a plane such as the Home Grid.

You usually produce 2D shapes in a drawing package like Adobe Illustrator or CorelDRAW. Max supports importing line drawings using the AI format.

CROSS-REF See Chapter 3, "Working with Files, Importing, and Exporting," to learn about importing AI files.

Whereas newly created or imported shapes are 2D and are confined to a single plane, splines can exist in 3D space. The Helix spline, for example, exists in 3D, having height as well as width values. Animation paths in particular typically move into 3D space.

Working with shape primitives

The shape primitive buttons are displayed in the Object Type rollout of the Create panel when either the Create ⇨ Shapes or the Create ⇨ Extended Shapes menu is selected. The Shapes category include many basic shapes, including Line, Circle, Arc, NGon (a polygon where you can set the number of sides), Text, Section, Rectangle, Ellipse, Donut, Star, and Helix, as shown in Figure 11.1. The Extended Shapes category includes several shapes that are useful to architects, including WRectangle, Channel, Angle, Tee, and Wide Flange, as shown in Figure 11.2. Clicking any of these shape buttons lets you create the shape by dragging in one of the viewports. After a shape is created, several new rollouts appear.

FIGURE 11.1

The shape primitives in all their 2D glory: Line, Circle, Arc, NGon, Text, Section, Rectangle, Ellipse, Donut, Star, and Helix

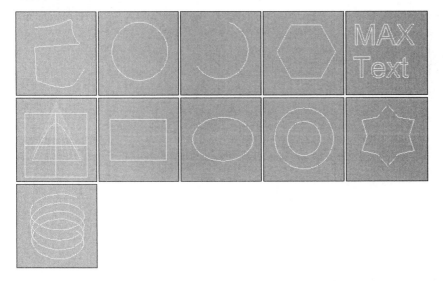

Above the Shape buttons are two check boxes: AutoGrid and Start New Shape. AutoGrid creates a temporary grid, which you can use to align the shape with the surface of the nearest object under the mouse at the time of creation. This feature is helpful for starting a new spline on the surface of an object.

FIGURE 11.2

The extended shape primitives: WRectangle, Channel, Angle, Tee, and Wide Flange

CROSS-REF For more details on AutoGrid, see Chapter 7, "Transforming Objects, Pivoting, Aligning, and Snapping."

The Start New Shape option creates a new object with every new shape drawn in a viewport. Leaving this option unchecked lets you create compound shapes, which consist of several shapes used to create one object. Because compound shapes consist of several shapes, the shapes are automatically converted to be an Editable Spline object and you cannot edit them using the Parameters rollout. For example, if you want to create a target from several concentric circles, keep the Start New Shape option unselected to make all the circles part of the same object.

Just as with the Geometric primitives, every shape that is created is given a name and a color. You can change either of these in the Name and Color rollout.

Most of the shape primitives have several common rollouts: Rendering, Interpolation, Creation Method, Keyboard Entry, and Parameters, as shown in Figure 11.3. I cover these rollouts initially and then present the individual shape primitives.

FIGURE 11.3

These rollouts are common for most of the shape primitives.

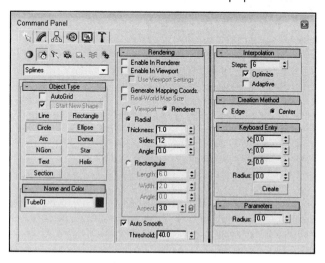

Rendering rollout

The Rendering rollout includes options for making a spline a renderable object. Making a spline a renderable object converts the spline into a 3D object that is visible when you render the scene. For renderable objects, you can choose to make the spline Radial or Rectangular. For the Radial option, you can specify a Thickness, the number of Sides, and the Angle values; for the Rectangular option, you can specify Length, Width, Angle, and Aspect values.

The Radial Thickness is the diameter of the renderable spline. The number of Sides sets the number of sides that make up the cross section of the renderable spline. The lowest value that is possible is 3, which creates a triangle cross section. The Length and Width values set the size along the Y-axis and the X-axis, respectively, of the rectangular sides. The Angle value determines where the corners of the cross section sides start, so you can set a three-sided spline to have a corner or an edge pointing upward. The Aspect value sets the ratio of the Length per Width. If the Lock icon to the right of the Aspect value is enabled, then the aspect ratio is locked, and changing one value affects the other.

> **NOTE** By default, a renderable spline has a 12-sided circle as its cross section.

You can choose different rendering values for the viewport and for the renderer using the Viewport and Renderer options above the Radial option. Each of these settings can be enabled or disabled using the Enable in Renderer and Enable in Viewport options at the top of the Rendering rollout. Renderable splines appear as normal splines in the viewport unless the Enable in Viewport option is selected. The Use Viewport Settings option gives the option of setting the spline render properties different in the viewport and the renderer.

The Auto Smooth option and Threshold value offer a way to smooth edges on the renderable spline. If the angle between two adjacent polygons is less than the Threshold value, then the edge between them is smoothed. If it is greater than the Threshold value, then the hard edge is preserved.

The Generate Mapping Coordinates option automatically generates mapping coordinates that are used to mark where a material map is placed, and the Real-World Map Size option allows real-world scaling to be used when mapping a texture onto the renderable spline.

> **CROSS-REF** To learn more about mapping coordinates and real-world scaling, see Chapter 17, "Adding Material Details with Maps."

Interpolation rollout

In the Interpolation rollout, you can define the number of interpolation steps or segments that make up the shape. The Steps value determines the number of segments to include between adjacent vertices. For example, a circle shape with a Steps value of 0 has only four segments and looks like a diamond. Increasing the Steps value to 1 makes a circle out of eight segments. For shapes composed of straight lines (like the Rectangle and simple NGons), the Steps value is set to 0, but for a shape with many sides (like a Circle or Ellipse), the Steps value can have a big effect. Larger step values result in smoother curves.

The Adaptive option automatically sets the number of steps to produce a smooth curve by adding more interpolation points to the spline based on the spline's curvature. When the Adaptive option is enabled, the Steps and Optimize options become disabled. The Optimize option attempts to reduce the number of steps to produce a simpler spline by eliminating all the extra segments associated with the shape.

>  The Section and Helix shape primitives have no Interpolation rollout.

Figure 11.4 shows the number 5 drawn with the Line primitive in the Front viewport. The line has been made renderable so that you can see the cross sections. The images from left to right show the line with Steps values of 0, 1, and 3. The fourth image has the Optimize option enabled. Notice that it uses only one segment for the straight edges. The fifth image has the Adaptive option enabled.

FIGURE 11.4

Using the Interpolation rollout, you can control the number of segments that make up a line.

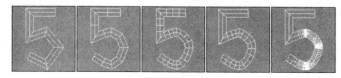

Creation Method and Keyboard Entry rollouts

Most shape primitives also include Creation Method and Keyboard Entry rollouts (Text, Section, and Star are the exceptions). The Creation Method rollout offers options for specifying different ways to create the spline by dragging in a viewport, such as from edge to edge or from the center out. Table 11.1 lists the various creation method options for each of the shapes and each of the extended shapes.

TABLE 11.1

Shape Primitive Creation Methods

Primitive Object	Number of Viewport Clicks to Create	Default Creation Method	Other Creation Method
Line	2 to Infinite	Corner Initial, Bézier Drag	Smooth, Initial, Corner, or Smooth Drag
Circle	1	Center	Edge
Arc	2	End-End-Middle	Center-End-End
NGon	1	Center	Edge
Text	1	none	none
Section	1	none	none

continued

TABLE 11.1 *(continued)*

Primitive Object	Number of Viewport Clicks to Create	Default Creation Method	Other Creation Method
Rectangle	1	Edge	Center
Ellipse	1	Edge	Center
Donut	2	Center	Edge
Star	2	none	none
Helix	3	Center	Edge
WRectangle	2	Edge	Center
Channel	2	Edge	Center
Angle	2	Edge	Center
Tee	2	Edge	Center
Wide Flange	2	Edge	Center

Some shape primitives such as Star, Text, and Section don't have any creation methods because Max offers only a single way to create these shapes.

The Keyboard Entry rollout offers a way to enter exact position and dimension values. After you enter the values, click the Create button to create the spline or shape in the active viewport. The settings are different for each shape.

The Parameters rollout includes such basic settings for the primitive as Radius, Length, and Width. You can alter these settings immediately after an object is created. However, after you deselect an object, the Parameters rollout moves to the Modify panel, and you must do any alterations to the shape there.

Line

The Line primitive includes several creation method settings, enabling you to create hard, sharp corners or smooth corners. You can set the Initial Type option to either Corner or Smooth to create a sharp or smooth corner for the first point created.

After clicking where the initial point is located, you can add points by clicking in the viewport. Dragging while creating a new point can make a point a Corner, Smooth, or Bézier based on the Drag Type option selected in the Creation Method rollout. The curvature created by the Smooth option is determined by the distance between adjacent vertices, whereas you can control the curvature created by the Bézier option by dragging with the mouse a desired distance after the point is created. Bézier corners have control handles associated with them, enabling you to change their curvature.

> **TIP**
> Holding down the Shift key while clicking creates points that are constrained vertically or horizontally. This makes it easy to create straight lines that are at right angles to each other. Holding down the Ctrl key snaps new points at an angle from the last segment, as determined by the Angle Snap setting.

After creating all the points, you exit line mode by clicking the right mouse button. If the last point is on top of the first point, then a dialog box asks whether you want to close the spline. Click Yes to create a closed spline or No to continue adding points. Even after creating a closed spline, you can add more points to the current selection to create a compound shape if the Start New Shape option isn't selected. If the first and last points don't correspond, then an open spline is created.

Figure 11.5 shows several splines created using the various creation method settings. The left spline was created with all the options set to Corner, and the second spline with all the options set to Smooth. The third spline uses the Corner Initial type and shows where dragging has smoothed many of the points. The last spline was created using the Bézier option.

FIGURE 11.5

The Line shape can create various combinations of shapes with smooth and sharp corners.

In the Keyboard Entry rollout, you can add points by entering their X, Y, and Z dimensions and clicking the Add Point button. You can close the spline at any time by clicking the Close button or keep it open by clicking the Finish button.

Rectangle

The Rectangle shape produces simple rectangles. In the Parameters rollout, you can specify the Length and Width and also a Corner Radius. Holding down the Ctrl key while dragging creates a perfect square shape.

Circle

The Circle button creates — you guessed it — circles. The only adjustable parameter in the Parameters rollout is the Radius. All other rollouts are the same, as explained earlier. Circles created with the Circle button have only four vertices.

Ellipse

Ellipses are simple variations of the Circle shape. You define them by Length and Width values. Holding down the Ctrl key while dragging creates a perfect circle (or you can use the Circle shape).

Arc

The Arc primitive has two creation methods. Use the End-End-Middle method to create an arc shape by clicking and dragging to specify the two end points and then dragging to complete the shape. Use the Center-End-End method to create an arc shape by clicking and dragging from the center to one of the end points and then dragging the arc length to the second end point.

Other parameters include the Radius and the From and To settings, where you can enter the value in degrees for the start and end of the arc. The Pie Slice option connects the end points of the arc to its center to create a pie-sliced shape, as shown in Figure 11.6. The Reverse option lets you reverse the arc's direction.

Enabling the Pie Slice option connects the arc ends with the center of the circle.

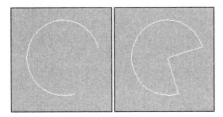

Donut

As another variation of the Circle shape, the Donut shape consists of two concentric circles; you can create it by dragging once to specify the outer circle and again to specify the inner circle. The parameters for this object are simply two radii.

NGon

The *NGon* shape lets you create regular polygons by specifying the Number of Sides and the Corner Radius. You can also specify whether the NGon is Inscribed or Circumscribed, as shown in Figure 11.7. Inscribed polygons are positioned within a circle that touches all the outer polygon's vertices. Circumscribed polygons are positioned outside of a circle that touches the midpoint of each polygon edge. The Circular option changes the polygon to a circle that inscribes the polygon.

An inscribed pentagon and a circumscribed pentagon

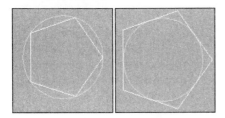

Star

The Star shape also includes two radii values — the larger Radius value defines the distance of the outer points of the Star shape from its center, and the smaller Radius value is the distance from the center of the star to the inner points. The Point setting indicates the number of points. This value can range from 3 to 100. The Distortion value causes the inner points to rotate relative to the outer points and can be used to create some interesting new star types. The Fillet Radius 1 and Fillet Radius 2 values adjust the Fillet for the inner and outer points. Figure 11.8 shows a sampling of what is possible with the Star shapes.

FIGURE 11.8

The Star primitive can be changed to create some amazing shapes.

Text

You can use the Text primitive to add outlined text to the scene. In the Parameters rollout, you can specify a Font by choosing one from the drop-down list at the top of the Parameters rollout. Under the Font drop-down list are six icons, shown in Table 11.2. The left two icons are for the Italic and Underline styles. Selecting either of these styles applies the style to all the text. The right four icons are for aligning the text to the left, centered, right, or justified.

TABLE 11.2

Text Font Attributes

Icon	Description
I	Italic
U	Underline
≡	Left
≡	Centered
≡	Right
≡	Justified

The list of available fonts includes only the Windows TrueType fonts and Type 1 PostScript fonts installed on your system and any extra fonts located in the font path listed in the Configure Paths dialog box. You need to restart Max before the fonts in the font path are recognized.

The size of the text is determined by the Size value. The Kerning (which is the space between adjacent characters) and Leading (which is the space between adjacent lines of text) values can actually be negative. Setting the Kerning value to a large negative number actually displays the text backwards. Figure 11.9 shows an example of some text and an example of kerning values in the Max interface.

FIGURE 11.9

The Text shape lets you control the space between letters, known as kerning.

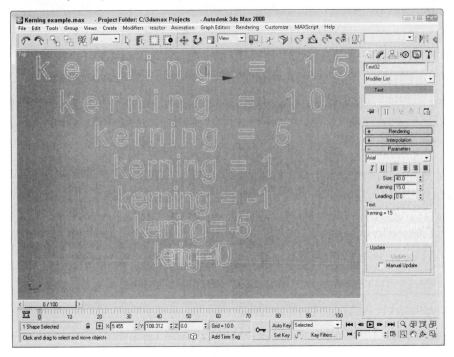

You can type the text to be created in the text area. You can cut, copy, and paste text into this text area from an external application if you right-click on the text area. After setting the parameters and typing the text, the text appears as soon as you click in one of the viewports. The Text is updated automatically when any of the parameters (including the text) are changed. To turn off automatic updating, select the Manual Update toggle. You can then update with the Update button.

To enter special characters into the text area, hold down the Alt key while typing the character code using the numeric keypad. For example, type 0188 in the numeric keypad with the Alt key held down and the ¼ symbol appears. If you open the Character Map application, you can see a complete list of special characters and the number combinations that make them appear. The Character Map application, shown in Figure 11.10, can be opened in Windows by selecting Start ➪ All Programs ➪ Accessories ➪ System Tools ➪ Character Map.

FIGURE 11.10

FIGURE 11.10

The Character Map application shows all the special characters that are available.

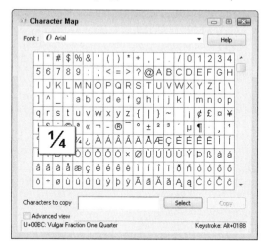

Helix

A Helix is like a spring coil shape, and it is the one shape of all the Shape primitives that exists in 3D. Helix parameters include two radii for specifying the inner and outer radius. These two values can be equal to create a coil or unequal to create a spiral. Parameters also exist for the Height and number of Turns. The Bias parameter causes the Helix turns to be gathered all together at the top or bottom of the shape. The CW and CCW options let you specify whether the Helix turns clockwise or counterclockwise.

Figure 11.11 shows a sampling of Helix shapes: The first Helix has equal radii values, the second one has a smaller second radius, the third Helix spirals to a second radius value of 0, and the last two Helix objects have Bias values of 0.8 and –0.8.

FIGURE 11.11

The Helix shape can be straight or spiral shaped.

Section

Section stands for cross section. The Section shape is a cross section of the edges of any 3D object through which the Section's cutting plane passes. The process consists of dragging in the viewport to create a cross-sectioning plane. You can then move, rotate, or scale the cross-sectioning plane to obtain the desired cross section. In the Section Parameters rollout is a Create Shape button. Clicking this button opens a dialog box where you can name the new shape. You can use one Section object to create multiple shapes.

> **NOTE**   You can make sections only from intersecting a 3D object. If the cross-sectioning plane doesn't intersect the 3D object, then it won't create a shape. You cannot use the Section primitive on shapes, even if it is a renderable spline.

The Parameters rollout includes settings for updating the Section shape. You can update it when the Section plane moves, when the Section is selected, or Manually (using the Update Section button). You can also set the Section Extents to Infinite, Section Boundary, or Off. The Infinite setting creates the cross-section spline as if the cross-sectioning plane were of infinite size, whereas the Section Boundary limits the plane's extents to the boundaries of the visible plane. The color swatch determines the color of the intersecting shape.

To give you an idea of what the Section shape can produce, Figure 11.12 shows the shapes resulting from sectioning two Cone objects, including a circle, an ellipse, a parabola, and a hyperbole. The shapes have been moved to the sides to be more visible.

FIGURE 11.12

You can use the Section shape primitive to create the conic sections (circle, ellipse, parabola, hyperbola) from a set of 3D cones.

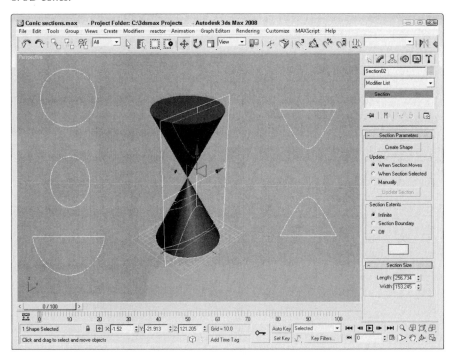

Tutorial: Drawing a company logo

One of the early uses for 3D graphics was to animate corporate logos, and although Max can still do this without any problems, it now has capabilities far beyond those available in the early days. The Shape tools can even be used to design the logo. In this example, we design and create a simple logo using the Shape tools for the fictitious company named Expeditions South.

To use the Shape tools to design and create a company logo, follow these steps:

1. Create a four-pointed star by clicking the Star button and dragging in the Top view to create a shape. Change the parameters for this star as follows: Radius1 = **60**, Radius2 = **20**, and Points = **4**.

2. Select and move the star shape to the left side of the viewport.

3. Now click the Text button, and change the font to Impact and the Size to **50**. In the Text area, type **Expeditions South** and include a line return and several spaces between the two words so they are offset. Click in the Top viewport to place the text.

4. Use the Select and Move button (W) to reposition the text next to the Star shape.

5. Click the Line button, and create several short highlighting lines around the bottom point of the star.

The finished logo is now ready to extrude and animate. Figure 11.13 shows the results.

FIGURE 11.13

A company logo created entirely in Max using shapes

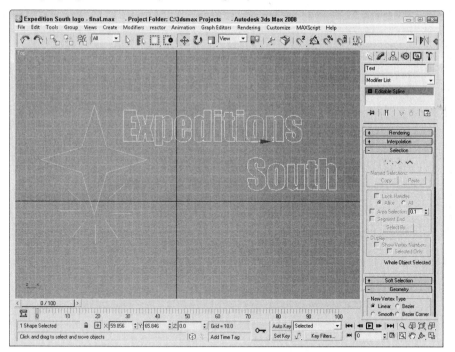

Tutorial: Viewing the interior of a heart

As an example of the Section primitive, let's explore a section of a Heart model. The model was created by Viewpoint Datalabs and is very realistic — so realistic, in fact, that it could be used to teach medical students the inner workings of the heart.

To create a spline from the cross section of the heart, follow these steps:

1. Open the Heart section.max file from the Chap 11 directory on the DVD.

   This file includes a physical model of a heart created by Viewpoint Datalabs.

2. Select Create ➪ Shapes ➪ Section, and drag a plane in the Front viewport that is large enough to cover the heart.

   This plane is your cross-sectioning plane.

3. Select the Select and Rotate button on the main toolbar (or press the E key), and rotate the cross-sectioning plane to cross the heart at the desired angle.

4. In the Parameters rollout of the Modify panel, click the Create Shape button and give the new shape the name **Heart Section**.

5. From the Select by Name dialog box (opened with the H key), select the section by name, separate it from the model, and reposition it to be visible.

Figure 11.14 shows the resulting model and section.

FIGURE 11.14

You can use the Section shape to view the interior area of the heart.

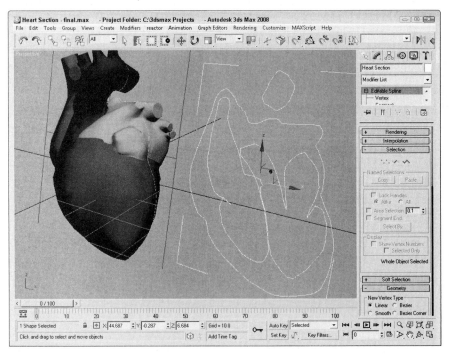

Editing Splines

After you create a shape primitive, you can edit it by modifying its parameters, but the parameters for shapes are fairly limited. For example, the only parameter for the Circle shape is Radius. All shapes can be converted to Editable Splines, or they can have the Edit Spline modifier applied to them. Doing either enables a host of editing features. Before you can use these editing features, you must convert the shape primitive to an Editable Spline (except for the Line shape). You can do so by right-clicking the spline shape in the viewport and choosing Convert to ➪ Convert to Editable Spline from the pop-up quadmenu, or by right-clicking on the Circle base object in the Modifier Stack and selecting Convert To Editable Spline in the pop-up menu. Another way to enable these features is to apply the Edit Spline modifier.

Editable Splines versus the Edit Spline modifier

After you convert the spline to an Editable Spline, you can edit individual subobjects within the spline, including Vertices, Segments, and Splines. There is a subtle difference between applying the Edit Spline modifier and converting the shape to an Editable Spline. Applying the Edit Spline modifier maintains the shape parameters and enables the editing features found in the Geometry rollout. However, an Editable Spline loses the ability to be able to change the base parameters associated with the spline shape.

NOTE When you create an object that contains two or more splines (such as when you create splines with the Start New Shape option disabled), all the splines in the object are automatically converted into Editable Splines.

Another difference is that the shape primitive base name is listed along with the Edit Spline modifier in the Modifier Stack. Selecting the shape primitive name makes the Rendering, Interpolation, and Parameters rollouts visible, and the Selection, Soft Selection, and Geometry rollouts are made visible when you select the Edit Spline modifier in the Modifier Stack. For Editable Splines, only a single base object name is visible in the Modifier Stack, and all rollouts are accessible under it.

NOTE Another key difference is that subobjects for the Edit Spline modifier cannot be animated.

Making splines renderable

Splines normally do not show up in a rendered image, but using the Renderable option in the Rendering rollout and assigning a thickness to the splines makes them appear in the rendered image. Figure 11.15 shows a rendered image of the Expeditions South logo after all shapes have been made renderable and assigned a Thickness of 3.0.

CROSS-REF The settings in the Rendering and Interpolation rollouts are the same as those used for newly created shapes, which were covered earlier in the chapter.

Selecting spline subobjects

When editing splines, you must choose the subobject level to work on. For example, when editing splines, you can work with Vertex (1), Segment (2), or Spline (3) subobjects. Before you can edit spline subobjects, you must select them. To select the subobject type, click the small plus sign icon to the left of the Editable Spline object in the Modifier Stack. This lists all the subobjects available for this object. Click the subobject in the Modifier Stack to select it. Alternatively, you can click the red-colored icons under the Selection rollout, shown in Figure 11.16. You can also select the different subobject modes using the 1, 2, and 3 keyboard shortcuts. When you select a subobject, the selection in the Modifier Stack and the associated icon in the Selection rollout turn yellow.

FIGURE 11.15

Using renderable splines with a Thickness of 3.0, the logo can be rendered.

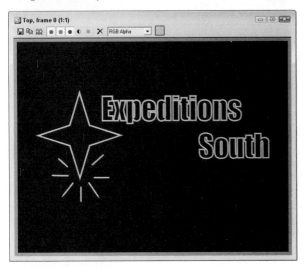

NOTE
The Sub-Object button turns yellow when selected to remind you that you are in subobject edit mode. Remember, you must exit this mode before you can select another object.

You can select many subobjects at once by dragging an outline over them in the viewports. You can also select and deselect vertices by holding down the Ctrl key while clicking them. Holding down the Alt key removes any selected vertices from the selection set.

After selecting several vertices, you can create a named selection set by typing a name in the Name Selection Sets drop-down list in the main toolbar. You can then copy and paste these selection sets onto other shapes using the buttons in the Selection rollout.

The Lock Handles option allows you to move the handles of all selected vertices together when enabled, but each handle moves by itself when disabled. With the Lock Handles and the All options selected, all selected handles move together. The Alike option causes all handles on one side to move together.

The Area Selection option selects all the vertices within a defined radius of where you click. The Segment End option, when enabled, allows you to select a vertex by clicking the segment. The closest vertex to the segment that you clicked is selected. This feature is useful when you are trying to select a vertex that lies near other vertices. The Select By button opens a dialog box with Segment and Spline buttons on it. These buttons allow you to select all the vertices on either a spline or segment that you choose.

The Selection rollout also has the Show Vertex Numbers option to display all the vertex numbers of a spline or to show the numbers of only the selected vertices. This can be convenient for understanding how a spline is put together and to help you find noncritical vertices. The Selected Only option displays the Vertex Numbers only for the selected subobjects when enabled.

FIGURE 11.16

The Selection rollout provides icons for entering the various subobject modes.

Segment subobject mode

Vertex subobject mode | Spline subobject mode

NOTE The vertex order is critical in determining the direction in which cross sections are swept when using the Loft and Sweep commands. You always can identify the first vertex in a spline because it is the one that is colored yellow.

Figure 11.17 shows a simple star shape that was converted to an Editable Spline. The left image shows the spline in Vertex subobject mode. All the vertices are marked with small plus signs, and the starting point is marked with a small square. The middle image has the Show Vertex Numbers option enabled. For the right image, the vertex numbers are shown after the Reverse button was used (in Spline subobject mode).

At the bottom of the Selection rollout, the Selection Information is displayed. This information tells you the number of the spline (or segment) and vertex selected, or the number of selected items and whether a spline is closed.

NOTE The Soft Selection rollout allows you to alter adjacent non-selected subobjects (to a lesser extent) when selected subobjects are moved, creating a smooth transition. See Chapter 10, "Learning Modeling Basics and Working with Subobjects and Helpers," for the details on this rollout.

FIGURE 11.17

Several spline shapes displayed with vertex numbering turned on

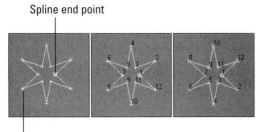

Controlling spline geometry

Much of the power of editing splines is contained within the Geometry rollout, shown in Figure 11.18, including the ability to add new splines, attach objects to the spline, weld vertices, use Boolean operations such as Trim and Extend, and many more. Some Geometry buttons may be disabled, depending on the subobject type that you've selected. Many of the features in the Geometry rollout can be used in all subobject modes. Some of these features do not even require that you be in a subobject mode. These features are covered first.

> **TIP** The quadmenu provides quick access to the main features for each subobject mode. After you are familiar with the various features, you can quickly access them through the quadmenu by simply right-clicking in the viewport.

FIGURE 11.18

For Editable Splines, the Geometry rollout holds most of the features.

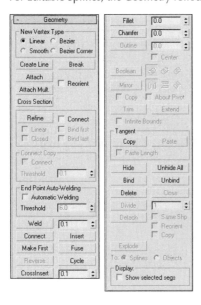

Create line

While editing splines, you can add new lines to a spline by clicking the Create Line button and then clicking in the one of the viewports. You can add several lines at the same time and all these new splines are part of the same object. Right-click in the viewport to exit this mode. Any new lines are their own spline, but you can weld them to the existing splines.

Break

Selecting a vertex and clicking the Break button in Vertex subobject mode breaks the segment at the selected vertex by creating two separate end points. You also can use the Break button in Segment subobject mode by clicking anywhere along the segment to add two separated vertices on the segment, thereby breaking the segment into two. You can also use the Break button in Vertex and Segment subobject modes.

Attach and Attach Multiple

The Attach button lets you attach any existing splines to the currently selected spline. The cursor changes when you're over the top of a spline that can be attached. Clicking an unselected object makes it part of the current object. The Reorient option aligns the coordinate system of the spline being attached with the selected spline's coordinate system.

For example, using the Boolean button requires that objects be part of the same object. You can use the Attach button to attach several splines into the same object.

The Attach Mult. button enables several splines to be attached at once. When you click the Attach Mult. button, the Attach Multiple dialog box (which looks much like the Select by Name dialog box) opens. Use this dialog box to select the objects you want to attach to the current selection. Click the Attach button in the dialog box when you're finished. You can use both the Attach and Attach Mult. buttons in all three subobject modes.

> **NOTE** If the spline object that is being attached has a material applied to it, then a dialog box appears that gives you options for handling the materials. These options include Match Material IDs to Material, Match Material to Material IDs, or Do Not Modify Material IDs or Material. Applying materials is covered in Chapter 14, "Exploring the Material Editor."

Cross Section

The Cross Section button works just like the Cross Section modifier by creating splines that run from one cross-section shape to another. For example, imagine creating a baseball bat by positioning circular cross sections for each diameter change and connecting each cross section from one end to the other. All the cross sections need to be part of the same Editable Spline object, and then using the Cross Section button, you can click from one cross section to another. The cursor changes when the mouse is over a shape that can be used. When you're finished selecting cross-section shapes, you can right-click to exit Cross Section mode.

The type of vertex used to create the new splines that run between the different cross sections is the type specified in the New Vertex Type section at the top of the Geometry rollout.

> **CAUTION** Although the splines that connect the cross sections are positioned alongside the cross section shape, they are not connected.

After the splines are created, you can use the Surface modifier to turn the splines into a 3D surface.

Auto Welding end points

To work with surfaces, you typically need a closed spline. When you enable the Automatic Welding option in the End Point Auto-Welding section and specify a Threshold, all end points within the threshold value are welded together, thus making a closed spline.

Insert

The Insert button adds vertices to a selected spline. Click the Insert button, and then click the spline to place the new vertex. At this point, you can reposition the new vertex and its attached segments — click again to set it in place. A single click adds a Corner type vertex, and a click-and-drag adds a Bézier type vertex.

After positioning the new vertex, you can add another vertex next to the first vertex by dragging the mouse and clicking. To add vertices to a different segment, right-click to release the currently selected segment, but stay in Insert mode. To exit Insert mode, right-click in the viewport again or click the Insert button to deselect it.

Tutorial: Working with cross sections to create a doorknob

You can work with cross sections in several ways. You can use the Cross Section feature for Editable Splines, the Cross Section modifier, or the Loft compound object. All these methods have advantages, but the first is probably the easiest and most forgiving method.

To create a simple doorknob using the Editable Spline Cross Section button, follow these steps:

1. Right-click any of the Snap toggle buttons on the main toolbar, and select Grid Points in the Grid and Snap Settings dialog box. Then click the Snap toggle button on the main toolbar (or press the S key) to enable grid snapping.

2. Select the Create ⇨ Shapes ⇨ Circle menu command, and drag from the center grid point in the Top viewport to create a small circle. Repeat this step to create two more circles: one the same size and one much larger.

3. Select the Create ⇨ Shapes ⇨ Rectangle menu command, and hold down the Ctrl key while dragging in the Top viewport to create a square that is smaller than the first circle. Repeat this step to create another square the same size. Aligning the squares is easier if you select the Center option in the Creation Method rollout.

4. Click the Select and Move (W) button on the main toolbar, and drag the shapes in the Left viewport upward in this order: square, square, small circle, large circle, small circle. Separate the squares by a distance equal to the width of a door, and spread the circles out to be the width of a doorknob.

5. Select the bottom-most square shape, and then right-click and select Convert To ⇨ Editable Spline in the pop-up quadmenu.

6. In the Geometry rollout, click the Attach button and then select the other shapes to add them to the selected Editable Spline object.

7. Rotate the Perspective viewport until all shapes are visible and easily selectable. Then select each and rotate each of the cross sections in the Top viewport so their first vertices are aligned. This helps prevent any twisting that may occur when the cross sections try to align the first vertices.

8. Select the Linear option in the New Vertex Type section in the Geometry rollout, and then click the Cross Section button. Click the lowest square shape in the Perspective viewport, followed by the higher square shape, and then the lower small circle. This creates a spline that runs linearly between these lowest three cross-section shapes. Right-click in the Perspective viewport to exit Cross Section mode.

9. Select the Bezier option in the New Vertex Type section, and then click the Cross Section button again. Click the lowest circle shape in the Perspective viewport, followed by the larger circle shape, and then the higher small circle. This creates a spline that runs smoothly between the last three cross-section shapes. Right-click in the Perspective viewport to exit Cross Section mode.

Figure 11.19 shows the splines running between the different cross sections. A key benefit to the Editable Spline approach is that you don't need to order the cross-section shapes exactly. You just need to click on them in the order that you want.

FIGURE 11.19

The Cross Section feature of Editable Splines can create splines that run between several cross-section shapes.

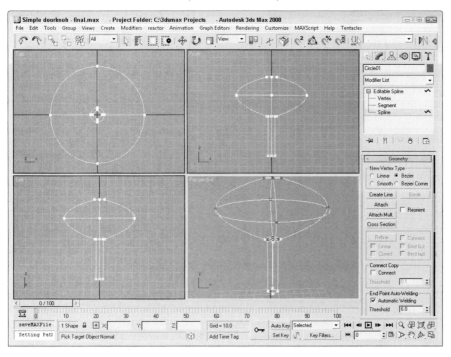

Editing vertices

To edit a vertex, click the Vertex subobject in the Modifier Stack or select the vertex icon from the Selection rollout (keyboard shortcut, 1). After the Vertex subobject type is selected, you can use the transform buttons on the main toolbar to move, rotate, and scale the selected vertex or vertices. Moving a vertex around causes the associated spline segments to follow.

With a vertex selected, you can change its type from Corner, Smooth, Bézier, or Bézier Corner by right-clicking and selecting the type from the pop-up quadmenu.

CAUTION   The New Vertex Type section in the top of the Geometry sets only the vertex type for new vertices created when you Shift-copy segments and splines or new vertices created with the Cross Section button. These options cannot be used to change vertex type for existing vertices.

Selecting the Bézier or Bézier Corner type vertex reveals green-colored handles on either side of the vertex. Dragging these handles away from the vertex alters the curvature of the segment. Bézier type vertices have both handles in the same line, but Corner Bézier type vertices do not. This allows them to create sharp angles.

NOTE Holding down the Shift key while clicking and dragging on a handle causes the handle to move independently of the other handle, turning it into a Bézier Corner type vertex instead of a plain Bézier. You can use it to create sharp corner points.

Figure 11.20 shows how the Bézier and Bézier Corner handles work. The first image shows all vertices of a circle selected where you can see the handles protruding from both sides of each vertex. The second image shows what happens to the circle when one of the handles is moved. The handles for Bézier vertices move together, so moving one upward causes the other to move downward. The third image shows a Bézier Corner vertex where the handles can move independently to create sharp points. The fourth image shows two Bézier Corner vertices moved with the Lock Handles and Alike options enabled. This causes the handles to the left of the vertices to move together. The final image has the Lock Handles and All options selected causing the handles of all selected vertices to move together.

FIGURE 11.20

Moving the vertex handles alters the spline around the vertex.

The pop-up quadmenu also includes a command to Reset Tangents. This option makes the tangents revert to their original orientation before the handles were moved.

Refine

The Refine button lets you add vertices to a spline without changing the curvature, giving you more control over the details of the spline. With the Refine button selected, just click on a spline where you want the new vertex and one is added.

The Connect option makes adds a new segment that connects each two successive points added with the Refine tool. These segments don't actually appear until the Refine button is disabled. This provides a method for copying part of an existing spline. When the Connect option is enabled, then the Linear, Closed, Bind First, and Bind Last options become enabled. The Linear option creates Corner type vertices resulting in linear segments. The Closed option closes the spline by connecting the first and last vertices. The Bind First and Bind Last options bind the first and last vertices to the center of the selected segment. Refine is available only for Vertex and Segment subobject modes.

Weld and Fuse

When two endpoint vertices are selected and are within the specified Weld Threshold, they can be welded into one vertex and moved to a position that is the average of the welded points using the Weld button. Several vertices can be welded simultaneously. Another way to weld vertices is to move one vertex on top of another. If they are within the threshold distance, a dialog box asks whether you want them to be welded. Click the Yes button to weld them.

CAUTION The Weld button can be used only to weld spline endpoints.

The Fuse button is similar to the Weld command, except that it doesn't delete any vertices. It just positions the two vertices on top of one another at a position that is the average of the selected vertices.

In Figure 11.21, the left image shows a star shape with all its lower vertices selected. The middle image is the same star shape after the selected vertices have been welded together, and the right image shows the star shape with the selected vertices fused. The Selection rollout shows five selected vertices for the fused version.

FIGURE 11.21

Using the Fuse and Weld buttons, several vertices in our star shape have been combined.

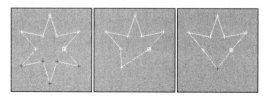

You can use the Fuse button to move the selected vertices to a single location. This is accomplished by selecting all the vertices to relocate and clicking the Fuse button. The average point between all the selected vertices becomes the new location. You can combine these vertices into one after they've been fused by clicking the Weld button.

Connect

The Connect button lets you connect end vertices to one another to create a new line. This works only on end vertices and not on connected points within a spline. To connect the ends, click the Connect button and drag the cursor from one end point to another (the cursor changes to a plus sign when it is over a valid end point) and release it. The first image in Figure 11.22 shows an incomplete star drawn with the Line primitive, the middle image shows a line being drawn between the end points (notice the cursor), and the third image is the resulting star.

FIGURE 11.22

You can use the Connect button to connect end points of shapes.

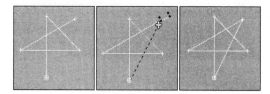

Make First

The Show Vertex Numbers option in the Selection rollout displays the number of each vertex. The first vertex is identified by the yellow color. The Make First button lets you change which vertex you want to be the first vertex in the spline. To do this, select a single vertex and click the Make First button. If more than one vertex is selected, Max ignores the command. If the selected spline is an open spline, again Max ignores the command; an end point must be selected.

 The vertex number is important because it determines the first key for path animations and where Loft objects start.

Cycle

If a single vertex is selected, the Cycle button causes the next vertex in the Vertex Number order to be selected. The Cycle button can be used on open and closed splines and can be repeated around the spline. The exact vertex number is shown at the bottom of the Selection rollout. This is very useful for locating individual vertices in groups that are close together, such as groups that have been fused.

CrossInsert

If two splines that are part of the same object overlap, you can use the CrossInsert button to create a vertex on each spline at the location where they intersect. The distance between the two splines must be closer than the Threshold value for this to work. Note that this button does not join the two splines; it only creates a vertex on each spline. Use the Weld button to join the splines. Figure 11.23 shows how you can use the CrossInsert button to add vertices at the intersection points of two elliptical splines. Notice that each ellipse now has eight vertices.

FIGURE 11.23

The CrossInsert button can add vertices to any overlapping splines of the same object.

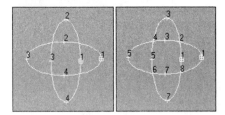

Fillet

The Fillet button is used to round the corners of a spline where two edges meet. To use the Fillet command, click the Fillet button and then drag on a corner vertex in the viewport. The more you drag, the larger the Fillet. You can also enter a Fillet value in the Fillet spinner for the vertices that are selected. The Fillet has a maximum value based on the geometry of the spline. Figure 11.24 shows the Fillet command applied to an eight-pointed star with values of 10, 15, and 20. Notice that each selected vertex has split into two.

CAUTION Be careful not to apply the fillet command multiple times to the selected vertices. If the new vertices cross over each other, then the normals will be misaligned, which will cause problems when you use modifiers.

NOTE You can fillet several vertices at once by selecting them and then clicking the Fillet button and dragging the Fillet distance.

FIGURE 11.24

The Fillet button can round the corners of a shape.

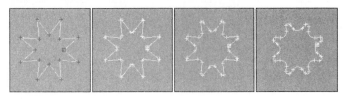

Chamfer

The Chamfer button works much like the Fillet button, except that the corners are replaced with straight-line segments instead of smooth curves. This keeps the resulting shape simpler and maintains hard corners. To use the Chamfer command, click the Chamfer button and drag on a vertex to create the Chamfer. You can also enter a Chamfer value in the rollout. Figure 11.25 shows chamfers applied to the same eight-pointed shape with the same values of 10, 15, and 20.

FIGURE 11.25

Chamfers alter the look of spline corners.

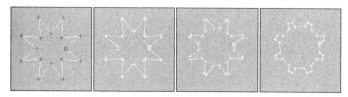

Tangent Copy and Tangent Paste

If you spend considerable time positioning the handles for the Bézier or Bézier Corner vertices just right, it can be tricky to repeat these precise positions again for other handles. Using the Tangent Copy and Tangent Paste buttons, you can copy the handle positions between different handles. To do so, simply select a handle that you wish to copy and click the Copy button, and then select the vertex to which you want to copy the handle and press the Paste button. The Paste Length button copies the handle length along with its orientation, if enabled.

Hide/Unhide All

The Hide and Unhide All buttons hide and unhide spline subobjects. They can be used in any subobject mode. To hide a subobject, select the subobject and click the Hide button. To unhide the hidden subobjects, click the Unhide All button.

Bind/Unbind

The Bind button attaches an end vertex to a segment. The bound vertex then cannot be moved independently, but only as part of the bound segment. The Unbind button removes the binding on the vertex and lets it move independently again. To bind a vertex, click the Bind button and then drag from the vertex to the segment to bind to. To exit Bind mode, right-click in the viewport or click the Bind button again.

For Figure 11.26, a circle shape is created and converted to an Editable Spline object. The right vertex is selected and then separated from the circle with the Break button. Then by clicking the Bind button and dragging the vertex to the opposite line segment, the vertex is bound to the segment. Any movement of the spline keeps this vertex bound to the segment.

Delete

The Delete button deletes the selected subobject. You can use it to delete vertices, segments, or splines. This button is available in all subobject modes. Pressing the Delete key when the subobject is selected has the same effect.

FIGURE 11.26

The Bind button attaches one end of the circle shape to a segment.

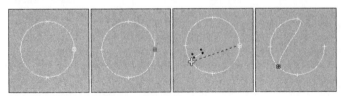

Show Selected Segments

The Show Selected Segs option causes any selected segments to continue to be highlighted in Vertex subobject mode as well as Segment subobject mode. This feature helps you keep track of the segments that you are working on when moving vertices.

Tutorial: Making a ninja star

If you're involved with fighting games, either creating or playing them, then chances are good that when you look at the Star primitive, you think, "Wow, this is perfect for creating a ninja star weapon." If not, then just pretend.

To create a ninja star using splines, follow these steps:

1. Right-click any of the Snap toggle buttons on the main toolbar, and select Grid Points in the Grid and Snap Settings dialog box. Then click the Snap toggle button (or press the S key) on the main toolbar to enable grid snapping.

2. Select the Create ⇨ Shapes ⇨ Circle menu command, and drag from the center grid point in the Top viewport to create a circle.

3. Select the Create ⇨ Shapes ⇨ Star menu command, and drag again from the center of the Top viewport to center align the star with the circle. Make the star shape about three times the size of the circle, and set the number of Points to **10**.

4. With the star shape selected, right-click in the Top viewport and select Convert To ⇨ Editable Spline. In the Modify panel, click the Attach button, and click the circle shape. Then click the Vertex icon in the Selection rollout (or press 1) to enter Vertex subobject mode.

5. Click the Create Line button in the Geometry rollout; then click the circle's top vertex and bottom vertex, then right-click to end the line, and right-click again to exit Create Line mode.

6. Select the top vertex of the line that you just created (be careful not to select the circle's top vertex; you can use the Cycle button to find the correct vertex). Right-click the vertex, and select the Bézier vertex type from the quadmenu. Then drag its lower handle until it is on top of the circle's left vertex. Repeat this step for the bottom vertex, and drag its handle to the circle's right vertex to create a yin-yang symbol in the center of the ninja star.

7. While holding down the Ctrl key, click on all the inner vertices of the star shape. Click the Chamfer button, enter the value of **15** in the Chamfer field, and press the Enter key.

Figure 11.27 shows the resulting ninja star.

FIGURE 11.27

The completed ninja star, ready for action (or extruding)

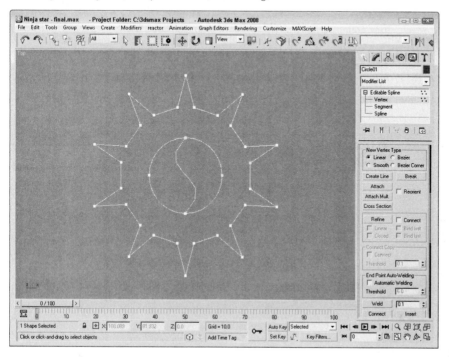

Editing segments

To edit a segment, click the Segment subobject in the Modifier Stack or select the segment icon from the Selection rollout to enter segment subobject mode. Clicking again on either exits this mode. *Segments* are the lines or edges that run between two vertices. Many of the editing options work in the same way as when editing Vertex subobjects. You can select multiple segments by holding down the Ctrl key while clicking the segments, or you can hold down the Alt key to remove selected segments from the selection set. You can also copy segments when they're being transformed by holding down the Shift key. The cloned segments break away from the original spline, but are still a part of the Editable Spline object.

You can change segments from straight lines to curves by right-clicking the segment and selecting Line or Curve from the pop-up quadmenu. Line segments created with the Corner type vertex option cannot be changed to Curves, but lines created with Smooth and Bézier type vertex options can be switched back and forth.

Several Geometry rollout buttons work on more than one subobject type.

Connect Copy

When you create a copy of a segment by moving a segment with the Shift key held down, you can enable the Connect Copy option to make segments that join the copied segment with its original. For example, if you have a single straight horizontal line segment, dragging it upward with the Copy Connect option enabled creates a copy that is joined to the original, resulting in a rectangle. Be aware that the vertices that connect to the original segment are not welded to the original segment.

Divide

When you select a segment, the Divide button becomes active. This button adds the number of vertices specified to the selected segment or segments. These new vertices are positioned based on the curvature of the segment with more vertices being added to the areas of greater curvature. Figure 11.28 shows the diamond shape (second row, second from right) after all four segments were selected, a value of 1 was entered into the spinner, and the Divide button was clicked.

FIGURE 11.28

The Divide button adds segments to the spline.

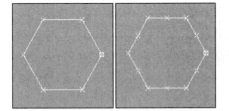

Detach

The Detach button separates the selected subobjects from the rest of the object (opposite of the Attach button). When you click this button, the Detach dialog box opens, enabling you to name the new detached subobject. When segments are detached, you can select the Same Shape option to keep them part of the original object. The Reorient option realigns the new detached subobject to match the position and orientation of the current active grid. The Copy option creates a new copy of the detached subobject.

You can use Detach on either selected Spline or Segment subobjects.

Tutorial: Using Connect Copy to create a simple flower

Connect Copy is one of the features that you'll use and wonder how you ever got along without it. For this tutorial, we create a simple flower from a circle shape using the Connect Copy feature.

To create a simple flower using the Connect Copy feature, follow these steps:

1. Select Create ➪ Shapes ➪ Circle, and drag in the Top viewport to create a simple circle shape.
2. Right-click on the circle, and select Convert to ➪ Editable Spline to convert the shape.
3. In the Modifier Stack, select the Segment subobject mode (keyboard shortcut, 2) and enable the Connect option in the Connect Copy section.
4. Select one of the circle segments, and with the Shift key held down, drag it outward away from the circle. Then repeat this step for each segment.

Figure 11.29 shows the results. With the Connect Copy option, you don't need to worry about the connecting lines.

FIGURE 11.29

The Connect Copy feature joins newly copied segments to the original.

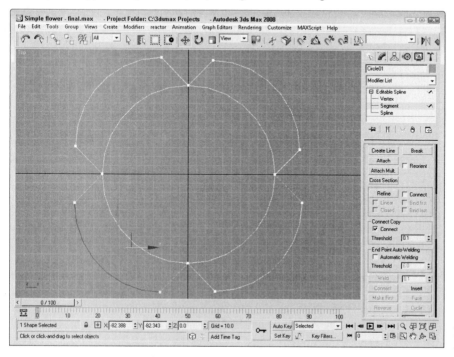

Surface Properties

For segment and spline subobjects, you can access a Surface Properties rollout that lets you assign a Material ID to the subobject. These Material IDs are used with the Multi/Sub-object Material available in the Material Editor. For example, suppose you've created a road from a bunch of splines that are part of the same object. You can assign one Material ID for the lines at the edge of the road that will be the curb and a different Material ID for the yellow lines running down the middle of the road. Separate materials then can be applied to each of the parts using the matching Material IDs.

CROSS-REF You can find information on Material IDs in Chapter 15, "Creating and Applying Standard Materials."

Using the Select ID button and drop-down list, you can locate and select all subobjects that have a certain Material ID. Simply select the Material ID that you are looking for and click the Select ID button, and all segments (or splines) with that Material ID are selected. Beneath the Select ID button is another drop-down list that lets you select segments by material name. The Clear Selection option clears all selections when the Select ID button is clicked. If disabled, then all new selections are added to the current selection set.

Editing Spline subobjects

To edit a spline, click the Spline subobject in the Modifier Stack or select the spline icon from the Selection rollout. Transforming a spline object containing only one spline works the same way in subobject mode as it does in a normal transformation. Working in spline subobject mode lets you move splines relative to one another. Right-clicking a spline in subobject mode opens a pop-up quadmenu that lets you convert it between Curve and Line types. The Curve type option changes all vertices to Bézier type, and the Line type option makes all vertices Corner type. Spline subobject mode includes many of the buttons previously discussed as well as some new ones in the Geometry rollout.

Reverse

The Reverse button is available only for Spline subobjects. It reverses the order of the vertex numbers. For example, a circle that is numbered clockwise from 1 to 4 is numbered counterclockwise after using the Reverse button. The vertex order is important for splines that are used for animation paths or loft compound objects.

Outline

The Outline button creates a spline that is identical to the one selected and offset by an amount specified by dragging or specified in the Offset value. The Center option creates an outline on either side of the selected spline, centered on the original spline. When the Center option is not selected, then an outline is created by offsetting a duplicate of the spline on only one side of the original spline. To exit Outline mode, click the Outline button again or right-click in the viewport. Figure 11.30 shows an arc that has had the Outline feature applied. In the right image, the Center option is enabled.

FIGURE 11.30

The Outline button creates a duplicate copy of the original spline and offsets it.

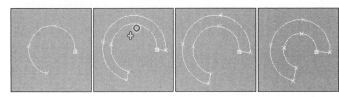

Boolean

Boolean operations work with two or more splines that overlap one another. There are three different operations that can happen: You can combine the splines to create a single spline (union), you can subtract the overlapping area from one of the splines (subtract), or you can throw away everything except the overlapping area (intersection).

CROSS-REF You can also use Booleans to combine or subtract 3D volumes, which are covered in Chapter 26, "Working with Compound Objects."

The Boolean button works on overlapping closed splines and has three different options — Union, Subtraction, and Intersection — shown in Table 11.3. The splines must all be part of the same object. The Union option combines the areas of both splines, the Subtraction option removes the second spline's area from the first, and the Intersection option keeps only the areas that overlap.

TABLE 11.3

Boolean Button Options

Button	Description
	Union
	Subtraction
	Intersection

To use the Boolean feature, select one of the splines and select one of the Boolean operation options. Then click the Boolean button, and select the second spline. Depending on which Boolean operation you chose, the overlapping area is deleted, the second spline acts to cut away the overlapping area on the first, or only the overlapping area remains. To exit Boolean mode, right-click in the viewport.

NOTE **Boolean operations can be performed only on closed splines that exist within a 2D plane.**

Figure 11.31 shows the results of applying the Spline Boolean operators on a circle and star shape. The first image consists of the circle and star shapes without any Boolean operations applied. The second image shows the result of the Union feature, the third (circle selected first) and fourth (star selected first) use the Subtraction feature, and the fifth image uses the Intersection feature.

FIGURE 11.31

Using the Boolean operations on two overlapping shapes

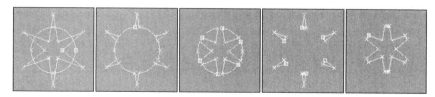

Mirror

You can use the Mirror button to mirror a spline object horizontally, vertically, or along both axes. To use this feature, select a spline object to mirror and then locate the Mirror button. To the right of the Mirror button are three smaller buttons, each of which indicates a direction—Mirror Horizontally, Mirror Vertically, and Mirror Both—shown in Table 11.4. Select a direction, and then click the Mirror button. If the Copy option is selected, a new spline is created and mirrored. The About Pivot option causes the mirroring to be completed about the pivot point axes.

TABLE 11.4

Mirror Button Options

Button	Description
▷◁	Mirror Horizontally
⊟	Mirror Vertically
◇	Mirror Both

Figure 11.32 shows a little critter that has been mirrored horizontally, vertically, and both. The right image was horizontally mirrored with the About Pivot option disabled. Notice that the eye spline was mirrored about its own pivot.

FIGURE 11.32

Mirroring a shape is as simple as selecting a direction and clicking the Mirror button.

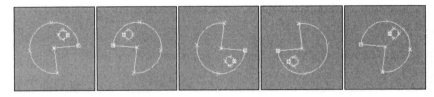

Trim and Extend

The Trim button cuts off any extending portion between two overlapping splines. The splines must be part of the same object. To use the Trim feature, select the spline that you want to keep, click the Trim button, and then click the segment to trim. The spline you click is trimmed back to the nearest intersecting point of the selected object. This button works only in Spline subobject mode. The trimming command is dependent on the viewport that is active. When the Perspective or a Camera view is active, this command uses the Top viewport to trim.

Figure 11.33 shows a circle intersected by two ellipse shapes. The Trim button was used to cut the center sections of the ellipse shapes away.

FIGURE 11.33

You can use the Trim button to cut away the excess of a spline.

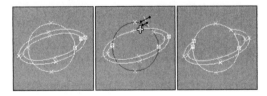

The Extend button works in the reverse manner compared to the Trim button. The Extend button lengthens the end of a spline until it encounters an intersection. (There must be a spline segment to intersect.) To use the Extend command, click the Extend button and then click the segment to extend. The spline you click is extended. To exit Extend mode, right-click in the viewport or click the Extend button again.

The Infinite Bounds option works for both the Trim and Extend buttons. When enabled, it treats all open splines as if they were infinite for the purpose of locating an intersecting point. The Extend command, like Trim, is dependent on the active viewport.

Close

The Close button completes an open spline and creates a closed spline by attaching a segment between the first and last vertices. You can check which vertex is first by enabling the Show Vertex Numbers in the Selection rollout. This is similar to the Connect feature (accessible in Vertex subobject mode), but the Connect feature can connect the end point of one spline to the end point of another as long as they are part of the same Editable Spline object. The Close feature works only in Spline subobject mode and connects only the end points of each given spline.

Explode

The Explode button performs the Detach command on all subobject splines at once. It separates each segment into a separate spline. You can select to explode all spline objects to separate Splines or Objects. If you select to explode to Objects, then a dialog box appears asking you for a name. Each spline uses the name you enter with a two-digit number appended to distinguish between the different splines.

Tutorial: Spinning a spider's web

Now that you're familiar with the many aspects of editing splines, let's try to mimic one of the best spline producers in the world — the spider. The spider is an expert at connecting lines together to create an intricate pattern. (Luckily, unlike the spider that depends on its web for food, we won't go hungry if this example fails.)

To create a spider web from splines, follow these steps:

1. Select Create ➪ Shapes ➪ Circle, and drag in the Front viewport to create a large circle for the perimeter of the web (let's pretend that the spider is building this web inside a tire swing). Right-click on the circle, and select Convert To ➪ Editable Spline to convert the circle shape.

2. Select the Spline subobject in the Modifier Stack (or press the 3 key) to enter Spline subobject mode.

3. Click the Create Line button in the Geometry rollout, and click in the center of the circle and again outside the circle to create a line. Then right-click to end the line. Repeat this step until 12 or so radial lines extend from the center of the circle outward.

4. Select and right-click on the 2D Snaps Toggle in the main toolbar. In the Grid and Snap Settings dialog box, enable the Vertex and Edge/Segment options and close the dialog box. While you're still in Create Line mode, click on the circle's center and create lines in a spiral pattern by clicking on each radial line that you intersect. Right-click to end the line when you finally reach the edge of the circle. Then right-click again to exit Create Line mode.

5. Select the circle shape, and click the Trim button. Then click on each line segment on the portion that extends beyond the circle. This trims the radial lines to the edge of the circle. Click the Trim button again when you are finished to exit Trim mode.

6. Change to Vertex subobject mode by clicking Vertex in the Modifier Stack (or by pressing 1). Then select all the vertices in the center of the circle, and click the Fuse button.

Figure 11.34 shows the finished spider web. (I have a new respect for spiders.)

FIGURE 11.34

A spider web made from Editable Splines

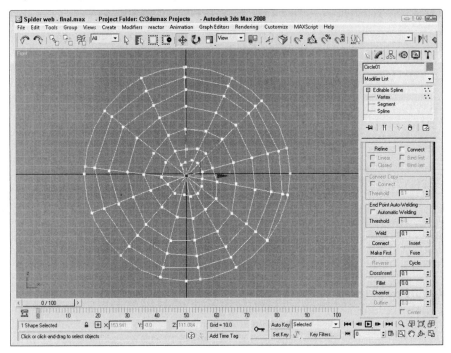

Using Spline Modifiers

In the Modifiers menu is a whole submenu of modifiers that apply strictly to splines. You can find these modifiers in the Modifiers ⇨ Patch/Spline Editing menu.

Spline-specific modifiers

Of the modifiers that work only on splines, several of these duplicate functionality that is available for Editable Splines, such as the Fillet/Chamfer modifier. Applying these features as modifiers gives you better control over the results because you can remove them using the Modifier Stack at any time.

Edit Spline modifier

The Modifiers ⇨ Patch/Spline Editing ⇨ Edit Spline modifier (mentioned at the start of the chapter) makes spline objects so they can be edited. It has all the same features as the Editable Spline object. The Edit Spline modifier isn't really a modifier, but an Object type. It shows up in the Modifier Stack above the base object. The key benefit of the Edit Spline modifier is that it enables you to edit spline subobjects while maintaining the parametric nature of the primitive object.

Spline Select modifier

This modifier enables you to select spline subobjects, including Vertex, Segment, and Spline. You can copy and paste named selection sets. The selection can then be passed up the Stack to the next modifier. The Spline Select modifier provides a way to apply a modifier to a subobject selection.

The Modifiers ⇨ Selection Modifiers ⇨ Spline Select modifier lets you select objects from any of the subobject modes available in the Editable Spline object. It also includes buttons for selecting subobjects based on the other subobject modes. For example, if you select Vertex subobject mode, then two buttons available in the Select Vertex rollout are Get Segment Selection and Get Spline Selection. Clicking either of these buttons gets all the vertices that are part of the other subobject mode.

You can also Copy and Paste selection sets using the Copy and Paste buttons.

Delete Spline modifier

You can use the Delete Spline modifier to delete spline subobjects. This is helpful if you want to remove a spline from an object so it doesn't render without destroying the curvature of the other splines in the object. To do this, simply select the splines to remove from the object in Spline subobject mode and then apply the Delete Spline modifier. The selection will be passed up the stack.

Normalize Spline modifier

The Normalize Spline modifier adds new points to the spline. These points are spaced regularly based on the Segment Length value. Figure 11.35 shows a simple flower shape with the Spline Select modifier applied so you can see the vertices. The Normalize Spline modifier was then applied with Segment Length values of 1, 5, 10, and 15. Notice that the shape is changing with fewer vertices.

FIGURE 11.35

The Normalize Spline modifier relaxes the shape by removing vertices.

Fillet/Chamfer modifier

You can use the Fillet/Chamfer modifier to Fillet or Chamfer the corners of shapes. Fillet creates smooth corners, and a Chamfer adds another segment where two edges meet. Parameters include the Fillet Radius and the Chamfer Distance. Both include an Apply button. The results of this modifier are the same as if you were to use the Fillet or Chamfer features of an Editable Spline.

Renderable Spline modifier

The Renderable Spline modifier lets you make any selected spline renderable. The Parameters rollout includes the same controls that are available for Editable Splines including Thickness, Sides, and Angle values.

Sweep modifier

The Sweep modifier works just like the loft compound object, letting you follow a spline path with a defined cross section, except that the Sweep modifier is a modifier, making it easier to apply and remove from splines and shapes. Another benefit of the Sweep modifier is that it has several Built-In Sections available that you can choose or you can pick your own. The built-in sections include many that are useful for architectural structures including Angle, Bar, Channel, Cylinder, Half Round, Pipe, Quarter Round, Tee, Tube, and Wide Flange.

Using the Merge From File button, you can choose a shape from another file. You can also set the number of interpolation steps. The Sweep Parameters rollout includes options for mirroring, offsetting, smoothing, aligning, and banking the generated sweep. The Union Intersecting option causes self-intersecting portions of the path to be combined using a union Boolean command. You also can select to have mapping coordinates generated on the sweep object.

Tutorial: Plumbing with pipes

If you want to create a shape that renders in the scene, you can use the Renderable Spline option or you can apply the Sweep modifier. In this example, we apply the Sweep modifier to a line that defines the path of a bathroom sink drain.

To create a pipe that follows a spline, follow these steps:

1. Open the Bathroom sink.max file from the Chap 11 directory on the DVD.

   This file includes a simple bathroom sink and a line that defines its drain path.

2. With the spline selected, choose the Modifiers ➪ Patch/Spline Editing ➪ Sweep menu command to apply the Sweep modifier.

3. In the Section Type rollout, choose the Cylinder option from the Built-In Section drop-down list. Then set the Radius value to 10.

Figure 11.36 shows the resulting sink complete with a drain created using a cylinder cross section.

Trim/Extend modifier

The Trim/Extend modifier lets you trim the extending end of a spline or extend a spline until it meets another spline at a vertex. The Pick Locations button turns on Pick mode, where the cursor changes when it is over a valid point. Operations include Auto, Trim Only, and Extend Only with an option to compute Infinite Boundaries. You can also set the Intersection Projection to View, Construction Plane, or None.

Using the Shape Check utility

The Shape Check utility is helpful in verifying that a shape doesn't intersect itself. Shapes that have this problem cannot be extruded, lofted, or lathed without problems. To use this utility, open the Utilities panel (the icon for the Utilities panel looks like a hammer) and click the More button. Select Shape Check from the Utilities dialog box list, and click OK.

 **The Shape Check utility is found in the Utilities panel and not in the Modifiers menu.**

The Shape Check rollout includes only two buttons: Pick Object and Close. Click the Pick Object button, and click the shape you want to check. Any intersection points are displayed as red squares, as shown in Figure 11.37, and the response field displays "Shape Self-Intersects." If the shape doesn't have any intersections, then the response field reports "Shape OK."

FIGURE 11.36

The resulting drain pipe was created using the Sweep modifier.

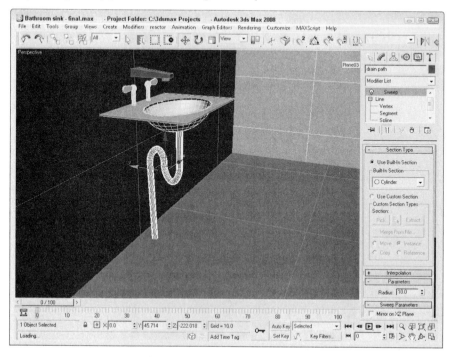

> **NOTE** You can use the Shape Check utility on normal splines and on NURBS splines.

Moving splines to 3D

Although splines can be rendered, the real benefit of splines in Max is to use them to create 3D objects and for animation paths. You can use splines in several ways as you model 3D objects including Loft objects and modifiers. One way to use splines to make 3D objects is with modifiers.

> **NOTE** As you build splines that will be used to create mesh objects, remember that the number of vertices in a spline determines the number of segments in the final mesh. For example, if you have a spline with 10 points that is extruded 5 times, then you'll end up with more than 50 polygons, but the same spline with 80 points would have more than 400 polygons.

> **CROSS-REF** Using splines to create an animation path is covered in Chapter 20, "Understanding Animation and Keyframe Basics," and Loft objects are covered in Chapter 26, "Working with Compound Objects." General information on working with modifiers is covered in Chapter 13, "Introducing Modifiers and Using the Modifier Stack."

Extruding splines

Because splines are drawn in a 2D plane, they already include two of the three dimensions. By adding a Height value to the shape, we can create a simple 3D object. The process of adding Height to a shape is called *extruding*.

FIGURE 11.37

The Shape Check utility can identify spline intersections.

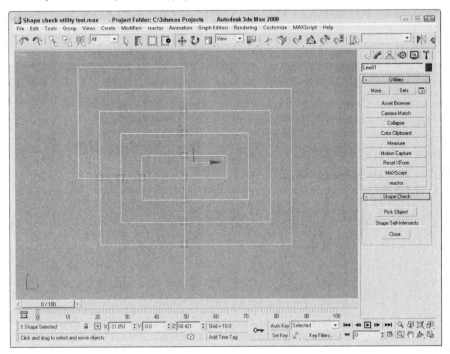

To extrude a shape, you need to apply the Extrude modifier. To do so, select a spline object and choose Modifiers ➪ Mesh Editing ➪ Extrude, or select the Extrude modifier from the Modifier Stack drop-down list. In the Parameters rollout, you can specify an Amount, which is the height value of the extrusion; the number of Segments; and the Capping options (caps fill in the surface at each end of the Extruded shape). You can also specify the final Output to be a Patch, Mesh, or NURBS object. Figure 11.38 shows our capital Es that modeled the various vertex types extruded to a depth of 10.0.

FIGURE 11.38

Extruding simple shapes adds depth to the spline.

Tutorial: Routing a custom shelf

In Woodshop 101, you use a router to add a designer edge to doorframes, window frames, and shelving of all sorts. In Woodshop 3D, the Boolean tools work nicely as we customize a bookshelf.

To create a custom bookshelf using spline Boolean operations, follow these steps:

1. Open the Bookshelf.max file from the Chap 11 directory on the DVD.

   This file includes a triangle shape drawn with the Line primitive that is overlapped by three circles. All these shapes have been converted and combined into a single Editable Spline object.

2. Select the shape, open the Modify panel, and select the Spline subobject mode (or press the 3 key) and select the triangle shape.

3. Select the Subtraction Boolean operation (the middle icon) in the Geometry rollout, and click the Boolean button. Then select each of the circles.

4. Click the Subtraction button next to the Boolean button (it's the middle one). Then select the triangle shape, and click the Boolean button. Right-click in the viewport to exit Boolean mode, and click Spline in the Modifier Stack again to exit subobject mode.

5. Back in the Modify panel, select the Extrude modifier from the Modifier drop-down list and enter an Amount of **1000**. Select Zoom Extents All to resize your viewports and view your bookshelf.

Figure 11.39 shows the finished bookshelf in the Perspective viewport ready to hang on the wall.

FIGURE 11.39

The finished bookshelf created with spline Boolean operations and the Extrude modifier

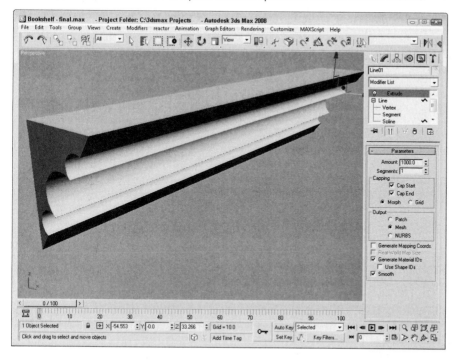

Lathing splines

Another useful modifier for 2D splines is the Lathe. This modifier rotates the spline about an axis to create an object with a circular cross section (such as a baseball bat). In the Parameters rollout, you can specify the

Degrees to rotate (a value of 360 makes a full rotation) and Cappings, which add ends to the resulting mesh. Additional options include Weld Core, which causes all vertices at the center of the lathe to be welded together, and Flip Normals, which realigns all the normals.

The Direction option determines the axis about which the rotation takes place. The rotation takes place about the object's pivot point.

 **If your shape is created in the Top view, then lathing about the screen Z-axis produces a thin disc without any depth.**

Tutorial: Lathing a crucible

As an example of the Lathe modifier, we create a simple crucible, although we could produce any object that has a circular cross section. A crucible is a thick porcelain cup used to melt chemicals. I chose this as an example because it is simple (and saying "crucible" sounds much more scientific than "cup").

To create a crucible using the Lathe modifier, follow these steps:

1. Open the Crucible.max file from the Chap 11 directory on the DVD.

   This file includes a rough profile cross-section line of the crucible that has been converted to an Editable Spline.

2. Select the line, and select the Modifiers ⇨ Patch/Spline Editing ⇨ Lathe menu command. Set the Degrees value in the Parameters rollout to **360**. Because you'll lathe a full revolution, you don't need to check the Cap options. In the Direction section, select the Y button (the Y-axis), and you're finished.

Figure 11.40 shows the finished product. You can easily make this into a coffee mug by adding a handle. To make a handle, simply loft an ellipse along a curved path.

Bevel and Bevel Profile modifiers

Another common set of modifiers that can be used with splines and shapes are the Bevel and Bevel Profile modifiers.

 **Both the Bevel and Bevel Profile modifiers are not found in the Modifiers menu. To apply them, use the Modifier List found in the Modifier Stack. They are among the Object-Space modifiers.**

Using the Bevel modifier, you can extrude and outline (scale) the shape in one operation. With the Bevel modifier, you can set the Height and Outline values for up to three different bevel levels. The Capping options let you select to cap either end of the beveled shape. The Cap Type can be either Morph or Grid. The Morph type is for objects that will be morphed. You can specify that the Surface use Linear or Curved Sides with a given number of segments. You can also select to Smooth Across Levels automatically. The Keep Lines from Crossing option avoids problems that may result from crossing lines.

The Bevel Profile modifier lets you select a spline to use for the bevel profile.

Tutorial: Modeling unique rings

If you were paying attention when we discussed primitive objects, you realize that you can create a simple ring using a Tube or Torus primitive object. If you want the ring to have a unique profile, then the Bevel and Bevel Profile modifiers are what you need.

FIGURE 11.40

Lathing a simple profile can create a circular object.

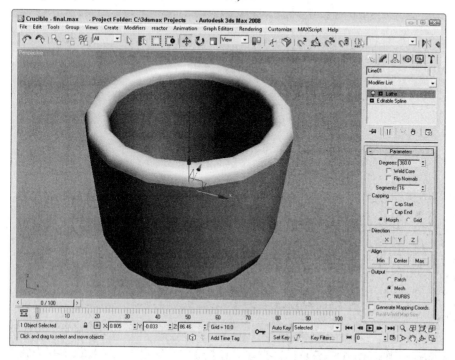

To create a couple of unique rings with the Bevel and Bevel Profile modifiers, follow these steps:

1. Select Create ➪ Shapes ➪ Donut, and drag in the Top viewport to create two donut objects that are positioned side by side. Set the Radius 1 value to **80** and the Radius 2 value to **75** for both rings.

2. Select the ring on the left in the Top viewport, open the Modify panel, and select the Bevel modifier from the Modifier List drop-down list in the Modifier Stack. In the Bevel Values rollout, set the Start Outline to **0**, the Height values for Levels 1, 2, and 3 to **20**, the Outline for Level 1 to **15**, and the Outline value for Level 3 to **–15**. Then enable the Smooth Across Levels option.

3. Select Create ➪ Shapes ➪ Line, and draw a profile curve in the Front viewport that is about the same height as the first ring.

4. Select the donut shape on the right, open the Modify panel, and choose the Bevel Profile modifier from the Modifier List in the Modifier Stack. In the Parameters rollout, click the Pick Profile button and select the profile curve.

Figure 11.41 shows the finished rings.

CrossSection modifier

The CrossSection modifier is one of two modifiers that collectively are referred to as the surface tools. The surface tools provide a way to cover a series of connected cross sections with a surface. It connects the vertices of several cross-sectional splines together with additional splines in preparation for the Surface modifier. These cross-sectional splines can have different numbers of vertices. Parameters include different spline types such as Linear, Smooth, Bézier, and Bézier Corner.

FIGURE 11.41

Bevels applied to a shape can give a unique profile edge.

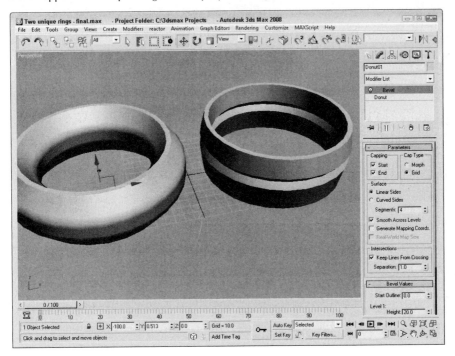

> **CROSS-REF** The second half of the surface tools is the Surface modifier. You can find this modifier and an example in Chapter 27, "Modeling with Patches and NURBS." The surface tools are similar in many ways to the Loft compound object, which is covered in Chapter 26, "Working with Compound Objects."

Summary

As this chapter has shown, there is much more to splines than just points, lines, and control handles. Splines in Max are one of the fundamental building blocks and the pathway to advanced modeling skills using NURBS.

This chapter covered the following spline topics:

- Understanding the various shape primitives
- Editing splines
- Working with the various spline subobjects
- Applying modifiers to splines

The next chapter continues our voyage down the modeling pathway with perhaps the most common modeling types — meshes and polys.

Chapter 12

Modeling with Polygons

Meshes (or, more specifically, polygon meshes) are perhaps the most popular and the default model type for most 3D programs. You create them by placing polygonal faces next to one another so the edges are joined. The polygons can then be smoothed from face to face during the rendering process. Using meshes, you can create almost any 3D object, including simple primitives such as a cube or a realistic dinosaur.

Meshes have lots of advantages. They are common, intuitive to work with, and supported by a large number of 3D software packages. In this chapter, you learn how to create and edit mesh and poly objects.

Understanding Poly Objects

Before continuing, you need to understand exactly what a Poly object is, how it differs from a regular mesh object, and why it is the featured modeling type in Max. To understand these issues, you'll need a quick history lesson. Initially, Max supported only mesh objects and all mesh objects had to be broken down into triangular faces. Subdividing the mesh into triangular faces ensured that all faces in the mesh object were coplanar, which prevented any hiccups with the rendering engine.

Over time, the rendering engines have been modified and upgraded to handle polygons that weren't subdivided (or whose subdivision was invisible to the user), and doing such actually makes the model more efficient by eliminating all the extra edges required to triangulate the mesh. Also, users can work with polygon objects more easily than individual faces. To take advantage of these new features, the Editable Poly object was added to Max.

As development has continued, many new features have been added to the Editable Poly object while the Editable Mesh remained mainly for backwards compatibility. The one advantage that the Editable Mesh object had over the

IN THIS CHAPTER

Creating Editable Poly objects

Working with the poly subobject modes

Editing poly geometry

Changing surface properties like NURMS

Editable Poly was that the Edit Mesh modifier could be applied, but as of version 7, Max has an Edit Poly modifier, which lets you make changes to an object as a modifier that can easily be removed.

Even with the addition of the Edit Poly modifier, the Editable Mesh object type still exists, and there are times when you'll want to use each type, shown in Figure 12.1. Editable Mesh objects split all polygons into triangular faces, but the Editable Poly object maintains four-sided (or more) polygon faces. Another key difference is found in the subobjects. Editable Meshes can work with Vertex, Edge, Face, Polygon, and Element subobjects; and Editable Poly objects can work with Vertex, Edge, Border, Polygon, and Element subobjects.

Some game engines still require that all faces be coplanar, and for such conditions you'll want to continue to use the Editable Mesh object. Another case where the Editable Mesh object is helpful is in performing certain face-oriented operations. In addition, normal meshes have a smaller memory footprint, which enables them to render more quickly, especially if you have many of them. Regardless, Max lets you convert seamlessly between these two modeling types.

Although many of the same features are available for both object types, the advance features available for the Editable Poly object make it the preferred object type to use for mesh modeling. This chapter focuses on working with Editable Poly objects. Although the specific features of the Editable Mesh object aren't covered, most of these same commands apply equally to the Editable Mesh object.

FIGURE 12.1

Editable Mesh objects have triangular faces; the Editable Poly object uses faces with four or more vertices.

Editable Mesh object　　　　　　Editable Poly object

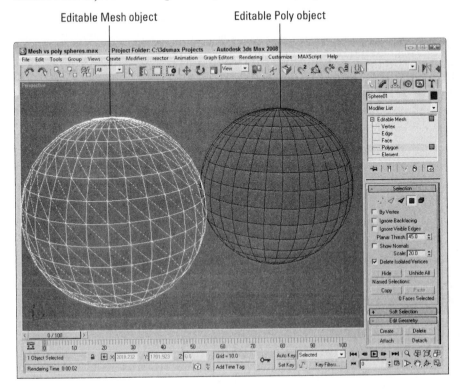

Creating Editable Poly Objects

The Create panel has no method for making mesh objects — mesh objects must be converted from another object type or produced as the result of a modifier. Object types that you can convert include shapes, primitives, Booleans, patches, and NURBS. Many models that are imported appear as mesh objects. Most 3D formats, including 3DS and DXF, import as mesh objects.

NOTE You can even convert spline shapes to editable poly objects, whether they are open or closed. Closed splines are filled with a polygon, whereas open splines are only a single edge and can be hard to see.

Before you can use many of the mesh editing functions discussed in this chapter, you need to convert the object to an Editable Poly object, collapse an object with modifiers applied, or apply the Edit Poly modifier.

Converting objects

To convert an object into an Editable Poly object, right-click the object and choose Convert To ➪ Convert to Editable Poly from the pop-up quadmenu. You can also convert an object by right-clicking the object within the Modifier Stack and selecting one of the convert options from the pop-up menu.

Collapsing to a mesh object

When an object is collapsed, it loses its parametric nature and the parameters associated with any applied modifiers. Only objects that have had modifiers applied to them can be collapsed. Objects are made into an Editable Poly object when you use the Collapse To option available from the right-click pop-up menu in the Modifier Stack or when you use the Collapse utility.

TIP You can also collapse objects using the Collapse utility found in the Utilities panel.

Most objects collapse to Editable Poly objects, but some objects, such as the compound objects, give you an option of which structure to collapse to.

Applying the Edit Poly modifier

Another way to enable the mesh editing features is to apply the Edit Poly modifier to an object. You apply this modifier by selecting the object and choosing Modifiers ➪ Mesh Editing ➪ Edit Poly, or selecting Edit Poly from the Modifier drop-down list in the Modify panel.

The Edit Poly modifier is different from the Editable Poly object in that, as an applied modifier, it maintains the parametric nature of the original object. For example, you cannot change the Radius value of a sphere object that has been converted to an Editable Poly, but you could if the Edit Poly modifier were applied.

Editing Poly Objects

After an object has been converted to an Editable Poly, you can alter its shape by applying modifiers, or you can work with the mesh subobjects. You can find the editing features for these objects in the Modify panel.

CROSS-REF Each of the mesh related modifiers are covered in Chapter 25, "Deforming Surfaces and Using the Mesh Modifiers."

Editable Poly subobject modes

Before you can edit poly subobjects, you must select them. To select a subobject mode, select Editable Poly in the Modifier Stack, click the small plus sign to its left to display a hierarchy of subobjects, and then click the subobject type with which you want to work. Another way to select a subobject type is to click on the appropriate subobject button in the Selection rollout. The subobject button in the Selection rollout and the subobject listed in the Modifier Stack both turn bright yellow when selected. You can also type a number from 1 to 5 to enter subobject mode with 1 for Vertex, 2 for Edge, 3 for Border, 4 for Polygon, and 5 for Element.

The Vertex subobject mode lets you select and work with all vertices in the object. Edge subobject mode makes all edges that run between two vertices available for selection. The Border subobject mode lets you select all edges that run around an opening in the object such as a hole. The Polygon subobject mode lets you work with individual polygon faces and the Element subobject mode picks individual objects if the object includes several different elements.

To exit subobject edit mode, click the subobject button (displayed in yellow) again. Remember, you must exit this mode before you can select another object.

NOTE Selected subobject edges appear in the viewports in red to distinguish them from edges of the selected object, which appear white when displayed as wireframes.

After you're in a subobject mode, you can click on a subobject (or drag over an area to select multiple subobjects) to select it and edit the subobject using the transformation buttons on the main toolbar. You can transform subobjects just like other objects.

CROSS-REF For more information on transforming objects, see Chapter 7, "Transforming Objects, Pivoting, Aligning, and Snapping."

When working with Editable Poly objects in subobject mode, you can use Press and Release keyboard shortcuts. These shortcuts are identified in bold in the Editable Poly group of the Keyboard panel of the Customize User Interface dialog box. When using these keyboard shortcuts, you can access a different editing mode without having to exit subobject mode. For example, if you press and hold Alt+C while in Polygon subobject mode, you can make a cut with the Cut tool and when you release the keyboard keys, you'll return to Polygon subobject mode.

CROSS-REF You can learn more about the Customize User Interface dialog box in Chapter 4, "Customizing the Max Interface and Setting Preferences."

You can select multiple subobjects at the same time by dragging an outline over them. You can also select multiple subobjects by holding down the Ctrl key while clicking them. The Ctrl key can also deselect selected subobjects while maintaining the rest of the selection. Holding down the Alt key removes any selected vertices from the current selection set.

With one of the transform buttons selected, hold down the Shift key while clicking and dragging on a subobject to clone it. During cloning, the Clone Part of Mesh dialog box appears, enabling you to Clone to Object or Clone to Element. Using the Clone to Object option makes the selection an entirely new object, and you are able to give the new object a name. If the Clone to Element option is selected, the clone remains part of the existing object but is a new element within that object.

If you hold down the Ctrl key while choosing a different subobject mode, the current selection is maintained for the new subobject type. For example, if you select all the polygons in the top half of a model using the Polygon subobject mode and click the Vertex subobject mode while holding down the Ctrl key, all vertices in the top half of the model are selected. This works only for the applicable subobjects. If the selection of polygons doesn't have any borders, then holding down the Ctrl key while clicking the Border subobject mode selects nothing.

You also can hold down the Shift key to select only those subobjects that lie on the borders of the current selection. For example, selecting all the polygons in the top half of a model using the Polygon subobject mode and clicking the Vertex subobject mode with the Shift key held down selects only those vertices that surround the selection and not the interior vertices.

Selection rollout

The Selection rollout, shown in Figure 12.2, includes options for selecting subobjects. The By Vertex option is available in all but the Vertex subobject mode. It requires that you click a vertex in order to select an edge, border, polygon, or element. It selects all edges and borders that are connected to a vertex when the vertex is selected. The Ignore Backfacing option selects only those subobjects with normals pointing toward the current viewport. For example, if you are trying to select some faces on a sphere, only the faces on the side closest to you are selected. If this option is off, then faces on both sides of the sphere are selected. This option is helpful if many subobjects are on top of one another in the viewport.

> **TIP** The select commands in the Edit menu also work with subobjects. For example, in Vertex subobject mode, you can select Edit ⇨ Select All (or press Ctrl+A) to select all vertices.

FIGURE 12.2

The Selection rollout includes options for determining which subobjects are selected.

The By Angle option selects adjacent polygons that are within the specified threshold. The threshold value is defined as the angle between the normals of adjacent polygons. For example, if you have a terrain mesh with a smooth, flat lake area in its middle, you can select the entire lake area if you set the Planar Threshold to 0 and click the lake.

The Selection rollout also includes four buttons. These buttons include Shrink, Grow, Ring, and Loop. Use the Grow button to increase the current selection around the perimeter of the current selection, as shown in Figure 12.3. Click the Shrink button to do the opposite.

The Ring and Loop buttons are available only in Edge and Border subobject modes. Use Ring and Loop to select all adjacent subobjects horizontally and vertically around the entire object. Ring selection looks for parallel edges, and Loop selection looks for all edges around an object that are aligned the same as the initial selection. For example, if you select a single edge of a sphere, the Ring button selects all edges going around the sphere and the Loop button selects all edges in a line from the top to the bottom of the sphere.

FIGURE 12.3

Using the Grow button, you can increase the subobject selection.

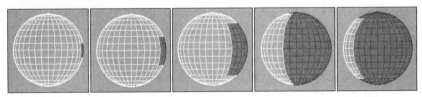

Next to the Ring and Loop buttons is a set of up/down arrows. These arrows are used to shift the current ring and/or loop selection left and right for the Ring selection, or up and down for the Loop selection. Holding down the Ctrl key adds the adjacent ring or loop to the current selection, and holding down the Alt key removes the adjacent selection. Figure 12.4 shows how the Ring and Loop buttons work. The first sphere shows a selection made using the Ring button; the second sphere has increased this selection by holding down the Ctrl key while clicking the up arrow next to the Loop button. The third sphere shows a selection made using the Loop button; the fourth sphere has increased this selection by holding down the Ctrl key while clicking the up arrow next to the Ring button.

FIGURE 12.4

The Ring and Loop buttons can select an entire row and/or column of edges.

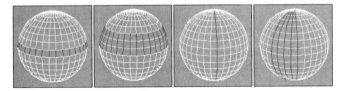

NOTE For Editable Poly objects, the Hide Selected, Unhide All, Copy, and Paste buttons are located at the bottom of the Edit Geometry rollout.

CROSS-REF The Soft Selection rollout allows you to alter adjacent non-selected subobjects when selected subobjects are moved, creating a smooth transition. For the details on this rollout, see Chapter 10, "Learning Modeling Basics and Working with Subobjects and Helpers."

The Preview Selection options let you quickly move among the different subobject modes by selecting the highlighted subobject in the viewports. When the SubObj preview option is enabled, the subobjects for the current mode are highlighted as you move the cursor over the object. For example, if you have Polygon subobject mode selected and the SubObj preview option enabled, moving the mouse cursor over the top of each polygon automatically highlights the polygon that the cursor is over. This provides vital feedback for ensuring that you are selecting the correct subobject.

Also while this preview mode is on, you can highlight multiple subobjects by holding down the Ctrl key while you move the mouse over the top of the object. This gives you an easy way to paint a selection. If you click when multiple subobjects are highlighted, then all the highlighted subobjects are selected.

NEW FEATURE The ability to interactively select multiple subobjects in the same mode is new to 3ds Max 2008.

Even if you like the SubObj previewing option, the Multi previewing option is even better, allowing Vertex, Edge, and Polygon subobjects to be highlighted as you move the cursor about. If you're in Polygon subobject mode and you select the highlighted edge subobject, Max automatically switches to Edge subobject mode. This previewing option lets you select any kind of subobject without having to switch to the different subobject modes using the Command Panel or a keyboard shortcut.

Holding down the Ctrl key locks you into the current subobject and lets you paint to highlight multiple subobject.

NOTE The space at the very bottom of the Selection rollout shows the number of subobjects currently selected or the number of the single selected subobject. It also lists the specific subobject that is highlighted.

Tutorial: Modeling a clown head

Now that you know how to select subobjects, you can use the transform tools to move them. In this example, you'll quickly deform a sphere to create a clown face by selecting, moving, and working with some vertices.

To create a clown head by moving vertices, follow these steps:

1. Select Create ➪ Standard Primitives ➪ Sphere, and drag in the Front viewport to create a sphere object. Then right-click the sphere, and select Convert To ➪ Editable Poly in the pop-up quad-menu.

2. Open the Modify panel. Now make a long, pointy nose by pulling a vertex outward from the sphere object. Click the small plus sign to the left of the Editable Poly object in the Modifier Stack, and select Vertex in the hierarchy (or press the 1 key). This activates the Vertex subobject mode. Enable the Ignore Backfacing option in the Selection rollout, and select the single vertex in the center of the Front viewport. Make sure that the Select and Move button (W) is selected, and in the Left viewport, drag the vertex along the Z-axis until it projects from the sphere.

3. Next, create the mouth by selecting and indenting a row of vertices in the Front viewport below the protruding nose. Holding down the Ctrl key makes selecting multiple vertices easy. Below the nose, select several vertices in a circular arc that make a smile. Then move the selected vertices along the negative Z-axis in the Left viewport.

4. For the eyes, select Create ➪ Standard Primitives ➪ Sphere and enable the AutoGrid option. Then drag in the Front viewport to create two eyes above the nose.

This clown head is just a simple example of what is possible by editing subobjects. Figure 12.5 shows the clown head in a shaded view.

Edit Geometry rollout

Much of the power of editing meshes is contained within the Edit Geometry rollout, shown in Figure 12.6. Features contained here include, among many others, the ability to create new subobjects, attach subobjects to the mesh, weld vertices, chamfer vertices, slice, explode, and align. Some Edit Geometry buttons are disabled depending on the subobject mode that you select. The features detailed in this section are enabled for the Editable Poly object before you enter a subobject mode.

FIGURE 12.5

A clown head created from an editable poly by selecting and moving vertices

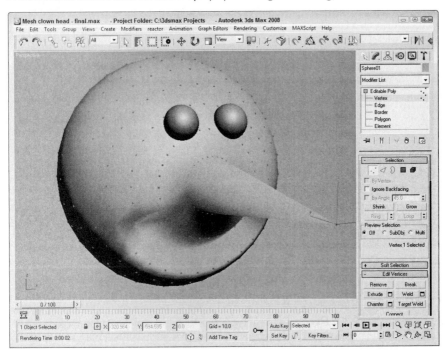

FIGURE 12.6

The Edit Geometry rollout includes many general-purpose editing features.

Many of the buttons for the Editable Poly include a small icon to the right of the button that opens a settings dialog box. These settings dialog boxes allow you to change the settings and immediately see the results in the viewports. The OK button applies the settings and closes the dialog box, and the Apply button applies the settings and leaves the dialog box open. These settings dialog boxes are included next to the Preserve UVs, Attach, MSmooth, Tessellate, and Relax buttons for all subobject modes and next to many of the subobject-specific buttons such as Extrude, Bevel, Outline, and Inset.

Editable Poly objects include all their common buttons in the Edit Geometry rollout and all subobject-specific buttons is a separate rollout named after the subobject mode, such as Edit Vertices or Edit Edges.

Repeat Last

The first button in the Edit Geometry rollout is the Repeat Last button. This button repeats the last subobject command. This button does not work on all features, but it's very convenient for certain actions.

 The tooltip for this button displays the last repeatable command.

Enabling constraints

The Constraints options limit the movement of subobjects to a specified subobject. The available constraints are None, Edge, Face, and Normal. For example, if you select and move a vertex with the Edge constraint enabled, then the movement is constrained to the adjacent edges.

NEW FEATURE The Normal constraint is new to 3ds Max 2008.

Tutorial: Creating a roof truss

When creating houses, modeling the roof can be tricky, but using an edge constraint makes it much easier.

To create a triangular roof truss, follow these steps:

1. Select Create ➪ Standard Primitives ➪ Box, and drag in the Top viewport to create a Box object centered over the Y-axis.
2. Right-click the box object, and select Convert To ➪ Editable Poly in the pop-up quadmenu.
3. Open the Modify panel, and choose the Vertex subobject mode. In the Constraints drop-down list of the Edit Geometry panel, select the Edge option.
4. With the Select and Move tool, drag over the top-left corners and drag them to the Y-axis; then repeat for the top-right corners.

Notice that the points are constrained to the top edge as they are dragged. Moving both sets of points results in a simple perfect triangle.

 An even easier way to create such a triangle would be to use the Gengon primitive found among the Extended Primitives.

Preserve UVs

UV coordinates define how a texture map is applied to an object's surface. These UV coordinates are tied closely to the surface subobject positions, so moving a subobject after a texture is applied moves the texture also. This could cause discontinuities to the texture map. The Preserve UVs option lets you make subobject changes without altering the UV coordinates for an existing texture.

The Settings dialog box for the Preserve UVs option lets you select a Vertex Color and Texture Channel to preserve. Figure 12.7 shows two block objects with a brick texture map applied. The inner vertices on the left block were scaled outward without the Preserve UVs option selected; the right block had this option enabled.

FIGURE 12.7

The Preserve UVs option lets you make subobject changes after texture maps have been applied.

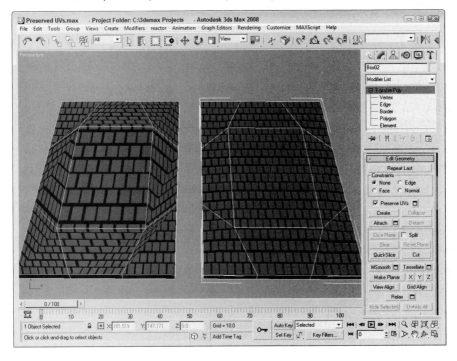

Create

The Create button lets you create new subobjects, specifically polygons, by connecting isolated vertices and border vertices. When the cursor is over a valid vertex, it changes to a crosshair, and you can click to create a polygon edge from the last clicked point. If no vertices are available, you can Shift click to create one. This creates a vertex where you click. Be aware that creating a vertex doesn't add it to any of the edges, but the Create button in Edge subobject mode can connect edges to these isolated vertices.

NEW FEATURE The ability to use snapping in Polygon Create mode is new to 3ds Max 2008.

TIP As you create new polygons, the normal is determined by the direction in which you create the polygon using the right-hand rule. If you bend the fingers of your right hand in the direction (clockwise or counterclockwise) that the vertices are clicked, then your thumb will point in the direction of the normal. If the normal is pointing away from you, then the backside of the polygon will be visible and the lighting could be off.

You can use the Create button to create new polygons based on new or existing vertices. To create a new face, click the Create button, which highlights all vertices in the selected mesh. Next, click a vertex to start the polygon; after you click two more vertices, a new face is created. You can also create a new vertex not based on any existing vertices by holding down the Shift key while clicking.

Polygons aren't limited to three vertices. You can click as many times as you want to add additional vertices to the polygon. Click the first vertex, or double-click to complete the polygon.

Collapse

The Collapse button is used to collapse all the selected subobjects to a single subobject located at the averaged center of the selection. This button is similar to the Weld button, except that the selected vertices don't need to be within a Threshold value to be combined. This button works in all subobject modes.

Attach and Detach

The Attach button is available with all subobject modes and even when you are not in subobject mode. Use the Attach button to add objects to the current Editable Poly object. You can add primitives, splines, patch objects, and other mesh objects. Any object attached to a mesh object is automatically converted into an editable poly and inherits the object color of the object to which it is attached. Any objects added to a poly object can be selected individually using the Element subobject mode.

CAUTION If you attach an object that is smoothed using NURMS, the NURMS are lost when the object is attached.

To use this feature, select the main object and click the Attach button. Move the mouse over the object to be attached; the cursor changes over acceptable objects. Click the object to select it. Click the Attach button again or right-click in the viewport to exit Attach mode.

NOTE If the object that you click to attach already has a material applied that is different from the current Editable Poly object, then a dialog box appears giving you options to Match Material IDs to Material, Match Material to Material IDs, or Do Not Modify Material IDs or Material. Materials and Material IDs are discussed in more detail in Chapter 14, "Exploring the Material Editor."

Clicking the Attach List button opens the Attach List dialog box (which looks just like the Select Objects (H) dialog box) where you can select from a list of all the objects to attach. The list contains only objects that you can attach.

NOTE When you enter a subobject mode, the Attach List button changes to a Detach button for poly objects.

Attaching objects is different from grouping objects because all attached objects act as a single object with the same object color, name, and transforms. You can access individual attached objects using the Element subobject mode.

Use the Detach button to separate the selected subobjects from the rest of the object. To use this button, select the subobject and click the Detach button. The Detach dialog box opens, enabling you to name the new detached subobject. You also have the options to Detach to Element or to Detach as Clone. All subobject modes except Edge have a Detach option. This button appears in place of the Attach List button in all subobject modes.

Slicing and cutting options

The Slice Plane button lets you split the poly object along a plane. When you click the Slice Plane button, a yellow slice plane gizmo appears on the selected object. You can move, rotate, and scale this gizmo using the transform buttons. After you properly position the plane and set all options, click the Slice button to finish slicing the mesh. All intersected faces split in two, and new vertices and edges are added to the mesh where the Slice Plane intersects the original mesh.

The Slice Plane mode stays active until you deselect the Slice Plane button or until you right-click in the viewport; this feature enables you to make several slices in one session. The Slice Plane button is enabled for all subobject modes. For the Editable Poly object, a Reset Plane button is located next to the Slice Plane button. Use this button to reset the slice plane to its original location. You use the Split option to double the number of vertices and edges along the Slice Plane, so each side can be separated from the other. When used in Element mode, the Split option breaks the sliced object into two separate elements.

The QuickSlice button lets you click anywhere on an Editable Poly object where you want a slicing line to be located. You can then move the mouse, and the QuickSlice line rotates about the point you clicked on. When you click the mouse again, a new vertex is added at every place where the QuickSlice line intersects an object edge. This is a very convenient tool for slicing objects because the slice line follows the surface of the object, so you can see exactly where the slice will take place.

For the QuickSlice and Cut tools, you can enable the Full Interactivity option (located near the bottom of the Edit Geometry rollout). With this option enabled, the slice lines are shown as you move the mouse about the surface. With Full Interactivity disabled, the resulting lines are shown only when the mouse is clicked.

For Editable Poly objects, the Cut button is interactive. If you click a polygon corner, the cut edge snaps to the corner, and a new edge extends from the corner to a nearby corner. As you move the mouse around, the edge moves until you click where the edge should end. If you click in the middle of an edge or face, then new edges appear to the nearest corner.

Tutorial: Combining, cutting and separating a car model

When dealing with a model that includes interior parts, you may want to slice the object and separate a portion to reveal the interior. Although this can be accomplished using a camera clipping plane, which is explained in Chapter 18, "Configuring and Aiming Cameras," a more permanent solution uses the QuickSlice and Detach operations.

To combine, slice, and detach a car model, follow these steps:

1. Open the Sliced car.max file from the Chap 12 directory on the DVD.

2. Before you can slice the car, you'll need to combine the entire car into a single Editable Poly object. Select one of the body parts, right-click on it, and select the Convert To ➪ Editable Poly in the pop-up quadmenu.

3. Open the Modify panel, and click on the dialog box icon next to the Attach button in the Edit Geometry rollout.

4. In the Attach List dialog box that opens, click the All button and select the Attach button. In the Attach Options dialog box that appears, select the Match Material IDs to Material option and click OK.

   All objects are now combined into a single Editable Poly object.

5. Click the QuickSlice button, and click in the Top viewport at the point where you want to slice the car. Then drag to align the slicing plane, and click again to make the slice. Click on the QuickSlice button again to exit QuickSlice mode.

6. Select the Polygon subobject mode, and drag over all the polygons below the slice line in the Top viewport. Then click the Detach button in the Edit Geometry rollout. In the Detach dialog box, enter the name **Car Front** and click the OK button.

7. Disable Polygon subobject mode, and use the Select and Move tool to separate the car front from the rest of the car.

Figure 12.8 shows the separated car front.

FIGURE 12.8

Using the Attach, QuickSlice, and Detach features, you can slice and separate mode parts.

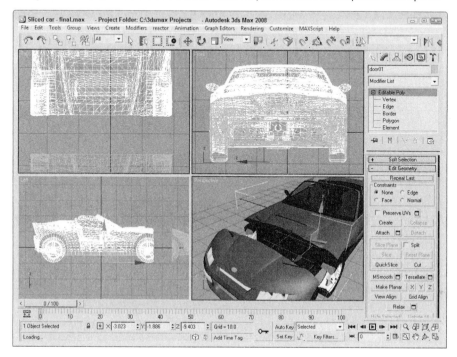

MSmooth

Both the MSmooth and Tessellate buttons include new settings dialog boxes, as shown in Figure 12.9. The MSmooth setting for Smoothness rounds all the sharp edges of an object. Tessellation can be done using Edges or Faces, and the Tension setting controls how tight the adjacent faces are.

FIGURE 12.9

The Settings dialog boxes for the MSmooth and Tessellate buttons let you interactively set the Smoothness and Tension values.

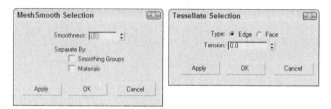

The MSmooth button can be used to smooth the selected subobjects in the same way as the MeshSmooth modifier. This button can be used several times. The Smoothness value determines which vertices are used to smooth the object. The higher the value, the more vertices are included and the smoother the result. You can also select that the smoothing is separated by Smoothing Groups or by Materials.

Figure 12.10 shows a simple diamond-shaped hedra that has been MeshSmoothed using the MSmooth button and then tessellated three consecutive times.

FIGURE 12.10

Using MSmooth reduces the sharp edges, and tessellating adds more editable faces.

Tessellate

Tessellation is used to increase the density of the faces or edges. When modeling, you may want more details in a select area. This is where the tessellation command comes in. Tessellation can be applied to individual selected subobjects or to the entire object.

You can use the Tessellate button to increase the resolution of a mesh by splitting a face or polygon into several faces or polygons. You have two options to do this: Edge and Face.

The Edge method splits each edge at its midpoint. For example, a triangular face would be split into three smaller triangles. The Tension spinner to the right of the Tessellate button specifies a value that is used to make the tessellated face concave or convex.

The Face option creates a vertex in the center of the face and also creates three new edges, which extend from the center vertex to each original vertex. For a square polygon, this option would create six new triangular faces. (Remember, a square polygon is actually composed of two triangular faces.)

Figure 12.11 shows the faces of a cube that has been tessellated once using the Edge option and then again using the Face-Center option.

Make Planar

A single vertex or two vertices don't define a plane, but three or more vertices do. If three or more vertices are selected, you can use the Make Planar button to make these vertices coplanar (which means that all vertices are on the same plane). Doing so positions the selected vertices so that they lie in the same plane. This is helpful if you want to build a new polygon face. Polygonal faces need to be coplanar. This button works in all subobject modes. The X, Y, and Z buttons let you collapse the current object or subobject selection to a single plane lying on the specified axis.

View and Grid Align

The View and Grid Align buttons move and orient all selected vertices to the current active viewport or to the current construction grid. These buttons can also be used in all subobject modes. This causes all the selected face normals to point directly at the grid or view.

FIGURE 12.11

A cube tessellated twice, using each option once

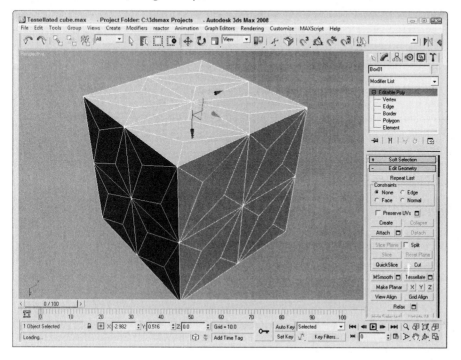

Relax

The Relax button works just like the Relax modifier by moving vertices so they are as far as possible from their adjacent vertices according to the Amount value listed in the Settings dialog box. The Settings dialog box also includes an Iterations value, which determines the number of times the operation is performed. You can also select to hold all Boundary and Outer points from being moved.

Hide, Copy, and Paste

The Hide button hides the selected subobjects. You can make hidden objects visible again with the Unhide All button.

After selecting several subobjects, you can create a named selection set by typing a name in the Name Selection Sets drop-down list in the main toolbar. You can then copy and paste these selection sets onto other shapes.

At the bottom of the Selection rollout is the Selection Information, which is a text line that automatically displays the number and subobject type of selected items.

Editing Vertex subobjects

When working with the Editable Poly objects, after you select a Vertex subobject mode (keyboard shortcut, 1) and select vertices, you can transform them using the transform buttons on the main toolbar. All vertex-specific commands are found within the Edit Vertices rollout.

Remove

The Remove button lets you delete the selected vertices. The Remove button automatically adjusts the surrounding subobjects to maintain the mesh integrity.

 **You can also delete Editable Poly subobjects using the Delete key.**

Figure 12.12 shows a sphere object with several vertex subobjects selected. The middle image is an Editable Mesh that used the Delete feature, and the right image is an Editable Poly that used the Remove feature.

FIGURE 12.12

Deleting vertices also deletes the adjoining faces and edges, but Remove maintains the mesh.

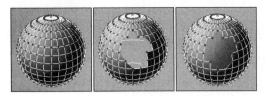

The Remove button also is available in Edge subobject mode. If you hold down the Ctrl key when clicking the Remove button when an edge is selected, vertices at either end of the deleted edge are also removed.

Break

You use the Break button to create a separate vertex for adjoining faces that are connected by a single vertex.

In a normal mesh, faces are all connected by vertices: Moving one vertex changes the position of all adjoining faces. The Break button enables you to move the vertex associated with each face independent of the others. The button is available only in Vertex subobject mode.

Figure 12.13 shows a Hedra object. The Break button was used to separate the center vertex into separate vertices for each face. The face vertices can be manipulated independently, as the figure shows.

Extrude

The Extrude button copies and moves the selected subobject perpendicular a given distance and connects the new copy with the original one. For example, four edges forming a square extruded would form a box with no lid. To use this feature, select an edge or edges, click the Extrude button, and then drag in a viewport. The edges interactively show the extrude depth. Release the button when you've reached the desired distance.

Alternatively, you can set an extrude depth in the Extrusion spinner. The Group option extrudes all selected edges in the direction of the average of all the normals for the group (the normal runs perpendicular to the face) and the Normal Local option moves each individual edge along its local normal. For polygons, you can extrude By Polygons, which extrudes each individual polygon along its normal as a separate extrusion. To exit Extrude mode, click the Extrude button again or right-click in the viewport.

The Extrude button is enabled for Face, Polygon, and Element subobject modes for the Editable Poly object. Figure 12.14 shows a GeoSphere object with all edges selected and extruded. The Group Normal option averages all the normals and extrudes the edges in the averaged direction. The Local Normal option extrudes each edge along its own normal.

FIGURE 12.13

You can use the Break button to give each face its own vertex.

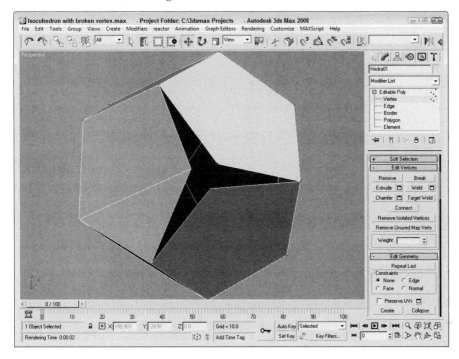

The Extrude settings dialog box includes options for setting the Extrusion Height and the Extrusion Base Width.

FIGURE 12.14

Subobjects can be extruded along an averaged normal or locally.

Weld and Chamfer

Vertices and edges that are close or on top of one another can be combined together into one using the Weld command. The Weld and Chamfer buttons include settings dialog boxes that let you interactively see the results of different settings. The Weld settings dialog box includes a weld Threshold value and displays the number of vertices before and after the welding process, which is very useful to check whether a weld was successful.

 **If you run into trouble with the Weld button and its Threshold value, try using the Collapse button.**

The Target Weld button lets you click on a single vertex and move the cursor over an adjacent vertex. A rubber band line stretches from the first selected vertex to the target weld vertex and the cursor changes to indicate that the vertex under the cursor may be selected. Clicking on the target vertex welds the two vertices together.

 **When two vertices are welded, the new vertex is positioned at a location that is halfway between both vertices, but when Target Weld is used, the first vertex is moved to the location of the second.**

The Chamfer button — which is enabled in Vertex, Edge, and Border subobject modes — lets you cut the edge off a corner and replace it with a face. Using the settings dialog box, you can interactively specify a Chamfer Amount and the number of segments. The settings dialog box also includes an Open option, which cuts a hole in the polygon face instead of replacing it with a new polygon. Figure 12.15 shows two plane objects that have been chamfered with the Open option enabled. The left plane had all its interior vertices selected, and the right plane had a selection of interior edges selected.

NEW FEATURE **The option to add more than one segment to a Chamfer is new to 3ds Max 2008.**

Connect

The Connect button can be used to add new edges to subobjects. In Vertex subobject mode, the button connects vertices on the opposite side of a face. In Edge and Border subobject mode, the button makes a settings dialog box available, which includes a setting to Connect Edge Segments. This value is the number of edge segments to add between the selected edges or borders. It also includes Pinch and Slide values. The Pinch value moves the segments closer or farther away from each other; the Slide value moves the segments along the original edge.

Remove Isolated and Unused Map Vertices

The Remove Isolated Vertices button deletes all isolated vertices. Vertices become isolated by some operations and add unneeded data to your file. You can search and delete them quickly with this button. Good examples of isolated vertices are those created using the Create button but never attached to an edge.

The Remove Unused Map Vertices button removes any leftover mapping vertices from the object.

Weight and Crease

The Weight settings control the amount of pull that a vertex has when NURMS subdivision or a MeshSmooth modifier is used. The higher the Weight value, the more resistant a vertex is to smoothing. For edge and border subobjects, the Weight value is followed by a Crease value that determines how visible the edge is when the mesh is smoothed. A value of 1.0 ensures that the crease is visible.

FIGURE 12.15

Enabling the Open option in the Chamfer settings dialog box removes a polygon instead of replacing it.

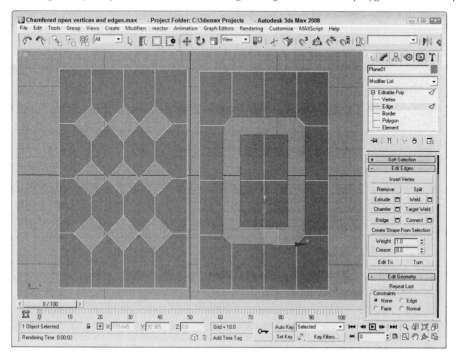

Editing Edge subobjects

Edges are the lines that run between two vertices. Edges can be *closed*, which means that each side of the edge is connected to a face, or *open*, which means that only one face connects to the edge. When a hole exists in a mesh, all edges that are adjacent to the hole are open edges. Mesh edges, such as in the interior of a shape that has been converted to a mesh, can also be *invisible*. These invisible edges appear as dotted lines that run across the face of the polygon.

You can select multiple edges by holding down either the Ctrl key while clicking the edges or the Alt key to remove selected edges from the selection set. You can also copy edges using the Shift key while transforming the edge. The cloned edge maintains connections to its vertices by creating new edges.

Many of the Edge subobject options work in the same way as the Vertex subobject options.

Split and Insert Vertex

The Split button adds a new vertex at the middle of the edge and splits the edge into two equal sections. This button is handy when you need to increase the resolution of a section quickly.

The Insert Vertex button lets you add a new vertex anywhere along an edge. The cursor changes to crosshairs when it is over an edge. Click to create a vertex. When in Edge, Border, Polygon, or Element subobject mode, this button also makes vertices visible.

Bridge Edges

The Bridge button for edges allows you to create a new set of polygons that connect the selected edges. If two edges are selected when the Bridge button is pressed, then they are automatically connected with a new polygon. If no edges are selected, then you can click the edges to bridge after clicking the Bridge button. The selected edges on either side of the bridge can be different in number.

You also can access the settings dialog box for the Bridge feature. This dialog box offers the options to Bridge Specific Edges or to Use Edge Selection. The Bridge Specific Edges option has two buttons for each edge. If you click one of these buttons, you can select an edge in the viewport. The Use Edge Selection option lets you drag a marquee in the viewport to select the edges. The Bridge Edges dialog box also includes options for setting the number of Segments, the Smooth value, and a Bridge Adjacent value, which increases the triangulation for angles above the given threshold.

Figure 12.16 shows a simple example of some edges that have been bridged. The letters before bridging are on the top and after bridging on the bottom.

FIGURE 12.16
_____

Selecting two opposite edges and clicking the Bridge button in Edge subobject mode creates new connecting polygons.

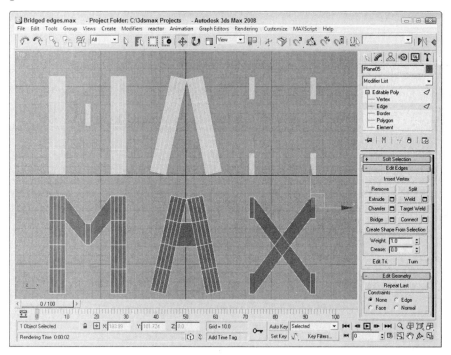

Create Shape from Selection

The Create Shape from Selection button creates a new spline shape from selected edges. The Create Shape dialog box appears, shown in Figure 12.17, enabling you to give the new shape a name. You can also select options for Smooth or Linear shape types.

FIGURE 12.17

The Create Shape dialog box lets you name shapes created from selected edge subobjects.

Edit Triangulation

For the Editable Poly object, the Edge, Border, Polygon, and Element subobjects include the Edit Triangulation button. The Edit Triangulation button lets you change the internal edges of the polygon by dragging from one vertex to another. When this button is clicked, all hidden edges appear. To edit the hidden edges, just click a vertex and then click again where you want the hidden edge to go. If you're dealing with multiple four-sided polygons, then the Turn button is quicker.

Turn

The Turn button rotates the hidden edges that break up the polygon into triangles (all polygonal faces include these hidden edges). For example, if a quadrilateral (four-sided) face has a hidden edge that runs between vertices 1 and 3, then the Turn button changes this hidden edge to run between vertices 2 and 4. This affects how the surface is smoothed when the polygon is not coplanar.

This button is available for all subobject modes except Vertex. When enabled, all subobjects that you click on are turned until the button is disabled again. Figure 12.18 shows the top face of a Box object with a hidden edge across it diagonally. The Turn button was used to turn this hidden edge.

 **TIP** Surfaces can deform only along places where there are edges, so as you create your models be aware of where you place edges and how the edges flow into one another. When building characters, it is important to have the edges follow the muscle flow to deform properly.

FIGURE 12.18

The Turn feature is used to change the direction of edges.

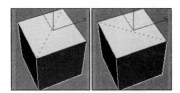

Editing Border subobjects

Editable Poly objects do not need the Face subobject that is found in the Editable Mesh objects because they support polygon faces. Instead, they have a Border subobject. Border subobjects are polygons with no faces that are actually holes within the geometry.

Cap

The Cap button causes the existing border selection to be filled in with a single coplanar polygon. After using this feature, the Border subobject is no longer identified as a Border subobject.

Bridge

The Bridge feature joins two selected Border subobjects with a tube of polygons that connect the two borders. The two selected borders must be part of the same object and need not have an equal number of segments.

The Bridge dialog box, shown in Figure 12.19, lets you specify twist values for each edge, the number of segments, and the Taper, Bias, and Smooth values.

FIGURE 12.19

The Bridge dialog box lets you specify options such as the number of segments, the Taper, and whether the bridge twists.

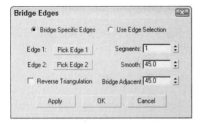

Tutorial: Bridging a forearm

The Bridge tool is great for working with two border selections, allowing you to create a smooth set of polygons that flow between them. For this example, you'll create a forearm by bridging a hi-res hand model with a simple cylinder. The polygons of the hand and the cylinder that are to be joined have already been removed.

To create a forearm object by bridging a cylinder with a hand model, follow these steps:

1. Open the Forearm bridge.max file from the Chap 12 directory on the DVD.
2. With the body parts selected, open the Modify panel, and select the Border subobject mode. Then press and hold the Ctrl key, and click on the borders for the hand and cylinder objects.
3. With both facing Border subobjects selected, click the dialog box icon next to the Bridge button in the Edit Geometry rollout.
4. In the Bridge dialog box, select the Use Border Selection and set the Segments value to **6**. Then click the OK button.

Figure 12.20 shows the resulting forearm object.

FIGURE 12.20

The Bridge feature can be used to quickly connect body parts such as this forearm.

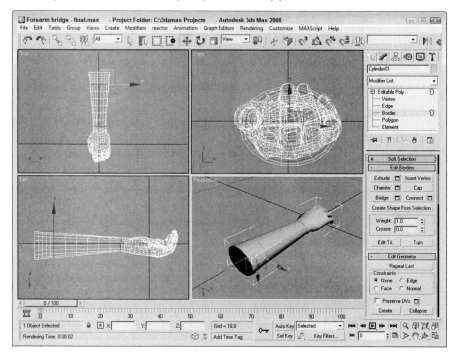

Editing Polygon and Element subobjects

Like the other subobject modes, Editable Polys can be edited at the polygon and element subobject level. The buttons for these modes are found in the Edit Polygons and Edit Elements rollouts.

Outline and Inset

The Outline button offsets the selected polygon a specified amount. This increases the size of the selected polygon or element. The Inset button creates another polygon set within the selected polygon and connects their edges. For both these buttons, a Settings dialog box is available that includes the Outline or Inset Amount values.

Bevel

The Bevel button extrudes the Polygon subobject selection and then lets you bevel the edges. To use this feature, select a polygon, click the Bevel button, drag up or down in a viewport to the Extrusion depth, and release the button. Drag again to specify the Bevel amount. The Bevel amount determines the relative size of the extruded face.

Figure 12.21 displays a poly dodecahedron. Each face has been locally extruded with a value of 20 and then locally beveled with a value of −10.

FIGURE 12.21

The top faces of this dodecahedron have been individually extruded and beveled.

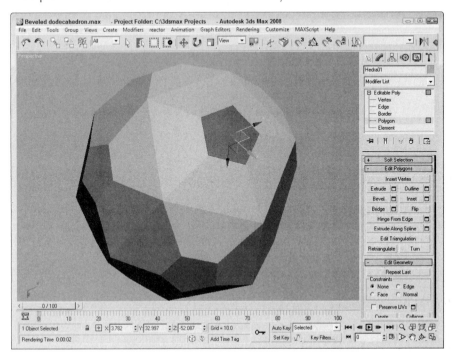

Flip

The Flip button flips the normal vectors for the selected subobjects. The Flip button is available only in Polygon and Element subobject modes.

Retriangulate

The Retriangulate button automatically computes all the internal edges for you for the selected subobjects.

Hinge From Edge

The Hinge From Edge button rotates a selected polygon as if one of its edges were a hinge. The angle of the hinge depends on the distance that you drag with the mouse, or you can use the available settings dialog box. In the settings dialog box, shown in Figure 12.22, you can specify an Angle value and the number of segments to use for the hinged section.

By default, one of the polygon's edges will be used as the hinge about which the section rotates, but in the settings dialog box, you can click the Pick Hinge button and select an edge (which doesn't need to be attached to the polygon). Figure 12.23 shows a sphere primitive with four polygon faces that have been hinged around an edge at the sphere's center.

FIGURE 12.22

The Hinge Polygons From Edge dialog box lets you select a hinge.

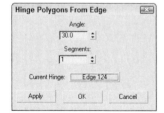

FIGURE 12.23

Several polygon faces in the sphere have been extruded along a hinge.

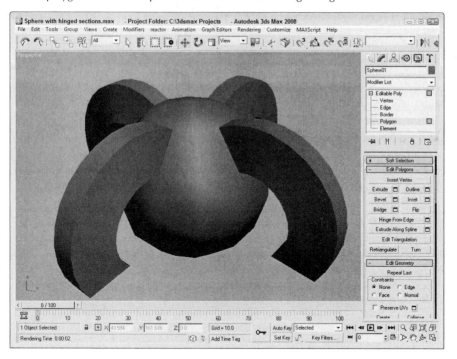

Extrude Along Spline

The Extrude Along Spline button can be used to extrude a selected polygon along the spline path. The settings dialog box, shown in Figure 12.24, includes a Pick Spline button that you can use to select the spline to use. You can also specify the number of segments, the Taper Amount and Curve, and a Twist value. You also have an option to Align the extrusion to the face normal or to rotate about the normal.

FIGURE 12.24

The Extrude Polygons Along Spline settings dialog box

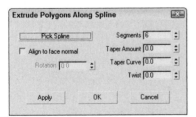

Tutorial: Building an octopus

The one thing about an octopus that makes it unique is the fact that it has eight tentacles. Creating these tentacles can be easily accomplished with the Extrude Along Spline feature.

To create an octopus using the Extrude Along Spline feature, follow these steps:

1. Open the Octopus.max file from the Chap 12 directory on the DVD.

   This file includes the base of an octopus created from a squashed sphere primitive that has been converted to an Editable Poly. Eight splines surround the object.

2. Select the octopus object to automatically open the Modify panel. In the Selection rollout, click the Polygon subobject button (keyboard shortcut, 4) and enable the Ignore Backfacing option in the Selection rollout.

3. Right-click the Perspective viewport title, and select the Edged Faces option from the pop-up menu (or press the F4 key).

   This makes the polygons easier to see.

4. Click a single face object at the base of the sphere object, and click the Extrude Along Spline settings dialog box button to open the Extrude Polygons Along Spline dialog box.

5. Click the Pick Spline button, and select the spline to the side of the face. Set the Segments to **6** and the Taper Amount to **−1.0**, and click the OK button. Make sure that the Align to Face Normal option isn't selected.

6. Repeat Steps 4 and 5 for each spline surrounding the octopus.

7. In the Subdivisions Surface rollout, enable the Use NURMS Subdivision option and set the Display Iterations value to **2** to smooth the entire octopus.

Figure 12.25 shows the resulting octopus.

Surface properties

Below the Edit Geometry rollout are several rollouts of options that enable you to set additional properties such as vertex colors, material IDs, Smoothing Groups, and NURMS Subdivision.

Vertex Surface properties

The Vertex Properties rollout in Vertex subobject mode lets you define the Color, Illumination, and Alpha value of object vertices. The color swatches enable you to select Color and Illumination colors for the selected vertices. The Alpha value sets the amount of transparency for the vertices. After you assign colors, you can then recall vertices with the same color by selecting a color (or illumination color) in the Select Vertices By section and clicking the Select button. The RGB values match all colors within the Range defined by these values.

FIGURE 12.25

The tentacles of this octopus were created easily with the Extrude Along Spline feature.

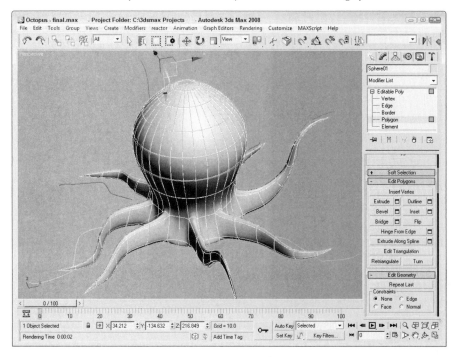

CROSS-REF You can find more information on vertex colors in Chapter 31, "Creating Baked Textures and Normal Maps."

Polygon and Element Surface properties

For Polygon and Element subobjects, the Polygon Properties rollout, shown in Figure 12.26, includes Material IDs and Smoothing Groups options. The Material IDs option settings are used by the Multi/Sub-Object material type to apply different materials to faces or polygons within an object. By selecting a polygon subobject, you can use these option settings to apply a unique material to the selected polygon. The Select ID button selects all subobjects that have the designated Material ID, or you can select subobjects using a material name in the drop-down list under the Select ID button.

CROSS-REF You can find more information on the Multi/Sub-Object material type in Chapter 15, "Creating and Applying Standard Materials."

You use the Smoothing Groups option to assign a subobject to a unique smoothing group. To do this, select a subobject and click a Smoothing Groups number. The Select By SG button, like the Select By ID button, opens a dialog box where you can enter a Smoothing Groups number, and all subobjects with that number are selected. The Clear All button clears all Smoothing Groups number assignments, and the Auto Smooth button automatically assigns Smoothing Groups numbers based on the angle between faces as set by the value to the right of the Auto Smooth button.

The Polygon Properties rollout also includes options for setting vertex Color, Illumination, and Alpha values.

FIGURE 12.26

The Polygon Properties rollout includes settings for Material IDs, Smoothing Groups, and Vertex Colors.

Subdivision Surface

Editable Poly objects include an extra rollout called Subdivision Surface that automatically smoothes the object when enabled. The Subdivision Surface rollout, shown in Figure 12.27, applies a smoothing algorithm known as NURMS, which stands for Non-Uniform Rational Mesh Smooth. It produces similar results to the MSmooth button but offers control over how aggressive the smoothing is applied; the settings can be different for the viewports and the renderer.

To enable NURMS subdivision, you need to enable the Use NURMS Subdivision option. The Smooth Result option places all polygons into the same smoothing group and applies the MeshSmooth to the entire object. Applying NURMS with a high Iterations value results in a very dense mesh, but the Isoline Display option displays a simplified number of edges, making the object easier to work with. The process of smoothing adds many edges to the object, and the Isoline Display option displays only the isolines. The Show Cage option makes the surrounding cage visible or invisible. The two color swatches to the right of the Show Cage option let you set the color of the cage and the selection.

The Iterations value determines how aggressive the smoothing is. The higher the Iterations value, the more time it takes to compute and the more complex the resulting object. The Smoothness value determines how sharp a corner must be before adding extra faces to smooth it. A value of 0 does not smooth any corners, and a maximum value of 1.0 smoothes all polygons.

CAUTION Each smoothing iteration quadruples the number of faces. If you raise the number of Iterations too high, the system can become unstable quickly.

The two check boxes in the Render section can be used to set the values differently for the Display and Render sections. If disabled, then both the viewports and the renderer use the same settings. The smoothing algorithm can be set to ignore smoothing across Smoothing Groups and Materials.

If the Show Cage option is enabled (at the bottom of the Edit Geometry rollout), an orange cage surrounds the NURMS object and shows the position of the polygon faces that exist if NURMS is disabled. This cage makes selecting the polygon faces easier.

FIGURE 12.27

The Subdivision Surface rollout includes controls for NURMS subdivision.

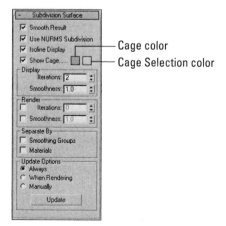
— Cage color
— Cage Selection color

Tutorial: Modeling a tooth

If you've ever had a root canal, then you know how much pain dental work can cause. Luckily, modeling a tooth isn't painful at all, as we see in this example.

To model a tooth using NURMS, follow these steps:

1. Select Create ➪ Standard Primitives ➪ Box, and drag in the Top viewport to create a Box object. Set its dimensions to 140 × 180 × 110 with Segments of 1 × 1 × 1. Then right-click, and select Convert To ➪ Editable Poly from the pop-up quadmenu.

2. Click the Polygon icon in the Selection rollout to enable Polygon subobject mode. Then select the Top viewport, and press B to change it to the Bottom viewport. Then click the box's bottom polygon in the Bottom viewport.

3. Click the Select and Scale button (R), and scale the bottom polygon 10%.

4. Drag over the entire object to select all polygons, and click the Tessellate button once to divide the polygon into more polygons. Then select Edit ➪ Region ➪ Window (or click the Window/Crossing button in the main toolbar) to enable the Window selection method, and drag over the bottom of the Box object in the Left viewport to select just the bottom polygons. Click the Tessellate button again.

5. Select the Vertex subobject mode in the Selection rollout, press and hold the Ctrl key, and select the vertices at the center of each quadrant. Then move these vertices downward in the Left viewport a distance about equal to the height of the Box.

6. Select the Bottom viewport again, and press T to change it back to the Top viewport. Select the single vertex in the center of the polygon with the Ignore Backfacing option enabled in the Selection rollout, and drag it slightly downward in the Left viewport.

7. Disable the Ignore Backfacing option in the Selection rollout, and select the entire second row of vertices in the Left viewport. With the Select and Scale tool, scale these vertices toward the center in the polygon in the Top viewport.

8. In the Subdivision Surface rollout, enable the Use NURMS Subdivision option and set the Iterations value to **2**.

Figure 12.28 shows the completed tooth.

FIGURE 12.28

The organic look for this tooth is accomplished with NURMS.

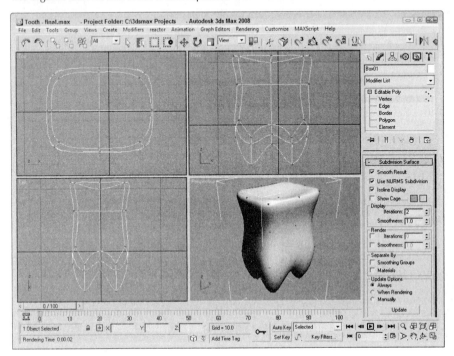

Summary

Meshes are probably the most common 3D modeling types. You can create them by converting objects to Editable Meshes or Editable Poly objects or by collapsing the Stack. Editable Poly objects in Max have a host of features for editing meshes, as you learned in this chapter. More specifically, this chapter covered the following topics:

- Creating Editable Poly objects by converting other objects or applying the Edit Poly modifier
- The features for editing Editable Poly objects
- How to select and use the various mesh subobject modes
- Editing mesh objects using the various features found in the Edit Geometry rollout
- Changing surface properties using features like NURMS

In the next chapter, you learn another excellent tool for deforming mesh objects. Modifiers allow specific types of deformation to be applied to an object such as bending, twisting or rippling a surface.

Chapter 13

Introducing Modifiers and Using the Modifier Stack

Think for a moment of a wood shop, with all its various (and expensive) tools and machines. Some tools are simple, like a screwdriver or a sander, and others, like a planer or router, are more complex, but they all change the wood (or models) in different ways. In some ways, you can think of modifiers as the tools and machines that work on 3D objects.

Each woodshop tool has different parameters that control how it works, such as how hard you turn the screwdriver or the coarseness of the sandpaper. Likewise, each modifier has parameters that you can set that determine how it affects the 3D object.

Modifiers can be used in a number of different ways, to reshape objects, apply material mappings, deform an object's surface, and perform many other actions. Many different types of modifiers exist. This chapter introduces you to the concept of modifiers and explains the basics on how to use them. The chapter concludes by exploring two different categories of modifiers that are used to deform geometry objects: Parametric Deformers and Free Form Deformers (FFD).

IN THIS CHAPTER

Using the Modifier Stack to manage modifiers

Learning to work with modifier gizmos

Exploring the Select modifiers

Deforming objects with the Parametric Deformer and FFD modifiers

Exploring the Modifier Stack

All modifiers applied to an object are listed together in a single location known as the Modifier Stack. This Stack is the manager for all modifiers applied to an object and can be found at the top of the Modify panel in the Command Panel. You can also use the Stack to apply and delete modifiers; cut, copy, and paste modifiers between objects; and reorder them.

Understanding Base Objects

The first entry in the Modifier Stack isn't a modifier at all; it is the Base Object. The Base Object is the original object type. The Base Object for a primitive is listed as its object type, such as Sphere or Torus. Editable meshes, polys, patches, and splines can also be Base Objects. NURBS Surfaces and NURBS Curves are also Base Objects.

You can also see the Base Objects using the Schematic View window if you enable the Base Objects option in the Display floater.

Applying modifiers

An object can have several modifiers applied to it. Modifiers can be applied using the Modifiers menu or by selecting the modifier from the Modifier List drop-down list located at the top of the Modify panel directly under the object name. Selecting a modifier in the Modifiers menu or from the Modifier List applies the modifier to the current selected object. Modifiers can be applied to multiple objects if several objects are selected.

TIP You can quickly jump to a specific modifier in the Modifier List by pressing the first letter of the modifier that you want to select. For example, pressing the T key when the Modifier List is open immediately selects the Taper modifier.

NOTE Some modifiers aren't available for some types of objects. For example, the Extrude and Lathe modifiers are enabled only when a spline or shape is selected.

Other Modifier Stack entities

Most modifiers are Object-Space modifiers, but another category called World-Space modifiers also exists. World-Space modifiers are similar to Object-Space modifiers, except they are applied using a global coordinate system instead of a coordinate system that is local to the object. More on World-Space modifiers is presented later in this chapter, but you should be aware that World-Space modifiers (identified with the initials, WSM) appear at the top of the Modifier Stack and are applied to the object after all Object-Space modifiers.

In addition to World-Space modifiers, Space Warp bindings also appear at the top of the Modifier Stack.

CROSS-REF Space Warps are covered in Chapter 37, "Using Space Warps."

Using the Modifier Stack

After a modifier is applied, its parameters appear in rollouts within the Command Panel. The Modifier Stack rollout, shown in Figure 13.1, lists the base object and all the modifiers that have been applied to an object. Any new modifiers applied to an object are placed at the top of the stack. By selecting a modifier from the list in the Modifier Stack, all the parameters for that specific modifier are displayed in rollouts.

TIP You can increase or decrease the size of the Modifier Stack by dragging the horizontal bar that appears beneath the Modifier Stack buttons.

Beneath the Modifier Stack are five buttons that affect the selected modifier. They are as described in Table 13.1.

CROSS-REF For more information on configuring modifier sets, see Chapter 4, "Customizing the Max Interface and Setting Preferences."

If you right-click on a modifier, a pop-up menu appears. This pop-up menu includes commands to rename the selected modifier, which you might want to do if the same modifier is applied to the same object multiple times. This pop-up menu also includes an option to delete the selected modifier among other commands.

FIGURE 13.1

The Modifier Stack rollout displays all modifiers applied to an object.

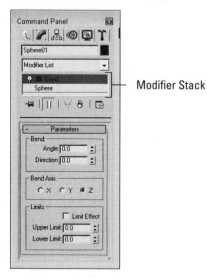

Modifier Stack

TABLE 13.1

Modifier Stack Buttons

Button	Name	Description
⊷	Pin Stack	Makes the parameters for the selected modifier available for editing even if another object is selected (like taking a physical pin and sticking it into the screen so it won't move).
∦	Show End Result On/Off Toggle	Shows the end results of all the modifiers in the entire Stack when enabled and only the modifiers up to the current selected modifier if disabled.
∀	Make Unique	Used to break any instance or reference links to the selected object. After you click this button, an object will no longer be modified along with the other objects for which it was an instance or reference. Works for Base Object and modifiers.
θ	Remove Modifier from the Stack	Used to delete a modifier from the Stack or unbind a Space Warp if one is selected. Deleting a modifier restores it to the same state it was in before the modifier was applied.
⊡	Configure Modifier Sets	Opens a pop-up menu where you can select to show a set of modifiers as buttons above the Modifier Stack. You can also select which modifier set appears at the top of the list of modifiers. The pop-up menu also includes an option to configure and define the various sets of modifiers.

Copying and pasting modifiers

The pop-up menu also includes options to Cut, Copy, Paste, and Paste Instance modifiers. The Cut command deletes the modifier from the current object but makes it available for pasting onto other objects. The Copy command retains the modifier for the current object and makes it available to paste onto another object. After you use the Cut or Copy command, you can use the Paste command to apply the modifier to another object. The Paste Instance command retains a link between the original modifier and the instanced modifier, so that any changes to either modifier affect the other instances.

You can also apply modifiers for the current object onto other objects by dragging the modifier from the Modifier Stack and dropping it on the other object in a viewport. Holding down the Ctrl key while dropping a modifier onto an object in a viewport applies the modifier as an instance (like the Paste Instance command). Holding down the Shift key while dragging and dropping a modifier on an object in the viewport removes the modifier from the current object and applies it to the object on which it is dropped (like the Cut and Paste commands).

> **CROSS-REF**   You can also cut, copy, and paste modifiers using the Schematic View window. See Chapter 24, "Working with the Schematic View," for more details.

Using instanced modifiers

When you apply a single modifier to several objects at the same time, the modifier shows up in the Modifier Stack for each object. These are *instanced modifiers* that maintain a connection to each other. If one of these instanced modifiers is changed, the change is propagated to all other instances. This feature is very helpful for modifying large groups of objects.

When a modifier is copied between different objects, you can select to make the copy an instance.

To see all the objects that are linked to a particular modifier, select an object in the viewport and choose Views ⇨ Show Dependencies. All objects with instanced modifiers that are connected to the current selection appear in bright pink. At any time, you can break the link between a particular instanced modifier and the rest of the objects using the Make Unique button in the Modifier Stack rollout.

Identifying instances and references in the Modifier Stack

If you look closely at the Modifier Stack, you will notice that it includes some visual clues that help you identify instances and references. Regular object and modifier copies appear in normal text, but instances appear in bold. This applies to both objects and modifiers. If a modifier is applied to two or more objects, then it appears in italic.

Referenced objects and modifiers can be identified by a Reference Object Bar that splits the Modifier Stack into two categories — ones that are unique to the referenced object (above the bar) and ones that are shared with the other references (below the bar).

Figure 13.2 shows each of these cases in the Modifier Stack.

Disabling and removing modifiers

Clicking the light bulb icon to the left of the modifier name toggles the modifier on and off. The right-click pop-up menu also offers options to turn the modifier off in the viewport or off for the renderer.

To remove a modifier from the Modifier Stack, just select the modifier and press the Remove Modifier button below the stack. This button removes the selected modifier only. You can select multiple modifiers at once by holding down the Ctrl key while clicking individually on the modifiers or by holding down the Shift key and clicking on the first and last modifiers in a range.

FIGURE 13.2

The Modifier Stack changes the text style to identify instances and references.

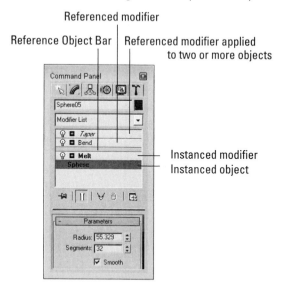

Referenced modifier

Reference Object Bar | Referenced modifier applied to two or more objects

Instanced modifier
Instanced object

Reordering the Stack

Modifiers are listed in the Modifier Stack with the first applied ones on the bottom and the newest applied ones on the top. The Stack order is important and can change the appearance of the object. Max applies the modifiers starting with the lowest one in the Stack first and the topmost modifier last. You can change the order of the modifiers in the Stack by selecting a modifier and dragging it above or below the other modifiers. You cannot drag it below the object type or above any World-Space modifiers or Space Warp bindings.

Tutorial: Creating a molecular chain

Whether you're working with DNA splices or creating an animation to show how molecular chains are formed, you can use the Lattice and Twist modifiers to quickly create a molecular chain. Using these chains shows how reordering the Modifier Stack can change the outcome.

To create a molecular chain using modifiers, follow these steps.

1. Select Create ➪ Standard Primitives ➪ Plane, and drag in the Top viewport to create a Plane object. Set its Length to **300**, its Width to **60**, its Length Segments to **11**, and its Width Segments to **1**.

2. With the Plane object selected, select Modifiers ➪ Parametric Deformers ➪ Lattice to apply the Lattice modifier. Enable the Apply to Entire Object option. Then set the Struts Radius value to **1.0** with **12** sides and the Joints Base Type to **Icosa** with a Radius of **6.0** and a Segments value of **6**.

3. Select Modifiers ➪ Parametric Deformers ➪ Twist, and set the Twist Angle to **360** about the Y-axis.

4. Notice that the Sphere objects have been twisted along with the Plane object. You can fix this by switching the modifier order in the Modifier Stack. Select the Lattice modifier, and drag and drop it above the Twist modifier in the stack.

    This step corrects the elongated spheres.

Figure 13.3 shows the corrected molecular chain.

FIGURE 13.3

Changing the order of the modifiers in the Stack can affect the end result.

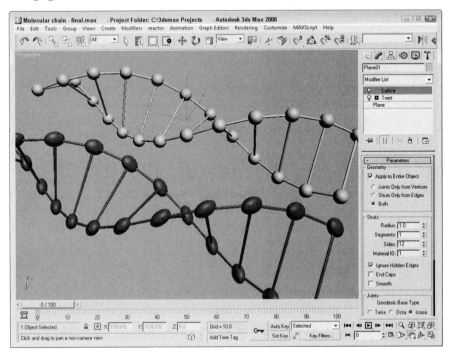

Holding and fetching a scene

Before going any farther, you need to know about an important feature in Max that allows you to set a stopping point for the current scene. The Hold command saves the scene into a temporary buffer for easy recovery. After a scene is set with the Hold command (Alt+Ctrl+H), you can bring it back instantly with the Fetch command (Alt+Ctrl+F). These commands provide a quick way to backtrack on modifications to a scene or project without your having to save and reload the project. If you use these commands before applying or deleting modifiers, you can avoid some potential headaches.

 **Along with saving your file often, using the Hold command before applying any complex modifier to an object is a good idea.**

Collapsing the Stack

Collapsing the Stack removes all its modifiers by permanently applying them to the object. It also resets the modification history to a baseline. All the individual modifiers in the Stack are combined into one single modification. This feature eliminates the ability to change any modifier parameters, but it simplifies the object. The right-click pop-up menu offers options to Collapse To and Collapse All. You can collapse the entire Stack with the Collapse All command, or you can collapse to the current selected modifier with the Collapse To command. Collapsed objects typically become Editable Mesh objects.

TIP Another huge advantage of collapsing the Modifier Stack is that it conserves memory and results in smaller file sizes, which makes larger scenes load much quicker. Collapsing the Modifier Stack also speeds up rendering because Max doesn't need to calculate the stack results before rendering.

When you apply a collapse command, a warning dialog box appears, shown in Figure 13.4, notifying you that this action will delete all the creation parameters. Click Yes to continue with the collapse.

NOTE In addition to the Yes and No buttons, the warning dialog box includes a Hold/Yes button. This button saves the current state of the object to the Hold buffer and then applies the Collapse All function. If you have any problems, you can retrieve the object's previous state before the collapse was applied by choosing Edit ➪ Fetch (Alt+Ctrl+F).

FIGURE 13.4

Because the Collapse operation cannot be undone, this warning dialog box offers a chance to Hold the scene.

Using the Collapse utility

You can also use the Collapse utility found on the Utility panel to collapse the Modifier Stack. This utility enables you to collapse an object or several objects to a Modifier Stack Result or to a Mesh object. Collapsing to a Modifier Stack Result doesn't necessarily produce a mesh but collapses the object to its base object state, which is displayed at the bottom of the Stack hierarchy. Depending on the Stack, this could result in a mesh, patch, spline, or other object type. You can also collapse to a Single Object or to Multiple Objects.

If the Mesh and Single Object options are selected, you can also select to perform a Boolean operation. The Boolean operations are available if you are collapsing several overlapping objects into one. The options are Union (which combines geometries together), Intersection (which combines only the overlapping geometries), and Subtraction (which subtracts one geometry from another).

CROSS-REF Boolean operations can also be performed using the Boolean compound object. See Chapter 26, "Working with Compound Objects," for details on this object type.

If multiple objects are selected, then a Boolean Intersection results in only the sections of the objects that are intersected by all objects; if no objects overlap, all objects disappear.

If you use the Boolean Subtraction option, you can specify which object is the base object from which the other objects are subtracted. To do so, select that object first and then select the other objects by holding down the Ctrl key and clicking them. Figure 13.5 shows an example of each of the Boolean operations.

FIGURE 13.5

Using the Collapse utility, you can select the following Boolean operations (shown from left to right): Union, Intersection, and Subtraction.

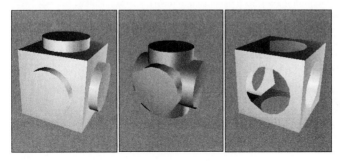

Using gizmo subobjects

As you've worked with modifiers, you've probably noticed the orange wireframe box that surrounds the object in the viewports when you apply the modifier. These boxes are called modifier gizmos, and they provide a visual control for how the modifier changes the geometry. If you want, you can work directly with these gizmos to affect the modifier.

Clicking the plus sign to the left of the modifier name reveals any subobjects associated with the modifier. To select the modifier subobjects, simply click the subobject name. The subobject name is highlighted in yellow when selected. Many modifiers create *gizmo subobjects*. Gizmos have an icon usually in the shape of a box that can be transformed and controlled like regular objects using the transformation buttons on the main toolbar. Another common modifier subobject is Center, which controls the point about which the gizmo is transformed.

Tutorial: Squeezing a plastic bottle

To get a feel for how the modifier gizmo and its center affect an object, this tutorial applies the Squeeze modifier to a plastic bottle; by moving its center, we can change the shape of the object.

To change a modifier's characteristics by moving its center, follow these steps:

1. Open the Plastic bottle.max file from the Chap 13 directory on the DVD.

   This file includes a plastic squirt bottle with all the parts attached into a single mesh object.

2. With the bottle selected, choose the Modifiers ➪ Parametric Deformers ➪ Squeeze menu command to apply the Squeeze modifier to the bottle. Set the Radial Squeeze Amount value to **1**.

3. In the Modifier Stack, click the plus sign to the left of the Squeeze modifier to see the modifier's subobjects. Select the Center subobject.

   The selected subobject is highlighted in yellow.

4. Click the Select and Move (W) button on the main toolbar, and drag the center point in the Perspective viewport upward.

   Notice how the bottle's shape changes.

Figure 13.6 shows several different bottle shapes created by moving the modifier's center point.

FIGURE 13.6

By changing the modifier's center point, the bottle's shape changes.

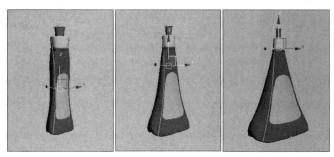

Modifying subobjects

In addition to being applied to complete objects, modifiers can also be applied and used to modify *subobjects*. A subobject is defined as a collection of object parts, such as vertices, edges, faces, or elements.

CROSS-REF To learn more about applying modifiers to subobject selections, see Chapter 10, "Learning Modeling Basics and Working with Subobjects and Helpers."

To work in subobject selection mode, click the plus sign to the left of the object name to see the subobjects. Several modifiers, including Mesh Select, Spline Select, and Volume Select, can select subobject areas for passing these selections up to the next modifier in the Stack. For example, you can use the Mesh Select modifier to select several faces on the front of a sphere and then apply the Face Extrude modifier to extrude just those faces.

Topology dependency

When you attempt to modify the parameters of a Base Object that has a modifier applied, you sometimes get a warning dialog box that tells you that the modifier depends on topology that may change. Max is telling you that the surface of the object with that particular modifier is dependent on the subobjects that are selected and if you change the underlying subobjects, you may change the resulting topology. For example, the CrossSection and Surface modifiers build the surface using a set of splines, but if you change the original spline, you can destroy the resulting surfaced object. You can eliminate this problem by collapsing the Modifier Stack.

You can disable the warning by selecting the "Do not show this message again" option on the dialog box or by opening the Preference Settings dialog box and turning off the Display Topology-Dependence Warning option in the General panel of the Preference Settings dialog box. Disabling the warning does not make the potential problem go away; it only prevents the warning dialog box from appearing.

Exploring Modifier Types

To keep all the various modifiers organized, Max has grouped them into several distinct modifier sets. The modifier sets, as listed in the Modifier menu, include those listed in Table 13.2.

TABLE 13.2

Modifiers Menu Items

Menu	Submenu Items
Selection Modifiers	FFD Select, Mesh Select, Patch Select, Poly Select, Select by Channel, Spline Select, Volume Select
Patch/Spline Editing	Cross Section, Delete Patch, Delete Spline, Edit Patch, Edit Spline, Fillet/Chamfer, Lathe, Normalize Spline, Renderable Spline Modifier, Surface, Sweep, Trim/Extend
Mesh Editing	Cap Holes, Delete Mesh, Edit Mesh, Edit Normals, Edit Poly, Extrude, Face Extrude, MultiRes, Normal Modifier, Optimize, Smooth, STL Check, Symmetry, Tessellate, Vertex Paint, Vertex Weld
Conversion	Turn to Mesh, Turn to Patch, Turn to Poly
Animation Modifiers	Attribute Holder, Flex, Linked XForm, Melt, Morpher, PatchDeform, PatchDeform (WSM), PathDeform, PathDeform (WSM), Skin, Skin Morph, Skin Wrap, Skin Wrap Patch, SplineIk Control, SurfDeform, SurfDeform (WSM)
Cloth	Cloth, Garment Maker
Hair and Fur	Hair and Fur (WSM)
UV Coordinates	Camera Map, Camera Map (WSM), MapScaler (WSM), Projection, Unwrap UVW, UVW Map, UVW Mapping Add, UVW Mapping Clear, UVW XForm
Cache Tools	Point Cache, Point Cache (WSM)
Subdivision Surfaces	HSDS Modifier, MeshSmooth, TurboSmooth
Free Form Deformers	FFD 2x2x2, FFD 3x3x3, FFD 4x4x4, FFD Box, FFD Cylinder
Parametric Deformers	Affect Region, Bend, Displace, Lattice, Mirror, Noise, Physique, Push, Preserve, Relax, Ripple, Shell, Slice, Skew, Stretch, Spherify, Squeeze, Twist, Taper, Substitute, XForm, Wave
Surface	Disp Approx, Displace Mesh (WSM), Material, Material By Element
NURBS Editing	Disp Approx, Surf Deform, Surface Select
Radiosity	Subdivide, Subdivide (WSM)
Cameras	Camera Correction

You can find roughly these same sets if you click the Configure Modifier Sets button in the Modifier Stack. Within this list is a single selected set. The selected set is marked with an arrow to the left of its name. The modifiers contained within the selected set appear at the very top of the Modifier List.

CROSS-REF Covering all the modifiers in a single chapter would result in a very long chapter. Instead, I decided to cover most of the modifiers in their respective chapters. For example, you can learn about the Mesh Editing modifiers in Chapter 25, "Deforming Surfaces and Using the Mesh Modifiers"; animation modifiers in Chapter 32, "Using Animation Modifiers"; the UV Coordinates modifiers in Chapter 30, "Unwrapping UVs and Using Pelt Mapping"; and so on. This chapter covers the Selection Modifiers, Parametric Deformers, and FFD modifiers.

Object-Space versus World-Space modifiers

If you view the modifiers listed in the Modifier List, they are divided into two categories: Object-Space and World-Space modifiers (except for the selected set of modifiers that appear at the very top for quick access).

Object-Space modifiers are more numerous than World-Space modifiers. For most World-Space modifiers, there is also an Object-Space version. World-Space modifiers are all identified with the abbreviation WSM, which appears next to the modifier's name.

Object-Space modifiers are modifiers that are applied to individual objects and that use the object's Local Coordinate System, so as the object is moved, the modifier goes with it.

World-Space modifiers are based on World-Space coordinates instead of on an object's Local Coordinate System, so after a World-Space modifier is applied, it stays put, no matter where the object with which it is associated moves.

Another key difference is that World-Space modifiers appear above all Object-Space modifiers in the Modifier Stack, so they affect the object only after all the other modifiers are applied.

CROSS-REF All Space Warps are also applied using World-Space coordinates, so they also have the WSM letters next to their name. You can get more information on Space Warps in Chapter 37, "Using Space Warps."

Selection modifiers

The first modifiers available in the Modifiers menu are the Selection modifiers. You can use these modifiers to select subobjects for the various object types. You can then apply other modifiers to these subobject selections. Any modifiers that appear above a Selection modifier in the Modifier Stack are applied to the subobject selection.

Selection modifiers are available for every modeling type, including Mesh Select, Poly Select, Patch Select, Spline Select, Volume Select, FFD Select, Select by Channel, and NURBS Surface Select. You can apply the Mesh Select, Poly Select, Patch Select, and Volume Select modifiers to any 3D object, but you can apply the Spline Select modifier only to spline and shape objects, the FFD Select modifier only to the FFD Space Warps objects, and the NURBS Surface Select modifier (found in the NURBS Editing submenu) only to NURBS objects. Any modifiers that appear above one of these Selection modifiers in the Modifier Stack are applied only to the selected subobjects.

CROSS-REF Each of the Selection modifiers is covered for the various modeling types in its respective chapter. For example, to learn about the Patch Select modifier, see Chapter 27, "Modeling with Patches and NURBS."

When a Selection modifier is applied to an object, the transform buttons on the main toolbar become inactive. If you want to transform the subobject selection, you can do so with the XForm modifier.

Volume Select modifier

Among the Selection modifiers, the Volume Select modifier is unique. It selects subobjects based on the area defined by the modifier's gizmo. The Volume Select modifier selects all subobjects within the volume from a single object or from multiple objects. One of the benefits of using this modifier is that the subobjects within the volume can change as the object is moved during an animation sequence. It also can work with several objects at once.

In the Parameters rollout for the Volume Select modifier, you can specify whether subobjects selected within a given volume should be Object, Vertex, or Face subobjects. Any new selection can Replace, be Added to, or be Subtracted from the current selection. You can use the Invert option to select the subobjects outside of the current volume. You can also choose either a Window or Crossing Selection Type.

The actual shape of the gizmo can be a Box, Sphere, Cylinder, or Mesh Object. To use a Mesh Object, click the button beneath the Mesh Object option and then click the object to use in a viewport. In addition to selecting by a gizmo-defined volume, you can also select subobjects based on certain surface characteristics, such as Material IDs, Smoothing Groups, or a Texture Map including Mapping Channel or Vertex Color. This makes it possible to quickly select all vertices that have a Vertex Color assigned to them.

The Alignment options can Fit or Center the gizmo on the current subobject selection. The Reset button moves the gizmo to its original position and orientation, which typically is the bounding box of the object. The Auto Fit option automatically changes the size and orientation of the gizmo as the object it encompasses changes.

NOTE The Volume Select modifier also includes a Soft Selection rollout. Soft Selection lets you select adjacent subobjects to a lesser extent. The result is a smoother selection over a broader surface area. The Soft Selection options are explained in Chapter 10, "Learning Modeling Basics and Working with Subobjects and Helpers."

Tutorial: Applying damage to a car

In this tutorial, we use the Volume Select modifier to select the front corner of a car and then apply Noise and XForm modifiers to make the corner look like it's been damaged in a collision.

To use modifiers to make a section of a car appear damaged, follow these steps:

1. Open the Damaged car.max file from the Chap 13 directory on the DVD.

   This file includes a car model created by Viewpoint Datalabs.

2. With the front end of the car selected, choose the Modifiers ⇨ Selection Modifiers ⇨ Volume Select menu command.

   This command applies the Volume Select modifier to the group.

3. In the Modifier Stack, click the plus icon to the left of the modifier name and select the Gizmo subobject. Move the gizmo in the Top viewport so only the front corner of the car is selected. In the Parameters rollout, select the Vertex option.

4. Choose the Modifiers ⇨ Parametric Deformers ⇨ Noise menu command to apply the Noise modifier to the selected volume. In the Parameters rollout, enable the Fractal option and set the X, Y, and Z Strength values to **30**.

5. Choose Modifiers ⇨ Parametric Deformers ⇨ XForm to apply the XForm modifier, and use its gizmo to push the selected area up and to the left in the Top viewport. This step makes the section look dented.

Figure 13.7 shows the resulting damaged car. Notice that the rest of the object is fine and only the selected volume area is damaged.

CROSS-REF You can see another example of how a Selection modifier can be used to select and apply a modifier to a subobject selection in Chapter 10, "Learning Modeling Basics and Working with Subobjects and Helpers."

Parametric Deformer modifiers

Perhaps the most representative group of modifiers are the Parametric Deformers. These modifiers affect the geometry of objects by pulling, pushing, and stretching them. They all can be applied to any of the modeling types, including primitive objects.

NOTE In the upcoming examples, you might start to get sick of seeing the hammer model used over and over, but using the same model enables you to more easily compare the effects of the various modifiers, and it's more interesting to look at than a simple box.

FIGURE 13.7

FIGURE 13.7

The Noise and XForm modifiers are applied to just the subobject selection.

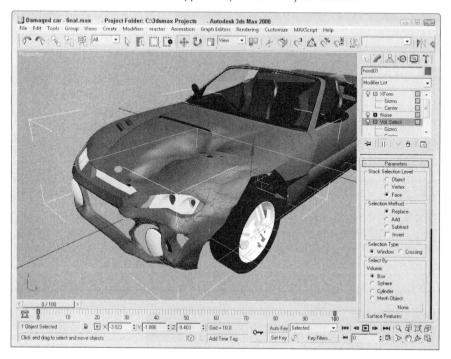

Affect Region modifier

The Affect Region modifier can cause a local surface region to bubble up or be indented. Affect Region parameters include Falloff, Pinch, and Bubble values. The Falloff value sets the size of the affected area. The Pinch value makes the region tall and thin, and the Bubble value rounds the affected region. You also can select the Ignore Back Facing option. Figure 13.8 shows the Affect Region modifier applied to a Quad Patch with a Falloff value of 80 on the left, and with a Bubble value of 1.0 on the right. The height and direction of the region are determined by the position of the modifier gizmo, which is a line connected by two points.

NOTE   The Affect Region modifier accomplishes the same effect as the Soft Selection feature, but Affect Region applies the effect as a modifier, making it easier to discard.

Bend modifier

The Bend modifier can bend an object along any axis. Bend parameters include the Bend Angle and Direction, Bend Axis, and Limits. The Bend Angle defines the bend in the vertical direction, and the Direction value defines the bend in the horizontal direction.

Limit settings are the boundaries beyond which the modifier has no effect. You can set Upper and Lower Limits relative to the object's center, which is placed at the object's pivot point. Limits are useful if you want the modifier applied to only one half of the object. The Upper and Lower Limits are visible as a simple plane on the modifier gizmo. For example, if you want to bend a tall cylinder object and have the top half remain straight, you can simply set an Upper Limit for the cylinder at the location where you want it to stay linear.

The Affect Region modifier can raise or lower the surface region of an object.

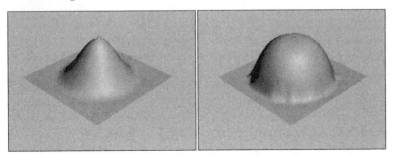

> **NOTE** Several modifiers have the option to impose limits on the modifier, including Upper and Lower Limit values.

The hammer in Figure 13.9 shows several bending options. The left hammer shows a bend value of 75 degrees around the Z-axis, the middle hammer also has a Direction value of 60, and the right hammer has an Upper Limit of 8.

FIGURE 13.9

The Bend modifier can bend objects about any axis.

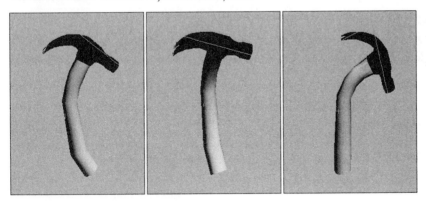

Tutorial: Bending a tree

If you have a tree model that you want to bend as if the wind were blowing, you can apply the Bend modifier. The tree then bends about its Pivot Point. Luckily, all the trees and plants found in the AEC Objects category have their Pivot Points set about their base, so bending a tree is really easy.

To bend a tree using the Bend modifier, follow these steps:

1. Select the Create ➪ AEC Objects ➪ Foliage menu command to access the available trees. Select a long thin tree like the Yucca, and click in the Top viewport to add it to the scene.

2. With the tree selected, select the Modifiers ⇨ Parametric Deformers ⇨ Bend menu command to apply the Bend modifier to the tree.

3. In the Parameters rollout found in the Modify panel, set the Bend Axis to **Z** and the Bend Angle to **60**.

   The tree bends as desired.

Figure 13.10 shows the bending Yucca plant. To animate this tree bending back and forth, just set keys for the Angle parameter.

FIGURE 13.10

The Bend modifier can be used to bend trees.

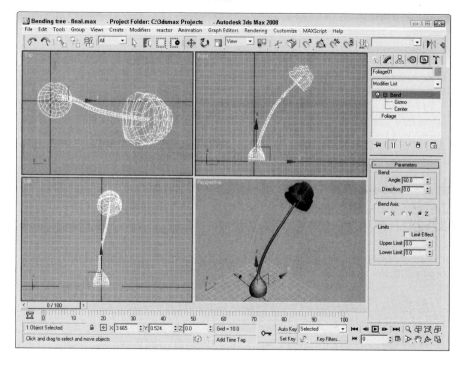

Displace modifier

The Displace modifier offers two unique sets of features. It can alter an object's geometry by displacing elements using a gizmo, or it can change the object's surface using a grayscale bitmap image. The Displace gizmo can have one of four different shapes: Planar, Cylindrical, Spherical, or Shrink Wrap. This gizmo can be placed exterior to an object or inside an object to push it from the inside.

CAUTION In order for the Displace modifier to work, the surface requires a dense mesh, which can lead to very high polygon counts.

The Displace modifier parameters include Strength and Decay values. You can also specify the dimensions of the gizmo. A cylindrical-shaped gizmo can be capped or uncapped. The alignment parameters let you align the gizmo to the X-axis, Y-axis, or Z-axis, or you can align it to the current view. The rest of the parameters deal with displacing the surface using a bitmap image. Figure 13.11 shows a Quad Patch with the Plane-shaped gizmo applied with a Strength value of 25. To the right is a Quad Patch with the Sphere-shaped gizmo.

FIGURE 13.11

You can use the Displace modifier's gizmo as a modeling tool to change the surface of an object.

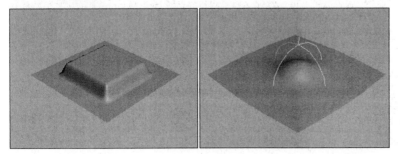

CROSS-REF   The Displace modifier can also alter an object's geometry using a grayscale bitmap image. This is similar to a Displacement map, which is covered in Chapter 17, "Adding Material Details with Maps." In many ways, the Displace gizmo works like the Conform compound object. You can learn about the Conform compound object in Chapter 26, "Working with Compound Objects."

Lattice modifier

The Lattice modifier changes an object into a lattice by creating struts where all the edges are located or by replacing each joint with an object. The Lattice modifier considers all edges as struts and all vertices as joints.

The parameters for this modifier include several options to determine how to apply the effect. These options include Apply to Entire Object, to Joints Only, to Struts Only, or Both (Struts and Joints). If the Apply to Entire Object option isn't selected, then the modifier is applied to the current subobject.

For struts, you can specify Radius, Segments, Sides, and Material ID values. You can also specify to Ignore Hidden Edges, to create End Caps, and to Smooth the Struts.

For joints, you can select Tetra, Octa, or Icosa types with Radius, Segments, and Material ID values. There are also controls for Mapping Coordinates.

NOTE   Although the joints settings enable you to select only one of three different types, you can use the Scatter compound object to place any type of object instead of the three defaults. To do this, apply the Lattice modifier and then select the Distribute Using All Vertices option in the Scatter Objects rollout.

Figure 13.12 shows the effect of the Lattice modifier. The left hammer has only joints applied, the middle hammer has only struts applied, and the right hammer has both applied.

FIGURE 13.12

The Lattice modifier divides an object into struts, joints, or both.

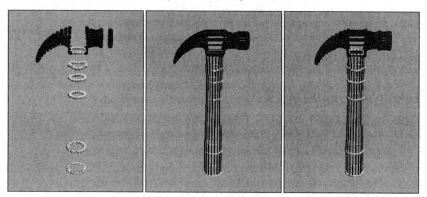

Mirror modifier

You can use the Mirror modifier to create a mirrored copy of an object or subobject. The Parameters rollout lets you pick a mirror axis or plane and an Offset value. The Copy option creates a copy of the mirrored object and retains the original selection.

> **NOTE** The Mirror modifier works the same as the Mirror command found in the Tools menu, but the modifier is handy if you want to be able to quickly discard the mirroring changes.

Noise modifier

The Noise modifier randomly varies the position of object vertices in the direction of the selected axes. Noise parameters include Seed and Scale values, a Fractal option with Roughness and Iterations settings, Strength about each axis, and Animation settings.

The Seed value sets the randomness of the noise. If two identical objects have the same settings and the same Seed value, they look exactly the same even though a random noise has been applied to them. If you alter the Seed value for one of them, then they will look dramatically different.

The Scale value determines the size of the position changes, so larger Scale values result in a smoother, less rough shape. The Fractal option enables fractal iterations, which result in more jagged surfaces. If Fractal is enabled, Roughness and Iterations become active. The Roughness value sets the amount of variation, and the Iterations value defines the number of times to complete the fractal computations. More iterations yield a wilder or chaotic surface, but require more computation time.

If the Animate Noise option is selected, the vertices positions will modulate for the duration of frames. The Frequency value determines how quickly the object's noise changes, and the Phase setting determines where the noise wave starts and ends.

Figure 13.13 shows the Noise modifier applied to several sphere objects. These spheres make the Noise modifier easier to see than on the hammer object. The left sphere has Seed, Scale, and Strength values along all three axes set to 1.0, the middle sphere has increased the Strength values to 2.0, and the right sphere has the Fractal option enabled with a Roughness value of 1.0 and an Iterations value of 6.0.

> **CROSS-REF** The Physique modifier is one of the original Character Studio tools. Although both modifiers still exist, the Skin modifier is preferred. It is covered in Chapter 43, "Skinning Characters."

FIGURE 13.13

The Noise modifier can apply a smooth or wild look to your objects.

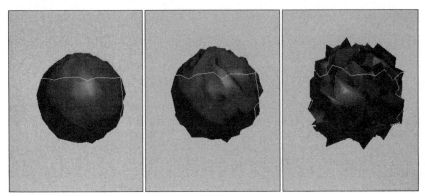

Push modifier

The Push modifier pushes an object's vertices inward or outward as if they were being filled with air. The Push modifier also has one parameter: the Push Value. This value is the distance to move with respect to the object's center.

The positive Push value pushes the vertices outward away from the center, and a negative Push value pulls the vertices in towards the center. The Push modifier can increase the size of characters or make an object thinner by pulling its vertices in. Figure 13.14 shows the hammer pushed with 0.05, 0.1, and 0.15 values.

FIGURE 13.14

The Push modifier can increase the volume of an object.

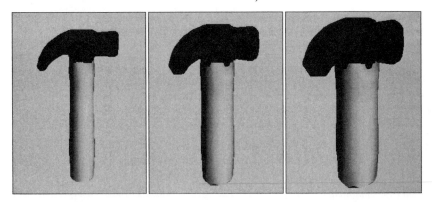

Preserve modifier

The Preserve modifier works to maintain Edge Lengths, Face Angles, and Volume as an object is deformed and edited. Before an object is modified, make an additional copy. Then edit one of the copies. To apply the Preserve modifier, click the Pick Original button; then click the unmodified object, and finally click the modified object. The object is modified to preserve the Edge Lengths, Face Angles, and Volume as defined in the Weight values. This helps prevent the topology of the modified object from becoming too irregular.

 **In order for the Preserve modifier to keep objects and modifiers in check, it must be placed above the objects and modifiers it is watching.**

The Iterations option determines the number of times the process is applied. You can also specify to apply to the Whole Mesh, to Selected Vertices Only, or to an Inverted Selection.

Relax modifier

The Relax modifier tends to smooth the overall geometry by separating vertices that lie closer than an average distance. Parameters include a Relax Value that is the percentage of the distance that the vertices move. Values can range between 1.0 and −1.0. A value of 0 has no effect on the object. Negative values have the opposite effect, causing an object to become tighter and more distorted.

TIP **As you model, it is common for meshes to have sections that are too tight, which are dense locations in the mesh where all a large concentration of vertices are close together. The Relax modifier can be used to cause the areas that are too tight to be relaxed.**

The Iterations value determines how many times this calculation is computed. The Keep Boundary Points Fixed option removes any points that are next to an open hole. Save Outer Corners maintains the vertex position of corners of an object.

Ripple modifier

The Ripple modifier creates ripples across the surface of an object. This modifier is best used on a single object; if several objects need a ripple effect, use the Ripple Space Warp. The ripple is applied via a gizmo that you can control. Parameters for this modifier include two Amplitude values and values for the Wave Length, Phase, and Decay of the ripple.

The two amplitude values cause an increase in the height of the ripples opposite one another. Figure 13.15 shows the Ripple modifier applied to a simple Quad Patch with values of 10 for Amplitude 1 and a Wave Length value of 50. The right Quad Patch also has an Amplitude 2 value of 20.

FIGURE 13.15

The Ripple modifier can make small waves appear over the surface of an object.

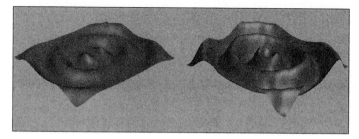

Shell modifier

When a mesh subobject is deleted, it leaves a hole in the surface that allows the inside of the object to be seen. This inside section doesn't have normals pointing the right direction, so the object appears blank unless the Force 2-Sided option in the Viewport Configuration dialog box is selected. The Shell modifier makes an object into a shell with a surface on the inside and outside of the object.

343

For the Shell modifier, you can specify Inner and Outer Amount values. This is the distance from the original position that the inner or outer surfaces are moved. These values together determine how thick the shell is. The Bevel Edges and Bevel Spline options let you bevel the edges of the shell. By clicking on the Bevel Spline button, you can select a spline to define the bevel shape.

For each Material ID, you can use the Material ID for the inner section or the outer section. The Auto Smooth Edge lets you smooth the edge for all edges that are within the Angle threshold. The edges can also be mapped using the Edge Mapping options. The options include Copy, None, Strip, and Interpolate. The Copy option uses the same mapping as the original face, None assigns new mapping coordinates, Strip maps the edges as one complete strip, and Interpolate interpolates the mapping between the inner and outer mapping.

The last options make selecting the edges, the inner faces, or the outer faces easy. The Straighten Corners option moves the vertices so the edges are straight.

Tutorial: Making a character from a sphere

Creating a little game character from a sphere is a good example of how the Shell modifier can be used.

To use the Shell modifier to create a character, follow these steps:

1. Open the Gobbleman shell.max file from the Chap 13 directory on the DVD.

   This file includes a simple sphere object that has had several faces deleted.

2. With the sphere object selected, select Modifiers ⇨ Parametric Deformers ⇨ Shell to apply the Shell modifier. Set the Outer Amount to **5.0**.

   This makes the hollow sphere into a thin shell. Notice that the lighting inside the sphere is now correct.

Figure 13.16 shows the resulting shell.

Slice modifier

You can use the Slice modifier to divide an object into two separate objects. Applying the Slice modifier creates a Slice gizmo. This gizmo looks like a simple plane and can be transformed and positioned to define the slice location. To transform the gizmo, you need to select it from the Stack hierarchy.

 You can use the Slice modifier to make objects slowly disappear a layer at a time.

The Slice parameters include four slice type options. Refine Mesh simply adds new vertices and edges where the gizmo intersects the object. The Split Mesh option creates two separate objects. The Remove Top and Remove Bottom options delete all faces and vertices above or below the gizmo intersection plane.

Using Triangular or Polygonal faces, you can also specify whether the faces are divided. Figure 13.17 shows the top and bottom halves of a hammer object. The right hammer is sliced at an angle.

 Editable Meshes also have a Slice tool that can produce similar results. The difference is that the Slice modifier can work on any type of object, not only on meshes.

Skew modifier

The Skew modifier changes the tilt of an object by moving its top portion while keeping the bottom half fixed. Skew parameters include Amount and Direction values, a Skew Axis, and Limits. Figure 13.18 shows the hammer on the left with a Skew value of 2.0, in the middle with a Skew value of 5, and on the right with an Upper Limit of 8.

FIGURE 13.16

The Shell modifier can add an inside to hollow objects.

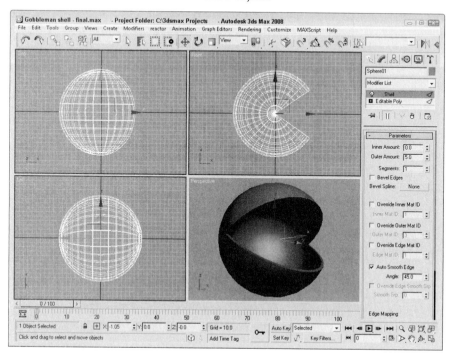

FIGURE 13.17

The Slice modifier can cut objects into two separate pieces.

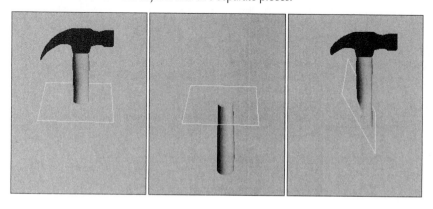

FIGURE 13.18

You can use the Skew modifier to tilt objects.

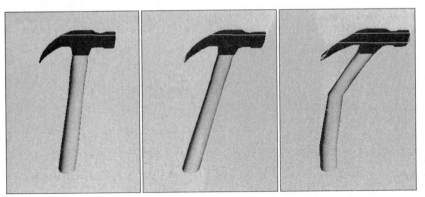

Stretch modifier

The Stretch modifier moves one axis in one direction while moving the other axes in the opposite direction, like pushing in on opposite sides of a balloon. Stretch parameters include Stretch and Amplify values, a Stretch Axis, and Limits.

The Stretch value equates the distance the object is pulled, and the Amplify value is a multiplier for the Stretch value. Positive values multiply the effect, and negative values reduce the stretch effect.

Figure 13.19 shows a Stretch value of 0.2 about the Z-axis applied to the hammer, the middle hammer also has an Amplify value of 2.0, and the right hammer has an Upper Limit value of 8.

FIGURE 13.19

The Stretch modifier pulls along one axis while pushing the other two.

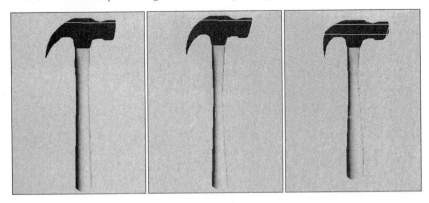

Spherify modifier

The Spherify modifier distorts an object into a spherical shape. The single Spherify parameter is the percent of the effect to apply. Figure 13.20 shows the hammer with Spherify values of 10, 20, and 30 percent.

The Spherify modifier is different from the Push modifier. Although they both are applied to the entire object, the Push modifier forces all vertices continuously outward, the Spherify modifier uses a sphere shape as a limiting boundary. The visible difference is that the Spherify modifier creates a bulging effect.

FIGURE 13.20

The Spherify modifier pushes all vertices outward like a sphere.

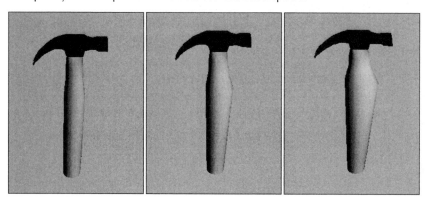

Tutorial: Making a fat crocodile

A good way to use the Spherify modifier is to add bulges to an object. For example, in this tutorial we make a plump crocodile even fatter by applying the Spherify modifier.

To fatten up a crocodile character with the Spherify modifier, follow these steps:

1. Open the Fat crocodile.max file from the Chap 13 directory on the DVD.

   This file includes a crocodile model created by Viewpoint Datalabs.

2. With the crocodile selected, select the Modifiers ⇨ Parametric Deformers ⇨ Spherify menu command to apply the Spherify modifier to the crocodile.

   The bulge appears around the object's pivot point.

3. In the Parameters rollout, set the Percent value to **15**.

Figure 13.21 shows the plump crocodile.

NOTE The drawback of the Spherify modifier is that you have no control over its placement because there isn't a gizmo that you can position. One way around this problem is to use the Volume Select modifier to select a specific volume that is passed up the stack to the Spherify modifier.

Squeeze modifier

The Squeeze modifier takes the points close to one axis and moves them away from the center of the object while it moves other points toward the center to create a bulging effect. Squeeze parameters include Amount and Curve values for Axial Bulge and Radial Squeeze, and Limits and Effect Balance settings.

The Effect Balance settings include a Bias value, which changes the object between the maximum Axial Bulge or the maximum Radial Squeeze. The Volume setting increases or decreases the volume of the object within the modifier's gizmo.

FIGURE 13.21

The Spherify modifier can fatten up a crocodile.

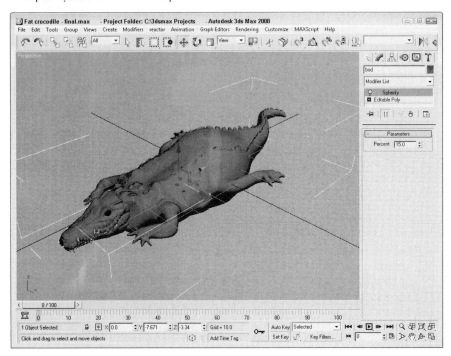

Axial Bulge is enabled with an Amount value of 0.2 and a Curve value of 2.0 in the left hammer in Figure 13.22, the middle hammer has also added Radial Squeeze values of 0.4 and 2.0, and the right hammer has an Upper Limit value of 8.

FIGURE 13.22

The Squeeze modifier can bulge or squeeze along two different axes.

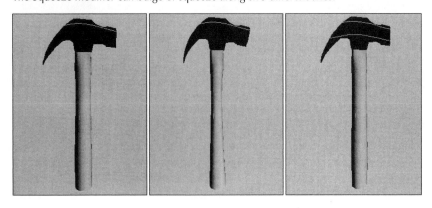

Twist modifier

The Twist modifier deforms an object by rotating one end of an axis in one direction and the other end in the opposite direction. Twist parameters include Angle and Bias values, a Twist Axis, and Limits.

The Angle value is the amount of twist in degrees that is applied to the object. The Bias value causes the twists to bunch up near the Pivot Point (for negative values) or away from the Pivot Point (for positive values).

The left hammer in Figure 13.23 shows a twist angle of 120 about the Z-axis, the middle hammer shows a Bias value of 20, and the right hammer has an Upper Limit value of 8.

FIGURE 13.23

The Twist modifiers can twist an object about an axis.

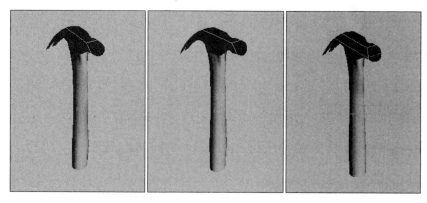

Taper modifier

The Taper modifier scales one end of an object. The tapered end is the end opposite the Pivot Point. Taper parameters include the Amount and Curve, Primary and Effect Axes, and Limits. The Amount value defines the amount of taper applied to the affected end. The Curve value bends the taper inward (for negative values) or outward (for positive values). You can see the curve clearly if you look at the modifier's gizmo. For example, you can create a simple vase or a bongo drum with the Taper modifier and a positive Curve value.

The Primary Axis defines the axis about which the taper is applied. The Effect axis can be a single axis or a plane, and the options change depending on your Primary Axis. This defines the axis or plane along which the object's end is scaled. For example, if the Z-axis is selected as the Primary Axis, then selecting the XY Effect plane scales the object equally along both the X-axis and the Y-axis. Selecting the Y Effect axis scales the end only along the Y-axis. You can also select a Symmetry option to taper both ends equally. Taper limits work just like the Bend modifier.

The left hammer in Figure 13.24 shows a taper of 1.0 about the Z-axis, the middle hammer has a Curve value of –2, and the right hammer has the Symmetry option selected.

FIGURE 13.24

The Taper modifier can proportionally scale one end of an object.

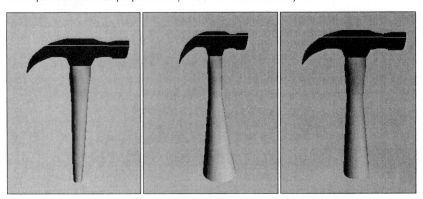

Tutorial: Creating a yo-yo

The Taper modifier can be used to create a variety of simple objects quickly, such as a yo-yo.

To create a yo-yo using the Taper modifier, follow these steps:

1. Select Create ➪ Standard Primitives ➪ Sphere, and drag in the Front viewport to create a sphere object.
2. With the sphere object selected, choose Modifiers ➪ Parametric Deformers ➪ Taper to apply the Taper modifier. Set the Taper Amount to **4.0** about the Primary Z-Axis and **XY** as the Effect plane, and enable the Symmetry option.

Figure 13.25 shows the resulting yo-yo; just add a string.

Substitute modifier

The Substitute modifier lets you place an object in the scene and substitute it with a higher-resolution object during render time. The substitute object may come from with the scene or from an XRef file. To remove the substitute object, simply remove the Substitute modifier from the stack.

XForm modifier

The XForm modifier enables you to apply transforms such as Move, Rotate, and Scale to objects and/or sub-objects. This modifier is applied by means of a gizmo that can be transformed using the transform buttons on the main toolbar. The XForm modifier has no parameters.

The XForm modifier solves a tricky problem that occurs during modeling. The problem happens when you scale, link, and animate objects in the scene, only to notice that the objects distort as they move. The distortion is caused because the transforms are the last action in the stack to be performed. So, when the object was first scaled and modifiers were applied, if you used the XForm modifier to do the scale transformation in the stack before the modifiers were applied, then the object's children won't inherit the scale transformation.

 XForm is short for the word *transform*.

FIGURE 13.25

The Taper modifier can be used to create a simple yo-yo.

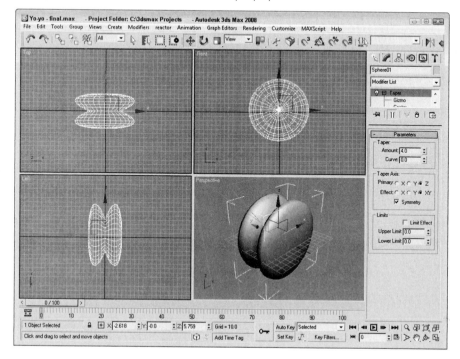

Wave modifier

The Wave modifier produces a wave-like effect across the surface of the object. All the parameters of the Wave Parameter are identical to the Ripple modifier parameters. The difference is that the waves produced by the Wave modifier are parallel, and they propagate in a straight line. Figure 13.26 shows the Wave modifier applied to a simple Quad Patch with values of 5 for Amplitude 1 and a Wave Length value of 50. The right Quad Patch also has an Amplitude 2 value of 20.

FIGURE 13.26

The Wave modifier produces parallel waves across the surface of an object.

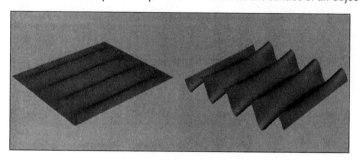

Tutorial: Waving a flag

The Wave modifier can add a gentle wave to an object such as a flag. If you animate the Phase value, you can show a flag unfurling in the breeze.

CROSS-REF For a more realistic looking flag, you can apply a Cloth modifier. See Chapter 28, "Adding and Styling Hair, Fur, and Cloth," for more information on the Cloth modifier.

To animate a flag waving with the Wave modifier, follow these steps:

1. Open the Waving US flag.max file from the Chap 13 directory on the DVD.

   This file includes a simple flag and flagpole made from primitive objects.

2. With the flag selected, select the Modifiers ⇨ Parametric Deformers ⇨ Wave menu command to apply the Wave modifier to the flag.

3. Notice how the waves run from the top of the flag to the bottom. You can change this by rotating the gizmo. Click the plus sign to the left of the Wave modifier in the Modifier Stack and select the Gizmo subobject. With the Select and Rotate tool (E), rotate the gizmo 90 degrees and then scale the gizmo with the Select and Scale tool (R) so it covers the flag object. Click the Gizmo subobject again to deselect gizmo subobject mode.

4. Set Amplitude 1 to **25**, Amplitude 2 to **0**, and the Wave Length to **50**. Then click the Auto Key button (N), drag the Time Slider to frame 100, and set the Phase value to **4**. Click the Auto Key button (N) again to exit key mode.

Figure 13.27 shows the waving flag.

FIGURE 13.27

The Wave modifier can gently wave a flag.

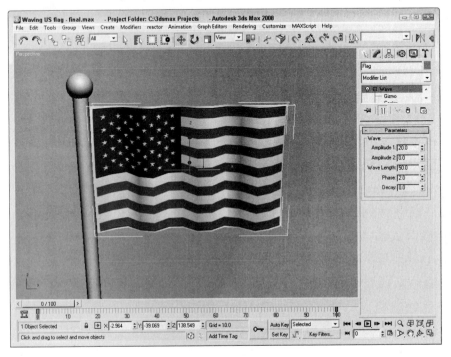

Free Form Deformer modifiers

The Free Form Deformers category of modifiers causes a lattice to appear around an object. This lattice is bound to the object, and you can alter the object's surface by moving the lattice control points. Modifiers include FFD (Free Form Deformation) and FFD (Box/Cyl).

FFD (Free Form Deformation) modifier

The Free Form Deformation modifiers create a lattice of control points around the object. The object's surface can deform the object when you move the control points. The object is deformed only if the object is within the volume of the FFD lattice. The three different resolutions of FFDs are 2×2, 3×3, and 4×4.

You can also select to display the lattice or the source volume, or both. If the Lattice option is disabled, only the control points are visible. The Source Volume option shows the original lattice before any vertices were moved.

The two deform options are Only In Volume and All Vertices. The Only In Volume option limits the vertices that can be moved to the interior vertices only. If the All Vertices option is selected, the Falloff value determines the point at which vertices are no longer affected by the FFD. Falloff values can range between 0 and 1. The Tension and Continuity values control how tight the lines of the lattice are when moved.

The three buttons at the bottom of the FFD Parameters rollout help in the selection of control points. If the All X button is selected, then when a single control point is selected, all the adjacent control points along the X-axis are also selected. This feature makes selecting an entire line of control points easier. The All Y and All Z buttons work in a similar manner in the other dimensions.

Use the Reset button to return the volume to its original shape if you make a mistake. The Conform to Shape button sets the offset of the Control Points with Inside Points, Outside Points, and Offset options.

To move the control points, select the Control Points subobject. This enables you to alter the control points individually.

FFD (Box/Cyl) modifier

The FFD (Box) and FFD (Cyl) modifiers can create a box-shaped or cylinder-shaped lattice of control points for deforming objects. The Set Number of Points button enables you to specify the number of points to be included in the FFD lattice. Figure 13.28 shows how you can use the FFD modifier to distort the hammer by selecting the Control Point's subobjects. The left hammer is distorted using a $2 \times 2 \times 2$ FFD, the middle hammer has a $4 \times 4 \times 4$ FFD, and the right hammer is surrounded with an FFD (Cyl) modifier.

FIGURE 13.28

The FFD modifier changes the shape of an object by moving the lattice of Control Points that surround it.

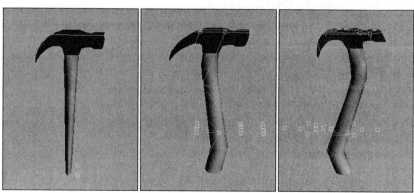

CROSS-REF The FFD (Box) and FFD (Cyl) lattices are also available as Space Warps. To learn more about Space Warps, see Chapter 37, "Using Space Warps."

Tutorial: Modeling a tire striking a curb

The FFD modifiers are great for changing the shape of a soft-body object being struck by a solid object. Soft-body objects deform around the rigid object when they make contact. In this tutorial, we deform a tire hitting a curb.

To deform a tire striking a curb using an FFD modifier, follow these steps:

1. Open the Tire hitting a curb.max file from the Chap 13 directory on the DVD.

   This file includes a simple tube object and a curb.

2. With the tire selected, choose the Modifiers ➪ Free Form Deformers ➪ FFD Cyl menu option.

   A cylinder gizmo appears around the tire.

3. Click the FFD name in the Modifier Stack, and select the Control Points subobject from the hierarchy list. Then select all the center control points in the Left viewport, and scale the control points outward with the Select and Scale tool (R) to add some roundness to the tire.

4. Then select all the control points in the lower-left corner of the Front viewport, and move these points diagonally up and to the right until the tire's edge lines up with the curb.

Figure 13.29 shows the tire as it strikes the hard curb.

FIGURE 13.29

This tire is being deformed via an FFD modifier.

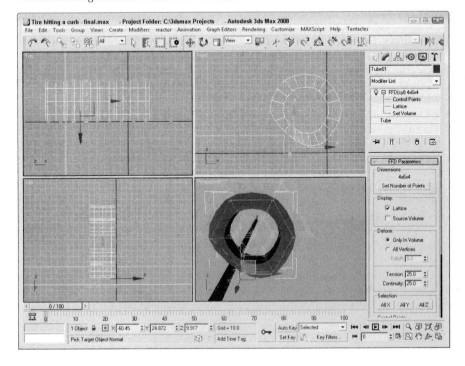

Summary

With the modifiers contained in the Modify panel, you can alter objects in a vast number of ways. Modifiers can work with every aspect of an object, including geometric deformations, materials, and general object maintenance. In this chapter, we looked at the Modifier Stack and how modifiers are applied, and examined several useful modifier sets. These topics were covered in this chapter:

- Working with the Modifier Stack to apply, reorder, and collapse modifiers
- Exploring the Selection modifiers
- Using the Parametric Deformer and FFD modifiers

This chapter concludes Part III, "Modeling Basics." You're now ready to learn about dressing up objects with materials, cameras, and lights. The next chapter covers the basics of applying materials.

Part IV

Materials, Cameras, and Lighting Basics

Chapter 14

Exploring the Material Editor

Materials are used to dress, color, and paint objects. Just as materials in real life can be described as scaly, soft, smooth, opaque, or blue, materials applied to 3D objects can mimic properties such as color, texture, transparency, shininess, and so on. In this chapter, you learn the basics of working with materials and all the features of the Material Editor.

Understanding Material Properties

Before jumping into the Material Editor, let's take a close look at the type of material properties that you will deal with. Understanding these properties will help you as you begin to create new materials.

Up until now, the only material property that has been applied to an object has been the default object color, randomly assigned by Max. The Material Editor can add a whole new level of realism using materials that simulate many different types of physical properties.

 NOTE Many of these material properties are not visible until the scene is rendered.

Colors

Color is probably the simplest material property and the easiest to identify. However, unlike the object color defined in the Create and Modify panels, there isn't a single color swatch that controls an object's color.

Consider a basket of shiny red apples. When you shine a bright blue spotlight on them, all the apples turn purple because the blue highlights from the light mix with the red of the apple's surface. So, even if the apples are assigned a red material, the final color in the image might be very different because the light makes the color change.

Within the Material Editor are several different color swatches that control different aspects of the object's color. The following list describes the types of color swatches that are available for various materials:

- **Ambient:** Defines an overall background lighting that affects all objects in the scene, including the color of the object when it is in the shadows. This color is locked to the Diffuse color by default so that they are changed together.
- **Diffuse:** The surface color of the object in normal, full, white light. The normal color of an object is typically defined by its Diffuse color.
- **Specular:** The color of the highlights where the light is focused on the surface of a shiny material.
- **Self-Illumination:** The color that the object glows from within. This color takes over any shadows on the object.
- **Filter:** The transmitted color caused by light shining through a transparent object.
- **Reflect:** The color reflected by a raytrace material to other objects in the scene.
- **Luminosity:** Causes an object to glow with the defined color. It is similar to Self-Illumination color but can be independent of the Diffuse color.

NOTE   Standard materials don't have Reflectivity and Luminosity color swatches, but these swatches are part of the Raytrace material.

If you ask someone the color of an object, he or she would respond by identifying the Diffuse color, but all these properties play an important part in bringing a sense of realism to the material. Try applying very different, bright materials to each of these color swatches and notice the results. This gives a sense of the contribution of each color.

TIP   For realistic materials, your choice of colors depends greatly on the scene lights. Indoor lights have a result different from an outdoor light like the sun. You can simulate objects in direct sunlight by giving their Specular color a yellow tint and their Ambient color a complementary, dark, almost black or purple color. For indoor objects, make the Specular color bright white and use an Ambient color that is the same as the Diffuse color, only much darker. Another option is to change the light colors instead of changing the specular colors.

Opacity and transparency

Opaque objects are objects that you cannot see through, such as rocks and trees. Transparent objects, on the other hand, are objects that you can see through, like glass and clear plastic. Max's materials include several controls for adjusting these properties, including Opacity and several Transparency controls.

Opacity is the amount that an object refuses to allow light to pass through it. It is the opposite of transparency and is typically measured as a percentage. An object with 0 percent opacity is completely transparent, and an object with an opacity of 100 percent doesn't let any light through.

Transparency is the amount of light that is allowed to pass through an object. Because this is the opposite of opacity, transparency can be defined by the opacity value. Several options enable you to control transparency, including Falloff, Amount, and Type. These options are discussed later in this chapter.

Reflection and refraction

A *reflection* is what you see when you look in the mirror. Shiny objects reflect their surroundings. By defining a material's reflection values, you can control how much it reflects its surroundings. A mirror, for example, reflects everything, but a rock won't reflect at all.

Reflection Dimming controls how much of the original reflection is lost as the surroundings are reflected within the scene.

Refraction is the bending of light as it moves through a transparent material. The amount of refraction that a material produces is expressed as a value called the Index of Refraction. The Index of Refraction is the amount that light bends as it goes through a transparent object. For example, a diamond bends light more than a glass of water, so it has a higher Index of Refraction value. The default Index of Refraction value is 1.0 for objects that don't bend light at all. Water has a value of 1.3, glass a value of around 1.5, and solid crystal a value of around 2.0.

Shininess and specular highlights

Shiny objects, such as polished metal or clean windows, include highlights where the lights reflect off their surfaces. These highlights are called *specular highlights* and are determined by the Specular settings. These settings include Specular Level, Glossiness, and Soften values.

The Specular Level is a setting for the intensity of the highlight. The Glossiness determines the size of the highlight: Higher Glossiness values result in a smaller highlight. The Soften value thins the highlight by lowering its intensity and increasing its size.

A rough material has the opposite properties of a shiny material and almost no highlights. The Roughness property sets how quickly the Diffuse color blends with the Ambient color. Cloth and fabric materials have a high Roughness value; plastic and metal Roughness values are small.

> **NOTE** Specularity is one of the most important properties that we sense to determine what kind of material the object is made from. For example, metallic objects have a specular color that is the same as their diffuse color. If the colors are different, then the objects look like plastic instead of metal.

Other properties

Max uses several miscellaneous properties to help define standard materials, including properties such as Diffuse Level and Metalness.

The Diffuse Level property controls the brightness of the Diffuse color. Decreasing this value darkens the material without affecting the specular highlights. The Metalness property controls the metallic look of the material. Some properties are available only for certain material types.

> **NOTE** Before proceeding, you need to understand the difference between a material and a map. A *material* is an effect that permeates the 3D object, but most *maps* are 2D images (although procedural 3D maps also exist) that can be wrapped on top of the object. Materials can contain maps, and maps can be made up of several materials. In the Material Editor, materials appear shaded in the sample slots, and maps appear as 2D images. Usually, you can tell whether you're working with a material or a map by looking at the default name. Maps show up in the name drop-down list as Map and a number (Map #1), and materials are named a number and Default (7- Default).

Working with the Material Editor

The Material Editor is the interface with which you define, create, and apply materials. You can access the Material Editor by choosing Rendering ➪ Material Editor, clicking the Material Editor button on the main toolbar (it has four small rendered spheres on the icon), or using the M keyboard shortcut.

Using the Material Editor controls

At the top of the default Material Editor window is a menu of options including Material, Navigation, Options, and Utilities. The menu commands found in these menus offer the same functionality as the tool-bar buttons, but the menus are often easier to find than the buttons with which you are unfamiliar.

Below the menus are six sample slots that display a preview of some available materials. Surrounding these slots are button icons for controlling the appearance of these sample slots and interacting with materials. Figure 14.1 shows the Material Editor.

The button icons to the right and below the sample slots control how the materials appear in the editor. These buttons are defined in Tables 14.1 and 14.2.

FIGURE 14.1

Use the Material Editor window to create, store, and work with materials.

Sample slots

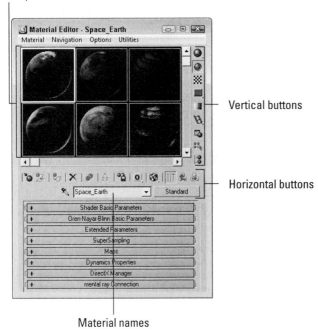

Vertical buttons

Horizontal buttons

Material names

TABLE 14.1

Material Editor Buttons — Vertical

Toolbar Button	Name	Description
	Sample Type (Sphere, Cylinder, Box, Custom)	Controls the type of object displayed in the sample slot. The default object is a sphere. Other options available as flyouts include a cylinder and a cube. You can also select a custom object to use as the preview object.
	Backlight (L)	Turns backlighting in the selected sample slot on or off.
	Background (B)	Displays a checkered background image (or a custom background) behind the material, which is helpful when displaying a transparent material.
	Sample UV Tiling (1×1, 2 × 2, 3 × 3, 4 × 4)	Sets UV tiling for the map in the sample slot. The default is 1 × 1. Additional options available as flyouts are 2 × 2, 3 × 3, and 4 × 4. This setting affects only maps.
	Video Color Check	Checks the current material for colors that are unsupported by the NTSC and PAL formats.
	Make Preview (P), Play Preview, Save Preview	Used to generate, view, and save material preview renderings. These animated material previews enable you to see the effect of an animated material before rendering.
	Options (O)	Opens the Material Editor Options dialog box. This dialog box includes settings for enabling material animation, loading a custom background, defining the light intensity and color, and specifying the number of sample slots.
	Select by Material	Selects all objects using the current material. This button opens the Select Objects dialog box with those objects selected.
	Material/ MapNavigator	Opens the Material/Map Navigator dialog box. This dialog box displays a tree of all the levels for the current material.

TABLE 14.2

Material Editor Buttons — Horizontal

Toolbar Button	Name	Description
	Get Material (G)	Opens the Material/Map Browser for selecting materials.
	Put Material in Scene	Updates the materials applied to objects in the viewport after materials have been edited.
	Assign Material to Selection	Applies the selected object with the selected material.
	Reset Map/Mtl to Default Settings	Removes any modified properties and resets the material properties to their defaults.
	Make Material Copy	Creates a copy of the current material in the selected sample slot.
	Make Unique	Makes instanced materials into a new stand-alone material.
	Put to Library	Opens a simple dialog box that lets you rename the material and saves it into the current open library.
	Material Effects Channel	Sets a unique channel ID for applying post-processing effects. This button includes channels 1–15 as flyouts. A material with channel 0 means that no effect will be applied.
	Show Map in Viewport, Show Hardware Map in Viewport	Displays 2D material maps and hardware maps on objects in the viewports.
	Show End Result	Displays the material in the sample slot with all levels applied. If this button is disabled, you will see only the level that is currently selected.
	Go to Parent	Moves up one level for the current material. This applies only to compound objects with several levels.
	Go Forward to Sibling	Selects the next map or material at the same level.
	Pick Material From Object	Enables you to select a material from an object in the scene and load the material into the selected sample slot.
 Metal_Brushed ▼	Material drop-down list	Lists the elements in the current material. You can change the material or map name by typing a new name in this field.
 Standard	Type button	Displays the current material or map type that is being used. Clicking this button opens the Material/Map Browser where you can select a new material or map type.

NEW FEATURE The Show Hardware Map in Viewport button is new to 3ds Max 2008.

Below the material name and type button is where the rollouts for the current material are opened. These rollouts change depending on the material type.

CROSS-REF The Material Effects Channel IDs are used with the Rendering Effects dialog box to apply specific effects, such as glow and blur, to a material. To learn more about these effects, see Chapter 45, "Using Atmospheric and Render Effects."

Using the sample slots

The Material Editor includes 24 sample slots that display materials and map examples. Each of these sample slots contains one material or map. Only one sample slot can be selected at a time: The selected slot is outlined with a white border. Click one of the material slots to select it.

NOTE Sample slots cannot be empty: They always contain some kind of material.

Sample slots are temporary placeholders for materials and maps. An actual scene can have hundreds of materials. By loading a material into a sample slot, you can change its parameters, apply it to other objects, or save it to a library for use in other scenes. When a file is saved, all materials in the Material Editor are saved with the file.

Twenty-four slots are available, but the default layout displays only six. You can access the other 18 slots using the scroll bars. You can also change the number of displayed slots. To change the number of slots, choose Options ➪ Cycle Sample Slots (or press the X key), or right-click any of the material slots and select 2 × 3, 3 × 5, or 4 × 6 from the pop-up menu. These options are also available in the Options dialog box (keyboard shortcut, O). Figure 14.2 shows the Material Editor with 24 sample slots displayed.

FIGURE 14.2

You can set the number of sample slots in the Material Editor to display 6, 15, or 24 slots.

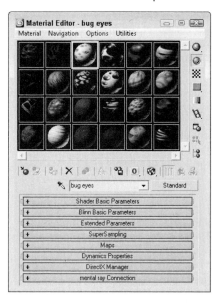

 The 24 default sample slots that are by default a dull gray are loaded from the medit.mat file in the \matlibs subdirectory. To load your own custom default materials, save them into this file.

Magnifying a sample slot

The Material ⇨ Launch Magnify Window menu command (also found in the right-click pop-up menu) opens the material in a magnified window. You can also open this window by double-clicking the sample slot. You can resize the window to view the material at any size, and you can set it to automatically update when changes are made. If the Auto option is disabled, you can update the material by clicking the Update button. Figure 14.3 shows the magnified window. This window is great for seeing the intricate details of a material.

FIGURE 14.3

Open materials in a magnified window by double-clicking them.

Using different sample objects

You can change the Sample Type object displayed in the sample slots to be a sphere, cylinder, or box using the Sample Type button at the top right of the Material Editor window.

The Options button (the seventh button from the top in the vertical column of buttons at the right) opens the Material Editor Options dialog box (also opened with the keyboard shortcut, O), where you can designate a custom sample object. The sample object must be contained in a .max file. To create a sample object, create and save a Max scene with a single object that fits inside a 100-unit cube.

The scene can also include custom lights and cameras. The object must have Mapping Coordinates enabled. You can enable them by selecting the Generate Mapping Coordinates option for primitive objects or by applying the UVW Map modifier. To make the object available, click the File Name button and select the option to Load Camera and/or Lights in the Material Editor Options dialog box. After the object loads, its name appears on the button in the Options dialog box. You can then select the custom object from the Object Type flyout button. Figure 14.4 shows the Material Editor with several different object types loaded, including a custom object.

Dragging materials

When you right-click the active sample slot, a pop-up menu appears. From this menu, you can select several commands. The Drag/Copy command is a toggle setting. This option also lets you drag and drop materials between the various sample slots. When the Drag/Copy option is enabled, it leaves a copy of the material when it's dragged to another slot. This option also allows you to drag a material to an object in the viewports. Dropping a material onto an object automatically assigns the material to that object.

FIGURE 14.4

You can load a custom sample object to be displayed in the sample slots.

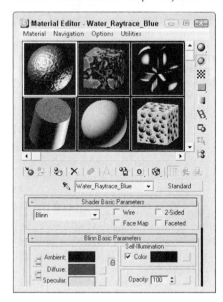

The Drag/Rotate pop-up menu command (also found in the Options menu) lets you rotate the material object in the sample slot when you drag with the mouse. Dragging on the object rotates it about its X-axis and Y-axis, and dragging from the corner of the sample slot rotates it about its Z-axis. This feature is useful for looking at how maps are applied. Holding down the Shift key constrains the rotation about a single axis. The Material ⟳ Reset Sample Slot Rotation menu command resets the material object to its original orientation.

You can also drag materials from the sample slots back and forth among the Material/Map Browser, the Asset Browser Utility, and any rollouts where you can specify maps, such as the Environment Map button (found in the Environment dialog box, accessed via Rendering ⟳ Environment) and the Projector and Shadow Map buttons (found in the rollouts for a selected light).

Naming materials

Every material has a name that appears beneath the sample slots in a drop-down list. This same name appears in the Material Editor's title bar. You can rename a material by typing a new name in the material name drop-down list. This name appears in the Material/Map Navigator dialog box and in the Track View. As you create materials, give each one a unique name that is easy to identify. When a material is saved to a Library with the Put to Library button, a dialog box opens that enables you to rename the material. You can see the name of any of the materials in the sample slots by moving the mouse over the top of the sample slot; the material name appears as a tooltip.

NOTE If you drag a material from one sample slot to another, a copy is made with the same name as the original. If one of these materials is changed and then applied to the scene, a warning dialog box appears stating that a material with the same name already exists in the scene. It also gives you the option of replacing or renaming the material.

Getting new materials

You load new materials into the sample slots by clicking the Get Material button (the leftmost button on the horizontal toolbar), choosing the Material ⇨ Get Material menu command, or pressing the G key. This opens the Material/Map Browser where you can select a new material by double-clicking it. The new material loads into the selected sample slot. The Material/Map Browser is covered later in this chapter.

CAUTION   The Material/Map Browser holds materials and maps. If you select a material map, a 2D map is loaded into the sample slot. 2D maps cannot be applied directly to an object in the viewport. You can tell the difference between maps and materials because maps are flat 2D bitmaps and materials are shown on an object like a sphere.

Assigning materials to objects

When you select a material, you can apply it to the selected object in the viewports with the Assign Material to Selection button (the third button from the left on the horizontal toolbar under the sample slots) or with the Material ⇨ Assign to Selection menu command. Alternatively, you can drag a material from its sample slot and drop it on an object.

When you assign a material to an object in the scene, the material becomes "Hot." A *Hot material* is automatically updated in the scene when the material parameters change. Hot materials have white corner brackets displayed around their sample slots. You can "cool" a material by clicking the Copy Material button (the fifth from the left) or choosing Material ⇨ Make Material Copy menu command. This detaches the sample slot from the material in the scene to which it is applied, so that any changes to the material aren't applied to the object.

Whenever a material is applied to an object in the scene, the material is added to a special library of materials that get saved with the scene. Materials do not need to be loaded in one of the sample slots to be in the scene library. You can also load materials into the scene library that aren't applied to an object using the Put Material to Scene button (the second button from the left) or the Material ⇨ Put to Scene menu command. You can see all the materials included in the scene library in the Material/Map Browser by selecting the Scene radio button.

In addition to the scene library, you can also put materials into a separate material library. The Put to Library button (the seventh from the left) or the Material ⇨ Put to Library menu command places the current selected material into the default library. Clicking the Get Material button opens the Material/Map Browser where you can see the current library by clicking the Material Library radio button.

Picking materials from a scene

Another useful option is obtaining a material from an object in the scene. Clicking the eyedropper button to the left of the Material Name or choosing the Material ⇨ Pick from Object menu command changes the cursor to an eyedropper. You can then click an object in one of the viewports, and the object's material is loaded into the current sample slot.

Selecting objects by material

If you want to select all the objects in your scene with a specific material applied (like the shiny gold material), then select the material in the sample slots and click on the Select by Material button in the vertical set of buttons, or choose the Utilities ⇨ Select Objects by Material menu command. This command opens the Select Objects dialog box with all the objects that have the selected material applied. Clicking the Select button selects these objects in the viewport.

Previewing materials and rendering maps

The Material ⇨ Make Preview menu command, along with the Make Preview button and the P keyboard shortcut, opens the Create Material Preview dialog box, shown in Figure 14.5. Using this dialog box, you can create a preview of an animated material. The dialog box lets you specify the Preview Range and Frame Rate, as well as the Image Size, which is a percentage of the default resolution.

 **Animated materials are covered in Chapter 20, "Understanding Animation and Keyframe Basics."**

After you create a material preview, you can view the preview with the Material ⇨ View Preview menu command. This opens the default media player and plays the animated preview. To save the preview as a file, use the Material ⇨ Save Preview menu command. Preview files are saved as .AVI files.

The Utilities ⇨ Render Map menu command (also found in the right-click pop-up menu) opens the Render Map dialog box, shown in Figure 14.5. This option is available only if the selected material has a map applied. The Render Map dialog box lets you select the Range of frames to include and the Dimensions of the rendered image. You can click the Files button to open a file dialog box where you can name the render map and specify the file type. The Render button renders the current map as a bitmap or an animation to the Rendered Frame Window and to the file (if selected).

FIGURE 14.5

The Create Material Preview and Render Map dialog boxes offer two ways to render a material.

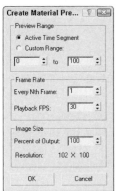
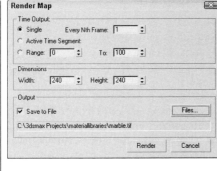

 **You can save render maps as .AVI, .BMP, .CIN, .EPS, .FLC, .HDR, .JPEG, .PNG, .MOV, .SGI, .RGB, .RLA, .RPF, .TGA, .jpg, and .DDS files.**

Setting Material Editor options

You open the Material Editor Options dialog box by clicking the Options button to the right of the sample slots, selecting Options from the Options menu, right-clicking the pop-up menu, or by just pressing the O key. Figure 14.6 shows this dialog box.

FIGURE 14.6

The Material Editor Options dialog box offers many options for controlling the Material Editor window.

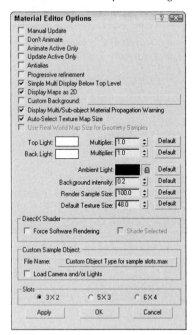

The Material Editor Options dialog box includes options that control how the materials are displayed in the sample slots. These options are as follows:

- **Manual Update:** Doesn't update any changes in the sample slot until the slot is clicked on.

- **Don't Animate:** Causes materials not to animate when an animation is played or the Time Slider is dragged. It does, however, update these materials to the current frame.

- **Animate Active Only:** Animates only the active sample slot if it contains an animated material. This option isn't available when the Don't Animate option is selected.

- **Update Active Only:** Updates only the active sample slot when changes are made to the material.

- **Antialias:** Enables anti-aliasing for all sample slots. Aliasing is a negative staircase-type effect that occurs for pixel-based images when adjacent pixels along the edges of an image are different colors. Anti-aliasing is a process for eliminating this distracting effect and smoothing the edges.

- **Progressive refinement:** Causes materials to be rendered progressively. This causes the material to appear quickly as blocky sections and then slowly in more detail. This gives you a rough idea of how the material looks before the rendering is finished.

- **Simple Multi Display Below Top Level:** Displays several different areas for only the top level when a Multi/Sub-Object material is applied.

- **Display Maps as 2D:** Displays stand-alone maps in 2D and not on the sample object. This feature helps you to know when you're looking at a map versus a material.

- **Custom Background:** Enables you to use a custom background behind the sample slots. You can load the background using the button to the right of the option. Once changed, the new background is used in all sample slots where the background is enabled.
- **Display Multi/Sub-object Material Propagation Warning:** Lets you to disable the warning screen that appears when you apply a Multi/Sub-object Material to an instanced object.
- **Auto-Select Texture Map Size:** Automatically scales Real-World textures on the sample sphere so that they appear correctly.
- **Use Real-World Map Size for Geometry Samples:** Causes all textures displayed within the sample slots to use Real-World mapping coordinates. This option is available when the Auto-Select Texture Map Size option is disabled.

This dialog box also offers options to adjust the color and intensity of the Top and Backlights used to render the materials in the sample slots. The intensity of these lights is determined by the Multiplier values. You use the Ambient Light Intensity value to control the brightness of the Ambient light in the sample slots; use the lock icon to set the color to the same as the Diffuse color. The Background Intensity value sets the brightness of the background: A value of 0 produces a black background, and 1 produces a white background. The Render Sample Size option scales the maps applied to the sample object for all slots. By scaling the map, you can match it up with the scale of an object in the scene. The Render Sample Size value lets you define the size of the sample slot object using the default units. Changing this value doesn't change the object size in the sample slots, but is used as a reference to the texture size. The Default Texture Size value sets the initial size of Real-World textures. This value applies only to Real-World textures and is ignored by textures using other mapping methods. You can reset all these options to their default values using the Default buttons on the right.

The Custom Sample Object button is for loading a Custom Sample Object (as discussed earlier). The Slots option is used to specify the number of sample slots.

Resetting materials

The Reset Material/Maps to Default Settings button (the fourth from the left) lets you reset the selected material to its default settings. If you apply the selected material to a material in the scene, then a dialog box appears that lets you reset just the sample slots or both the sample slots and the material applied to objects in the scene.

The Utilities ⇨ Reset Material Editor Slots menu command is used to reset all sample slots to the default material. You can also set all unused material sample slots to the default material using the Utilities ⇨ Condense Material Editor Slots menu command. This replaces all materials that aren't applied to a scene object. It also moves all used materials to the top of the Material Editor sample slots. Both the Reset and Condense commands can be restored to their previous set of materials using the Utilities ⇨ Restore Material Editor Slots menu command.

Removing materials and maps

If you accidentally apply an unwanted material to an object, you can replace the material with another material by dragging the new material onto the object. If you want to view the object color within the viewport, then open the Display panel, and in the Display Color rollout, select the Object color option for Wireframe and Shaded. The Material Color options display the material color in the viewports.

371

If you apply a material or map to an object that doesn't look just right and tweaking it won't help, you can always return to square one by removing the material or any mappings that have been applied to the object. The tool to remove materials and maps is the UVW Remove utility. You can access this utility by clicking the More button in the Utility panel and selecting UVW Remove from the list of utilities.

This utility includes a single rollout that lists the number of objects selected. It also includes two buttons. The UVW button removes any mapping coordinates from the selected objects, and the Materials button removes any materials from the selected objects. This button restores the original object color to the selected objects. Alternatively, you can select the Set Gray option, which makes the selected object gray when the materials are removed.

Using the Fix Ambient utility

Standard material types always have their Ambient and Diffuse colors locked together. If you have older files with unlocked Diffuse and Ambient colors, the Fix Ambient utility can be used to locate and fix all materials in the scene with this condition. To access this utility, open the Utilities panel, click the More button, and select the Fix Ambient utility. Clicking the Find All button opens a dialog box that lists all materials in the scene with unlocked Diffuse and Ambient colors.

Tutorial: Coloring Easter eggs

Everyone loves spring with its bright colors and newness of life. One of the highlights of the season is the tradition of coloring Easter eggs. In this tutorial, we use virtual eggs — no messy dyes and no egg salad sandwiches for the next two weeks.

To create our virtual Easter eggs and apply different colors to them, follow these steps:

1. Open the Easter eggs.max file from the Chap 14 directory on the DVD.

   This file contains several egg-shaped objects.

2. Open the Material Editor by choosing Rendering ⇨ Material Editor (or press the M key).

3. Increase the number of sample slots by right-clicking the active material and selecting 5 × 3 Sample Windows from the pop-up menu (or press the X key).

4. Select the first sample slot, and click the Diffuse color swatch in the rollout below it. From the Color Selector that appears, drag the cursor around the color palette until you find the color you want and then click Close.

5. In any viewport, select an egg and then click the Assign Material to Selection button in the Material Editor, or you can simply drag the material from its sample slot to the viewport object.

6. Repeat Steps 4 and 5 for all the eggs.

Figure 14.7 shows the assortment of eggs that we just created.

FIGURE 14.7

These eggs have been assigned materials with different Diffuse colors.

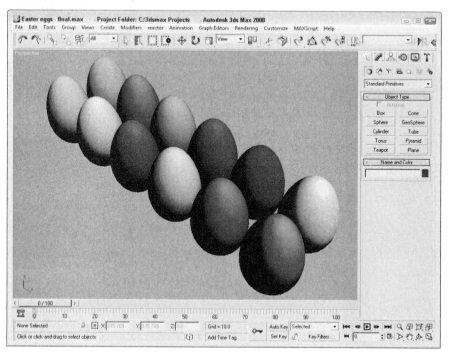

Using the Material/Map Browser

Now that you know how to apply materials to objects, the easiest way to get materials is from the Material/Map Browser. Max ships with several libraries of materials that you can access. If you click the Get Material button (or press the G key), the Material/Map Browser, shown in Figure 14.8, appears.

The Material/Map Browser is the place where all your materials are stored. They are stored in sets called libraries. These libraries are saved along with the scene file or they can be saved as a separate file. The Material/Map Browser opens whenever you change material types (by clicking on the material type button), choose a new map, or click the Get Material button. Materials are indicated with a blue sphere icon, and material maps have a green parallelogram next to them. Mental ray materials and maps are indicated in yellow, a red sphere appears for materials that have the Show Map in Viewport option enabled, and DirectX Shaders are shown in magenta.

FIGURE 14.8

The Material/Map Browser lets you select new materials from a library of materials.

View options

Material icon | Material Library name

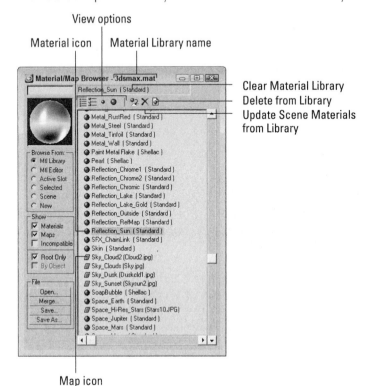

Clear Material Library
Delete from Library
Update Scene Materials
from Library

Map icon

The Material/Map Browser includes several browse options accessible as radio buttons on the left of the dialog box. The browse options include Material Library, Material Editor, Active Slot, Selected, Scene, and New. The Material Library options list all the materials available in the open material library. The current library set is listed in the title bar of the Material/Map Browser. The Material Editor options lists the 24 materials found in the current sample slots. The Active Slot option lists the single material found in the selected sample slot. The Selected and Scene options list the materials applied to the selected viewport objects or all the materials found in the current scene. The New option is the default and lists all the available material types and maps.

You can also limit the material list to show only materials, only maps, or both. The Incompatible option displays all materials and maps that will not work with the current assigned renderer. For example, the mental ray materials are not compatible with the default Scanline renderer. Incompatible materials and maps are shown in gray. You can also specify to see all the pieces that make up a material or only the base material with the Root Only option.

> **NOTE** All instanced materials are listed in bold within the Material/Map Browser and within the Material/Map Navigator interfaces.

The view options buttons above the material list enable you to display the materials and maps in different ways. They include List, List + Icons, Small Icons, and Large Icons. Figure 14.9 shows two different display methods.

FIGURE 14.9

You can use the Material/Map Browser to view the materials in many different ways, such as View List + Icons and Large Icons.

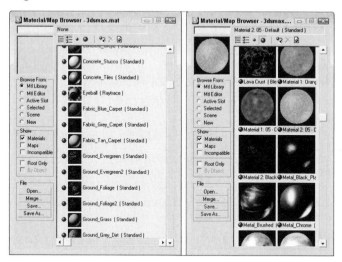

The text field directly above the material sample slot in the Material/Map Browser is a selection field. By typing a name in this field, you can search and select materials. Above the material list, three additional buttons become enabled when you open a material library. These buttons let you update the scene, delete the selected material from the library, and clear the entire library.

Working with libraries

Anytime you adjust a material or a map parameter, a new material is created and the material's sample slot is updated. Although newly created materials are saved along with the scene file, you can make them available for reuse by including them in a library.

NOTE   Max ships with several different material libraries, including Backgrounds, Bricks, Concrete, Fabric, Ground, Metal, Nature, RayTraced, ReflectionMaps, Skys, Space, Stones, Wood, and several architecture material sets. You can find all these libraries in the matlibs directory.

You can save new materials to a new library or to the default library. Select the material's sample slot, and click the Put in Library button to open a simple dialog box in which you can name the material and add it to the current library.

To see which library is current, open the Material/Map Browser by clicking the Get Material button. Select the Mtl Library option in the Browse From section: The library name is shown in the title bar. The File section includes four buttons for opening, merging, and saving material libraries. After you've created all the materials you want to keep to a library, the Save button lets you save the library as a file. Material libraries are saved with the .mat extension.

CROSS-REF   Although materials can be saved out as libraries, perhaps the easiest way to share materials between applications is using the Material XML Export utility. To learn about this utility, see Chapter 3, "Working with Files, Importing, and Exporting."

Tutorial: Loading a custom material library

To practice loading a material library, I've created a custom library of materials using various textures created with Kai's Power Tools.

To load a custom material library, follow these steps:

1. Choose Rendering ⇨ Material Editor (or press the M key) to open the Material Editor. Then click the Get Material button, which is the leftmost button on the horizontal toolbar (or press the G key), to open the Material/Map Browser.

2. In the Browse From section, select the Mtl Library option and click the Open button.

3. Select and open the KPT samples.mat file from the Chap 14 directory on the DVD.

   The library loads into the Material/Map Browser.

4. In the selection field (above the sample slot), type **Bug** to locate and select the bug eyes material.

Figure 14.10 shows the Material/Map Browser with the custom material library open.

FIGURE 14.10

The Material/Map Browser also lets you work with saved custom material libraries.

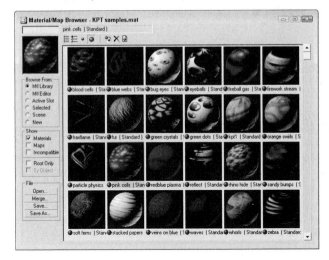

Using the Material/Map Navigator

Each material can consist of several submaterials. For example, anytime a map is added to a material, it becomes a submaterial. A single material can consist of many submaterials, which may be maps or materials. You can edit each submaterial by accessing the rollouts associated with it. The trick is being able to locate the various submaterials. This is where the Material/Map Navigator comes in handy.

The Material/Map Navigator, shown in Figure 14.11, shows all the submaterials that make up a material in a hierarchy list. Double-clicking a submaterial opens the submaterial and all of its associated rollouts in the Material Editor.

The Material/Map Navigator shows the layered material as a hierarchy.

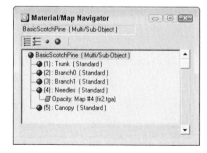

The Material/Map Navigator, like the Material/Map Browser, offers several viewing methods for the submaterials, including View List, View List + Icons, View Small Icons, and View Large Icons.

When you select a submaterial, its object type is displayed on the Object Type button. Directly above this button are three buttons that become active when you select a submaterial. These buttons, shown in Table 14.3, enable you to navigate the submaterial hierarchy. The rightmost button is Go Forward to Sibling. This moves to the next adjacent submaterial on the same level. The Go to Parent button (the second from the right) selects the submaterial's parent. The Show End Result button is a toggle button that shows the selected submaterial or the resulting material with all submaterials included. These options are also available from the Navigation menu. The keyboard shortcuts for these buttons are the arrow keys — Up arrow for Go to Parent, Right arrow for Go Forward to Sibling, and Left arrow for Go Backward to Sibling.

TABLE 14.3

Submaterial Navigation Buttons

Button	Description
	Go Forward to Sibling
	Go to Parent
	Show End Result

If the submaterial is itself a material, such as one of the submaterials for the Multi/Sub-object material, then you can separate the submaterial from the base material using the Make Unique button.

Summary

Materials can add much to the realism of your models. Learning to use the Material Editor, the Material/Map Browser, and the Material/Map Navigator enables you to work with materials. This chapter covered the following topics:

- Understanding various material properties
- Working with the Material Editor buttons and sample slots
- Using the Material/Map Browser and material libraries
- Using the Material/Map Navigator to view submaterials

The next chapter delves more into the topic of material, including the standard material and all its settings.

Chapter 15

Creating and Applying Standard Materials

N ow that you've learned the basic material properties and acquainted yourself with the Material Editor, this chapter gives you a chance to create some simple original materials and apply them to objects in the scene. The simplest material is based on the Standard material type, which is the default material type. Several external tools can be very helpful when you create materials. These tools include an image-editing package such as Photoshop, a digital camera, and a scanner. With these tools, you can create and capture bitmap images that can be applied as materials to the surface of the object.

IN THIS CHAPTER

Using standard materials

Learning the various shaders

Exploring the Material rollouts

Creating textures with Photoshop

Using the Standard Material

Standard materials are the default Max material type. They provide a single, uniform color determined by the Ambient, Diffuse, Specular, and Filter color swatches. Standard materials can use any one of several different shaders. *Shaders* are algorithms used to compute how the material should look, given its parameters.

Standard materials have parameters for controlling highlights, opacity, and self-illumination. It also includes many other parameters sprinkled throughout many different rollouts. With all the various rollouts, even a standard material has an infinite number of possibilities.

Using Shading Types

Max includes several different shader types. These shaders are all available in a drop-down list in the Shader Basic Parameters rollout. Each shader type displays different options in its respective Basic Parameters rollout. Figure 15.1 shows the basic parameters for the Blinn shader. Other available shaders include Anisotropic, Metal, Multi-Layer, Oren-Nayar-Blinn, Phong, Strauss, and Translucent Shader.

The Shader Basic Parameters rollout also includes several options for shading the material, including Wire, 2-Sided, Face Map, and Faceted, as shown in Figure 15.1. Wire mode causes the model to appear as a wireframe model. The 2-Sided option makes the material appear on both sides of the face and is typically used in conjunction with the Wire option or with transparent materials. The Face Map mode applies maps to each single face on the object. Faceted ignores the smoothing between faces.

 Using the Wire option or the 2-Sided option is different from the wireframe display option in the viewports. The Wire and 2-Sided options define how the object looks when rendered.

FIGURE 15.1

Basic parameter options include (from left to right) Wire, 2-Sided, Face Map, and Faceted.

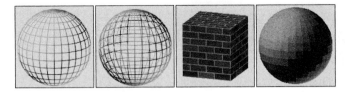

Blinn shader

This shader is the default. It renders simple circular highlights and smoothes adjacent faces.

The Blinn shader includes color swatches for setting Ambient, Diffuse, Specular, and Self-Illumination colors. To change the color, click the color swatch and select a new color in the Color Selector dialog box.

 You can drag colors among the various color swatches. When you do so, the Copy or Swap Colors dialog box appears, which enables you to copy or swap the colors.

You can use the Lock buttons to the left of the color swatches to lock the colors together so that both colors are identical and a change to one automatically changes the other. You can lock Ambient to Diffuse and Diffuse to Specular.

The small square buttons to the right of the Ambient, Diffuse, Specular, Self-Illumination, Opacity, Specular Level, and Glossiness controls are shortcut buttons for adding a map in place of the respective parameter. Clicking these buttons opens the Material/Map Browser where you can select the map type. You can also lock the Ambient and Diffuse maps together with the lock icon to the right of the map buttons. The Ambient and Diffuse colors are locked together by default.

When a map is loaded and active, it appears in the Maps rollout and an uppercase letter *M* appears on its button. When a map is loaded but inactive, a lowercase *m* appears. After you apply a map, these buttons open to make the map the active level and display its parameters in the rollouts. Figure 15.2 shows these map buttons.

 For more on Maps and the various map types, see Chapter 17, "Adding Material Details with Maps."

FIGURE 15.2

The Blinn Basic Parameters rollout lets you select and control properties for the Blinn shader.

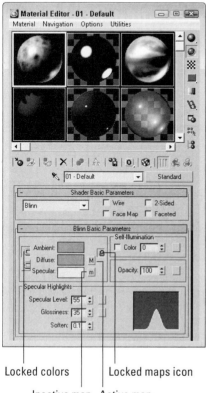

Locked colors   Locked maps icon

Inactive map   Active map

Self-Illumination can use a color if the Color option is enabled. If this option is disabled, a spinner appears that enables you to adjust the amount of default color used for illumination. Materials with a Self-Illumination value of 100 or a bright color like white lose all shadows and appear to glow from within. This happens because the self-illumination color replaces the ambient color, but a material with self-illumination can still have specular highlights. To remove the effect of Self-Illumination, set the spinner to 0 or the color to black. Figure 15.3 shows a sphere with Self-Illumination values (from left to right) of 0, 25, 50, 75, and 100.

FIGURE 15.3

Increasing the Self-Illumination value reduces the shadows in an object.

The Opacity spinner sets the level of transparency of an object. A value of 100 makes a material completely opaque, while a value of 0 makes the material completely transparent. Use the Background button (located on the upper-right side of the Material Editor) to enable a patterned background image to make it easier to view the effects of the Opacity setting. Figure 15.4 shows materials with Opacity values of 10, 25, 50, 75, and 90.

FIGURE 15.4

The Opacity value sets how transparent a material is.

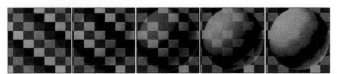

Specular highlights are the bright points on the surface where the light is reflected at a maximum value. The Specular Level value determines how bright the highlight is. Its values can range from 0, where there is no highlight, to 100, where the highlight is at a maximum. The graph to the right of the values displays the intensity per distance for a cross section of the highlight. The Specular Level defines the height of the curve or the value at the center of the highlight where it is the brightest. This value can be overloaded to accept numbers greater than 100. Overloaded values create a larger, wider highlight.

The Glossiness value determines the size of the highlight. A value of 100 produces a pinpoint highlight, and a value of 0 increases the highlight to the edges of the graph. The Soften value doesn't affect the graph, but it spreads the highlight across the area defined by the Glossiness value. It can range from 0 (wider) to 1 (thinner). Figure 15.5 shows a sampling of materials with specular highlights. The left image has a Specular Level of 20 and a Glossiness of 10, the second image has the Specular Level increased to 80, the third image has the Specular Level overloaded with a value of 150, and the last two images have the Glossiness value increased to 50 and 80, respectively.

FIGURE 15.5

You can control specular highlights by altering brightness and size.

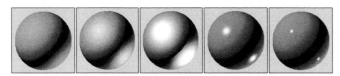

Phong shader

The Phong shader creates smooth surfaces like Blinn without the quality highlights, but it renders more quickly than the Blinn shader does. The parameters for the Phong shader are identical to those for the Blinn shader. The differences between Blinn and Phong are very subtle, but Blinn can produce highlights for lights at low angles to the surface, and its highlights are generally softer.

 **TIP** The Blinn shader is typically used to simulate softer materials like rubber, but the Phong shader is better for hard materials like plastic.

Anisotropic shader

The Anisotropic shader is characterized by non-circular highlights. The Anisotropy value is the difference between the two axes that make up the highlight. A value of 0 is circular, but higher values increase the difference between the axes, and the highlights are more elliptical.

Most of the parameters for this shader are the same as those for the Blinn shader, but several parameters of the Anisotropic type are unique. The Diffuse Level value determines how bright the Diffuse color appears. This is similar to Self-Illumination, but it doesn't affect the specular highlights or the shadows. Values can range from 0 to 400.

Compared with the Blinn shader, the Specular Highlight graph looks very different. That is because it displays two highlight components that intersect at the middle. The Specular Level value still controls the height of the curve, and the Glossiness still controls the width, but the Anisotropy value changes the width of one axis relative to the other, creating elliptical highlights. The Orientation value rotates the highlight. Figure 15.6 compares the Specular Highlight graphs for the Blinn and Anisotropic shaders.

TIP Because the Anisotrophy shader can produce elliptical highlights, it is often used on surfaces with strong grooves and strands, like fabrics and stainless steel objects.

FIGURE 15.6

The Specular Highlight graph for the Blinn and Anisotropic shaders

Figure 15.7 shows several materials with the Anisotropic shader applied. The first three images have Anisotropic values of 30, 60, and 90, and the last two images have Orientation values of 30 and 60.

FIGURE 15.7

Materials with the Anisotropic shader applied have elliptical highlights.

Multi-Layer shader

The Multi-Layer shader includes two Anisotropic highlights. Each of these highlights can have a different color. All parameters for this shader are the same as the Anisotropic shader described previously, except that there are two Specular Layers and one additional parameter: Roughness. The Roughness parameter defines how well the Diffuse color blends into the Ambient color. When Roughness is set to a value of 0, an object appears the same as with the Blinn shader, but with higher values, up to 100, the material grows darker.

Figure 15.8 shows several materials with a Multi-Layer shader applied. The first two images have two specular highlights each with an Orientation value of 60 and Anisotropy values of 60 and 90. The third image

383

has an increased Specular Level of 110 and a decrease in the Glossiness to 10. The fourth image has a change in the Orientation value for one of the highlights to 20, and the final image has a drop in the Anisotrophy value to 10.

 **TIP** The Multi-Layer shader is useful to give a material a sense of surface depth. For example, it can give the illusion of a layer of shellac on wood or a layer of wax on tile.

FIGURE 15.8

Materials with a Multi-Layer shader applied can have two crossing highlights.

Oren-Nayar-Blinn shader

The Oren-Nayar-Blinn shader is useful for creating materials for matte surfaces such as cloth and fabric. The parameters are identical to the Blinn shader, with the addition of the Diffuse Level and Roughness values.

Metal shader

The Metal shader simulates the luster of metallic surfaces. The Highlight curve has a shape that is different from that of the other shaders. It is rounder at the top and doesn't include a Soften value. It can also accept a much higher Specular Level value (up to 999) than the other shaders. Also, you cannot specify a Specular color. All other parameters are similar to those of the Blinn shader. Figure 15.9 shows several materials with the Metal shader applied. These materials differ in Specular Level values, which are (from left to right) 50, 100, 200, 400, and 800.

 **NOTE** For the Metal shader, the specular color is always the same as the material's diffuse color.

FIGURE 15.9

A material with a Metal shader applied generates its own highlights.

Strauss shader

The Strauss shader provides another alternative for creating metal materials. This shader has only four parameters: Color, Glossiness, Metalness, and Opacity. Glossiness controls the entire highlight shape. The Metalness value makes the material appear more metal-like by affecting the primary and secondary highlights. Both of these values can range between 0 and 100.

 **TIP** The Strauss shader is often better at making metal than the Metal shader because of its smoothness value and the ability to mix colors with the Metalness property.

Translucent shader

The Translucent shader allows light to easily pass through an object. It is intended to be used on thin, flat plane objects, such as a bed sheet used for displaying shadow puppets. Most of the settings for this shader are the same as the others, except that it includes a Translucent color. This color is the color that the light becomes as it passes through an object with this material applied. This shader also includes a Filter color and an option for disabling the specular highlights on the backside of the object.

Tutorial: Making curtains translucent

The Translucent shader can be used to create an interesting effect. Not only does light shine through an object with this shader applied, but shadows also are visible.

To make window curtains translucent, follow these steps:

1. Open the Translucent curtains.max file from the Chap 15 directory on the DVD.

   This file contains a simple scene of a tree positioned outside a window.

2. Open the Material Editor by choosing Rendering ⇨ Material Editor, by clicking the Material Editor button on the main toolbar, or by pressing the M key.

3. In the Material Editor, select the first sample slot; in the Name field, name the material **Curtains**. Select the Translucent Shader from the Shader Basic Parameters rollout. Click the Diffuse color swatch, and select a light blue color. Click the Close button to exit the Color Selector.

4. Click the Translucent Color swatch, change its color to a light gray, and set the Opacity to **75**.

5. Drag the Curtains material onto the curtain object in the Left viewport.

Figure 15.10 shows the resulting image. Notice that the tree's shadow is cast on the curtains.

FIGURE 15.10

These translucent window curtains show shadows.

Accessing Other Parameters

In addition to the basic shader parameters, several other rollouts of options can add to the look of a material.

Extended Parameters rollout

The Material Editor includes several settings, in addition to the basic parameters, that are common for most shaders. The Extended Parameters rollout, shown in Figure 15.11, includes Advanced Transparency, Reflection Dimming, and Wire controls. All shaders include these parameters.

FIGURE 15.11

The Extended Parameters rollout includes Advanced Transparency, Reflection Dimming, and Wire settings.

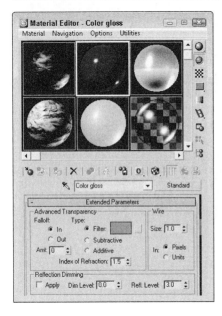

You can use the Advanced Transparency controls to set the Falloff to be In, Out, or a specified Amount. The In option increases the transparency as you get farther inside the object, and the Out option does the opposite. The Amount value sets the transparency for the inner or outer edge. Figure 15.12 shows two materials that use the Transparency Falloff options on a gray background and on a patterned background. The two materials on the left use the In option, and the two on the right use the Out option. Both are set at Amount values of 100.

The three transparency types are Filter, Subtractive, and Additive. The Filter type multiplies the Filter color with any color surface that appears behind the transparent object. With this option, you can select a Filter color to use. The Subtractive and Additive types subtract from or add to the color behind the transparent object.

FIGURE 15.12

Materials with the In and Out Falloff options applied

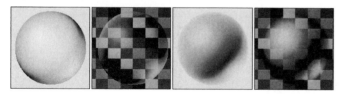

The Index of Refraction is a measure of the amount of distortion caused by light passing through a transparent object. Different physical materials have different Index of Refraction values. The amount of distortion also depends on the thickness of the transparent object. The Index of Refraction for water is 1.33 and for glass is 1.5. The default of 1.0 has no effect.

The Wire section lets you specify a wire size or thickness. Use this setting if the Wire option or the 2-Sided option is enabled in the Shaders Basic Parameters rollout. The size can be measured in either Pixels or Units. Figure 15.13 shows materials with different Wire values from 1 to 5 pixels.

FIGURE 15.13

Three materials with Wire values of (from left to right) 1, 2, 3, 4, and 5 pixels

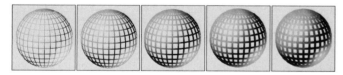

Reflection Dimming controls how intense a reflection is. You enable it by using the Apply option. The Dim Level setting controls the intensity of the reflection within a shadow, and the Refl Level sets the intensity for all reflections not in the shadow.

SuperSampling rollout

Pixels are small square dots that collectively make up the entire screen. At the edges of objects where the material color changes from the object to the background, these square pixels can cause jagged edges to appear. These edges are called *artifacts* and can ruin an image. Anti-aliasing is the process through which these artifacts are removed by softening the transition between colors.

Max includes anti-aliasing filters as part of the rendering process. SuperSampling is an additional anti-aliasing pass that can improve image quality that is applied at the material level. You have several SuperSampling methods from which to choose. The SuperSampling method can be defined in the Material Editor or you can choose the settings in the Default Scanline Renderer rollout of the Render Scene dialog box by enabling the Use Global Settings option.

 Anti-aliasing happens before raytracing when rendering, so even if the anti-aliasing option is enabled, the reflections and/or refractions will still be aliased.

CROSS-REF For more about the various anti-aliasing filters, see Chapter 22, "Learning to Render a Scene."

SuperSampling is calculated only if the Anti-Aliasing option in the Render Scene dialog box is enabled. The raytrace material type has its own SuperSampling pass that is required in order to get clean reflections.

NOTE Using SuperSampling can greatly increase the time it takes to render an image.

In a SuperSampling pass, the colors at different points around the center of a pixel are sampled. These samples are then used to compute the final color of each pixel. These four SuperSampling methods are available:

- **Adaptive Halton:** Takes semi-random samples along both the pixel's X-axis and Y-axis. It can take from 4 to 40 samples.
- **Adaptive Uniform:** Takes samples at regular intervals around the pixel's center. It takes from 4 to 26 samples.
- **Hammersley:** Takes samples at regular intervals along the X-axis but takes random samples along the Y-axis. It takes from 4 to 40 samples.
- **Max 2.5 Star:** Takes four samples along each axis.

The first three methods enable you to select a Quality setting. This setting specifies the number of samples to be taken. The more samples taken, the higher the resolution, but the longer it takes to render. The two Adaptive methods (Adaptive Halton and Adaptive Uniform) offer an Adaptive option with a Threshold spinner. This option takes more samples if the change in color is within the Threshold value. The SuperSample Texture option includes maps in the SuperSampling process along with materials.

TIP To get good reflections and refractions, enable supersampling for final renders.

Maps rollout

A *map* is a bitmap image that is wrapped about an object. The Maps rollout includes a list of the maps that you can apply to an object. Using this rollout, you can enable or disable maps, specify the intensity of the map in the Amount field, and load maps. Clicking the Map buttons opens the Material/Map Browser where you can select the map type.

CROSS-REF Find out more about maps in Chapter 17, "Adding Material Details with Maps."

Dynamic Properties rollout

The properties in the Dynamic Properties rollout, including Bounce Coefficient, Static Friction, and Sliding Friction, are used along with the Dynamics utility in simulations. These properties define how the object is animated during collisions. If these properties are not specified for an object, then the default material settings, which are similar to steel, are used.

CAUTION These dynamic properties are used only with the Dynamic utility. reactor is a more versatile and robust dynamics solution making these properties obsolete; they are included only for backward compatibility.

DirectX Manager rollout

The DirectX Manager rollout lets you display the current material in the viewport as a DirectX shader when the DX Display of Standard Material option is enabled. The current material also can be saved as a .FX material file. Many game engines render using DirectX, so this option lets you view your materials in the viewport as they will appear within the game.

CAUTION The DirectX Manager rollout appears only when the Direct3D display driver is selected.

At the bottom of the DirectX Manager rollout is a drop-down list for selecting to use the available DirectX shaders. The two available DirectX shaders are LightMap and Metal Bump 9. These shaders are generic to be used on a many different types of objects. The Light Map shader includes a parameter for loading a custom light map, and the Metal Bump 9 shader includes parameters for specifying two texture maps; specularity; and normal, bump, and reflection maps.

mental ray connection rollout

The mental ray connection rollout includes options for enabling different properties that are used by the mental ray rendering engine. The properties include Surface and Shadow Shaders, Photon and Photon Volume, and Extended Shaders and Advanced Shaders, including Contour and Light Map.

CROSS-REF The mental ray rendering engine and its properties are covered in Chapter 46, "Raytracing and mental ray."

Tutorial: Coloring a dolphin

As a quick example of applying materials, we take a dolphin model created by Zygote Media and position it over a watery plane. We then apply custom materials to both objects.

To add materials to a dolphin, follow these steps:

1. Open the Dolphin.max file from the Chap 15 directory on the DVD.

    This file contains a simple plane object and a dolphin mesh.

2. Open the Material Editor by choosing Rendering ⇨ Material Editor, clicking the Material Editor button on the main toolbar, or pressing the M key.

3. In the Material Editor, select the first sample slot; in the Name field (to the right of the Pick Material from Object button), rename the material **Dolphin Skin**. Click the Diffuse color swatch, and select a light gray color. Then click the Specular color swatch, and select a light yellow color. Click the Close button to exit the Color Selector. In the Specular Highlights section, increase the Specular Level to **45**.

4. Drag the Dolphin Skin material from the first sample slot to the second sample slot, and name it **Ocean Surface**. Click the Diffuse color swatch, and select a light blue color. Set the Specular Level and Opacity values to **80**. In the Maps rollout, click the None button to the right of the Bump selection. In the Material/Map Browser that opens, double-click the Noise selection, then enable the Fractal option and set the Size value to **15** in the Noise Parameters rollout.

5. Drag the Ocean Surface material onto the plane object in the Top viewport. Then drag the Dolphin Skin material onto the dolphin model.

NOTE This model also includes separate objects for the eyes, mouth, and tongue. These objects could have different materials applied to them, but they are so small in this image that we won't worry about them.

6. Choose Rendering ⇨ Environment (keyboard shortcut, 8), click the Background Color swatch, and change it to a light sky blue.

Figure 15.14 shows the resulting image.

FIGURE 15.14

A dolphin over the water with applied materials

Using External Tools

Several external tools can be valuable when you create material textures. These tools can include an image-editing program like Photoshop, a digital camera or camcorder, and a scanner. With these tools, you can create or capture images that can be applied as maps to a material using the map channels.

After the image is created or captured, you can apply it to a material by clicking a map shortcut button or by selecting a map in the Maps rollout. This opens the Material/Map Browser, where you can select the Bitmap map type and load the image file from the file dialog box that appears.

Creating material textures using Photoshop

When you begin creating texture images, Photoshop becomes your best friend. Using Photoshop's filters enables you to quickly create a huge variety of textures that add life and realism to your textures.

Table 15.1 is a recipe book of several common textures that you can create in Photoshop. The table provides only a quick sampling of some simple textures. Many other features and effects are possible with Photoshop.

TABLE 15.1

Photoshop Texture Recipes

Texture	Technique	Create in Photoshop	Apply in Max as
	Faded color	Decrease the image saturation value (Image ➪ Adjustments ➪ Hue/Saturation) by 20 to 30%.	Diffuse map
	Surface scratches	Apply the Chalk & Charcoal filter (Filter ➪ Sketch ➪ Chalk & Charcoal) with a Stroke Pressure of 2, to a blank white image, and then apply the Film Grain (Filter ➪ Artistic ➪ Film Grain) filter with maximum Grain and Intensity.	Bump map
	Adding stains to fabric	Use the Dodge and Burn tools to add stains to a fabric bitmap.	Diffuse map
	Surface relief texture	Apply Dark Strokes filter (Filter ➪ Brush Strokes ➪ Dark Strokes) to a texture bitmap, and save the image as a separate bump image.	Diffuse map (original texture), Bump map (Dark Strokes version)
	Planar hair	Apply the Fibers filter (Filter ➪ Render ➪ Fibers).	Diffuse, Bump, and Specular maps
	Clouds or fog background	Apply the Clouds filter (Filter ➪ Render ➪ Clouds).	Diffuse map
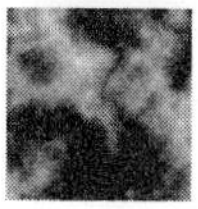	Nebula or plasma cloud	Apply the Difference Clouds filter (Filter ➪ Render ➪ Difference Clouds). Then switch black and white color positions, and apply the Difference Clouds filter again.	Diffuse map
	Rock wall	Apply the Clouds filter (Filter ➪ Render ➪ Clouds), and then apply the Bas Relief (Filter ➪ Sketch ➪ Bas Relief) filter.	Diffuse and Bump maps

continued

TABLE 15.1   *(continued)*

Texture	Technique	Create in Photoshop	Apply in Max as
	Burlap sack	Apply the Add Noise filter (Filter ⇨ Noise ⇨ Add Noise), followed by the Texturizer filter (Filter ⇨ Texture ⇨ Texturizer) with the Burlap setting.	Diffuse and Bump maps
	Tile floor	Apply the Add Noise filter (Filter ⇨ Noise ⇨ Add Noise), followed by the Stained Glass filter (Filter ⇨ Texture ⇨ Stained Glass).	Diffuse map
	Brushed metal	Apply the Add Noise filter (Filter ⇨ Noise ⇨ Add Noise), followed by the Angled Strokes filter (Filter ⇨ Brush Strokes ⇨ Angled Strokes).	Diffuse and Bump maps
	Frosted glass	Apply the Clouds filter (Filter ⇨ Render ⇨ Clouds), and then apply the Glass (Filter ⇨ Distort ⇨ Glass) filter and select the Frosted option.	Diffuse map
	Pumice stone	Apply the Add Noise filter (Filter ⇨ Noise ⇨ Add Noise), followed by the Chalk & Charcoal filter (Filter ⇨ Sketch ⇨ Chalk & Charcoal).	Diffuse and Bump maps
	Planet islands	Apply the Difference Clouds filter (Filter ⇨ Render ⇨ Difference Clouds), and then apply the Note Paper (Filter ⇨ Sketch ⇨ Note Paper) filter.	Diffuse and Shininess maps
	Netting	Apply the Mosaic Tiles filter (Filter ⇨ Texture ⇨ Mosaic Tiles), followed by the Stamp (Filter ⇨ Sketch ⇨ Stamp) filter.	Diffuse and Opacity maps
	Leopard skin	Apply the Grain filter (Filter ⇨ Texture ⇨ Grain) with the Clumped option, followed by the Poster Edges (Filter ⇨ Artistic ⇨ Poster Edges) filter applied twice.	Diffuse and Opacity maps

Capturing digital images

Digital cameras and camcorders are inexpensive enough that they really are a necessary item when creating material textures. Although Photoshop can be used to create many unique and interesting textures, a digital image of riverbed stones is much more realistic than anything that can be created with Photoshop. The world is full of interesting textures that can be used in creating images.

Avoiding specular highlights

Nothing can ruin a good texture taken with a digital camera faster than the camera's flash. Taking a picture of a highly reflective surface like the surface of a table can reflect back to the camera, thereby ruining the texture.

You can counter this in several ways. One is to block the flash and make sure that you have enough ambient light to capture the texture. Taking pictures outside can help with this because they don't need the flash. Another technique is to take the image at an angle, but this might skew the texture. A third technique is to take the image and then crop away the unwanted highlights.

 **The best time to take outdoor photos that are to be used for materials is on an overcast day. This eliminates the direct shadows from the sun, which are very difficult to remove. It also makes the light gradient across the surface much cleaner for tiling the photo.**

Adjusting brightness

Digital images that are taken with a digital camera are typically pre-lit, meaning that they already have a light source lighting them. When these pre-lit images are added to a Max scene that includes lights, the image gets a double dose of light that typically washes out the images.

You can remedy this problem by adjusting the brightness of the image prior to loading it into Max. For images taken in normal indoor light, you'll want to decrease the brightness value by 10 to 20 percent. For outdoor scenes in full sunlight, you may want to decrease the brightness even more.

You can find the Brightness/Contrast control in Photoshop in the Image ➪ Adjustments ➪ Brightness/Contrast menu.

Scanning images

In addition to taking digital images with a digital camera, you can scan images from other sources. For example, the maple leaf that was modeled using patches in Chapter 27 was scanned from a real leaf found in my yard.

When scanning images, use the scanner's descreen option to remove any dithering from the printed image. If you place the image on a piece of matte black construction paper, then the internal glare from the scanning bulb gets a more uniform light distribution.

CAUTION **Most magazine and book images are copyrighted and cannot be scanned and used without permission.**

Tutorial: Creating a fishing net

Some modeling tasks can be solved more easily with a material than with geometry changes. A fishing net is a good example. Using geometry to create the holes in the net would be tricky, but a simple Opacity map makes this complex modeling task easy.

To create a fishing net, follow these steps:

1. Before working in Max, create the needed texture in Photoshop. In Photoshop, select File ⇨ New, enter the dimensions of 512 pixels × 512 pixels in the New dialog box, and click OK to create a new image file.

2. Select the Filter ⇨ Texture ⇨ Mosaic Tiles menu command to apply the Mosaic Tiles filter. Set the Tile Size to **30** and the Grout Width to **3**, and click the OK button. Then select the Filter ⇨ Sketch ⇨ Stamp menu command to apply the Stamp filter with a Light/Dark Balance value of **49** and a Smooth value of **50**.

3. Choose File ⇨ Save As, and save the file as **Netting.tif**.

   A copy of this file is available in the Chap 15 directory on the DVD.

4. Open the Fish net.max file from the Chap 15 directory on the DVD.

   This file includes a fishing net model created by stretching half a sphere with the Shell modifier applied.

5. Select the Rendering ⇨ Material Editor menu command (or press the M key) to open the Material Editor, and select the first sample slot. Name the material **net**.

6. Click the map shortcut to the right of the Opacity value in the Blinn Basic Parameters rollout, and double-click the Bitmap map type. This opens a file dialog box where you can select the netting texture. Then drag the material from its sample slot to the net object in the viewports.

7. If you were to render the viewport, the net would look rather funny because the black lines are transparent instead of the white spaces. To fix this, open the Output rollout and enable the Invert option. This inverts the texture image.

 Although you can enable the Show Map in Viewport button in the Material Editor, the transparency is not displayed until you render the scene.

Figure 15.15 shows the rendered net.

FIGURE 15.15

A fishing net completed easily with the net texture applied as an Opacity map

Summary

This chapter presented the Standard material and gave you a chance to create some simple original materials.

In this chapter, you did the following:

- Learned about various material types
- Discovered and learned to use the various material parameters
- Discovered the basics of using standard materials
- Learned how to use the various shaders
- Explored the other Material rollouts
- Learned how to create materials using external tools such as Photoshop and a digital camera

This chapter should have been enough to whet your appetite for materials, and yet it really covered only one material — the Standard material. Many other materials are available, and we dive into those in the next chapter.

Chapter 16

Creating Compound Materials and Using Material Modifiers

Now that you've learned to create materials using the Standard material type, you get a chance to see the variety of material types that you can create in Max. You can select all the various Max materials from the Material/Map Browser. Open this browser automatically by clicking the Material Type button beneath the sample slots.

Although many of these materials are called Compound materials, they are really just collections of materials that work together as one. Just like a mesh object can include multiple elements, materials also can be made up of several materials. Using Material IDs, you can apply a multiple materials to the subobject selections of a single mesh object. The chapter concludes with a quick look at the various modifiers that are applied to materials.

Using Compound Materials

Compound materials combine several different materials into one. You select a compound object type by clicking the Type button in the Material Editor and then selecting the material type from the Material/Map Browser. The Type button is the button to the right of the material name. It lists the current material on the button, such as Standard, which is the default material. Most of the entries in the Material/Map Browser are compound objects.

Whenever compound materials are selected, the Replace Material dialog box appears, asking whether you want to discard the current material or make the old material a submaterial. This feature enables you to change a normal material into a compound material while retaining the current material.

Compound materials usually include several different levels. For example, a Top/Bottom material includes a separate material for the top and the bottom. Each of these submaterials can then include another Top/Bottom material, and so on. The Material/Map Navigator dialog box (accessed by clicking the Material/Map Navigator button) displays the material as a hierarchical list. This list lets you easily choose the level you want to work with.

CROSS-REF Chapter 14, "Exploring the Material Editor," covers the Material/Map Navigator in more detail.

Each compound material includes a customized rollout for specifying the submaterials associated with the compound material.

CROSS-REF Some of the material types work closely with specific objects and other Max features. These materials are covered in their respective chapters. The Advanced Lighting Override and Lightscape materials are presented in Chapter 44, "Working with Advanced Lighting, Light Tracing, and Radiosity," the raytracing and various mental ray material settings are covered in detail in Chapter 46, "Raytracing and mental ray," and the XRef material is covered in Chapter 23, "Building Complex Scenes with XRefs and Using Vault."

Blend

The Blend material blends two separate materials on a surface. The Blend Basic Parameters rollout, shown in Figure 16.1, includes buttons for loading the two submaterials. The check boxes to the right of these buttons enable or disable each submaterial. The Interactive option enables you to select one of the submaterials to be viewed in the viewports.

The Mask button (which appears below the two submaterial buttons) lets you load a map to specify how the submaterials are mixed. Gray areas on the map are well blended, white areas show Material 1, and black areas show Material 2. As an alternative to a mask, the Mix Amount determines how much of each submaterial to display. A value of 0 displays only Material 1, and a value of 100 displays only Material 2. This value can be animated, allowing an object to gradually change between materials.

FIGURE 16.1

The Blend material can include a mask to define the areas that are blended.

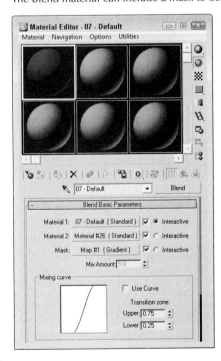

The Mixing Curve defines the transition between edges of the two materials. The Upper and Lower spinners help you control the curve.

Composite

The Composite material mixes up to ten different materials by adding, subtracting, or mixing the opacity. The Composite Basic Parameters rollout, shown in Figure 16.2, includes buttons for the base material and nine additional materials that can be composited on top of the base material. The materials are applied from top to bottom.

FIGURE 16.2

Composite materials are applied from top to bottom, with the last layer being placed on top of the rest.

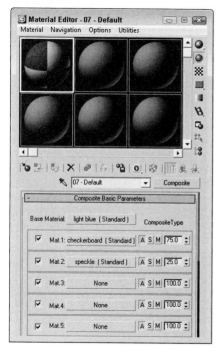

You enable or disable each material using the check box to its left. The buttons labeled with the letters A, S, and M specify the opacity type: Additive, Subtractive, or Mix. The Additive option brightens the material by adding the background colors to the current material. The Subtractive option has the opposite effect and subtracts the background colors from the current material. The Mix option blends the materials based on their Amount values.

To the right of the A, S, and M buttons is the Mix amount. This value can range from 0 to 200. At 0, none of the materials below it will be visible. At 100, full compositing occurs. Values greater than 100 cause transparent regions to become more opaque.

CROSS-REF You can learn more about compositing and the Video Post interface in Chapter 48, "Compositing with Render Elements and the Video Post Interface."

Double Sided

The Double Sided material specifies different materials for the front and back of object faces. You also have an option to make the material translucent. This material is for objects that have holes in their surface. Typically, objects with surface holes do not appear correctly because only the surfaces with normals pointing outward are visible. Applying the Double Sided material shows the interior and exterior of such an object.

The Double Sided Basic Parameters rollout includes two buttons, one for the Facing material and one for the Back material. The Translucency value sets how much of one material shows through the other.

Multi/Sub-Object

You can use the Multi/Sub-Object material to assign several different materials to a single object via the material IDs. You can use the Mesh Select modifier to select each subobject area to receive the different materials.

At the top of the Multi/Sub-Object Basic Parameters rollout, shown in Figure 16.3, is a Set Number button that lets you select the number of subobject materials to include. This number is displayed in a text field to the left of the button. Each submaterial is displayed as a separate area on the sample object in the sample slots. Using the Add and Delete buttons, you can selectively add or delete submaterials from the list.

FIGURE 16.3

The Multi/Sub-Object material defines materials according to material IDs.

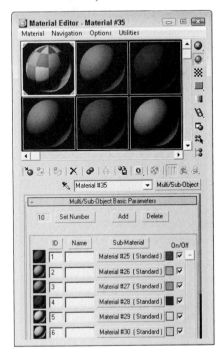

Each submaterial includes a sample preview of the submaterial and an index number listed to the left, a Name field where you can type the name of the submaterial, a button for selecting the material, a color swatch for creating solid color materials, and a check box for enabling or disabling the submaterial. You can sort the submaterials by clicking the ID, Name, or Sub-Material buttons at the top of each column.

After you apply a Multi/Sub-Object material to an object, use the Mesh Select modifier to make a subobject selection. In the Material section for this subobject selection, choose a material ID to associate with a sub-material ID or select the material by name from the drop-down list.

Tutorial: Creating a patchwork quilt

When I think of patches, I think of a 3D Max object type, but for many people, "patches" instead bring to mind small scraps of cloth used to make a quilt. Because they share the same name, maybe we can use Max patches to create a quilt. We can then use the Multi/Sub-Object material to color the various patches appropriately.

CROSS-REF You can learn more about modeling with patches in Chapter 27, "Modeling with Patches and NURBS."

To create a quilt using patches, follow these steps:

1. Open the Patch quilt.max file from the Chap 16 directory on the DVD.

   This file contains a quilt made of patch objects that have been combined into one object.

2. Open the Material Editor by choosing Rendering ⇨ Material Editor (or press M), and click the first sample slot. Then click the Type button. The Material/Map Browser opens. In the list of materials, locate and double-click the Multi/Sub-Object material (or select it and press the OK button). In the dialog box that appears, select Discard old material and click OK.

   The Multi/Sub-Object material loads into the selected sample slot, and the Multi/Sub-Object Basic Parameters rollout displays in the Material Editor.

3. In the Multi/Sub-Object Basic Parameters rollout, click the color swatches to the right of the Material button to open the Color Selector. Select different colors for each of the first ten material ID slots.

4. Drag the Multi/Sub-Object material from its sample slot in the Material Editor, and drop it onto the patch object. Close the Material/Map Browser and the Material Editor.

5. In the Modify panel, select the Patch subobject and scroll to the bottom of the Modify panel to the Surface Properties rollout.

6. Assign each patch a separate material ID by clicking a patch and changing the ID number in the rollout field.

Figure 16.4 shows the finished quilt. Because it's a patch, you can drape it over objects easily.

Morpher

The Morpher material type works with the Morpher modifier to change materials as an object morphs. For example, you can associate a blushing effect with light red applied to the cheeks of a facial expression to show embarrassment. You can use this material only on an object that has the Morpher modifier in its Stack. The Morpher modifier includes a button called Assign New Material in the Global Parameters rollout for loading the Material Editor with the Morpher material type.

FIGURE 16.4

A quilt composed of patches and colored using the Multi/Sub-Object material

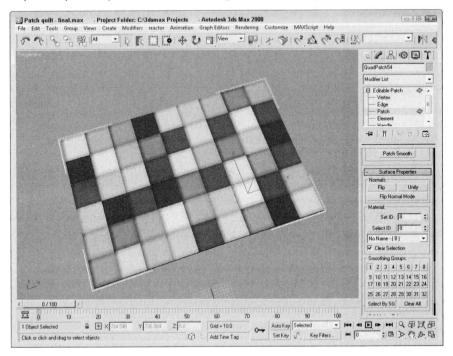

CROSS-REF   Discover more about the Morpher modifier in Chapter 32, "Using Animation Modifiers."

For the Morpher material, the Choose Morph Object button in the Morpher Basic Parameters rollout lets you pick a morpher object in the viewports and then open a dialog box used to bind the Morpher material to an object with the Morpher modifier applied. The Refresh button updates all the channels. The base material is the material used before any channel effects are used.

The Morpher material includes 100 channels that correlate to the channels included in the Morpher modifier. Each channel can be turned on and off. At the bottom of the parameters rollout are three Mixing Calculation options that can be used to determine how often the blending is calculated. The Always setting can consume lots of memory and can slow down the system. Other options are When Rendering and Never Calculate.

Shell

The Shell material consists of an original material and a baked material. For each of these materials, you can specify which appear in the Viewport and which are rendered.

CROSS-REF More on baked materials is found in Chapter 31, "Creating Baked Textures and Normal Maps."

Shellac

The Shellac material is added on top of the Base material. The Shellac Basic Parameters rollout includes only two buttons for each material, along with a Color Blend value. The Blend value has no upper limit.

Top/Bottom

The Top/Bottom material assigns different materials to the top and bottom of an object. The Top and Bottom areas are determined by the direction in which the face normals point. These normals can be according to the World or Local Coordinate System. You can also blend the two materials.

The Top/Bottom Basic Parameters rollout includes two buttons for loading the Top and Bottom materials. You can use the Swap button to switch the two materials. Using World coordinates enables you to rotate the object without changing the material positions. Local coordinates tie the material to the object.

The Blend value can range from 0 to 100, with 0 being a hard edge and 100 being a smooth transition. The Position value sets the location where the two materials meet. A value of 0 represents the bottom of the object and displays only the top material. A value of 100 represents the top of the object, and only the Bottom material is displayed.

Tutorial: Surfing the waves

There's nothing like hitting the surf early in the morning, unless you consider hitting the virtual surf early in the morning. As an example of a compound material, we apply the Top/Bottom material to a surfboard.

To apply a Top/Bottom compound material to a surfboard, follow these steps:

1. Open the Surfboard.max file from the Chap 16 directory on the DVD.

   This file contains a surfboard model and an infinite plane to represent the ocean.

2. Apply the Ocean Surface material, which is already created in the Material Editor, to the plane object by dragging the material from the Material Editor to the Plane object.

3. In the Material Editor, select the second sample slot and click the Type button. From the Material/Map Browser, select the Browse From New option and double-click the Top/Bottom material.

4. When the Replace Material dialog box appears, select the Discard Old Material option. Type the name **Surfboard** for the new material. Then click the Top Material button, name the material **Surfboard Top**, and change the Diffuse color to White. In the material drop-down list, select Surfboard and then click the Bottom Material button. Give this material the name **Surfboard Bottom**, and change the Diffuse color to Black.

5. Click the Material/Map Navigator button to view the hierarchy of the material. Then drag this material to the surfboard object.

Figure 16.5 shows the resulting image.

FIGURE 16.5

A rendered image of a surfboard with the Top/Bottom compound material applied

Applying Multiple Materials

Most complex models are divided into multiple parts, each distinguished by the material type that is applied to it. For example, a car model would be separated into windows, tires, and the body, so that each part can have a unique material applied to it.

Using material IDs

Sometimes you may want to apply multiple materials to a single part. Selecting subobject areas and using material IDs can help you accomplish this task.

Many of the standard primitives have material IDs automatically assigned: Spheres get a single material ID, boxes get six (one for each side), and cylinders get three (one for the cylinder and one for each end cap). In addition to the standard primitives, you can assign material IDs to Editable Mesh objects. You also can assign these material IDs to any object or subobject using the Material modifier. These material IDs correspond to the various materials specified in the Multi/Sub-Object material.

NOTE   Don't confuse these material IDs with the material effect IDs, which are selected using the Material Effect flyout buttons under the sample slots. Material IDs are used only with the Multi/Sub-Object material type, whereas the effect IDs are used with the Render Effects and Video Post dialog boxes for adding effects such as glows to a material.

Tutorial: Mapping die faces

As an example of mapping multiple materials to a single object, consider a die. Splitting the cube object that makes up the die into several different parts wouldn't make sense, so we'll use the Multi/Sub-Object material instead.

To create a die model, follow these steps:

1. Open the Pair of dice.max file from the Chap 16 directory on the DVD.

   This file contains two simple cube primitives that represent a pair of dice. I also used Adobe Photoshop and created six images with the dots of a die on them. All of these images are the same size.

2. Open the Material Editor, and select the first sample slot. Name the material Die Faces, and click the Type button. Select the Multi/Sub-Object material from the Material/Map Browser. In the dialog box that opens, select to discard the current map and click OK.

3. In the Multi/Sub-Object Basic Parameters rollout, click the Set Number button and enter a value of **6**.

4. Name the first material **face 1**, and click the material button to open the parameter rollouts for the first material. Then click the map button to the right of the Diffuse color swatch to open the Material/Map Browser, and double-click the Bitmap map. In the Select Bitmap Image File dialog box, choose the dieface1.tif image from the Chap 16 directory on the DVD and click Open.

5. Back in the Material Editor, click the Go to Parent button twice to return to the Multi/Sub-Object Basic Parameters rollout and repeat Step 4 for each of the die faces.

6. When the Multi/Sub-Object material is defined, select the cube object and click the Assign Material to Selection button.

NOTE Because the cube object used in this example is a box primitive, we didn't need to assign the material IDs to different subobject selections. The box primitive automatically assigned a different material ID to each face of the cube. When material IDs do need to be assigned, you can specify them in the Surface Properties rollout for editable meshes.

Figure 16.6 shows a rendered image of two dice being rolled.

TIP If you enable the Show Map in Viewport option in the Material Editor, then the subobject materials are visible; you also can enable them using the Views ⇨ Activate All Maps menu command.

Using the Clean MultiMaterial utility

All compound materials have submaterials that are used to add layers of detail to the material, but if these submaterials aren't used, they can take up memory and disk space. You can locate and eliminate unused submaterials in the scene using the Clean MultiMaterial utility. This utility can be accessed from the Utility panel or from the Utilities menu in the Material Editor. For example, if you create a Multi/Sub-Object material with seven submaterials but later as you are modeling find that you need only five, the two unneeded submaterials can be cleaned.

Clicking the Find All button finds all submaterials that aren't used and presents them in a list where you can select the ones to clean.

FIGURE 16.6

These dice have different bitmaps applied to each face.

Material Modifiers

Of the many available modifiers, most modifiers change the geometry of an object, but several work specifically with materials and maps, including the Material, MaterialByElement, UVW Map, UVW XForm, Unwrap UVW, and Vertex Paint modifiers. In this section, you get a chance to use several material-specific modifiers. The Surface modifiers set includes several modifiers for working with materials.

CROSS-REF   Find out more about the modifiers that apply to maps in Chapter 17, "Adding Material Details with Maps." Another common texture-applying technique uses the Vertex Paint modifier, which is covered in Chapter 31, "Creating Baked Textures and Normal Maps."

Material modifier

The Material modifier lets you change the material ID of an object. The only parameter for this modifier is the Material ID. When you select a subobject and apply this modifier, the material ID is applied only to the subobject selection. This modifier is used in conjunction with the Multi/Sub-Object Material type to create a single object with multiple materials.

MaterialByElement modifier

The MaterialByElement modifier enables you to change material IDs randomly. You can apply this modifier to an object with several elements. The object needs to have the Multi/Sub-Object material applied to it.

The parameters for this modifier can be set to assign material IDs randomly with the Random Distribution option or according to a desired Frequency. The ID Count is the minimum number of material IDs to use. You can specify the percentage of each ID to use in the fields under the List Frequency option. The Seed option alters the randomness of the materials.

Tutorial: Creating random marquee lights with the MaterialByElement modifier

The MaterialByElement modifier enables you to change material IDs randomly. In this tutorial, we reproduce the effect of lights randomly turning a marquee on and off by using the Multi/Sub-Object material together with the MaterialByElement modifier.

To create a randomly lighted marquee, follow these steps:

1. Open the Marquee Lights.max file from the Chap 16 directory on the DVD.

    This file includes some text displayed on a rectangular object surrounded by spheres that represent lights.

2. Open the Material Editor, and select the first sample slot. Then click the Type button, and select the Multi/Sub-Object material from the Material/Map Browser. Select to discard the current material, and click OK. Give the material the name **Random Lights**.

3. In the Multi/Sub-Object Basic Parameters rollout, click the Set Number button and change its value to **2**. Then click the Material 1 button, and in the Material name field, give the material the name **Light On**. Set the Diffuse color to yellow and Self-Illumination to yellow. Then click the Go Forward to Sibling button to access the second material.

4. Name the second material **Light Off**, and select a gray Diffuse color. Then click the Go to Parent button to return to the Multi/Sub-Object material.

5. Select all the spheres, and click the Assign Material to Selection button to assign the material to the spheres.

6. With all the spheres selected, open the Modify panel and select the MaterialByElement modifier from the Modifier List drop-down list. In the Parameters rollout, select the Random Distribution option and set the ID Count to **2**.

Figure 16.7 shows the marquee with its random lights. (I've always wanted to see my name in lights!)

Disp Approx and Displace Mesh modifiers

You can change the geometry of an object in several ways using a bitmap. One way is to use the Displace modifier (found in the Modifiers ⇨ Parametric Deformers menu). The Displace modifier lets you specify a bitmap and a map to use to alter the object's geometry. Black areas on the bitmap are left unmoved, gray areas are indented, and white areas are indented a greater distance. Several controls are available for specifying how the image is mapped to the object and how it tiles, and buttons are available for setting its alignment, including Fit, Center, Bitmap Fit, Normal Align, View Align, Region Fit, Reset, and Acquire.

Another way to displace geometry with a bitmap is to use a displacement map. Displacement maps can be applied directly to Editable Poly and Mesh, NURBS, and Patch objects. If you want to apply a displacement map to another object type, such as a primitive, you first need to apply the Modifiers ⇨ Surface ⇨ Disp Approx modifier, which is short for Displacement Approximation. This modifier includes three default presets for Low, Medium, and High that make it easy to use.

CROSS-REF More details on working with maps are covered in Chapter 17, "Adding Material Details with Maps."

FIGURE 16.7

This marquee is randomly lighted, thanks to the MaterialByElement modifier.

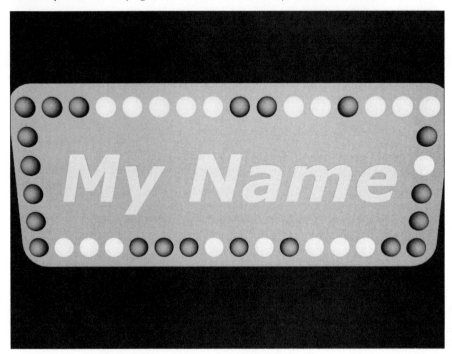

One drawback to using displacement maps is that you cannot see their result in the viewport, but if you apply the Modifiers ➪ Surface ➪ Displace Mesh (WSM) modifier, then the displacement map becomes visible in the viewports. If you change any of the displacement map settings, you can update the results by clicking the Update Mesh button in the Displacement Approx. rollout.

 The Displace modifier requires a dense mesh in order to see the results of the displacement map, but the Disp Approx modifier creates the required density at render time.

Tutorial: Displacing geometry with a bitmap

When faced with how to displace an object using a bitmap, Max once again comes through with several ways to accomplish the task. The method you choose depends on the pipeline. You can choose to keep the displacement in the Modifier Stack or on the material level. This simple tutorial compares using both these methods.

To compare the Displace modifier with a displacement map, follow these steps:

1. Create two square-shaped plane objects side by side in the Top viewport using the Create ➪ Standard Primitives ➪ Plane menu command. Then set the Length and Width Segments to 150 for the left plane object and to 20 for the right plane object.

 When displacing geometry using a bitmap, make sure the object faces that will be displaced have sufficient resolution to represent the displacement.

2. Select the first plane object and apply the Displace modifier with the Modifiers ➪ Parametric Deformers ➪ Displace menu command. In the Parameters rollout, set the Strength value to 2 and click the Bitmap button. In the Select Displacement Image dialog box, select the Tulip logo.tif file from the Chap 16 directory on the DVD.

3. Select the second plane object and open the Material Editor by pressing the M key. In the Material Editor, open the Maps rollout, set the Displacement Map Amount value to 10, and click the Displacement map button. Then double-click on the Bitmap option in the Material/Map Browser, and load the same Tulip logo.tif file from the Chap 16 directory on the DVD. Then apply the material to the second plane object by pressing the Assign Material to Selection button, and close the Material Editor.

4. With the second plane still selected, choose the Modifiers ➪ Surface ➪ Displace Mesh (WSM) menu command. In the Displacement Approx. rollout, enable the Custom Settings option and click on the High subdivision preset.

Figure 16.8 shows the resulting displacement on both plane objects.

FIGURE 16.8

Objects can be displaced using the Displace modifier or a displacement map.

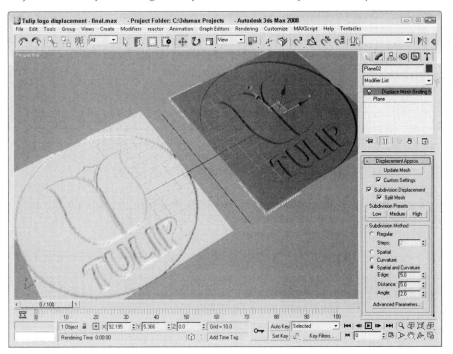

Using Vertex Colors

When creating models that are for games, the size of the texture map can be prohibitive. I mean, what model that weighs in at 16KB or less wants to carry around a 2MB texture map? The solution that much of the gaming world relies on is to apply a single color to a vertex. Having each vertex remember its color (or even several colors) requires very little additional information for the mesh and can create some good shading. Colors are then interpolated across the face of the polygon between two different colors on adjacent vertices.

The results aren't as clean and detailed as a texture map, but for their size, vertex colors are worth the price.

Assigning vertex colors

Vertex colors can be assigned in the Surface Properties rollout for Editable Mesh and Editable Patch objects, and in the Vertex and Polygon Properties rollouts for Editable Poly objects. They also can be assigned in Face, Polygon, and Element subobject modes using a little rollout section called Edit Vertex Colors. Within this section are two color swatches for selecting Color and Illumination values. The Alpha value sets the alpha transparency value for the vertex.

Painting vertices with the Vertex Paint modifier

Another, more interactive way to color vertices is with the Vertex Paint modifier. This modifier lets you paint on an object by specifying a color for each vertex. If adjacent vertices have different colors assigned, then a gradient is created across the face. The benefit of this coloring option is that it is very efficient and requires almost no memory.

The Vertex Paint modifier lets you specify a color and paint directly on the surface of an object by painting the vertices. The color is applied with a paintbrush-shaped cursor. The modifier can be applied multiple times to an object, giving you the ability to blend several layers of vertex paints together. You can find this modifier in the Modifiers ⇨ Mesh Editing submenu.

NOTE Once the VertexPaint modifier has been applied to an object, the Paintbox automatically reappears whenever the object is reselected.

Applying this modifier opens a VertexPaint dialog box called the Paintbox, shown in Figure 16.9. At the top of the Paintbox are four icons that can be used to show the visible results of the painting in the viewports. The options include Vertex Color Display–Unshaded, Vertex Color Display–Shaded, Disable Vertex Color Display, and Toggle Texture Display On/Off.

The Vertex Color icon flyout lets you work on the Vertex Color, Illumination, Alpha, or any one of the 99 available map channels. The lock icon locks the display to the selected channel, or you could be looking at a different channel than the one you are painting.

The large Paint and Erase buttons let you add or remove vertex colors using the color specified in the color swatch. You can also select colors from objects in the viewports using the eyedropper tool and then set the Opacity.

The Size value determines the size of the brush used to paint. Max supports pressure-sensitive devices such as a graphics tablet, and you can set the brush options using the Brush Options dialog box. When paining on the surface of an object, a blue normal line appears. This line guides you as you paint so that you know you're on the correct surface.

CROSS-REF The Painter Options dialog box also is used by the Skin modifier and the Paint Deformation tool. It is described in detail in Chapter 12, "Modeling with Polygons."

Beneath the Brush Options button is a Palette button that opens the Color Palette interface, shown in Figure 16.10. The Color Palette holds custom colors and lets you copy and paste colors between the different swatches. Collections of colors can be saved by right-clicking the Color Palette and selecting the Save As command. Color palettes are saved as Color Clipboard files with the .ccb extension.

FIGURE 16.9

The Paintbox palette for the Vertex Paint modifier includes a wealth of features.

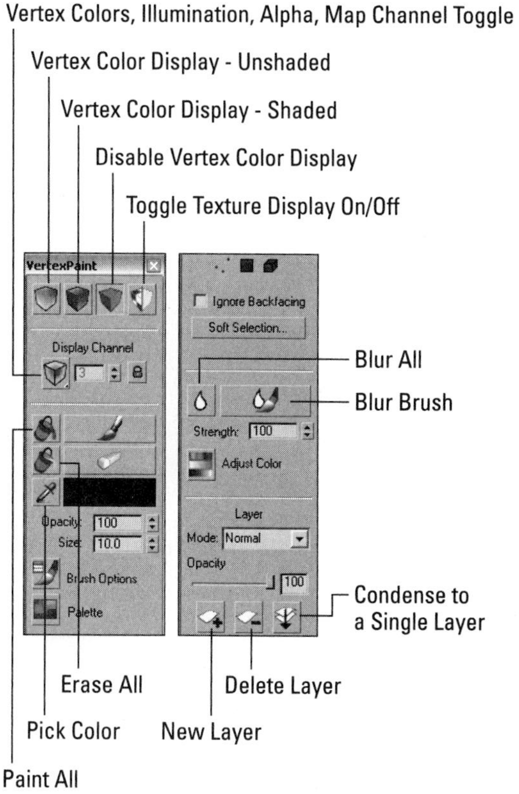

Vertex Colors, Illumination, Alpha, Map Channel Toggle

    Vertex Color Display - Unshaded

        Vertex Color Display - Shaded

            Disable Vertex Color Display

                Toggle Texture Display On/Off

Blur All

Blur Brush

Condense to a Single Layer

Delete Layer

Erase All

New Layer

Pick Color

Paint All

The Paintbox also includes three subobject selection icons. These icons can be used to select certain Vertices, Faces, or Elements to be painted. This limits the painting to the selected subobjects only. You also can select to Ignore Backfacing and use Soft Selection.

The Blur brush button lets you blur colors across polygons using a brush that works just like the Paint and Erase brushes.

The Adjust Color dialog box lets you change all the painted colors applied to an object using HSV or RGB color sliders. The Preview option makes the color adjustment visible in the viewports if selected. Below the Adjust Color icon is the Blur Selected icon that blurs together all the vertex colors based on the designated Amount value.

Colors can be mixed between layers using the various blending modes. Clicking the New Layer button adds a new instance of the Vertex Paint modifier to the Modifier Stack; the Delete Layer button does the opposite. Click the Condense to a Single Layer button to merge all the consecutive Vertex Paint modifiers to a single instance using the selected blending mode.

FIGURE 16.10

The Color Palette can display colors as a list or as swatches.

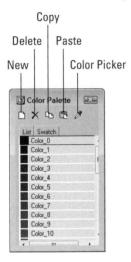

Copy

Delete | Paste

New | Color Picker

NOTE   Any files that are opened within 3ds Max 2008 that have an older version of the Vertex Paint modifier are displayed as OldVertexPaint in the Modifier Stack.

Tutorial: Marking heart tension

As an example of using the Vertex Paint modifier, imagine a doctor who has a 3D model of the human heart. While discussing the results of the latest test with a patient, the doctor can color parts of the heart model to illustrate the various points.

To color on a human heart using the Vertex Paint modifier, follow these steps:

1. Open the Vertex paint on heart.max file from the Chap 16 directory on the DVD.

   This file includes a heart mesh created by Viewpoint Datalabs.

2. Select a portion of the heart model, and choose Modifiers ➪ Mesh Editing ➪ Vertex Paint to apply the Vertex Paint modifier.

3. In the Paintbox that opens, choose the Vertex Color Display–Shaded button at the top of the VertexPaint dialog box, select the red color, and click the Paint button. Then drag the mouse over the surface of the Perspective view.

Figure 16.11 shows the resulting color.

The Assign Vertex Color utility

The Assign Vertex Color utility works a little differently. It converts any existing material colors to vertex colors. To use this utility, select the utility from the Utilities list that opens when the More button in the Utility panel is clicked, select an object, choose a Channel, choose a Light Model (Lighting + Diffuse, Lighting Only, or Diffuse Only), and click the Assign to Selected button.

FIGURE 16.11

The Vertex Paint modifier can apply color to an object by assigning a color to its vertices.

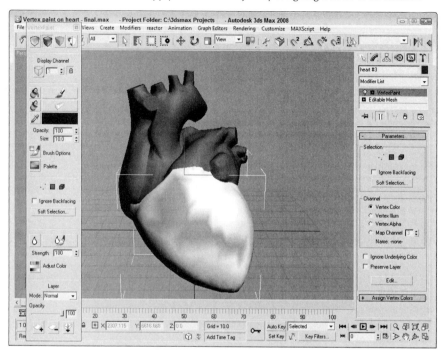

Summary

This chapter introduced the great variety of materials that you can create in Max. The chapter presented various material types, including compound, matte/shadow, and Ink 'n' Paint materials.

The following topics were covered in this chapter:

- Various compound material types
- Applying multiple materials to an object with material IDs
- Exploring several material modifiers, including the Material and MaterialByElement
- Comparing the different displacement methods
- Using Vertex Colors to paint models

The one big rollout that was skipped as we investigated materials deals with maps. The next chapter delves into the topic of material maps.

FIGURE 17.1

Use the Material/Map Browser to list all the maps available for assigning to materials.

2D maps

A two-dimensional map can be wrapped onto the surface of an object or used as an environment map for a scene's background image. Because they have no depth, 2D maps appear only on the surface. The Bitmap map is perhaps the most common 2D map. It enables you to load any image, which can be wrapped around an object's surface in a number of different ways.

Many maps have several rollouts in common. These include Coordinates, Noise, and Time. In addition to these rollouts, each individual map type has its own parameters rollout.

The Coordinates rollout

Every map that is applied to an object needs to have mapping coordinates that define how the map lines up with the object. For example, with the soup can label example mentioned earlier, you probably would want to align the top edge of the label with the top edge of the can, but you could position the top edge of the map at the middle of the can. Mapping coordinates define where the map's upper-right corner is located on the object.

All map coordinates are based on a UVW coordinate system that equates to the familiar XYZ coordinate system, except that it is named uniquely so as not to be confused with transformation coordinates. For UVW coordinates, U represents the horizontal coordinate, V is the vertical coordinate and W, is along the surface normal. To keep them straight, remember that the UVW coordinate system applies to surfaces and that the XYZ coordinate system applies to spatial objects. These coordinates are required for every object to which a map is applied. In most cases, you can generate these coordinates automatically when you create an object by selecting the Generate Mapping Coordinates option in the object's Parameter rollout.

 **Editable meshes don't have any default mapping coordinates, but you can generate mapping coordinates using the UVW Map modifier.**

In the Coordinates rollout for 2D Maps, shown in Figure 17.2, you can specify whether the map will be a texture map or an environment map. The Texture option applies the map to the surface of an object as a texture. This texture moves with the object as the object moves. The Environ option creates an environment map. Environment maps are locked to the world and not to an object. Moving an object with an environment map applied to it scrolls the map across the surface of the object.

FIGURE 17.2

The Coordinates rollout lets you offset and tile a map.

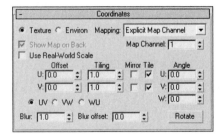

Different mapping types are available for both the Texture and Environ options. Mapping types for the Texture option include Explicit Map Channel, Vertex Color Channel, Planar from Object XYZ, and Planar from World XYZ. The Explicit Map Channel option is the default. It applies the map using the designated Map Channel. The Vertex Color Channel uses specified vertex colors as its channel. The two planar mapping types place the map in a plane based on the Local or World coordinate systems.

The Environ option includes Spherical Environment, Cylindrical Environment, Shrink-Wrap Environment, and Screen mapping types. The Spherical Environment mapping type is applied as if the entire scene were contained within a giant sphere. The same applies for the Cylindrical Environment mapping type, except that the shape is a cylinder. The Shrink-Wrap Environment plasters the map directly on the scene as if it were covering it like a blanket. All four corners of the bitmap are pulled together to the back of the wrapped object. The Screen mapping type just projects the map flatly on the background.

The Show Map on Back option causes planar maps to project through the object and be rendered on the object's back.

The U and V coordinates define the X and Y positions for the map. For each coordinate, you can specify an Offset value, which is the distance from the origin. The Tiling value is the number of times to repeat the image and is used only if the Tile option is selected. If the Use Real-World Scale option is selected, then the Offset fields change to Height and Width and the Tiling fields change to Size. The Mirror option inverts the map. The UV, VW, and WU options apply the map onto different planes.

Tiling is the process of placing a copy of the applied map next to the current one and so on until the entire surface is covered with the map placed edge to edge. You will often want to use tiled images that are seamless or that repeat from edge to edge.

 **TIP** Tiling can be enabled within the material itself or in the UVW Map modifier.

Figure 17.3 shows an image tile that is seamless. Notice how the horizontal and vertical seams line up. This figure shows three tiles positioned side by side, but because the opposite edges line up, the seams between the tiles aren't evident.

FIGURE 17.3

Seamless image tiles are a useful way to cover an entire surface with a small map.

The Material Editor includes a button that you can use to check the Tiling and Mirror settings. The Sample UV Tiling button (fourth from the top) is a flyout button that you can switch to 2 × 2, 3 × 3, or 4 × 4.

You can also rotate the map about each of the U, V, and W axes by entering values in the respective fields, or by clicking the Rotate button, which opens the Rotate Mapping Coordinates dialog box, shown in Figure 17.4. Using this dialog box, you can drag the mouse to rotate the mapping coordinates. Dragging within the circle rotates about all three coordinates, and dragging outside the circle rotates the mapping coordinates about their center point.

FIGURE 17.4

The Rotate Mapping Coordinates dialog box appears when you click the Rotate button in the Coordinates rollout.

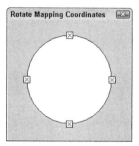

The Blur and Blur Offset values affect the blurriness of the image. The Blur value blurs the image based on its distance from the view, whereas the Blur Offset value blurs the image regardless of its distance.

 **TIP** You can use the Blur setting to help make tile seams less noticeable.

The Noise rollout

You can use the Noise rollout to randomly alter the map settings in a pre-defined manner. Noise can be thought of as static that you see on the television added to a bitmap. This feature is helpful for making textures more grainy, which is useful for certain materials.

The Amount value is the strength of the noise function applied; the value ranges from 0 for no noise through 100 for maximum noise. You can disable this noise function at any time, using the On option.

The Levels value defines the number of times the noise function is applied. The Size value determines the extent of the noise function based on the geometry. You can also Animate the noise. The Phase value controls how quickly the noise changes over time.

The Time rollout

Maps, such as bitmaps, that can load animations also include a Time rollout for controlling animation files. In this rollout, you can choose a Start Frame and the Playback Rate. The default Playback Rate is 1.0; higher values run the animation faster, and lower values run it slower. You also can set the animation to Loop, Ping-Pong, or Hold on the last frame.

The Output rollout

The Output rollout includes settings for controlling the final look of the map. The Invert option creates a negative version of the bitmap. The Clamp option prevents any colors from exceeding a value of 1.0 and prevents maps from becoming self-illuminating if the brightness is increased.

The Alpha From RGB Intensity option generates an alpha channel based on the intensity of the map. Black areas become transparent and white areas opaque.

 **NOTE** For materials that don't include an Output rollout, you can apply an Output map, which accepts a submaterial.

The Output Amount value controls how much of the map should be mixed when it is part of a composite material. You use the RGB Offset value to increase or decrease the map's tonal values. Use the RGB Level value to increase or decrease the saturation level of the map. The Bump Amount value is used only if the map is being used as a bump map—it determines the height of the bumps.

The Enable Color Map option enables the Color Map graph at the bottom of the Output rollout. This graph displays the tonal range of the map. Adjusting this graph affects the highlights, midtones, and shadows of the map. Figure 17.5 shows a Color Map graph.

The left end of the graph equates to the shadows, and the right end is for the highlights. The RGB and Mono options let you display the graphs as independent red, green, and blue curves or as a single mono-color curve. The Copy CurvePoints option copies any existing points from Mono mode over to RGB mode, and vice versa. The buttons across the top of the graph are used to manage the graph points.

The buttons above the graph include Move (with flyout buttons for Move Horizontally and Move Vertically), Scale Point, Add Point (with a flyout button for adding a point with handles), Delete Point, and Reset Curves. Along the bottom of the graph are buttons for managing the graph view. The two fields at the bottom left contain the horizontal and vertical values for the current selected point. The other buttons are to Pan and Zoom the graph.

FIGURE 17.5

The Color Map graph enables you to adjust the highlights, midtones, and shadows of a map.

Move

Scale Point

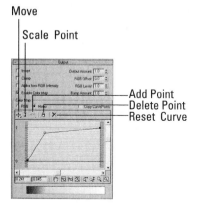

Add Point
Delete Point
Reset Curve

Bitmap map

Selecting the Bitmap map from the Material/Map Browser opens the Select Bitmap Image File dialog box, shown in Figure 17.6, where you can locate an image file. Various image and animation formats are supported, including AVI, MPEG, BMP, CIN, CWS, DDF, EXR, GIF, HDRI, IFL, IPP, FLC, JPEG, MOV, PNG, PSD, RGB, RLA, RPF, TGA, TIF, and YUV.

FIGURE 17.6

The Select Bitmap Image File dialog box lets you preview images before opening them.

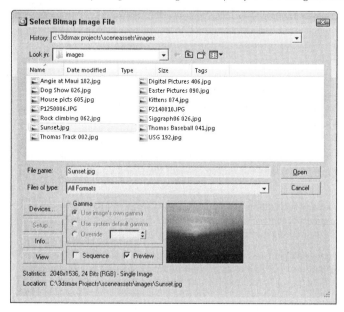

Video sequences saved in the AVI, MPEG, and MOV formats can be loaded as a map.

The name of the current bitmap file is displayed on the button in the Bitmap Parameters rollout, shown in Figure 17.7. If you need to change the bitmap file, click the Bitmap button and select the new file. Use the Reload button to update the bitmap if you've made changes to the bitmap image by an external program.

FIGURE 17.7

The Bitmap Parameters rollout offers several settings for controlling a bitmap map.

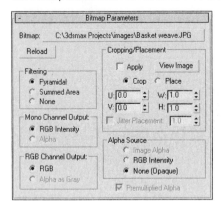

The Bitmap Parameters rollout includes three Filtering options: Pyramidal, Summed Area, and None. These methods perform a pixel-averaging operation to anti-alias the image. The Summed Area option requires more memory but produces better results.

You can also specify the output for a mono channel or for an RGB channel. For maps that use only the monochrome information in the image (such as an opacity map), the Mono Channel as RGB Intensity or Alpha option can be used. For maps that use color information (for example, a diffuse map), the RGB Channel can be RGB (full color) or Alpha as Gray.

The Cropping/Placement controls enable you to crop or place the image. *Cropping* is the process of cutting out a portion of the image, and *Placing* is resizing the image while maintaining the entire image and positioning it. The View Image button opens the image in a Cropping/Placement dialog box, shown in Figure 17.8. The rectangle is available within the image when Crop mode is selected. You can move the handles of this rectangle to specify the crop region.

 When the Crop option is selected, a UV button is displayed in the upper right of the Cropping/Placement dialog box. Clicking this button changes the U and V values to X and Y pixels.

You can also adjust the U and V parameters, which define the upper-left corner of the cropping rectangle, and the W and H parameters, which define the crop or placement width and height. The Jitter Placement option works with the Place option to randomly place and size the image.

 The U and V values are a percentage of the total image. For example, a U value of 0.25 positions the image's left edge at a location that is 25 percent of the distance of the total width from the left edge of the original image.

FIGURE 17.8

Viewing an image in the Cropping/Placement dialog box enables you to set the crop marks.

If the bitmap has an alpha channel, you can specify whether it is to be used with the Image Alpha option, or you can define the alpha values as RGB Intensity or as None. You can also select to use Premultiplied Alphas. Premultiplied Alphas are images that use the transparency information stored in the image.

Checker map

The Checker map creates a checkerboard image with two colors. The Checker Parameters rollout includes two color swatches for changing the checker colors. You can also load maps in place of each color. Use the Swap button to switch the position of the two colors and the Soften value to blur the edges between the two colors.

Figure 17.9 shows three Checker maps with Tiling values of 2 for the U and V directions and Soften values of (from left to right) 0, 0.2, and 0.5.

FIGURE 17.9

The Checker map can be softened as these three maps are with Soften values of 0, 0.2, and 0.5.

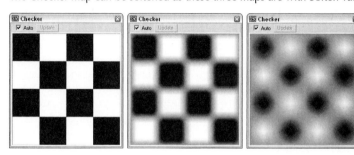

Combustion map

This map works with Autodesk's Combustion package, which is used for post-processing compositing. The Combustion map enables you to include Combustion-produced effects as a material map.

The Project button lets you load a file to paint on. These files are limited to the types that Combustion supports. Use the Edit button to load the Combustion interface.

In the Live Edit section, the Unwrap Selected button places markings on the bitmap image to show where the mapping coordinates are located. The UV button lets you change from among UV, VW, and UW coordinate systems. The Track Time button lets you change the current frame, which enables you to paint materials that change over time. The Paint button changes the viewport cursor to enable you to paint interactively in the viewport. The Operator button lets you select a composition operator from within Combustion.

The Combustion map also includes information about current project settings for specifying a custom resolution. You can also control the Start Frame and Duration of an animation sequence. The Filtering options are Pyramidal, Summed Area, or None, and the End Conditions can be set to Loop, Ping Pong (which moves back and forth between the start and end positions), or Hold.

CAUTION   To use this map type, you must have the Combustion program. If the program isn't installed, the text "Error: Combustion Engine DLL Not Found" displays at the top of the Combustion Parameters rollout.

Gradient map

The Gradient map creates a gradient image using three colors. The Gradient Parameters rollout includes a color swatch and map button for each color. You can position the center color at any location between the two ends using the Color 2 Position value spinner. The value can range from 0 through 1. The rollout lets you choose between Linear and Radial gradient types.

The Noise Amount adds noise to the gradient if its value is nonzero. The Size value scales the noise effect, and the Phase controls how quickly the noise changes over time. The three types of noise that you can select are Regular, Fractal, and Turbulence. The Levels value determines how many times the noise function is applied. The High and Low Threshold and Smooth values set the limits of the noise function to eliminate discontinuities.

Figure 17.10 shows linear and radial Gradient maps.

FIGURE 17.10

A Gradient map can be linear (left) or radial (right).

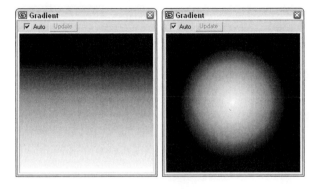

Gradient Ramp map

This advanced version of the Gradient map can use many different colors. The Gradient Ramp Parameters rollout, shown in Figure 17.11, includes a color bar with several flags along its bottom edge. You can add flags by simply clicking along the bottom edge. You can also drag flags to reposition them or delete the interior flags by dragging them all the way to either end until they turn red.

To define the color for each flag, right-click the flag and then select Edit Properties from the pop-up menu. The Flag Properties dialog box, also shown in Figure 17.11, opens so you can select a color or texture to use.

FIGURE 17.11

The Flag Properties dialog box enables you to specify a color and its position to use in the Gradient Ramp.

Gradient Marker

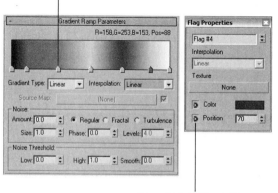

Show/hide in Track View

The Gradient Type drop-down in the Gradient Ramp Parameters rollout offers various Gradient Types, including 4 Corner, Box, Diagonal, Lighting, Linear, Mapped, Normal, Pong, Radial, Spiral, Sweep, and Tartan. You can also select from several Interpolation Types, including Custom, Ease In, Ease In Out, Ease Out, Linear, and Solid.

Figure 17.12 shows several of the gradient types available for the Gradient Ramp map.

Swirl map

The Swirl map creates a swirled image of two colors: Base and Swirl. The Swirl Parameters rollout includes two color swatches and map buttons to specify these colors. The Swap button switches the two colors. Other options include Color Contrast, which controls the contrast between the two colors; Swirl Intensity, which defines the strength of the swirl color; and Swirl Amount, which is how much of the Swirl color gets mixed into the Base color.

 All maps that use two colors include a Swap button for switching between the colors.

The Twist value sets the number of swirls. Negative values cause the swirl to change direction. The Constant Detail value determines how much detail is included in the swirl.

FIGURE 17.12

The Gradient Ramp map offers several different gradient types, including (from top left to bottom right) Box, Diagonal, Normal, Pong, Spiral, and Tartan.

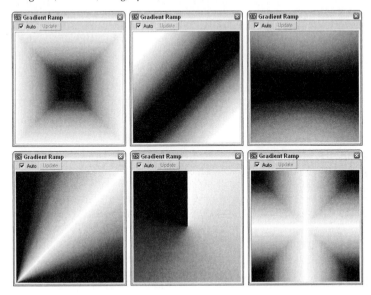

With the Swirl Location X and Y values, you can move the center of the swirl. As the center is moved far from the materials center, the swirl rings become tighter. The Lock button causes both values to change equally. If the lock is disabled, then the values can be changed independently.

The Random Seed sets the randomness of the swirl effect.

Figure 17.13 shows the Swirl map with three different Twist values. From left to right, the Twist values are 1, 5, and 10.

FIGURE 17.13

The Swirl map combines two colors in a swirling pattern.

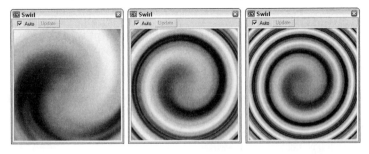

Tiles map

The Tile map creates brick patterns. The Standard Controls rollout contains a Preset Type drop-down list with a list of preset tile patterns. These patterns are popular tile patterns including Running Bond, Common Flemish Bond, English Bond, ½ Running Bond, Stack Bond, Fine Running Bond, and Fine Stack Bond.

In the Advanced Controls rollout under both the Tile and Grout Setup sections, you can use a custom texture map and color. You can specify the Horizontal and Vertical Count of the Tiles and the Grout's Horizontal and Vertical Gaps, as well as Color and Fade Variance values for both. The Horizontal and Vertical Gaps can be locked to always be equal. For Grout, you can also define the Percentage of Holes. Holes are where tiles have been left out. A Rough value controls the roughness of the mortar.

The Random Seed value controls the randomness of the patterns, and the Swap Texture Entries option exchanges the tile texture with the grout texture.

In the Stacking Layout section, the Line Shift and Random Shift values are used to move each row of tiles a defined or random distance.

The Row and Column Editing section offers options that let you change the number of tiles Per Row or Column and the Change (or leftover) in each row or column.

Figure 17.14 shows three different Tile map styles.

FIGURE 17.14

From the Standard Controls rollout, you can select from several preset Tile styles, including Running Bond, English Bond, and Fine Running Bond.

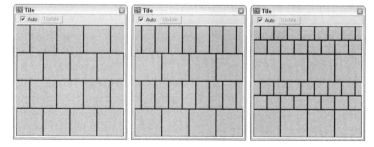

3D maps

3D maps are procedurally created, which means that these maps are more than just a grouping of pixels; they are actually created using a mathematical algorithm. This algorithm defines the map in three dimensions, so that if a portion of the object were to be cut away, the map would line up along each edge.

The Coordinates rollout for 3D maps is similar to the Coordinates rollout for 2D maps with a few exceptions; differences include Coordinate Source options of Object XYZ, World XYZ, Explicit Map Channel, and Vertex Color Channel. There are also Offset, Tiling, and Angle values for the X-, Y-, and Z-axes as well as Blur and Blur offset options.

Cellular map

The Cellular 3D map creates patterns of small objects referred to as cells. In the Cell Color section of the Cellular Parameters rollout, you can specify the color for the individual cells or apply a map. Setting the Variation value can vary the cell color.

In the Division Colors section, two color swatches are used to define the colors that appear between the cells. This space is a gradient between the two colors.

In the Cell Characteristics section, you can control the shape of the cells by selecting Circular or Chips, a Size, and how the cells are Spread. The Bump Smoothing value smoothes the jaggedness of the cells. The Fractal option causes the cells to be generated using a fractal algorithm. The Iterations value determines the number of times that the algorithm is applied. The Adaptive option determines automatically the number of iterations to complete. The Roughness setting determines how rough the surfaces of the cells are.

The Size value affects the overall scale of the map, while the Threshold values specify the specific size of the individual cells. Settings include Low, Mid, and High.

Figure 17.15 shows three Cellular maps: the first with Circular cells and a Size value of 20, the second with Chips cells, and the final one with the Fractal option enabled.

FIGURE 17.15

The Cellular map creates small, regular-shaped cells.

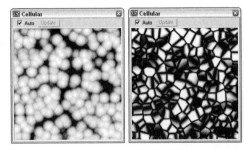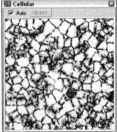

Dent map

The Dent 3D map works as a bump map to create indentations across the surface of an object. In the Dent Parameters rollout, the Size value sets the overall size of the dents. The Strength value determines how deep the dents are, and the Iterations value sets how many times the algorithm is to be computed. You can also specify the colors for the Dent map. The default colors are black and white. Black defines the areas that are indented.

Figure 17.16 shows three spheres with the Dent map applied as bump mapping. The three spheres, from left to right, have Size values of 500, 1000, and 2000.

Falloff map

The Falloff 3D map creates a grayscale image based on the direction of the surface normals. Areas with normals that are parallel to the view are black, and areas whose normals are perpendicular to the view are white. This map is usually applied as an opacity map, giving you greater control over the opacity of the object.

 **TIP** The Falloff map is also useful for creating a Fresnel effect on a glazed surface through its reflections.

FIGURE 17.16

The Dent map causes dents in the object when applied as bump mapping.

 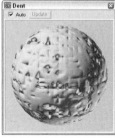 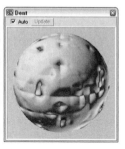

The Falloff Parameters rollout includes two color swatches, a Strength value of each, and an optional map. There are also drop-down lists for setting the Falloff Type and the Falloff Direction. Falloff Types include Perpendicular/Parallel, Towards/Away, Fresnel, Shadow/Light, and Distance Blend. The Falloff Direction options include Viewing Direction (Camera Z axis); Camera X Axis; Camera Y Axis; Object; Local X, Y, and Z Axis; and World X, Y, and Z Axis.

In the Mode Specific Parameters section, several parameters are based on the Falloff Type and Direction. If Object is selected as the Falloff Direction, then a button that lets you select the object becomes active. The Fresnel Falloff Type is based on the Index of Refraction and provides an option to override the material's Index of Refraction value. The Distance Blend Falloff Type offers values for Near and Far distances.

The Falloff map also includes a Mix Curve graph and rollout that give you precise control over the falloff gradient. Points at the top of the graph have a value of 1 and represent the white areas of falloff. Points at the bottom of the graph have a value of 0 and are black.

Marble map

The Marble 3D map creates a marbled material with random colored veins. The Marble Parameters rollout includes two color swatches: Color #1 is the vein color and Color #2 is the base color. You also have the option of loading maps for each color. The Swap button switches the two colors. The Size value determines how far the veins are from each other, and the Vein Width defines the vein thickness.

Figure 17.17 shows three Marble maps with Vein Width values of (from left to right) 0.01, 0.025, and 0.05.

FIGURE 17.17

The Marble map creates a marbled surface.

 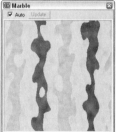 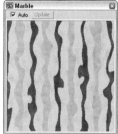

Noise map

The Noise 3D map randomly alters the surface of an object using two colors. The Noise Parameters rollout offers three Noise types: Regular, Fractal, and Turbulence. Each type uses a different algorithm for computing noise. The two color swatches let you alter the colors used to represent the noise. You also have the option of loading maps for each color. The Size value scales the noise effect. To prevent discontinuities, the High and Low Noise Threshold can be used to set noise limits.

Figure 17.18 shows Noise maps with the (from left to right) Regular, Fractal, and Turbulence options enabled.

FIGURE 17.18

The Noise map produces a random noise pattern on the surface of the object.

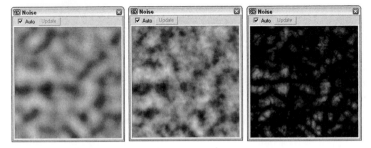

Particle Age map

The Particle Age map is used with particle systems to change the color of particles over their lifetime. The Particle Age Parameters rollout includes three different color swatches and age values.

Particle MBlur map

The Particle MBlur map is also used with particle systems. This map is used to blur particles as they increase in velocity. The Particle Motion Blur Parameters rollout includes two colors: The first color is the one used for the slower portions of the particle, and the second color is used for the fast portions. When you apply this map as an opacity map, the particles are blurred. The Sharpness value determines the amount of blur.

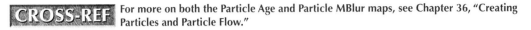

CROSS-REF   For more on both the Particle Age and Particle MBlur maps, see Chapter 36, "Creating Particles and Particle Flow."

Perlin Marble map

This map creates marble textures using a different algorithm. Perlin Marble is more chaotic and random than the Marble map. The Perlin Marble Parameters rollout includes a Size parameter, which adjusts the size of the marble pattern, and a Levels parameter, which determines how many times the algorithm is applied. The two color swatches determine the base and vein colors, or you can assign a map. There are also values for the Saturation of the colors.

Figure 17.19 shows the Perlin Marble map Size values of (from left to right) 50, 100, and 200.

FIGURE 17.19

The Perlin Marble map creates a marble pattern with random veins.

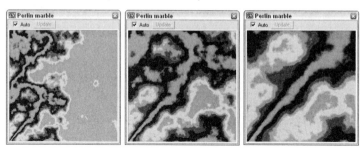

Planet map

The Planet map is especially designed to create random areas of land and water. The Planet Parameters roll-out includes three color swatches for the water areas and five color swatches for the land areas. These colors are displayed successively to simulate the elevation of the map. Other options include the Continent Size, the Island Factor (which determines the number of islands), an Ocean percentage, and a Random Seed. There is also an option to Blend Water and Land.

Figure 17.20 shows Planet map with Island Factor values of (from left to right) 0, 10, and 30.

FIGURE 17.20

You can use the Planet map to create planets with landmasses and oceans.

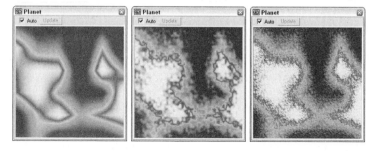

Smoke map

The Smoke map can create random fractal-based patterns such as those you would see in smoke. In the Smoke Parameters rollout, you can set the Size of the smoke areas and the number of Iterations (how many times the fractal algorithm is computed). The Phase value shifts the smoke about, and the Exponent value produces thin, wispy lines of smoke. The rollout also includes two colors for the smoke particles and the area between the smoke particles, or you can load maps instead.

Figure 17.21 shows the Smoke map with Size values of (from left to right) 40, 80, and 200.

FIGURE 17.21

The Smoke map simulates the look of smoke when applied as opacity mapping.

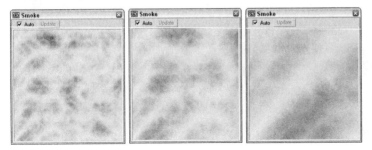

Speckle map

The Speckle map produces small randomly positioned specks. The Speckle Parameters rollout lets you control the Size and color of the specks. Two color swatches are for the base and speck colors.

Figure 17.22 shows the Speckle map with Size values of (from left to right) 100, 200, and 400.

FIGURE 17.22

The Speckle map paints small random specks on the surface of an object.

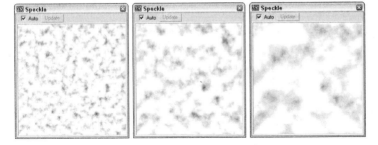

Splat map

The Splat map can create the look of covering an object with splattered paint. In the Splat Parameters rollout, you can set the Size of the splattered areas and the number of Iterations, which is how many times the fractal algorithm is computed. For each additional Iteration, a smaller set of spatters appears. The Threshold value determines how much of each color to mix. The rollout also includes two colors for the splattered sections, or you can load maps instead.

Figure 17.23 shows the Splat map with a Size value of 60, 6 Iterations, and Threshold values of (from left to right) 0.2, 0.3, and 0.4.

FIGURE 17.23

The Splat map splatters paint randomly across the surface of an object.

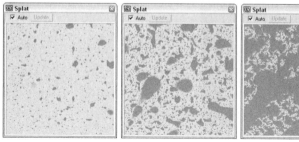

Stucco map

The Stucco map generates random patches of gradients that create the look of a stucco surface if applied as a bump map. In the Stucco Parameters rollout, the Size value determines the size of these areas. The Thickness value determines how blurry the patches are, which changes the sharpness of the bumps for a bump map. The Threshold value determines how much of each color to mix. The rollout also includes two colors for the patchy sections, or you can load maps instead.

Figure 17.24 shows the Stucco map with a Threshold value of 0.5, Thickness of 0.02, and Size values of (from left to right) 10, 20, and 40.

FIGURE 17.24

The Stucco map creates soft indentations when applied as bump mapping.

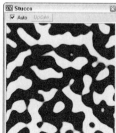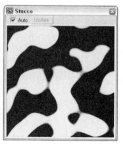

Waves map

This map creates wavy, watery-looking maps and can be used as both a diffuse map and a bump map to create a water surface. You can use several values to set the wave characteristics in the Water Parameters rollout, including the number of Wave Sets, the Wave Radius, the minimum and maximum Wave Length, the Amplitude, and the Phase. You can also Distribute the waves as 2D or 3D, and a Random Seed value is available.

Figure 17.25 shows the Water map with the Num Wave Sets value set to (from left to right) 1, 3, and 9.

FIGURE 17.25

You can use the Water map to create watery surfaces.

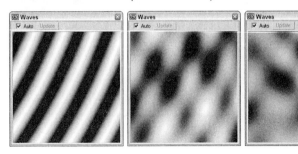

Wood map

The Wood map produces a two-color wood grain. The Wood Parameters rollout options include Grain Thickness, Radial, and Axial Noise. You can select the two colors to use for the wood grain.

Figure 17.26 shows the Wood map with Grain Thickness values of (from left to right) 8, 16, and 30.

FIGURE 17.26

The Wood map creates a map with a wood grain.

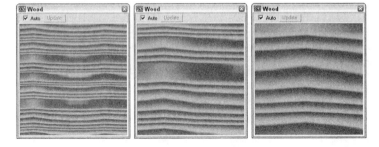

Compositor maps

Compositor maps are made by combining several maps into one. Compositor map types include Composite, Mask, Mix, and RGB Multiply.

Composite map

Composite maps combine a specified number of maps into a single map using the alpha channel. The Composite Parameters rollout enables you to specify the number of maps and has buttons for loading each.

In order for the maps to be specified, at least one of them must contain an alpha channel. If the submaterials contain an Output rollout, then you can select the Alpha from RGB Intensity option. If the submaterial doesn't have an Output rollout, then you can apply the Output map and keep the submaterial as a submap. This enables the same options found in the Output rollout.

Figure 17.27 shows three different uses for the Composite map. The left image combines a Checker map with a Gradient map. The Gradient map includes an Output rollout with the Alpha from RGB Intensity option enabled. The last two images combine a Swirl map with Checker and Cellular maps. To enable the alpha channel for these last two, the Output map was used.

FIGURE 17.27

The Composite map can use multiple maps.

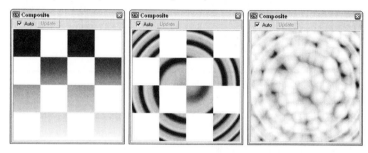

Mask map

In the Mask Parameters rollout, you can select one map to use as a Mask and another one to display through the holes in the mask simply called Map. You also have an option to Invert the Mask. The black areas of the masking map are the areas that hide the underlying map. The white areas allow the underlying map to show through. The result of the Mask map is visible only when rendered.

Mix map

You can use the Mix map to combine two maps or colors. It is similar to the Composite map, except that it uses a Mix Amount value to combine the two colors or maps instead of using the alpha channel. In the Mix Parameters rollout, the Mix Amount value of 0 includes only Color #1, and a value of 100 includes only Color #2. You can also use a Mixing Curve to define how the colors are mixed. The curve shape is controlled by altering its Upper and Lower values.

Figure 17.28 shows the Mix map with Perlin marble and Checker maps applied as sub-maps and Mix values of (from left to right) 25, 50, and 75.

FIGURE 17.28

The Mix map lets you combine two maps and define the Mix Amount.

RGB Multiply map

The RGB Multiply map multiplies the RGB values for two separate maps and combines them to create a single map. Did you notice in the preceding figure that the Mix map fades both maps? The RGB Multiply map keeps the saturation of the individual maps by using each map's alpha channel to combine the maps.

The RGB Multiply Parameters rollout includes an option to use the Alpha from either Map #1 or Map #2 or to Multiply the Alphas.

Figure 17.29 shows three samples of the RGB Multiply map. Each of these images combines a Wood map with (from left to right) a Checker map, a Gradient map, and a Stucco map. Notice that the colors aren't faded for this map type.

FIGURE 17.29

The RGB Multiply map combines maps at full saturation using alpha channels.

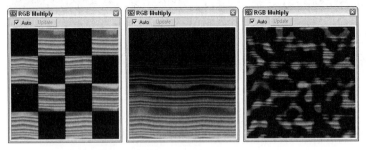

Color Modifier maps

You can use this group of maps to change the color of different materials. Color Modifier map types include Output, RGB Tint, and Vertex Color.

Output map

The Output map provides a way to add the functions of the Output rollout to maps that don't include an output rollout. Details on this map type are presented in the earlier section that covers the Output rollout.

RGB Tint map

The RGB Tint map includes color swatches for the red, green, and blue channel values. Adjusting these colors alters the amount of tint in the map. For example, setting the red color swatch in the RGB Tint Parameters rollout to white and the green and blue color swatches to black creates a map with a heavy red tint. You can also load maps in place of the colors.

Vertex Color map

The Vertex Color map makes the vertex colors assigned to an Editable Mesh, Poly, or Patch object visible when the object is rendered. When an Editable Mesh, Poly, or Patch object is in Vertex subobject mode, you can assign the selected vertices a Color, an Illumination color, and an Alpha value. These settings are in the Surface Properties rollout. You can also assign vertex colors using the Assign Vertex Colors utility. Use this utility to assign color to the current object or to assign material colors to the object's vertices using the given lights. A third way to assign vertex colors is with the Vertex Paint modifier, which you access using the Modifiers ➪ Mesh Editing ➪ Vertex Paint menu command. This modifier lets you color vertices by painting directly on an object.

 For more detail on the Vertex Paint modifier, see Chapter 31, "Creating Baked Textures and Normal Maps."

After vertex colors are assigned, you need to apply the Vertex Color map to the diffuse color in the Material Editor and apply it to the object for the object to render the vertex colors. This map doesn't have any settings.

Miscellaneous maps

These maps are actually grouped into a category called *Other*, but they mostly deal with reflection and refraction effects. Maps in this category include Camera Map Per Pixel, Flat Mirror, Normal Bump, Raytrace, Reflect/Refract, and Thin Wall Refraction.

Camera Map Per Pixel map

The Camera Map Per Pixel map lets you project a map from the location of a camera. You use this map by rendering the scene, editing the rendered image in an image-editing program, and projecting the image back onto the scene.

The Camera Map Parameters rollout includes buttons that let you select the Camera, Texture, ZBuffer Mask, and Mask.

Flat Mirror map

The Flat Mirror map reflects the surroundings using a coplanar group of faces. In the Flat Mirror Parameters rollout, you can select a Blur amount to apply. You can specify whether to Render the First Frame Only or Every Nth Frame. You also have an option to Use the Environment Map or to apply to Faces with a given ID.

NOTE Flat Mirror maps are applied only to selected coplanar faces using the material ID.

The Distortion options include None, Use Bump Map, and Use Built-In Noise. If the Bump Map option is selected, you can define a Distortion Amount. If the Noise option is selected, you can choose Regular, Fractal, or Turbulence noise types with Phase, Size, and Levels values.

Tutorial: Creating a mirrored surface

Mirror, mirror on the wall, who's the best modeler of them all? Using the Flat Mirror map, you can create, believe it or not, mirrors. To create and configure a flat mirror map, follow these steps:

1. Open the Reflection in mirror.max file from the Chap 17 directory on the DVD.

   This file includes a mesh of a man standing in front of a mirror. The mirror subobject faces have been selected and applied a material ID of 1.

2. Choose Rendering ➪ Material Editor (or press the M key) to open the Material Editor.

3. Select the second sample slot, name the material **Mirror** and open the Maps rollout. Click the mapping button for the Reflection map. In the Material/Map Browser that opens, double-click the Flat Mirror map to select it.

NOTE If the Flat Mirror map isn't available, select the Map radio button in the Show section.

4. In the Flat Mirror Parameters rollout, deselect the Apply Blur and Use Environment Map options and select the Apply to Faces with ID option. Then set the ID value to 1.

5. Drag the sample slot to the mirror object in the viewport to apply the material to the mirror.

Figure 17.30 shows a model being reflected off a simple patch object with a Flat Mirror map applied to it. The reflection is visible only in the final rendered image.

FIGURE 17.30

A Flat Mirror map causes the object to reflect its surroundings.

Normal Bump map

The Normal Bump map lets you alter the appearance of the details on the surface using a Normal map. Normal maps can be created using the Render to Texture dialog box. The Parameters rollout for this map type lets you specify a normal map along with another additional bump map. You also can set the amount each map is displaced. Additional options let you flip and swap the red and green channel directions, which define the X and Y axes.

CROSS-REF The Render to Texture dialog box and Normal maps are covered in more detail in Chapter 31, "Creating Baked Textures and Normal Maps."

Raytrace map

The Raytrace map is an alternative to the raytrace material and, as a map, can be used in places where the raytrace material cannot.

CROSS-REF Check out Chapter 46, "Raytracing and mental ray," for more on the Raytrace materials and maps.

Reflect/Refract map

Reflect/Refract maps are yet another way to create reflections and refractions on objects. These maps work by producing a rendering from each axis of the object, like one for each face of a cube. These rendered images, called *cubic maps*, are then projected onto the object.

These rendered images can be created automatically or loaded from pre-rendered images using the Reflect/Refract Parameters rollout. Using automatic cubic maps is easier, but they take considerably more time. If you select the Automatic option, you can select to render the First Frame Only or Every Nth Frame. If you select the From File option, then you are offered six buttons that can load cubic maps for each of the different directions.

In the Reflect/Refract Parameters rollout, you can also specify the Blur settings and the Atmospheric Ranges.

Thin Wall Refraction map

The Thin Wall Refraction map simulates the refraction caused by a piece of glass, such as a magnifying glass. The same result is possible with the Reflect/Refract map, but the Thin Wall Refraction map achieves this result in a fraction of the time.

The Thin Wall Refraction Parameters rollout includes options for setting the Blur, the frames to render, and Refraction values. The Thickness Offset determines the amount of offset and can range from 0 through 10. The Bump Map Effect value changes the refraction based on the presence of a bump map.

Tutorial: Creating a magnifying glass effect

Another common property of glass besides reflection is refraction. Refraction can enlarge items when the glass is thick, such as when you look at the other side of the room through a glass of water. Using the Thin Wall Refraction map, you can simulate the effects of a magnifying glass.

To create a magnifying glass effect, follow these steps:

1. Open the Magnifying glass.max file from the Chap 17 directory on the DVD.

   This file includes a simple sphere with a Perlin Marble map applied to it and a magnifying glass modeled from primitive objects.

2. Choose Rendering ➪ Material Editor (or press the M key) to open the Material Editor.

3. Select the fourth sample slot, name the material **Magnifying Glass** and open the Maps rollout. Click the map button for the Refraction map. In the Material/Map Browser that opens, double-click the Thin Wall Refraction map. In the Thin Wall Refraction Parameters rollout, set the Thickness Offset to **10** to increase the amount of magnification.

4. Drag the Magnifying Glass material to the magnifying glass object in the viewport to apply the material to the object.

Figure 17.31 shows the resulting rendered image. Notice that the texture in the magnifying glass appears magnified.

FIGURE 17.31

The Thin Wall Refraction map is applied to a magnifying glass.

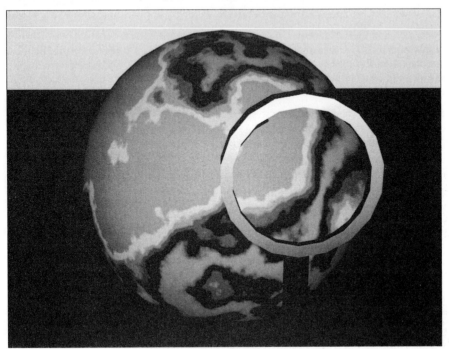

Using the Maps Rollout

Now that you've seen the different types of maps, we'll revisit the Maps rollout (introduced in Chapter 14), shown in Figure 17.32, and cover it in more detail.

The Maps rollout is where you apply maps to the various materials. To use a map, click the Map button; this opens the Material/Map Browser where you can select the map to use. The Amount spinner sets the intensity of the map, and an option to enable or disable the map is available. For example, a white diffuse color with a red Diffuse map set at 50 percent Intensity results in a pink material.

The available maps in the Maps rollout depend on the type of material and the Shader that you are using. Raytrace materials have many more available maps than the standard material. Some of the common mapping types found in the Maps rollout are discussed in Table 17.1.

The Maps rollout can turn maps on or off.

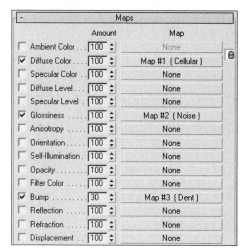

TABLE 17.1

Material Properties for Maps

Material Property	Description
Ambient Color	Replaces the ambient color component of the base material. You can use this feature to make an object's shadow appear as a map. Diffuse mapping (discussed next) also affects the Ambient color. A lock button in the Maps rollout enables you to lock these two mappings together.
Diffuse Color	Replaces the diffuse color component of the base material. This is the main color used for the object. When you select a map such as Wood, the object appears to be created out of wood. As mentioned previously, diffuse mapping also can affect the Ambient color if the lock button is selected.
Diffuse Level	Changes the diffuse color level from 0, where the map is black, to a maximum, where the map is white. This mapping is available only with the Anisotropic, Oren-Nayar-Blinn, and Multi-Level Shaders.
Diffuse Roughness	Sets the roughness value of the material from 0, where the map is black, to a maximum, where the map is white. This mapping is available only with the Oren-Nayar-Blinn and Multi-Layer Shaders.
Specular Color	Replaces the specular color component of the base material. This option enables you to include a different color or image in place of the specular color. It is different from the Specular Level and Glossiness mappings, which also affect the specular highlights.

continued

TABLE 17.1   *(continued)*

Material Property	Description
Specular Level	Controls the intensity of the specular highlights from 0, where the map is black, to 1, where the map is white. For the best effect, apply this mapping along with the Glossiness mapping.
Glossiness	Defines where the specular highlights will appear. You can use this option to make an object appear older by diminishing certain areas. Black areas on the map show the non-glossy areas, and white areas are where the glossiness is at a maximum.
Self-Illumination	Makes certain areas of an object glow, and because they glow, they won't receive any lighting effects, such as highlights or shadows. Black areas represent areas that have no self-illumination, and white areas receive full self-illumination.
Opacity	Determines which areas are visible and which are transparent. Black areas for this map are transparent, and white areas are opaque. This mapping works in conjunction with the Opacity value in the Basic Parameters rollout. Transparent areas, even if perfectly transparent, still receive specular highlights.
Filter Color	Colors transparent areas for creating materials such as colored glass. White light that is cast through an object using filter color mapping is colored with the filter color.
Anisotropy	Controls the shape of an anisotropy highlight. This mapping is available only with the Anisotropic and Multi-Layer Shaders.
Orientation	Controls an anisotropic highlight's position. Anisotropic highlights are elliptical, and this mapping can position them at a different angle. Orientation mapping is available only with the Anisotropic and Multi-Layer Shaders.
Metalness	Controls how metallic an area looks. It specifies metalness values from 0, where the map is black, to a maximum, where the map is white. This mapping is available only with the Strauss Shader.
Bump	Uses the intensity of the bitmap to raise or indent the surface of an object. The white areas of the map are raised, and darker areas are lowered. Although bump mapping appears to alter the geometry, it actually doesn't affect the surface geometry.
Reflection	Reflects images off the surface as a mirror does. The three types of Reflection mapping are Basic, Automatic, and Flat Mirror. Basic reflection mapping simulates the reflection of an object's surroundings. Automatic reflection mapping projects the map outward from the center of the object. Flat-Mirror reflection mapping reflects a mirror image off a series of coplanar faces. Reflection mapping doesn't need mapping coordinates because the coordinates are based on world coordinates and not on object coordinates. Therefore, the map appears different if the object is moved, which is how reflections work in the real world.
Refraction	Bends light and displays images through a transparent object, in the same way a room appears through a glass of water. The amount of this effect is controlled by a value called the Index of Refraction. This value is set in the parent material's Extended Parameters rollout.
Displacement	Changes the geometry of an object. The white areas of the map are pushed outward, and the dark areas pushed in. The amount of the surface displaced is based on a percentage of the diagonal that makes up the bounding box of the object. Displacement mapping isn't visible in the viewports unless the Displace NURBS (for NURBS objects) or the Displace Mesh (for Editable Meshes) modifiers have been applied.

Tutorial: Aging objects for realism

I don't know whether your toolbox is well worn like mine — it must be the hostile environment that it is always in (or all the things I keep dropping in and on it). To render a toolbox with nice specular highlights just doesn't feel right. This tutorial shows a few ways to age an object so that it looks older and worn.

To add maps to make an object look old, follow these steps:

1. Open the Toolbox.max file from the Chap 17 directory on the DVD.

   This file contains a simple toolbox mesh created using extruded splines.

2. Press the M key to open the Material Editor, and select the first sample slot. Select the Metal shader from the drop-down list in the Shader Basic Parameters rollout. In the Metal Basic Parameters rollout, set the Diffuse color to a nice, shiny red and increase the Specular Level to **97** and the Glossiness value to **59**. Name the material **Toolbox**.

3. In the Maps rollout, click the button for the Glossiness mapping and double-click the Splat map from the Material/Map Browser. In the Splat Parameters rollout, set the Size value to **100** and change Color #1 to a rust color and Color #2 to white.

4. Click the Go to Parent button (which is located above the material Type button) to get back the Maps rollout for the base material. In the Maps rollout, click the Bump mapping button and double-click the Dent map from the Material/Map Browser. In the Dent Parameters rollout, set the Size value to **200**, Color #1 to black, and Color #2 to white.

5. At the top of the Material Editor, select the second sample slot and name it **Hinge**. Select the Metal shader from the Shader Basic Parameters rollout for this material also, and increase the Specular Level in the Metal Basic Parameters rollout to **26** and the Glossiness value to **71**. Also change the Diffuse color to a light gray. Click the map button next to the Glossiness value, and double-click the Noise map in the Material/Map Browser. In the Noise Parameters rollout, set the Noise map to Fractal with a Size of **10**.

6. Drag the "Toolbox" material to the toolbox object and the "Hinge" material to the hinge and the handle.

 **Bump and glossiness mappings are not visible until the scene is rendered. To see the material's results, choose Rendering ⇨ Render and click the Render button.**

Figure 17.33 shows the well-used toolbox.

Using the Map Path Utility

After you have all your maps in place, losing them can really make life troublesome. However, Max includes a utility that helps you determine which maps are missing and lets you edit the path to them to quickly and easily locate them. The Bitmap/Photometric Path Editor utility is available in the Utility panel. To find it, click the More button and select Bitmap/Photometric Path Editor from the list of utilities.

CROSS-REF **This utility is used for bitmaps as well as photometric lights. You can learn about photometric lights in Chapter 19, "Using Lights and Basic Lighting Techniques."**

When opened, the Path Editor rollout includes the Edit Resources button that opens the Bitmap/Photometric Path Editor window, shown in Figure 17.34. The rollout also includes two options for displaying the Materials Editor and Material Library bitmap paths. The Close button closes the rollout.

FIGURE 17.33

This toolbox shows its age with Glossiness and Bump mappings.

FIGURE 17.34

The Bitmap/Photometric Path Editor window lets you alter map paths.

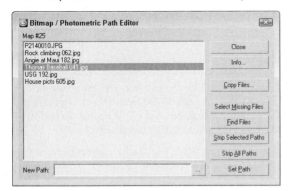

The Info button in the Bitmap/Photometric Path Editor dialog box lists all the nodes that use the selected map. The Copy Files button opens a File dialog in which you can select a location to which to copy the selected map. The Select Missing Files option selects any maps in the list that can't be located. The Find Files button lists the maps in the current selection that can be located and the number that are missing. Stripping paths removes the path information and leaves only the map name. The New Path field lets you enter the path information to apply to the selected maps. The button with three dots to the right of the New Path field lets you browse for a path, and the Set Path button applies the path designated in the New Path field to the selected maps.

Using Map Instances

Using the same bitmap for many different map channels is common. For example, you may use the same bitmap for the Diffuse and Bump map channels. If a file includes the same bitmaps over and over, the file size can increase, and replacing a bitmap when you make changes can become difficult. This potential problem can be fixed easily by making the maps into instances instead of copies. If you have an existing Max file, you can use the Instance Duplicate Maps utility to find all the common maps and make them instances automatically.

Access this utility from the Utilities menu in the Material Editor or from the Utilities panel. Both commands open the same dialog box, shown in Figure 17.35. From this dialog box, you can select which maps to make instances or click Instance All to consolidate all the found maps into instances.

FIGURE 17.35

The Instance Duplicate Maps dialog box lets you consolidate maps into a single instance.

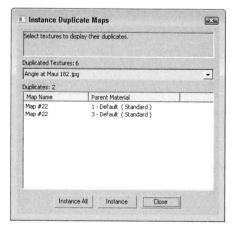

Summary

We've covered lots of ground in this chapter because Max has lots of different maps. Learning to use these maps will make a big difference in the realism of your materials.

In this chapter, you learned about the following:

- All the different map types in several different categories, including 2D, 3D, Compositors, Color Mods, and Reflection/Refraction
- The various mapping possibilities provided in the Maps rollout
- Using the Bitmap Path Editor to change map paths
- Using the Duplicate Map Instances utility

In the next chapter, you gain some experience with using cameras to create and capture a unique view into the scene.

Chapter 18

Configuring and Aiming Cameras

D o you remember as a kid when you first got your own camera? After taking the usual pictures of your dog and the neighbor's fence, you quickly learned how much fun you could have with camera placement, such as a picture of a flagpole from the top of the flagpole or your mom's timeless expression when she found you inside the dryer. Cameras in Max can also offer all kinds of amusing views of your scene.

The benefit of cameras is that you can position them anywhere within a scene to offer a custom view. Camera views are fixed so they won't get lost as a Perspective view can sometimes do. You can open camera views in a viewport, and you can also use them to render images or animated sequences. Cameras in Max can also be animated (without damaging the camera, even if your mischievous older brother turns on the dryer).

In the Camera Parameters rollout is a section for enabling Multi-Pass Camera Effects. These effects include Motion Blur and Depth of Field. Essentially, these effects are accomplished by taking several rendered images of a scene and combining them with some processing.

Learning to Work with Cameras

If you're a photography hobbyist or like to take your video camera out and shoot your own footage, then many of the terms in this section will be familiar to you. The cameras used in Max to get custom views of a scene behave in many respects just like real-world cameras.

Max and real-world cameras both work with different lens settings, which are measured and defined in millimeters. You can select from a variety of preset stock lenses, including 35mm, 80mm, and even 200mm. Max cameras also offer complete control over the camera's focal length, field of view, and perspective for wide-angle or telephoto shots. The big difference is that you never have to worry about setting flashes, replacing batteries, or loading film.

Light coming into a camera is bent through the camera lens and focused on the film, where the image is captured. The distance between the film and the lens is known as the *focal length*. This distance is measured in millimeters, and you can change it by switching to a different lens. On a camera that shoots 35mm film, a lens with a focal length of 50mm produces a view similar to what your eyes would see. A lens with a focal length less than 50mm is known as a wide-angle lens because it displays a wider view of the scene. A lens longer than 50mm is called a telephoto lens because it has the ability to give a closer view of objects for more detail, as a telescope does.

Field of view is directly related to focal length and is a measurement of how much of the scene is visible. It is measured in degrees. The shorter the focal length, the wider the field of view.

When we look at a scene, objects appear larger if they are up close than they would be lying at a farther distance. This effect is referred to as *perspective* and helps us to interpret distances. As mentioned, a 50mm lens gives a perspective similar to what our eyes give. Images taken with a wide field of view look distorted because the effect of perspective is increased.

Creating a camera object

To create a camera object, you can use the Create ⇨ Cameras menu, or you can open the familiar Create panel and click the Cameras category button. The two types of cameras that you can create are a Free camera and a Target camera.

Camera objects are visible as icons in the viewports, but they aren't rendered. The camera icon looks like a box with a smaller box in front of it, which represents the lens or front end of the camera. Both the Free and Target camera types include a rectangular cone that shows where the camera is pointing.

Free camera

The Free camera object offers a view of the area that is directly in front of the camera and is the better choice if the camera will be animated. When a Free camera is initially created, it points at the negative Z-axis of the active viewport.

Target camera

A Target camera always points at a controllable target point some distance in front of the camera. Target cameras are easy to aim and are useful for situations where the camera won't move. To create this type of camera, click a viewport to position the camera and drag to the location of its target. The target can be named along with the camera. When a target is created, Max automatically names the target by attaching ".target" to the end of the camera name. You can change this default name by typing a different name in the Name field.

Creating a camera view

You can change any viewport to show a camera's viewpoint. To do so, right-click the viewport's title, and select View and the camera's name from the pop-up menu. Any movements done to the camera are reflected immediately in the viewport.

Another way to select a camera for a viewport is to press the C key. This keyboard shortcut makes the active viewport into a camera view. If several cameras exist in a scene, then the Select Camera dialog box appears, from which you can select a camera to use. You also can select a camera and choose the Set View to Selected Camera from the right-click pop-up menu. Figure 18.1 shows two Target cameras pointing at a car. The two viewports on the right are the views from these cameras.

FIGURE 18.1

A car as seen by two different cameras

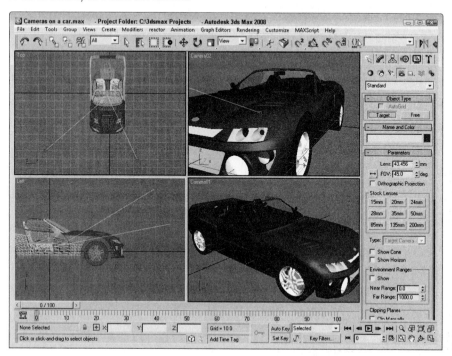

You can turn off the camera object icons using the Display panel. In the Display panel, under the Hide by Category rollout, select the Cameras option. When selected, the camera icons are not visible in the viewports.

> **NOTE** Cameras are usually positioned at some distance away from the rest of the scene. Their distant position can make scene objects appear very small when the Zoom Extents button is used. If the visibility of the camera icons is turned off, Zoom Extents does not include them in the zoom. You can also enable the Ignore Extents option in the camera's Object Properties dialog box.

Tutorial: Setting up an opponent's view

There is no limit to the number of cameras that you can place in a scene. Placing two cameras in a scene showing a game of checkers lets you see the game from the perspective of either player.

To create a new aligned view from the opponent's perspective, follow these steps:

1. Open the Checkers game.max file from the Chap 18 directory on the DVD.

2. Select Create ⇨ Cameras ⇨ Target Camera, and drag in the Top viewport to create the camera. Then give the new camera the name **Opponents Camera**.

3. Position the new target camera behind the opponent's pieces roughly symmetrical to the other camera.

4. With the new camera selected, drag the target point and position it on top of the other camera's target point somewhere below the center of the board.

To see the new camera view, right-click the Perspective viewport title and choose View ⇨ Black Camera (or select the camera and the Perspective viewport, and press the C key). Figure 18.2 shows the view from this camera.

FIGURE 18.2

Positioning an additional camera behind the Black player's pieces offers the opponent's view.

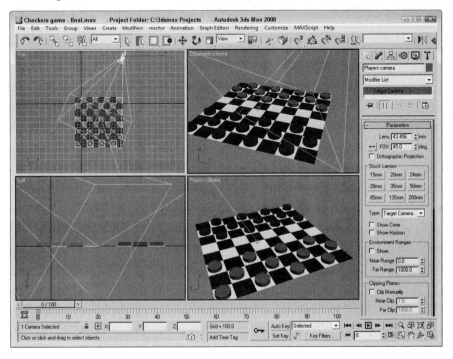

> **TIP**   Because viewports can be resized, the view you see in the viewport isn't necessarily the view that will be rendered. Using the Safe Frames feature found in the Safe Frames panel of the Viewport Configuration dialog box, you can see a border around exactly what will be rendered.

Controlling a camera

I was once on a ride at Disneyland when a person behind me decided to blatantly disregard the signs not to take photographs. As he leaned over to snap another picture, I heard a fumbling noise, a faint, "Oh no," and then the distinct sound of his camera falling into the depths of the ride. (That was actually more enjoyable than the ride. It served him right.) As this example shows, controlling a camera can be difficult. This chapter offers many tips and tricks for dealing with the cameras in Max, and you won't have to worry about dropping them.

You control the camera view in a viewport by means of the Camera Navigation controls located in the lower-right corner of the screen. These controls replace the viewport controls when a camera view is selected and are different from the normal Viewport Navigation controls. The Camera Navigation controls are identified and defined in Table 18.1.

Many of these controls are identical to the controls for lights.

You can constrain the movements to a single axis by holding down the Shift key. The Ctrl key causes the movements to increase rapidly. For example, holding down the Ctrl key while dragging the Perspective tool magnifies the amount of perspective applied to the viewport.

You can undo changes in the normal viewports using the Views ⇨ Undo (Shift+Z) command, but you undo camera viewport changes with the regular Edit ⇨ Undo command because it involves the movement of an object.

TABLE 18.1

Camera Navigation Control Buttons

Control Button	Name	Description
✛	Dolly Camera, Dolly Target, Dolly Camera + Target	Moves the camera, its target, or both the camera and its target closer to or farther away from the scene in the direction it is pointing.
◇	Perspective	Increases or decreases the viewport's perspective by dollying the camera and altering its field of view.
↻	Roll Camera	Spins the camera about its local Z-axis.
⊞	Zoom Extents All, Zoom Extents All Selected	Zooms in on all objects or the selected objects by reducing the field of view until the objects fill the viewport.
▷	Field of View	Changes the width of the view, similar to changing the camera lens or zooming without moving the camera.
✋ ░	Truck Camera, Walk Through	The Truck Camera button moves the camera perpendicular to the line of sight, and the Walk Through button enables a mode in which you can control the camera using the arrow keys and the mouse.
♁ ⊃	Orbit, Pan Camera	The Orbit button rotates the camera around the target, and the Pan button rotates the target around the camera.
⧉	Min/Max Toggle	Makes the current viewport fill the screen. Clicking this button a second time returns the display to several viewports.

 If a Free camera is selected, then the Dolly Target and Dolly Camera + Target buttons are not available.

Aiming a camera

In addition to the Camera Navigation buttons, you can use the Transformation buttons on the main toolbar to reposition the camera object. To move a camera, select the camera object and click the Select and Move button (W). Then drag in the viewports to move the camera.

Using the Select and Rotate (E) button changes the direction in which a camera points, but only Free cameras rotate in all directions. When applied to a Target camera, the rotate transformation spins only the camera about the axis pointing to the target. You aim Target cameras by moving their targets.

> **CAUTION**   Don't try to rotate a Target camera so that it is pointing directly up or down, or the camera will flip.

Select the target for a Target camera by selecting its camera object, right-clicking to open the pop-up menu, and selecting Select Camera Target.

Tutorial: Watching a rocket

Because cameras can be transformed like any other geometry, they can also be set to watch the movements of any other geometry. In this tutorial, we aim a camera at a distant rocket and watch it as it flies past us and on into the sky. Zygote Media created the rocket model used in this tutorial.

To aim a camera at a rocket as it hurtles into the sky, follow these steps:

1. Open the Following a rocket.max file from the Chap 18 directory on the DVD.

   This file includes a rocket mesh.

2. Select Create ➪ Cameras ➪ Target Camera, and drag in the Front viewport from the top to the bottom of the viewport to create a camera. Set the Field of View value to **2.0** degrees. The corresponding Lens value is around 1031mm.

3. Select the camera target, click the Select and Link button in the main toolbar, and drag from the target to the rocket object.

4. To view the scene from the camera's viewpoint, right-click the Perspective viewport title and choose Views ➪ Camera01 from the pop-up menu (or press the C button). Then click the Play Animation button to see how well the camera follows the target.

Figure 18.3 shows some frames from this animation.

Aligning cameras

Another way to aim a camera is with the Tools ➪ Align Camera menu command or by clicking the Align Camera button on the main toolbar (under the Align flyout). After selecting this command, click an object face and hold down the mouse button; the normal to the object face that is currently under the cursor icon is displayed as a blue arrow. When you've located the point at which you want the camera to point, release the mouse button. The camera is repositioned to point directly at the selected point on the selected face along the normal. The Align Camera command requires that a camera be selected before the command is used.

> **CROSS-REF**   The Align Camera command does the same thing for cameras that the Place Highlight command does for lights. A discussion of the Place Highlight command appears in Chapter 19, "Using Lights and Basic Lighting Techniques."

Cameras can be positioned automatically to match any view that a viewport can display, including lights and the Perspective view. The Views ➪ Create Camera From View (Ctrl+C) menu command creates a new Free camera if one doesn't already exist, matches the current active viewport, and makes the active viewport a camera view. This provides you with the ability to position the view using the Viewport Navigation Controls, and it automatically makes a camera that shows that view. If a camera already exists in the scene and is selected, this command uses the selected camera for the view.

> **CAUTION**   If you use the Match Camera to View command while a camera view is the active viewport, the two cameras are positioned on top of each other.

FIGURE 18.3

Positioning the camera's target on the rocket enables the camera to follow the rocket's ascent.

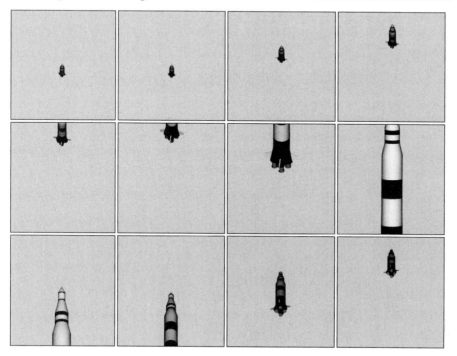

Tutorial: Seeing the dinosaur's good side

Using the Align Camera tool, you can place a camera so that it points directly at an item or the face of an object, such as the dinosaur's good side (if a dinosaur has a good side). To align a camera with an object point, follow these steps:

1. Open the Dinosaur.max file from the Chap 18 directory on the DVD.

   This file includes a dinosaur model created by Viewpoint Datalabs.

2. Select Create ➪ Cameras ➪ Free Camera, and click in the Top viewport to create a new Free camera in the scene.

3. With the camera selected, choose Tools ➪ Align Camera or click the Align Camera flyout button on the main toolbar.

   The cursor changes to a small camera icon.

4. Click the cursor on the dinosaur's face just under its eye in the Perspective viewport.

   This point is where the camera will point.

5. To see the new camera view, right-click the viewport title and choose Views ➪ Camera01 (or press C).

   Although the camera is pointing at the selected point, you may need to change the field of view or dolly the camera to correct the zoom ratios.

Figure 18.4 shows our dinosaur from the newly aligned camera.

FIGURE 18.4

This new camera view of the dinosaur shows his best side.

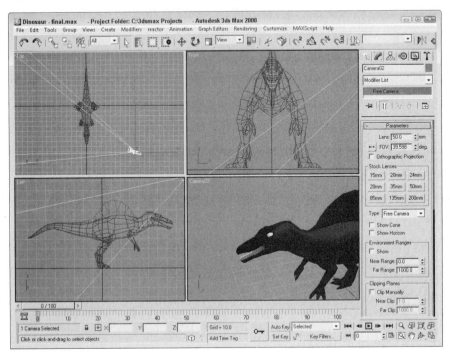

The Align Camera command points a camera at an object only for the current frame. It does not follow an object if it moves during an animation. To have a camera follow an object, you need to use the Look At Controller, which is covered in Chapter 21, "Animating with Constraints and Controllers."

Setting Camera Parameters

When a camera is first created, you can modify the camera parameters directly in the Create panel as long as the new camera is selected. After the camera object has been deselected, you can make modifications in the Modify panel's Parameters rollout for the camera.

Lens settings and field of view

The first parameter in the Parameters rollout sets the Lens value or, more simply, the camera's focal length in millimeters.

The second parameter, FOV (which stands for field of view), sets the width of the area that the camera displays. The value is specified in degrees and can be set to represent a Horizontal, Vertical, or Diagonal distance using the flyout button to its left, as shown in Table 18.2.

TABLE 18.2	

Field of View Buttons

Button	Description
↔	Horizontal distance
↕	Vertical distance
↗	Diagonal distance

The Orthographic Projection option displays the camera view in a manner similar to any of the orthographic viewports such as Top, Left, or Front. This eliminates any perspective distortion of objects farther back in the scene and displays true dimensions for all edges in the scene. This type of view is used heavily in architecture.

Professional photographers and film crews use standard stock lenses in the course of their work. These lenses can be simulated in Max by clicking one of the Stock Lens buttons. Preset stock lenses include 15, 20, 24, 28, 35, 50, 85, 135, and 200mm lengths. The Lens and FOV fields are automatically updated on stock lens selection.

 On cameras that use 35mm film, the typical default lens is 50mm.

Camera type and display options

The Type option enables you to change a Free camera to a Target camera and then change back at any time.

The Show Cone option enables you to display the camera's cone, showing the boundaries of the camera view when the camera isn't selected. (The camera cone is always visible when a camera is selected.) The Show Horizon option sets a horizon line within the camera view, which is a dark gray line where the horizon is located.

Environment ranges and clipping planes

You use the Near and Far Range values to specify the volume within which atmospheric effects like fog and volume lights are to be contained. The Show option causes these limits to be displayed as yellow rectangles within the camera's cone.

You use clipping planes to designate the closest and farthest object that the camera can see. In Max, they are displayed as red rectangles with crossing diagonals in the camera cone. If the Clip Manually option is disabled, then the clipping planes are set automatically with the Near Clip Plane set to 3 units. Figure 18.5 shows a camera with Clipping Planes specified. The front Clipping Plane intersects the car and chops off its front end. The far Clipping Plane is far behind the car.

 Clipping planes can be used to create a cutaway view of your model.

FIGURE 18.5

A camera cone displaying Clipping Planes

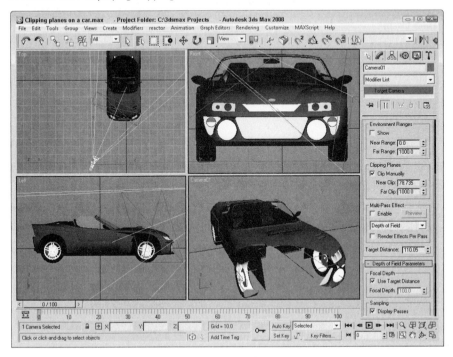

Camera Correction modifier

To understand the Camera Correction modifier, you first need to understand what two-point perspective is. Default cameras in Max use three-point perspective, which causes all lines to converge to a vanishing point off in the distance, but two-point perspective causes all vertical lines to remain vertical.

The visual effect of this modifier is that extra tall objects appear to bend toward the camera when corrected. For example, if you have a camera pointed at a skyscraper, then correcting the camera with the Camera Correction modifier makes the top of the building appear closer rather than having it recede away.

The Camera Correction modifier has an Amount value that lets you specify how much correction to apply and a Direction value that orients the angle of vertical lines in the scene. There is also a Guess button, which automatically sets the correction values for you based on the Z-axis vertical.

 The Camera Correction modifier doesn't appear in the Modifier List in the Modifier Stack, but you can select it from the Modifiers menu.

Creating multi-pass camera effects

All cameras have the option to enable them to become multi-pass cameras. You can find these settings in the Parameters rollout when a camera object is selected. Multi-pass cameras are created by checking the Enable button and selecting the effect from the drop-down list. The current available effects include Depth of Field (mental ray), Depth of Field, and Motion Blur. For each, an associated rollout of parameters opens.

CROSS-REF   The Depth of Field (mental ray) effect option is covered in Chapter 46, "Raytracing and mental ray."

The Multi-Pass Effect section of the Parameters rollout also includes a Preview button. This button makes the effect visible in the viewports for the current frame. This feature can save you a significant amount of time that normally would be spent test-rendering the scene. The Preview button is worth its weight in render speed. Using this button, you can preview the effect without having to render the entire sequence.

CAUTION   The Preview button does not work unless the Camera view is the active viewport.

The Render Effect Per Pass option causes any applied Render Effect to be applied at each pass. If disabled, then any applied Render Effect is applied after the passes are completed.

CROSS-REF   You can also apply these multi-pass effects as Render Effects. See Chapter 45, "Using Atmospheric and Render Effects."

Using the Depth of Field effect

The Depth of Field Parameters rollout, shown in Figure 18.6, appears when the Depth of Field option is selected in the Multi-Pass Effect section of the Parameters rollout. It includes settings for controlling the Depth of Field multi-pass effect.

FIGURE 18.6

Use the Depth of Field Parameters rollout to set the number of passes.

You can select to use the Target Distance (which is the distance to the camera's target), or you can specify a separate Focal Depth distance. This location is the point where the camera is in focus. All scene objects closer and further from this location are blurred to an extent, depending in their distance from the focal point.

NOTE   Even Free cameras have a Target Distance. This distance is displayed at the bottom of the Parameters rollout.

Within the Depth of Field Parameters rollout, you also have the option to display each separate pass in the Rendered Frame Window with the Display Passes option and to use the camera's original location for the first rendering pass by enabling the Use Original Location option.

The Total Passes is the number of times the scene is rendered to produce the effect, and the Sample Radius is the potential distance that the scene can move during the passes. By moving the scene about the radius value and re-rendering a pass, the object becomes blurred more away from the focal distance. If you have a fairly tight scene, the default Radius value does not produce very visible results. Try increasing the Sample Radius value and re-rendering. Figure 18.7 shows a scene with Sample Radius values of 1 and 5.

FIGURE 18.7

Changing the Sample Radius value changes the amount of blur added to the scene.

> **NOTE**   The Depth of Field effect is applied only to rendered scene objects. It is not applied to any background images.

The Sample Bias value moves the blurring closer to the focal point (for higher values) or away from the focal point (for lower values). If you want to highlight the focal point and radically blur the other objects in the scene, set the Sample Bias to 1.0. A Sample Bias setting of 0 results in a more even blurring.

The Normalize Weights option allows you to control how the various passes are blended. When enabled, you can avoid streaking along the object edges. The Dither Strength value controls the amount of dither taking place. Higher Dither Strength values make the image grainier. The Tile Size value also controls dither by specifying the dither pattern size.

With lots of passes specified, the render time can be fairly steep. To lower the overall rendering time, you can disable the Anti-alias and filtering computations. These speed up the rendering time at the cost of image quality.

Tutorial: Applying a Depth of Field effect to a row of windmills

In the dry plains of Southwest America, the wind blows fiercely. Rows of windmills are lined up in an effort to harness this energy. For this example, we use the Depth of Field effect to display the windmills.

To apply a Depth of Field effect to a row of windmills, follow these steps:

1. Open the Depth of field windmills.max file from the Chap 18 directory on the DVD.

    This file includes a windmill object (created by Viewpoint Datalabs) duplicated multiple times and positioned in a row.

2. Select Create ➪ Cameras ➪ Target Camera, and drag in the Top viewport from the lower-left corner to the center of the windmills. In the Left vewpoint, select the camera and move it upward, and then select the Camera Target and also move it upward to the upper third of the windmill's height, so the entire row of windmills can be seen. If the windmills don't fill the camera view, adjust the Field of View (FOV) setting.

TIP You can select both the camera and its target by clicking on the line that connects them.

3. Select the Perspective viewport, right-click on the viewport title, and select Views ➪ Camera01 (or just press the C key) to make this viewport the Camera view.

4. With the Camera selected, open the Modify panel, enable the Multi-Pass Effect option, and then select Depth of Field in the drop-down list.

5. In the Depth of Field Parameters rollout, enable the Use Target Distance option and set the Total Passes to **15**, the Sample Radius to **3.0**, and the Sample Bias to **1.0**.

6. Select the Camera viewport, and click the Preview button in the Parameters rollout.

   This shows the Depth of Field effect in the viewport.

Figure 18.8 shows the resulting Depth of Field effect in the viewport for the row of windmills.

FIGURE 18.8

Multi-Pass camera effects can be viewed in the viewport using the Preview button.

Using the Motion Blur effect

Motion Blur is an effect that shows motion by blurring objects that are moving. If a stationary object is surrounded by several moving objects, the Motion Blur effect blurs the moving objects and the stationary object remains in clear view, regardless of their positions in the scene. The faster an object moves, the more blurry it becomes.

This blurring is accomplished in several ways, but with a multi-pass camera, the camera renders subsequent frames of an animation and then blurs the images together.

The Motion Blur Parameters rollout, shown in Figure 18.9, appears when the Motion Blur option is selected in the Multi-Pass Effect section of the Parameters rollout. Many of its parameters work the same as the Depth of Field effect.

FIGURE 18.9

For the Motion Blur effect, you can set the number of frames to include.

The Display Passes option displays the different frames as they are being rendered, and Total Passes is the number of frames that are included in the averaging. You can also select the Duration, which is the number of frames to include in the effect. The Bias option weights the averaging toward the current frame. Higher Bias values weight the average more toward the latter frames, and lower values lean toward the earlier frames.

The remaining options all work the same as for the Depth of Field effect.

Tutorial: Using a Motion Blur multi-pass camera effect

The Motion Blur effect works only on objects that are moving. Applying this effect to a stationary 2D shape does not produce any noticeable results. For this tutorial, you apply this effect to a speeding car model created by Viewpoint Datalabs.

To apply a Motion Blur multi-pass effect to the camera looking at a car mesh, follow these steps:

1. Open the Car at a stop sign.max file from the Chap 18 directory on the DVD.

   This file includes a car mesh (created by Viewpoint Datalabs), a camera, and a simple stop sign made of primitives. The car is animated.

2. Click the Select by Name button on the main toolbar to open the Select by Name dialog box (or press the H key). Double-click the Camera01 object to select it.

3. With the camera object selected, open the Modify panel. In the Multi-Pass Effect section of the Parameters rollout, click the Enable check box and select the Motion Blur effect from the drop-down list.

4. In the Motion Blur Parameters rollout, set the Total Passes to **10**, the Duration to **1.0**, and the Bias to **0.9**.

5. Drag the Time Slider to frame 57. This is the location where the car just passes the stop sign.

6. With the Camera viewport active, click the Preview button in the Parameters rollout.

Figure 18.10 shows the results of the Motion Blur effect. This effect has been exaggerated to show its result. Notice that the stop sign isn't blurred. The only problem with this example is that, with the Motion Blur effect enabled, you can't make out the license plate number, so you can't send this speeder a ticket.

Using the Motion Blur multi-pass effect for a camera, you can blur objects moving in the scene.

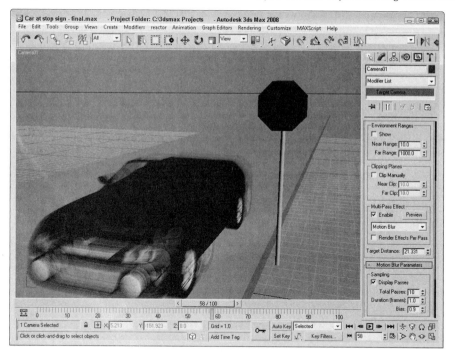

Summary

Cameras can offer a unique look at your scene. You can position and move them anywhere. In this chapter, you discovered how cameras work and how to control and aim them at objects. With Multi-Pass camera effects, you can add Depth of Field and Motion Blur effects.

In this chapter, you've accomplished the following:

- Learned the basics of cameras
- Created a camera object and view
- Discovered how to control a camera
- Aimed a camera at objects
- Changed camera parameters
- Learned to correct camera perspective with the Camera Correction modifier
- Used a multi-pass camera to create a Depth of Field effect
- Used a multi-pass camera to create a Motion Blur effect

Although the director typically says, "Lights, camera, action," we've switched the order to be cameras and then lights (action comes with animation later in the book). We just finished cameras, so next we move on to lights.

Chapter 19

Using Lights and Basic Lighting Techniques

L ights play an important part in the visual process. Have you ever looked at a blank page and been told it was a picture of a polar bear in a blizzard or looked at a completely black image and been told it was a rendering of a black spider crawling down a chimney covered in soot? The point of these two examples is that with too much or too little light, you really can't see anything.

Light in the 3D world figures into every rendering calculation, and 3D artists often struggle with the same problem of too much or too little light. This chapter covers creating and controlling lights in your scene.

Understanding the Basics of Lighting

Lighting plays a critical part of any Max scene. Understanding the basics of light-ing can make a big difference in the overall feeling and mood of your rendered scenes. Most Max scenes typically use one of two types of lighting: natural light or artificial light. *Natural light* is used for outside scenes and uses the sun and moon for its light source. *Artificial light* is usually reserved for indoor scenes where light bulbs provide the light. However, when working with lights, you'll sometimes use natural light indoors, such as sunlight streaming through a win-dow, or artificial light outdoors, such as a streetlight.

Natural and artificial light

Natural light is best created using lights that have parallel light rays coming from a single direction: You can create this type of light using a Direct Light. The inten-sity of natural light is also dependent on the time, date, and location of the sun: You can control this intensity precisely using Max's Sunlight or Daylight systems.

The weather can also make a difference in the light color. In clear weather, the color of sunlight is pale yellow; in clouds, sunlight has a blue tint; and in dark, stormy weather, sunlight is dark gray. The colors of light at sunrise and sunset are more orange and red. Moonlight is typically white.

IN THIS CHAPTER

Lighting basics

Understanding Max's light types

Creating and positioning light objects

Viewing a scene from a light

Altering light parameters

Using the Sunlight and Daylight systems

Using the Volume light effect

Using projector maps and raytraced shadows

Artificial light is typically produced with multiple lights of lower intensity. The Omni light is usually a good choice for indoor lighting because it casts light rays in all directions from a single source. Standard white fluorescent lights usually have a light green or light blue tint.

A standard lighting method

When lighting a scene, not relying on a single light is best. A good lighting method includes one key light and several secondary lights.

A spotlight is good to use for the main key light. It should be positioned in front of and slightly above the subject, and it should usually be set to cast shadows, because it will be the main shadow-casting light in the scene.

The secondary lights fill in the lighting gaps and holes. You can position these at floor level on either side of the subject, with the intensity set at considerably less than the key light and set to cast no shadows. You can place one additional light behind the scene to backlight the subjects. This light should be very dim and also cast no shadows. From the user's perspective, all the objects in the scene will be illuminated, but the casual user will identify only the main spotlight as the light source, because it casts shadows.

Figure 19.1 shows the position of the lights that are included in the standard lighting model using a key light, two secondary lights, and a backlight. This model works for most standard scenes, but if you want to highlight a specific object, additional lights are needed.

FIGURE 19.1

A standard lighting model includes a key light, two secondary lights, and a backlight.

Key light

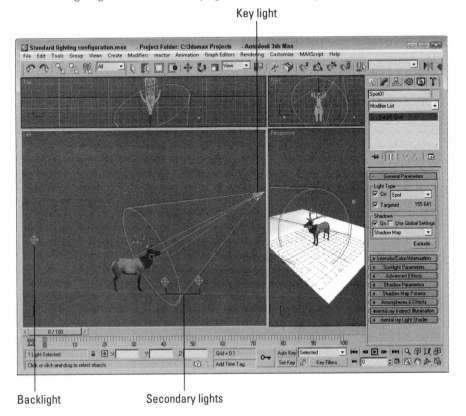

Backlight   Secondary lights

Figure 19.2 shows an elk model that was rendered using different levels of the standard lighting model. The upper-left image uses the default lighting with no lights. The upper-right image uses only the key light. This makes a shadow visible, but the details around the head are hard to define. The lower-left image includes the secondary lights, making the head details more easily visible and adding some highlights to the antlers. The bottom-right image includes the backlight, which highlights the back end of the model and casts a halo around the edges if viewed from the front.

FIGURE 19.2

An elk model rendered using default lighting, a single key light, two secondary lights, and a backlight

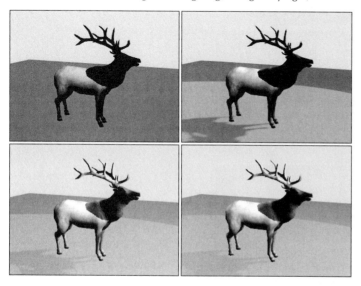

The final type of light to keep in mind is *ambient light*. Ambient light is not from a direct source but is created by light that is deflected off walls and objects. It provides overall lighting to the entire scene and keeps shadows from becoming completely black. Global Lighting (including Ambient light) is set in the Environment panel.

Shadows

Shadows are the areas behind an object where the light is obscured. Max supports several types of shadows, including Area Shadows, Shadow Maps, and Raytraced Shadows.

Area Shadows create shadows based on an area that casts a light. It doesn't require lots of memory and results in a soft shadow that is created from multiple light rays that blur the shadows. Shadow maps are actual bitmaps that the renderer produces and combines with the finished scene to produce an image. These maps can have different resolutions, but higher resolutions require more memory. Shadow maps typically create fairly realistic, softer shadows, but they don't support transparency.

Max calculates raytraced shadows by following the path of every light ray striking a scene. This process takes a significant amount of processing cycles but can produce very accurate, hard-edged shadows. Raytracing enables you to create shadows for objects that shadow maps can't, such as transparent glass. The Shadows drop-down list also includes an option called Advanced Raytraced Shadows, which uses memory more efficiently than the standard Raytraced Shadows. Another option is the mental ray Shadow Map.

CROSS-REF You can learn more about raytracing and mental ray in Chapter 46, "Raytracing and mental ray."

Figure 19.3 shows several images rendered with the different shadow types. The image in the upper left includes no shadows. The upper-right image uses Area Shadows. The lower-left image uses a Shadow Map, and the lower-right image uses Advanced Raytraced Shadows. The last two images took considerably longer to create. Viewpoint Datalabs created the elk model shown in this figure.

FIGURE 19.3

Images rendered with different shadow types, including no shadow (upper left), Area Shadows (upper right), a Shadow Map (lower left), and Raytraced Shadows (lower right)

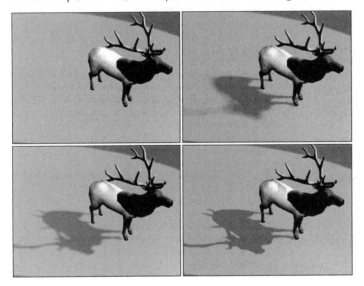

Getting to Know the Light Types

Max includes several different types of lights. The main difference in these types is how the light rays are cast into the scene. Light can come from the default lights that are present when no other user-created lights have been added to the scene. Light can also come from ambient light, which is light that bounces off other objects. Max includes several standard light objects that can be added where needed to a scene, including Omni, Direct, Spot, and skylights, each having its own characteristics. Max also includes a category of Photometric lights, which are based on real-world lights. Understanding these sources of light will help you to know where to look to control the lighting.

Default lighting

So you get Max installed, and you eagerly start the application, throw some objects in a scene, and render it . . . and you'll be disappointed in the output, because you forgot to put lights in the scene. Right? Wrong! Max is smart enough to place default lighting in the scene that does not have any light.

The default lighting disappears as soon as a light is created in a scene (even if the light is turned off). When all the lights in a scene are deleted, default lighting magically reappears. So you can always be sure that your objects are rendered using some sort of lighting. Default lighting actually consists of two lights: The first light is positioned above and to the left, and the bottom light is positioned below and to the right.

The Viewport Configuration dialog box has an option to enable default lighting for any viewport or set the default lighting to use only one light. You can open this dialog box by choosing Customize ⇨ Viewport Configuration or by right-clicking the viewport title and selecting Configuration from the pop-up menu.

If you want to access the default lights in your scene, you can use the Views ⇨ Add Default Lights to Scene command to convert the default lights into actual light objects that you can control and reposition. This feature lets you start with the default lights and modify them as needed.

 **The Views ⇨ Add Default Lights to Scene menu command is enabled only if the Default Lighting and 2 Lights options are selected in the Viewport Configuration dialog box.**

Ambient light

Ambient light is general lighting that uniformly illuminates the entire scene. It is caused by light that bounces off other objects. Using the Environment dialog box, you can set the ambient light color. You can also set the default ambient light color in the Rendering panel of the Preference Settings dialog box. This is the darkest color that can appear in the scene, generally in the shadows.

In addition to these global ambient settings, each material can have an ambient color selected in the Material Editor.

CAUTION **Don't rely on ambient light to fill in unlit sections of your scene. If you use a heavy dose of ambient light instead of placing secondary lights, your scene objects appear flat, and you won't get the needed contrast to make your objects stand out.**

Standard lights

Within the Create panel, the available lights are split into two subcategories: Standard and Photometric. Each subcategory has its own unique set of properties. The Standard light types include Omni, Spot and Direct (Spot and Free), Skylight, and two area lights (Spot and Omni) that work with mental ray.

Omni light

The Omni light is like a light bulb: It casts light rays in all directions. The two default lights are Omni lights.

Spotlight

Spotlights are directional: They can be pointed and sized. The two spotlights available in Max are a Target Spot and a Free Spot. A Target Spot light consists of a light object and a target marker at which the spotlight points. A Free Spot light has no target, which enables it to be rotated in any direction using the Select and Rotate transform button. Spotlights always are displayed in the viewport as a cone with the light positioned at the cone apex.

CROSS-REF **Both Target Spot and Target Direct lights are very similar in functionality to the Target Camera object, which you learn about in Chapter 18, "Configuring and Aiming Cameras."**

Direct light

Direct lights cast parallel light rays in a single direction, like the sun. Just like spotlights, direct lights come in two types: a Target Direct light and a Free Direct light. The position of the Target Direct light always points toward the target, which you can move within the scene using the Select and Move button. A Free Direct light can be rotated to determine where it points. Direct lights are always displayed in the viewport as cylinders.

Skylight

The Skylight is like a controllable ambient light. You can move it about the scene just like the other lights, and you can select to use the Scene Environment settings or select a Sky Color.

Area Omni and Area Spot

The Area lights project light from a defined area instead of from a single point. This has the effect of casting light along a wider area with more cumulative intensity that a point light source. Area lights are supported only by the mental ray renderer. If you use the Scanline renderer, these lights behave like simple point lights.

The Area Omni light lets you set its shape as a Sphere or a Cylinder in the Area Light Parameters rollout. Area Spot lights can be set to be either Rectangular or Disc-shaped. Be aware that area lights can take significantly longer to render than point lights.

CROSS-REF   For more details on the mental ray renderer, see Chapter 46, "Raytracing and mental ray."

Photometric lights

The standard Max lights rely on parameters like Multiplier, Decay, and Attenuation, but the last time I was in the hardware store looking for a light bulb with a 2.5 Multiplier value, I was disappointed. Lights in the real world have their own set of measurements that define the type of light that is produced. Photometric lights are lights that are based on real-world light measurement values such as Intensity in Lumens and temperatures in degrees Kelvin.

If you select the Lights menu or the Lights category in the Create panel, you'll notice another subcategory called Photometric. Photometric lights are based on photometric values, which are the values of light energy. The lights found in this subcategory include Point, Linear, and Area (both Free and Target), and IES and mental ray Sun and Sky.

Target and Free photometric lights

Target photometric lights come in three shapes — Point, Linear, and Area. Selecting a different-shaped light causes the light to be spread over a wider area, so in most cases, the Point light results in the brightest intensity. Figure 19.4 shows the three different shapes. The General Parameters rollout in the Modify panel includes a drop-down list that you can use to change the light shape and specify whether it is targeted.

FIGURE 19.4

Photometric lights can be Point, Linear, or Area (left to right).

The gizmo for point photometric lights is a simple sphere, the gizmo for linear lights is a sphere and a line, and the gizmo for area lights is a sphere and a rectangle. For targeted lights, the target extends from the gizmo to the target. The dimensions for the light are in the Linear (Area) Light Parameters rollout.

Sun and Sky photometric lights

The Photometric light subcategory also includes additional light types: Sky and Sun. The IES Sky light simulates ambient light. In the Sky Parameters rollout, you can specify the sky as Clear, Partly Cloudy, or Cloudy. These same parameters are found in the Daylight system.

The IES Sun light simulates the bright outdoor light of the sun. It is a single light with a great deal of power. It can be targeted and can have an Intensity value of 50 billion lux. This type of light is very valuable in architecture renderings.

Sun and Sky lights also are available for mental ray. These mental ray lights have several additional settings. The mental ray Sun and Sky lights are typically used in conjunction with the Daylight system.

Creating and Positioning Light Objects

Max, in its default setup, can create many different types of light. Each has different properties and features. To create a light, just select Create ⇨ Lights and choose the lights type or click the Lights category button in the Create panel. Then click the button for the type of light you want to create and drag in a viewport to create it. Most light types are created with a single click, but you create Target lights by clicking at the light's position and dragging to the position of the target.

Transforming lights

Lights can be transformed just like other geometric objects. To transform a light, click one of the transformation buttons and then select and drag the light.

Target lights can have the light and the target transformed independently, or you can select both the light and target by clicking the line that connects them. Target lights can be rotated around the X and Y axes only if the light and target are selected together. A target light can spin about its local Z-axis even if the target isn't selected. Scaling a target light increases its cone or cylinder. Scaling a Target Direct light with only the light selected increases the diameter of the light's beam, but if the light and target are selected, then the diameter and distance are scaled.

An easy way to select or deselect the target is to right-click the light and choose Select Target from the pop-up menu. All transformations work on free lights.

Viewing lights and shadows in the viewport

Lights and shadows can be displayed in the viewports if you are using the Direct3D display driver. You can check to see if your video card supports interactive lights and shadows using the Views ⇨ Diagnose Video Hardware menu command. This command runs a script and returns the results to the MAXScript Listener window.

NEW FEATURE The ability to interactively view lights and shadows in the viewport is new to 3ds Max 2008.

If your graphics card supports viewport shading, you can enable viewport shading using the Viewport Lighting and Shadows ⇨ Viewport Shading ⇨ Good or Best menu commands from the right-click pop-up quadmenu. The Good option uses the Direct3D Shading Model 2.0 for fast shadowing and the Best option uses the Direct3D Shading Model 3.0 for per pixel quality shadows.

The Viewport Lighting and Shadows quadmenu also includes options to lock and unlock the selected light, commands to enable and disable shadows for the selected light, a command to select all lights displaying shadows and all lights displaying lighting, and options to auto display the selected lights and to display only the selected lights.

Listing lights

The Tools ➪ Light Lister menu command opens the Light Lister dialog box, shown in Figure 19.5, where you can see at a quick glance all the details for all the lights in the scene. This dialog box also lets you change the light settings. It includes two rollouts: Configuration, which lets you select to see All Lights, the Selected Lights, or the General Settings that apply to all lights; and Lights, which holds details on each individual light.

The Light Lister dialog box includes a comprehensive list of light settings in one place.

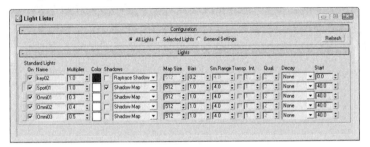

If the General Settings option is selected, then a separate rollout opens with all the typical settings, including Multiplier, Color, Shadows, Map Size, and so on. You can apply these changes to the Selected Lights or to All Lights. The Light Lister provides an easy way to change the parameters of many lights at once.

If either the All Lights option or the Selected Lights option is selected, then the parameters are listed in the Lights rollout. Using this rollout, you can change the settings for any of the listed lights that affect all lights. The Refresh button updates the Light Lister dialog box if a new light has been added to the scene or if any parameters have been altered in the Modify panel.

 NOTE If several lights are instanced, then only one of the instanced lights appears in the Light Lister dialog box, but each of the instanced lights can be selected from a drop-down list.

Placing highlights

The Place Highlight (Ctrl+H) feature enables you to control the position and orientation of a light in order to achieve a highlight in a precise location. To use this feature, you must select a light object in the scene and then choose Tools ➪ Place Highlight, or click the Place Highlight flyout button on the toolbar. The cursor changes to the Place Highlight icon. Click a point on the object in the scene where you want the highlight to be positioned, and the selected light repositions itself to create a specular highlight at the exact location where you clicked. The light's position is determined by the Angle of Incidence between the highlight point and the light.

Tutorial: Lighting the snowman's face

You can use the Place Highlight feature to position a light for our snowman. To place a highlight, follow these steps:

1. Open the Snowman.max file from the Chap 19 directory on the DVD.

   This file contains a simple snowman created using primitive objects.

2. Select the Create ➪ Lights ➪ Standard Lights ➪ Target Spotlight menu command, and position the spot light below and to the left of the Snowman model.

3. To place the highlight so it shows the Snowman's face, select the spot light and then choose Tools ➪ Place Highlight (or press Ctrl+H). Then click the Snowman's face where the highlight should be located, just above his right eye.

Figure 19.6 shows the results.

FIGURE 19.6

The snowman, after the lights have been automatically repositioned using the Place Highlights command

> **NOTE**   The effect of lights can be fully seen in the viewport if the Best or Good shading option is enabled.

Viewing a Scene from a Light

You can configure viewports to display the view from any light, with the exception of an Omni light. To do so, right-click the viewport title and then select Views and the light name at the top of the pop-up menu.

> **NOTE** The keyboard shortcut for making the active viewport a Light view is the $ (the dollar sign that appears above the 4) key. If more than one light exists, then the Select Light dialog box appears and lets you select which light to use. This can be used only on spot and direct lights.

Light viewport controls

When a viewport is changed to show a light view, the Viewport Navigation buttons in the lower-right corner of the screen change into Light Navigation controls. Table 19.1 describes these controls.

> **NOTE** Many of these controls are identical for viewports displaying lights or cameras.

Light Navigation Control Buttons

Toolbar Button	Name	Description
	Dolly, Target, Both	Moves the light, its target, or both the light and its target closer to or farther away from the scene in the direction it is pointing.
	Light Hotspot	Adjusts the angle of the light's hotspot, which is displayed as a blue cone.
	Roll Light	Spins the light about its local Z-axis.
	Zoom Extents All, Zoom Extents All Selected	Zooms in on all objects or the selected objects until they fill the viewport.
	Light Falloff	Changes the angle of the light's falloff cone.
	Truck Light	Moves the light perpendicular to the line of sight.
	Orbit, Pan Light	The Orbit button rotates the light around the target, whereas the Pan Light button rotates the target around the light.
	Min/Max Toggle	Makes the current viewport fill the screen. Clicking this button a second time returns the display to several viewports.

If you hold down the Ctrl key while using the Light Hotspot or Falloff buttons, Max maintains the distance between the hotspot and falloff cones. Holding down the Alt key causes the size to change at a much slower rate. The Hotspot cone cannot grow any larger than the Falloff cone, but if you hold down the Shift key, then trying to make the size of the hotspot larger than the falloff causes both to increase, and vice-versa.

You can constrain any light movements to a single axis by holding down the Shift key. The Ctrl key causes the movements to increase rapidly.

For Free lights, an invisible target is determined by the distance computed from the other light properties. You can use the Shift key to constrain rotations to be vertical or horizontal.

NOTE You can undo changes in the normal viewports using the Views ⇨ Undo command, but you undo light viewport changes with the regular Edit ⇨ Undo command.

Tutorial: Lighting a lamp

To practice using lights, let's try to get a lamp model to work as it should.

To add a light to a lamp model, follow these steps:

1. Open the Lamp.max file from the Chap 19 directory on the DVD.

   This file includes a lamp mesh surrounded by some plane objects used to create the walls and floor. The lamp model was created by Zygote Media. It looks like a standard living room lamp that you could buy in any department store.

2. Select the Create ⇨ Lights ⇨ Standard Lights ⇨ Omni menu command, and click in any viewport.

3. Use the Select and Move transform button (W) to position the light object inside the lamp's light bulb.

The resulting image is shown in Figure 19.7. Notice that the light intensity is greater at places closer to the light.

FIGURE 19.7

The rendered lighted-lamp image

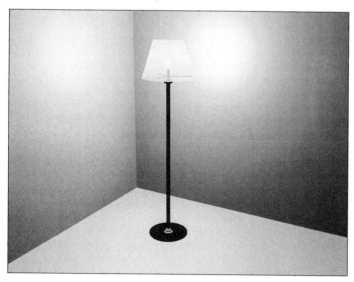

Altering Light Parameters

Lights affect every object in a scene and can really make or break a rendered image, so it shouldn't be surprising that each light comes with many controls and parameters. Several different rollouts work with lights.

If you're looking for a light switch to turn lights on and off, look no further than the Modify panel. When a light is selected, several different rollouts appear. The options contained in these rollouts enable you to turn the lights on and off, select a light color and intensity, and determine how a light affects object surfaces.

General parameters

The Light Type drop-down list in the General Parameters rollout lets you change the type of light instantly, so that you can switch from Omni light to Spotlight with little effort. You can also switch between targeted and untargeted lights. To the right of the Targeted option is the distance in scene units between the light and the target. This feature provides an easy way to look at the results of using a different type of light. When you change the type of light, you lose the settings for the previous light.

The General Parameters rollout also includes some settings for shadows. Shadows can be easily turned on or off. In this rollout, you can defer to the global settings by selecting the Use Global Settings option. This option helps to maintain consistent settings across several lights. It applies the same settings to all lights, so that changing the value for one light changes that same value for all lights that have this option selected.

You can also select from a drop-down list whether the shadows are created using Area Shadows, a Shadow Map, regular or advanced raytraced shadows, or a mental ray shadow map. A new rollout appears, depending on the selection that you make.

The Exclude button opens the Exclude/Include dialog box, where you can select objects to be included or excluded from illumination and/or shadows. The pane on the left includes a list of all the current objects in the scene. To exclude objects from being lit, select the Exclude option, select the objects to be excluded from the pane on the left, and click the double arrow icon pointing to the right to move the objects to the pane on the right.

Figure 19.8 shows the Exclude/Include dialog box. This dialog box also recognizes any Selection Sets that you've previously defined. You select them from the Selection Sets drop-down list.

FIGURE 19.8

The Exclude/Include dialog box lets you set which objects are excluded or included from being illuminated.

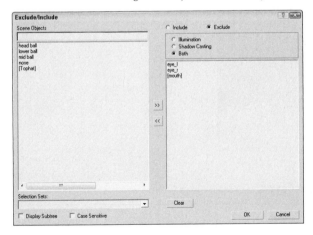

As an example of the Exclude/Include feature, Figure 19.9 shows the elk model with the antlers (left) and its body (right) excluded from the shadows pass.

FIGURE 19.9

Using the Exclude/Include dialog box, you can exclude objects from casting shadows.

The Intensity/Color/Attenuation rollout

In the Intensity/Color/Attenuation rollout, the Multiplier value controls the light intensity. A light with a Multiplier set to 2 is twice as bright as a light with its Multiplier set to 1. Higher Multiplier values make a light appear white regardless of the light color. The Multiplier value can also be negative. A negative value can be used to pull light from a scene but should be used with caution.

 **TIP** Adding and positioning another light typically is better than increasing the multiplier.

To the right of the Multiplier value is a color swatch. Clicking the color swatch opens a color selector where you can choose a new light color.

Attenuation is a property that determines how light fades over distance. An example of this is a candle set in a room. The farther you get from the candle, the less the light shines.

You use three basic parameters to simulate realistic attenuation. Near Attenuation sets the distance at which the light begins to fade, and Far Attenuation sets the distance at which the light falls to 0. Both these properties are ranges that include Start and End values. The third parameter sets the Decay value, which simulates attenuation using a mathematical formula to compute the drop in light intensity over time.

Selecting the Use option enables the Near and Far Attenuation values; both have Start and End values that set the range for these attenuation types. The Show option makes the attenuation distances and decay values visible in the viewports. The three types of decay from which you can choose are None, Inverse, and Inverse Square. The Inverse type decays linearly with the distance away from the light. The Inverse Square type decays exponentially with distance.

 **NOTE** The Inverse Square type approximates real lights the best, but it is often too dim for computer graphic images. You can compensate for this by increasing the Multiplier value.

Spotlight and directional light parameters

The Spotlight Parameters rollout includes values to set the angular distance of both the Hot Spot and Falloff cones. The Show Cone option makes the Hotspot and Falloff cones visible in the viewport when the light is not selected. The Overshoot option makes the light shine in all directions like an Omni light, but projections and shadows occur only within the Falloff cone. You can also set the light shape to be circular or rectangular. For a rectangular-shaped spotlight, you can control the aspect ratio. You can use the Bitmap Fit button to make the aspect ratio match a particular bitmap.

The Directional Light Parameters rollout, which appears for Direct light types, is identical to the Spotlight Parameters rollout and also includes settings for the Hot Spot and Falloff values.

Advanced Effects

Options in the Affect Surface section of the Advanced Effects rollout control how light interacts with an object's surface. The Contrast value alters the contrast between the diffuse and the ambient surface areas. The Soften Diffuse Edge value blurs the edges between the diffuse and ambient areas of a surface. The Diffuse and Specular options let you disable these properties of an object's surface. When the Ambient Only option is turned on, the light affects only the ambient properties of the surface.

CROSS-REF Find more detail on the Diffuse, Specular, and Ambient properties in Chapter 14, "Exploring the Material Editor."

You can use any light as a projector; you find this option in the Advanced Effects rollouts. Selecting the Map option enables you to use the light as a projector. You can select a map to project by clicking the button to the right of the map option. You can drag a material map directly from the Material/Map Browser onto the Projector Map button.

Shadow parameters

All light types have a Shadow Parameters rollout that you can use to select a shadow color by clicking the color swatch. The default color is black. The Dens setting stands for "Density" and controls how dark the shadow appears. Lower values produce light shadows, and higher values produce dark shadows. This value can also be negative.

The Map option, like the Projection Map, can be used to project a map along with the shadow color. The Light Affects Shadow Color option alters the Shadow Color by blending it with the light color if selected.

In the Atmosphere Shadows section, the On button lets you determine whether atmospheric effects, such as fog, can cast shadows. You can also control the Opacity and the degree to which atmospheric colors blend with the Shadow Color.

When you select a light and open the Modify panel, one additional rollout is available: the Atmospheres and Effects rollout. This rollout is a shortcut to the Environment dialog box, where you can specify atmospheric effects such as fog and volume lights.

 The only effects that can be used with lights are Volume Light and Lens Effects.

CROSS-REF Chapter 45, "Using Atmospheric and Render Effects," covers atmospheric effects.

If the Area Shadows option is selected in the General Parameters rollout, then the Area Shadows rollout appears, which includes several settings for controlling this shadow type. In the drop-down list at the top of the rollout, you can select from several Basic Options including Simple, Rectangle Light, Disc Light, Box Light, and Sphere Light. You can select dimensions depending on which option is selected. You can also set the Integrity, Quality, Spread, Bias, and Jitter amounts.

For the Shadow Map option, the Shadow Map Params rollout includes values for the Bias, Size, and Sample Range. The Sample Range value softens the shadow edges. You can also select to use an Absolute Map Bias and 2 Sided Shadows.

If the Ray Traced Shadows option is selected in the Shadow Parameters rollout, the Ray Traced Shadows Parameters rollout appears below it. This simple rollout includes only two values: Bias and Max Quadtree Depth. The Bias settings cause the shadow to move toward or away from the object that casts the shadow. The Max Quadtree Depth determines the accuracy of the shadows by controlling how long the ray paths are followed. There is also an option to enable 2 Sided Shadows, which enables both sides of a face to cast shadows including backfacing objects.

For the Advanced Raytraced Shadows options, the rollout includes many more options, including Simple, 1-Pass, or 2-Pass Anti-aliasing. This rollout also includes the same quality values found in the Area Shadows rollout.

 NOTE Depending on the number of objects in your scene, shadows can take a long time to render. Enabling raytraced shadows for a complex scene can greatly increase the render time.

Optimizing lights

If you select either the Area Shadows type or the Advanced Raytracing Shadows type, then a separate Optimizations rollout appears. This rollout includes settings that help speed up the shadow rendering process. Using this rollout, you can enable Transparent Shadows. You can also specify a color that is used at the Anti-aliasing Threshold. You can also turn off anti-aliasing for materials that have SuperSampling or Reflection/Refraction enabled. Or you can have the shadow renderer skip coplanar faces with a given threshold.

Manipulating Hotspot and Falloff cones

When the Select and Manipulate mode is enabled on the main toolbar, the end of the Hotspot and Falloff cones appear green for a selected spotlight. When you move the mouse over these lines, the lines turn red, allowing you to drag the lines and make the Hotspot and/or Falloff angle values greater. These manipulators provide visual feedback as you resize the spotlight cone.

Photometric light parameters

Most of the light rollouts for photometric lights are the same as those for the standard lights, but the Intensity/Color/Distribution rollout, as shown in Figure 19.10, is unique.

FIGURE 19.10

The Intensity/Color/Distribution rollout for photometric lights uses real-world intensity values.

Distribution options

The Distribution options are listed in the drop-down list at the top of the rollout. The options include Isotropic, Spotlight, and Web for the Point lights and Diffuse and Web for the Linear and Area lights.

The Isotropic option distributes light equally in all directions. The Diffuse option has its greatest distribution at right angles to the surface it is emitted from and gradually decreases in intensity at increasing angles from the normal. For both options, the light gradually becomes weaker as the distance from the light increases.

The Spotlight option is available only for Point lights. It concentrates the light energy into a cone that emits from the light. This cone of light energy is directional and can be controlled with the Hotspot and Falloff values.

The Web option is a custom option that lets you open a separate file describing the light's emission pattern. These files have the .IES, .CIBSE, or .LTLI extensions. Light manufacturers have this data for the various real-world lights that they sell. You load these files using the Web File button found in the Web Parameters rollout. You can also specify the X-, Y-, and Z-axis rotation values.

Color options

The Color section of the Intensity/Color/Distribution rollout includes two ways to specify a light's color. The first is a drop-down list of options. The options found in the list include standard real-world light types such as Cool White, Mercury, and Halogen. Table 19.2 lists each of these types and its approximate color.

TABLE 19.2

Photometric Light Colors

Light Type	Color
Cool White	Yellow-white
Custom	Any color
D65White	White
Daylight Fluorescent	Mostly white with a slight gray tint
Fluorescent	Yellow-white
Halogen	Beige-white
High-Pressure Sodium	Tan
Incandescent	Beige-white
Low Pressure Sodium	Light orange
Mercury	Green-white
Metal Halide	Yellow-white
Phosphor Mercury	Light green
Quartz	Yellow-white
White Fluorescent	Yellow-white
Xenon	White

In addition to a list of available light types, you can specify a color based on temperature expressed in degrees Kelvin. Temperature-based colors run from a cool 1,000 degrees, which is a mauve-pink color, through light yellow and white (at 6,000 degrees Kelvin) to a hot light blue at 20,000 degrees Kelvin. Typical indoor lighting is fairly low on the Kelvin scale at around 3300 degrees K. Direct sunlight is around 5500 degrees K. Thunderbolts, arc welders, and electric bolts run much hotter, from 10,000 to 20,000 degrees Kelvin.

You also can set a Filter Color using the color swatch found in this section. The Filter Color simulates the color caused by colored cellophane placed in front of the light.

Intensity options

The Intensity options can be specified in Lumens, Candelas, or Lux at a given distance. Light manufacturers have this information available. You also can specify a Multiplier value, which determines how effective the light is.

Using the Sunlight and Daylight Systems

The Sunlight and Daylight systems, accessed through the Systems category of the Create panel, create a light that simulates the sun for a specific geographic location, date, time, and compass direction.

NOTE The Daylight system can be created using the Create ➪ Lights menu or the Create ➪ Systems menu, but the Sunlight system cannot be created using a menu.

To create either of these systems, open the Create panel and click the Systems category button. Then click the Sunlight (or Daylight) button, and drag the mouse in a viewport. A Compass helper object appears. Click again to create a Direct light (or Skylight) representing the sun. Figure 19.11 shows the Compass helper created as part of the Sunlight system. The main difference between these two systems is that the Sunlight system uses a Directional light and the Daylight system uses the IES Sun and Sky lights.

TIP The best results for the Daylight system are realized when you use the mr Sun and mr Sky options. Using the Daylight system with these options also enables the mr Physical Sky environment settings. More on this system is covered in Chapter 46, "Raytracing and mental ray."

Using the Compass helper

The Compass helper is useful when working with a Sunlight system. It can be used to define the map directions of North, East, South, and West. The Sunlight system uses these directions to orient the system light. This helper is not renderable and is created automatically when you define a sunlight object.

After you create a Sunlight system, you can alter the point that the sun is pointing at by transforming the Compass helper. Doing so causes the direct light object to move appropriately. The light's position in the sky is controlled by the Time, Date, and Location parameters, but if you want to move the light independent of these parameters, you can select the Manual option and move the light using the transform tools.

NOTE You can change the settings for the light that is the sun by selecting the light from the Select by Name dialog box and opening the Modify panel. The sunlight object uses raytraced shadows by default.

Once created, the light parameters for the Daylight system including light intensity and shadows are located in the Modify panel, but the Date, Time, and Location parameters are in the Motion panel when the light object is selected. You can access the Motion panel parameters by clicking on the Setup button in the Daylight Parameters rollout.

FIGURE 19.11

The Compass helper provides an orientation for positioning the sun in a Sunlight system.

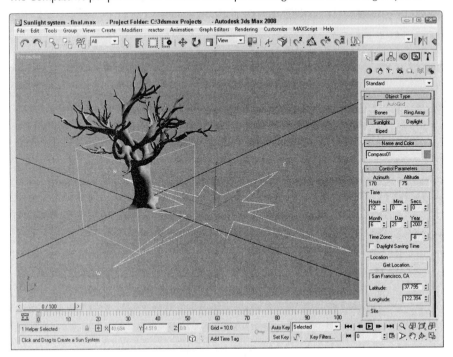

Understanding Azimuth and Altitude

Azimuth and Altitude are two values that help define the location of the sun in the sky. Both are measured in degrees. *Azimuth* refers to the compass direction and can range from 0 to 360, with 0 degrees being North, 90 degrees being East, 180 degrees being South, and 270 degrees being West. *Altitude* is the angle in degrees between the sun and the horizon. This value ranges typically between 0 and 90, with 0 degrees being either sunrise or sunset and 90 when the sun is directly overhead.

Specifying date and time

The Time section of the Control Parameters rollout lets you define a time and date. The Time Zone value is the number of offset hours for your current time zone. You can also set the time to be converted for Daylight Saving Time.

Specifying location

Clicking the Get Location button in the Control Parameters rollout opens the Geographic Location dialog box, shown in Figure 19.12, which displays a map or a list of cities. Selecting a location using this dialog box automatically updates the Latitude and Longitude values. In addition to the Get Location button, you can enter Latitude and Longitude values directly in the Control Parameters rollout.

FIGURE 19.12

The Geographic Location dialog box lets you specify where you want to use the Sunlight system. You have many different cities to choose from.

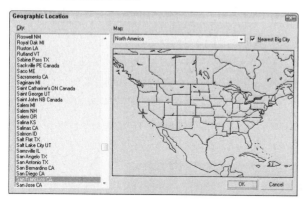

The Daylight system also includes an option to set the Sky value from Clear to Partly Cloudy to Cloudy.

Tutorial: Animating a day in 20 seconds

You can animate the Sunlight system to show an entire day from sunrise to sundown in a short number of frames. In this tutorial, we focus on an old tree positioned somewhere in Phoenix, Arizona, on Christmas. The tree certainly won't move, but watch its shadows.

To use the Sunlight system to animate shadows, follow these steps:

1. Open the Sunlight system.max file from the Chap 19 directory on the DVD.

   This file includes a tree mesh created by Zygote.

2. Add a Sunlight System by selecting the Systems category in the Create panel and clicking the Sunlight button. Then drag in the Top view to create the Compass helper, and click again to create the light. In the Control Parameters rollout (found in the Motion panel), enter **12/25** and the current year for the Date and an early morning hour for the Time.

3. Click the Get Location button, locate Phoenix in the Cities list, and click OK. Rotate the compass helper in the Top view so that north is pointing toward the top of the viewport.

4. Click the Auto Key button (or press the N key), and move the Time slider to frame 100.

5. In the Control Parameters rollout, change the Time value to an evening hour. Then click the Auto Key button (N) again to disable animation mode.

NOTE You can tell when the sun comes up and goes down by looking at the Altitude value for each hour. A negative Altitude value indicates that the sun is below the horizon.

Figure 19.13 shows a snapshot of this quick day. The upper-left image shows the animation at frame 20, the upper-right image shows it at frame 40, the lower-left image shows it at frame 60, and the final image shows it at frame 80.

FIGURE 19.13

Several frames of an animation showing a tree scene from sunrise to sunset

Using Volume Lights

When light shines through fog, smoke, or dust, the beam of the light becomes visible. The effect is known as a *Volume Light*. To add a Volume Light to a scene, choose Rendering ➪ Environment (or press the 8 key) to open the Environment dialog box. Then click the Add button in the Atmosphere rollout to open the Add Atmospheric Effect dialog box, and select Volume Light. The parameters for the volume light are presented in the Volume Light Parameters rollout.

You can also access the Volume Light effect from the Atmospheres and Effects rollout in the Modify panel when a light is selected.

CROSS-REF   Chapter 45, "Using Atmospheric and Render Effects," covers the other atmospheric effects.

Volume light parameters

At the top of the Volume Light Parameters rollout, shown in Figure 19.14, is a Pick Light button, which enables you to select a light to apply the effect to. You can select several lights, which then appear in a drop-down list. You can remove lights from this list with the Remove Light button.

FIGURE 19.14

The Volume Light Parameters rollout in the Environment dialog box lets you choose which lights to include in the effect.

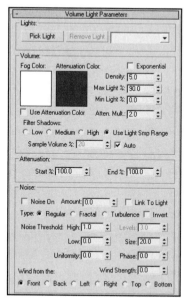

In the Volume section, the Fog Color swatch lets you select a color for the fog that is seen within the light. This color is combined with the color of the light. The Attenuation Color is the color the fog appears to have at a distance far from the light source. This color also combines with the Fog Color and is best set to a dark color.

The Density value determines the thickness of the fog. The Exponential option causes the density to increase exponentially with the distance. The Max and Min Light Percentage values determine the amount of glow that the volume light causes, and the Attenuation Multiplier controls the strength of the attenuation color.

You have four options for filtering shadows: Low, Medium, High, and Use Light Smp Range. The Low option renders shadows quickly but isn't very accurate. The High option takes a while but produces the best quality. The Use Light Smp Range option bases the filtering on the Sample Volume value and can be set to Auto. The Sample Volume can range from 1 to 10,000. The Low option has a Sample Volume value of 8; Medium, 25; and High, 50.

NOTE   Only Shadow Map type shadows cast shadows through volume fog.

The Start and End Attenuation values are percentages of the Start and End range values for the light's attenuation. These values have an impact only if attenuation is turned on for the light.

The Noise settings help to determine the randomness of Volume Light. Noise effects can be turned on and given an Amount. You can also Link the noise to the light instead of using world coordinates. Noise types include Regular, Fractal, and Turbulence. Another option inverts the noise pattern. The Noise Threshold limits the effect of noise. Wind settings affect how the light moves as determined by the wind's direction, Wind Strength, and Phase.

Figure 19.15 shows several volume light possibilities. The left image includes the Volume Light effect, the middle image enables shadows, and the right image includes some Turbulent Noise.

The Volume Light effect makes the light visible.

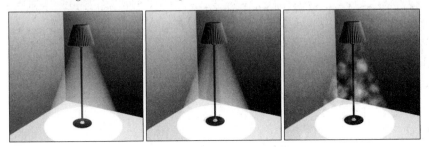

Tutorial: Showing car headlights

One popular way to use volume lights is to display the headlights of cars. For this tutorial, we're going to use the Delfino Feroce 2001 car model created by Viewpoint Datalabs.

To display the headlights of a car, follow these steps:

1. Open the Car headlights.max file from the Chap 19 directory on the DVD.

   This file includes a model of a car.

2. Select the Create ➪ Lights ➪ Standard Lights ➪ Target Spotlight menu command, and drag in the Left viewport to create a spotlight object. Select and move the spotlight and the target to be positioned to look as if a light is shining out from the left headlight.

3. Open the Modify panel, and in the Spotlight Parameters rollout, set the Hotspot value to **20**, the Falloff to **25** and the Decay setting to Inverse Square with a Start value of **3.0**. In the Atmospheres and Effects rollout, click the Add button, select Volume Light from the Add Atmosphere or Effect dialog box that appears, and click OK.

 **NOTE**   When a light is added to the scene, the default lights are automatically turned off. To provide any additional lighting, add some Omni lights above the car.

4. Select the Volume Light effect in the list within the Atmospheres and Effects rollout, and click the Setup button. The Environment dialog box opens, in which you can edit the Volume Light parameters for the newly created light. Set the Density value to **100**.

5. Now create three more headlights. To do this, select both the first spotlight object and its target, and create a cloned copy by holding down the Shift key while moving it toward the right headlight. Position the other spotlights so that they shine outward from the other headlights.

Figure 19.16 shows the resulting car with its headlights illuminated.

Tutorial: Creating laser beams

Laser beams are extremely useful lights. From your CD-ROM drive to your laser printer, lasers are found throughout a modern-day office. They also are great to use in fantasy and science fiction images. You can easily create laser beams using direct lights and the Volume Light effect. In this tutorial, we add some lasers to the spaceship model created by Viewpoint Datalabs.

FIGURE 19.16

The car now has headlights, thanks to spotlights and the Volume Light effect.

To add some laser beams to a scene, follow these steps:

1. Open the Spaceship laser.max file from the Chap 19 directory on the DVD.
    This file includes a spaceship model.

2. Select the Create ➪ Lights ➪ Standard Lights ➪ Directional menu command, and add a Free Direct light to the end of one of the laser guns in the Front viewport. Scale the light down until the cylinder is the size of the desired laser beam and rotate it so it points away from the laser beam.

3. With the light selected, open the Modify panel. In the Atmospheres and Effects rollout, click the Add button and double-click the Volume Light selection. Then select the Volume Light option in the list, and click the Setup button to open the Environment dialog box. Change the Fog Color to red and the Density value to **50** and make sure that the Use Attenuation Color is disabled.

4. With the direct lights added to the scene, the default lights are deactivated, so you need to add some Omni lights above the spaceship to illuminate it. To do this, select the Create ➪ Lights ➪ Standard Lights ➪ Omni menu command, and click above the spaceship in the Front view three times to create three lights. Set the Multiplier on the first light to **1.0**, and position it directly above the spaceship. Set the other two lights to **0.5**, and position them on either side of the spaceship and lower than the first light.

Figure 19.17 shows the resulting laser beams shooting forth from the spaceship.

Using projector maps and raytraced shadows

If a map is added to a light in the Parameters rollout, the light becomes a projector. Projector maps can be simple images, animated images, or black-and-white masks to cast shadows. To load a projector map, select a light and open the Modify panel. Under the Spotlight Parameters rollout, click the Projector Map button and select the map to use from the Material/Map Browser.

FIGURE 19.17

You can create laser beams using direct lights and the Volume Light effect.

Raytraced shadows take longer to render than the Shadow Maps or Area Shadows option, but the shadows always have a hard edge and are an accurate representation of the object.

 **You can create shadows for wireframe objects with transparency only by using raytraced shadows.**

In the Shadow Parameters rollout, you can select whether shadows are computed using shadow maps or raytraced shadows. Using the latter selection lets you project a transparent object's color onto the shadow.

Tutorial: Projecting a trumpet image on a scene

As an example of a projector light, we create a musical scene with several musical notes and project the image of a trumpet on them.

To project an image onto a rendered scene, follow these steps:

1. Open the Trumpet mask.max file from the Chap 19 directory on the DVD.

   This file includes a trumpet model shown in the maximized Left viewport. This file is used to generate a project map.

2. Choose Rendering ➪ Render (or press the F10 key) to open the Render dialog box; set the resolution to 640 × 480, and select the Left viewport. Then select the Render Elements tab, and click the Add button. Select Alpha from the Render Elements dialog box, click OK, and then click the Render button. The side view of the trumpet in the Rendered Frame Window renders along with an alpha channel rendering of the trumpet. When the rendering completes, click the Save File button in the Rendered Frame Window for the alpha channel and save the file as **trumpet mask.tif**.

3. Open the Musical notes.max file from the Chap 19 directory on the DVD.

   This file contains several musical notes created from primitive objects.

4. Select the Create ➪ Lights ➪ Standard Lights ➪ Target Spotlight menu command, and drag to create two lights in the Top viewport. Position the first spotlight to be perpendicular to the scene and to shine down on it from above.

5. Open the Modify panel; in the Advanced Effects rollout, click the Projector Map button and double-click Bitmap from the Material/Map Browser. Locate and select the Trumpet Mask.tif file, and click Open. This projects a silhouette of a trumpet onto the scene. Use the second spotlight to light the music notes.

Figure 19.18 shows the musical notes with the trumpet projection map.

FIGURE 19.18

You can use projection maps to project an image in the scene, like this trumpet.

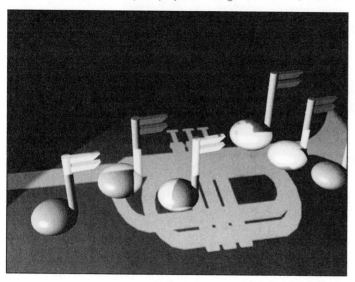

Tutorial: Creating a stained-glass window

When a light that uses raytraced shadows shines through an object with transparent materials, the Filter color of the material is projected onto objects behind. In this tutorial, we create a stained-glass window and shine a light through it using raytraced shadows.

To create a stained-glass window, follow these steps:

1. Open the Stained glass window.max file from the Chap 19 directory on the DVD.

   This file includes a stained-glass window for a fish market (don't ask me why a fish market has a stained-glass window).

2. Select the Create ➪ Lights ➪ Standard Lights ➪ Target Spotlight menu command, and drag in the Left view from a position to the right and above the window to the window.

   This creates a target spotlight that shines through the stained-glass window onto the floor behind it.

3. In the General Parameters rollout, make sure that the On option is enabled in the Shadows section and select Ray Traced Shadows from the drop-down list.

Figure 19.19 shows the stained-glass window with the colored shadow cast on the scene floor.

FIGURE 19.19

A stained-glass window effect created with raytraced shadows

Summary

I hope you have found this chapter enlightening. (Sorry about the bad pun, but I need to work them in where I can.) Max has many different lights, each with plenty of controls. Learning to master these controls can take you a long way toward increasing the realism of the scene. In this chapter, you've accomplished the following:

- Learned the basics of lighting
- Discovered Max's standard and photometric light types
- Created and positioned light objects
- Learned to change the viewport view to a light
- Used the Sunlight and Daylight systems
- Used the Volume Light atmospheric effect
- Added projection maps to lights
- Used raytraced shadows to create a stained-glass window

In the next chapter we finally start animating objects, beginning with the basics including keyframing.

Part V

Animation and Rendering Basics

Chapter 20

Understanding Animation and Keyframe Basics

Max can be used to create some really amazing images, but I bet more of you go to the movies than go to see images in a museum. The difference is in seeing moving images versus static images.

In this chapter, we start discussing what is probably one of the main reasons you decided to learn 3ds Max in the first place — animation. Max includes many different features to create animations. This chapter covers the easiest and most basic of these features — keyframe animation.

Along the way, we examine all the various controls that are used to create, edit, and control animation keys, including the Time Controls, the Track Bar, and the Motion panel. Keyframes can be used to animate object transformations, but they also can be used to animate other parameters such as materials. If you get finished with this chapter in time, you may have time to watch a movie.

Using the Time Controls

Before jumping into animation, you need to understand the controls that make it possible. These controls collectively are called the Time Controls and can be found on the lower interface bar between the key controls and the Viewport Navigation Controls. The Time Controls also include the Time Slider found directly under the viewports.

The Time Slider provides an easy way to move through the frames of an animation. To do this, just drag the Time Slider button in either direction. The Time Slider button is labeled with the current frame number and the total number of frames. The arrow buttons on either side of this button work the same as the Previous and Next Frame (Key) buttons.

The Time Control buttons include buttons to jump to the Start or End of the animation, or to step forward or back by a single frame. You can also jump to an exact frame by entering the frame number in the frame number field. The Time Controls are presented in Table 20.1.

TABLE 20.1

Time Controls

Toolbar Button	Name	Description
	Go to Start	Sets the time to frame 1.
	Previous Frame/Key	Decreases the time by one frame or selects the previous key.
	Play Animation, Play Selected	Cycles through the frames; this button becomes a Stop button when an animation is playing.
	Next Frame/Key	Advances the time by one frame or selects the next key.
	Go to End	Sets the time to the final frame.
	Key Mode Toggle	Toggles between key and frame modes; with Key Mode on, the icon turns light blue and the Previous Frame and Next Frame buttons change to Previous Key and Next Key.
	Current Frame field	Indicates the current frame; a frame number can be typed in this field for more exact control than the Time Slider.
	Time Configuration	Opens the Time Configuration dialog box where settings like frame rate, time display, and animation length can be set.

The default scene starts with 100 frames, but this is seldom what you actually need. You can change the number of frames at any time by clicking the Time Configuration button, which is to the right of the frame number field. Clicking this button opens the Time Configuration dialog box, shown in Figure 20.1. You can also access this dialog box by right-clicking any of the Time Control buttons.

Setting frame rate

Within this dialog box, you can set several options, including the Frame Rate. *Frame rate* provides the connection between the number of frames and time. It is measured in frames per second. The options include standard frame rates such as NTSC (National Television Standards Committee, around 30 frames per second), Film (around 24 frames per second), and PAL (Phase Alternate Line, used by European countries, around 25 frames per second), or you can select Custom and enter your own frame rate.

The Time Display section lets you set how time is displayed on the Time Slider. The options include Frames, SMPTE (Society of Motion Picture Technical Engineers), Frame:Ticks, or MM:SS:Ticks (Minutes and Seconds). *SMPTE* is a standard time measurement used in video and television. A *Tick* is $\frac{1}{4800}$ of a second.

FIGURE 20.1

The Time Configuration dialog box lets you set the number of frames to include in a scene.

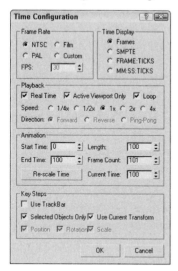

Setting speed and direction

The Playback section sets options for how the animation sequence is played back. The Real Time option skips frames to maintain the specified frame rate. The Active Viewport Only option causes the animation to play only in a single viewport, which speeds up the animation. The Loop option repeats the animation over and over. The Loop option is available only if the Real Time option is disabled. If the Loop option is set, then you can specify the Direction as Forward, Reverse, or Ping-Pong (which repeats playing forward and then reverse). The Speed setting can be ¼, ½, 1, 2, or 4 times normal.

The Time Configuration dialog box also lets you specify the Start Time, End Time, Length, and Current Time values. These values are all interrelated, so setting the Length and the Start Time, for example, auto-matically changes the End Time. These values can be changed at any time without destroying any keys. For example, if you have an animation of 500 frames and you set the Start and End Time to 30 and 50, the Time Slider controls only those 21 frames. Keys before or after this time are still available and can be accessed by resetting the Start and End Time values to 0 and 500.

The Re-scale Time button fits all the keys into the active time segment by stretching or shrinking the num-ber of frames between keys. You can use this feature to resize the animation to the number of frames defined by Start and End Time values.

The Key Steps group lets you set which key objects are navigated using key mode. If you select Use Track Bar, key mode moves through only the keys on the Track Bar. If you select the Selected Objects Only option, key mode jumps only to the keys for the currently selected object. You can also filter to move between Position, Rotation, and Scale keys. The Use Current Transform option locates only those keys that are the same as the current selected transform button.

Using Time Tags

To the right of the Prompt Line is a field marked Add Time Tag. Clicking this field pops up a menu with options to Add or Edit a Time Tag. Time Tags can be set for each frame in the scene. Once set, the Time Tags are visible in the Time Tag field whenever that time is selected.

Working with Keys

It isn't just a coincidence that the largest button in the entire Max interface has a key on it. Creating and working with keys is how animations are accomplished. Keys define a particular state of an object at a particular time. Animations are created as the object moves or changes between two different key states. Complex animations can be generated with only a handful of keys.

You can create keys in numerous ways, but the easiest is with the Key Controls found on the lower interface bar. These controls are located to the left of the Time Controls. Table 20.2 displays and explains all these controls. Closely related to the Key Controls is the Track Bar, which is located under the Time Slider.

TABLE 20.2

Key Controls

Toolbar Button	Name	Description
o—r	Set Key (K)	Creates animation keys in Set Key mode.
Auto Key	Toggle Auto Key Mode (N)	Sets keys automatically for the selected object when enabled.
Set Key	Toggle Set Key Mode (')	Sets keys as specified by the key filters for the selected object when enabled.
Selected ▼	Selection Set drop-down list	Specifies a selection set to use for the given keys.
⟋	Default In/Out Tangents for New Keys	Assigns the default tangents that are used on all new keys.
Key Filters...	Open Filters Dialog box	Contains pop-up options for the filtering keys.

Max includes two animation modes: Auto Key (N) and Set Key ('). You can select either of these modes by clicking the respective buttons at the bottom of the interface. When active, the button turns bright red, and the border around the active viewport also turns red to remind you that you are in animate mode. Red also appears around a spinner for any animated parameters.

Auto Key mode

With the Auto Key button enabled, every transformation or parameter change creates a key that defines where and how an object should look at that specific frame.

To create a key, drag the Time Slider to a frame where you want to create a key and then move the selected object or change the parameter, and a key is automatically created. When the first key is created, Max automatically goes back and creates a key for frame 0 that holds the object's original position or parameter.

Upon setting the key, Max then interpolates all the positions and changes between the keys. The keys are displayed in the Track Bar.

Each frame can hold several different keys, but only one for each type of transform and each parameter. For example, if you move, rotate, scale, and change the Radius parameter for a sphere object with the Auto Key mode enabled, then separate keys are created for position, rotation, scaling, and a parameter change.

Set Key mode

The Set Key button (') offers more control over key creation and sets keys only when you click the Set Key button (K). It also creates keys only for the key types enabled in the Key Filters dialog box. You can open the Key Filters dialog box, shown in Figure 20.2, by clicking the Key Filters button. Available key types include All, Position, Rotation, Scale, IK Parameters, Object Parameters, Custom Attributes, Modifiers, Materials, and Other (which allows keys to be set for manipulator values).

FIGURE 20.2

Use the Set Key Filters dialog box to specify the types of keys to create.

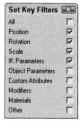

Tutorial: Rotating a windmill's blades

The best way to learn is to practice, and there's no better time to practice than now. For this quick example, you animate a set of blades on a windmill.

To animate a set of windmill blades rotating, follow these steps:

1. Open the Rotating windmill blades.max file from the Chap 20 directory on the DVD.

   This file includes a windmill model created by Viewpoint Datalabs.

2. Click the Auto Key button (or press the N key) at the bottom of the Max window, and drag the Time Slider to frame 50.

3. Select the "prop" object at the top of the windmill in the Front viewport. The blades are attached to the center prop and rotate about its Pivot Point. Then click the Select and Rotate button on the main toolbar (or press E key), and rotate the "prop" object about its Y-axis.

4. Click the Auto Key button (or press the N key) again to disable animation mode. Select the key in the Track Bar located at frame 1, hold down the Shift key, and drag the key to frame 100 (or press the End key).

   This step copies the key from frame 1 to frame 100. Doing so ensures a smooth looping animation (even though it spins the prop forward and then backward; I guess it must be a strange wind that's blowing).

5. Click the Play Animation button in the Time Controls to see the animation.

Figure 20.3 shows frame 50 of this simple animation.

Frame 50 of this simple windmill animation

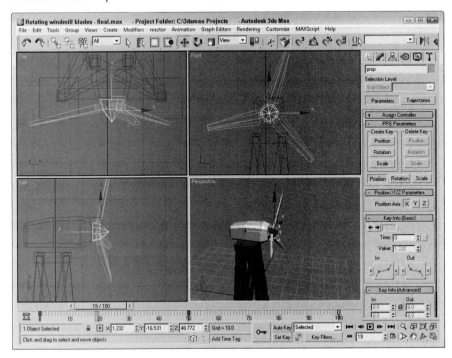

Creating keys with the Time Slider

Another way to create keys is to select the object to be animated and right-click the Time Slider button. This opens the Create Key dialog box, shown in Figure 20.4, where you can set Position, Rotation, and Scale keys for the currently selected object. You can use this method only to create transform keys.

The Create Key dialog box enables you to create a Position, Rotation, or Scale key quickly.

If a key already exists, you can clone it by dragging the selected key with the Shift key held down. Dragging the Track Bar with the Ctrl and Alt keys held down changes the active time segment.

Copying parameter animation keys

If a parameter is changed while the Auto Key mode is enabled, then keys are set for that parameter. You can tell when a parameter has a key set because the arrows to the right of its spinner are outlined in red when the Time Slider is on the frame where the key is set. If you change the parameter value when the spinner is highlighted red, then the key value is changed (and the Auto Key mode doesn't need to be enabled).

If you highlight and right-click the parameter value, a pop-up menu of options appears. Using this pop-up menu, you can Cut, Copy, Paste, and Delete the parameter value. You can also select Copy Animation, which copies all the keys associated with this parameter and lets you paste them to another parameter. Pasting the animation keys can be done as a Copy, an Instance, or a Wire. A Copy is independent; an Instance ties the animation keys to the original copy so that they both are changed when either changes; and a Wire lets one parameter control some other parameter.

> **CAUTION** To copy a parameter value, be sure to select and right-click the value. If you right-click the parameter's spinner, the value is set to 0.

The right-click pop-up menu also includes commands to let you Edit a wired parameter, show the parameter in the Track View, or show the parameter in the Parameter Wire dialog box.

> **CROSS-REF** Parameter wiring and the Parameter Wire dialog box are discussed in more detail in Chapter 32, "Using Animation Modifiers."

Deleting all object animation keys

Individual keys can be selected and deleted using the Track Bar or the right-click pop-up menu, but if an object has many keys, this can be time consuming. To delete all animation keys for the selected object quickly, choose the Animation ⇨ Delete Selected Animation menu command.

Using the Track Bar

The Max interface includes a simple way to work with keys: with the Track Bar, which is situated directly under the Time Slider. The Track Bar displays a rectangular marker for every key for the selected object. These markers are color-coded, depending on the type of key. Position keys are red, rotation keys are green, scale keys are blue, and parameter keys are dark gray.

> **CAUTION** In the Track View — Dope Sheet interface, position, rotation, and scale keys are red, green, and blue, but parameter keys are yellow.

The current frame is also shown in the Track Bar as a light blue, transparent rectangle, as shown in Figure 20.5. The icon at the left end of the Track Bar is the Open Mini Curve Editor button, which opens a mini Track View.

> **CROSS-REF** For more on the Track View interface, see Chapter 34, "Working with Function Curves in the Track View."

Using the Track Bar, you can move, copy, and delete keys. The Track Bar shows key markers only for the currently selected object or objects, and each marker can represent several different keys. When the mouse is moved over the top of these markers, the cursor changes to a plus sign, and you can select a marker by clicking it (selected markers turn white). Using the Ctrl key, you can select multiple keys at the same time. You can also select multiple key markers by clicking an area of the Track Bar that contains no keys and then dragging an outline over all the keys you want to select. If you move the cursor over the top of a selected key, the cursor is displayed as a set of arrows enabling you to drag the selected key to the left or right. Holding down the Shift key while dragging a key creates a copy of the key. Pressing the Delete key deletes the selected key.

FIGURE 20.5

The Track Bar displays all keys for the selected object.

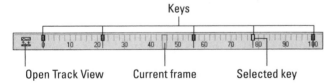

Open Track View   Current frame   Selected key

> **TIP**
>
> If you drag a key off the end of the Track Bar, the frame number is displayed on the Prompt Line at the bottom of the interface and the key is not included in the current time range. If you ever want to hide a key without deleting it, you can drag it off the end of the Track Bar and recover it by resetting the time in the Time Configuration dialog box.

Because each marker can represent several keys, you can view all the keys associated with the marker in a pop-up menu by right-clicking the marker.

> **NOTE**
>
> In the pop-up menu, a check mark next to a key indicates that the key is shared with another instance.

The marker pop-up menu also offers options for deleting selected keys or filtering the keys. In addition, there is a Goto Time command, which automatically moves the Time Slider to the key's location when selected.

To delete a key marker with all of its keys, right-click to open the pop-up menu and choose Delete Key ➪ All, or select the key marker and press the Delete key.

Viewing and Editing Key Values

At the top of the marker's right-click pop-up menu is a list of current keys for the selected object (or if there are too many keys for a marker, they are placed under the Key Properties menu). When you select one of these keys, a key information dialog box opens. This dialog box displays different controls depending on the type of key selected. Figure 20.6 shows the dialog box for the Position key. There are slight variations in this dialog box, depending on the key type.

FIGURE 20.6

Key dialog boxes enable you to change the key parameters.

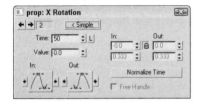

> **NOTE**
>
> You can also access key-specific dialog boxes in the Motion panel for a selected object by clicking the Parameters button.

Within each of these key dialog boxes is a Time value that shows the current frame. Next to the Time value are two arrows that enable you to move easily to the other keys in the scene. The dialog box also includes several text fields, where you can change the key parameters.

Most of the key dialog boxes also include flyout buttons for selecting Key Tangents. Key Tangents determine how the animation moves into and out of the key. For example, if the In Key Tangent is set to Slow and the Out Key Tangent is set to Fast, the object approaches the key position in a slow manner but accelerates as it leaves the key position. The arrow buttons on either side of the Key Tangent buttons can copy the current Key Tangent selection to the previous or next key.

The available types of Tangents are detailed in Table 20.3.

TABLE 20.3

Key Tangents

Toolbar Button	Name	Description
	Smooth	Produces straight, smooth motion; this is the default type.
	Linear	Moves at a constant rate between keys.
	Step	Causes discontinuous motion between keys; it occurs only between matching In-Out pairs.
	Slow	Decelerates as you approach the key.
	Fast	Accelerates as you approach the key.
	Custom	Lets you control the Tangent handles in function curves mode.
	Custom – Locked Handles	Lets you control the Tangent handles in function curves mode with the handles locked.

Using the Motion Panel

You have yet another way to create keys: by using the Motion panel. The Motion panel in the Command Panel includes settings and controls for animating objects. At the top of the Motion panel are two buttons: Parameters and Trajectories.

Setting parameters

The Parameters button on the Motion panel lets you assign controllers and create and delete keys. *Controllers* are custom key-creating algorithms that can be defined through the Parameters rollout, shown in Figure 20.7. These controllers are assigned by selecting the position, rotation, or scaling track and clicking the Assign Controller button to open a list of applicable controllers that you can select.

CROSS-REF For more information on controllers, see Chapter 21, "Animating with Constraints and Controllers."

FIGURE 20.7

The Parameters section of the Motion panel lets you assign controllers and create keys.

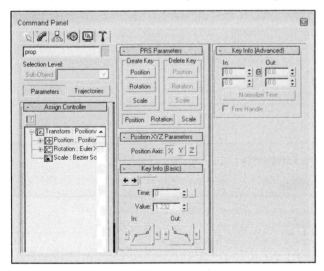

Below the Assign Controllers rollout is the PRS Parameters rollout, where you can create and delete Position, Rotation, and Scale keys. You can use this rollout to create Position, Rotation, and Scale keys whether or not the Auto Key or Set Key buttons are enabled. Additional rollouts may be available, depending upon the selected controller.

Below the PRS Parameters rollout are two Key Info rollouts: Basic and Advanced. These rollouts include the same key-specific information that you can access using the right-click pop-up menu found in the Track Bar.

Using trajectories

A *trajectory* is the actual path that the animation follows. When you click the Trajectories button in the Motion panel, the animation trajectory is shown as a spline with each key displayed as a node and each frame shown as a white dot. You can then edit the trajectory and its nodes by clicking the Sub-Object button at the top of the Motion panel, shown in Figure 20.8. The only subobject available is Keys. With the Sub-Object button enabled, you can use the transform buttons to move and reposition the trajectory nodes. You can also add and delete keys with the Add Key and Delete Key buttons.

For more control over the trajectory path, you can convert the trajectory path to a normal editable spline with the Convert To button. You can also convert an existing spline into a trajectory with the Convert From button.

To use the Convert From button, select an object, click the Convert From button, and then click a spline path in the scene. This creates a new trajectory path for the selected object. The first key of this path is placed at the spline's first vertex, and the final key is placed as the spline's final vertex position. Additional keys are spaced out along the spline based on the spline's curvature as determined by the Samples value listed in the Sample Range group. All these new keys are roughly spaced between the Start and End times, but smaller Bézier handles result in more closely packed keys.

FIGURE 20.8

The Trajectories rollout in the Motion panel enables you to see the animation path as a spline.

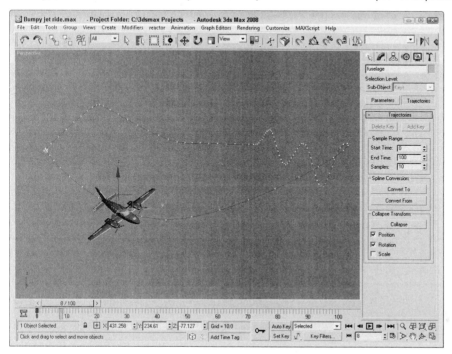

Click the Collapse button at the bottom of the Trajectories rollout to reduce all transform keys into a single editable path. You can select which transformations to collapse including Position, Rotation, and Scale using the options under the Collapse button. For example, an object with several Controllers assigned can be collapsed, thereby reducing the complexity of all the keys.

 If you collapse all keys, you cannot alter their parameters via the controller rollouts.

The Views menu includes an option to Show Key Times. The Show Key Times command displays frame numbers along the trajectory path where every animation key is located. Enabling this option causes the display of the frame numbers next to any key along a trajectory path. You can make the trajectory visible for any object by enabling the Trajectory option in the Object Properties dialog box.

Tutorial: Making an airplane follow a looping path

Airplanes that perform aerobatic stunts often follow paths that are smooth. You can see this clearly when watching a sky writer. In this example, I've created a simple looping path using the Line spline primitive, and we use this path to make a plane complete a loop.

To make an airplane follow a looping path, follow these steps:

1. Open the Looping airplane.max file from the Chap 20 directory on the DVD.

   This file includes a simple looping spline path and an airplane created by Viewpoint Datalabs.

2. With the airplane selected, open the Motion panel and click the Trajectories button. Then click the Convert From button in the Trajectories rollout, and select the path in the Front viewport.

3. If you drag the Time Slider, you'll notice that the plane moves along the path, but it doesn't rotate with the path. To fix this, click the Key Mode Toggle button in the Time Controls to easily move from key to key. Click the Key Filters button, select only Rotation, and then click the Set Key button (or press the ' key) to enter Set Key mode.

4. Before moving the Time Slider, click the Set Keys button to create a rotation key at frame 0. Then, click the Select and Rotate button, click the Next Key button, rotate the plane in the Front viewport to match the path, and click the large Set Keys button (or press the K key) to create a rotation key. Click the Next Key button to move to the next key, and repeat this step until rotation keys have been set for the entire path.

5. Drag the Time Slider, and watch the airplane circle about the loop.

CROSS-REF Max provides an easier way to make the plane follow the path using the Path constraint. To learn more about constraints, see Chapter 21, "Animating with Constraints and Controllers."

Figure 20.9 shows the plane's trajectory.

FIGURE 20.9

When you use a spline path, the position keys are automatically set for this plane.

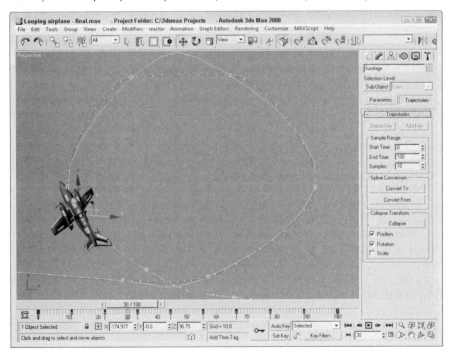

Using the Follow/Bank utility

When an object travels along a path that defines its trajectory, it maintains its same orientation without rotating. Imagine a roller coaster car; it rotates and banks as it moves around the track. This rotation and banking motion can be added to an object following a path using the Follow/Bank utility. You can access this utility by opening the Utilities panel and clicking the More button. Double-click the Follow/Bank utility to load it into the Utilities panel.

CAUTION The Follow/Bank utility aligns the local X-axis of the object with the local Z-axis of the spline when the utility is applied, so you need to correctly orient the object's pivot point before applying the utility. If you don't, the object will be aligned at right angles to the path.

The Follow/Bank utility lets you enable a Bank option and set its Amount and Smoothness. Another option allows the object to turn upside down (not recommended for a traditional roller coaster car). Click the Apply Follow button to add the keys to cause the object to follow and bank. The Samples section determines how many keys are created.

Using Ghosting

As you're trying to animate objects, using the ghosting feature can be very helpful. This feature displays a copy of the object being animated before and after its current position. To enable ghosting, choose Views ➪ Show Ghosting. The Show Ghosting command displays the position of the selected object in the previous several frames, the next several frames, or both. This command uses the options set in the Preference Settings dialog box. Access this dialog box by choosing Customize ➪ Preferences. In the Viewports panel of this dialog box is a Ghosting section.

You use this Ghosting section to set how many ghosted objects are to appear; whether the ghosted objects appear before, after, or both before and after the current frame; and whether frame numbers should be shown. You can also specify every Nth frame to be displayed. You also have an option to display the ghost object in wireframe (they are displayed as shaded if this option is not enabled) and an option to Show Frame Numbers. Objects before the current frame are colored yellow, and objects after are colored light blue.

Figure 20.10 shows a lion toy object that is animated to travel in a bumpy circle with ghosting enabled. The Preference settings are set to show three ghosting frames at every five frames before and after the current frame. The Trajectory path has also been enabled.

FIGURE 20.10

Enabling ghosting lets you know where an object is and where it's going.

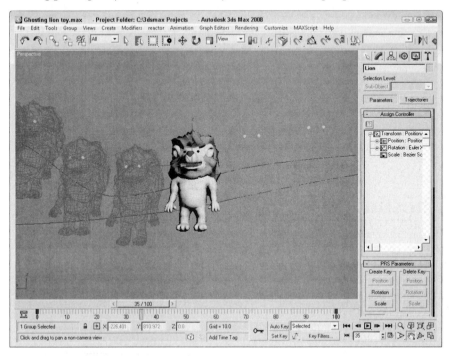

Animation Preferences

The Animation panel of the Preference Settings dialog box, shown in Figure 20.11, contains several preference options dealing with animations. When a specific frame is selected, all objects with keys for that frame are surrounded with white brackets. The Animation panel offers options that specify which objects get these brackets. Options include All Objects, Selected Objects, and None. You also can limit the brackets to only those objects with certain transform keys.

 **TIP** The Key Bracket Display option is helpful when you need to locate specific keys. When the selected object for the given frame has a key, the object is surrounded with brackets.

The Local Center During Animate option causes all objects to be animated about their local centers. Turning this option off enables animations about other centers (such as screen and world).

The MIDI Time Slider Controls include an On option and a Setup button. The Setup button opens the MIDI Time Slider Control Setup dialog box shown in Figure 20.12. After this control is set up, you can control an animation using a MIDI device.

You can use the Animation panel to assign a new Sound Plug-In to use, as well as to set the default values of all animation controllers. The Override Parametric Controller Range by Default option causes controllers to be active for the entire animation sequence instead of just their designated range. The Spring Quick Edit option lets you change the accuracy of all Spring controllers in the entire scene in one place. The Rollback setting is the number of frames that the Spring controller uses to return to its original position.

FIGURE 20.11

FIGURE 20.11

The Animation panel includes settings for displaying Key Brackets.

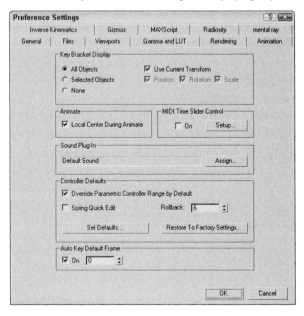

FIGURE 20.12

The MIDI Time Slider Control Setup dialog box lets you set up specific notes to start, stop, and step through an animation.

Clicking the Set Defaults button opens the Set Controller Defaults dialog box. This dialog box includes a list of all the controllers and a Set button. When you select a controller and click the Set button, another dialog box appears with all the values for that controller.

When you first start up Max, the default first frame on the Timeline is frame 0, but if you enable the Auto Key Default Frame option, you can set the first frame to be any frame you want. This is convenient if you like to use some frames to set up a shot or if the starting frame of the shot is not at frame 0.

CROSS-REF You can learn more about specific controllers in Chapter 21, "Animating with Constraints and Controllers."

NEW FEATURE The preference to change the Auto Key Default Frame is new to 3ds Max 2008.

Animating Objects

Many different objects in Max can be animated, including geometric objects, cameras, lights, and materials. In this section, we look at several types of objects and parameters that can be animated.

Animating cameras

You can animate cameras using the standard transform buttons found on the main toolbar. When animating a camera that actually moves in the scene, using a Free camera is best. A Target camera can be pointed by moving its target, but you risk its being flipped over if the target is ever directly above the camera. If you want to use a Target camera, attach both the camera and its target to a Dummy object using the Link button and move the Dummy object.

Two useful constraints when animating cameras are the Path constraint and the Look At constraint. You can find both of these in the Animation ⇨ Constraints menu. The Path constraint can make a camera follow a spline path, and the Look At constraint can direct the focus of a camera to follow an object as the camera or the object moves through the scene.

CROSS-REF For more on constraints, including these two, see Chapter 21, "Animating with Constraints and Controllers."

Tutorial: Animating darts hitting a dartboard

As a simple example of animating objects using the Auto Key button, we animate several darts hitting a dartboard.

To animate darts hitting a dartboard, follow these steps:

1. Open the Dart and dartboard.max file from the Chap 20 directory on the DVD.

   This file includes a dart and dartboard objects created by Zygote Media.

2. Click the Auto Key button (or press the N key) to enable animation mode. Drag the Time Slider to frame 25, and click the Select and Move button on the main toolbar (or press the W key).

3. Select the first dart in the Left viewport, and drag it to the left until its tip just touches the dartboard.

   This step creates a key in the Track Bar for frames 0 and 25.

4. Click the Select and Rotate button on the main toolbar, set the reference coordinate system to Local, and constrain the rotation to the Y-axis. Then drag the selected dart in the Front viewport to rotate it about its local Y-axis.

   This step also sets a key in the Track Bar.

5. Select the second dart, and click the Select and Move button again. Right-click the Time Slider to make the Create Key dialog box appear. Make sure that the check boxes for Position and Rotation are selected, and click OK.

   This step creates a key that keeps the second dart from moving before it's ready.

6. With the second dart still selected, drag the Time Slider to frame 50 and move the dart to the dartboard as shown in Step 3. Then repeat Step 4 to set the rotation key for the second dart.

7. Repeat Steps 3, 4, and 5 for the last two darts.

8. Click the Auto Key button (or press the N key) again to disable animation mode, maximize the Perspective viewport, and click the Play Animation button to see the animation. Figure 20.13 shows the darts as they're flying toward the dartboard.

FIGURE 20.13

One frame of the dart animation

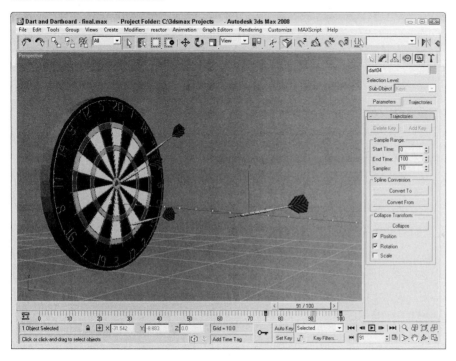

Animating lights

The process for animating lights includes many of the same techniques as that for animating cameras. For moving lights, use a Free Spot light or attach a Target Spot light to a Dummy object. You can also use the Look At and Path controllers with lights.

CROSS-REF If you need to animate the Sun at different times in the day, use the Daylight or Sunlight systems, which are discussed in Chapter 19, "Using Lights and Basic Lighting Techniques."

To flash lights on and off, enable and disable the On parameter at different frames and assign a Step Tangent. To dim lights, just alter the Multiplier value over several frames.

Animating materials

Materials can be animated if their properties are altered while the Auto Key button is active. Max interpolates between the values as the animation progresses. The material must be consistent for the entire animation: You cannot change materials at different keys; you can only alter the existing materials parameters.

If you want to change materials as the animation progresses, you can use a material that combines multiple materials, such as the Blend material. This material includes a Mix Amount value that can change at different keyframes. The next tutorial shows how to use the Blend material in this manner.

Several maps include a Phase value, including all maps that have a Noise rollout. This value provides the means to animate the map. For example, using a Noise map and changing the Phase value over many keys animates the noise effect.

A useful way to view animated materials is to click the Make Preview button (the sixth button from the top) to open the Create Material Preview dialog box, shown in Figure 20.14. Select the Active Time Segment option, and click OK. The material renders every frame and automatically opens and plays the material preview.

FIGURE 20.14

The Create Material Preview dialog box can render the entire range of frames or a select number of frames.

Tutorial: Dimming lights

Occasionally, you'll want to change materials in a scene to gradually alter it in some way, such as dimming a light. You can easily accomplish this task with the Blend material.

To create a light that dims with time, follow these steps:

1. Open the Dimming light.max file from the Chap 20 directory on the DVD.

   This file contains a simple lamp object with a sphere to represent a light bulb.

2. Open the Material Editor by pressing the M key, and select the first sample slot. Then click the Type button, and select the Blend material from the Material/Map Browser. Select the Discard Old Material option in the Replace Material dialog box that appears. Give the material the name **Dimming Light**.

> **NOTE** When using composite materials, a dialog box appears asking whether you want to discard the old material or keep it as a submaterial. If you choose to keep it, the current material in the sample slot becomes one of the maps for the composite material.

3. Click the Material 1 button in the Blend Basic Parameters rollout, and name the material **Light On**. Set the Diffuse color in the Blinn Basic Parameters rollout to yellow and the Self-Illumination to yellow. Then click the Go Forward to Sibling button.

NOTE Composite materials such as Blend include several submaterials. When one of these submaterials is selected, you can move quickly to the other submaterials by clicking the Go Forward to Sibling button. To access the root material, click the Go to Parent button.

4. Name the second material **Light Off**, and select a gray Diffuse color. Then click the Go to Parent button to return to the Blend material.

5. With the Time Slider at frame 0, click the Auto Key button (or press the N key). Then drag the Time Slider to frame 100, and change the Mix Amount to 100. Click the Auto Key button again to deactivate it. The material changes gradually from the "Light On" material to the "Light Off" material. By dragging the Time Slider, you can see the material in the sample slot change.

6. Select the light bulb object, and click the Assign Material to Selection button to assign the material to the bulb object.

Figure 20.15 shows a simple lamp object with a dimming sphere in its center. The actual dimming effect isn't visible in the viewport — only when the image is rendered.

FIGURE 20.15

This lamp object dims as the animation proceeds.

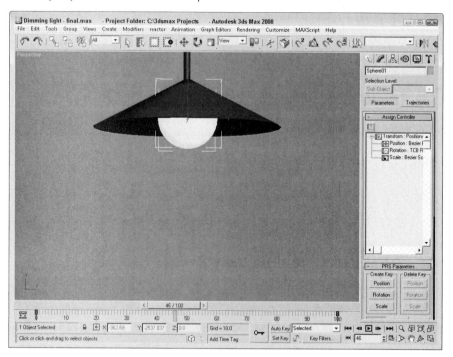

Creating Image File Lists

Anywhere you can load a bitmap map, you can also load an animation file such as a Microsoft Video (AVI) or a QuickTime (MOV) file. Another way to create animated material is with Image File Lists, which is a text file that lists each separate image file contained in an animation. Max supports two different image file formats — Autodesk ME Image Sequence File (IMSQ) and 3ds Max Image File List (IFL) files.

IMSQ and *IFL files* are text files that list which images should appear and for which frames. You save them with the .IMSQ or .IFL extension and load them using the Bitmap map. Image file lists can be created during the render process by selecting the Put Image File List in Output Path option in the Common Parameter rollout of the Render Scene dialog box. There is also a Create Now button to create an image file list at any time.

To manually create an IMSQ or IFL file, open a text editor and type the name of the image followed by the number of frames for which it should appear. Be sure to include a space between the name and the number of frames. The images are displayed in the order they are listed and repeated until all frames have been displayed. Once applied, the image file list is visible in the sample slot if you drag the Time slider, or you can create a material preview.

NOTE   You can also use the * and ? wildcard characters within an IFL file. For example, flyby* includes any image file that begins with "flyby," and flyby? includes any image file that begins with "flyby" and has one additional character.

Generating IFL files with the IFL Manager Utility

If you don't want to create text files by yourself, you can use the IFL Manager Utility to generate IFL files for you. To use this utility, open the Utilities panel and click the More button. Then select the IFL Manager Utility, and click OK.

In the IFL Manager rollout, shown in Figure 20.16, the Select button opens a File dialog box where you can select a sequential list of images to include in an IFL file. After you select a list of images, you can specify the Start and End images. You can cause the images to be displayed in reverse by placing a greater number in the Start field than is in the End field. The Every Nth field can specify to use every Nth image. You use the Multiplier field to specify in how many frames each image should appear.

FIGURE 20.16

IFL Manager Utility can help to create IFL files.

The Create button opens a File dialog box where you can save the IFL file. The Edit button opens an IFL text file in the system's default text editor for editing.

Tutorial: What's on TV?

Animated files such as AVI and MOV can be opened and mapped to an object to animate the texture, but you can also use IFL files.

To create an IFL file that will be mapped on the front of a television model, follow these steps:

1. Open the Windows standard Notepad text editor, and type the following:

```
; these frames will be positioned on a television screen.
static.tif 20
Exploding planet - frame 10.tif 2
Exploding planet - frame 15.tif 2
Exploding planet - frame 20.tif 2
Exploding planet - frame 25.tif 2
Exploding planet - frame 30.tif 2
Exploding planet - frame 35.tif 2
Exploding planet - frame 40.tif 2
Exploding planet - frame 45.tif 2
Exploding planet - frame 50.tif 2
Exploding planet - frame 55.tif 2
static.tif 60
```

> **NOTE** The first line of text is referred to as a *comment line*. You enter comments into the IFL file by starting the line with a semicolon (;) character.

2. Save the file as **tv.ifl**. Make sure that your text editor doesn't add the extension .TXT on the end of the file.

   You can check your file with the one I created, which you can find in the Chap 20 directory on the DVD.

> **NOTE** The IFL file as described earlier looks for the image files in the same directory as the IFL file. Make sure that the images are included in this directory.

3. Open the Television — IFL File.max file from the Chap 20 directory on the DVD.

   This file includes a television model created by Zygote Media.

4. Select the television front screen object, open the Material Editor, and select the first sample slot. Name the material **Television Screen**. Click the map button to the right of the Diffuse color swatch. Double-click the Bitmap map. In the File dialog box, locate the tv.ifl file and click OK. Then click the Assign Material to Selection button to apply the material to the screen.

> **TIP** To see the map in the viewport, click the Show Map in Viewport button. This button makes the frames of the IFL file visible in the viewport.

5. Because the screen object is a mesh object, you need to use the UVW Map modifier to create some mapping coordinates for the map. Open the Modify panel, and click the UVW Map button. Set the mapping option to Planar. Then click the Sub-Object button, and transform the planar gizmo until it covers the screen.

6. Click the Play button (/) to see the final animation.

Figure 20.17 shows one rendered frame of the television with the IFL file applied.

Working with Previews

More than likely, your final output will be rendered using the highest-quality settings with all effects enabled, and you can count on this taking a fair amount of time. After waiting several days for a sequence to render is a terrible time to find out that your animation keys are off. Even viewing animation sequences in the viewports with the Play Animation button cannot catch all problems.

FIGURE 20.17

IFL files are commonly used to animate materials via a list of images such as the image on the front of this television.

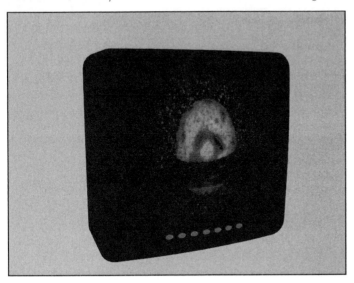

One way to catch potential problems is to create a sample preview animation. Previews are test animation sequences that render quickly to give you an idea of the final output. The Animation menu includes several commands for creating, renaming, and viewing previews. The rendering options available for previews are the same as the shading options available in the viewports.

Creating previews

You create previews by choosing Animation ➪ Make Preview to open the Make Preview dialog box, shown in Figure 20.18.

In the Make Preview dialog box, you can specify what frames to include using the Active Time Segment or Custom Range options. You can also choose Every Nth Frame or select a specific frame rate in the Playback FPS field. The image size is determined by the Percent of Output value, which is a percentage of the final output size. The resolution is also displayed.

The Display in Preview section offers a variety of options to include in the preview. These options include Geometry, Shapes, Lights, Cameras, Helpers, Space Warps, Particle Systems, Active Grid, Safe Frames, Frame Numbers, Background, and Bone Objects. Because the preview output is rendered like the viewports, certain selected objects such as Lights and Cameras actually display their icons as part of the file. The Frame Numbers option prints the frame number in the upper-left corner of each frame.

The Rendering Level drop-down list includes the same shading options used to display objects in the viewports, including Smooth, Smooth + Highlights, Facets, Facets + Highlights, Lit Wireframes, Wireframe, and Bounding Box.

Output options include the default AVI option; a Custom File Type option, which enables you to choose your own format; and the Use Device option, which you can use to render the preview to a different device. For the AVI option, you can select a CODEC, which is used to compress the resulting file. Options include Cinepak Codec by Radius, Logitech Video (1420), Intel IYUV, Microsoft Video 1, Intel Indeo Video 4.5, DivX 5.0.5, and

Full Frames (uncompressed), depending on the CODECs that are installed on your system. When the Use Device option is selected, the Choose Device button becomes active. Clicking this button opens the Select Output Image Device dialog box, where you can select and configure output devices such as a Digital Recorder.

FIGURE 20.18

The Make Preview dialog box lets you specify the range, size, and output of a preview file.

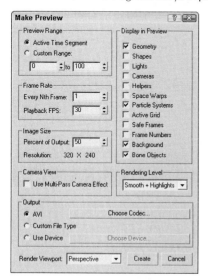

At the bottom of the dialog box is a Render Viewport drop-down list, where you can select which viewport to use to create your preview file. The Create button starts the rendering process. When a preview is being rendered, the viewports are replaced with a single image of the current render frame, and the Status bar is replaced by a Progress bar and a Cancel button. Figure 20.19 shows a preview file being created.

 **You can use the Esc key on your keyboard to cancel a rendering job.**

If you cancel the rendering, the Make Preview alert box offers the options Stop and Play, Stop and Don't Play, and Don't Stop.

Viewing previews

When a preview file is finished rendering, the default Media Player for your system loads and displays the preview file. You can disable this autoplay feature using the Autoplay Preview File option in the General panel of the Preference Settings dialog box.

At any time, you can replay the preview file using the Animation ➪ View Preview menu command. This command loads the latest preview file and displays it in the Media Player.

Renaming previews

The preview file is actually saved as a file named scene.avi and is saved by default in the previews subdirectory. Be aware that this file is automatically overwritten when a new preview is created. To save a preview file by renaming it, choose Animation ➪ Rename Preview File. This command opens the Save Preview As dialog box, where you can give the preview file a name.

513

FIGURE 20.19

When a preview file is being created, the viewports are replaced with a single view of the current frame.

Summary

This chapter covered the basics of animating objects in Max, including working with time and keys. You also learned about the two key creation modes and editing keys. Several animation helps are available, such as trajectories and ghosting. This chapter also discussed how to animate materials and how to create preview animations. In this chapter, you learned how to do the following:

- Control time and work with keys
- Use the two key creation modes
- Work with the Track Bar and the Motion panel
- View and edit key values
- Use trajectories and ghosting
- Animate materials and use IFL files
- Create preview animations

The next chapter shows how to automate the creation of animation keys with constraints and controllers.

Chapter 21

Animating with Constraints and Controllers

When you first begin animating and working with keys, having Max figure out all the frames between the start and end keys seems amazing, especially if you've ever animated in 2D by drawing every frame. But soon you realize that animating with keys can be time-consuming for complex realistic motions, and again, Max comes to the rescue. You can use animation constraints and controllers to automate the creation of keys for certain types of motions.

Constraints and controllers store and manage the key values for all animations in Max. When you animate an object using the Auto Key button, the default controller is automatically assigned. You can change the assigned controller or alter its parameters using the Motion panel or the Track View.

This chapter explains how to work with constraints and controllers and examines all the various types that are available. For example, you can use the Noise controller to add random motion to a flag blowing in the wind, the Surface constraint to keep a bumper car moving over the surface, or the Waveform controller to produce regular repeating motions such as a sine or square wave.

Restricting Movement with Constraints

The trick of animating an object is to make it go where you want it to go. Animating objects deals not only with controlling the motion of the object, but also with controlling its lack of motion. Constraints are a type of animation controller that you can use to restrict the motion of an object.

Using these constraints, you can force objects to stay attached to another object or follow a path. For example, the Attachment constraint can be used to make a robot's feet stay connected to a ground plane as it moves. The purpose of these constraints is to make animating your objects easier.

IN THIS CHAPTER

Using constraints

Attaching an object to the surface of an object

Making an object travel along a path with the Path constraint

Controlling the weighted position and orientation of objects

Shifting between two controlling objects using the Link constraint

Following objects with the LookAt constraint

Understanding the controller types

Assigning controllers using the Motion panel and the Track View

Setting default controllers

515

Using constraints

You can apply constraints to selected objects using the Animation ➪ Constraints menu. The constraints contained within this menu include Attachment, Surface, Path, Position, Link, LookAt, and Orientation.

 All constraints have the same controller icon displayed in the Motion panel or the Track View.

After you select one of the constraints from the Animation ➪ Constraints menu, a dotted link line extends from the current selected object to the mouse cursor. You can select a target object in any of the viewports to apply the constraint. The cursor changes to a plus sign when it is over a target object that can be selected. Selecting a constraint from the Constraints menu also opens the Motion panel, where the settings of the constraint can be modified.

 You can also apply constraints using the Assign Controller button found in the Motion panel and in the Track View window.

 **Find out more about the Track View window in Chapter 34, "Working with Function Curves in the Track View."**

The ability to apply animation constraints to several objects at once is new to 3ds Max 2008.

Working with the constraints

Each constraint is slightly different, but learning how to use these constraints will help you control the animated objects within a scene. You can apply several constraints to a single object. All constraints that are applied to an object are displayed in a list found in the Motion panel. From this list, you can select which constraint to make active and which to delete. You can also cut and paste constraints between objects.

Attachment constraint

The Attachment constraint determines an object's position by attaching it to the face of another object. This constraint lets you attach an object to the surface of another object. For example, you could animate the launch of a rocket ship with booster rockets that are attached with the Attachment constraint. The booster rockets would move along with the ship until the time when they are jettisoned.

The pivot point of the object that the constraint is applied to is attached to the target object. At the top of the Attachment Parameters rollout is a Pick Object button for selecting the target object to attach to. You can use this button to change the target object or to select the target object if the Animation ➪ Constraints menu wasn't used. There is also an option to align the object to the surface. The Update section enables you to manually or automatically update the attachment values.

NOTE **The Attachment constraint shows up in the Position track of the Assign Controller rollout as the Position List controller. To minimize the effect of other controllers, set their Weight values in the Position List rollout to 0.**

The Key Info section of the Attachment Parameters rollout displays the key number and lets you move between the various keys. The Time value is the current key value. In the Face field, you can specify the exact number of the face to attach to. To set this face, click the Set Position button and drag over the target object. The A and B values represent Barycentric coordinates for defining how the object lies on the face. You can change these coordinate values by entering values or by dragging the red crosshairs in the box below the A and B values. The easiest way to position an object is to use the Set Position button to place the object and then to enhance its position with the A and B values. The Set Position button stays active until you click it again.

The TCB section sets the Tension, Continuity, and Bias values for the constraint. You can also set the Ease To and Ease From values.

Tutorial: Attaching eyes to a melting snowman

When part of a model is deformed, such as applying the Melt modifier to a snowman's body, smaller parts like the eyes either get left behind or get the full weight of the modifier applied to them. If the Melt modifier weren't applied to these items, they would stay floating in the air while the rest of the snowman melted about them. This problem can be fixed with the Attachment constraint, which causes the eyes to remain attached to the snowball as it melts.

 **CROSS-REF** The tutorial where the Melt modifier is applied to the snowman is included in Chapter 32, "Using Animation Modifiers."

To constrain the solid objects to a melting snowman, follow these steps:

1. Open the Melting snowman.max file from the Chap 21 directory on the DVD.

   This file includes the melting snowman file from the previous chapter with the Melt modifier applied to all objects.

2. Select the left eye object in the scene. In the Modifier Stack, select the Melt modifier and click the Remove Modifier button to throw that modifier away.

3. With the left eye still selected, select Animation ➪ Constraints ➪ Attachment Constraint. A connecting line appears in the active viewport. Click the top snowball to select it as the attachment object. This moves the eye object to the top of the snowball where the snowball's first face is located.

4. In the Attachment Parameters rollout, change the Face value until the eye is positioned where it should be. This should be around face 315. Then change the A and B values (or drag in the Position graph) to position the eye where it looks good.

5. Repeat Step 5 for the right eye and for any other objects in the scene that you want to attach.

6. Click the Play button (/), and notice that the snow melts, but the eye objects stay the same size.

Figure 21.1 shows the resulting melted snowman.

Surface constraint

The Surface constraint moves an object so that it is on the surface of another object. The object with Surface constraint applied to it is positioned so that its pivot point is on the surface of the target object. You can use this constraint only on certain objects, including Spheres, Cones, Cylinders, Toruses, Quad Patches, Loft objects, and NURBS objects.

In the Surface Controller Parameters rollout is the name of the target object that was selected after the menu command. The Pick Surface button enables you to select a different surface to attach to. You can also select specific U and V Position values. Alignment options include No Alignment, Align to U, Align to V, and a Flip toggle.

NOTE Don't be confused because the rollout is named Surface Controller Parameters instead of Surface Constraint Parameters. The developers at Autodesk must have missed this one.

Tutorial: Rolling a tire down a hill with the Surface constraint

Moving a vehicle across a landscape can be a difficult procedure if you need to place every rotation and position key, but with the Surface constraint, it becomes easy. In this tutorial, we use the Surface constraint to roll a tire down a hill.

FIGURE 21.1

The Attachment constraint sticks one object to the surface of another.

To roll a tire down a hill with the Surface constraint, follow these steps:

1. Open the Tire rolling on a hill.max file from the Chap 21 directory on the DVD.

   This file includes a patch grid hill and a wheel object made from primitives.

2. Create a dummy object from the Helpers category, and link the tire object to it as a child. This causes the tire to move along with the dummy object. Position the dummy object's pivot point at the bottom of the tire and the top of the hill.

3. Select the dummy object, choose Animation ➪ Constraints ➪ Surface Constraint, and select the hill object.

4. In the Surface Controller Parameters rollout, select the Align to V and Flip options to position the dummy and tire objects at the top of the hill. Set the V Position value to **50** to move the tire down the hill.

5. Click the Auto Key button (or press the N key), drag the Time Slider to frame 100, and change the U Position to **100**. Click the Animate button again to deactivate it, and click the Play Animation button to see the tire move down the hill.

Figure 21.2 shows the tire as it moves down the hill. In the Top view, you can see the function curves for this motion.

FIGURE 21.2

The Surface constraint can animate one object moving across the surface of another.

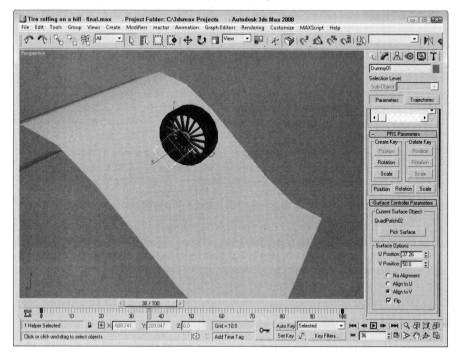

Path constraint

The Path constraint lets you select a spline path for the object to follow. The object is locked to the path and follows it even if the spline is changed. This is one of the most useful constraints because you can control the exact motion of an object using a spline. With Max's spline features, you can control very precisely the motions of objects that are constrained with the Path constraint. A good example of this constraint is an animated train following a track. Using a spline to create the train tracks, you can easily animate the train using the Path constraint.

When you choose the Animation ➪ Constraints ➪ Path Constraint menu command, you can select a single path for the object to follow. This path is added to a list of paths in the Path Parameters rollout.

The Path Parameters rollout also includes Add and Delete Path buttons for adding and deleting paths to and from the list. If two paths are added to the list, then the object follows the position centered between these two paths. By adjusting the Weight value for each path, you can make the object favor a specific path.

The Path Options include a % Along Path value for defining the object's position along the path. This value ranges from 0 at one end to 100 at the other end. The Follow option causes the object to be aligned with the path as it moves, and the Bank option causes the object to rotate to simulate a banking motion.

The Bank Amount value sets the depth of the bank, and the Smoothness value determines how smooth the bank is. The Allow Upside Down option lets the object spin completely about the axis, and the Constant

Velocity option keeps the speed regular. The Loop option returns the object to its original position for the last frame of the animation setting up a looping animation sequence. The Relative option lets the object maintain its current position and does not move the object to the start of the path. From its original position, it follows the path from its relative position. At the bottom of the Path Parameters rollout, you can select the axis to use.

Tutorial: Creating a spaceship flight path

Another way to use splines is to create animation paths. As an example, we use a Line spline to create an animation path. You can use splines for animation paths in two ways. One way is to create a spline and have an object follow it using either the Path constraint or the Path Follow Space Warp. The first vertex of the spline marks the first frame of the animation. The other way is to animate an object and then edit the Trajectory path.

In this tutorial, we use a simple path and attach it to a spaceship model. Viewpoint Datalabs provided the spaceship model.

To attach an object to a spline path, follow these steps:

1. Open the Spaceship and asteroids.max file from the Chap 21 directory on the DVD.

    This file contains the spaceship model and several asteroid objects.

2. Select Create ➪ Shapes ➪ Line, and click and drag in the Top viewport to create an animation path that moves the spaceship through the asteroids. Right-click when the path is complete. Then select the Modify panel, click the Vertex button in the Selection rollout to enable Vertex subobject mode, and edit several vertices in the Front viewport.

3. With the spaceship selected, choose Animation ➪ Constraints ➪ Path Constraint. Then click the animation path to select it as the path to follow. Select the Follow option in the Path Parameters rollout, and choose the Y-Axis option.

4. Click the Play Animation button in the Time Controls to see the spaceship follow the path.

Figure 21.3 shows the spaceship as it moves between the asteroids.

Position constraint

You can use the Position constraint to tie the position of an object to the weighted position of several target objects. For example, you could animate a formation of fighter jets by animating one of the jets and using Position constraints on all adjacent jets.

The Position constraint menu option lets you select a single target object, enabling you to place the pivot points of the two objects on top of one another. To add another target object, click the Add Position Target button in the Position Constraint rollout in the Motion panel. This button enables you to select another target object in the viewports; the target name appears within the target list in the rollout.

If you select a target name in the target list, you can assign a weight to the target. The constrained object is positioned close to the object with the higher weighted value. The Weight value provides a way to center objects between several other objects. The Keep Initial Offset option lets the object stay in its current location, but centers it relative to this position.

Figure 21.4 shows a sled positioned between four tree objects using the Position constraint. Notice how the weight of the downhill tree object is weighted higher than the other targets, and the sled is close to it.

FIGURE 21.3

The spaceship object has been attached to a spline path that it follows.

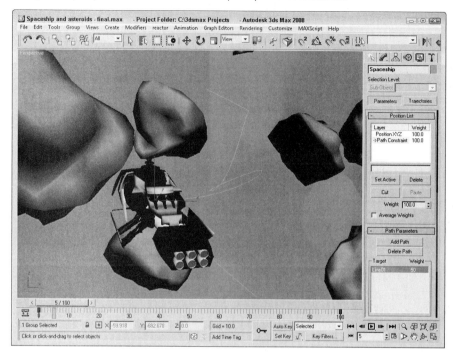

Link constraint

The Link constraint can transfer hierarchical links between objects. This constraint can cause a child's link to be switched during an animation. Anytime you animate a complex model with a dummy object, the Link constraint makes it possible to switch control from one dummy object to another during the animation sequence. This keeps the motions of the dummy objects simple.

The Link Params rollout includes Add Link and Delete Link buttons, a list of linked objects, and the Start Time field. To switch the link of an object, enter for the Start Time the frame where you want the link to switch, or drag the Time Slider and click the Add Link button. Then select the new parent object. The Delete key becomes active when you select a link in the list.

NOTE If you create a link using the Link constraint, the object is not recognized as a child in any hierarchies.

All links are kept in a list in the Link Params rollout. You can add links to this list with the Add Link button, create a link to the world with the Link to World button or delete links with the Delete Link button. The Start Time field specifies when the selected object takes control of the link. The object listed in the list is the parent object, so the Start Time setting determines when each parent object takes control.

FIGURE 21.4

You can use the Position constraint to control the position of an object in relation to its targets.

The Key Mode section lets you choose a No Key option. This option does not write any keyframes for the object. If you want to set keys, you can choose the Key Nodes options and set keys for the object itself (Child option) or for the entire hierarchy (Parent option). The Key Entire Hierarchy sets keys for the object and its parents (Child option) or for the object and its targets and their hierarchies (Parent option).

This constraint also includes the PRS Parameters and Key Info rollouts.

 **You cannot use Link constraints with Inverse Kinematics systems.**

Tutorial: Skating a figure eight

For an animated object to switch its link from one parent to another halfway through an animation, you need to use the Link constraint. Rotating an object about a static point is easy enough: Simply link the object to a dummy object, and rotate the dummy object. The figure-eight motion is more complex, but you can do it with the Link constraint.

To move an object in a figure eight, follow these steps:

1. Open the Figure skater skating a figure eight.max file from the Chap 21 directory on the DVD.

   This file includes a figure skater model imported from Poser and two dummy objects. The figure skater is linked to the first dummy object.

2. Click the Auto Key button (or press the N key), drag the Time Slider to frame 100, and rotate the first dummy object two full revolutions in the Top viewport.

3. Select the second dummy object, and rotate it two full revolutions in the opposite direction. Click the Auto Key button again to deactivate it.

4. With the figure skater selected, choose Animation ⇨ Constraints ⇨ Link Constraint. Then click the first dummy object (the top one in the Top viewport).

   The Link constraint is assigned to the figure skater.

5. In the Link Params rollout, click the Add Link button. With the first dummy object selected in the viewport, set the Start Time value to **0**. Then click the second dummy object, and set the Start Time to **25**. Finally, click the first dummy object again, and set the Start Time to **75**.

6. Click the Play Animation button (or press the / key) to see the animation play.

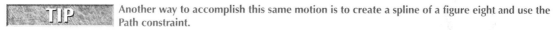

TIP　Another way to accomplish this same motion is to create a spline of a figure eight and use the Path constraint.

Figure 21.5 shows the skater as she makes her path around the two dummy objects.

FIGURE 21.5

With the Link constraint, the figure skater can move in a figure eight by rotating about two dummy objects.

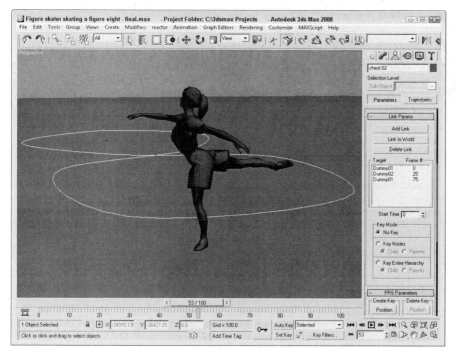

LookAt constraint

The LookAt constraint won't move an object, but it rotates the object so it is always orientated toward the target object. For example, you could use the LookAt constraint to animate a character's head that is watching a flying bumblebee. It is also very useful to apply to camera objects that follow a specific object throughout the animation.

After you select a target object, a single line extends from the object and points at the target object. This line, called the Viewline, is visible only within the viewports.

The LookAt Constraint rollout, like many of the other constraints, includes a list of targets. With the Add and Delete LookAt Target buttons, you can add and remove targets from the list. If several targets are on the list, the object is centered on a location between them. Using the Weight value, you can cause the various targets to have more of an influence over the orientation of the object. The Keep Initial Offset option prevents the object from reorienting itself when the constraint is applied. Any movement is relative to its original position.

You can set the Viewline length, which is the distance that the Viewline extends from the object. The Viewline Length Absolute option draws the Viewline from the object to its target, ignoring the length value.

The Set Orientation button lets you change the offset orientation of the object using the Select and Rotation button on the main toolbar. If you get lost, the Reset Orientation button returns the orientation to its original position. You can select which local axis points at the target object.

The Upnode is an object that defines the up direction. If the LookAt axis ever lines up with the Upnode axis, then the object flips upside-down. To prevent this, you can select which local axis is used as the LookAt axis and which axis points at the Upnode. The World is the default Upnode object, but you can select any object as the Upnode object by deselecting the World object and clicking the button to its right.

To control the Upnode, you can select the LookAt option or the Axis Alignment option, which enables the Align to Upnode Axis option. Using this option, you can specify which axis points toward the Upnode.

 The object using the LookAt constraint flips when the target point is positioned directly above or below the object's pivot point.

When you assign the LookAt constraint, the Create Key button for rotation changes to Roll. This is because the camera is locked to point at the assigned object and cannot rotate; rather, it can only roll about the axis.

You can use the LookAt constraint to let cameras follow objects as they move around a scene. It is the default transform controller for Target camera objects.

Orientation constraint

You can use the Orientation constraint to lock the rotation of an object to another object. You can move and scale the objects independently, but the constrained object rotates along with the target object. A good example of an animation that uses this type of constraint is a satellite that orbits the Earth. You can offset the satellite and still constrain it to the Earth's surface. Then, as the Earth moves, the satellite follows.

In the Orientation Constraint rollout, you can select several orientation targets and weight them in the same manner as with the Position constraint. The target with the greatest weight value has the most influence over the object's orientation. You can also constrain an object to the World object. The Keep Initial Offset option maintains the object's original orientation and rotates it relative to this original orientation. The Transform Rule setting determines whether the object rotates using the Local or World Coordinate Systems.

Understanding Controller Types

Controllers are used to set the keys for animation sequences. Every object and parameter that is animated has a controller assigned, and almost every controller has parameters that you can alter to change its functionality. Some controllers present these parameters as rollouts in the Motion panel, and others use a Properties dialog box.

Max has five basic controller types that work with only a single parameter or track and one specialized controller type that manages several tracks at once (the Transform controllers). The type depends on the type of values the controller works with. The types include the following:

- **Transform controllers** are a special controller type that applies to all transforms (position, rotation, and scale) at the same time, such as the Position, Rotation, Scale (PRS) controllers.
- **Position controllers** control the position coordinates for objects, consisting of X, Y, and Z values.
- **Rotation controllers** control the rotation values for objects along all three axes.
- **Scale controllers** control the scale values for objects as percentages for each axis.
- **Float controllers** are used for all parameters with a single numeric value, such as Wind Strength and Sphere Radius.
- **Point3 controllers** consist of color components for red, green, and blue, such as Diffuse and Background colors.

 **NOTE** Understanding the different controller types is important. When you copy and paste controller parameters between different tracks, both tracks must have the same controller type.

Float controllers work with parameters that use float numbers, such as a sphere's Radius or a plane object's Scale Multiplier value. Float values are numbers with a decimal value, such as 2.3 or 10.99. A Float controller is assigned to any parameter that is animated. After it is assigned, you can access the function curves and keys for this controller in the Track View and in the Track Bar.

Assigning Controllers

Any object or parameter that is animated is automatically assigned a controller. The controller that is assigned is the default controller. The Animation panel in the Preference Settings dialog box lists the default controllers and lets you change them. You can change this automatic default controller using the Track View window or the transformation tracks located in the Motion panel.

NEW FEATURE The ability to apply animation controllers to several objects at once is new to 3ds Max 2008.

Automatically assigned controllers

The default controllers are automatically assigned for an object's transformation tracks when the object is created. For example, if you create a simple sphere and then open the Motion panel (which has the icon that looks like a wheel), you can find the transformation tracks in the Assign Controller rollout. The default Position controller is Position XYZ, the default Rotation controller is Euler XYZ, and the default Scale controller is the Bézier Scale controller.

The default controller depends on the type of object. For example, the Barycentric Morph controller is automatically assigned when you create a morph compound object, and the Master Point controller is automatically assigned to any vertices or control points subobjects that are animated.

NOTE Because controllers are automatically assigned to animation tracks, they cannot be removed; they can only be changed to a different controller. There is no function to delete controllers.

Assigning controllers with the Animation menu

The easiest way to assign a controller to an object is with the Animation menu. Located under the Animation menu are four controller submenus consisting of Transform, Position, Rotation, and Scale.

NOTE Although constraints are contained within a separate menu, they control the animating of keys just like controllers.

When a controller is assigned to an object using the Animation menu, the existing controller is not removed, but the new controller is added as part of a list along with the other controllers. You can see all these controllers in the Motion panel.

For example, Figure 21.6 shows the Motion panel for a sphere object that has the default Position XYZ controller assigned to the Position track. If you choose Animation ⇨ Position Controllers ⇨ Noise, then the Position List controller is added to the Position track, of which Position XYZ and Noise are two available controllers. This lets you animate multiple motions such as the shimmy of a car with a bad carburetor as it moves down the road.

FIGURE 21.6

The Motion panel displays all transform controllers applied to an object.

The List controller allows you to set Weights for each of its controllers. Using the Position List rollout, you can set the active controller and delete controllers from the list. You can also Cut and Paste controllers to other tracks.

Assigning controllers in the Motion panel

The top of the Motion panel includes two buttons: Parameters and Trajectories. Clicking the Parameters button makes the Assign Controller rollout available.

 To change a transformation track's controller, select the track and click the Assign Controller button positioned directly above the list. An Assign Controller dialog box opens that is specific to the track you selected.

CROSS-REF For more about the Trajectories button, see Chapter 20, "Understanding Animation and Keyframe Basics."

For example, Figure 21.7 shows the Assign Position Controller dialog box for selecting a controller for the Position track. The arrow mark (>) shows the current selected controller. At the bottom of the dialog box, the default controller type is listed. Select a new controller from the list, and click OK. This new controller now is listed in the track, and the controller's rollouts appear beneath the Assign Controller rollout.

FIGURE 21.7

The Assign Position Controller dialog box lets you select a controller to assign.

 NOTE Transformation controllers can be applied in the Motion panel, but the Track View can be used to apply controllers to all parameters including transforms.

Assigning controllers in the Track View

 You can also use the Track View to assign controllers. To do this, locate and select the track to apply a controller to, and then click the Assign Controller button on the Controllers toolbar, choose the Controller ⇨ Assign (keyboard shortcut, C) menu command, or right-click on the track and select Assign Controller from the pop-up menu. An Assign Controller dialog box opens in which you can select the controller to use.

 **CROSS-REF**   Chapter 34, "Working with Function Curves in the Track View," covers the details of the Track View.

You can also use the Controller toolbar to copy and paste controllers between tracks, but you can paste controllers only to similar types of tracks. When you paste controllers, the Paste dialog box lets you choose to paste the controller as a copy or as an instance. Changing an instanced controller's parameters changes the parameters for all instances. The Paste dialog box also includes an option to replace all instances. This option replaces all instances of the controller, whether or not they are selected.

Setting Default Controllers

When you assign controllers using the Track View, the Assign Controller dialog box includes the option Make Default. With this option, the selected controller becomes the default for the selected track.

You can also set the global default controller for each type of track by choosing Customize ➪ Preferences, selecting the Animation panel, and then clicking the Set Defaults button. The Set Controller Defaults dialog box opens, in which you can set the default parameter settings, such as the In and Out curves for the controller. To set the default controller, select a controller from the list and click the Set Defaults button to open a controller-specific dialog box where you can adjust the controller parameters. The Animation panel also includes a button to revert to the original settings.

 **NOTE**   Changing a default controller does not change any currently assigned controllers.

Examining the Various Controllers

Now that you've learned how to assign controllers, let's look at the available controllers. Max includes a vast assortment of controllers, and you can add more controllers as plug-ins.

Earlier in the chapter, I mentioned six specific controller types. These types define the type of data that the controller works with. This section covers the various controllers according to the types of tracks with which they work.

 **NOTE**   Looking at the function curves for a controller provides a good idea of how you can control it, so many of the figures that follow show the various function curves for the different controllers.

Each of these controllers has a unique icon to represent it in the Track View. This makes them easy to identify.

Transform controllers

Multi-track transform controllers work with the Position, Rotation, and Scale tracks all at the same time. You access them by selecting the Transform track in the Motion panel and then clicking the Assign Controller button, or by choosing the Animation ➪ Transform Controllers menu command.

 NOTE   Each of the available constraints is listed again in the appropriate controller submenu.

Position/Rotation/Scale Transform controller

The Position/Rotation/Scale Transform controller is the default controller for all transforms. This controller includes a Bézier controller for the Position and Scale tracks and a Euler XYZ controller for the Rotation track.

The PRS Parameters rollout, shown in Figure 21.8, lets you create and delete keys for Position, Rotation, and Scale transforms. The Position, Rotation, and Scale buttons control the fields that appear in the Key Info rollouts positioned below the PRS Parameters rollout.

FIGURE 21.8

The PRS Parameters rollout is the default transform controller.

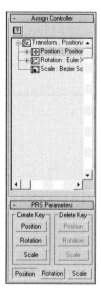

Script controller

The Script controller is similar to the Expression controller, except that it can work with the MAXScript lines of code for controlling the scene. Right-clicking a track with the Script controller assigned and selecting Properties opens the Script Controller dialog box. Script controllers are available for all transform tracks including Transform, Position, Rotation, and Scale. The flexibility of the Script controller is quite robust. The Script controller is covered in more detail at the end of this chapter, as is the Expression controller.

CROSS-REF For more information on MAXScript, see Chapter 49, "Automating with MAXScript."

XRef controller

If you have a defined motion used by an object in another file that you want to access, you can use the XRef controller. This controller can only be assigned to the Transform track. When this controller is assigned, a file dialog box opens where you can select the XRef file; then in the Merge Object dialog box, you can select a specific object that has the controller and motion you want to use.

In the Parameters rollout for the XRef controller is a button to open the XRef Object dialog box with the XRef Record highlighted. The Parameters rollout also lists the XRef file, object, and status.

CROSS-REF XRefs are covered in detail in Chapter 3, "Working with Files, Importing, and Exporting."

Position track controllers

Position track controller types include some of the common default controllers and can be assigned to the Position track. They typically work with three unique values representing the X-, Y-, and Z-axes. These controllers can be assigned from the Animation ➪ Position Controllers menu. Many of the controllers found in this menu are also found in the Rotation and Scale Controllers menu.

Audio controller

 The Audio controller can control an object's transform, color, or parameter value in response to the amplitude of a sound file. The Audio Controller dialog box, shown in Figure 21.9, includes Choose Sound and Remove Sound buttons for loading or removing sound files.

FIGURE 21.9

The Audio Controller dialog box lets you change values based on the amplitude of a sound file.

The Real Time Control drop-down list lets you specify a device to control the system. To control the sound input, you can specify a Sample Threshold and Oversampling rate. You can also set Base Point and Target Point values for each axis. The Channel options let you specify which channel to use: Left, Right, or Mix.

Bézier controller

 The Bézier controller is the default controller for many parameters. It enables you to interpolate between values using an adjustable Bézier spline. By dragging its tangent vertex handles, you can control the spline's curvature. Tangent handles produce a smooth transition when they lie on the same line, or you can create an angle between them for a sharp point. Figure 21.10 shows the Bézier controller assigned to a Position track.

The Bézier controller parameters are displayed in the Motion panel under two rollouts: Key Info (Basic) and Key Info (Advanced).

At the top of the Key Info (Basic) rollout are two arrows and a field that shows the key number. The arrows let you move between the Previous and Next keys. Each vertex shown in the function curve represents a key. The Time field displays the frame number where the key is located. The Time Lock button next to the Time field can be set to prevent the key from being dragged in Track View. The value fields show the values for the selected track; the number of fields changes depending on the type of track that is selected.

FIGURE 21.10

FIGURE 21.10

The Bézier controller produces smooth animation curves.

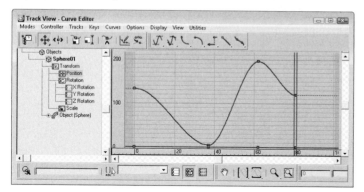

At the bottom of the Key Info (Basic) rollout are two flyout buttons for specifying the In and Out curves for the key. The arrows to the sides of these buttons move between the various In/Out curve types. The curve types include Smooth, Linear, Step, Slow, Fast, Custom, and Tangent Copy.

 CROSS-REF Chapter 34, "Working with Function Curves in the Track View," describes these various In/Out curve types.

The In and Out values in the Key Info (Advanced) rollout are enabled only when the Custom curve type is selected. These fields let you define the rate applied to each axis of the curve. The Lock button changes the two values by equal and opposite amounts. The Normalize Time button averages the positions of all keys. The Constant Velocity option interpolates the key between its neighboring keys to provide smoother motion.

Linear controller

 The Linear controller interpolates between two values to create a straight line by changing its value at a constant rate over time.

The Linear controller doesn't include any parameters and can be applied to time or values. Figure 21.11 shows the curves from the previous example after the Linear controller is assigned — all curves have been replaced with straight lines.

Motion Clip Slave controller

The Motion Clip Slave controller lets the object's transform be controlled by a linked motion clip that is loaded and defined in the Motion Mixer.

 **CROSS-REF** The Motion Mixer and using Motion Clips are covered in Chapter 35, "Using Animation Layers and the Motion Mixer."

Noise controller

The Noise controller applies random variations in a track's values. In the Noise Controller dialog box, shown in Figure 21.12, the Seed value determines the randomness of the noise and the Frequency value determines how jagged the noise is. You also can set the Strength along each axis: The > (greater than) 0 option for each axis makes the noise values remain positive.

FIGURE 21.11

The Linear controller uses straight lines.

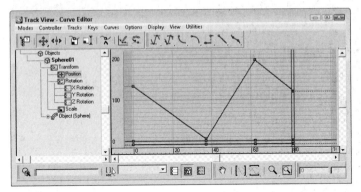

FIGURE 21.12

The Noise controller properties let you set the noise strength for each axis.

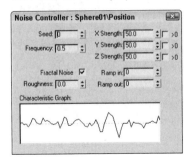

You also have an option to enable Fractal Noise with a Roughness setting.

The Ramp in and Ramp out values determine the length of time before or until the noise can reach full value. The Characteristic Graph gives a visual look at the noise over the range. Figure 21.13 shows the Noise controller assigned to the Position track. If you need to change any Noise properties, right-click the Noise track and select Properties from the pop-up menu.

Motion Capture controller

 The Motion Capture controller allows you to control an object's transforms using an external device such as a mouse, keyboard, joystick, or MIDI device. This controller works with the Motion Capture utility to capture motion data.

After you assign the Motion Capture controller to a track, right-click the track and select Properties from the pop-up menu to open the Motion Capture panel, shown in Figure 21.14. This dialog box lets you select the devices to use to control the motion of the track values. Options include Keyboard, Mouse, Joystick, and MIDI devices.

FIGURE 21.13

The Noise controller lets you randomly alter track values.

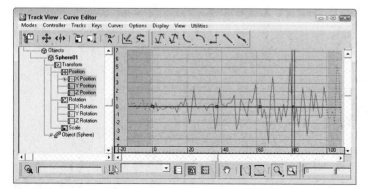

FIGURE 21.14

The Motion Capture controller lets you control track values using external devices.

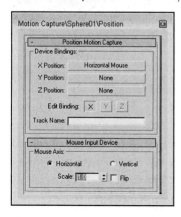

For the Keyboard control, the Keyboard Input Device rollout appears, as shown in Figure 21.15. The Assign button lets you select a keyboard key to track. The other settings control the Envelope Graph, which defines how quickly key presses are tracked.

The Motion Capture dialog box defines only which device controls which values. The actual capturing of data is accomplished using the Motion Capture utility. Selecting the Motion Capture utility in the Utility panel displays the Motion Capture rollout. This rollout includes buttons to Start, Stop, and Test the data-capturing process.

Before you can use the Start, Stop, and Test buttons, you need to select the tracks to capture from the Tracks list. The Record Range section lets you set the Preroll, In, and Out values, which are the frame numbers to include. You can also set the number of Samples Per Frame. The Reduce Keys option removes any unnecessary keys, if enabled.

FIGURE 21.15

The Keyboard Input Device rollout lets you select which key press is captured.

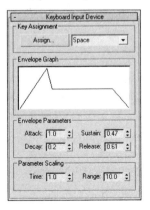

Tutorial: Drawing with a pencil with the Motion Capture controller

Some motions, such as drawing with a pencil, are natural motions for our hands, but they become very difficult when you're trying to animate using keyframes. This tutorial uses the Motion Capture controller and utility to animate the natural motion of drawing with a pencil.

To animate a pencil drawing on paper, follow these steps:

1. Open the Drawing with a pencil.max file from the Chap 21 directory on the DVD.

   This file has a pencil object positioned on a piece of paper.

2. Select the pencil object, open the Motion panel, and select the Position track for the pencil object. Then click the Assign Controller button, and double-click the Position Motion Capture selection.

   The Motion Capture dialog box opens.

3. Click the X Position button, and double-click the Mouse Input Device selection. Then click the Y Position button, and double-click the Mouse Input Device selection again. In the Mouse Input Device rollout, select the Vertical option. This sets the X Position to the Horizontal Mouse movement and the Y Position to the Vertical Mouse movement. Close the Motion Capture dialog box.

4. Open the Utilities panel, and click the Motion Capture button. In the Motion Capture rollout, select the Position track, and get the mouse ready to move. Then click the Start button in the Record Controls section, and move the mouse as if you were drawing with the mouse. The pencil object moves in the viewport along with your mouse movements.

   The Motion Capture utility creates a key for each frame. It quits capturing the motion when it reaches frame 100.

5. Click the Play Animation button (or press the / key) to see the results.

Figure 21.16 shows the scene after the Motion Capture controller has computed all the frames.

FIGURE 21.16

The Motion Capture controller and utility let you animate with a mouse, keyboard, joystick, or MIDI device.

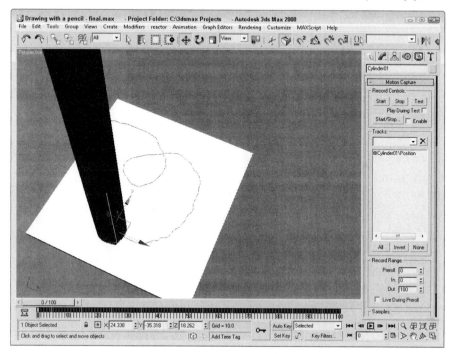

Quaternion (TCB) controller

The Quaternion (TCB) controller produces curved animation paths similar to the Bézier controller, but it uses the values for Tension, Continuity, and Bias to define their curvature. The benefit of this controller is that it enables objects to be rotated without having the problem of Gimbal lock, which can happen when the Euler XYZ controller is used. Gimbal lock can occur when two of the rotation axes become aligned, causing the object to lose one of its degrees of freedom.

The parameters for this controller are displayed in a single Key Info rollout. Like the Bézier controller rollouts, the Quarternion (TCB) controller rollout includes arrows and Key, Time, and Value fields. It also includes a graph of the TCB values; the red plus sign represents the current key's position, while the rest of the graph shows the regular increments of time as black plus signs. Changing the Tension, Continuity, and Bias values in the fields below the graph changes its shape. Right-clicking the track and selecting Properties from the pop-up menu opens the TCB graph dialog box, shown in Figure 21.17.

The Tension value controls the amount of curvature: High Tension values produce a straight line leading into and away from the key, and low Tension values produce a round curve. The Continuity value controls how continuous, or smooth, the curve is around the key: The default value of 25 produces the smoothest curves, whereas high and low Continuity values produce sharp peaks from the top or bottom. The Bias value controls how the curve comes into and leaves the key point, with high Bias values causing a bump to the right of the key and low Bias values causing a bump to the left.

FIGURE 21.17

This dialog box shows and lets you control a curve defined by the Tension, Continuity, and Bias values.

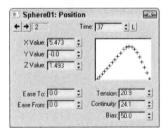

The Ease To and Ease From values control how quickly the key is approached or left.

 NOTE Enabling the trajectory path by clicking the Trajectory button in the Motion panel lets you see the changes to the path as they are made in the Key Info rollout.

Figure 21.18 shows three TCB curves assigned to the Position track of an object.

FIGURE 21.18

The TCB controller offers a different way to work with curves.

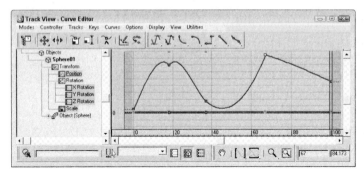

Reaction controller

The Reaction controller changes its values as a reaction to another controller. This controller is different from the Attachment controller in that the motions don't need to be in the same direction. For example, you can have one object rise as another object moves to the side.

CROSS-REF Don't confuse the Reaction controller with the reactor plug-in, which computes motion based on physical dynamics. The reactor plug-in is covered in Chapter 38, "Simulating Physics-Based Motion with reactor."

After the Reaction controller is assigned to a track, you can define the reactions using the Reaction Manager dialog box, shown in Figure 21.19. Selecting and right-clicking the track with this controller assigned and selecting Properties from the pop-up menu opens this dialog box. You can also open the Reaction Manager dialog box using the Animation ⇨ Reaction Manager menu.

FIGURE 21.19

The Reaction Manager dialog box lets you set the parameters of a reaction.

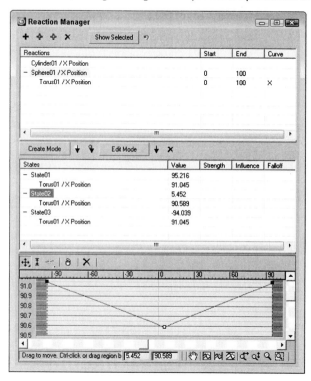

The Reaction Manager is made up of two lists and a graph of function curves. The top list holds all the object values that are involved in reactions. These are listed in a hierarchy with the master object listed above the slave object. A single master object can control several slave parameters.

The buttons above the Reactions list let you add new masters, slaves, and selected objects to the list. The cursor changes after you click any of these buttons, allowing you to click an object in the viewport and select a value from a pop-up menu.

For the slave objects selected in the Reactions list, you can set states using the buttons above the States list. To set a state, click the Create Mode button, drag the Time Slider to appropriate frame, and change the slave object's value. Then click the Add State button to create the target object state. Several unique states can be defined for each slave object.

State values can be changed by accessing the Edit Mode button or by editing the curves displayed at the bottom of the Reaction Manager dialog box.

Tutorial: Rotating gears with the Reaction controller

Many mechanical devices use gears, and animating these gears can be tricky because every adjacent gear rotates in the opposite direction. Animating by linking the gears together causes one gear to rotate around the other one. You can achieve this motion by animating the rotation of every gear individually, or you can use the Reaction controller to make the gears work like they are supposed to — which is what we do in this tutorial.

To rotate gears using the Reaction controller, follow these steps:

1. Open the Reaction rotating gears.max file from the Chap 21 directory on the DVD.

    This file contains some gears created using the Ringwave primitive. The lower gear is animated rotating about its center.

2. Select the upper gear, open the Motion panel, and click the Rotation track. Then click the Assign Controller button located in the Assign Controller rollout, and select Rotation Reaction from the dialog box that appears.

    The Reaction Manager dialog box opens.

3. In the Reactions list of the Reaction Manager, select the Unassigned item, right-click, and choose Replace Master from the pop-up menu to enter pick mode. Then click the lower gear object in the viewport, and choose Transform ⇨ Rotation from the pop-up menu that appears.

    This adds both gears to the Reaction Manager with Gear2/Rotation being the master and Gear1/Rotation being the slave.

4. Drag the Time Slider to frame 100 (or press the End key), select the upper gear, choose the Select and Rotation tool, and click the Create Mode button in the Reaction Manager. Rotate the upper gear about its Z-axis 180 degrees counterclockwise. Then click the Create State button to create a new state. Then click the Create Mode button again to disable it.

    This creates another reaction called State02 in the list.

5. Click the Play Animation button (or press the / key) to see the gears move together.

Figure 21.20 shows the two gears and the Reaction Manager dialog box. The second gear rotates in the opposite direction of the first gear.

Spring controller

 The Spring controller is similar in many ways to the Flex modifier in that it adds secondary motion associated with the wiggle of a spring after a force has been applied and then removed. When the Spring controller is applied, a panel with two rollouts appears. These rollouts, shown in Figure 21.21, let you control the physical properties of the spring and the forces that influence it.

FIGURE 21.20

The Reaction controller animates these two opposite rotating gears.

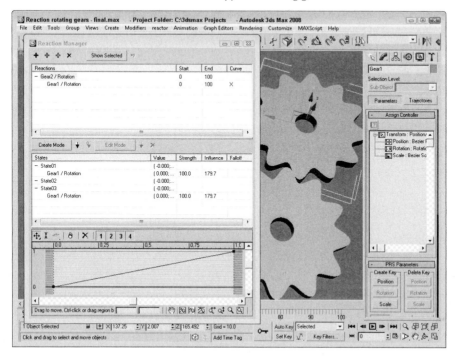

In the Spring Dynamics rollout, you can change the Mass and Drag values. Higher mass values result in greater secondary motion as the object is moved, and the Drag value controls how quickly the bouncing motion stops. You can add multiple springs, each with its own Tension and Damping values to be applied Relative or Absolute.

The Forces, Limits, and Precision rollout lets you add forces that affect the spring motion. The Add button lets you identify these forces, which are typically Space Warps, and you can limit the effect to specific axes.

Tutorial: Wagging a tail with the Spring controller

One of the best uses of the Spring controller is to gain the secondary motion associated with an existing motion. For example, if a character moves, then an appendage such as a tail can easily follow if you apply a Spring controller to it.

FIGURE 21.21

The Spring controller rollouts can add additional springs and forces.

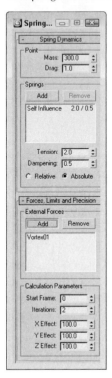

To wag a row of spheres using the Spring controller, follow these steps:

1. Open the Dog wagging tail.max file from the Chap 21 directory on the DVD.

   This file contains a linked row of spheres with the head sphere animated rotating back and forth.

2. Select the smallest sphere, and choose the Animation ➪ Position Controllers ➪ Spring menu command. This moves the sphere to its parent. Choose the Select and Move button (or press the W key), and return the sphere to its original position.

3. Repeat Step 2 for the remaining spheres, moving from smallest to largest.

4. Click the Play Animation button (or press the / key) to see the resulting motion.

Figure 21.22 shows a frame of the final motion. Notice that the spheres aren't lined up exactly. The smallest sphere is moving the greatest distance because all the springs are adding their effect.

Position XYZ controller

 The Position XYZ controller splits position transforms into three separate tracks, one for each axis. Each axis has a Bézier controller applied to it, but each component track can be assigned a different controller. The Position XYZ Parameters rollout lets you switch between the component axes.

The Rotation tracks use a variety of controllers, many of them common to the Position track. This section lists the controllers that can be used only with the Rotation track.

FIGURE 21.22

The Spring controller adds secondary motion to the existing motion of the largest sphere.

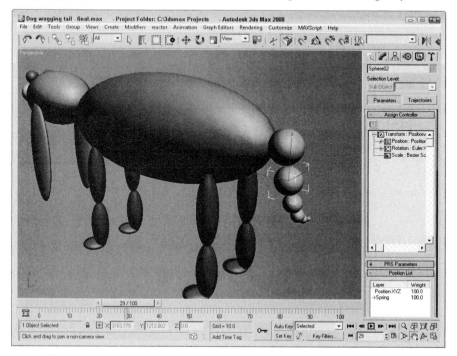

Rotation and Scale track controllers

The Rotation and Scale track controller types include some of the common default controllers and can be assigned to the Rotation and Scale tracks. They typically work with three unique values representing the X-, Y-, and Z-axes. These controllers can be assigned from the Animation ➪ Rotation (Scale) Controllers menu. Many of the controllers found in this menu are also found in the Position Controllers menu. Only the controllers unique to the Rotation and Scale tracks are covered here.

Euler XYZ Rotation controller

 The Euler XYZ Rotation controller lets you control the rotation angle along the X-, Y-, and Z-axes based on a single float value for each frame. Euler rotation is different from Max's default rotation method (which is quaternion rotation and not as smooth).

The main difference is that Euler rotation gives you access to the function curves. Using these curves, you can smoothly define the rotation motion of the object.

NOTE Euler XYZ Rotation values are in radians instead of degrees. If using these as part of an expression, be sure to use radians and not degrees. Radians are much smaller values than degrees. A full revolution is 360 degrees or 2 times Pi radians, so one degree equals about 0.0174 radians.

The Euler Parameters rollout lets you choose the Axis Order, which is the order in which the axes are calculated. You can also choose which axis to work with.

CAUTION The Euler XYZ controller is susceptible to Gimbal lock, which occurs when two of the three axes align to each other causing the object to lose a degree of freedom. This can be minimized by making the axis that rotates the least, the middle axis. You also can use the Euler Filter utility in the Track View to avoid Gimbal lock or you can use the Quaternion controller instead.

Smooth Rotation controller

 The Smooth Rotation controller automatically produces a smooth rotation. This controller doesn't add any new keys; it simply changes the timing of the existing keys to produce a smooth rotation. It does not have any parameters.

Scale XYZ controller

Max has one controller that you can use only in Scale tracks. The Scale XYZ controller breaks scale transforms into three separate tracks, one for each axis. This feature enables you to precisely control the scaling of an object along separate axes. It is a better alternative to using Select and Non-Uniform Scale from the main toolbar because it is independent of the object geometry.

The Scale XYZ Parameters rollout lets you select which axis to work with. This controller works the same way as the other position and rotation XYZ controllers.

Parameter controllers

Other controllers are used to affect the animated changes of parameters whether they are float, point3, or other parameter types. Many of these controllers combine several controllers into one, such as the List and Block controllers. Others include separate interfaces, such as the Waveform controller for defining the controller's functions.

Most of these special-purpose controllers can be assigned only by using the Track View window. The Motion panel contains only the tracks for transformations.

Boolean controller

 The Boolean controller, like the On/Off controller, can hold one of two states: 0 for off and 1 for on. But, unlike the On/Off controller, the Boolean controller changes only when a different state is encountered.

Limit controller

 The Limit controller sets limits for the motion or parameters of the selected controller. It is applied on top of the existing controller and opens the Limit Controller dialog box, shown in Figure 21.23, when applied.

FIGURE 21.23

The Limit controller dialog box lets you set upper and lower limits for the current controller value.

The upper limit is the maximum value to which the controller can be set, and the lower limit is the minimum value that the controller uses. Controller values may exceed the upper and lower limit values, but the object's motion stops at the limit values when the Limit controller is enabled. The Smoothing Buffer value provides a range that gradually alters the value as it approaches the limit value.

After a Limit controller is applied to an object, you can quickly change its upper and lower limit values by right-clicking the object in the Track View and accessing the Limit Controller option in the quadmenu.

 You can disable all limits at once using the Animation ➪ Toggle Limits menu command.

List controller

 You can use the List controller to apply several controllers at once. This feature enables you to produce smaller, subtler deviations, such as adding some noise to a normal Path controller.

When the List controller is applied, the default track appears as a subtrack along with another subtrack labeled Available. By selecting the Available subtrack and clicking the Assign Controller button, you can assign additional controllers to the current track.

All subtrack controllers are included in the List rollout of the Motion panel. You also can access this list by right-clicking the track and selecting Properties from the pop-up menu. The order of the list is important because it defines which controllers are computed first.

The Set Active button lets you specify which controller you can interactively control in the viewport; the active controller is marked with an arrow, which is displayed to the left of the name. You also can cut and paste controllers from and to the list. Because you can use the same controller type multiple times, you can distinguish each one by entering a name in the Name field.

On/Off controller

 The On/Off controller works on tracks that hold a binary value, such as the Visibility track; you can use it to turn the track on and off or to enable and disable options. In the Track View, each On section is displayed in blue, with keys alternating between on and off. No parameters exist for this controller. Figure 21.24 shows a Visibility track that has been added to a sphere object. This track was added using the Tracks ➪ Visibility Track ➪ Add menu command. You can add keys with the Add Keys button. Each new key toggles the track on and off.

 You can also add a Visibility track by changing the Visibility value in the Object Properties dialog box.

FIGURE 21.24

The On/Off controller lets you make objects appear and disappear.

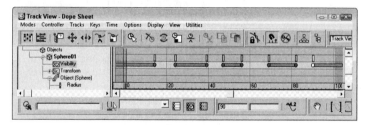

Waveform controller

The Waveform controller can produce regular periodic waveforms, such as a sinusoidal wave. Several different waveform types can make up a complete waveform. The Waveform Controller dialog box, shown in Figure 21.25, includes a list of all the combined waveforms. To add a waveform to this list, click the Add button.

When you select a waveform in the list, you can give it a name and edit its shape using the buttons and values. Preset waveform shapes include Sine, Square, Triangle, Sawtooth, and Half Sine. You can also invert and flip these shapes.

FIGURE 21.25

The Waveform Controller dialog box lets you produce sinusoidal motions.

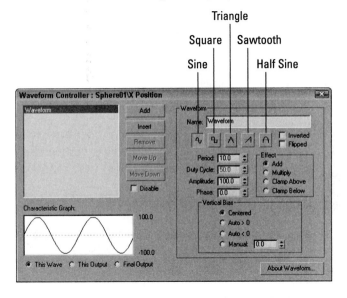

The Period value defines the number of frames required to complete one full pattern. The Amplitude value sets the height of the wave, and the Phase value determines its location at the start of the cycle. The Duty Cycle value is used only for the square wave to define how long it stays enabled.

You can use the Vertical Bias options to set the values range for the waveform. Options include Centered, which sets the center of the waveform at 0; Auto > 0, which causes all values to be positive; Auto < 0, which causes all values to be negative; and Manual, which lets you set a value for the center of the waveform.

The Effect option determines how different waveforms in the list are combined. They can be added, multiplied, clamped above, or clamped below. The Add option simply adds the waveform values together, and the Multiply option multiplies the separate values. The Clamp Above and Clamp Below options force the values of one curve to its maximum or minimum while not exceeding the values of the other curve. The Characteristic Graph shows the selected waveform, the output, or the final resulting curve. Figure 21.26 shows the Characteristic Graph for each Effect option when a sine wave and a square wave are combined.

FIGURE 21.26

Combining sine and square waves with the Add, Multiply, Clamp Above, and Clamp Below Effect options.

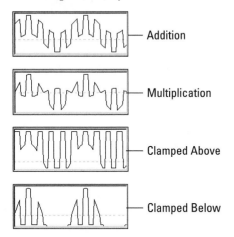

— Addition

— Multiplication

— Clamped Above

— Clamped Below

Color RGB controller

 You can use the Color RGB controller to animate colors. Color values are different from regular float values in that they include three values that represent the amounts of red, green, and blue (referred to as RGB values) present in the color. This data value type is known as Point3.

The Color RGB controller splits a track with color information into its component RGB tracks. You can use this controller to apply a different controller to each color component and also to animate any color swatch in Max.

Figure 21.27 shows the function curves for the Color RGB controller assigned to the Diffuse Color track under the Material #1 track, including subtracks for Red, Green, and Blue. The figure shows the Bézier controller applied to the Red track, the Noise controller that is assigned to the Green track, and the Waveform controller with a triangle wave applied to the Blue track.

FIGURE 21.27

The Color RGB controller lets you assign different controllers to each color component.

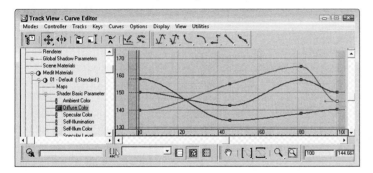

Cubic Morph controller

You can assign the Cubic Morph controller to a morph compound object. You can find the track for this object under the Objects track. A subtrack of the morph object is the Morph track, which holds the morph keys.

The Cubic Morph controller uses Tension, Continuity, and Bias values to control how targets blend with one another. You can access these TCB values in the Key Info dialog box by right-clicking any morph key or by right-clicking the Morph track and selecting Properties from the pop-up menu.

 **You can also access the TCB values by right-clicking the keys in the Track Bar.**

Barycentric Morph controller

The Barycentric Morph controller is automatically applied when a morph compound object is created. Keys are created for this controller based on the morph targets set in the Modify panel under the Current Targets rollout for the morph compound object. You can edit these keys using the Barycentric controller Key Info dialog box, which you can open by right-clicking a morph key in the Track View or in the Track Bar.

The main difference between the Cubic Morph controller and the Barycentric Morph controller is that the latter can have weights applied to the various morph keys.

The Barycentric Morph controller Key Info dialog box includes a list of morph targets. If a target is selected, its Percentage value sets the influence of the target. The Time value is the frame where this key is located. The TCB values and displayed curve control the Tension, Continuity, and Bias parameters for this controller. The Constrain to 100% option causes all weights to equal 100 percent; changing one value changes the other values proportionally if this option is selected.

Block controller

 The Block controller combines several tracks into one block so you can handle them all together. This controller is located in the Global Tracks track. If a track is added to a Block controller, a Slave controller is placed in the track's original location.

To add a Block controller, select the Available track under the Block Control track under the Global Tracks track, and click the Assign Controller button. From the Assign Constant Controller dialog box that opens, select Master Block and click OK. Right-click the Master Block track and select Properties to open the Master Block Parameters dialog box, shown in Figure 21.28.

FIGURE 21.28

The Master Block Parameters dialog box lists all the tracks applied to a Block controller.

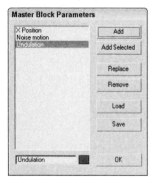

In the Master Block Parameters dialog box, you can add a track to the Block controller with the Add button. All tracks added are displayed in the list on the left. You can give each track a name by using the Name field. You can also use the Add Selected button to add any selected tracks. The Replace button lets you select a new controller to replace the currently selected track. The Load and Save buttons enable you to load or save blocks as separate files.

The Add button opens the Track View Pick dialog box, shown in Figure 21.29. This dialog box displays all valid tracks in a darker color to make them easier to see, while graying out invalid tracks.

FIGURE 21.29

The Track View Pick dialog box lets you select the tracks you want to include in the Block controller.

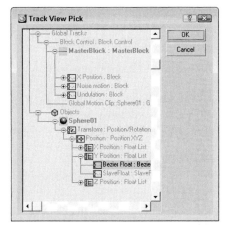

Select the tracks that you want to include, and click the OK button. The Block Parameters dialog box opens, shown in Figure 21.30, in which you can name the block, specify Start and End frames, and choose a color. Click OK when you've finished with this dialog box.

FIGURE 21.30

The Block Parameters dialog box lets you name a block.

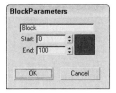

Back in the Master Block Parameters dialog box, click the Load button to open a file dialog box where you can load a saved block of animation parameters. The saved block files have the .BLK extension. After the parameters have loaded, the Attach Controls dialog box opens, as shown in Figure 21.31. This dialog box includes two panes. The Incoming Controls pane on the left lists all motions in the saved block. By clicking the Add button, you can add tracks from the current scene, to which you can copy the saved block motions.

FIGURE 21.31

The Attach Controls dialog box lets you attach saved tracks to the Block controller.

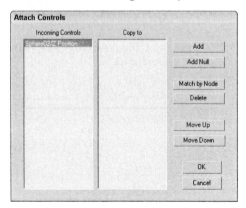

Because the saved motions in the Incoming Controls pane will match up with the Copy to entries in the right pane, the Add Null button adds a space in place of a specific track if you don't want a motion to be copied. The Match by Node button matches tracks by means of the Track View Pick dialog box.

IK controller

The IK controller works on a bones system for controlling the bone objects of an IK system. The IK controller includes many different rollouts for defining joint constraints and other parameters.

 Find out more about the IK controller in Chapter 40, "Understanding Rigging and Working with Bones."

Master Point controller

 The Master Point controller controls the transforms of any point or vertex subobject selections. The Master Point controller gets added as a track to an object whose subobjects are transformed. Subtracks under this track are listed for each subobject. The keys in the Master track are colored green.

Right-clicking a green master key opens the Master Track Key Info dialog box, shown in Figure 21.32. This dialog box shows the Key number with arrows for selecting the previous or next key, a Time field that displays the current frame number, and a list of all the vertices. Selecting a vertex from the list displays its parameters at the bottom of the dialog box.

Figure 21.33 shows the Master Point controller that was automatically assigned when a selection of vertex subobjects was moved with the Auto Key button enabled. A separate track is created for each vertex.

FIGURE 21.32

The Master Track Key Info dialog box lets you change the key values for each vertex.

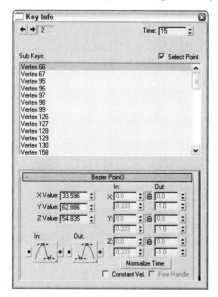

FIGURE 21.33

The Master Point controller defines tracks for each subobject element that is animated.

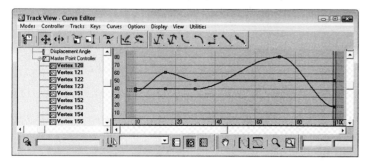

Summary

Using the Animation ⇨ Constraints menu, you can apply constraints to objects. This menu also lets you select a target object. You can use the various constraints to limit the motion of objects, which is helpful as you begin to animate. If you're an animator, you should thank your lucky stars for controllers. Controllers offer power flexibility for animating objects — and just think of all those keys that you don't have to set by hand.

This chapter covered the basics of using the Expression controller. Using mathematical formulas to control the animation of an object's transformation and parameters offers lots of power. You can also use the values of one object to control another object.

In this chapter, you accomplished the following:

- Constrained an object to the surface of another object using the Attachment and Surface constraints
- Forced an object to travel along a path with the Path constraint
- Controlled the position and orientation of objects with weighted Position and Orientation constraints
- Shifted between two different controlling objects using the Link constraint
- Followed objects with the LookAt constraint
- Learned about the various controller types
- Discovered how to assign controllers using the Motion panel and the Track View
- Set default controllers in the Preference Settings dialog box
- Examined the various controllers in several different categories
- Saw a few examples of using controllers

In the next chapter, you learn to final render a scene so you can have some output to hang on Mom's fridge.

Chapter 22

Learning to Render a Scene

fter hours of long, hard work, the next step — rendering — is where the "rubber hits the road" and you get to see what you've worked on so hard. After modeling, applying materials, positioning lights and cameras, and animating your scene, you're finally ready to render the final output. Rendering deals with outputting the objects that make up a scene at various levels of detail.

Max includes a Scanline Renderer that is optimized to speed up this process, and several settings exist that you can use to make this process even faster. Understanding the Render Scene dialog box and its functions can save you many headaches and computer cycles. However, other rendering options are available.

The need for all these different rendering engines comes about because of a trade-off between speed and quality. For example, the renderer used to display objects in the viewports is optimized for speed, but the renderer used to output final images leans toward quality. Each renderer includes many settings that you can use to speed the rendering process or improve the quality of the results.

IN THIS CHAPTER

Working with the ActiveShade window

Setting render parameters and preferences

Using the Rendered Frame Window and the RAM Player

Understanding render types

Creating an environment

Previewing with ActiveShade

The ActiveShade window gives a quick semi-rendered look at the current scene. You can open ActiveShade within a viewport by right-clicking the viewport title in the upper-left corner of each viewport and choosing Views ➪ ActiveShade from the pop-up menu. Figure 22.1 shows the ActiveShade view visible for the Perspective view.

CAUTION The ActiveShade window doesn't display a complete rendered image. Although it includes lighting effects and material maps, it does not include many other features such as Render Effects and Atmospheric effects.

FIGURE 22.1

The ActiveShade window can be opened within a viewport.

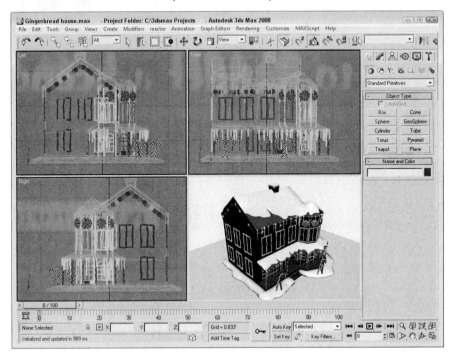

Only one ActiveShade viewport can be open at a time. If you try to open more than one window, a warning dialog box lets you know that opening it will close the previous window. Right-clicking the ActiveShade window opens a quadmenu of commands. The Render quadmenu in the upper right contains the common rendering menu options. The View quadmenu in the upper left contains the command to close the ActiveShade window.

> **CAUTION**   If the active viewport is maximized, then the ActiveShade view option is disabled.

In the lower-left quadmenu, the Act Only on Mouse Up option waits to update the rendered scene until the mouse is released. If disabled, the window updates immediately. Auto Initialization updates as soon as a new mapped material is applied, and the Auto Update option updates any time a non-mapped material is applied or when the lights are altered.

> **TIP**   You can drag materials from the Material Editor and drop them directly on the ActiveShade window.

The Draw Region option (keyboard shortcut, D) changes the cursor to look like a pen. Using this pen cursor, you can select a region in the ActiveShade window by dragging from corner to corner. Within a selected region, only that section is updated. The Initialize option (keyboard shortcut, P) reinitializes the window if the Auto Initialization option isn't enabled. The Update option is a manual update if the Auto Update option isn't selected. The Select Object option lets you pick an object in the ActiveShade window: The selected object is bounded by brackets, and any initialization updates the mapped material on the selected object only.

There is also a command to Toggle Toolbar. The ActiveShade window has access to the same toolbar that is found in the Rendered Frame Window. The buttons on this toolbar are covered in "Using the Rendered Frame Window," later in this chapter.

Render Parameters

Commands and settings for rendering an image are contained within the Render Scene dialog box. This dialog box includes several tabbed panels.

After you're comfortable with the scene file and you're ready to render a file, you need to open the Render Scene dialog box, shown in Figure 22.2, by means of the Rendering ➪ Render menu command (F10) or by clicking the Render Scene button on the main toolbar. This dialog box has several panels: Common, Renderer, Render Elements, Raytracer, and Advanced Lighting. The Common panel includes commands that are common for all renderers, but the Renderer panel includes specific settings for the selected renderer.

CROSS-REF The Common and Renderer panels for the Default Scanline Renderer are covered in this chapter. The Raytracer and Renderer panel for the mental ray renderer are covered in Chapter 46, "Raytracing and mental ray," the Render Elements panel is covered in Chapter 48, "Compositing with Render Elements and the Video Post Interface," and the Advanced Lighting panel is covered in Chapter 44, "Working with Advanced Lighting, Light Tracing, and Radiosity."

FIGURE 22.2

You use the Render Scene dialog box to render the final output.

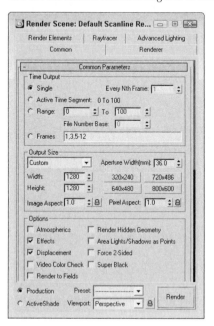

Initiating a render job

At the bottom of the Render Scene dialog box are several controls that are visible for all panels; these controls let you initiate a render job. The render modes are Production and ActiveShade. Each of these modes can use a different renderer with different render settings as defined using the Assign Renderer rollout.

> **NOTE**   If any objects in the rendered scene are missing mapping coordinates, then a dialog box appears as you try to the render the scene with options to Continue or Cancel. A similar dialog box appears for any missing external files or any missing XRefs with options to continue, cancel, or browse from the missing file.

The Preset option lets you save and load a saved preset of renderer settings. When saving or loading a preset, the Select Preset Categories dialog box, shown in Figure 22.3, opens (after you select a preset file in a file dialog box). In this dialog box, you can select which panels of settings to include in the preset. The panels listed will depend on the selected renderer. All presets are saved with the .RPS file extension.

FIGURE 22.3

The Select Preset Categories dialog box lets you choose which settings to include in the preset.

The Viewport drop-down list includes all the available viewports. When the Render Scene dialog box opens, the currently active viewport appears in the Viewport drop-down list. The one selected is the one that gets rendered when you click the Render button. The Render button starts the rendering process. You can click the Render button without changing any settings, and the default parameters are used.

> **TIP**   The little lock icon next to the Viewport indicates that the selected viewport is always rendered when the Render button is clicked, regardless of the active viewport.

When you click the Render button, the Rendering dialog box appears. This dialog box, shown in Figure 22.4, displays all the settings for the current render job and tracks its progress. The Rendering dialog box also includes Pause and Cancel buttons for halting the rendering process. If the rendering is stopped, the Rendering dialog box disappears, but the Rendered Frame Window stays open.

> **CAUTION**   If you close the Rendered Frame Window, the render job still continues. To cancel the rendering, click the Pause or Cancel button, or press the Esc key on your keyboard.

> **TIP**   After you've set up the render settings for an image, you can re-render an image without opening the Render Scene dialog box by clicking the Quick Render button on the main toolbar, by using the Shift+Q keyboard shortcut or by selecting a render option from the Render Shortcuts toolbar. The F9 shortcut renders the last viewport again.

FIGURE 22.4

The Rendering dialog box displays the current render settings and progress of the render job.

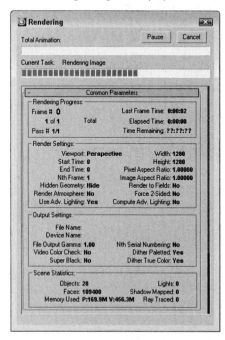

Common parameters

The Common Parameters rollout in the Render Scene dialog box includes the same controls regardless of the renderer being used.

Specifying range and size

The Time Output section defines which animation frames to include in the output. The Single option renders the current frame specified by the Time Slider. The Active Time Segment option renders the complete range of frames. The Range option lets you set a unique range of frames to render by entering the beginning and ending frame numbers. The last option is Frames, where you can enter individual frames and ranges using commas and hyphens. For example, entering "1, 6, 8-12" renders frames 1, 6, and 8 through 12. The Every Nth Frame value is active for the Active Time Segment and Range options. It renders every nth frame in the active segment. For example, entering 3 would cause every third frame to be rendered. This option is useful for sped-up animations. The File Number Base is the number to add to or subtract from the current frame number for the reference numbers attached to the end of each image file. For example, a File Number Base value of 10 for a Range value of 1–10 would label the files as image0011, image0012, and so on.

TIP Don't render long animation sequences using the .AVI, .MPEG, or .MOV formats. If the rendering has trouble, the entire file will be corrupt. Instead, choose to render the frames as individual images. These individual images can then be reassembled into a video format using Max's RAM Player, the Video Post interface or an external package like Adobe's Premiere.

The Output Size section defines the resolution of the rendered images or animation. The drop-down list includes a list of standard film and video resolutions, including various 35mm and 70mm options, Anamorphic, Panavision, IMAX, VistaVision, NTSC, PAL, and HDTV standards. A Custom option allows you to select your own resolution.

> **TIP** Setting up the aspect ratio of the final rendering at the start of the project is helpful. Once an aspect ratio is established, you can use the Safe Frames panel in the Viewport Configuration dialog box to display the borders of the render region in the viewport.

Aperture Width is a property of cameras that defines the relationship between the lens and the field of view. The resolutions listed in the Aperture Width drop-down list alter this value without changing the view by modifying the Lens value in the scene.

For each resolution, you can change the Width and Height values. Each resolution also has six preset buttons for setting these values.

> **TIP** You can set the resolutions of any of the preset buttons by right-clicking the button that you want to change. The Configure Preset dialog box opens, where you can set the button's Width, Height, and Pixel Aspect values.

The Image Aspect is the ratio of the image width to its height. You can also set the Pixel Aspect ratio to correct rendering on different devices. Both of these values have lock icons to their left that lock the aspect ratio for the set resolution. Locking the aspect ratio automatically changes the Width dimension whenever the Height value is changed and vice versa. The Aperture Width, Image Aspect, and Pixel Aspect values can be set only when Custom is selected in the drop-down list.

Render options

The Options section includes the following options:

- **Atmospherics:** Renders any atmospheric effects that are set up in the Environment dialog box.
- **Effects:** Enables any Render Effects that have been set up.
- **Displacement:** Enables any surface displacement caused by an applied displacement map.
- **Video Color Check:** Displays any colors that cannot be displayed in the HSV color space used by television in black.
- **Render to Fields:** Enables animations to be rendered as fields. Fields are used by video formats. Video animations include one field with every odd scan line and one field with every even scan line. These fields are composited when displayed.
- **Render Hidden Geometry:** Renders all objects in the scene, including hidden objects. Using this option, you can hide objects for quick viewport updates and include them in the final rendering.
- **Area Lights/Shadows as Points:** Rendering area lights and shadows can be time consuming, but point lights render much more quickly. By enabling this option, you can speed the rendering process.
- **Force 2-Sided:** Renders both sides of every face. This option essentially doubles the render time and should be used only if singular faces or the inside of an object are visible.
- **Super Black:** Enables Super Black, which is used for video compositing. Rendered images with black backgrounds have trouble in some video formats. The Super Black option prevents these problems.

The Advanced Lighting panel offers options to use Advanced Lighting or Computer Advanced Lighting when Required. Advanced lighting can take a long time to compute, so these two options give you the ability to turn advanced lighting on or off.

CROSS-REF Advanced lighting is covered in more detail in Chapter 44, "Working with Advanced Lighting, Light Tracing, and Radiosity."

Bitmap Proxies

The Bitmap Proxies section includes a Setup button to enable a feature that can downscale all maps for the current scene. Clicking the Setup button opens the Global Settings and Defaults for Bitmap Proxies dialog box, shown in Figure 22.5.

The Bitmap Proxies dialog box lets you replace all texture maps with proxy images.

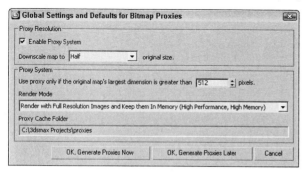

The Downscale Map option lets you select to downscale all maps to Half, Third, Quarter, or Eighth, or to their current size. This lets you create your scene with high-quality maps and quickly reduce their sizes as needed without having to open and scale each individual map. The Proxy System lets you select to use a proxy image if the current map is larger than a specified size in pixels.

This dialog box also lets you set the Render Mode to be optimized for performance or memory. The options include Render with Proxies, Render with Full Resolution and Keep them [image maps] In Memory, and Render with Full Resolution and Free up the Memory once Rendered.

Choosing a Render Output option

The Render Output section enables you to output the image or animations to a file, a device, or the Rendered Frame Window. To save the output to a file, click the Files button and select a location in the Render Output File dialog box. Supported formats include .AVI, .BMP, .DDS, Postscript (.EPS), JPEG, Kodak Cineon (.CIN), Open EXR, Radiance Image File (.HDRI), QuickTime (.MOV), .PNG, .RLA, .RPF, SGI's Format (.RGB), Targa (.TGA), and .TIF. The Device button can output to a device such as a video recorder. If the Rendered Frame Window option is selected, then both the Files and Devices buttons are disabled. (The Rendered Frame Window is discussed later in this chapter.)

TIP Each of these output formats has its advantages. For example, Targa files are good for compositing because they have an alpha channel. TIFF and EPS files are good for files to be printed. JPEG, PNG, and GIF files are used for Web images. DDS images are used in many game engines.

You also have an option to Put Image File List in Output Path, which creates a list of image files in the same location as the rendered file. You also have the choice of choosing Max's IFL standard or the Autodesk ME Image Sequence File (IMSQ). The Create Now button creates an image list instantly.

CROSS-REF   More on using Image File Lists is covered in Chapter 20, "Understanding Animation and Keyframe Basics."

The Net Render option enables network rendering. The Skip Existing Images option doesn't replace any images with the same filename, a feature that you can use to continue a rendering job that has been canceled.

CROSS-REF   For more information on network rendering, see Chapter 47, "Batch and Network Rendering."

E-mail notifications

The process of rendering an animation (or even a single frame) can be brief or it can take several days, depending on the complexity of the scene. For complex scenes that will take a while to render, you can configure Max to send you an e-mail message when your rendering is complete or if it fails. These options are in the Email Notifications rollout, shown in Figure 22.6.

In addition to the options, you can enter whom the e-mail is from, whom it is to, and an SMTP Server.

FIGURE 22.6

The Email Notifications rollout includes options for sending an e-mail message to report on rendering status.

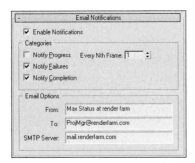

Adding pre-render and post-render scripts

The Scripts rollout includes File buttons for adding pre-render and post-render scripts. The scripts must be .ms scripts and are executed before and after the rendering of each file. These scripts can be used to compile information about the render or to do some post-processing work. Above each script file button is an Execute Now button that can be used to check the script before rendering.

Assigning renderers

Max performs rendering operations in several different places: The Render Scene dialog box renders to the Render Frame Window or to files; the sample slots in the Material Editor also are rendered; and the ActiveShade windows show another level of rendering.

The plug-in nature of Max enables you to select the renderer to use to output images. To change the default renderer, look in the Assign Renderers rollout in the Common panel of the Render Scene dialog box (F10). You can select different renderers for the Production, Material Editor, and ActiveShade modes. For each, you can select from the Default Scanline Renderer, the mental ray Renderer, and the VUE File Renderer.

CROSS-REF   The VUE File Renderer is covered later in this chapter, and the mental ray rendering engine is covered in Chapter 46, "Raytracing and mental ray."

The lock next to the Material Editor option indicates that the same renderer is used for both Production and Material Editor.

Scanline A-Buffer renderer

The Default Scanline Renderer rollout, found in the Renderer panel and shown in Figure 22.7, is the default renderer rollout that appears in the Render Scene dialog box. If a different renderer is loaded, then a different rollout for that renderer is displayed in the Renderer panel.

FIGURE 22.7

The Default Scanline Renderer rollout includes settings unique to this renderer.

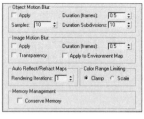

You can use the Options section at the top of the Default Scanline Renderer rollout to quickly disable various render options for quicker results. These options include Mapping, Shadows, Auto Reflect/Refract and Mirrors, and Force Wireframe. For the Force Wireframe option, you can define a Wire Thickness value in pixels. The Enabled SSE option uses Streaming SIMD (Single Instruction, Multiple Data) Extensions to speed up the rendering process by processing more data per instruction.

 Intel Pentium III and later processors include the SSE instructions and can benefit from enabling this option.

Anti-alias filters

Another way to speed up rendering is to disable the Anti-aliasing and Filter Maps features. Anti-aliasing smoothes jagged edges that appear where colors change. The Filter Maps option allows you to disable the computationally expensive process of filtering material maps. The Filter drop-down list lets you select image filters that are applied at the pixel level during rendering. Below the drop-down list is a description of the current filter. The Filter Size value applies only to the Soften filter. Available filters include the following:

- **Area:** Does an anti-aliasing sweep using the designated area specified by the Filter Size value.
- **Blackman:** Sharpens the image within a 25-pixel area; provides no edge enhancement.
- **Blend:** Somewhere between a sharp and a coarse Soften filter; includes Filter Size and Blend values.
- **Catmull-Rom:** Sharpens with a 25-pixel filter and includes edge enhancement.
- **Cook Variable:** Can produce sharp results for small Filter Size values and blurred images for larger values.
- **Cubic:** Based on cubic-spline curves; produces a blurring effect.

- **Mitchell-Netravali:** Includes Blur and Ringing parameters.
- **Plate Match/MAX R2:** Matches mapped objects against background plates as used in Max R2.
- **Quadratic:** Based on a quadratic spline; produces blurring within a 9-pixel area.
- **Sharp Quadratic:** Produces sharp effects from a 9-pixel area.
- **Soften:** Causes mild blurring and includes a Filter Size value.
- **Video:** Blurs the image using a 25-pixel filter optimized for NTSC and PAL video.

SuperSampling

Global SuperSampling is an additional anti-aliasing process that you can apply to materials. This process can improve image quality, but it can take a long time to render; you can disable it using the Disable all Samplers option. Supersampling can be enabled in the Material Editor for specific materials, but the SuperSampling rollout in the Material Editor also includes an option to Use Global Settings. The Global Settings are defined in the Default Scanline Renderer rollout.

Max includes anti-aliasing filters as part of the rendering process. You have several SuperSampling methods from which to choose.

SuperSampling is disabled if the Antialiasing option is disabled. Global Supersampling can be enabled using the Enable Global Supersampler option.

In a SuperSampling pass, the colors at different points around the center of a pixel are sampled. These samples are then used to compute the final color of each pixel. Max has four available SuperSampling methods: Max 2.5 Star, Hammersley, Adaptive Halton, and Adaptive Uniform.

 You can find more information on each of these sampling methods in Chapter 15, "Creating and Applying Standard Materials."

Motion Blur

The Default Scanline Renderer rollout also offers two different types of motion blur: Object Motion Blur and Image Motion Blur. You can enable either of these using the Apply options.

Object Motion Blur is set in the Properties dialog box for each object. The renderer completes this blur by rendering the object over several frames. The movement of the camera doesn't affect this type of blur. The Duration value determines how long the object is blurred between frames. The Samples value specifies how many Duration units are sampled. The Duration Subdivision value is the number of copies rendered within each Duration segment. All these values can have a maximum setting of 16. The smoothest blurs occur when the Duration and Samples values are equal.

Image Motion Blur is also set in the Properties dialog box for each object. This type of blur is affected by the movement of the camera and is applied after the image has been rendered. You achieve this blur by smearing the image in proportion to the movement of the various objects. The Duration value determines the time length of the blur between frames. The Apply to Environment Map option lets you apply the blurring effect to the background as well as the objects. The Work with Transparency option blurs transparent objects without affecting their transparent regions. Using this option adds time to the rendering process.

 You can add two additional blur effects to a scene: the Blur Render Effect, found in the Rendering Effects dialog box (covered in Chapter 45, "Using Atmospheric and Render Effects") and the Scene Motion Blur effect, available through the Video Post dialog box (covered in Chapter 48, "Compositing with Render Elements and the Video Post Interface").

Other options

The Auto Reflect/Refract Maps section lets you specify a Rendering Iterations value for reflection maps within the scene. The higher the value, the more objects are included in the reflection computations, and the longer the rendering time.

Color Range Limiting offers two methods for correcting over-brightness caused by applying filters. The Clamp method lowers any value above a relative ceiling of 1 to 1 and raises any values below 0 to 0. The Scale method scales all colors between the maximum and minimum values.

The Conserve Memory option optimizes the rendering process to use the least amount of memory possible. If you plan on using Max (or some other program) while it is rendering, you should enable this option.

Rendering Preferences

In addition to the settings available in the Render Scene dialog box, the Rendering panel in the Preference Settings dialog box includes many global rendering settings. The Preference Settings dialog box can be opened using the Customize ➡ Preferences menu command. Figure 22.8 shows this panel.

FIGURE 22.8

The Rendering panel in the Preference Settings dialog box lets you set global rendering settings.

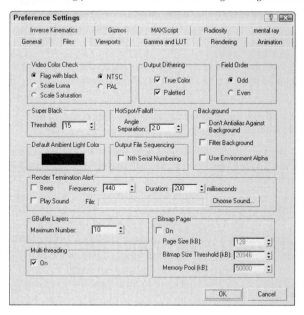

The Video Color Check options specify how unsafe video colors are flagged or corrected. The Flag with black option shows the unsafe colors, and the Scale Luma and Scale Saturation options correct them by scaling either the luminance or the saturation until they are in range. You can also choose to check NTSC or PAL formats.

CAUTION Be aware that the Scale options can discolor some objects.

Output Dithering options can enable or disable dithering of colors. The options include True Color for 24-bit images and Paletted for 8-bit images.

The Field Order options let you select which field is rendered first. Some video devices use even first, and others use odd first. Check your specific device to see which setting is correct.

The Super Black Threshold setting is the level below which black is displayed as Super Black.

The Angle Separation value sets the angle between the Hotspot and Falloff cones of a light. If the Hotspot angle equals the Falloff angle, then alias artifacts will appear.

The Don't Anti-alias Against Background option should be enabled if you plan on using a rendered object as part of a composite image. The Filter Background option includes the background image in the anti-aliasing calculations. The Use Environment Alpha option combines the background image's alpha channel with the scene object's alpha channel.

The Default Ambient Light Color is the darkest color for rendered shadows in the scene. Selecting a color other than black brightens the shadows.

You can set the Output File Sequencing option to list the frames in order if the Nth Serial Numbering option is enabled. If the Nth Serial Numbering option is disabled, the sequence uses the actual frame numbers.

In the Render Termination Alert section, you can elect to have a beep triggered when a rendering job is finished. The Frequency value changes the pitch of the sound, and the Duration value changes its length. You can also choose to load and play a different sound. The Choose Sound button opens a File dialog box where you can select the sound file to play.

The GBuffer Layers value is the maximum number of graphics buffers to allow during rendering. This value can range between 1 and 1000. The value you can use depends on the memory of your system.

The Multi-threading option enables the renderer to complete different rendering tasks as separate threads. Threads use the available processor cycles more efficiently by subdividing tasks. This option should be enabled, especially if you're rendering on a multiprocessor computer.

The Bitmap Pager option breaks rendered images into pages with a specified size. This keeps images from becoming so large that they become difficult to work with. Once enabled, you can specify the Page Size, the Bitmap Size Threshold, and the size in KB of the Memory Pool.

Using the Rendered Frame Window

The Rendered Frame Window is a temporary window that holds any rendered images. Often when developing a scene, you want to test-render an image to view the shadows or transparency not visible in the viewports. The Rendered Frame Window, shown in Figure 22.9, enables you to view these test renderings without saving any data to the network or hard drive.

This buffer opens when you select the Rendered Frame Window option and click the Render button in the Render Scene dialog box. You can also view images from a local hard drive or a network drive in the Rendered Frame Window using the File ⇨ View Image File menu command.

To zoom in on the buffer, hold down the Ctrl key and click the buffer. Right-click while holding down the Ctrl key to zoom out. The Shift key enables you to pan the buffer image. You can also use the mouse wheel (if you have a scrolling mouse) to zoom and pan within the frame buffer.

FIGURE 22.9

The Rendered Frame Window displays rendered images without saving them to a file.

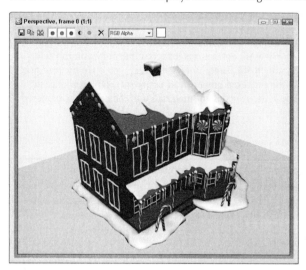

 You can zoom and pan the image while it is rendering.

 At the top of the frame buffer dialog box are several icon buttons. The first is the Save Bitmap button, which enables you to save the current frame buffer image.

 The Copy Bitmap button copies the image in the Rendered Frame Window to the Windows clipboard where you can paste it into another application like Photoshop.

 The Copy Bitmap button in the Rendered Frame Window is new to 3ds Max 2008.

The Clone Rendered Frame Window button creates another frame buffer dialog box. Any new rendering is rendered to this new dialog box, which is useful for comparing two images.

The next four buttons enable the red, green, blue, and alpha channels. The alpha channel holds any transparency information for the image. The alpha channel is a grayscale map, with black showing the transparent areas and white showing the opaque areas. Next to the Display Alpha Channel button is the Monochrome button, which displays the image as a grayscale image.

 The Clear button erases the image from the window.

The Channel Display drop-down list lets you select the channel to display. The color swatch at the right shows the color of the currently selected pixel. You can select new pixels by right-clicking and holding on the image. This temporarily displays a small dialog box with the image dimensions and the RGB value of the pixel directly under the cursor. The color in the color swatch can then be dragged and dropped in other dialog boxes such as the Material Editor.

Using the RAM Player

Just as you can use the Rendered Frame Window to view and compare rendered images, the RAM Player enables you to view rendered animations in memory. With animations loaded in memory, you can selectively change the frame rates. Figure 22.10 shows the RAM Player interface, which you open by choosing Rendering ➪ RAM Player. You see two images of the rendered gingerbread house placed on top of each other with half of each showing. One was rendered using its default materials and the other was rendered using Ink 'n' Paint materials.

FIGURE 22.10

The RAM Player interface lets you load two different images or animations for comparison.

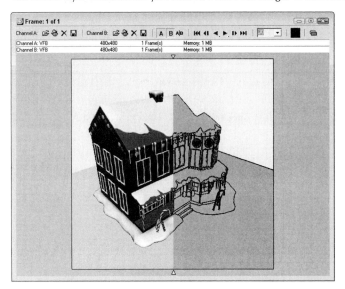

The buttons at the top of the RAM Player interface window, shown in Table 22.1, enable you to load an image to two different channels named A and B. The two Open Channel buttons open a file dialog box where you can select the file to load. Notice that the image on the right side of the RAM Player is a different frame from the left side.

TABLE 22.1

RAM Player Interface Buttons

Button	Description
🖿	Open Channel
🫖	Open Last Rendered Image
✕	Close Channel
💾	Save Channel
A|B	Horizontal/Vertical Screen Split
⧉	Double Buffer

The Open Last Rendered Image button in the RAM Player interface window provides quick access to the last rendered image. The Close Channel button clears the channel. The Save Channel button opens a file dialog box for saving the current file.

CAUTION All files that load into the RAM Player are converted to 24-bit images.

The Channel A and Channel B (toggle) buttons enable either channel or both. The Horizontal/Vertical Screen Split button switches the dividing line between the two channels to a horizontal or vertical line. When the images are aligned one on top of the other, two small triangles mark where one channel leaves off and the other begins. You can drag these triangles to alter the space for each channel.

The frame controls let you move between the frames. You can move to the first, previous, next, or last frame and play the animation forward or in reverse. The drop-down list to the right of the frame controls displays the current frame rate setting.

You can capture the color of any pixel in the image by holding down the Ctrl key while clicking the image with the right mouse button. This puts the selected color in the color swatch. The RGB value for this pixel is displayed in the blue title bar.

The Double Buffer button synchronizes the frames of the two channels.

TIP You can use the arrow keys and Page Up and Page Down keys to move through the frames of the animation. The A and B keys are used to enable the two channels.

Tutorial: Using the RAM Player to combine rendered images into a video file

Not only can the RAM Player be used to load and compare images, but it can handle animation files. It also can load in multiple frames of an animation that were saved as individual image files and save them back out as an animated file.

To combine multiple rendered image files into a video file using the RAM Player, follow these steps:

1. Select the Rendering ➪ RAM Player menu command to open the RAM Player. Then click on the Open Channel A button and locate the Exploding Planet - frame 10.tif file from the Chap 22 directory on the DVD.

   This file is the first rendered frame of a 10-frame animation.

2. The Image File List Control dialog box opens. Using this dialog box you can specify the Start and End Frames to load. You also can select to load every nth frame. Select 0 as the Start Frame and 9 as the End Frame and click the OK button.

3. The RAM Player Configuration dialog box loads next, letting you set the Resolution and Memory Usage for the loaded files. Click OK to accept the default values.

   All of the image files that share the same base name as the selected file are loaded into the RAM Player sequentially. Press the Play button to see the loaded animation.

4. Click on the Save Channel A button to access the file dialog box, where you can save the loaded animation using the AVI, MPEG, or MOV video formats.

Figure 22.11 shows one frame of the loaded animation files.

FIGURE 22.11

This rendered image is just one of a series of rendered animation frames that can be viewed in the RAM Player.

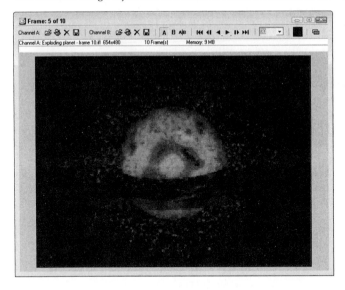

Reviewing the Render Types

From the main toolbar, the Render Type drop-down list enables you to render subsections of the scene. The default setting is View. After you pick a selection from the list, click the Quick Render button or the Render button in the Render Scene dialog box to begin the rendering. The available Render Types are described in Table 22.2.

TABLE 22.2

Render Type Options

Render Type	Description
View	Renders the entire view as shown in the active viewport.
Selected	Renders only the selected objects in the active viewport.
Region	Places a frame of dotted lines with handles in the active viewport. This frame lets you define a region to render. You can resize the frame by dragging the handles. When you have defined the region, click the OK button that appears in the lower-right corner of the active viewport.
Crop	Similar to Region in that it uses a frame to define a region, but the Crop setting doesn't include the areas outside the defined frame.
Blowup	Takes the defined region and increases its size to fill the render window. The frame for Blowup is constrained to the aspect ratio of the final resolution.
Box Selected	Renders the selected objects, but it presents a dialog box where you can specify the dimensions for rendering the bounding box of the selected objects. Constrain the Aspect Ratio is an additional option.
Region Selected	Renders only the objects within the boundary box of the selected object. The rest of the scene is unchanged.
Crop Selected	Renders the objects within the boundary box of the selected object and crops the scene to this area.

Using Command-Line Rendering

Within the default installation directory is a file named 3dsmaxcmd.exe. This file lets you initiate the rendering of files using a command-line interface. This feature enables you to create batch files that can be used to start Max, load several scenes, and render them automatically during the night while you sleep. You can find a command prompt interface in Windows XP using Start ⇨ All Programs ⇨ Accessories ⇨ Command Prompt.

CROSS-REF If you're not comfortable with executing commands using the command line, you can set up batch rendering using the Batch Render feature covered in Chapter 47, "Batch and Network Rendering."

If you type **3dsmaxcmd -?**, the command line returns a list of available parameters that you can use. Typing **3dsmaxcmd –x** returns several sample commands. The simplest command to render a scene called cool-stuff.max would be **3dsmaxcmd coolstuff.max**.

Using the various command-line flags, you can specify an image size and format, use Render Preset files to control the renderer settings and even submit a job for network rendering.

Creating Panoramic Images

The Panorama Exporter tool (found in the Rendering menu and in the Utilities panel) can be used to create a panoramic scene consisting of images rendering in all six directions from the current camera and stitched together.

A camera needs to be added to the scene at the center of the panoramic view, and the camera needs to be selected. You can quickly create a camera using the Perspective view with the Views ➪ Create Camera From View (Ctrl+C) command. Then click the Render button in the Panorama Exporter rollout. This opens a Render Scene dialog box where you can specify the size of the images and the rest of the Render parameters. Click the Render button to render the panoramic scene.

Once rendered, the panoramic scene is opened within a Viewer, as shown in Figure 22.12, where you can move about the scene using the mouse. Dragging with the left mouse button spins the scene about its center point. Dragging with the middle mouse button zooms in and out of the scene. Dragging with the right mouse button pans the scene. The Viewer interface includes a File menu that can be used to open or export the scene file. Export options include a Cylinder, Sphere, and QuickTime VR.

FIGURE 22.12

The Panoramic Viewer lets you zoom, pan, and spin the scene about its center location.

Getting Printer Help

Printing still images from Max has always been a problem because you never knew quite what you would get. To solve this problem, Max now includes a Print Size Wizard located in the Rendering menu. This menu command opens the Print Size Wizard, as shown in Figure 22.13. This wizard sizes the output of the rendered image to one of the many paper sizes.

 Although the Print Size Wizard can size the rendered image, it cannot print rendered images.

Using this Print Size Wizard, you can select a Paper Size and Orientation, and a DPI setting and the Image dimensions are computed automatically. You can then click the Render Scene Dialog button to open the Render Scene dialog box with these dimensions. You also can select a filename using the Files button and click the Quick Render button to render an image using the specified dimensions. The only available image format is TIFF.

FIGURE 22.13

The Print Size Wizard lets you set the image dimensions based on paper size and DPI settings.

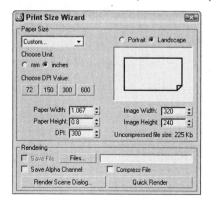

Creating an Environment

Whether it's a beautiful landscape or just clouds drifting by, the environment behind the scene can do much to make the scene more believable. In this section, you learn to define an environment using the Rendering ⇨ Environment (8) menu command.

Environment maps are used as background for the scene and can also be used as images reflected off shiny objects. Environment maps are displayed only in the final rendering and not in the viewports, but you can add a background to any viewport and even set the environment map to be displayed as the viewport backdrop.

CROSS-REF Chapter 2, "Controlling and Configuring the Viewports," covers adding a background image to a viewport.

But there is more to an environment than just a background. It also involves altering the global lighting, controlling exposure, and introducing atmosphere effects.

Defining the rendered environment

You create environments in the Environment and Effects dialog box, shown in Figure 22.14, which you can open by choosing Rendering ⇨ Environment (or by pressing the 8 key). Several settings make up an environment, including a background color or image, global lighting, exposure control, and atmospheric effects.

Setting a background color

The first color swatch in the Environment panel lets you specify a background color. This color appears by default if no environment map is specified or if the Use Map option is disabled (and is black by default). The background color is animatable, so you can set the background color to start black and slowly fade to white.

FIGURE 22.14

The Environment and Effects dialog box lets you select a background color or image, define global lighting, control exposure, and work with atmospheric effects.

Using a background image

To select a background image to be used as an environment map, click the Environment Map button in the Environment panel to open the Material/Map browser. If you want to load a bitmap image as the background image, double-click the Bitmap selection to open the Select Bitmap Image dialog box. Locate the bitmap to use, and click OK. The bitmap name appears on the Environment Map button.

> **TIP** If the environment map that you want to use is already displayed in one of the Material Editor sample slots, you can drag it directly from the Material Editor and drop it on the Map button in the Environment panel.

To change any of the environment map parameters (such as the mapping coordinates), you need to load the environment map into the Material Editor. You can do so by dragging the map button from the Environment panel onto one of the sample slots in the Material Editor. After releasing the material, the Instance (Copy) Map dialog box asks whether you want to create an Instance or a Copy. If you select Instance, any parameter changes that you make to the material automatically update the map in the Environment panel.

Once in the Material Editor, you can use the Environment Map to create a Spherical Environment map that is used to reflect off objects in the scene.

> **CROSS-REF** For more information about the types of available mapping parameters, see Chapter 17, "Adding Material Details with Maps."

The background image doesn't need to be an image: You can also load animations. Supported formats include AVI, MPEG, MOV, and IFL files.

Figure 22.15 shows a scene with an image of the Golden Gate Bridge loaded as the environment map. Viewpoint Datalabs created the airplane model.

FIGURE 22.15

The results of a background image loaded into the Environment panel

Setting global lighting

The Tint color swatch in the Global Lighting section of the Environment panel specifies a color used to tint all lights. The Level value increases or decreases the overall lighting level for all lights in the scene. The Ambient color swatch sets the color for the ambient light in the scene, which is the darkest color that any shadows in the scene can be. You can animate all these settings.

Summary

This chapter covered the basics of producing output using the Render Scene dialog box. Although rendering a scene can take a long time to complete, Max includes many settings that can speed up the process and helpful tools such as the Rendered Frame Window and the RAM Player.

In this chapter, you accomplished the following:

- Working with the ActiveShade window
- Discovering how to control the various render parameters
- Configuring the global rendering preferences
- Learning about the command-line rendering interface
- Creating VUE files
- Using the Rendered Frame Window and the RAM Player
- Understanding the different render types
- Exploring the Panoramic Exporter and Print Size Wizard tools
- Using the Environment panel to change the background color and image

The next chapter covers atmospheric effects such as fog and fire, along with the various render effects.

Part VI

Advanced Modeling

Chapter 23

Building Complex Scenes with XRefs and Using Vault

U sing external references (XRefs), you can pull multiple scenes, objects, materials, and controllers together into a single scene. XRefs allow a diverse team to work on separate parts of a scene at the same time. They also provide a great way to reuse existing resources.

How often do you go into your garage during the winter months? Unless you have a pair of the warm overalls or a space heater, you probably just throw in any tools you use, the Christmas lights, spare quarts of oil, and the kids' bikes wherever they fit as you make a mad dash back into the warm house, and then when spring comes, you have a real mess on your hands.

Max projects can be the same. During an aggressive project, Max files, textures, and render passes get saved all over the network. By the time the project is finished, you may have a hard time reusing things simply because you can't find anything. This dilemma is compounded when you work on a team with several individuals throwing stuff all over the place.

An asset management system can help with this problem by introducing a system that acts as a little secretary logging every object thrown to the network. This little secretary is also smart enough to keep track of the latest updates of all files, making sure that each accessed file includes the latest updates. It also locks any file that is being used to keep unwanted fingers out of the pie.

Referencing External Objects

No man is an island, and if Autodesk has its way, no Max user will be an island either. XRefs (which stands for eXternal References) make it easy for creative teams to collaborate on a project without having to wait for another group member to finish his or her respective production task. External references are objects and scenes contained in separate Max files and made available for reference during a Max session. This arrangement enables several artists on a team to work on separate sections of a project without interfering with one another or altering each other's work.

Max includes two different types of XRefs: XRef scenes and XRef objects. You also can use XRef for materials, modifiers, and controllers.

Using XRef scenes

An externally referenced scene is one that appears in the current Max session, but that is not accessible for editing or changing. The scene can be positioned and transformed when linked to a parent object and can be set to update automatically as changes are made to the source file.

As an example of how XRef scenes facilitate a project, let's say that a design team is in the midst of creating an environment for a project while the animator is animating a character model. The animator can access the in-production environment as an XRef scene in order to help him move the character correctly about the environment. The design team members are happy because the animator didn't modify any of their lights, terrain models, maps, and props. The animator is happy because he won't have to wait for the design team members to finish all their tweaking before he can get started. The end result is one large, happy production team (if they can meet their deadlines).

Choose File ➪ XRef Scenes to open the XRef Scenes dialog box (shown in Figure 23.1), which you use to load XRef scenes into a file.

FIGURE 23.1

The XRef Scenes dialog box lets you specify which scenes to load as external references.

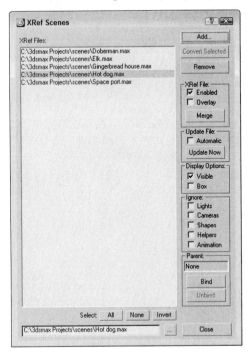

XRef scene options

In the XRef Scenes dialog box are several options for controlling the appearance of the scene objects, how often the scene is updated, and to which object the scene is bound. This dialog box is modeless, and you can open and change the options in this dialog box at any time.

The pane on the left lists all XRef scenes in the current scene. These scenes are displayed using their full path unless the Convert Local File Paths to Relative option in the Files panel of the Preference Settings dialog box is enabled. To the right are the settings, which can be different for each XRef scene in the list. To view or apply a setting, you first need to select the scene from the list. You can remove any scene by selecting it from the list and clicking the Remove button.

 **If an XRef scene in the list is displayed in red, then the scene could not be loaded. If the path or name is incorrect, you can change it in the Path field at the bottom of the list.**

The Convert Selected button converts any selected objects in the current scene to XRef objects by saving them as a separate file. This button opens a dialog box to let you name and save the new file. If no objects are selected in the current scene, then this option is disabled.

Use the Enabled option to enable or disable all XRef scenes. Disabled scenes are displayed in gray. The Merge button lets you insert the current XRef scene into the current scene. This button removes the scene from the list and acts the same way as the File ➪ Merge command.

Updating an external scene

Automatic is a key option that can set any XRef scene to be automatically updated. Enable this option by selecting a scene from the list and checking the Automatic option box; thereafter, the scene is updated anytime the source file is updated. This option can slow the system if the external scene is updated frequently, but the benefit is that you can work with the latest update.

The Update Now button is for manually updating the XRef scene. Click this button to update the external scene to the latest saved version.

External scene appearance

Other options let you decide how the scene is displayed in the viewports. You can choose to make the external scene invisible or to display it as a box. Making an external scene invisible removes it from the viewports, but the scene is still included in the rendered output. To remove a scene from the rendered output, deselect the Enabled option.

The Ignore section lists objects such as lights, cameras, shapes, helpers, and animation; selecting them causes them to be ignored and to have no effect in the scene. If an external scene's animation is ignored, then the scene appears as it does in frame 0.

Positioning an external scene

Positioning an external scene is accomplished by binding the scene to an object in the current scene (a dummy object, for example). The XRef Scenes dialog box is modeless, so you can select the object to bind to without closing the dialog box. After a binding object is selected, the external scene transforms to the binding object's pivot point. The name of the parent object is also displayed in the XRef Scenes dialog box.

Transforming the object to which the scene is bound can control how the external scene is repositioned. To unbind an object, click the Unbind button in the XRef Scenes dialog box. Unbound scenes are positioned at the World origin for the current scene.

Specifying an XRef as an Overlay

The Overlay option in the XRef Scenes dialog box makes the XRef visible to the current scene, but not to any other scenes that XRef the scene including the overlay. This provides a way to hide XRef content from more than one level. Overlay XRefs also make it possible to avoid circular dependencies. For example, in previous Max versions, Max wouldn't allow two designers to XRef one another's scenes, but if one of the scenes is an overlay, then this can be done.

Working with XRef scenes

You can't edit XRef scenes in the current scene. Their objects are not visible in the Select by Name dialog box or in the Track and Schematic Views. You also cannot access the Modifier Stack of external scenes' objects. However, you can make use of external scene objects in other ways. For example, you can change a viewport to show the view from any camera or light in the external scene. External scene objects are included in the Summary Info dialog box.

> **TIP** Another way to use XRef scenes is to create a scene with lights and/or cameras positioned at regular intervals around the scene. You can then use the XRef Scenes dialog box to turn these lights on and off or to select from a number of different views without creating new cameras.

You can also nest XRef scenes within each other, so you can have one XRef scene for the distant mountains that includes another XRef for a castle.

> **NOTE** If a Max file is loaded with XRef files that cannot be located, a warning dialog box appears, enabling you to browse to the file's new location. If you click OK or Cancel, the scene still loads, but the external scenes are missing.

Tutorial: Adding an XRef scene

As an example of a project that would benefit from XRefs, I've created a maze environment. I open a new Max file and animate a simple mouse moving through this maze that is opened as an XRef scene.

To set up an XRef scene, follow these steps:

1. Create a new Max file by choosing File ➪ New.

2. Choose File ➪ XRef Scenes to open the XRef Scenes dialog box.

3. Click the Add button, locate the Maze.max file from the Chap 23 directory on the DVD, and click Open to add it to the XRef Scene dialog box list, but don't close the dialog box just yet.

> **TIP** You can add several XRef scenes by clicking the Add button again. You can also add a scene to the XRef Scene dialog box by dragging a .max file from Windows Explorer or from the Asset Manager window.

4. Select Create ➪ Helpers ➪ Dummy, and drag in the Perspective viewport to create a new Dummy object.

5. In the XRef Scenes dialog box, click the Bind button and select the dummy object.

   This enables you to reposition the XRef scene as needed.

6. Select the Automatic update option, and then click the Close button to exit the XRef Scene dialog box.

7. Now animate objects moving through the maze.

Figure 23.2 shows the Maze.max scene included in the current Max file as an XRef.

 With the simple mouse animated, you can replace it at a later time with a detailed model of a furry mouse using the File ⌐ Replace command.

FIGURE 23.2

The maze.max file loaded into the current file as an XRef scene

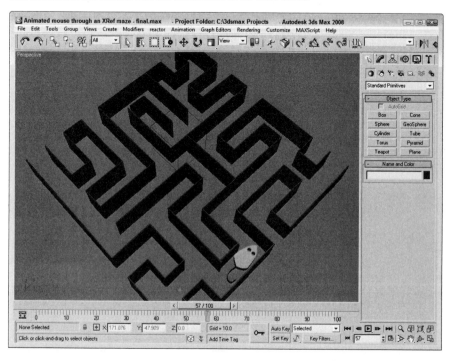

Using XRef objects

XRef objects are slightly different from XRef scenes. XRef objects appear in a scene and can be transformed and animated, but the original object's structure and Modifier Stack cannot be changed.

An innovative way to use this feature would be to create a library of objects that you could load on the fly as needed. For example, if you had a furniture library, you could load several different styles until you got just the look you wanted.

You can also use XRef objects to load low-resolution proxies of complex models in order to lighten the system load during a Max session. This method increases the viewport refresh rate.

Many of the options in the XRef Objects dialog box, shown in Figure 23.3, are the same as in the XRef Scenes dialog box.

579

FIGURE 23.3

The XRef Objects dialog box lets you choose which files to look in for external objects.

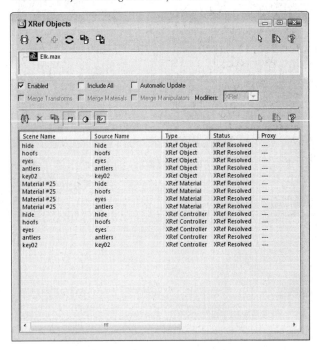

The interface buttons for the XRef Objects dialog box are listed in Table 23.1.

TABLE 23.1

XRef Objects Dialog Box

Button	Name	Description
	Create XRef Record from File	Opens the XRef Merge dialog box where you can select the XRef source file.
	Remove XRef Record	Deletes the selected XRef record.
	Combine XRef Record	Allows two or more selected XRef records pointing to the same file to be combined into a single record.
	Update	Updates the content of all XRefs.
	Merge in Scene	Makes all XRefs for the selected record part of the scene file. This also removes the XRef record from the dialog box.

Fabricio Moraes created this character study of Don Quixote. He modeled and textured the scene in Max, rendered it using mental ray, and touched it up using Photoshop. It is an excellent example of texturing, lighting, and atmospheric ambiance.

Bryan Jumarang (enigma3dv@hotmail.com) produced the two architectural images on this page. The condo interior above includes an amazing amount of detail, exquisite textures, and effective lighting. The lower image uses glass and metal beams along with reflections to create a museum hallway.

The images on the opposite page are the work of Wolfgang Ortner. The top image uses only external lights to light the scene. The lower image effectively uses background images to place the house in its location. Subtle additions like the flowers and grass make the image look like a photograph. You can find more of Wolfgang's work at www.mm-vis.at.

www.jieanu.com

Dragos Jieanu created the top image, "Keyholder." Notice how the flowing cloth and the use of perspective make the character intimidating. You can view more of Dragos' work at www.jieanu.com.

In the lower image, "Templar Angel," Luciano Neves used subtle overhead lighting and a weathered texture to give the statue a realistic, worn look. Luciano's site is www. infinitecg.com.

In "The Diviners," right, Joel LeLievre gave his characters an eerie feel using translucent and self-illuminating materials. He used the paint deformation brush to give the ribs an organic look. Joel's site is www.intrinsia.net.

Giuseppe Guzzardi based the evocative portrait below on a reference photo. He modeled it in Maya and rendered it in Max using the Scanline renderer. You can find more of Giuseppe's work at www.giuseppeguzzardi.com.

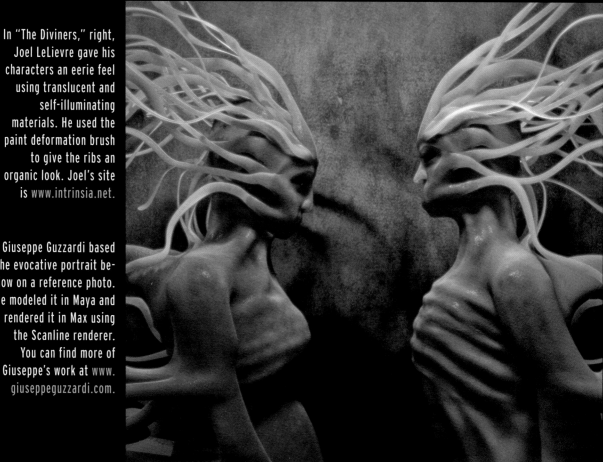

Gustavo Groppo
(driven9@hotmail.com)
titled this image "The
Audience is Listening."
The view angle makes
the guitar loom over
the scene. Notice the
cracks, scratches, and
nicks that give the
guitar a used look and
make it more realistic.
This image is based on
the actual guitar used
by Steve Vai.

Andre Kutscherauer created this clever image and rendered it using mental ray. The reflections and bulb transparency give it a realistic look. Notice the depth of field effect that focuses your attention on the

Till Nowak produced this humorous scene titled "Dishes." Till used multiple instances of several satellite dishes to create the resulting image. More of Till's work, including a detailed explanation of how this image was created, is available at www.framebox.de.

Luciano Neves' rendering of Big Ben on the facing page includes an amazing amount of detail. Luciano's site is www.infinitecg.com.

These furry creatures by Patrick Beaulieu show off Max's hair and fur features. See more of Patrick's creatures at www.squeezestudio.com.

PATRICK BEAULIEU

PATRICK BEAULIEU

This fearsome warrior and his friend on the opposing page were created by Robin Benes. Notice the attention to detail—the fiery eyes and bloody knuckles on this image, and the projected light, drooling mouth, and peeling paint on the other image. You can find more of Robin's awesome work at www.tes3d.com

Saeed Maghboul created the fun cow scenes featured on this page and the facing page. Although the cow model is reused in each image, Saeed has changed the cow's pose and expression to give each scene a unique look.

"The Journey Begins–Take Care Daddy" is by Lombardo Simone. He tweaked the render settings to produce an anime-like style. See more of his work at www.superxcm.com.

Button	Name	Description
	Convert Selected Objects to Xrefs	Opens a save dialog box, and saves the selected scene objects as a separate scene file, which is an XRef in the current scene.
	Select	Selects the objects that are part of the selected XRef record.
	Select by Name	Opens the Select Objects dialog box listing all objects that are part of the selected XRef record.
	Highlight Selected Object's XRef Records	Highlights the XRef record that contains the objects selected in the viewport.
	Add Objects	Opens the XRef Merge dialog box where additional objects from the selected XRef record can be loaded.
	Delete XRef Entity	Deletes the current object from the XRef record.
	Merge in Scene	Merges the selected object to the current scene and removes its XRef.
	List Objects	Filters the display to show the XRef objects.
	List Materials	Filters the display to show the XRef materials.
	List Controllers	Filters the display to show the XRef controllers.

The XRef Objects dialog box is divided into two sections. The top section displays the externally referenced source files (or records), and the lower section displays the objects, materials, or controllers selected from the source file. If multiple files are referenced, then a file needs to be selected in the top pane in order for its objects and materials to be displayed in the lower pane.

The Convert Selected button works the same as in the XRef Scenes dialog box. It enables you to save the selected objects in the current scene to a separate file just like the File ➪ Save Selected command and to have them instantly made into XRefs.

In the XRef Objects dialog box, you can choose to automatically update the external referenced objects or use the Update button or you can enable the Automatic Update option. You can also enable or disable all objects in a file with the Enabled option. The Include All option skips the XRef Merge dialog box and automatically includes all objects in the source file.

If the Merge Transforms, Merge Materials, and Merge Manipulators options are enabled before an XRef file is added, then all transforms, materials, and manipulators are automatically combined with the current scene instead of being referenced. When merged, the link between the source file is broken so that changes to the source file aren't propagated.

Using material XRefs

When a source file is loaded into the XRef Objects dialog box, both its objects and materials are loaded and included. If the Merge Materials option is selected before the source file is loaded, then the materials are included with the objects, but if the Merge Materials option isn't enabled, then the objects and the materials appear as separate entities. You can use the List Objects and the List Materials buttons to list just one type of entity.

Materials also can be referenced from directly within the Material Editor. If you used a material in a previous scene that would be perfect in your current scene, you can just select the XRef Material from the Material/Map Browser. This material type includes fields where you can browse to an external scene file and select a specific object. The selected material is added automatically to the XRef Objects dialog box.

CROSS-REF You can learn more about applying materials and using the Material Editor in Chapter 14, "Exploring the Material Editor."

Merging modifiers

If the Merge Manipulators option is enabled before loading the XRef file, then any manipulator that is part of the XRef object is merged and loaded along with the object. You also can specify how modifiers are included with XRef objects, but you must select the option from the Modifier drop-down list before the file is selected. The XRef option loads all modifiers with the XRef object, but hides them from being edited. New modifiers can be added to the object. The Merge option adds all modifiers to the XRef object and makes these modifiers accessible via the Modifier Stack. The Ignore option strips all modifiers from the XRef object.

XRef objects appear and act like any other object in the scene. You may see a slight difference if you open the Modifier Stack. The Stack displays "XRef Object" as its only entry.

Using proxies

When an XRef object is selected in the viewport, all details concerning the XRef object — including its source file name, Object Name, and status — are listed in the Modify panel. The Modify panel also includes a Proxy Object rollout, where you can select a separate object in a separate file as a proxy object. The File or Object Name buttons open a file dialog box where you can select a low-resolution proxy object in place of a more complex object. This feature saves memory by not requiring the more complex object to be kept in memory. You also can select to enable or disable the proxy or use the proxy in rendering.

TIP The real benefit of using proxies is to replace complex referenced objects with simpler objects that update quickly. When creating a complex object, remember to also create a low-resolution version to use as a proxy.

Controller XRefs

In addition to objects, materials, and modifiers, controllers also can be externally referenced. This means that you can borrow the controller motions of an object in a separate scene and save some animation time. To reference an external controller, select the Transform track and choose the XRef Controller option. This opens a File dialog box followed by a Select Object dialog box where you can choose with the controller the object that you want to reference. XRef controllers also appear as records in the XRef Objects dialog box.

CROSS-REF You can learn more about applying and using controllers in Chapter 21, "Animating with Constraints and Controllers."

Tutorial: Using an XRef proxy

To set up an XRef proxy, follow these steps:

1. Open the Post box with XRef tree.max file from the Chap 23 directory on the DVD.

   This file includes the post box model produced by Zygote Media.

2. Open the XRef Objects dialog box by choosing File ➪ XRef Objects.

3. Click the Create XRef Record from File button, and locate the Park bench under a tree.max file from the Chap 23 directory on the DVD.

This file includes the old tree and park bench models made by Zygote Media. The XRef Merge dialog box, shown in Figure 23.4, automatically opens and displays a list of all the objects in the file just added.

FIGURE 23.4

The XRef Merge dialog box lets you choose specific objects from a scene.

4. Select the Tree object to add to the current scene, and click OK.

NOTE If an object you've selected has the same name as an object that is currently in the scene, the Duplicate Name dialog box appears and lets you rename the object, merge it anyway, skip the new object, or delete the old version.

5. Select the Tree object in the lower pane of the XRef Objects dialog box, and click the Select button. The tree object is selected in the viewport. Close the XRef Objects dialog box.

6. With the tree object selected, open the Modify panel, check the Enable option in the Proxy rollout, and click the button under the File Name field to open a file dialog box. Select the Tree Lo-Res.max file from the Chap 23 directory on the DVD, and click the Open button.

The Merge dialog box opens.

7. Select the Cylinder01 object, and click OK.

CAUTION If the proxy object has a different offset than the original object, a warning dialog box appears instructing you to use the Reset XForm utility to reset the transform of the objects.

8. With the Tree object still selected, disable the Enable option in the Proxy Object rollout to see the actual object.

XRef objects that you add to a scene instantly appear in the current scene as you add them. Figure 23.5 shows the post box with the actual tree object. The Modify panel lets you switch to the proxy object at any time.

FIGURE 23.5

The tree object is an XRef from another scene. Its proxy is a simple cylinder.

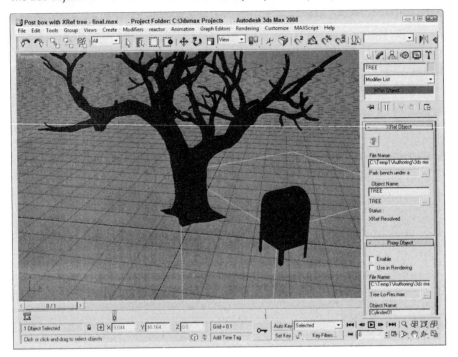

Configuring XRef paths

The Configure Paths dialog box includes an XRefs tab for setting the paths for XRef scenes and objects, shown in Figure 23.6. Choose Customize ➪ Configure User Paths to open the XRefs panel.

Max keeps track of the path of any XRefs used in a scene, but if it cannot find them, it looks at the paths designated in the XRefs panel of the Configure Paths dialog box. For projects that use lots of XRefs, populating this list with potential paths is a good idea. Paths are scanned in the order they are listed, so place the most likely paths at the top of the list.

To add a new path to the panel, click the Add button. You can also modify or delete paths in this panel with the Modify and Delete buttons.

FIGURE 23.6

The XRefs panel in the Configure User Paths dialog box lets you specify paths to be searched when an XRef cannot be located.

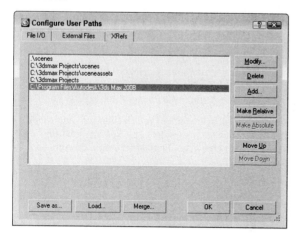

Setting Up Asset Tracking

Max's asset tracking features provides support for several different systems including Autodesk's Vault, Microsoft's Visual SourceSafe, CVS, and Perforce. Each of these systems can be accessed using Server ➪ Launch Provider menu command in the Asset Tracking interface. This interface is opened with the File ➪ Asset Tracking menu command (Shift+T).

> **NOTE** In order for an asset tracking system to work with Max, it must conform to the MSSCC standard.

For project teams that don't currently use an asset tracking system, you'll be happy to know that Autodesk has included a copy of its Vault system on the 3ds Max 2008 install disc. Both the Vault Server and a Vault Client can be installed from the install discs. Vault installation requires a separate setup from the standard 3ds Max 2008 setup. Just locate the Vault setup link on the first page of the install wizard under the Install Tools & Utilities section.

> **NOTE** Installation and configuration of the Vault Server should be left to your network administrator. The administrator is also responsible for setting up user profiles, issuing usernames and passwords for accessing the system, and creating project folders.

For an asset tracking system, assets are defined as any file that is used as part of a project. This could include Max scene files, XRefs, bitmap textures, MAXScript files, and so on. One of the key benefits to the Vault asset management system is that is stores data in a hierarchical structure including files such as textures as dependents of the Max scene file.

> **NEW FEATURE** 3ds Max 2008 includes support and installations for Vault 5 and Vault 2008.

Checking in and checking out

To request an asset from the asset tracking system, you "check out" the file. This command locks the file so you can edit it without worrying about others making changes at the same time. If another user tries to check out a file that is already checked out, he receives a polite message stating that the requested file is available for read-only access and lists you as the person who has the file checked out. The requested file can be loaded and viewed, but it cannot be edited.

When you're finished editing the file, you can "check in" the file, making it available for other users. As a file is checked in, a comment dialog box appears where you can enter a message about the latest changes. Over time, these comments are compiled into a historical list that marks the changes over the life of the file. The asset tracking system can also be used to recall the file at any point in its history.

NOTE   Asset tracking systems such as Vault are very good at reminding you to check out and check in files so changes aren't lost. For example, if you make changes to a checked out Vault file and try to open another file, a dialog box appears reminding you to check the file back in before opening another file.

Logging in

The first step in using an asset tracking system is to log into the system. This lets the system know who you are, the access rights you have, and which name to place beside the assets you're editing. If you select either the File ➪ Open from Vault menu command or the File ➪ Asset Tracking menu command, the Vault Log In dialog box opens, as shown in Figure 23.7.

FIGURE 23.7

The Vault Log In dialog box opens when the File ➪ Open from Vault menu command is used.

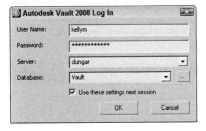

The Vault Log In dialog box requires a username and password. It also includes drop-down lists for selecting the Server and Database. A production facility may have several different asset tracking instances running at the same time, and a separate database would be established for each project.

TIP   If you enable the Use these settings next session option, then the Vault Log In dialog box won't open again until Max is started again.

Selecting a working folder

When files are checked out from the asset tracking system, they are copied to a local directory on your current machine where the changes are saved until the file is checked back in. The first time you try to check out a file from the asset tracking system, the system asks you to select a working folder. This folder is a temporary folder where the checked out files are saved while being worked on. You can manually set the working folder by selecting the Server ➪ Options menu command in the Asset Tracking interface.

Using Autodesk Vault

Max's asset tracking system, Vault, is a long-standing Autodesk product used extensively by AutoCAD teams around the world. It is a robust, stable product that fits well into any production pipeline that uses Max.

After a Vault server has been installed and configured on your network and you know your username, password, server, and project name, you can log in and access Vault files.

Opening Vault files

Any Vault project files can be opened using the File ⇨ Open from Vault menu command. This opens a special file dialog box, shown in Figure 23.8, listing all the files in the folder where you logged in.

 The Open from Vault menu command appears in the File menu only after the Vault client has been installed on your local computer.

FIGURE 23.8

The Open File from Vault dialog box lists the available Vault files.

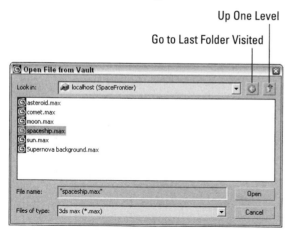

Opening a Vault file is different from checking the file out, but whenever a file is selected from the Open File from Vault dialog box, a warning dialog box, shown in Figure 23.9, opens and asks if you want to check out the file. This dialog box includes an option to Always perform this action. If this option is enabled, then the action of checking out when a Vault file is opened happens automatically.

FIGURE 23.9

Warning dialog boxes such as this one remind you to check out files.

You can set which warning dialog boxes appear and which are handled automatically using the Options ⇨ Prompts menu command in the Asset Tracking interface. This command presents a list of all the available prompt dialog boxes and lets you right-click on each to have it appear or not appear.

Using the Asset Tracking interface

Although the Vault client, called Vault Explorer, can be installed using the install DVD and used to check out Vault files, the Asset Tracking interface, shown in Figure 23.10, is part of the Max interface and takes the place of the Vault client for Max users. The Asset Tracking interface is opened using the File ⇨ Asset Tracking menu command. It also may be opened using the Shift+T keyboard shortcut. This interface also allows you to access commands in the main Max interface while it is open.

Vault files that are opened appear in this interface including all dependent files such as texture bitmaps, XRefs, photometric files, render files, and so on. Using the buttons at the top of the interface, you can Refresh the current list to see the latest updates, view the Status Log (which is a running list of all Vault commands), and change the view between a Tree view and a Table view.

To the left of each filename is a small icon that marks the status of the file. These icons are handy when the Tree view is enabled, or you can read the status as text in the Table view. The Table view includes separate columns for displaying the Name, Full Path, Status, Proxy Resolution, and Proxy Status of the various files.

On the left side of the interface are two buttons for filtering the assets. The first button highlights the material and map assets. The second button highlights the assets for the selected object.

FIGURE 23.10

The Asset Tracking interface shows all the checked out files and the status of each.

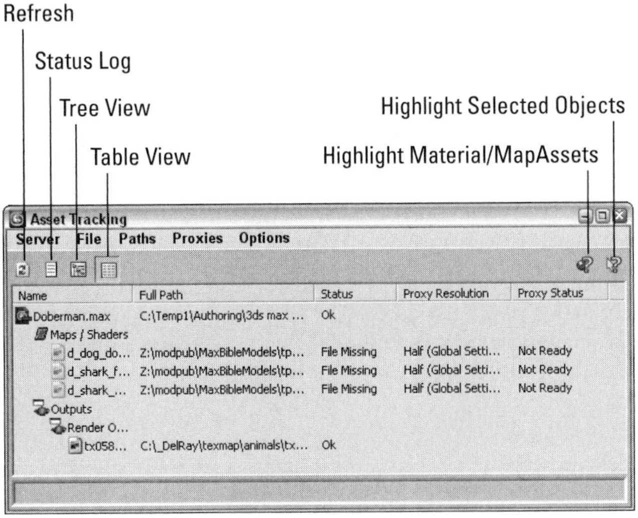

The Asset Tracking dialog box has commands for checking files in and out under the File menu. Each time a file is checked in a confirmation dialog box appears, as shown in Figure 23.11. In this dialog box, you can enter a comment about the latest changes. The file is then saved to the Vault server with an incremented version number. The ability to save and keep track of different versions of a file is known as "version control" and is one of the key features of an asset management system.

FIGURE 23.11

The dialog box where comments on the latest changes are entered appears every time a Vault file is checked in.

An Undo Checkout command is available in the File menu that throws away the current changes and restores the current Vault file.

Getting and adding Vault files

After a database is created for a project and you've logged in, you can add open files to the Vault server using File ⇨ Add Files menu command. This command adds the current file to the Vault project folder, but the file must be saved to the local working folder before it can be added to the Vault folder. Multiple files such as bitmap textures can be selected by holding down the Ctrl key while clicking on them; you also can add multiple files at the same time using this command.

The File ⇨ Get from Provider menu command does the opposite. It downloads any selected files from the Vault folder to your local working folder.

If you're missing files, such as a texture that has been moved to a different local folder, you can use the File ⇨ Browse menu command to locate the missing file.

Loading older file versions

Each time a file is checked in, it is given a new version number. This makes it possible to load older versions of a file. For example, if you want to reuse a character made for a previous game, but you want to access the character before any textures were applied, you can locate and load the version saved just before textures were applied.

Older file versions can be found in the History dialog box, which is also found in the File menu. This dialog box, shown in Figure 23.12, lists all the different versions of a file along with their creation dates, their creator, and any comments entered when the file was checked in. To load an older version, simply select the file from the list and click the Get Version button.

FIGURE 23.12

The History dialog box lets you access older versions of a file.

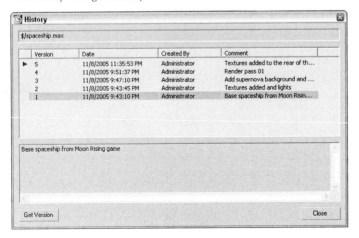

Changing asset paths

The Path menu includes options for setting and changing the paths for the various assets. The Highlight Editable Assets command selects all assets in the Asset Tracking interface that have paths that can change. Typically, only the base Max file loaded from the Vault cannot be edited. The Set Path command opens a simple dialog box where you can browse to a new path for an asset. This is helpful if the asset has moved and is marked as missing. The Path menu also includes commands for retargeting the root path, which is the path that all assets have in common, stripping the path from an asset so that only the filenames are visible, making the path absolute or relative to the project folder, and converting paths to the Universal Naming Convention (UNC).

Working with proxies

The Proxy System lets you use proxy texture maps in place of high-resolution maps across all objects in the scene. Using the Proxies menu, you can enable the use of proxies, set the global settings for the proxy system, and set the proxy resolution to use. The table view also displays the current proxy resolution for each asset and its status.

CROSS-REF   Bitmap Proxies can be used outside of Vault. For information on using them, see Chapter 22, "Learning to Render a Scene."

Tutorial: Editing a Vault asset

The real advantage of an asset tracking system comes when working with a team. It allows only one person to work on an asset at a time, but still lets other view the file as needed.

To edit a Vault asset, follow these steps:

1. Select the File ⇨ Open from Vault menu command. In the Vault Log In dialog box that appears, enter the correct Username, Password, Server, and Database, and then press the OK button.

2. In the Open File from Vault dialog box that appears, select the asset file that you want to edit and click the Open button. A dialog box appears asking if you want to check out the requested file. Click the Yes button, and the asset is loaded into the Max interface.

3. Select the File ⇨ Asset Tracking menu command (or press the Shift+T shortcut) to open the Asset Tracking interface. The opened file appears in the interface with all its dependents and a small check mark icon to the left of its name to indicate that it is checked out, as shown in Figure 23.13.

4. Make the desired edits to the Max file, and save the file with the File ⇨ Save menu command. This saves the file in the working folder.

5. In the Asset Tracking interface, select the File ⇨ Checkin menu command. A dialog box appears where you can enter comments concerning the changes you've just made. Enter the comments, and press OK. The file is updated on the server and made available for others to edit it.

FIGURE 23.13

The Asset Tracking interface shows the checked out file along with its dependents.

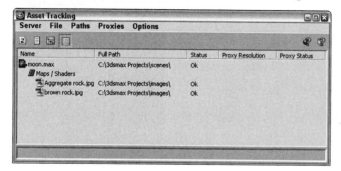

Summary

Working with XRefs lets you combine the work of several users and creatively collaborate across teams. This chapter covered the features typically found in an asset tracking system and looked at the specific features involved in setting up and using Autodesk's Vault asset tracking system. This chapter covered the following topics:

- Using externally referenced scenes and objects to work on the same project at the same time as your fellow team members without interfering with their work (or they with yours)
- Configuring XRef paths to help Max track your XRef Scenes and Objects
- Understanding what an asset management system is
- Setting up an asset tracking system to work with Max by logging in and selecting a working folder
- Using the Open from Vault menu command and the Asset Tracking interface to work with Vault assets

The next chapter looks closely at a valuable tool in seeing the big picture of your scene. The Schematic View lets you see all scene objects as individual nodes that are easy to select and connect with other nodes.

Chapter 24

Working with the Schematic View

A valuable tool for selecting, linking, and organizing scene objects is the Schematic View window. This window offers a 1,000-foot view of the objects in your scene. From this whole scene perspective, you can find the exact item you seek.

The Schematic View window shows all objects as simple nodes and uses arrows to show relationships between objects. This structure makes the Schematic View window the easiest place to establish links and to wire parameters. You can also use this view to quickly see all the instances of an object.

Using the Schematic View Window

A great way to organize and select objects is by using the Schematic View window. Every object in the Schematic View is displayed as a labeled rectangular box. These boxes, or nodes, are connected to show the relationships among them. You can rearrange them and save the customized views for later access.

 You access the Schematic View window via the Graph Editors menu command or by clicking its button on the main toolbar. When the window opens, it floats on top of the Max interface and can be moved by dragging its title bar. You can also resize the window by dragging on its borders. The window is modeless and lets you access the viewports and buttons in the interface beneath it.

The Graph Editors menu options

The Schematic View menu options enable you to manage several different views. The Graph Editors ➪ New Schematic View command opens the Schematic View window, shown in Figure 24.1. If you enter a name in the View Name field at the top of the window, you can name and save the current view. This name then appears in the Graph Editors ➪ Saved Schematic Views submenu and also in the title bar when the saved view is open.

Every time the Graph Editors ➪ New Schematic View menu command is used, a new view name is created and another view is added to the Saved Schematic Views submenu. The Schematic View ➪ Delete Schematic View command opens a dialog box in which you can select the view you want to delete.

TIP   You can open any saved Schematic View window (or a new Schematic View window) within a viewport by right-clicking the viewport title, choosing Views ➪ Schematic, and clicking the view name in the pop-up menu.

FIGURE 24.1

The Schematic View window displays all objects as nodes.

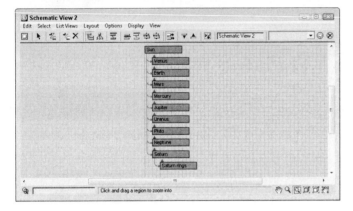

The Schematic View interface

The Schematic View window includes several common interface elements including menus, toolbar buttons, and a right-click quadmenu. Just like the main interface, you can access the commands in many ways.

Using the Schematic View menus

The Schematic View window includes menus at the top of its interface, including Edit, Select, List Views, Layout, Options, Display, and View.

The Edit menu includes commands to Connect (C) and Unlink Selected object nodes. It also includes a Delete command, which deletes an object from the viewports as well as from the object node. The Edit menu includes features to Assign Controllers, Wire Parameters, and edit Object Properties.

NOTE   Many of the keyboard shortcuts for the Schematic View window are the same as those in the main interface. If you enable the Keyboard Shortcut Override Toggle, then you can use the Schematic View keyboard shortcuts.

The Select menu includes commands for accessing the Select tool (S); selecting All (Ctrl+A), None (Ctrl+D), and Invert (Ctrl+I); selecting (Ctrl+C) and deselecting children; and commands to synch the selected nodes in the Schematic View with the scene (Select From Scene) and vice versa (Select to Scene).

The List Views menu determines what is shown in the Schematic View. Options include All Relationships, Selected Relationships, All Instances, Selected Instances, Show Occurrences, and All Animated Controllers. Many of these options are also available in the Display Floater.

The Layout menu includes various options for controlling how the nodes are arranged. The Align submenu lets you align selected nodes to the Left, Right, Top, Bottom, Center Horizontal, or Center Vertical. You can also Arrange Children, or Arrange Selected. The Free Selected (Alt+S) and Free All (Alt+F) commands remove nodes from being auto arranged. With the Layout menu, you can also Shrink Selected, Unshrink Selected, Unshrink All, and Toggle Shrink (Ctrl+S).

The Options menu lets you select the Always Arrange option and view mode (either Hierarchy and Reference modes). You can also select the Move Children (Alt+C) option and open the Schematic View Preferences dialog box.

The Display menu provides access to the Display Floater. The Display Floater (D) command opens the Display floater, which can be used to select the types of nodes to display. You also can hide and unhide nodes and Expand or Collapse the selected node.

The View menu includes commands for selecting the Pan, Zoom, and Zoom Region tools. You also can access the Zoom Extents, Zoom Extents Selected (Z), and Pan to Selected commands. The View menu also includes options to Show/Hide Grid (G), Show/Hide Background, and Refresh View.

Learning the toolbar buttons

You can also select most of these commands from the toolbar. Many of the toolbar buttons are toggle switches that enable and disable certain viewing modes. The background of these toggle buttons is highlighted yellow when selected. You'll also find some buttons along the bottom of the window. All Schematic View icon buttons are shown in Table 24.1 and are described in the following sections.

NOTE The Schematic View toolbar buttons are permanently docked to the interface and cannot be removed.

TABLE 24.1

Schematic View Toolbar Buttons

Toolbar Button	Name	Description
	Display Floater	Opens the Display Floater, where you can toggle which items are displayed or hidden.
	Select (S)	Toggles selection mode on, where nodes can be selected by clicking.
	Connect (C)	Enables you to create links between objects in the Schematic View window; also used to copy modifiers and materials between objects.
	Unlink Selected	Destroys the link between the selected object and its parent.
	Delete Objects	Deletes the selected object in both the Schematic View and in the viewports.
	Hierarchy Mode	Displays all child objects indented under their parents.
	References Mode	Displays all object references and instances. This mode displays all materials and modifiers associated with the objects.

continued

TABLE 24.1   (continued)

Toolbar Button	Name	Description
	Always Arrange	Causes all nodes to be automatically arranged in a hierarchy or in references mode, and disables moving of individual nodes.
	Arrange Children	Automatically rearranges the children of the selected object nodes.
	Arrange Selected	Automatically rearranges the selected object nodes.
	Free All	Allows all objects to be freely moved without being automatically arranged.
	Free Selected	Allows selected objects to be freely moved without being automatically arranged.
	Move Children	Causes children to move along with their parent node.
	Expand Selected	Reveals all nodes below the selected node.
	Collapse Selected	Rolls up all nodes below the selected node.
	Preferences	Opens the Schematic View Preferences dialog box.
My Saved View	View Name field	Allows you to name the current display. Named displays show up underneath the Graph Editors ⇨ Saved Schematic View submenu.
My Bookmark ▼	Bookmark Name	Marks a selection of nodes to which you can return later.
	Go to Bookmark	Zooms and pans to the selected bookmarked objects.
	Delete Bookmark	Removes the bookmark from the Bookmark selection list.

As you navigate the Schematic View window, you can save specific views as bookmarks by typing an identifying name in the Bookmark drop-down list. To recall these views later, select them from the drop-down list and click the Go to Bookmark icon in the Schematic View toolbar. Bookmarks can be deleted with the Delete Bookmark button.

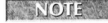 **NOTE**   Most of the menu commands and toolbar buttons are available in a pop-up menu that you can access by right-clicking in the Schematic View window.

Navigating the Schematic View window

As the number of nodes increases, it can become tricky to locate and see the correct node to work with. Along the bottom edge of the Schematic View window are several navigation buttons that work similarly to the Viewport Navigation Control buttons. Using these buttons, you can pan, zoom, and zoom to the extents of all nodes. These buttons are described in Table 24.2.

The Schematic View navigation buttons can also be accessed from within the View menu. These menu commands include Pan Tool, Zoom Tool, Zoom Region Tool, Zoom Extents, Zoom Extents Selected (Z), and Pan to Selected.

TIP You can also navigate the Schematic View window using the mouse and its scroll wheel. Scrubbing the mouse wheel zooms in and out of the window in steps. Holding down the Ctrl key and dragging with the scroll wheel button zooms smoothly in and out of the window. Dragging the scroll wheel pans within the window.

TABLE 24.2

Schematic View Navigation Buttons

Toolbar Button	Name	Description
	Zoom Selected Viewport Object	Zooms in on the nodes that correspond to the selected viewport objects.
Search	Search Name field	Locates an object node when you type its name.
	Pan	Moves the node view when you drag in the window.
	Zoom	Zooms when you drag the mouse in the window.
	Region Zoom	Zooms to an area selected when you drag an outline.
	Zoom Extents	Increases the window view until all nodes are visible.
	Zoom Extents Selected	Increases the window view until all selected nodes are visible.
	Pan to Selected	Moves the node view at the current zoom level to the selected objects.

Working with Schematic View nodes

Every object displayed in the scene has a *node* — a simple rectangular box that represents the object or attribute. Each node contains a label, and the color of the node depends on the node type.

Node colors

Nodes have a color scheme to help identify them. The colors of various nodes are listed in Table 24.3.

TABLE 24.3

Schematic View Node Colors

Color	Name
White	Selected node
Blue	Geometry Object node
Cyan	Shape Object node
Yellow	Light Object node
Dark Blue	Camera Object node
Green	Helper Object node
Purple	Space Warp Object node
Goldenrod	Modifier node
Dark Yellow	Base Object node
Brown	Material node
Dark Green	Map node
Salmon	Controller node
Magenta	Parameter Wires

 If you don't like any of these colors, you can set the colors used in the Schematic View using the Colors panel of the Customize User Interface dialog box.

Selecting nodes

The Select (S) button enters select mode, which lets you select nodes within the Schematic View window by clicking the object node. You can select multiple objects by dragging an outline over them. Holding down the Ctrl key while clicking an object node selects or deselects it. Selected nodes are shown in white.

The Select menu includes several selection commands that enable you to quickly select (or deselect) many nodes, including Select All (Ctrl+A), Select None (Ctrl+D), Select Invert (Ctlr+I), Select Children (Ctrl+C), and Deselect Children.

If the Select ⇨ Sync Selection option in the Select menu is enabled, then the node of any object that is selected in the viewports is also selected in the Schematic View window, and vice versa. If you disable the Sync Selection option, then you can select different objects in the viewports and in the Schematic View at the same time. The node of the object selected in the viewports is outlined in white, and the interior of selected nodes is white. To select all the objects in the viewports that match the selected nodes without the Sync Selection option enabled, just use Select ⇨ Select to Scene. Select ⇨ Select From Scene selects the nodes for all objects selected in the viewports.

 All animated objects have their node border drawn in red.

Rearranging nodes

The Schematic View includes several options for arranging nodes. In the Options menu, you can toggle between Hierarchy and Reference modes. Hierarchy mode displays the nodes vertically with child objects indented under their parent. Reference mode displays the nodes horizontally allowing for plenty of room to display all the various reference nodes under each parent node. Figure 24.2 shows these modes side by side.

FIGURE 24.2

The Schematic View window can automatically arrange nodes in two different modes: Hierarchy and Reference.

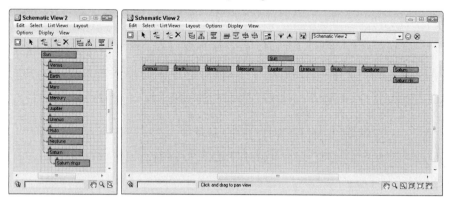

You can move nodes and rearrange them in any order. To move a node, simply click and drag it to a new location. When a node is dragged, all selected nodes move together, and any links follow the node movement. If a child node is moved, all remaining child nodes collapse together to maintain the specified arrangement mode. The moved node then becomes free, which is designated by an open rectangle on the left edge of the node. Figure 24.3 shows two nodes that were moved and thereby became free. The other children automatically moved closer together to close the gaps made by the moving nodes.

FIGURE 24.3

Free nodes are moved independent of the arranging mode.

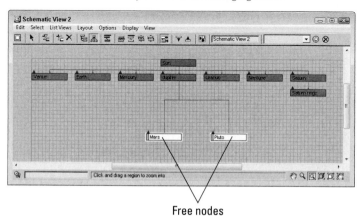

Free nodes

Using the Layout ⇨ Free Selected (Alt+S) and Free All (Alt+F) menu commands, you can free the selected nodes or all nodes. You can also designate that all the children of a node be auto arranged with the Layout ⇨ Arrange Children menu command or that just the selected nodes be arranged (Layout ⇨ Arrange Selected). The Options ⇨ Move Children (Alt+C) command causes all children to be moved along with their parent when the parent is moved. This causes free and non-free nodes to move with their parent.

If the Options ⇨ Always Arrange option is enabled, then Max automatically arranges all the nodes using either the Hierarchy or Reference mode, but you cannot move any of the nodes while this option is enabled. If you've moved any nodes when the Always Arrange option is selected, a dialog box appears telling you that your custom layout will be lost. If the Always Arrange option is enabled, the Arrange Children, Free All (Alt+F), Free Selected (Alt+S), Move Children (Alt+C), and all the Align options are all disabled. If two or more nodes are selected, you can align them using the Layout ⇨ Align menu. The options include Left, Right, Top, Bottom, Center Horizontal, and Center Vertical.

Hiding, shrinking, and deleting nodes

If your Schematic View window starts to get cluttered, you can always hide nodes to simplify the view. To hide a node, select the nodes to hide and use the Display ⇨ Hide Selected menu command. The Display ⇨ Unhide All menu command can be used to make the hidden nodes visible again.

 **If you hide a parent object, its children nodes are also hidden.**

Another useful way to reduce clutter in the Schematic View window is with the Layout ⇨ Shrink Selected command. This command replaces the rectangular node with a simple dot, but all hierarchical lines to the node are kept intact. Figure 24.4 shows a Schematic View with several shrunk nodes. Shrunk nodes can be unshrunk with the Layout ⇨ Unshrink Selected and Unshrink All menu commands.

 **The Shrink commands work only when Layout ⇨ Toggle Shrink (Ctrl+S) is enabled. With this command, you can turn on and off the visibility of shrunken nodes.**

FIGURE 24.4

Shrunken nodes appear as simple dots in the Schematic View.

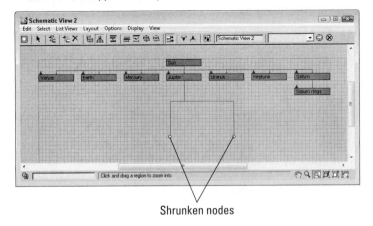

Shrunken nodes

To delete a node, select the node and click the Delete Objects button on the Schematic View toolbar or press the Delete key. If several nodes are selected, they are all deleted. This deletes the object in the viewports also.

Renaming objects

In the Schematic View window, you can rename objects quickly and conveniently. To rename an object, click a selected node and click again to highlight the text. When the text is highlighted, you can type the new name for the object. This works only for nodes that have a name, which includes materials.

Tutorial: Rearranging the Solar System

To practice moving nodes around, we order the solar system model. When Max places nodes in the Schematic View, it really doesn't follow any specific order, but you can move them as needed by hand.

To rearrange the solar system nodes, follow these steps.

1. Open the Ordered solar system.max file from the Chap 24 directory on the DVD.

   This file includes several named spheres representing the solar system.

2. Select Graph Editors ⇨ New Schematic View to open the Schematic View window.

   All planets are displayed as blue nodes under the Sun object.

3. Select Options ⇨ Reference Mode (if it is not already selected) to position all the nodes horizontally. Click the Select tool on the main toolbar (or press the S key).

4. Make sure that the Options ⇨ Always Arrange option is disabled. Then click and drag the Mercury node to the left, and place it front of the Venus node.

5. Select the Options ⇨ Move Children (Alt+C) menu command, and drag and drop the Saturn node between the Jupiter and Uranus nodes.

   With the Move Children option enabled, the Saturn rings node moves with its parent.

6. Drag and drop the Pluto node beyond the Neptune node.

7. Select all the planet nodes, and choose Layout ⇨ Align ⇨ Top to align all the nodes together.

 **Although astronomers no longer classify Pluto as a planet, I doubt that this book is required reading for astronomers. I think we can get away with calling Pluto a planet.**

Figure 24.5 shows the rearranged hierarchy with all the planets lined up in order.

FIGURE 24.5

After rearranging nodes to the correct order, the planets are easy to locate.

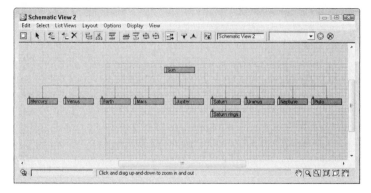

Working with Hierarchies

Another key benefit of the Schematic View is to see the relationships between different objects. With the Schematic View open, you can quickly tell which objects are children and which are parents. You can also see which objects have modifiers and which have materials applied. You can get a wealth of knowledge from the Schematic View.

Using the Display floater

With all relationships enabled, the Schematic View becomes a mess. Luckily, you can control which Relationships and which Entities are displayed using the Display floater, shown in Figure 24.6.

The Display floater can turn nodes and lines on and off in the Schematic View.

The top section of the Display floater shows or hides relationships between nodes, which are displayed as lines. The relationships that you can control include Constraints, Controllers, Param Wires, Light Inclusion, and Modifiers. If you hold the mouse over these relationship lines, the details of the relationship are shown in the tooltip that appears.

TIP   **For some relationships, you can double-click on the relationship line to open a dialog box where you can edit the relationship. For example, double-clicking on a Parameter Wire relationship line opens the Parameter Wiring dialog box.**

The lower section of the Display Floater lets you show or hide entities that are displayed as nodes, including Base Objects, Modifier Stack, Materials, and Controllers. The P, R, and S buttons let you turn on Positional, Rotational, and Scale controllers. When a node has a relationship with another node, the right end of the node displays an arrow. Clicking this arrow toggles the relationship lines on and off.

The Expand button shows the actual nodes when enabled, but only an arrow that can be clicked on to access the nodes if disabled. The Focus button shows all related objects as colored nodes, and all other nodes are unshaded.

Figure 24.7 shows a Schematic View with the Base Objects and Controllers Entities selected in the Display floater. The Expand button is also disabled. This makes up and down arrows appear above each node. Clicking the up arrow collapses the node, rolling it up into its parent. Clicking the down arrow expands the node and displays the Base Object and Controller nodes for the node that you clicked on, such as the Earth node in Figure 24.7. You can also expand and collapse nodes with the Display ⇨ Expand Selected and Collapse Selected menu commands.

FIGURE 24.7

Schematic View nodes can be collapsed or expanded by clicking the up and down arrows.

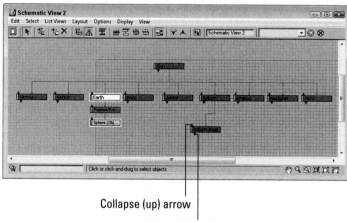

Collapse (up) arrow

Expand (down) arrow

Hierarchical relationships are shown as lines that connect the nodes. Even if the nodes are moved, the lines follow as needed to show the relationship between the nodes.

Connecting nodes

To create a hierarchy, use the Edit ⇨ Connect (or press the C shortcut) menu command or click the Connect button on the Schematic View toolbar. This enters Connect mode, which lets you link objects together; copy modifiers, materials, or controllers between nodes; or even wire parameters.

For linking nodes, the Connect button works the same way here as it does on the main toolbar — selecting the child node and dragging a line from the child node to its parent. You can even select multiple nodes and link them all at once.

The Edit ⇨ Unlink Selected menu command (and toolbar button) destroys the link between any object and its immediate parent. Remember that every child object can have only one parent.

Copying modifiers and materials between nodes

Before you can copy materials or modifiers between nodes, you need to make sure that they are visible. Material nodes and modifier nodes show up only if they are enabled in the Display floater. You can access this floater by clicking the Display floater button (or by pressing the D key).

To copy a material or modifier, select the material node for one object, click the Connect (C) button, and drag the material to another object node.

NOTE In the Schematic View, materials can be copied only between objects — you cannot apply new materials from the Material Editor to Schematic View nodes.

When modifiers are copied between nodes, a dialog box appears giving you the chance to Copy, Move, or Instance the modifier. You can also use the Schematic View window to reorder the Modifier Stack. Using the Connect tool, just drag the modifier node to the modifier node that you want to be beneath and the stack is reordered.

> **CROSS-REF**   You can learn more about applying modifiers and the Modifier Stack in Chapter 13, "Introducing Modifiers and Using the Modifier Stack."

Assigning controllers and wiring parameters

If controller nodes are visible, you can copy them to another node using the same technique used for materials and modifiers using the Connect (C) button. You can also assign a controller to an object node that doesn't have a controller using the Edit ➪ Assign Controller menu command. This opens the Assign Controller dialog box, shown in Figure 24.8, where you can select the controller to apply.

FIGURE 24.8

Controllers can be assigned using the Schematic View window.

Nodes can be wired using the Schematic View window. To wire parameters, just select the node that you want to wire and select Edit ➪ Wire Parameters. A pop-up menu of wire parameters appears that works the same as in the viewports. All parameter wiring relationships are shown in magenta.

> **CROSS-REF**   You can learn more about parameter wiring in Chapter 20, "Understanding Animation and Keyframe Basics."

Tutorial: Linking a character with the Schematic View

Perhaps one of the greatest benefits of the Schematic View is its ability to link objects. This can be tricky in the viewports because some objects are small and hidden behind other items. The Schematic View with its nodes that are all the same size makes it easy, but only if the objects are named correctly.

To link a character model using the Schematic View, follow these steps:

1. Open the Futuristic man.max file from the Chap 24 directory on the DVD.

   This file includes a simplified version of a futuristic man created by Viewpoint Datalabs with no links between the various parts.

2. Select Graph Editors ➪ New Schematic View to open a Schematic View window, and name the view **Linked character**. Click the Region Zoom button in the lower-right corner, and drag over the nodes at the left end of the Schematic View.

   For this model, we want the pelvis to be the parent node.

3. Click the Connect button on the toolbar (or press the C key), and drag from the handr node to the armr node to link the two nodes. Continue linking by connecting the following nodes: handl to arml, head to neck, pupil to eyes, bootr to legr, bootl to legl, and torso to pelvis.

4. Select the eyes, mask, patch, and hair nodes, and drag them all to the head node.

5. Finally, grab the armr, arml, neck, and katana nodes, and drag them to the torso node and the legr and legl nodes to the pelvis node.

   This completes the hierarchy.

 **Typically, when rigging characters, you want the pelvis to be the parent object because it is the center of most of the character movement.**

Figure 24.9 shows the final geometry object nodes of the linked character. If you move the pelvis part in the viewports, all the parts move together.

FIGURE 24.9

All character parts are now linked to the man's pelvis part.

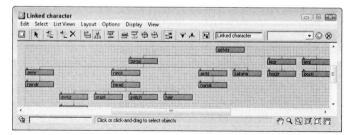

Setting Schematic View Preferences

The Preferences button opens the Schematic View Preferences dialog box, shown in Figure 24.10, where you can set which items are displayed or hidden, set up grids and background images, and specify how the Schematic View window looks.

Limiting nodes

When the Schematic View window is opened, Max traverses the entire hierarchy looking for objects and features that can be presented as nodes. If you have a complex scene and don't intend on using the Schematic View to see materials or modifiers, you can disable them in the Include in Calculation section of the Schematic View Preferences dialog box. This provides a way to simplify the data that is presented. With less data, locating and manipulating what you are looking for becomes easier.

FIGURE 24.10

The Schematic View Preferences dialog box lets you customize many aspects of the Schematic View window.

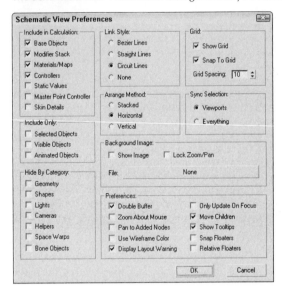

The Include in Calculation section includes options for limiting the following:

- **Base Objects:** The geometry type that makes up a node. The node is the named object, such as Earth; the Base Object is its primitive, such as Sphere (Object).
- **Modifier Stack:** Identifies all nodes with modifiers applied.
- **Materials/Maps:** Identifies all nodes with materials and maps applied.
- **Controllers:** Identifies all nodes that have controllers applied.
- **Static Values:** Displays unanimated parameter values.
- **Master Point Controller:** Displays nodes for any subobject selections that include controllers.
- **Skin Details:** Displays nodes for the modifiers and controllers that are used when the Skin modifier is applied to a bones system.

You can also limit the number of nodes using the Include Only options. The Selected Objects option shows only the objects selected in the viewports. The nodes change as new objects are selected in the viewports. The Visible Objects option displays only the nodes for those objects that are not hidden in the viewports, and the Animated Objects option displays only the nodes of the objects that are animated.

Object categories that can be hidden include Geometry, Shapes, Lights, Cameras, Helpers, Space Warps, and Bone Objects. Figure 24.11 shows a single sphere object in the Schematic View window with all the Include in Calculation options selected.

Working with grids and backgrounds

The Schematic View Preferences dialog box includes settings to Show Grid, Snap to Grid, and set Grid Spacing. The keyboard shortcut for toggling the grid on and off is G. Enabling the Snap to Grid option makes the nodes snap to the closest grid intersection. This helps keep the nodes aligned and looking neat.

FIGURE 24.11

Without limiting nodes, the Schematic View window can get very busy.

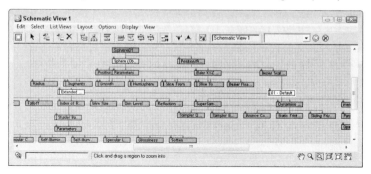

The Background Image section of the Schematic View Preferences dialog box includes a File button that opens a file dialog box when clicked. Selecting an image file opens and displays the image as a background image. This is helpful as you arrange nodes. You need to select the Show Image option to see the background image, and the Lock Zoom/Pan option locks the nodes to the background image so zooming in on a set of nodes also zooms in on the background image.

> **TIP** One of the easiest ways to get a background image of a model to use in the Schematic View is to render a single frame and save it from the Rendered Frame Window to a location where you can reopen it as the Schematic View background. If you want to print the hierarchy, you can do a screen capture of the Schematic View window, but it would be nice to have a print feature added to the window.

Display preferences

In the Schematic View Preferences dialog box, you can select the style to use for relationship lines. The options include Bezier, Straight, Circuit, and None. When the Always Arrange, Arrange Children, or Arrange Selected options are used, you can select to have the nodes arranged Stacked, Horizontal, or Vertical. The Sync Selection options enable you to synch the selection between the Schematic View and the Viewports or between Everything. If the Everything option is selected, then not only are geometry objects in the viewports selected, but if a material is selected in the Schematic View, then the material is selected in the Material Editor also. Sync Selection Everything also affects the Modifier Stack, the Controller pane in the Display panel, and the Wiring Parameters dialog box.

The Schematic View Preferences dialog box also includes a Preferences section. These preference settings include Double Buffer, which enables a double-buffer display and helps improve the viewport update performance. The Zoom About Mouse Pointer preference enables zooming by using the scroll wheel on your mouse or by pressing the middle mouse button while holding down the Ctrl key. The Move Children option causes children nodes to move along with their parent. The Pan to Added Nodes preference automatically resizes and moves the nodes to enable you to view any additional nodes that have been added.

The Use Wireframe Color option changes the node colors to be the same as the viewport object color. The Display Layout Warning lets you disable the warning that appears every time you use the Always Arrange feature. The Only Update on Focus option causes the Schematic View to update only when the window is selected. Until then, any changes are not propagated to the window. This can be a timesaver when complex scenes require redraws.

The Show Tooltips option allows you to disable tooltips if you desire. Tooltips show in the Schematic View window when you hover the cursor over the top of a node. Tooltips can be handy if you've zoomed out so far that you can't read the node labels; just move the cursor over a node, and its label appears. The Snap Floater option enables the Display and List floaters to be snapped to the edge of the window for easy access, and the Relative Floaters option moves and resizes the floaters along with the Schematic View window.

Tutorial: Adding a background image to the Schematic View

You can position nodes anywhere within the Schematic View window. For example, you can position the nodes to look something like the shape of the model that you're linking. When positioning the different objects, having a background image is really handy.

To add a background image for the Schematic View, follow these steps:

1. Open the Futuristic man with background.max file in the Chap 24 directory on the DVD.

   This file uses the same futuristic man model used in the preceding example.

2. With the Perspective viewport maximized, select Tools ⇨ Grab Viewport. Give the viewport the name of futuristic man — front view, and click the Grab button.

   The viewport image opens the Rendered Frame Window.

3. Click the Save Bitmap button in the upper-left corner. Save the image as Futuristic man — front view. Then close the Rendered Frame Window.

4. Select Graph Editors ⇨ New Schematic View to open a Schematic View window, and name the view **Background**. Click the Preferences button on the Schematic View toolbar, and click the File button in the Background Image section.

5. Locate the saved image, and open it. Select the Show Image option in the Schematic View Preferences dialog box and click the OK button.

   You can perform this step using the image file saved in the Chap 24 directory on the DVD, if you so choose.

6. Select the View ⇨ Show Grid menu command (or press the G key) to turn off the grid. Drag on the corner of the Schematic View interface to increase the size of the window so that the whole background image is visible.

7. Before moving any of the nodes, enable the Lock Zoom/Pan option in the Schematic View Preferences dialog box so the image resizes with the nodes. Then, select each of the nodes, and drag them so that they are roughly positioned on top of the part that they represent. Start by moving the parent objects first, and then work to their children.

Figure 24.12 shows all the nodes aligned over their respective parts. From this arrangement, you can clearly see how the links are organized.

Using List Views

One of the last uses of the Schematic View is to list all nodes that have things in common. Using the List Views menu, you can select to see All Relationships, Selected Relationships, All Instances, Selected Instances, Show Occurrences, and All Animated Controllers.

The List Views ⇨ All Relationships menu command displays a separate dialog box, shown in Figure 24.13, containing a list of nodes and their relationships. The Selected Relationships menu command limits the list to only selected objects with relationships. The List Views dialog box also includes a Detach button to remove the relationships if desired. Double-clicking on a relationship in the list opens its dialog box, where you can edit the relationship.

FIGURE 24.12

Using a background image, you can see how the links relate to the model.

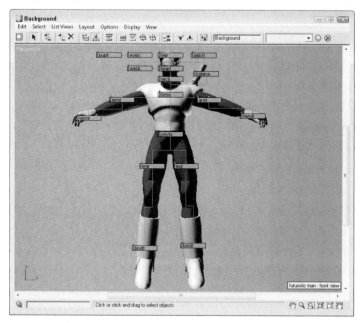

 **TIP** You can click each column head to sort the entries.

FIGURE 24.13

The List Views dialog box includes a list of nodes with relationships.

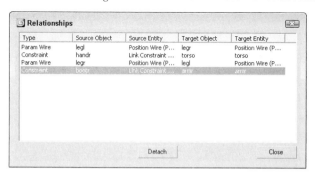

The List Views ➪ All Instances menu command displays all the instances found in the scene. This includes all types of instances, including geometry, modifiers, controllers, and so on. For the Instances list view, the Detach button is replaced with a Make Unique button.

Another way to identify instances is to look for bold text in the node. All label text for all instanced nodes is displayed in bold.

If a node is selected and you want to see all other nodes that share the same type of relationship or that share a property, the List Views ➪ Show Occurrences displays them. The final list view shows All Animated Controllers.

Summary

Some tasks in the viewport, such as linking objects into a hierarchy, can be difficult. The Schematic View represents all data as simple rectangular nodes. These nodes make easy work of accomplishing a variety of tasks.

In this chapter, you've done the following:

- Viewed all objects as nodes using the Schematic View window
- Learned the Schematic View interface
- Used the Schematic View window to select, delete, and copy objects, materials, and modifiers
- Used the Schematic View to assign controllers and wire parameters
- Set preferences for the Schematic View window
- Listed views of nodes with common properties

In the next chapter, you learn more about features that enable deforming meshes, including the Paint Deformation tool and various modifiers that may be applied to mesh objects.

Chapter 25

Deforming Surfaces and Using the Mesh Modifiers

W hen an Editable Poly object is selected, three specific deformation brushes may be selected in the Paint Deformation rollout. Using these brushes, you can deform the surface of an object by dragging over the surface with the selected brush.

In addition to the editing features available for Editable Mesh and Editable Poly objects and the Paint Deformation brushes, you also can modify mesh geometries using modifiers. The Modifiers menu includes a submenu of modifiers that are specific to mesh (and poly) objects. These modifiers are found in the Mesh Editing submenu and can be used to enhance the features available for these objects.

Another set of modifiers that apply specifically to mesh objects are the Subdivision Surface modifiers. These modifiers are also covered in this chapter.

IN THIS CHAPTER

Using the Paint Deformation brush

Maintaining primitive objects with the Edit Mesh and Edit Poly modifiers

Changing mesh geometry with modifiers

Editing mesh normals

Working with Subdivision Surfaces

The Basics of Deformation Painting

The first thing to remember about the Paint Deformation feature is that it is available only for Editable Poly objects (or objects with the Edit Poly modifier applied). When an Editable Poly object is selected, the Paint Deformation rollout appears at the very bottom of the Command Panel.

Painting deformations

At the top of the Paint Deformation rollout are three buttons used to select the type of deformation brush to use. These three brushes are the Push/Pull brush, the Relax brush, and the Revert brush.

When one of these brushes is selected, the mouse cursor changes to a circular brush, shown in Figure 25.1, that follows the surface of the object as you move the mouse over the object. A single line points outward from the center of the circle in the direction of the surface normal. Dragging the mouse affects the surface in a certain manner, depending on the brush that is selected.

The Paint Deformation brush looks like a circle that follows the surface.

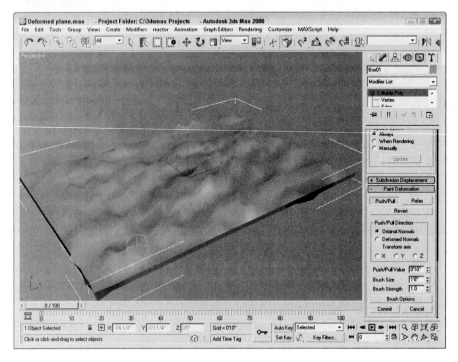

Dragging the Paint Deformation brush over the object surface deforms the surface by moving the vertices within the brush's area. The direction that the vertices are moved follows the surface normals by default, or you can have the deformation follow a deformed normal or along a specified transform axis. For example, if you select to deform vertices along the X-axis, then all vertices underneath the brush are moved along the X-axis as the brush is dragged over the surface.

NOTE Deformations created using the Paint Deformation brushes cannot be animated. For objects with the Edit Poly modifier applied, the Paint Deformation brushes are disabled when in Animate mode.

The Push/Pull value determines the distance that the vertices are moved, thereby setting the amount of the deformation. The Brush Size sets the size (or radius) of the brush and determines the area that is deformed. The Brush Strength value sets the rate at which the vertices are moved. For example, if the Push/Pull Value is set to 100 mm, then a Brush Strength value of 1.0 causes the vertices directly under the brush center to move 100 mm; a Brush Strength value of 0.4 causes the same vertices to move only 40 mm.

TIP Holding down the Shift and Alt keys while dragging in the viewports lets you interactively change the Brush Strength value.

Accessing brush presets

If you right-click the main toolbar away from any of the buttons, you can access the Brush Presets toolbar, shown in Figure 25.2, from the pop-up menu.

FIGURE 25.2

FIGURE 25.2

The Brush Presets toolbar lets you quickly select from a selection of predefined brushes.

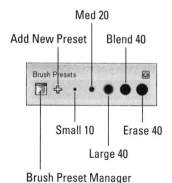

The first toolbar button opens the Brush Preset Manager, shown in Figure 25.3. From this interface, you can choose to create preset brushes for each of the different features that use brushes — Vertex Paint, Paint Deformation, Paint Soft Selection, and Paint Skin Weights. The Add button works the same as the Add New Preset toolbar button. It opens a dialog box where you can name the new preset. The new preset is then added to the list of presets.

FIGURE 25.3

The Brush Preset Manager lets you create new preset brushes.

When a brush preset is selected on the Brush Presets toolbar, you can change its attributes using the Brush Options dialog box. Any changes to the brush attributes are automatically updated in the Brush Preset Manager. The Load and Save buttons in the Brush Preset Manager dialog box let you save and load brush preset sets.

Using the Deformation Brushes

The Push/Pull brush may be used to pull vertices away from the object surface or to indent the surface by moving the surface toward the object's center. The difference is determined by the Push/Pull value. Positive values pull vertices, and negative values push vertices.

 Holding down the Alt key while dragging reverses the direction of the Push/Pull brush, causing a pull brush to push and vice versa.

Controlling the deformation direction

By default, dragging over vertices with the Push/Pull brush causes the affected vertices to be moved inward or outward along their normals. If you drag over the same vertices several times, they are still deformed using the original face normals.

The Deformed Normals option causes the vertices to be moved in the direction of the normal as the normals are deformed. Using the Original Normals option causes the deformed area to rise from the surface like a hill with a gradual increasing height. The Deformed Normals option causes the deformed area to bubble out from the surface.

The Transform Axis option causes the vertices to be moved in the direction of the selected transform axis. This option is useful if you want to skew or shift the deformed area.

Limiting the deformation

If a subobject selection exists, then the vertices that are moved are limited to the subobject area that is selected. You can use this to your advantage if you want to make sure that only a certain area is deformed.

Committing any changes

After you make some deformation changes, the Commit and Cancel buttons become active. Pressing the Commit button makes the changes permanent, which means that you can no longer return the vertices to their original location with the Revert brush. The Cancel button rejects all the recent deformation changes.

Using the Relax and Revert brushes

The Relax brush provides a much more subtle change. It moves vertices that are too close together farther apart, causing a general smoothing of any sharp points. It works the same way as the Relax feature for the Editable Poly object and the Relax modifier.

The Revert brush is used to return to their original position any vertices that have moved. For example, if you pushed and pulled several vertices, the Revert brush can undo all of these changes for the area under the brush cursor.

 Holding down the Ctrl key while dragging with the Push/Pull brush lets you temporarily access the Revert brush.

Tutorial: Adding veins to a forearm

The Paint Deformation feature is very useful in adding surface details to organic objects such as the veins of a forearm.

To add veins to a forearm object, follow these steps:

1. Open the Forearm with veins.max file from the Chap 25 directory on the DVD.

   The polygons that make up the forearm object have been selected and tessellated to increase its resolution.

2. With the forearm object selected, open the Modify panel and in the Paint Deformation rollout, click the Relax button. Set the Brush Size to **1.0**, and drag over the entire forearm.

   This smoothes out some of the vertical lines that run along the forearm.

3. Click the Push/Pull button, and set the Push/Pull Value to **0.15**, the Brush Size to **0.08**, and the Brush Strength to **0.5**. Then draw in some veins extending from the elbow toward the hand.

4. Lower the Brush Strength value to **0.25**, and extend the vein further down the arm. Then drop the Brush Strength to **0.1**, and finish the veins.

5. With the Push/Pull brush still selected, hold down the Alt key and drag near the wrist to indent the surface around the area where the hand tendons are located.

Figure 25.4 shows the resulting forearm.

FIGURE 25.4

The Paint Deformation brushes are helpful in painting on raised and indented surface features.

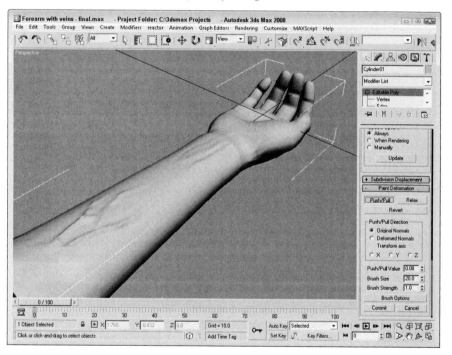

Setting Brush Options

At the bottom of the Paint Deformation rollout is a button labeled Brush Options. Clicking this button opens the Painter Options dialog box, shown in Figure 25.5. Using this dialog box, you can set several customized brush options including the sensitivity of the brush.

CROSS-REF The Painter Options dialog box is also used by the brushes to paint vertex colors for the Vertex Paint modifier and to paint skin weights as part of the Skin modifier. The Vertex Paint modifier is covered in Chapter 31, "Creating Baked Textures and Normal Maps," and the Skin modifier is covered in Chapter 43, "Skinning Characters."

FIGURE 25.5

The Painter Options dialog box includes a graph for defining the minimum and maximum brush strengths and sizes.

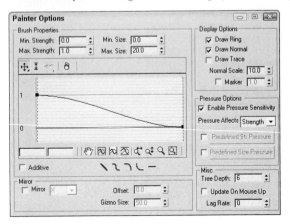

The Min/Max Strength and Min/Max Size values determine the minimum and maximum weight values and paint gizmo sizes. You can define the brush falloff using the curve. This keeps the weights from making an abrupt change (muscles tend to look funny when this happens). Under the curve are several buttons for quickly defining the shape of the falloff curve, including Linear, Smooth, Slow, Fast, and Flat.

The Display Options section includes options that determine the look of the painting gizmo. The Draw Ring, Draw Normal, and Draw Trace options make a ring; the surface normal or an arrow showing the trace direction appears. The Normal can be scaled, and the Marker option displays a small circular marker at the end of the normal.

The Pressure Options let you paint using a graphics tablet with the pressure applied to affect the Strength, Size, or a combination. You can enable Pressure Sensitivity for the brush gizmo. The options include None, Strength, Size, and Both. Using the graph, you can predefine Strength and Size pressure curves and then select to use them.

The Mirror option paints symmetrically on the opposite side of the gizmo across the specified axis. You can also set an Offset and the Gizmo Size. This is handy for muscles that you want to deform symmetrically.

In the Miscellaneous section, the Tree Depth, Update on Mouse Up, and Lag Rate options control how often the scene and the painted strokes are updated.

Primitive Maintenance Modifiers

Included among the Mesh Editing modifiers are two unique modifiers that can be applied to primitive objects, allowing them to maintain their parametric nature.

 Using the Edit Mesh or Edit Poly modifiers increases the file size and memory required to work with the object. You can reduce the overhead by collapsing the modifier stack.

Edit Mesh modifier

All mesh objects are by default Editable Mesh objects. This modifier enables objects to be modified using the Editable Mesh features while maintaining their basic creation parameters.

When an object is converted to an Editable Mesh, its parametric nature is eliminated. However, if you use the Edit Mesh modifier, you can still retain the same object type and its parametric nature while having access to all the Editable Mesh features. For example, if you create a sphere and apply the Edit Mesh modifier and then extrude several faces, you can still change the radius of the sphere by selecting the Sphere object in the Modifier Stack and changing the Radius value in the Parameters rollout.

If the Sphere base object is selected after a modifier has been applied, the Topology Dependence warning dialog box appears. This dialog box doesn't prevent you from making any changes to the base object parameters, but it reminds you that changes you make to the base object's parameters may disrupt the changes to the surface accomplished by the modifiers. The warning dialog box also includes a Hold button to load the current scene in a buffer in case you don't like the results.

 One drawback of the Edit Mesh modifier is that its subobjects cannot be animated.

Edit Poly modifier

The Edit Poly modifier lets you work with primitive objects using the operators found in the Editable Poly rollouts. A huge benefit of this modifier is that you can remove it at any time if the changes don't work out.

The Edit Poly modifier includes two separate modes: Model and Animate. You can select these modes in the Edit Poly Mode rollout, shown in Figure 25.6.

FIGURE 25.6

The Edit Poly Mode rollout lets you switch between Model and Animate modes.

Model mode lets you access the same features available for Editable Poly objects. Animate mode lets you animate subobject changes made with the features used to edit the object. To animate these subobject changes, you use the Auto Key or Set Key buttons to set the keys.

The Commit button lets you freeze the changes and set the keyframe for the current change. The current change is listed directly above the Commit button. The Settings button lets you access the dialog box used to make the changes. The Cancel button cancels the last change, and the Show Cage option displays an orange cage around the object; you can change the color of the cage using the color swatch. The cage is useful when using the MeshSmooth modifier to see the original shape of the object before being smoothed.

The differences between the features available for the Edit Poly modifier and the Editable Poly object are subtle. In the Selection rollout is a Get Stack Selection button. Clicking this button passes the subobject selection up from the stack. Also, the Edit Poly modifier doesn't include the Subdivision Surfaces rollout, but you can use the MeshSmooth modifier to get this functionality.

Edit Geometry Modifiers

Most of the Mesh Editing modifiers are used to change the geometry of objects. Some of these modifiers, such as Extrude and Tessellate, perform the same operation as buttons available for the Editable Mesh or Editable Poly objects. Applying them as modifiers separates the operation from the base geometry.

 You can find a more general explanation of modifiers in Chapter 13, "Introducing Modifiers and Using the Modifier Stack."

Cap Holes modifier

The Cap Holes modifier patches any holes found in a geometry object. Sometimes when objects are imported, they are missing faces. This modifier can detect and eliminate these holes by creating a face along open edges.

For example, if a spline is extruded and you don't specify Caps, then the extruded spline has holes at its end. The Cap Holes modifier detects these holes and creates a Cap. Cap Holes parameters include Smooth New Faces, Smooth with Old Faces, and Triangulate Cap. Smooth with Old Faces applies the same smoothing group as that used on the bordering faces.

Delete Mesh modifier

You can use the Delete Mesh modifier to delete mesh subobjects. Subobjects that you can delete include Vertices, Edges, Faces, and Objects. The nice part about the Delete Mesh modifier is that it remains in the Modifier Stack and can be removed to reinstate the deleted subobjects.

The Delete Mesh modifier deletes the current selection as defined by the Mesh Select (or Poly Select) modifier. It can be used to delete a selection of Vertices, Edges, Faces, Polygons, or even the entire mesh if no subobject selection exists. The Delete Mesh modifier has no parameters.

NOTE Even if the entire mesh is deleted using the Delete Mesh modifier, the object still remains. To completely delete an object, use the Delete key.

Extrude modifier

The Extrude modifier can be applied only to spline or shape objects, but the resulting extrusion can be a Patch, Mesh, or NURBS object. This modifier copies the spline, moves it a given distance, and connects the two splines to form a 3D shape. Parameters for this modifier include an Amount value, which is the distance to extrude, and the number of segments to use to define the height. The Capping options let you select a Start Cap and/or an End Cap using either a Morph or Grid option. The Morph option divides the caps into long, thin polygons suitable for morph targets, and the Grid option divides the caps into a tight grid of polygons suitable for deformation operations. The Cap fills the spline area and can be made as a Patch, Mesh, or NURBS object. Only closed splines that are extruded can be capped. You can also have mapping coordinates and Material IDs generated automatically. The Smooth option smoothes the extrusion.

CROSS-REF Chapter 11, "Drawing and Editing 2D Splines and Shapes," includes a good example of the Extrude modifier.

Face Extrude modifier

The Face Extrude modifier extrudes the selected faces in the same direction as their normals. Face Extrude parameters include Amount and Scale values and an option to Extrude From Center. Figure 25.7 shows a mesh object with several extruded faces. The Mesh Select modifier was used to select the faces, and the extrude Amount was set to **30**.

FIGURE 25.7

Extruded faces are moved in the direction of the face normal.

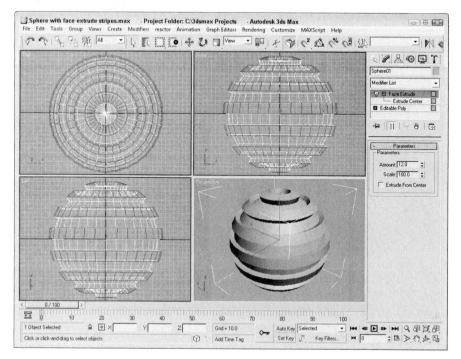

Tutorial: Extruding a bullet

As a simple example that uses a couple of Mesh modifiers, we create a single bullet using a hemisphere object. You can create this simple object in other ways, but this offers some good practice.

To create a bullet using the Face Extrude modifier, follow these steps:

1. Select Create ⇨ Standard Primitives ⇨ Sphere, and drag in the Top viewport to create a sphere object. Set the Radius value to **60** and the Hemisphere value to **0.5** to create half a sphere.

2. Right-click on the sphere object, and select Convert To ⇨ Editable Poly in the pop-up quadmenu to convert the hemisphere to an Editable Poly object.

3. Select the Top viewport, right-click on the viewport name, and select Views ⇨ Bottom from the pop-up menu (or press the B key) to switch to the Bottom view.

4. In the Selection rollout, click the Vertex button to enter Vertex subobject mode and enable the Ignore Backfacing option. Then select the single vertex in the center of the hemisphere, and press the Delete key.

5. In the Selection rollout, click the Border button to enter Border subobject mode, and then click the edge of the hemisphere to select the border of the hole that was created by deleting the center vertex. Then click the Cap button in the Edit Borders rollout.

6. Select the Polygon button in the Selection rollout to enter Polygon subobject mode and select the bottom polygon subobject. Then select Modifiers ⇨ Mesh Editing ⇨ Face Extrude to apply the Face Extrude modifier to the selected polygon face. Set the Amount value to **200**.

619

7. Select Create ➪ Standard Primitives ➪ Cylinder, and drag in the Bottom viewport to create a thin Cylinder object that is just wider than the extruded hemisphere. Then move the new Cylinder object until it is positioned at the end of the bullet object.

Figure 25.8 shows the completed simple bullet.

FIGURE 25.8

A simple bullet can be created by extruding one face of a hemisphere.

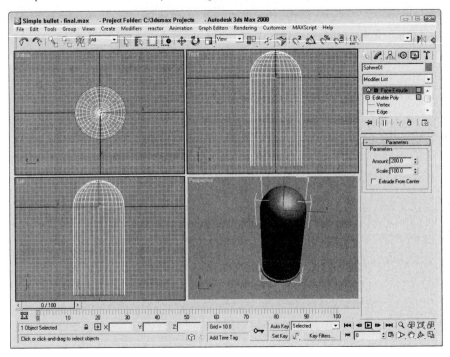

Optimize modifier

The Optimize modifier isn't as robust as the MultiRes modifier, but it roughly accomplishes the same function — reducing the overall number of polygons. It does the opposite of the Tessellation modifier. It simplifies models by reducing the number of faces, edges, and vertices. The Level of Detail can be set differently for the Renderer and the Viewports. Face and Edge Thresholds determine whether elements should be collapsed. Other options include Bias and Maximum Edge Length. Parameters can also be set to Preserve Material and Smooth Boundaries. The Update button enables manual updating of the object, and the text field at the bottom of the rollout displays the number of vertices and faces for the current optimization.

Figure 25.9 shows an alligator model that has been optimized. Notice the dramatic reduction in the number of faces from the left to the right. Viewpoint Datalabs, known for producing high-resolution models, created this model. At the bottom of the Modify panel, you can see that the number of faces has been reduced from 34,404 to 10,140 faces by setting the Face Threshold to **15** and the Edge Threshold to **3.0**. (I guess that would make the gator on the right "lean and mean.")

FIGURE 25.9

You can use the Optimize modifier to reduce the complexity of the alligator model.

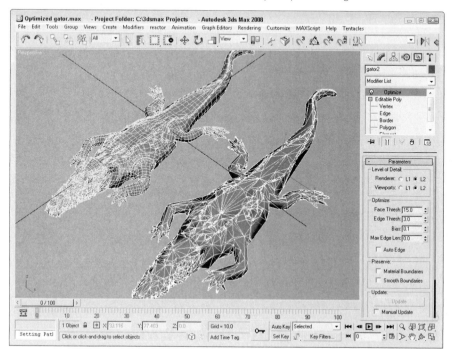

MultiRes modifier

You can use the MultiRes modifier to create lower-resolution versions of a mesh object. This modifier is especially useful for creating real-time updated meshes for the gaming market. Once applied to a mesh object using the Modifier List in the Modify panel, you can set the desired options in the Generation Parameters section of the MultiRes Parameters rollout and click the Generate button to apply the MultiRes solution to the selected object.

The Vertex Merging option maintains continuity between vertices within the mesh. When enabled, vertices within the Threshold value are welded as the mesh is reduced. The Within Mesh option collapses the boundaries of adjacent elements. The Boundary Metric option looks for boundaries where different materials are applied and tries to maintain these boundaries.

The MultiRes modifier includes a single subobject: Vertex. Using this subobject mode, you can select vertices that you don't want to change. These selected subobject vertices are not altered if the Maintain Base Vertices option is enabled. The Crease Angle value can be used to maintain sharp edges. If any of the options are changed, you can update the solution by clicking the Generation button again.

Once generated, you can use the Vertex Percent and Vertex Count spinners to control the mesh complexity. The viewport displays the updated mesh as you change its complexity. The rollout displays the number of vertices and faces. The Max Vertex and Max Face fields are the number of vertices and faces in the original mesh; the Face Count is the current number of faces.

Tutorial: Creating a MultiRes hand

You can use the Optimize modifier to quickly create the lower-resolution models, but the MultiRes modifier offers more functionality and enables you to dynamically dial down the resolution to exactly what you want. In this example, we use the MultiRes modifier on a high-res hand model created by Viewpoint Datalabs. The hand weighs in at 2,906 polygons, which is a little heavy for any game engine.

To create a MultiRes hand, follow these steps:

1. Open the MultiRes hand.max file from the Chap 25 directory on the DVD.

   This file contains a simple hand model.

2. With the hand selected, choose MultiRes from the Modifier List to apply the modifier to the hand model.

3. In the MultiRes Parameters rollout, enable the Vertex Merging option and set the Threshold to **0.05**. Also enable the Boundary Metric and Multiple Vertex Normals options, and set the Crease Angle to **75**. Then click the Generate button.

4. Create a copy of the hand by holding down the Shift key and dragging the hand to the right. In the Clone Options dialog box that appears, select Copy, name the clone **Hand – Lo**, and click OK.

5. With the cloned hand selected, set the Vert Percent to **10**.

   Notice that the number of faces has dropped from over 2,906 to 302.

Figure 25.10 shows the results of the MultiRes modifier. If you look closely, you can see that the hand on the right isn't as smooth, but it still looks pretty good and the game engine won't complain.

CAUTION   Reducing mesh density on the fly should not be done with animated objects such as characters because the mesh can become chaotic and dirty, resulting in poor deformations. However, the Multi-Res modifier does work very well with static background objects.

Smooth modifier

You can use the Smooth modifier to auto-smooth an object. This automates the creation of different smoothing groups based on the angular threshold. Smooth parameters include options for Auto Smooth and Prevent Indirect Smoothing along with a Threshold value. The Parameters rollout also includes a set of 32 Smoothing Groups buttons labeled 1 through 32. These same Smoothing Groups are available as options for the Polygon and Element subobjects.

Symmetry modifier

The Symmetry modifier allows you to mirror a mesh object across a single axis. You can also select to Slice Along Mirror and weld along the seam with a defined Threshold. The gizmo for this modifier is a plane, which matches the selected axis and the arrow vector that extends from the plane.

Tutorial: Creating symmetrical antlers

Using symmetry, you can create one half of a model and then use the mirror tool to create the other half. If you need to see the changes as you make them, you can use the Symmetry modifier. In this example, we've taken the antlers off an elk model so you can practice putting them back on.

FIGURE 25.10

You can use the MultiRes modifier to dynamically dial back the complexity of a mesh.

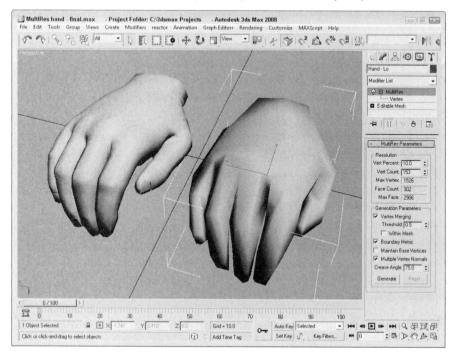

To create a set of symmetrical antlers, follow these steps:

1. Open the Elk with short antlers.max file from the Chap 25 directory on the DVD.

   This file contains an elk model created by Viewpoint Datalabs with its antlers removed.

2. With the hide object selected, select the Modifiers ➪ Mesh Editing ➪ Symmetry menu command to apply the Symmetry modifier. Its default setting has the X-axis selected, which places a plane running down the center of the elk model, but you need to enable the Flip option so the symmetry goes the right way.

3. In the Modifier Stack, select the Editable Poly object and enable the Polygon subobject mode. Then rotate the view until you're looking at the elk from behind its head. Select a polygon on the left side of the elk where the antler should be located.

4. In the Edit Polygons rollout, click the option dialog box button for the Bevel tool. Set the Height value to **2.0**, the Outline Amount to **-0.15**, and click OK.

5. With the polygon still selected, move the beveled polygon outward away from the elk's head.

6. Disable the polygon subobject mode and click on the Symmetry modifier in the Modifier Stack to see the symmetrical antler.

> **TIP** If you toggle the Show End Result button in the Modifier Stack, then you can see the results of the Symmetry modifier in real time.

Figure 25.11 shows the results of the Symmetry modifier.

FIGURE 25.11

When you use the Symmetry modifier, you have to model certain objects only once.

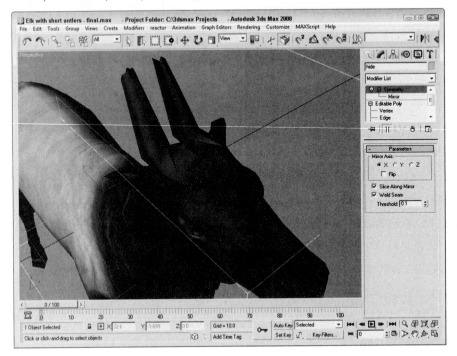

Tessellate modifier

You use the Tessellate modifier to subdivide the selected faces for higher-resolution models. You can apply tessellation to either Triangle or Polygonal faces. The Edge option creates new faces by dividing the face from the face center to the middle of the edges. The Face-Center option divides each face from the face center to the corners of the face. The Tension setting determines whether the faces are convex or concave. The Iterations setting is the number of times the modifier is applied.

 Applying the Tessellate modifier to an object with a high Iterations value produces objects with many times the original number of faces.

Vertex Weld modifier

The Vertex Weld modifier is a simple modifier that welds all vertices within a certain Threshold value. This is a convenient modifier for cleaning up mesh objects.

Miscellaneous Modifiers

Several of the Mesh Editing modifiers are unique, special-purpose modifiers. The Edit Normals modifier, for example, lets you change the direction of face normals, which doesn't really change the geometry, but it can have a big impact on how the object is smoothed and shaded.

Edit Normals

The Edit Normals modifier enables you to select and move normals. Normals appear as blue lines that extend from the vertex of each face. The Edit Normal modifier includes a Normals subobject that you can select and change its direction. To move (or rotate) a normal, you can use the transform tools on the main toolbar. If your viewport has shading enabled, you can see the effect of moving the normals.

> **TIP** The Edit Normals modifier can be used to create the illusion of surface geometry. For example, by selecting and flipping specific localized normals, you can create what look like dents in a metal plate.

You can select normals by Normal, Edge, Vertex, or Face. Selecting normals by Face, for example, selects all normals attached to a face when you click on a face. Moving a normal then moves all selected normals together.

You also have options to Ignore Backfacing and to Show Handles. Handles appear as small squares at the top of the normal vector. The Display Length value defines the length of the normals displayed in the viewports. Figure 25.12 shows all the normals extending from a simple Box object.

FIGURE 25.12

The Edit Normals Parameters let you work with normals.

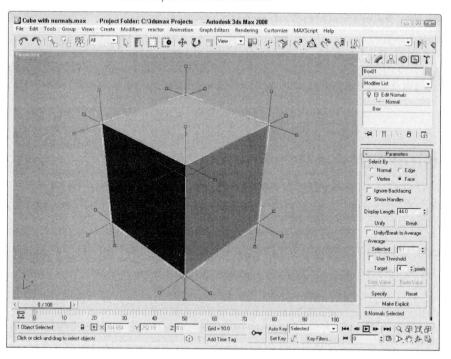

The modifier also includes buttons to Unify and to Break selected normals. Unify causes all selected normals to be combined to a single normal, and Break splits unified normals into their separate components again. The direction of the unified normal is an average of the surface points when unified or an average of the normals if the Unify/Break to Average option is enabled.

The Average Selected button averages all selected normals that are within the specified value if the Use Threshold value is enabled. If it is not enabled, then all selected normals are averaged. The Average Target button lets you interactively select a normal and then click on another normal to average. The Target normal must be within the specified Target value.

The direction of selected normals can be copied and pasted between normals. The Specify button marks a normal as a Specified normal. These normals appear cyan in the viewport and ignore any smoothing group information associated with the vertex. Explicit normals are green in the viewport, which denotes a normal that has deviated from its regular position. The Make Explicit button can be used to make normals explicit, thereby removing them from the normal computation task. The Reset button returns a normal to its regular type and position. At the bottom of the Parameters rollout is an information line that displays which normal is selected or how many normals are selected.

Normal modifier

The Normal modifier is the precursor to the Edit Normals modifier. It enables object normals to be flipped or unified. When some objects are imported, their normals can become erratic, producing holes in the geometry. By unifying and flipping the normals, you can restore an object's consistency. This modifier includes only two options: Unify Normals and Flip Normals.

STL Check modifier

The STL Check modifier checks a model in preparation for exporting it to the StereoLithography (STL) format. StereoLithography files require a closed surface: Geometry with holes or gaps can cause problems. Any problems are reported in the Status area of the Parameters rollout.

This modifier can check for several common errors, including Open Edge, Double Face, Spike, or Multiple Edge. Spikes are island faces with only one connected edge. You can select any or all of these options. If found, you can have the modifier select the problem Edges or Faces, or neither, or you can change the Material ID of the problem area.

Subdivision Surface Modifiers

The Modifiers menu also includes a submenu of modifiers for subdividing surfaces. These include the MeshSmooth and HSDS Modifiers. You can use these modifiers to smooth and subdivide the surface of an object. Subdividing a surface increases the resolution of the object, allowing for more detailed modeling.

MeshSmooth modifier

The MeshSmooth modifier smoothes the entire surface of an object by applying a chamfer function to both vertices and edges at the same time. This modifier has the greatest effect on sharp corners and edges. With this modifier, you can create a NURMS object. NURMS stands for Non-Uniform Rational MeshSmooth. NURMS can weight each control point. The Parameters rollout includes three MeshSmooth types: Classic, NURMS, and Quad Output. You can set it to operate on triangular or polygonal faces. Smoothing parameters include Strength and Relax values.

Settings for the number of Subdivision Iterations to run and controls for weighting selected control points are also available. Update Options can be set to Always, When Rendering, and Manually using the Update button. You can also select and work with either Vertex or Edge subobjects. These subobjects give you local control over the MeshSmooth object. Included within the Local Control rollout is a Crease value, which is available in Edge subobject mode. Selecting an Edge subobject and applying a 1.0 value causes a hard edge to be retained while the rest of the object is smoothed. The MeshSmooth modifier also makes the Soft Selection rollout available. The Reset rollout is included to quickly reset any crease and weight values.

TurboSmooth modifier

The TurboSmooth modifier works just like the MeshSmooth modifier, except that it is much faster and doesn't require as much memory.

Tutorial: Smoothing a birdbath

One effective way to model is to block out the details of a model using the Editable Poly features and then smooth the resulting model using the TurboSmooth modifier. This gives the model a polished look and increases the resolution.

To create a smoothed birdbath object, follow these steps:

1. Open the Birdbath.max file from the Chap 25 directory on the DVD.

    This file includes a simple birdbath created by selecting and scaling rows of cylinder vertices. The water is simply an inverted cone.

2. Select and clone the existing birdbath by pressing the Shift key and moving the birdbath.

3. Select the cloned birdbath, and apply the TurboSmooth modifier with the Modifiers ⇨ Subdivision Surfaces ⇨ TurboSmooth menu.

4. In the TurboSmooth rollout, set the Iterations value to 2.

    Notice that the entire birdbath is smooth and the resolution is greatly increased, as shown in Figure 25.13.

HSDS modifier

You use the HSDS (Hierarchical SubDivision Surfaces) modifier to increase the resolution and smoothing of a localized area. It works like the Tessellate modifier, except that it can work with small subobject sections instead of the entire object surface. The HSDS modifier lets you work with Vertex, Edge, Polygon, and Element subobjects. After a subobject area is selected, you can click the Subdivide button to subdivide the area. Each time you press the Subdivide button, the selected subobjects are subdivided again, and each subdivision level appears in the list above the Subdivide button.

Using the subdivision list, you can move back and forth between the various subdivision hierarchy levels. When edges are selected, you can specify a Crease value to maintain sharp edges. In the Advanced Options rollout, you can select to Smooth Result, Hide, or Delete Polygon. The Adaptive Subdivision button opens the Adaptive Subdivision dialog box, in which you can specify the detail parameters. This modifier also includes a Soft Selection rollout.

FIGURE 25.13

The TurboSmooth modifier can make a model flow better.

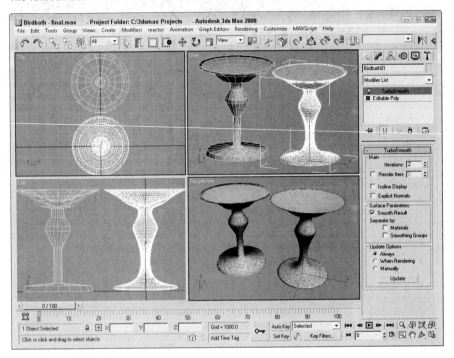

Summary

The Paint Deformation feature is a welcome addition, allowing you to add surface details using an intuitive and easy-to-use interface. Max includes several unique modifiers that apply specifically to mesh objects. This chapter covered these topics:

- Using the various Paint Deformation brushes
- Setting brush options with the Brush Options dialog box
- How the Edit Mesh and Edit Poly modifiers can be used to edit a primitive object using the Editable Mesh and Editable Poly features while maintaining its parametric nature
- How several mesh modifiers are used to edit surface geometry
- How to edit normals and what the effects are
- Working with the Subdivision Surface modifiers to smooth mesh objects

The next chapter focuses on working with a miscellaneous group of mutant objects called compound objects. These objects are unique and used for special purposes.

Chapter 26

Working with Compound Objects

So far, we have covered a variety of modeling types, including shapes, meshes, and polys. The Compound Objects subcategory includes several additional modeling types that don't seem to fit anywhere else. As you will see in this chapter, these modeling types provide several new and unique ways to model objects, such as working with Boolean objects, scattering objects across the surface of another object, or lofting a cross section along a spline path.

Understanding Compound Object Types

The Compound Objects subcategory includes several unique object types. You can access these object types with the Create ➪ Compound menu or by clicking the Geometry category button in the Create panel and selecting Compound Objects in the subcategory drop-down list. All the object types included in the Compound Objects subcategory are displayed as buttons at the top of the Create panel. They include the following:

- **Morph:** Consists of two or more objects with the same number of vertices. The vertices are interpolated from one object to the other over several frames.

- **Scatter:** Randomly scatters a source object about the scene. You can also select a Distribution object that defines the volume or surface where the objects scatter.

- **Conform:** Wraps the vertices of one object onto another. You can use this option to simulate a morph between objects with different numbers of vertices.

- **Connect:** Connects two objects with open faces by joining the holes with additional faces.

- **BlobMesh:** Creates a metaball object that flows from one object to the next like water.
- **ShapeMerge:** Lets you embed a spline into a mesh object or subtract the area of a spline from a mesh object.
- **Boolean:** Created by performing Boolean operations on two or more overlapping objects. The operations include Union, Subtraction, Intersection, and Cut.
- **Terrain:** Creates terrains from the elevation contour lines like those found on topographical maps.
- **Loft:** Sweeps a cross-section shape along a spline path.
- **Mesher:** Creates an object that converts particle systems into mesh objects as the frames progress. This makes assigning modifiers to particle systems possible.
- **ProBoolean:** Replaces the original Boolean compound object with the ability to perform Boolean operations on multiple objects at a time.
- **ProCutter:** Cuts a single stock object into multiple objects using several cutter objects.

> **NOTE** When two or more objects are combined into a single compound object, they use a single object material. The Multi/Sub-Object Material type can be used to apply different materials to the various parts.

Morphing Objects

Morph objects are used to create a Morph animation by interpolating the vertices in one object to the vertex positions of a second object. The original object is called the *Base object,* and the second object is called the *Target object.* The Base and Target objects must have the same number of vertices. One Base object can be morphed into several targets.

> **CAUTION** To ensure that the Base and Target objects have the same number of vertices, create a copy of one object and modify it to be a target. Be sure to avoid such modifiers as Tessellate and Optimize, which change the number of vertices.

To morph a Base object into a Target, select the Base object and select Create ➪ Compound ➪ Morph. Then click the Pick Target button in the Pick Targets rollout, shown in Figure 26.1, and select a Target object in the viewport. The cursor changes to a plus sign when it is over an acceptable object. Unavailable objects (that have a different number of vertices) cannot be selected. Pick Target options include Copy, Instance, Reference, and Move. (The Move option deletes the original object that is selected.) The Target object appears under the Current Targets rollout in the Morph Targets list.

Each Morph object can have several Target objects. You can use the Pick Target button to select several targets, and the order in which these targets appear in the list is the order in which they are morphed. To delete a Target object, select it from the list and click the Delete Morph Target button. Beneath the list is a Name field where you can change the name of the selected Target object.

Creating Morph keys

With a Target object name selected in the Morph Targets list, you can drag the Time Slider to a frame and set a Morph key by clicking the Create Morph Key button found at the bottom of the rollout. This option sets the number of frames used to interpolate among the different morph states.

FIGURE 26.1

A Morph rollout lets you pick targets and create morph keys.

> **NOTE** If the Morph object changes dramatically, set the Morph Keys to include enough frames to interpolate smoothly.

If a frame other than 0 is selected when a Target object is picked, a Morph Key is automatically created.

Morph objects versus the Morph modifier

Max includes two different ways to morph an object. You can create a Morph object or apply the Morph modifier to an existing object. The Morph object is different from the Morph modifier, but the results are the same; however, some subtle differences exist between these two.

A Morph object can include multiple Morph targets, but it can be created only once. Each target can have several Morph keys, which makes it easy to control. For example, you could set an object to morph to a different shape and return to its original form with only two Morph keys.

The Morph modifier, on the other hand, can be applied multiple times and works well with other modifiers, but the control for each modifier is buried in the Stack. The Parameters rollout options available for the Morph modifier are much more extensive than for the Morph object, and they include channels and support for a Morph material.

> **CROSS-REF** You can find more information on the Morph modifier in Chapter 20, "Understanding Animation and Keyframe Basics."

For the best of both worlds, apply the Morph modifier to a Morph object.

Tutorial: Morphing a woman's face

Although this example is fairly simple, it demonstrates a powerful technique that can be very helpful as you begin to animate characters. One of the key uses of morphing is to copy a character and move it about to create a new pose. You can then morph between the different poses to create smooth actions, gestures, or face motions.

To morph a woman's face, follow these steps:

1. Open the Greek woman head morph.max file from the Chap 26 directory on the DVD.

    This file includes a woman's head. All objects have been attached to the face object to make working with it easy.

2. Select the head object, and hold down the Shift key while dragging to the right in the Top viewport. In the Clone Options dialog box that opens, select Copy and set the Number of Copies to **2**. Name one copy **frown face** and the other **smiling face.**

3. Select the object named "smiling face," and open the Modify panel. Zoom in around the mouth area, and enable Vertex subobject mode. Enable the Ignore Backfacing option in the Selection rollout, and turn on the Use Soft Selection option in the Soft Selection rollout with a Falloff value of **1.4**. Then select the vertex at the corner of the mouth, and drag it upward in the Front viewport to make the woman smile. Repeat this action for the vertex on the opposite side of the mouth. Click on the Vertex subobject button again to exit subobject mode.

4. Select the original head object, and choose Create ➪ Compound ➪ Morph to make this object into a morph object. In the Pick Targets rollout, select the Copy option and click the Pick Target button. Then click the "frown face" object, or press the H key, and select it from the Select Objects dialog box (actually, it is the only object that you can select). Then click the "smiling face" object. Both targets are now added to the list. Click the Pick Target button again to disable pick mode.

5. In the Morph Targets list, select the "frown face" object and click the Create Morph Key button. Then drag the Time Slider (below the viewports) to frame 50, select the "smiling face" object, and press the Create Morph Key button again.

6. Click the Play button (in the Time Controls section at the bottom of the Max window) to see the morph. The woman's head object morphs when you move the Time Slider between frame 0 and 50. Figure 26.2 shows different stages of the morph object.

FIGURE 26.2

A woman's face being morphed to a smile

Creating Conform Objects

Conform compound objects mold one object over the surface of another. This compound object is useful for adding geometric details to objects, such as stitches to a baseball or a quilt.

The object that is modified is called the *Wrapper object.* The other object is the *Wrap-To object.* These objects need to be either mesh objects or objects that you can convert to mesh objects.

CROSS-REF Another way to mold one object over the surface of another is with the Conform Space Warp. Find out more about this Space Warp in Chapter 37, "Using Space Warps."

To create a Conform object, select an object to be the Wrapper object and select Create ➪ Compound ➪ Conform. To select the Wrap-To object, click the Pick Wrap-To Object button in the Pick Wrap-To Object rollout and choose one of the options below the button (Reference, Move, Copy, or Instance).

CAUTION Shapes and splines cannot be used as either the Wrapper or Wrap-To objects, even if they are renderable.

In the Parameters rollout, shown in Figure 26.3, the Objects section lists both the Wrapper and Wrap-To objects. Name fields are also available for changing the names of both objects.

FIGURE 26.3

The Parameters rollout of the Conform object lets you define how the object is wrapped.

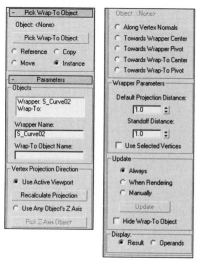

The Wrapper Parameters section includes two adjustable values: Default Projection Distance, which is the distance that the Wrapper moves if it doesn't intersect with the Wrap-To object, and Standoff Distance, which is the distance between the Wrapper and the Wrap-To object. The Use Selected Vertices option causes only the selected vertices passed up the Stack to be moved.

Setting a vertex projection direction

The Parameters rollout also includes controls for specifying the Vertex Projection Direction settings. You can select to project the vertices based on the current active viewport with the Use Active Viewport option. If the view changes, you can use the Recalculate Projection button to compute the new projection direction.

You can also use the local Z-axis of any object in the scene as the projection direction. The Pick Z-Axis Object button lets you select the object to use. After you have selected it, rotating this object can alter the projection direction. The name of the object is displayed below the Pick Z-Axis Object button.

Other projection options include Along Vertex Normals, Towards Wrapper Center, Towards Wrapper Pivot, Towards Wrap-To Center, and Towards Wrap-To Pivot. The Along Vertex Normals option sets the projection direction opposite the Wrapper's normals. The other options set the direction toward the center or pivot of the Wrapper or Wrap-To objects.

Tutorial: Placing a facial scar

As an example of the Conform object, let's add a gruesome scar to the face of a character. Using the Conform compound object, details like this scar can be a mesh object and still perfectly match the contour of the face object.

To create a facial scar using the Conform object, follow these steps:

1. Open the Facial scar.max file from the Chap 26 directory on the DVD.

   This file includes a face mesh with a mesh scar placed to its side. The face mesh was created by Viewpoint Datalabs.

2. Click the Select and Move button on the main toolbar, and select and move the scar to position it in front of the face mesh in the Front and Top viewports.

3. With the scar selected, choose the Create ⇨ Compound ⇨ Conform menu command.

4. Click the Pick Wrap-To Object button, and click the face mesh. Select the Move option.

5. Under the Parameters rollout, select the Use Active Viewport option and make sure that the Front viewport is active. In the Wrapper Parameters section, set the Standoff Distance value to **1.0**.

Figure 26.4 shows a close-up of our surgery in the maximized Perspective view.

FIGURE 26.4

A patch grid being conformed to the front of a face object

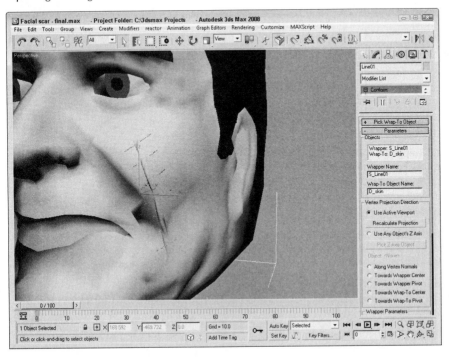

Creating a ShapeMerge Object

The ShapeMerge compound object enables you to use a spline shape as a cookie cutter to extract a portion of a mesh object. This button is enabled only if a mesh object and a spline exist in the scene. To use this object, select a mesh object and click the Pick Shape button in the Pick Operand rollout, and then select a spline shape. The shape can be a Reference, Move, Instance, or Copy.

The spline shape is always projected toward its negative Z-axis. By rotating and positioning the spline before selecting it, you can apply it to different sides of an object. You can apply multiple shapes to the same mesh object.

The Parameters rollout, shown in Figure 26.5, displays each mesh and shape object in a list. You can also rename either object using the Name field. The Extract Operand button lets you separate either object as an Instance or a Copy.

FIGURE 26.5

Use the Parameters rollout for the ShapeMerge compound object to cut or merge a shape.

Cookie Cutter and Merge options

The Operations group includes options for cutting the mesh, including Cookie Cutter and Merge. The Cookie Cutter option cuts the shape out of the mesh surface, and the Merge option combines the spline with the mesh. You can also Invert the operation to remove the inside or outside of the selected area.

Like the Boolean Subtraction operations, the Cookie Cutter option can remove sections of the mesh, but it uses the area defined by a spline instead of a volume defined by a mesh object. The Merge option is useful for marking an area for selection. Figure 26.6 shows a ShapeMerge object with the Cookie Cutter option selected.

NOTE You can use the Merge option to create a precise face object that can be used with the Connect object.

The Output Sub-Mesh Selection option lets you pass the selection up the Stack for additional modifiers. Options include None, Face, Edge, and Vertex.

NOTE To see the backsides of the faces, right-click the object, select Properties from the pop-up menu, and disable the Backface Cull option.

FIGURE 26.6

A ShapeMerge object using the Cookie Cutter option

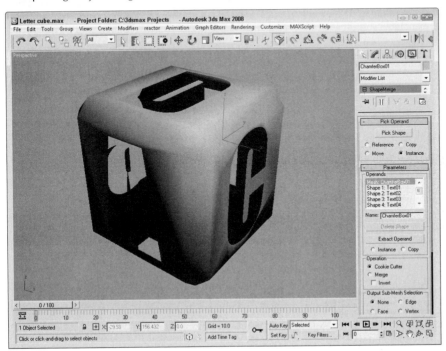

Tutorial: Using the ShapeMerge compound object

When outlined text is imported into Max, it typically contains letters that have shapes within shapes. For example, the letter *p*, when outlined, includes the outline of the letter *p* and a circle shape to denote the interior section of the letter. When outline text like this is converted to a mesh object, both the letter outline and its interior section are covered, making the text illegible. You can use the ShapeMerge compound object to remedy this tricky situation.

You can practice handling this situation using the logo for the fictional Box It Up company. Before this logo can be extruded, you need to do some work involving the ShapeMerge object.

To use the ShapeMerge object to remove the center area from an extrusion, follow these steps:

1. Open the Box It Up Co logo.max file from the Chap 26 directory on the DVD.

2. Select all the letters in the logo, press the Ctrl key, and deselect the interior shapes in the B, O, and P letters. Then apply the Extrude modifier with an Amount value of 0.010 feet.

3. Select the letter B shape again. Then select the Create ⇨ Compound ⇨ ShapeMerge menu command.

4. Set the Operation to Cookie Cutter, and click the Pick Shape button in the Pick Operand rollout with the Copy option. Select the two interior shapes for the letter B. Then click the Select Object button on the main toolbar again to exit ShapeMerge mode. Then repeat this step for the letters O and P.

Figure 26.7 shows the finished logo. Notice that the letters have the interior sections removed.

The logo with the interior centers removed from extruded letters using the ShapeMerge object

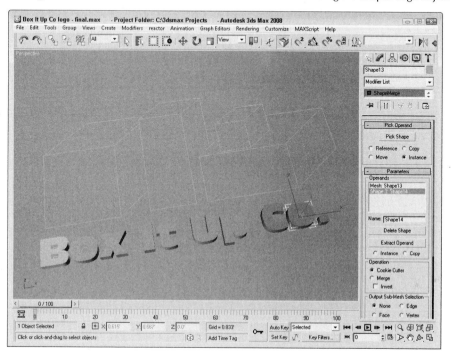

Creating a Terrain Object

The Terrain object is a great object that enables you to create terrains from splines representing elevation contours. These contour splines can be created in Max or imported using a format like AutoCAD's DWG. If the splines are created in Max, make sure that each contour spline is a separate object. The splines all must be closed splines. If all the splines have an equal number of vertices, then the resulting terrain object is much cleaner. You can insure this by copying and scaling the base spline.

To create a terrain, create splines at varying elevations, select all the splines, and click the Terrain button. You can use the Pick Operand button in the Pick Operand rollout to select additional splines to add to the Terrain object. All splines in the object become operands and are displayed in the Operands list.

The Form group includes three options that determine how the terrain is formed: Graded Surface, Graded Solid, and Layered Solid. The Graded Surface option displays a surface grid over the contour splines; the Graded Solid adds a bottom to the object; and the Layered Solid displays each contour as a flat, terraced area. The Stitch Border option causes polygons to be created to close open splines by creating a single edge that closes the spline. The Retriangulate option optimizes how the polygons are divided to better represent the contours.

The Display group includes options to display the Terrain mesh, the Contour lines, or Both. You can also specify how you want to update the terrain.

The Simplification rollout lets you alter the resolution of the terrain by selecting how many vertical and horizontal points and lines to use. Options include using all points (no simplification), half of the points, a quarter of the points, twice the points, or four times the points.

Coloring elevations

The Color by Elevation rollout, shown in Figure 26.8, displays as reference the Maximum and Minimum Elevations. Between these is a Reference Elevation value, which is the location where the landmass meets the water. Entering a Reference Elevation and clicking the Create Defaults button automatically creates several separate color zones. You can add, modify, or delete zones using the Add, Modify, or Delete Zone buttons.

FIGURE 26.8

The Color by Elevation rollout lets you change the color for different elevations.

You can access each color zone from a list. To change a zone's color, select it and click the color swatch. You can set colors to Blend to the Color Above or to be Solid to Top of Zone.

Tutorial: Creating an island with the Terrain compound object

In this tutorial, we create a simple island. The Color by Elevation rollout makes distinguishing the water from the land easy.

To create an island using the Terrain object, follow these steps:

1. Select Create ➪ Shapes ➪ Ellipse, and drag in the Top view to create several ellipses of various sizes representing the contours of the island.

   The first ellipse you create should be the largest, and they should get progressively smaller.

2. In the Left view, select and move the ellipses up and down so that the largest one is on the bottom and the smallest one is on top. You can create two smaller hills by including two ellipses at the same level.

3. Use the Edit ➪ Select All (Ctrl+A) menu command to select all the ellipses, and select Create ➪ Compound ➪ Terrain.

   The ellipses automatically join together. Joining all the ellipses forms the island.

4. In the Color by Elevation rollout, select a Reference Elevation of **5** and click the Create Defaults button.

   This automatically creates color zones for the island. The elevation values for each zone are displayed in a list within the Color by Elevation rollout. Selecting an elevation value in the list displays its color in the color swatch.

5. Select each elevation value individually, and set all Zones to Blend to the Color Above option for all zones, except for the Zone with the lightest blue.

   This creates a distinct break between the sea and the land of the island.

Figure 26.9 shows the final terrain. In an example later in this chapter, we use the Scatter compound object to add trees to the small terrain island.

FIGURE 26.9

A Terrain island created with the Terrain compound object

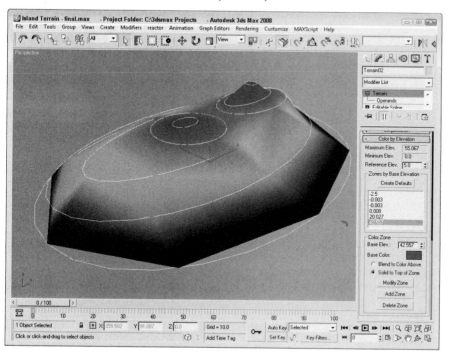

Using the Mesher Object

You can use the Mesher compound object to convert objects to mesh objects on the fly as an animation progresses. This feature is useful for objects such as particle systems. After you convert the object to a mesh object, you can apply modifiers that weren't possible before, such as Optimize, UVW Map, and others.

Another benefit of the Mesher object is that you can apply several complex modifiers to a single Mesher object and load it to a particle system rather than applying the modifiers to all the pieces that make up a particle system.

The Parameters rollout of the Mesher object includes a Pick Object button. Click this button, and select an object in the viewport to make the selected object an instance of the Mesher object. This action does not delete the original object, and the Mesher instance is oriented to the Mesher object's coordinate system. The object name then appears on the button. You can change the object by clicking the button again and selecting a new object.

CAUTION Do not delete the original object, or the Mesher instance also disappears. If you want to render only the Mesher instance, then select the original object and hide it using the Tools ⇨ Display Floater command.

The Time Offset is the number of the frames ahead (values can be negative) or behind the original object that the animation should progress. If the Build Only at Render Time option is set, then the Mesher instance is not visible in the viewports but shows up in the final rendered image. You can use the Update button to manually force an update of the Mesher instance after the settings for the original object have been modified.

When you use the Mesher object to create an instance of a particle system, the bounding box of the particle system as it streams the particles becomes long and thin over time. This long, thin bounding box can potentially cause problems with certain modifiers. You can prevent these problems by selecting an alternative bounding box that doesn't change over time. To select a new bounding box, select the Custom Bounding Box option, click the Pick Bounding Box button, and click an object in the viewport. You can select the original object as the new bounding box. With the Mesher object selected, the bounding box is shown in orange wherever it is located. The corner coordinates of the custom bounding box are displayed under the Pick Bounding Box button. Mesher objects can also be used as Particle Flow events using the Add and Remove buttons at the bottom of the Parameters rollout.

CROSS-REF Chapter 36, "Creating Particles and Particle Flow," provides more information on working with particle systems.

Working with BlobMesh Objects

BlobMesh objects are simple spheres. If you have only one of them, they aren't interesting at all, but if you get them together, they run into each other much like the metal mercury. This makes them an ideal choice for modeling flowing liquids and soft organic shapes.

BlobMesh objects are used as sets of objects rather than as individual objects. If you click the BlobMesh button in the Compound Objects subcategory and then create a BlobMesh in the viewports, it appears as a sphere with the radius set using the Size parameter. The real benefit comes from clicking the Pick or Add buttons below the Blob Objects list and selecting an object in the scene.

NOTE The Pick, Add, and Remove buttons become enabled only in the Modify panel.

The object that is picked is added to the Blob Objects list, and each vertex of the object gets a BlobMesh added to it. If the BlobMesh objects are large enough to overlap, then the entire object is covered with these objects and they run together to form a flowing mass of particles.

Setting BlobMesh parameters

The Size value sets the radius of the BlobMesh object. Larger sizes result in more overlapping of surrounding objects. For particle systems, the Size is discounted and the size of the particles determines the size of the BlobMesh objects. The Tension value sets how loose or tight the surface of the BlobMesh object is. Small tension values result in looser objects that more readily flow together.

The Evaluation Coarseness value sets how dense the BlobMesh objects will be. By enabling the Relative Coarseness option, the density of the objects changes as the size of the objects changes. The Coarseness values can be different for the viewport and the Render engine.

When a BlobMesh object is selected and applied to the picked object, each vertex has an object attached to it, but if you apply a selection modifier, such as the Mesh Select modifier, to the picked object, then only the selected subobjects get a MeshBlob object. You can also use the Soft Selection option to select those subobjects adjacent to the selected subobjects. The Minimum Size value is the smallest-sized BlobMesh object that is used when Soft Selection is enabled.

The Large Data Optimization option is a quicker, more efficient way of rendering a huge set of BlobMesh objects. The benefit from this method comes when more than 2,000 BlobMesh objects need to be rendered. If the viewport updates are slow because of the number of BlobMesh objects, you can select to turn them Off in Viewport.

> **CROSS-REF** When BlobMesh objects are applied to a particle system, they can be used as part of a Particle Flow workflow. The Particle Flow Parameters rollout includes a list of events to apply to the BlobMesh objects. Particle Flow is covered in detail in Chapter 36, "Creating Particles and Particle Flow."

Tutorial: Creating icy geometry with BlobMesh

The BlobMesh object can be combined with a geometry object to create the effect of an object that has been frozen in ice. Using the BlobMesh's Pick feature, you can select a geometry object, and a BlobMesh is placed at each vertex of the object. I suggest using an object with a fairly limited number of vertices.

To create the effect of an object covered in ice, follow these steps:

1. Open the Icy sled.max file from the Chap 26 directory on the DVD.

   This file includes a sled model created by Viewpoint Datalabs.

2. With the sled selected, choose Create ➪ Compound ➪ BlobMesh, and create a simple BlobMesh in the Top viewport. Set the Size value to 6.0. Then click the Pick button in the Parameters rollout, and select the Sled object.

3. Press the M key to open the Material Editor, and select the first sample slot. Change the Diffuse color to a light blue, and set the Opacity to 20. Then increase the Specular Level to **90** and the Glossiness to **40**, and apply the material to the BlobMesh object.

Figure 26.10 shows the resulting sled, all ready to be defrosted.

FIGURE 26.10

BlobMesh objects can be used to cover objects in ice.

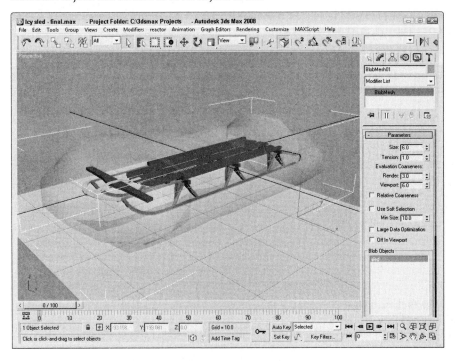

Creating a Scatter Object

A Scatter object spreads multiple copies of the object about the scene or within a defined area. The object that is scattered is called the *Source object*, and the area where the scatter objects can be placed is defined by a *Distribution object*.

CROSS-REF   Particle systems, which are discussed in Chapter 36, "Creating Particles and Particle Flow," can also create many duplicate objects, but you have more control over the placement of objects with a Scatter object.

To create a Scatter object, choose an object that will be scattered over the surface and select the Create ⇨ Compound ⇨ Scatter menu command. The selected object becomes the Source object. A rollout then opens, in which you can select the Distribution object or use defined transforms.

Under the Scatter Objects rollout, the Objects section lists the Source and Distribution objects. Name fields are also available for changing the name of either object. The Extract Operand button is available only in the Modify panel; it lets you select an operand from the list and make a copy or instance of it.

NOTE   The placement of the source object on the distribution object is determined by the source object's pivot point.

Working with Source objects

The Source object is the object that is to be duplicated. Figure 26.11 shows a Cylinder primitive scattered over a spherical Distribution object with 500 duplicates. The Perpendicular and Distribute Using Even options are set.

FIGURE 26.11

A Scatter object made of a Cylinder spread over an area defined by a sphere

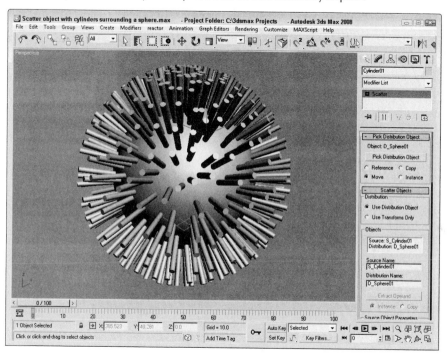

In the Scatter Objects rollout are several parameters for controlling the Source object. In the Source Object Parameters section, the Duplicates value specifies how many objects to scatter. You can also specify a Base Scale and the Vertex Chaos values. The Base Scale is the value that the object is scaled to before being scattered. All new objects are scaled equally to this value. The Vertex Chaos button randomly distributes the object vertices.

The Animation Offset defines the number of frames between a new duplicate and the previous one.

NOTE If you look closely at a Scatter object, you'll notice that both the Source and Distribution objects have the same object color. To color them differently, use the Multi/Sub-Object Material.

Working with Distribution objects

To select a Distribution object, click the Pick Distribution Object button and select an object in the viewport. (Make sure that the Use Distribution Object option is selected in the Scatter Objects rollout.) You can specify the Distribution object as a Copy, Instance, Reference, or Move.

Under the Distribution Object Parameters rollout are several options for controlling the Distribution object. The Perpendicular option causes the Source objects to be aligned perpendicular to the Distribution object. If the Perpendicular option is disabled, the orientation remains the same as that of the default Source object. Figure 26.12 shows the same Scatter object as in the preceding figure, but with several different options.

FIGURE 26.12

A Scatter object with different options: Base Scale at 20%, Vertex Chaos at 2.0, Perpendicular option disabled, and Duplicates at 100

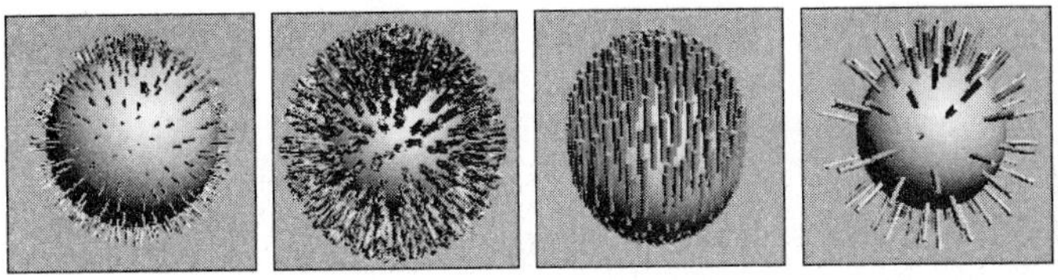

The Use Selected Faces Only option enables you to select the faces over which the duplicates are positioned. The Selected Faces are those passed up the Stack by the Mesh Select modifier.

Other Distribution object parameter options include Area, Even, Skip N, Random Faces, Along Edges, All Vertices, All Edge Midpoints, All Face Centers, and Volume. The Area option evenly distributes the objects over the surface area, and the Even option places duplicates over every other face. The Skip N option lets you specify how many faces to skip before placing an object. The Random Faces and Along Edges options randomly distribute the duplicates around the Distribution object. The All Vertices, All Edge Midpoints, and All Face Centers options ignore the Duplicates value (which specifies the number of duplicates) and place a duplicate at every vertex, edge midpoint, and face. Figure 26.13 shows several of these options.

FIGURE 26.13

A Scatter object with different distribution options: Area, Skip N where N=7, Random Faces, All Vertices, and All Face Centers

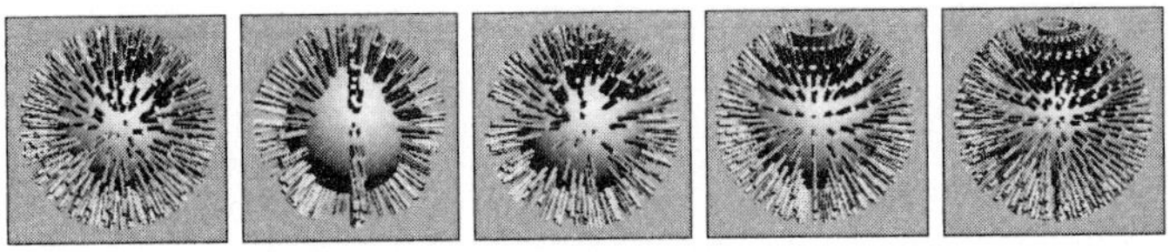

All the options described thus far place the duplicates on the surface of the object, but the Volume option scatters the duplicates inside the Distribution object's volume.

Setting Transforms

The Transforms rollout is used to specify the individual transformation limits of the duplicate objects. For example, if the Z-axis value is set to 90, then each new duplicate is randomly rotated about its local Z-axis at a distance somewhere between –90 and 90.

You can use these transformations with a Distribution object or by themselves if the Use Transforms Only option is selected under the Scatter Objects rollout. The Use Maximum Range option causes all three axes to adopt the same value. The Lock Aspect Ratio option maintains the relative dimensions of the Source object to ensure uniform scaling.

Speeding updates with a proxy

Working with a large number of duplicates can slow the viewport updates to a crawl. To speed these updates, select the Proxy option in the Display rollout. This option replaces each duplicate with a wedge-shaped object. For example, if you used the Scatter object to place people on a sidewalk, you can use the Proxy option to display simple cylinders in the viewports instead of the details of the person mesh.

Another way to speed the viewport updates is to use the Display spinner. Using this spinner, you can select a percentage of the total number of duplicates to display in the viewport. The rendered image still uses the actual number specified.

The Hide Distribution Object option lets you make the Distribution object visible or invisible. The Seed value is used to determine the randomness of the objects.

Loading and saving presets

With all the various parameters, the Load/Save Presets rollout enables you to Save, Load, or Delete various presets. You can use saved presets with another Source object.

Tutorial: Covering the island with trees

You can combine several different types of compound objects to create interesting effects. In this tutorial, we use the Scatter object to add trees to the Terrain object island created earlier in this chapter.

To add trees to the island with the Scatter object, follow these steps:

1. Open the Island terrain with trees.max file from the Chap 26 directory on the DVD.

   This file is the same island terrain example that you completed earlier in this chapter, but it also has a simple tree added to it.

2. With the tree object selected, select the Create ➪ Compound ➪ Scatter menu command.

3. Click the Pick Distribution Object button, and select the island terrain. Set the number of Duplicates to **100**, and disable the Perpendicular option.

   All the trees now stand upright.

4. Select the Random Faces option.

   The trees become denser around the hills where there are more faces.

Figure 26.14 shows the island with the trees.

FIGURE 26.14

Using the Scatter object, we can add trees to our island terrain.

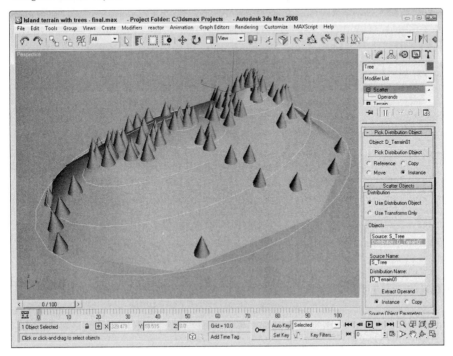

Creating Connect Objects

A Connect object is useful for building a connecting bridge between two separate objects. Each object must have an open face or hole that specifies where the two objects are to be connected.

To use this object, delete a face on two Editable Mesh objects and then position the holes across from each other. Select one of the objects, and choose the Create ➪ Compound ➪ Connect menu command. Then, click the Pick Operand button, and select the second object. The Connect object builds the additional faces required to connect the two holes.

Filling object holes

If multiple holes exist between the objects, the Connect object attempts to patch them all. You can also use the button several times to connect a single object to multiple objects.

 The Connect object doesn't work well with NURBS objects.

The Parameters rollout includes a list of all the operands or objects involved in the connection. You can delete any of these with the Delete Operand button. The Extract Operand button lets you separate the Operand object from the Connect object.

In the Interpolation section, the Segments value is the number of segments used to create the bridge section, and the Tension value is the amount of curvature to use in an attempt to smooth the connected bridge.

The Bridge Smoothing option smoothes the faces of the bridge, and the Ends option smoothes where the bridge and the original objects connect.

Tutorial: Creating a park bench

The Connect object is best used between two symmetrical copies of an object that need to be attached, as with a table or bridge. For this tutorial, we use the Connect object to create a park bench between two end pieces.

 Although the Connect compound object works fine, it requires both holes to have the same number of vertices. A more robust solution is the Editable Poly's Bridge feature.

To connect two ends of a park bench, follow these steps:

1. Open the Park bench.max file from the Chap 26 directory on the DVD.

   This file includes symmetrical ends of the park bench. One end was created by extruding a spline shape and using the ShapeMerge tool to cut matching holes on the inner facing surfaces. The Mirror tool was then used to create and rotate the symmetrical clone.

2. Select one end of the park bench, and select the Create ⇨ Compound ⇨ Connect menu command.

3. In the Pick Operand rollout, click the Pick Operand button, select the Move option, and click on the opposite side of the park bench.

   The two end pieces connect.

4. In the Parameters rollout, select the Smoothing: Bridge option to smooth the seat of the bench.

Figure 26.15 shows the resulting park bench.

FIGURE 26.15

A Connect compound object can join two open holes in separate objects.

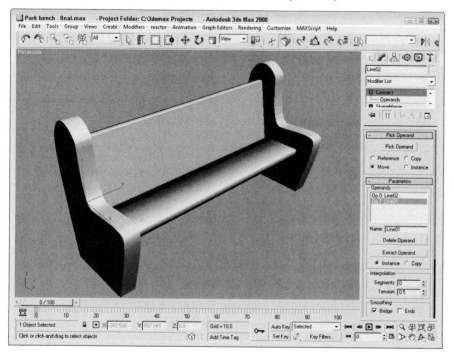

Creating a Loft Object

Lofting is a term that comes from the shipbuilding industry. It describes a method for building ships that creates and positions the cross sections and then attaches a surface or skin along the length of the cross sections.

To create a Loft object, you need to have at least two spline shapes: one shape that defines the path of the Loft and a second shape that defines its cross section. After the shapes are created, select the Create ➪ Compound menu command. A Loft button is enabled if two or more splines are present in the viewport.

> **TIP**   Be aware of the orientation of the cross section shape and the loft path before the loft is applied. The cross section's local Z-axis is always aligned with the path's local Y-axis. By making the correct orientations before applying the loft you can save some headache. If the orientations aren't correct, you can edit the pivot on either object.

Using the Get Shape and Get Path buttons

After you click the Loft button, the Creation Method rollout displays the Get Path and Get Shape buttons, which you use to specify which spline is the path and which spline is the cross section. Select a spline, and then click either the Get Path button or the Get Shape button. If you click the Get Shape button, the selected spline is the path and the next spline shape you select is the cross section. If you click the Get Path button, the selected spline is the shape and the next spline shape you select is the path.

> **NOTE**   After you click the Get Path or Get Shape button, although the cursor changes when you're over a valid spline, not all spline shapes can be used to create Loft objects. For example, you cannot use a spline created with the Donut button as a path.

When creating a Loft object with the Get Shape and Get Path buttons, you can specify either to Move the spline shape or to create a Copy or an Instance of it. The Move option replaces both splines with a Loft object. The Copy option leaves both splines in the viewport and creates a new Loft object. The Instance option maintains a link between the spline and the Loft object. This link enables you to modify the original spline. The Loft object is updated automatically.

The vertex order of the path spline is important. The Loft object is created starting at the vertex numbered 1.

> **NOTE**   You can tell which vertex is the first by enabling Vertex Numbering in the Selection rollout of an editable spline. The first vertex is also identified with a yellow box.

Controlling surface parameters

All Loft objects include the Surface Parameters rollout. Using this rollout, you can set the smoothing of the Loft object with two different options: Smooth Length and Smooth Width. You can use the Mapping options to control the mapping of textures by setting values for the number of times the map repeats over the Length or Width of the Loft. The Normalize option applies the map to the surface evenly or proportionately according to the shape's vertex spacing. You can set the Loft object to automatically generate Material and Shape IDs, and you can specify the output of the Loft to be either a Patch or Mesh.

Changing path parameters

The Path Parameters rollout, shown in Figure 26.16, lets you position several different cross-sectional shapes at different positions along the Loft path. The Path value indicates either the Distance or Percentage along the path where this new shape should be located. The Snap option, if turned on, enables you to snap to consistent distances along the path. The Path Steps option enables you to place new shapes at steps along the path where the vertices are located. Each path will have a different number of steps depending on its complexity.

FIGURE 26.16

FIGURE 26.16

The Loft compound object rollouts

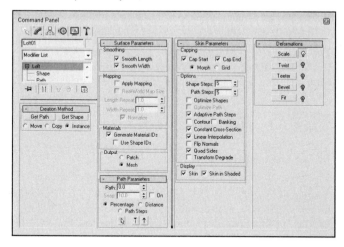

The viewport displays a small yellow X at the location where the new cross-sectional shape will be inserted. At the bottom of the rollout are three buttons, which are illustrated and described in Table 26.1.

TABLE 26.1

Path Rollout Buttons

Toolbar Button	Name	Description
⬉	Pick Shape	Selects a new cross-section spline to be inserted at the specified location
⬇	Previous Shape	Moves to the previous cross-section shape along the Loft path
⬆	Next Shape	Moves to the next cross-section shape along the Loft path

Setting skin parameters

The Skin Parameters rollout includes many options for determining the complexity of the Loft skin. You can specify whether to cap either end of the Loft using the Cap Start and/or Cap End options. The caps can be either Morph or Grid type.

This rollout also includes the following options for controlling the look of the skin:

- **Shape and Path Steps:** Sets the number of segments that appear in each spline's cross-sectional shape and between each division along the path. The straight segments are ignored if the Optimize Path option is selected.

- **Optimize Shapes and Paths:** Reduces the Loft's complexity by deleting any unneeded edges or vertices.

- **Adaptive Path Steps:** Automatically determines the number of steps to use for the path in order to maintain a smooth curve.
- **Contour:** Determines how the cross-sectional shapes line up with the path. If this option is enabled, the cross section is aligned to be perpendicular to the path at all times. If disabled, this option causes the cross-sectional shapes to maintain their orientation as the path is traversed.
- **Banking:** Causes the cross-section shape to rotate as the path bends.
- **Constant Cross-Section:** Scales the cross-sectional shapes in order to maintain a uniform width along the path. Turning off this option causes the cross sections to pinch at any sharp angles along the path.
- **Linear Interpolation:** Causes straight linear edges to appear between different cross-sectional shapes. Turning off this option causes smooth curves to connect various shapes.
- **Flip Normals:** Used to correct difficulties that would appear with the normals. Often the normals are flipped accidentally when the Loft is created.
- **Quad Sides:** Creates four-sided polygons to connect to adjacent cross-section shapes with the same number of sides.
- **Transform Degrade:** Makes the Loft skin disappear when subobjects are transformed. This feature can help you better visualize the cross-sectional area while it is being moved.

The Display options at the bottom of the Skin Parameters rollout give you the choice of displaying the skin in all viewports or displaying the Loft skin only in the viewports with shading turned on.

Tutorial: Designing a slip-proof hanger

As an example of creating a Loft object with different cross-sectional shapes, we design a new hanger that includes some rough edges along its bottom section to keep slacks from sliding off.

To design a hanger Loft object with different cross sections, follow these steps:

1. Open the Lofted slip-proof hanger.max file from the Chap 26 directory on the DVD.

   This file includes a spline outline of a hanger and two simple shapes.

2. Select the hanger spline, and choose the Create ➪ Compound ➪ Loft menu command.

3. In the Creation Method rollout, click the Get Shape button and then click the small circle shape (make sure that the Copy option is selected).

   This lofts the entire hanger with a circular cross section.

4. In the Path Parameters rollout, select the Path Steps option. A dialog box appears warning that this may change the relocate shapes. Click Yes to continue. Increment the Path value until the yellow X marker in the viewport is positioned at the beginning of the hanger's bottom bar (at Step 53 for this tutorial). Click the Get Shape button again, and click the small circular shape again.

   This extends the circular cross section from the start at Step 0 to Step 53.

5. Increment the Path value by 1 to Step 54, click the Get Shape button, and select the star shape. This makes the remainder of the hanger use a star-shaped cross section. Increment the Path value again to the end of the hanger's bottom bar (at Step 60), click the Get Shape button, and select the star shape again to end the star cross section.

> **NOTE**   If you forget to start and end a section with the same cross section, the loft blends between the two different cross sections.

6. In the Path Parameters rollout, increment the Path value a final time to Step 61, click the Get Shape button, and click the circular shape. Click the Pick Shape icon button at the bottom of the Path Parameters dialog box to change the cross section of the hanger to the end of the path. Right-click in the viewport to exit Get Shape mode.

Figure 26.17 shows the finished designer hanger.

FIGURE 26.17

A lofted hanger created with two different cross-sectional shapes

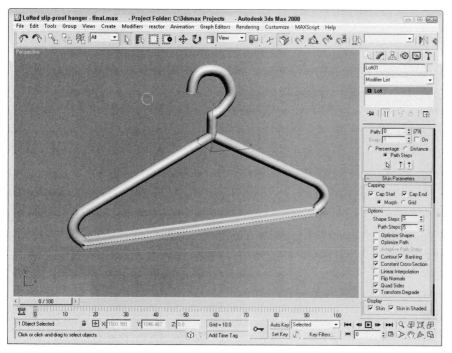

Deforming Loft objects

When you select a Loft object and open the Modify panel, the Deformation rollout appears. This rollout includes five buttons that let you Scale, Twist, Teeter, Bevel, and Fit the cross-section shapes along the path. All five buttons open similar graph windows that include control points and a line that represents the amount of the effect to apply. Next to each button is a toggle button with a light switch on it. This button enables or disables the respective effect.

The Deformation window interface

All five deformation options use the same basic window and controls. The vertical lines within the window represent the placement of vertices on the loft path. As an example of the Deformation window interface, Figure 26.18 shows the Scale Deformation window.

FIGURE 26.18

The Deformation dialog box interface lets you control the cross section over the length of the path.

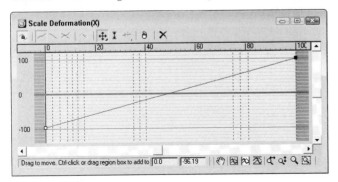

Dragging the curve directly can modify the deformation curve. You can also insert control points at any location along the curve. These control points can be one of three different types: Corner, Bézier Corner, or Bézier Smooth. Bézier type points have handles for controlling the curvature at the point. To change the point type, select the point and right-click. Then make your selection from the pop-up menu. The end points must always be either Corner or Bézier Corner type.

To move a control point, select and drag it or enter a horizontal and/or vertical value in the fields at the bottom of the window.

Table 26.2 describes the buttons at the top of the Deformation window.

TABLE 26.2

Deformation Dialog Box Buttons

Toolbar Button	Name	Description
	Make Symmetrical	Links the two curves so that changes made to one curve are also made to the other
	Display X-Axis	Makes the line controlling the X-axis visible
	Display Y-Axis	Makes the line controlling the Y-axis visible
	Display XY axes	Makes both lines visible
	Swap Deform Curves	Switches the lines
	Move Control Point	Enables you to move control points, and includes flyouts for horizontal and vertical movements
	Scale Control Point	Scales the selected control point

Toolbar Button	Name	Description
	Insert Corner Point,	Inserts new points on a deformation curve
	Insert Bézier Point	
	Delete Control Point	Deletes the current control point
	Reset Curve	Returns the original curve
	Pan	Pans the curve as the mouse is dragged
	Zoom Extents	Zooms to display the entire curve
	Zoom Extents Horizontal	Zooms to display the entire horizontal curve range
	Zoom Extents Vertical	Zooms to display the entire vertical curve range
	Zoom Horizontal	Zooms on the horizontal curve range
	Zoom Vertical	Zooms on the vertical curve range
	Zoom	Zooms in and out as the mouse is dragged
	Zoom Region	Zooms to the region specified by the mouse

NOTE Several buttons are disabled on the Twist and Bevel Deformation windows because these dialog boxes have only one deformation curve.

At the bottom of the Deformation dialog boxes are two value fields. The value fields display the X and Y coordinate values for the currently selected point. The navigation buttons enable you to pan and zoom within the dialog box.

Figure 26.19 and Figure 26.20 show each of the various deformation options applied to a lofted column.

Scale Deformation

The Scale Deformation window can alter the relative scale of the Loft object at any point along its path. This window includes two lines: one red and one green. The red line displays the X-axis scale, and the green line displays the Y-axis scale. By default, both lines are positioned equally at the 100 percent value. Specifying a value greater than 100 percent increases the scale, and specifying a value less than 100 percent has the opposite effect.

FIGURE 26.19

The Loft compound object deformation options: Scale, Twist, and Teeter

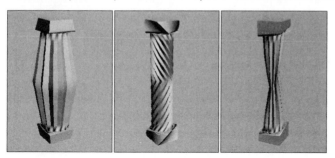

FIGURE 26.20

The Loft compound object deformation options: Bevel and Fit

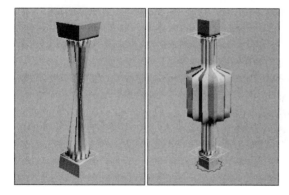

Twist Deformation

The Twist Deformation rotates one cross section relative to the others along the shape's local Z-axis and can be used to create an object that spirals along its path. This option is similar to the Banking option, which can also produce rotations about the path.

The Twist Deformation window includes only one red line representing the rotation value. By default, this line is set to a 0-degree rotation value. Positive values result in counterclockwise rotations, and negative values have the opposite effect.

Teeter Deformation

Teeter Deformation rotates a cross section so that its outer edges move closer to the path. This is done by rotating the cross section about its local X-axis or Y-axis. The result is similar to that produced by the Contour option.

The Teeter Deformation window includes two lines: one red and one green. The red line displays the X-axis rotation, and the green line displays the Y-axis rotation. By default, both lines are positioned equally at the 0 degree value. Positive values result in counterclockwise rotations, and negative values have the opposite effect.

Bevel Deformation

Bevel Deformation bevels the cross-section shapes. To bevel an edge is to round the edge so it is smooth by adding more parallel edges. The Bevel Deformation window includes only one red line representing the amount of bevel applied. By default, this line is set to a 0 value. Positive values increase the bevel amount, which equals a reduction in the shape area, and negative values have the opposite effect.

You can also use the Bevel Deformation window to select three different types of beveling: Normal, Adaptive Linear, and Adaptive Cubic. Table 26.3 shows and describes the buttons for these three beveling types. You can select them from a flyout at the right end of the window.

TABLE 26.3

Bevel Deformation Buttons

Toolbar Button	Name	Description
	Normal Bevel	Produces a normal bevel with parallel edges, regardless of the path angle
	Adaptive (Linear)	Alters the bevel linearly, based on the path angle
	Adaptive (Cubic)	Alters the bevel using a cubic spline, based on the path angle

Fit Deformation

The Fit Deformation window, shown in Figure 26.21, lets you specify a profile for the outer edges of the cross-section shapes to follow. This window includes two lines: one red and one green. The red line displays the X-axis scale, and the green line displays the Y-axis scale. By default, both lines are positioned equally at the 100 percent value. Specifying a value that is greater than 100 percent increases the scale, and specifying a value less than 100 percent has the opposite effect.

 **When using the Fit deformation, you cannot make the surface go backward on the path.**

The Fit Deformation window includes ten buttons unique to it that are used to control the profile curves. These buttons are illustrated and described in Table 26.4.

FIGURE 26.21

A Loft object with Fit Deformation applied

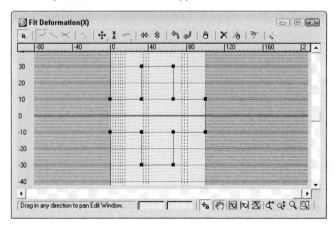

TABLE 26.4

Fit Deformation Dialog Box Buttons

Toolbar Button	Name	Description
	Mirror Horizontally	Mirrors the selection horizontally
	Mirror Vertically	Mirrors the selection vertically
	Rotate 90 degrees CCW	Rotates the selection 90 degrees counterclockwise
	Rotate 90 degrees CW	Rotates the selection 90 degrees clockwise
	Delete Control Point	Deletes the selected control point
	Reset Curve	Returns the curve to its original form
	Delete Curve	Deletes the selected curve
	Get Shape	Selects a separate spline to use as a profile
	Generate Path	Replaces the current path with a straight line
	Lock Aspect	Maintains the relationship between height and width

Modifying Loft subobjects

When you select a Loft object, you can work with its subobjects in the Modify panel. The subobjects for a Loft include Path and Shape. The Path subobject opens the Path Commands rollout. This rollout has only a single button — Put — for creating a copy of the Loft path. If you click this button, the Put To Scene dialog box appears, enabling you to give the path a name and select to create it as a Copy or an Instance.

If your path is created as an Instance, you can edit the instance to control the Loft path.

TIP Scaling or transforming a cross section has no effect on the Loft because there isn't any way to access the shape transform. If you add an XForm modifier on the cross section, then you can control its transform after it is lofted.

The Shape subobject opens the Shape Commands rollout. This rollout also includes a Put button along with some additional controls. The Path Level value adjusts the shape's position on the path. The Compare button opens the Compare dialog box, which is discussed in the following section. The Reset button returns the shape to its former state before any rotation or scaling has taken place, and the Delete button deletes the shape entirely.

NOTE You cannot delete a shape if it is the only shape in the Loft object.

The Shape Commands rollout also includes six Align buttons for aligning the shape to the Center, Default, Left, Right, Top, and Bottom. For the Loft object local coordinates, Left and Right move the shape along the X-axis, and Top and Bottom move it along the Y-axis.

Comparing shapes

The Compare dialog box superimposes selected cross-sectional shapes included in a Loft object on top of one another to check their center alignment. The button in the upper-left corner is the Pick Shape button. This button lets you select which shapes to display in the dialog box. The button to its right is the Delete Shape button, for removing a shape from the dialog box. Figure 26.22 shows the Compare dialog box with the two shapes from the pillar example selected. Notice that the first vertices on these two shapes are in different locations. This causes the strange twisting at both the top and bottom of the pillar.

FIGURE 26.22

You can use the Compare dialog box to align shapes included in a Loft.

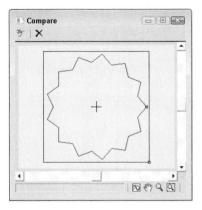

 You can align these two vertices by subdividing the square shape in Edit Spline mode and selecting a new first vertex with the Make First button.

While the Compare dialog box is open, the Align buttons in the Shape Commands rollout are still active and can be used to move and position the shapes. The first vertex on each shape is shown as a small square. If these vertices aren't correctly aligned on top of one another, then the resulting Loft object will have skewed edges. The lower-right corner of the dialog box includes buttons to View Extents, Pan, Zoom, and Zoom Region.

Editing Loft paths

The original shapes that were used to create the Loft object can be edited at any time. These updates also modify the Loft object. The shapes, if not visible, can be selected using the Select by Name button. The shapes maintain their base parameters, or they can be converted to an Editable Spline.

Tutorial: Creating drapes

Modeling home interiors is a task commonly performed by professional architects and interior designers, but creating the drapes can be tricky. In this tutorial, we create some simple drapes using a Loft object.

To create drapes using a Loft object, follow these steps:

1. Open the Lofted drapes.max file from the Chap 26 directory on the DVD.

   This file contains two splines that can be used to create the loft.

2. Select the straight line spline, and select the Create ➪ Compound ➪ Loft menu command. In the Creation Method rollout, click the Get Shape button and then click the cross-section spline.

3. Open the Modify panel, and under the Skin Parameters rollout, turn off the Contour and Banking options.

4. Use the Deformation functions to add more control to the drapes, such as tying them together as shown in Figure 26.23.

Loft objects versus surface tools

You can create compound loft objects completely from 2D shape splines: One open spline is typically used as the Loft path, and other, closed splines are used as the cross sections. You can have several different cross sections, and these can change as you travel the path. Loft cross sections aren't required to have the same number of vertices, and you can modify the scale and rotation of the cross sections with the Deformation options.

CROSS-REF See Chapter 27, "Modeling with Patches and NURBS," for more detail on the surface tools.

The surface tools, which include the CrossSection and Surface modifiers, provide another way to model that is similar to lofting. The CrossSection modifier takes several cross-section shapes and connects their vertices with additional splines to create a spline framework. You can then use the Surface modifier to cover this framework with a skin.

Although similar in nature, Loft objects and the surface tools have different subtleties and strengths.

One difference is that the CrossSection modifier connects spline cross sections according to their order. This can cause strange results if the order is incorrect. A Loft always follows a path, so the cross-section order isn't a problem.

FIGURE 26.23

Drapes that have been modeled using a Loft object

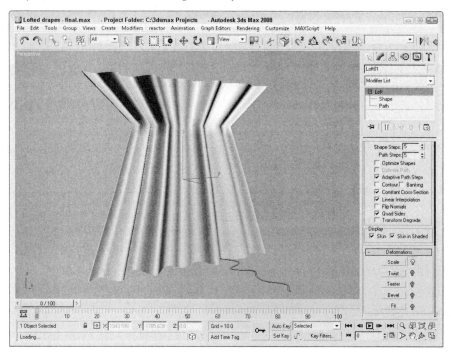

Another difference is that surface tools give you more control over the surface of a created object. Because the underlying structure is a series of splines, you can add new branches and objects without much difficulty. This can be hard to do with Loft objects.

As a general guideline, Loft objects are better suited to modeling rigid objects with relatively uniform cross sections, whereas the surface tools are better for modeling more organic model types.

Working with ProBoolean and ProCutter Objects

The original Boolean compound object worked well enough for combining, subtracting, and intersecting objects, but it had some limitations that have been overcome with the ProBoolean and ProCutter compound objects. The original Boolean could combine only two operands together, but the ProBoolean object can perform multiple Boolean operations simultaneously. ProBoolean also can subdivide the result into quad faces. The results of the ProBoolean and ProCutter objects are much cleaner and more accurate than the original Boolean object.

The original Boolean compound object still is available for backward compatibility, but if you perform a new Boolean operation, you really should use the ProBoolean object.

Using ProBoolean

When two objects overlap, you can perform different Boolean operations on them to create a unique object. The ProBoolean operations include Union, Intersection, Subtraction, and Merge. Two additional options are available: Imprint and Cookie.

The Union operation combines two objects into one. The Intersection operation retains only the overlapping sections of two objects. The Subtraction operation subtracts the overlapping portions of one object from another. The Merge operation combines objects without removing the interior faces and adds new edges where the objects overlap. Figure 26.24 shows the original objects and each of the possible Boolean operators.

> **NOTE** Unlike many CAD packages that deal with solid objects, Max's Booleans are applied to surfaces, so if the surfaces of the two objects don't overlap, all Boolean operations (except for Union) will have no effect.

FIGURE 26.24

Object before any operations and Boolean operations: Union, Intersection, Subtraction, and Merge with the Imprint option enabled

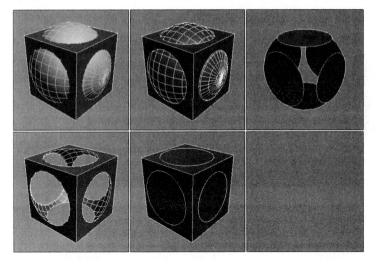

The Cookie option causes the operation to cut the original object without adding any of the faces from the picked object to the original object. The Imprint option causes the outline of the operation to appear on the original object.

All Boolean operations are added in the order in which they are applied to a list in the Parameters rollout. You can select any of the operations in the list at any time and change the operation. For example, if you select the Subtraction operation from the list and then change the operation type to Union and click the Change Operation button, the Subtraction changes to a Union. With an operation selected in the list, the Extract Selected button restores the original object. When using this button, you can choose to Remove, Copy, or Instance the operation.

The order in which the operations are applied affects the result. You can reorder the operations in the list by selecting an operation, choosing its position in the list, and clicking the Reorder Ops button.

CROSS-REF You also can apply Boolean operations to shapes using the Boolean operators available for Editable Meshes in the Geometry rollout. Chapter 11, "Drawing and Editing 2D Splines and Shapes," covers these 2D Boolean operators.

The materials that get applied to a ProBoolean result can be set to use the Operand Material or to retain the Original Material. If you use the Operand Material with the subtraction operation, then the surface that touches the picked object retains the removed object's material and the rest of the object has the original object's material. If the Retain Original Material option is selected, then the entire result gets the original object's material.

In the Advanced Options rollout are options for updating the scene and for reducing the complexity of the object. The Decimation value is the percentage of edges to remove from the result. If you plan on smoothing the object or converting it to an Editable Poly object, then you want to enable the Make Quadrilaterals option, which causes the polygon reduction to avoid triangles in favor of quads. You also can set the Quad Size, and you can select how planar edges are handled.

NOTE If you plan to deform the mesh as part of a skinned object or a cloth simulation, the resulting mesh has to be clean or the deformation will have problems.

Tutorial: Creating a keyhole

What was it that Alice saw when she looked through the keyhole? The ProBoolean feature is the perfect tool for cutting a keyhole through a doorknob plate.

To use the ProBoolean object to create a keyhole, follow these steps:

1. Open the Doorknob.max file from the Chap 26 directory on the DVD.
2. Select the doorknob plate object positioned where the keyhole is, and choose the Create ⇨ Compound ⇨ ProBoolean menu command. In the Parameters rollout, select the Subtraction option.
3. In the Pick Boolean rollout, click the Start Picking button and select the Box and Cylinder objects positioned where the keyhole should be.

Figure 26.25 shows the finished keyhole.

Using ProCutter

The original Boolean compound object included a Cut option. This feature has been replaced with ProCutter that offers many more features than the original option. ProCutter allows you to cut a single object (known as the Stock object) with multiple cutter objects.

You can pick both the Stock and Cutter objects using the buttons found in the Cutter Picking Parameters rollout. You have four options with each selection: Reference, Move, Copy, or Instance. The Auto Extract Mode option automatically replaces the selected stock object with the extracted result. The Explode by Elements option works only when the Auto Extract Mode option is enabled. It separates each cut element into an object.

Within the Cutter Parameters rollout, you can select from three Cutting Options. The Stock Outside Cutter option keeps the portion of the stock object that is on the outside of the cutter. The Stock Inside Cutter option is the opposite, keeping the stock portion inside the cutters. The Cutters Outside Stock option maintains those portions of the cutters that are outside of the stock.

FIGURE 26.25

A keyhole built using the ProBoolean object

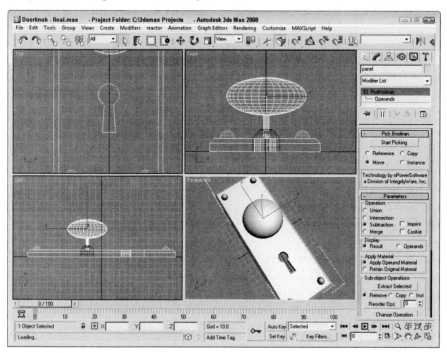

All selected cutters and stock objects are added to a list in the Cutter Parameters. Using the Extract Selected button, you can restore any cutter or stock object that has been operated on as a Copy or Instance. Materials and Decimation also work the same as for ProBoolean objects.

 **TIP** The ProCutter features are helpful for dividing an object that will be animated exploding into pieces.

Tutorial: Creating a jigsaw puzzle

The ProCutter is useful for creating destructive scenes just as shattering glass to pieces and breaking down buildings, but it also can be used for constructive cutting such as creating a jigsaw puzzle.

To use the ProCutter compound object to divide an object into a jigsaw puzzle, follow these steps:

1. Open the ProCutter puzzle.max file from the Chap 26 directory on the DVD. This file includes a simple box mapped with a scenic image and several extruded lines that mark the jigsaw puzzle's edges.

2. Select one of the extruded lines that mark where the cuts should be (known as a cutter), and choose the Create ⇨ Compound ⇨ ProCutter menu command.

3. Then, click the Pick Cutter Objects button and select all of the remaining cutter objects. In the Cutter Parameters rollout, enable the Stock Outside Cutter along with the Stock Inside Cutter options. Select the Retain Original Material option also.

4. In the Cutter Picking Parameters rollout, enable the Auto Extract Mesh and Explode By Elements options; then select the Pick Stock Objects button and choose the Box object in the viewport.

5. Select the final cutter and repeat steps 2 and 3. Enable the Auto Extract Mesh and Explode By Elements options. Then click the Pick Stock Objects button and select the three objects that haven't been cut to complete the cuts.

6. Open the Material Editor and drag the image material onto each puzzle piece.

Figure 26.26 shows the final puzzle with one piece moved away from the others.

FIGURE 26.26

A puzzle cut using the ProCutter compound object

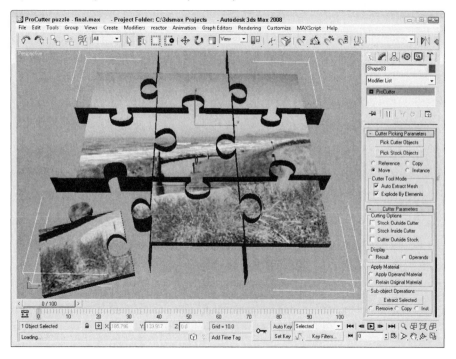

Summary

Compound objects provide several additional modeling types to our bulging modeling toolkit. From morph objects to complex deformed lofts, you can use these special-purpose types to model many different objects. This chapter covered these topics:

- The various compound object types
- Morphing objects with the same number of vertices
- Creating a Conform object with differing numbers of vertices
- Using splines and mesh objects to create a ShapeMerge object

- Creating a Terrain object using splines
- The Mesher object
- Using the BlobMesh object to simulate water
- Creating a Scatter object
- Creating a Connect object to join two objects
- Creating a Loft object
- How to control Loft parameters
- Using Loft deformations
- Modifying Loft subobjects
- Comparing the strengths of loft objects versus surface tools
- Modeling with the ProBoolean and ProCutter objects

As an alternative to polygon modeling, you can try your hand using two other modeling constructs — patches and its cousin, NURBS. These types are covered in the next chapter.

Chapter 27

Modeling with Patches and NURBS

Patches are a modeling type that exists somewhere between polygon meshes and NURBS. They are essentially polygon surfaces stretched along a closed spline. Modifying the spline alters the surface of the patch.

In many ways, patches have advantages over the more common mesh objects. They take less memory to store, are easier to edit at the edges, and are easy to join to one another.

NURBS is an acronym for Non-Uniform Rational B-Splines. They are the ideal modeling tool for creating organic characters because they are easy to work with, they give you good interactive control, they blend together seamlessly, and their surfaces remain smooth even when distorted. NURBS are superior to polygonal modeling methods when building models with smooth flowing contours such as plants, flowers, animals, and skin.

 **NOTE** For real-time applications, neither of these methods is widely used.

In this chapter, we explore different methods of NURBS model construction and then look at some advanced NURBS tutorials.

Introducing Patch Grids

Because patches have splines along their edges, a patch can be deformed in ways that a normal polygon cannot. For example, a polygon always needs to be coplanar, meaning that if you look at it on edge, it appears as a line. A patch doesn't have this requirement and can actually bend, which permits greater control over the surface and makes it better for modeling things like clothes and natural objects like leaves.

Another key advantage of Patch objects is that they efficiently represent the object geometry. If you examine some mesh objects, you'll notice that they contain a discrete vertex at the intersection of every edge at the corner of every face. Patch grids, on the other hand, have a vertex only at the corner of every patch. Each patch can consist of several faces. This reduction of vertices makes patches much cleaner and less cumbersome objects to work with.

 Even though the patch object looks simple, the resulting surface generates a large number of faces.

Creating a patch grid

Patches are named according to the number of vertices at their edges; for example, a Tri Patch has three vertices, a Quad Patch has four vertices, and so on. The default Quad Patch is made up of 36 visible rectangular faces, and the default Tri Patch has 72 triangular faces, as shown in Figure 27.1.

FIGURE 27.1

A Quad Patch and a Tri Patch

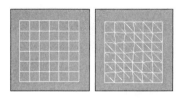

To create patches, select the Create ⇨ Patch Grids ⇨ Quad Patch or Tri Patch menu commands. This opens the Create panel. Select the Geometry category, and then select Patch Grids in the drop-down list. To create a patch grid, click in a viewport and drag to specify the dimensions of the grid.

You can also use the Keyboard Entry rollout to create patch grids with precise dimensions. To use this rollout, enter the grid's position coordinates and its dimensions and click the Create button. The X, Y, and Z coordinates define the location of the center of the grid.

The Patch Grid Parameters rollout includes Length and Width values and values for the number of Segments for each dimension (but only for the Quad Patch). A Segment value of 1 creates six rows or columns of segments, so the total number of polygons for a Quad Patch never drops below 36. Tri Patches do not have a Segments parameter. You can also select to automatically Generate Mapping Coordinates.

Newly created patches are always flat.

Tutorial: Creating a checkerboard

In this tutorial, we create a simple checkerboard. To keep the white squares separate from the black squares, we use Quad and Tri Patches.

To create a checkerboard from patch surfaces, follow these steps:

1. Right-click the Snap button on the main toolbar; in the Grid and Snap Settings dialog box that appears, make sure that the Grid Points option is enabled. Then enable the Snap button on the main toolbar (keyboard shortcut, S).

2. Select Create ⇨ Patch Grids ⇨ Quad Patch, and in the Top view, create a perfect square using the grid points. Click the color swatch in the Name and Color rollout, and select the color black.

3. In the Command Panel, click the Tri Patch button and drag in the Top view to create an equally sized patch to the right of the first object. Select the Tri Patch, click its color swatch, and change its object color to white.

CAUTION With the Tri Patch's object color set to white, telling when it is selected can be difficult.

4. Repeat Steps 2 and 3, alternating which color comes first until the entire 8 × 8 checkerboard is complete.

TIP An easier way to accomplish the checkerboard would be to create the first two squares and then to use the Array dialog box to create the rest. Find out more about the Array dialog box in Chapter 8, "Cloning Objects and Creating Object Arrays."

Figure 27.2 shows the completed checkerboard.

FIGURE 27.2

A checkerboard created using patch grids

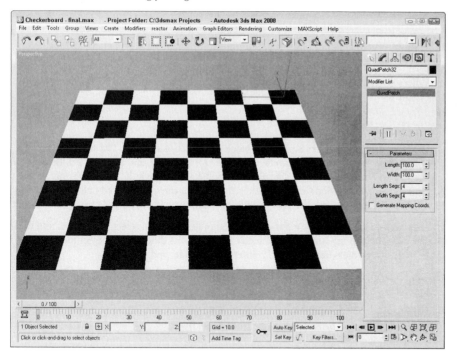

Editing Patches

Creating and working with patches is easy, but because they are always flat, they have limited functionality. The key to making patches really useful is to convert the object into an Editable Patch object. Any type of geometric object can be converted to an Editable Patch object. Even patch grids created with the Quad

Patch and Tri Patch buttons described earlier need to be converted before they can be edited at the subobject level.

You have several ways to convert an object to an Editable Patch. One way is to right-click a selected object and choose Convert To ➪ Convert to Editable Patch from the pop-up quadmenu. Another way is to apply the Edit Patch modifier by selecting it from the Modifier List in the Modifier Stack, or by choosing Modifiers ➪ Patch/Spline Editing ➪ Edit Patch. These two methods create slightly different Editable Patches.

Editable patches versus the Edit Patch modifier

The differences between Editable Patches and objects with the Edit Patch modifier applied are subtle. The main difference between these two appears in the Modifier Stack. Editable Patch objects have the type Editable Patch displayed in the Stack. Patch grids with the Edit Patch modifier applied maintain their creation parameters, and the Edit Patch modifier is displayed in the Stack above the object type, where you can move or remove it at any time.

The other big difference is that the transformation of an Editable Patch subobject can be animated, whereas patch grids with the Edit Patch modifier cannot.

Editable patches and patch grids with the Edit Patch modifier applied both access subobjects and their parameters in the same way. These are covered in the next section.

 **Using the Edit Patch modifier offers more flexibility during the modeling phase and the object can be collapsed down to an Editable Patch object after the modeling is completed for speed.**

The Edit Patch modifier also can be applied to a closed spline. This makes the spline a surface in one step instead of applying the Cross Section and Surface modifiers.

Selecting patch subobjects

Editable patches and the Edit Patch modifier both make patch subobjects accessible. The subobjects for patches include Vertex (keyboard shortcut, 1), Handle (5), Edge (2), Patch (3), and Element (4). Before you can edit patch subobjects, you must select them. To select a subobject type, click the small plus sign to the left of the Editable Patch object in the Modifier Stack. Alternatively, you can click the red-colored icons under the Selection rollout. When selected, the subobject button and hierarchy turn yellow.

A third way to enter subobject edit mode is to right-click the Editable Patch and select Sub-Object and the subobject type to edit from the pop-up quadmenu. You can also select the different subobject modes using the 1–5 keyboard shortcuts—1 enters Vertex mode, 2 enters Edge mode, and so on.

Clicking either the subobject button or the hierarchy object again exits subobject mode. Remember, you must exit this mode before you can select another object. This is called Top Level in the quadmenu.

To select many subobjects at once, drag an outline over them. You can also select and deselect many subobjects by holding down the Ctrl key while clicking them. Hold down the Alt key to remove any selected vertices from the current selection set.

With subobjects selected, the options in the Selection rollout become enabled. Using these controls enables you to more easily select the desired subobjects. Figure 27.3 shows the Selection and Soft Selection rollouts.

After selecting several subobjects, you can create a named selection set by typing a name in the Name Selection Sets drop-down list on the main toolbar. You can then copy and paste these selection sets onto other patch objects using the Copy and Paste buttons in the Selection rollout. In Vertex subobject mode, the Selection rollout lets you see, when selected, just Vertices, just Vectors, or both. The Lock Handles option causes all selected Bézier handles to move together when one handle is moved.

FIGURE 27.3

The Selection rollout includes icon buttons for selecting the various subobject modes.

Handle subobject mode

Vertex
subobject
mode

Patch
subobject
mode

Element
subobject
mode

Edge subobject mode

The By Vertex option is available in all but the Vertex subobject mode. It requires that you click a vertex in order to select an Edge, Face, Polygon, or Element. It selects all edges and faces that are connected to a vertex when the vertex is selected. This is handy because selecting a vertex is often easier than selecting numerous faces or edges.

The Ignore Backfacing option selects only those subobjects with normals pointing toward the current viewport. This option is helpful if many subobjects are on top of one another in the viewport. For example, if a sphere object were converted into an Editable Patch, you could enable the Ignore Backfacing option, and then selecting subobjects on the front of the sphere would not select the subobjects on the back of the sphere at the same time.

The Shrink and Grow buttons decrease or increase the selected subobjects by adding or deleting all adjacent subobjects to the current selection. The Ring and Loop buttons are available only in Edge subobject mode. Ring selects all edges that are parallel to the current edge, and Loop selects all other edges that have the same alignment as the current edge.

The Select Open Edges option is active only in Edge subobject mode. This button lets you select all the edges in the patch that are connected only to one face. This provides an easy way to quickly locate all the holes in your current model.

At the bottom of the Selection rollout is some information on the current selection. This lists the current subobject type and number selected.

CROSS-REF   The Soft Selection rollout allows you to alter (to a lesser extent) adjacent non-selected subobjects when selected subobjects are moved, creating a smooth transition. Check out the details of this rollout in Chapter 10, "Learning Modeling Basics and Working with Subobjects and Helpers."

Working with Patch Geometry

Much of the power of editing patches is contained within the Geometry rollout, shown in Figure 27.4. You can use this rollout to attach new patches, weld and delete vertices, and bind and hide elements. Some Geometry rollout buttons may be disabled in the various subobject modes but are enabled in one of the other subobject editing modes.

FIGURE 27.4

The Geometry rollout (shown in two parts) includes controls for editing patches.

Attach

The Attach button is available in all subobject modes, even when you're not in subobject mode. You use it to add objects to the current Editable Patch object, such as primitives, mesh objects, and other patch objects. Be aware that you cannot attach a spline. Objects that are attached to an Editable Patch also become Editable Patches. Most Editable Patch features work only if all the involved patch pieces are attached as part of the same patch object.

To use this feature, select an object, click the Attach button, and move the mouse over the object to attach. The cursor changes over acceptable objects. Click the object to be attached. Click the Attach button again or right-click in the viewport to exit Attach mode. The Reorient option aligns the attached object's Local Coordinate System with the Local Coordinate System of the patch to which it is being attached.

 Converting mesh objects to patch objects results in objects with many vertices.

Surface settings

The View Steps value determines the resolution of the patch grid that is displayed in the viewport. You can change this resolution for rendering using the Render Steps value. You can turn off the Interior Edges altogether using the Show Interior Edges option. The Use True Patch Normals option sets the type of normal used to smooth between patch objects. Enabling this option results in more accurate shading.

A Quad Patch with a View Steps value of 0 is a simple square. Figure 27.5 shows four spheres that have all been cloned from one, converted to Editable Patches, and set with different View Steps. From left to right, the View Steps values are 0, 2, 4, 6, and 10.

FIGURE 27.5

The only differences in these patch spheres are the View Steps values.

Patch Smooth

The Patch Smooth button adjusts all vertex handles to smooth the surface of the Editable Patch object. Be aware that patch smoothing may cause an abrupt change in the surface of the patch object.

Relaxing a patch

When the Editable Patch object is selected without any subobject modes, the Surface Properties rollout includes an option to Relax the patch. Enabling this option moves vertices that are too close to neighboring vertices slightly apart. The net result is to smooth the areas of tension, making the entire patch more continuous and less abrupt.

With the Relax option enabled, the other options in the rollout become available. The Relax Viewports option displays the results of the Relax option in the viewports. The Relax Value determines how far the vertices move. The Iterations value sets how many times the relax function is performed. The Keep Boundary Points Fixed and Save Outer Corners options can be used to maintain the exterior profile of the patch and prevent edges and corners from being relaxed.

Editing vertices

After you select Vertex subobject mode, you can transform selected vertices using the transform buttons on the main toolbar, or you can also distort the faces around the selected vertex by transforming the handles, shown as small green squares. Dragging these handles changes the surface of the patch, as shown in Figure 27.6. The first patch shows the handles before being moved, the second patch shows the effect of moving the handles with the Lock Handles option enabled, the third patch has moved a single handle, and the fourth patch shows where both handles have been moved.

FIGURE 27.6

Moving the Vertex handles alters the adjacent faces.

Selected vertex

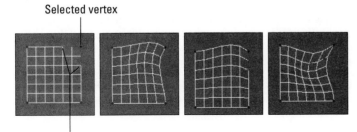

Vertex handles

Patch vertices can be either of two types: Coplanar or Corner. Coplanar vertices maintain a smooth transition from vertex to vertex because their handles are locked. This causes the handles to always move so as to prevent any surface discontinuities. You can drag the handles of corner vertices to create gaps and seams in the surface.

You can switch between these two vertex types by right-clicking a vertex while in vertex subobject mode and selecting the desired type from the pop-up quadmenu.

 **NOTE** Holding down the Shift key while clicking and dragging on a handle unlocks the handles and automatically changes the vertex type to Corner.

Bind and Unbind

You can use the Bind button to connect edge vertices of one patch to an edge of another patch, which is useful for connecting edges with a different number of vertices. Be aware that the two patches must be part of the same object (you can make them part of the same object using the Attach button) and that the corner vertices must be welded together first. If you try to bind a vertex before welding the corner vertices, the Bind action won't work. To use the Bind feature, click the Bind button and then drag a line from a vertex to the edge where it should join.

The Bind button attaches vertices to edges; to attach vertices to vertices, use one of the Weld buttons. When you bind vertices, the point of contact between the two patches is seamless and the vertex becomes part of the interior. To exit Bind mode, click the Bind button again or right-click in a viewport.

You use the Unbind button to detach vertices that have been connected using the Bind button.

Create

You can use the Create button in the Vertex subobject mode to create patch vertices by clicking in the viewport. Use the Create button in Patch or Element subobject mode to connect the created vertices into three-sided or four-sided patches. Right-click in the viewport or click again on the Create button to exit Create mode.

The order in which you click on the vertices determines the direction of the normal vector, which determines the visibility of the patch in the viewports (unless the Force 2-Sided display option is enabled). If you click on the vertices in a clockwise direction, then the normal vector points away from the current viewport. The counterclockwise order points the normal vector out toward the user (which makes it visible).

> **TIP** An easy way to determine the direction of the normal vector is to curl the fingers on your right hand in the direction that the vertices were clicked. Your thumb points toward the direction of the normal vector. This is called the right-hand rule.

Delete

The Delete button (or pressing the Delete key) deletes the selected vertices. This button works for all the subobject types.

> **NOTE** Deleting a vertex also deletes all faces and edges connected to that vertex. For example, deleting a single (top) vertex from a sphere that has been converted to an Editable Patch object leaves only a hemisphere.

Break

Click the Break button to create a separate vertex for adjoining faces that are connected by a single vertex.

Patches are all connected by vertices: Moving one vertex changes the position of all adjoining patches. The Break button enables you to move the vertex associated with each patch independent of the others. The button is available only in Vertex subobject mode.

Hide and Unhide All

The Hide and Unhide All buttons hide and unhide selected vertices. They can be used in any subobject mode. To hide a subobject, select the subobject and click the Hide button. To unhide the hidden subobjects, click the Unhide All button. Clicking the Unhide All button makes all subobjects, regardless of type, visible.

Weld Selected and Weld Target

The Weld button enables you to weld two or more vertices into one vertex. To use this feature, move the vertices close to one another, drag an outline over them to select them, and then click the Weld button. You can tell whether the weld was successful by looking at the number of vertices selected at the bottom of the Selection rollout. If the weld was unsuccessful, increase the Weld Threshold specified by the spinner and try again.

The Weld Target button lets you select a vertex and drag and drop it on top of another vertex. If the target vertex is within the number of pixels specified by the Target value, the vertices are welded into one vertex. To exit Weld Target mode, click the Target button again or right-click in the viewport.

Figure 27.7 shows two inverted sloping patches that have been combined. The resolution of the patch on the right is twice that of the patch on the left. The Bind button was used to attach the center vertex to the edge of the other patch. Notice that the seam between the two patches is smooth.

Copy and Paste Tangents

Getting the handle positions between vertices just right can be tricky, but after you get it right, the Copy and Paste buttons in the Tangent section let you copy the handle orientation between vertices. The Paste Length option enables you to paste the length of the handle as well.

Vertex surface properties

In Vertex subobject mode, the Surface Properties rollout that appears lets you color the object by assigning colors to its vertices. For each vertex, you can also specify an Illumination color and an Alpha value, which sets the transparency. You can also specify vertex colors in Patch and Element subobject modes.

FIGURE 27.7

Two patches of different resolutions have been combined using the Bind and Weld buttons.

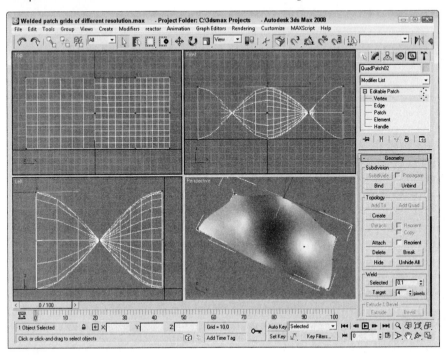

CROSS-REF You can find more information on vertex colors in Chapter 31, "Creating Baked Textures and Normal Maps."

After you assign colors, you can recall vertices with the same color by selecting a color (or illumination color) in the Select Vertices By section and clicking the Select button. The RGB values match all colors within the Range defined by these values. For example, if the RGB Range values are all set to 255, then every vertex is selected.

Editing handles

The Handle subobject mode gives you direct access to the vertex handles without the vertices or edges getting in the way. You can still work with handles in Vertex subobject mode, but the Handle subobject mode is more convenient and you don't need to worry about accidentally moving the vertex in the process.

When the Handle subobject mode is enabled, all vertex handles for the entire patch object are visible. Multiple handles can be selected and transformed at the same time. The Copy and Paste Tangent options are available for this mode also.

Editing edges

Edges are the lines that run between two vertices. You can select multiple edges by holding down the Ctrl key while clicking the edges or by holding down the Alt key to remove selected edges from the current selection set.

Many of the features in the Geometry rollout work in the same way as the Vertex subobjects, but the Geometry rollout also includes some features that are enabled in Edge subobject mode, like the ones in the following sections.

Subdivide

You use the Subdivide button to increase the resolution of a patch. This is done by splitting an edge into two separate edges, divided at the original edge's center. To use this feature, select an edge or edges and click the Subdivide button. The Propagate option causes the edges or neighboring patches to also be subdivided. Using Subdivide without the Propagate option enabled can cause cracks to appear in the patch. The Subdivide button also works in Patch subobject mode.

In Figure 27.8, I've subdivided a Quad Patch edge three times after selecting the upper-right corner edges.

FIGURE 27.8

By subdividing edge subobjects, you can control where the greatest resolution is located.

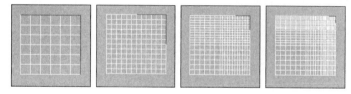

Add Tri and Add Quad

You can add Quad and Tri Patches to any open edge of a patch. To do this, select the open edge or edges and click the Add Tri or Add Quad button. You can locate all open edges using the Select Open Edges button in the Selection rollout. The new patch extends along the current curvature of the patch. To add a patch to a closed surface, like a box, you first need to detach one of the patches to create an open edge. This feature provides a way to extend the current patch.

Figure 27.9 shows a simple quad patch that was subdivided and then added to using the Add Quad button. This provides an easy way to quickly create a rough outline of an object that you want to model.

Create Shape

You can use the Create Shape button that appears at the bottom of the Geometry rollout in Edge subobject mode to create spline shapes from all the selected edges. To use this button, select several edge subobjects and click the button. A dialog box appears that allows you to name the new shape. You can then use the Select by Name dialog box (keyboard shortcut, H) to select the newly created shape.

Tutorial: Modeling a shell

Now that you've seen all the various tools, let's try out some of them. A Patch object can be used to create a common beach shell, as we do in this tutorial.

FIGURE 27.9

A quick outline of a key was created by selecting edge subobjects and adding Quad patches.

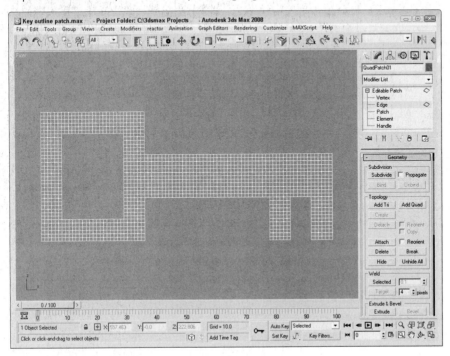

To model a shell using a patch, follow these steps:

1. Open the Patch seashell.max file from the Chap 27 directory on the DVD.

   This file includes a simple disk that has been converted to an Editable Patch object and all the lower vertices have been welded together.

2. Select the shell object, and open the Modify panel. Click the small plus icon to the left of the Editable Patch object in the Modifier Stack, and select Edge from the hierarchy (or press 2).

   You are now in Edge subobject mode.

3. Select every other interior set of radial edges in the Front viewport along the shell while holding down the Ctrl key. Make sure that you select both the front and back edges. The Info line at the bottom of the Selection rollout tells you what is selected (14 edges should be selected). When you have the edges selected, press the spacebar to lock the selection.

4. Click the Select and Move button (or press W), and move the edges upward in the Top view.

   A zigzag pattern appears on the surface of the patch.

Figure 27.10 shows the completed shell.

FIGURE 27.10

This shell is an Editable Patch created by moving every other interior edge.

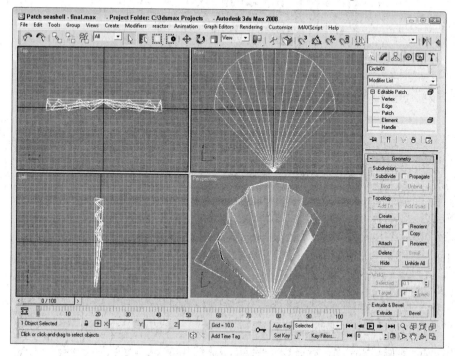

Editing patch and element subobjects

Transforming a patch object containing only one patch works the same way in subobject mode as it works for normal transformations. Working with the patch subobject on an object that contains several patches lets you transform individual patches. A key advantage of working with the patch subobjects is controlling their Geometry using the buttons in the Geometry rollout. The following sections discuss the additional features available in patch subobject mode.

Detach

The Detach button separates the selected patch or element subobjects from the rest of the object. Using this button opens the Detach dialog box, which enables you to name the detached subobject. The Reorient option realigns the detached subobject patch to match the position and orientation of the current active patch. The Copy option creates a new copy of the detached subobject.

 This feature is different from Delete. Detach maintains the subobject and gives it a separate name, but the Delete function eliminates the subobject.

Extrude

The Extrude button adds depth to a patch by replicating a patch surface and creating sides to connect the new patch surface to the original. For example, a square patch grid that is extruded forms a cube. To use this feature, select a patch, click the Extrude button, and then drag in a viewport — the patch interactively shows the extrude depth. Release the button when you reach the desired distance.

Alternatively, you can specify an extrude depth in the Extrusion spinner. The Outlining value lets you resize the extruded patch. Positive outlining values cause the extrusion to get larger, whereas negative values reduce its size. The Normal Group option extrudes all selected patches along the normal for the group, and the Normal Local option moves each individual patch along its local normal. To exit extrude mode, click the Extrude button again or right-click in the viewport.

> **TIP** One place to use this function is to add arms to the torso of a character. If you've created a torso model out of patches, you can add arms by detaching a patch and extruding the area where the arms go.

Figure 27.11 shows the key-shaped patch that has been extruded using the Extrude button.

FIGURE 27.11

The simple key-shaped patch has been extruded.

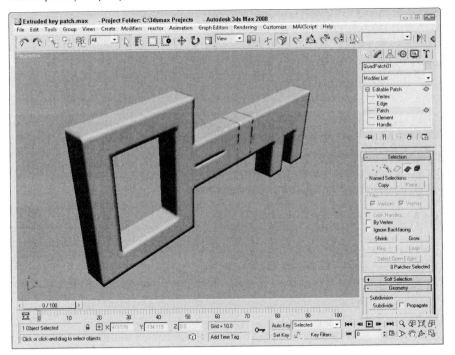

Bevel

The Bevel button extrudes a patch and then lets you bevel the edges. To use this feature, select a patch, click the Bevel button, and then drag in a viewport to the Extrusion depth and release the button. Then drag again to specify the Outlining amount.

You can use the same options for the Bevel button as for the Extrude button described previously. In addition, the Bevel button includes Smoothing options for the bevel. Set the Start and End Smoothing options to Smooth, Linear, or None.

Figure 27.12 displays a sphere that has been converted to an Editable Patch object. Each corner of the sphere object was selected and beveled with an Extrusion value of 25 and an Outline value of –5.

FIGURE 27.12

A patch sphere whose corner patches have been beveled

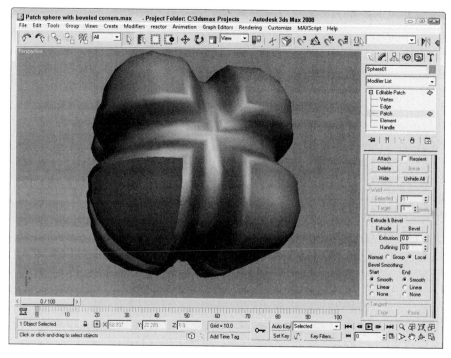

Patch and element surface properties

If either the patch or element subobject mode is selected, the Surface Properties rollout appears. You can use this rollout to control normal vectors and assign Material IDs and Smoothing Groups.

The Surface Properties rollout includes Flip and Unify buttons to control the direction of the normal vectors. Flip reverses the direction of the normals of each selected face; Unify makes all normals face in the same direction based on the majority. The Flip Normal Mode button activates a mode where you can click individual faces and flip their normals. This mode stays active until you click the Flip Normal Mode button again or right-click in the viewport.

Material IDs are used by the Multi/Sub-Object material type to apply different materials to different patches within an object. By selecting a patch subobject, you can use this control to apply a unique material to each patch.

CROSS-REF   **You can find more information on the Multi/Sub-Object material type in Chapter 15, "Creating and Applying Standard Materials."**

You can also assign a patch to a unique Smoothing Group. To do this, select a patch and click a Smoothing Group number.

Tutorial: Creating a maple leaf from patches

Because patches are a good modeling type for organic objects, let's put it to the test by trying to create a maple leaf. Because of the symmetry of the leaf, we really need to create only half of the leaf. We can then use the Mirror tool to create the other half.

To model a maple leaf using patches, follow these steps:

1. Open the Maple leaf.max file from the Chap 27 directory on the DVD.

   This file includes a background image of a real maple leaf loaded into the Front viewport.

2. Select Create ⇨ Patch Grids ⇨ Tri Patch, and drag in the Front viewport to create a square patch grid from the base where the stem is to the upper-left interior area of the leaf. The right edge of the patch should run about halfway up along the midline of the leaf.

3. In the Modify panel, right-click the Tri Patch name and select Convert to Editable Patch from the pop-up menu.

4. In the Modifier Stack, select the Element subobject mode (or press the 4 key) and then select the patch element. With the Propagate option selected, click the Subdivide button.

5. Select the Edge subobject mode (or press the 2 key), and select one of the edges that is completely within the interior area of the background leaf image. Then press the Add Tri button to extend the patch. Repeat this step until you have added a patch for each point around the outer perimeter of the leaf.

6. Select Vertex subobject mode (or press the 1 key). With the Select and Move button on the main toolbar, select and drag the edge vertices so they align with the corners of the background leaf. Move all internal vertices so they lie within the leaf area. Select each vertex that lies along the outer edge of the leaf, and move its handles so the patch edge aligns with the background leaf's border. If the handles move together, hold down the Shift key to move them individually.

7. Deselect the Vertex subobject mode. In the Surface Properties rollout, enable all the options, and set the Relax Value to **1.0** and the Iterations to **50**. This smoothes out the wrinkles in the patch.

Figure 27.13 shows the completed maple leaf patch (half of it, anyway). To complete this leaf, use the Mirror tool and add a spline object for the stem.

FIGURE 27.13

FIGURE 27.13

By repositioning the vertex handles, you can make the patch object match the leaf's edges precisely.

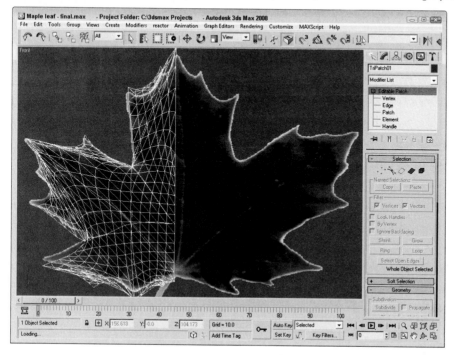

Using Modifiers on Patch Objects

Several modifiers work specifically on patch objects. The Modifiers ⇨ Patch/Spline Editing submenu contains most of these modifiers.

 Many other modifiers work on patch objects. To see which modifiers work on patch objects, select the patch object and check the Modifiers menu to see which modifiers are enabled.

Patch Select modifier

The Patch Select modifier enables you to select patch subobjects, including Vertex, Edge, Patch, and Element. You can copy and paste named selection sets. The selection can then be passed up the Stack to the next modifier. The Patch Select modifier provides a way to apply a separate modifier to a subobject selection.

Edit Patch modifier

This modifier includes tools for editing patch objects. The features of this modifier are the same as those of the Editable Patch object. If you want to animate the features of an Editable Patch, use the Edit Patch modifier. You can even apply the Edit Patch modifier to an Editable Patch. The key benefit of the Edit Patch modifier is that it enables you to edit patch subobjects while maintaining the parametric nature of the object.

Delete Patch modifier

You can use the Delete Patch modifier to delete a patch subobject from a patch object. You use the Patch Select modifier to select the patch subobjects to delete, and you apply the Delete Patch modifier to the Patch Select modifier.

Using the Surface tools

The surface tools, which include the CrossSection and Surface modifiers, provide a way to model that is similar to lofting. The CrossSection modifier takes several cross-section shapes and connects their vertices with additional splines to create a spline framework. You can then use the Surface modifier to cover this framework with a skin.

 Lofting is accomplished with the Loft compound object. For more information on it, see Chapter 26, "Working with Compound Objects."

CrossSection modifier

The CrossSection modifier and the Surface modifier are the key reason why the spline and patch modifiers have been combined into a single submenu.

The CrossSection modifier works only on spline objects. This modifier connects the vertices of several cross-sectional splines together with another spline that runs along their edges like a backbone. The various cross-sectional splines can have different numbers of vertices. Parameters include different spline types such as Linear, Smooth, Bézier, and Bézier Corner.

To apply this modifier, all the cross-section splines need to belong to the same Editable Spline object. You can connect them using the Attach button. The cross-section splines are attached in the order they exist, which can be a problem if you create them in a different order. Figure 27.14 shows a spline network that has been created with the CrossSection modifier.

 Editable Splines include a CrossSection feature that works just like the CrossSection modifier.

Surface modifier

The Surface modifier is the other part of the surface tools. It creates a surface from several combined splines. It can use any spline network but works best with structures created with the CrossSection modifier. The surface created with this modifier is a patch surface.

Parameters for this modifier include a Spline Threshold value and options to Flip Normals, Remove Interior Patches, and Use Only Selected Segments. You can also specify the steps used to create the patch topology. After the surface is created, you can apply the Edit Patch modifier to further edit and refine the patch surface.

FIGURE 27.14

The CrossSection modifier joins several cross-section splines into a network of splines ready for a surface.

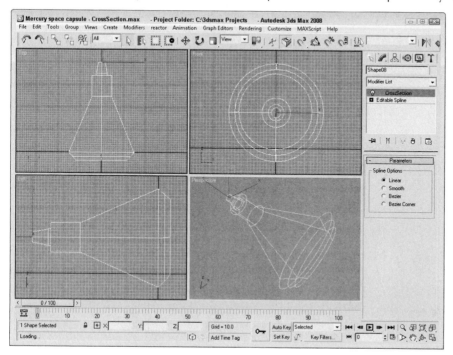

In order for the surface to be created correctly, the vertices of the spline cage should be as close to coincident as possible. The Threshold value represents how close they have to be before they are considered coincident. In addition, any closed loop in the spline cage can have no more than four vertices or a patch will not be created.

NOTE If the structure is already created, you can create a surface from the splines by simply applying the Edit Patch modifier.

Figure 27.15 shows the spline structure illustrated in the preceding figure with the Surface modifier applied.

FIGURE 27.15

The Surface modifier applies a surface to the cross-section spline network.

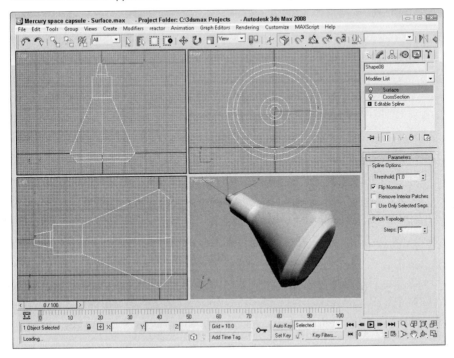

Tutorial: Modeling a brass swan

Chapter 2 included a tutorial that added a background image of a brass swan to the viewports. In this tutorial, we use the CrossSection and Surface modifiers to create a swan based on these background images.

To create a brass swan, follow these steps:

1. Open the Brass swan.max file from the Chap 27 directory on the DVD.

   This file includes the background images needed to create the swan model.

2. Select Create ➪ Shapes ➪ Ellipse, and drag in the Top viewport to create a simple ellipse that is roughly the shape of the swan's nose. Use the transform tools to move, rotate, and scale the ellipse to match the cross section of the background image.

3. Hold down the Shift key, and drag the ellipse shape to the base of the swan's nose to create a clone. Use the transform tools to align this clone to the background image in the Front and Left viewports.

> **NOTE**   Although background images have been loaded for the Top, Front, and Left viewports, you really need only two viewports to align all the cross sections. In this example, the Top viewport is misaligned with the other two viewports.

4. Continue to create cloned copies of the ellipse shape, and match them to each changing cross section in the background images.

5. For the base cross sections, right-click the ellipse shape and select Convert to ➪ Editable Spline from the pop-up quadmenu. Then enable Vertex subobject mode, click the Refine button in the Geometry rollout, and click the lower-left and lower-right corners of the ellipse to add two new vertices to the shape. Select and right-click these new vertices, and change their vertex type to Bézier Corner to make the bottom of their cross-section shapes flat.

6. Select the first cross-section shape at the swan's nose, and convert it to an Editable Spline. Then click the Attach button, and select each cloned cross-section shape in order from the nose to the tail. This makes all the shapes part of the same Editable Spline object.

7. Choose Modifiers ➪ Patch/Spline Editing ➪ CrossSection to apply the CrossSection modifier to the Editable Spline object. Then choose Modifiers ➪ Patch/Spline Editing ➪ Surface to apply the Surface modifier. Next, enable the Flip Normals option to see the final swan model. This command creates a surface that covers the spline framework. The surface created is a patch object.

> **NOTE** You may not need to enable the Flip Normals option depending on how you created your initial splines.

Figure 27.16 shows the completed swan model. Using the surface tools to create patch objects results in objects that are easy to modify. You can change any patch subobject by applying the Edit Patch modifier and using the rollouts in the Modify panel.

Another way to create this swan model is to use the CrossSection feature for the Editable Spline and then apply the Edit Patch modifier to create the finished surface. This method is cleaner and involves fewer modifiers.

FIGURE 27.16

The brass swan was created using the CrossSection and Surface modifiers.

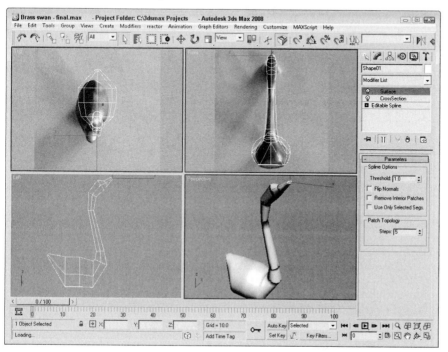

 Another common modifier that is used with patch objects is the PatchDeform modifier. Learn more about this modifier in Chapter 20, "Understanding Animation and Keyframe Basics."

Creating NURBS Curves and Surfaces

If you boil down any complex NURBS object, you'll find a collection of fundamental building pieces. These fundamental pieces consist of curves and surfaces. From these simple pieces, you can form complex models. You can create both of these fundamental pieces using the Create menu.

 A large benefit of modeling with NURBS is that all points, curves, and surfaces are contained with a single object. This enables you to attach a NURBS curve to a NURBS surface and vice versa.

From the Create menu, you can create two types of NURBS curves and two types of NURBS surfaces. For both curves and surfaces, one type works with points and the other type works with control vertices (referred to as CVs). The point type includes lines that always run through the points that make up the curves or surfaces. The CV type is different. It has a lattice of points that control how the lines run. The lines do not run through the CVs but are affected by their distance, much like how Bézier curves work.

NURBS curves

The two kinds of NURBS curves are CV curves and point curves. CV curves are the most commonly used NURBS curves. You can create both of these curves by selecting the Create ➪ NURBS menu command or by opening the Create panel, selecting the Shapes category, and selecting the NURBS Curves subcategory. Then click and drag in the viewport to set the first point, and begin drawing the curve. After each click, drag the mouse to a new location, click again to continue extending the curve, and then right-click to end the curve.

Figure 27.17 shows a NURBS point curve on the left and a NURBS CV curve on the right.

 You can also create NURBS curves and surfaces using the NURBS Creation Toolbox, which you find out more about later in this chapter.

CV curves versus Point curves

CV curves have a *CV control lattice* with points (shown in the viewports as yellow) that let you control the shape of an individual curve or the entire surface. The *point curve* is similar to a CV curve, except that the NURBS curve passes through the points. Point curves give you more intuitive control over the shape of a curve or surface, but they are not as stable as CV curves, and point surfaces do not have as many modification options. Notice that NURBS curves are automatically smoothed, but, unlike splines, they do not have Bézier control handles to adjust their shape. You can adjust the shape of a NURBS curve by moving the control vertices or by adjusting the weights (strengths of attraction) of individual CVs.

Rendering NURBS curves

The Rendering rollout includes many of the same rendering options that apply for splines. You can make the curves renderable and give them a Thickness value. The Sides value defines the number of edges that are included in the curve cross section, and the Angle value determines how the cross section is oriented. You can also make the curves appear in the renderer and/or the viewports and have Max generate mapping coordinates. If the Display Render Mesh option is selected, then you can select to Use Viewport Settings, and the renderer will use the settings for the Viewport.

FIGURE 27.17

NURBS curves come in two different types: point and CV curves.

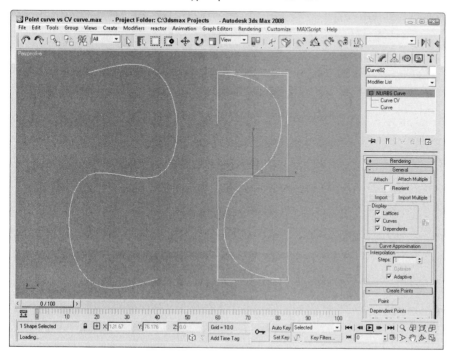

NURBS surfaces

You can also create NURBS point surfaces and CV surfaces using the Create ⇨ NURBS menu or by opening the Create panel, selecting the Geometry category, and selecting the NURBS Surfaces subcategory. Then, to create the surface, you simply click and drag to make a rectangular shape in any viewport. When you release the mouse button, the surface is built. These rectangles, also referred to as NURBS patches, are easy to form into shapes by moving, scaling, and rotating the CVs. You can build a large model by assembling a group of these NURBS patches and attaching them with various NURBS surface tools.

The Create Parameters rollout includes settings to specify the Length and Width of the surface. You can also specify the number of points or CVs the surface will have. This rollout also includes options to Generate Mapping Coordinates and Flip Normals. For CV surfaces, you can set Automatic Reparameterization to None, Chord Length, or Uniform.

CV surfaces versus Point surfaces

You can create different types of NURBS surfaces from NURBS curves and patches using the various buttons found in the Create Surfaces rollout in the Modify panel. You learn more about these buttons in the sections that follow. Figure 27.18 shows a NURBS point surface on the left and a NURBS CV surface on the right.

FIGURE 27.18

NURBS surfaces also come in two different types: point and CV surfaces.

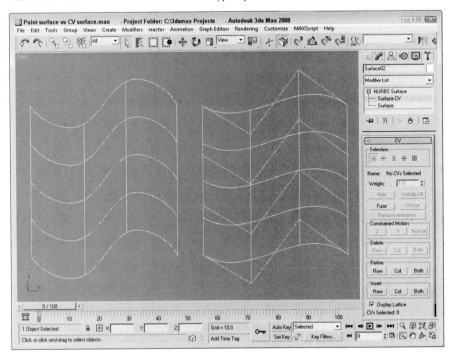

When a surface is created from two or more NURBS curves using the buttons in the Create Surfaces rollout, the surface is displayed in the form of U and V isoparms. *Isoparms* are lines that span the distance from one curve to the next and establish the NURBS surface. Isoparms are displayed in the viewport as green lines when a NURBS surface is selected.

> **TIP**   When building some models such as a human head, using point surfaces is often easier because you can adjust the surface interactively, and you avoid the confusion of having a complex control vertex lattice floating on top of your model, obscuring the area on which you are working.

Accessing NURBS subobjects

You can modify CV surfaces by selecting the Surface CV subobject in the Modifier Stack and moving the control vertices that surround the surface or by adjusting the weight of the individual CVs in the CV rollout. Point surfaces have no lattice, but you can shape them directly by selecting the Point subobject and moving the points on the surface.

Converting objects to NURBS

To convert a standard primitive object to a NURBS object, select the primitive object, right-click in the viewport, and choose Convert To ⇨ Convert to NURBS in the pop-up quadmenu. Another option for converting primitives is to right-click the object title in the Modifier Stack and select the Convert to NURBS option from the pop-up menu.

Figure 27.19 shows two spheres. The one on the left is a normal primitive sphere, and the one on the right has been converted to a NURBS surface.

FIGURE 27.19

Standard primitives, like the sphere on the left, can be converted to NURBS surfaces.

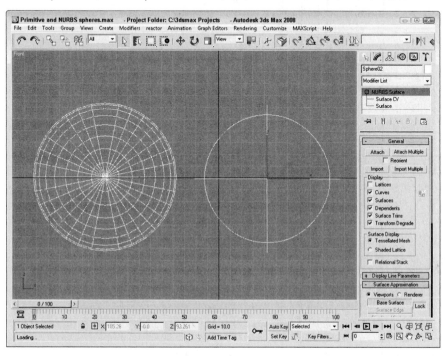

Another method to convert a standard primitive to a NURBS object is to attach it to a NURBS object. To do this, select the NURBS object, open the Modify panel, and under the General rollout, click the Attach button and select the polygon object to attach. Any object that is attached to a NURBS object is automatically converted to a NURBS object.

Some modifiers, such as the Lathe modifier, give you the option of creating a patch, mesh, or NURBS as the output type. However, after a lathed object has been output as a polygonal mesh or a patch object, it can no longer be converted to a NURBS object.

You can also convert splines to NURBS curves, but not all types of splines convert to one-piece NURBS curves. For example, a line created using the Corner Initial type and Drag type options converts to a series of separate NURBS curves. If you want the spline to convert to a single curve, you must set the Drag type option to Smooth or Bézier. Of the many types of splines available in the Shapes category, only the Helix cannot be converted to a NURBS curve. The Rectangle, NGon, and Text shapes yield segmented NURBS curves, and closed shapes such as the Circle, Star, Ellipse, and Donut yield one-piece NURBS curves when converted.

 If you plan to use multiple-piece curve shapes as cross sections in a 1-rail or 2-rail sweep (discussed later in the chapter) or as NURBS Extrusion curves, considering whether or not a curve is closed is important. To function properly, multiple-piece curve shapes need to be welded into a single NURBS curve after conversion.

Editing NURBS

You can edit and model NURBS curves and surfaces into desired shapes using the rollouts in the Modify panel, using the tools in the NURBS Creation Toolbox, or by working with the NURBS subobjects.

Attach and Import

When a NURBS curve or surface is selected, the General rollout includes buttons to attach and import NURBS. The Attach Multiple and Import Multiple buttons let you select from a dialog box several objects to attach or import. When attaching NURBS, you have the option of reorienting the attached object.

Display options

The General rollout, shown in Figure 27.20, also includes a Display section where you can select which elements get displayed. For curves, the options include Lattices, Curves, and Dependents. For surfaces, you have further options to display Surfaces, Surface Trims, and Transform Degrade, and you can also choose the surface display to be a Tessellated Mesh or a Shaded Lattice. Next to the Display section is the NURBS Creation Toolbox button. This button opens a floating window of buttons that make working with NURBS easy. You find out more about the NURBS Creation Toolbox buttons in the next section.

For NURBS surfaces, the Display Line Parameters rollout lets you specify the number of U and V isoparms to use to display the NURBS surface. These isoparms are the lines that make the NURBS object visible in the viewport. You can also select to display Iso Only, Iso and Mesh, or Mesh Only.

 You can set the number of U and V isoparms to 0, which makes the NURBS surface invisible.

Surface and Curve Approximation

Using the Curve Approximation rollout, which becomes available when you choose the CV Curve option, you can set the Interpolation Steps value. The Optimize and Adaptive options automatically reduce the number of points required for the curve.

When you're working with NURBS surfaces, the Surface Approximation rollout lets you control the surface details for both the viewport and the renderer. For Base Surface, Surface Edge, and Displaced Surface, you can set the Tessellation Method. The three Tessellation Presets are Low, Medium, and High. These presets set the parameters for the various tessellation methods, with Low representing the values that produce the lowest-quality surface. You can also select which tessellation method to use — Regular, Parametric, Spatial, Curvature, or Spatial and Curvature. Each of these methods uses a different algorithm to compute the surface.

The Merge value determines the space between surfaces that should be combined to eliminate gaps when the surface is rendered. In most cases, the default value is acceptable for eliminating surface gaps. The Advanced Parameters button opens an additional dialog box of parameters, shown in Figure 27.21, where you can choose the tessellation method to use. The options include Grid (which divides the surface using a regular grid), Tree (which divides the surface using a binary tree), and Delaunay (which subdivides the surface into equilateral triangles). The selected tessellation option is used by the Spatial, Curvature, and Spatial and Curvature tessellation methods. Use the Clear Surface Level button to eliminate all Surface Approximation settings.

The General rollout includes options for determining what is displayed in the viewports.

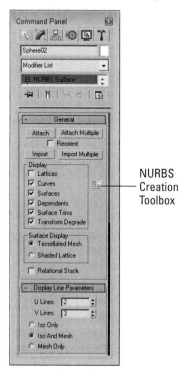

NURBS
Creation
Toolbox

The Advanced Surface Approximation dialog box lets you specify subdivision levels.

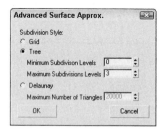

 The Delaunay tessellation option is particularly useful in preparing objects to be dynamic cloth objects.

The Curve Approximation rollout lets you select the number of interpolation steps to use. You can also select the Optimize or Adaptive option. These options define the number of segments used to represent the curve.

If you have several NURBS surfaces whose approximation settings you'd like to change at once, you can use the Surface Approximation Utility found in the Utility panel. This utility includes the same settings found in the Surface Approximation and Surface Display rollouts, but can be applied to multiple NURBS objects at once.

The NURBS Creation Toolbox

Clicking the NURBS Creation Toolbox button in the General rollout opens the toolbox shown in Figure 27.22. Clicking the button a second time closes the toolbox. This toolbox has three sections: Points, Curves, and Surfaces. All of the NURBS editing tools are contained within the NURBS Creation Toolbox.

NOTE   You can also open the NURBS Creation Toolbox by using the Ctrl+T keyboard shortcut.

FIGURE 27.22

The NURBS Creation Toolbox lets you work with NURBS points, curves, and surfaces.

Each of these sections includes buttons that create dependent subobjects. Dependent subobjects are objects that depend on other points, curves, or surfaces. When the parent object is changed, the dependent subobjects are changed also.

The Points section includes buttons for creating dependent NURBS points. Table 27.1 describes these point types and their respective buttons.

TABLE 27.1

Points NURBS Creation Toolbox Buttons

Toolbar Button	Name	Description
	Create Point	Creates a free independent point
	Create Offset Point	Creates a point that is offset from another point
	Create Curve Point	Creates a point that is on a curve
	Create Curve-Curve Point	Creates a point that intersects two curves

Toolbar Button	Name	Description
	Create Surf Point	Creates a point that is on a surface
	Create Surface Curve Point	Creates a point that intersects a curve and a surface

Creating freestanding or dependent NURBS points gives you another way to build curves. When one of these buttons is selected, the cursor changes when it is positioned over a place where the point can be created. For example, clicking the Create Surf Point button causes the cursor in the viewport to change when it is over a NURBS surface.

The Curves section includes many more buttons than the Points section. You can use these buttons to create dependent NURBS curves. Table 27.2 describes each of these buttons.

TABLE 27.2

Curves NURBS Creation Toolbox Buttons

Toolbar Button	Name	Description
	Create CV Curve	Creates a CV curve
	Create Point Curve	Creates a point curve
	Create Fit Curve	Creates a point curve that fits the selected points
	Create Transform Curve	Creates a copy of a curve that is transformed
	Create Blend Curve	Blends or smoothly connects the ends of two NURBS curves
	Create Offset Curve	Creates a copy of the original curve that is larger or smaller and moved to one side according to the distance setting
	Create Mirror Curve	Creates a mirrored copy of the original curve in the selected axis at a user-set distance
	Create Chamfer Curve	Creates a bevel where two curves meet
	Create Fillet Curve	Creates a radius line to make a smooth transition between two curves that cross each other
	Create Surface-Surface Intersection Curve	Creates a curve along the edge created when two NURBS surfaces intersect each other
	Create U Iso Curve	Creates a dependent curve from the U isoparm that makes up the NURBS surface
	Create V Iso Curve	Creates a dependent curve from the V isoparm that makes up the NURBS surface

continued

TABLE 27.2   *(continued)*

Toolbar Button	Name	Description
	Create Normal Projected Curve	Projects a curve on a NURBS surface by projecting along a surface normal
	Create Vector Projected Curve	Projects a curve on a NURBS surface by projecting along a vector
	Create CV Curve on Surface	Enables the user to create a CV curve directly on a NURBS surface
	Create Point Curve on Surface	Enables the user to create a point curve directly on a NURBS surface
	Create Surface Offset Curve	Creates a curve that is offset from a surface curve
	Create Surface Edge Curve	Creates a curve that lies on the surface edge

You can create dependent curve subobjects from points, curves, or surfaces. The cursor indicates when these can be created. Some dependent curves require two objects. For example, the Create Blend Curve button can attach two curves together. Selecting the first and then selecting the second does this. Each curve is highlighted blue as it is selected. The curves must be part of the same object.

The Surfaces section includes buttons for creating dependent NURBS surfaces. Table 27.3 describes each of these buttons.

TABLE 27.3

Surfaces NURBS Creation Toolbox Buttons

Toolbar Button	Name	Description
	Create CV Surface	Creates a CV surface
	Create Point Surface	Creates a point surface
	Create Transform Surface	Creates a copy of a surface that is transformed
	Create Blend Surface	Connects one surface to another with a smooth surface between them
	Create Offset Surface	Creates a copy of the original curve that is moved to one side according to the distance setting
	Create Mirror Surface	Creates a mirrored copy of the original surface in the selected axis at a user set distance
	Create Extrude Surface	Creates a NURBS surface at right angles to the construction plane

Toolbar Button	Name	Description
	Create Lathed Surface	Creates a NURBS surface by rotating a curve about an axis
	Create Ruled Surface	Creates a straight surface that joins the edges of two separate surfaces; one edge can be curved and the other straight
	Create Cap Surface	Creates a surface that closes the edges of a closed surface
	Create U Loft Surface	Creates a surface by linking multiple closed curved contours along the U axis
	Create UV Loft Surface	Creates a surface by linking multiple closed curved contours along the U and V axes
	Create 1-Rail Sweep	Creates a surface using an edge defined by one curve with a cross section defined by another
	Create 2-Rail Sweep	Creates a surface using an edge defined by two curves with a cross section defined by another
	Create a Multisided Blend Surface	Creates a surface by blending several curves and surfaces
	Create a Multicurved Trimmed Surface	Creates a surface that is trimmed by several curves that form a loop
	Create Fillet Surface	Creates a surface with rounded corners where the surfaces meet

The buttons included in the NURBS Creation Toolbox give you a wide variety of possible NURBS objects with which to work. We use many of these NURBS objects in the tutorials later in this chapter.

Using NURBS subobject editing tools

Max provides you with many tools that you can use to edit the various NURBS points, curves, and surfaces. To access these tools, select a NURBS object, open the Modify panel, select the object name in the Modifier Stack, and click the small plus sign icon to its left. A hierarchical list of subobjects appears in the Modifier Stack. The rollouts present the available editing tools. For example, if you select CV Surface in the Modifier Stack list, you can then adjust the position of the control vertices (or points on a point surface) using Max's standard transform buttons to change the shape of any NURBS surface.

The rollouts change depending on the type of NURBS object and subobject selected. The tools in these rollouts let you select and name specific areas, as well as hide, delete, break, and detach NURBS elements, and even work with a Soft Selection.

Many details of these various subobject tools are demonstrated in the tutorials that follow.

Working with NURBS

You'll learn many of the details of working with NURBS as you dive in and start building NURBS objects. This section includes several tutorials that can help as you try to grasp the power and flexibility of modeling with NURBS.

Lofting a NURBS surface

U Loft is one of the most versatile NURBS surface tools: You can use it to create simple or very complex surfaces. In the following tutorial, we create a spoon by U Lofting a NURBS surface over a series of point curve cross sections. The U Loft tool requires sections in the horizontal (U) direction.

Tutorial: Creating a U Loft NURBS spoon

Lofting a skin over a series of cross-section curves can create NURBS surfaces. In this tutorial, we create the point curves necessary for modeling a NURBS spoon. Then we use the U Loft tool to skin the surface and create the finished spoon.

To create a NURBS spoon using the U Loft feature, follow these steps:

1. Open the U-Loft spoon.max file from the Chap 27 directory on the DVD.

   This file includes 10 cross-section NURBS point curves that are correctly positioned to form a spoon.

2. Select one of the curves, and open the Modify panel. In the General rollout, click the Attach Multiple button to open the Attach Multiple dialog box, click the All button to select all the curves, and then click the Attach button to attach all the curves to the first curve you selected.

3. You are now ready to U Loft the spoon's surface. In the General rollout, click the NURBS Creation Toolbox icon to open the NURBS Toolbox window. In the Surfaces section, select the Create U Loft Surface icon.

   The cursor changes to a pointer accompanied by the U Loft Surface icon. (Notice that when you place the cursor over a cross section, it changes to a cross and the curve turns blue.)

NOTE You can also create this surface using the U Loft button found in the Create Surfaces rollout.

4. Click the smallest cross section at the tip of the spoon, drag to the next adjacent curve, and click again.

   The first section of the U Lofted NURBS surface is then generated as indicated by the green isoparm lines displayed in the viewport.

5. Continue clicking each curve in sequential order until you have lofted the entire spoon. After you've clicked the final section, right-click to exit this mode.

6. Now cap the ends by returning to the NURBS Toolbox window, selecting the Create Cap Surface tool, and clicking each small end curve.

Figure 27.23 shows the completed NURBS spoon.

Creating a UV Loft surface

A UV Loft surface can have more complex contours than a U Loft surface. UV Lofts are created from several curves spanning two dimensions; the U dimension is horizontal and the V dimension is vertical. To use this tool, select the cross-section curves in the order that they will be skinned along the U dimension, right-click in the viewport, and click the cross-sectional curves for the V dimension. The resulting surface is made up of cross-sectional curves for both dimensions to create a complex NURBS surface. Just like the U Loft surface, all curves need to be attached to the same NURBS object.

FIGURE 27.23

A NURBS spoon created with the U Loft tool

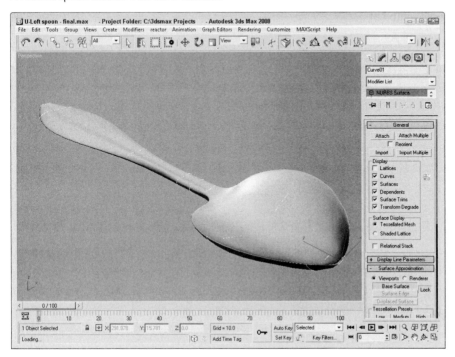

As an example, Figure 27.24 shows a chair seat that has been UV Lofted using three curves in the U direction and five curves in the V direction, thus enabling the surface to be contoured to fit a human being without your having to go back later and modify it by moving control vertices.

This technique is very useful for building mechanical shapes, automobiles, and spaceships, and for modeling product designs.

Lathing a NURBS surface

Lathing a NURBS curve works the same way as lathing a spline. You simply need to select a curve, click the Lathe button in the Create Surface rollout (or click the Create Lathe Surface button in the NURBS Creation Toolbox), and then click the curve. You can change the Degrees value and the axis of rotation in the Lathe Surface rollout that appears under the Create Surfaces rollout in the Modify panel.

Tutorial: Lathing a NURBS CV curve to create a vase

In this tutorial, we create a NURBS CV curve profile shape. We then use this curve with the Lathe modifier to create a vase.

FIGURE 27.24

A UV Loft surface lofted from two sets of curves

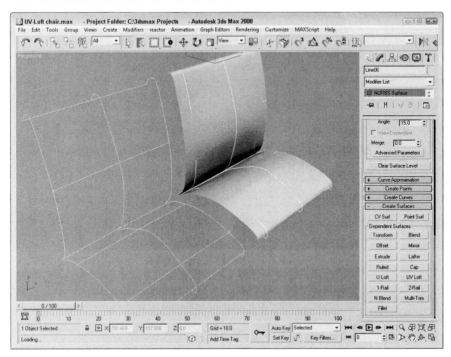

To create a Lathed NURBS surface, follow these steps:

1. Open the Lathed NURBS vase.max file from the Chap 27 directory on the DVD.

   This file includes two CV curves that you can lathe to create a vase.

2. Select one of the CV curves, open the Modify panel, and click the Lathe button in the Create Surfaces rollout (or click the Create Lathe Surface button in the NURBS Creation Toolbox). In the Lathe Surface rollout that appears at the bottom of the Modify panel, enter a value of **360** in the Degrees field and click the Y-axis button. Then click on both CV curves to complete the lathe. Click the Lathe button again to exit Lathe mode.

Figure 27.25 shows the completed vase produced using the Lathe tool.

Creating a 1-rail and 2-rail sweep surface

The 1-rail sweep surface tool lets you create a NURBS surface by using one NURBS curve to act as a side rail and one or more profile shape curves to sweep along the rail to generate the surface. A 2-rail sweep surface is similar, except that it uses two NURBS curves as side rails.

FIGURE 27.25

The lathed CV surface vase

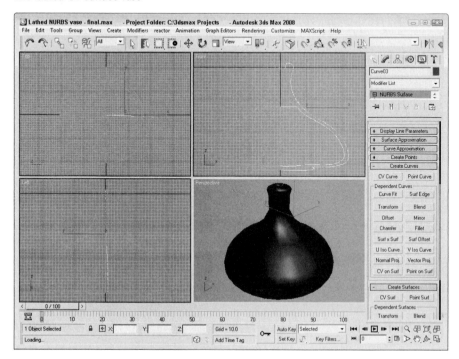

Tutorial: Creating a flower stem

Now that we have carefully constructed a flower vase, we need to create some flowers to place in the vase. We start with the flower stem.

To create a NURBS point surface using a 1-rail sweep, follow these steps:

1. Open the Flower stem.max file from the Chap 27 directory on the DVD.

   This file includes three cross sections and a curve correctly positioned that you can sweep to form a flower stem.

2. Select the long stem curve. Open the Modify panel, click the Attach button, and click the three cross-section shapes. Then click the Attach button again to exit attach mode.

3. Open the Create Surfaces rollout, and click the 1-Rail (Sweep) button (or click the Create 1-Rail Sweep button in the NURBS Creation Toolbox). Click the long stem curve, and then click the cross-section shapes in order from the bottom to the top. Right-click to end the creation of the 1-rail sweep.

The NURBS skin is generated on the stem, as shown in Figure 27.26.

FIGURE 27.26

A stem created with a 1-rail sweep

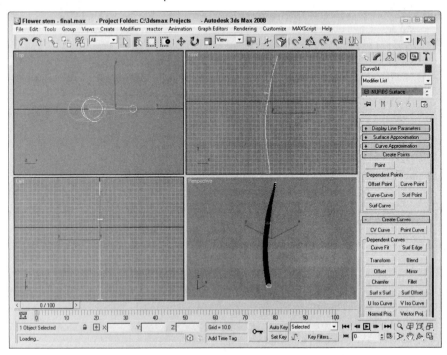

Sculpting a rectangular NURBS surface

NURBS patches are a quick way to create a surface that can be sculpted using the subobject elements, such as a control lattice. For each subobject type, you can use many different tools to form the patch.

Tutorial: Creating a NURBS leaf

In this tutorial, we create a NURBS CV surface plane sculpted into a leaf for the NURBS flower. To do this, we work in the Surface CV subobject level and use the Select and Move transform tool to move CVs and sculpt the NURBS rectangle into a leaf shape.

To create a rectangular NURBS CV surface, follow these steps:

1. Select Create ➪ NURBS ➪ CV Surface, and in the Create Parameters rollout, increase the Length CVs to **6** and Width CVs to **6**. Click the Generate Mapping Coords check box.

2. In the Top viewport, click and drag to create the NURBS surface. In the Create Parameters rollout, set both the Length and Width to **180**. While still in the Top viewport, rotate the NURBS surface 45 degrees along the Z-axis using the Select and Rotate tool so that it looks like a diamond shape.

3. With the NURBS surface selected, open the Modify panel and click the plus sign to the left of the NURBS Surface object to gain access to the subobjects. Select the Surface CV subobject.

   The CV lattice is displayed in the Top viewport.

4. Select the Non-Uniform Scale tool (R), constrain it to the X-axis (F5), and then drag-select the middle horizontal row of CVs. Scale them down (narrower) to 85 percent.

5. Select the middle three horizontal rows of CVs (including the one just scaled), and scale them down to 90 percent. Then select the middle five horizontal rows, and scale them down to 90 percent.

   This step gently rounds the outside contours of the NURBS surface.

6. In the Front viewport, you should see the edge of the NURBS surface. Maximize the viewport, and then select the Rotate tool, constrain it to the Z-axis, and select the right half of the CVs, but do not select the CVs at the very center. Rotate the CVs upward –60 degrees.

7. Repeat the select-and-rotate process with the CV on the left half of the center, but do not alter the CVs at the very center.

   The leaf should now be U-shaped.

8. Click the Move tool (W), constrain it to the Y-axis (F6), and then select the center row of CVs and move them downward –40 units to make a deep V shape.

Figure 27.27 shows the NURBS leaf with the control lattice visible.

FIGURE 27.27

Translating CVs to sculpt a NURBS leaf

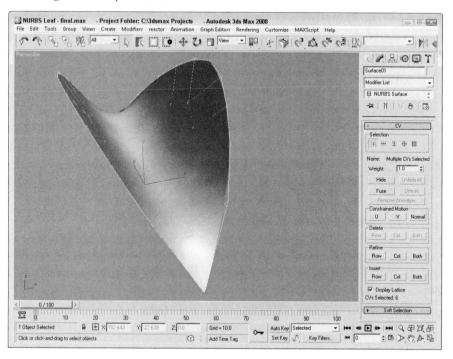

Tutorial: Sculpting a flower petal

Continuing to build our flower, we now sculpt a second rectangular NURBS surface into the shape of a flower petal. In this case, the center CVs of the surface are raised to create a soft, rounded shape. We sculpt one end of the NURBS rectangle into a blossom petal shape, and then scale and clone it to create three more petals.

To sculpt the flower petal shape, follow these steps:

1. Select Create ⇨ NURBS ⇨ CV Surface, and in the Keyboard Entry rollout, create a NURBS rectangular surface 80 units long and 80 units wide, with 6 Length CVs and 6 Width CVs.

2. Select the Rotate tool (or press the E key), and in the Top view, rotate the surface 45 degrees. Open the Modify panel, click the plus sign to the left of the NURBS Surface object, and select the Surface CV subobject.

3. Select the Non-Uniform Scale tool (R), constrain it to the X-axis (F5), and then select the center horizontal row of CVs and scale it down (narrower) to 86 percent.

   This step rounds the outside corners of the petal.

4. Drag-select the six CVs that make up the upper tip of the petal. Non-uniform-scale the triangle of CVs in the Y-axis down to 35 percent to blunt the point at the top of the petal.

5. Click and drag a selection box around all the CVs in the center of the petal (don't select any CVs on the edges). You can use the Ctrl key to add CVs to the selection and the Alt key to remove CVs from the selection. In the Front viewport, select the Move tool and move the CVs upward 6 units in the Y-axis to round the top of the petal.

6. In the Top viewport, select the lower half of the center vertical column of CVs, click the Lock Selection icon (or press the spacebar), and then in the Front viewport use the Move tool to move the CVs 7 units downward in the Y-axis. When a groove appears halfway down the center of the petal, unlock the selection set.

7. To clone the petal, turn off subobject mode and activate the Top viewport. Select World from the Reference Coordinate System drop-down list. Click the Mirror icon to open the Mirror: Screen Coordinates dialog box, and then clone the petal by selecting the Y-axis and Copy options. Move the new petal downward in the Y-axis so that the points of the petals touch.

8. Now clone the petals again, but make them smaller. Select the Uniform Scale button (or press the R key), select both petals in the Top viewport, and then press the Shift key and scale the petals down to 40 percent to create smaller cloned versions of the petals. Lock the selection set (press the spacebar), click Rotate (E), and then rotate the small petals 90 degrees to finish the blossom.

Figure 27.28 shows the completed flower.

To finish the flower and vase model, you need to merge all the parts of the flower vase project into one scene. Clone and position the leaves next to the stem. Position the stem in the throat of the vase at a slight angle. Position the leaves midway up the stem, and then place the flower at the top of the stem, at right angles to the leaves. Finally, apply texture maps to all objects, using a glass material for the vase, dark green for the leaves and stem, and a yellow radial gradient for each petal of the blossom. The finished flower is shown in Figure 27.29.

NURBS modifiers

The Modifiers ⇨ NURBS Editing menu includes a set of modifiers unique to NURBS objects. This set includes the following modifiers: NURBS Surface Select, Surf Deform, and Disp Approx. There is also a World-Space modifier called Displace NURBS.

FIGURE 27.28

Flower petals that were sculpted using NURBS

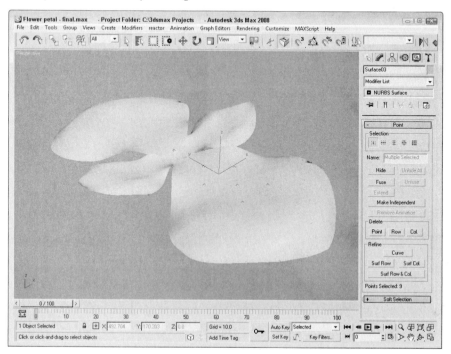

The NURBS Surface Select modifier (known in the Modifier List as NSurfSel) lets you make a subobject selection for the selected NURBS object. This selection is then passed up the Modifier Stack to the next modifier. The two subobjects for this modifier are Surface CV and Surface.

The Surf Deform modifier works on NURBS surfaces just like the PatchDeform and PathDeform modifiers. After applying this modifier, you can select another NURBS object with the Pick Object button to deform the selected NURBS object. This modifier also has a World-Space version.

The Displacement Approximation (or Disp Approx) modifier makes displacement mapping (which is applied using materials) available in the Modifier Stack. This modifier alters the surface of an object based on displacement mapping. This modifier can work with any object that can be converted to an Editable Mesh, including primitives, NURBS, and Patches. Parameters for this modifier include Subdivision Preset settings of Low, Medium, and High.

The Displace NURBS World-Space modifier is similar to the Disp Approx modifier. It can convert a NURBS object into a mesh object and includes the effect of a displacement map. In the Displace NURBS rollout, you can select the Tessellation method to be Regular, Parametric, Curvature, Spatial, or both Spatial and Curvature.

NOTE   Because U and V curves implicitly define a NURBS object's surface, they don't require mapping modifiers.

FIGURE 27.29

A vase and flower built completely from NURBS

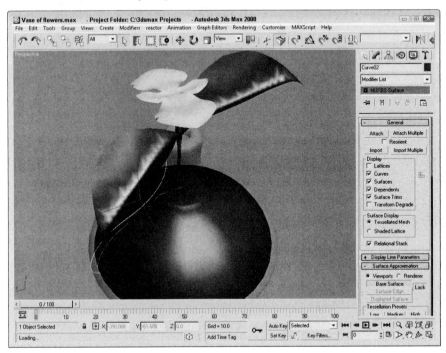

Summary

Patches don't have the overhead of NURBS objects and are better optimized than mesh objects. Editable Patch objects include a huge list of tools that you can use to edit and modify them. In addition to Patches, NURBS are an ideal method for modeling if you require free-flowing models. This chapter covered the following topics:

- Creating Quad and Tri Patch grids
- Discovering the features of an Editable Patch object
- Working with the Editable Patch subobjects
- Working with patch-specific modifiers such as the surface tools
- Creating CV and point curves
- Discovering how to convert primitives to NURBS objects
- Creating NURBS surfaces from curves
- Learning to edit NURBS curves and surfaces
- Using NURBS subobject tools
- Lofting surfaces from point and CV curves
- Creating NURBS surfaces by lathing and sweeping

The next chapter is really hairy. In fact, it is all about adding hair, fur, and cloth to your models.

Chapter 28

Adding and Styling Hair, Fur, and Cloth

I want to start this chapter with a bold statement, "Bald Is Beautiful." I make this statement because I have a brother who, upon discovering his hair had started thinning, decided that bald was the way to go. But, after seeing far too many 3D models that were bald because of the unavailability of a decent hair plug-in in Max, I can also declare that "Bald Is Boring."

Now that Max has hair and fur, I expect to see the level of realism for a number of Max artists, including myself, take a quantum leap forward.

Creating cloth isn't that difficult. In fact, with a plane primitive, you can easily create a perfectly straight blanket, towel, or flag. However, animating cloth that drapes realistically over a character is very difficult and best left to dynamic engines like reactor.

Although you can still animate cloth collections using reactor, Max also has a separate stand-alone cloth simulation system aptly named Cloth that you can use to create deformable cloth and to animate it as well.

CROSS-REF The hair and cloth systems in Max are dynamic, meaning that they are affected by forces in the scene such as wind and gravity. The dynamic nature of hair and cloth is covered in Chapter 39, "Animating Hair and Cloth."

Understanding Hair

Although a section titled "Understanding Hair" sounds like it would be taken from a beauty salon guide, the way Max deals with hair is unique and needs some explanation. Hair, like particle systems, deals with thousands of small items that can bring even the most powerful computer screeching to a halt if not managed.

In Max, hair doesn't exist as geometry, but is applied to scene objects as a separate modifier. This level of separation keeps the hair solution independent of the geometry and makes removing or turning off the hair solution as needed easy.

It also keeps the viewport display from bogging down. The Hair and Fur modifier is a World-Space Modifier (WSM), meaning that it is applied using the World Space coordinates instead of local ones.

The other half of the Hair and Fur solution is a render effect that allows the hair to be rendered. This render effect is applied and configured automatically when the Hair and Fur modifier is applied to an object. This causes the scene with hair to be rendered in two passes. The geometry is rendered first, followed by the hair.

NOTE   Hair can be rendered only when a Perspective or Camera view is selected. Hair cannot be rendered in any of the orthogonal views.

Another similarity to particle systems is that the hair follicles can be replaced by instanced geometry, so you can create a matchstick head character by replacing hairs with an instance of a matchstick.

TIP   Using instanced geometry with a fur system is a great way to create and position plants and ground cover.

The materials that are used on hair are defined in the Material Parameters rollout in the Modify panel instead of in the Material Editor. Many of the hair parameters have a square button to their right that lets you apply a map to the parameter.

When the Hair and Fur modifier is added to an object in the scene, a Hair and Fur render element becomes available that you can use to render out just the hair for compositing.

Working with Hair

Applying hair to an object is as easy as selecting an object and choosing the Hair and Fur WSM modifier, which is found in the Modifiers ➪ Hair and Fur ➪ Hair and Fur WSM. After hair is applied to an object, you can use the parameters in the Modify panel to change the hair's properties.

Growing hair

Hair can be grown on any geometry surface, including splines, by simply applying the Hair and Fur WSM to the selected object. When the Hair and Fur modifier is first applied to an object, it is applied to the entire surface of the selected object and when it is applied to set of splines, the hair appears between the first and last spline.

If you want to localize the hair growth to a specific area of the object, you can make a subobject selection using the controls in the Selection rollout. The available subobjects include Face, Polygon, Element, and Guides. After making a subobject selection, click the Update Selection to display the guide hairs only in the selected area in the viewports. Figure 28.1 shows hair grown on a man's face to create a beard.

TIP   After taking the time to make a subobject selection, create a selection set for the hair area for quick recall.

Applying hair to a single spline doesn't create any hair, but if multiple splines are included as part of the same Editable Spline object, then the hair is interpolated between the various splines in the order they are attached following the spline's curvature. This provides a great way to add special features like a ringlet to an existing set of hair.

FIGURE 28.1

By making a subobject selection, you can control precisely where hair is grown.

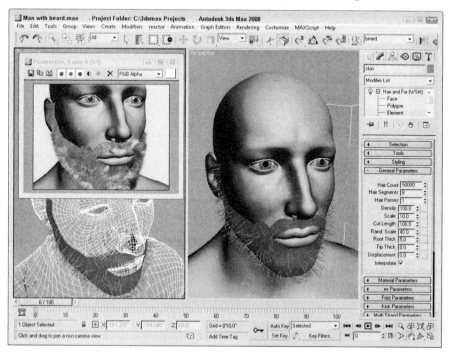

Setting hair properties

Several rollouts of properties can be used to change the look of the hair. The General Parameters rollout, shown in Figure 28.2, includes settings for the overall Hair Count, the number of Hair Segments between adjacent splines, the number of Hair Passes, Density, Scale, Cut Length, Random Scale, Root and Tip Thickness, and Displacement. The Hair Count value sets the total number of hairs for the given geometry. Higher values take longer to render but produce more realistic hair. The Hair Passes sets the number of render passes to use for determining hair transparency. The higher the Hair Passes value, the more wispy the hair looks. The Rand Scale value provides a random amount of scaling for a percentage of hairs to look more natural. The Displacement value sets how far from the source object the hairs grow and can be a negative value.

CAUTION Although the Hair Count value can accept huge numbers, adding a large number of hairs takes a long time to render and can really slow your system.

The buttons to the right of most of the parameters in the General Parameters rollout lets you add a map to control the property with a grayscale bitmap. Figure 28.3 shows a simple plane object mapped with a bitmap used to control the hair density. The black areas of the bitmap have no hair growth, but the white areas have maximum growth. This provides a way to create patchy hair on a character or creature.

FIGURE 28.2

Hair properties can be altered using the General and Material Parameters rollouts.

Map button

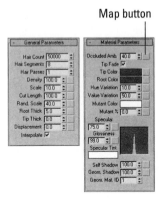

FIGURE 28.3

Many of the hair properties can be defined using maps.

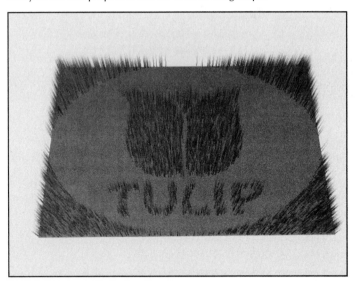

The Material Parameters rollout, also shown in Figure 28.2, includes settings for the Occluded Ambient value, controlling the tip and root colors, Hue and Value Variations, the addition of mutant hairs, percentage to include, and specular and glossiness settings. The Occluded Ambient value sets the contrast for the hair lighting. Smaller values have a stronger contrast, and higher values appear more washed out. The Hue and Value Variation values define a percentage that the hair color can deviate from the specified color to give the hair a more natural coloring. The Mutant percentage defines the percentage and color of hairs that are discolored, such as white hairs.

 The Occluded Ambient property is applied as an effect, so it is actually a fake global illumination pass.

The Tip Fade option causes the hair to be more transparent toward the tip. The Specular Tint color changes the color of specular highlights. The Tip Fade and Specular Tint options apply only to hairs rendered with mental ray. The Self Shadow value sets how much the individual hairs cast shadows on other hairs, and the Geometry Shadow settings determines how much shadow is contributed by other geometry objects. The Geometry Material ID is used to assign a material to geometry-rendered hair.

Many of the properties in the Material Parameters rollout also can be controlled using map buttons located to the right.

 Map colors are multiplied with the base color value, so set the base color to white before using a map.

In addition to the general and material parameters, rollouts also are available for controlling the amount of Frizz and Kink, and for the Multi-Strand nature of hair. Frizz causes the hair to curl at its tip or root. Kink parameters cause the hair to be zigzagged in shape; the Multi-Strand parameters cause hair to separate into groups like grass does. Figure 28.4 shows four areas with different hair properties applied, including normal straight hair with no frizz or kink, a section with Frizz, one with Kink, and Multi-Strand.

FIGURE 28.4

Changing hair properties can drastically alter the hair's look from normal to frizz, kink, and multi-strand.

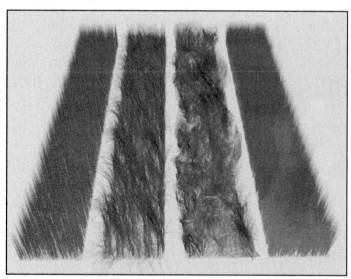

Tutorial: Adding a spline fringe to a quilt

Quilts are designed to make you feel all warm and fuzzy, and what could be fuzzier than some soft fringe surrounding a quilt. Fringe makes grabbing the quilt easy.

To add hairy fringe to a quilt using splines, follow these steps:

1. Open the Patch quilt.max file from the Chap 28 directory on the DVD.

2. Select the Create ➪ Shapes ➪ Line menu command, and draw a couple of simple spline that extends at right angles from every corner of the quilt in the Top view. These splines will be used to designate the start and end splines for the quilt fringe. Hair strands will be placed between these two simple splines. Start at one corner, and proceed in turn clockwise around each of the corners. Add a second line on top of the first line to complete the set of splines.

3. Select the first spline, and convert it to an Editable Spline object using the right-click quadmenu. Then click the Attach button, and select the splines in the order they were created.

4. With all the splines selected, choose the Modifiers ➪ Hair and Fur ➪ Hair and Fur WSM menu command to apply the Hair and Fur modifier to the splines.

5. Open the Modify panel, and in the General Parameters rollout, set the Random Scale value to 10, and the Tip and Root Thickness to 5.0. Then open the Material Parameters rollout, and change the Tip and Root colors to white.

Figure 28.5 shows the resulting quilt with its fringe, all warm and fuzzy.

FIGURE 28.5

Hair can be added to only a subobject selection or to the entire object.

Styling Hair

The Display rollout (located way at the bottom of the rollouts) includes settings for controlling how many hairs are displayed in the viewports. To see all the hairs, you need to render the scene. You can select to display Guide Hairs and actual hairs and set a color for each. The Override option causes the color specified in the color swatch to be used instead of the render color. You also can select a Percentage value of the total hairs to display in the viewport up to the number in the Max Hairs value. Enabling the As Geometry option causes the hairs to appear as geometry objects instead of lines.

Guide hairs control the position of all adjacent hairs. Guides hairs extend from each vertex in the attached object. Guide hairs are yellow by default, and viewport hairs are red, but you can change the color for each in the Display rollout.

Guide hairs provide a simple way to style, comb, and brush hair. By positioning the guide hairs, you can control what the rest of the hair looks like.

> **NOTE** No guide hairs are available when the Hair and Fur modifier is applied to a selection of splines because the splines act as guides.

Using the Style interface

In addition to the hair properties, you can change the look of hair by using the various hair styling features. These features are found in the Styling rollout. The Style Hair button activates an interactive styling mode in the viewport where you can brush, comb, and manipulate the individual hairs. The Style Hair button is activated automatically when the Guides subobject mode is selected.

Within the Styling rollouts are several icon buttons. These buttons are described in Table 28.1. The brush size can be interactively set by holding down the Ctrl and Shift keys while dragging the mouse when in Brush mode, or you can change the brush size using the slider located under the Ignore Back Hairs option. The Distance Fade option causes the brushing effect to fade as it gets closer to the edge, resulting in a softer effect at the hair tips.

TABLE 28.1

Light Navigation Control Buttons

Toolbar Button	Name	Description
	Select by Hair Ends (Ctrl+1)	Selects the end vertex when you drag over hairs.
	Select the Whole Guide (Ctrl+2)	Selects all vertices in the whole strand when you drag over hairs.
	Select Guide Vertices (Ctrl+3)	Selects specific vertices when you drag over hairs.
	Select Guide by Root (Ctrl+4)	Selects the entire hair by selecting only the root vertex when you drag over hairs.
	Marker Style drop-down list	Choose the style to mark the selected vertices. Options include Box, Plus, X, and Dot.

continued

TABLE 19.1 *(continued)*

Toolbar Button	Name	Description
	Invert Selection (Shift+Ctrl+N)	Deselects the current selection, and selects all hairs not currently selected.
	Rotate Selection (Shift+Ctrl+R)	Rotates the current selection.
	Expand Selection (Shift+Ctrl+E)	Adds to the current selection set by increasing the selection area.
	Hide Selected (Shift+Ctrl+H)	Hides the selected vertices.
	Show Hidden (Shift+Ctrl+W)	Unhides all hidden vertices.
	Hair Brush (Ctrl+B)	Moves all selected vertices in the direction of the brush. Press Escape to exit this mode.
	Hair Cut (Ctrl+C)	Cuts the hair in length.
	Select (Ctrl+S)	Enters selection mode where you can select hairs by dragging over them.
☑ Distance Fade	Distance Fade (Shift+Ctrl+F)	Causes the brush effect to fade with distance. Available only in Hair Brush mode.
☑ Ignore Back Hairs	Ignore Back Hairs (Shift+Ctrl+B)	Causes only hairs facing the camera to be affected.
	Brush Size slider (Ctrl+Shift+mouse drag)	Changes the size of the brush.
	Translate (Shift+Ctrl+1, Ctrl+T)	Moves the selected guides in the direction of the brush when you drag.
	Stand (Shift+Ctrl+2, Ctrl+N)	Stands the selected guides up straight.
	Puff Roots (Shift+Ctrl+3, Ctrl+P)	Causes small deviations to appear at the root of each selected guide.
	Clump (Shift+Ctrl+4, Ctrl+M)	Pulls the selected guides together to the center of the brush.
	Rotate (Shift+Ctrl+5, Ctrl+R)	Rotates and spins the selected guides about the center of the brush.
	Scale (Shift+Ctrl+6, Ctrl+E)	Scales the selected guides when you drag with the brush.
	Attenuate (Shift+Ctrl+A)	Scales the hairs based on the size of the polygon.
	Pop Selected (Shift+Ctrl+P)	Lengthens the selected hairs along the surface normal.
	Pop Zero Sized (Shift+Ctrl+Z)	Lengthens any zero length hairs along the surface normal.

Toolbar Button	Name	Description
	Recomb (Shift+Ctrl+M)	Combs the hair from the top downward.
	Reset Rest (Shift+Ctrl+T)	Relaxes the hair by averaging the position of hairs.
	Toggle Collisions (Shift+Ctrl+C)	Turns collisions of hairs on and off.
	Toggle Hair (Shift+Ctrl+I)	Toggles the display of hairs on and off.
	Lock (Shift+Ctrl+L)	Locks the selected vertices so they cannot be moved by other tools.
	Unlock (Shift+Ctrl+U)	Unlocks any locked vertices.
	Undo (Ctrl+Z)	Undoes the last command.
	Split Selected Hair Groups (Shift+Ctrl+-)	Separates the selected hairs into separate groups.
	Merge Selected Hair Groups (Shift+Ctrl+=)	Combines the selected hairs into groups.

When you're finished styling, click the Finish Styling button in the Styling rollout to exit styling mode.

Tutorial: Creating a set of fuzzy dice

Fuzzy dice. What could be cooler?

To style the fur applied to a set of fuzzy dice, follow these steps:

1. Open the Fuzzy dice.max file from the Chap 28 directory on the DVD.

2. Select one of the dice, and choose the Modifiers ➪ Hair and Fur ➪ Hair and Fur (WSM) menu command to apply hair to the selected dice.

3. Open the General Parameters rollout, and set the Hair Count to 20000 and the Scale value to 50. Then open the Material Parameters rollout, and change the Tip Color to white and the Root Color to Red. Then open the Frizz Parameters rollout, and set the Frizz Root and Frizz Tip values to 0. This makes the hair strands straight and red.

4. Open the Styling rollout, and click the Style Hair button. In the Utilities section, click the Pop Selected button to make all the hair stand out. Then select the Hair Brush icon, and drag downward in the viewport near the guides at each of the top corners.

5. Drag the Hair and Fur (WSM) modifier from the Modifier Stack, and drop it on the unselected die.

Figure 28.6 shows the resulting pair of dice.

FIGURE 28.6

Hair can be styled by changing the position and orientation of the guide hairs.

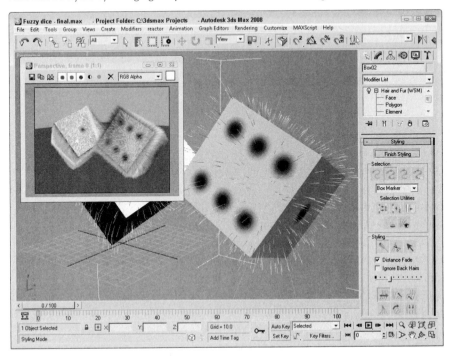

Using hair presets

If you have a specific set of parameters that create a unique hair look that you're happy with, you can save it using the Save Presets button in the Tools rollout. Hair preset files are rendered on the spot and added to the Hair and Fur Presets dialog box, shown in Figure 28.7. To add a preset configuration to the current object, simply double-click it.

In addition to presets, hairdos—created by styling the hair—also can be copied and pasted onto other hair selections.

 If you ever get into trouble styling hair, you can click on the Regrow Hair button in the Tools rollout to reset all the styling to its original state.

Using hair instances

Although the default hair looks great, if you ever wanted to replace the hair splines with an instanced geometry, you can do so by using the Pick Instance Node in the Tools rollout. The X button to the right of the Instance Node Pick button is used to remove the instance. Figure 28.8 shows a funny head created using a matchstick for a hair instance.

 Be sure to adjust the Hair Count value before selecting an instanced object. Complex instanced objects should be used only with manageable numbers.

FIGURE 28.7

The Hair and Fur Presets dialog box shows rendered thumbnails of the available presets.

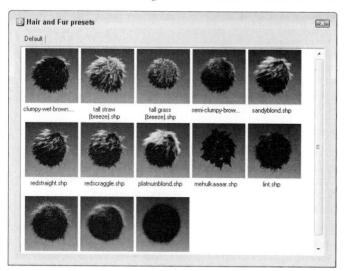

FIGURE 28.8

Mr. Matchstick head has all his hair replaced with matchsticks, an instance.

Rendering Hair

You can change the hair render settings by opening the Effects panel using the Rendering ⇨ Effects menu. The Render Settings button in the Tools rollout provides quick access to the Effects panel. The Hair and Fur rollout includes settings for the Hairs and Lighting rendering methods.

Hairs can be rendered using three options. The Buffer method renders each hair individually and combines the effect. It uses minimal memory requirements. When the buffer method is selected, you can choose the Raytrace Reflections/Refractions option for better quality. The Geometry method converts each hair into a geometry object that is rendered. The mr Prim method renders hair using the mental ray renderer. For this option, you can set the Voxel Resolution used to render hairs.

CROSS-REF   More on mental ray is covered in Chapter 46, "Raytracing and mental ray."

Motion Blur can be enabled to make hairs that are moving fast appeared blurred. The Oversampling setting adds an anti-aliasing pass to the rendering. The options include Draft, Low, Medium, High, and Maximum. The Composite Method option depends on the rendering method that is selected. A list of occlusion objects and a setting for Shadow Density also are available.

By default, all lights (except for direct lights and daylight systems) are used to light hair, but if a spotlight is added to the scene, you can select the spotlight and click the Add Hair Properties button at the bottom of the Hair and Fur rollout. This adds a Hair Light Attributes rollout to the Modify panel for the selected spotlight where you can set the Resolution and Fuzz of the shadow map for the hair object cast by the light.

Understanding Cloth

If you drop a shirt over a chair, how does it land? It folds and bunches as it drapes over the solid object. Also notice how different types of cloth drape differently. Compare how silk reacts verses a terry-cloth towel. Being able to accurately simulate how cloth reacts to scene objects and forces is yet another critical element that can really make a difference in your final scenes.

Cloth in Max is created using a modifier. This modifier can be applied to any object to make it a cloth object, or you can specifically create a set of clothes using the Garment Maker modifier. During the process of making an object into a cloth object, the object is divided into multiple faces using one of several subdivision methods. This provides the mesh with enough resolution to be deformed accurately.

Cloth objects are endowed with characteristics that let them respond to external forces within the scene including gravity, wind, and collisions with other scene objects. After all the scene objects, forces, and cloth objects are added to the scene, you can start a simulation that defines how the cloth moves within the scene under the effect of the other scene objects and forces.

CROSS-REF   This chapter focuses on creating and defining cloth objects. The dynamic nature of cloth is covered in Chapter 39, "Animating Hair and Cloth."

Creating Cloth

When you start to model a cloth object, keep in mind that the model must have enough resolution so that it can accurately fold over itself several times. If the resolution isn't defined enough, then the bending of the cloth is not believable.

> **NOTE** Although dynamic cloth can be deformed under the effect of forces applied to it, cloth cannot apply a force back against the deforming object. This is a scenario that reactor can handle because it deals with all objects in the scene. A trampoline, for example, is a good example of deformable cloth surface that can apply a force back on the deforming object using reactor.

You can increase the resolution of a model in several ways. The Garment Maker modifier includes parameters that can increase the resolution of a mesh, or you can use the HSDS modifier to increase an object's resolution.

> **TIP** When making cloth objects, use a single-sided Plane object instead of a Box object. Using a Box object needlessly doubles the number of polygons to be included in the simulation.

Using Garment Maker to define cloth

Clothes can be added to models using a method that is similar to the way real clothes are made. Each section of cloth, called a panel, is outlined using lines and splines in the Top viewport. Clothes patterns also can be imported and used. Include a break at each corner of the panel or the modifier will round the corner. After you have all the various panels created, convert one of the panels to an Editable Spline object and attach all the panels into a single object. You can apply the Modifiers ➪ Cloth ➪ Garment Maker to the set of panels.

> **TIP** The easiest way to create cloth panels is to draw the entire cloth panel and then use the Break Vertex command in Vertex subobject mode to break each corner.

When the Garment Maker modifier is first applied, the panel outlines are made into mesh objects and subdivided using the Delaunay algorithm, as shown in Figure 28.9. This algorithm uses random triangulation and divides the triangles into roughly equal shapes. This helps keep the cloth from folding along common lines caused by regular patterns. You can alter the number of polygons in the subdivided mesh using the Density value. If the Auto Mesh option is disabled, then you can update the density change using the Mesh It button. The Preserve option maintains the 3D shape of the object. If Preserve is disabled, then the panel is made flat.

The next step is to position the panels so they surround the model that they will be draped over. The subject that is to receive the clothes can be selected by clicking the Figure button in the Main Parameters rollout. After an object is selected, clicking the Mark Points on Figure button makes a small figure outline appear in the upper-left corner of the viewport, as shown in Figure 28.10. This figure outline has markers corresponding to the chest, neck, pelvis, shoulder, and wrists. Dragging over the body of the character lets you mark corresponding locations on the character.

After body parts are marked, you can select a cloth panel and use the Panel Position buttons in the Panel rollout to position the various cloth panels around the body. The Panel Position buttons include Front Center, Front Right, Back Center, Right Arm, etc. You also can position the panels manually.

FIGURE 28.9

FIGURE 28.9

The Garment Maker modifier uses the Delaunay algorithm for subdividing cloth meshes.

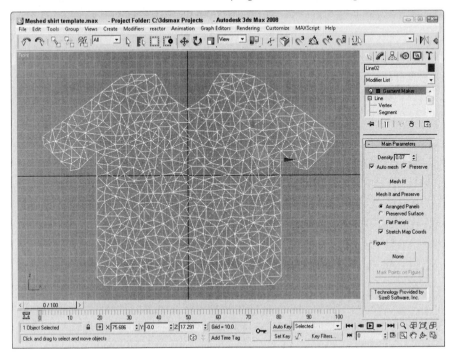

The Garment Maker modifier has three subobjects: Curves, Panels, and Seams. With the panels in place, you can stitch seams between the panels using the Curves subobject mode for flat drawn panels or with the Seams subobject mode for panels that are positioned about a model. Each seam edge should be relatively the same length. The Seam Tolerance value sets how far apart the two edges can deviate. For each seam, you can set a Crease Angle and Strength. The Sewing Stiffness value determines the strength that the seams are pulled together.

After the seams are defined, you can apply the Modifiers ➪ Cloth ➪ Cloth modifier to pull the panels together and simulate the cloth's motion.

Creating cloth from geometry objects

Any geometry object can be made into a cloth object using the Cloth modifier available by selecting the Modifiers ➪ Cloth ➪ Cloth menu command. Although the modifier is added to the object, it is set to Inactive by default. To activate the cloth, you need to open the Object Properties dialog box, shown in Figure 28.11.

FIGURE 28.10

The figure outline lets you identify corresponding body markers on the character model for positioning cloth panels.

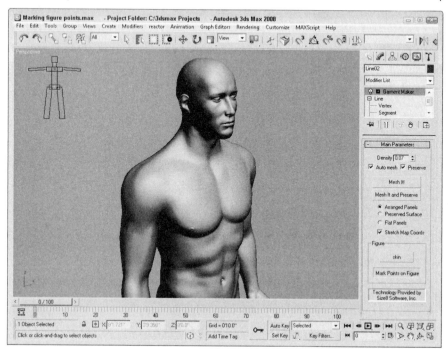

The list at the left holds all the objects that are involved in the cloth simulation. New objects can be added to the list using the Add Objects button. Each object can be set to Inactive, Cloth, or Collision Object, and properties can be set for each type. For cloth, the properties include Bend, Stretch, Shear, Density, Thickness, Friction, and Scale values. Defined cloth settings can be saved and recalled. Cloth property files are saved using the .STI file extension. Max also includes a sizable list of presets in a drop-down list, including Burlap, Cashmere, Cotton, Flannel, Rubber, Satin, Silk, Terrycloth, and Wool, among others.

NEW FEATURE The U Compress and V Compress properties are new to 3ds Max 2008.

In addition to objects added to the scene, a cloth simulation also can include forces. The Cloth Forces button opens a dialog box where you can select which forces in the scene can be added to the cloth simulation. Gravity is added by default automatically to the simulation. You can set the Gravity value in the Simulation Parameters rollout along with several other parameters, including the Start and End Frames.

With all the objects and forces added, click the Simulate Local button to set the initial state of the cloth simulation. This drapes the cloth over the scene objects and pulls all defined seams from the Garment Maker modifier together. Sometimes the Simulate Local button moves the cloth panels together too fast, so you can use the Simulate Local (damped) button to add lots of damping to the scene to prevent problems from panels moving too fast.

FIGURE 28.11

The Object Properties dialog box includes all the parameters for the cloth and collision objects.

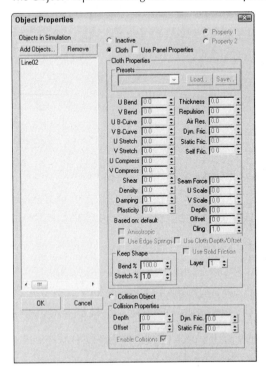

Tutorial: Clothing a 3D model

If you've ever wanted to design and outfit a set of models with a custom-made line of clothing, here's your chance. Using Garment Maker and the Cloth modifiers, we outfit our 3D model with a set of clothes. Watch for this new line next spring at your local retailers. This excellent female character was supplied by Zygote Media.

To create and apply a set of clothes to a 3D character, follow these steps:

1. Open the Zygote woman with clothes.max file from the Chap 28 directory on the DVD.

2. Select the Create ⇨ Shapes ⇨ Line menu command, and draw in the Top viewport the front outline of a simple tank top and a simple skirt. Make sure the panels are closed splines.

3. Select the Tools ⇨ Mirror menu command, and create mirrored copies of the clothes for the back side. Then convert one of the panels to an Editable Spline, and attach all the other panels together into a single object. In Vertex subobject mode, select all the corner vertices in all panels and click the Break button.

4. With the clothes selected, choose the Modifiers ⇨ Cloth ⇨ Garment Maker modifier. This automatically subdivides all the cloth panels into multiple polygons.

5. In the Main Parameters rollout, click the Figure button and select the female character. Then click the Mark Points on Figure button. A small figure appears in the upper-left corner of each viewport with the upper chest area marked in red. Drag the cursor over the character until the matching

upper chest area is located, and click. Repeat for all the marked positions. When all points are marked, click the Mark Points on Figure button again to exit marking mode.

6. In the Modify panel, select the Panels subobject mode and choose the tank top's front panel. Select the Top at Neck level, and click the Front Center button. This places the tank top's front in front of the character. Repeat the placement for the other panels. If the placement isn't correct, manually move the panels until they are in front of and behind the character, as shown in Figure 28.12.

FIGURE 28.12

Using figure markers, you can approximate where the clothes are positioned on a character.

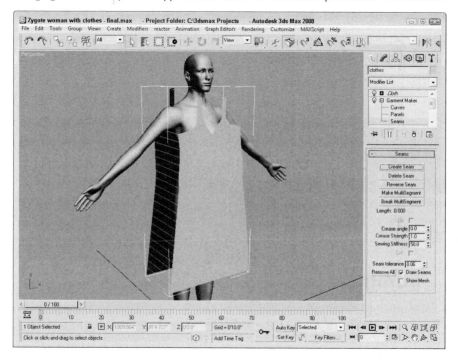

7. In the Modify panel, select the Seams subobject mode. In the Front viewport, select two edges that should be connected and click the Create Seam button. Repeat this for all seams including the sides of the skirt and shirt and the top of the shirt. Connecting lines are drawn between both sides of the seam. If the seam boundaries are crossed, then click the Reverse Seam button.

8. With the seams defined, select Modifiers ⇨ Cloth ⇨ Cloth to apply the Cloth modifier. In the Object rollout, click the Object Properties button. In the Object Properties dialog box, select the clothes object and enable the Cloth option. Then click the Add Objects button, select the character mesh, and mark it as a Collision Object. Set the Offset value for the clothes to 0.3, and close the Object Properties dialog box.

9. Click the Simulate Local button. The cloth seams are pulled together, and the clothes are draped over the character.

Figure 28.13 shows the female character in a simple gown.

FIGURE 28.13

The Simulate Local button causes the clothes to be draped over the body.

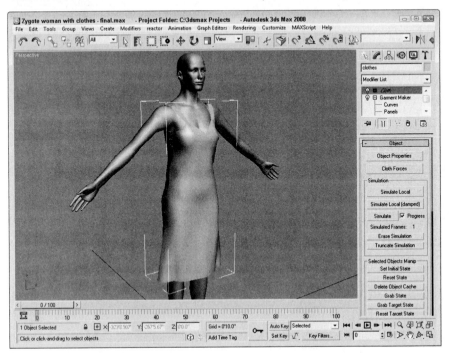

Summary

The Hair and Fur modifier allows you to add hair to scene objects. Using the parameters found in the various rollouts, you can define the type of hair that is created. The Cloth modifier enables a cloth dynamic system that can simulate the complex motion of cloth as it interacts with objects and forces in the scene.

Specifically, this chapter covered the following topics:

- Growing hair and setting hair parameters
- Styling hair and using the hair presets
- Understanding how cloth systems work
- Using the Garment Maker modifier
- Creating cloth objects from geometry objects using the Cloth modifier

Part VII, "Advanced Materials," is next. The first chapter in this part covers the tricky topic of unwrapping UV coordinates.

Part VII

Advanced Materials

Chapter 29

Using Specialized Material Types

You probably noticed back in the chapter on compound materials that a number of intriguing material types listed in the Materia/Map Browser were not discussed. These material types are important, but they can't be classified as compound materials.

These specialized materials are sort of like your waffle iron. They're meant to be pulled out of your arsenal when you have a specific need. You wouldn't cook eggs on a waffle iron, would you?

The specialized materials include the Matte/Shadow material, the Ink 'n' Paint material, the Architectural materials, and the DirectX Shader material. These materials let you hide things in the scene, render the scene as a cartoon, use building materials, and view objects as they'll be seen in a game.

Even more special material types are listed after you enable the mental ray renderer. These materials are so specialized that they require a change in the rendering engine. These mental ray materials include an updated set of architectural materials, a Car Paint material, and several subsurface scattering materials.

With these specialized materials, you can create some really advanced, realistic results. Unfortunately they don't make waffles.

IN THIS CHAPTER

Using matte/shadow materials

Using Ink 'n' Paint materials

Using the architectural materials

Using the DirectX Shader material

Using the Matte/Shadow Material

You can apply matte/shadow materials to objects to make portions of the model invisible. This lets any objects behind the object or in the background show through. This material is also helpful for compositing 3D objects into a photographic background. Objects with matte/shadow materials applied can also cast and receive shadows. The effect of these materials is visible only when the object is rendered.

Matte/Shadow Basic Parameters rollout

You can apply a matte/shadow material by clicking the Type button and selecting Matte/Shadow from the Material/Map Browser. Matte/shadow materials include only a single rollout: the Matte/Shadow Basic Parameters.

The Opaque Alpha option causes the matte material to appear in an alpha channel. This essentially is a switch for turning Matte objects on and off.

You can apply atmospheric effects such as fog and volume light to Matte materials. The At Background Depth option applies the fog to the background image. The At Object Depth option applies the fog as if the object were rendered.

CROSS-REF Find out about Atmospheric effects in Chapter 45, "Using Atmospheric and Render Effects."

The Receive Shadows section enables shadows to be cast on a Matte object. You can also specify the Shadow Brightness and color. Increasing Shadow Brightness values makes the shadow more transparent. The Affect Alpha option makes the shadows part of the alpha channel.

Matte objects can also have reflections. The Amount spinner controls how much reflection is used, and the Map button opens the Material/Map Browser.

Tutorial: Adding 3D objects to a scene

A common use of the Matte/Shadow map is to add 3D objects to a background image. For example, if you add a Plane object that is aligned with the ground plane in the background image that has a Matte/Shadow material applied to it, then the Plane object can capture the shadows of the 3D objects, but the Matte/Shadow material allows the background to be seen through the Plane object. The result is that the 3D object appears added to the background image scene.

To use a matte/shadow material to add an object to a background image, follow these steps:

1. Open the Xylophone on shadow matte.max file from the Chap 29 directory on the DVD.

    This file contains a background image of a cow statue taken in front of the Boston Convention Center. The scene also includes a xylophone positioned on the Plane object. The Plane object has a Scale multiplier of 4 to make a complete ground plane when the scene is rendered.

2. Open the Material Editor by pressing the M keyboard shortcut. Click on the Standard material button and select the Matte/Shadow option from the Material/Map Browser. Name the material **Shadow plane** and drag it onto the Plane object in the Perspective viewport.

3. Select the Create ⇨ Lights ⇨ Standard Lights ⇨ Omni menu and click in the Top viewport to create a light. In the General Parameters rollout, enable the Shadows option. Then in the Shadow Parameters rollout, click on the Color swatch. In the Color Selector that opens, select the Sample Screen Color eyedropper tool and click on the cow's shadow color to select it.

4. With the Omni light selected, right click on the Perspective viewport and select the Viewport Lighting and Shadows ⇨ Viewport Shading ⇨ Best option from the quadmenu. Then select the Viewport Lighting and Shadows ⇨ Enable Viewport Shadows Selected option.

    This makes the shadows appear in the viewport on the Plane object.

5. Move the Omni light in the Left and Top views until the shadows are projected along the same path as the cow's shadows.

 **TIP** One way to help align the shadows is to make the shadows of parallel geometry objects, like the xylophone's vertical leg and the cow's leg, parallel.

6. To see the final result, you need to render the image. To do this, select Rendering ⇨ Render (or press F10) to open the Render Scene dialog box. Click the Render button at the bottom of the dialog box, and the image is rendered in the Rendered Frame Window.

Figure 29.1 shows the resulting rendered image.

FIGURE 29.1

A rendered xylophone fits into the scene because its shadows are cast on an object with a matte/shadow material applied.

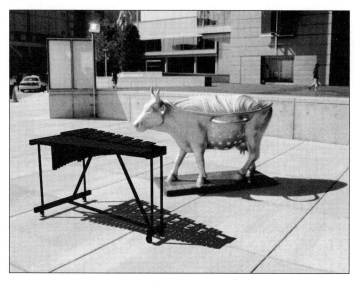

Using the Ink 'n' Paint Material

Although it may seem silly, many different production houses use Max to create 2D line-drawn cartoons. This is accomplished using the Ink 'n' Paint material. Traditionally, cartoons have been drawn by hand using a paper and pen. Then animation houses found that, using computers, you can fill in a cartoon feature easily, but using a 3D program like Max with its ability to animate using keyframes simplifies the animation task even further. The difference is in how the objects are rendered; the Ink 'n' Paint material controls this.

With the Ink 'n' Paint material selected, several rollouts appear, including the Basic Material Extensions. This rollout includes options for making the material 2-Sided, enabling a Face Map, and making the material Faceted. Other options cause the background to be foggy when not painting and make the alpha channel opaque. Maps are available for Bump and Displacement.

Controlling paint and ink

The Paint Controls rollout includes settings for how the paint (or colors inside the ink outline) is applied. You can specify colors for the Lighted, Shaded, and Highlight colors. The Lighted color is used for sections of the material that face the scene lights, the Shaded color is used for sections that are in the shadows, and the Highlight color is for the specular highlights. For each color, you also can select a map with an amount value. The Paint Levels value sets the number of colors that are used to color the material. The Glossiness value determines the size of the highlight. Figure 29.2 shows materials with Paint Level values of 2-6.

FIGURE 29.2

Use the Paint Level value to set the number of colors used in the material.

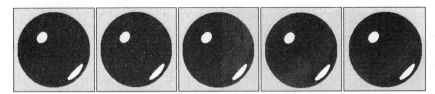

The Ink Controls rollout includes an Ink option that you can use to turn off the outlining ink completely. You also can set the Ink Quality to values between 1 and 3. The higher quality values trace the edges better, but require more time to complete. The width of the ink strokes can be set to Variable Width or a Clamped width. For each option, you can select a Minimum ink width and if Variable Width is enabled, you can choose a Maximum ink width. For the Variable Width option, the stroke changes so that the minimum setting is used in lighted areas and the maximum width is used in shaded areas. This helps to accentuate the lighting. You can also apply the ink width as a map. Figure 29.3 shows the Ink 'n' Paint material applied to a cube. The first image shows a standard material; the second image has the Ink option disabled. The last three images have Width values of 1, 10, and 30.

 **Placing a noise map on the Ink Width property is a great way to give the ink outline a hand-drawn look.**

FIGURE 29.3

The Paint Level value sets the number of colors used in the material.

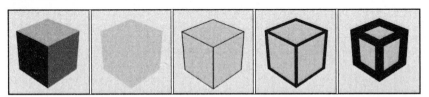

The rest of the options in the Ink Controls rollout are enabled to control where the ink is applied to the object. Options include Outline, Overlap, Underlap, Smoothing Group, and Material ID. For each of these options (except for Smoothing Group), you can alter a Bias value that can adjust intersecting edges. Each of these options can be applied as a map.

Tutorial: Cartooning a turtle

As an example of the Ink 'n' Paint material, we'll render a cartoonish turtle model created by Zygote Media as a cartoon that is fit for the Sunday papers.

To apply the Ink 'n' Paint material to a turtle model, follow these steps:

1. Open the Cartoon turtle.max file from the Chap 29 directory on the DVD.

   This file includes a simple turtle model.

2. With the turtle model selected, open the Material Editor by choosing the Rendering ⇨ Material Editor menu command (or by pressing the M key).

   The turtle's current materials are displayed.

3. In the Utility panel, select the Color Clipboard button, and in the Color Clipboard rollout, click the New Floater button. A palette of colors opens. Drag the Diffuse colors from each current material to the Color Clipboard for each of the five materials.

4. Select the first sample slot, and click on the Material Type button to open the Material/Map Browser. Double-click the Ink 'n' Paint material type from the list. Then drag the corresponding color from the Color Clipboard, and copy it in the Lighted color swatch of the Paint Controls rollout. Repeat this for each of the five materials.

5. Open and render the Perspective viewport using the Render Scene dialog box.

Figure 29.4 shows the resulting cartoon.

FIGURE 29.4

Cartooning made easy with the Ink 'n' Paint material

Using Architectural Materials

If you look in the Material/Map Browser, you'll notice an Architectural material. This material is specifically designed for creating realistic materials that can be applied to buildings and interiors. The Architectural material uses predefined templates to create almost any type of material that you'd find in a building, including ceramic, fabric, metal, glass, stone, wood, and water. The real benefit of using the Architectural materials is how they interact with real-world lights. Using Photometric lights and Radiosity produces realistic results.

CROSS-REF If you've selected the mental ray renderer, then the Arch & Design material becomes available. The Arch & Design material is a more powerful and extensive set of architectural materials. You can learn more about this and other mental ray materials later in this chapter.

Figure 29.5 shows a house that uses several of these architectural materials. Notice how the shingles on the roof are consistent.

FIGURE 29.5

Architectural materials make adding textures to a building easy.

Using the DirectX Shader Material

The Material Editor includes support for DirectX 9 and 10 shaders using the DirectX Shader material. These shaders are saved as .fx files and are available only if the Direct3D display driver is enabled. FX files are text files created using the Higher-Level Shader Language (HLSL).

NOTE The DirectX Shader material is available only if you are using the DirectX display driver.

In the 3dsmax9/maps/fx directory where Max is installed are several example DirectX shaders. You can load these example shaders using the button in the DirectX Shader rollout. The available parameters are different for each shader. Figure 29.6 shows several rifles with various FX shaders applied.

FIGURE 29.6

The Direct X Shader material lets you view game assets in the viewport.

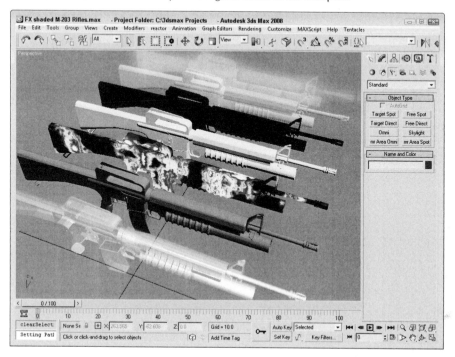

FX shaders are commonly used in games and applying an FX shader to an object displays the shader in the viewport. This display looks the same as if the object were rendered in the game engine. However, if you render an object with an FX shader applied, it will appear as default gray unless you specify a material to appear using the Software Render Style rollout.

Using mental ray Materials and Shaders

If the mental ray renderer is enabled, you can open the Material/Map Browser in the Material Editor and be greeted with about twice as many available material types. Mental ray includes a good number of its own custom shaders and materials that can be accessed and used only when the mental ray renderer is enabled. All of the mental ray materials and maps are identified by a yellow sphere or shape next to their names.

 **NOTE**   If you enable the Incompatible option in the Material/Map Browser, then you can view the list of mental ray materials even if the mental ray renderer isn't enabled.

CROSS-REF   You can learn more about enabling the mental ray renderer in Chapter 46, "Raytracing and mental ray."

Understanding shaders

A shader is an algorithm that defines the surface color for all pixels in the scene. Surface Shaders come to this conclusion by factoring in such details as texture files, reflection, refraction, and atmospheric effects.

Atmospheric Shaders change the light properties as they move through a volume. Shaders can be programmed and applied to objects and scenes, and renderers like mental ray render the scene based on these shaders.

Accessing mental ray materials and shaders

With the mental ray renderer selected, all materials include an additional rollout labeled mental ray Connection. This rollout, shown in Figure 29.7, is available only if the mental ray extensions are enabled in the mental ray panel of the Preference Settings dialog box. They let you override the existing shaders used by the Scanline renderer and enable additional shaders that the mental ray renderer will use.

FIGURE 29.7

The mental ray Connection rollout in the Material Editor lets you override the default shaders.

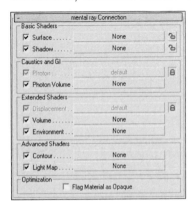

The lock icons to the right of the shader buttons are the default shaders used by the Scanline renderer. To select a new shader, simply unlock these shaders by clicking the lock button. If a material is opaque, you can speed up the rendering process by flagging the material as Opaque using the option at the bottom of the rollout.

If you want to get direct access to the shaders used by mental ray, use the mental ray material type, which presents all the shaders listed in the mental ray Connection rollout.

In addition to modifying the default materials to take advantage of mental ray, a number of mental ray materials and maps (shaders) are available from the Material/Map Browser, shown in Figure 29.8. These materials and maps show up only if the mental ray renderer is the assigned renderer and are marked in the Material/Map Browser with a yellow icon. All the mental ray materials and maps are split into different libraries, which are displayed in parentheses beside their name.

NOTE Several materials and maps in the Material/Map Browser do not work with mental ray. These items are marked with a gray icon. You can hide all these items by disabling the Incompatible option in the Show section of the Material/Map Browser.

A complete list of the mental ray materials and maps appears in Table 29.1.

NEW FEATURE The Glare shader is new to 3ds Max 2008.

FIGURE 29.8

The Material/Map Browser includes many additional mental ray materials and maps.

TABLE 29.1

mental ray Materials and Maps

Type	List
mental ray materials	Arch & Design, Car Paint Material, DGS Material, Glass, mental ray, SSS Fast Material, SSS Fast Skin Material, SSS Fast Skin Material+Displace, SSS Physical Material
mental ray maps	3D Displacement, Ambient/Reflective Occlusion, Beam, Bump, Car Paint Shader, Combi, Contour Composite, Contour Contrast Function Levels, Contour Only, Contour PS, Contour Store Function, Curvature, Depth Fade, DGS Material, Dielectric, Dielectric Material, Distortion, Edge, Edge Shadow, Environment, Façade, Factor Color, Glare, Glass, Glow, Height Map Displacement, Landscape, Layer Thinner, Light Infinite, Light Point, Light Spot, Material to Shader, Metal, Mist, mr Physical Sky, Night, Ocean, Opacity, Parti Volume, Parti Volume Photon, Photon Basic, Reflect, Refract, Shader List, Shadow Transparency, shaveMRGeom and Hair, Simple, SSS Physical Shader, Stain, Submerge, Texture Remap, Texture Rotate, Texture Wave, Translucency, Transmat, Transmat Photon, Transparency, Two-Sided, UV Coordinate, UV Generator, Water Surface, Water Surface Shadow, Wet-Dry Mixer, Width from Color, Width From Light, Width form Light Direction, Wrap Around, XYZ Coordinate, XYZ Generator

Using the Arch & Design materials

The Arch & Design materials are a set of advanced mental ray materials designed for architects to add to buildings and surfaces found in architecture renderings. All of these materials are based on physical properties that are typically found in environments lighted with global illumination. For example, the Satin Varnished Wood template includes slightly blurred reflections and a high glossiness to give it a realistic look.

Many of the Arch & Design materials are already defined and available in the Templates rollout. The available presets include Pearl Finish, Satin Varnished Wood, Glazed Ceramic, Glossy Plastic, Masonry, Leather, Frosted Glass, Translucent Plastic Film, Brushed Metal, and Patterned Copper.

 Arch & Design materials can be viewed in the viewport if you enable the Show Hardware Map in Viewport option in the Material Editor. This button is a flyout underneath the Show Standard Map in Viewport button.

NEW FEATURE The ability to view Architectural & Design materials interactively in the viewport is new to 3ds Max 2008.

For each template, several rollouts of parameters are available for defining the Diffuse, Reflection, Refraction, Translucency, Anisotropy, Fresnel Reflections, Bumps, and Self-Illumination properties along with a full selection of maps. Figure 29.9 shows a sampling of the available materials.

FIGURE 29.9

The materials in the mental ray Arch & Design collection include a broad set of physical properties.

Within the Special Effects rollout are two specialized options that add to the render realism. Ambient Occlusion lights the scene based on how accessible ambient light is to scene objects. It is a material shader solution and is not based on lights. Areas that face a wall or that are blocked by other objects are recessed in shadow. Areas facing the lights are highlighted more. Using the Samples and Max Distance, you can control the contrast of the resulting image. By default, ambient occlusion uses black and gray tones to show occluded areas, but if you enable the Use Color From Other Materials (Exact AO), then the object's diffuse color is reflected into the occluded areas. Figure 29.10 shows an example of Ambient Occlusion.

NEW FEATURE The ability to reflect material color into the occluded areas is new to 3ds Max 2008.

FIGURE 29.10

Ambient Occlusion lets you light the scene by controlling the ambient light that get bounced around the scene.

The other useful special effect option is Round Corners. When you apply this option to a mechanical object, the object's edge is rounded so the light source highlights the edge, but no change is made to the object's geometry. This creates a realistic soft edge without the time or extra polygons to create it using geometry.

Using the Self Illumination (Glow) rollout, you can make a material act as a light source to the scene. This rollout includes presets for photometric properties based on real-world values such as degrees Kelvin.

NEW FEATURE The Self Illumination attribute is new to 3ds Max 2008.

Using the Car Paint material

When cars are painted in the factory, the paint is composed of two layers that give the car its unique look. The undercoat is called the flake layer and it shines through the top layer. The mental ray Car Paint material includes settings for defining both of these layers. Figure 29.11 shows a car painted with this material.

Using the Subsurface Scattering materials

The four mental ray materials that begin with "SSS" are Subsurface Scattering materials used to shade human skin. Skin has an interesting property that allows it to become slightly translucent when it is placed in front of a strong light source. The ears in particular are a good example of this because they allow light to penetrate and highlight their features. Most organic objects including leaves, rubber, milk and skin can benefit from these materials.

FIGURE 29.11

Cars rendered with the mental ray Car Paint shader use multiple layers just like real cars.

Summary

This chapter covered an assortment of specialized materials that enable specific types of effects. These specialized materials include matte/shadow, Ink 'n' Paint, DirectX Shader, and the various mental ray materials including the Arch & Design, Car Paint, and SubSurface Scattering materials.

In this chapter, you've learned about the following:

- Using the Matte/shadow material to hide objects
- Creating a cartoon rendering with the Ink 'n' Paint materials
- Viewing game assets with the DirectX Shader
- Using the Arch & Design materials
- Applying a multi-layer car paint material
- Using the Subsurface Scattering materials

In the next chapter you learn how the Unwrap UVW modifier can be used to customize the mapping coordinates for an object. We also explore one specific type of mapping a little closer. The Pelt mapping method lets you split and unwrap complicated models by using seams.

Chapter 30

Unwrapping UVs and Using Pelt Mapping

Throughout the modeling chapter, as you created objects, the Generate Mapping Coordinates option appeared for almost all objects. Now you find out what mapping coordinates are and how to use them.

Mapping coordinates define how a texture map is aligned to an object. These coordinates are expressed using U, V, and W dimensions. U is a horizontal direction, V is a vertical direction, and W is depth.

When you enable the Generate Mapping Coordinates option for new objects, Max takes its best guess at where these coordinates should be located. For example, a Box primitive applies a texture map to each face. This works well in some cases, but you won't have to wait long until you'll want to change the coordinates.

Control over the mapping coordinates is accomplished using many different modifiers, including the granddaddy of them all — UVW Unwrap.

Pelts remind me of early turn-of-the-century explorers and trappers who captured and skinned critters such as foxes and wolves and preserved their fur pelts on a circular rack. These furs were valuable commodities that could be traded for whatever the trapper needed. The market for such furs has diminished significantly, but the concept works well for the virtual world as a mapping method for applying textures to 3D objects.

Pelt mapping is simply another mapping method available within the Unwrap UVW modifier. You can access it from the Map Parameters rollout when the Face subobject mode is selected.

Mapping Modifiers

Among the many modifiers found in the Modifiers menu are several that are specific to material maps. These modifiers are mainly found in the UV Coordinates submenu and are used to define the coordinates for positioning material maps.

These modifiers include the UVW Map, UVW Mapping Add, UVW Mapping Clear, UVW XForm, MapScaler (WSM), Projection, Unwrap UVW, Camera Map (WSM), and Camera Map.

CROSS-REF The Projection modifier is used to create normal maps and is covered in Chapter 31, "Creating Baked Textures and Normal Maps."

UVW Map modifier

The UVW Map modifier lets you specify the mapping coordinates for an object. Primitives, Loft Objects, and NURBS can generate their own mapping coordinates, but you need to use this modifier to apply mapping coordinates to mesh objects and patches.

NOTE Objects that create their own mapping coordinates apply them to Map Channel 1. If you apply the UVW Map modifier to Map Channel 1 of an object that already has mapping coordinates, then the applied coordinates overwrite the existing ones.

You can apply the UVW Map modifier to different map channels. Applying this modifier places a map gizmo on the object. You can move, scale, or rotate this gizmo. To transform a UVW Map gizmo, you must select it from the subobject list. Gizmos that are scaled smaller than the object can be tiled.

Many different types of mappings exist, and the parameter rollout for this modifier lets you select which one to use. The Length, Width, and Height values are the dimensions for the UVW Map gizmo. You can also set tiling values in all directions.

NOTE It is better to adjust the tiling within the UVW Map modifier than in the Material Editor because changes in the Material Editor affect all objects that have that material applied, but changes to a modifier affect only the object.

The Alignment section offers eight buttons for controlling the alignment of the gizmo. The Fit button fits the gizmo to the edges of the object. The Center button aligns the gizmo center with the object's center. The Bitmap Fit button opens a File dialog box where you can align the gizmo to the resolution of the selected bitmaps. The Normal Align button lets you drag on the surface of the object, and when you release the mouse button, the gizmo origin is aligned with the normal. The View Align button aligns the gizmo to match the current viewport. The Region Fit button lets you drag a region in the viewport and match the gizmo to this region. The Reset button moves the gizmo to its original location. The Acquire button aligns the gizmo with the same coordinates as another object.

Figure 30.1 displays a brick map applied to an umbrella using spherical mapping.

Tutorial: Using the UVW Map modifier to apply decals

After mapping coordinates have been applied either automatically or with the UVW Map modifier, you can use the UVW XForm modifier to move, rotate, and scale the mapping coordinates.

Most objects can automatically generate mapping coordinates — with the exception of meshes. For meshes, you need to use the UVW Map modifier. The UVW Map modifier includes seven different mapping options. Each mapping option wraps the map in a different way. The options include Planar, Cylindrical, Spherical, Shrink Wrap, Box, Face, and XYZ to UVW.

In this tutorial, we use the UVW Map modifier to apply a decal to a rocket model. Zygote Media created the rocket model.

FIGURE 30.1

The UVW Map modifier lets you specify various mapping coordinates for material maps.

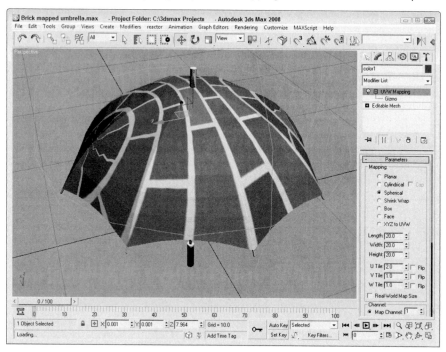

To use the UVW Map modifier, follow these steps:

1. Open the Nasa decal on rocket.max file from the Chap 30 directory on the DVD.

   This file includes a model of a rocket with the appropriate materials applied. The Chap 30 directory on the DVD also includes a 300 × 600 image of the word NASA in black capital letters on a white background. The background color of this image was set to be transparent, and the image was saved as a .GIF.

NOTE   The GIF format, typically used for Web pages, can easily make areas of the image transparent. These transparent areas become the alpha channel when loaded into Max.

2. Open the Material Editor (or press the M key), and select the first sample slot. Name the material **NASA Logo**. Click the Diffuse color swatch, and select a white color. Then click the map button to the right of the Diffuse color swatch, and from the Material/Map Browser, double-click the Bitmap map. Locate the NASA image from the Chap 30 directory on the DVD, and click Open. The bitmap image loads, and the Bitmap parameters display in the rollouts. In the Coordinates rollout, enter a value of **–90** in the W Angle field. The letters rotate vertically. Then, in the Bitmap Parameters rollout, select the Image Alpha option.

3. Select the lower white section of the rocket in the viewport, and open the Modify panel. At the top of the Modify panel, click the Modifier List and select the UVW Map modifier. Select the Cylindrical Mapping option, but don't select the Cap option in the Parameters rollout.

4. With the cylinder section selected, open the Material Editor again, select the first sample slot, and click the Assign Material to Selection button.

TIP When a bitmap is applied to an object using the UVW Map modifier, you can change the length, width, and tiling of the bitmap using the UVW Map manipulator. If you enable the Select and Manipulate button on the main toolbar the manipulator appears as green lines. When you move the mouse over the top of these green lines, they turn red, and you can drag them to alter the map dimensions. Use the small green circles at the edges of the map to change the tiling values. As you use the manipulator, the map is updated in real time within the viewports if you have enabled the Show Map in Viewport option in the Material Editor.

Figure 30.2 shows the resulting rendered image.

FIGURE 30.2

You can use the UVW Map modifier to apply decals to objects.

UVW Mapping Add and Clear modifiers

The UVW Mapping Add and the UVW Mapping Clear modifiers are added to the Modifier Stack when you add or clear a channel using the Channel Info utility. More on this utility is covered in Chapter 31, "Creating Baked Textures and Normal Maps."

UVW XForm modifier

The UVW XForm modifier enables you to adjust mapping coordinates. It can be applied to mapping coordinates that are automatically created or to mapping coordinates created with the UVW Map modifier. The parameter rollout includes values for the UVW Tile and UVW Offsets. You can also select the Map Channel to use.

Map Scaler modifier

The Map Scaler modifier is available as both an Object-Space modifier and a World-Space modifier. The World-Space version of this modifier maintains the size of all maps applied to an object if the object itself is resized. The Object-Space version ties the map to the object, so the map scales along with the object. The Wrap Texture option wraps the texture around the object by placing it end-to-end until the whole object is covered.

Camera Map modifier

The Camera Map modifier creates planar mapping coordinates based on the camera's position. It comes in two flavors — one applied using Object-Space and another applied using World-Space.

The single parameter for this modifier is Pick Camera. To use this modifier, click the Pick Camera button and select a camera. The mapping coordinates are applied to the selected object.

Using the Unwrap UVW Modifier

The Unwrap UVW modifier lets you control how a map is applied to a subobject selection. It also can be used to unwrap the existing mapping coordinates of an object. You then can edit these coordinates as needed. You also can use the Unwrap UVW modifier to apply multiple planar maps to an object. You accomplish this task by creating planar maps for various sides of an object and then editing the mapping coordinates in the Edit UVWs interface.

The Unwrap UVW modifier lets you control precisely how a map is applied to an object. The Unwrap UVW modifier has Vertex, Edge, and Face subobject modes. In subobject mode, you can select a subobject, and the same selection is displayed in the Edit UVWs interface and vice versa. This synchronization between the Edit UVW window and the viewports helps to ensure that you're working on the same subobjects all the time. When Edge subobjects are selected, the Ring and Loop buttons become active.

In the Modify panel you find two rollouts: Selection Parameters and Parameters. The Selection Parameters rollout includes a button with a plus sign and one with a minus sign. These buttons grow or shrink the current selected subobject selection. You can also select to Ignore Backfacing, Select by Element (instead of faces), set the Planar Angle, or select by Material ID or Smoothing Group.

The Edit UVWs interface

The Parameters rollout includes a button named Edit. This button opens the Edit UVWs interface, shown in Figure 30.3 for a simple cube. You also can load and save the edited mapping coordinates using the Save and Load buttons in the Parameters rollout, and the Reset UVWs button resets all the mapped coordinates. Saved mapping coordinate files have the .UVW extension. The Display section of the Parameters rollout lets you set how the edges of the planar maps are displayed. The options include Show No Seam, Thin Seam Display, and Thick Seam Display. By making the seams visible, you can easily tell where the textures don't match the object's creases.

FIGURE 30.3

The Edit UVWs interface lets you control how different planar maps line up with the model.

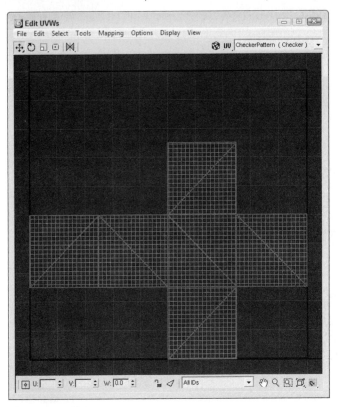

Table 30.1 shows and describes the buttons in the Edit UVWs dialog box.

TABLE 30.1

Edit UVW Interface Buttons

Buttons	Name	Description
	Move,	Moves the selected vertices when dragged.
	Move Horizontal,	
	Move Vertical	
	Rotate	Rotates the selected vertices when dragged.

Buttons	Name	Description
	Scale,	Scales the selected vertices when dragged.
	Scale Horizontal,	
	Scale Vertical	
	Freeform Mode	Displays a gizmo that you can use to transform the subobject selection.
	Mirror Horizontal,	Mirrors or flips the selected vertices about the center of the selection.
	Mirror Vertical,	
	Flip Horizontal,	
	Flip Vertical	
	Show Map	Toggles the display of the map in the dialog box.
	Coordinates	Displays the vertices for the UV, UW, and WU axes.
MAP # 1 (CELLULAR) ▼	Pick Texture drop-down list	Displays a drop-down list of all the maps applied to this object. You can display new maps by using the Pick Texture option.
	Absolute/Relative Toggle	Lets you enter U, V, and W values as absolute values or relative offsets.
U: 0.0 V: 0.0 W: 0.0	U, V, W values	Displays the coordinates of the selected vertex. You can use these values to move a vertex.
	Lock Selected Vertices	Locks the selected vertices and prevents additional vertices from being selected.
	Filter Selected Faces	Displays vertices for only the selected faces.
All IDs ▼	All IDs drop-down list	Filters selected material IDs.

The buttons in the lower-right corner of the Edit UVWs dialog box work just like the Viewport Navigation buttons described in earlier chapters including buttons to snap to grid and snap to pixel.

Within the Pick Texture drop-down list is a Checker Pattern option. This option applies a checker map to the mesh without having to assign a material. The checker pattern makes easy work of looking for stretching on the model.

Using the Options panel

Many of the commands found in the menus also can be found in the Options panel at the bottom of the interface. You can expand these controls by clicking the Options button, as shown in Figure 30.4. Using these controls, you can enable Soft Selection with a specified Falloff value. The UV and XY options let you switch between texture coordinates and object coordinates for the falloff. The Edge Distance lets you specify the Soft Selection falloff in terms of the number of edges from the selection instead of a falloff value. You also can choose the falloff profile as Smooth, Linear, Slow Out, or Fast Out.

FIGURE 30.4

The Options pop-up interface includes many of the same features as the menus.

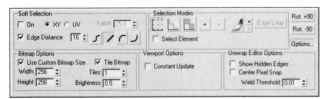

To the right of the Soft Selection controls are the Selection Modes with buttons for selecting Vertex, Edge, and Face subobjects. Selected subobjects in the Edit UVW interface are highlighted red. Using the + and – buttons, you can expand or contract the current selection. The paintbrush icon button is used to Paint Select subobjects, and the small + and – buttons to its immediate right allow you to increase and decrease the brush size. The Edge Loop button automatically selects all edges that form a loop with the current selected edges. The Select Element option selects all subobjects in the given cluster. This happens only when the Select Face subobject mode is enabled in the Modifier Stack. The Rotate +90 and Rotate –90 buttons rotate the selected subobjects 90 degrees in the Edit UVW interface.

The Bitmap Options section lets you specify the exact size of the loaded bitmap. This only affects how the bitmap is displayed in the interface and doesn't change the actual bitmap file dimensions. The Tile Bitmap option places the bitmap end-to-end for the specified number of tiles. The Constant Update option causes the viewport to update along with the texture map. The Show Hidden Edges option lets you make the hidden edges visible or invisible. The Center Pixel Snap causes the Pixel Snap button at the bottom right of the interface to snap to the center of the background pixels instead of to its edges.

Using the Edit UVW interface's menu commands

The File menu can also be used to load (Alt+Shift+Ctrl+L), save, and reset UV coordinates. The Edit menu lets you specify the mode to use to transform subobject selections. These modes include Move (W), Rotate (E), Scale (R), and Freeform, which lets you use the gizmo to transform subobjects. Corresponding buttons are available on the toolbar. The Edit menu also includes Copy and Paste and a Paste Weld command. The Copy and Paste commands let you copy a mapping and paste it to another set of faces. The Paste Weld command welds vertices as it pastes the mapping.

The gizmo is simply a rectangle gizmo that surrounds the current selection. Move the selection by clicking in the gizmo and dragging; Shift+dragging constrains the selection to move horizontally or vertically. The plus sign in the center marks the rotation and scale center point. Scale the selection by dragging on one of its handles. Ctrl+dragging on a handle maintains the aspect ratio of the selection. Click and drag the middle handles to rotate the selection. Ctrl+dragging snaps to 5-degree positions, and Alt+dragging snaps to 1-degree positions.

Within the Edit UVWs interface, you can select vertices, edges, or faces. The Select menu commands let you convert selections between vertices, edges, and faces. Additional options let you to select all inverted and overlapped faces, allowing you to find potential problem areas. Subobjects that are selected in one planar map are also highlighted in the other planar maps. This makes it easy to stitch elements together. The Stitch dialog box also includes an option to scale the entire cluster instead of scaling only the selected edges.

The Tools menu includes commands for flipping, mirroring, welding, breaking, and detaching subobjects. The Tools ➪ Stitch Selected menu command lets you stitch mapped segments together into a single cluster, and the Pack UVs menu command lets you combine UVs into a smaller space. Packed UVs are easy to move and work with because they use a smaller resolution bitmap. Within the Pack dialog box, the Spacing value sets the amount of space between each segment, and the Normalize Clusters option fits all clusters into the given space. The Rotate Clusters option allows segments to be rotated to fit better, and the Fill Holes option places smaller segments within open larger segments.

The Tools ➪ Sketch Vertices command lets you select vertices by dragging over them. The vertices can then be aligned to a shape including Line, Circle, Box, or Freeform. You can also set the cursor size used to select vertices. This tool is available only in Vertex selection mode.

The Mapping menu includes three auto-mapping options: Flatten, Normal, and Unfold Mapping. The Flatten Mapping option breaks the mesh into segments based on the angle between adjacent faces. This option is good for objects that have sharp angles like a robot or a machine. Figure 30.5 shows a plastic bottle with Flatten Mapping applied.

FIGURE 30.5

The Flatten Mapping option displays every part of a model as a separate segment.

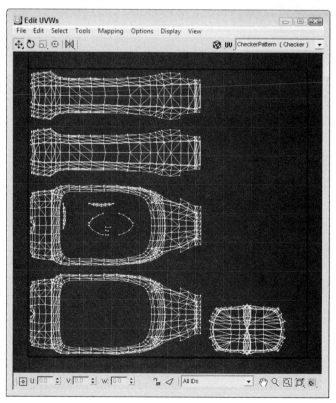

The Normal Mapping option lets you select to map a mesh using only specific views, including Top/Bottom, Front/Back, Left/Right, Box, Box No Top, and Diamond. These views are based on the direction of the normals from the faces of the mesh. It is helpful for thin models like butterfly wings or a coin.

The Unfold Mapping option is unique because it starts at one face and slowly unwraps all the adjacent faces into a single segment if possible. Figure 30.6 shows a simple cylinder that has been unwrapped using this method. The advantage of this mapping is that it results in a map with no distortions. It includes two options: Walk to Closest Face and Walk to Farthest Face. You'll almost always want to use the Walk to Closest Face option.

NOTE   Within a single mesh, multiple different mapping methods can be used. For example, a car's wheel will use cylindrical mapping, but its hood might use planar mapping. Even a subobject selection can use different mapping methods.

FIGURE 30.6

The Unfold Mapping option splits the model and unfolds it by adjacent faces into a single segment.

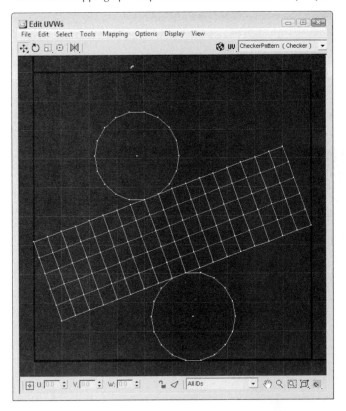

The Options ➪ Preferences (Ctrl+O) menu command opens the Unwrap Options dialog box, shown in Figure 30.7, and lets you set the Line and Selection Colors as well as the preferences for the Edit UVWs dialog box. You can load and tile background images at a specified map resolution or use the Use Custom Bitmap Size option. There is also a setting for the Weld Threshold and options to constantly update, show selected vertices in the viewport, and snap to the center pixel.

In the Unwrap Options dialog box, you can set the preferences for the Edit UVWs dialog box.

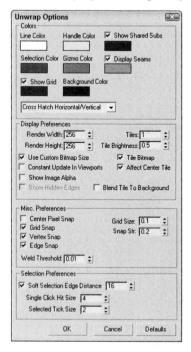

Tutorial: Controlling the mapping of a covered wagon

The covered wagon model created by Viewpoint Datalabs is strong enough to carry the pioneers across the plains, but you can add a motivating slogan to the wagon using the Unwrap UVW modifier. In this tutorial, we add and edit the mapping coordinates for the covered wagon using the Unwrap UVW modifier.

To control how planar maps are applied to the side of a covered wagon, follow these steps:

1. Open the Covered wagon.max file from the Chap 30 directory on the DVD.

   This file includes a covered wagon model. The Chap 30 directory also includes a 256 × 256 image, created in Photoshop, of the paint that we want to apply to its side. The file is saved as Oregon or bust.tif (note that the spelling in the image is rough).

2. With the covered section selected, choose Modifiers ➪ UV Coordinates ➪ Unwrap UVW. In the Parameters rollout, click the Edit button.

   The Edit UVWs interface opens. In the Modifier Stack, select the Polygon subobject mode.

3. In the Edit UVWs interface, choose Mapping ➪ Normal Mapping. In the Normal Mapping dialog box, select the Left/Right Mapping option from the drop-down list and click OK.

   The left and right views of the wagon's top are displayed in the Edit UVWs interface.

4. From the drop-down list at the top of the interface, select the Pick Texture option. The Material/Map Browser opens. Double-click on the Bitmap option, and select the Oregon or bust.tif image from the Chap 30 directory on the DVD.

   The texture appears in the window.

5. Drag the mouse over all the faces for the lower half of the wagon's cover, and select the Tools ⇨ Flip Horizontal menu command to flip the UVs so they match the top unselected UVs. Then drag and place the selected UVs on top of the unselected ones.

   By matching these two UV sections together, you can apply the same texture to both sides of the covering.

6. Then select all the UV faces, and with the Move tool, drag them to the center of the Edit UVWs window. Click and hold over the Scale tool, and select the Vertical Scale tool. Then drag in the window to vertically scale the vertices until they fit over the texture. Then horizontally scale the vertices slightly until the background texture is positioned within the wagon's top.

   Figure 30.8 shows the covered wagon with the mapped bitmap.

FIGURE 30.8

The Edit UVWs interface lets you transform the mapping coordinates by moving vertices.

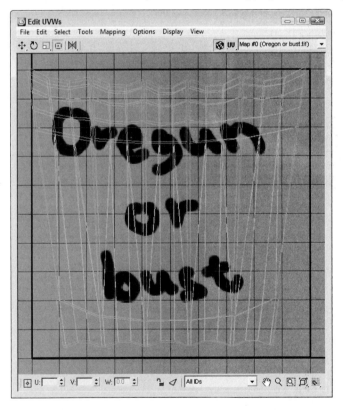

7. Press the M key to open the Material Editor. Click on the mapping button next to the Diffuse color, and double-click on the Bitmap type in the Material/Map Browser. Then select the Oregon or bust.tif file from the Chap 30 directory on the DVD. Apply this material to the covered wagon top. Click the Show Map in Viewport button (the small checkerboard cube icon) to see the map on the covered wagon.

Figure 30.9 shows the results of the new mapping coordinates.

FIGURE 30.9

The position of covered wagon's texture map has been set using the Unwrap UVW modifier.

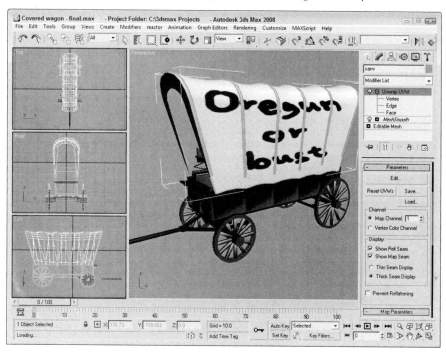

Relaxing vertices

If your mapping coordinates are too tight and you're having a tough time moving them, you can use the Relax Dialog menu command (found in the Tools menu of the Edit UVW interface) to equally space the vertices. This tool works like the Relax modifier, pushing close vertices away and pulling far vertices closer together. Selecting this menu option opens the Relax Tool dialog box, shown in Figure 30.10, which offers three different relax methods: Relax by Face Angles, Relax by Edge Angles, and Relax by Centers. The Iterations value is the number of times to apply the relax algorithm. The Amount value is how aggressive the movements of the vertices are, and the Stretch value controls how much vertices are allowed to move. You also have options to Keep Boundary Points Fixed and Save Outer Corners.

Using the Quick Planar Map

One of the easiest way to isolate mapping surfaces is with the Quick Planar Map button found in the Map Parameters rollout. If you select a set of faces either in the viewports or in the Edit UVW window, you can click on this button and a planar map based on the X, Y, Z or an Averaged Normals is separated and the selected area is marked with a map seam.

FIGURE 30.10

The Relax tool can make working with vertices easier.

Tutorial: Creating a mapping for a swan mesh

An early chapter created a swan based on scanned images of an actual model. This irregular shape can be tricky to separate into maps, but the Quick Planar Map button makes it easy.

To create maps for a swan model, follow these steps:

1. Open the Brass swan.max file from the Chap 30 directory on the DVD.

   This file includes the simple swan modeled in an early chapter. The model has been converted to an Editable Poly object.

2. With the swan mesh selected, choose Modifiers ⇨ UV Coordinates ⇨ Unwrap UVW. In the Parameters rollout, click the Edit button to open the Edit UVW window.

3. Rotate the swan to its side and select the Polygon subobject mode. Then drag over the swan's side in the viewport with the Ignore Backfacing option in the Selection Parameters rollout enabled.

4. Click the Quick Planar Map button with the Averaged Normals option enabled in the Map Parameters rollout. In the Edit UVW window, drag the selected faces away from the rest of the faces to separate it.

5. Back in the viewport, rotate the swan around and select all the faces on its opposite side. Then click the Quick Planar Map button again. Drag these faces away from the others in the Edit UVW window.

6. In the Edit UVW window, enable the Select Element button and drag over all the vertices that haven't been separated. Then click the Quick Planar Map button again.

7. If any stray polygons exist, select them and notice which elements they are next to. Then select the stray polygon and the major element that it should be connected to and press the Quick Planar Map button to combine them.

8. Once all the stray polygons have been attached, you can position each of the elements for the final map.

Figure 30.11 shows the results of the swan mapping.

Mapping multiple objects

If your model is divided into several different pieces, you're in luck because Max allows you to apply the Unwrap UVW modifier to several pieces at once. When loaded into the Edit UVW window, the wireframe for each piece is displayed using its object color, which makes identifying the various separate pieces easy.

FIGURE 30.11

The Quick Planar Map button makes separating the faces into elements easy.

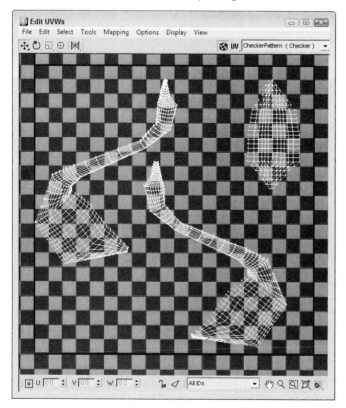

NEW FEATURE The ability to apply a texture map to multiple objects simultaneously is new to 3ds Max 2008.

Tutorial: Creating a mapping for a fighter plane

As a final example of unwrapping, we add a Navy logo to a P-28 Trojan fighter plane. This plane was created by Viewpoint Datalabs. The logo was created and saved as a PNG file, which allowed the background to be saved as transparent. This allows the shiny metallic material to show through the applied logo.

For this tutorial, we add the logo to one of the wings. The tricky part of this tutorial that we didn't have for the rocket tutorial earlier is that the wing's ailerons are separated from the wing. This makes it possible to animate the ailerons.

NOTE I realize that all you military aircraft enthusiasts out there know that the logo actually belongs on the fuselage and not on the wing, but the fuselage isn't divided into separate parts like the wing, so I'm taking creative license for the sake of the tutorial.

To add a texture map to several pieces of an airplane, follow these steps:

1. Open the T-28 Trojan plane.max file from the Chap 30 directory on the DVD.

2. In the Perspective view, select the wing and the aileron and flaps. Don't select the molding between the wing and the ailerons.

3. Select the Modifiers ⇨ UV Coordinates ⇨ Unwrap UVW menu to apply the modifier to all the selected pieces. Then click the Edit button in the Parameters rollout to open the Edit UVWs window.

4. From the drop-down list at the top of the Edit UVWs interface, select the Pick Texture option. The Material/Map Browser opens. Double-click the Bitmap option, and select the T-28 Trojan logo.png image from the Chap 30 directory on the DVD. To focus the bitmap, disable the Tile Bitmap option in the Options panel of the Edit UVWs window.

   The texture appears in the window.

5. Select Face subobject mode in the Modifier Stack and click in the viewport on the center of the right wing. Then click the Expand Selection button (the one with the plus sign) at the bottom of the Edit UVWs window to grow the selection. Keep clicking the Expand Selection button until the entire right half of the wing is selected. Then select the Tools ⇨ Break command. Then zoom out in the Edit UVWs window, and move the separated wing to the top of the window so it doesn't overlap any other sections.

   The selected wing UVs are separated from the rest of the wing object, which includes both wings.

> **TIP** Another way to select the faces is to use the Planar Angle value, which selects all the polygons on one side of the wing.

6. Select the center of one of the right ailerons, and click the Expand Selection button until the entire part is selected. Then click the Planar button in the Map Parameters rollout in the Command Panel to orient the part to match the wing. Then move the aileron up to the top of the Edit UVWs window near the wing UVs. Repeat this step for the other right aileron.

7. Enable the Select Element option at the bottom of the Edit UVWs window so you can select the entire part by clicking it. Then use the Freeform mode button to move and scale the ailerons to fit next to the wing.

> **TIP** If you need to seamlessly fit two separate parts together, you can use the Welding feature in Vertex subobject mode to weld the vertices on each part.

8. Select all the remaining UVs, and move them to the bottom of the window where they don't overlap the logo. Then select the positioned wing and ailerons, and click the Rot -90 button to rotate the wing to align with the logo. Then scale and position the UVs over the logo, as shown in Figure 30.12. Then close the Edit UVWs window.

FIGURE 30.12

The UVs are positioned to match the loaded bitmap.

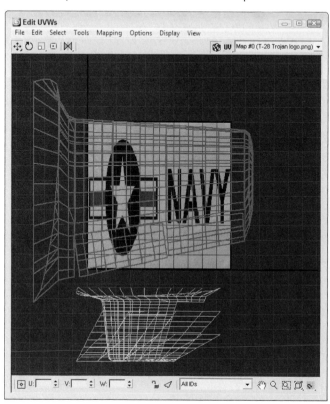

9. Press the M key to open the Material Editor. Click the mapping button next to the Diffuse color, and double-click the Bitmap type in the Material/Map Browser. Then select the T-28 Trojan logo.png file from the Chap 30 directory on the DVD. Apply this material to the selected wing and ailerons. Click the Show Map in Viewport button (the small checkerboard cube icon) to see the map on the plane.

Figure 30.13 shows the results of the plane mapping. After the map is applied to the plane and visible in the viewports, you can open the Edit UVWs window again and tweak the mapping coordinates.

FIGURE 30.13

The logo map is positioned on the wing and spreads over to the ailerons also, even though they are separate parts.

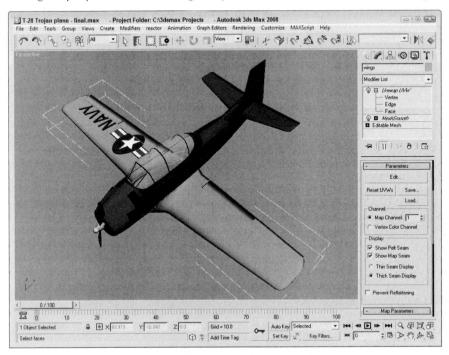

Using Pelt Mapping

Consider mapping a complex mesh like the human head. Using traditional mapping methods, you would divide the head into sections based on planar projections like those in Figure 30.14. The UVs for this head include planar views of the front and back of the head. These provide good UV coordinates for those features that are straight on with the projection, but the ears and the sides of the nose are all wrong using this method. You could divide the mesh into more projections including one for each side of the head and for under the chin, but then you need to deal with matching the seams between the different parts, which is a tough challenge.

Pelt mapping overcomes these difficulties by allowing the user to define the seams for the mesh. These seams can be located along material boundaries or along mesh borders. The vertices along these defined seams are then positioned around the edges of a circle called the Stretcher and pulled until the mesh UVs are pulled flat. This results in clearly displaying and flattening all the UVs for the selected part, allowing you to easily paint and apply a texture map.

Before you can start pulling the pelt tight, you need to define the seams that will be used to cut the model. These seams should be located in areas of the model that won't be clearly visible. For example, if you are unwrapping a head model, the back and top of the head is a good choice since it probably will be covered with hair that will hide the seam. Locating a seam on the midline up the front of the face is a terrible choice, because lining up face details like the lips and the nose on opposite ends of the map is difficult.

FIGURE 30.14

Planar mapping isn't a good solution for a complex head mesh.

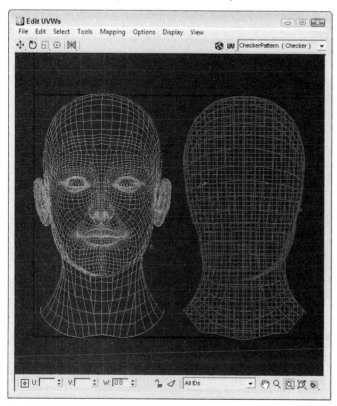

Selecting seams

The first step of pelt mapping is to select the seams for the map. To do this, click the Face subobject mode and then use the four buttons located in the Map Parameters rollout to define the pelt seams. These seams are displayed in light blue as they are created.

NOTE All open borders are automatically made into seams.

The Edit Seams button lets you click edges to highlight them as seams. This can be time consuming if you have a complex mesh. The Point to Point Seam button lets you click a starting point; a rubber band line then appears that lets you extend to an ending point. A seam is created between these two points using the shortest possible route. After an ending point is selected, the rubber band remains, letting you add to the seam. Right-click to exit the rubber band and to choose a new starting point. Figure 30.15 shows the seams added to the head model.

TIP When placing pelt mapping seams, try to position the seams where they aren't readily visible, such as under the arms and legs or down the middle of the back.

FIGURE 30.15

Seams define where the mesh can be split.

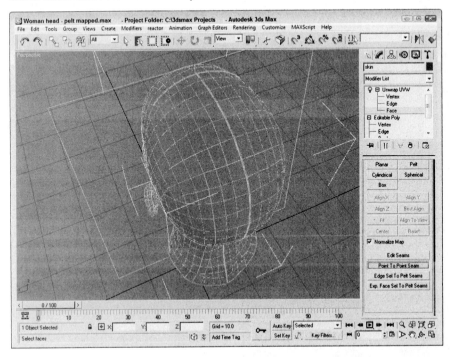

The Edge Sel to Pelt Seams button converts an existing edge selection to a pelt seam, and the Expand Face Selection to Pelt Seams button selects all faces that are next to the pelt seams.

The Parameters rollout contains an option to Always Show Pelt Seam. If this option is enabled, then the pelt seam is clearly shown. You also can set the size of the seams to thin or thick.

Positioning the projection gizmo

After the seams are defined, select all the faces that are to be mapped and click the Pelt button in the Map Parameters rollout. A rectangular projection gizmo appears. Orient this gizmo so that it is projected at the flattest part of the map away from the major seam.

Stretching the pelt mapping

With the projection gizmo oriented correctly, click the Edit Pelt Map button. The Edit UVWs window opens with the front projection displayed, and all seam points are positioned in a circle around the selected faces, as shown in Figure 30.16. The circle of seam points is called the Stretcher, and the lines connecting the Stretcher points to the selected faces are springs. The Pelt Map Parameters dialog box, shown in Figure 30.17, also opens.

The Simulate Pelt Pulling button causes the springs to pull at the selected UV faces causing them to stretch toward the Stretcher using the defined spring properties. Based on the Iterations and Spring properties, you may need to click the Simulate Pelt Pulling button several times. Figure 30.18 shows the UV faces after being stretched.

FIGURE 30.16

Pelt mapping positions all seam points in a circle around the selected faces.

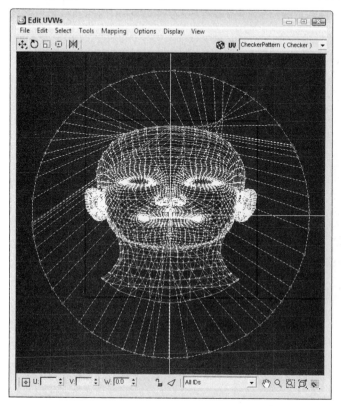

FIGURE 30.17

The Pelt Map Parameters dialog box includes commands for stretching the pelt mapping.

FIGURE 30.18

After being stretched, the UV faces are lined up quite well.

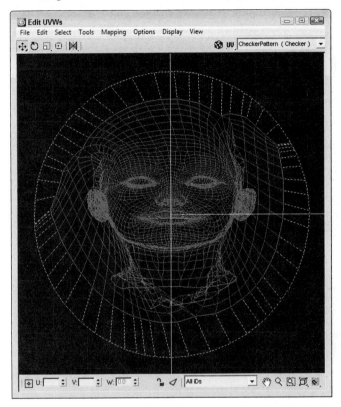

The Select Stretcher and Select Pelt UVs buttons let you select and manipulate both the selected faces and the Stretcher points. You can also straighten and mirror the stretcher, or have the UVs snap to seams. If you get confused, the Reset Stretcher button returns the mapping to its starting positions. The Relax buttons can be used to further move the UVs to eliminate any tension in the mapping.

Tutorial: Using pelt mapping

Pelt mapping is especially helpful on characters because they have irregular seams and surfaces. The Pelt mapping method works well for smoothing out character textures.

To use pelt mapping on a character's face, follow these steps:

1. Open the Lion toy face.max file from the Chap 30 directory on the DVD.

   This file includes just the face of a lion toy model.

2. With the face mesh selected, choose Modifiers ➪ UV Coordinates ➪ Unwrap UVW. Choose the Face subobject mode and select all the face subobjects in the face mesh.

3. In the Map Parameters rollout, click on the Pelt mapping button.

   A planar gizmo appears in the center of the viewport. Rotate and move the gizmo so it is parallel to the face mesh and in front of it (or press the Align Y button). Click on the Expand Face Selection to Pelt Seams button to ensure that all face polygons are selected.

4. Click on the Edit Pelt Map button. The Edit UVWs dialog box appears with each seam positioned along the Stretcher. Select and rotate the Stretcher about 10 degrees clockwise so the pelt is stretched out straight. In the Pelt Map Parameters dialog box that appears, click on the Simulate Pelt Pulling button several times until the face is stretched out.

Figure 30.19 shows the UVs for the face mesh stretched and ready to paint.

FIGURE 30.19

Using Pelt mapping, you can stretch the UVs for a mesh object.

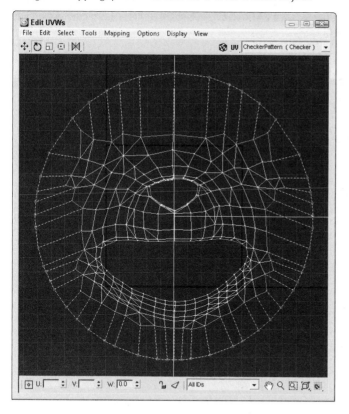

Rendering UV Templates

After all the UV coordinates are mapped onto a model, you can paint the desired textures in an external paint program like Photoshop and then load the texture back into the Edit UVWs window, where they can be aligned to the correct UVs. Using the Tools ⇨ Render UVs menu command, you can create a template that can be saved and loaded into Photoshop showing you exactly where the UV boundaries are.

The Tools ⇨ Render UVW Template menu command opens the Render UVs dialog box, shown in Figure 30.20. This dialog box lets you set the template's dimensions, set the template's Fill and Edges colors, and show overlaps and seams. The Fill mode can be set to None, Solid, Normals and Shaded, providing more information about the object.

FIGURE 30.20

The Render UVs dialog box lets you render and save a template for painting textures.

Clicking the Render UV Template button renders the template into the Render Frame Buffer window where it can be saved to the needed image format.

Summary

We've covered lots of ground in this chapter because there are lots of different maps. Learning to use these maps will make a big difference in the realism of your materials.

In this chapter, you've learned about the following:

- Understanding the basics of mapping coordinates
- Using mapping modifiers
- Applying labels with the UVW Map modifier
- Controlling mapping coordinates with the Unwrap UVW modifier
- Editing pelt seams
- Using the Pelt mapping method
- Rendering a UV template

In the next chapter, you learn how to use the Render to Texture interface to bake textures into an object. Creating normal maps is also covered.

Chapter 31

Creating Baked Textures and Normal Maps

3D games pose an interesting dilemma — creating interactive scenes that are displayed in real-time with the highest quality graphics. To achieve this, game developers use a number of tricks designed to speed up the rendering time. One of these tricks is pre-rendering textures that include all the lighting information and applying these pre-rendered textures as texture maps. This allows advanced lighting solutions such as global illumination to be included within a game without requiring extra time to rendering such a complex solution. The process of applying pre-rendered textures as maps is called baking a texture.

Rendering textures is a significant part of the rendering process, and baking a texture doesn't remove this step; it simply completes the step beforehand, so that the game engine doesn't need to do the texture calculations.

Another common efficiency trick is to use normal maps. Normal maps calculate the lighting results used to light small details that stick out from the surface of an object. These details are then recreated using a normal map that is applied back onto a simplified version of the object. The normal map allows these details to be simulated without the extra polygons used to create them. By allowing simple base objects to have details such as bolts and rivets without the extra polygons, the objects can be redrawn quickly without losing their visual quality.

This chapter covers some of the features found in Max that enable the amazing graphics that are found in the latest real-time games.

Using Channels

When 3D models are used in games, the color and material data for the model is stored in channels. The game engine then knows if it wants to change the color of a group of vertices because of an explosion that has happened, it just looks in the preset channel, finds the vertices it needs, changes the color, and then goes on with the game.

Working with channels is a very efficient way to interface with the gaming engine, but a sloppy game developer can introduce a model to the game engine with all sorts of unneeded or exaggerated channels. If this happens, the game engine can ignore the extra channels and get the wrong information, which can cause your hero to march off into battle without a weapon. Worse, it can crash the system.

To prevent problems and to streamline the number of channels that are included with game models, Max includes a Map Channel Info editor that you can use to manipulate the various channel data. This editor, shown in Figure 31.1, can be opened using the Tools ⇨ Channel Info menu command.

FIGURE 31.1

The Map Channel Info dialog box lets you edit channel data.

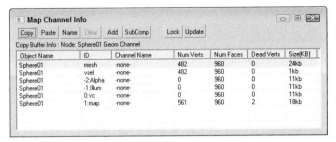

Using the Map Channel Info dialog box

The Map Channel Info dialog box shows lots of information including the Object Name; its ID; its Channel Name; the number of Vertices, Faces, and Dead Vertices (unattached vertices); and its Size. With this information, you can quickly determine which channels are taking up the most space and eliminate them.

All objects include some default channels for mesh, which holds the geometry; vsel, which holds the selected vertices; -2:Alpha, which holds the alpha channel information; -1:Illum, which holds illumination values; and channel 0:vc, which holds vertex color information. Objects also include at least one default map channel (even if it is empty). These channels cannot be deleted.

 **NOTE** Vertex colors are covered along with painting on objects in Chapter 16, "Creating Compound Materials and Using Material Modifiers."

The interface lets you Copy and Paste selected channels. You can give each channel a name with the Name button. Beneath the Copy button, text appears that lists the information currently copied in the Copy Buffer. Channels can be copied only between channels that have the same number of vertices.

The Clear button clears out the selected channels, but you cannot clear a map channel if there is another map channel above it. The Add button adds a new map channel to the object. Objects can hold as many as 99 map channels. The Clear and Add buttons also apply UVW Mapping Clear or UVW Mapping Add modifiers to the Modifier Stack. The Paste command also adds a modifier. These modifiers are convenient because they can easily be removed or reordered in the Stack. If changes have been made in the Modifier Stack, the Update button reflects these changes in the Map Channel Info dialog box.

The SubComp button shows the channel components if they exist. For example, map channels can be broken into X, Y, and Z components, and other channels like Alpha have R, G, and B components. The Lock button holds the current channels even if another object is selected.

Select by Channel modifier

After new channels have been created, you can recall them at any time using the Select by Channel modifier. This modifier is found in the Create ➪ Selection Modifiers ➪ Select by Channel menu command. Using this modifier, you can choose to Replace, Add, or Subtract a given channel from the selection. The available channels for the selection are listed by their channel name in a drop-down list.

Rendering to a Texture

When working with a game engine, game designers are always looking for ways to increase the speed and detail of objects in the game. One common way to speed game calculations is to pre-render the textures used in a game and then to save these textures as texture maps. The texture map takes more memory to save, but can greatly speed the rendering time required by the game engine. This process of pre-rendering a texture is called texture baking.

 **If you bake a texture into an object and then render it with the rest of the scene, the object gets a double dose of light.**

Texture baking can be accomplished in Max using the Rendering ➪ Render to Texture menu command (or by pressing the 0 key). This opens the Render to Texture dialog box. In several ways, the Render to Texture dialog box, shown in Figure 31.2, resembles the Render Scene dialog box, including a Render button at the bottom edge of the interface.

FIGURE 31.2

The General Settings rollout of the Render to Textures panel includes settings for all objects.

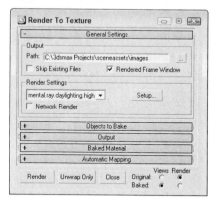

To create a baked texture, select a Texture Element from the Output rollout and click the Render button. Clicking the Render button creates the baked texture for the selected object and saves it in the directory specified in the General Settings rollout. It also applies an Automatic Flatten UVs modifier to the Modifier Stack and applies a Shell material to the object. The Shell material contains the object's original material along with the new baked material. You can select which material is displayed in the viewport and which is rendered using the options to the bottom right of the Render to Texture dialog box.

> **NOTE** You also can select Use an Existing Channel for mapping coordinates. This is a good choice because the Auto Unwrap option doesn't have the control over the UV coordinates that you may want and sometimes it does a poor job of unwrapping the mesh.

The interface also includes an Unwrap Only button. This button can be used to flatten the UVW Coordinates for the selected objects and to automatically create a map channel.

General Settings

The General Settings rollout includes an output path where the baked texture is saved. The file is saved by default using the Targa file format. The Skip Existing Files option renders only those elements that don't already exist in the designated directory. The Rendered Frame Window option displays the resulting map in the Rendered Frame Window along with saving the image as a file. For the render pass, you can select which rendering settings to use, including the mental ray rendering engine. The Setup button opens the Render Scene panel, where you can change the render settings.

Selecting objects to bake

In the Objects to Bake rollout, shown in Figure 31.3, a list displays exactly which objects, subobjects, and channels will be included in the rendered texture. The Edge Padding defines the overlap in pixels of the texture. The Objects to Bake rollout also includes a Presets list that lets you save and reload defined settings.

> **NEW FEATURE** The ability to save and load presets is new to 3ds Max 2008.

FIGURE 31.3

The Objects to Bake rollout of the Render to Textures panel lets you specify which objects are baked into the texture map.

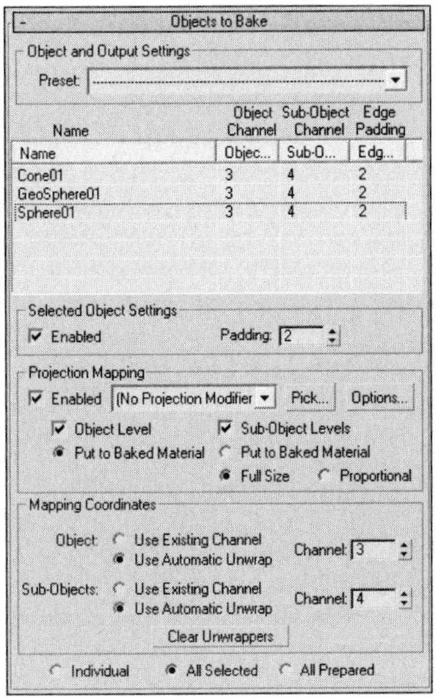

The Projection Mapping section lets you enable the creation of a normal map using a Projection modifier. These settings are covered in detail in the Normal Map section that appears later in this chapter.

The Mapping Coordinates section lets you choose to use the mapping coordinates of the Object or the Subobject selection contained within a specified channel or you can select to use the Use Automatic Unwrap feature, which automatically flattens the mapping coordinates. If the Use Automatic Unwrap option is selected, you can set the mapping options in the Automatic Mapping rollout. By default, unwrap mapping uses channel 3, but you can change this channel if you wish. If a different mapping uses channel 3 and you don't change this, the new mapping replaces the old one. The Clear Unwrappers button removes any existing Unwrap UVW modifiers from the object's stack.

You can select to bake an Individual object, All Selected objects, or All Prepared objects, which are all objects with at least one texture element.

Output settings

The Output rollout, shown in Figure 31.4, lists the texture elements that are included in the texture map. The Enable option can be used to disable the selected texture element or elements can be deleted with the Delete button.

FIGURE 31.4

The Output rollout of the Render to Textures panel lets you choose which texture elements are baked.

Clicking the Add button lets you select the type of texture elements that you can render. You'll want to use different maps depending on the purpose of the map, and you may want to render several at a time. The available types are CompleteMap, SpecularMap, DiffuseMap, ShadowsMap, LightingMap, NormalsMap, BlendMap, AlphaMap, and HeightMap. You can also change the map size or use the Automatic Map Size option, which bases the map size on the object size. Some map elements present a list of components to include in the map. These components appear below the size settings.

> **TIP** If the mental ray renderer is selected, then Ambient Occlusion is added to the list of available texture elements. The Ambient Occlusion option creates a map that recreates effects created by limited light bounces resulting from surrounding objects. This option is new to 3ds Max 2008.

Baked Material and Automatic Mapping settings

The Baked Material and Automatic Mapping rollouts, shown in Figure 31.5, provide a way to keep the existing object material using the Shell material. The Clear Shell Materials button removes the Shell materials for the baked objects and restores their original materials.

FIGURE 31.5

The final two rollouts of the Render to Textures panel include settings for handling the baked material and how the texture is mapped.

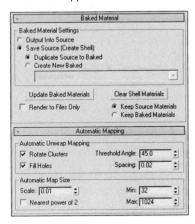

In the Automatic Mapping rollout, you can set how the mapping is applied. If the Use Automatic Unwrap option in the Objects to Bake rollout is enabled, then the object to be baked has the Automatic Flatten UVs modifier applied. For this type, you can set the Threshold Angle (which is the difference between the normals of adjacent faces; if the angular value is greater than the Threshold Angle value, then a hard edge is created between the faces), the Spacing (which is the amount of space between different map pieces), and whether map pieces can be rotated and used to fill in holes of larger map pieces.

The size of the texture map depends on the size of the object, but you can set a Scale value for greater resolution and set Min and Max values to keep the maps within reason. By default, maps are saved to the /images directory, but you can select a different directory if you prefer. The Nearest Power of 2 option causes the map to be optimized for use in memory to a square pixel size that is a power of 2, such as 8×8, 16×16, 32×32, or 64×64.

NOTE   Most game engines require square texture maps because they are efficiently loaded into memory. Main characters can use texture maps that are 1024×1024 or even 2048×2048, but background characters and props usually only have textures maps that are 256×256 or 512×512 so clustering is important to get as much into the textures as you can.

Tutorial: Baking the textures for a dog model

To practice baking textures, we bake a complete map of just the dog's head. Now I need to find a game engine to run it in.

To bake a dog's head texture, follow these steps:

1. Open the Doberman.max file from the Chap 31 directory on the DVD.

   This file includes a dog model created by Viewpoint Datalabs.

2. Select Rendering ⇨ Render to Texture (or press the 0 key) to open the Render to Textures dialog box.

3. Select the dog's body object. In the Render to Textures dialog box, set the Threshold Angle to **75** in the Automatic Mapping rollout, and make sure that the Rendered Frame Window option in the General Settings rollout is set. In the Output rollout, click the Add button and double-click the CompleteMap option. Set the Map Size to **512**, select the Diffuse Color option as the Target Map Slot, and click the Render button.

Figure 31.6 shows the resulting texture map. If you look in the Modify panel, you'll see that the Automatic Flatten UVs modifier has been applied to the object. If you look at the material applied to the object, you'll see that it consists of a Shell material.

FIGURE 31.6

A texture map created with the Render to Textures panel

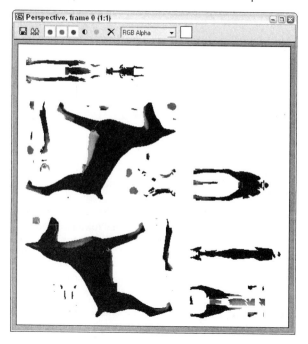

Creating Normal Maps

Normal maps are becoming more common in games because they offer a way to increase the bump details of a model by mapping high-detail bump information onto a low-resolution model. Normal maps are created using the Render to Texture interface and applied to an object using the Normal Bump map type found in the Material Editor.

The Normal Bump map type is typically applied as a bump map in the Maps rollout and includes a separate button, shown in Figure 31.7, to apply an additional bump map.

CAUTION   Normal maps can be displayed in the viewports only if the DirectX display driver is selected.

FIGURE 31.7

Although normal maps are created using the Render to Texture dialog box, they are applied using the Material Editor.

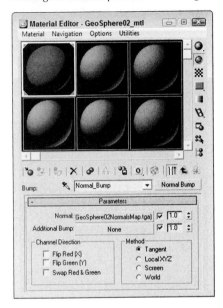

Using the Projection modifier

The Projection modifier is used to create a normal map. It works by being applied to a low-resolution object and then picking a high-resolution object that is similar to the low-resolution one. The Projection modifier surrounds the object with a cage that can be manipulated to include all the object details.

Within the Modifier Stack, the Projection modifier includes three subobject modes: Cage, Face, and Element. The Geometry Selection rollout includes a list of objects, a Pick button, and a Pick List for selecting the high-resolution object to be used.

The Cage rollout includes settings for displaying and pushing the cage out from the surface of the object. A Tolerance setting is used for wrapping the cage about the surface. The Selection Check rollout informs you if the Material IDs or Geometry faces are overlapping.

Setting Projection Mapping options

With a Projection modifier applied to a selected object, the Projection Mapping option can be enabled in the Objects to Bake rollout of the Render to Texture dialog box. The object can actually include several Projection modifiers, so a drop-down list lets you select the one to use or you can use the Pick button to select a target object in the viewports.

NEW FEATURE The Cage Reset button allows you to reset the cage before projection. This feature is new to 3ds Max 2008.

The Options button opens the Projection Options dialog box, shown in Figure 31.8. Using this dialog box, you can set the projection method, determine how to resolve hits, and define the Map Space.

FIGURE 31.8

The Projection Options dialog box lets you specify how the projection values are determined.

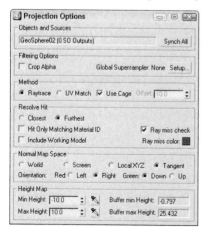

At the top of the Projection Options dialog box is the Source object. The Synch All button causes each object to use its active source for the projection. The two projection methods are Raytrace, which traces each normal line from its source to its target, and UV Match, which works by matching the UV coordinates between the source and the target objects.

For transparent objects, two projection rays may hit the same point. The Resolve Hit options let you set which one is selected, either the Closest or the Furthest. Most projections use the Tangent Map Space, but you can select to use the World, Screen, or Local Map Spaces also.

 **NOTE** Before the Projection modifier is applied, you need to have the high-res object and the low-res object positioned at the same place.

Tutorial: Creating a normal map for a spikey sphere

For this example, I've created two sphere objects, extruded the vertices on one of them, and called it Spikey ball. The other is a plain GeoSphere. The spikey ball sphere weighs in at 1280 polygons, while the normal GeoSphere is only 320 polygons. Although the spikey ball includes many more polygons, many of these details can be reclaimed using a normal map.

To create a normal map for the spikey ball model, follow these steps:

1. Open the Spikey ball.max file from the Chap 31 directory on the DVD.

2. Select and move the spikey ball object over the top of the low-res sphere object in the Top viewport.

3. Select the normal GeoSphere object, and select the Rendering ➪ Render to Texture menu command (or press the 0 key) to open the Render to Texture dialog box. In the General Settings rollout, select the Scanline renderer, no advanced lighting option as the Render Settings. In the Select Preset Categories dialog box that appears, click the Load button.

4. In the Objects to Bake rollout, click the Pick button, select the spikey ball object in the Select Targets dialog box that appears, and click the Add button. Then enable Projection Mapping.

5. In the Output rollout, click on the Add button and select the Normals map. From the Target Map Slot drop-down list, select the Bump option. Click the 512 button to set the map size, and enable the Output into Normal Bump option.

6. Click the Render button at the bottom of the Render to Texture dialog box.

7. To see the normal map when rendered, open the Material Editor and use the Pick Material from Object eyedropper tool and click on the Geosphere object. Then set the low-res sphere's render material to be the baked material.

8. Drag the normal Geosphere away from the spikey ball object and render the Perspective viewport.

Figure 31.9 shows the resulting normal map rendered on the GeoSphere.

FIGURE 31.9

The normal map for the spikey ball can be applied as a bump map to reclaim the high-res details.

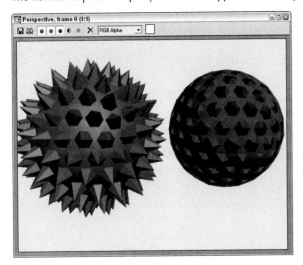

Summary

If you're working with games, then you'll want to use these features to help keep your models small and fleet. This chapter covers the following topics:

■ Discovering what channels the models have

■ Learning how to bake textures

■ Creating normal maps using the Projection modifier

The next part takes up the topic of animation again starting with animation modifiers.

Part VIII

Advanced Animation Techniques

Chapter 32

Using Animation Modifiers

odifiers can be used to deform and otherwise alter the geometry of objects, but they also can be used to affect other aspects of an object, including animated changes. Once such important animation modifier is the Point Cache modifier. This modifier lets the movement of each vertex in the scene be saved to a cached file for immediate recall and for animating multiple objects simultaneously.

The Modifiers menu also includes an Animation submenu that contains many such modifiers. These modifiers are unique in that each of them changes with time. They can be useful as an alternate to controllers, but their resulting effects are very specific. Included with this submenu are modifiers such as Morpher, which allows an object to move through several different preset shapes, and Flex, which is used to add soft-body dynamics to your scene. Other animation modifiers include Melt and PathDeform.

Baking Animation Keys with the Point Cache Modifier

When you add keys to an object to control its animation using modifiers, the modifiers remain with the object and can be revisited and altered as needed. However, if you have multiple objects that follow the same set of keys, such as for a crowd scene, then including a set of modifiers for each object can increase the overhead many times over. A simple solution is to bake all the keys into the object, allowing all the keys to be pulled from an external file. This frees the resources required to animate multiple objects and makes the animated keys portable. The Point Cache modifier makes this possible.

You also can use the Point Cache modifier when playback in the viewport is too slow because Max needs to compute the vertex positions of a huge number of vertices. Reading their position from a separate file increases the playback speed. You also can use the file on a cloned object to control its motion at a different speed.

NEW FEATURE   3ds Max 2008 includes version 3 of the Point Cache modifier, which includes the ability to save cached files using the XML file format.

The Point Cache modifier records the movement of every vertex of an object to a file. Point Cache files have the .XML extension, but they can also be saved using the older .pc2 extension. To create a Point Cache file, click the New button and name a new file on the hard drive. Then set the range of the animation to capture and click the Record button. Once recorded, the total number of points along with the sample rate and range are displayed for the active cache.

CAUTION   Point Cache files can be loaded and used only on objects with the same number of vertices as the original used to record the file.

If you select the Disable Modifiers Below option, then all modifiers below the Point Cache in the Modifier Stack are disabled. You can enable the Relative Offset option and set the Strength value to cause the cached animation to be exaggerated or even reversed. In the Playback Type section, you can control the range of the animation.

Tutorial: Trees in a hurricane

As an example of using the Point Cache modifier, we'll use a tree that is bending under violent forces such as a hurricane and duplicate it many times.

To create a forest of trees in a hurricane, follow these steps:

1. Open the Bending tree.max file from the Chap 32 directory on the DVD.

   This file includes an animated tree swaying back and forth using the Bend modifier.

2. Select the tree and choose the Modifiers ⇨ Cache Tools ⇨ Point Cache menu to apply the Point Cache modifier to the tree.

3. In the Parameters rollout, click the New button and create a file named "Bending tree.pct." Then click the Record button to save all the animation data to the file.

4. Select the tree and delete its Bend modifier. Then use the Tools ⇨ Array dialog box to create several rows of trees. Be sure to create the trees as copies and not instances.

5. Select several random trees and change the Playback Type to Custom Start and change the Start Frame to cause some random motion.

6. Press the Play Animation button to see the results.

Figure 32.1 shows several of the trees being moved about by the storm.

FIGURE 32.1

Using the Point Cache modifier, you can animate a whole forest of trees.

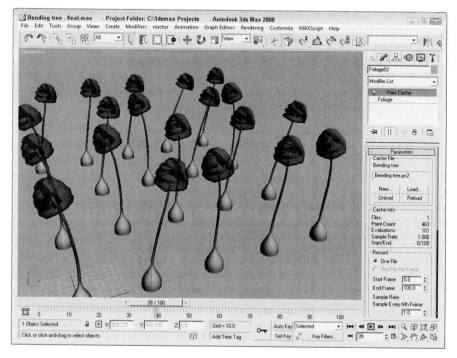

Using the Animation Modifiers

Animation is more than just moving an object from here to there. All objects move not only with major transformations, but with lots of secondary motions also. When a human character walks, the motions of his arms and legs are major, but the secondary motions of his swinging hips and bobbing shoulders make the walk realistic. Many of the animation modifiers enable these key secondary motions.

All the animation modifiers presented in this chapter are located in the Modifiers ➪ Animation submenu.

CROSS-REF Also included among the Animation modifiers are several Skin modifiers, which are used to make an object move by attaching it to an underlying skeleton. The Skin modifiers are covered in Chapter 43, "Skinning Characters."

Morpher modifier

The Morpher modifier lets you change a shape from one form into another. You can apply this modifier only to objects with the same number of vertices.

CROSS-REF In many ways, the Morpher modifier is similar to the Morph compound object, which is covered in Chapter 26, "Working with Compound Objects."

The Morpher modifier can be very useful for creating facial expressions and character lip-synching. You can also use it to morph materials. Max makes 100 separate channels available for morph targets, and channels can be mixed. You can use the Morpher modifier in conjunction with the Morph material. For example, you could use the Morph material to blush a character for an embarrassed expression.

TIP When it comes to making facial expressions, a mirror and your own face can be the biggest help. Coworkers may look at you funny, but your facial expressions will benefit from the exercise.

The first task before using this modifier is to create all the different morph targets. Because the morph targets need to contain the same number of vertices as the base object, make a copy of the base object for each morph target that you are going to create. As you create these targets, be careful not to add or delete any vertices from the object.

NOTE Because morph targets deal with each vertex independently, you cannot mirror morph targets, so if you want a morph target for raising the left eyebrow and a morph target for raising the right eyebrow, you need to create each morph target by hand.

After all your morph targets are created, select a channel in the Channel Parameters rollout, shown in Figure 32.2, and use the Pick Object from Scene button to select the morph target for that channel. Another option for picking is to Capture Current State. After a morph target has been added to a channel, you can view it in the Channel List rollout.

FIGURE 32.2

The Morpher modifier's rollouts

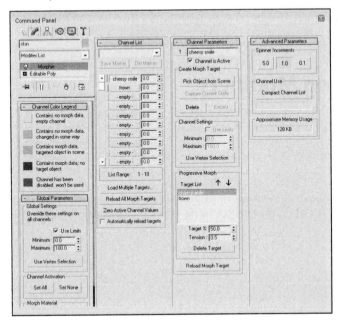

As you animate, you can specify the amount of each morph target to include in the frame using the value to the right of the channel name in the Channel List rollout. The slim color bar to the left of the channel name designates the status of the channel. You can find information on what each color represents in the Channel Color Legend rollout.

The Channel Parameters rollout also includes a Progressive Morph section. This feature lets you define an intermediate step for how the morph is to progress, with the final step being the morph target. Using these intermediate steps, you can control how the object morphs.

Tutorial: Morphing facial expressions

The Morpher modifier is very helpful when you're trying to morph facial expressions, such as those to make a character talk. With the various sounds added to the different channels, you can quickly morph between them. In this example, we use the Morpher modifier to change the facial expressions of the general character.

 When creating facial expressions, be sure to enable the Soft Selection features, which make modifying the face meshes much easier.

To change facial expressions using the Morpher modifier, follow these steps:

1. Open the Morphing facial expressions.max file from the Chap 32 directory on the DVD.

   This file includes a head model created by Viewpoint Datalabs. The model has been copied twice, and the morph targets have already been created by modifying the subobjects around the mouth.

2. Select the face on the left, and select the Modifiers ⇨ Animation Modifiers ⇨ Morpher menu command to apply the Morpher modifier.

3. In the Channel List rollout, select channel 1, click the Pick Object from Scene button, and select the middle face object. Then select the second empty channel from the Channel List rollout; in the Channel Parameters rollout, again click the Pick Object from Scene button and select the face on the right.

   If you look in the Channel List rollout, you'll see "cheesy smile" in Channel 1 and "frown" in Channel 2.

4. Click the Auto Key button (or press the N key), drag the Time Slider to frame 50, and then increase the "cheesy smile" channel in the Channel List rollout to **50**. Drag the Time Slider to frame 100, and increase the "frown" channel to **100** and the "cheesy smile" channel to **0**. Then return the Time Slider to 50, and set the "frown" channel to **0**.

5. Click the Play Animation button in the Time Controls to see the resulting animation.

Figure 32.3 shows the three facial expressions. The Morpher modifier is applied to the left face.

 Be sure to keep the morph target objects around. You can hide them in the scene or select them and save them to a separate file with the File ⇨ Save Selected menu command.

Using the Flex Modifier

The Flex modifier can add soft body dynamic characteristics to an object. The characteristic of a *soft body* is one that moves freely under a force. Examples of soft body objects are clothes, hair, and balloons. The opposite of soft body dynamics is *rigid body* dynamics. Think of a statue in the park. When the wind blows, it doesn't move. The statue is an example of a rigid body. On the other hand, the flag flying over the library moves all over when the wind blows. The flag is an example of a soft body.

FIGURE 32.3

Using the Morpher modifier, you can morph one facial expression into another.

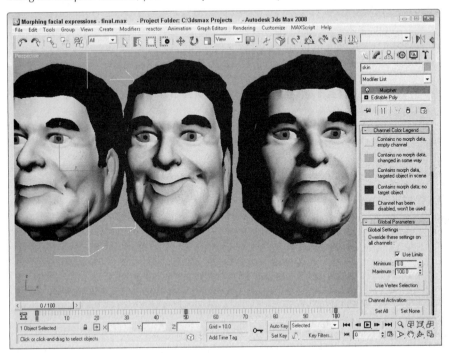

CROSS-REF   Soft body objects can also be defined and simulated using reactor, which is covered in Chapter 38, "Simulating Physics-Based Motion with reactor."

Another way to think of soft bodies is to think of things that can flex. Objects such as a clothesline flex under very little stress, but other objects like a CD flex only a little when you apply a significant force. The settings of the Flex modifier make it possible to represent all kinds of soft body objects.

Figure 32.4 shows many of the rollouts available for the Flex modifier.

Flex subobjects

In the Modifier Stack, the Flex modifier has three subobjects that you can access: Center, Edge Vertices, and Weights and Springs. The Center subobject is a simple box gizmo that marks the center of the flex effect. Portions of the object that are farther from the center move a greater distance. The Edge Vertices subobject can be selected to control the direction and falloff of the flex effect. The Weights and Springs rollout controls the Weights and Springs subobject.

Setting flex strength

The Parameters rollout includes a Flex value, which controls the amount of bending the object does; a Strength value, which controls the rigidity of the object; and a Sway value, which controls how long the flexing object moves back and forth before coming to a stop. An antenna on a car is an example of an object that has fairly high Flex and Sway values and a low Strength value.

FIGURE 32.4

The Flex modifier rollout lets you control the flex settings.

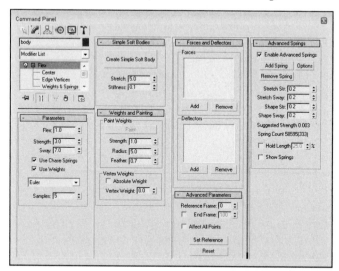

Chase Springs cause an object to return to its original position when the force is removed. A twig on a tree is an example of an object with Chase Springs. The Use Chase Springs option lets you disable these springs. A piece of cloth is an example of when you would want Chase Springs disabled.

Selecting the Weights and Springs subobject lets you apply weights to certain selected springs. You can disable these weights using the Use Weights option. If you disable these weights, the entire object acts together.

The Flex modifier offers three solution methods to compute the motions of objects. These are presented in a drop-down list. The Euler solution is the simplest method, but it typically requires five samples to complete an accurate solution. The Midpoint and Runge-Kutta4 solutions are more accurate and require fewer samples, but they require more computational time. Setting the Samples value higher produces a more accurate solution.

Creating simple soft bodies

In the Simple Soft Bodies rollout, use the Create Simple Soft Body button to automatically set the springs for the selected object to act like a soft body. You can also set the amount of Stretch and Stiffness the object has. For cloth, you want to use a high Stretch value and a low Stiffness value, but a racquetball would have both high Stretch and Stiffness values.

 You can manually set the spring settings for the object using the Advanced Springs rollout.

Painting weights

When you select the Weights and Springs subobject mode, the spring vertices are displayed on the object. The vertices are colored to reflect their weight. By default, the vertices that are farthest from the object's pivot point have the lowest weight value. Vertices with the greatest weight value (closest to 1) are colored

red, and spring vertices with the lowest weight value (closest to –1) are blue. Vertices in between these two values are orange and yellow. The lower-weighted vertices move the greatest distance, and the higher-weighted vertices move the least.

Selecting the Weights and Springs subobject also enables the Paint button in the Weights and Springs roll-out. Clicking this button puts you in Paint mode, where you can change the weight of the spring vertices by dragging a paint gizmo over the top of the object in the viewports. As you paint the spring vertices, they change color to reflect their new weight.

The Strength value sets the amount of weight applied to the vertices. This value can be negative. The Radius and Feather settings change the size and softness of the Paint brush. Figure 32.5 shows a dinosaur model with the Flex modifier applied. The dinosaur has had some weights painted so its tail, arms, and neck move under the influence of the Flex modifier. The blue vertices are the weights that don't move as much.

FIGURE 32.5

Use the Paint button to change the weight of the spring vertices.

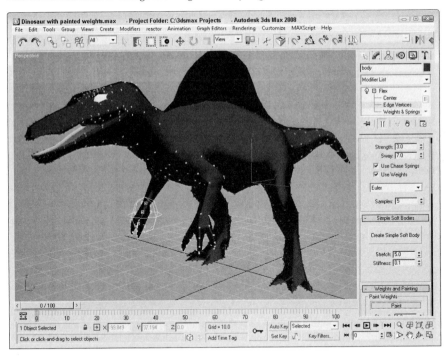

The weights applied using the Paint button are relative to the existing vertex weight. If you select the Absolute Weight option, then the Vertex Weight value is applied to the selected vertices.

Adding Forces and Deflectors

To see the effect of the Flex modifier, you need to add some motion to the scene. The flex object flexes only when it is moving. One of the easiest ways to add motion to the scene is with Space Warps.

The Forces and Deflectors rollout includes two lists: one for Forces and one for Deflectors. Below each are Add and Remove buttons. Using these buttons, you can add and remove Space Warps from the list. The Forces list can use any of the Space Warps in the Forces subcategory (except for Path Follow). The Deflector list can include any of the Space Warps in the Defectors subcategory.

 When you add Space Warps to the Forces and Deflectors list for the Flex modifier, they do not need to be bound to the object.

Manually creating springs

The final two rollouts for the Flex modifier are Advanced Parameters and Advanced Springs. The Advanced Parameters rollout includes settings for controlling the Start and End frames where the Flex modifier has an effect. The Affect All Points option ignores any subobject selections and applies the modifier to the entire object. The Set Reference button updates all viewports, and the Reset button resets all the vertices' weights to their default values.

You can use the Advanced Springs rollout to manually add and configure springs to the object. Clicking the Options button opens a dialog box where you can select the type of spring to add to the selected vertices, including Edge and Shape Springs. Edge springs are applied to vertices at the edges of an object, and Shape springs are applied between vertices. For these advanced springs, you can set the Stretch Strength, Stretch Sway, Shape Strength, and Shape Sway.

Tutorial: Making a flag wave

A good example of a soft body object is a flag. By making a flag wave in the wind, you can practice using the Flex modifier. In this example, you also apply the Flex modifier to subobjects.

To make a flag wave in the wind using the Flex modifier, follow these steps:

1. Open the Soft body flex flag.max file from the Chap 32 directory on the DVD.

   This file includes a simple plane object that has been converted to an Editable Mesh.

2. With the Flag object selected, open the Modify panel and select the Vertex subobject mode in the Selection rollout. In the Front viewport, drag over all the vertices, except the left column where the flag touches the flagpole.

3. With all the vertices on the right selected, click the Modifier List and select the Flex modifier (or you can choose the Modifiers ➪ Animation Modifiers ➪ Flex menu command).

4. In the Parameters rollout, set the Flex value to **3.0**, set the Sway value to **50**, and disable the Use Weights option. In the Simple Soft Bodies rollout, click the Create Simple Soft Body button. Finally, click the Add button for the Forces list in the Forces and Deflectors rollout, and select the Wind Space Warp in the Top viewport.

5. To see the final results, click the Play Animation button to see the flag wave in the viewport.

Figure 32.6 shows the flag waving.

Melt modifier

The Melt modifier simulates an object melting by sagging and spreading edges over time. Melt parameters include Amount and Spread values, Solidity (which can be Ice, Glass, Jelly, or Plastic), and a Melt Axis.

Figure 32.7 shows the Melt modifier applied to the snowman model (it was inevitable).

FIGURE 32.6

You can use the Flex modifier to simulate the motion of soft body objects like cloth.

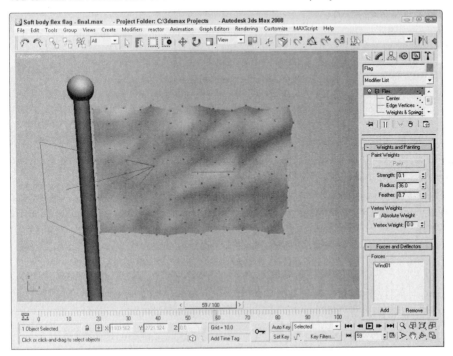

PatchDeform and SurfDeform modifiers

Among the animation modifiers are several that are similar in function but that work on different types of objects. The PatchDeform modifier uses patches, and the SurfDeform modifier deforms an object according to a NURBS surface.

In the Parameters rollout for each of these modifiers is a Pick Patch (or Surface) button that lets you select an object to use in the deformation process. After the object is selected, you can enter the Percent and Stretch values for the U and V directions, along with a Rotation value.

NOTE   The PatchDeform modifier is also available as a World Space Modifier (WSM). WSMs are similar to the normal Object Space Modifiers (OSM), except that they use World Space coordinates instead of Object Space coordinates. The most noticeable differences are that WSMs don't use gizmos and that the OSM moves the patch to the object, while the WSM causes the object to move to the patch.

Tutorial: Deforming a car going over a hill

Have you seen those commercials that use rubber cars to follow the curvature of the road as they drive? In this tutorial, we use the PatchDeform modifier to bend a car over a hill made from a patch.

FIGURE 32.7

The Melt modifier slowly deforms objects to a flat plane.

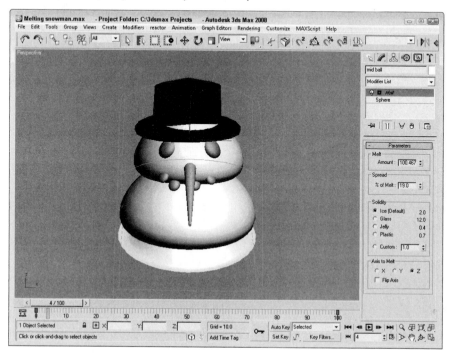

To deform a car according to a patch surface, follow these steps:

1. Open the Car bending over a hill.max file from the Chap 32 directory on the DVD.

    This file contains a simple hill made from patch objects and a car model created by Viewpoint Datalabs.

2. Select the car model, and choose Modifiers ➪ Animation Modifiers ➪ PatchDeform (WSM). Then click the Pick Patch button in the Parameters rollout, and select the hill object.

    This applies the World Space PatchDeform modifier (WSM) to the car object and moves the car to align with the hill.

3. Set the V Percent value to 0 in the Parameters rollout. Then, click the Auto Key button (or press the N key) to enable key mode, and drag the Time Slider to frame 100. Then set the V Percent value to **–50**, and click the Auto Key button again to disable key mode.

4. Click the Play button (or press the / key) to see the car deform over the hill.

Figure 32.8 shows the results of this tutorial.

FIGURE 32.8

Our car model hugs the road, thanks to the PatchDeform modifier.

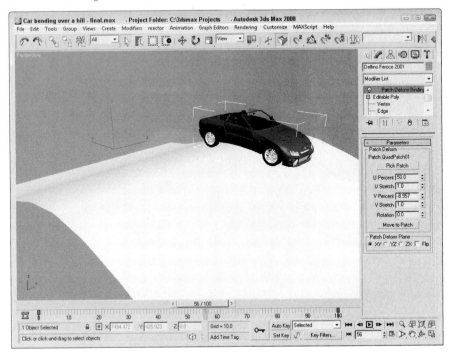

PathDeform modifier

The PathDeform modifier uses a spline path to deform an object. The Pick Path button lets you select a spline to use in the deformation process. You can select either an open or closed spline. The Parameters rollout also includes spinners for controlling the Percent, Stretch, Rotation, and Twist of the object. The Percent value is the distance the object moves along the path.

 If you use the PathDeform modifier, you can benefit from using the Follow/Bank utility, which gives you control over how the object follows and banks along the path.

Figure 32.9 shows some text wrapped around a spline path.

Linked XForm modifier

The Linked XForm modifier passes all transformations of one object onto another, but not vice versa. The object that controls the transformation is designated as the Control Object and is selected via the Pick Control Object button (which is the only control in the Parameters rollout for this modifier). After the Control object is selected, the Control Object controls the selected object's transforms, but the object that is being controlled can move independent of the control object without affecting the control object.

FIGURE 32.9

The text in this example has been deformed around a spline path using the PathDeform modifier.

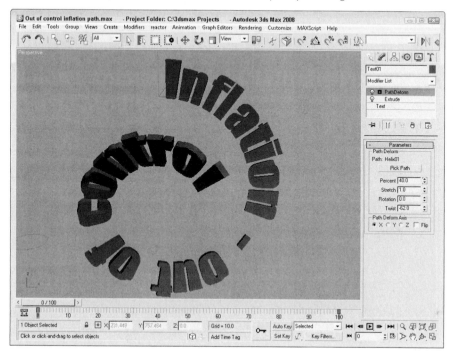

SplineIK Control modifier

The SplineIK Control modifier can be applied only to spline objects. In the Spline IK Control Parameters rollout, you can click the Create Helpers button, which adds a dummy object to every vertex on the spline, as shown in Figure 32.10. These dummy objects make it much easier to control the spline without having to enter vertex subobject mode. You can also specify how the dummy objects are linked and how they are displayed.

Attribute Holder modifier

The Attribute Holder modifier displays all custom defined attributes in their own rollout. Creating custom attributes and wiring attributes is discussed in the next section.

FIGURE 32.10

The SplineIK Control modifier may be applied only to spline objects.

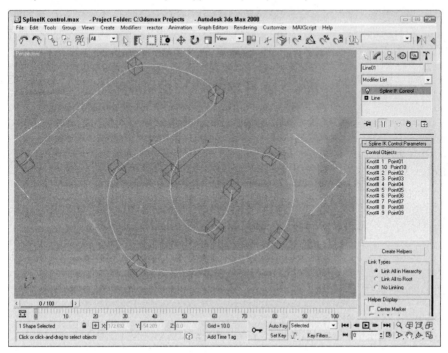

Summary

This chapter introduced all the available animation modifiers and showed you how to use several of them. Through custom attributes and wiring parameters, the animator's job can be accomplished by tweaking some controls. In this chapter, you accomplished the following:

- Used the Point Cache modifier
- Used the Morpher modifier to deform a face
- Learned about the Flex modifier and the other deformation modifiers
- Used the various miscellaneous animation modifiers

The next chapter takes a close look at the Expression Controller that gives you the ability to script the controller's behavior. It also covers wiring parameters so that one parameter can control another and creating custom parameters.

Chapter 33

Animating with the Expression Controller and Wiring Parameters

Expressions are looks that you make in the mirror when you're trying to wake up, but in Max they are a series of equations that define how an object acts. Max expressions can be as simple as adding two numbers together or as complex as several lines of MAXScript. But expressions enable you to create customized animated reactions.

Although Max expressions can be used with any Max spinner, they are mainly used within MAXScript scripts or in the Expression controller. The Expression controller is a specialized controller that lets you control the object's behavior using scripted expressions.

This chapter then looks at a unique way to drive animations based on object parameters. Parameters of one object can be wired to another parameter so that when one parameter changes, the wired parameter changes with it. For example, you can wire the On/Off parameter of a light to the movement of a switch. All parameters that can be animated can be wired.

As long as you are working with parameters, Max includes several helpful tools for viewing and working with the available parameters including the Parameter Collector. If the Parameter Collector doesn't gather the exact parameters that you need, you can create your own custom parameters also.

Working with Expressions in Spinners

Although much of this chapter focuses on using the Expression controller, the Expression Controller Interface isn't the only place where you can play with expressions. Expressions can also be entered into spinner controls using the Numerical Expression Evaluator, shown in Figure 33.1. This simple dialog box is accessed by selecting a spinner and pressing Ctrl+N.

CROSS-REF Another place that commonly uses expressions is the Parameter Wiring dialog box, which is covered later in this chapter.

FIGURE 33.1

The Numerical Expression Evaluator dialog box lets you enter expressions for a spinner.

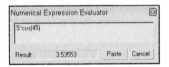

To use this evaluator, just type the expression in the field; the result is displayed in the result field. The result field is updated as you type the expression. If you make a mistake, the Result is blanked out. The Paste button places the result value in the spinner, and the Cancel button closes the dialog box without a change.

TIP   You can enter a relative value in a spinner by typing the letter R and a value. For example, if the Segments value of a sphere object is 32, then typing R20 changes the value to 52 and R-20 changes the value to 12.

Understanding the Expression Controller Interface

The term *expression* refers to a mathematical expression or simple formula that computes a value based on other values. These expressions can be simple, as with moving a bicycle based on the rotation of the pedals, or they can be complex, as with computing the sinusoidal translation of a boat on the sea as a function of the waves beneath it.

You can use almost any value as a variable in an expression, from object coordinates and modifier parameters to light and material settings. The results of the expression are computed for every frame and used to affect various parameters in the scene. You can include the number of frames and time variables in the expression to cause the animation results to repeat for the entire sequence.

NOTE   Although it is not as powerful as the Script controller, the Expression controller is much faster than the Script controller because it doesn't require any compile time.

Of all the controllers that are available, the Expression controller has limitless possibilities that could fill an entire book. This section covers the basics of building expressions and includes several examples.

The Expression controller is just one of the many controllers that are available for automating animations. This controller enables you to define how the object is transformed by means of a mathematical formula or expression, which you can apply to any of the object's tracks. It shows up in the controller list, based on the type of track to which it is assigned, as a Position Expression, Rotation Expression, Scale Expression, Float Expression, or Point3 Expression controller.

Before you can use the Expression controller on a track, you must assign it to a track. You can assign controllers to the Position, Rotation, and Scale tracks using the Motion panel or the Track View or you can apply a controller by right-clicking on a track in the Track View and selecting the Assign Controller option. After you assign a controller, the Expression Controller dialog box immediately opens, or you can access this dialog box at any time by right-clicking the track and selecting Properties from the pop-up menu. For example, select an object in your scene, open the Motion panel, and select the Position track. Then click the Assign Controller button at the top of the Assign Controller rollout, and select Position Expression from the list of Controllers. This causes the Expression Controller dialog box to appear.

You can use this dialog box to define variables and write expressions. The dialog box, shown in Figure 33.2, includes four separate panes used to display a list of Scalar and Vector variables, build an expression, and enter a description of the expression.

FIGURE 33.2

You can use the Expression controller to build expressions and define their results.

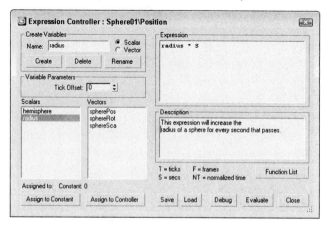

Defining variables

Variables are placeholders for different values. For example, creating a variable for a sphere's radius called "r" would simplify an expression for doubling its size from "take the sphere's radius and multiply it by two," to simply "r times 2."

To add Variables to the list panes in the Expression Controller dialog box, type a name in the Name field, select the Scalar or Vector option type, and click the Create button; the new variable appears in the Scalars or Vectors list. To delete a variable, select it from the list and click the Delete button. The Tick Offset value is the time added to the current time and can be used to delay variables.

You can assign any new variable either to a constant or to a controller. Assigning a variable to a constant does the same thing as typing the constant's value in the expression. Constant variables are simply for convenience in writing expressions. The Assign to Controller button opens the Track View Pick dialog box, shown in Figure 33.3, where you can select the specific controller track for the variable, such as the position of an object.

Assigning a variable to a controller enables you to animate the selected object based on other objects in the scene. To do this, create a variable and assign it to an animated track of another object. For example, if you create a Vector variable named boxPos and assign it to the Position track for a box object, then within the expression you can use this variable to base the motion of the assigned object on the box's position.

FIGURE 33.3

The Track View Pick dialog box displays all the tracks for the scene. Tracks that you can select are displayed in black.

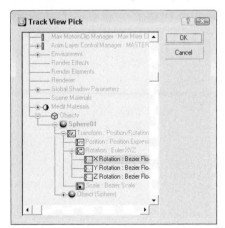

Building expressions

You can type expressions directly into the Expression pane of the Expression Controller dialog box. To use a named variable from one of the variable lists (Scalars or Vectors), type its name in the Expression pane. Predefined variables (presented later in the chapter) such as F and NT do not need to be defined in the variable panes. The Function List button opens a list of functions, shown in Figure 33.4, where you can view the functions that can be included in the expression. This list is for display only; you still need to type the function in the Expression pane.

 **TIP** One way to learn the syntax for different expressions is to enable the MacroRecorder in the MAXScript Listener window and look in the upper pane while performing a task in the viewports.

 **NOTE** The Expression pane ignores any white space, so you can use line returns and spaces to make the expression easier to see and read.

Debugging and evaluating expressions

After typing an expression in the Expression pane, you can check the values of all variables at any frame by clicking the Debug button. This opens the Expression Debug window, shown in Figure 33.5. This window displays the values for all variables, as well as the return value. The values are automatically updated as you move the Time Slider.

The Evaluate button in the Expression Controller dialog box commits the results of the expression to the current frame segment. If the expression contains an error, an alert dialog box warns you of the error. Replacing the controller with a different one can erase the animation resulting from an Expression controller.

FIGURE 33.4

The Function List dialog box lets you view all the available functions that you can use in an expression.

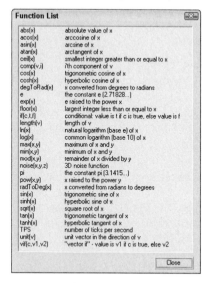

FIGURE 33.5

The Expression Debug window offers a way to test the expression before applying it.

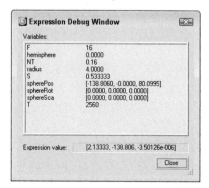

Managing expressions

You can use the Save and Load button to save and recall expressions. Saved expressions are saved as files with an .XPR extension. Expression files do not save variable definitions.

> **CAUTION** If you load a saved expression into the Expression Controller dialog box, you need to reassign all variables before you can use the loaded expression.

Tutorial: Creating following eyes

As a quick example, we start with a simple expression. The Expression controller is very useful for setting the eye pupil objects to move along with the ball's motion. This same functionality can be accomplished using a manipulator and wiring the parameter, but we show it with the Float Expression controller.

To make eye pupil objects follow a moving ball object, follow these steps:

1. Open the Following eyes.max file from the Chap 33 directory on the DVD.

   This file includes a face taken from a Greek model made by Viewpoint Datalabs, along with a ball that is animated to move back and forth.

2. Select the left eye pupil object named "pupil_l" (the right pupil has been linked to move with the left pupil), and open the Motion panel. Select the Position track, and click the Assign Controller button. Select the Position Expression controller, and click OK.

   The Expression Controller dialog box opens.

3. Create a new vector variable named **ballPos** by typing its name in the Name field, selecting the Vector option, and clicking the Create button.

4. With the ballPos variable selected, click the Assign to Controller button. In the Track View Pick dialog box, locate and select the Position track for the Sphere01 object, as shown in Figure 33.6, and click OK.

FIGURE 33.6

Select the Position track for the Sphere01 object in the Track View Pick dialog box.

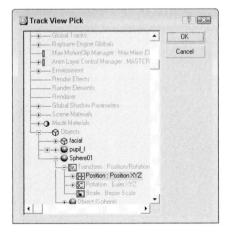

5. In the Expression pane, erase the existing expression and type the following:

   ```
   [ -3.1 + ballPos.x/20, -2.9, 41.0 ]
   ```

   Then click the Debug button. The Expression Debug window appears, in which you can see the variable values change as items in the scene change. With the expression complete, you can drag the Time Slider back and forth and watch the pupil follow the ball from side to side. If you're happy with the motion, click the Evaluate button and then the Close button to exit the interface.

This is a simple example, but it demonstrates what is possible. Figure 33.7 shows the resulting face.

FIGURE 33.7

The Expression controller was used to animate the eyes following the ball in this example.

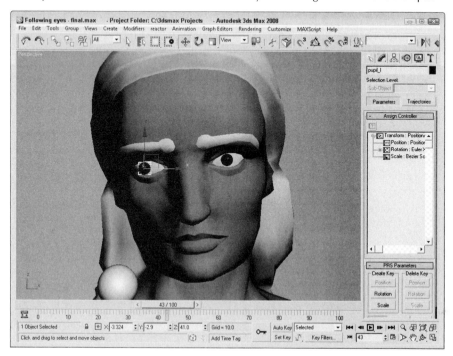

Using Expression Controllers

You can use expressions to control the transforms of objects. You can access these transforms from the Track View or from the Motion panel. You can also use expressions to control object parameters such as a box's length or material properties such as the amount of illumination applied to a material. You can access all these parameters from the Track View.

Animating transforms with the Expression controller

After you assign a controller to a transform track, the Expression pane in the Expression Controller dialog box includes the current values of the selected object. Position transforms display the X, Y, and Z coordinates of the object; Rotation transforms display the rotation value in radians; and Scale transforms display values describing the relative scaling values for each axis.

> **NOTE** Radians are another way to measure angles. A full revolution equals 360 degrees, which equates to 2 × pi radians. The Expression dialog box includes the `degToRad` and `radToDeg` functions to convert back and forth between these two measurement systems.

Animating parameters with the Float Expression controller

To assign the Float Expression controller, select an object with a parameter or Modifier applied and open the Track View. Find the track for the parameter that you want to change, and click the Assign Controller button. Select the Float Controller from the list, and click OK.

The actual controller type depends on the parameter selected. Many parameters use float expressions, but some use Transform controllers.

After you assign the Expression controller, the Expression Controller dialog box opens, or you can open it by right-clicking the track and selecting Properties from the pop-up menu to load the dialog box. Within this dialog box, the Expression pane includes the current value of the selected parameter.

Tutorial: Inflating a balloon

The Push Modifier mimics filling a balloon with air by pushing all its vertices outward. In this tutorial, we use a balloon model created by Zygote Media to demonstrate how you can use the Float Expression controller to control the parameters of a modifier.

To inflate a balloon using the Float Expression controller, follow these steps:

1. Open the Balloon and pump.max file from the Chap 33 directory on the DVD.

   This file includes a pump created from primitives and the balloon model with the Push modifier applied.

2. Next, open the Track View by choosing Graph Editors ➪ Track View — Curve Editor. Navigate the balloon object's tracks until you find the Push Value track (found under Objects ➪ b3 ➪ Modified Object ➪ Push ➪ Push Value). Select the Push Value track, and click the Assign Controller button (or select it from the right-click popup menu). From the list of controllers, select Float Expression and click OK.

   The Expression Controller dialog box opens.

3. In the Expression pane, you should see a single scalar value of 0. Modify the expression to read like this:

   ```
   2 * NT
   ```

   Click the Debug button to see the value results. With the Expression Debug window open, drag the Time Slider and notice that the balloon inflates.

 **If you use a parameter such as Radius as part of an Expression, then the parameter is unavailable in the Modify panel if you try to change it by hand.**

Figure 33.8 shows the balloon as it is being inflated.

Animating materials with the Expression controller

You can locate the material's parameter in the Track View and assign the Expression controller to it to control material parameters. Some of these parameters are scalar values, but any material parameter set with a color swatch has a Point3 return type.

When using material parameters and color values, be sure not to combine them in expressions with vector values.

Tutorial: Controlling a stoplight

In this example, we use the `if` function to turn the colors of a sphere on and off to simulate a traffic light. We accomplish this task by applying the Expression controller to the Diffuse color track. The goal is to show the color green for the first third of the animation, yellow for the second third, and red for the last third.

FIGURE 33.8

A balloon being inflated using an Expression controller to control the Push modifier

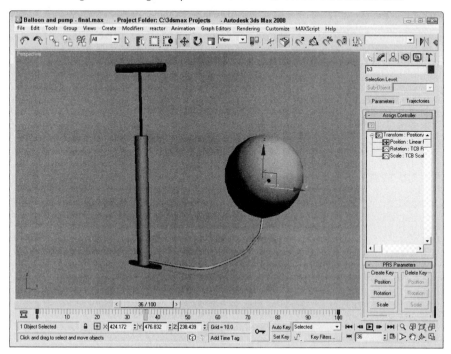

To change the colors of stoplight spheres using the Expression controller, follow these steps:

1. Open the Stoplight.max file from the Chap 33 directory on the DVD.

   This file includes a simple stoplight created using primitives. One of the spheres moves between the three light positions and has had a green material applied to it.

2. Open the Track View — Curve Editor, and locate and select the Diffuse Color track, which you can find under Objects ⇨ Sphere03 ⇨ Material #1 ⇨ Shader Basic Parameters tracks. Click the Assign Controller button, and double-click the Point3 Expression selection.

   This assigns the Point3 Expression controller to the Diffuse Color track.

3. Open the Expression Controller dialog box by right-clicking the Diffuse Color track and selecting Properties from the pop-up menu.

4. In the Expression pane, enter the following:

   ```
   [if(NT>=.33,255,0), if(NT<.66,255,0), 0]
   ```

   Then click the Evaluate button, and close the Expression Controller dialog box.

Click the Play Animation button to see the results. Figure 33.9 shows the stoplight alongside the Dope Sheet for this stoplight.

FIGURE 33.9

The Expression controller animates the diffuse color for this object.

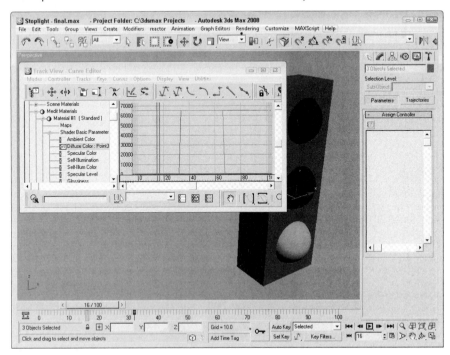

Before leaving this example, let's examine the expression. The expression works with a Point3 number that includes the values of red, green, and blue. The first Point3 value represents red. Because yellow, in the RGB color system, is composed of equal parts of red and green, we want red to be visible for the last two-thirds of the time. To do this, we make the expression include the following statement:

```
if (NT >= .33, 255, 0)
```

This basically says that if the Normalized Time falls in the last two-thirds of the time, then set the red value to 255; if it does not, then set red to 0.

NOTE   Normalized time takes the entire time range and scales it to fit between values of 0 and 1, so the beginning is at time 0 and the end is where time equals 1.

The second Point3 value is green, which appears for the first third of the animation and along with red for the second third to make yellow. So the following expression needs to go where the green value would be located:

```
if (NT < .66, 255, 0)
```

This expression says that if the Normalized Time is less than two-thirds of the time, then set the green value to its maximum; if it isn't, then set its value to 0.

The third Point3 value is for blue. Blue doesn't appear at all in green, yellow, or red, so its value is set to 0 for the entire animation.

The completed expression for the entire animation (which you entered in Step 4 of the tutorial) looks like this:

```
[if (NT >= .33, 255, 0), if (NT < .66, 255, 0), 0]
```

Wiring Parameters

When parameters are wired together, the value of one parameter controls the value of the parameter to which it is wired. This is a powerful animation technique that lets a change in one part of the scene control another aspect of the scene. Another way to use wired parameters is to create custom animation controls such as a slider that dims a light source that animators can use as needed.

Using the Parameter Wiring dialog box

You can access the Parameter Wiring dialog box in several places. The Animation ⇨ Wire Parameters ⇨ Wire Parameters (Ctrl+5) menu makes a pop-up menu of parameters appear. Selecting a parameter from the menu changes the cursor to a dotted line (like the one used when linking objects). Click the object that you want to wire to, and another pop-up menu lets you choose the parameter to wire to. The Parameter Wiring dialog box appears with the parameter for each object selected from a hierarchy tree.

You can also wire parameters by right-clicking the quadmenu and selecting Wire Parameters. The Wire Parameters option is disabled if multiple objects are selected.

The Parameter Wiring dialog box (Alt+5), shown in Figure 33.10, displays two tree lists containing all the available parameters. This tree list looks very similar to the Track View and lets you connect parameters in either direction or to each other. If you used the Wire Parameters feature to open the Parameter Wiring dialog box, then the parameter for each object is already selected and highlighted in yellow.

FIGURE 33.10

The Parameter Wiring dialog box can work with expressions.

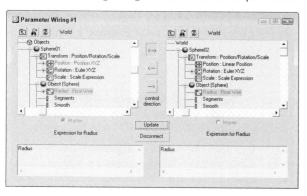

The three arrow buttons between the two tree lists let you specify the connection direction. These buttons connect the parameter in one pane to the selected parameter in the opposite pane. The direction determines whether the parameter in the left pane controls the parameter in the right pane, or vice versa. You can also select the top bidirectional button to make the parameters mutually affect each other. Below each tree list is a text area where you can enter an expression. An *expression* is a mathematical statement that follows a specific syntax for defining how one parameter controls the other. These expressions can be any valid expression that is accepted in the Animation Controller dialog box or in MAXScript.

CROSS-REF   You can learn more about creating and using expressions in Chapter 21, "Animating with Constraints and Controllers."

After an expression is entered, click the Connect button to complete the wiring. Based on the connection direction, the Master radio button indicates which object controls the other. You can also use this dialog box to disconnect existing wired parameters. You can use the icon buttons at the top of the dialog box, shown in Table 33.1, to Show All Tracks, to find the next wired parameter, and to refresh the tree view.

TABLE 33.1

Parameter Wiring Dialog Box Icons

Button	Description
	Show All Tracks
	Next Wired Parameter
	Refresh Tree View

After the wiring is completed, the Parameter Wiring dialog box remains open. You can try out the wiring by moving the master object. If the results aren't what you wanted, you can edit the expression and click the Update button (the Connect button changes to an Update button).

NOTE   When you select objects to be wired, the order in which the objects are selected doesn't matter because in the Parameter Wiring dialog box, you can select the direction of control.

Once you've made a connection in the Parameter Wiring dialog box, the track name for the controlling object turns green and the track name of the object being controlled turns red. If you make a bi-directional connection, then both tracks turn green.

Manipulator helpers

To create general-use controls that can be wired to control various properties, Max includes three Manipulator Helpers. These helpers are Cone Angle, Plane Angle, and Slider. They are available as a subcategory under the Helpers category of the Create panel or in the Create ➪ Helpers ➪ Manipulators menu.

For the Cone Angle helper, you can set the Angle, Distance, and Aspect settings. The default cone is a circle, but you can make it a square. The Plane Angle helper includes settings for Angle, Distance, and Size.

You can name the Slider helper. This name appears in the viewports above the slider object. You can also set a default value along with maximum and minimum values. To position the object, you can set the X Position, Y Position, and Width settings. You can also set a snap value for the slider.

Once created, you can use these manipulator helpers when the Select and Manipulate button on the main toolbar is enabled (this button must be disabled before the manipulator helpers can be created). The advantage of these helpers is in wiring parameters to be controlled using the helpers.

Tutorial: Controlling a crocodile's bite

One way to use manipulator helpers and wired parameters is to control within limits certain parameters that can be animated. This gives your animation team controls they can use to quickly build animation sequences. In this example, you use a slider to control a crocodile's jaw movement.

To create a slider to control a crocodile's bite, follow these steps:

1. Open the Biting crocodile.max file from the Chap 33 directory on the DVD.

   This file includes a crocodile model created by Viewpoint Datalabs. For this model, the head, eyes, and upper teeth have been joined into a single object, and the pivot point for this object has been moved to where the jaw hinges.

2. Select Create ➪ Helpers ➪ Manipulators ➪ Slider, and click in the Perspective view above the crocodile. Name the slider **Croc Bite**, and set the Maximum value to **60**.

3. With the Slider selected, choose Animation ➪ Wire Parameter ➪ Wire Parameter (or press the Ctrl+5) to access the pop-up menu. Choose Object (Slider) ➪ value option, drag the dotted line to the crocodile's head object, and click. Choose Transform ➪ Rotation ➪ Y Rotation.

   The Parameter Wiring dialog box appears.

4. In the Parameter Wiring dialog box, click the direction arrow that points from the Slider to the head so that the slider is set to control the head. Then click the Connect button and drag the Slider.

> **NOTE** Before you can drag the slider, you need to enable the Select and Manipulate button in the main toolbar.

   The crocodile's jaw spins around erratically. This happens because the rotation values are in radians and we need them in degrees.

5. In the expression text area under the head object, enter the expression **degToRad(value)** and click the Update button. The drag the Slider again.

   Now the values are in degrees and the range is correct, but the croc's upper jaw rotates unrealistically through the bottom jaw. This can be fixed by multiplying by a negative 1.

6. In the expression text area under the head object, update the expression to be -1*degToRad(value) and click the Update button.

7. Click the Select and Manipulate button on the main toolbar, and drag the slider to the right.

   The crocodile's mouth opens.

Figure 33.11 shows the crocodile biting using the slider control.

FIGURE 33.11

A slider control is wired to open the crocodile's mouth.

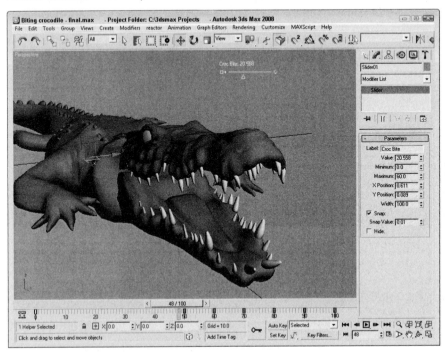

Collecting Parameters

To help in organizing the various parameters that you use to animate a scene, you can use the Parameter Collector to gather all custom and animated parameters used in the scene. The Parameter Editor can be used to create custom attributes and parameters, but the custom attributes are attached to the specific object or element that was selected when the attribute was created. This can make finding the custom attributes difficult, but Max includes another tool that you can use to collect all these custom attributes into a single location—the Parameter Collector.

Open the Parameter Collector dialog box, shown in Figure 33.12, with the Animation ➪ Parameter Collector (Alt+2) menu command. This dialog box lets you gather a set of parameters into a custom rollout that can be opened and accessed from anywhere. This provides a convenient way to compile and look at only the parameters that you need to animate a certain task. Under the menus are several toolbar buttons, explained in Table 33.2.

FIGURE 33.12

The Parameter Collector dialog box is used to gather several different parameters into a custom rollout.

Select rollout marker

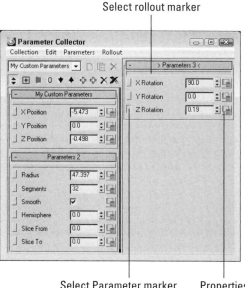

Select Parameter marker   Properties

TABLE 33.2

Parameter Collector Toolbar Buttons

Toolbar Button	Name	Description
Sphere Collection ▼	Collection Name	Enters a name for the current collection or selects an existing collection.
▯	New Collection	Creates a new collection of parameters.
▤	Duplicate Collection	Creates a copy of the existing collection.
✕	Delete Collection	Deletes the current collection.
⬍	Multiple Edits	Toggle button that allows multiple parameters to be changed at once when enabled.
◉	Absolute/Relative	Toggle button that maintains the current value in Absolute mode and resets the value to 0 when the mouse is released in Relative mode.
▯	Key Selected	Creates a key for the selected parameters when the Auto Key mode is enabled.

continued

TABLE 33.2	(continued)	
Toolbar Button	**Name**	**Description**
0	Reset Selected	Sets the selected parameter values to 0.
▼	Move Parameters Down	Moves the selected parameters downward in the rollout order.
▲	Move Parameters Up	Moves the selected parameters upward in the rollout order.
✛	Add to Selected Rollout	Opens a Track View Pick dialog box where you can select the parameter to add to the selected rollout.
✛	Add to New Rollout	Opens a Track View Pick dialog box where you can select the parameter to add to a new rollout.
✕	Delete Selected	Deletes the selected parameters.
✖	Delete All	Deletes all parameters in the current collection.
⬚	Properties	Opens the Key Info dialog box for the selected parameter if a key is set. This button is found to the right of a parameter.

Within the Parameter Collection dialog box, you can create and name new rollouts, add parameters to these rollouts using a Track View Pick dialog box, and save multiple rollouts into collections that can be recalled.

Collections are named by typing a new name in the drop-down list located in the upper-left corner of the interface. This drop-down list holds all available collections. The Collection menu (or the toolbar buttons) may be used to create, rename, duplicate, or delete a collection.

A Parameter Collection can include multiple rollouts. The current active rollout is marked with a yellow bar directly under the rollout title and with brackets that surround the rollout name. Using the Rollout menu (or the toolbar buttons) you can create a new rollout or rename, reorder, or delete existing rollouts.

Parameters are added to the rollouts using the Parameters ➪ Add to Selected and the Parameters ➪ Add to New Rollout menu commands. Both of these commands open a Pick Track View dialog box where you can select the specific parameter to add to the current rollout. To the left of each parameter is a small box that can be used to select the parameter. You can also select parameters using the Edit menu commands.

If multiple parameters are selected, then you can change the values for all selected parameters at the same time by enabling the Edit ➪ Multiple Edits option. With the Multiple Edits option enabled, changing any parameter value also changes all other selected parameters.

CAUTION   **Multiple parameters' values can be changed together only if they are of the same type.**

At the bottom of the Edit menu is the Edit Notes menu command. Using this menu command, you can change the parameter's name, link it to a URL, and type some notes about how this parameter works.

The Parameter Collector dialog box can also be used to create animation keys. To create a key for the selected parameters, you'll need to enable the Auto Key button and then select the Parameters ➪ Key Selected or Parameters ➪ Key All menu commands. If a key exists for the selected parameter, the Properties button to the right of the parameter becomes active and displays the Key Info dialog box when clicked.

Using the Collection ⇨ Show Selected Keys in Track Bar menu command, you can see the keys for the selected parameters regardless of whether the objects are selected in the viewports.

Adding Custom Parameters

Another useful way to expand the number of parameters is to create custom parameters. These custom parameters can define some aspect of the scene that makes sense to you. For example, if you create a model of a bicycle, you can define a custom parameter for the pedal rotation. You can add your own custom parameters using the Parameter Editor dialog box, shown in Figure 33.13. You can open this modeless panel by choosing Animation ⇨ Parameter Editor (or by pressing the Alt+1 keys).

FIGURE 33.13

You can use the Parameter Editor dialog box to create custom parameters.

Pick Explicit Track

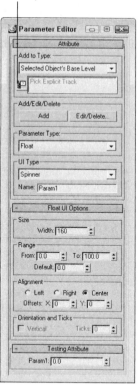

The Add to Type drop-down list at the top of the Attribute rollout in the Parameter Editor dialog box lets you select where the custom attribute shows up. Custom attributes can be created for an object, for the selected modifier, for the object's material, or for any track found in the Track View. The Pick Explicit Track button opens a dialog box where you can select a specific track.

The Add button creates the custom attribute and adds it to a rollout named Custom Attributes for the specified element. If the specified element is selected, you can click the Edit/Delete button to open the Edit Attributes/Parameters dialog box, shown in Figure 33.14. All custom attributes associated with the selected element are displayed.

> **NOTE** Custom attributes show up in a rollout named Custom Attributes positioned beneath all the other rollouts, but if you add the Attribute Holder modifier to the object before creating the new attribute, then the Custom Attributes rollout appears under the Attribute Holder modifier.

FIGURE 33.14

The Edit Attributes/Parameters dialog box lets you edit or delete custom attributes.

The Edit Attributes/Parameters dialog lets you select and reorder the custom attributes within their rollout. Selecting a custom attribute also loads its settings into the Parameter Editor where they can be changed.

The Parameter Type drop-down list lets you choose the parameter format. Possibilities include Angle, Array, Boolean (true or false), Color, Float (a decimal-point number), fRGBA, Integer, Material, Node, Percent, String, TextureMap, and WorldUnits. The UI Type drop-down list defines how the parameter is displayed in the rollout. How the parameter looks depends on the type of parameter. Float and integer values can be spinners or sliders, Boolean values can be check boxes or radio buttons, array values are drop-down lists, nodes are pick buttons (allowing you to select an object in the viewports), color and RGB values are color pickers, and texture maps are map buttons. You can also name the parameter.

The Options rollout changes depending on which parameter type was selected. These rollouts contain settings for the interface's Width, value ranges, default values, Alignment (left, right, or center), and list items.

The Testing Attribute rollout shows what the interface element will look like and lets you change the attribute to see how the custom parameter works.

The value of custom attributes becomes apparent when you start wiring parameters.

Summary

This chapter covered the basics of using the Expression controller. Using mathematical formulas to control the animation of an object's transformation and parameters offers lots of power. You also can use the values of one object to control another object.

Along with the Expression controller, the ability to wire parameters together in the Parameter Wire dialog box opens up a whole new way to control objects. This chapter also covered how you can create new parameters with the Parameter Collector dialog box. All of these tools give you lots of control over the scene using parameters and expressions. In this chapter, you accomplished the following:

- Practiced building expressions in the Expression Controller dialog box
- Learned about expressions and what they can do
- Reviewed the available operators, variables, and functions
- Tried out examples of controlling object transformations and parameters
- Created and wired parameters
- Gathered and edited several parameters at once with the Parameter Collector
- Created custom parameters with the Parameter Editor

In the next chapter, you learn to use the Track View to display and manage all the details of the current scene.

Chapter 34

Working with Function Curves in the Track View

As you move objects around in a viewport, you often find yourself eye-balling the precise location of an object in the scene. If you've ever found yourself wishing that you could precisely see all the values behind the scene, then you need to find the Track View. The Track View can be viewed using three different layouts: Curve Editor, Dope Sheet, and Track Bar. Each of these interfaces offers a unique view into the details of the scene.

These Track View layouts can display all the details of the current scene, including all the parameters and keys. This view lets you manage and control all these parameters and keys without having to look in several different places.

The Track View also includes additional features that enable you to edit key ranges, add and synchronize sound to your scene, and work with animation controllers using function curves.

Learning the Track View Interface

Although the Track View can be viewed using different layouts, the basic interface elements are the same. They all have menus, toolbars, a Controller pane, a Key pane, and a Time Ruler. Figure 34.1 shows these interface elements. You can hide any of these interface elements using the Show UI Elements option in the pop-up menu that appears when you right-click the title bar.

The Track View layouts

The Track View includes three different layouts: a Curve Editor, a Dope Sheet, and the Track Bar. The Curve Editor layout displays all parameter and motion changes as graphs that change over time. You manipulate these curves just like normal splines. You can use the Dope Sheet layout to coordinate key ranges between the different parameter tracks. And the Track Bar layout offers a way to quickly view the Track View within the viewports.

FIGURE 34.1

The Track View interface offers a complete hierarchical look at your scene.

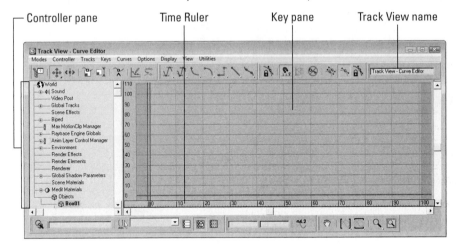

Controller pane   Time Ruler   Key pane   Track View name

You can open the Curve Editor and Dope Sheet layouts using the Graph Editors menu. You can open the Curve Editor window by choosing Graph Editors ⇨ Track View–Curve Editor or by clicking the Curve Editor button on the main toolbar. You open the Dope Sheet interface in a similar manner by choosing Graph Editors ⇨ Track View–Dope Sheet.

CROSS-REF You also use the Graph Editors menu to access the Schematic View interface. For more on the Schematic View interface, see Chapter 24, "Working with the Schematic View."

After the Track View opens, you can give it a unique name using the Track View–Curve Editor field found on the Name: Track View toolbar. If the Name toolbar isn't visible, right-click the title bar and select Show Toolbars ⇨ Name: Track View from the pop-up menu. These named views are then listed in the Graph Editors ⇨ Saved Track Views menu. Any saved Track Views that are named are saved along with the scene file.

To open the Track Bar layout in the viewports, expand the Track Bar using the Open Mini Curve Editor button at the left end of the Timeline. Close the Track Bar layout by clicking the Close button on the toolbar. Figure 34.2 shows this Track View.

After you open a Track View, you can switch between the Curve Editor and the Dope Sheet using the Modes menu or by right-clicking the menu bar or toolbar (away from the buttons) and selecting a new layout from the Load Layout menu. You can also save customized layouts using the Save Layout or Save Layout As menu commands.

Track View menus and toolbars

In many cases, the menus and the toolbars provide access to the same functionality. One difference is the Modes menu, which lets you switch the current interface between the Curve Editor and the Dope Sheet layouts. The Curve Editor menus include Modes, Controller, Tracks, Keys, Curves, Options, Display, View, and Utilities. The Dope Sheet menu loses the Curves menus and adds a Time menu in its place. The Track Bar menus are the same as the Curve Editor menus, except that the Modes menu is absent.

The Track Bar offers quick access to the Track View.

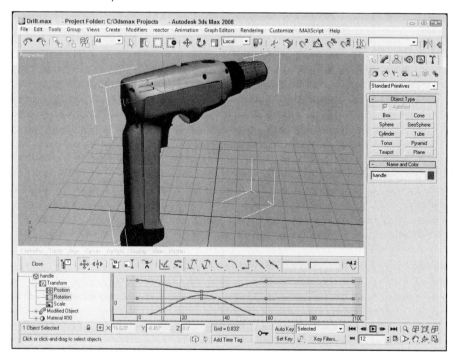

The Track View consists of several toolbars. You can open these toolbars by right-clicking the toolbar (away from the buttons) and selecting the Show Toolbars submenu. The available toolbars depend on the layout (either Curve Editor or Dope Sheet), but they can include Name, Navigation, Key Stats, Key Tangents, Controllers, Track Selection, Keys, Time, Ranges, Display, Extras, Curves, Tools, and Biped. All these toolbars can be docked, floated, and hidden. You can also add and delete new toolbars using the right-click pop-up menu.

CROSS-REF You can learn more about docking and floating toolbars in Chapter 1, "Exploring the Max Interface."

For the Track View–Curve Editor layout, four toolbars appear by default at the top of the interface. These toolbars include the Keys, Curves, Key Tangents, and Name toolbars. For the Track View–Dope Sheet, the default toolbars at the top of the interface include the Keys, Time, Display, and Name toolbars.

NOTE Depending on the size of the Track View window, you may need to drag the toolbar to the left to see the buttons at the right end of the toolbar.

Keys toolbar

The Keys toolbar is one of the default toolbars for the Curve Editor and for the Dope Sheet. The toolbar is slightly different in each layout. Table 34.1 describes these buttons.

TABLE 34.1

Keys Toolbar Buttons

Toolbar Button	Name	Description
	Filters	Opens the Filter dialog box, where you can specify which tracks will appear
  	Move Keys, Move Keys Horizontal, Move Keys Vertical	Enables you to move the selected keys or limit their movement to horizontal or vertical
	Slide Keys	Enables you to slide the selected keys
	Scale Keys	Enables you to scale the selected keys
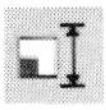	Scale Values	Scales the selected keys' values vertically; Curve Editor layout only
	Add Keys	Enables you to add new keys to a track
	Draw Curves	Creates a function curve by dragging the mouse; Curve Editor layout only
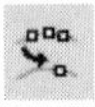	Reduce Keys	Optimizes the current time selection by eliminating unnecessary keys; Curve Editor layout only
	Edit Keys	Enables edit keys mode; Dope Sheet layout only
	Edit Ranges	Enables edit ranges mode; Dope Sheet layout only

Curves toolbar

The Curves toolbar is another of the default toolbars for the Curve Editor. This toolbar shares some buttons with the Display toolbar, which is a default toolbar in the Dope Sheet layout. Table 34.2 describes these buttons.

TABLE 34.2

Curves and Display Toolbar Buttons

Toolbar Button	Name	Description
	Lock Selection	Prevents any changes to the current selection
	Snap Frames	Causes moved tracks to snap to the nearest frame

Toolbar Button	Name	Description
	Parameter Curve Out-of-Range Types	Opens the Parameter Curve Out-of-Range Types dialog box, where you can make tracks loop and cycle; Curve Editor layout only
	Show Keyable Icons	Displays a key icon next to all tracks that can be animated
	Show All Tangents	Displays the Bézier curve handles for all keys; Curve Editor layout only
	Show Tangents	Displays the Bézier curve handles for the selected keys; Curve Editor layout only
	Lock Tangents	Prevents the curve handles from moving; Curve Editor layout only
	Modify Subtree	Causes changes to a parent to affect all tracks beneath the parent in the hierarchy; Dope Sheet layout only
	Modify Child Keys	Causes changes to child keys when parent keys are changed; Dope Sheet layout only

Key Tangents toolbar

The Key Tangents toolbar is another of the default toolbars for the Curve Editor. It is used to set the In and Out curve types. This toolbar is also available in the Dope Sheet layout. Table 34.3 describes these buttons.

TABLE 34.3

Key Tangents Toolbar Buttons

Toolbar Button	Name	Description
	Set Tangents to Auto, Set In Tangents to Auto, Set Out Tangents to Auto	Sets curve to approach and leave the key in an automatic manner
	Set Tangents to Custom, Set In Tangents to Custom, Set Out Tangents to Custom	Sets curve to approach and leave the key in a custom manner defined by the handle positions
	Set Tangents to Fast, Set In Tangents to Fast, Set Out Tangents to Fast	Sets curve to approach and leave the key in an ascending manner

continued

TABLE 34.3 *(continued)*

Toolbar Button	Name	Description
	Set Tangents to Slow,	Sets curve to approach and leave the key in a descending manner
	Set In Tangents to Slow,	
	Set Out Tangents to Slow	
	Set Tangents to Step,	Sets curve to approach and leave the key in a stepping manner
	Set In Tangents to Step,	
	Set Out Tangents to Step	
	Set Tangents to Linear,	Sets curve to approach and leave the key in a linear manner
	Set In Tangents to Linear,	
	Set Out Tangents to Linear	
	Set Tangents to Smooth,	Sets curve to approach and leave the key in a smooth manner
	Set In Tangents to Smooth,	
	Set Out Tangents to Smooth	

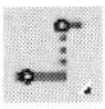

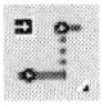

Time toolbar

The Time toolbar is one of the default toolbars for the Dope Sheet. It is used to work with time ranges. Table 34.4 describes these buttons.

TABLE 34.4

Time Toolbar Buttons

Toolbar Button	Name	Description
	Select Time	Enables you to select a block of time by clicking and dragging
	Delete Time	Deletes the selected block of time
	Reverse Time	Reverses the order of the selected time block
	Scale Time	Scales the current time block

Toolbar Button	Name	Description
	Insert Time	Inserts an additional amount of time
	Cut Time	Deletes the selected block of time and places it on the clipboard for pasting
	Copy Time	Makes a copy of the selected block of time and places it on the clipboard for pasting
	Paste Time	Inserts the current clipboard time selection

Controllers toolbar

The Controllers toolbar is available in both the Curve Editor and the Dope Sheet. It is used to assign controllers to tracks. Table 34.5 describes these buttons.

TABLE 34.5

Controllers Toolbar Buttons

Toolbar Button	Name	Description
	Filters	Opens the Filter dialog box, where you can specify which tracks will appear; same button as found in the Keys toolbar
	Copy Controller	Copies the selected track for pasting elsewhere
	Paste Controller	Pastes the last copied track
	Assign Controller	Enables you to assign a controller to the selected track
	Delete Controller	Removes the current controller
	Make Controller Unique	Changes an instanced track to one that is unique

Tools toolbar

The Tools toolbar is available in the Curve Editor and includes buttons to add some additional tracks such as the Notes and Visibility. Table 34.6 describes these buttons.

TABLE 34.6

Tools Toolbar Buttons

Toolbar Button	Name	Description
	Add Note Track	Adds a note track to the current track for recording information
	Delete Note Track	Deletes an associated note track
	Add Visibility Track	Adds a track to an object for controlling its visibility
	Snap Frames	Causes moved tracks to snap to the nearest frame; also found in the Curves toolbar
	Lock Selection	Locks the current selection of keys so that no other keys can be selected
	Properties	Displays a dialog box of properties associated with the track
	Track View Utilities	Opens a dialog box of available Track View utilities

Biped toolbar

The Biped toolbar is available only in the Curve Editor and includes buttons to display the various biped tracks. Table 34.7 describes these buttons.

TABLE 34.7

Biped Toolbar Buttons

Toolbar Button	Name	Description
	Show Biped Position Curves	Displays the position curves for the selected biped
	Show Biped Rotation Curves	Displays the rotation curves for the selected biped
	Show Biped X Curves	Displays the X-axis curves for the selected biped
	Show Biped Y Curves	Displays the Y-axis curves for the selected biped
	Show Biped Z Curves	Displays the Z-axis curves for the selected biped

Other toolbars

The Dope Sheet layout includes two additional toolbars: Ranges and Extras. Table 34.8 describes these buttons.

TABLE 34.8

Ranges and Extras Toolbar Buttons

Toolbar Button	Name	Description
	Edit Ranges	Enables edit ranges mode; same button as found in the Keys toolbar
	Position Ranges	Enables position ranges mode
	Recouple Ranges	Lines up the keys with the range
[	Exclude Left End Point	Leaves the left end point out of the current time block
]	Exclude Right End Point	Leaves the right end point out of the current time block

Controller and Key panes

Below the menus (and below the topped docked toolbars) are two panes. The left pane, called the Controller pane, presents a hierarchical list of all the tracks. The right pane is called the Key pane, and it displays the time range, keys, or function curves, depending on the layout. You can pan the Controller pane by clicking and dragging on a blank section of the pane: The cursor changes to a hand to indicate when you can pan the pane.

Each track can include several subtracks. To display these subtracks, click the plus sign (+) to the left of the track name. To collapse a track, click the minus sign (−). You can also use the Settings menu to Auto Expand a selected hierarchy. Under the Options ➪ Auto Expand menu are options for Selected Objects Only, Transforms, XYZ Components, Limits, Keyable, Animated, Base Objects, Modifiers, Materials, and Children. For example, if the Auto Expand ➪ Transforms option is enabled, then the Transform tracks for all objects is automatically expanded in the Track View. Using these settings can enable you to quickly find the track you're looking for.

The Options ➪ Auto Select ➪ Animated toggle automatically selects all tracks that are animated. You can also auto select Position, Rotation, and/or Scale tracks. The Options ➪ Auto Scroll menu command can be set for Selected and/or Objects tracks. This command automatically moves either the Selected tracks or the Objects track to the top of the Controller pane.

 **NOTE** You can also select, expand, and collapse tracks using the right-click pop-up quadmenu.

The Controller pane includes many different types of tracks. By default, every scene includes the following tracks: World, Sound, Global Tracks, Video Post, Anim Layer Control Manager, Raytrace Engine Globals, Max MotionClip Manager, Environment, Render Effects, Render Elements, Renderer, Global Shadow Parameters, Scene Materials, Medit Materials (for materials in the Material Editor), and Objects, as shown in Figure 34.3.

FIGURE 34.3

Several tracks are available by default.

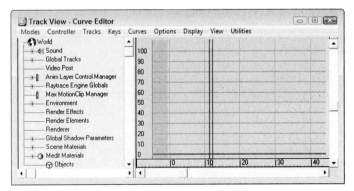

The Shift, Ctrl, and Alt keys make selecting and deselecting multiple tracks possible. To select a contiguous range of tracks, select a single track and then select another track while holding down the Shift key. This selects the two tracks and all tracks in between. Hold down the Ctrl key while selecting tracks to select multiple tracks that are not contiguous. The Alt key removes selected items from the selection set.

Below the right pane is the Time Ruler, which displays the current time as specified in the Time Configuration dialog box. The current frame is marked with a light blue time bar. This time bar is linked to the Time Slider, and moving one updates the other automatically.

At the top right of the Key pane (above the vertical scroll bar) is a split tab that you can use to split the Controller and Key pane into two separate views, as shown in Figure 34.4. Using this feature, you can look at two different sections of the tree at the same time. This makes it easy to copy and paste keys between different tracks.

 You can drag the Time Ruler vertically in the right pane.

FIGURE 34.4

Drag the tab above the vertical scroll tab to split the Track View into two views.

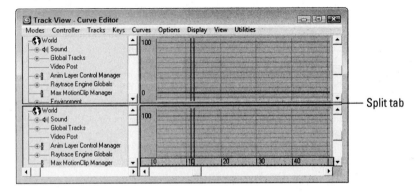

Split tab

Lower interface toolbars

At the bottom edge of the Track View window are three toolbars that appear by default. These toolbars are the Track Selection, Key Stats, and Navigation. Using these toolbars, you can locate specific tracks, see information on the various keys, and navigate the interface.

In the Track Selection toolbar is the Zoom Selected Object button and the Select by Name field, in which you can type a name to locate any tracks with that name.

NOTE In the Select by Name field, you can also use wildcard characters such as * (asterisk) and ? (question mark) to find several tracks.

The Key Stats toolbar includes Key Time and Value Display fields that display the current time and value. You can enter values in these fields to change the value for the current time. You can also enter an expression in these fields in which the variable n equals the key time or value. For example, to specify a key value that is 20 frames from the current frame, enter $n + 20$ (where you supply the current value in place of n). You can also include any function valid for the Expression controller, such as sin( ) or log( ). Click the Show Selected Key Stats button to display the key value in the Key pane.

CROSS-REF Chapter 21, "Animating with Constraints and Controllers," presents the functions that are part of the Expression controller.

Table 34.9 describes the buttons found in the lower interface toolbars consisting of the Track Selection, Key Stats, and Navigation toolbars.

TABLE 34.9

Track Selection, Key Stats, and Navigation Toolbar Buttons

Status Bar Button	Name	Description
	Zoom Selected Object	Places current selection at the top of the hierarchy
	Edit Track Set	Opens a dialog box where selected sets of tracks can be edited
	Filter Selected Tracks	Toggle to show only the selected tracks in the Controller pane
	Filter Selected Objects	Toggle to show the tracks for the selected objects in the Controller pane
	Filter Animated Tracks	Toggle to show only the animated tracks in the Controller pane
	Show Selected Key Statistics	Displays the frame number and values next to each key
	Pan	Pans the view
	Zoom Horizontal Extents, Zoom Horizontal Extents Keys	Displays the entire horizontal track or keys

continued

TABLE 34.9	*(continued)*	
Status Bar Button	**Name**	**Description**
	Zoom Value Extents	Displays the entire vertical track
	Zoom, Zoom Time, Zoom Values	Zooms in and out of the view
	Zoom Region	Zooms within a region selected by dragging the mouse

NEW FEATURE   The Filter buttons at the bottom of the Track View interface for filtering selected tracks, selected objects, and animated tracks are new to 3ds Max 2008. Another new feature is that zooming in the Track View zooms about the mouse and not about the view center.

Working with Keys

Keys define the main animation points in an animation. Max interpolates all the positions and values between the key points to generate the animation. Using the Track View, you can edit these animation keys with precision. Keys can be edited in either layout, but are probably easiest to edit in the Dope Sheet layout with the Edit Keys button enabled.

CROSS-REF   Chapter 20, "Understanding Animation and Keyframe Basics," covers key creation in more detail.

In the Curve Editor, keys are shown as small squares positioned along the curve. In the Dope Sheet, keys are shown as colored lines that extend across the applicable tracks, as shown in Figure 34.5. The keys for the Position track are red, the Rotation track keys are green, the Scale track keys are blue, and the parameter tracks (all non-transformation keys) are gray. Parent tracks (such as an object's name) are colored gray. Selecting a parent key selects all its children keys. Any selected keys appear white. A track title that includes a key is highlighted yellow.

CAUTION   If the Key pane is not wide enough, then a key is shown as a thick, black line.

Selecting keys

Before you can move and edit keys, you need to be able to select them. Just like selecting keys on the Track Bar, you select keys by clicking them. Selected keys turn white. To select multiple keys, hold down the Ctrl key while clicking several keys, or drag an outline over several keys to select them. Click away from the keys to deselect all the selected keys.

With a key or multiple keys selected, you can lock the selection with the Lock Selection button. The spacebar is the keyboard shortcut for this button. With the selection locked, you cannot select any new keys.

TIP   If you want to access a specific parameter in the Track View, you can right-click the parameter and select the Show in Track View command from the pop-up menu, and the Track View loads with the parameter visible.

FIGURE 34.5

In the Dope Sheet, Position keys are red, Rotation keys are green, Scale keys are blue, and parameter keys are gray.

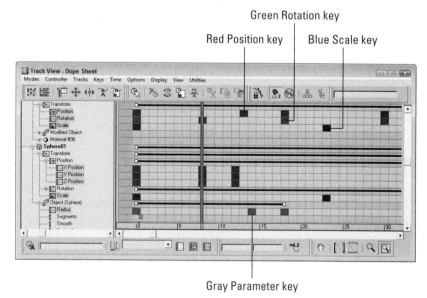

Green Rotation key

Red Position key   Blue Scale key

Gray Parameter key

Using soft selection

The Keys menu also includes a Use Soft Select option. This feature is similar to the soft selection found in the Modify panel when working on a subobject, except that it works with keys. The Keys ⇨ Use Soft Select menu command opens a simple toolbar where you can enable soft selection and set the Range and Falloff values.

When enabled, all keys within a specified range are also selected and moved to a lesser degree than the selected key. When enabled, the function curve is displayed with a gradient for the Curve Editor layout and as a gradient across the key markers in the Dope Sheet layout. This shows the range and falloff for the curve.

The Keys ⇨ Soft Select Settings menu opens a hidden toolbar that lets you enable and disable the soft selection feature with a single button labeled Soft. The Range value sets how many frames the soft selection covers.

Adding and deleting keys

You can add a key by clicking the Add Keys button (or pressing the A key) and clicking the location where the new key should appear. Each new key is set with the interpolated value between the existing keys.

To delete keys, select the keys, and click the Delete Keys button or press the Delete key on the keyboard. By selecting the track name and pressing the Delete key, you can delete all keys in a track.

Moving, sliding, and scaling keys

The Move Keys button (keyboard shortcut, M) lets you select and move a key to a new location. You can clone keys by holding down the Shift key while moving a key. Using the flyout buttons, you can select to restrict the movement horizontally or vertically. You can also move the selected key to the cursor's location with the Keys ⇨ Align to Cursor menu command.

The Slide Keys button lets you select a key and move all adjacent keys in unison to the left or right. If the selected key is moved to the right, all keys from that key to the end of the animation slide to the right. If the key is moved to the left, then all keys to the beginning of the animation slide to the left.

The Scale Keys button lets you move a group of keys closer together or farther apart. The scale center is the current frame. You can use the Shift key to clone keys while dragging.

If the Snap Frames button (keyboard shortcut, S) is enabled, then the selected key snaps to the nearest key as it is moved. This makes aligning keys to the same frame easy.

Editing keys

To edit the key parameters for any controller, click the Properties button; this opens the Key Info dialog box for most controllers. You can also access this dialog box by right-clicking a key and selecting Properties from the pop-up menu. These commands can also be used when multiple keys on the same or on different tracks are selected.

Using the Randomize Keys utility

The Randomize Keys utility lets you generate random time or key positions with an offset value. To access this utility, select the track of keys that you want to randomize and choose Utilities ⇨ Track View Utilities to open the Track View Utilities dialog box. From this dialog box, select Randomize Keys from the list of utilities and click OK; the Randomize Keys utility dialog box opens, as shown in Figure 34.6.

Use the Randomize Keys utility to create random key positions and values.

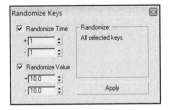

In this dialog box, you can specify positive and negative shift values for both Time and Value. Click the Apply button to apply the randomization process.

Using the Euler Filter utility

Euler rotations are easy to understand and use. They provide rotations about each of the three axis or can be thought of as yaw, pitch, and roll, but they have an inherit flaw — they are susceptible to Gimbal flipping and Gimbal lock. Gimbal flipping can occur when the rotation is directed straight up or straight down. This causes the object to instantly flip 180 degrees to continue its rotation. Gimbal lock can occur when two Euler rotation angles are aligned causing the object to lose a degree of freedom.

To counter these problems, Max has the ability to use Quaternions instead of Euler angles. Quaternions are vector-based instead of angle-based, so they aren't susceptible to the Gimbal flipping and lock problems, but many animators find Quaternions difficult to understand and use, so they stick to Euler rotations and are watchful for potential problems.

The Track View has a utility that can help if you're dealing with Euler rotations. The Euler Filter utility analyzes the current frame range and corrects any Gimbal flipping that it detects. Selecting this utility from the Track View Utilities dialog box opens a simple dialog box where you can set the range to analyze. You also have an option to Add Keys if Needed.

NEW FEATURE The Euler Filter utility is new to 3ds Max 2008.

Displaying keyable icons

If you're not careful, you could animate a track that you didn't mean to (especially with the Auto Key mode enabled). By marking a track as non-keyable or keyable, you can control which tracks can be animated. To do this, open the Curves toolbar and click the Show Keyable Icons button, or choose the Display ➪ Keyable Icons menu. This places a small red key icon to the left of each track that can be animated. You can then click the icon to change it to a non-keyable track. Figure 34.7 shows the Curve Editor with this feature enabled.

FIGURE 34.7

The Keyable Icons feature displays an icon next to all tracks that can be keyed.

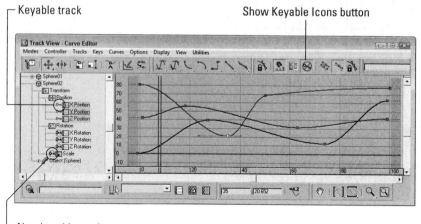

— Keyable track   Show Keyable Icons button

— Non-keyable track

Editing Time

In some cases, directly working with keys isn't what you want to do. For example, if you need to change the animation length from six seconds to five seconds, you want to work in the Dope Sheet's Edit Ranges mode. To switch to this mode, click the Edit Ranges button on the Keys toolbar. In this mode, the key ranges are displayed as black lines with square markers on either end, as shown in Figure 34.8.

FIGURE 34.8

FIGURE 34.8

Click the Edit Ranges button to display the key ranges in the Key pane.

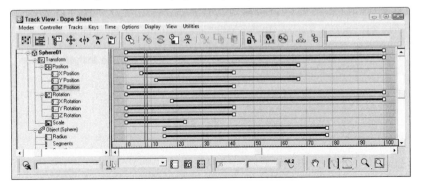

Selecting time and the Select Keys by Time utility

Before you can scale, cut, copy, or paste time, you need to select a track and then select a time block. To select a section of time, click the Select Time button and drag the mouse over the time block.

The Select Keys by Time utility lets you select all the keys within a given time block by entering the frame or time values. To use this utility, click the Track View Utilities button to open the Track View Utilities dialog box, and choose the Select Keys by Time utility from the list. Then in the Select Keys by Time dialog box, enter the Start and End values to complete the selection.

Deleting, cutting, copying, and pasting time

After you select a block of time, you can delete it by clicking the Delete Time button. Another way to delete a block of time is to use the Cut Time button, which removes the selected time block but places a copy of it on the clipboard for pasting. The Copy Time button also adds the time block to the clipboard for pasting, but it leaves the selected time in the track.

After you copy a time block to the clipboard, you can paste it to a different location within the Track View. The track where you paste it must be of the same type as the one from which you copied it.

All keys within the time block are also pasted, and you can select whether they are pasted relatively or absolutely. *Absolute* pasting adds keys with the exact values as the ones on the clipboard. *Relative* pasting adds the key value to the current initial value at the place where the key is pasted.

You can enable the Exclude Left End Point and Exclude Right End Point buttons on the Extras toolbar when pasting multiple sections next to each other. By excluding either end point, the time block loops seamlessly.

Reversing, inserting, and scaling time

The Reverse Time button flips the keys within the selected time block.

The Insert Time button lets you insert a section of time anywhere within the current track. To insert time, click and drag to specify the amount of time to insert; all keys beyond the current insertion point slide to accommodate the inserted time.

The Scale Time button scales the selected time block. This feature causes all keys to be pushed closer together or farther apart. The scaling takes place around the current frame.

Setting ranges

The Position Ranges button on the Ranges toolbar enables you to move ranges without moving keys. In this mode, you can move and scale a range bar independently of its keys, ignoring any keys that are out of range. For example, this button, when enabled, lets you remove the first several frames of an animation without moving the keys. The Recouple Ranges button can be used to line up the keys with the range again. The left end of the range aligns with the first key, and the right end aligns with the last key.

Editing Curves

When an object is moving through the scene, estimating the exact point where its position changes direction can sometimes be difficult. Function curves provide this information by presenting a controller's value as a function of time. The slope of the function curve shows the value's rate of change. Steep curves show quick movements. Shallow lines are slow-moving values. Each key is a vertex in the curve. Function curves are visible only in the Curve Editor and the Track Bar layout.

Function curves mode lets you edit and work with these curves for complete control over the animation parameters. Figure 34.9 shows the Position curves for a sphere that moves about the scene.

FIGURE 34.9

Function curves display keys as square markers along the curve.

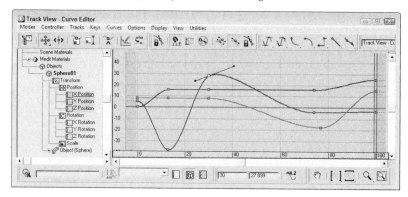

Inserting new keys and moving keys

Function curves with only two keys have slow in and out tangents, making the animation start slow, speed up, and then slow down. You can add more curvature to the line with the addition of another key. To add another key, click the Add Keys button, and then click the curve where you want to place the key.

TIP Keep the total number of keys to a minimum. More keys make editing more difficult.

If the curve contains multiple curves, such as a curve for the Position or RGB color values, then a point is added to each curve. The Move Keys button enables you to move individual keys by dragging them. It also includes flyouts for constraining the key movement to a horizontal or vertical direction.

Click the Scale Keys button to move the selected keys toward or away from the current time. The keys move only horizontally. Click the Scale Values button to move the selected keys toward or away from the zero value. The keys move only vertically.

Tutorial: Animating a monorail

As an example of working with function curves, you animate a monorail that moves around its track, changing speeds, and stopping for passengers.

To animate the monorail using function curves, follow these steps:

1. Open the Monorail.max file from the Chap 34 directory on the DVD.

   This file contains a simple monorail setup made from primitives.

2. Click the Play button, and watch the train move around the track.

   As a default, the Path Constraint's Percent track has a Linear controller that causes the train to move at a constant speed. To refine the animation, you need to change it.

3. Open the Track View–Curve Editor, and locate the train group's Percent track. (You can find this track under the Objects ⇨ Train ⇨ Transform ⇨ Path Constraint ⇨ Percent menu command.) Click the Assign Controller button to open the Assign Float Controller dialog box. Select the Bézier Float controller, and click OK.

 **NOTE** If the Objects track isn't visible, open the Filter Tracks dialog box and make sure the Objects option is enabled.

4. Click the Play button. The train starts slowly (represented by the flattish part of the curve), accelerates (the steeper part of the curve), and slows down again (another flattish part).

TIP When "reading" function curves, remember that a steep curve produces fast animation, shallow curves produce slow animation, horizontal produces no movement or value change, and a straight curve produces a constant animation.

5. We need the train to stop for passengers at the station, so click the Add Keys button (or right-click and choose Add Keys) and add a key somewhere around frame 115 when the train is near the dock.

6. Select the newly created key, and choose the Move Keys Horizontal button from the Move Keys flyout. Hold down the Shift key, and drag right to copy the key to frame 135.

   The curve is flat, so the train stops at the station.

7. To adjust the actual position where the train stops, choose the Move Keys Vertical button from the Move Keys flyout, select both keys, and move them up or down until the train's position at the station is correct.

   Because the default in and out tangent types cause the curve to flatten out at the keys, the train slows as it reaches the station and then starts out slow and picks up speed as it leaves the station. Anyone who has ever ridden on a train knows that stopping and starting are not always smooth operations. Next, you add a few more keys to make the train shudder to a stop and lurch as it starts out again.

8. Click the Add Keys button (or right-click and choose Add Keys), and add keys somewhere around frames 105, 109, 113, 142, and 150. Use Zoom Region to zoom in on the keys where the train pulls into the station to stop.

9. Change the Move Keys Vertical button back to Move Keys by selecting it from the flyout, and move the keys slightly up or down to send the train backward and forward along the path.

10. As you can see, a little movement goes a long way, so the keys need only to be offset a very small amount. Use the Zoom Values button from the Zoom flyout and the Pan button to help in making the small changes to the animation. Figure 34.10 shows the zoomed in view of this section of the curve.

Using Zoom Values to see the stopping position keys

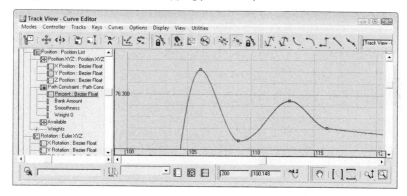

11. Repeat for the keys where the train leaves the station.

    The train also needs to slow down to look at one of the famous buildings in "Primitive Town," the Tubular "building" on the far side of the track.

12. Add a couple more keys somewhere around frames 18 and 50. Lower the second of the new keys until the curve is shallower but not horizontal. Again, adjust the train's position on the track (Percent along the path) by raising or lowering the two new keys.

13. Adjust the Out tangent handle of the very first key and the In tangent handle of the very last key to produce a smooth looping animation.

Figure 34.11 shows the final curve after you've completed the editing, and Figure 34.12 shows the monorail along its path.

The finished Percent curve for the train's position along the path

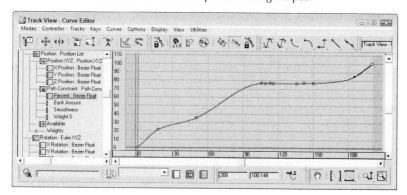

FIGURE 34.12

The monorail and "Primitive Town"

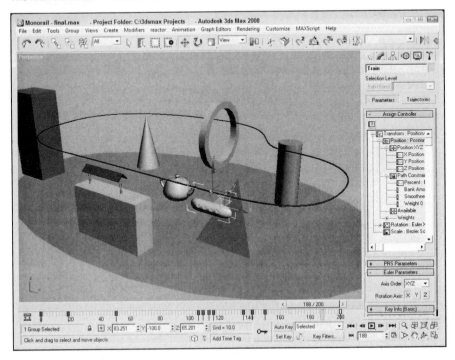

Drawing curves

If you know what the curve you want is supposed to look like, you can actually draw the curve in the Key pane with the Draw Curves button enabled. This mode adds a key for every change in the curve. You may want to use the Reduce Keys optimization after drawing a curve.

 **TIP** If you make a mistake, you can just draw over the top of the existing curve to make corrections.

Figure 34.13 shows a curve that was created with the Draw Curves feature.

Reducing keys

The Reduce Keys button enables you to optimize the number of keys used in an animation. Certain IK methods and the Dynamics utility calculate keys for every frame in the scene, which can increase your file size greatly. By optimizing with the Reduce Keys button, you can reduce the file size and complexity of your animations.

Clicking the Reduce Keys button opens the Reduce Keys dialog box. The threshold value determines how close to the actual position the solution must be to eliminate the key. Figure 34.14 shows the same curve created with the Draw Curves feature after it has been optimized with a Threshold value of 0.5 using the Reduce Keys button.

FIGURE 34.13

Drawing curves results in numerous keys.

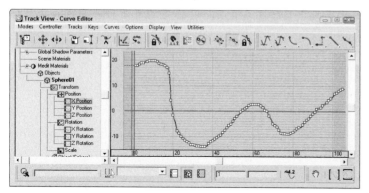

FIGURE 34.14

The Reduce Keys button optimizes the curve by reducing keys.

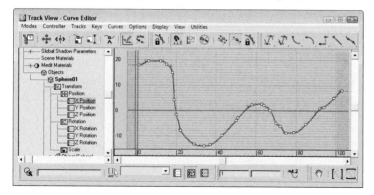

Working with tangents

Function curves for the Bézier controller have tangents associated with every key. To view and edit these tangents, click the Show All Tangents button. These tangents are lines that extend from the key point with a handle on each end. By moving these handles, you can alter the curvature of the curve around the key.

You can select the type of tangent from the Key Tangents toolbar. These can be different for the In and Out portion of the curve. You can also select them using the Key dialog box. The default tangent type for all new keys is set using the button to the left of the Key Filters button at the bottom of the Max interface. Using this button, you can quickly select from any of the available tangent types.

You open the Key dialog box, shown in Figure 34.15, by selecting a key and clicking the Properties button or by right-clicking the key. It lets you specify two different types of tangent points: Continuous and Discontinuous. *Continuous* tangents are points with two handles that are on the same line. The curvature for continuous tangents is always smooth. *Discontinuous* tangents have any angle between the two handle lines. These tangents form a sharp point.

 Holding down the Shift key while dragging a handle lets you drag the handle independently of the other handle.

FIGURE 34.15

The Key dialog box lets you change the key's Time, Value, or In and Out tangent curves.

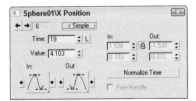

The Lock Tangents button lets you change the handles of several keys at the same time. If this button is disabled, adjusting a tangent handle affects only the key of that handle.

Tutorial: Animating a flowing river

The default auto-tangent types create a function curve that has ease-in and ease-out built into the curve. This causes the animation to start slowly, speed up, and then slow to a stop. While this may be a good starting point for many animations, it won't work for those that should have a constant speed. This example shows how to create a river with a material animated to a constant speed.

To create a flowing river, follow these steps:

1. Open the River.max file from the Chap 34 directory on the DVD.

   This file contains a river surface made from a loft. The V Offset for the River Water material's diffuse channel has been animated to simulate flowing water (yes, this river has a checkered past . . .).

2. Click the Play button.

   The river flow starts out slow, speeds up, and then slows to a stop.

3. Open the Track View–Curve Editor, and locate and select the V Offset track for the river's material. (You can find this track under the Objects ➪ Checkered River ➪ River Water ➪ Maps ➪ Diffuse Color: Map #2 (Checker) ➪ Coordinates ➪ V Offset menu command.)

4. You have two easy options for creating an animation with a constant speed. The first changes the entire controller type; the second changes the individual key's tangent types.

   Option 1: Right-click over the V Offset track, and choose Assign Controller or choose Assign from Controller on the menu bar to open the Assign Float Controller dialog box. Select Linear Float, and click OK.

   or

   Option 2: Select both keys by clicking one key, holding down the Ctrl button, and clicking the other, or by dragging an outline around both keys. Click the Set Tangents to Linear button.

   Whichever method you use, the line between the two keys is now straight.

5. Click the Play button.

   The river now flows at a constant speed.

6. To increase the speed of the flow, select Move Keys Vertical from the Move Keys button flyout, and select and move the end key higher in the graph.

   The river flows faster.

Figure 34.16 shows the river as it flows along.

FIGURE 34.16

The Checkered River flows evenly.

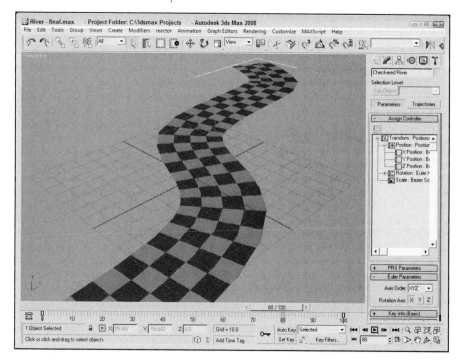

Applying out-of-range, ease, and multiplier curves

Out-of-range curves define what the curve should do when it is beyond the range of specified keys. For example, you could tell the curve to loop or repeat its previous range of keys. To apply these curves, select a track and click the Parameter Curve Out-of-Range Types button on the Curves toolbar (or select the Out-of-Range menu command from the Controller menu). This opens a dialog box, shown in Figure 34.17, where you can select from the available curve types.

NOTE You can also apply an out-of-range curve to a select range of frames using the Create Out-of-Range Keys utility. This utility is available via the Track View Utilities button.

FIGURE 34.17

The Param Curve Out-of-Range Types dialog box lets you select the type of out-of-range curve to use.

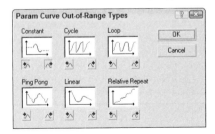

By clicking the buttons below the types, you can specify a curve for the beginning and end. This Out-of-Range dialog box includes six options:

- **Constant:** Holds the value constant for all out-of-range frames
- **Cycle:** Repeats the track values as soon as the range ends
- **Loop:** Repeats the range values, like the Cycle option, except that the beginning and end points are interpolated to provide a smooth transition
- **Ping Pong:** Repeats the range values in reverse order after the range end is reached
- **Linear:** Projects the range values in a linear manner when out of range
- **Relative Repeat:** Repeats the range values offset by the distance between the start and end values

You can apply ease curves (choose Curves ⇨ Apply Ease Curve, or press Ctrl+E) to smooth the timing of a function curve. You can apply multiplier curves (Curves ⇨ Apply Multiplier Curve, Ctrl+M) to alter the scaling of a function curve. You can use ease and multiplier curves to automatically smooth or scale an animation's motion. Each of these buttons adds a new track and function curve to the selected controller track.

Ease and Multiplier curves add another layer of control on top of the existing animation and allow you to edit the existing animation curves without changing the original animation keys. For example, if you have a standard walk cycle, you can use an ease curve to add a limp to the walk cycle or you can reuse the walk cycle for a taller character by adding a multiplier curve.

 Not all controllers can have an ease or multiplier curve applied.

You can delete these tracks and curves using the Delete Ease/Multiplier Curve button. You can also enable or disable these curves with the Enable Ease/Multiplier Curve Toggle button.

After you apply an ease or multiplier curve, you can assign the type of curve to use with the Ease Curve Out-of-Range Types button. This button opens the Ease Curve Out-of-Range Types dialog box, which includes the same curve types as the Out-of-Range curves, except for the addition of an Identity curve type.

 In the Ease Curve Out-of-Range Types dialog box is an Identity option that isn't present in the Parameter Curve Out-of-Range Types dialog box. The Identity option begins or ends the curve with a linear slope that produces a gradual, constant rate increase.

When editing ranges, you can make the range of a selected track smaller than the range of the whole animation. These tracks then go out of range at some point during the animation. The Ease/Multiplier Curve Out-of-Range Types buttons are used to tell the track how to handle its out-of-range time.

Tutorial: Animating a wind-up teapot

As an example of working with multiplier curves, we create a wind-up teapot that vibrates its way across a surface.

To animate the vibrations in the Track View, follow these steps:

1. Open the Wind-up teapot.max file from the Chap 34 directory on the DVD.

   This file contains a teapot with legs.

2. Click the Play button.

   The teapot's key winds up to about frame 40 and then runs down again as the teapot moves around a bit. To add the random movement and rotation to make the vibrations, you use Noise controllers and Multiplier curves to limit the noise.

3. Open the Track View–Curve Editor, and navigate down to the Wind-up Key's X Rotation track. Take a moment to observe the shape of the curve, shown in Figure 34.18.

   The key is "wound up" in short spurts and then runs down, slowing until it stops. The vibration, then, should start midway and then taper off as the key runs down.

FIGURE 34.18

The rotation of the Wind-up Key object

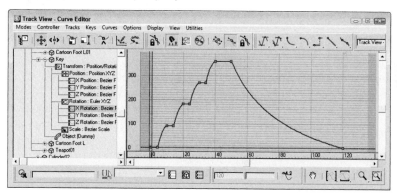

---

4. Click the teapot in the viewport to have the curves for its transforms selected and centered in the Track View.

   When adding the Noise controller, you should assign a List controller first to retain the ability to transform the object independently of the Noise.

> **NOTE**   Assigning controllers through the Animation menu automatically creates a List controller first.

5. Select the Position track, and click the C key to access the Assign Controller dialog box. Choose Position List. Under the Position track are now the X, Y, and Z Position tracks and an Available track. Select the Available track, access the Assign Controller dialog box again, and choose Noise Position. The default controller should remain the Position XYZ controller, so close the List Controller dialog box. Click Play.

   The teapot vibrates the entire animation. You add a multiplier curve to correct the situation.

6. Select the Noise Position track, and choose Curves ⇨ Apply-Multiplier Curve. Select the Multiplier curve track. Assign the first key a value of **0**. Change its Out tangent to Stepped so it holds its value until the next key. Click the Add Keys button, and add a key at frame 50 with a value of **1**. Move the last key to frame 120, and set a value of **0**. The Multiplier curve should now look like the curve in Figure 34.19. Select the Noise Position track.

The noise curve now conforms to the multiplier track.

FIGURE 34.19

The Multiplier curve keeps the Noise track in check.

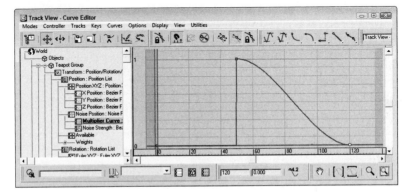

7. With the Noise Position track still selected, right-click and choose Properties. In the Noise Position dialog box, set the X and Y Strength to **30**, set the Z strength to **20**, and check the >0 check box to keep the teapot from going through the floor. Close the dialog box, and click Play.

The animation is much better. Next, you add some noise to the Rotation track.

8. Select the Rotation track, right-click, and choose Assign controller or click the C key to bring up the Assign Controller dialog box. Select Rotation List, and click OK. Select the Available track, access the Assign Controller dialog box again, and choose Noise Rotation.

Click Play. Again, the noise is out of control.

9. This time, select the Noise Strength track and add a multiplier curve.

You already have a perfectly good multiplier curve, so you can instance it into the new track.

10. Select the position multiplier track, right-click, and choose Copy. Now select the rotation Noise Strength multiplier track, right-click, and choose Paste. Choose Instance, and close the dialog box.

11. Click the Play button, and watch the Teapot wind up and then vibrate itself along until it winds down.

Figure 34.20 shows the teapot as it dances about, compliments of a controlled noise controller.

FIGURE 34.20

The wind-up teapot moves about the scene.

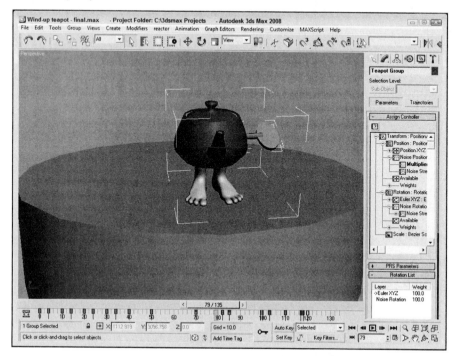

Filtering Tracks and Creating Track Sets

With all the information included in the Track View, finding the exact tracks you need can be difficult. The Filters button on the Keys toolbar (or on the Controllers toolbar) can help. Clicking this button opens the Filters dialog box, shown in Figure 34.21.

 Right-clicking the Filters button reveals a quick list of filter items.

Using the Filters dialog box

Using this dialog box, you can limit the number of tracks that are displayed in the Track View. The Show section contains many display options. The Hide by Controller Type pane lists all the available controllers. Any controller types selected from this list do not show up in the Track View. You can also elect to not display objects by making selections from the check boxes in the Hide By Category section.

FIGURE 34.21

The Filters dialog box lets you focus on the specific tracks.

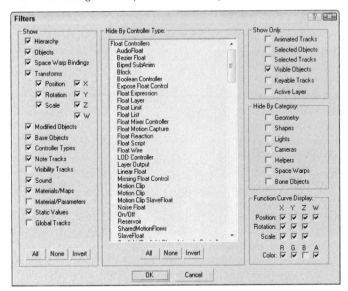

The Show Only group includes options for displaying only the Animated Tracks, Selected Objects, Selected Tracks, Visible Objects, Keyable Tracks, or any combination of these. For example, if you wanted to see the animation track for a selected object, select the Animated Tracks option and click the OK button; then open the Filters dialog box again, choose Selected Objects, and click OK.

You can also specify whether the function curve display includes the Position, Rotation, and Scale components for each axis or the RGB color components.

Creating a Track Set

A selection of tracks can be saved into a track set by clicking the Edit Track Set button located at the bottom of the Track View interface. This button opens the Track Sets Editor, shown in Figure 34.22. Clicking the Create a New Track Set button in the Track Sets Editor creates a new track set containing all the currently selected tracks and lists it in the editor window. Selected tracks can be added, removed, and selected using the other editor buttons.

After a track set is created, its tracks can be instantly selected by choosing the track set's name from the drop-down list located next to the Edit Track Set button at the bottom of the Track View window.

FIGURE 34.22

The Track Sets Editor dialog box lets you name track selections for easy recall.

Add the Track View selection
to the current Track Set

Remove the Track View selection
from the current Track Set

Delete Track
Sets or Tracks

Highlight Tracks selected
in the Track View

Create a
New Track Set

Select the current Track or
Track Set in the Track View

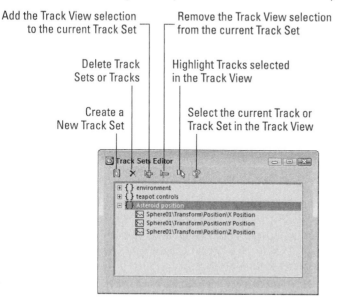

Working with Controllers

Controllers offer an alternative to positioning keys manually. Each controller can automatically control a key's position or a parameter's value. The Controller toolbar includes several buttons for working with controllers. The Copy Controller and Paste Controller buttons let you move existing controllers between different tracks, and the Assign Controller button lets you add a new controller to a track.

CROSS-REF   Chapter 21, "Animating with Constraints and Controllers," covers all the various controllers used to automate animated sequences.

Although the buttons are labeled Copy Controller and Paste Controller, they can be used to copy different tracks. Tracks can be copied and pasted only if they are of the same type. You can copy only one track at a time, but that single controller can be pasted to multiple tracks. A pasted track can be a copy or an instance, and you have the option to replace all instances. For example, if you have several objects that move together, using the Replace All Instances option when modifying the track for one object modifies the tracks for all objects that share the same motion.

All instanced copies of a track change when any instance of that track is modified. To break the linking between instances, you can use the Make Controller Unique button.

Clicking the Assign Controller button opens the Assign Controller dialog box, where you can select the controller to apply. If the controller types are similar, the keys are maintained, but a completely different controller replaces any existing keys in the track.

Using visibility tracks

When an object track is selected, you can add a visibility track using the Add Visibility Track button or the Object Properties dialog box. This track enables you to make the object visible or invisible. The selected track is automatically assigned the Bézier controller, but you can change it to an On/Off controller if you want that type of control. You can use function curves mode to edit the visibility track.

Adding Note Tracks

You can add note tracks to any track and use them to attach information about the track. The Add Note Track button is used to add a note track, which is marked with a yellow triangle and cannot be animated.

After you've added a note track in the Controller pane, use the Add Keys button to position a note key in the Key pane by clicking in the note track. This adds a small note icon. Right-clicking the note icon opens the Notes dialog box, where you can enter the notes, as shown in Figure 34.23. Each note track can include several note keys.

The Notes dialog box includes arrow controls that you can use to move between the various notes. The field to the right of the arrows displays the current note key number. The Time value displays the frame where a selected note is located, and the Lock Key option locks the note to the frame so it can't be moved or scaled.

You can use the Tracks ➪ Note Track ➪ Remove menu command to delete a selected note track.

FIGURE 34.23

_____

The Notes dialog box lets you enter notes and position them next to keys.

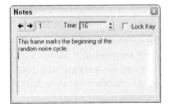

Tutorial: Animating a hazard light

As an example of working with the Track View, you animate a flashing hazard light in this tutorial.

To animate a flashing hazard light using function curves, follow these steps:

1. Open the Hazard.max file from the Chap 34 directory on the DVD.

   This file contains a hazard barrier with a light.

2. Select Omni01, open the Track View–Curve Editor, and locate the omni light's Multiplier track. (You can find this track under the Objects ➪ Omni01 ➪ Object(Omni Light) ➪ Multiplier menu command.) Click the Add Keys button (or press the A key), and create a key on the dotted line (its current multiplier value) at frame 0 and at frame 15. Set the end key to a value of **1.2**.

3. Select the first key and set its position to 0 by moving the key down or by typing **0** in the value display field. Click the Zoom Value Extends button to better see the shape of the curve. Click the Play button.

The light comes on slowly. It should be either on or off, so you need to change the tangent types to Stepped.

4. Select both keys, and click the Set Tangents to Stepped button. Click the Play button.

   The light turns on at frame 15.

5. Select the first key, and choose the Move Keys Horizontal button from the Move Keys flyout. Hold down the Shift key, and drag right to copy the key at frame 30.

   The light now turns off at frame 30. You can continue to make the rest of the keys in that fashion, but using the Parameter Out of Range feature to complete the animation is easier.

6. With the Multiplier curve selected, click the Parameter Curves Out-of-Range Types button or Choose Out-of-Range Types from the Controller menu item. The Out-of-Range Types dialog box appears. Choose Cycle, and click OK.

   Figure 34.24 shows the Stepped tangents.

FIGURE 34.24

The curve with Stepped in and out tangents and a Cycle Parameter Out-of-Range type

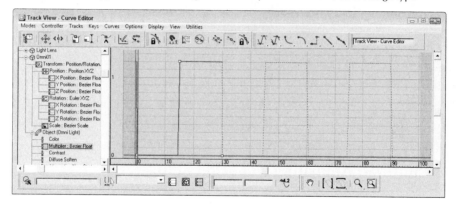

7. Click Play.

   The light flashes off and on. The animation would be more convincing if the light lens object appeared to turn off and on as well. Next, you animate the self-illumination of the lens material.

8. With the omni light's multiplier track still selected, right-click over the track in the controller pane and choose Copy. Locate and select the Light Lens material's Self-Illumination track. (You can find this track under the Objects ⇨ Light Lens ⇨ Lens ⇨ Shader Basic Parameters ⇨ Self-Illumination menu command.) Right-click, choose Paste, and paste as Copy.

9. Because the Self-Illumination should top out at 100 percent, not 120 percent, select the second key and change its value to **100**. Click the Play button.

   The Omni light and lens flash off and on together.

Figure 34.25 shows the hazard light as it repeatedly blinks on and off.

FIGURE 34.25

The hazard light flashing on

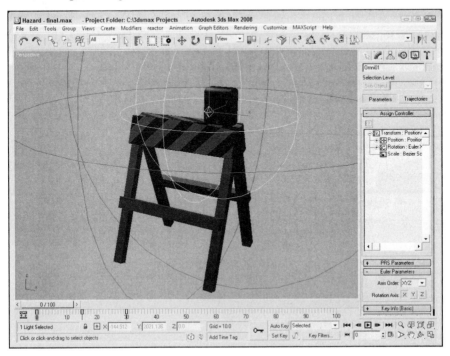

Tutorial: Animating a checkers move

As an example of working with function curves, we animate a checkers move in this tutorial. It is often easiest to block in the animation using key-framing and then to refine the animation in the Track View.

To animate a white checker making its moves, follow these steps:

1. Open the Checkers.max file from the Chap 34 directory on the DVD.

    This file contains a simple checkerboard with one white piece and three red pieces.

    The white checker is on the wrong colored square to start, so first you move it into place and then to each successive position.

2. Turn on Auto Key. Move the time slider to frame 25, and move the white checker to the square with the "1" text object (visible in the Top viewport). Move the time slider to 50, and move the white piece to the "2" position. At frame 75, move it to the "3" position, and at 100, move it to the "4" position. Turn off Auto Key.

3. Right-click over the white piece, and choose Curve Editor to open the Track View–Curve Editor. The white piece's X, Y, and Z Position tracks should be highlighted, and you should be able to see the function curves in the graph editor. If not, find them by choosing Objects ➪ White Piece ➪ Transform ➪ Position ➪ X, Y and Z Position.

    Keeping in mind that RGB (red, green, blue) = XYZ, you can see the white checker's movement across the board. From 0 to 25, it moves only in the X direction. From 25 to 100, it moves diagonally across the board as indicated by the slope of both the X and Y curves. Note that when the object goes back the other way in the X direction at frame 75, the curve goes in the opposite direction, as shown in Figure 34.26.

The blocked-in animation curves for the white piece

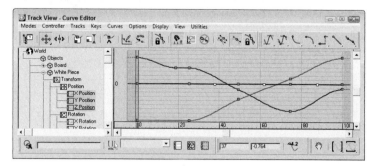

4. Click the Play button.

The white piece slides sloppily around the board. Next, you create keys to make it hop over the red pieces.

5. Click the Add Keys button, or select Add Keys from the right-click menu. Click to add keys on the Z-position track between the second, third, fourth, and fifth keys.

6. Select Move Keys Vertical from the Move Keys flyout, and select the three new keys. Move them up about 50 units, as shown in Figure 34.27.

The new keys are moved up.

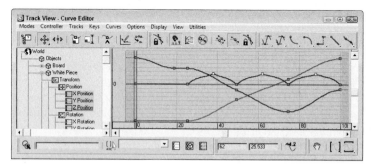

The white piece hops over the red pieces, but the motion is not correct. The In and Out tangents should be fast so the piece does not spend much time on the board.

7. Hold the Shift key down, and move the handles on the keys to make them discontinuous tangent types, as shown in Figure 34.28.

FIGURE 34.28

The In and Out tangents corrected for the new keys

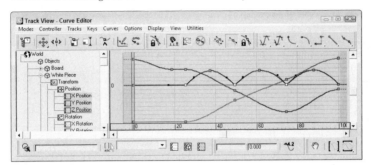

The hopping looks better, but the sliding motion would look better with a slight pause before hopping over the first red piece.

8. Select Move Keys Horizontal from the Move Keys flyout, and choose the second X-position track key. Hold down the Shift key, and move the key a few frames to the left to make a copy of the original key. Click the play button.

The red pieces should disappear as the white piece hops over them.

9. Scroll down the Controller pane on the left, and select the three red pieces. Under Tracks on the menu bar, choose Visibility ➪ Add.

A visibility track has been added to each of the red pieces, directly below the root name.

With visibility, a value of 0 is invisible, and a value of 1 is visible. You could change the tangent types to Stepped to turn the red pieces invisible from one frame to the next, but changing the entire track to an On/Off controller helps to visualize what is happening.

10. Select the visibility track for Red Piece 01. Right-click, and choose Assign Controller. Choose On/Off.

Nothing seems to have happened. The Off/On controller is best used in Dope Sheet mode.

11. Choose Dope Sheet from the Modes menu. The On/Off controller track is represented with a blue bar. Blue indicates "on" or visible. Click the Add Keys button, and click to add a key at frame 50. The blue bar stops at the key at frame 50. Click Play.

The first red piece disappears at frame 50. You can copy and paste tracks to save yourself a bit of work.

12. Select Red Piece 01's visibility track in the Controller pane. Right-click, and choose Copy. Select the visibility tracks for Red Piece 02 and Red Piece 03 (hold down the Ctrl key to add to the selection). Right-click, and choose Paste.

Paste as a Copy because the other pieces should disappear at different times.

13. Move Red Piece 02's key to 75 and Red Piece 03's key to 100. Click Play.

Things are looking pretty good, but the animation would look better if the whole thing were faster.

14. Click the Edit Ranges button and the Modify Subtree button. A World track bar appears at the top of the Key Pane. Click and drag the rightmost end of the range bar to frame 75 to scale all the tracks at one time. Click Play.

The animation is quite respectable as the white piece slides into the correct square and then hops over and captures the three red pieces.

Figure 34.29 shows the checkerboard.

FIGURE 34.29

The checker pieces on the checkerboard

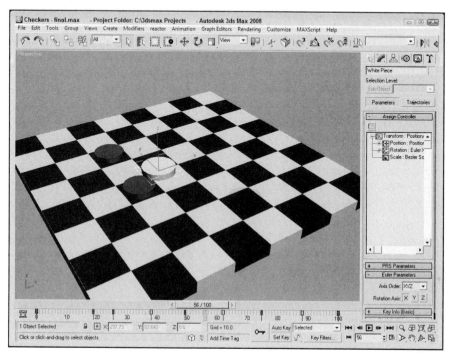

Synchronizing to a Sound Track

One of the default tracks for any scene is the sound track. Included in the Sound hierarchy is the metronome track. You can also set up a sound file using the Sound Options dialog box, shown in Figure 34.30. You can open this dialog box by right-clicking the Metronome track and selecting Properties from the pop-up menu.

You can make the sound track appear as a waveform curve under the Track Bar. This helps as you try to synchronize the sound to the movements in the viewports. To see this sound track, right-click the Track Bar and choose Configure ➪ Show Sound Track from the pop-up menu.

Using the Sound Options dialog box

You can use the Audio section of the Sound Options dialog box to load a sound or remove an existing sound. The Active option causes the sound file to play when the animation is played. The Choose Sound button can load AVI, WAV, and FLC file types. The dialog box also includes buttons to Remove Sound and Reload Sound.

FIGURE 34.30

The Sound Options dialog box lets you select a sound to play during the animation.

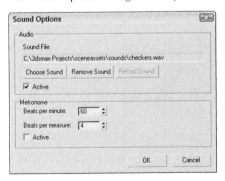

You can also set up a regular metronome beat with two tones. For a metronome, you can specify the beats per minute and the beats per measure. The first option sets how often the beats occur, and the second option determines how often a different tone is played. This dialog box also contains an Active option for turning the metronome on and off.

Tutorial: Adding sound to an animation

As an example of adding sound to an animation, we work with a hyper pogo stick and synchronize its animation to a sound clip.

To synchronize an animation to a sound clip, follow these steps:

1. Open the Hyper pogo stick with sound.max file from the Chap 34 directory on the DVD.

2. In the Track View–Dope Sheet window, right-click one of the sound tracks and select Properties from the pop-up menu to open the Sound Options dialog box. In this dialog box, click the Choose Sound button. Then locate the boing.wav file from the Chap 34 directory on the DVD, and click OK. Make sure the Active option is selected.

   The sound file appears as a waveform in the Track View, as shown in Figure 34.31.

FIGURE 34.31

Sounds loaded into the sound track appear as waveforms.

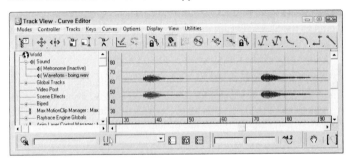

 The Open Sound dialog box includes a play button that lets you play the sound before loading it.

Although it can't be edited in Max, the sound file can be shifted left or right to change its starting point.

3. Click the Move Keys button (or press the M key), and move the pogo stick position keys to line up with the waveforms in the sound track.

4. Click the Play Animation button, and the sound file plays with the animation.

Figure 34.32 shows the sound track under the Track Bar for this example.

FIGURE 34.32

To help synchronize sound, the audio track can be made visible under the Track Bar.

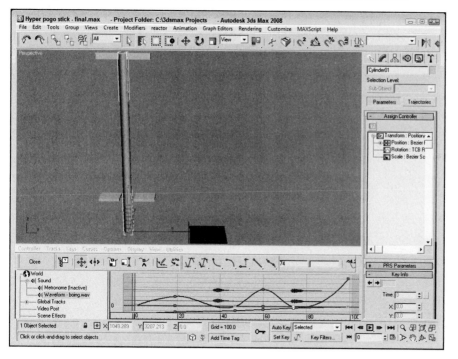

Summary

Using the Track View, you have access to all the keys, parameters, and objects in a scene in one convenient location. Different features are available in the different layouts. In this chapter, you accomplished the following:

- Learned the Track View interface elements
- Learned about the different Track View layouts, including the Curve Editor, Dope Sheet, and Track Bar

- Discovered how to work with keys, times, and ranges
- Controlled and adjusted function curves
- Selected specific tracks using the Filter dialog box
- Assigned controllers
- Explored the different out-of-range types
- Added notes to a track
- Synchronized animation to a sound track

The next chapter shows how the Motion Mixer can be used to create new animation sequences by combining existing animations.

Chapter 35

Using Animation Layers and the Motion Mixer

J ust as layers can be used to organize a scene by placing unique objects on different layers, you also can separate the various animation motions into different layers. This gives you great control over how motions are organized.

The animation layers feature isn't new to Max, but it was previously available only for Biped animations. All animation sequences can now take advantage of layers.

If you've worked to animate a biped or some other Max object and are pleased with the result, you can save the animation clip and reuse it. Several animation clips can be mixed together to create an entirely new animation sequence.

The Motion Mixer lets you add several different animations to the interface comprising both biped and non-biped objects. The animations then can be blended and transitioned between the loaded animation clips. You also can modify clips as needed.

Now that you've learned how to animate characters using a variety of techniques from Biped's Footstep and Freeform modes to custom bone systems with IK solutions, it's time for you to explore Max's set of features that enable you to reuse animation clips between characters. This technique is called Retargeting, which involves scaling the animation keys so that a single character animation can be reused on other characters that are different in size and width.

Using the Animation Layers Toolbar

Behind the scenes, animation layers add several new controller tracks to objects that are visible in the Motion panel and in the Track View interface, but the front end is accessible through a simple toolbar. The Animation Layers toolbar, shown in Figure 35.1, is similar in many ways to the Layers toolbar.

CROSS-REF The Layers toolbar is covered in Chapter 6, "Selecting Objects, Setting Object Properties, and Using Layers and the Scene Explorer."

FIGURE 35.1

The Animation Layers toolbar includes icons for defining and merging layers.

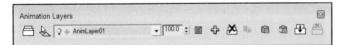

You can open the Animation Layers toolbar by right-clicking the main toolbar away from the buttons and selecting Animation Layers from the pop-up menu. Each of the toolbar buttons is labeled and explained in Table 35.1.

TABLE 35.1

Animation Layers Toolbar Controls

Toolbar Button	Name	Description
	Enable Animation Layers	Turns the animation layers system on.
	Select Active Layer Objects	Selects the objects in the viewport that are on the active animation layer.
AnimLayer01	Layer Selection drop-down list	Presents a selection list of all the available animation layers.
100.0	Animation Layer Weight	Displays the weight value for the current animation layer.
	Animation Layer Properties	Opens the Animation Layer Properties dialog box.
	Add Animation Layer	Adds another animation layer.
	Delete Animation Layer	Deletes the current animation layer.
	Copy Animation Layer	Copies the current animation layer.
	Paste Active Animation Layer	Pastes the keys from the current animation layer to the selected object.
	Paste New Layer	Pastes the copied animation layer keys to a new layer.
	Collapse Animation Layer	Combines and deletes the current animation layer with the layer above it.
	Disable Animation Layer	Turns the current animation layer off.

When a new animation layer is created using the Add Animation Layer button, a new entry is added to the Animation Layer Selection List. This list displays the default name of the animation layer as AnimLayer with a number. The original layer is named Base Layer. To the left of the animation layer name is a small light bulb icon that indicates whether the animation layer is enabled or disabled.

 You cannot rename animation layer names.

Each layer can have a weight assigned to it. These weight values control how much influence the current animation layer has. The weight value also can be animated. For example, if a car is animated moving forward 100 meters over 50 frames, then weighting the animation layer to 30 causes the car to move forward only 30 meters over the 50 frames.

Working with Animation Layers

Animation layers are good for organizing motions into sets that can be easily turned on and off, but you also can use them to blend between motions to create an entirely new set of motions.

NOTE Animations can be divided into primary motions, which are the major motions, and secondary motions, which are derivative motions that depend on the animation of other parts. Using animation layers, you can separate primary motions, like foot placement, from secondary motions, like a swinging arm, and adjust them independently.

Enabling animation layers

The first button on the Animation Layers toolbar is the Enable Animation Layers button. Clicking this button opens a dialog box, shown in Figure 35.2, where you can filter the type of keys to include in the animation layer.

FIGURE 35.2

The Enable Animation Layers dialog box lets you limit which type of keys are included.

The base animation layer can be disabled using the Disable Animation Layer button. This button is available only when you collapse all its layers. This changes the light bulb icon on the Selection list to indicate that the layer is disabled.

NOTE If Animation Layers are enabled for an object whose animation is loaded into the Motion Mixer, then a dialog box automatically appears asking if you want to create a new map file for the animation.

NEW FEATURE The ability to automatically create a new map file if Animation Layers are enabled is new to 3ds Max 2008.

Setting animation layers properties

The button to the right of the Weight value opens the Layer Properties dialog box, shown in Figure 35.3. This dialog box lets you specify the type of controller to which the layers are collapsed. The options include Bézier (for Position and Scale tracks) or Euler (for Rotation tracks), Linear or TCB, and Default. You also can specify a range to collapse.

FIGURE 35.3

The Layers Properties dialog box lets you set the controller type to collapse to.

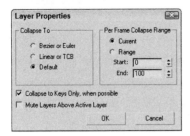

Collapsing animation layers

By collapsing layers, you combine the animation keys on each layer into a single set of keys that includes all the various motions. Be careful when collapsing; the results can be unexpected. Collapsing animation layers is accomplished with the Collapse Animation Layers button.

Tutorial: Using animation layers for a plane takeoff

Have you ever been to a small airport and watched the commuter planes take off? Sometimes they leave the ground and then return to the ground and then finally take off. It's like they need to get a good bounce to overcome gravity. This is a good example of when animation layers come in handy.

To animate a jet's takeoff using animation layers, follow these steps:

1. Open the Mig take-off.max file from the Chap 35 directory on the DVD.

   This file includes a detailed Mig-29 jet model created by Viewpoint Datalabs.

2. With the jet selected, open the Animation Layers toolbar by right-clicking the main toolbar away from the buttons and choosing Animation Layers from the pop-up menu.

3. Click the Enable Animation Layers button, and enable the Position track. This adds a Base Layer to the Selection list.

4. Click the Auto Key, drag the Time Slider to frame 100, and move the jet to the far end of the runway. Then disable the Auto Key button. Set the Weight value for this layer to 0.

5. In the Animation Layer toolbar, click the Add Animation Layer button to add a new layer. In the Create New Animation Layer dialog box that appears, select the Duplicate the Active Controller Type option and click OK. A new layer labeled AnimLayer01 is added to the Selection list.

6. Click the Auto Key button again, drag the Time Slider to frame 100, and move the jet upward away from the runway. Then disable the Auto Key button again.

7. Select the Base Layer from the Selection list in the Animation Layers toolbar, and set its Weight value to 100. Then drag the Time Slider, and notice that the jet moves up at an angle over the 100 frames.

8. Click the Auto Key button again, drag the Time Slider to frame 0, and set the Weight value for AnimLayer01 to 0; drag the Time Slider to frame 30, and set the Weight to 60; drag the Time Slider to frame 50, and set the Weight back to 0; and finally drag the Time Slider to frame 80, and set the Weight to 80. Then disable the Auto Key button again.

Dragging the Time Slider shows the jet bounce down the runway before taking off, as shown in Figure 35.4.

FIGURE 35.4

The Animation Layers feature provides a single parameter for controlling the plane's height.

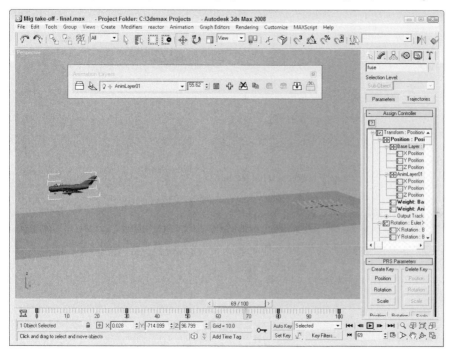

Saving Animation Files

Before an animation sequence can be mixed in the Motion Mixer, it must be saved. The Motion Mixer easily can load any existing animation sequence in the current opened Max file, but saving a sequence to the local hard disk makes it accessible for other Max scenes. The Motion Mixer can be accessed using the Graph Editors ⇨ Motion Mixer menu command.

Saving biped animations

Biped animations are saved to the hard disk as .bip files using the Save File button found in the Biped rollout. This opens a Save As dialog box, shown in Figure 35.5. For the animation sequence, you can select the range of frames to save. For .bip files, you also can save additional Max objects and controllers with the file, such as a target object that the head follows.

NOTE The Save File button in the Biped rollout may be used to save .fig, .bip, and .stp files, but only .bip files save the motion information that can be loaded into the Motion Mixer. fig files save only the structure and position of the biped, and .stp files save footstep timing and location data, but no keys.

CROSS-REF Bipeds are skeleton rigs that have their own unique set of animation controls specific to animating human characters. More on using bipeds is covered in Chapter 42,"Creating and Animating Bipeds and Crowds."

FIGURE 35.5

The Biped Save As dialog box is used to save biped animations.

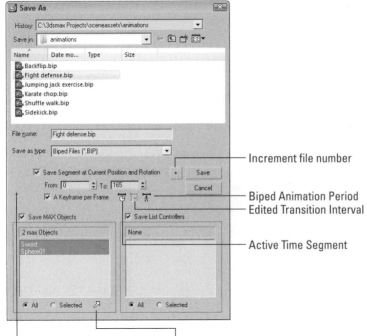

Expand/Contract dialog box   Open Select dialog box

Saving general animations

In addition to biped animation sequences, the animation of other objects also can be saved using the XML Animation File (XAF) format. To save the animation for the selected object, open the Save XML Animation File dialog box, shown in Figure 35.6, using the File ➪ Save Animation.

For general animations, you can select to include tracks, constraints, only keyable tracks, and a specific range. The User Data fields let you enter notes or specific data used by plug-ins about the animation sequence.

Loading Animation Sequences

The Load XML Animation File dialog box, shown in Figure 35.7, is opened using the File ➪ Load Animation menu command. It looks like a normal file dialog box, but it has some additional features.

FIGURE 35.6

The Save XML Animation File dialog box is used to save animations of the selected object.

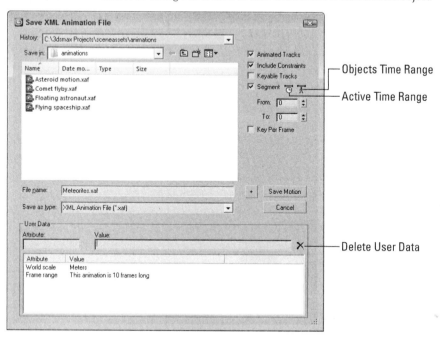

Within the Character Assembly rollout for Character objects is a button to Save Animation. **CAUTION** This button saves character animations using the ANM file format, which cannot be opened using the File ➪ Load Animation menu command.

The Relative and Absolute options determine whether the animation is loaded relative to the object's current location or whether it is loaded into the frames where it was saved. The Replace and Insert options let the new keys overwrite the existing ones or move them out to insert the loaded keys. You can even select the frame where the new keys are loaded. The Load Motion button lets you load an existing mapping file named the same as the animation file if one exists or create a new one.

NOTE The File ➪ Load Animation and File ➪ Save Animation menu commands are active only when an object is selected.

Mapping files are listed in the drop-down list for easy selection, or you can use the Get Mapping button to select a different mapping file to load. Mapping files are saved with the .XMM file extension. The Edit Mapping button in the Load Animation dialog box opens the Map Animation dialog box, where you can define the mapping between objects in the two scenes.

Mapping animated objects

Mapping files define a relationship between objects in the saved animation file and objects in the current Max file. These relationships allow the animation keys to be transferred from one scene object to another.

FIGURE 35.7

The Load XML Animation File dialog box lets you load animation files from one scene and apply them to another.

Using the Map Animation dialog box

The Map Animation dialog box, shown in Figure 35.8, includes several rollouts. The Motion Mapping Parameters rollout includes options for allowing Max to make its best guess at mapping objects. If the scenes are fairly similar, then this option may be just the ticket. The Exact Names, Closest Names, and Hierarchy buttons allow Max to attempt the mapping on its own. This works especially well on bipeds that use the default naming conventions. You also can select to have Max look at the various controllers that are used when trying to match up objects.

The Filters section lets you filter out the tracks that you don't want to see. The Lock button applies the selected filters to both the Current and Incoming lists.

The Map Track to Track rollout consists of three lists. The left list contains all the tracks for the current scene objects, the middle list contains all the mapped tracks, and the right list contains all the tracks from the incoming animation file. Select tracks and click the button with the left-pointing arrow to add tracks to the Mapped list; click the other arrow button to remove them.

At the bottom of the Map Animation dialog box are buttons for saving the current mapping file.

Retargeting animations

The Retargeting rollout, shown in Figure 35.9, lets you specify how the scale changes between certain mapped objects. Scale values can be entered for the mapped nodes as Absolute or Derived Scale values for each axis. Derived scale values can be obtained from a specific origin object. After the settings are right, the Set button applies the scaling to the selected mapping.

FIGURE 35.8

The Map Animation dialog box lets you map objects to receive animation.

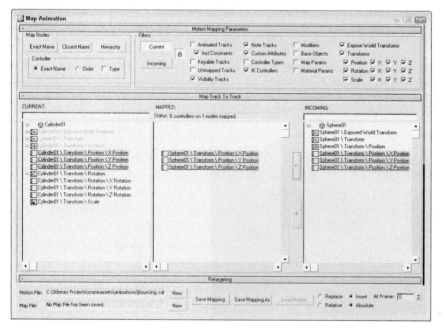

FIGURE 35.9

Use the Retargeting rollout to specify how the scale changes between mapped objects.

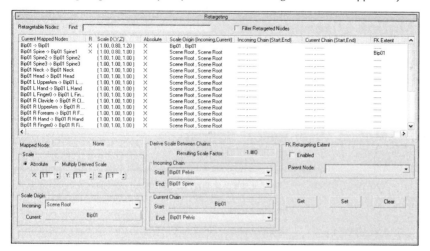

Using the Motion Mixer

The Motion Mixer is a completely separate interface, shown in Figure 35.10. This interface is accessed using the Graph Editors ⇨ Motion Mixer menu command. The same interface also is opened using the Mixer button found in the Biped Apps rollout of the Motion panel when a biped is selected. If the Mixer button is used, then the Motion Mixer opens with the biped already added as a track to the mixer interface.

The Motion Mixer interface shows each loaded animation on a separate track.

Transition track

Layer track

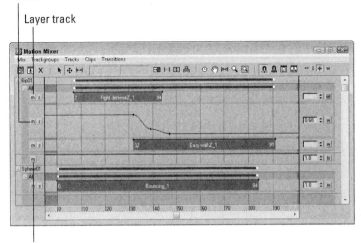

Balance track

Learning the Motion Mixer interface

Along the top edge of the Motion Mixer interface are several menus and a row of toolbar buttons. Many of these buttons perform the same commands that are found in the menus. You also can access these commands using the right-click pop-up menus. The toolbar buttons are described in Table 35.2.

Motion Mixer Toolbar Buttons

Toolbar Button	Name	Description
	Add Max Objects	Opens a select dialog box listing all the Max objects in the current scene. Selected objects are added as tracks to the Motion Mixer.
	Add Bipeds	Opens a select dialog box listing all the biped objects in the current scene. Selected objects are added as tracks to the Motion Mixer.
X	Delete	Deletes the selected track from the interface.

Toolbar Button	Name	Description
	Select	Enables select mode for selecting tracks. Multiple tracks can be selected at once.
	Move Clips	Allows the movement of tracks and clips within tracks. Holding down the Shift key clones the selection.
	Slide Clips	Allows the horizontal movement of a clip within its own track.
Offset: 0 Frame: 44	Offset and Frame fields	Displays the number of frames from its original position that a clip has moved and the current frame number.
	Trim Clips	Displays the original clip as a gray bar under the actual clipped track. Clips are trimmed by dragging on either end of a clip.
	Editable Time Warps	Displays any Time Warp markers added to a clip.
	Draggable Tracks	Enables clips to be dragged between tracks.
	Lock Transitions	Locks the transition track so it doesn't change when the clips are edited.
	Set Range	Sets the range for the selected track to equal the entire range.
	Pan	Pans within the interface.
	Zoom Extents	Zooms to show the full range of all tracks.
	Zoom	Zooms in on the tracks.
	Zoom Region	Zooms in on the region selected by dragging a rectangular area with the cursor.
	Snap Frames	Causes all clips to snap to the nearest frame.
	Snap Clips	Causes clips on the same track to be joined end to end when moved.
	Preferences	Opens the Motion Mixer preferences dialog box.
	Reservoir	Opens the Reservoir dialog box that lists available animation clips.
	Horizontal, Vertical, Horizontal Vertical	Makes the horizontal and vertical editing of weight possible.
	Weight Mode	Makes the editing of Weight curves accessible.

To the left of the interface, each track is listed under its controlling object or biped name. The small *m* button is used to mute a track, which removes its effect from the interface and the small *s* button is the solo button, which displays only the animation clip on that track. The right end of the interface shows the weight value for each track. The small *w* button lets you edit the weight values for the selected track, and the small *b* button lets you edit the weight of the balance track.

855

Adding layer and transition tracks

If the Mixer button in the Biped Apps rollout is used to open the Motion Mixer, then the selected biped is automatically added as a track to the mixer interface. After the Motion Mixer is open, additional biped tracks may be added using the Add Biped button, which opens a dialog box listing the available bipeds in the scene.

NEW FEATURE A group of clips can be named for easy selection in the main toolbar. This feature is new to 3ds Max 2008.

Biped tracks that are added to the Motion Mixer include an additional balance track that isn't available for non-biped tracks.

TIP To see the mixed motion applied to the selected biped, click the Mixer Mode button in the Biped rollout.

Non-biped tracks are added using the Add Max Objects button on the toolbar. This button also opens a dialog box listing the available scene objects.

TIP Biped tracks are dark yellow and non-biped tracks are light blue, but the track colors can be changed using the dialog box opened with the Mix ➪ Track Color menu command.

Additional tracks can be added to the interface using the Tracks ➪ Add Layer Track Above or the Tracks ➪ Add Layer Track Below menu commands. Transition tracks also are added to the interface using the Tracks menu. Transition tracks are taller than layer tracks and let you define the transition between overlapping clips.

TIP All animation clips that are added to the Motion Mixer during a session are automatically copied to the Reservoir, which is a separate dialog box, like a library, that lets you quickly access various clips. The Reservoir even displays previews of any .bip files that are loaded.

Editing clips

Tracks can be trimmed easily from their original length by dragging on either end of the clip. The cursor changes when the cursor is positioned over the end of a clip. To see the clip's original size, click the Trim Clips button. The original clip size is shown in gray.

NOTE Editing clips in the Motion Mixer is similar to using a Non-Linear Editor such as Adobe Premiere or Final Cut Pro.

Editing track weights

Each track is associated with a weight value. The weight values define the influence of the track when two or more clips overlap. Weight values can range between 1.0 for full influence and 0.0 for no influence. If two overlapping clips both have a weight value of 1.0, then the topmost clip is used.

To edit a track weight, click the small *w* button to the right of the track. This enables the weight value, which appears as a red line for the track. If you position the cursor over the weight line, the cursor changes and lets you add an edit point if you click. This edit point may be selected and moved horizontally, vertically, or both horizontally and vertically depending on which button is selected on the right end of the toolbar. The weight value for the selected weight point is displayed in the value field to the right of the track. Several weight points may be selected and edited simultaneously.

Adding Time Warps

A Time Warp is just what it sounds like: a way to alter time or speed up and slow down animation clips. To add a Time Warp, select a clip and choose the Clips ⇨ Add Time Warp. The cursor changes and lets you click the track to place the location of the Time Warp, which appears as a thin, vertical white line.

After a Time Warp has been added to a clip, you can enable Time Warp editing mode by clicking the Editable Time Warp button in the toolbar. A dashed line is overlaid on the clip. This dashed line gives you an idea of how the clip's time is being altered. Then click and drag the top of the Time Warp marker to crunch time in one direction, or click and drag the bottom half of the Time Warp marker to crunch time in another direction. The dashed lines show the relative effect. Figure 35.11 shows two layer tracks separated by a transition track. The top track shows the default spacing for a Time Warp, and the bottom track shows time compressed to the right.

FIGURE 35.11

Time Warps can be added to clips to compress time.

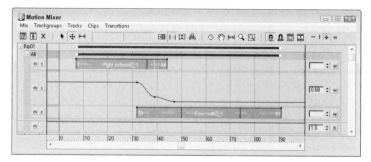

Copying mixed animation to a biped

After the mixed animation is complete, you can create a new track that includes all the mixed animation clips called a Mixdown using the Mix ⇨ Compute Mixdown menu command. The Mixdown shows up as a new track and can be copied to a biped using the Mix ⇨ Copy Mixdown to Biped menu command.

Saving and loading Mix files

All the clips loaded and edited in the Motion Mixer can be saved to an external file as a .mix file using the Mix ⇨ Save Mix File and reloaded into the Motion Mixer using the Mix ⇨ Load Mix File menu command.

Tutorial: Mixing biped animations

Mixing biped animations together can create some really interesting effects. For example, try mixing a back flip with a front flip, and you'll get a really dizzy biped, but for more common motions — such as a character transitioning from a walking animation to a fighting stance — the Motion Mixer can be extremely helpful and save you lots of time.

To mix two animation clips into a single motion, follow these steps:

1. Click the Systems icon in the Create panel, and select the Biped button. Then drag in the Left viewport to create a biped.

2. With the biped selected, open the Motion panel and click the Mixer button in the Biped Apps rollout to open the Motion Mixer. Notice that the Mixer Mode button in the Biped rollout is activated automatically.

3. Click the first biped track in the Motion Mixer to select it, and choose the Tracks ➪ New Clips ➪ From Files menu command. In the Open dialog box that appears, locate and select the Walking.bip file from the DVD. The animation clip is added to the Motion Mixer and is 78 frames long.

4. With the new clip selected, choose the Tracks ➪ Add Layer Track Below menu command to create a new layer track.

5. Select the new layer track, and choose the Tracks ➪ New Clips ➪ From Files menu command again. In the Open dialog box that appears, locate and select the Fighting stance.bip file from the DVD. This clip is only 10 frames long.

6. Select the Walking track, and choose the Tracks ➪ Convert to Transition Track menu command. Then select and drag the Fighting stance clip to the bottom level of the transition track at frame 79. A transition between the two clips is added automatically, as shown in Figure 35.12.

FIGURE 35.12

Two biped clips have been combined to produce a new animation.

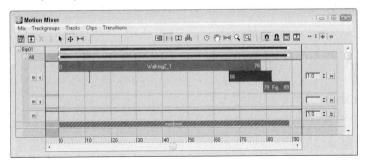

7. Drag the Time Slider to see the resulting mixed animation. Then select the Biped root track, and choose the Mix ➪ Compute Mixdown menu command followed by the Mix ➪ Copy Mixdown to Biped menu command.

Summary

The Animation Layers feature provides a simple way to organize animated motions into an easy-to-manage method. The Animation Layers toolbar includes all the tools you need to manage these unique layers. The Motion Mixer interface is used to combine multiple separate animation clips into a single smooth, new animation. Biped clips and animation clips for standard non-biped objects can be added and mixed in the Motion Mixer. The File ➪ Load Animation option, along with its mapping and retargeting features, lets you reuse saved animations by applying them to other scenes.

Specifically, this chapter covered the following topics:

- Using the Animation Layers toolbar
- Creating new layers and using weights
- Collapsing animation layers
- Saving animation assets into formats that can be loaded into the Motion Mixer
- Loading saved XML animation files
- Remapping animation tracks between objects
- Retargeting to adjust for a change in scale
- Using the Motion Mixer to edit tracks, add transitions, and adjust weight values

With all these different modeling types, you've probably started to create lots of different objects, but get ready to really start creating lots with particle systems. The next chapter begins a part on dynamic animation starting with particle systems.

Part IX

Dynamic Animation

Chapter 36

Creating Particles and Particle Flow

very object that you add to the scene slows down Max to a small degree because Max needs to keep track of every object. If you add thousands of objects to a scene, not only does Max slow down noticeably, but the objects become difficult to identify. For example, if you had to create thousands of simple snowflakes for a snowstorm scene, the system would become unwieldy, and the number wouldn't get very high before you ran out of memory.

Particle systems are specialized groups of objects that are managed as a single entity. By grouping all the particle objects into a single controllable system, you can easily make modifications to all the objects with a single parameter. This chapter discusses using these special systems to produce rain and snow effects, fireworks sparks, sparkling butterfly wings, and even fire-breathing dragons.

Understanding the Various Particle Systems

A *particle* is a small, simple object that is duplicated en masse, like snow, rain, or dust. Just as in real life, Max includes many different types of particles that can vary in size, shape, texture, color, and motion. These different particle types are included in various particle systems.

When a particle system is created, all you can see in the viewport is a single gizmo known as an *emitter icon*. An emitter icon is the object (typically a gizmo, but it can be a scene object) where the particles originate. Selecting a particle system gizmo makes the parameters for the particle system appear in the Modify panel.

Max includes the following particle systems:

- **Particle Flow Source:** Particles that can be defined using the Particle Flow window and controlled using actions and events.

- ■ **Spray:** Simulates drops of water. These drops can be Drops, Dots, or Ticks. The particles travel in a straight line from the emitter's surface after they are created.

- ■ **Snow:** Similar to the Spray system, with the addition of some fields to make the particles Tumble as they fall. You can also render the particles as Six Pointed shapes that look like snowflakes.

- ■ **Blizzard:** An advanced version of the Snow system that can use the same mesh object types as the Super Spray system. Binding the system to the Wind Space Warp can create storms.

- ■ **PArray:** Can use a separate Distribution Object as the source for the particles. For this system, you can set the particle type to Fragment and bind it to the PBomb Space Warp to create explosions.

- ■ **PCloud:** Confines all generated particles to a certain volume. A good use of this system is to reproduce bubbles in a glass or cars on the road.

- ■ **Super Spray:** An advanced version of the Spray system that can use different mesh objects, closely packed particles called MetaParticles, or an instanced object as its particles. Super Spray is useful for rain and fountains. Binding it to the Path Follow Space Warp can create waterfalls.

Creating a Particle System

You can find all the various particle systems under the Create panel and also in the Create menu. To access these systems, click the Geometry category and select the Particle Systems subcategory from the drop-down list. All the particle systems then appear as buttons. Or you can select the Create ⇨ Particles menu.

With the Particle Systems subcategory selected, click the button for the type of particle system that you want to use, and then click in a viewport to create the particle system emitter icon. The emitter icon is a gizmo that looks like a plane or a sphere and that defines the location in the system where the particles all originate. Attached to the icon is a single line that indicates the direction in which the particles move when generated. This line points by default toward the construction grid's negative Z-axis when first created. Figure 36.1 shows the emitter icons for each particle system type including, from left to right, Particle Flow Source; Super Spray; Spray, Snow, and Blizzard (which all have the same emitter icon); PArray; and PCloud.

FIGURE 36.1

The emitter icons for each particle system type

You can transform these icons using the standard transform buttons on the main toolbar. Rotating an emitter changes the direction in which the particles initially move.

After an icon is created, you can set the number, shape, and size of the particles and define their motion in the Parameter rollouts. To apply a material to the particles, simply apply the material to the system's icon. This material is applied to all particles included in the system.

 Be aware that the particles are displayed as simple objects such as ticks or dots in the viewports. To see the actual resulting particles, you need to render the scene file.

You can set the parameters for the Max particle systems in the Create panel when they are first created or in the Modify panel at any time. The simpler systems, Spray and Snow, have a single Parameters rollout, but the advanced systems — Particle Flow Source, Super Spray, and Blizzard — include multiple Parameters rollouts. The PArray and PCloud systems have similar multiple rollouts, with a few subtle differences, and the Particle Flow system includes several rollouts, but most of the action is with the Particle Flow window. The following sections describe how to use these rollouts to set the parameters for the various particle systems.

Using the Spray and Snow Particle Systems

All I can say about the Spray and Snow particle systems is that when it rains, it pours. The Spray Parameters rollout, shown in Figure 36.2, includes values for the number of particles to be included in the system. These values can be different for the viewport and the renderer. By limiting the number of particles displayed in the viewport, you can make the viewport updates quicker. You can also specify the drop size, initial speed, and variation. The Variation value alters the spread of the particles' initial speed and direction. A Variation value of 0 makes the particles travel in a straight line away from the emitter.

FIGURE 36.2

The Spray Parameters rollout holds the parameters for the Spray particle system.

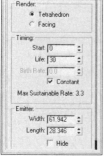

Spray particles can be Drops, Dots, or Ticks, which affect how the particles look only in the viewport. Drops appear as streaks, Dots are simple points, and Ticks are small plus signs. You can also set how the particles are rendered — as Tetrahedron objects or as Facing objects (square faces that always face the viewer).

 The Facing option is visible only in the Perspective view, but can be rendered using any viewport including a camera viewport.

The Timing values determine when the particles appear and how long the particles stay around. The Start Frame is the first frame where particles begin to appear, and the Life value determines the number of frames in which the particles are visible. When a particle's lifetime is up, it disappears. The Birth Rate value lets you set how many new particles appear in each frame; you can use this setting or select the Constant option. The Constant option determines the Birth Rate value by dividing the total number of particles by the number of frames.

The emitter dimensions specify the width and height of the emitter gizmo. You can also hide the emitter with the Hide option.

 The Hide option hides the emitter only in the viewports. Emitters are never rendered.

The parameters for the Snow particle system are similar to the Spray particle system, except for a few unique settings. Snow can be set with a Tumble and Tumble Rate. The Tumble value can range from 0 to 1, with 1 causing a maximum amount of rotation. The Tumble Rate determines the speed of the rotation.

The Render options are also different for the Snow particle system. The three options are Six Point, Triangle, and Facing. The Six Point option renders the particle as a six-pointed star. Triangles and Facing objects are single faces.

Tutorial: Creating rain showers

One of the simplest uses for particle systems is to simulate rain or snow. In this tutorial, you use the Spray system to create rain and then learn how to use the Snow system to create snow.

To create a scene with rain using the Spray particle system, follow these steps:

1. Open the Simple rain.max file from the Chap 36 directory on the DVD.

   This file includes an umbrella model created by Zygote Media.

2. Select the Create ➪ Particles ➪ Spray menu command, and drag the icon in the Top viewport to cover the entire scene. Position the icon above the objects, and make sure that the vector is pointing down toward the scene objects.

3. Open the Modify panel, and in the Parameters rollout, set the Render Count to **1000** and the Drop Size to **2**. Keep the default speed of **10**, and select the Drops option; these settings make the particles appear as streaks. Select the Tetrahedron Render method, and set the Start and Life values to **0** and **100**, respectively.

 NOTE To cover the entire scene with an average downpour, set the number of particles to 1000 for a 100-frame animation.

4. Open the Material Editor (by pressing the M key), and drag a light-blue-colored material to the particle system icon.

Figure 36.3 shows the results of this tutorial.

Tutorial: Creating a snowstorm

Creating a snowstorm is very similar to what you did in the preceding tutorial. To create a snowstorm, use the Snow particle system with the same number of particles and apply a white material to the particle system.

To create a scene with snow using the Snow particle system, follow these steps:

1. Open the Snowman in snowstorm.max file from the Chap 36 directory on the DVD.

   This file includes a snowman created using primitive objects.

2. Select the Create ➪ Particles ➪ Snow menu command, and drag the icon in the Top viewport to cover the entire scene. Position the icon above the objects, and make sure that the vector is pointing down toward the scene objects.

3. Open the Modify panel, and in the Parameters rollout, set the Render Count to **1000** and the Flake Size to **6**, and use the Six Point Render option. Set the Start and Life values to **0** and **100**, respectively.

4. Open the Material Editor (by pressing the M key), and drag a white-colored material with some self-illumination added to the particle system gizmo.

Figure 36.4 shows the results of this tutorial.

FIGURE 36.3

Rain created with the Spray particle system

FIGURE 36.4

A simple snowstorm created with the Snow particle system

Using the Super Spray Particle System

If you think of the Spray particle system as a light summer rain shower, then the Super Spray particle system is like a fire hose. The Super Spray particle system is considerably more complex than its Spray and Snow counterparts. With this complexity comes a host of features that make this one of the most robust effects creation tools in Max.

Unlike the Spray and Snow particle systems, the Super Spray particle system includes several rollouts.

Super Spray Basic Parameters rollout

The Super Spray particle system emits all particles from the center of the emitter icon. The emitter icon is a simple cylinder and an arrow that points in the direction in which the particles will travel. In the Basic Parameters rollout, shown in Figure 36.5, the Off Axis value sets how far away from the icon's arrow the stream of particles will travel. A value of 0 lines up the particle stream with the icon's arrow, and a value of 180 emits particles in the opposite direction. The Spread value can also range from 0 to 180 degrees and fans the particles equally about the specified axis. The Off Plane value spins the particles about its center axis, and the Spread value sets the distance from this center axis that particles can be created. If all these values are left at 0, then the particle system emits a single, straight stream of particles, and if all values are 180, then particles go in all directions from the center of the emitter icon.

FIGURE 36.5

The Basic Parameters rollout lets you specify where and how the particles appear in the viewports.

The icon size can be set or the icon can be hidden in the viewport. You can also set the particles to be displayed in the viewport as Dots, Ticks, Meshes, or Bounding Boxes. The Percentage value is the number of the total particles that are visible in the viewport and should be kept low to ensure rapid viewport updates.

Particle Generation rollout

The Particle Generation rollout, shown in Figure 36.6, is where you set the number of particles to include in a system as either a Rate or Total value. The Rate value is the number of particles per frame that are generated. The Total value is the number of particles generated over the total number of frames. Use the Rate value if you want the animation to have a steady stream of particles throughout the animation; use the Total value if you want to set the total number of particles that will appear throughout the entire range of frames.

FIGURE 36.6

The Particle Generation rollout lets you control the particle motion.

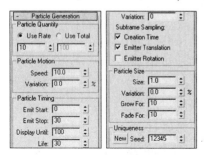

In the Particle Motion group, the Speed value determines the initial speed and direction of particles. The Variation value alters this initial speed as a percentage of the Speed value. A high Variation value results in particles with all sorts of different speeds.

 **Be sure to use the Variation values liberally to get more realistic particle behavior.**

In the Particle Timing group, you can set when the emitting process starts and stops. Using the Display Until value, you can also cause the particles to continue displaying after the emitting has stopped. The Life value is how long particles stay around, which can vary based on another Variation setting.

When an emitter is animated (such as moving back and forth), the particles can clump together where the system changes direction. This clumping effect is called *puffing*. The Subframe Sampling options help reduce this effect. The three options are Creation Time (which controls emitting particles over time), Emitter Translation (which controls emitting particles as the emitter is moved), and Emitter Rotation (which controls emitting particles as the emitter is rotated). All three options can be enabled, but each one that is enabled adds the computation time required to the render.

 **The Subframe Sampling options increase the rendering time and should be used only if necessary.**

You can specify the particle size along with a Variation value. You can also cause the particles to grow and fade for a certain number of frames.

The Seed value helps determine the randomness of the particles. Clicking the New button automatically generates a new Seed value.

NOTE **If you clone a particle system and each system has the same seed value, then the two systems will be exactly the same. Two cloned particle systems with different seed values will be unique.**

Particle Type rollout

The Particle Type rollout, shown in Figure 36.7, lets you define the look of the particles. At the top of the rollout are three Particle Type options: Standard Particles, MetaParticles, and Instanced Geometry.

If you select Standard Particles as the particle type, you can select which geometric shape you want to use from the Standard Particles section. The options are Triangle, Special, Constant, Six Point, Cube, Facing, Tetra, and Sphere.

FIGURE 36.7

The Particle Type rollout (shown in four parts) lets you define how the particles look.

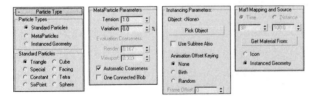

The Special type consists of three intersecting planes, which are useful if you apply maps to them. The Facing type is also useful with maps; it creates a simple, square face that always faces the viewer. The Constant type maintains the same pixel size, regardless of the distance from the camera or viewer. The Six Point option renders each particle as a 2D six-pointed star. All other types are common geometric objects.

Tutorial: Creating a fireworks fountain

For an example of the Super Spray particle system, you create a fireworks fountain. Fireworks are essentially just lots of particles with a short life span and a high amount of self-illumination. (Tell yourself that the next time you watch a fireworks display.)

CROSS-REF The ready-made material for this example uses the Glow Render effect to make the particles glow. You can learn more about render effects in Chapter 45, "Using Atmospheric and Render Effects."

To create a fireworks fountain using a particle system, follow these steps:

1. Open the Fireworks fountain.max file from the Chap 36 directory on the DVD.

   This file includes a simple fountain base and the Gravity space warp to cause the particles to curve back toward the ground.

TIP Some of the most amazing special effects are made possible by combining particle systems with Space Warps.

2. Select the Create ➪ Particles ➪ Super Spray menu command, drag in the Top view, and position the system at the top of the cylinder with the direction arrow pointing toward the sky.

3. Open the Modify panel, and set the Off Axis Spread to **45** and the Off Plane Spread to **90**. In the Particle Generation rollout, set the Total of particles to **2000** with a Speed of **20** and a Variation of **100**. Set the Emit Start to **0** and the Emit Stop to **100**. Set the Display Until to **100** and the Life to **25** with a Variation of **20**. The Size of the particles should be **5**.

4. Open the Material Editor (by pressing the M key), and select the first sample slot. This slot includes a material named Spark. Drag the material from the Material Editor to the particle system's icon.

5. Select the Super Spray icon, right-click it to open the pop-up menu, and select the Properties menu option. In the Object Properties dialog box, select the Object Motion Blur option.

CAUTION When viewing the animation, maximize a single viewport. If Max tries to update all four viewports at once with this many particle objects, the update is slow.

Figure 36.8 shows sparks emitting from the fireworks fountain.

FIGURE 36.8

The Super Spray particle system is used to create fireworks sparks.

Tutorial: Adding spray to a spray can

The Super Spray particle system is complex enough to warrant another example. What good is a spray can without any spray? In this tutorial, we create a spray can model and then use the Super Spray particle system to create the spray coming from it.

To create a stream of spray for a spray can, follow these steps:

1. Open the Spray can.max file from the Chap 36 directory on the DVD.

   This file includes a simple spray can object created using a cylinder for the can base and the nozzle and a lathed spline for the top of the can.

2. Select the Particle Systems subcategory button from the drop-down list, and click the Super Spray button. Drag in the Top viewport to create the Super Spray icon, and position it at the mouth of the nozzle.

3. In the Basic Parameters rollout, set the Off Axis Spread to **20** and the Off Plane Spread to **90**. In the Particle Generation rollout, set the Emit Rate to **1000**, the Speed to **20**, and the Life to **30**. Set the Size of the particles to **5**.

4. Open the Material Editor (by pressing M), and select the material named Spray Mist. Then drag this material onto the Super Spray icon to apply this material to the Super Spray particle system.

Figure 36.9 shows the fine spray from an aerosol can.

Using the MetaParticles option

The MetaParticles option in the Particle Type rollout makes the particle system release Metaball objects. *Metaballs* are viscous spheres that, like mercury, flow into each other when close. These particles take a little longer to render but are effective for simulating water and liquids. The MetaParticles type is available for the Super Spray, Blizzard, PArray, and PCloud particle systems.

FIGURE 36.9

Using a mostly transparent material, you can create a fine mist spray.

Selecting the MetaParticles option in the Particle Types section enables the MetaParticle Parameters group. In this group are options for controlling how the MetaParticles behave. The Tension value determines how easily objects blend together. MetaParticles with a high-tension resist merging with other particles. You can vary the amount of tension with the Variation value. The Tension value can range between 0.1 and 10 and the Variation can range from 0 to 100 percent.

Because MetaParticles can take a long time to render, the Evaluation Coarseness settings enable you to set how computationally intensive the rendering process is. This can be set differently for the viewport and the renderer — the higher the value, the quicker the results. You can also set this to Automatic Coarseness, which automatically controls the coarseness settings based on the speed and ability of the renderer. The One Connected Blob option speeds the rendering process by ignoring all particles that aren't connected.

Tutorial: Spilling soda from a can

MetaParticles are a good option to use to create drops of liquid, like those from a soda can.

To create liquid flowing from a can, follow these steps:

1. Open the MetaParticles from a soda can.max file from the Chap 36 directory on the DVD.

   This file includes a soda can model created by Zygote Media positioned so the can is on its side.

2. Select the Create ➪ Particles ➪ Super Spray menu command, and drag the icon in the Front viewport. Position the icon so that its origin is at the opening of the can and the directional vector is pointing outward.

3. With the Super Spray icon selected, open the Modify panel, and in the Basic Parameters rollout, set the Off Axis and Off Plane Spread values to **40**.

4. In the Particle Generation rollout, keep the default Rate and Speed values, but set the Speed Variation to **50** to alter the speed of the various particles. Set the Particle Size to **20**.

5. In the Particle Type rollout, select the MetaParticles option, set the Tension value to **1**, and make sure that the Automatic Coarseness option is selected.

6. Open the Material Editor (by pressing the M key), and drag the Purple Soda material to the particle system icon.

Figure 36.10 shows a rendered image of the MetaParticles spilling from a soda can at frame 25.

FIGURE 36.10

MetaParticles emitting from the opening of a soda can

Instanced Geometry

Using the Particle Type rollout, you can select an object to use as the particle. If the Instanced Geometry option is selected as the particle type, you can select an object to use as the particle. To choose an object to use as a particle, click the Pick Object button and then select an object from the viewport. If the Use Subtree Also option is selected, then all child objects are also included.

CAUTION Using complicated objects as particles can slow down a system and increase the rendering time.

The Animation Offset Keying option determines how an animated object that is selected as the particle is animated. The None option animates all objects the same, regardless of when they are born. The Birth option starts the animation for each object when it is created, and the Random option offsets the timing randomly based on the Frame Offset value. For example, if you have selected an animated bee that flaps its wings as the particle, and you select None as the Animation Offset Keying option, all the bees flap their wings in concert. Selecting the Birth option instead starts them flapping their wings when they are born, and selecting Random offsets each instance differently.

For materials, the Time and Distance values determine the number of frames or the distance traveled before a particle is completely mapped. You can apply materials to the icon that appears when the particle system is created. The Get Material From button lets you select the object from which to get the material. The options include the icon and the Instanced Geometry.

Rotation and Collision rollout

In the Rotation and Collision rollout is an option to enable interparticle collisions. This option causes objects to bounce away from one another when their object boundaries overlap.

The Rotation and Collision rollout, shown in Figure 36.11, contains several controls to alter the rotation of individual particles. The Spin Time is the number of frames required to rotate a full revolution. The Phase value is the initial rotation of the particle. You can vary both of these values with Variation values.

 The Rotation and Collision rollout options can also increase the rendering time of a scene.

FIGURE 36.11

The Rotation and Collision rollout options can control how objects collide with one another.

You can also set the axis about which the particles rotate. Options include Random, Direction of Travel/MBlur, and User Defined. The Stretch value under the Direction of Travel option causes the object to elongate in the direction of travel. The User Defined option lets you specify the degrees of rotation about each axis.

Interparticle collisions are computationally intensive and can easily be enabled or disabled with the Enable option. You can also set how often the collisions are calculated. The Bounce value determines the speed of particles after collisions as a percentage of their collision speed. You can vary the amount of Bounce with the Variation value.

Tutorial: Basketball shooting practice

When an entire team is warming up before a basketball game, the space around the basketball hoop is quite chaotic — with basketballs flying in all directions. In this tutorial, we use a basketball object as a particle and spread it around a hoop. (Watch out for flying basketballs!)

To use a basketball object as a particle, follow these steps:

1. Open the Basketballs at a hoop.max file from the Chap 36 directory on the DVD.

   This file includes basketball and basketball hoop models created by Zygote Media.

2. Select the Create ⇨ Particles ⇨ Super Spray menu command, and drag the icon in the viewport. Position the icon in the Front view so that its origin is above and slightly in front of the hoop and the directional vector is pointing down (you need to rotate the emitter icon).

3. Open the Modify panel, and in the Basic Parameters rollout, set the Off Axis Spread value to **90** and the Off Plane Spread value to **40**; this randomly spreads the basketballs around the hoop. In the Viewport Display group of the Basic Parameters rollout, select the Mesh option. Set the Percentage of Particles to **100** percent to see the position of each basketball object in the viewport.

> **CAUTION** Because the basketball is a fairly complex model, using the Mesh option severely slows down the viewport update. You can speed the viewport display using the Bbox (Bounding Box) option, but you'll need to choose it after selecting the Instanced Geometry option.

4. In the Particle Generation rollout, select the Use Total option, and enter **30** for the value. (This number is reasonable and not uncommon during warm-ups.) Set the Speed value to **0.2** and the Life value to **100** because we don't want basketballs to disappear. Because of the low number of particles, you can disable the Subframe Sampling option. Set the Grow For and Fade For values to **0**.

5. In the Particle Type rollout, select the Instanced Geometry option and click the Pick Object button. Make sure that the Use Subtree Also option is selected to get the entire group, and then select the basketball group in the viewport. At the bottom of this rollout, select the Instanced Geometry option and click the Get Material From button to give all the particles the same material as the original object.

6. In the Rotation and Collision rollout, set the Spin Time to **100** to make the basketballs spin as they move about the scene. Set the Spin Axis Control to Random. Also enable the Interparticle Collisions option, and set the Calculation Interval to **1** and the Bounce value to **100**.

   With the Collisions option enabled, the basketballs are prevented from overlapping one another.

7. At the floor of the basketball hoop is a Deflector Space Warp. Click the Bind to Space Warp button on the main toolbar, and drag from this floor deflector to the Super Spray icon.

   This makes the basketballs bounce off the floor.

Figure 36.12 shows a rendered image of the scene at frame 30 with several basketballs bouncing chaotically around a hoop.

Object Motion Inheritance rollout

The settings on the Object Motion Inheritance rollout, shown in Figure 36.13, determine how the particles move when the emitter is moving. The Influence value defines how closely the particles follow the emitter's motion; a value of 100 has particles follow exactly, and a value of 0 means they don't follow at all.

The Multiplier value can exaggerate or diminish the effect of the emitter's motion. Particles with a high multiplier can actually precede the emitter.

FIGURE 36.12

Multiple basketball particles flying around a hoop

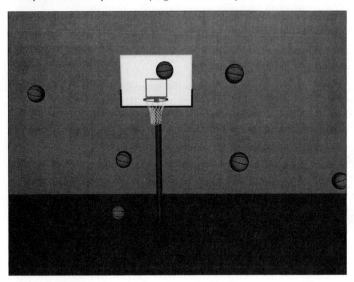

FIGURE 36.13

The Object Motion Inheritance rollout sets how the particles inherit the motion of their emitter.

Bubble Motion rollout

The Bubble Motion rollout, also shown in Figure 36.13, simulates the wobbling motion of bubbles as they rise in a liquid. Three values define this motion, each with variation values. Amplitude is the distance that the particle moves from side to side. Period is the time that it takes to complete one side-to-side motion cycle. The Phase value defines where the particle starts along the amplitude curve.

Particle Spawn rollout

The Particle Spawn rollout, shown in Figure 36.14, sets options for spawning new particles when a particle dies or collides with another particle. If the setting is None, colliding particles bounce off one another and dying particles simply disappear. The Die After Collision option causes a particle to disappear after it collides. The Persist value sets how long the particle stays around before disappearing. The Variation value causes the Persist value to vary by a defined percentage.

FIGURE 36.14

The Particle Spawn rollout (shown in two parts) can cause particles to spawn new particles.

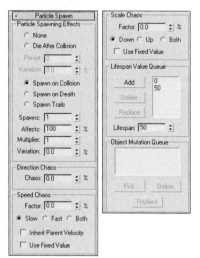

The Spawn on Collision, Spawn on Death, and Spawn Trails options all enable the spawn controls and define when particles spawn new particles. The Spawns value is the number of times a particle can spawn other particles. The Affects value is the percentage of particles that can spawn new particles; lowering this value creates some duds that do not spawn. The Multiplier value determines the number of new particles created.

> **NOTE** The Spawn Trails option causes every particle to spawn a new particle at every frame. This option can quickly create an enormous number of particles and should be used with caution.

The Chaos settings define the direction and speed of the spawned particles. A Direction Chaos value of 100 gives the spawned particles the freedom to travel in any direction, whereas a setting of 0 moves them in the same direction as their originator.

The Chaos Speed Factor is the difference in speed between the spawned particle and its originator. This factor can be faster or slower than the original. Selecting the Both option speeds up some particles and slows others randomly. You can also choose to have spawned particles use their parent's velocity or use the factor value as a fixed value.

The Scale Chaos Factor works similarly to the Chaos Speed Factor, except that it scales particles to be larger or smaller than their originator.

The Lifespan Value Queue lets you define different lifespan levels. Original particles have a lifespan equal to the first entry in the queue. The particles that are spawned from those spawned particles last as long as the second value, and so on. To add a value to the list, enter the value in the Lifespan spinner and click the Add button. The Delete button removes values from the list, and the Replace button switches value positions.

If Instanced Geometry is the selected particle type, you can fill the Object Mutation Queue with additional objects to use at each spawn level. These objects appear after a particle is spawned. To pick a new object to add to the queue, use the Pick button. You can select several objects, and they are used in the order in which they are listed.

Load/Save Presets rollout

You can save and load each particle configuration using the Load/Save Presets rollout, shown in Figure 36.15. To save a configuration, type a name in the Preset Name field and click the Save button. All saved presets are displayed in the list. To use one of these preset configurations, select it and click the Load button.

FIGURE 36.15

The Load/Save Presets rollout enables you to save different parameter settings.

> **NOTE**   A saved preset is valid only for the type of particle system used to save it. For example, you cannot save a Super Spray preset and load it for a Blizzard system.

Max includes several default presets that can be used as you get started. These presets include Bubbles, Fireworks, Hose, Shockwave, Trail, Welding Sparks, and Default (which produces a straight line of particles).

Using the Blizzard Particle System

The Blizzard particle system uses the same rollouts as the Super Spray system, with some slightly different options. The Blizzard emitter icon is a plane with a line pointing in the direction of the particles (similar to the Spray and Snow particle systems). Particles are emitted across the entire plane surface.

The differences between the Blizzard and Super Spray parameters include dimensions for the Blizzard icon. In the Particle Generation rollout, you'll find values for Tumble and Tumble Rate. Another difference is the Emitter Fit Planar option under the Material Mapping group of the Particle Type rollout. This option sets particles to be mapped at birth, depending on where they appear on the emitter. The other big difference is that the Blizzard particle system has no Bubble Motion rollout, because snowflakes don't make very good bubbles. Finally, you'll find a different set of presets in the Load/Save Presets rollout, including Blizzard, Rain, Mist, and Snowfall.

Using the PArray Particle System

The PArray particle system is a unique particle system. It emits particles from the surface of a selected object. These particles can be emitted from the object's surface, edges, or vertices. The particles are emitted from an object separate from the emitter icon.

The PArray particle system includes many of the same rollouts as the Super Spray particle system. The PArray particle system's emitter icon is a cube with three tetrahedron objects inside it. This system has some interesting parameter differences, starting with the Basic Parameters rollout, shown in Figure 36.16.

FIGURE 36.16

The Basic Parameters rollout for the PArray particle system lets you select the location where the particles form.

In the PArray system, you can select separate objects as emitters with the Pick Object button. You can also select the location on the object where the particles are formed. Options include Over Entire Surface, Along Visible Edges, At All Vertices, At Distinct Points, and At Face Centers. For the At Distinct Points option, you can select the number of points to use.

The Use Selected Sub-Object option forms particles in the locations selected with the Pick Object button, but only within the subobject selection passed up the Stack. This is useful if you want to emit particles only from a certain selection of a mesh, such as a dragon's mouth or the end of a fire hose. The other options in the PArray system's Basic Parameters rollout are the same as in the other systems.

The Particle Generation rollout includes a Divergence value. This value is the angular variation of the velocity of each particle from the emitter's normal.

Splitting an object into fragments

The Particle Type rollout for the PArray system contains a unique particle type: Object Fragments. This type breaks the selected object into several fragments. Object Fragment settings include a Thickness value. This value gives each fragment a depth. If the value is set to 0, the fragments are all single-sided polygons.

Also in the Particle Type rollout, the All Faces option separates each individual triangular face into a separate fragment. An alternative to this option is to use the Number of Chunks option, which enables you to divide the object into chunks and define how many chunks to use. A third option splits up an object based on the smoothing angle, which can be specified.

In the Material section of the Particle Type rollout, you can select material IDs to use for the fragment's inside, outside, and backside.

The Load/Save Presets rollout includes a host of interesting presets, including the likes of Blast, Disintegrate, Geyser, and Comet.

Tutorial: Creating rising steam

In this tutorial, we create the effect of steam rising from a street vent. Using the PArray particle system, you can control the precise location of the steam.

To create the effect of steam rising from a vent, follow these steps:

1. Open the Street vent.max file from the Chap 36 directory on the DVD.

   This file includes a street scene with a vent. The car model was created by Viewpoint Datalabs.

2. Select the Create ➪ Particles ➪ PArray menu command, and drag in the Front viewport to create the system.

3. In the Basic Parameters rollout, click the Pick Object button and select the Quadpatch object that is positioned directly beneath the vent object. Set the Particle Formation option to Over Entire Surface.

   Because the Plane object only has a single face, the particles travel in the direction of the Plane's normal.

4. In the Particle Generation rollout, set the Emit Stop value to **100** and the Life value to **60** with a Variation of **50**. Set the Particle Size value to **5.0** with a Variation of **30**.

5. In the Particle Type rollout, select the Standard Particles and the Constant options.

6. Open the Material Editor (by selecting the M key), and name the selected sample slot **steam**. Click the map button to the right of the Opacity value, and double-click the Mask map type from the Material/Map Browser. In the Mask Parameters rollout, click the Map button and select the Noise map type. Then click the Go to Parent button to return to the Mask map, click the Mask button, and select the Gradient map type. For the Gradient material, drag the black color swatch to the white color swatch, select Swap in the dialog box that appears, and enable the Radial option. Finally, drag the steam material to the PArray icon.

Figure 36.17 shows the steam vent at frame 60.

FIGURE 36.17

A Plane object positioned beneath the vent is an emitter for the particle system.

Using the PCloud Particle System

The PCloud particle system keeps all emitted particles within a selected volume. This volume can be a box, sphere, cylinder, or a selected object. The emitter icon is shaped as the selected volume. This particle system includes the same rollouts as the Super Spray system, with some subtle differences.

The options on the Basic Parameters rollout are unique to this system. This system can use a separate mesh object as an emitter. To select this emitter object, click the Pick Object button and select the object to use. Other options include Box, Sphere, and Cylinder Emitter. For these emitters, the Rad/Len, Width, and Height values are active for defining its dimensions.

In addition to these differences in the Basic Parameters rollout, several Particle Motion options in the Particle Generation rollout are different for the PCloud system as well. Particle Motion can be set to a random direction, a specified vector, or in the direction of a reference object's Z-axis.

The only two presets for this particle system in the Load/Save Presets rollout are Cloud/Smoke and Default.

Using Particle System Maps

Using material maps on particles is another way to add detail to a particle system without increasing its geometric complexity. You can apply all materials and maps available in the Material Editor to particle systems. To apply them, select the particle system icon and click the Assign Material to Selection button in the Material Editor.

CROSS-REF For more details on using maps, see Chapter 17, "Adding Material Details with Maps."

Two map types are specifically designed to work with particle systems: Particle Age and Particle MBlur. You can find these maps in the Material/Map Browser. You can access the Material/Map Browser using the Rendering ➪ Material Map Browser menu command or from the Material Editor by clicking on the Get Material button.

Using the Particle Age map

The Particle Age map parameters include three different colors that can be applied at different times, depending on the Life value of the particles. Each color includes a color swatch, a map button, an Enable check box, and an Age value for when this color should appear.

This map typically is applied as a Diffuse map because it affects the color.

Using the Particle MBlur map

The Particle MBlur map changes the opacity of the front and back of a particle, depending on the color values and sharpness specified in its parameters rollout. This results in an effect of blurred motion if applied as an Opacity map.

 **MBlur does not work with the Constant, Facing, MetaParticles, or PArray object fragments.**

Tutorial: Creating jet engine flames

The Particle Age and MBlur maps work well for adding opacity and colors that change over time, such as hot jets of flames, to a particle system.

To create jet engine flames, follow these steps:

1. Open the Jet airplane flames.max file from the Chap 36 directory on the DVD.

   This file includes an A-10 airplane model created by Viewpoint Datalabs.

2. Select the Create ➪ Particles ➪ Super Spray menu command, and drag the icon in the viewport. Rotate and position the emitter icon so that its origin is right in the jet's exhaust port and the directional vector is pointing outward away from the jet.

3. Open the Modify panel, and in the Basic Parameters rollout, set the Off Axis Spread value to **20** and the Off Plane Spread value to **90**.

   These settings focus the flames shooting from the jet's exhaust.

4. In the Particle Generation rollout, set the Emit Stop to **100**, the Life value to **30**, and the Particle Size to **5.0**.

5. In the Particle Type rollout, select the Standard Particles option and select the Sphere type.

6. Open the Material Editor by pressing the M key, and select the first sample slot. Name this material **Jet's Exhaust**, and click the map button to the right of the Diffuse color.

7. From the Material/Map Browser that opens, select the Particle Age map. In the Particle Age Parameters rollout, select dark red, dark yellow, and black as colors for the ages 0, 50, and 100.

   You should use darker colors because the scene is lighted.

8. Click the Go to Parent button to access the Jet's Exhaust material again, and then click the map button to the right of the Opacity setting. Select the Particle MBlur map.

9. In the Particle MBlur Parameters rollout, make Color #1 white and Color #2 black with a Sharpness value of **0.1**. Then drag this material from its sample slot onto the particle system's icon to apply the material (or click the Assign Material to Selection button if the emitter icon is still selected).

10. With the Shift key held down, drag the Super Spray icon in the Front viewport to the other exhaust port. Make the new Super Spray an instance of the original.

Figure 36.18 shows the jet at frame 30 with its fiery exhaust.

FIGURE 36.18

Realistic jet flames created using the Particle Age and MBlur maps

Controlling Particles with Particle Flow

Particle systems like Super Spray are great for certain applications, but they suffer from an inflexibility. Each system has lots of parameters, but once the parameters are set, the particles follow the set parameters without changing. The Particle Flow system is an event-driven system that constantly tests its particles for certain criteria and alters its actions based on these defined criteria. This gives you the ability to program the particles to react in unique and different ways not possible with the other systems.

The Particle Flow Source option in the Create ➪ Particles menu is more than just a new particle system: It is a whole new interface and paradigm that you can use to control particles throughout their life. This is accomplished using the Particle View window where you can visually program the flow of particles.

The Particle View window

The Particle View window, shown in Figure 36.19, is opened by clicking on the Particle View button in the Setup rollout when a Particle Flow Source icon is selected or by pressing the keyboard shortcut, 6. Pressing 6 opens the Particle View window even if its icon isn't selected.

FIGURE 36.19

The Particle View window lets you program the flow of particles using a visual editor.

Event display   Parameters

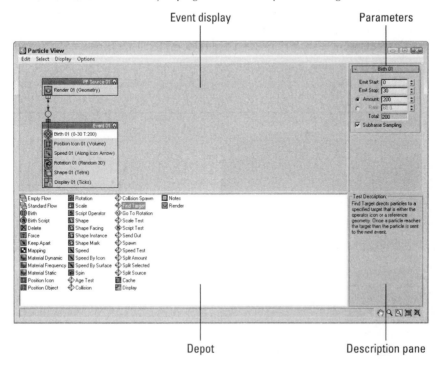

Depot   Description pane

The Particle View window is divided into four panes. The Event display contains all the event nodes. These nodes contain individual actions, and nodes can be wired to one another to define the flow. The Parameter pane in the upper-right corner displays the parameters in rollouts for the action selected in the Event display. The Depot pane is below the Event display pane and contains all the possible actions that can work with particles. In the lower right is a Description pane that offers a brief description of the action that is selected in the Depot pane. Except for the Event display pane, you can turn off the other panes using the Display menu.

In the lower-right corner of the window are several display tools. These tools can be used to navigate the Event display. The Display tools include Pan, Zoom, Region Zoom, Zoom Extents, and No Zoom. The No Zoom button eliminates all zooming and displays the nodes at their normal size.

 With the Particle View window open, you can Pan the Event display by dragging the scroll wheel on the mouse.

The Standard Flow

When the Particle Flow Source icon is created and the Particle View window is first opened, two nodes appear in the Event display. These nodes are called a Standard Flow. These two nodes identify the Particle Flow Source and are wired to an event node containing a Birth action. The Birth action defines when particles Start and Stop and the Amount or Rate. You can change these values by selecting the Birth event in the Event display and changing its parameters in the rollout that appears in the Parameters pane.

Several other default actions appear in this default event node, including Position Icon, Speed, Rotation, Shape, and Display. Each of these events has parameters that you can alter that appear in the Parameters pane when the action is selected, and each event and action is identified with a number (such as 01) that appears next to its name. Each new event or action gets an incremented number. You can also rename any of these events if you right-click on the event and select Rename from the pop-up menu.

A new Standard Flow can be created using the Edit ➪ New ➪ Particle System ➪ Standard Flow menu command. An Empty Flow includes only the PF Source node. When a new Standard Flow (or Empty Flow) is created in the Particle Flow window, a PF Source icon is added to the viewports. And if the PF Source icon is deleted in the viewports, the associated event nodes are also deleted in the Particle Flow window.

Working with actions

The Depot pane includes all the different actions that can affect particles. These actions can be categorized into Birth actions (identified with green icons), Operator actions (identified with blue icons), Test actions (identified with yellow icons), and Miscellaneous actions (which are also blue). Each of these categories can also be found in the Edit ➪ New menu.

New events can be dragged from the Depot pane to the Event display. If you place them within an existing node, a blue line appears at the location where the action will appear when dropped. The particles are affected within a node in the order from top to bottom in which they appear. If a new action from the Depot is dragged over the top of an existing action in the Event display, a red line appears on top of the existing action. When you drop the new action, it replaces the existing action.

Actions can also be dropped away from an event node, making it a new event node. If an event is a new node, then you can wire certain actions that are tested as true. For example, if you have a set of particles with a random speed assigned, then you could use a Test event to determine which particles are moving faster than a certain speed and wire those particles to change size using the new event node.

Clicking on the action's icon disables the action. Table 36.1 provides a complete list of actions and their descriptions.

TABLE 36.1

Particle View Actions

Toolbar Button	Name	Description
	Empty Flow	Creates an emitter icon, but includes no actions
	Standard Flow	Creates an emitter icon wired to an event that includes default actions including Birth, Position Icon, Speed, Rotation, Shape, and Display
	Birth	Emits particles and defines the start, stop, and amount or rate
	Birth Script	Emits particles based on a script
	Delete	Removes particles from the flow, either All, Selected, or by Age
	Force	Adds and subjects particles to Space Warp forces

continued

TABLE 36.1	*(continued)*	
Toolbar Button	**Name**	**Description**
	Keep Apart	Prevents particle collisions by controlling particle speed
	Mapping	Defines the mapping coordinates for the particles
	Material Dynamic	Assigns material to a particle that can change during the life of a particle
	Material Frequency	Assigns materials to subobjects based on defined amounts per Material ID
	Material Static	Assign a material to a particle that is constant for the event
	Position Icon	Defines the particle's position relative to the emitter icon
	Position Object	Defines the particles position relative to a scene object that acts as an emitter
	Rotation	Defines the rotation of the particles
	Scale	Defines the scale of the particles
	Script	Allows the particles to be controlled with a script
	Shape	Defines the shape of the particles; options include Vertex, Tetra, Cube, and Sphere
	Shape Facing	Causes the particles to always face the camera's view; lets you select a camera or object to look at
	Shape Instance	Allows the particle to be a separate scene object
	Shape Mark	Creates a spot mark on a specified contact object
	Speed	Defines the speed of the particles
	Speed By Icon	Causes the particles to follow the trajectory of the viewport icon
	Speed By Surface	Sets the speed of a particle based on an object's surface normals or to be parallel to its surface
	Spin	Defines the amount of spin and the axis about which the particle spins
	Age Test	Tests for the particle's age or its age in the current event
	Collision	Yields true if the particle collides with a selected deflector object

Toolbar Button	Name	Description
	Collision Spawn	Yields true if the particle collides with a selected deflector object; new particles are then spawned
	Find Target	Yields true if the particle is within the specified threshold of the target icon
	Go To Rotation	Yields true when the current rotation action ends and transitions to the next rotation
	Scale Test	Yields true if the particle is scaled to a specified size
	Script Operator	Tests the particles based on a script
	Send Out	Sets all particles to true and moves them to the next event
	Spawn	Creates new particles and moves them to the next event
	Speed Test	Yields true if a particle exceeds a specified speed
	Split Amount	Sends a fraction or every *n*th particle to the next event
	Split Selected	Yields true if particle is selected
	Split Source	Yields true based on the particle's origin emitter
	Cache	Records particle positions for quicker viewport playback
	Display	Defines how the particles are displayed in the viewports
	Notes	Allows notes to be added to the event node
	Render	Defines how the particles are rendered

Tutorial: Creating an avalanche

One of the cautions that come with particles is that if you're not careful, you can quickly spawn enough particles to bring any system to its knees. Using the particle spawn feature is one of the worst offenders. For this tutorial, we use a Collision Spawn action to create an avalanche, but we must be sure to keep the number of spawned particles in check.

To use Particle Flow to make an avalanche effect, follow these steps:

1. Open the Avalanche.max file from the Chap 36 directory on the DVD.

   This file includes a simple hillside covered with snow.

887

2.   Select Create ➪ Space Warps ➪ Deflectors ➪ SomniFlect, and drag in the Top viewport to create a spherical deflector that covers the entire hill. Click the Select and Scale tool, and in the Z-axis, scale the SOmniFlect sphere down in the Left viewport until it is roughly the same thickness as the hill object. Then rotate the SOmniFlect until it is aligned parallel to the hill. This deflector is going to keep the snowball particles on top of the hill.

3.   Select Create ➪ Particles ➪ Particle Flow Source, and drag in the Top viewport to create the emitter icon. Scale and rotate the emitter icon so it is positioned inside the SOmniFlect object on the uphill side pointing downhill. The emitter can be fairly small so it fits inside the deflector.

4.   Click the Particle View button in the Command Panel to open the Particle View window (or press 6). Select the Shape01 action, and set the Shape to Sphere and the Size to **5.0**. Select the Speed01 action, and set the Speed value to **100**. Click the colored dot to the right of the Display01 action, and select white as the new color.

5.   Select the Collision Spawn action from the Depot pane, and drop it in Event01 beneath the Display01 action. Then select the Collision Spawn action, click the By List button in the Parameters pane, and select the SOmniFlect object. Then disable the Test True for Parent and Spawn Particles option, enable the Spawn On Each Collision option, and set the Offspring value to **10**.

Figure 36.20 shows an avalanche of snowballs as it rages down a snowy hillside.

FIGURE 36.20

Using the Collision Spawn and a well-placed deflector, you can create an avalanche effect.

Using Particle Flow helpers

In addition to the Standard Flow event, several other actions create icons in the viewports that are controlled using the action parameters. One of these helpers appears when the Find Target action is added to an event node. This helper is a simple sphere, but all particles in the scene are attracted to it. It can also be animated.

The Speed By Icon action creates an icon that forces particles to follow its trajectory path.

Wiring events

Each new event node that is created has an input that extends from the upper-left corner of the node, and each Test event that is added has an output that extends to the left of its icon, as shown in Figure 36.21. Test action outputs can be wired to event inputs by dragging from one to the other. The cursor changes when it is over each.

FIGURE 36.21

Event outputs can be wired to event inputs.

Event output

Event input

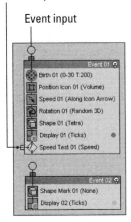

Once wired, all particles that are tested to be true are transferred to the new event node and are subject to the actions in the wired event node.

Tutorial: Moths chasing a light

Another cool feature that the Particle Flow interface makes available is the ability to have particles chase a target object. In this example, we use the Target event to make some annoying bugs follow a lantern's light.

To use Particle Flow to make several bugs chase a light, follow these steps:

1. Open the Moths chasing light.max file from the Chap 36 directory on the DVD.

   This file includes a simple lantern created from primitives that is suspended from a chain and animated rocking back and forth. The file also includes a simple moth.

2. Select Create ➪ Particles ➪ Particle Flow Source, and drag in the Front viewport to create the emitter icon. Click the Particle View button to open the Particle View interface.

3. In the Event01 node, select the Birth01 action and set the Emit Stop to **100** with an Amount of **50**.

4. Drag the Position Object action from the Depot pane, and drop it on top of the Position Icon action to replace it. Select the new Position Object action, click the By List button under the Emitter Objects list in the Parameters pane, and select the Sphere01 object.

   This sphere surrounds the lantern and is the source of the moths. It has a material with an Opacity setting of 0 applied so that it is not visible in the scene.

5. Select the Rotation action in the Event01 node, and change the Orientation Matrix option to Speed Space Follow.

   This rotates the moths as they follow the swinging lantern.

6. Drag the Shape Instance action from the Depot pane, and drop it on top of the Shape action to replace it. Select the new Shape Instance action, click the Particle Geometry Object button in the Parameters pane, and select the moth object in the viewports.

7. Drag the Find Target action from the Depot pane, and drop it at the bottom of the Event01 node. This adds a new Find Target icon to the viewports. Select the Find Target icon in the viewports, and move it to the lantern flame's position. Select Group ⇨ Attach, and click the lantern object to add the Find Target icon to the lantern group. This makes the target move with the lantern. Enable the Use Cruise Speed option, and then set the Speed to **1000** with a Variation of **50** and the Accel Limit to **5000** with an Ease % of **50**. You also need to enable the Follow Target Animation option.

8. Drag the Material Dynamic from the Depot pane to the Event Display pane, and drop it outside the Event01 node to create a new node called Event02. In the Parameters pane, enable the Assign Material button and click the material button. Select the Flash material from the Material/Map Browser (select the Material Editor option to see the sample slot materials). Then drag a wire from Event01 to Event02.

9. Drag the Age Test action from the Depot pane, and drop it below the Material Dynamic action. Then select Event Age from the drop-down list in the Parameters pane, and set the Test Value to **2**.

10. Finally, drag the Delete action from the Depot pane, and drop it away from the other events. Then wire Event02 to the new event node, and select the Selected Particles Only option in the Parameters pane.

Figure 36.22 shows several moths eagerly pursuing the swinging lantern.

FIGURE 36.22

All the moths in this scene are particles and are following a target linked to the lantern.

Debugging test actions

Any test action can be made to return a True or False value if you click the left (for True) or right (for False) side of the test action's icon in the Particle View interface. This lets you debug the particle flow. Tests set to be true show an icon with a green light, and tests set to be false show a red light icon.

Tutorial: Firing at a fleeing spaceship

Well, it is about time for a space scene, and we all know that lots of particles float around out in space — stars, asteroids, comets, and so forth. It's all great stuff to animate. For this scene, we use the Particle Flow feature to fire laser blasts on a fleeing spaceship.

To use Particle Flow to fire on a fleeing spaceship, follow these steps:

1. Open the Fleeing spaceship.max file from the Chap 36 directory on the DVD.

   This file includes a spaceship model created by Viewpoint Datalabs that has been animated as if it were fleeing.

2. Select Create ⇨ Particles ⇨ Particle Flow Source, and drag in the Front viewport to create the emitter. With the Select and Move (W) button selected, move the emitter until it is aligned with the end of the laser gun. Then click the Select and Link button, and drag from the emitter to the gun object to bind the emitter to the gun.

   The emitter now moves with the animated laser gun.

3. With the Particle Flow Source icon selected, open the Modify panel and click on the Particle View button in the Setup rollout (or press the 6 key) to open the Particle View interface.

4. In the Event01 node, select the Birth 03 event; in the Parameters panel, set the Emit Stop to **100** and the Amount to **50**. This produces a laser blast every two frames. Click the blue dot in the lower-right corner of the Event node, and select a red color from the Color Selector that appears.

5. Select Create ⇨ Standard Primitives ⇨ Cylinder, and drag in the Front viewport to create a Cylinder object. In the Hierarchy panel, select the Affect Pivot Only button and rotate the Cylinder's Pivot Point until its Y-axis points at the spaceship. Then in the Particle View window, drag the Shape Instance event from the depot and drop it on top of the Shape event in the Event 01 node. This replaces the Shape event with a Shape Instance event. In the Parameters rollout, click the Particle Geometry Object button and select the Cylinder object. Select the Rotation event, and delete it with the Delete key.

6. Select Create ⇨ Space Warps ⇨ Deflectors ⇨ SOmniFlect, and drag in the Top viewport to create a spherical deflector that encompasses the spaceship. Click the Select and Non-Uniform Scale button, and scale the X- and Z-axes until the deflector just fits around the spaceship. Then link the deflector Space Warp to the spaceship.

7. In the Particle View window, drag the Collision event from the depot to the bottom of the Event 01 node. In the rollout, below the Deflectors list, click the Add button and select the SOmniFlect01 object surrounding the spaceship.

8. Drag a Spawn event from the depot to the event display, and then connect the Collision event by dragging from its output to the input of the new Spawn event. Then click the color for the new event particles, and change it to orange. Select the Spawn 01 event, enable the Delete Parent option, and set the Offspring to **200** and the Variation % to **20**. Then set the Inherited % to **50** with a Variation of **30**.

9. Drag the Delete event to the bottom of the Event 02 node, select the By Particle Age option, and set the Life Span to **20** and the Variation to **30**. Drag a Shape event to the Event 02 node, and set the Shape to Sphere and the Size to **0.5**.

10. Finally, click the Play button to see the resulting animation.

Figure 36.23 shows the final Particle View flow, and Figure 36.24 shows a frame of the animation in the viewport. You can still do several things to improve this animation, such as adding a Glow Render Effect to the laser blasts and using the Particle Age material with some transparency to improve the explosion's look.

The Particle View window shows the flow of the particles in the animation.

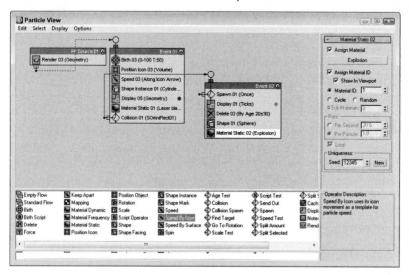

Tutorial: Creating a black hole using Particle Flow

Particle systems are one of the best sources for special effects, and with the Particle Flow interface, you can control them more easily. In this tutorial, we create an array of particle systems and have all their particles flow together to form a black hole.

To create a black hole using the Particle Flow interface, follow these steps:

1. Select Create ➪ Particles ➪ Particle Flow Source, and drag in the Left viewport to create the icon. The icon's direction arrow should point to the right in the Top viewport. With the icon selected, click the Affect Pivot Only button in the Hierarchy panel and move the icon to the origin location in the Top viewport. Then click the Affect Pivot Only button again to disable pivot mode.

2. Select Create ➪ Standard Primitives ➪ Sphere, and create a small sphere in the Top viewport at the grid origin in the center of the viewport.

3. Click the Auto Key button at the bottom of the interface, and drag the Time Slider to frame 100. Then select the sphere object in the Left viewport, and move it downward a little. Then select the Particle Flow Source icon in the Top viewport, and rotate it about 60 degrees. Then disable the Auto Key button to leave key mode.

4. With the Particle Flow icon selected, click the Particle View button in the Modify panel (or press the 6 key) to open the Particle Flow window. Select the Birth event, and change the Emit Stop value to **100** and the Amount to **200**. Select the Shape event, and change the Shape to Sphere and the Size value to **2.0**. In the Display event, change the Visible % to **10**.

FIGURE 36.24

The spaceship is trying to outrun the laser blasts.

5. Drag the Speed by Surface event from the Depot window, and drop it on top of the Speed event in the Event node. Select the Control Speed Continuously option from the drop-down list, enable the Speed option, and set the Speed value to **100** and the Speed Variation to **20**. Then click the Add button, and select the small Sphere object in the Top viewport or you can select the sphere from a dialog box using the By List button.

6. Select the Particle Flow icon; with the Shift key held down, rotate the icon about 52 degrees and enter **6** for the Number of Copies in the Clone Options dialog box that appears.

   This creates particle flow icons that surround and feed the black hole.

Figure 36.25 shows the resulting black hole with no materials or Render Effects applied after the Particle Amount is set to 500. For materials, I recommend using the Particle Age map along with a high Self-Illumination value and a Glow Render Effect.

This same structure can be modified to produce a tornado or hurricane.

One spiraling black hole accomplished with the Particle Flow interface

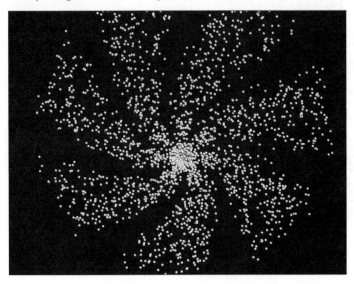

Summary

This chapter presented particle systems and showed how you can use them. The chapter also took a close look at each system, including Spray, Snow, Super Spray, Blizzard, PArray, PCloud, and Particle Flow. This chapter covered these topics:

- Learning about the various particle systems
- Creating a particle system for producing rain and snow
- Using the Super Spray particle system
- Working with MetaParticles
- Specifying an object to use as a particle and an object to use as an emitter
- Using the PArray and PCloud particle systems
- Using the Particle Age and Particle MBlur maps on particles
- Controlling and programming the flow of particles with the Particle Flow window

The next chapter explains working with Space Warps to add forces to a scene. These forces can be used to control the motion of objects in the scene.

Chapter 37

Using Space Warps

S pace Warps sound like a special effect from a science fiction movie, but actually they are non-renderable objects that let you affect another object in many unique ways to create special effects.

You can think of Space Warps as the unseen forces that control the movement of objects in the scene such as gravity, wind, and waves. Several Space Warps, such as Push and Motor, deal with dynamic simulations and can define forces in real-world units. Some Space Warps can deform an object's surface; others provide the same functionality as certain modifiers.

Space Warps are particularly useful when combined with particle systems. This chapter includes some examples of Space Warps that have been combined with particle systems.

Creating and Binding Space Warps

Space Warps are a way to add forces to the scene that can act on an object. Space Warps are not renderable and must be bound to an object to have an effect. A single Space Warp can be bound to several objects, and a single object can be bound to several Space Warps.

In many ways, Space Warps are similar to modifiers, but modifiers typically apply to individual objects, whereas Space Warps can be applied to many objects at the same time and are applied using World Space Coordinates. This ability to work with multiple objects makes Space Warps the preferred way to alter particle systems and to add forces to dynamic hair and cloth systems.

Creating a Space Warp

Space Warps are found in the Create ➪ Space Warps menu, which opens the Space Warps category (the icon is three wavy lines) in the Create panel. From the subcategory drop-down list, you can select from four different subcategories. Each subcategory has buttons to enable several different Space Warps, or you can select them using the Create ⇨ Space Warps menu command. To create a Space Warp, click a button or select a menu option, and then click and drag in a viewport.

When a Space Warp is created, a gizmo is placed in the scene. This gizmo can be transformed as other objects can: by using the standard transformation buttons. The size and position of the Space Warp gizmo often affects its results. After a Space Warp is created, it affects only the objects to which it is bound.

Binding a Space Warp to an object

A Space Warp's influence is felt only by its bound objects, so you can selectively apply gravity only to certain objects. The Bind to Space Warp button is on the main toolbar next to the Unlink button. After clicking the Bind to Space Warp button, drag from the Space Warp to the object to which you want to link it or vice versa.

All Space Warp bindings appear in the Modifier Stack. You can use the Edit Modifier Stack dialog box to copy and paste Space Warps between objects.

Some Space Warps can be bound only to certain types of objects. Each Space Warp has a Supports Objects of Type rollout that lists the supported objects. If you're having trouble binding a Space Warp to an object, check this rollout to see whether the object is supported.

Understanding Space Warp Types

Just as many different types of forces exist in nature, many different Space Warp types exist. These appear in several different subcategories, based on their function. The subcategories are Forces, Deflectors, Geometric/Deformable, Modifier-Based, Particles & Dynamics, and reactor.

CROSS-REF The Particles & Dynamics subcategory includes a Vector Field button that is used with biped crowds, discussed in Chapter 42, "Creating and Animating Bipeds and Crowds." Although it is not available in the Create ⇨ Space Warps menu, the Create panel includes a reactor category that makes the Water button available. The Water reactor object is discussed with the rest of the reactor objects in Chapter 38, "Simulating Physics-Based Motion with reactor."

Force Space Warps

The Forces subcategory of Space Warps is mainly used with particle systems and dynamic simulations. Space Warps in this subcategory include Motor, Vortex, Path Follow, Displace, Wind, Push, Drag, PBomb, and Gravity. Figure 37.1 shows the gizmos for these Space Warps.

Motor

The Motor Space Warp applies a rotational torque to objects. This force accelerates objects radially instead of linearly. The Basic Torque value is a measurement of torque in newton-meters, foot-pounds, or inch-pounds.

The On Time and Off Time options set the frames where the force is applied and disabled, respectively. Many of the Space Warps have these same values.

FIGURE 37.1

The Force Space Warps: Motor, Vortex, Path Follow, Displace, Wind, Push, Drag, PBomb, and Gravity

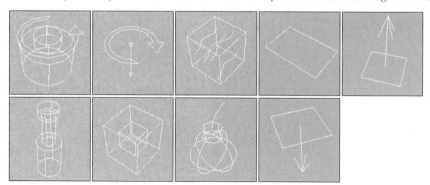

The Feedback On option causes the force to change as the object's speed changes. When this option is off, the force stays constant. You can also set a Target Revolution units in revolutions per hour (RPH), revolutions per minute (RPM), or revolutions per second (RPS), which is the speed at which the force begins to change if the Feedback option is enabled. The Reversible option causes the force to change directions if the Target Speed is reached, and the Gain value is how quickly the force adjusts.

The motor force can also be adjusted with Periodic Variations, which cause the motor force to increase and then decrease in a regular pattern. You can define two different sets of Periodic Variation parameters: Period 1, Amplitude 1, Phase 1; and Period 2, Amplitude 2, Phase 2.

For particle systems, you can enable and set a Range value. The Motor Space Warp doesn't affect particles outside this distance. At the bottom of the Parameters rollout, you can set the size of the gizmo icon. You can find this same value for all Space Warps.

Figure 37.2 shows the Motor Space Warp twisting the particles being emitted from the Super Spray particle system in the direction of the icon's arrow.

Push

The Push Space Warp accelerates objects in the direction of the Space Warp's icon from the large cylinder to the small cylinder. Many of the parameters for the Push Space Warp are similar to those for the Motor Space Warp. Using the Parameters rollout, you can specify the force Strength in units of newtons or pounds.

The Feedback On option causes the force to change as the object's speed changes, except that it deals with Target Speed instead of Target Revolution like the Motor Space Warp does.

FIGURE 37.2

You can use the Motor Space Warp to apply a twisting force to particles and dynamic objects.

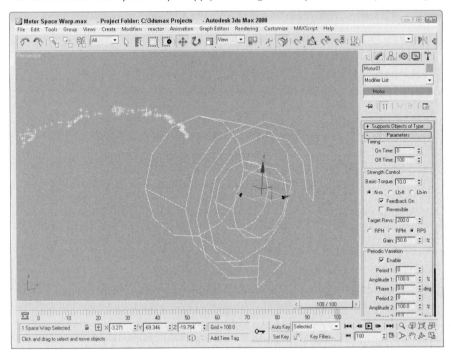

The push force can also be set to include Periodic Variations that are the same as with the Motor Space Warp. Figure 37.3 shows the Push Space Warp pushing the particles being emitted from the Super Spray particle system.

Vortex

You can use the Vortex Space Warp on particle systems to make particles spin around in a spiral like going down a whirlpool. You can use the Timing settings to set the beginning and ending frames where the effect takes place.

You can also specify Taper Length and Curve values, which determine the shape of the vortex. Lower Taper Length values wind the vortex tighter, and the Taper Curve values can range between 1.0 and 4.0 and control the ratio between the spiral diameter at the top of the vortex versus the bottom of the vortex.

FIGURE 37.3

You can use the Push Space Warp to apply a controlled force to particles and dynamic objects.

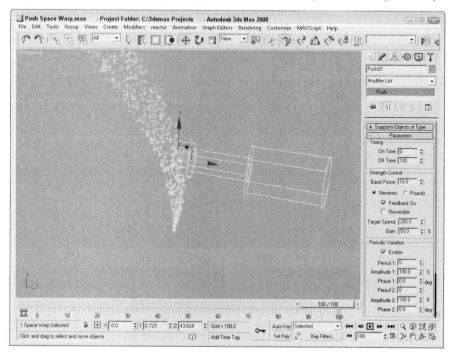

The Axial Drop value specifies how far each turn of the spiral is from the adjacent turn. The Damping value sets how quickly the Axial Drop value takes effect. The Orbital Speed is how fast the particles rotate away from the center. The Radial Pull value is the distance from the center of each spiral path that the particles can rotate. If the Unlimited Range option is disabled, then Range and Falloff values are included for each setting. You can also specify whether the vortex spins clockwise or counterclockwise.

Figure 37.4 shows a Vortex Space Warp being bound to a particle system.

FIGURE 37.4

You can use the Vortex Space Warp to force a particle system into a spiral like a whirlpool.

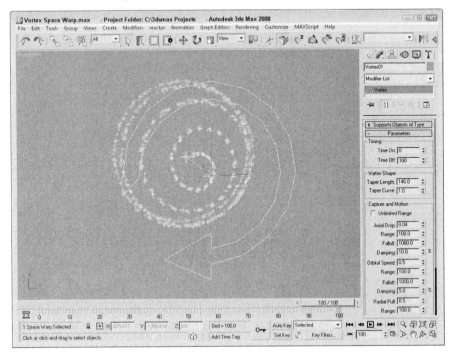

Drag

Drag is another common force that can be simulated with a Space Warp. The Drag Space Warp can be Linear, Spherical, or Cylindrical. This Space Warp causes particle velocity to be decreased, such as when simulating air resistance or fluid viscosity. Use the Time On and Time Off options to set the frame where the Space Warp is in effect.

For each of the Damping shape types — Linear, Spherical, and Cylindrical — you can set the drag, which can be along each axis for the Linear shape or in the Radial, Tangential, and Axial direction for the Spherical and Cylindrical shapes. If the Unlimited Range option is not selected, then the Range and Falloff values are available.

Figure 37.5 shows a Drag Space Warp surrounding a particle system. Notice how the particles are slowed and moved to the side as they pass through the Drag space warp.

PBomb

The PBomb (particle bomb) Space Warp was designed specifically for the PArray particle system, but it can be used with any particle system. To blow up an object with the PBomb Space Warp, create an object, make it a PArray emitter, and then bind the PBomb Space Warp to the PArray.

FIGURE 37.5

You can use the Drag Space Warp to slow the velocity of particles.

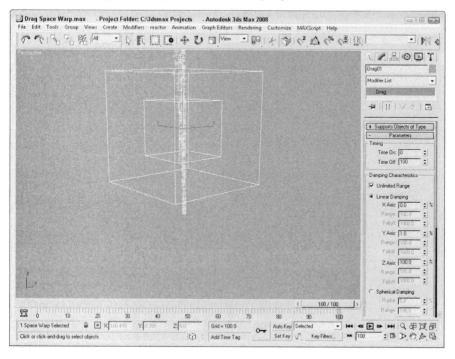

CROSS-REF You can find more information on the PArray particle system in Chapter 36, "Creating Particles and Particle Flow."

Basic parameters for this Space Warp include three blast symmetry types: Spherical, Cylindrical, and Planar. You can also set the Chaos value as a percentage.

In the Explosion Parameters section, the Start Time is the frame where the explosion takes place, and the Duration defines how long the explosion forces are applied. The Strength value is the power of the explosion.

A Range value can be set to determine the extent of the explosion. It is measured from the center of the Space Warp icon. If the Unlimited Range option is selected, the Range value is disabled. The Linear and Exponential options change how the explosion forces die out. The Range Indicator option displays the effective blast range of the PBomb.

Figure 37.6 shows a box selected as an emitter for a PArray. The PBomb is bound to the PArray and not to the box object. The Speed value for the PArray has been set to 0, and the Particle Type is set to Fragments. Notice that the PBomb's icon determines the center of the blast.

FIGURE 37.6

You can use the PBomb Space Warp with the PArray particle system to create explosions.

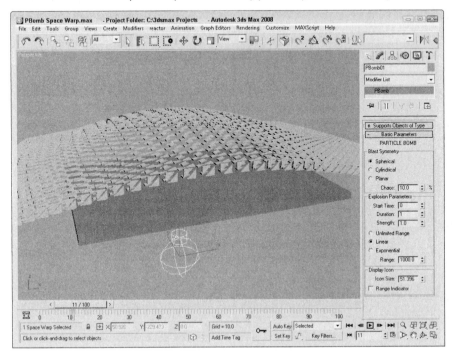

Path Follow

The Path Follow Space Warp causes particles to follow a path defined by a spline. The Basic Parameters rollout for this Space Warp includes a Pick Shape Object button for selecting the spline path to use. You can also specify a Range value or the Unlimited Range option. The Range distance is measured from the path to the particle.

CROSS-REF The Path Follow Space Warp is similar to the Path Constraint, which is discussed in Chapter 21, "Animating with Constraints and Controllers."

In the Motion Timing section, the Start Frame value is the frame where the particles start following the path, the Travel Time is the number of frames required to travel the entire path, and the Last Frame is where the particles no longer follow the path. There is also a Variation value to add some randomness to the movement of the particles.

The Basic Parameters rollout also includes a Particle Motion section with two options for controlling how the particles proceed down the path: Along Offset Splines and Along Parallel Splines. The first causes the particles to move along splines that are offset from the original, and the second moves all particles from their initial location along parallel path splines. The Constant Speed option makes all particles move at the same speed.

Also in the Particle Motion section is the Stream Taper value. This value is the amount by which the particles move away from the path over time. Options include Converge, Diverge, or Both. Converging streams move all particles closer to the path, and diverging streams do the opposite. The Stream Swirl value is the number of spiral turns that the particles take along the path. This swirling motion can be Clockwise, Counterclockwise, or Bidirectional. The Seed value determines the randomness of the stream settings.

Figure 37.7 shows a Path Follow Space Warp bound to a Super Spray particle system. A Helix shape has been selected as the path.

FIGURE 37.7

A Path Follow Space Warp bound to an emitter from the Super Spray particle system and following a Helix path

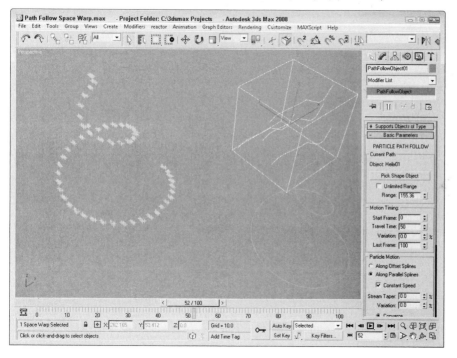

Gravity

The Gravity Space Warp adds the effect of gravity to a scene. This causes objects to accelerate in the direction specified by the Gravity Space Warp, like the Wind Space Warp. The Parameters rollout includes Strength and Decay values. Additional options make the gravity planar or spherical. You can turn on the Range Indicators to display a plane or sphere where the gravity is half its maximum value.

Wind

The Wind Space Warp causes objects to accelerate. The Parameters rollout includes Strength and Decay values. Additional options make the gravity planar or spherical. The Turbulence value randomly moves the objects in different directions, and the Frequency value controls how often these random turbulent changes occur. Larger Scale values cause turbulence to affect larger areas, but smaller values are wilder and more chaotic.

You can turn on the Range Indicators just like the Gravity Space Warp. Figure 37.8 shows the Wind Space Warp pushing the particles being emitted from a Super Spray particle system.

FIGURE 37.8

You can use the Wind Space Warp to blow particles and dynamic objects.

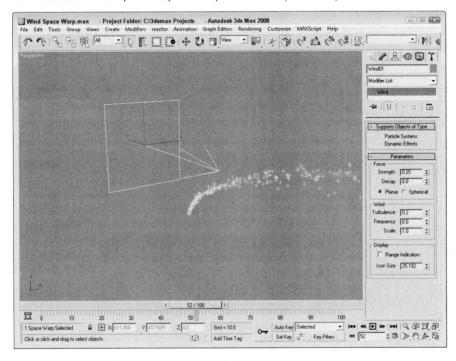

Displace

The Displace Space Warp is like a force field: It pushes objects and is useful when applied to a particle system. It can also work on any deformable object in addition to particle systems. The strength of the displacement can be defined with Strength and Decay values or with a grayscale bitmap.

The Strength value is the distance that the geometry is displaced and can be positive or negative. The Decay value causes the displacement to decrease as the distance increases. The Luminance Center is the grayscale point where no displacement occurs; any color darker than this center value is moved away, and any brighter areas move closer.

The Bitmap and Map buttons let you load images to use as a displacement map; the amount of displacement corresponds with the brightness of the image. A Blur setting blurs the image. You can apply these maps with different mapping options, including Planar, Cylindrical, Spherical, and Shrink Wrap. You can also adjust the Length, Width, and Height dimensions and the U, V, and W Tile values.

CROSS-REF The Displace Space Warp is similar in function to the Displace modifier. The Displace modifier is discussed in Chapter 17, "Adding Material Details with Maps."

Figure 37.9 shows two Displace Space Warps with opposite Strength values.

FIGURE 37.9

The Displace Space Warp can raise or indent the surface of a patch grid.

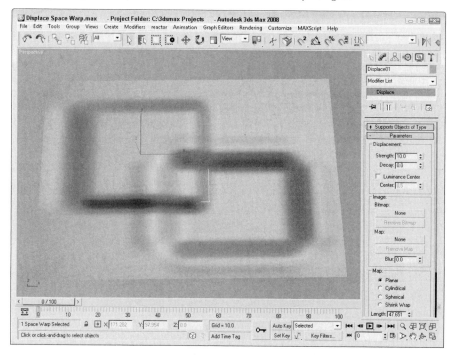

Deflector Space Warps

The Deflectors subcategory of Space Warps includes PDynaFlect, SDynaFlect, UDynaFlect, POmniFlect, SOmniFlect, UOmniFlect, Deflector, SDeflector, and UDeflector. You use them all with particle systems, but only the DynaFlect Space Warps can be used with dynamic objects. This category includes several different types of deflectors starting with P, S, and U. The difference between these types is their shape. P-type (planar) deflectors are box shaped, S-type (spherical) deflectors are spherical, and U-type (universal) deflectors include a Pick Object button that you can use to select any object as a deflector.

Figure 37.10 shows the icons for each of these Space Warps. All the P-type deflectors are in the first row, the S-type deflectors are in the second row, and the U-type deflectors are in the third row.

> **TIP** When you use deflector objects, the number of polygons makes a big difference. The deflector object uses the normal to calculate the bounce direction, so if the deflector object includes lots of polygon faces, then the system slows way down. A solution to this, especially if you're using a simple plane deflector, because all its polygon normals are the same anyway, is to use a simplified proxy object as the deflector and hide it so the particles look like they are hitting the complex object.

> **NOTE** The PDynaFlect, SDynaFlect, and UDynaFlect space warps allow the particles that strike the deflector object to exert a force on the deflector, but this force is detected only when the Dynamics utility is used to create a dynamic simulation. If a dynamic simulation is included, then the deflectors act just like the OmniFlect deflectors. Since reactor is much more powerful and helpful than the Dynamics utility, it is recommended that the OmniFlect deflectors be used instead of these DynmFlect deflectors as the DynaFlect deflectors require more memory and are slower to respond than their OmniFlect counterparts.

FIGURE 37.10

The Deflector Space Warps: POmniFlect, SOmniFlect, UOmniFlect, PDynaFlect, SDynaFlect, UDynaFlect, Deflector, SDeflector, and UDeflector

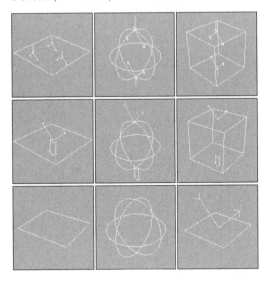

POmniFlect, SOmniFlect, and UOmniFlect

The POmniFlect Space Warp is a planar deflector that defines how particles reflect and bounce off other objects. The SOmniFlect Space Warp is just like the POmniFlect Space Warp, except that it is spherical in shape. The UOmniFlect Space Warp is another deflector, but this one can assume the shape of another object using the Pick Object button in the Parameters rollout. Its Parameters rollout includes a Timing section with Time On and Time Off values and a Reflection section.

The difference between this type of Space Warp and the DynaFlect Space Warp is the addition of refraction. Particles bound to this Space Warp can be refracted through an object. The values entered in the Refraction section of the Parameters rollout change the velocity and direction of a particle. The Refracts value is the percentage of particles that are refracted. The Pass Vel (velocity) is the amount that the particle speed changes when entering the object; a value of 100 maintains the same speed. The Distortion value affects the angle of refraction; a value of 0 maintains the same angle, and a value of 100 causes the particle to move along the surface of the struck object. The Diffusion value spreads the particles throughout the struck object. You can vary each of these values by using its respective Variation value.

 If the Refracts value is set to 100 percent, no particles are available to be refracted.

You can also specify Friction and Inherit Velocity values. In the Spawn Effects Only section, the Spawns and Pass Velocity values control how many particle spawns are available and their velocity upon entering the struck object. Figure 37.11 shows each of these Space Warps bound to a Super Spray particle system. The Reflect percentage for each of the Space Warps is set to 50, and the remaining particles are refracted through the Space Warp's plane. Notice that the particles are also reflecting off the opposite side of the refracting object.

FIGURE 37.11

The POmniFlect, SOmniFlect, and UOmniFlect Space Warps reflecting and refracting particles emitted from the Super Spray particle system

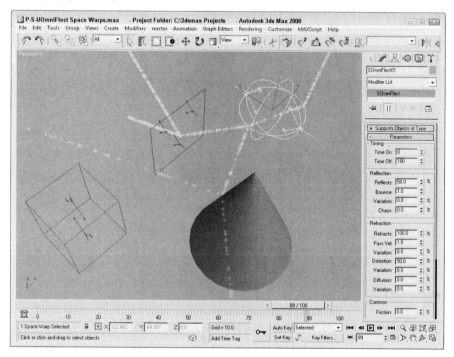

Deflector, SDeflector, and UDeflector

The Deflector and SDeflector Space Warps are simplified versions of the POmniFlect and SOmniFlect Space Warps. Their parameters include values for Bounce, Variation, Chaos, Friction, and Inherit Velocity. The UDeflector Space Warp is a simplified version of the UOmniFlect Space Warp. It has a Pick Object button for selecting the object to act as the deflector and all the same parameters as the SDeflector Space Warp.

Geometric/Deformable Space Warps

You use Geometric/Deformable Space Warps to deform the geometry of an object. Space Warps in this sub-category include FFD (Box), FFD (Cyl), Wave, Ripple, Displace, Conform, and Bomb. These Space Warps can be applied to any deformable object. Figure 37.12 shows the icons for each of these Space Warps.

FFD (Box) and FFD (Cyl)

The FFD (Box) and FFD (Cyl) Space Warps show up as a lattice of control points in the shape of a box and a cylinder; you can select and move the control points that make up the Space Warp to deform an object that is bound to the Space Warp. The object is deformed only if the bound object is within the volume of the Space Warp.

These Space Warps have the same parameters as the modifiers with the same name found in the Modifiers ⇨ Free Form Deformers menu. The difference is that the Space Warps act in World coordinates and aren't tied to a specific object. This allows a single FFD Space Warp to affect multiple objects.

FIGURE 37.12

The Geometric/Deformable Space Warps: FFD (Box), FFD (Cyl), Wave, Ripple, Displace, Conform, and Bomb

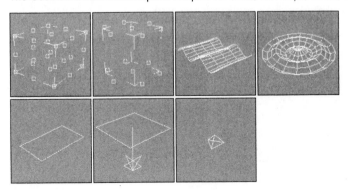

 To learn about the FFD (Box) and FFD (Cyl) modifiers, see Chapter 13, "Introducing Modifiers and Using the Modifier Stack."

To move the control points, select the Space Warp object, open the Modify panel, and select the Control Points subobject, which lets you alter the control points individually.

FFD Select modifier

The FFD Select modifier is another unique selection modifier. It enables you to select a group of control point subobjects for the FFD (Box) or the FFD (Cyl) Space Warps and apply additional modifiers to the selection. When an FFD Space Warp is applied to an object, you can select the Control Points subobjects and apply modifiers to the selection. The FFD Select modifier lets you select a different set of control points for a different modifier.

Wave and Ripple

The Wave and Ripple Space Warps create linear and radial waves in the objects to which they are bound. Parameters in the rollout help define the shape of the wave. Amplitude 1 is the wave's height along the X-axis, and Amplitude 2 is the wave's height along its Y-axis. The Wave Length value defines how long each wave is. The Phase value determines how the wave starts at its origin. The Decay value sets how quickly the wave dies out. A Decay value of 0 maintains the same amplitude for the entire wave.

The Sides (Circles) and Segments values determine the number of segments for the X- and Y-axes. The Division value changes the icon's size without altering the wave effect. Figure 37.13 shows a Wave Space Warp applied to a simple Box primitive. Notice that the Space Warp icon is smaller than the box, yet it affects the entire object.

NOTE Be sure to include enough segments in the bound object, or the effect won't be visible.

FIGURE 37.13

The Wave and Ripple Space Warps applied to a patch grid object

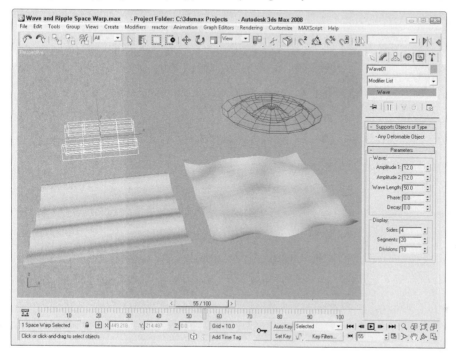

Tutorial: Creating pond ripples

For this tutorial, we position a patch object so it aligns with a background image and apply the Ripple Space Warp to it.

To add ripples to a pond, follow these steps:

1. Open the Pond ripple.max file from the Chap 37 directory on the DVD.

   This file includes a background image of a bridge matched to a patch grid where the pond is located with a reflective material assigned to it.

2. Select the Create ➪ Space Warps ➪ Geometric/Deformable ➪ Ripple menu command. Drag in the Perspective view to create a Space Warp object. In the Parameters rollout, set the Amplitudes to **2** and the Wave Length to **30**.

3. Click the Bind to Space Warp button, and drag from the patch object to the Space Warp.

Figure 37.14 shows the resulting image.

FIGURE 37.14

A ripple in a pond produced using the Ripple Space Warp

Conform

The Conform Space Warp pushes all object vertices until they hit another target object called the Wrap To Object, or until they've moved a preset amount. The Conform Parameters rollout includes a Pick Object button that lets you pick the Wrap To Object. The object vertices move no farther than this Wrap To Object.

You can also specify a Default Projection Distance and a Standoff Distance. The Default Projection Distance is the maximum distance that the vertices move if they don't intersect with the Wrap To Object. The Standoff Distance is the separation amount maintained between the Wrap To Object and the moved vertices. Another option, Use Selected Vertices, moves only a subobject selection.

CROSS-REF The Conform Space Warp is similar in function to the Conform compound object that is covered in Chapter 26, "Working with Compound Objects."

Figure 37.15 shows some text being deformed with the Conform Space Warp. A warped quad patch has been selected as the Wrap To Object.

FIGURE 37.15

The Conform Space Warp wraps the surface of one object around another object.

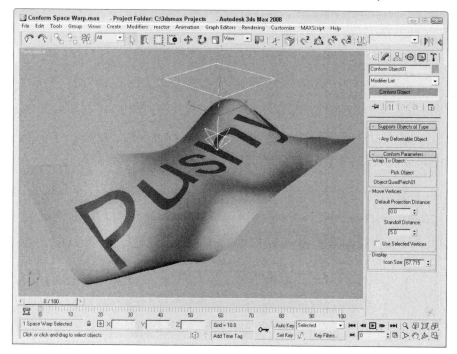

Bomb

The Bomb Space Warp causes an object to explode from its individual faces. The Strength value is the power of the bomb and determines how far objects travel when exploded. The Spin value is the rate at which the individual pieces rotate. The Falloff value defines the boundaries of faces affected by the bomb. Object faces beyond this distance remain unaffected. You must select Falloff On for the Falloff value to work.

The Min and Max Fragment Size values set the minimum and maximum number of faces caused by the explosion.

The Gravity value determines the strength of gravity and can be positive or negative. Gravity always points toward the world's Z-axis. The Chaos value can range between 0 and 10 to add variety to the explosion. The Detonation value is the number of the frame where the explosion should take place, and the Seed value alters the randomness of the event. Figure 37.16 shows frame 20 of an explosion produced by the Bomb Space Warp.

 The Bomb Space Warp is seen over time. At frame 0, the object shows no effect.

Tutorial: Blowing a dandelion puff

You can use Space Warps with other types of objects besides particle systems. The Scatter object, for example, can quickly create many unique objects that can be controlled by a Space Warp. In this tutorial, we create a simple, crude dandelion puff that can blow away in the wind.

FIGURE 37.16

The Bomb Space Warp causes an object to explode.

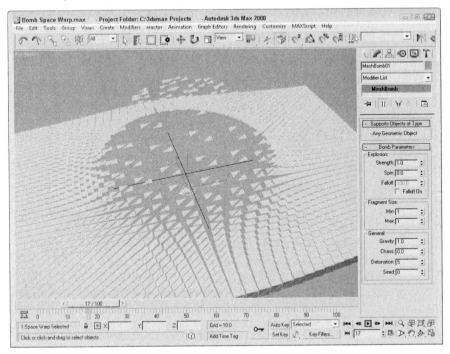

To create and blow away a dandelion puff, follow these steps:

1. Open the Dandelion puff.max file from the Chap 37 directory on the DVD.

    This file includes a sphere covered with a Scatter compound object representing the seeds of a dandelion.

2. Select the Create ➪ Space Warps ➪ Geometric/Deformable ➪ Bomb menu command. Click in the Front viewport, and position the Bomb icon to the left and slightly below the dandelion object. In the Bomb Parameters rollout, set the Strength to **10**, the Spin to **0.5**, the Min and Max Fragment Size values to **24**, the Gravity to **0.2**, and the Chaos to **2.0**.

    This is the total number of faces included in the dandelion object.

3. Click the Bind to Space Warp button on the main toolbar, and drag from the dandelion object to the Space Warp.

Figure 37.17 shows one frame of the dandelion puff being blown away.

Modifier-Based Space Warps

Modifier-Based Space Warps produce the same effects as many of the standard modifiers, but because they are Space Warps, they can be applied to many objects simultaneously. Space Warps in this subcategory include Bend, Noise, Skew, Taper, Twist, and Stretch, as shown in Figure 37.18. All Modifier-Based Space Warp gizmos are simple box shapes. The parameters for all Modifier-Based Space Warps are identical to the modifiers (found in the Parametric Deformers category) of the same name. These Space Warps don't include a Supports Objects of Type rollout because they can be applied to all objects.

> **CROSS-REF** For details on the Bend, Noise, Skew, Taper, Twist, and Stretch modifiers and their parameters, see Chapter 13, "Introducing Modifiers and Using the Modifier Stack."

FIGURE 37.17

You can use Space Warps on Scatter objects as well as particle systems.

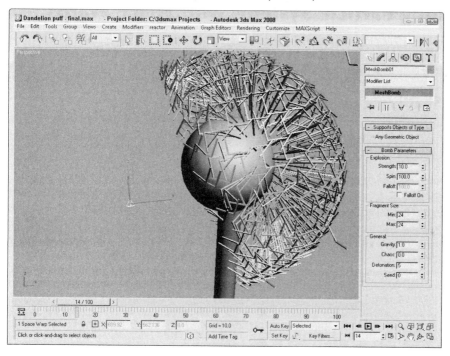

FIGURE 37.18

The Modifier-Based Space Warps: Bend, Noise, Skew, Taper, Twist, and Stretch

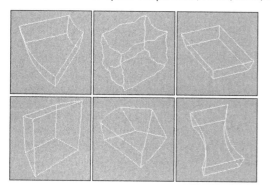

These Space Warps include a Gizmo Parameters rollout with values for the Length, Width, and Height of the gizmo. You can also specify the deformation decay. The Decay value causes the Space Warp's effect to diminish with distance from the bound object.

You can reposition the Modifier-Based Space Warp's gizmo as a separate object, but the normal modifiers require that you select the gizmo subobject to reposition it. Unlike modifiers, Space Warps don't have any subobjects.

Combining Particle Systems with Space Warps

To conclude this chapter, let's look at some examples that use Space Warps along with particle systems. With all these Space Warps and their various parameters combined with particle systems, the possibilities are endless. These examples are only a small representation of what is possible.

Tutorial: Shattering glass

When glass shatters, it is very chaotic, sending pieces in every direction. For this tutorial, we shatter a glass mirror on a wall. The wall keeps the pieces from flying off, and most pieces fall straight to the floor.

To shatter glass, follow these steps:

1. Open the Shattering glass.max file from the Chap 37 directory on the DVD.

    This file includes a simple mirror created from patch grid objects. The file also includes a simple sphere that is animated striking the mirror.

2. Select the Create ➪ Particles ➪ PArray menu command. Then drag in the Front viewport to create the PArray icon. In the Basic Parameters rollout, click the Pick Object button and select the first patch object. In the Viewport Display section, select the Mesh option. In the Particle Generation rollout, set the Speed and Divergence to 0. Also set the Emit Start to **30** and the Life value to **100**, so it matches the last frame. In the Particle Type rollout, select the Object Fragments option, and set the Thickness to **1.0**. Then in the Object Fragment Controls section, select the Number of Chunks option with a Minimum value of **30**. In the Rotation and Collision rollout, set the Spin Time to **100** and the Variation to **50**.

    These settings cause the patch to emit 30 object fragments with a slow, gradual rotation.

3. Select the Space Warps category button, and choose the Forces subcategory from the drop-down list. Click the PBomb button, and create a PBomb Space Warp in the Top view, then center it above the Mirror patch. In the Modify panel, set the Blast Symmetry option to Spherical with a Chaos value of **50** percent. Set the Start Time to **30** with a Strength value of **0.2**. Then click the Bind to Space Warp button, and drag from the PBomb Space Warp to the PArray icon.

4. Select the Create ➪ Space Warps ➪ Forces ➪ Gravity menu command, and drag in the Front viewport to create a Gravity Space Warp. Position the Gravity Space Warp so that the icon arrow is pointing down in the Front viewport. In the Modify panel, set the Strength value to **0.1**. Then bind this Space Warp to the PArray icon.

5. Select the Create ➪ Space Warps ➪ Deflectors ➪ PDynaFlect menu command. Drag this Space Warp in the Top view, and make it wide enough to be completely under the mirror object. Rotate the PDynaFlect Space Warp so that a single large arrow is pointing up at the mirror. Position it so that it lies in the same plane as the plane object that makes up the floor. In the Modify panel, set the Reflects value to **100** percent and the Bounce value to **0**. Bind this Space Warp to the PArray as well; this keeps the pieces from falling through the floor.

Figure 37.19 shows the mirror immediately after being struck by a ball.

FIGURE 37.19

A shattering mirror

Tutorial: Making water flow down a trough

That should be enough destruction for a while. In this final example, we'll make some water particles flow down a trough. This is accomplished using the Path Follow Space Warp.

To make water flow down a trough, follow these steps:

1. Open the Water flowing down a trough.max file from the Chap 37 directory on the DVD.

   This file includes a simple trough made from primitives and a spline path that the water will follow.

2. Select Particle Systems from the subcategory drop-down list, and click the Super Spray button. Create a Super Spray object in the Front viewport and position it where you want the particles to first appear. In the Viewport Display section, select the Ticks particles option. In the Particle Generation rollout, set the Speed to **10** and the Variation to **100**. Then set the Emit Start to **0** and the Display Until and Life values to **100**. In the Particle Type rollout, select MetaParticles and enable the Automatic Coarseness option.

3. Select the Space Warps category button, and choose Forces from the subcategory drop-down list. Click the Path Follow button, and create a Path Follow objects; then click the Bind to Space Warp button on the main toolbar, and drag from the Path Follow icon to the first Super Spray icon. Open the Modify panel, select the Path Follow icon, click the Pick Shape Object button, and select the path in the viewports. Set the Start Frame to **0** and the Travel Time to **100**.

Figure 37.20 shows the rendered result.

FIGURE 37.20

Water flowing down a trough using the Path Follow Space Warp

Summary

Space Warps are useful for adding forces and effects to objects in the scene. Max has several different types of Space Warps, and most of them can be applied only to certain object types. In this chapter, you learned the following:

- How to create Space Warps
- How to bind Space Warps to objects
- How to use all the various Space Warps in several subcategories
- How to combine Space Warps with particle systems to shatter glass and explode a planet

You can have Max dynamically compute all the animation frames in a scene using the physics-based reactor engine, which is covered in the next chapter.

Chapter 38

Simulating Physics-Based Motion with reactor

When you speak of reactor in Max, you really are speaking of physics. Physics is one of the coolest arms of science because it deals with the science of matter and energy and includes laws that govern the motions and interactions between objects. For animators, this is great news because what you are trying to do is to animate the motions and interactions between objects.

So, should all animators study physics? The answer is absolutely. Understanding these laws through study and experience will sharpen your animating skills. But you can also take advantage of the work that other animators have done in understanding the laws of physics and turning them into a product that ships with Max. The other animators are a group called Havok, and the product is reactor.

The Havok physics engine included in Max is the same engine commonly used in games to simulate game-world physics such as the reactions in Value's Half Life 2.

Using reactor, you can simulate many physical properties and automatically capture keyframes as the objects interact. It's like getting a physics degree for free.

The reactor menu includes everything you need to access the reactor physics simulation engine. With reactor, you can define objects as rigid bodies like chairs or bowling balls or as soft bodies like stuffed animals. You can also define specialized objects including cloth and rope.

After physical properties are defined, you can define physical forces to act on these objects and simulate the resulting animation. Not only does reactor make difficult physical motions realistic, but it also is fun to play with.

Understanding Dynamics

Dynamics is a branch of physics that deals with forces and the motions they cause, and regardless of your experience in school, physics is your friend — especially in the world of 3D. Dynamics in Max can automate the creation of animation keys by calculating the position, rotation, and collisions between objects based on physics equations.

Consider the motion of a simple yo-yo. Animating this motion with keys is fairly simple: Set rotation and position keys halfway through the animation and again at the end, and you're finished.

Now think of the forces controlling the yo-yo. Gravity causes the yo-yo to accelerate toward the ground, causing the string to unwind, which makes the yo-yo spin about its axis. When it reaches the end of the string, the rotation reverses and the yo-yo rises. Using Gravity and Motor Space Warps, you can simulate this motion, but setting the keys manually is probably easier for these few objects.

But before you write off dynamics, think of the motion of popcorn popping. With all the pieces involved, setting all the position and rotation keys would take a long time. For this system, using dynamics makes sense.

Dynamic tools let you specify objects to include in a simulation, the forces they interact with, and the objects to be involved in collisions. After the system is defined, the Dynamics utility automatically calculates the movement and collisions of these objects according to the forces involved, and then it sets the keys for you.

> **NOTE** Max includes several different dynamic tools, including dynamic objects such as a spring and damper, dynamic material properties found in the Material Editor, specialized dynamic Space Warps, and the Dynamics utility. Before investing too much time in the Dynamics utility, please realize that for dynamic simulations, the reactor features are more robust and easier to set up. The Dynamics utility still exists only for backwards compatibility.

Using reactor

The reactor plug-in was developed by a company named Havok. reactor is a complex piece of software with a huge assortment of features that enable you to define physical properties and forces and have the scene automatically generate the resulting animation keys as the objects interact while following the laws of physics.

> **NOTE** Be aware that the reactor plug-in is different from the Reaction controller, discussed in Chapter 21, "Animating with Constraints and Controllers."

The reactor plug-in interface exists in the Utilities panel and is one of the default utilities, but you can also access it from the reactor menu and the reactor toolbar, shown in Figure 38.1. The reactor menu and the reactor toolbar provide a quick and easy way to access the various reactor elements. For example, clicking the Rope Collection button opens the Helper category in the Command Panel, selects the reactor sub-category, and selects the RP Collection button.

FIGURE 38.1

Use the reactor toolbar to define physical object properties.

The reactor process

Before getting into the details of reactor, I want to briefly explain the process involved in using reactor. reactor works with geometry that is defined with certain physical properties. After these properties are defined, the reactor engine can take over and determine how all the various objects interact with one another. In the reactor utility, you can select to use the reactor version 1 engine (Havok 1) or the reactor version 3 engine

(Havok 3). Version 3 of the reactor engine is much more accurate and considerably faster than version 1, but if your simulation includes cloth, rope, or soft body objects, then you need to stick with version 1.

Within the Utilities panel are several rollouts of options for controlling the simulation. In the Preview & Animation rollout, you can set the simulation range, number of frames, and substeps per key. In the Havok 1 World rollout, you can set the global gravity values, the World Scale, and Collision Tolerance. The Add Deactivator option lets you remove objects from the simulation that are considered at rest. This keeps them from wiggling around, which happens when they are still part of the simulation. The Short and Long Frequency values help determine when an object is at rest.

If the Havok 3 option is selected, then you can choose to compute the object's motion on a Continuous basis or on a Discrete basis, which only checks the object motion at the beginning and end of each step and interpolates between these two states. You also can set a Maximum Linear Velocity for objects and a Stiffness value.

The Collisions rollout lets you specify how collisions are stored. By storing collisions, you can trigger an event to make particles show sparks, but enabling the storing of collisions can slow down a simulation. A window for Defining Collisions lets you ensure that certain objects won't collide and others will.

The Display panel lets you specify a camera, clipping planes, lights, and textures to use in the Preview window for displaying the simulated objects.

The Utils panel includes an Analyze World button that you can use before starting a simulation. There are also controls for reducing the total number of keys and for testing the convexity of objects.

Defining geometry with physical properties happens in several different ways. Objects can be added to a collection. A collection is a type of reactor object that has several inherited physical properties such as a Rigid Body collection. Objects can also be linked with reactor objects such as a Spring or Motor. These objects are affected by forces that are preset for the different reactor objects. Finally, you can set properties using the Object Property rollout that lets you define properties such as mass, friction, and elasticity. After all the objects are defined and attached to the correct reaction collection or object, you can open a Preview window that lets you see how the object will react under the current forces. You can also interactively play with the various objects in the Preview window.

When you're comfortable with the animation, the reactor ⇨ Create Animation menu command creates all the keys for the animation sequence.

Tutorial: Filling a glass bowl

Imagine trying to animate a bunch of marbles falling into a glass bowl. If you were using keyframes, determining whether an object overlaps another would be difficult, but with this quick example, we see the power of reactor.

To animate marbles falling into a glass bowl, follow these steps:

1. Open the Glass bowl of marbles.max file from the Chap 38 directory on the DVD.

   This file includes a glass bowl and several marbles positioned above its opening.

2. Select reactor ⇨ Create Objects ⇨ Rigid Body Collection, and click in the Front viewport to create the icon. In the RB Collection Properties rollout, click the Add button to open the Select Objects dialog box.

3. In the Select Objects dialog box, click the Select All button and then the Select button to select and make all objects in the scene rigid body objects. Then right click to exit Rigid Body Collector mode.

4. Select the Box and sphere objects that make up the floor and bowl, select reactor ➪ Open Property Editor, and enable the Unyielding option. This prevents these two objects from moving. Then select the sphere bowl object, and enable the Concave Mesh option.

5. Select all the marble objects in the scene, and set the Mass value to **5.0**.

6. Then select reactor ➪ Preview Animation to open the Preview window, and press the P key to start the simulation.

7. If the animation looks fine, select reactor ➪ Create Animation to have reactor compute all the keys.

Figure 38.2 shows the bowl full of marbles positioned using reactor.

FIGURE 38.2

reactor can compute all the collisions between all these marbles.

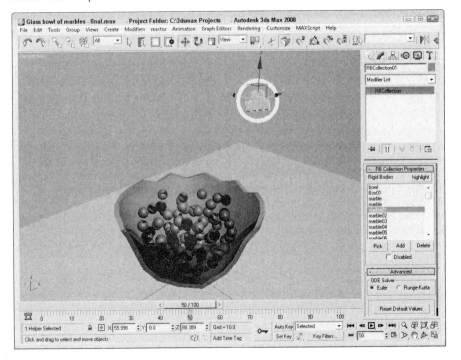

Using reactor Collections

One of the first steps in creating with a simulation is defining the object properties. For example, a simple sphere object in Max could represent a bowling ball, an orange, or a tennis ball. Each of these objects responds very differently when being animated to drop on the floor.

In reactor, the simulation identifies the various objects by the type of collection that it is part of. reactor has five types of collections: Rigid Body, Cloth, Soft Body, Rope, and Deforming Mesh, as described in Table 38.1.

TABLE 38.1

reactor Collections

Toolbar Button	Name	Description
	Rigid Body Collection	Rigid bodies resist a force.
	Cloth Collection	Cloth objects flow and bend to all forces.
	Soft Body Collection	Soft bodies flex when they come in contact with a force.
	Rope Collection	Rope objects support tension, but not compression.
	Deforming Mesh Collection	Meshes can be deformed by forces.

Rigid bodies are objects that keep their shape when pushed; soft bodies deform when pushed. Cloth and rope are intuitive, and deformable meshes are any object with keyed animation including bones and skin systems.

> **NOTE** Remember that cloth, rope, and soft body objects are only as flexible as the number of segments that make up the object. For example, a rope made from a spline with three vertices bends only in the middle.

All objects that are included in one of these collections behave with similar properties. To include a collection in the scene, select the reactor ⇨ Create Objects menu or click one of the collection buttons in the reactor toolbar and then click in the active viewport to add the collection icon. Figure 38.3 shows the gizmos for each of these collections.

FIGURE 38.3

The gizmo icons for each of the collections

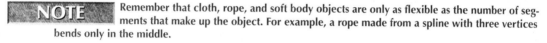

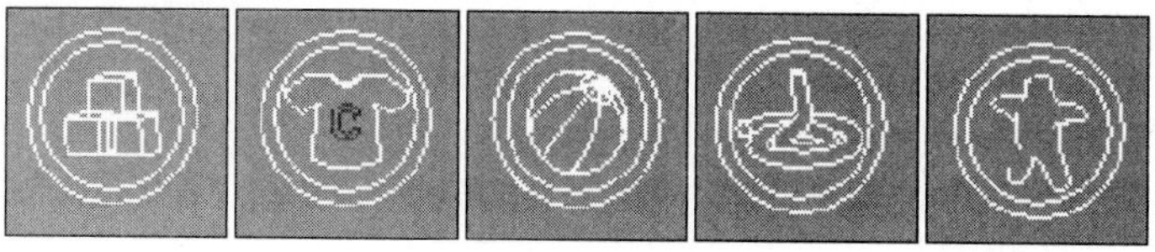

Collection gizmos in the scene are not rendered and appear red when first created. When selected, the gizmo appears white; when an object has been added to the collections, it appears blue. This makes it easy to see which collections are empty.

After a collection is added to the scene, you can use its Pick button in the Properties rollout to select a single object to the collection. The cursor changes into crosshairs when it is over an object that can be added to the collection. Or you could click the Add button to open a Select Object dialog box where you can select objects from a list. The collection objects are then displayed in a list found in the Properties rollout. Clicking the highlight button in the Properties rollout briefly turns white all objects that are part of the collection.

 A single object can be added to multiple collections, but this causes a warning to appear when you try to preview the animation.

If an object is selected before you create a collection icon, then the selected object is automatically added to the collection and the collection icon is positioned at the Pivot Point of the selected object or objects.

Collection modifiers

If you tried several times to add an object to a Cloth collection with no luck, then this section is for you. Before you can add objects to the Cloth, Rope, or Soft Bodies collections, you need to apply the Cloth, Rope, or Soft Body modifiers to the object. To apply a modifier to an object, select the object in the viewport, choose reactor ➪ Apply Modifier, and choose the modifier type to apply. Table 38.2 shows the three reactor modifiers.

 The Rope modifier can be applied only to splines or shapes.

TABLE 38.2

reactor Modifiers

Toolbar Button	Name	Description
	Cloth Modifier	Allows objects to be simulated as cloth
	Soft Body Modifier	Allows objects to be simulated as soft bodies
	Rope Modifier	Allows objects to be simulated as rope

Each of the reactor modifiers has a Vertex subobject mode available in the Modifier Stack. Selecting a vertex allows you to give it different physical properties than the rest of the vertices. For example, you could select the vertices at one end of a rope to have a higher Mass value where it connects with a hook. This end would then fall under gravity before the other end.

Setting object properties

After collections have been added to the scene and objects have been added to the collection, you can define the physical properties using the Property Editor, shown in Figure 38.4. You can open the Property Editor by selecting reactor ➪ Open Property Editor. To set the properties for the objects, you need to select the object and not the collection icon. The Property Editor lets you set the properties for many selected objects at the same time. The title bar of the Property Editor identifies the collection whose properties you are setting.

Mass, friction, and elasticity

The Mass property defines how heavy the object is. For example, a bowling ball has a higher mass value than a Ping-Pong ball. The Elasticity value defines how springy the object is; a tennis ball is more elastic than a marble. The Friction value defines how resistant the object is to rolling or sliding along the floor. For example, a brick has a higher friction value than an ice cube.

FIGURE 38.4

The Property Editor can set the physical properties for geometric objects included in the scene.

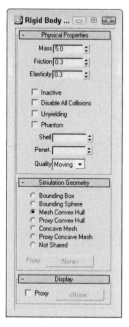

 A rigid body with a Mass value of 0 is left out of all calculations and remains stuck in the simulation.

The Property Editor also includes several other options. The Inactive option removes the object from the simulation calculations. The Disable All Collisions option causes the object to not collide with other objects. The Unyielding option makes the object immovable and is good to use for floor and wall objects, and the Phantom option makes objects so they have no impact on other objects in the scene.

The Shell value defines an additional radius that surrounds convex shapes and is used for collision detection. If you specify a shell value, the simulation runs much more quickly and the likelihood that objects will interpenetrate each other is much less. The Penetration value is the amount of penetration that is allowed between objects. By providing a non-zero value, the simulation can be solved much more quickly. The Quality settings lets you set how important the object's motion is to the animation. The options include Debris, for objects of low importance; Moving, for objects of medium importance; Critical, for objects that should never penetrate other objects; and Bullet, for objects that move rapidly. The Shell, Penetration, and Quality values work only with the version 3 reactor engine.

Defining collision boundaries

Another common property that you can set pertains to how the object deals with collision detection. You can select the volume to use to determine when two objects collide with each other. If this sounds a bit funny because any collision volume that doesn't use the actual mesh would be inaccurate, then you need to realize that a complex simulation with lots of collisions of complex objects could take a long time to compute. If reactor has only to compute collisions based on the object's bounding box instead of the actual mesh object, the simulation runs much more quickly and the inaccuracies aren't even noticeable.

Before deciding on the collision boundary to use, you need to determine whether an object is convex or concave. A concave object is one that you can penetrate with a ray and cross its mesh boundary only twice. Convex objects require more than two crossings with an imaginary ray. You can test whether an object is convex using the reactor ➪ Utilities ➪ Convexity Test menu command or in the Utils rollout of the Utilities panel with a button named Test Convexity.

A convex object can use any of the options found in the Simulation Geometry rollout of the Object Properties dialog box, including Bounding Box, Bounding Sphere, Mesh Convex Hull, Proxy Convex Hull, Concave Mesh, Proxy Concave Mesh, or Not Shared as its collision boundary. If a Proxy option is selected, you can select the proxy object using the Proxy button found in the Simulation Geometry rollout. A proxy is a just a low-resolution version of an object used here for collision detection.

> **NOTE** The Material Editor includes a Dynamics Properties rollout with values for Bounce Coefficient, Static, and Sliding Friction. These values are used with the Dynamics utility but are not used with the reactor engine.

Modifier properties

In addition to the properties found in the Property Editor, objects that have one of the reactor modifiers applied to it have additional properties that are specific to the collection types. These properties show up in the Modify panel when the object is selected.

> **NOTE** All the modifiers include an option to Avoid Self-Intersections. Because these object types are flexible, they often move and bunch up together. This option prevents an object from turning inside out and intersecting with itself.

For the Cloth modifier, these additional properties include Mass, Friction, Relative Density, and Air Resistance. You can also select to use the Simple Force Model or the Complex Force Model, which enables Stretch, Bend, Shear, and Damping values. You can also define a Fold Stiffness, which determines how stiff the fold in the cloth is.

> **NOTE** When similar properties exist for an object in the Property Editor and the Modify panel, the value in the Modify panel takes precedence. Actually, the properties in the Property Editor apply only to rigid body objects.

The Soft Body modifier adds value for Stiffness and Damping to the Mass and Friction values. You can also select to have the object deform using a Mesh-based or an FFD-based algorithm. The FFD-based algorithm uses control points and is a simpler method that doesn't require as much memory.

The Rope modifier includes Mass, Thickness, Friction, and Air Resistance values. You can also select the rope to be a Spring or Constraint type. Spring ropes act like bungee cords or rubber bands.

Tutorial: Throwing a shirt over a chair

In the preceding example, we looked at something that reactor made much easier, but in this example, we see some animations that would be impossible without reactor. Cloth deformation is very difficult to animate, but the laws of physics know lots about how to describe this motion. In this simple example, we throw a stiff shirt over a stationary chair to see how it reacts.

To animate cloth falling over a hard object, follow these steps:

1. Open the Shirt over chair.max file from the Chap 38 directory on the DVD.

   This file includes a chair object and a shirt that is nothing more than an extruded shape that has been sufficiently subdivided.

2. Select reactor ⇨ Create Object ⇨ Rigid Body Collection, and click in the Front viewport to create the collection icon. Click the Add button, and select the chair and the floor objects to add them both to the Rigid Body Collection.

3. Select the chair and floor object, and choose reactor ⇨ Open Property Editor. Select the Unyielding option. Then right-click to exit Rigid Body Collector mode.

4. Select the shirt object, and choose reactor ⇨ Apply Modifier ⇨ Cloth Modifier.

5. With the shirt object still selected, choose reactor ⇨ Create Object ⇨ Cloth Collection to create a Cloth collection that contains the shirt object.

6. Now let's preview the animation before computing it. Select reactor ⇨ Preview Animation to open the Preview window, and press the P button. When the animation finishes (and the shirt falls on the chair), close the Preview window.

7. Select reactor ⇨ Create Animation to have the keys computed for this animation. Then click the Play button to see the final animation.

Figure 38.5 shows one frame of the finished animation.

FIGURE 38.5

reactor can be used to simulate cloth falling realistically over a chair.

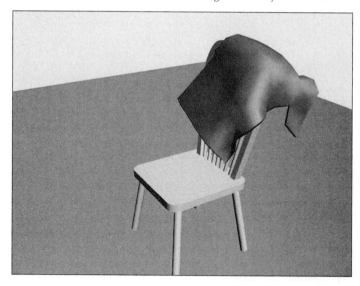

Creating reactor Objects

In addition to collections, reactor also includes several default objects that react with the scene in unique defined ways. These objects can be created using the reactor ⇨ Create Object menu commands or by clicking its icon in the reactor toolbar and dragging in one of the viewports.

The default objects include Spring, Plane, Linear Dashpot, Angular Dashpot, Motor, Wind, Toy Car, Fracture, and Water as listed in Table 38.3.

TABLE 38.3

reactor Objects

Toolbar Button	Name	Description
	Spring	Acts to bring connected child and parent objects closer together
	Plane	Adds a solid plane object to the scene
	Linear Dashpot	Acts to limit linear motion between connected child and parent objects
	Angular Dashpot	Acts to limit angular motion between connected child and parent objects
	Motor	Used to add angular force to the scene
	Wind	Used to add linear force to the scene
	Toy Car	Simulates a simple car with rotating wheels and linear motion
	Fracture	Identifies objects that can be broken into pieces
	Water	Adds water to the scene that conforms to concave surface

The gizmos for these objects, like the collection gizmos, appear red when first created for most of these objects and then turn white when selected and blue when connected to a geometry object. Figure 38.6 shows the gizmo icons for each of these reactor objects.

FIGURE 38.6

The gizmo icons for each of the reactor objects

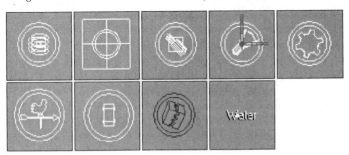

Most of these objects need to be associated with an object to be included in reactor. For example, the Toy Car reactor object must be connected to a geometry object for its chassis and up to four geometry objects for its wheels. This is done by clicking on the respective buttons in the Properties rollout and selecting the geometry object in the viewport. For example, you can connect a Spring object to both a Child and a Parent object. Other reactor objects, like the Plane and Wind objects, do not need to be connected to an object to work.

Springs and dashpots

The Spring and Dashpot objects can be linked between a child and parent object. Simply select the Child button in the Spring Properties rollout, and click the scene object to make the Spring's child. If no parent is selected, the Spring is connected between the child object and the Spring object gizmo's location.

The Align options let you move the Spring to the Child or Parent Body and to use the Child or Parent Space. Selecting the Each Body option positions the Spring object equally spaced between the child and parent.

For the Spring object, you can set the Stiffness, Rest Length, and Damping values and whether it acts on Compression or Extension. The farther the child and parent objects are from the Spring object icon, the stronger the pull toward the icon, so changing the Rest Length value to a small value causes the two objects to be pulled quickly together.

 **The child and parent objects still need to be added to a collection such as the Rigid Body collection to be used in the simulation.**

Dashpot objects work in a similar manner to Springs. They can be linked to child and parent objects and include values for Strength and Damping. Linear dashpots forces the parent and child objects to maintain their position as if they were connected by a springy bar. The Angular dashpot forces two objects to retain the same orientation; rotating one causes the other to rotate the same way.

Plane

A Plane object creates a solid wall that objects cannot penetrate if the object belongs to the Rigid Body collection, but only the face with the normal extending from it is solid. This object can be scaled, and its only property is a Show Normal option. Also note that these objects are not renderable and are not visible in the Preview window.

Motor and Wind

The Motor object can be used to spin objects belonging to the Rigid Body collection in the scene. For these objects, you can select a Rotation Axis value, as well as Angular Speed and Gain values.

The Wind object can be used to add a linear force to the scene. The force is directed globally in the direction that is displayed on the Wind object icon, so you need to be careful to place this icon in the correct viewport in order to get the wind blowing in the right direction. The strength of the wind is determined by the Wind Speed value. The wind's ability to move objects depends on its strength and the object's Mass value. Heavier objects are harder to blow away.

The Perturb Speed option lets you make the wind gusty. The Variance is how different its strength is from the base value, and the Time Scale determines how often these gusts take place. You can also set a Ripple option to cause a variance in wind strength Left/Right, Up/Down, or Back/Forward with a given Magnitude and Frequency. You can also perturb time.

The Use Range lets you specify a range on which the wind has an effect. All objects within the set range are influenced by the wind, but objects beyond the range are not. The Enable Sheltering option lets objects positioned behind other objects be sheltered from the wind. You can choose which objects the wind can affect, including Rigid Bodies, Cloth, Soft Bodies, and Ropes.

Toy Car

The Toy Car reactor object is a specific object type that simulates a driving car that produces linear motion by rotating wheels. For this object, you can select a Chassis object that represents the car body and pick a list of objects to act as wheels. For this system, you can specify Angular and Linear Strength values and a Suspension value.

You can also specify the car's orientation using the icon (an arrow points in the direction the car will travel) or using a Common Local Orientation. For the wheels, you can specify to Allow Wheel Penetration, which lets the system have some give as it moves over a rough surface and whether the wheels spin. To give the car some power, you can set the Angular Speed and Gain of the wheels.

For the reactor version 3 engine, an additional set of parameters is available.

> **TIP** If you use the reactor version 3 engine with the Toy Car object, then a new set of parameters for controlling its strength, suspension, and breakable threshold are available. This option is new to 3ds Max 2008.

Fracture

The Fracture reactor object offers a way to have reactor objects blown apart. The Properties rollout includes a list of Pieces that are to be involved in the fracturing. If you select a Piece from the list, you can designate it as Broken, Normal, Unbreakable, or Keystone, or to Break at Time. The Now button sets the break time to the current frame.

The Use Connectivity option enables linked objects to stay together, such as two parts connected to a spring. You can also select to Break On and set an Impulse value or a Velocity value. The Energy Loss is the amount of energy lost with every collision.

Tutorial: Smashing a gingerbread house

It doesn't matter how many times your mother asks you to not play ball in the house, you always forget. And Murphy's Law says that you'll forget at just the wrong time, like when the gingerbread house has just been finished.

To smash a gingerbread house, follow these steps:

1. Open the Smashed gingerbread house.max file from the Chap 38 directory on the DVD.

    This file includes a gingerbread house model created by Viewpoint Datalabs.

2. Select reactor ⇨ Create Objects ⇨ Rigid Body Collection, and click in the Top viewport to create the collection icon. Then click the Add button to open the Select Objects dialog box. Click the All button, and close the dialog box with the Select button.

3. Select reactor ⇨ Create Objects ⇨ Fracture, and click in the Top viewport to create the Fracture icon. Click the Add button in the Properties rollout, select all the objects except for the "Sphere01" and the "ground" objects, and click Select. In the Pieces list of the Properties rollout, select all the objects, enable the Break at Time option, and set the time to **30**.

4. Select the "ground" object in the scene, choose reactor ⇨ Open Property Editor, and enable the Unyielding option. Then select the "Sphere01" object, and set its Mass value to 60. Finally, select all the gingerbread house objects, and set their Mass values to **20** and the Friction value to **1.0**. To be more realistic, you should set the Mass value on the smaller pieces to a smaller value, but for this example, they can all be the same.

5. Select reactor ⇨ Preview Animation to open the Preview window. A dialog box appears stating that many of the smaller pieces have a density value that likely is too high, which we already know, so click the Continue button to close the warning window. Then press the P button to see the animation.

   The ball falls, and the house explodes into pieces.

6. Select reactor ⇨ Create Animation. A warning dialog box appears reminding you that this action cannot be undone. Click OK. Then after the animation is finished, click the Play button to see the final results.

Figure 38.7 shows the gingerbread house as it fractures into pieces.

FIGURE 38.7

The fracture object in reactor can be used to compute realistic explosions.

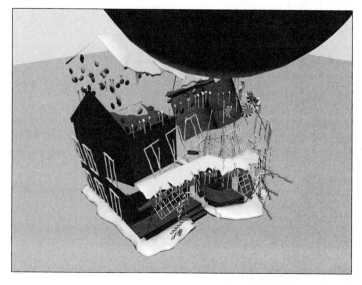

Water

The Water reactor object creates a realistic surface that acts and behaves like a liquid. For water, you can specify its size in X- and Y-coordinate values and its Subdivisions. Be aware that with inadequate subdivisions, the water does not work realistically. The Landscape option lets you select a surround object that acts like an object with which the water interacts.

You can also set the Wave Speed, Minimum and Maximum Ripple sizes, Density, Viscosity, and Depth. If the Depth option is disabled, then the water has only surface effects.

reactor water is applied as a Space Warp. Space Warps aren't rendered, so to see the water surface, you need to create a Plane object and bind it to the Space Warp using the Bind to Space Warp icon on the main toolbar.

Tutorial: Working with water

One of the coolest features of reactor is its ability to create and simulate the effects of water. Before you can use water, you must have a model that can hold water.

To use reactor to create a body of water, follow these steps:

1. Open the Pool of water.max file from the Chap 38 directory on the DVD.

    This file includes a pool to hold water created from primitives, along with three spheres of different mass.

2. Select reactor ➪ Create Objects ➪ Rigid Body Collection, and click in the Front viewport. In the RB Collection Properties rollout, click the Add button and select all the Box and Sphere objects. Then right-click to exit Rigid Body Collector mode.

3. Select reactor ➪ Create Objects ➪ Water, and click and drag in the Top viewport to create the water plane that fills the box. Then drag the water plane upward in the Left viewport to move the water level toward the top of the box.

4. Select the left sphere in the Front viewport, and open the Property Editor with the reactor ➪ Open Property Editor menu command. Set the Mass value to **3 kg**. Select the middle sphere, and set its Mass to **100 kg**, and then set the right sphere to **5000 kg**.

5. Check the animation in the Preview window by selecting reactor ➪ Preview Animation. Press P to start the animation.

6. Record the animation keys with the reactor ➪ Create Animation menu command.

7. Select Create ➪ Standard Primitives ➪ Plane, and drag in the Top viewport to create a Plane object that is the same size and density as the Water plane. Then click the Bind to Space Warp button on the main toolbar, and drag from the Plane to the Water Space Warp. Open the Material Editor, and create a material that is light blue with an Opacity value of **20** and a Specular value of **75**. Drag this material to the Plane object.

Figure 38.8 shows the simulation in the Preview window. Notice how the mass values determine whether the sphere floats or sinks.

FIGURE 38.8

Depending on the mass property, objects sink or float.

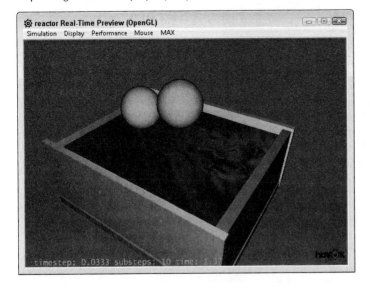

Calculating and Previewing a Simulation

Although you've already had some experience with the Preview window in the examples, more controls are available than just playing the animation. To preview the simulation, select reactor ⇨ Preview Animation or click the Preview Animation button on the reactor toolbar. This opens a Havok window like the one shown in Figure 38.9. This window lets you play with your simulation. The Simulation ⇨ Play/Pause menu (keyboard shortcut, P) executes the simulation. Dragging with the left mouse button rotates the scene, and you can zoom in and out with the scroll wheel.

 The Preview window runs only if the OpenGL or the Direct3D display drivers are used. The window uses OpenGL by default, or you can set it to use DirectX with the DirectX option in the Display rollout. The display driver being used is displayed in the title bar of the Preview window.

Using the Preview window

The fun part of the preview window is that you can interact with the objects. Right-clicking (when the simulation is playing) and dragging on the object moves it. If you find a position that you want to capture for Max, you can use the MAX ⇨ Update Max menu command to set the starting positions of the objects in Max.

TIP If the reactor version 3 engine is selected, then you can interact with the objects in the Preview window by holding down the Spacebar and dragging the mouse.

FIGURE 38.9

The Preview window is a fun place to play with a simulation.

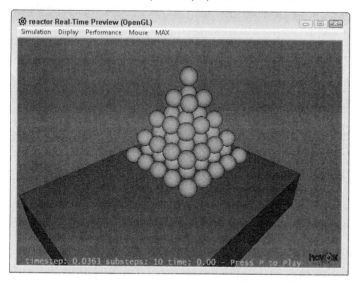

If you want to reset the animation to its starting positions, you can use the Simulation ⇨ Reset menu command. The Display menu includes several options that you can turn on to change the display. Objects can be seen as Faces or Wireframes. If you have a particularly complex scene to preview, then wireframes may be easy to work with. You can also display the Simulation Edges (which shows the collision boundaries of the objects), Grids, the Origin, and a Flashlight to add light to the scene. The Display menu also includes a Camera Settings option that you can use to set the near and far Clipping Planes and the Preview window's Field of View.

The Performance menu includes options for setting the frames per second and the number of substeps used to compute the simulation. For most animations, the default of 10 substeps is sufficient, but if you want Max to spend more time computing an accurate solution, you can try a higher substep value.

 Don't use a high substep value with water.

Creating animation keys

To compute the animation keys for the simulation, select the reactor ⇨ Create Animation menu command or press the Create Animation button in the reactor toolbar. The progress is displayed at the bottom of the Max interface. You can cancel the simulation at any time with the Esc key.

 After you've clicked the Create Animation menu command, a warning appears stating that the operation cannot be undone.

Analyzing the scene

After the Preview window is opened, a warning dialog box appears if the scene has any errors or warnings that could cause trouble with the simulation. It also warns of unrealistic data, such as property settings that are too high or too low.

 The one warning that isn't included in the warning dialog box is if objects have no Mass value. If objects in your simulation are just sitting there, then make sure that they have a Mass value.

If you want to check your scene without opening the Preview window, you can use the reactor ⇨ Utilities ⇨ Analyze World menu command. This command checks your scene for any trouble and presents problems in a dialog box. If no problems are found, then a separate dialog box tells you that no problems were found.

Tutorial: Dropping a plate of donuts

All the great books have an element of tragedy, so consider a policeman carrying a dozen donuts on a plate when he stumbles and drops the plate. Donuts everywhere, how tragic! This animation sequence would be difficult or at least time-consuming, but not with reactor.

To use reactor to animate a falling plate of donuts, follow these steps:

1. Open the Falling plate of donuts.max file from the Chap 38 directory on the DVD.

   This file includes a simple plate of donuts created from primitives.

2. Select the reactor ⇨ Create Objects ⇨ Rigid Body Collection menu command, and click in the Front viewport. In the RB Collection Properties rollout, click the Pick button and select the plate object. Click the Pick button again, and select the Box object that represents the floor.

3. Select the Torus objects, and choose reactor ⇨ Apply Modifier ⇨ Soft Body Modifier (or click the Soft Body Modifier button in the reactor toolbar).

4. Then select reactor ⇨ Create Objects ⇨ Soft Body Collection, and click again in the Front viewport. In the SB Collection Properties rollout, click the Add button and select all the Torus objects again.

5. Select reactor ⇨ Open Property Editor, and select the Box object; in the Properties rollout, enable the Unyielding option. Select the plate object, and make its Mass value **5.0**. Then select all the donuts, and make their Mass value **0.25**. Enable the Mesh Convex Hull option.

6. The last step is to execute the simulation: Select the reactor ⇨ Create Animation menu command. It takes some time to compute a solution for this example. When it completes, press the Play Animation button (or press the / key) to see the results.

Figure 38.10 shows the upturned plate of donuts.

FIGURE 38.10

Animating these falling donuts, simulated as soft body objects, was easy with reactor.

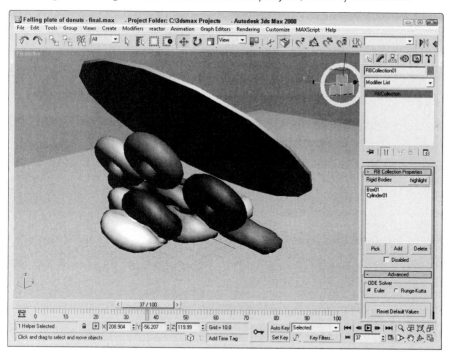

933

Constraining Objects

Constraints are ways to limit the amount of motion that an object can do. Using constraints can help control objects in the scene as they interact with other objects. Perhaps the simplest constraint isn't a constraint at all. If you enable the Unyielding option in the Property Editor the rigid body is set so that won't move and is a good option for the ground plane. It also allows hand-keyed animated objects to interact with rigid body objects instead of relying on the dynamics engine.

Other constraints are found in the reactor ⇨ Create Objects menu and consist of Constraint Solver, Rag Doll Constraint, Hinge Constraint, Point-Point Constraint, Prismatic Constraint, Car-Wheel Constraint, and Point-Path Constraint, as listed in Table 38.4.

TABLE 38.4

reactor Constraints

Toolbar Button	Name	Description
	Constraint Solver	Contains all active constraints used in the scene
	Rag Doll Constraint	Causes a model to act as a human figure
	Hinge Constraint	Allows angular rotation like a hinge
	Point-Point Constraint	Links two points together; good for rope ends
	Prismatic Constraint	Used to constrain the motion of two rigid bodies to a single axis with no rotation
	Car-Wheel Constraint	Causes a car to move linearly as a wheel object is rotated
	Point-Path Constraint	Limits a point to move only along a path

After a constraint object is added to the scene, you can select the objects that will be included as child and parent objects using the buttons in the Properties rollout. The Properties rollout also includes buttons to align the constraint to the Child Body, Parent Body, Child Space, or Parent Space. For each constraint, you can set the Strength and Tau of the connection. This determines how strong the link is and how easily broken. In addition to the Strength and Tau values, you can set Limits and allow the hinge to be Breakable under a defined Linear or Angular force value. The Threshold value defines the breakability of the constraint. Higher Threshold values make it less likely to break. The Threshold value works only with reactor, version 3.

When a constraint's Child is first selected, the Constraint's icon is positioned at the pivot point of the child object. If you look in the Modifier Stack for the Constraint object, you'll find subobject modes for Child Space and Parent Space. If you select these subobject modes, you can change the position of the constraint's child and parent objects.

Using a Constraint Solver

In order to use most constraints, you need to add a Constraint Solver to the scene. Then you can use the Modify panel to add Constraints to the list to be solved. The Constraint Solver needs to know about any Rigid Body Collections that are attached to any Constraints in the scene. To identify all the Constraints that are part of the Constraint Solver, click the Highlight button.

 **If the simulation includes any constraints that the Constraint Solver doesn't know about, the Constraint Solver icon appears red in the viewports.**

Rag Doll constraint

The Rag Doll constraint defines all the joint limits common in a human figure. It can be used to animate a lifeless body colliding with various rigid body objects. Using the Rag Doll constraint, you can manually define how the body joints can twist, rotate, and move.

These joints are fairly common for human bodies. Autodesk has created a script to create a human body proxy that creates a rag doll with the correct constraints already defined. The script is named rctRagdollScript.ms. It can be found in the scripts directory where 3ds Max is installed.

You can execute this script by opening the Utilities panel, clicking the MAXScript button, and clicking the Run Script button. This opens a file dialog box. Locate the script and click Open, and the script runs. Running this script opens the Rag Doll dialog box, shown in Figure 38.11. Using this dialog box, you can provide a Name for the rag doll and set its Height and the number of Vertebra. The Create Humanoid button makes the rag doll appear in the viewports.

Once positioned, you can press the Constrain Humanoid button in the Constrain Humanoid rollout. This adds all the necessary constrains to the rag doll.

 **You can use the rag doll script to place reactor constraints on a Biped object.**

FIGURE 38.11

Fully constrained humanoid figures can be created using the rctRagdollScript.ms script.

The Point-to-Point constraint lets you attach two objects together by a common point. The attach point is the pivot point of the child and parent objects. It can be used to animate a lifeless body colliding with various rigid body objects. Using the Rag Doll constraint, you can manually define how the body joints can twist, rotate, and move.

Tutorial: Swinging into a wall

Playing with the rag doll object is just plain fun. Remember that in the Preview window you can use the right-click button to throw the doll around. For this example, we use a couple of Point-to-Point Constraints along with a Rag Doll constraint to create a simple scene where the rag doll swings from a rope into a brick wall.

To animate a rag doll swinging on a rope, follow these steps:

1. Open the Swinging into a wall.max file from the Chap 38 directory on the DVD.

    This file includes a simple scene consisting of several Boxes, a Cylinder for the rope, and a brick wall.

2. Open the Utilities panel, and click the MAXScript button. Click the Run Script button in the MAXScript rollout. In the file dialog box, locate the Scripts directory where Max is installed. Select the rctRagdollScript.ms file, and click the Open button. The script file opens in a MAXScript window. In the MAXScript window, select the File ➪ Evaluate All menu command to make the Rag Doll panel appear.

3. In the Rag Doll panel that appears, open the Create Humanoid rollout and click the Create Humanoid button. Then move the Rag Doll panel to the side, but don't close it. Select the rag doll that appears at the origin, and move it so that one of its hands is positioned close to the end of the Cylinder object.

4. In the Rag Doll panel, open the Constrain Humanoid rollout and click the Constrain Humanoid button. This automatically adds all the needed constraints for the rag doll. Then close the Rag Doll panel.

5. Select the long Cylinder object, choose reactor ➪ Create Object ➪ Point-Point Constraint, and click in the Left viewport close to the rag doll. In the Properties rollout, click the Child button and select the hand object that is close to the Cylinder. Then enable the Parent option, click the Parent button, and select the Cylinder. Open the Modify panel, select the Parent Space subobject mode, and move the gizmo in the Front viewport to be on the Cylinder. Do the same for the Child Space subobject.

    This defines where the two objects will be attached.

6. Repeat Step 5 to create a Point-to-Point Constraint where the Cylinder touches the roof object with the Cylinder as the Child object and the roof as the Parent object. With the second Point-to-Point Constraint selected, click on the Align Spaces to Parent Body button in the Modify panel.

7. Press the H key to open the Select Objects dialog box, and select the RagdollRBCollection object. Then click the Add button in the RB Collection Properties rollout. Click the All button in the Select Rigid Bodies dialog box, and click Select. Repeat this step for the RagdollCSolver icon to add the two new Point-to-Point Constraints.

8. Select all three Box objects in the scene, and choose reactor ➪ Open Property Editor. In the Physical Properties rollout, enable the Unyielding option. Then select the Cylinder object, and set its Mass value to **0.5**.

9. Select reactor ➪ Preview Animation to see the resulting preview. Then select reactor ➪ Create Animation to create the animation keys.

Figure 38.12 shows the swinging rag doll.

Using constraints gives you control over the animation motion.

reactor Troubleshooting

reactor identifies problems before you try to preview or compute the simulation. These problems are displayed in an error window. The following are some common errors that you can avoid. Use the Analyze World button to look for warnings.

- **Don't use the default Plane primitive:** reactor complains if the plane object is co-planar. The problem is that without any depth, reactor can't accurately compute collisions. Instead, use a Box primitive or use reactor's Plane Primitive object (found in its toolbar). However, you can use a plane object if you make it a Concave Mesh.

- **Watch for low Mass values:** reactor complains if the Mass value for any objects is too low. To fix this problem, increase the Mass value for the identified object.

- **Don't have interpenetrating objects:** Objects that intersect cause an error in reactor. Make sure that none of the objects intersect with each other.

- **Build all reactor objects to scale:** reactor tends to work well when all objects are within one meter of each other. Objects that are too small or too big tend to have issues with collisions.

Summary

This chapter covered the basics of animating a dynamic simulation using the reactor. In this chapter, you accomplished the following:

- Experimented with the reactor plug-in
- Worked with collections
- Applied reactor modifiers
- Used reactor objects
- Previewed reactor animations
- Used constraints

The next chapter covers the dynamic abilities of Max's hair and cloth systems.

Chapter 39

Animating Hair and Cloth

The specialized hair and cloth systems can create believable, realistic hair, but the real benefit to making hair and cloth come alive is found in the dynamic abilities of both.

In this chapter, we look at the dynamic abilities of both the hair and cloth systems. Using these systems, you can simulate hair that is blown by the wind and cloth that drapes over and around underlying objects.

ROSS-REF Creating and defining both the Hair and Cloth systems is covered in Chapter 28, "Adding and Styling Hair, Fur, and Cloth."

Using Hair Dynamics

Being able to style hair is great, but have you ever left the barbershop and had the wind do its own styling job on your hair? The Dynamics rollout for Hair and Fur lets you define specific forces and let the hair fall where it may.

TIP Be conservative with the forces that are applied to a hair system. Too many forces or too extreme forces can easily destroy any styling that you've created.

Making Hair Live

The Dynamics rollout is available only if the Hair and Fur (WSM) modifier has been applied to an object. At the top of the Dynamics rollout are three modes: None, Live, and Precomputed. If you select the Live mode, then the hair around the growth object immediately becomes subject to gravity and other forces in real-time, causing the hair to droop about the growth object. Moreover, if you move the object within the viewport, the hair flows about the object as if you were moving a real object with hair attached. Figure 39.1 shows a simple mouse with hair attached. The image on the left shows the hair particles with the None mode enabled and the image on the right shows the hair after the Live mode is enabled. Notice how the hair particles fall around the mouse object.

FIGURE 39.1

The Live dynamic mode makes the hair react in real time to the scene forces.

If you press the Escape key while in Live mode, a dialog box appears, giving you the option to Freeze, Stop, or Continue. If you choose the Freeze button, then the hair stays in its current position.

The Precomputed mode is available only after you've specified a Stat File name. This mode lets you save the hair motions into a separate stat file.

Setting properties

Only a few properties need to be defined to enable hair dynamics. In the Dynamics rollout, you find values for Gravity, Stiffness, Springiness, Root Hold, and Dampen. These properties control how the hair behaves in response to the environment forces. The Gravity value can be negative if you want the hair to rise instead of fall. You can simulate space environments by setting the gravity to 0. The Stiffness value eliminates all dynamic movement if set to 1.0. If you want the hair to move only slightly as the object moves, then a Stiffness value close to 1.0 should work. The Root Hold value is like stiffness, but applies only to the root. The Dampen value causes motions to die out quickly.

All dynamic properties except Gravity can be controlled using a grayscale map, using the small button to the right of the value field.

Enabling collisions

The first type of dynamic force to address is to enable collisions between the hair and the other scene objects. To enable collisions between the growth object and its hair, simply enable the Use Growth Object option. In addition to the growth object, other scene objects can be added to the list with which the hair will collide. To add other objects, click the Add button and pick the object to add in the viewport. Each collision object can use either a boundary Sphere to define its collision volume or a Polygon, which bases collisions on the actual surface geometry. The latter takes longer to compute, but it's more accurate.

Enabling forces

In addition to the ubiquitous gravity, you can enable collisions between the hairs and the growth object and any other scene objects. To add another scene object to the collision calculations, click the Add button and select the new collision object. The External Forces list lets you add Space Warps for additional forces such as Wind.

Running a simulation

The Precomputed mode lets you save the hair dynamics to a separate stat file. If you want to capture the dynamic simulation, you first must specify a stat file by clicking the button to the right of the Stat File section. With a stat file specified, click the Run button in the Simulation section to calculate the dynamic solution. The Start and End fields let you enter the range for the simulation. A separate stat file is generated for every frame of the animation.

If you enable the Precomputed mode option before you render, then the stat file is read and used during the rendering process. You can delete all stat files quickly with the scarily named Delete all files button.

Tutorial: Simulating hair dynamics

Dynamic hair moves and flows around the other objects in the scene that are animated. As an example of this, we move a female character's head back and forth and simulate how the hair moves. I selected the Mohawk hairstyle because I'm hip and cool, a real rebel. Actually, the Mohawk is a simple style and gives us a chance to play with the Stiffness property.

To simulate the dynamics of a hair system, follow these steps:

1. Open the Female head with mohawk.max file from the Chap 39 directory on the DVD.

    This file includes the head from a female character model created by Zygote Media. The hair modifier already has been added to this character and styled.

2. Click the Auto Key button, drag the Time Slider to frame 5, and move the character to the right in the Top viewport. Then drag the Time Slider to frame 10, and move the character back to the left. This simple motion should be enough to bend the hair over. Then disable the Auto Key mode.

3. With the head selected, open the Dynamics rollout and set the Stiffness value to 0.8. This should keep the hair standing straight up. To check this, enable the Live mode and watch how the hair reacts.

4. Set the Simulation to run from 0 to 10 frames, and then open and specify a stat file location. The path of the stat file location is displayed. Then click the Run button to start the simulation. The precomputed values are saved to stat files.

5. Select the Precomputed mode option and drag through the animation frames to see how the hair reacts.

Figure 39.2 shows the hair bending to one side as the female head moves.

FIGURE 39.2

Using precomputed hair can save you a bundle of time when rendering.

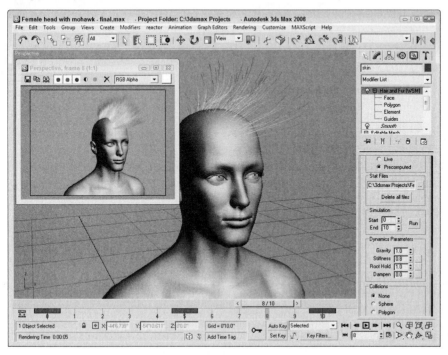

Simulating Cloth Dynamics

Hair isn't the only system that has the benefit of dynamic motion. Cloth can also benefit from dynamic simulations. The steps for setting up a dynamic cloth simulation are similar to those for hair. First, define the cloth properties and the environmental forces acting on the cloth. Then run the simulation.

Defining cloth properties and forces

To add objects (both cloth and collision objects) to the simulation, click on the Object Properties button in the Object rollout. This opens the Object Properties dialog box, shown in Figure 39.3. Clicking the Add Objects button lets you select scene objects to add to the simulation. Only objects added to the scene are included in the simulation. If an object isn't added, it is ignored. All objects added to the simulation are added to the list at the left. Selected objects in the list can be specified as Inactive, Cloth, or Collision Object. For Cloth and Collision Objects, you can set properties. You also can load and save cloth presets. Cloth presets are saved using the .sti extension.

 **TIP** If the cloth tends to pass through objects, then you can increase the Offset value for the collision object.

FIGURE 39.3

The Object Properties dialog box lets you define the properties of cloth and collision objects.

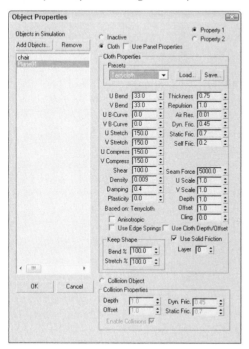

After all the objects involved in the simulation are included and defined, you can set the simulation range in the Simulation Parameters rollout. The initial state for the object to be draped may be set using the Set Initial State button. The Cloth Forces button, in the Object rollout, opens a simple dialog box where you can select to add additional forces to the simulation. Gravity is added by default, but you can change its value in the Simulation Parameters rollout.

Creating a Cloth simulation

After completing the initial setup, clicking the Simulate button starts the simulation process. The objects are updated in the viewport as each frame is calculated. After every frame is calculated, you can see the entire dynamic simulation by dragging the Time Slider or clicking the Play Animation button. If you want to drape the cloth without running it over several frames, you can use the Simulate Local button. The Simulate Local (damped) button causes the simulation to run local with a large amount of damping, which is useful if the cloth tends to drape too fast. If you want to remove the current simulation because some properties have changed, click the Erase Simulation button, or you can remove all frames after the current simulation frame with the Truncate Simulation button.

 If the simulation is taking too long to compute, you can cancel the simulation by pressing the Escape button.

If you need to change a cloth or force property, click Erase Simulation, make the change, and run the simulation again. Simulation motions can be saved as keys with the Create Keys button. Figure 39.4 shows a simple plane object that has been draped over a chair over the course of 100 frames.

FIGURE 39.4

After you've defined cloth and force properties, an executed simulation drapes the cloth over a chair.

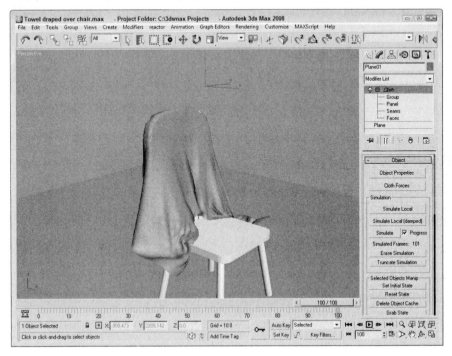

Viewing cloth tension

For cloth objects created using the Garment Maker modifier, you can view the tension in the cloth using the Tension option in the Simulation Parameters rollout. This option shows the areas of greatest tension in shaded colors. Figure 39.5 shows the tension in the dress draped over the female model from Chapter 28, "Adding and Styling Hair, Fur, and Cloth."

Tutorial: Draping cloth over a jet

For a larger example of a cloth system, we drape a drop cloth over a jet.

To simulate the dynamics of a cloth object, follow these steps:

1. Open the Sheet over Mig jet.max file from the Chap 39 directory on the DVD.

    This file includes a Mig-29 jet model created by Viewpoint Datalabs.

2. Choose the Create ➪ Standard Primitives ➪ Plane menu command, and drag in the Top viewport to create a plane object that covers the jet. Set the Length and Width Segment values to 100 to make the sufficient resolution for the cloth, and drag the plane object upward in the Front viewport, so it sits above the jet.

FIGURE 39.5

You can view the tension for cloth created with the Garment Maker modifier.

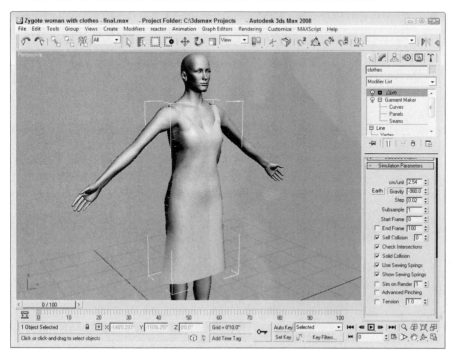

> **NOTE** You also can create the cloth from a rectangular spline that has the Garment Maker modifier applied to it. This approach uses the Delaunay tessellation, which is better for simulating cloth than the rectangular sections in the Plane object.

3. With the plane object selected, choose the Modifiers ➪ Cloth ➪ Cloth menu command to apply the Cloth modifier to the object.

4. Open the Modifier panel, and click the Object Properties button in the Object rollout to open the Object Properties dialog box. Select the Plane01 object in the left list, and choose the Cloth option. Then select the Silk option from the Presets drop-down list, and set the Thickness to 0.5.

5. With the Object Properties dialog box still open, click the Add Objects button, select the All button, and click the Add button. With all added properties in the left list selected, choose the Collision Object option and click the OK button to close the dialog box.

6. In the Simulation Parameters rollout, enable the End Frame option and set the end frame to 100. Then click the Simulate button in the Object rollout. The plane object descends and covers the jet being draped as it falls.

Figure 39.6 shows the sheet draped over the jet.

FIGURE 39.6

Computing the dynamics of a cloth object is possible with a cloth system.

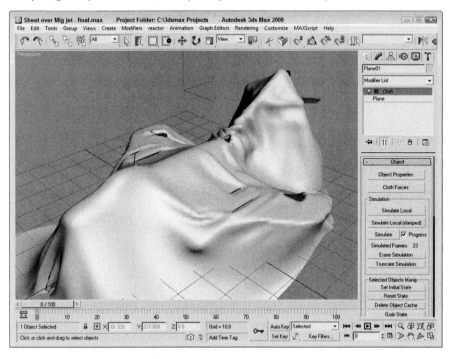

Summary

Using dynamic simulations you can control and compute the motions of hair, fur, and cloth. These motions take into account the various forces and collision objects included in the scene.

Specifically, this chapter covered the following topics:

- Enabling hair dynamics
- Simulating cloth dynamic motion by initiating a simulation process

Part X, "Working with Characters," is up next. It includes coverage of creating, rigging, and skinning characters in preparation for the animation process. The first chapter jumps into working with bones.

Part X

Working with Characters

Chapter 40

Understanding Rigging and Working with Bones

What does a graveyard have in common with animated characters? The answer is bones. Bones are used as an underlying structure attached to a character that is to be animated. By using a bones structure, you can produce complex character motions by simply animating the bones and not having to move all the vertices associated with a high-resolution character.

Although Max includes a prebuilt skeleton with its Biped system, at times you may want to build a custom bones system because not all characters stand on two feet. Have you ever seen a sci-fi movie in which the alien was less than human-like? If your character can't be created by modifying a biped, then you need to use the traditional manual methods of rigging.

This chapter focuses on the process of manually rigging a character, which, depending on the complexity of your character, could end up being even easier than working with bipeds. It also gives you a clear idea of concepts of rigging.

IN THIS CHAPTER

Creating a rigging workflow

Building a bones system

Setting bone parameters and IK Solvers

Making linked objects into a bones system

Creating a Rigging Workflow

A rigged character starts with a linked hierarchy. A linked hierarchy attaches, or links, one object to another and makes it possible to transform the attached object by moving the one to which it is linked. The arm is a classic example of a linked hierarchy: When the shoulder rotates, so do the elbow, wrist, and fingers. Establishing linked hierarchies can make moving, positioning, and animating many objects easy.

A bones system is a unique case of a linked hierarchy that has a specific structure. You can create a structure of bones from an existing hierarchy, or you can create a bones system and attach objects to it. A key advantage of a bones system is that you can use IK Solvers to manipulate and animate the structure. These IK Solvers enable the parents to rotate when the children are moved. In this way, the

IK Solver maintains the chain integrity. Another advantage of a bones structure is that you can constrain the motion of bones so the motion is forced to be realistic, just like a real character.

CROSS-REF IK Solvers are covered in Chapter 41, "Working with Inverse Kinematics."

After the bone structure is created, it needs to be edited to fit the skin mesh that it will control. You also need to define the limits of each bone and joint. This helps prevent the skeleton from moving in unrealistic ways. Applying IK systems is another way to control the motion of the bones and joints. This process of creating a skeleton structure and defining its limits is called rigging.

After you've edited a system of bones, you can cover the bones with objects that have the Skin modifier applied. This modifier lets the covering object move and bend with the bones structure underneath. The process of attaching a model to a bones system is called *skinning*.

CROSS-REF The Skin modifier is covered along with other aspects of skinning a character in Chapter 43, "Skinning Characters."

After a character is rigged and skinned, the character is ready to be animated.

Building a Bones System

In some instances, establishing a hierarchy of objects before linking objects is easier. By building the hierarchy first, you can be sure of the links between objects. One way to build this hierarchy is to use a *bones system*. A bones system consists of many bone objects that are linked together. These bone objects are normally not rendered, but you can set them to be renderable, like splines. You can also assign an IK Solver to the bones system for controlling their motion.

To create a bones system, select Create ➡ Systems ➡ Bones IK Chain, click in a viewport to create a root bone, click a short distance away to create another bone, and repeat this a few more times. Each subsequent click creates another bone linked to the previous one. When you're finished adding bones, right-click to exit bone creation mode. In this manner, you can create a long chain of bone objects all linked together.

These bones are actually linked joints. Moving one bone pulls its neighbors in the chain along with it. Bones can also be rotated, scaled, and stretched. Scaling a bones system affects the distance between the bones.

CAUTION Bones should never be scaled without the XForm modifier applied or all animation keys will behave erratically.

To branch the hierarchy of bones, simply click the bone where you want the branch to start while still in bone creation mode. A new branching bone is created automatically. Click the Bones button again to create a new bone. Then continue to click to add new bones to the branch.

Figure 40.1 shows the rollouts that are available for creating bones.

FIGURE 40.1

The Bone rollouts lets you specify which bones get assigned an IK Controller.

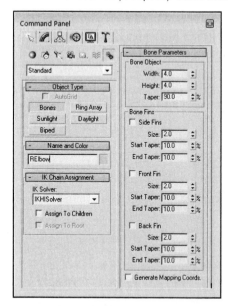

Assigning an IK Solver

In the IK Chain Assignment rollout (found in the Modify panel when a bone is selected), you can select from four IK Solvers: History Dependent, IKHISolver, IKLimb, and SplineIK Solver. You can assign each of these solver types to children and to the root bone using the available options. You need to select both the Assign to Children and the Assign to Root options to assign the IK Controller to all bones in the system. If the Assign to Children option is deselected, then the Assign to Root option is disabled.

CROSS-REF   Chapter 41, "Working with Inverse Kinematics," presents details on each of these IK Solvers.

Setting bone parameters

The Bone Parameters rollout (also in the Modify panel) includes parameters for setting the size of each individual bone, including its Width and Height. You can also set the percentage of Taper applied to the bone.

TIP   Because bones are simple geometry objects, you can apply an Edit Poly modifier to it and edit the bone shape to be whatever you'd like. Custom bone geometry doesn't always work with the Bone Tools.

Fins can be displayed on the front, back, and/or sides of each bone. For each fin, you can specify its size and start and end taper values. Including fins on your bones makes correctly positioning and rotating the bone objects easier. Figure 40.2 shows a simple bones system containing two bones. The first bone has fins.

FIGURE 40.2

This bone includes fins that make understanding its orientation easier.

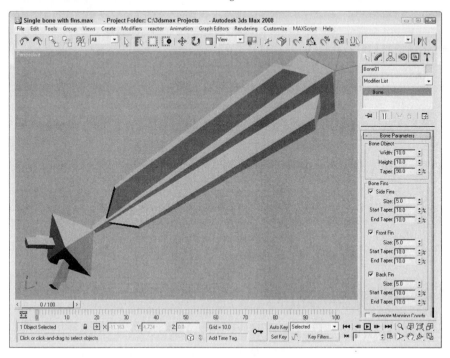

At the bottom of the Bone Parameters rollout is an option to Generate Mapping Coordinates. Bones are renderable objects, so this option lets you apply texture maps to them.

Tutorial: Creating a bones system for an alligator

To practice creating a bones system, we take a trip to the deep South to gator country. The main movement for this gator is going to be in its tail so we need the most bones there. The front legs are smaller and can be controlled with only two simple bones. We also won't worry about fingers.

To create a bones system for an alligator, follow these steps:

1. Open the Alligator bones.max file from the Chap 40 directory on the DVD.

   This file includes an alligator model created by Viewpoint Datalabs.

2. Select Create ➪ Systems ➪ Bones IK Chain, and in the IK Chain Assignment rollout, select IK Limb from the IK Solver drop-down list. Then set the Width and Height values to **10** and enable all the bone fins and set their Size to **5**.

3. In the Top viewport, click once at the pelvis and then again at the mid-abdomen, the base of the neck, and the end of the nose. Then right-click to end the bones chain.

4. While still in Bones mode, click below the pelvis and create an additional five bones to define the tail. Then right-click to end the chain. Select the first bone in the tail chain and link it to the first joint that moves from the pelvis to the nose, which is the root joint.

 If you can't see the bones to make the link, then hide the body so the bones are clearly visible.

5. Click on the Bones button in the Create panel and select the bone just in front of the legs in the Top viewport (the cursor changes to a crosshair when it is over a bone) and drag to the top to form the left shoulder, left upper arm and left lower arm bones. Right-click to end the chain. Repeat to create bones for the left leg.

6. Select the Animation ⇨ Bone Tools menu command to open the Bone Tools dialog box. Select all the bones in the left arm and leg and click the Mirror button. In the Bone Mirror dialog box, select the Y axis and click OK.

7. Click the Select Objects button on the main toolbar to exit Bones mode, and select and name each bone object so it can be easily identified later.

TIP The Schematic View window is a good interface for quickly labeling bones.

Figure 40.3 shows the completed bones system for the alligator.

FIGURE 40.3

This bones system for an alligator was easy to create.

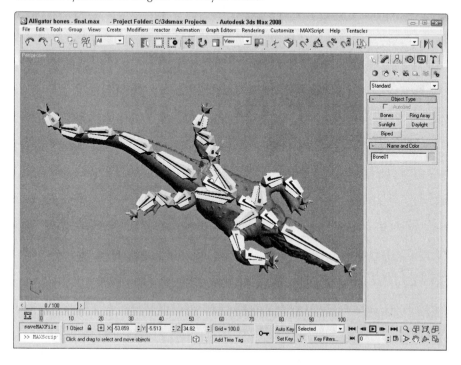

Using the Bone Tools

After you've created a bones system, you can use the Bone Tools to edit and work with the bones system. You access these tools from a panel that is opened using the Tools ⇨ Bone Tools menu command. Figure 40.4 shows this panel of tools that includes three separate rollouts: Bone Editing Tools, Fin Adjustment Tools, and Object Properties.

The Bone Tools palette includes several buttons for working with bones systems.

Reordering bones

You can use the transform buttons on the main toolbar to move, rotate, and scale a bone along with all its children, but if you want to transform the parent without affecting any of the children you need to open the Bone Tools panel using the Tools ⇨ Bone Tools menu command. Bone Edit Mode lets you move and realign a bone without affecting its children.

Clicking the Remove Bone button removes the selected bone and reconnects the bone chain by stretching the child bone. If you hold down the Shift key while removing a bone, the parent is stretched. Clicking the Delete Bone button deletes the selected bone and adds an End bone to the last child.

 **CAUTION** Using the Delete key to delete a bone does not add an End bone, and the bone chain does not work correctly with an IK Solver.

If a bone exists that isn't connected to another bone, you can add an End bone to the bone using the Create End button. The bone chain must end with an End bone in order to be used by an IK Solver.

The Connect Bones button lets you connect the selected bone with another bone. After clicking this button, you can drag a line from the selected bone to another bone to connect the two bones.

Use the Reassign Root button to reverse the chain and move the End bone from the parent to the last child.

Refining and mirroring bones

As you start to work with a bones system that you've created, you may discover that the one long bone for the backbone of your monster is too long to allow the monster to move like you want. If this happens, you can refine individual bones using the Refine button. This button appears at the bottom of the Bone Tools section of the Bone Editing Tools rollout.

Clicking the Refine button enables you to select bones in the viewport. Every bone that you select is divided into two bones at the location where you click. Click on the Refine button again to exit Refine mode.

The Mirror button lets you create a mirror copy of the selected bones. This button makes the Bone Mirror dialog box appear where you can select the Mirror Axis and the Bone Axis to Flip. You also can specify an Offset value. In the previous example, we created arms and legs manually, but you could have created one of them and used the Mirror button to create its opposite.

Coloring bones

Bones, like any other objects, are assigned a default object color and materials can be applied from the Material Editor. For each separate bone, its object color can be changed in the Modify panel or in the Bone Tools panel.

You can also apply a gradient to a bone chain using the Bone Tools palette. This option is available only if two or more bones are selected. The Start Color is applied to the chain's head and the End Color is applied to the last selected child. The colors are applied or updated when the Apply Gradient button is clicked. Figure 40.5 shows a long spiral bone chain with a white-to-black gradient applied.

FIGURE 40.5

A white-to-black gradient was applied to this spiral bone chain.

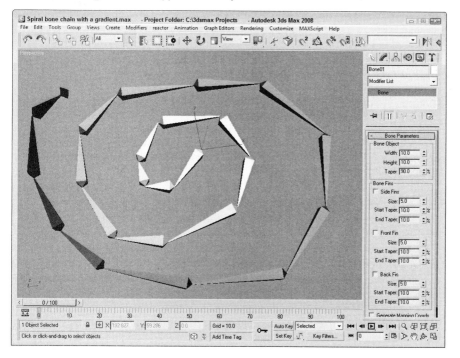

Adjusting fins

The Fin Adjustment Tools rollout includes the same parameters as those found in the Bone Parameters rollout. You can specify the dimensions and taper of a bone and its fins. But you can also specify that the parameters are applied using Absolute or Relative values. Relative values are based on the parameters of the bone that is above the current bone in the chain.

This rollout also includes Copy and Paste buttons that you can use to copy the bone parameters from one bone to another.

Making objects into bones

You can make any object act like a bone. To make an object into a bone, you need to open the Object Properties rollout in the Bone Tools panel. The Object Properties rollout includes a setting for Bone On. If enabled, the object acts like a bone. When the Bone On/Off option is enabled, the remaining Bone controls become available. The Auto-Align option causes the pivot points of adjacent bones to be aligned automatically. The Freeze Length option causes a bone to keep its length as the bones system is moved. If the Freeze Length is disabled, you can specify a Stretch type. None prevents any stretching from occurring, and Scale changes the size along one axis, but Squash causes the bone to get wider as its length is decreased and thinner as it is elongated. You can also select to stretch an axis and choose whether to Flip the axis.

You can use the Realign button to realign a bone; click the Reset Stretch button to normalize the stretch value to its current value.

Summary

The benefits of a bones system become more apparent in the next chapter when we cover inverse kinematics. In this chapter, you learned how to create and work with bones systems and the Bone Tools. This chapter covered the following topics:

- Creating bones systems
- Setting bone parameters and the IK Solver
- Using the Bone Tools
- Making objects into bones systems

If you're feeling pretty good about the skeleton you've created, the next part of rigging is applying the IK Solver that is used to tell the bones how to move relative to one another. This also gives you the chance to constrain the bone's movement. The second part of rigging characters is covered in the next chapter along with Inverse Kinematics.

Chapter 41

Working with Inverse Kinematics

Kinematics is a branch of mechanics that deals with the motions of a system of objects, so inverse kinematics would be its evil twin brother that deals with the non-motion of a system of objects. Well, not exactly.

In Max, a system of objects is a bunch of objects that are linked together. After a system is built and the parameters of the links are defined, the motions of all the pieces below the parent object can be determined as the parent moves using kinematics formulas.

Inverse kinematics (IK) is similar, except that it determines all the motions of objects in a system when the last object in the hierarchy chain is moved. The position of the last object, such as a finger or a foot, is typically the one you're concerned with. Using IK, you can then use these solutions to animate the system of objects by moving the last object in the system.

Forward Kinematics versus Inverse Kinematics

Before you can understand inverse kinematics (IK), you need to realize that another type of kinematics exists — forward kinematics. Kinematics solutions work only on a kinematics chain, which you can create by linking children objects to their parents.

ROSS-REF Chapter 9, "Grouping, Linking, and Parenting Objects," covers linking objects and creating kinematics chains.

Forward kinematics causes objects at the bottom of a linked structure to move along with their parents. For example, consider the linked structure of an arm, where the upper arm is connected to a forearm, which is connected to a hand, and finally to some fingers. Using forward kinematics, the lower arm, hand, and fingers all move when the upper arm is moved.

FIN THIS CHAPTER

Understanding forward and inverse kinematics

Using interactive and applied IK methods

Setting thresholds in the IK panel of the Preference Settings dialog box

Learning to work with the HI, HD, and IK Limb solvers

Having the linked children move with their parent is what you would expect and want, but suppose the actual object that you wanted to place is the hand. *Inverse kinematics* (IK) enables child objects to control their parent objects. So, using inverse kinematics, you can drag the hand to the exact position you want, and all other parts in the system follow.

Forward kinematics in Max involves simply transforming linked hierarchies. Any time you move, rotate, or scale a linked hierarchy, the children move with the parent, but the child object can also be transformed independent of its parent.

Creating an Inverse Kinematics System

Before you can animate an inverse kinematics system, you need to build and link the system, define joints by positioning pivot points, and define any joint constraints you want.

Building and linking a system

The first step in creating an inverse kinematics system is to create and link several objects together. You can create links using the Link button on the main toolbar.

With the linked system created, position the child object's pivot point at the center of the joint between it and its parent. For example, the joint between an upper and lower arm would be at the elbow, so this is where the pivot point for the lower arm should be located.

CROSS-REF Chapter 9, "Grouping, Linking, and Parenting Objects," covers creating linked systems, and Chapter 7, "Transforming Objects, Pivoting, Aligning, and Snapping," covers moving pivot points.

After you create the linked system and correctly position your pivot points, open the Hierarchy panel and click the IK button. Several rollouts open that let you control the IK system, including the Object Parameters rollout shown in Figure 41.1.

FIGURE 41.1

The IK rollouts let you control the binding of an IK system.

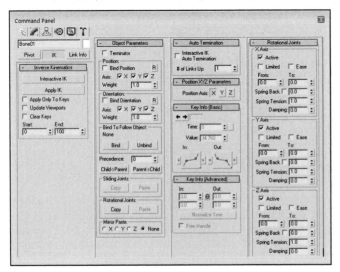

Selecting a terminator

Because child objects in an inverse kinematics system can cause their parents to move, moving a child could cause unwanted movements all the way up the system to the root object. For example, pulling on the little finger of a human model could actually move the head. To prevent this, you can select an object in the system to be a terminator.

A *terminator* is the last object in the IK system that is affected by the child's movement. Making the upper arm a terminator would prevent the finger's movement from affecting any objects above the arm.

To set a terminator, select an object and then enable the Terminator option in the Object Parameters rollout.

For Interactive IK mode, you can also enable the Auto Termination option included in the Auto Termination rollout. The Number (#) of Links Up value sets the terminator a specified number of links above the current selection.

Defining joint constraints

The next step is to define the joint constraints, which you specify in the Sliding Joints and Rotational Joints rollouts. By default, each joint has six degrees of freedom, meaning that the two objects that make up the joint can each move or rotate along the X-, Y-, or Z-axes. The axis settings for all other sliding and rotational joints are identical. Defining joint constraints enables you to constrain these motions in order to prevent unnatural motions, such as an elbow bending backward. To constrain an axis, select the object that includes the pivot point for the joint, locate in the appropriate rollout the section for the axis that you want to restrict, and deselect the Active option. If an axis's Active option is deselected, the axis is constrained. You can also limit the motion of joints by selecting the Limited option.

When the Limited option is selected, the object can move only within the bounds set by the From and To values. The Ease option causes the motion of the object to slow as it approaches either limit. The Spring Back option lets you set a rest position for the object; the object returns to this position when pulled away. The Spring Tension sets the amount of force that the object uses to resist being moved from its rest position. The Damping value sets the friction in the joint, which is the value with which the object resists any motion.

NOTE As you enter values in the From and To fields, the object moves to that value to show visually the location specified. You can also hold down the mouse on the From and To values to cause the object to move temporally to its limits. These settings are based on the current Reference Coordinate system.

Copying, pasting, and mirroring joints

Defining joint constraints can be lots of work — work that you wouldn't want to have to duplicate if you didn't have to. The Copy and Paste buttons in the Object Parameters rollout enable you to copy Sliding Joints or Rotational Joints constraints from one IK joint to another.

To use these buttons, select an IK system and click the Copy button; then select each of the joints to be constrained in a similar manner, and click the Paste button. You also have an option to mirror the joints about an axis. It is useful for duplicating an IK system for opposite arms or legs of a human or animal model.

Binding objects

When using applied IK, you need to bind an object in the IK system to a follow object. The IK joint that is bound to the follow object then follows the follow object around the scene. The bind controls are located in the Hierarchy panel under the Object Parameters rollout. To bind an object to a follow object, click the Bind button in the Object Parameters rollout and select the follow object.

In addition to binding to a follow object, IK joints can also be bound to the world for each axis by position and orientation. This causes the object to be locked in its current position so it won't move or rotate along the axis that is selected. You can also assign a Weight value. When the IK computations determine that two objects need to move in opposite directions, the solution favors the object with the largest Weight value.

The Unbind button eliminates the binding.

Understanding precedence

When Max computes an IK solution, the order in which the joints are solved determines the end result. The Precedence value (located in the Object Parameters rollout) lets you set the order in which joints are solved. To set the precedence for an object, select the object and enter a value in the Precedence value setting. Max computes the object with a higher precedence value first.

The default joint precedence for all objects is 0. This assumes that the objects farthest down the linkage move the most. The Object Parameters rollout also includes two default precedence settings. The Child to Parent button sets the precedence value for the root object to 0 and increments the precedence of each level under the root by 10. The Parent to Child button sets the opposite precedence, with the root object having a value of 0 and the precedence value of each successive object decreasing by 10.

Tutorial: Controlling a backhoe

As an example of a kinematics system, we start with a backhoe, which is a simple linkage system with tracks that can move forward, a chair housing that can rotate independently, and an arm and bucket that can rotate about a pivot. When you're finished with this tutorial, you can take the backhoe out and dig a hole for a swimming pool. I think you deserve it.

To create an inverse kinematics system for a backhoe, follow these steps:

1. Open the Backhoe.max file from the Chap 41 directory on the DVD.
2. Open the Schematic View window with the Graph Editors ➪ New Schematic View menu. Click the Connect button, and connect the tracks to the base plate, the base plate and the housing to the base cylinder, and the bucket to the arm to the housing. The connections should look like those in Figure 41.2.

 **CROSS-REF**   You can learn more about the Schematic View window in Chapter 24, "Working with the Schematic View."

FIGURE 41.2

The Schematic View window is helpful for linking hierarchies.

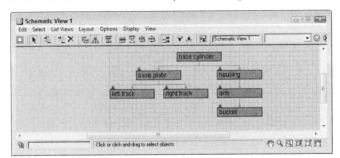

3. Next, we need to define the pivots for the objects that can rotate. Select the housing, and notice that its pivot is already located in the center of the base cylinder where it should be. Then select the arm, open the Hierarchy panel, and click the Pivot button. Click the Affect Pivot Only button, and move the pivot to the center of the cylinder that connects it to the housing. Then do the same for the bucket. Click the Affect Pivot Only button again to exit pivot-editing mode.

4. The next step is to define the joint constraints for the system. Open the Hierarchy panel, and click the IK button. In the Object Parameters rollout, select the base cylinder and enable the Terminator, Bind Position, and Bind Orientation options; doing so prevents the base cylinder from moving anywhere. In the Rotational Joint rollout, deactivate all the axes.

5. Select the housing object, and enable the Bind Position axes and the X and Y Orientation axes. Then disable the X and Y Rotation axes. Select the arm object, enable all the Bind Position axes and the X and Z Orientation axes. Then disable the X and Z Rotational axes. Then click the Copy button for the Rotational joint type in the Object Parameters rollout, select the bucket object, and click the Paste button. This copies the joint constraints from the arm object to the bucket object.

6. To test the system, select the Interactive IK button in the Inverse Kinematics rollout and select and move the bucket.

   As the bucket is moved, the arm rotates and the housing spins about its axis just as you'd expect.

Figure 41.3 shows the bucket moving. With the Interactive IK mode disabled, any object can be moved and/or rotated, and only the links are enforced.

FIGURE 41.3

The objects in this scene are part of an inverse kinematics system.

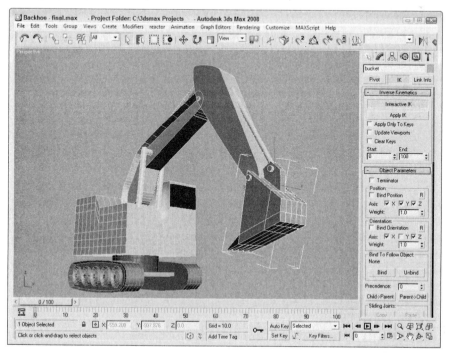

Using the Various Inverse Kinematics Methods

After you create a linked hierarchy chain, you need to apply an IK method to the chain before you can animate it. Max includes several different methods for animating using inverse kinematics. The traditional methods of Interactive and Applied IK are now joined with IK solvers. The Interactive and Applied IK methods are applied using the Hierarchy panel; the IK solvers can be applied to a bones system, or you can use the Animation ⇨ IK Solvers menu.

An IK solver is a specialized controller that computes an inverse kinematics solution. This solution is used to automatically set all the required keys needed for the animation. Max offers four different IK solvers: History Dependent (HD) IK, History Independent (HI) IK, IK Limb, and SplineIK solvers.

Interactive IK

Interactive IK is the method that lets you position a linked hierarchy of objects at different frames. Max then interpolates all the keyframes between the various keys. This method isn't as precise, but it uses a minimum number of keys and is useful for an animation sequence involving many frames. Interactive IK interpolates positions between the two different keys, whereas Applied IK computes positions for every key. Because the motions are simple interpolations between two keys, the result may not be accurate, but the motion is smooth.

After your IK system is established, animating using the Interactive IK method is simple. First, you need to enable the Auto Key button and select the Interactive IK button in the Inverse Kinematics rollout of the Hierarchy panel. Enabling this button places you in Interactive IK mode, causing the system to move together as a hierarchy. Then reposition the system in a different frame; Max automatically interpolates between the two positions and creates the animation keys. To exit Interactive IK mode, simply click the Interactive IK button again.

The Inverse Kinematics rollout includes several options. The Apply Only to Keys option forces Max to solve IK positions for only those frames that currently have keys. The Update Viewports option shows the animation solutions in the viewports as it progresses, and the Clear Keys option removes any existing keys as the solution is calculated. The Start and End values mark the frames to include in the solution.

IK Preference settings

The required accuracy of the IK solution can be set using the Inverse Kinematics panel in the Preference Settings dialog box, shown in Figure 41.4. You can open this dialog box by choosing Customize ⇨ Preferences. For the Interactive and Applied IK methods, you can set Position and Rotation Thresholds. These Threshold values determine how close the moving object must be to the defined position for the solution to be valid.

You can also set an Iterations limit for both methods. The Iterations value is the maximum number of times the calculations are performed. This value limits the time that Max spends looking for a valid solution. The Iterations settings control the speed and accuracy of each IK solution.

 If the Iterations value is reached without a valid solution, Max uses the last calculated iteration.

The Use Secondary Threshold option provides a backup method for determining whether Max should continue to look for a valid solution. This method should be used if you want Max to bail out of a particularly difficult solution rather than to continue to try to find a solution. If you are working with very small thresholds, you want to enable this option.

The Always Transform Children of the World option enables you to move the root object when it is selected by itself but constrains its movement when any of its children are moved.

FIGURE 41.4

The Inverse Kinematics panel of the Preference Settings dialog box lets you set the global Threshold values.

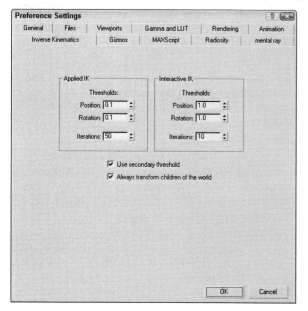

Tutorial: Animating a simple IK propeller system

Machines are good examples of a kinematics system. In this example, you animate a simple gear-and-propeller system using the Applied IK method.

To animate an inverse kinematics system with a propeller, follow these steps:

1. Open the Gear and prop.max file from the Chap 41 directory on the DVD.

   This file includes a simple handle and prop system.

2. The first task is to link the model. Click the Select and Link button on the main toolbar. Then drag from each child object to its parent. Connect the propeller to the shaft, the shaft to the gear, and the gear to the handle.

3. Open the Hierarchy panel, and click the IK button. We next constrain the motions of the parts by selecting the handle object. All Sliding Joints can be deactivated, and only the Z Axis Rotational Joint needs to be activated. To do this, make sure that a check mark is next to the Active option. When this is set for the handle object, click the Copy button for both joint types, select the gear object, and click Paste to copy these constraints. Then select the shaft object, click both Paste buttons again, and repeat this process for the propeller.

4. Finally, enable the Auto Key button (or press the N key), drag the Time Slider to frame 100 (or press the End key), and click the Interactive IK button in the Inverse Kinematics rollout of the Hierarchy panel. Then select the Select and Rotate button (E), and drag in the Left viewport to rotate the handle about its Z-axis.

Figure 41.5 shows the propeller system.

FIGURE 41.5

The propeller rotates by turning the handle and using inverse kinematics.

Applied IK

Applied IK applies a solution over a range of frames, computing the keys for every frame. This task is accomplished by binding the IK system to an object that it follows. This method is more precise than the interactive IK method, but it creates lots of keys. Because keys are set for every object and every transform, this solution sets lots of keys, which increases the size and complexity of the scene. Each frame has its own set of keys, which could result in jerky and non-smooth results.

 **NOTE**   Because the Applied IK method is more accurate, you want to set its Threshold values lower than those of the Interactive IK method.

To animate using the Applied IK method, you need to bind one or more parts of the system to a follow object, which can be a dummy object or an object in the scene. You do so by clicking the Bind button in the Object Parameters rollout of the Hierarchy panel and selecting an object in one of the viewports. After the system has a bound follow object, select an object in the system. Open the Hierarchy panel; in the Inverse Kinematics rollout, click the Apply IK button. Max then computes the keys for every frame between the Start and End frames specified in the rollout. Click the Apply IK button to start the computation process that sets all the animation keys for the range of frames indicated.

 If you plan on using the Applied IK method, set the Threshold values in the Inverse Kinematics panel of the Preference Settings dialog box to small values in order to ensure accurate results.

History Independent IK solver

The History Independent (HI) IK solver looks at each keyframe independently when making its solution. You can animate linked chains with this IK solver applied by positioning the goal object; the solver then keyframes the position of the pivot point of the last object in the chain to match the goal object.

You can apply IK solvers to any hierarchy of objects. IK solvers are applied automatically to a bones system when you create the system. You can also choose Animation ⇨ IK Solvers to select an IK solver.

When you choose Animation ⇨ IK Solver, a dotted line appears from the selected object. You can drag this line within a viewport and click another object within the hierarchy to be the end joint. A white line is drawn between the beginning and ending joints. The pivot point of the end joint is the goal for the IK solver. It is known as the End Effector. The End Effector of the IK solver is marked by a blue cross. Several rollouts within the Hierarchy panel also appear. These rollouts let you set the parameters for the IK solver.

The first rollout is the IK Solver rollout, shown in Figure 41.6. Using this rollout, you can select to switch between the HI IK solver and the IK Limb solver. The Enabled button lets you disable the solver. By disabling the solver, you can use forward kinematics to move the objects. To return to the IK solution, simply click the Enabled button again. The IK for FK Pose option enables IK control even if the IK solver is disabled. This lets you manipulate the hierarchy of objects using forward kinematics while still working with the IK solution. If both the IK for FK Pose and the Enabled buttons are disabled, then the goal can move without affecting the hierarchy of objects.

FIGURE 41.6

The IK Solver rollout lets you enable or disable the IK solver.

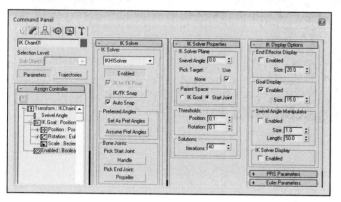

If the goal ever gets moved away from the end link, clicking the IK/FK Snap button automatically moves the goal to match the end links position. Auto Snap automatically keeps the goal and the end link together. The Set as Preferred Angle button remembers the angles for the IK system. These angles can be recalled at any time using the Assume Preferred Angle button.

When you choose Animation ⇨ IK Solvers ⇨ HI Solver, the start joint is the selected object, and the end joint is the object to which you drag the dotted line. If you want to change these objects, you can click the Pick Start Joint or Pick End Joint buttons.

> **TIP** The best way to select an object using the Pick Start or End Joint buttons is to open the Select by Name dialog box by pressing the H key. Using this dialog box, you can select an exact object without having to miss selecting it in a complex viewport.

> **CAUTION** If you select a child as the start joint and an object above the child as the end joint, then moving the goal has no effect on the IK chain.

Defining a swivel angle

The IK Solver Properties rollout includes the Swivel Angle value. The swivel angle defines the plane that includes the joint objects and the line that connects the starting and ending joints. This plane is key because it defines the direction that the joint moves when bent.

The Swivel Angle value can change during an animation. Using the Pick Target button, you can also select a Target object to control the swivel angle. The Use button turns the target on and off. The Parent Space group defines whether the IK Goal's parent object or the Start Joint's parent object is used to define the plane. Having an option lets you select two different parent objects that control the swivel plane if two or more IK solvers are applied to a single IK chain.

You can also change the Swivel Angle value by using a manipulator. To view the manipulator, click the Select and Manipulate button on the main toolbar. This manipulator is a green line with a square on the end of it. Dragging this manipulator in the viewports causes the swivel angle to change.

To understand the swivel angle, consider the two puppet bones systems displayed in Figure 41.7. The HI solver has been applied to the right arms of both puppets with the upper arm as the beginning joint and the hand as the end joint. The swivel angle for the left bones system is 90 degrees, and the swivel angle for the right bones system is 180. You can see the manipulators for both bones systems. The left one is pointing upward, and the right one is pointing straight out from the puppet's head. Notice that the swivel angle determines the direction the elbow joint is pointing. The left bones system's elbow is pointing up and away from the spine, and the right bones system's elbow is pointing painfully out in front of the puppet in the direction of the manipulator.

The IK Solver Properties rollout also includes Threshold values. These values determine how close the end joint and the goal must be before the solution is pronounced valid. You can set thresholds for Position and Rotation. The Iterations value sets the number of times the solution is tried.

> **TIP** Setting the Iterations value to a higher number produces smoother (less jerky) results, but it increases the time required to find a solution.

Displaying IK controls

The IK Display Options rollouts can enable, disable, and set the size of the gizmos used when working with IK solvers. Using this rollout, you can Enable the End Effector, the Goal, the Swivel Angle Manipulator, and the IK solver (which is the line connecting the start and end joints).

FIGURE 41.7

The swivel angle defines the plane along which the joint moves.

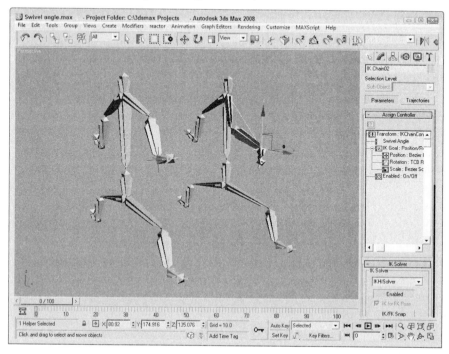

Tutorial: Animating a puppet with the HI IK solver

The HI solver is probably the best solver to use for animating characters. This fine fellow made of bones makes a good candidate for trying out the HI solver.

To animate an alligator with the HI IK solver, follow these steps:

1. Open the Dancing puppet.max file from the Chap 41 directory on the DVD.

   This file is the same file that was created using the bones system.

2. Apply the HI solver to the arm chains by selecting the left upper arm and choosing Animation ⇨ IK Solvers ⇨ HI Solver. A dotted line appears in the viewports extending from the selected object. Move the cursor over the left hand object, and click.

3. Repeat Step 2 for the right arm and both leg chains.

4. Click the Auto Key button, and drag the Time Slider to frame 20. Select the goal for the left leg IK chain, click the Select and Move button on the main toolbar (or press the W key), and move the left leg goal upward.

5. Repeat Step 4 for frames 40, 60, 80, and 100, moving the various IK chains in different directions.

6. Move the Time Slider to frame 50, and select all objects by choosing Edit ⇨ Select All (Ctrl+A). Then drag all the objects upward a short distance. Drag the Time Slider to frame 100 (or press the End key), and drag all the objects back down again.

7. Click the Play Animation button (/) to see the resulting dance.

Figure 41.8 shows one frame of the dancing puppet.

History Dependent IK solver

The History Dependent (HD) IK solver takes into account the previous keyframes as it makes a solution. This solver makes having very smooth motion possible, but the cost of time to compute the solution is increased significantly. You can also assign this IK solver to bones systems by specifying the History Dependent solver in the IK Chain Assignment rollout or by choosing Animation ⇨ IK Solvers ⇨ HD Solver.

This IK solver shows up as a controller in the Motion panel. The settings are contained in a rollout named IK Controller Parameters, which is visible in the Motion panel if you select one of the end effector gizmos. The end effector gizmo is the object that you move to control the IK chain. It is displayed as a set of crossing axes.

FIGURE 41.8

Moving the goal for each IK chain makes animating a character easy.

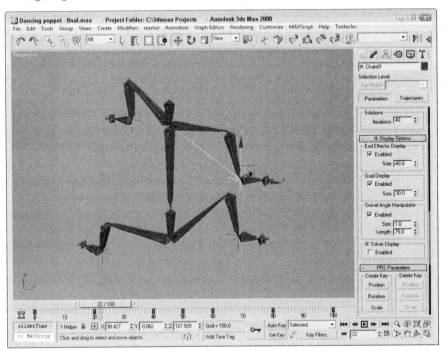

You can access the IK Controller Parameters rollout, shown in Figure 41.9, in the Motion panel. Any parameter changes affect all bones in the current structure. In the Thresholds section, the Position and Rotation values set how close the end effector must be to its destination before the solution is complete. In the Solution section, the Iterations value determines the maximum number of times the solution is attempted. These Thresholds and Iterations values are the same as those in the Preference Settings dialog box, except that they affect only the current linkage. The Start Time and End Time values set the frame range for the IK solution.

FIGURE 41.9

The IK Controller Parameters rollout sets the boundaries of the IK solution.

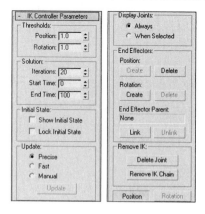

The Show Initial State option displays the initial state of the linkage and enables you to move it by dragging the end effector object. The Lock Initial State option prevents any linkage other than the end effector from moving.

The Update section enables you to set how the IK solution is updated with Precise, Fast, and Manual options. The Precise option solves for every frame, Fast solves for only the current frame, and Manual solves only when the Update button is clicked. The Display Joints options determine whether joints are Always displayed or only When Selected.

When you first create a bones system, an end effector is set to the last joint automatically. In the End Effectors section, at the bottom of the IK Controller Parameters rollout, you can set any joint to be a Positional or Rotational end effector. To make a bone an end effector, select the bone and click the Create button. If the bone already is an end effector, then the Delete button is active. You can also link the bone to another parent object outside of the linkage with the Link button. The linked object then inherits the transformations of this new parent.

Click the Delete Joint button in the Remove IK section to delete a joint. If a bone is set to be an end effector, the Position or Rotation button displays the Key Info parameters for the selected bone.

Tutorial: Animating a spyglass with the HD IK solver

A telescoping spyglass is a good example of a kinematics system that we can use to show off the HD solver. The modeling of this example is also easy because it consists of a bunch of cylinders that gradually get smaller.

To animate a spyglass with the HD IK solver, follow these steps:

1. Open the Spyglass.max file from the Chap 41 directory on the DVD.

   This file includes a simple spyglass made from primitive objects. The pieces of the spyglass are linked from the smallest section to the largest section. At the end of the spyglass is a dummy object linked to the last tube object.

2. First, you need to define the joint properties. Select the largest tube object, open the Hierarchy panel, and click the IK button. In the Object Properties rollout, select the Terminator, Bind Position, and Bind Orientation options to keep this joint from moving.

3. With the largest tube section selected, make the Z Axis option active in the Sliding Joints rollout, and disable all the axes in the Rotational Joints rollout. Then click the Copy button for both Sliding Joints and Rotational Joints in the Object Properties rollout.

4. Select each remaining tube object individually, and click the Paste buttons for both the Sliding Joints and Rotational Joints.

   This enables the local Z-axis sliding motion for all tube objects.

5. Select the largest tube section again, and choose Animation ⇨ IK Solvers ⇨ HD Solver. Then drag the dotted line to the dummy object at the end of the spyglass.

6. Select the second tube object, and for the Sliding Z Axis, select the Limited option with values from **0.0** to **−80**. Then click on the Copy button for the Sliding Joints in the Object Parameters rollout. Then select tubes 3 through 6 individually, and click the Paste button for the Sliding Joints to apply these same limits to the other tube objects.

7. Click the Auto Key button (N), drag the Time Slider to frame 100 (End), select the Select and Move button on the main toolbar (W), and drag the dummy object away from the largest tube object.

Figure 41.10 shows the end tube segment collapsing within the spyglass.

IK Limb solver

The IK Limb solver was specifically created to work with limbs. It is used on chains of three bones such as a hip, upper leg, and lower leg. Only two of the bones in the chain actually move. The goal for these three joints is located at the pivot point for the third bone. This solver is ideal for game character rigging.

The way this solver works is that it considers the first joint as being a spherical joint that can rotate along three different axes, like a hip or shoulder joint. The second joint can bend only in one direction, such as an elbow or knee joint.

The rollouts and controls for the IK Limb solver are exactly the same as those used for the HI solver covered earlier in this chapter.

FIGURE 41.10

The HD IK solver is used to control the spyglass.

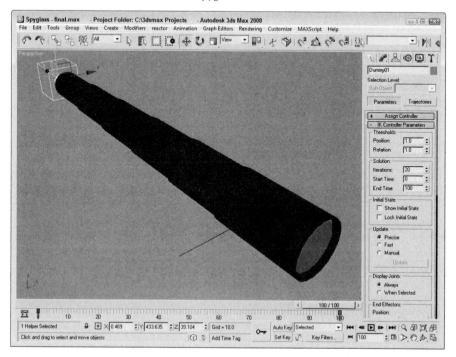

Tutorial: Animating a spider's leg with the IK Limb solver

As an example of the IK Limb solver, we should probably animate a limb, so I've created a simple spider skeleton with not two limbs, but eight. This skeleton was created fairly quickly using four bones for the abdomen; then I created one limb and cloned it three times. Then I used the Bone Tools to connect the leg bones to the abdomen bones, and finally I selected and mirrored the bones on all four legs to get the opposite legs. The hardest part was naming all the bones.

To animate a spider skeleton's leg using the IK Limb solver, follow these steps:

1. Open the Spider skeleton.max file from the Chap 41 directory on the DVD.

2. Click the Select by Name button on the main toolbar (or press the H key) to open the Select Objects dialog box. Double-click the "RUpperlegBone01" object to select the upper leg bone object.

3. With the upper leg bone selected, choose Animation ➪ IK Solvers ➪ IK Limb Solver. A dotted line appears in the viewport. Press the H key again to open the Pick Object dialog box, and double-click the "RFootBone01" object to select it.

    This bone corresponds to the foot bone, which is the end of the limb hierarchy.

4. With the IK Chain01 object selected, click the Auto Key button (or press the N key) and drag the Time Slider to frame 100 (End). With the Select and Move button (W), move the IK chain in the viewport.

The leg chain bends as you move the end effector.

Figure 41.11 shows the spider's leg being moved via the IK Limb solver. The IK Limb Solver provides a simple and quick way to add an effector to the end of a limb, giving you a good control for animating the spider's walk cycles.

Spline IK solver

The Limb IK solver works well for arms and legs that have a joint in their middle, but it doesn't work well for tails. Tails are unique because they require multiple bones to deform correctly. The Spline IK solver works well for tails, but it also works well for rigging tentacles, chains, and rope.

To use the Spline IK solver, you need to create a chain of bones and a spline path. By selecting the first and last bone and then selecting the spline, the bone chain moves to the spline. Each control point on the spline has a dummy object associated with it. By moving these dummy objects, you can control the position of the bones. At either end of the spline are manipulators that you can use to twist and rotate the bones.

FIGURE 41.11

You can use the IK Limb solver to control limbs such as legs and arms.

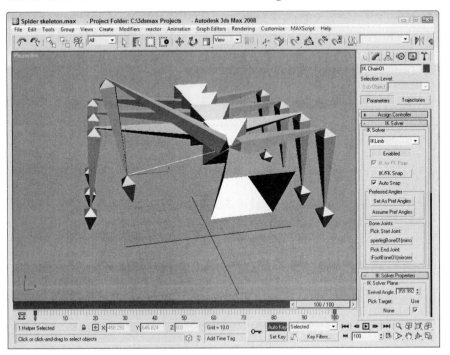

The easiest way to use this IK solver is to select SplineIKSolver from the drop-down list in the IK Chain Assignment rollout while you're creating the bone structure. After the bone structure is complete, the Spline IK Solver dialog box appears. With this dialog box, you can select a name for the IK chain, specify the curve type, and set the number of spline knots. The curve type options include Bézier, NURBS Point, and NURBS CV. You can also select to Create Helpers and to display several different options.

Another way to use this IK solver is with an existing bone structure. To do this, you need a spline curve in the scene that matches how you want the bone chain to look. Then select the first bone where you want the solver to be applied, and choose Animation ⇨ IK Solvers ⇨ Spline IK. In the viewports, a dragging line appears; move the line to the last bone that you want to include, and then drag a second time to the spline that you want to use.

The bone structure then assumes the shape of the spline curve. A helper object is positioned at the location of each curve vertex. These helper objects let you refine the shape of the curve.

Tutorial: Building an IK Spline alligator

The IK Spline solver is perfect for creating long, winding objects like snakes or an alligator's tail. For this example, we take an existing bone structure and, using the Spline IK solver, make it match a spline.

To create a bone structure for an alligator that follows a spline using the IK Spline solver, follow these steps:

1. Open the Alligator spline IK.max file from the Chap 41 directory on the DVD.

   This file includes an alligator model created by Viewpoint Datalabs, a simple bone chain, the Skin modifier, and a spline.

TIP If you're having trouble seeing the bones located inside the alligator, you can enable the See Through option in the Object Properties dialog box or press the Alt+X keyboard shortcut.

2. With the first bone in the tail chain selected, choose Animation ⇨ IK Solvers ⇨ SplineIK Solver.

   A dragging line appears in the viewport extending from the first bone.

3. Drag and click the cursor on the last bone in the bone tail chain.

4. Another dragging line appears; drag and click on the spline, and the bone structure moves to match the spline's curve.

Figure 41.12 shows the bone structure for the gator's tail. You can now control the gator's tail by moving the dummy objects along the spline.

FIGURE 41.12

The IK Spline solver is perfect for creating objects like snakes and animal tails.

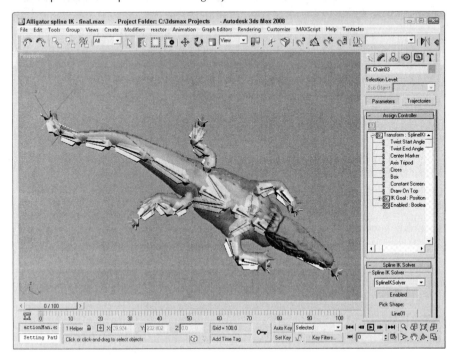

Summary

Inverse kinematics provides a unique way to control and animate hierarchical structures by transforming the child node. In this chapter, you accomplished the following:

- Learned the basic concepts behind inverse kinematics
- Explored the difference between interactive and applied IK methods
- Created and animated an inverse kinematics system
- Used the IK settings in the Preference Settings dialog box
- Learned how to use IK solvers

Now that you've learned the process for rigging a character and using IK, we'll take a look at Biped next and discover the benefits of using a pre-rigged skeleton.

Chapter 42

Creating and Animating Bipeds and Crowds

Max has always had a great way to create and animate characters, but in early versions of Max, it was available only as a separate plug-in known as Character Studio. Happily, Character Studio has been integrated into Max to the point that it isn't distinguishable as a separate package. In fact, some of Max's original features have overgrown Character Studio, but much of Character Studio's original, innovative features still exist and are extremely useful, including Biped.

Using Biped, you can create a fully linked and constrained human-form skeleton by simply dragging in the viewport. Biped objects can be altered in many ways while retaining their benefit. The major benefit of bipeds is that you can realistically animate them by simply positioning their footprints or setting freeform keys.

Although Max includes other features for rigging characters, which are covered in the next chapter, if you plan on animating a character that walks on two legs and has two arms, then biped is definitely the way to go. It's an incredible timesaver.

Nobody likes crowds (except for certain types of bugs), but with the Character Studio's Crowd Animation tools, controlling crowds can be lots of fun. The fun comes when you realize that you would spend weeks animating by hand all the actions that are possible with the Crowd animation tools.

Characters included in a crowd simulation are called delegates, and these delegates can have assigned behaviors that tell them to follow a certain object or a certain path and to avoid designated objects. As you begin to simulate crowds, you'll delight in how much it is like taking the whole family shopping together, except the delegates actually do what you say.

Character Creation Workflow

A typical workflow for creating characters in Max involves first creating a skin mesh object. After the skin mesh is complete, you can create a biped object to drive its animation. The biped consists of a pre-rigged skeleton of bones that provide an underlying structure to the character. Animating these bones provides an easy way to give life to the character.

With a biped created, position the biped within the skin mesh and match the bone links to the relative size and position inside the skin mesh. The bones do not need to be completely within the skin mesh since you can set the biped objects to not be rendered, but the closer they are to the skin mesh, the more accurate the movements of the character are.

After the biped is sized and matched to the skin mesh, use the Skin modifier to attach the skin mesh to the biped. This automatically sets all the envelopes that govern which skin parts move with which bones. You can also use the Skin modifier settings to deform the skin at certain bone angles, such as bulging a muscle when the arm is raised.

NOTE   The original Character Studio package used the Physique modifier to bind the mesh skin to the biped. Although this modifier still exists and can be used, the Skin modifier includes many new features and is the preferred method for binding a mesh skin to the biped.

The next step is to animate the biped using its animation tools, which can include walk, run, and jump cycles by placing footsteps or freeform animation using keys. Along the way, you can save, load, and reuse animation sequences including motion capture files. Animated sequences can be combined and mixed together to form a smooth-flowing animation using the Motion Mixer.

Creating a Biped

Creating a hierarchical skeleton that is used to control the animation of the mesh skin that is draped over it is quite easy when you create a biped. The skeleton can be set to be invisible in the final render and exists only to make the process of animating easier. Although Max includes a robust set of tools that can be used to create a skeleton of bones, the Biped feature automates this entire process using prebuilt skeletons.

CROSS-REF   For some characters, manipulating a biped is more work than building a custom skeleton. For these occasions, you can manually create a skeleton structure. Building a skeleton system by hand is covered in Chapter 40, "Understanding Rigging and Working with Bones."

To create a biped, simply select the Create ➪ Systems ➪ Biped menu command and drag in a viewport. The Biped menu command accesses the Biped button found in the Systems category of the Create panel. Figure 42.1 shows a default biped created by dragging in a viewport.

The Create Biped rollout includes two creation methods: Drag Height and Drag Position. The Drag Height creation method lets you set the height of the biped by dragging in the viewport, and the Drag Position creation method creates a standard-sized biped and lets you position it by dragging about the viewport.

NOTE   To precisely position a biped on the surface of any existing object, enable the AutoGrid option at the top of the Object Type rollout.

In the Root Name field, you can name the biped. Every biped bone is given a unique name, and this root name is attached to the front of the unique bone name. For example, if you specify Gloop as the root name, then the right calf bone is given the name, Gloop R Calf.

Below the Biped Name field is the Body Type drop-down list. In this list, you can select from Skeleton, Female, Male, and Classic body types. The differences among these body types relate to the size and shape of the bones. The Classic body type was used in previous versions of Character Studio and exists for backward compatibility. Figure 42.2 shows each of these body types.

FIGURE 42.1

The default biped includes all the basic body parts for a human character.

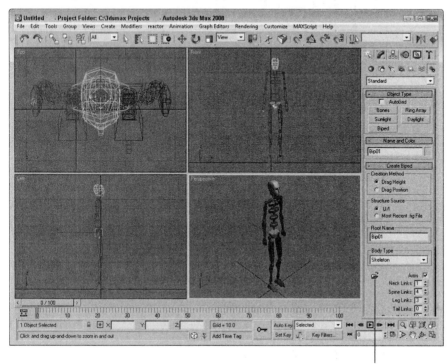

Open Fig File

FIGURE 42.2

The four available body types include Skeleton, Female, Male, and Classic.

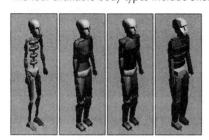

By default, all biped bones are color coded, with all bones on the right side colored green and all bones on the left side colored blue. The pelvis, which is the root bone, is colored yellow, and the head is light blue. These colors help keep the different bones straight, and the same colors are used for the footprints that define the biped's motion.

Customizing a biped

Although the standard biped resembles a human form, you can use the settings in the Create panel to radically change the biped to resemble whatever creature you've created.

Customized biped skeletons can be saved using the Save File button found in the Motion panel when Figure Mode is enabled. Biped files are saved with the .fig file extension. Saved biped files can then be recalled when a new biped is being created using the Open Fig File button in the Create Biped rollout. You can also select to create any new bipeds using the user interface settings or using the Most Recent .fig File.

NOTE The Save File button saves the skeleton structure as a .fig file when Figure Mode is enabled and saves the animation sequence as a .bip file when Figure Mode is disabled.

The Create Biped rollout includes settings for toggling the arms on and off. Settings are available for controlling the number of links used to represent all the various body parts listed in Table 42.1. These same settings are available in the Structure rollout of the Motion panel, which is available when Figure Mode is enabled.

TABLE 42.1

Biped Parts

Body Part	Link Limits
Arms	On or Off
Neck Links	1 to 25
Spine Links	1 to 10
Leg Links	3 to 4
Tail Links	0 to 25
Ponytail1 Links	0 to 25
Ponytail2 Links	0 to 25
Fingers	0 to 5
Finger Links	1 to 3
Toes	1 to 5
Toe Links	1 to 3
Props	Up to 3 enabled
Ankle Attach	0.0 (back of foot) to 1.0 (front of foot)
Height	unlimited
Triangle Pelvis	On or Off
Twist Links	On or Off
Upper Arm Twist Links	0 to 10
Forearm Twist Links	0 to 10
Thigh Twist Links	0 to 10
Calf Twist Links	0 to 10
Horse Link Twist Links	0 to 10 (Leg links must be set to 4 to use Horse Links)

Ponytail links are located on the back on the head and, like the arms, will naturally hang down when the spine bones are rotated. Tail links extend as expected off the back of the pelvis bone. Enabled Props appear as tall rectangular boxes attached to the hands. Prop1 is attached to the right hand, Prop2 is attached to the left hand, and Prop3 floats on the left side of the body.

Figure 42.3 shows a biped with two ponytails, a tail, and a single prop.

TIP　Ponytail objects can be used to represent ears, horns, or a unique haircut that moves independently of the head.

The Triangle Pelvis option isn't initially visible when creating a biped, but if enabled, the pelvis consists of two links that extend from the spine to where the leg links are located. This helps keep the leg joints from intersecting directly under the spine. The twist links feature allows body parts to twist during animation. The Twists option needs to be enabled before twist links can be used, and the twist links are frozen by default. For example, if you hold your arm out to the side with your palm facing forward, the ulna and radius bones that make up your forearm are actually rotated 90 degrees.

NOTE　The twist links feature, located at the bottom of the Structure rollouts, cannot be animated individually; it can be used only to deform the skin as the body part is animated.

FIGURE 42.3

This biped includes two ponytails, a tail, and a prop object attached to its right hand.

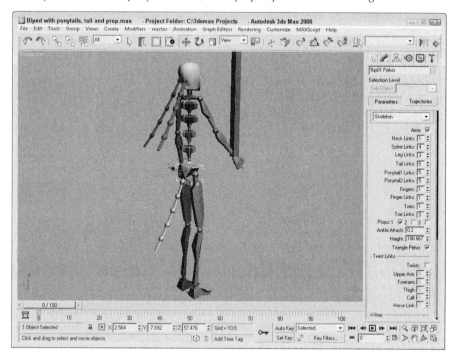

Using Xtras

If your character has some other specialized body parts that can't be covered using the typical Biped structure elements, you can use the Xtras section to add custom structures that are parented to any existing biped part, even to other Xtras. For example, if you're creating a flying monkey with a tail and wings sticking out from the monkey's shoulders, Xtras can be used to add the new wings.

NEW FEATURE   The addition of Xtras to build custom Bipeds is new to 3ds Max 2008.

Each new Xtra added to the biped can have up to 25 links, and you can select the biped object to link the Xtra part to. The Xtras controls, shown in Figure 42.4, also include buttons to automatically select and/or create a symmetrical part. New Xtras are highlighted red and yellow until an opposite is created. Then they become blue and green to match the biped's left and right sides. New Xtras can be renamed using the name field.

FIGURE 42.4

The Xtras section can add new structures attached at any part to the biped.

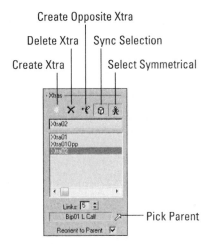

Create Opposite Xtra

Delete Xtra | Sync Selection

Create Xtra | Select Symmetrical

Pick Parent

Modifying a biped

After a biped is created, you may look to the Modify panel to change the biped, but the Modify panel is empty. Don't be surprised: All the controls for modifying a biped are located in the Motion panel. This is because biped deals with animation and not just with modifying structures.

In the Biped rollout of the Motion panel, you see several icons. These icons are described in Table 42.2.

TABLE 42.2

Biped Rollout Buttons

Toolbar Button	Name	Description
	Figure Mode	Enables Figure Mode where you can edit the skeleton structure.
	Footstep Mode	Enables Footstep Mode where you can animate the biped by placing footsteps to follow.
	Motion Flow Mode	Enables Motion Flow Mode where you can create scripts of motions for a biped to follow.
	Mixer Mode	Enables Mixer Mode where you can load and save Mixer files.
	Biped Playback	Plays the animated biped in the viewport in real time showing only the bones.
	Load File	Opens .fig, .bip, and .stp files.
	Save File	Saves .fig, .bip, and .stp files.
	Convert	Converts footstep animation sequences to freeform animation keys.
	Move All Mode	Enables a mode where the biped can be moved along with all its animation footsteps.

The first icon button of a little character is the Figure Mode button. When this button is selected, the button turns light blue, indicating that you are in Figure Mode, and a Structure rollout appears.

The Structure rollout includes all the same settings that were available in the Create panel when the biped was first created.

In Figure Mode, all bones can be moved, rotated, and scaled as needed to match the required skin mesh. You also need to set the initial position of the biped in Figure mode. If you look closely at the Biped rollout, you'll notice a title called Modes and Display with a plus sign to its left. If you click this title, several additional buttons appear. The Mode buttons are used to manipulate bones in certain ways and the Display buttons are used to set which biped objects are displayed. The Mode buttons are described in Table 42.3.

TABLE 42.3

Biped Mode Buttons

Toolbar Button	Name	Description
	Buffer Mode	Displays the latest footstep copied into the copy buffer.
	Rubber Band Mode	Allows a parent object to be moved without altering its child hand or foot. Typically results in stretching.

continued

TABLE 42.3 *(continued)*

Toolbar Button	Name	Description
	Scale Stride Mode	Scales the biped's stride in proportion to the biped's height.
	In Place Mode,	Makes the character go through the keyed actions without transforming its center of mass.
	In Place X Mode,	
	In Place Y Mode	

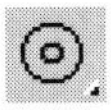

The second button in the Modes section is used to enable Rubber Band Mode. In this mode, you can move a parent bone without moving its children along with it. For example, if you've positioned the left foot exactly where it needs to be, then in Rubber Band Mode, the upper leg can be moved without affecting the foot's position. This is accomplished by stretching the upper and lower leg bones like a rubber band.

NOTE The Buffer Mode, Scale Stride Mode, and In Place Mode all work with animation sequences and are covered later in the chapter.

Although most body parts are attached to their adjacent body parts, the head can be moved in Figure mode independent of the rest of the body. This makes creating a headless character easy.

NEW FEATURE The ability to move a biped's head independent of its body is new to 3ds Max 2008.

Setting the Biped display options

The Display buttons in the Biped rollout let you show or hide certain items in order to speed up the display in the viewports. These controls become critical when working with crowds of bipeds. The display buttons are explained in Table 42.4.

TABLE 42.4

Biped Display Buttons

Toolbar Button	Name	Description
 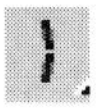 	Objects, Bones, Bones/Objects	Shows only the objects, only the bones (which appear as simple lines),or both.

Toolbar Button	Name	Description
	Show Footsteps, Show Footsteps and Numbers, Hide Footsteps	Shows the footsteps, the footsteps with numbers, or neither.
	Twist Links	Displays the forearm as a twisted bone.
	Leg States	Displays the foot motion type for each step as Move, Slide, or Plant.
	Trajectories	Shows the trajectory of the selected bone.
	Preferences	Opens the Display Preferences dialog box.

NOTE Biped body objects are rendered, but bone objects are not rendered. Enable the Bones display option to ensure that the biped body objects aren't rendered along with the skin mesh.

The Preferences option opens the Display Preferences dialog box, shown in Figure 42.5. Using this dialog box, you can set the options for how trajectories and footsteps are displayed, and you can set playback options.

NOTE The Biped Display Preferences dialog box is different from the Preference Settings dialog box.

FIGURE 42.5

The Display Preferences dialog box lets you set the options for displaying biped elements.

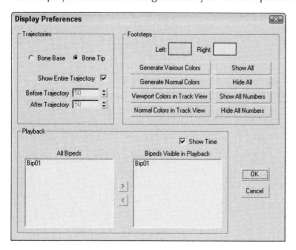

Selecting tracks

The Track Selection rollout is helpful as you begin to move bipeds and bones about. Its buttons select the biped's Center of Mass (COM) located at the pelvis root. With these buttons, you can key COM tracks for moving and rotating the biped. The buttons are detailed in Table 42.5.

TABLE 42.5

Biped Track Selection Buttons

Toolbar Button	Name	Description
↔	Body Horizontal	Selects the entire biped and constrains its movement to the horizontal plane.
↕	Body Vertical	Selects the entire biped and constrains its movement to the vertical plane.
↻	Body Rotation	Selects the entire biped and allows it to be rotated.
🔒	Lock COM Keying	Allows the Body Horizontal, Body Vertical, and Body Rotation buttons to be used simultaneously.
🧍	Symmetrical	Selects the symmetrical body part and allows both to be transformed together.
→🧍	Opposite	Selects the opposite body part and deselects the current one.

The Body Horizontal, Body Vertical, and Body Rotation buttons let you quickly select and move the entire biped in a horizontal or vertical direction or to rotate the entire biped using the common transform gizmos. Body Horizontal keys are displayed in red, Body Vertical keys are displayed in yellow, and Body Rotation keys are displayed in green. If the Lock COM Keying button is enabled, then multiple COM keying tracks can be selected at the same time.

The Symmetrical button instantly selects the symmetrical body part along with the current selection so that both can be transformed together. The Opposite button selects the symmetrical body part to the current selected bone and deselects the current bone. For example, if the right leg bone is selected, then clicking the Opposite button selects the left leg bone instead, and if the right arm bone is selected, then clicking the Symmetrical button also selects the left arm bone so both are selected together.

Bending links

The Bend Links rollout includes buttons that let you control the rotation and twist of link sets. Table 42.6 lists each of these buttons.

TABLE 42.6

Bend Links Buttons

Toolbar Button	Name	Description
	Bend Links Mode	Transfers rotation information onto children links to create a smooth rotation.
	Twist Links Mode	Allows constrained rotations about the link's local X-axis.
	Twist Individual Mode	Allows rotation of a single link without affecting the other links.
	Smooth Twist Mode	Propagates the rotation of the first and last links to all links to create a smooth twist.
	Zero Twist	Resets the rotation along the local X-axis to 0.
	Zero All	Resets the rotation along all local axes to 0.

The Bend Links Mode button causes all adjacent bones in a series of links to be adjusted in a realistic manner when one of the bones in the series is moved. Figure 42.6 shows two identical bipeds, each with a
rotated tail. The third link in the right biped's tail was rotated with the Bend Links Mode disabled; the left
biped has the Bend Links Mode enabled. Notice how the entire tail linkage is affected.

FIGURE 42.6

When links are rotated with the Bend Links Mode enabled, the entire link chain is affected.

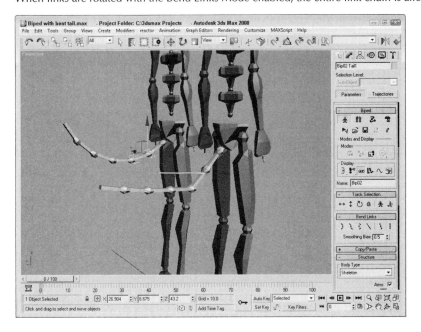

The Twist Links Mode button works in a similar manner to the Bend Links Mode, except it applies to twisting links. The Twist Links Mode button smoothly twists the entire link chain regardless of which link is rotated. The Twist Individual Mode allows only the selected bone to be twisted, and the Smooth Twist Mode bases the twisting of the entire link chain on the rotation of the first or last link. The Smoothing Bias moves the greater area of twisting toward the first link with a value of 0.0 and toward the last link with a value of 1.0.

Figure 42.7 shows how the Twist Links Mode works. The left biped has its fifth spine link rotated, and all other links have gradually been twisted resulting in a smooth rotation over the whole spine. The right biped has had the same link rotated with the Twist Links Mode turned off. Notice how all the links above have been rotated and those below haven't.

FIGURE 42.7

When a single spine link is rotated with the Twist Links Mode enabled, the entire link chain is affected.

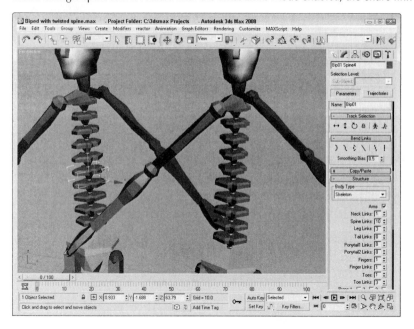

Working with postures and poses

The Copy/Paste rollout includes an interface for saving and reusing different postures, poses, and tracks. Sets of each can be saved into collections. This lets you break up all the poses for a certain character into logical collection sets such as standing poses, sitting poses, action poses, and so on. You can switch among these modes using the buttons at the top of the Copy/Paste rollout. Posture Mode records the position and orientation of a single bone object. Pose Mode records the position and orientation of the entire biped object, and Track Mode records the animation of a single bone object.

 The Track button in the Copy/Paste rollout is available only when Figure Mode is disabled.

New collections are created using the Create Collection button. You can rename the collection by typing a new name in the Copy Collections drop-down list at the top of the Copy/Paste rollout. Collections of postures, poses, and tracks can be saved as files using the Save Collection button and reloaded using the Load Collections button found in the Copy/Paste rollout. All saved postures, poses, and tracks are saved using the .cpy extension. Buttons are available for deleting the current collection or all collections. The Max Load Preferences button opens a simple dialog box with options to Keep Existing Collections and Load Collections when a Max file is loaded.

Postures, poses, and tracks can also be copied to the interface using the Copy button. Once copied, they appear in a preview window, as shown for the selected pose in Figure 42.8. All copied postures, poses, and tracks are saved with the Max file. Snapshots shown in the Preview window can be taken from the viewport, taken automatically, not taken at all, or hidden using the buttons located directly under the Preview window.

FIGURE 42.8

A Preview window in the Copy/Paste rollout lets you select the exact pose you want to use.

Delete Collection

Save Collection

Load Collections   Delete All Collections

Create Collection   Max Load Preferences

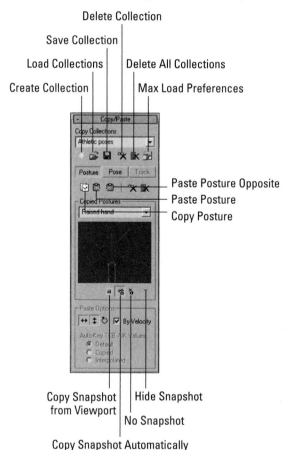

Paste Posture Opposite
Paste Posture
Copy Posture

Copy Snapshot | Hide Snapshot
from Viewport |
No Snapshot

Copy Snapshot Automatically

The selected posture, pose, or track may then be pasted to another bone or biped using the Paste button or using the Paste Opposite button to paste it to the opposite, symmetrical bone. When the Paste Opposite button is used in Pose Mode, the biped that receives a copied pose appears facing the opposite direction to the original. For each mode, there are also buttons to delete the current selection or delete all copies.

The Paste Horizontal, Paste Vertical, and Paste Rotate buttons at the bottom of the Copy/Paste rollout let you paste the COM track keys along with the posture, pose, or track. The By Velocity option pastes the biped's position based on the trajectory of its motion. You can also select to auto-key any TCB and IK values using the Default, Copied, or Interpolated methods.

Tutorial: Creating a four-footed biped

Biped means a two-footed structure, so creating a four-footed biped is actually an oxymoron. This tutorial should really be called "Creating a biped that is hunched over so its hands are touching the ground," but that would be too long.

To create a four-footed biped, follow these steps:

1. Select the Create ➪ Systems ➪ Biped menu command, and drag in the viewport to create a biped.
2. In the Create Biped rollout, set the number of Neck Links to **2**, the number of Tail Links to **5**, and the Ponytail1 and Ponytail2 Links to **1**.
3. Open the Motion panel, and click the Figure Mode button in the Biped rollout to enter Figure Mode.
4. In the Bend Links rollout, click the Bend Links Mode button.
5. Select and rotate the lowest spine bone so the upper torso leans forward.
6. Select one of the thigh bones, and click the Symmetrical button in the Track Selection rollout to select both thigh bones. Then rotate the thighs to come forward toward the head.

   The lower legs will follow.
7. Select one of the lower leg bones, and click the Symmetrical button in the Track Selection rollout. Then rotate the lower leg bones backward until the feet are in the same vertical position as the hands.
8. Select one of the ponytail links, and move and rotate it to the position of an ear. Then repeat for the other ponytail link. Make sure that the green ponytail link is on the left side, and the blue one is on the right.
9. With the Bend Links Mode button selected in the Biped rollout, select and rotate the top tail link away from the body.
10. Open the Copy/Paste rollout, click the Create Collection button and select the Pose button. Then click the Copy Pose button to add the pose to the list. Then click the Save Collection button, and save the file as Cat pose.cpy.

Figure 42.9 shows the resulting cat pose.

FIGURE 42.9

This cat pose was created by manipulating the biped bones.

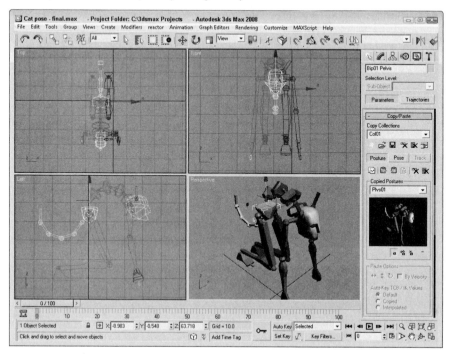

Animating a Biped

When it comes time to animate a biped, there are two modes that you can use: Footstep Mode and Freeform Mode. Both have advantages. Footstep Mode is useful for characters that need to walk, run, or jump. It ensures that the feet stay parallel to the ground at all times and can be used to walk over rough terrain. Freeform Mode doesn't constrain the biped and is used for all other actions. Most animation sequences use a combination of both modes.

Using Footstep Mode

In Footstep Mode, you animate the movement of the biped by placing footprints for the biped to follow. These footprints can be positioned anywhere within the scene, and the biped automatically creates the motion required to have the biped follow the footprints including all the realistic secondary motion such as swinging arms. You can also select to have the biped motion be walking, running, or jumping using the buttons in the Footstep Creation rollout.

NOTE When you create a Footstep animation sequence, the feet timing is controlled by the footstep icons. If you want to alter or customize the animation, you need to convert the footsteps into keys.

Using the Walk Footstep and Double Support values located under the Walk button, you can set how quickly the footstep animation happens. The Walk Footstep value is the number of frames for which the foot remains within the footstep, and the Double Support value is the number of frames during which both feet are touching the ground.

For the Run and Jump options, the Run Footstep and 2 Feet Down values define the number of frames in which the foot is (or feet are) within the footstep, and the Airborne values define the number of frames in which both feet are in the air.

Footstep Mode is enabled by clicking the Footstep Mode button in the Biped rollout of the Motion panel. This button turns light yellow when enabled and opens several additional rollouts.

 The easiest way to create footsteps is to click the Create Footsteps (at current frame) button in the Footstep Creation rollout and then click in the viewport where the footprints are to be located. By default, the left foot is placed first and the footprints alternate between right and left. Left footprints are marked in blue, and right footprints are marked in green. Until keys are created, you can select, move, and rotate footsteps.

TIP If you look closely at the cursor, you can see which footstep will be created with the next click. If you press the Q key and then reselect the Create Footsteps button, the opposite foot is placed with the first click.

 After several footprints are added to the scene, clicking the Create Keys for Inactive Footsteps button in the Footstep Operations rollout creates the keys for the biped following the footsteps. After the keys are created, the biped is moved to the location of the first footprint, and dragging the Time Slider (or clicking the Play Animation button) moves the biped through the available footsteps.

 After a sequence of footprints exists, you can add more footsteps using the Create Footsteps (Append) button in the Footstep Creation rollout. This button lets you place more footsteps, continuing the sequence already laid out.

 To automatically create multiple footsteps that are equally spaced, click the Create Multiple Footsteps button in the Footstep Creation rollout. This opens a dialog box, shown in Figure 42.10, that lets you specify which foot is first, the total number of footsteps, the stride width, and many other settings associated with the first and last steps.

If a footstep is selected, the Footstep Operations rollout includes buttons to deactivate, delete, or copy the selected footstep. If you copy a footstep and then forget what is in the copy buffer, you can enable the Buffer Mode button in the Biped rollout to see the motion of the footstep that is in the buffer.

The Dynamics & Adaptation rollout includes a GravAccel value. This value is used to determine how quickly the body returns to ground during a run or jump cycle. To simulate a character jumping on the moon, reduce the GravAccel value. There are also several Footstep Adapt Locks that can be set.

FIGURE 42.10

The Create Multiple Footsteps dialog box lets you specify details such as Stride Length.

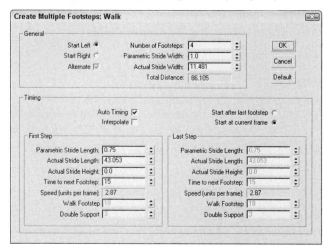

Tutorial: Making a biped jump on a box

Although we could easily make our biped dance the two-step, this tutorial has the biped walk a few steps, transition to a run, and then jump on top of a stationary box.

To make biped jump on a box, follow these steps:

1. Select the Create ➪ Standard Primitives ➪ Box menu command, and drag in the Top viewport to create a simple box.

2. Select the Create ➪ Systems ➪ Biped menu command, and drag in the Top viewport to create a biped object. Be sure to leave enough room between the biped and the box so the biped can get a running start.

3. Open the Motion panel, and click the Footstep Mode button in the Biped rollout to enter Footstep Mode.

4. In the Footstep Creation rollout, select the Walk button and click the Create Footsteps button. Then click in the Top viewport to create four footsteps in front of the biped object starting with the right foot.

5. Choose the Run option in the Footstep Creation rollout, select the Create Footsteps (append) button, and add four more steps that are spread out slightly more than the first steps.

6. Choose the Jump option in the Footstep Creation rollout, and click the Create Multiple Footsteps button. In the Create Multiple Footsteps dialog box that opens, set the Number of Footsteps to **2**, and click the OK button.

   The two footsteps where the biped lands should be in the center of the box object.

7. Select and move the final two footsteps upward in the Left viewport to be on top of the Box object.

8. Click the Create Keys for Inactive Footsteps button in the Footstep Operations rollout to create the keys for the available footsteps.

9. Click the Play Animation button to see the biped walk, run, and jump on the box.

Figure 42.11 shows the biped as he hops onto a box object.

Converting biped animation clips

 The Convert button in the Biped rollout lets you convert all footstep animations to Freeform keys. If you don't plan to append any additional steps to a biped, then converting the keys makes it easier to work in Freeform Mode.

Clicking the Convert button opens a simple dialog box with the option to generate a keyframe for every frame.

Using Freeform Mode

Freeform Mode is enabled by default when none of the other buttons in the Biped rollout are enabled. Using Freeform Mode, you can select and set keys for any of the biped bones, blend several animations into one using Layers, import Motion Capture data, and define Dynamic properties.

FIGURE 42.11

By positioning footsteps, you can control exactly where the biped moves.

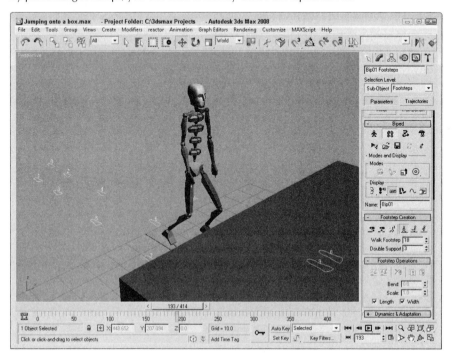

Setting Freeform keys

The easiest way to set biped keys is to drag the Time Slider to the frame where you want the key to be, select and transform the bone, and then click the Set Key button in the Key Info rollout, shown in Figure 42.12. The Key Info rollout also includes buttons for deleting keys; setting a planted, sliding, or free key; and viewing trajectories.

 **The Auto Key and Set Key tools don't work very well with bipeds because they use TCB controllers. Use the biped controls in the Motion panel to set keys instead.**

FIGURE 42.12

The Key Info rollout includes specialized buttons for setting biped keys.

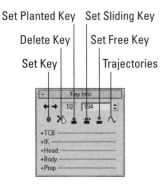

Set Planted Key   Set Sliding Key

Delete Key   Set Free Key

Set Key   Trajectories

The Key Info rollout also includes several expandable sets of controls including TCB, IK, Head, Body, and Prop. The TCB controls let you configure the Ease To and Ease From curves of the selected key using a Tension, Continuity, and Bias curve.

The IK controls let you set IK Blend and Ankle Tension values and select a pivot about which to apply the IK solution. The Head section lets you select a Look At Target. The Body controls include a Balance Factor that is used to determine the amount of sway in the biped's motion. The Prop controls lets you select which bone the current prop is linked to for position and rotation.

Using the Keyframing Tools, Layers, and Motion Capture

The Keyframing Tools rollout, shown in Figure 42.13, includes several useful buttons for enabling and manipulating subanimations. You can also delete a range of keys or all keys, mirror keys, set multiple keys, and anchor the right hand, left hand, right foot, or left foot. By default, the animation key for each bone is rolled up to its parent, but you can have the key for each individual bone appear as a separate track using the check boxes in the Keyframing Tools rollout.

The Layers rollout lets you layer sets of animations while maintaining existing animations. For example, if a character is animated walking about a scene, then adding a layer with the character's arms held straight up will have the character walk about the scene in the same manner with its arms held up.

After several layers are added onto a biped, you can use the Activate Only Me button to see the animation of a single layer or the Activate All button to view all layer animations.

FIGURE 42.13

The Keyframing Tools rollout includes a variety of features.

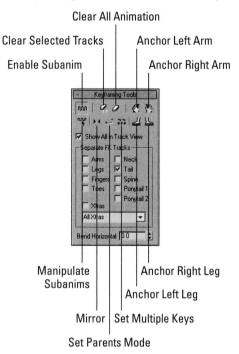

Clear All Animation

Clear Selected Tracks　　Anchor Left Arm

Enable Subanim　　　　Anchor Right Arm

Manipulate
Subanims　　　Anchor Right Leg

　　　　　Anchor Left Leg

Mirror │ Set Multiple Keys

Set Parents Mode

The Motion Capture rollout lets you load, apply, and manipulate motion capture data. Motion capture data is saved using the .bip file extension.

Loading and saving biped animation clips

In addition to creating an animation, you can simply load an existing animation using the Load File button in the Biped rollout. This button opens a file dialog box where you can select the .bip file to load. A preview of the selected biped animation sequence is displayed in the Open dialog box, and you can select to restructure the biped to match the file.

Animation sequences can also be saved using the Save File button. All biped animations are saved using the .bip file extension, and you can select to save any Max objects and List Controllers along with the file.

Using Motion Flow Mode

The Motion Flow Mode button in the Biped rollout opens a rollout of options that let you create a graphical flow of animation sequences that flow together to create a large animation sequence.

With the Motion Flow Mode button enabled, click the Show Graph button in the Motion Flow rollout. This opens the Motion Flow Graph dialog box, shown in Figure 42.14.

FIGURE 42.14

The Motion Flow Graph interface displays each motion clip as a separate node.

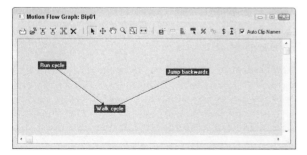

Using the Create Clips button, you can add a node to the graph window. Right-clicking the node lets you open a .bip file. The name of the clip file appears in the node. The Create Transition button can be used to define transitions between nodes, which are represented by arrowed lines. After a transition is defined between two nodes, clicking the Create All Transitions button causes transitions to be created for each defined transition that ensures smooth motion between the various motion clips.

After the nodes of the motion are established, you can use these same nodes to create a motion script that creates the keys needed to view the animation in the viewports. To create a script, click the Define Script button in the Motion Flow rollout and then select the nodes in the order that you want them to appear. Each selected node is added to the rollout list, and dragging the Time Slider displays the biped's motion in the viewports.

Scripts can be saved and loaded using the Load and Save buttons in the Motion Flow rollout. The Motion Flow Graph interface also includes buttons for optimizing, randomizing, and checking all motion clips and their transitions.

Previewing a biped animation

After a biped has been animated using footsteps of Freeform keys, you can preview the animation in the viewport using the Biped Playback button found in the Biped rollout. This animates the biped as a stick figure moving through the various keys and is useful for understanding the timing of the biped's motion.

Moving a biped with its footsteps

When footsteps are created, the biped and its footsteps can be moved independent of one another. The Move All Mode button lets you select and move a biped along with all its footsteps all together to a new location.

Creating Crowds

Crowd systems are composed of two helper objects called Crowd and Delegate, but the system can also use other scene objects that act as objects to avoid or follow.

Using Crowd and Delegate helpers

Crowd and Delegate helper objects are created using the Create ➪ Helper ➪ Crowd or Delegate menu commands. The Crowd object looks like a simple dummy object and the Delegates are simple pyramids. Objects can be linked to a behavior object that travels along with it.

Several of the tools that you need to define the crowd system are accessed from the Setup rollout, shown in Figure 42.15.

FIGURE 42.15

Use the Setup rollout to define the crowd system.

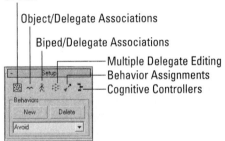

Scatter
Object/Delegate Associations
Biped/Delegate Associations
Multiple Delegate Editing
Behavior Assignments
Cognitive Controllers

Scattering delegates

If only a single delegate is created, it is not much of a crowd. Multiple delegates can be created using the various cloning methods or using the Scatter button located in the Setup rollout in the Modify panel when the Crowd object is selected.

CROSS-REF The various cloning methods are covered in Chapter 8, "Cloning Objects and Creating Object Arrays."

Clicking the Scatter button causes the Scatter Objects dialog box, shown in Figure 42.16, to open. This dialog box includes several panels used to randomize the Position, Rotation, and Scale of the cloned delegates. In the Clone panel, you can select the Object to Clone and How Many clones to create. After the settings are correct, click the Generate Clones button to create the duplicates.

FIGURE 42.16

The Scatter Objects dialog box lets you quickly create crowds of objects.

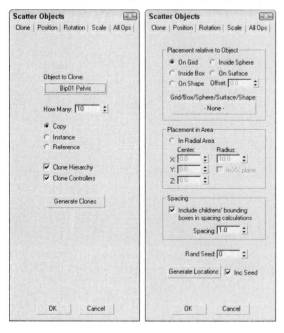

Setting delegate parameters

 Each selected delegate has parameters that can be set in the Modify panel including its dimensions, Speed, Acceleration, and Turning values. With the Crowd object selected, you can click the Multiple Delegate Editing button to open a dialog box, shown in Figure 42.17, that lets you change the parameters of multiple delegates simultaneously.

In the upper-left corner, you can select the delegate objects to change using the Add button. You can then specify two values for the parameters. If the Random option is specified, the parameter falls somewhere between the two values. You can also save sets of settings using the drop-down list in the lower-left corner of the interface.

FIGURE 42.17

The Edit Multiple Delegates dialog box lets you quickly set the parameters of multiple delegates.

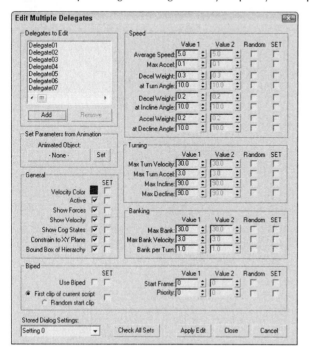

Assigning behaviors

Within the Setup rollout of the Crowd object is a New button that lets you add new behaviors that can be used with the crowd system. All behaviors that are added to the crowd system appear in a drop-down list. By typing a new name in the list, you can name each behavior. The available behaviors include the following:

- **Avoid:** Prevents collisions between scene objects and other delegates.
- **Orientation:** Controls the direction in which the delegates face.
- **Path Follow:** Forces delegates to move only along a designated path.
- **Repel:** Forces delegates to move away from a target object.
- **Scripted:** Makes a delegate behave using a MAXScript.
- **Seek:** Moves delegates toward a target object.
- **Space Warp:** Uses a Space Warp object to control behavior.
- **Speed Vary:** Changes the speed of delegates as they move about the scene.
- **Surface Arrive:** Moves delegates toward a surface.
- **Surface Follow:** Moves delegates across a surface.
- **Wall Repel:** Uses a grid object to repel delegates.
- **Wall Seek:** Uses a grid object to attract delegates.
- **Wander:** Makes delegates move randomly.

When a behavior is selected from the Setup rollout, a custom rollout of parameters for the selected behavior appears. Using these parameters, you can govern how the behavior acts and select which objects are targets.

 After the behavior's parameters are set, you can assign specific delegates or teams of delegates to use certain behaviors in the Behavior Assignments and Teams dialog box, shown in Figure 42.18. This dialog box is opened using the Behavior Assignment button found in the Setup rollout.

FIGURE 42.18

The Behavior Assignments and Teams dialog box lets you organize teams of delegates and assign them to behaviors.

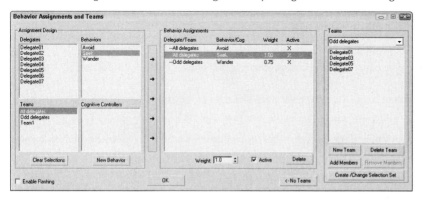

All behavior assignments are listed in the center pane, and each assignment can be given a weight. If the delegate has two conflicting behaviors to follow, then it follows the one with the greatest weight value.

Solving the simulation

The final step in the process is to solve the simulation. This step creates keyframes for all the motion in the scene. To solve the simulation, click the Solve button in the Solve rollout or click the Step Solve button to solve for a single frame at a time. By default, the solution saves keyframes for every frame, but you can increase the Positions and Rotations values to compute the simulation faster.

Tutorial: Rabbits in the forest

This example uses the delegate primitives linked to rabbit meshes to navigate through a forest. Moving several objects through an array of objects can be time consuming when done by hand, but the Crowd system makes it easy.

To move a group of rabbit delegates through an array of trees, follow these steps:

1. Open the Bunny in the forest.max file from the Chap 42 directory on the DVD. This file includes several pine trees and a bunch of bunnies.

2. Select the Create ➪ Helpers ➪ Crowd menu command, and drag in the viewport to create a Crowd object. Make the Crowd object big enough to be easily selected.

3. Select the Create ➪ Helpers ➪ Delegate menu command, and drag in the Left viewport to create a Delegate object positioned outside the trees. Orient and link the bunny to the delegate object. Then, shift+drag the delegate to create six total delegate bunnies positioned about the cubes.

4. Select the crowd object, click the New button in the Setup rollout of the Modify panel, select the Avoid behavior, and name it **Avoid trees**. In the Avoid Behavior rollout, click the Multiple Selection button. In the Select dialog box that appears, choose all tree objects and click the Select button. Enable the Display Hard Radius button, and then decrease the Hard Radius value to 0.2 so that bunnies can travel through the trees.

5. Click the New button again. This time, select the Seek behavior and name it **Seek hole**. In the Seek Behavior rollout, click the None button and choose the red box object that represents the hole.

6. In the Setup rollout, click the Behavior Assignment button to open the Behavior Assignment and Teams dialog box. Click the New Team button, select all delegate objects, and click the OK button. Then select the Team0 team and the Avoid cubes behavior, and click the center New Assignment button (the long, thin button with the right-pointing arrows). Select the Team0 team again with the Seek goal behavior, and click the New Assignment button again. Both assignments are listed in the center pane; click the OK button.

7. Set the Solve time equal to the animation length of 300 frames. In the Solve rollout, click the Solve button.

   The crowd system solves the movement of all delegates as they move toward the goal.

8. Click the Play Animation button to see the resulting solution.

Figure 42.19 shows the position of the delegates after the simulation has ended. Notice the random position of the various delegates.

FIGURE 42.19

The Crowd simulation automatically figures out how to move the delegate bunnies to reach the goal while avoiding the trees.

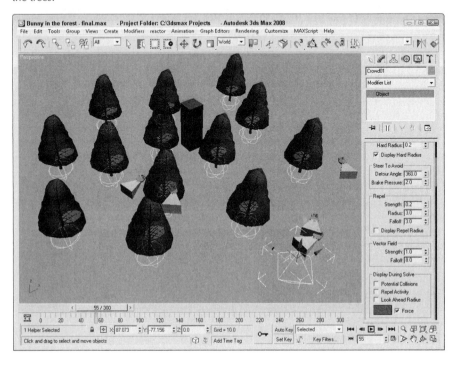

Creating a Crowd of Bipeds

Working with delegates is simple enough, but you probably don't have much need for an animation of several pyramids moving about the scene. The real advantage of the crowd system comes when working with objects and bipeds.

Associating delegates with objects

 The second button in the Setup rollout is called the Object/Delegate Associations button. It is used to open a dialog box of the same name. Using this dialog box, shown in Figure 42.20, you can specify which scene objects get associated with which delegates.

FIGURE 42.20

The Object/Delegate Associations dialog box lets you link objects to delegates.

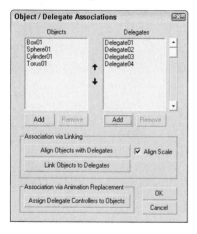

Click the Add buttons to add Objects and Delegates to their respective lists. The arrow buttons between the columns can be used to reorder items in the list. After all objects are matched with their correct delegates, click the Align Objects button or the Link Objects button to complete the linking.

Associating delegates with objects

 The third button in the Setup rollout is called the Biped/Delegate Association button. It is used just like the Object/Delegate Association button to open a dialog box to associate biped objects with delegates.

Summary

This chapter serves as an introduction to Character Studio and covers all aspects of working with bipeds. The Crowd features of Character Studio are useful for animating the motion of delegates following specified behaviors. The following topics were covered:

- Learning the basic workflow for creating characters
- Creating and editing biped skeletons
- Animating bipeds using footsteps and freeform keys
- Creating crowds with helper objects
- Assigning behaviors
- Using bipeds with crowds

Whether you're using a custom rig or a Biped, the next step is to begin the skinning process, which is covered next. Skinning surrounds the skeleton with a mesh skin and matches the way the skin aligns and moves with the underlying rig.

Chapter 43

Skinning Characters

In the taxidermy world, skinning an animal usually involves removing its skin, but in the Max world, skinning a character involves adding a skin mesh to a group of controlling bones. Skinning a character also involves defining how the skin deforms as the bones are moved.

A character skin created in Max can be any type of object and is attached to a biped or a bones skeleton using the Skin modifier. The Skin modifier isn't alone. Max includes other modifiers like the Skin Wrap and Skin Morph modifiers that make your skin portable. This chapter covers explains how the various Skin modifiers are attached to a skeleton and used to aid in animating your character.

Understanding Your Character

What are the main aspects of your character? Is it strong and upright, or does it hunch over and move with slow, twisted jerks? Before you begin modeling a character, you need to understand the character. It is helpful to sketch the character before you begin. This step gives you a design that you can return to as needed.

> **TIP** The sketched design also can be loaded and planar mapped to a plane object to provide a guide to modeling.

You have an infinite number of reference characters available to you (just walk down a city street if you can't think of anything new). If you don't know where to start, then try starting with a human figure. The nice thing about modeling a human is that an example is close by (try looking in the mirror).

We all know the basic structure of humans: two arms, two legs, one head, and no tail. If your character is human, then starting with a human character and changing elements as needed is the easiest way to go. As you begin to model human figures, being familiar with anatomy is helpful. Understanding the structure of muscles and skeletal systems helps explain the funny bumps you see in your elbow and why muscles bulge in certain ways.

IN THIS CHAPTER

Planning your character

Using the Skin modifier

Painting skin weights

Using the Weight Tool

Working with the Skin Wrap and Skin Morph modifiers

 If you don't have the model physique, then a copy of *Gray's Anatomy* can help. With its detailed pictures of the underlying muscular and skeletal systems, you'll have all the details you need without having to pull your own skin back.

The curse and blessing of symmetry

The other benefit of the human body is that it is symmetrical. You can use this to your benefit as you build your characters, but be aware that unless you're creating a band of killer robots, it is often the imperfections in the characters that give them, well, character. Positioning an eye a little off normal might give your character that menacing look you need.

Dealing with details

When you start to model a human figure, you quickly realize that the body includes lots of detail, but before you start naming an object "toenail lint on left foot," look for details you won't need. For example, modeling toes is pointless if your character will be wearing shoes and won't be taking them off. (In fact, I think shoes were invented so that animators wouldn't have to model toes.)

At the same time, details in the right places add to your character. Look for the right details to help give your character life — a pirate with an earring, a clown with a big red nose, a tiger with claws, a robot with rivets, and so on.

Figure 43.1 shows two good examples. The ninja warrior on the left doesn't need the details of a mouth or teeth because they are hidden behind his mask. In fact, if you were to remove his mask, the model would leave a large gaping hole. The Greek woman statue model on the right includes many necessary details including fingernails, toes, a bellybutton, and, uh, well, uh, other details.

NOTE You can actually find these two character models on the DVD at the back of the book, compliments of Viewpoint Datalabs.

FIGURE 43.1

These two characters have details modeled where needed.

Animated Skin Modifiers

Of all the animation modifiers, several specifically are used to deal with Skin. The Skin modifier is a key modifier for enabling character animation. The Skin Morph modifier lets you deform a skin object and create a morph target. It is designed to help fix problem areas, such as shoulders and hips, that have trouble with the standard Skin modifier. The Skin Wrap offers a way to animate a low-res proxy and then apply the same animation to a high-res wrapped object.

A Physique modifier left over from the Character Studio suite of tools has been integrated into Max. The Physique modifier also is used to bind skin meshes to skeletons, but the Skin modifier is easier to use and more powerful. The Physique modifier remains for backward compatibility.

Understanding the Skinning Process

Unless you like animating using only a skeleton or a biped by itself, a bones system will have a skin attached to it. Any mesh can be made into a skin using the Skin modifier. The Skin modifier is used to bind a skin mesh to a bones system and to define the associations between the skin vertices and the bones. The first step is to bind the skin mesh to the skeleton object. With a skin attached to a bones system, you can move the bones system and the skin follows, but just how well it follows the skeleton's motion depends on a process called skinning.

CROSS-REF Creating a bones system is covered in more detail in Chapter 40, "Understanding Rigging and Working with Bones." Bipeds are covered in Chapter 42, "Creating and Animating Bipeds and Crowds."

Skinning is where you tell which parts of the skin mesh to move with which bones. Obviously, you'd want all the skin vertices in the hand to move with the hand bone, but the skin vertices around the waist and shoulders are more tricky.

Each skin area that surrounds a bone gets encompassed by a capsule-shaped envelope. All vertices within this envelope move along with the bone. When two of these envelopes overlap, their surfaces blend together like skin around a bone joint. Most of the skinning process involves getting the skin vertices into the right envelope. The Skin modifier includes several tools to help make this easier, including the Skin Weight table and a painting weights feature.

Binding to a skeleton

After you have both a skeleton and a skin mesh, you need to bind the skin to the skeleton before you can edit the influence envelopes. The binding process is fairly easy: Simply select the skin mesh, and apply the Skin modifier to it using the Modifiers ➪ Animation ➪ Skin menu command.

TIP Before binding a skeleton to a skin mesh, take some time to match the size and dimensions of the bones close to the skin mesh. The skin mesh is bound to the skeleton, and the envelopes are created automatically. If the bones match the skin, then the new envelopes are pretty close to what they need to be.

In the Parameters rollout, click the Add button above the bones list. This opens a Select Bones dialog box where you can select the bones to use to animate this skin. The selected bones appear in the bones list. The text field directly under the bones list lets you locate specific bones in the list by typing the name. Only one bone at a time may be selected from the list. The Remove button removes the selected bone from the bone list.

Tutorial: Attaching skin to a biped

For human figures, using a biped skeleton saves lots of time. For this example, because he's human in form, we bind a biped skeleton to the Future man model.

To bind the skin of a model to a biped skeleton, follow these steps:

1. Open the Future man.max file from the Chap 42 directory on the DVD.

   This file includes a futuristic man model.

2. Select the pelvis object, and convert it to an Editable Poly object using the right-click quadmenu. In the Modify panel that opens, click the setting dialog box button next to the Attach button in

the Edit Geometry rollout. The Attach List dialog box opens. Click the All button to select all objects, and then click the Attach button. In the Attach Options dialog box that appears, choose the Match Material to Material IDs option and click the OK button. This makes the entire skin a single object and retains its materials.

3. Select Create ⇨ Systems ⇨ Biped. Click and drag in the Front viewport to create a new biped that is roughly the same height as the future man model.

4. Select the future man model, and choose the Freeze Selection option from the right-click quad-menu. Then press the G key to turn off the grid display and maximize the viewport.

5. Select the biped object, and open the Motion panel. Then click the Figure Mode button in the Biped rollout. Click the Body Horizontal button in the Track Selection rollout to select the biped's Center of Mass (COM) object instantly. Then position the biped so its pelvis lines up with the future man model.

6. Select the left thigh bone, and rotate and scale it until the biped's foot aligns with the future man model. Then click the Opposite button in the Track Selection rollout to select the right thigh bone, and align the foot in the same manner.

7. Press and hold the Ctrl key, and select each of the spine objects. Then scale the spine objects until the head is correctly aligned in the Front viewport. Select the right shoulder bone, click the Symmetrical button in the Track Selection rollout, and scale the shoulders to make them broader. Finally, rotate each upper arm into correct alignment.

8. Switch to the Right and Top views, and adjust the bones to better align with the future man model including performing these tasks: Move the entire biped forward, rotate the neck forward, rotate and scale the forearms in the Top viewport, and scale the feet.

9. After the biped is correctly aligned to the future man model, select Unfreeze All from the right-click quadmenu. Select the future man model, and choose Modifiers ⇨ Animation Modifiers ⇨ Skin to apply the Skin modifier.

10. In the Parameters rollout, click the Add button. The Select Bones dialog box opens. Click the All button to select all the bones, and click Select.

11. In the Parameters rollout, select each of the bones in the list and click the Edit Envelopes button. Zoom in on the highlighted bone (which is the left shin bone), select the cross-section handles for this bone, and set the Radius values to **0.15** near the body and **0.1** for the other end.

After the Skin modifier is applied and bound to the skin mesh, every bone includes an area of influence called an envelope that defines the skin vertices that it controls. If any of the skin mesh vertices are outside of the bone's envelope or are included in an envelope for the wrong bone, then the vertices are left behind when the bone is moved. This causes an odd stretching of the skin that is easy to identify.

To check the envelopes, select and rotate several of the skeleton's key bones. If any envelope problems exist, they are easy to spot, as shown in Figure 43.2. The incorrect stretching of the vertices for the boot simply means that the envelopes need to be adjusted.

Editing envelopes

When the Skin modifier is selected, the Parameters rollout includes an Edit Envelopes button that places you in a special mode that lets you edit the envelope for the selected bone in the bone list. This mode is also enabled by selecting the Envelope subobject under the Skin modifier at the top of the Modifier Stack.

When the Edit Envelopes mode is enabled, the entire skin mesh is colored with a gradient of colors to visually show the influence of the envelope. Areas of red are completely inside the envelope's influence, areas of green are somewhat affected by the bone, and areas of gray are completely outside the envelope's influence.

FIGURE 43.2

If the envelopes are off for any of the skin vertices, the skin stretches incorrectly.

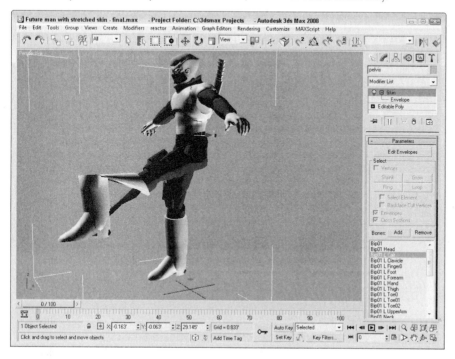

Figure 43.3 shows a simple loft object surrounding three bone objects with a Skin modifier applied. The Add Bone button was used to include the three bones within the Skin modifier list. The skin has been set to See Through in the Properties dialog box, so the bones are visible. The first bone was selected in the bone list, and the Edit Envelope button was clicked, revealing the envelope for the first bone.

An envelope consists of two capsule-shaped volumes within each other called the Inner and Outer Envelopes. Any vertices within the inner envelope are controlled exclusively by that bone. Any vertices positioned between the inner and outer envelopes are controlled by a falloff where the influence is shared between bones.

At either end of these envelopes are four small handles that can be dragged to change the cross-section radius. The cross-section area changes to pink when selected. The radius of the selected cross section is displayed in the Radius field within the Envelope Properties section of the Parameters rollout. The Squash value determines the amount of squash applied to the object for bones that can stretch. You can change an envelope's size by changing its Radius value or by dragging the cross-section handles. Within the Select section of the Parameters rollout, you can choose to select and edit Vertices, Envelopes, and/or Cross Sections. If you choose the Vertices option, selected vertices are shown as small squares, and the Shrink, Grow, Ring, and Loop buttons become active. These buttons allow you to select a desired set of vertices easily. If the Select Element option is enabled, then all vertices in the element are selected and the Backface Cull Vertices option prevents vertices on the backside of the object from being selected.

FIGURE 43.3

Envelopes define which Skin vertices move with the underlying bone.

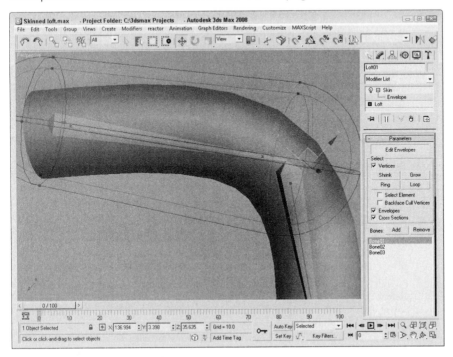

If a cross section is selected, you can add a different cross-section shape using the Add button. This button lets you select a cross-section shape within the viewports. The Remove Cross Section button removes an added cross section from the envelope.

> **NOTE** The orientation of the envelope spline is set by the longest dimension of the bone. This works well for arm and leg bones, but the pelvis or clavicle may end up with the wrong orientation.

The Envelope Properties section of the Parameters rollout (just below the Radius and Squash buttons) includes five icon buttons, shown in Table 43.1. The first toggles between Absolute and Relative. All vertices that fall within the outer envelope are fully weighted when the Absolute toggle is set, but only those within both envelopes are fully weighted when the Relative toggle is selected.

TABLE 43.1

Envelope Properties

Button	Name	Description
A	Absolute/Relative	Toggles between Absolute and Relative.
/	Envelope Visibility	Makes envelopes remain visible when another bone is selected.

Button	Name	Description
	Falloff Linear,	Sets Falloff curve shape.
	Falloff Sinual,	
	Falloff Fast Out,	
	Falloff Slow Out	
	Copy envelope	Copies envelope settings to a temporary buffer.
	Paste envelope,	Pastes envelope settings to the selected bone, to all bones, or to multiple bones chosen from a dialog box.
	Paste to All Bones,	
	Paste to Multiple Bones	

The second icon button enables envelopes to be visible even when not selected. This helps you see how adjacent bones overlap. The third icon button sets the Falloff curve for the envelopes. The options within this flyout are Linear, Sinual, Fast Out, and Slow Out. The last two icon buttons can be used to Copy and Paste envelope settings to other bones. The flyout options for the Paste button include Paste (to a single bone), Paste to All Bones, and Paste to Multiple Bones (which opens a selection dialog box).

Working with weights

For a selection of vertices, you can set its influence value (called its Weight value) between 0 for no influence and 1.0 for maximum influence. This provides a way to blend the motion of vertices between two or more bones. For example, the vertices on the top of a character's shoulder could have a weight value of 1.0 for the shoulder bone, a weight value of 0.5 for the upper arm bone, and a weight value of 0 for all other bones. This lets the shoulder skin area move completely when the shoulder bone moves and only halfway when the upper arm moves.

NOTE The shading in the viewport changes as vertices are weighted between 0 and 1. Weight values around 0.125 are colored blue, weight values around 0.25 are colored green, weight values around 0.5 are colored yellow, and weight values around 0.75 are colored orange.

The Absolute Effect field lets you specify a weight value for the selected vertices. The Rigid option makes the selected vertices move only with a single bone. The Rigid Handles causes the handles of the selected vertices for a patch object to move only with a single bone. This is important if the character is wearing a hard item such as armor plates. By enabling this options, you can be sure that the armor plates doesn't deform. The Normalize option requires that all the weights assigned to the selected vertices add up to 1.0.

The other buttons found in the Weight Properties section of the Parameters rollout are defined in Table 43.2. Include Vertices and Exclude Vertices buttons let you remove the selected vertices from those being affected by the selected bone. The Select Exclude Verts button selects all excluded vertices.

TABLE 43.2

Envelope Properties

Button	Name	Description
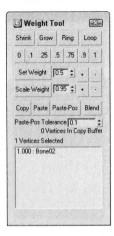	Exclude Selected Vertices	Excludes the selected vertices from the influence of the current bone.
	Include Selected Vertices	Includes all selected vertices in the bone's influence.
	Select Excluded Vertices	Selects all excluded vertices.
	Bake Selected Verts	Bakes the vertex weights into the model so they aren't changed with the envelope. Baked vertices can be changed using the Weight Table or the Absolute Effect value.
	Weight Tool	Opens the Weight Tool interface.

Using the Weight Tool

The Weight Tool button in the Parameters rollout opens the Weight Tool dialog box, shown in Figure 43.4. The Shrink, Grow, Ring, and Loop buttons work the same as those in the Select section, and they let you quickly select precise groups of vertices. The value buttons on the second row allow you to change weight values with a click of the button or by adding or subtracting from the current value.

FIGURE 43.4

The Weight Tool dialog box includes buttons for quickly altering weight values and for blending the weights of adjacent vertices.

The Copy, Paste, and Paste Position buttons let you copy weights between vertices quickly. The Paste Position button pastes the given weight to the surrounding vertices based on the Tolerance value. The Blend button quickly blends all the surrounding vertices from the current weight value to 0, creating a smooth blend weight. The Weight Tool dialog box also lists the number of vertices in the copy buffer and currently selected. The list at the bottom of the dialog box lists the weight and bone for the selected vertices.

Using the Weight Table

The Weight Table button opens the Weight Table interface, shown in Figure 43.5. This table displays all the vertices for the skinned object by ID in a column on the left side of the interface. All bones are listed in a row along the top. For each vertex and bone, you can set a weight.

FIGURE 43.5

The Weight Table lets you specify weight values for each vertex and for each bone.

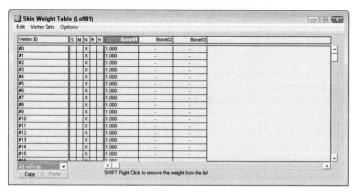

The Edit menu includes commands to Copy and Paste weights. It also includes commands to Select All, Invert, and None. A selection of vertices can be combined into a Vertex Set and named. The Vertex Sets menu lets you create and delete these sets.

The Options menu lets you flip the interface so that bones are displayed in the first column and the vertex IDs are along the top row. The Update On Mouse Up option limits the updates until the mouse is released. Several options for showing and hiding interface elements are included. The Show Affected Bones option lists only the bones that are affected. The Show Attributes option displays a column of attributes labeled S, M, N, R, and H. The Show Exclusions option makes a check box available in each cell. When checked, the vertex is excluded. The Show Global option makes a drop-down list available that enables you to set an attribute for all vertices. The Show Locks option (like the Show Exclusions option) makes a check box available for each cell. Enabling this check box (the left one) locks the weight so it can't change. The Set Sets UI makes available two buttons for creating and deleting vertex sets.

The S attribute is marked if a vertex is selected, the M attribute marks a vertex weight that has been modified, the N attribute marks a normalized weight, the R attribute marks rigid vertices, and an H attribute marks a vertex with rigid handles.

To set a weight, just locate the vertex for the bone, click in the cell, and type the new value. If you click a cell and drag to the left or right, the weight value changes. Weight values can be dragged between cells. Right-clicking a cell sets its value to 0, and right-clicking with the Ctrl key held down sets its value to 1.0.

After the vertex weights are set, you can click the Bake Selected Vertices to lock down the weight values. Changes to envelopes do not affect baked vertices.

Painting weights

Using the Paint Weights button, you can paint with a brush over the surface of the skin object. The Paint Strength value sets the value of each brush stroke. This value can be positive (up to 1.0) for vertices that will move with the bone or negative (to −1.0) for vertices that will not move with the bone.

To the right of the Paint Weights button is the Painter Options button (it has three dots on it), which opens the Painter Options dialog box.

CROSS-REF The Painter Options dialog box also is used by the Vertex Paint modifier and the Paint Deformation tool. It is described in detail in Chapter 12, "Modeling with Polygons."

Tutorial: Applying skin weights

In this example, we change the skin weights of the future man character in an attempt to fix the problem we saw with his boots.

To apply the skin weights to a character, follow these steps:

1. Open the Future man with skin.max file from the Chap 43 directory on the DVD.

2. With the mesh skin selected, open the Modify panel and choose the Bip01 L Foot bone in the bone list. Then click the Edit Envelopes button at the top of the Parameters rollout. This displays the envelopes around the foot object. Zoom in on the foot object, and change the display option to Smooth + Highlights so you can see the weight shading.

3. Make sure the Cross Sections option in the Select section of the Parameters rollout is selected. Then select the cross-section handles on the outer envelope and pull them in toward the foot. Rotate the side to make sure that the toe and heel of the boot are still covered.

4. Click the Vertices option in the Parameters rollout, and disable the Backface Cull Vertices option. Drag over all the vertices that are contained in the lower part of the boot, and enable the Rigid option. Then select the vertices above the boot in the shin. You can use the Loop button to select all vertices about the upper part of the boot and press and hold the Alt key to remove any vertices that are part of the lower boot.

5. In the Weight Properties section of the Parameters rollout, click the Weight Tool button. In the Weight Tool dialog box, click the .25 button. This changes the weight of the selected vertices. Then click the Blend button to smooth the transition areas.

6. Click the Edit Envelopes button to exit Edit Envelopes mode. Then select and rotate the upper leg to see whether the problem has been fixed. As I rotated my model, I noticed that some vertices on the back of the boot were left behind, which means that they aren't being influenced by the foot bone.

CAUTION Be sure to undo the upper leg rotation before making changes to the envelopes, or the envelopes will move along with the rotation.

7. Enter Edit Envelopes mode again, and click the Paint Weights button. The cursor changes to a round brush. Click the Brush Options button (which is next to the Paint Weights button with three dots). This opens the Brush Options dialog box. Set the Max Strength value to **1.0**, and close the dialog box. Then paint in the viewport over the vertices on the back of the boot heel, including those areas that aren't shaded red. Figure 43.6 shows the correct boot with its envelopes.

8. Exit Edit Envelopes mode again, and check the changes by rotating the upper leg bone.

FIGURE 43.6

Vertices' weights can be fixed with the Weight Tool and by Painting Weights.

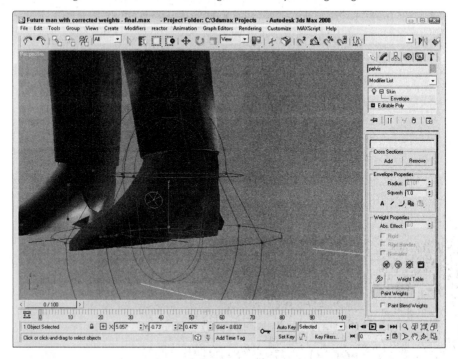

Mirror settings

Most characters have a natural symmetry, and you can use this symmetry to mirror envelopes and vertex weights between different sides of a model. You can use this feature by clicking the Mirror Mode button in the Mirror Parameters rollout. This button is active only when the Edit Envelope button is active.

In Mirror Mode, you see an orange plane gizmo that marks the symmetrical line for the model. You can move and orient this plane using the Mirror Offset and Mirror Plane controls. Once oriented, Max computes the matching vertices based on the volumes from the mirror plane. All vertices on one half of the character appear blue, and all the matching vertices appear green. All vertices that cannot be matched appear red.

If you drag over bones or vertices in the viewports, you can select them. Clicking the Mirror Paste button pastes the envelopes and vertex weights of the selected vertices to their matches. Or you can select the Paste Green to Blue Bones button or one of its neighbors to copy all the green bones or vertices to their matches, or vice versa.

The Display Projection drop-down list projects the position of the selected vertices onto the Mirror Plane so you can compare their locations relative to each other. With lots of vertices in your skin, you want to enable the Manual Update, or the viewport refreshes become slow.

Tutorial: Mirroring skin weights

Now that you have spent the time correcting the skin weights for the left boot, we use the Mirror Weights feature to apply the same weights to the opposite foot.

To apply the skin weights to a character, follow these steps:

1. Open the Future man with corrected weights - final.max file from the Chap 43 directory on the DVD.

2. With envelope mode turned on, click the Mirror Mode button in the Mirror Parameters rollout. An orange gizmo is added to the viewport that divides the model, as shown in Figure 43.7.

3. Drag over all the vertices that make up the left boot, and then click the Paste Blue to Green Verts button. All the vertex weights on the left side of the model are copied to the right side.

FIGURE 43.7

In Mirror mode, matched bones and vertices appear green and blue.

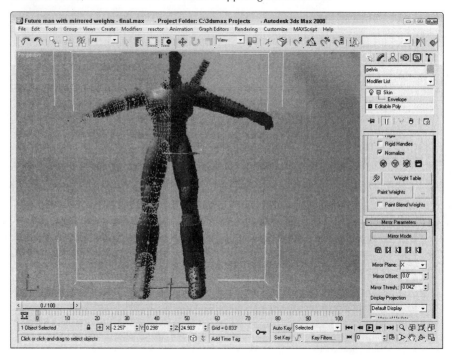

Display and Advanced settings

The Display rollout controls which features are visible within the viewports. Options include Show Colored Vertices, Show Colored Faces, Color All Weights, Show All Envelopes, Show All Vertices, Show All Gizmos, Show No Envelopes, Show Hidden Vertices, Draw On Top Cross Sections, and Draw On Top Envelopes.

With these display options, you can turn on and off the weight color shading on vertices and faces. You can also select to show all envelopes, vertices, and gizmos. The Color All Weights option is unique. It assigns every bone a different color and shows how the weights blend together between bones.

The Advanced Parameters rollout includes an option to Back Transform Vertices. This option avoids applying transform keys to the skin because the bones control the motion. The Rigid Vertices and Rigid Patch Handles options set the vertices so that they are controlled by only one bone. This rollout also includes buttons to Reset Selected Vertices, Reset Selected Bones, and Reset All Bones. This is handy if you really mess up a skinning job, because it gives you a chance to start over. It also includes buttons for saving and loading envelopes. The envelopes are saved as files with the .ENV extension.

The Animatable Envelopes option lets you create keys for envelopes. Weight All Vertices is a useful option that automatically applies a weight to the nearest bone of all vertices that have no weight. The Remove Zero Weights button removes the vertex weight of any vertex that has a value lower than the Zero Limit. This can be used to remove lots of unnecessary data from your model if you need to put it on a diet.

Using deformers

Below the Advanced Parameters rollout is the Gizmos rollout. You use this rollout to apply deformers to selected skin object vertices. Three deformers are available in the Gizmos rollout: a Joint Angle Deformer, a Bulge Angle Deformer, and a Morph Angle Deformer.

Each of these deformers is unique. They include the following features:

- **Joint Angle Deformer:** Deforms the vertices around the joint between two bones where the skin can bunch up and cause problems. This deformer moves vertices on both the parent and child bones.

- **Bulge Angle Deformer:** Moves vertices away from the bone to simulate a bulging muscle. This deformer works only on the parent bone.

- **Morph Angle Deformer:** Can be used on vertices for both the parent and child bones to move the vertices to a morph position.

All deformers added to a skin object are listed in the Gizmo rollout. You can add deformers to and remove deformers from this list using the Add and Remove Gizmo buttons. You can also Copy and Paste the deformers to other sets of vertices. Before a deformer gizmo can be applied, you need to select vertices within the skin object. To select vertices, enable the Vertices check box of the Parameters rollout and drag over the vertices in the viewport to select the vertices.

The parameters for the deformer selected in the Gizmo rollout's list appear when the deformer is selected in the Deformer Parameters rollout. This rollout lists the Parent and Child bones for the selected vertices and the Angle between them. This rollout changes depending on the type of deformer selected.

For the Joint and Bulge Angle Deformers, a new rollout labeled Gizmo Parameters or Deformer Parameters appears. The Gizmo Parameters rollout includes buttons to edit the control Lattice and to edit the deformer Key Curves. The Edit Lattice button lets you move the lattice control points in the viewports. The Edit Angle Keys Curves opens a Graph window that displays the transformation curves for the deformation.

Using the Skin Wrap modifiers

If you've created a high-resolution model that you want to animate as a skin object, but the mesh is too complex to move around, then the Skin Wrap modifier might be just what you need. The Skin Wrap modifier may be applied to a high-resolution mesh, and with the Parameters rollout you can select a low-resolution control object. Any movements made by the low-resolution control object automatically are applied to high-resolution mesh.

 Skin Wrap is also very useful for animating clothes on a character.

The Skin Wrap modifier has two available Deformation Engines: Face Deformation and Vertex Deformation. Each vertex contained with the control object acts as a control vertex. The Vertex Deformation option moves the vertices closest to each control vertex when the control vertex is moved, and the Face Deformation option moves the faces that are closest.

For each deformation mode, you can set a Falloff value, which moves vertices farther from the moved control vertex to a lesser extent to ensure a smoother surface. For the Vertex Deformation mode, you can also set a Distance Influence value and Face Limit values to increase the extent of influence for a control vertex.

The Reset button can be used to reset the control object to the high-resolution mesh object. This is useful if you need to realign the control object to the Skin Wrap object. When you're finished animating the control object, the Convert to Skin button may be used to transfer the animation keys to the high-resolution objects.

The Advanced Parameters rollout includes a button for mirroring the selected vertices to the opposite side of the control object.

The Modifiers menu also includes a Skin Wrap Patch modifier, which works the same as the Skin Wrap modifier, but it allows the control object to be a patch.

Tutorial: Making a simple squirt bottle walk

Creating a bones structure and applying a Skin modifier works well for characters with structure, but to animate the motion of an amorphous object such as a squirt bottle, the Skin Wrap modifier works much better than bones.

To animate a squirt bottle object walking using the Skin Wrap modifier, follow these steps:

1. Open the Walking squirt bottle.max file from the Chap 43 directory on the DVD.

   This file includes a squirt bottle model with all its parts attached together. The file also includes a simple box object that is roughly the same shape as the squirt bottle. The box object has been animated walking forward.

2. With the squirt bottle object selected, choose the Modifiers ➪ Animation ➪ Skin Wrap menu command to apply the Skin Wrap modifier.

3. In the Parameters rollout, click the Add button and select the Box object. The Box object is added to the Skin Wrap list in the Parameters rollout.

4. Select the Box object and hide it in the scene.

5. Click the Play Animation button, and the hi-res bottle follows the same animation as the box object.

Figure 43.8 shows the squirt bottle as it moves through the scene.

Using the Skin Morph modifier

Using the deformation options found in the Skin modifier, you can deform any part of the skin, but this feature relies on using gizmos found in an already complex envelope-editing mode. Skin Morph offers another way to deform a skin object using the underlying bones. The Skin Morph modifier is applied on top of a Skin modifier and lets you pick which bones to use in the deformation. For example, for bulging muscles, the forearm bone is rotated and should be added to the list in the Parameters rollout.

After selecting a bone from the Parameters rollout list, select the frame where the deformation is at maximum. Then click the Create Morph button in the Local Properties rollout to create the morph target. Morph targets can be given names to make them easy to select later. The Edit button in the Local Properties rollout then lets you move the vertices for the deformation.

Tutorial: Bulging arm muscles

Perhaps the most common bulging deformation for characters is making the bicep muscle bulge as the forearm is raised. This effect can be simplified using the Skin Morph modifier.

FIGURE 43.8

Not all objects that are animated need a bones structure.

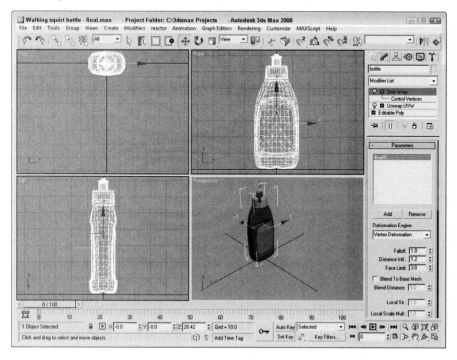

To bulge an arm muscle using the Skin Morph modifier, follow these steps:

1. Open the Bulging bicep.max file from the Chap 43 directory on the DVD.

   This file includes a rough arm model with a Skin modifier applied attached to a four-bone chain.

2. With the arm skin selected, choose the Modifiers ⇨ Animation ⇨ Skin Morph menu command to apply the Skin Morph modifier on top of the Skin modifier.

3. In the Parameters rollout, click the Add button and select the forearm bone object.

   The bone object is added to the Skin Morph list in the Parameters rollout.

4. Select and rotate the forearm bone to the location where the deformation is at its maximum. Then select the bone object from the list in the Parameters rollout, and click the Create Morph button in the Local Properties rollout. Name the morph **Bulging bicep**.

5. In the Local Properties rollout, click the Edit button. This enables the Points subobject mode. Then enable the Edge Limit option so the vertices on the forearm aren't accidentally selected. Drag over the points on the front of the bicep muscle in the Left viewport, and enable the Use Soft Selection option in the Selection rollout. Set the Radius value to **0.5**, and move the points to the right in the Left viewport to form a bulge. Click the Edit button again to exit Edit mode.

6. Select and rotate the forearm bone to see the bulging bicep muscle.

Figure 43.9 shows the arm muscle as it bulges along with the rotating forearm.

FIGURE 43.9

Using the Skin Morph, you can set a muscle to bulge as the forearm is rotated.

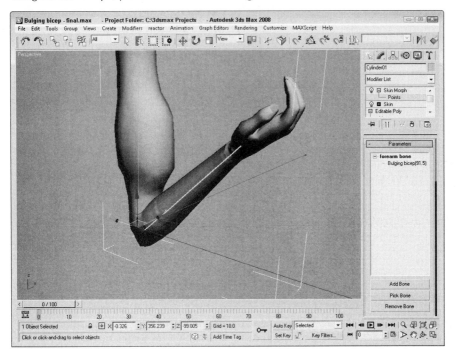

Using Character Animation Techniques

When it comes to character animation, several techniques can really help. Keeping these points in mind as you animate characters can make a difference:

- **Use Biped:** Manual rigging is useful for those cases where Biped won't work, but the tools and features found in Biped make it silly to look elsewhere for human characters.

- **Use Dynamics:** Dynamic packages like reactor can provide incredibly realistic motion based on physical properties. Learning to use this powerful tool for even the most basic animation sequences is worth the effort.

- **Learn by Example:** If you're working on a cartoon character, then by all means, watch cartoons. Traditional cartoons understand and invented the language of cartoon motion including squash and stretch, exaggerated motion, or scaling eyes large to indicate surprise. If your character motion is more realistic, find the motion, videotape it, and watch it over and over to catch the subtle secondary motion.

- **Use Background Animations:** The Viewport Background can load animation clips, which can make positioning characters to match real motion easy. This is a poor man's motion capture system.

- **Include Secondary Motion:** The primary motion of a character is often the main focus, but you can enhance the animation by looking for secondary motion. For example, when a person walks, you see his legs take the steps and his arms moving opposite the legs' motion, but secondary motion includes his hair swishing back and forth and shoelaces flopping about.

- **Use the Flex Modifier:** The Flex modifier gives soft bodies, such as tails, hair, ears, and clothing, the realistic secondary motion needed to make them believable.

- **Use the Morph Modifier:** The Morph modifier can be used to morph a character between two poses or to morph its face between the different phonemes as the character talks.

- **Use IK:** The next chapter covers this in detail, but here's a quick tip: Having a character move by positioning its foot or hand is often much easier than pushing it into position.

- **Use the Spring Controller:** Another good way to get secondary motion is to use the Spring Controller. This controller works well with limbs.

- **Add Randomness with the Noise Controller:** Often, perfect animation sequences don't look realistic, and using the Noise Controller can help to make a sequence look more realistic, whether the Noise Controller is applied to a walking sequence or to the subtle movement of the eyes.

- **Use Manipulators:** Manipulators can be created and wired to give you control over the animation values of a single motion, such as opening and closing the character's eyes.

Summary

Characters are becoming more and more important in the Max world and can be saved as separate files just like Max scene files. Combining a detailed skin mesh with a skeletal biped lets you take advantage of Character Studio's unique animation features. This chapter covered the following topics:

- Designing your character before building
- Working with the Skin modifier
- Reusing animations with Skin Wrap
- Bulging muscles with Skin Morph

In the next part, "Advanced Lighting and Rendering," we examine many of the high-end lighting and rendering features beginning with the Advanced Lighting system.

Part XI

Advanced Lighting and Rendering

Chapter 44

Working with Advanced Lighting, Light Tracing, and Radiosity

I f you were to walk into a dark room and reach for the light switch, you would be confused if you found a separate switch that controlled the advanced lighting. But in Max the advanced lighting controls are worth the trouble. They enable you to take your lighting solution to the next level.

The advanced lighting controls in Max enable you to light scenes using two separate global illumination techniques known as light tracing and radiosity. Both solutions deal with the effect of light bouncing off objects and being reflected to the environment.

Light tracing is typically used for outdoor scenes where the light consists of a single powerful light source at a far distance from the scene. Light tracing includes support for color bleeding between surfaces. Another aspect of light tracing is that the shadows are softer.

Radiosity computes lighting solutions that are much more realistic than using standard lights. As you learn to use Radiosity, you quickly discover that it is a complex system that takes lots of tweaking to get just right.

Selecting Advanced Lighting

You control the advanced lighting settings for the scene in the Advanced Lighting panel, which is part of the Render Scene dialog box. You can access this panel by selecting Rendering ⇨ Advanced Lighting ⇨ Light Tracer (or by pressing the 9 key). The Advanced Lighting panel includes a rollout with a single drop-down list where you can select the lighting plug-in to use. The options are None, Light Tracer, and Radiosity.

NOTE The Light Tracer and Radiosity options aren't available if the mental ray renderer is enabled.

Light Tracer and Radiosity are two different techniques for applying advanced lighting to a scene. Although they are fundamentally different, they both simulate a critical piece of the lighting puzzle that adds dramatically to the realism of the lights in the scene — light bouncing. When light strikes a surface in real life, a portion of the light bounces off the surface and illuminates other surfaces. Traditionally, Max hasn't worried about this, which required that users add more lights to the scene to account for this additional lighting. Both the Light Tracer and the Radiosity solutions include light bouncing in their calculations.

NEW FEATURE The ability to view lights and shadows interactively in the viewport is new to 3ds Max 2008.

How light tracing works

The Light Tracer is a Global Illumination (GI) system that is similar to raytracing, but it focuses more on calculating how light bounces off surfaces in the scene. The results are fairly realistic without being computationally expensive, and its solutions are rendered much quicker than a radiosity solution.

CROSS-REF The Light Tracer is similar in many ways to raytracing. Chapter 46, "Raytracing and mental ray," presents more information on raytracing.

The Light Tracer works by dividing the scene into sample points. These sample points are more heavily concentrated along the edges of objects in the scene. An imaginary light ray is then shot at each sample point, and the light intensity at the location of contact is recorded; then it is computed where the light ray would bounce to, and a reduced intensity value is recorded. One of the settings is how many times the light rays will bounce within the scene, and this value increases the amount of time required to compute the solution. When all the rays and light bounces have been computed, the total light intensity value for each sample point is totaled and averaged.

CAUTION Transparent objects split each ray in two. One ray bounces, and the second ray is projected through the transparent object. Transparent objects in the scene quickly double the amount of time required to compute a solution.

The end result of a light tracing solution is that objects that are typically hidden in the shadows become much easier to see. Figure 44.1 shows a house model that was rendered using the standard lighting solution with raytraced shadows and then again using the Light Tracer opened side by side in the RAM Player. Notice that many of the details hidden in the shadows of one figure are visible in the other.

Enabling light tracing

To enable light tracing in a scene, select Rendering ⇨ Advanced Lighting ⇨ Light Tracer to open the Advanced Lighting panel in the Render Scene dialog box, as shown in Figure 44.2.

The Global Multiplier value increases the overall effect of the Light Tracer, much like increasing the multiplier of a light. The net result is to brighten the scene. You can also increase the multiplier of skylights with the Sky Lights values. The Object Multiplier sets the amount of light energy that bounces off the objects.

Color bleeding

Another characteristic of global illumination is color bleeding. As a light ray strikes the surface of an object and bounces, it carries the color of the object that is struck with it to the next object. The result of this is that colors from one object bleed onto adjacent objects. You can control this effect using the Color Bleed setting. You can greatly exaggerate the amount of color bleeding by increasing the Object Multiplier along with the Color Bleed value. You can also select colors to use for a color filter and for extra ambient light.

NOTE The color bleeding effect doesn't happen unless the Bounce value is set to 2 or greater.

FIGURE 44.1

A house scene rendered using standard lighting (left) and light tracing (right)

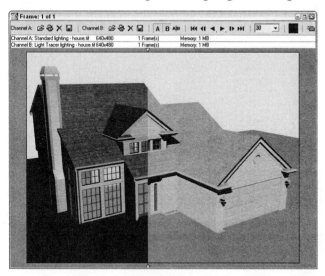

FIGURE 44.2

The Light Tracer Parameters rollout sets values for GI lighting.

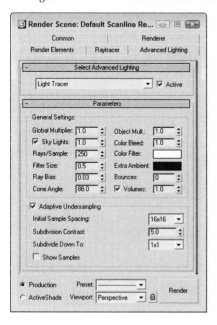

When using color bleeding, you want also to enable the Exposure Control to the scene. Exposure Control is found in the Environment panel (keyboard shortcut, 8), which can be opened with the Rendering ➪ Environment menu command.

CROSS-REF The Exposure Control features are discussed in Chapter 22, "Learning to Render a Scene."

Figure 44.3 shows an example of color bleeding with several colored cylinders projecting from a gray Box object. The Object Multiplier value was set to 4.0, and the Color Bleed was set a maximum value of 25.0 with a Bounce value of 3. Using the Exposure Control settings, you can isolate the color bleed.

FIGURE 44.3

Color bleeding spreads color about the scene. Exposure Control can highlight it with Automatic (left) and Logarithmic (right).

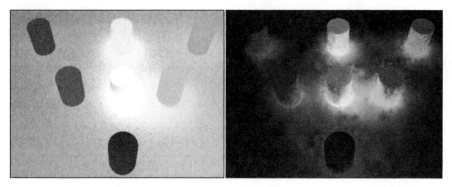

Quality versus speed

The big trade-off of global illumination is between quality and render time. The more rays per sample that you specify, the better the quality and the longer the render time. This is controlled with the Rays/Sample setting. The Rays/Sample setting and the number of Bounces dramatically increase the rendering time. The Ray Bias setting biases rays toward object edges versus flat areas.

TIP If you want to see a preview of your scene using light tracing, set the Rays/Sample value to around 10 percent of its normal value and render the scene. The resulting image is grainy, but it shows a rough approximation of the scene lighting without having to change the Bounce value.

If you don't include enough rays in the scene, then noise patterns appear within the scene. The Filter Size can help control the amount of noise that appears in the scene.

The number of Bounces value specifies the number of times the ray bounces before being dropped from the solution. A setting of 0 is the same as disabling the Light Tracer, and the maximum value of 10 requires a long time to compute. The Cone Angle defines the cone region within which the rays are projected. The Volumes option is a multiplier for the Volume Light and Volume Fog atmosphere effects.

Adaptive undersampling

With the Adaptive Undersampling option enabled, the Light Tracer focuses on the areas of most contrast, which usually occur along the edges of objects. When this option is enabled, you can specify the spacing of the samples and how finely the samples get subdivided. The Initial Sample Spacing options range from 1 × 1 to a very dense 32 × 32. The Subdivision Contrast affects the density for contrast edges between objects and shadows. This value is a minimum amount of contrast that is allowed. If the amount of contrast is greater than this value, then the area is further subdivided into more samples. These high-contrast areas use the Subdivide Down To setting. The Show Samples option displays each sample as a red dot on the rendered image.

Tutorial: Viewing color bleeding

One of the easiest effects of the Light Tracer to see is color bleeding. Although this is often undesirable, it is a telltale sign of global illumination.

To compare the differences between a regular rendering and the Light Tracer, follow these steps:

1. Open the Hotplate.max file from the Chap 44 directory on the DVD.

    This file includes a simple model of a hotplate.

2. Open the Advanced Lighting panel by selecting Rendering ⇨ Advanced Lighting ⇨ Light Tracer (or press the 9 key). In the Parameters rollout, set the Object Multiplier to **10**, the Color Bleed to **25**, and the Bounces to **1**.

3. Select the Rendering ⇨ Environment (8) menu command to open the Environment and Effects panel. In the Exposure Control rollout, select the Linear Exposure Control option and enable the Process Background and Environment Maps option.

4. In the Render Scene dialog box, click the Render button.

    This renders the scene in the Rendered Frame Window.

> **CAUTION** Remember that selecting an advanced lighting option greatly increases the render time.

Figure 44.4 shows the scene rendered with advanced lighting.

FIGURE 44.4

Color bleeding happens only when global illumination is enabled.

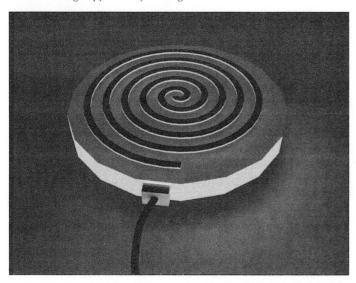

Using Local Advanced Lighting Settings

You can set advanced lighting settings locally for specific objects using the Object Properties dialog box, as shown in Figure 44.5.

At the top of the Advanced Lighting panel in the Object Properties dialog box is the number of selected objects and lights. This dialog box lets you specify whether this object should be excluded from the advanced lighting calculations. The properties can be set By Object or By Layer. If included, you can select whether the object casts shadows, whether it receives illumination, and how it handles Radiosity. The Number Regathering Rays Multiplier option sets the number of rays cast by the selected object. For large smooth surfaces, reducing artifacts by increasing this value can be helpful. The rest of the settings in this panel deal with Radiosity.

FIGURE 44.5

Use the Advanced Lighting panel in the Object Properties dialog box to disable advanced lighting.

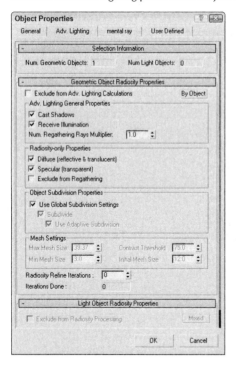

Tutorial: Excluding Objects from Light Tracing

Using the Object Properties dialog box, you can exclude certain objects from the light tracing calculations.

To exclude objects from the Light Tracer, follow these steps:

1. Open the Hotplate.max file from the Chap 44 directory on the DVD.

   This file includes a simple model of a hotplate.

2. Open the Advanced Lighting panel by selecting Rendering ⇨ Advanced Lighting ⇨ Light Tracer (or press the 9 key). In the Parameters rollout, set the Bounces value to **2**.

3. In the Front viewport, select the plug, cord, and floor objects, and then select Edit ⇨ Object Properties to open the Properties dialog box for these objects. In the Object Properties dialog box, open the Advanced Lighting panel and enable the Exclude from Advanced Lighting Calculations option. Then click the OK button.

4. In the Render Scene dialog box, click the Render button.

   This renders the scene in the Rendered Frame Window.

Figure 44.6 shows the scene rendered with advanced lighting that excludes certain objects.

FIGURE 44.6

Color bleeding becomes much stronger with a higher Bounce value.

Understanding Radiosity

Imagine a scene that includes an umbrella with a light source directly overhead. If you rendered the scene, the object caught in the umbrella's shadow would be too dark to see clearly. To fix this situation, you would need to add some extra lights under the umbrella and set them to not cast shadows. Although this workaround provides the solution we want, it is interesting to note that this isn't the case in real life.

The difference between the workaround and real life has to do with the effect of light energy being reflected (or bounced) off the lit objects. It is this phenomenon that allows me to look down the hall and see whether my children's light is still on past bedtime. Even though I can't see the light directly, I know it is on because of the light that reflects off the other walls.

Radiosity is a lighting algorithm that is based on how heat or energy transfers across surfaces. Every time a bit of light energy, called a photon, strikes a surface, the light energy is reduced, but the light energy is bounced onto the surrounding faces. The number of bounces that are computed, the more realistic the lighting solution, but the longer it takes to compute. So, using radiosity, the objects under the umbrella are visible even if they are in the shadows. Because of the way the light is computed, radiosity solutions are not capable of generating direct specular highlights.

Radiosity is mostly used to light indoor scenes because that is where the effect of light bouncing is most evident. Radiosity, along with light tracing, is another method for computing global illumination. Figure 44.7 shows the dinosaur exhibit in a museum with and without radiosity. Notice how dark the shadows are in the normal lighting image.

FIGURE 44.7

This scene is lighted using normal lighting (left) and radiosity lighting (right).

Lighting for radiosity

The Advanced Lighting panel in Max includes light tracing and radiosity options. You can choose either option from the Advanced Lighting panel in the Render Scene dialog box. You can open this panel with the Radiosity option selected using the Rendering ➪ Advanced Lighting ➪ Radiosity menu command. Pressing the 9 key opens the Render Scene dialog box with the Advanced Lighting panel open.

Radiosity lighting is not displayed until you have Max compute it by clicking the Start button in the Radiosity Processing Parameters rollout. After a radiosity solution is calculated, the results are saved as light maps. These maps are easy to apply to a scene and can be viewed within the viewports. However, when the geometry or lights of the scene change, you need to recalculate the lighting solution.

The Radiosity Processing Parameters rollout, shown in Figure 44.8, lets you set the quality of the radiosity solution. You can also specify the number of iterations to use for the scene and for the selected objects. These are different steps in the radiosity computation. The Initial Quality defines the accuracy of the rays that are bounced around the scene. This stage sets the brightness for the scene. The Refine Iterations improves the general quality of the lighting solution for each iteration. You can refine iterations only for the selected object. This lets you target the iterations instead of computing them for the entire scene.

The Interactive Tools section lets you specify a Filtering value. A greater Filtering value eliminates noise between adjacent surfaces by averaging the lighting coming from all surrounding surfaces. The Setup button offers access to the Exposure Control rollout in the Environment panel. You can also turn off Radiosity in the viewports.

FIGURE 44.8

The Radiosity Processing Parameters rollout includes buttons for computing a solution.

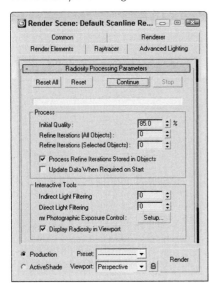

 Chapter 22, "Learning to Render a Scene," includes coverage of the Exposure Control rollout.

Subdividing a mesh for radiosity

As you begin to play with radiosity, you'll quickly find that to get accurate results, you need to have good, clean models. If any models have long, thin faces, then the results are unpredictable.

The Radiosity Meshing Parameters rollout includes an option to enable meshing and a Meshing Size value. This setting is the same as the Size value parameter for the Subdivide modifier, except that it is applied globally.

TIP If you're creating an indoor room using the Box object, be aware that Box objects have only one external face surface with normals, so the interior of a Box object will not have the correct lighting. You can easily fix this by applying the Shell modifier to the Box object. This adds an interior set of faces to the Box object.

Using the Subdivide modifier

The Modifiers menu includes a submenu for Radiosity modifiers. This submenu includes only the Subdivide modifier and a World-Space version of the Subdivide modifier. This modifier accomplishes a simple task — creating a mesh that has regular, equally shaped triangular faces that work well when computing a radiosity solution.

TIP Although this modifier was created to help with radiosity solutions, it also helps with other commands that require regular mesh faces such as the Boolean and Terrain compound objects.

The Parameters rollout includes a Size value that determines the density of the mesh. The lower the value, the denser the mesh and the better the resulting radiosity solution, but the longer the solution takes. This same Subdivision Size setting can also be found (and set globally) in the Radiosity Meshing Parameters rollout of the Advanced Lighting panel. It is also found in the Advanced Lighting panel of the Object Properties

1031

dialog box. Figure 44.9 shows a simple cube with the Subdivide modifier applied and the Size value set to (from left to right) 50, 30, 25, 20, and 12.

TIP   If you drag the Size value, you'll probably want to set the Update option to Manual or you'll find yourself waiting while Max computes some seriously dense mesh, or you can just disable the Display Subdivision option.

FIGURE 44.9

The Subdivide modifier changes all mesh faces into regularly shaped triangular faces.

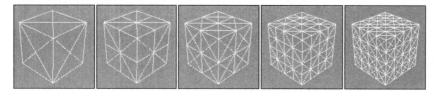

Tutorial: Preparing a mesh for radiosity

When it comes to meshes that have long, thin, and irregular faces, you don't have to look any further than Boolean compound objects. These objects typically are divided along strange angles producing ugly meshes. The good news is that these meshes are easy to subdivide.

To subdivide an irregular mesh in preparation for a radiosity solution, follow these steps:

1. Open the Boolean object.max file from the Chap 44 directory on the DVD.

   This file includes two copies of a Box object with an arch shape Boolean subtracted from it.

2. Select the top object, and choose the Modifiers ⇨ Radiosity Modifiers ⇨ Subdivide menu command.

   This applies the Subdivide modifier to the object.

3. In the Parameters rollout, select the Manual update option, set the Size value to **5.0**, and click Update Now.

   If the Display Subdivision option is enabled, then the changes are visible in the viewport.

4. Open the Advanced Lighting panel with the Rendering ⇨ Advanced Lighting menu command (or press the 9 key). Select Radiosity from the drop-down menu.

Figure 44.10 shows the two objects with and without the Subdivide modifier applied. The top object is ready for a radiosity solution.

Painting with light

The Light Painting rollout (found in the Advanced Lighting panel of the Render Scene dialog box), shown in Figure 44.11, includes buttons for Adding Illumination, Subtracting Illumination, and Picking an Illumination value from the scene. Using these tools, you can paint lighting on the objects in the scene. The Clear button removes all the changes you've made using the Light Painting tool.

Rendering parameters and statistics

Settings in the Rendering Parameters rollout (shown in Figure 44.12) are used during the rendering process. The Re-Use and Render Direct Illumination options give you the chance to re-use the existing radiosity solution when rendering or to recalculate it as part of the rendering process. This can save some time during rendering.

FIGURE 44.10

Subdividing an irregular mesh prepares it for radiosity lighting.

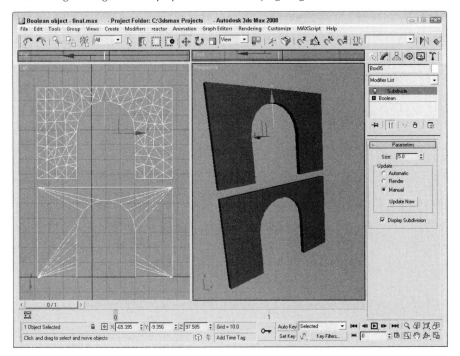

FIGURE 44.11

Because lighting is saved as a light map, you can add or subtract light from the scene using a brush tool.

FIGURE 44.12

The Rendering Parameters and Statistics rollouts offer rendering options and statistics for radiosity solutions.

The Regather Indirect Illumination option enables a Light-Tracer-like step along with the radiosity solution and produces an image that has the best of both solutions. The regathering options are the same as those defined for the light tracer.

The Statistics rollout includes information about the Radiosity process. Using this information, you can judge whether the settings are too high or too low.

Tutorial: Lighting a house interior with radiosity

Radiosity works best in indoor scenes or scenes that are mostly interior. The only light source for this scene is an Daylight system and a single Omni light in the front hallway.

To light a house interior with Radiosity, follow these steps:

1. Open the House interior.max file from the Chap 44 directory on the DVD.

2. Open the Advanced Lighting panel with the Rendering ⇨ Advanced Lighting menu command (or press the 9 key). Select Radiosity from the drop-down list in the Select Advanced Lighting rollout.

3. In the Radiosity Processing Parameters rollout, set the Refine Iterations value to **2** and click the Start button to have Max compute the radiosity solution.

4. In the Rendering Parameters rollout, enable the Render Direct Illumination, the Regather Indirect Illumination, and the Adaptive Sampling options. Then click the Render button to begin the rendering process.

Figure 44.13 shows the finished rendered house interior. Notice that all surfaces are well lit even though the scene has a limited number of lights.

CROSS-REF This same house interior is rendered with mental ray in Chapter 46, "Raytracing and mental ray."

FIGURE 44.13

The radiosity solution for this scene adds to the lighting levels for the entire room.

Using Local and Global Advanced Lighting Settings

Just like with the Light Tracer, you can set advanced lighting settings locally for specific objects using the Object Properties dialog box, opened with the Edit ➪ Object Properties menu command. This dialog box includes an Advanced Lighting panel, and several of the settings are specific to Radiosity.

For the selected objects, you can specify whether they Cast Shadows and Receive Illumination. For a radiosity solution, you can also select to enable or disable Diffuse, Specular, Regathering, and Subdividing. The Radiosity Refine Iterations value lets you set the number of iterations for the current selection. Think of Refine Iterations as the quality setting. You can set it for all objects or just for the selected object. It works by comparing the variance between adjacent faces.

If any light objects are selected, you can select to exclude them from radiosity processing or to store the illumination values with the mesh.

The Preference Settings dialog box also includes a panel for Radiosity. Using this panel, shown in Figure 44.14, you can set the advanced lighting settings that apply to all objects globally.

FIGURE 44.14

Use the Radiosity panel of the Preference Settings dialog box to set global parameters.

In the Radiosity panel of the Preference Settings dialog box is an option to Display Reflectance & Transmittance Information. If this option is enabled, this information (average and maximum percent values) appears directly below the sample slots. You can also select to have the radiosity solution displayed in the viewports and to automatically process any refine iterations noted in the Object Properties dialog box for a given object. Radiosity processing includes a couple of warning dialog boxes that appear — one when the current solution is reset, and another to update the solution when the Start button is clicked. You can disable both of these warnings. The final option is to save the radiosity solution with the Max file. This slightly increases the file size, but it doesn't require that you recalculate the radiosity solution when the file is opened again.

Working with Advanced Lighting Materials

Applying an advanced lighting solution can have a direct impact on the materials in the scene. The Material Editor includes two materials that are useful for working with advanced lighting: Advanced Lighting Override and Lightscape materials.

Advanced Lighting Override

The Advanced Lighting Override material type includes material parameters that override the global Advanced Lighting solution. These parameters let you set the amount of Reflectance, Color Bleed, Transmittance, Luminance, and Bump Map Scale that the material uses. This offers a way to make a specific material have its own defined lighting parameters.

 **The Advanced Lighting Override material does not need to be applied to all objects that are to receive advanced lighting. It is used only to override the existing scene settings for certain materials.**

As an example of how this material can be used, consider the hot plate example. Rather than excluding objects from the Advanced Lighting calculations, you can instead use the Light Tracer panel to set the global settings for the scene and apply the Advanced Lighting Override material to the hotplate coils with a higher Color Bleed value. This causes the coils to bleed, but not the rest of the scene.

Another common use for this material is to use the Luminance Scale value to cause self-illuminating materials to add light energy to the global illumination calculations. In other words, increasing this value makes self-illuminating materials act as lights to the scene.

The Advanced Lighting Override material parameters, shown in Figure 44.15, let you set the amount of Reflectance, Color Bleed, Transmittance, Luminance, and Indirect Light Bump Scale that the material uses.

FIGURE 44.15

The Advanced Lighting Override Material rollout defines how light interacts with the material.

Lightscape material

The Lightscape material type lets you apply a material to objects that are imported from Lightscape. They are used to control how the radiosity is mapped to objects. The Basic Parameters rollout includes values for Brightness, Contrast, Ambient Light, and Bump Amount. You also can enable Daylight and Exterior Scene options. These values are applied in addition to the base material.

Using Lighting Analysis

To get information about the current lighting solution, you can use the Lighting Analysis tool. The scene must include a lighting solution before this tool is available. You can access this tool by selecting the Rendering ⇨ Advanced Lighting ⇨ Lighting Analysis menu command. This opens the Lighting Analysis dialog box, shown in Figure 44.16.

FIGURE 44.16

The Lighting Analysis dialog box displays the light values at the specified location.

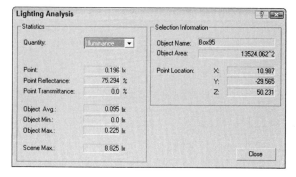

From the Quantity drop-down list, you can select to view light values for Illuminance and Luminance. The cursor also changes into an eyedropper while the dialog box is open. Clicking with the eyedropper in one of the viewports displays the lighting values for that point in the Lighting Analysis dialog box.

Summary

Advanced lighting offers a new way to shine lights on your scenes. With these features, many new lighting options are available. Advanced lighting enables two global illumination methods: light tracing and radiosity. In this chapter, you accomplished the following:

- Enabling advanced lighting
- Discovering light tracing
- Setting local advanced lighting settings
- Discovering radiosity

- Using the Subdivide modifier
- Setting local and global advanced lighting settings
- Using advanced lighting materials and the Lighting Analysis tool

The next chapter deals with fire and smoke and other Atmospheric effects. It also deals with the various Render Effects that Max can generate.

Chapter 45

Using Atmospheric and Render Effects

In the real world, an environment of some kind surrounds all objects. The environment does much to set the ambiance of the scene. For example, an animation set at night in the woods has a very different environment than one set at the horse races during the middle of the day. Max includes dialog boxes for setting the color, background images, and lighting environment; these features can help define your scene.

This chapter covers exposure controls, atmospheric effects, including the likes of clouds, fog, and fire. These effects can be seen only when the scene is rendered.

Max also has a class of effects that you can interactively render to the Rendered Frame window without using any post-production features such as the Video Post dialog box. These effects are called *render effects*. Render effects can save you lots of time that you would normally spend rendering an image, touching it up, and repeating the process again and again.

Using Exposure Controls

The Exposure Control rollout of the Environment panel lets you control output levels and color rendering ranges. Controlling the exposure of film is a common procedure when working with film and can result in a different look for your scene. Enabling the Exposure Controls can add dynamic range to your rendered images that is more comparable to what the eyes actually see. If you've worked with a Histogram in Photoshop, then you'll understand the impact that the Exposure Controls can have. The default selection is Automatic Exposure Control.

The Active option lets you turn this feature on and off. The Process Background and Environment Maps option causes the exposure settings to affect the background and environment images. When this option is disabled, only the scene objects are affected by the exposure control settings. The Exposure Control rollout also includes a Render Preview button that displays the rendered scene in a tiny pane. The preview pane is small, but for most types of exposure control settings, it is enough. When you click the Render Preview button, the scene is rendered. This preview is then automatically updated whenever a setting is changed.

Automatic, Linear, and Logarithmic Exposure Control

Selecting Automatic Exposure Control from the drop-down list automatically adjusts your rendered output to be closer to what your eyes can detect. Monitors are notoriously bad at reducing the dynamic range of the colors in your rendered image. This setting provides the needed adjustments to match the expanded dynamic range of your eyes.

When the Automatic Exposure Control option is selected, a new rollout appears in the Environment panel. This rollout includes settings for Brightness, Contrast, Exposure Value, and Physical Scale. You also can enable Color Correction, select a color, and select an option to Desaturate Low Levels. The Brightness and Contrast settings can range from 0 to 100. A Contrast value of 0 displays all scene objects with the same flat gray color, and a Brightness value of 100 displays all scene objects with the same flat white color. The Exposure Value can range from –5 to 5 and determines the amount of light allowed in the scene.

Another exposure control option is Linear Exposure Control. Although this option presents the same settings as the Automatic Exposure Control, the differences between the minimum and maximum values are a straight line across the light spectrum.

> **TIP** The tricky part is to know when to use which Exposure Control. For still images, the Automatic Exposure Control is your best bet, but for animations, you should use the Logarithmic Exposure Control. Automatic is also a good choice for any scenes that use many lighting effects. Using any of the exposure controls besides the Logarithmic Exposure Control when animating can lead to flickering. The Linear Exposure Control should be used for low dynamic range scenes such as nighttime or cloudy scenes.

The Logarithmic Exposure Control option replaces the Exposure Value setting with a Mid Tones setting. This setting controls the colors between the lowest and highest values. This exposure control option also includes options to Affect Indirect Only and Exterior Daylight. You should enable the Affect Indirect Only option if you use only standard lights in the scene, but if your scene includes an IES Sun light, then enable the Exterior Daylight option to tone down the intensity of the light.

> **CROSS-REF** You should always use the Logarithmic Exposure Control setting when enabling the advanced lighting features because it works well with low-level light. You can learn more about the advanced lighting radiosity features in Chapter 44, "Working with Advanced Lighting, Light Tracing, and Radiosity."

Pseudo Color Exposure Control

As you work with advanced lighting solutions and with radiosity, determining whether interior spaces and objects have too much light or not enough light can be difficult, especially when comparing objects on opposite sides of the scene. This is where the Pseudo Color Exposure Control option comes in handy.

This exposure control option projects a band of colors (or grayscale) in place of the material and object colors that represent the illumination or luminance values for the scene. With these pseudo-colors, you can quickly determine where all the lighting is consistent and where it needs to be addressed.

In the Pseudo Color Exposure Control rollout, shown in Figure 45.1, you can select to apply the colors to show Illumination or Luminance. You also can select to use a Colored or Grayscale style and to make the Scale Linear or Logarithmic. The Min and Max settings let you control the ranges of the colors, and a Physical Scale setting is included. The color (or grayscale) band is shown across the bottom of the rollout with the values for each color underneath.

FIGURE 45.1

The Pseudo Color Exposure Control rollout can display illumination and luminance values as colors.

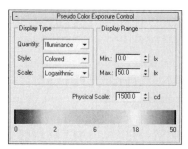

When this exposure control is used, the associated render element is automatically set in the Render Elements rollout of the Render Scene dialog box. If the scene is rendered, then the appropriate (Illumination or Luminance) render element is also rendered.

CROSS-REF See Chapter 48, "Compositing with Render Elements and the Video Post Interface" for more on render elements.

Photographic Exposure Control

If you're comfortable working with camera settings such as Shutter Speed, Aperture, and Film Speed, then the Photographic Exposure Control puts these settings at your fingertips using real-world values. Even if you're not familiar with camera settings, you can use one of the available presets from the list at the top of the rollout, shown in Figure 45.2.

NOTE The Photographic Exposure Control is available only for the mental ray render engine.

FIGURE 45.2

The Photographic Exposure Control rollout works with real-world camera settings.

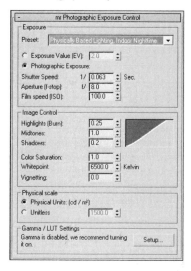

NEW FEATURE The Photographic Exposure Control is new to 3ds Max 2008.

Tutorial: Using the Logarithmic Exposure Control

As you start to use the new photometric lights, you may find it difficult to get the settings just right. The results are over-saturation or under-saturation, but luckily the Logarithmic Exposure Control can quickly fix any problems that appear.

To adjust the effect of a photometric light using the Logarithmic Exposure Control, follow these steps:

1. Open the Array of chrome spheres.max file from the Chap 45 directory on the DVD.

    This file contains lots and lots of chrome mapped spheres with advanced lighting enabled.

2. Choose Rendering ⇨ Render (or press the F10 key) to open the Render Scene dialog box, and click the Render button.

    It takes a while to render, but notice the results, shown on the left in Figure 45.3.

3. Choose Rendering ⇨ Environment (or press the 8 key) to open the Environment & Effects dialog box. In the Exposure Control rollout, select Logarithmic Exposure Control from the drop-down list, and enable the Active and Process Background and Environment Maps options. Then click the Render Preview button.

4. In the Logarithmic Exposure Control rollout, set the Brightness value to **60**, set the Contrast value to **100**, and enable the Desaturate Low Levels option.

5. In the Render Scene dialog box, click the Render button again to see the updated rendering.

The image on the right in Figure 45.3 shows the rendered image with exposure control enabled.

FIGURE 45.3

This rendered image shows an image before and after exposure control was enabled.

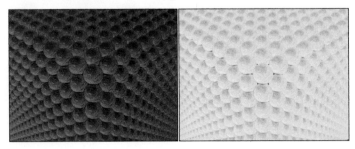

Creating Atmospheric Effects

The Environment and Effects dialog box (keyboard shortcut, 8) contains rollouts for adding atmospheric effects to your scene, but the first question is where. Atmospheric effects are placed within a container called an Atmospheric Apparatus gizmo, which tells the effect where it should be located. However, only the Fire and the Volume Fog effects need Atmospheric Apparatus gizmos. To create an Atmospheric Apparatus gizmo, select Create ⇨ Helpers ⇨ Atmospherics and choose the apparatus type.

The three different Atmospheric Apparatus gizmos are BoxGizmo, SphereGizmo, and CylGizmo. Each has a different shape similar to the primitives.

Working with the Atmospheric Apparatus

Selecting a gizmo and opening the Modify panel reveals two different rollouts: one for defining the basic parameters such as the gizmo dimensions, and another labeled Atmospheres & Effects, which you can use to Add or Delete an Environment Effect to the gizmo. Each gizmo parameters rollout also includes a Seed value and a New Seed button. The Seed value sets a random number used to compute the atmospheric effect, and the New Seed button automatically generates a random seed. Two gizmos with the same seed values have nearly identical results.

Adding effects to a scene

The Add button opens the Add Atmosphere dialog box, where you can select an atmospheric effect. The selected effect is then included in a list in the Atmospheres & Effects rollout. You can delete these atmospheres by selecting them from the list and clicking the Delete button. The Setup button is active if an effect is selected in the list. It opens the Environment and Effects dialog box. Adding Atmospheric Effects in the Modify panel is purely for convenience. They can also be added using the Environment and Effects dialog box.

In addition to the Modify panel, you can add atmospheric effects to the scene using the Atmosphere rollout in the Environment and Effects dialog box, shown in Figure 45.4. This rollout is pretty boring until you add an effect to it. You can add an effect by clicking on the Add button. This opens the Add Atmospheric Effect dialog box, which includes by default four atmospheric effects: Fire Effect, Fog, Volume Fog, and Volume Light. With plug-ins, you can increase the number of effects in this list. The selected effect is added to the Effects list in the Atmosphere rollout.

FIGURE 45.4

The Add Atmospheric Effect dialog box lets you select atmospheric effects.

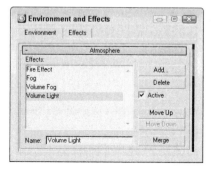

You can delete an effect from the current Effects list in the Environment and Effects dialog box by selecting the effect and clicking the Delete button. The effects are applied in the order in which they are listed, so the effects at the bottom of the list are layered on top of all other effects. To the right of the Effects pane are the Move Up and Move Down buttons, used to position the effects in the list. Below the Effects pane is a Name field where you can type a new name for any effect in this field. This enables you to use the same effect multiple times. The Merge button opens the Merge Atmospheric Effects dialog box, where you can select a separate Max file. You can then select and load any render effects from the other file.

Using the Fire Effect

To add the Fire effect to the scene, select the Rendering ➪ Environment (8) menu command and open the Environment panel; then click the Add button and select the Fire Effect selection. This opens the Fire Effect Parameters rollout, shown in Figure 45.5. At the top of the Fire Effect Parameters rollout is the Pick Gizmo button; clicking this button lets you select a gizmo in the scene. The selected gizmo appears in the drop-down list to the right. You can select multiple gizmos. To remove a gizmo from the list, select it and click the Remove Gizmo button.

FIGURE 45.5

The Fire Effect Parameters rollout lets you define the look of the effect.

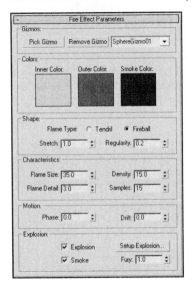

> **NOTE**   The Fire effect renders only in non-orthographic views such as Perspective or a camera view.

The three color swatches define the color of the fire effect and include an Inner Color, an Outer Color, and a Smoke Color. The Smoke Color is used only when the Explosion option is set. The default red and yellow colors make fairly realistic fire.

The Shape section includes two Flame Type options: Tendril and Fireball. The Tendril shape produces veins of flames, and the Fireball shape is rounder and puffier. Figure 45.6 shows four fire effects. The left two have the Tendril shape, and the two on the right are set to Fireball. The difference is in the Density and Flame Detail settings.

The Regularity value determines how much of the Atmospheric Apparatus is filled. The spherical gizmos in the previous figures were all set to 0.2, so the entire sphere shape wasn't filled. A setting of 1.0 adds a spherical look to the Fire effect because the entire gizmo is filled. For a more random shape, use a small Regularity value.

The Flame Size value affects the overall size of each individual flame (though this is dependent on the gizmo size as well). The Flame Detail value controls the edge sharpness of each flame and can range from 1 to 10. Lower values produce fuzzy, smooth flames, but higher values result in sharper, more distinct flames.

FIGURE 45.6

The Fire atmospheric effect can be either Tendril or Fireball shaped.

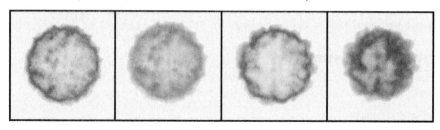

The Stretch value elongates the individual flames along the gizmo's Z-axis. Figure 45.7 shows the results of using the Stretch value. The Stretch values for these gizmos, from left to right, are 0.1, 1.0, 5.0, and 50.

The Density value determines the thickness of each flame in its center; higher Density values result in flames that are brighter at the center, while lower values produce thinner, wispy flames. Figure 45.8 shows the difference caused by Density values of, from left to right, 10, 20, 50, and 100.

The Samples value sets the rate at which the effect is sampled. Higher sample values are required for more detail, but they increase the render time.

The Motion section includes options for setting the Phase and Drift of a fire effect. The Phase value determines how wildly the fire burns. For a wild, out-of-control fire, animate the Phase value to change rapidly. For a constant, steady fire, keep the value constant throughout the frames. The Drift value sets the height of the flames. High Drift values produce high, hot-burning flames.

FIGURE 45.7

The Stretch value can elongate flames.

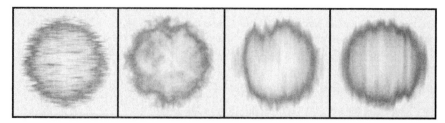

FIGURE 45.8

The Fire effect brightness is tied closely to the flame Density value.

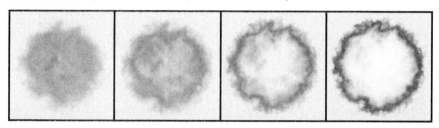

When the Explosion check box is selected, the fire is set to explode. The Start and End Times for the explosion are set in the Setup Explosion Phase Curve dialog box that opens when the Setup Explosion button is clicked. If the Smoke option is checked, then the fire colors change to the smoke color for Phase values between 100 and 200. The Fury value varies the churning of the flames. Values greater than 1.0 cause faster churning, and values lower than 1.0 cause slower churning.

Tutorial: Creating the sun

You can use the Fire effect to create a realistic sun. The modeling part is easy — all it requires is a simple sphere — but the real effects come from the materials and the Fire effect.

To create a sun, follow these steps:

1. Open the Sun.max file from the Chap 45 directory on the DVD.

   This file contains a simple sphere with a bright yellow material applied to it.

2. Select Create ⇨ Helpers ⇨ Atmospherics ⇨ Sphere Gizmo, and drag a sphere in the Front viewport that encompasses the "sun" sphere.

3. With the SphereGizmo still selected, open the Modify panel and click the Add button in the Atmospheres rollout of the Atmospherics and Effects dialog box, which is opened using the Rendering ⇨ Environment menu command or by pressing the 8 key. Select Fire Effect from the Add Atmospheres & Effects dialog box, and click OK. Then select the Fire effect, and click the Setup button.

   The Environment and Effects dialog box opens.

4. In the Fire Effects Parameters rollout, leave the default colors as they are — Inner Color yellow, Outer Color red, and Smoke Color black. For the Flame Type, select Tendril with Stretch and Regularity values of **1**. Set the Flame Size to **30**, the Density to **15**, the Flame Detail to **10**, and the Samples to **15**.

Figure 45.9 shows the resulting sun after it's been rendered.

Tutorial: Creating clouds

Sky images are fairly easy to find, or you can just take your camera outside and capture your own. The trick comes when you are trying to weave an object in and out of clouds. Although you can do this with a Shadow/Matte mask, it would be easier if the clouds were actual 3D objects. In this tutorial, we create some simple clouds using the Fire effect.

To create some clouds for a sky backdrop, follow these steps:

1. Open the Clouds.max file from the Chap 45 directory on the DVD.

   This file includes several hemispherical-shaped atmospheric apparatus gizmos.

2. Choose Rendering ⇨ Environment (or press the 8 key) to open the Environment and Effects dialog box. Click the Background Color swatch, and select a light blue color. In the Atmosphere section, click the Add button, select Fire Effect from the Add Atmospheric Effect list, and click OK.

FIGURE 45.9

A sun image created with a simple sphere, a material with a Noise Bump map, and the Fire effect

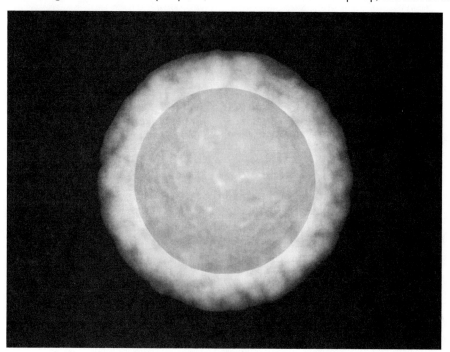

3. Name the effect **Clouds**, and click each of the color swatches. Change the Inner Color to a dark gray, the Outer Color to a light gray, and the Smoke Color to white. Set the Shape to Fireball with a Stretch of **1** and a Regularity of **0.2**. Set the Flame Size to **35**, the Flame Detail to **3**, the Density to **15**, and the Samples to **15**.

TIP If you want to add some motion to the clouds, click the Animate button, drag the Time Slider to the last frame, and change the Phase value to 45 and the Drift value to 30. The clouds slowly drift through the sky. Disable the Animate button when you're finished.

4. In the Fire Effect Parameters rollout, click the Pick Gizmo button and then click one of the gizmos in the viewports. Repeat this step until you've selected all the gizmos.

Figure 45.10 shows the resulting sky backdrop. By altering the Fire parameters, you can create different types of clouds.

FIGURE 45.10

You can use the Fire atmospheric effect to create clouds.

Using the Fog Effect

Fog is an atmospheric effect that obscures objects or backgrounds by introducing a hazy layer; objects farther from view are less visible. The normal Fog effect is used without an Atmospheric Apparatus gizmo and appears between the camera's environment range values. The camera's Near and Far Range settings set these values.

In the Environment and Effects dialog box, the Fog Parameters rollout appears when the Fog effect is added to the Effects list. This rollout, shown in Figure 45.11, includes a color swatch for setting the fog color. It also includes an Environment Color Map button for loading a map. If a map is selected, the Use Map option turns it on or off. You can also select a map for the Environment Opacity, which affects the fog density.

The Fog Background option applies fog to the background image. The Type options include Standard and Layered fog. Selecting one of these fog background options enables its corresponding parameters.

The Standard parameters include an Exponential option for increasing density as a function of distance. If this option is disabled, the density is linear with distance. The Near and Far values are used to set the range densities.

Layered fog simulates layers of fog that move from dense areas to light areas. The Top and Bottom values set the limits of the fog, and the Density value sets its thickness. The Falloff option lets you set where the fog density goes to 0. The Horizon Noise option adds noise to the layer of fog at the horizon as determined by the Size, Angle, and Phase values.

FIGURE 45.11

The Fog Parameters rollout lets you use either Standard fog or Layered fog.

Figure 45.12 shows several different fog options. The upper-left image shows the scene with no fog, the upper-right image uses the Standard option, and the lower-left image uses the Layered option with a Density of 50. The lower-right image has the Horizon Noise option enabled.

FIGURE 45.12

A rendered image with several different Fog effect options applied

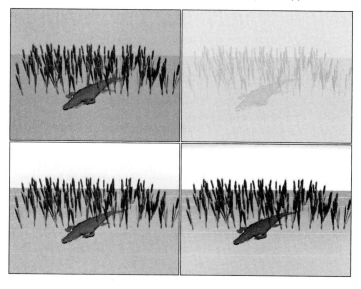

Using the Volume Fog effect

You can add the Volume Fog effect to a scene by clicking the Add button and selecting the Volume Fog selection. This effect is different from the Fog effect in that it gives you more control over the exact position of the fog. This position is set by an Atmospheric Apparatus gizmo. The Volume Fog Parameters rollout, shown in Figure 45.13, lets you select a gizmo to use with the Pick Gizmo button. The selected gizmo is included in the drop-down list to the right of the buttons. Multiple gizmos can be selected. The Remove Gizmo button removes the selected gizmo from the list.

NOTE The Atmospheric Apparatus gizmo contains only a portion of the total Volume Fog effect. If the gizmo is moved or scaled it displays a different cropped portion of fog.

FIGURE 45.13

The Volume Fog Parameters rollout includes parameters for controlling the fog density and type.

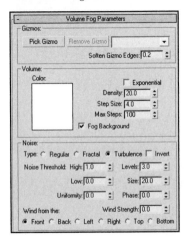

The Soften Gizmo Edges value feathers the fog effect at each edge. This value can range from 0 to 1.

Many of the settings for Volume Fog are the same as those for the Fog effect, but Volume Fog has several settings that are unique to it. These settings help set the patchy nature of Volume Fog. Step Size determines how small the patches of fog are. The Max Steps value limits the sampling of these small steps to keep the render time in check.

The Noise section settings also help determine the randomness of Volume Fog. Noise types include Regular, Fractal, Turbulence, and Invert. The Noise Threshold limits the effect of noise. Wind settings include direction and strength. The Phase value determines how the fog moves.

Tutorial: Creating a swamp scene

When I think of fog, I think of swamps. In this tutorial, we model a swamp scene. To use the Volume Fog effect to create the scene, follow these steps:

1. Open the Dragonfly in a foggy swamp.max file from the Chap 45 directory on the DVD.

   This file includes several cattail plants and a dragonfly positioned on top of one of the cattails.

2. Select Create ➪ Helpers ➪ Atmospherics ➪ Box Gizmo, and drag a box that covers the lower half of the cattails in the Top viewport.

3. Choose Rendering ⇨ Environment (or press the 8 key) to open the Environment and Effects dialog box. Click the Add button to open the Add Atmospheric Effect dialog box, and then select Volume Fog. Click OK. In the Volume Fog Parameters rollout, click the Pick Gizmo button and select the BoxGizmo in a viewport.

4. Set the Density to **0.5**, enable the Exponential option and the Noise Type to Turbulence. Then set the Uniformity to **1.0** and the Wind Strength to **10** from the Left.

Figure 45.14 shows the finished image. Using Atmospheric Apparatus gizmos, you can position the fog in the exact place where you want it.

FIGURE 45.14

A rendered image that uses the Volume Fog effect

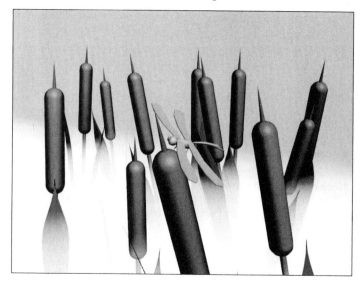

Using the Volume Light effect

The final choice in the Environment and Effects dialog box is the Volume Light effect. This effect shares many of the same parameters as the other atmospheric effects. Although this is one of the atmospheric effects, it deals with lights and fits better in that section.

> **CROSS-REF** To learn about the Volume Light atmospheric effect, see Chapter 19, "Using Lights and Basic Lighting Techniques."

Adding Render Effects

Rendering a scene in many cases is only the start of the work to produce some final output. The post-production process is often used to add lots of different effects, as you'll see when we discuss the Video Post interface. But just because you can add it in post-production doesn't mean you have to add it in post-production. Render effects let you apply certain effects as part of the rendering process.

You can set up all render effects from the Rendering Effects panel, which you open by choosing Rendering ⇨ Effects. Figure 45.15 shows this dialog box.

FIGURE 45.15

The Rendering Effects panel lets you apply interactive post-production effects to an image.

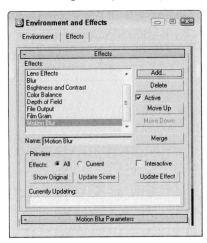

The Effects pane displays all the effects that are included in the current scene. To add a new effect, click the Add button to open the Add Effect dialog box, in which you can select from a default list of nine effects, including Hair and Fur, Lens Effects, Blur, Brightness and Contrast, Color Balance, Depth of Field, File Output, Film Grain, and Motion Blur. You can delete an effect from the current list by selecting that effect and clicking the Delete button.

Below the Effects pane is a Name field. You can type a new name for any effect in this field; doing so enables you to use the same effect multiple times. The effects are applied in the order in which they are listed in the Effects pane. To the right of the Effects pane are the Move Up and Move Down buttons, which you use to reposition the effects in the list. The effects are added to the scene in the order that they are listed.

CAUTION It is possible for one effect to cover another effect. Rearranging the order can help resolve this problem.

The Merge button opens the Merge Effect dialog box where you can select a separate Max file. If you select a Max file and click Open, the Merge Rendering Effects dialog box presents you with a list of render effects used in the opened Max file. You can then select and load any of these render effects into the current scene.

The Preview section holds the controls for interactively viewing the various effects. Previews are displayed in the Rendered Frame Window and can be set to view All the effects or only the Current one. The Show Original button displays the scene before any effects are applied, and the Update Scene button updates the rendered image if any changes have been made to the scene.

NOTE If the Rendered Frame Window isn't open, any of these buttons opens it and renders the scene with the current settings in the Render Scene dialog box.

The Interactive option automatically updates the image whenever an effect parameter or scene object is changed. If this option is disabled, you can use the Update Effect button to manually update the image.

CAUTION If the Interactive option is enabled and the Rendering Effects panel is open, the image is re-rendered in the Rendered Frame Window every time a change is made to the scene. This can slow down the system dramatically.

The Currently Updating bar shows the progress of the rendering update.

The remainder of the Rendering Effects panel contains global parameters and rollouts for the selected render effect. These rollouts are covered in this chapter, along with their corresponding effects.

CROSS-REF The Hair and Fur render effect offers the ability to add hair and fur to models. The Hair and Fur features — including the render effect — are covered in Chapter 28, "Adding and Styling Hair, Fur, and Cloth."

Creating Lens Effects

Of the eight available render effects, the first one of the list will be used perhaps more often than all the others combined. The Lens Effects option includes several different effects itself ranging from glows and rings to streaks and stars.

Lens Effects simulate the types of lighting effects that are possible with actual camera lenses and filters. When the Lens Effects selection is added to the Effects list and selected, several different effects become available in the Lens Effects Parameters rollout, including Glow, Ring, Ray, Auto Secondary, Manual Secondary, Star, and Streak. When one of these effects is included in a scene, rollouts and parameters for that effect are added to the panel as well.

Several of these Lens Effects can be used simultaneously. To include an effect, open the Environment and Effects dialog box with the Rendering ➪ Effects menu command, click the Add button, and select Lens Effect from the available effects. Then go to the Lens Effects Parameters rollout, select the desired effect from the list on the left, and click the arrow button pointing to the right. The pane on the right lists the included effects. Use the left-pointing arrow button to remove effects from the list.

Global Lens Effects Parameters

Under the Lens Effects Parameters rollout in the Rendering Effects panel is the Lens Effects Globals rollout. All effects available in Lens Effects use the two common tabbed panels in this rollout: Parameters and Scene. These two tabbed panels are shown side by side in Figure 45.16.

FIGURE 45.16

The Parameters tabbed panel of the Lens Effects Globals rollout lets you load and save parameter settings. The Scene tabbed panel lets you set the effect's Size and Intensity.

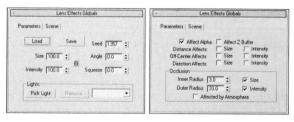

The Global Parameters tabbed panel

The Parameters panel of the Lens Effects Globals rollout includes Load and Save buttons for loading and saving parameter settings specified in the various rollouts. These settings are saved as LZV files.

The Size value determines the overall size of the effect as a percentage of the rendered image. Figure 45.17 shows the center of the Star Lens Effects with an Intensity value of 500 and Size values of 5, 10, 20, 50, and 100. The Size value increases the entire effect diameter and also the width of each radial line.

FIGURE 45.17

These Star Lens Effects vary in size.

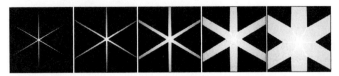

The Intensity value controls the brightness and opacity of the effect. Large values are brighter and more opaque, and small values are dimmer and more transparent. The Size and Intensity values can be locked together. Intensity and Size values can range from 0 to 500. Figure 45.18 shows a glow effect with Intensity values of (from left to right) 50, 100, 200, 350, and 500.

FIGURE 45.18

Lens Effects also can vary in intensity like these glows.

The Seed value provides the randomness of the effect. Changing the Seed value changes the effect's look. The Angle value spins the effect about the camera's axis. The Squeeze value lengthens the horizontal axis for positive values and lengthens the vertical axis for negative values. Squeeze values can range from −100 to 100. Figure 45.19 shows a Ring effect with Squeeze values of (from left to right) −30, −15, 0, 10, and 20.

FIGURE 45.19

These Ring effects vary in Stretch values.

All effects are applied to light sources, and the Pick Light button lets you select a light in the viewport to apply the effect to. Each selected light is displayed in a drop-down list. You can remove any of these lights with the Remove Light button.

The Global Scene tabbed panel

The second Lens Effects Globals tabbed panel common to all effects is the Scene panel. This rollout includes an Affect Alpha option that lets the effect work with the image's alpha channel. The alpha channel holds the transparency information for the rendered objects and for effects if this option is enabled. If you plan on using the effect in a composite image, then enable this option.

 **Click the Display Alpha Channel button in the Rendered Frame Window to view the alpha channel.**

The Affect Z Buffer option stores the effect information in the Z Buffer, which is used to determine the depth of objects from the camera's viewpoint.

The Distance Affects option alters the effect's Size and/or Intensity based on its distance from the camera. The Off-Center Affects option is similar, except that it affects the effect's Size and Intensity based on its Off-Center distance. The Direction Affects options can affect the size and intensity of an effect based on the direction in which a spotlight is pointing.

The Occlusion settings can be used to cause an effect to be hidden by an object that lies between the effect and the camera. The Inner Radius value defines the area that an object must block in order to hide the effect. The Outer Radius value defines where the effect begins to be occluded. You can also set the Size and Intensity options for the effect. The Affected by Atmospheres option allows effects to be occluded by atmospheric effects.

Glow

The Glow Element rollout, shown in Figure 45.20, includes parameters for controlling the look of the Glow Lens Effect. This rollout has two tabbed panels: Parameters and Options.

FIGURE 45.20

The Glow Element rollout lets you set the parameters for the Glow effect.

The Glow Element Parameters tabbed panel

In the Parameters tabbed panel of the Glow Element rollout, there is a Name field. Several glow effects can be added to a scene, and each one can have a different name. The On option can turn each glow on and off.

The Parameters panel also includes Size and Intensity values. These work with the Global settings to determine the size of the glow and can be set to any positive value. The Occlusion and Use Source Color values are percentages. The Occlusion value determines how much of the occlusion set in the Scene panel of the Lens Effects Globals rollout is to be used. If the Use Source Color is at 100 percent, then the glow color is determined by the light color; if it is set to any value below 100, then the colors specified in the Source and Circular Color sections are combined with the light's color.

This panel also includes Glow Behind and Squeeze options. Glow Behind makes the glow effect visible behind objects. The Squeeze option enables any squeeze settings specified in the Parameters panel.

If the Use Source Color value is set to 0 percent, only the Radial Color swatches determine the glow colors. Radial colors proceed from the center of the glow circle to the outer edge. The first swatch is the inner color, and the second is the outer color. The Falloff Curve button opens the Radial Falloff function curve dialog box, shown in Figure 45.21, where you can use a curve to set how quickly or slowly the colors change.

FIGURE 45.21

The Radial Falloff dialog box lets you control how the inner radial color changes to the outer radial color.

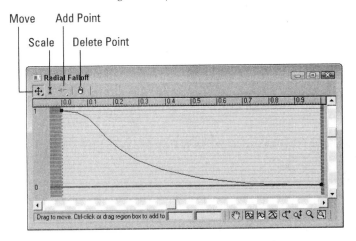

The Circular Color swatches specify the glow color around the glow circle starting from the top point and proceeding clockwise. The Mix value is the percentage to mix the Circular colors with the Radial Colors; a value of 0 displays only the Radial colors, and a value of 100 displays only the Circular colors. You can also access the Falloff Curve dialog box for the Circular Color Falloff curve.

You can also control the Radial Size using a curve by clicking the Size Curve button. Clicking the Size Curve button accesses the Radial Size dialog box. Figure 45.22 shows several glow effects where the radial size curve has been altered. The curves are, from left to right, roughly a descending linear curve, a v-shaped curve, a wide u-shaped curve, an m-shaped curve, and a sine curve.

FIGURE 45.22

These glow effects are distorted using the Radial Size function curves.

All these colors and function curves have map buttons (initially labeled None) that enable you to load maps. Useful maps to use include Falloff, Gradient and Gradient Ramp, Noise, and Swirl. You can enable a map by using the check box to its immediate right.

The Glow Element Options tabbed panel

The Options panel of the Glow Element rollout defines where to apply the glow effect. In the Apply Element To section, the first option is to apply a glow to the Lights. These lights are selected in the Lights section of the Lens Effects Globals rollout using the Pick Light button. The other two options — Image and Image Centers — apply glows using settings contained in the Options panel.

In the Image Sources section, you can apply glows to specific objects using the Object ID option and settings. Object IDs are set for objects in the Object Properties dialog box. If the corresponding Object ID is selected and enabled in the Options panel, the object is endowed with the Glow Lens Effect.

The Effects ID option and settings work in a manner similar to Object IDs, except that they are assigned to materials in the Material Editor. You can use Effects IDs to make a subobject selection glow.

The Unclamp option and settings enable colors to be brighter than pure white. Pure White is a value of 1. The Unclamp value is the lowest value that glows. The Surf Norm (Surface Normal) option and value let you set object areas to glow based on the angle between the surface normal and the camera. The "I" button to the right inverts the value.

Figure 45.23 shows an array of spheres with the Surf Norm glow enabled. Because the glows multiply, a value of only 2 was applied. Notice that the spheres in the center have a stronger glow.

FIGURE 45.23

The Surf Norm option causes objects to glow, based on the angle between their surface normals and the camera.

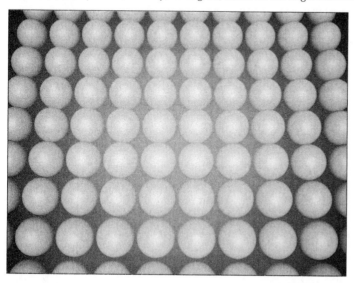

In the Image Sources section, options enable these glows to be applied to the Whole scene, the Alpha channel, or the Z buffer with specified Hi and Lo values.

The Image Filters section can further refine which objects to apply the glow effect to. Options include All, Edge, Perim (Perimeter) Alpha, Perim, Brightness, and Hue. The All option applies the effect to all pixels that are part of the source. The Edge, Perim Alpha, and Perim options apply the effect only to the edges, perimeter of the alpha channel, or perimeter of the source. The Brightness option includes a value and an "I" invert button. This applies the effect only to areas with a brightness greater than the specified value. The Hue option also includes a value and a color swatch for setting the hue, which receives the effect.

The Additional Effects section lets you apply a map to the Glow Lens Effect with an Apply option and a map button. You can also control the Radial Density function curve or add a map for the Radial Density.

Tutorial: Creating shocking electricity from a plug outlet

In addition to the light objects, lighting in a scene can be provided by self-illuminating an object and using a Glow render effect. Self-illuminating an object is accomplished by applying a material with a Self-Illumination value greater than 0 or a color other than black. You can create glows by using the Render Effects dialog box or the Video Post dialog box.

CROSS-REF   For more information on applying glows using the Video Post interface, see Chapter 48, "Compositing with Render Elements and the Video Post Interface."

Working with a faulty electrical outlet can be a shocking experience. In this tutorial, we create an electric arc that runs from an outlet to a plug. To create the effect of electricity, you can use a renderable spline with several vertices and apply the Noise modifier to make it dance around. You can set the light by using a self-illuminating material and a Glow render effect.

To create an electric arc that runs between an outlet and a plug, follow these steps:

1. Open the Electricity.max file from the Chap 45 directory on the DVD.

   This file includes an outlet and an electric plug. A spline runs between the outline and the plug with a Noise modifier applied to it, which will be our electric arc.

2. Open the Material Editor by pressing the M key, and select the first sample slot. Select a yellow Diffuse color and an equally bright yellow for the Self-Illumination color. Set the Material Effects Channel to 1 by clicking the Material Effects ID button and holding it down until a pop-up array of numbers appears, and then drag to the number 1 and release the mouse. Drag this new material to the electric arc.

3. Open the Render Effects dialog box by choosing Rendering ➪ Effects. Click the Add button, select the Lens Effects option, and click OK. Then select Lens Effects from the list, and double-click Glow in the Lens Effects Parameters rollout. Select Glow from the list; in the Glow Element rollout, set the Size to **1** and the Intensity value to **50**. Then open the Options panel, set the Material ID to **1**, and enable it.

Figure 45.24 shows the resulting electric arc.

Tutorial: Creating neon

You can also use the Glow render effect to create neon signs. The letters for these signs can be simple renderable splines, as this tutorial shows.

FIGURE 45.24

You can create electricity using a simple spline, the Noise modifier, and the Glow render effect.

To create a neon sign, follow these steps:

1. Open the Blues neon.max file from the Chap 45 directory on the DVD.

   This file includes a simple sign that reads "Blues."

2. Open the Material Editor with the M key, select the first sample slot, and name it **Blue Neon**. Set its Diffuse color to blue and its Self-Illumination color to dark blue. Set the Material Effects Channel to **1**, and apply the material to the sign.

3. Open the Rendering Effects panel, and click the Add button. Double-click the Lens Effects option to add it to the Effects list. In the Lens Effects rollout, double-click the Glow option and select it in the list to enable its rollouts. In the Lens Effects Globals rollout, set the Size and Intensity values to **1**. In the Glow Element rollout, set the Size to **10** and the Intensity to **100**, and make sure that the Glow Behind option is selected. For the neon color, set the Use Source Color to **100**. Finally, open the Options panel, set the Material ID to **1**, and enable it.

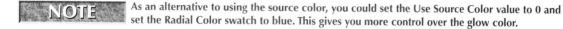

NOTE As an alternative to using the source color, you could set the Use Source Color value to 0 and set the Radial Color swatch to blue. This gives you more control over the glow color.

Figure 45.25 shows the rendered neon effect.

FIGURE 45.25

The glow of neon lights, easily created with render effects

Ring

The Ring Lens Effect is also circular and includes all the same controls and settings as the Glow Lens Effect. The only additional values are the Plane and Thickness values. The Plane value positions the Ring center relative to the center of the screen, and the Thickness value determines the width of the Ring's band.

Figure 45.26 shows several Ring effects with various Thickness values (from left to right): 1, 3, 6, 12, and 24.

FIGURE 45.26

Ring effects can vary in thickness.

Ray

The Ray Lens Effect emits bright, semitransparent rays in all directions from the source. It also uses the same settings as the Glow effect, except for the Num (Number) and Sharp values. The Num value is the number of rays, and the Sharp value can range from 0 to 10 and determines how blurry the rays are.

Figure 45.27 shows the Ray effect applied to a simple omni light with increasing Num values: 6, 12, 50, 100, and 200. Notice that the rays aren't symmetrical and are randomly placed.

FIGURE 45.27

The Ray effect extends a given number of rays out from the effect center.

Star

The Star Lens Effect radiates semitransparent bands of light at regular intervals from the center of the effect. It uses the same controls as the Glow effect, with the addition of Width, Taper, Qty (Quantity), and Sharp values. The Width sets the width of each band. The Taper value determines how quickly the width angles to a point. The Qty value is the number of bands, and the Sharp value determines how blurry the bands are.

Figure 45.28 shows several Star effects with (from left to right) 3, 4, 5, 6, and 12 bands.

FIGURE 45.28

The Star effect lets you set the number of bands emitting from the center.

Streak

The Streak Lens Effect adds a horizontal band through the center of the selected object. It is similar to the Star effect, except it has only two bands that extend in opposite directions.

Figure 45.29 shows several Streak effects angled at 45 degrees with Width values of (from left to right) 2, 4, 10, 15, and 20.

FIGURE 45.29

The Streak effect enables you to create horizontal bands.

Auto Secondary

When a camera is moved past a bright light, several small circles appear lined up in a row proceeding from the center of the light. These secondary lens flares are caused by light refracting off the lens. You can simulate this effect by using the Auto Secondary Lens Effect.

Many of the settings in the Auto Secondary Element rollout are the same as in the Glow effect rollout described previously, but it has several unique values. Figure 45.30 shows this rollout.

The Auto Secondary Element rollout sets the parameters for this effect.

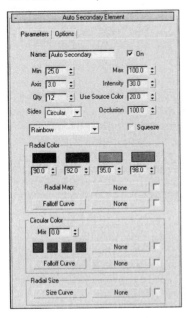

The Min and Max values define the minimum and maximum size of the flares. The Axis is the length of the axis along which the flares are positioned. Larger values spread the flares out more than smaller values. The actual angle of the flares depends on the angle between the camera and the effect object.

The Quantity value is the number of flares to include. The Sides drop-down list lets you select a Circular flare or flares with Three to Eight sides. Below the Sides drop-down list are several preset options in another drop-down list. These include options such as Brown Ring, Blue Circle, and Green Rainbow, among others.

You can also use four Radial Colors to define the flares. The color swatches from left to right define the colors from the inside out. The spinners below each color swatch indicate where the color should end.

Figure 45.31 shows the Auto Secondary Effect with the Rainbow preset and the Intensity increased to 50.

Manual Secondary

In addition to the Auto Secondary Lens Effect, you can add a Manual Secondary Lens Effect to add some more flares with a different size and look. This effect includes a Plane value that places the flare in front of (positive value) or behind (negative value) the flare source.

Figure 45.32 shows the same flares from the previous figure with an additional Manual Secondary Effect added.

FIGURE 45.31

The Auto Secondary Effect displays several flares extending at an angle from the center of the effect.

FIGURE 45.32

The Manual Secondary Effect can add some randomness to a flare lineup.

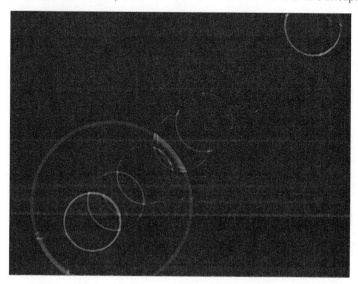

Tutorial: Making an airplane sparkle

When shiny metal planes fly through the sky, they often give off sparkling light effects. Adding some Lens Effects to an airplane scene can simulate this effect.

To make an object bright and shiny using Lens Effects, follow these steps:

1. Open the Spruce Goose.max file from the Chap 45 directory on the DVD.

   This file includes an airplane model of the famous Spruce Goose created by Viewpoint Datalabs.

2. Open the Create panel, and click the Lights category button. Create several Omni lights, and position them around the scene to provide adequate lighting. Position a single light close to the plane's surface where you want the highlight to be located — make it near the surface, and set the Multiplier value to **0.5**.

3. Open the Rendering Effects panel by choosing Rendering ⇨ Effects (or press the 8 key). Click the Add button, and select Lens Effects. Then, in the Lens Effects Parameters rollout, select the Glow effect in the left pane and click the button pointing to the right pane.

4. In the Parameters panel, click the Pick Light button and select the light close to the surface. Set the Size around **30** and the Intensity at **100**. Go to the Glow Element rollout, and in the Parameters panel, set the Use Source Color to **0**. Then, in the Radial Color section, click the second Radial Color swatch, and in the Color Selector dialog box, select a color like yellow and click the Close button.

5. Back in the Lens Effects Parameters rollout, select Star, and add it to the list of effects. It automatically uses the same light specified for the Glow effect. In the Star Element rollout, set the Quantity (Qty) value to **6**, the Size to **200**, and the Intensity to **100**.

Figure 45.33 shows the resulting airplane with a nice shine.

FIGURE 45.33

The Spruce Goose has had a sparkle added to it using the Glow and Star Lens Effects.

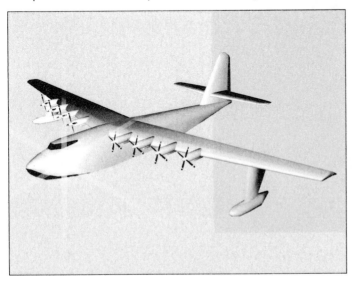

Using Other Render Effects

Now that the big brother of the render effects is covered, let's return to the Add Effect dialog box where six other render effects are available. If these selections aren't enough, Max also enables you to add even more options to this list via plug-ins.

Blur render effect

The Blur render effect displays three different blurring methods in the Blur Type panel: Uniform, Directional, and Radial. You can find these options in the Blur Type tabbed panel in the Blur Parameters rollout, shown in Figure 45.34.

FIGURE 45.34

The Blur Parameters rollout lets you select a Uniform, Directional, or Radial blur type.

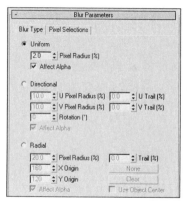

The Uniform blur method applies the blur evenly across the whole image. The Pixel Radius value defines the amount of the blur. The Directional blur method can be used to blur the image along a certain direction. The U Pixel Radius and U Trail values define the blur in the horizontal direction, and the V Pixel Radius and V Trail values blur in a vertical direction. The Rotation value rotates the axis of the blur.

The Radial blur method creates concentric blurred rings determined by the Radius and Trail values. When the Use Object Center option is selected, the None and Clear buttons become active. Clicking the None button lets you select an object about which you want to center the radial blur. The Clear button clears this selection.

Figure 45.35 shows a dinosaur model created by Viewpoint Datalabs. The actual rendered image shows the sharp edges of the polygons. The Blur effect can help this by softening all the hard edges. The left image is the original dinosaur, and the right image has a Directional blur applied.

The Blur Parameters rollout also includes a Pixel Selections tabbed panel, shown in Figure 45.36, that contains parameters for specifying which parts of the image get blurred. Options include the Whole Image, Non-Background, Luminance, Map Mask, Material ID, and Object ID.

You can use the Feather Falloff curve at the bottom of the Blur Parameters rollout to define the Brighten and Blend curves. The buttons above this curve are for adding points, scaling, and moving them within the curve interface.

FIGURE 45.35

The Blur effect can soften an otherwise hard model.

FIGURE 45.36

The Pixel Selections tabbed panel (shown in two parts) of the Blur Parameters rollout lets you select the parts of the image that get the Blur effect.

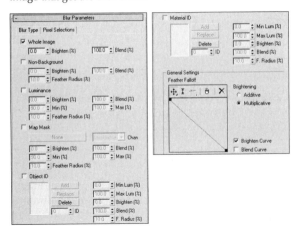

Brightness and Contrast render effect

The Brightness and Contrast render effect can alter these amounts in the image. The Brightness and Contrast Parameters rollout is a simple rollout with values for both the brightness and contrast that can range from 0 to 1. It also contains an Ignore Background option.

Color Balance render effect

The Color Balance effect enables you to tint the image using separate Cyan/Red, Magenta/Green, and Yellow/Blue channels. To change the color balance, drag the sliders in the Color Balance Parameters rollout. Other options include Preserve Luminosity and Ignore Background. The Preserve Luminosity option tints the image while maintaining the luminosity of the image, and the Ignore Background option tints the rendered objects but not the background image.

File Output render effect

The File Output render effect enables you to save the rendered file to a File or to a Device at any point during the render effect's post-processing. Figure 45.37 shows the File Output Parameters rollout.

FIGURE 45.37

The File Output Parameters rollout lets you save a rendered image before a render effect is applied.

Using the Channel drop-down list in the Parameters section, you can save out Whole Images, as well as grayscale Luminance, Depth, and Alpha images.

Film Grain render effect

The Film Grain effect gives an image a grained look, which hardens the overall look of the image. You can also use this effect to match rendered objects to the grain of the background image. This helps the objects blend into the scene better. Figure 45.38 shows the effect.

The Grain value can range from 0 to 1. The Ignore Background option applies the grain effect only to the objects in the scene and not to the background.

FIGURE 45.38

The Film Grain render effect applies a noise filter to the rendered image.

Motion Blur render effect

The Motion Blur effect applies a simple image motion blur to the rendered output. The Motion Blur Parameters rollout includes settings for working with Transparency and a value for the Duration of the blur. Objects that move rapidly within the scene are blurred.

Depth of Field render effect

The Depth of Field effect enhances the sense of depth by blurring objects close to or far from the camera. The Pick Cam button in the Depth of Field Parameters rollout, shown in Figure 45.39, lets you select a camera in the viewport to use for this effect. Multiple cameras can be selected, and all selected cameras are displayed in the drop-down list. A Remove button lets you remove cameras.

FIGURE 45.39

The Depth of Field Parameters rollout lets you select a camera or a Focal Point to apply the effect to.

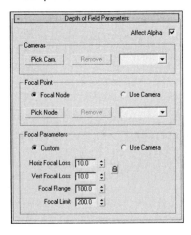

In the Focal Point section, the Pick Node button lets you select an object to use as the focal point. This object is where the camera focuses. Objects far from this object are blurred. These nodes are also listed in a drop-down list. You can remove objects from the list by selecting them and clicking the Remove button. The Use Camera option uses the camera's own settings to determine the focal point.

In the Focal Parameters section, if you select the Custom option, then you can specify values for the Horizontal and Vertical Focal Loss, the Focal Range, and the Focal Limit. The Loss values indicate how much blur occurs. The Focal Range is where the image starts to blur, and the Focal Limit is where the image stops blurring.

Figure 45.40 shows a beach scene created by Viewpoint Datalabs. For this figure, the Depth of Field effect has been applied using the Pick Node button and selecting some leaves on the tree. Then I set the Focal Range to 100, the Focal Limit to 200, and the Focal Loss values to 10 for both the Horizontal and Vertical.

CROSS-REF   The Depth of Field and Motion Blur effects can also be applied using a Multi-Pass camera, as discussed in Chapter 18, "Configuring and Aiming Cameras."

FIGURE 45.40

The Depth of Field effect focuses a camera on an object in the middle and blurs objects closer or farther away.

Summary

Creating the right environment can add lots of realism to any rendered scene. Using the Environment and Effects dialog box, you can work with atmospheric effects. Atmospheric effects include Fire, Fog, Volume Fog, and Volume Light.

Render effects are useful because they enable you to create effects and update them interactively. This gives a level of control that was previously unavailable. This chapter explained how to use render elements and render effects and described the various types.

This chapter covered these topics:

- Creating Atmospheric Apparatus gizmos for positioning atmospheric effects
- Working with the Fire atmospheric effects
- Creating fog and volume fog effects
- Applying render effects
- Using the Lens Effects to create glows, rays, and stars
- Working with the remaining render effects to control brightness and contrast, film grain, blurs, and more
- Learning how exposure controls can work

The next chapter delves into one of the advanced topics of 3D graphics — raytracing. It also covers the amazing mental ray rendering engine.

Chapter 46

Raytracing and mental ray

When computer-generated 3D images started to appear, it was the ray-traced images that really got the wow factor. These images were amazing in their clarity and perfect in reflecting and refracting light through the scene. Raytracing isn't new in Max, but making sense of all the ray-tracing features can be confusing.

Raytracing in Max can be used with the Default Scanline Renderer using the traditional Raytracing materials and controls, or it can be enabled at the renderer level using the mental ray settings.

To help you generate raytraced scenes, you can also use the mental ray rendering engine. This engine takes the rendering in Max to a new level, enabling you to render your scenes with amazing accuracy, but mental ray doesn't only enable raytracing. It also includes a host of advanced rendering features including caustics and global illumination that are physically realistic.

Using Raytrace Materials

Raytracing is a rendering method that calculates image colors by following imaginary light rays as they move through a scene. These rays can travel through transparent objects and reflect realistically off shiny materials. The results are stunning realistic images, but the drawback is the amount of time it takes to render using raytrace materials. Scenes with lots of lights and reflecting materials take even longer.

Raytrace materials also support special effects such as fog, color density, translucency, and fluorescence. They include the following rollouts (some of which are similar to the standard materials): Raytrace Basic Parameters, Extended Parameters, Raytracer Controls, SuperSampling, Maps, Dynamic Properties, and mental ray Connection. Figure 46.1 shows the Raytrace Basic Parameters and the Extended Parameters rollouts.

 Raytracing can take a long time to complete. As an alternative, you can use a Reflect/Refract map to simulate raytracing.

FIGURE 46.1

Many of the raytrace material settings are the same as those for the standard material.

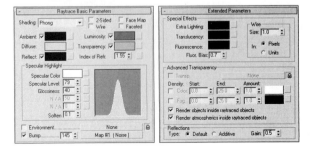

Raytrace Basic Parameters

The raytrace material doesn't have a shader rollout. Instead, shading is determined by a drop-down list at the top of the Raytrace Basic Parameters rollout. The options include Phong, Blinn, Metal, Oren-Nayar-Blinn, and Anisotropic. These shaders are similar to the shaders with the same names for standard materials.

The colors for a raytrace material (except for the Diffuse color) can switch between color swatches and a color value by enabling the check box to the left of the label. The spinners can range between 0 and 100, which equate to black and white. The Ambient color is different from that for the standard material although it is named the same. For raytrace materials, the Ambient value is the amount of ambient light that is absorbed. A setting of white is like locking a standard material's Diffuse and Ambient colors together.

The Reflect color is the color that is added to reflections. For example, if the background color is set to yellow and the Reflect color is red, then the reflections for this object are tinted orange. This is different from the Specular highlight color, which is set in the Specular Highlight group.

The Luminosity color makes an object glow with this color, similar to the Self-Illumination color for the standard material. In fact, when the Luminosity setting is disabled, the text label changes to Self-Illumination.

The Transparency color sets the color that filters light passing through the transparent material. When the color swatch is white, the material is transparent, and when it is black, the material is opaque.

At the bottom of the Raytrace Basic Parameters rollout are two map options for Environment and Bump maps. These maps, which are also included in the Maps rollout, are here for convenience. The Environment map for raytrace materials overrides the global Environment map set in the Environment dialog box. The Environment map is visible only if the Reflect color is enabled or its value is not 0. Figure 46.2 shows a sphere with an Environment map of a mountain meadow applied. The image is from Corel's Photo CD library.

CROSS-REF For more information on Environment, Bump, and other maps, see Chapter 17, "Adding Material Details with Maps."

FIGURE 46.2

A sphere with an Environment map reflected off a raytrace material

Extended Parameters rollout

The Extended Parameters rollout holds the settings for all the special material effects that are possible with the raytrace material. Only the Wire settings are the same as the standard material.

The Extra Lighting color swatch increases the effect of Ambient light. Use it to increase the ambient light for a single object or subobject area and to simulate radiosity. *Radiosity* is a rendering method that creates realistic lighting by calculating how light reflects off objects.

Translucent objects, like wax, lets light penetrate an object, but the objects on the other side are unclear or semitransparent causing the light to scatter. You can use this effect to create frosted glass. Fluorescence makes materials glow like fluorescent colors under a black light. This happens when a material appears one color when illuminated by another color light. The Fluorescence Bias field, which can range between 0 and 1, controls the amount of this effect that is applied.

The Advanced Transparency group includes a shortcut for the Transparent Environment map. This map is refracted through a transparent object and is visible only if the Environment map is enabled. You can use the lock icon to the right of the Transparency map button to lock the Environment map above with this map.

Raytrace materials that are transparent can also have Color and Fog Density settings. You can use Color Density to create tinted glass: The amount of color depends on how thick the object is and the Amount setting. The Start value is where the color starts, and the End value is the distance at which the color reaches a maximum. Fog Density works the same way as Color Density and is based on object thickness. You can use this effect to create smoky glass. You also have options to render any objects or atmospheric effects contained within raytraced objects.

The Reflections section offers a Default Reflection Type and an Additive Reflection Type. The Default type layers the reflection on top of the current Diffuse color, and the Additive type adds the reflection to the Diffuse color. The Gain value controls the brightness of the reflection and can range between 0 and 1.

Raytracer Control rollout

Raytracing can take a long time, but the Raytracer Control rollout, shown in Figure 46.3, lets you control several Raytracer options that can speed up the process. These options are all local options, including Enable Raytracing, Enable Self Reflect/Refract, Raytrace Atmospherics, and Reflect/Refract Material ID.

FIGURE 46.3

The Raytracer Controls rollout lets you set the raytracing options.

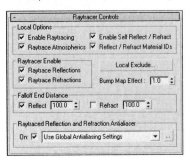

You can use this rollout to turn Raytrace Reflections or Refractions on or off. The Falloff values determine the distance at which the reflections or refractions fade to black. The Bump Map Effect increases or decreases the effect of bump maps on the reflections or refractions.

The Raytraced Reflection and Refraction Antialiaser drop-down list includes three options: Use Global Antialiasing Settings, Fast Adaptive Antialiaser, and Multiresolution Adaptive Antialiaser. This drop-down list is available only if the Global Ray Antialiaser option found in the Global Raytracer Settings dialog box is enabled. The first selection opens the Global Raytracer Settings dialog box.

In the Raytracer Controls rollout, you can also select to include or exclude objects from the effect of a local raytraced object. The Local Exclude button opens the Exclude/Include dialog box that is the same as the Global Exclude/Include dialog box.

Additional rollouts

Raytrace materials include three additional rollouts: SuperSampling, Maps, and Dynamic Properties. The SuperSampling rollout lets you defer to the Global Settings for changes to the SuperSampler settings for the selected material. The Maps rollout works the same for raytrace materials as it does with standard materials, but the raytrace material includes several unique maps that aren't found in standard materials. The Dynamic Properties rollout for raytrace materials is identical to the Dynamic Properties rollout for standard materials.

Tutorial: Coming up roses

Raytrace examples often include glasses or vases because shiny, highly reflective glass surfaces show off the effects of raytracing best. Zygote Media has an object that is perfect for this task — a vase of roses. (Zygote also created the table used in this tutorial.)

To apply raytrace materials to a vase of roses, follow these steps:

1. Open the Roses on table.max file from the Chap 46 directory on the DVD.

   The file includes some rose meshes in a vase on a table.

2. Press the M key to open the Material Editor, select the first sample slot, and name the material **Raytrace Glass**. Click the Type button, and double-click the raytrace material type in the Material/Map Browser. Deselect the Transparency option, and set its value to **100**. Set the Index of Refraction to **1.5**, and raise the Specular Level to **100**. Select the vase object, and click the Assign Material to Selection button.

3. Select the second sample slot, and name it **Leaves**. In the Shader Basic Parameters rollout, select the Oren-Nayar-Blinn shader from the drop-down list. Then click the Diffuse color swatch, and select a dark green color. Set the Diffuse Level, Opacity, and Roughness to **100** and the Specular Level to **10**. Then select the stems and leaves, and apply this material.

4. Select the third sample slot, click the Pick Material from Object tool to the left of the Name field, and then click the roses. Doing so loads the material already applied to the roses into the sample slot. Disable the Faceted option, and reapply the material using the Assign Material to Selection button.

5. Select the fourth sample slot, and click the square button to the right of the Diffuse color swatch to open the Material/Map Browser. Double-click the Wood map to apply this map instead of the Diffuse color and to display the map parameter rollouts. Set the Y-axis Tiling value to **20** in the Coordinates rollout. Then click the Go to Parent button, and in the Blinn Basic Parameters rollout, increase the Specular Level to **75**. Name the material **Tabletop**, and drag the material to the tabletop.

6. In a graphics program such as Adobe Photoshop, create and save a 200 × 200 image with some repeating colored vertical stripes that can be used as wallpaper. Select the fifth sample slot, and click the map button to the right of the Diffuse color. In the Material/Map Browser, double-click the Bitmap selection. A File dialog box loads, in which you can locate the wallpaper image. In the Coordinates rollout, set the U-coordinate Tiling value to **100** and drag the material to the wall plane object.

Figure 46.4 shows the rendered image.

FIGURE 46.4

A rendered image with raytrace materials applied to the vase and table

Using a Raytrace Map

The raytrace map is an alternative to the raytrace material discussed previously and, as a map, can be used in places where the raytrace material cannot.

The raytrace map includes several similar rollouts and several unique rollouts. In the Raytracer Parameters rollout, the Local Options section lets you select to Enable Raytracing, enable Raytrace Atmospherics, Enable Self Reflect/Refract, and use Reflect/Refract Material IDs. The Trace Mode determines how the rays are cast through the scene. Options include Auto Detect, Reflection, and Refraction. You can also use the Environment Settings or specify a color or map to use for the Background.

Setting raytrace parameters

The Local Exclude button opens the Exclude/Include dialog box where you can select which items to include or exclude in the raytracing calculations. The Raytracing Antialiasing drop-down list is enabled using the Global Raytracing Settings dialog box.

 You set global raytracing options using the Rendering ⊂ Raytracer Settings menu command.

The Attenuation rollout lets you select from one of several Falloff Types. The options include Linear, Inverse Square, Exponential, and Custom Falloff. You can also set values for the Start and End distances. The Custom Falloff type lets you set a graph by adjusting Near, Far, and two Control values.

The Basic Material Extensions rollout lets you set the Reflectivity/Opacity Map and its strength. You can also set a Basic Tinting color or map. The Refractive Material Extensions rollout includes settings for specifying the Color Density (Filter color) and Fog.

Understanding Global Raytracing Settings

When you use the Default Scanline Renderer, raytracing is added to a scene to be rendered by applying the Raytrace material found in the Material Editor. Applying a raytrace material to an object sets the local ray-tracing parameters for the object to which the material is applied, but other settings determine how the ray-tracing is applied globally to a scene. These settings are found in the Raytracer Global Parameters rollout of the Raytracer panel of the Render Scene dialog box, shown in Figure 46.5. You access it directly using the Rendering ⇨ Raytracer Settings menu command.

 The Raytracer Settings and Raytrace Global Include/Exclude options in the Rendering menu are available only if the Default Scanline Renderer is assigned in the Render Scene dialog box.

Figure 46.6 gives you an idea of what is possible with the raytrace settings. The scene includes several crystal birdbaths with a raytrace transparent material applied. The image on the left was rendered without enabling raytracing, and the image on the right has raytracing enabled. Both were rendered using the Default Scanline renderer. Notice that the reflections are much more pronounced in the raytraced image.

Controlling the raytracer

Suppose you have a scene with two mirrors that face one another. If the raytracer is allowed to track the bouncing of light rays through the scene, then it never completes because some light rays would bounce back and forth off the mirrors and never end.

The Maximum Depth setting tells the raytracer how long to follow each ray, or you can set a Cutoff Threshold. (Lower numbers speed up render times at the expense of quality.) You can also specify a color (or select to use the background color) to use for rays that reach the Max Depth, which is useful for identifying lost rays. Lost rays are raytraced lines that don't bounce as expected and can result in a less-than-accurate solution.

CAUTION The movement of a ray through the scene depends on the face normals. If the normals are flipped or pointing in the wrong direction, then the results are unpredictable.

FIGURE 46.5

The Raytracer Global Parameters rollout includes raytracing settings that affect the entire scene.

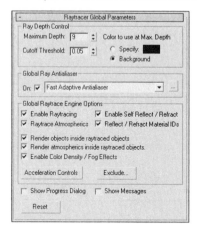

FIGURE 46.6

This simple scene of crystal birdbaths was rendered without raytracing (left) and with raytracing (right).

The Global Ray Antialiaser group includes a drop-down list with two options: Fast Adaptive Antialiaser and Multiresolution Adaptive Antialiaser. These two options open separate dialog boxes, shown in Figure 46.7. The Fast Adaptive Antialiaser is quicker than its partner and offers settings for Blur and Defocus. The Multiresolution Adaptive Antialiaser takes much longer than the other option, but you can limit it with the Threshold and Max Rays values.

NOTE If SuperSampling is enabled for a local raytracing material, then enabling a raytracing anti-aliasing option isn't needed, and vice versa, unless you want to apply a blur or defocus effect.

The Options section includes settings to Enable Raytracing, enable Raytrace Atmospherics, Enable Self Reflect/Refract, and Reflect/Refract Material IDs. There are also options to render the objects contained within raytraced objects, to render Atmospheric effects within raytraced objects, and to enable Color Density and Fog effects. The Show Progress Dialog and the Show Messages options let you see the progress of the raytracing engine along with any messages that the raytracing image may output. Figure 46.8 shows an example of the Message dialog box. This dialog box contains some useful information, including the total number of rays traced. From this info, you can determine whether the number of rays is too many or not enough.

FIGURE 46.7

Additional anti-aliasing settings are available by clicking the button to the right of the drop-down list.

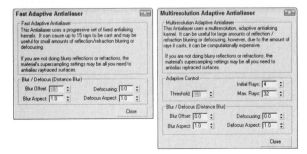

FIGURE 46.8

The Raytrace Messages window outputs all the data from the raytracing engine.

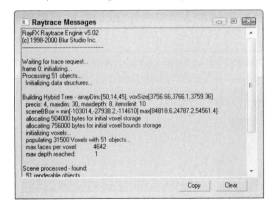

Raytracing can take a long time, but the Acceleration Controls (opened by clicking the Acceleration Controls button), shown in Figure 46.9, offer you several raytracer options that can control the speed of the process. These settings override the existing settings. Before sending rays into the scene, the scene is subdivided into a tree of nodes called a *voxel tree*. The complexity of this voxel tree determines how long the raytracing solution takes. The Face Limit is the number of faces to include in a voxel node before subdividing. The Balance value defines how the scene gets subdivided. The Max Division sets the size of the voxel subdivisions, and the Max Depth value limits how many times a subdivision takes place.

FIGURE 46.9

The Raytracing Acceleration Parameters options control the speed of the raytracing by limiting the number of faces and divisions that must be processed.

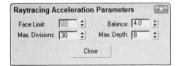

Excluding objects

One of the easiest ways to increase the speed of the raytracer is to reduce the number of objects that it has to deal with. You open the Exclude/Include dialog box for raytraced objects using the Rendering ⇨ Raytrace Global Include/Exclude menu command (or by clicking the Exclude button in the Raytracer Global Parameters rollout). From within this dialog box, shown in Figure 46.10, you can select objects to be excluded from the raytracer.

The Exclude/Include dialog box lets you select objects to be removed from the raytracer.

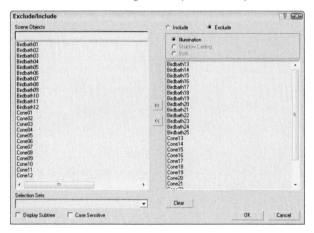

The Exclude/Include dialog box includes two panes. The pane on the left lists all the objects within the scene, and the one on the right lists the objects to Include or Exclude, depending on which option is selected.

 You use the same Exclude/Include dialog box to exclude objects from the effects of lights.

Enabling mental ray

If you're accustomed to using the Default Scanline Renderer and you're wondering if the mental ray rendering engine is good for you, the answer is yes. Actually, you should try a couple of test renderings first and play with the different settings, but in working with mental ray, I've been amazed at its results. One of the chief benefits of mental ray is its speed. It can render a fully raytraced scene in a fraction of the time without sacrificing quality.

NOTE mental ray is an external rendering engine that plugs into 3ds Max. It was developed by a company named mental images, so its development is separate from Max. Versions of the mental ray rendering engine also can be found in Maya and Softimage as well as a stand-alone version.

mental ray also includes support for global illumination without your having to enable the Advanced Lighting settings. In addition, mental ray can use all of Max's existing materials without having to use a limited specialized material like the Raytrace material. Each material has a new rollout that lets you specialize mental ray settings.

 **NOTE** mental ray can't use the Advanced Lighting settings. mental ray has its own lighting solution that is independent of Advance Lighting.

CROSS-REF Many of the available mental ray materials are covered in Chapter 29, "Using Specialized Material Types."

mental ray also includes native support for Area Lights, Shaders, Depth of Field, and Motion Blur. It also includes some specialized lights that offer functionality, such as caustics, that are unavailable in the Scanline Renderer.

To choose mental ray as the renderer for your scene, simply select it from the list of available renderers in the Assign Renderer rollout of the Common panel of the Render Scene dialog box. You can set a different renderer for Production, the Material Editor, and the ActiveShade viewer. To make mental ray your default renderer, click the Save as Defaults button in this rollout.

Once selected as your Production renderer, you don't need to modify any other settings for the renderer to work. The mental ray settings in the Material Editor, Lights category, and Object Properties dialog box enable additional features that mental ray can take advantage of, but they aren't required to render the scene. The current mental ray version is 3.6.

NEW FEATURE Support for mental ray 3.6 is new to 3ds Max 2008.

mental ray preferences

In the Preference Settings dialog box is a panel of global mental ray settings, shown in Figure 46.11. In this panel, you can select to Enable mental ray Extensions. These extensions add some additional controls to several of the various mental ray panels.

FIGURE 46.11

The Preference Settings dialog box includes a panel of mental ray settings.

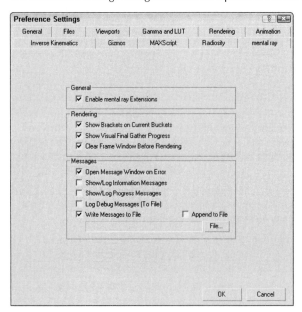

When the Scanline Renderer renders a scene, it progresses one line of pixels at a time down the image, but mental ray renders the image by breaking it up into blocks and rendering a block at a time. The Show Brackets on Current Buckets option displays white brackets around the current block as the image renders.

NOTE Multiple white brackets may be visible if you're rendering across a network or using a computer with multiple processors.

The Show Visual Final Gather Progress option displays a rough approximation of the render scene as it is being rendered before waiting for a Final Gather solution. This gives a quick look at the scene before taking the time to compute a Final Gather solution. You can also select to clear the frame before rendering.

The Messages section lets you specify which messages are displayed as the file renders. Options include Errors, Log Information, Log Progress, Debug Messages, and whether to write this information to a file.

mental ray lights and shadows

If you look in the Lights category of the Create ➪ Lights ➪ Standard Lights menu, you'll see two mental ray specific lights: mental ray Area Omni and mental ray Area Spot. These area lights spread light from a defined area in the Area Light Parameters rollout. By default, all mental lights use the Global Settings for their illumination values, but by using the mental ray Indirect Illumination rollout, shown in Figure 46.12, found in the Modify panel, you can override the global settings for the selected light.

FIGURE 46.12

The mental ray Indirect Illumination rollout lets you define the light settings for individual lights.

Enabling mental ray Shadow Maps

In the Shadows drop-down list is an option to enable mental ray Shadow Maps. These shadow maps are more accurate than normal shadow maps.

Using mental ray Sun & Sky

If you want to quickly create an outdoor scene and render it using mental ray, then the Daylight system that uses the mr Sun and Sky is an easy quality solution. Before adding the Daylight system to your scene, switch the renderer to mental ray in the Render dialog box. Then add the Daylight system to the scene and in the Modify panel, select mr Sun in the Sunlight drop-down list and mr Sky in the Skylight drop-down list. When you first select the Daylight system, a dialog box appears recommending that you use the Logarithmic Exposure Control with Exterior Daylight Flag enabled. Click the Yes button to enable this control. When your select the mr Sky option, another dialog box appears asking if you want to enable the mr Physical Sky environment map. Click Yes to this also.

If you look in the Environment panel, you can see the mr Physical Sky material applied. This material defines how the sky and ground planes look. The default settings look pretty good.

The Daylight system includes controls for positioning the sun in the sky based on a physical location, day of the year, and time of the day. By changing these controls, you can manipulate the sun's position in the sky relative to the scene objects. If the sun appears in the viewport, it is rendered with lens flares, as shown in Figure 46.13.

FIGURE 46.13

The Daylight can be endowed with mr Sun and mr Sky.

When a Sky & Sun system is in place, you can ensure that it displays within the viewport if you open the Views ➪ Viewport Background dialog box and enable the Use Environment Background settings. Make sure also that the Display Background option is set. Using this method makes the Sun & Sky system visible even if the Viewport Shading option is set to Off.

NEW FEATURE   The ability to view Sun & Sky interactively in the viewport is new to 3ds Max 2008.

Selecting the sun light object and moving it about the scene or changing the Time and Date parameters automatically updates the background and the scene. This provides a good way to precisely position the sun where you want it, as shown in Figure 46.14.

FIGURE 46.14

The Sun & Sky system can be viewed and interactively updated in the viewport.

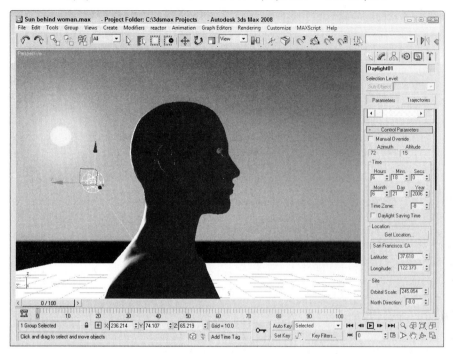

Using mental ray Sky Portal

If you look closely at the Photometric light category, you'll notice another light type sandwiched between the mr Sky and mr Sun lights. The mr Sky Portal provides a way to focus light streaming into an interior space from an external source using a designated portal. This can be thought of as a sky light that causes all Final Gather light rays to be focused on a specific area. It results in a better Final Gather result with fewer light rays. The Sky Portal is direct light giving you one bounce for free if Final Gather is disabled.

NEW FEATURE The ability to focus the light rays using the Sky Portal light is new to 3ds Max 2008.

To use a Sky Portal, you must have mental ray enabled, include a skylight or a Sun & Sky system, and have Final Gather turned on. Then simply drag over the area where the window is located, and all light rays entering the interior space are focused on those areas defined by the Sky Portal. The gizmo for the Sky Portal is a simple rectangular box with an arrow pointing in the direction of the light rays. If the light rays are pointing outward, you can use the Flip Light Flux Direction option to change their direction.

TIP For better results for interior scenes using exterior lighting, enable the mr Photographic Exposure Control and use the Physically Based Lighting, Indoor Daylight preset.

Within the mr Skylight Portal Parameters rollout, you can enable or disable the Sky Portal. A Multiplier value and a Filter Color work just like other lights. If the image appears grainy, you can increase the

Shadow Samples value to remove any splotchy effect on the walls, but this increases the render time. Within the Advanced Parameters rollout, the Visible to Renderer makes the Sky Portal visible in the rendered image, causing exterior objects to be blotted out.

You also can set the Color Source to Use the Scene Environment if you want light to be pulled from the environment map. Sky Portals also support HDRI maps as lighting sources. Figure 46.15 shows a house interior lighted using mental ray, Final Gather, and two Sky Portals.

FIGURE 46.15

Sky Portals can focus all rays coming from an external light source to speed up Final Gather passes.

Understanding caustics and photons

Light properties for the mental ray renderer include four unique properties: Energy, Decay, Caustic Photons, and Global Illumination (GI) Photons. You can find the settings for these properties in the mental ray Indirect Illumination rollout. Before learning about these properties, you need to understand what caustics and photons are.

Caustics are those strange glowing lines that you see at the bottom of an indoor swimming pool caused by the light refracting through the water. Caustics are common in nature, and now with mental ray, you can add these effects to your scenes. Photons are small bundles of light energy, and like the raytracing rays they are emitted from a light source with a given amount of energy. This energy is lost as the photon travels and as it hits objects in the scene.

The Energy value is the amount of light energy that each photon starts out with, and the Decay value specifies how quickly that energy dissipates. The number of Caustic and GI Photons determines the resulting accuracy of the lighting. More photons yield a better solution, but the greater number also increases the render time substantially. The Multiplier and color swatch lets you set the intensity and color of the caustics.

Figure 46.16 shows a swimming pool with caustics glowing on the side of the wall. The left image shows the pool scene with caustics disabled, and the right image shows them enabled.

FIGURE 46.16

FIGURE 46.16

This indoor swimming pool scene is rendered without caustics (left) and with caustics (right).

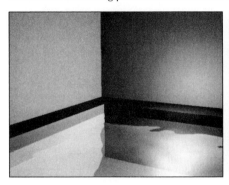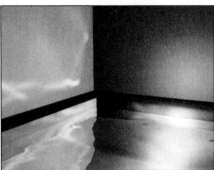

To get caustics to work in your scene, you need to add a Raytrace, Flat Mirror, or Reflect/Refract map to the Reflection map channel for the material that you want to generate caustics.

Tutorial: Using Caustic Photons to create a disco ball

When using the mental ray renderer, you can see the caustic photons as they are reflected around the room to help you determine the correct settings you need, but these photons themselves can be used to make a good disco ball effect.

 **TIP**   A common way to get a good, crisp caustic effect is to use significantly more photons than you would need for global illumination — on the order of millions of photons — for good results.

To create a disco ball effect using caustic photons, follow these steps:

1. Open the Disco ball.max file from the Chap 46 directory on the DVD.

   This file includes a simple room.

2. Select Create ➪ Standard Primitives ➪ Sphere, and click in the Top viewport to create a sphere positioned toward the top of the room.

3. Press the M key to open the Material Editor, and select the first sample slot. Select the map shortcut for the Diffuse color, and select the Raytrace map type in the Material/Map Browser. Then drag the Raytrace map in the Map rollout from the Diffuse Color to the Reflection map, and select the Instance option in the Copy Map dialog box that appears. Then enable the Faceted option; set the Opacity to **50**, the Specular Level to **95**, and the Glossiness to **30**; and drag the material to the sphere object.

4. Select Create Lights ➪ Standard Lights ➪ mr Area Omni, and click in the Top viewport to create four lights that surround the sphere object. In the Modify panel, change the Multiplier value to **0.3** for each of these lights, and offset each light vertically from the others.

5. Open the Render Scene dialog box (F10), and switch the Production Renderer in the Assign Renderer rollout of the Common panel to the mental ray Renderer. In the Indirect Illumination panel, enable the Caustics option and the Radius option, and set the Radius value to **1.0**. Enable the All Objects Generate and Receive Caustics & GI option. Then click the Render button.

Figure 46.17 shows the resulting disco scene with thousands of lights visible on the walls.

FIGURE 46.17

This disco ball simply reflects the caustic photons around the room.

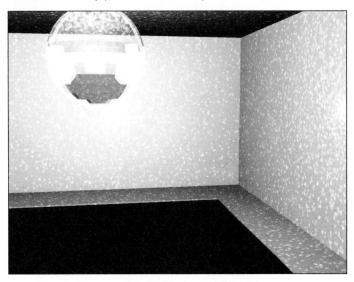

Enabling caustics and global illumination for objects

Another "gotcha" when dealing with caustics and global illumination is that each object can be specified to generate and/or receive caustics and global illumination. These settings are found in the mental ray panel of the Object Properties dialog box, shown in Figure 46.18. This dialog box can be opened using the Edit ➪ Properties menu command. If your scene isn't generating caustics and you can't figure out why, check this dialog box, because the Generate Caustics option is disabled by default.

TIP　The Indirect Illumination panel of the Render Scene dialog box includes an option that can be used to cause All Objects to Generate and Receive Caustics and GI. Enabling this option enables these options for all objects regardless of their Object Properties settings.

Controlling Indirect Illumination

In addition to the light settings, you can set many of the properties that control how caustics, global illumination, and Final Gather are computed in two rollouts of the Indirect Illumination panel of the Render Scene dialog box, shown in Figure 46.19. These two rollouts are the Final Gather rollout and the Caustics and Global Illumination (GI) rollout.

The Final Gather rollout is split into two parts. The top part features a set of Basic settings with several Presets that take the guesswork out of the settings. Simply choose one of the presets from the drop-down list and all the key settings are automatically made for you. The preset options include Draft, Low, Medium, High, and Very High. The Multiplier and color swatch changes the intensity and color of the indirect light. The Weight value sets how much indirect light affect the Final Gather solution.

For caustics and for global illumination, the Maximum Number of Photons per Sample value determines how the caustic photons are blended. A higher value results in more blending and softer edges. The Maximum Sampling Radius value sets the size of each photon. This value is set automatically depending on the size of the scene. However, you can enable the Radius value and enter a new value manually.

FIGURE 46.18

The Object Properties dialog box includes options for generating and receiving caustics and global illumination.

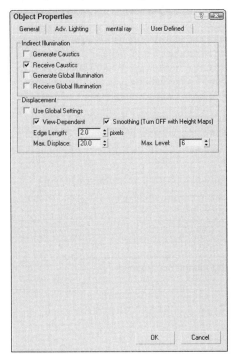

FIGURE 46.19

The Indirect Illumination panel includes settings for caustics, global illumination, and Final Gather.

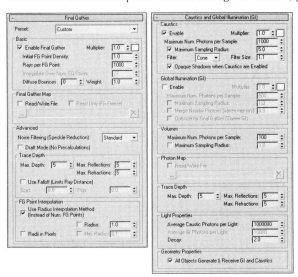

The Volumes setting is used by Volume material shaders to set the photon's size. The Trace Depth settings determine the maximum number of reflections and refractions that a photon can take before it is ignored.

Photon maps can take a while to generate for a complicated scene, but once computed, they can be saved and reloaded. These files are saved using the .PMAP extension.

Final Gather sends out rays to a scene that has computed caustics and global illumination already and computes the light at that location. All these rays are then combined to produce a total lighting picture of the scene and then blended to help fix any lighting abnormalities that may exist in the scene. The Samples value determines how many rays are cast into the scene. The Final Gather lighting pass can then be saved to a file after it is computed.

 Final Gather has been updated with the ability to use self-illuminated materials as a light source. These materials are in the Arch & Design materials. This feature is new to 3ds Max 2008.

Rendering control

The core rendering settings for the mental ray renderer are contained within the Renderer panel of the Render Scene dialog box, shown in Figure 46.20. Using these settings, you can increase the speed of the renderer (at the expense of image quality).

FIGURE 46.20

The Renderer panel includes several rollouts of settings for controlling the mental ray renderer.

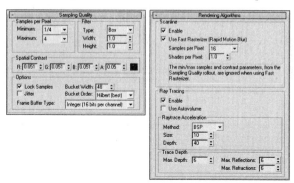

The Sampling settings are used to apply an anti-aliasing pass to the rendered image. These samples can be filtered, and you can control the details of the contrast between the samples. The Bucket Width is the size of the blocks that are identified and rendered. Smaller buckets do not take as long to render and provide quicker feedback in the Render window.

The mental ray renderer uses several different algorithms, and you can specify which ones to ignore in order to speed up the rendering cycle. If a needed algorithm is disabled, the features that rely on that algorithm are skipped. You can also set the Trace Depth for Reflections and Refractions and control the Raytrace Acceleration values.

Advanced mental ray

The mental ray renderer also includes many additional features that you can take advantage of, including Depth of Field, Motion Blur, Contours, Displacement, and Camera Shaders. The settings for these additional features are located in rollouts at the bottom of the Renderer panel. For example, if you add the Glare map to the Output map in the Camera Shader section, then you can get a strong glare from light in the scene, as shown for the house interior in Figure 46.21.

FIGURE 46.21

Placing the Glare map in the Output Camera Shader, you can get a strong glare from the light in the window.

Summary

If you're looking for a rendering option that perfectly calculates reflections, refractions, and transparencies, then raytracing is what you need. Raytracing settings can be set globally and applied to selected materials using materials and maps. And when raytracing needs an additional push, the mental ray renderer can be selected to render the scene.

In this chapter, you accomplished the following:

- Learned about the global raytracing settings
- Explored the raytrace material
- Worked with raytraced maps
- Learned to enable the mental ray renderer
- Created mental ray lights
- Worked with caustics and photons

Now that I've told you how to overload the rendering engine, the next chapter offers a way to get some help by batch rendering and rendering over the network.

Chapter 47

Batch and Network Rendering

M ax can help you create some incredible images and animations, but that power comes at a significant price — time. Modeling scenes and animation sequences takes enough time on its own, but after you're finished, you still have to wait for the rendering to take place, which for a final rendering at the highest detail settings can literally take days. Because the time rendering takes is directly proportional to the amount of processing power you have access to, Max lets you use network rendering to add more hardware to the equation and speed up those painfully slow jobs.

This chapter shows you how to set up Max to distribute the rendering workload across an entire network of computers, helping you finish big rendering jobs in record time.

Batch Rendering Scenes

If you work all day modeling, texturing, and animating sequences only to find that most of your day is shot waiting for a sequence to be rendered, then happily you have several solutions. You can get a second system and use it for rendering while you work on the first system, or you can use the network rendering feature to render over the network, but a third possibility is also available.

Unless you are working around the clock (which is common for many game productions), you can set up a batch rendering queue before you leave for the evening using the Batch Render tool. This queue runs through the night, giving you a set of takes to review in the morning.

Using the Batch Render tool

The Batch Render window, shown in Figure 47.1, is accessed from the Rendering menu. Render tasks can be added to the list by clicking the Add button. Render tasks can be disabled by selecting the check box to the left of the task name.

FIGURE 47.1

The Batch Render window lets you define render tasks to be run as a batch process.

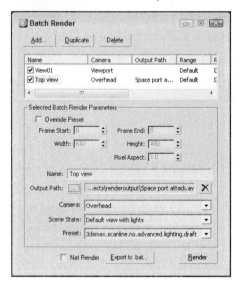

For each task, you can set the task's Name, Camera, Output Path, and render Preset. The Scene State drop-down list lets you select any scene states that are defined using the Tools ➪ Manage Scene States command.

Each new task that is added to the Batch Render window uses the default render parameters for its frame range, dimensions, and pixel aspect, but if you enable the Override Preset option, then you can customize each of these parameters for the selected task.

The Batch Render queue can be rendered over the network by enabling the Net Render option at the bottom of the Batch Render window.

Managing scene states

A single scene file may have many different settings that you'd like to try as different renderings. For example, you can set up a scene with different light settings, with different camera properties, or with unique materials.. Scene states let you define different sets of properties that can be recalled prior to a batch rendering. Each of these scene states can be part of a single Max file.

When the Tools ➪ Manage Scene States menu command is selected, the Manage Scene States dialog box appears, as shown in Figure 47.2, which lets you Save, Restore, Rename, and Delete the existing list of scene states. Clicking the Save button, opens the Save Scene State dialog box, also shown in Figure 47.2. In the Save Scene State dialog box, you can enter the name for the scene state and select which group of settings to use. The options include Light Properties, Light Transforms, Object Properties, Camera Transforms, Camera Properties, Layer Properties, Layer Assignment, Materials, and Environment.

Creating a standalone executable

After a batch render queue is established, you can click the Export to .bat button to open the Batch Render Export to Batch File dialog box, where you can save the batch file as a .bat file. This saved file can be executed from the command line or by using an agent.

FIGURE 47.2

The Manage Scene States and Save Scene State dialog boxes let you define which properties to save as a state that can be recalled for a batch render task.

Understanding Network Rendering

When you use network rendering to render your animation, Max divides the work among several machines connected via a network, with each machine rendering some of the frames. The increase in speed depends on how many machines you can devote to rendering frames: Add just one computer, and you double the rate at which you can render. Add seven or eight machines, and instead of missing that important deadline by a week, you can get done early and take an extra day off.

The price of all this (besides the extra machines) is a time investment on your part. It does take a little work to get things set up properly, but it's an investment that you have to make only once. If you take the time now to make sure that you do things right, you should be up and running fairly quickly and have far fewer headaches down the road.

Machines connected to handle network rendering are often referred to collectively as a *rendering farm*. The basic process during a network rendering goes like this: One machine manages the entire process and distributes the work among all the computers in the farm. Each machine signals the managing computer when it is ready to work on another frame. The manager then sends or "farms out" a new frame, which gets worked on by a computer in the rendering farm, and the finished frame gets saved in whatever format you've chosen.

The software in Max that makes network rendering possible is called Backburner. You may have noticed that it was installed when Max was installed. Max has several features to make the network rendering process easier. If one of the computers in your rendering farm crashes or loses its connection with the manager, the manager reclaims the frame that was assigned to the down computer and farms it out to a different machine. You can monitor the status of any rendering job you have running, and you can even have Max e-mail you when a job is complete.

In this chapter, we step through the process of setting up network rendering on a small network. You find out firsthand what's involved so that setting up your own network can go smoothly.

NOTE One additional caveat to using network rendering is that you have no guarantee that the frames of your animation will be rendered in order. Each participating computer renders frames as quickly as possible and saves them as separate files, so you cannot use network rendering to create .AVI or .MOV files. Instead, you have to render the scene with each frame saved as a separate bitmap file, and then use the RAM Player, Video Post, or a third-party program (such as Adobe Premiere) to combine them into an animation file format such as .AVI.

Network Requirements

Now that you're eager to get things under way, let's look at what you need to set up a rendering farm:

- **Computers:** First, of course, you need computers. The more the merrier, but they all must be connected via some sort of network and must be running TCP/IP, a very common communications protocol (we talk more about TCP/IP and setting it up later). As with most things related to computers, the more powerful the hardware you can get your hands on, the faster things go. All computers in your farm should meet at least the basic requirements for Max, but if they have more memory, more disk space, and faster processors, you're better off. Also, having nothing else running on the machines is preferable. Rendering is a CPU-intensive process, so any other programs you have running compete for the processor and increase the time needed to finish your rendering job.

- **Networking hardware:** Each computer needs some way to connect to the network. The most common way is to use a network adapter card in the computer and a cable that connects it to the rest of the network. The network also can work over a wireless connection, but the speed at which you can render will be determined by the speed of your network. If a computer is connected via a dial-up connection, then its networking hardware is a modem.

- **Windows Vista or XP:** According to the Max documentation, each computer in your rendering farm must be running under Windows Vista or XP.

- **3ds Max:** Obviously, you need Max to do all this, but the good news is that only one machine in your farm needs to have an *authorized* copy of Max installed.

> **NOTE** No authorization whatsoever is needed on machines used for network rendering only. Simply install Max, and each network rendering machine gets its authorization from the computer that launched the render job.

Basically that's all you need to network render with Max. But before we move on, you should remember two important things.

First, the display capabilities of the machines in your rendering farm are irrelevant. Max uses its own rendering engine, so in network rendering, a top-of-the-line graphics adapter won't give you any better performance or quality than the cheap, factory-installed adapters that often come built into the motherboard. In fact, you can even omit the monitor on each rendering farm computer, which can really cut down on how much you have to invest to set up a good network rendering farm.

Second, if you don't have access to a bunch of computers that can be exclusively dedicated to network rendering, don't give up. Max has some great scheduling features that enable you to configure each computer so that it's available to render at certain times of the day. If you have administrative access to additional computers at work or a university lab, you can use those computers at night or on weekends, when they are generally not being used.

Setting up a Network Rendering System

Before we get into the details of setting up Max and the network itself, understanding the different parts of the network rendering system is important. This list shows the major players involved:

- **Manager:** The *manager* is a program (manager.exe) that acts as the network manager. It's the network manager's job to coordinate the efforts of all the other computers in your rendering farm. Only one machine on your network needs to be running the manager, and that same machine can also be used to render.

- **Server:** A rendering server is any computer on your network that is used to render frames of your animation. When you run the server program (server.exe), it contacts the network manager and informs it that this particular computer is available to render. The server starts up Max when the manager sends a frame to be rendered.

- **3ds Max:** At least one computer in your rendering farm must have an authorized copy of Max running, although it does not need to be the same computer that is running the manager. It is from this machine that you initiate a rendering job.

- **Monitor:** The Monitor (monitor.exe) is a special program that lets you monitor your rendering farm. You can use it to check the current state of jobs that are running or that have been queued. You can also use it to schedule network rendering times. The Monitor is completely independent from the actual rendering process, so you can use it on one of the machines in your rendering farm, or you can use it to remotely check the status of things by connecting over the network.

We address the task of setting up the network rendering system in three stages. The first thing you need is a functioning network, so we first go through the steps of how to get it working. Next, we look at setting up the Max software on each computer, and finally I describe how to tell Max where to find scene data it needs and where to put the finished scenes.

Setting up the network

To communicate with the different machines on the network, Max uses *TCP/IP* (Transmission Control Protocol/Internet Protocol), a very common network protocol. It's so common, in fact, that if your computers are already set up with some sort of network, you might already have TCP/IP installed and configured properly. If so, you are saved from several hours of work. Each machine on a network is identified by an IP address, which is a series of four numbers, each between 0 and 255, separated by periods, such as:

```
192.1.17.5
```

Each computer on a network has a unique IP address as well as a unique, human-readable name. To use Max to do network rendering, you need to find the IP address and name of each computer used on the network.

The precise details of what constitutes a "correct" IP address are too long and boring to go into here, but for a nonpublic network, all the addresses start with 192 or 10. The second and third numbers can be anything between 0 and 255 inclusive, and the last number can be between 1 and 254 inclusive (0 and 255 have special meanings). As an example, I've chosen to set up my home network as follows:

```
Machine Name    IP Address
Dungar          10.0.0.1
Ramrod          10.0.0.2
Slazenger       10.0.0.3
Romulus         10.0.0.4
```

Notice that each address is unique and that because it's a private network, the first number in each address is 10.

Tutorial: Locating TCP/IP and gathering IP addresses

To get the computers to talk to one another, you need to make sure that each computer has the TCP/IP protocol installed, and you need to gather the IP addresses for all the machines on the network.

To see whether you already have TCP/IP installed and to find out the IP address and name of each computer, follow these steps:

1. Right-click the Computer icon in Explorer, and select Properties from the pop-up menu. The System information window opens. About halfway down the window is the Full computer name. Write the computer name in a list of all the computers that you are using to render via a network. Each computer on your network needs a unique name, so if the field is blank, enter a unique name and add the computer to your list.

> **CAUTION** Remember that there are differences between Windows Vista and Windows XP. These steps were written for Windows Vista.

2. Open the Control Panel by going to the Windows taskbar and choosing Start ➪ Control Panel.

3. Click the Network and Internet icon, and then click the Network and Sharing Center link to open the network connections window.

   This window displays a list of network connections.

4. Select the network connection identified as Local Area Connection, and select the View Status link. The Local Area Connection Status dialog box displays the status of the current connection. If you click the Details button, you see a dialog box that lists the current IP address being used if your network is already installed. You also can click the Properties button to open a dialog box, which lists the installed protocols. At the top of the Local Area Connection Properties dialog box, you should see your network adapter (such as the brand and model of your Ethernet card). If it is not listed, you need to get it set up before proceeding. Under the network adapter is a list of installed network protocols, similar to the list in Figure 47.3. Look through the list until you find the Internet (TCP/IP) Protocol. If you find it, double-click it to bring up the TCP/IP Properties dialog box. If you don't see the TCP/IP protocol anywhere, then you have to add it yourself in order to do network rendering.

> **NOTE** Two different versions (version 4 or version 6) of TCP/IP may be installed on your computer. Max's network rendering can work with either version.

FIGURE 47.3

A list of the network protocols installed on this computer

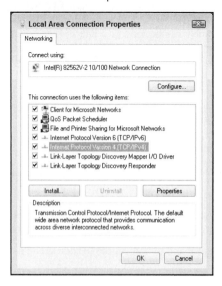

5. The Internet (TCP/IP) Protocol Properties dialog box has an important piece of information, called IP Address, shown in Figure 47.4. Do one of the following:

   - If Obtain an IP address automatically is selected, you don't have to worry about the exact IP address of this computer, because each time the computer connects to the network it gets an IP address from a server, and the address it gets may be different every time.

   - If Specify an IP address is selected, add the IP address to your written list of computers on the network. In the IP Address panel shown in the figure, the IP address has been statically assigned, which means that this computer will always have the same IP address.

FIGURE 47.4

You can find the IP address in the Internet Protocol (TCP/IP) Properties dialog box.

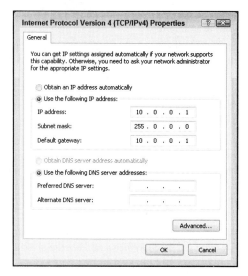

6. Repeat this procedure for each computer that will participate in your rendering farm. If you're lucky and all your machines have TCP/IP installed and ready to go, you can skip the next section and move on to setting up Max on your network. If not, then follow the steps for configuring TCP/IP in the next section.

Tutorial: Installing and configuring TCP/IP

If your computer doesn't already have TCP/IP installed, you have to install it in order to render via a network in Max.

CAUTION   Be careful about changing the TCP/IP settings of computers that are on a public network or are part of a large corporate network. Incorrect settings can not only keep your computers from communicating properly but can also cause problems in many other computers on the network.

If the computers you plan on using for your rendering farm are part of a public or corporate network, seek the assistance of the network administrator. If you're in charge of the computers yourself, dig out your Windows Vista installation DVD-ROM, because you're going to need it.

To install and configure TCP/IP, follow these steps:

1. Go to the Networking panel on the Local Area Connection Properties dialog box. To get there, choose Start ⇨ Control Panel. Double-click the Network and Internet icon, and select the Network and Sharing Center links to open the network connections window. Click the View Status link for the network connection identified as Local Area Connection, and select Properties from the pop-up menu.

2. Click the Install button to open the Select Network Component Type dialog box. Select Protocol, and click the Add button. From the list of protocols, select Internet (TCP/IP) Protocol and click OK.

3. At this point, Windows asks whether you want to use DHCP. DHCP is a server that automatically assigns an IP address to you computer. If you know for sure that there is a DHCP server running, choose Yes. If you're setting up the network yourself or you have no idea what DHCP is, choose No.

   If DHCP is already set up and working, it can save you lots of time, but if not and if you're setting up the network yourself, I recommend steering away from it. You can change the settings to use DHCP at a later time if you're feeling ambitious.

4. Now Windows starts looking for the files that it needs to install, and it pops up a dialog box asking for their location. The default path it lists is probably the right one, so you can just click OK and continue. If Windows guessed wrong, or if you have the CD-ROM in a different drive, correct the path and then click OK.

5. After Windows finishes copying the files, TCP/IP is installed but not configured. To configure the protocol, select it and click the Properties button.

   The Internet (TCP/IP) Protocol Properties dialog box, shown earlier in Figure 47.2, opens.

6. In the General panel is a section where you choose whether you want to have an IP address assigned automatically using DHCP. If you're not using DHCP, choose Specify an IP address and enter an IP address for this machine. Refer to the beginning of this section if you need help choosing a valid IP address. (If you're a little confused about what numbers to use, you should be safe using the same numbers that I did.)

> **CAUTION** It's extremely important that you choose an IP address that is unique on the network. (Duplicate IP addresses are a great way to guarantee a nonfunctional rendering farm.)

7. Below the IP address section, you have to enter a subnet mask. Enter

   ```
   255.255.255.0
   ```

   The subnet mask is used in conjunction with the IP address to identify different networks within the entire domain of every network in the world. If you do have to change this, be sure to change it in the 3dsnet.ini file that each rendering server creates (see "Configuring the Network Manager and Servers" later in this chapter).

8. Now select the Obtain DNS server address automatically option unless you know the IP address of your network's DNS server.

   This setting allows you to configure the TCP/IP protocol to check your local DNS when looking up addresses.

9. Click OK in the TCP/IP Properties dialog box to close it, and then click Close on the Local Area Connection Properties dialog box to close it.

   Windows needs to be shut down and restarted in order for the changes to take effect. This computer now has the proper network setup for your rendering farm.

Remember to repeat these instructions for every computer that you want to use in your rendering farm. Each computer must be properly connected to the network and have TCP/IP installed and configured. This may seem like lots of work, but fortunately it's a one-time investment.

Tutorial: Setting up Max on the networked computers

If you've made it this far, then you'll be happy to know that the worst is behind you. We've covered the most difficult parts of setting up a network rendering system; by comparison, everything else is relatively simple.

At this point, you should have a complete list of all the computers used in your network rendering system. Each computer should have a unique name and a unique IP address, and all should have TCP/IP installed and configured. You are now ready to move on to the actual Max installation for your rendering servers.

You have to set up Max on each computer in your rendering farm. Fortunately, this is as simple as a normal installation. To set up Max on each computer, follow these steps:

1. Run the setup.exe program on the Max installation CD-ROM.

NOTE You don't need to have a CD-ROM drive in every computer in your rendering farm. After your computers are networked, you can map a drive from your current machine to a computer that has the Max CD-ROM in its CD-ROM drive. In Windows Explorer, choose Tools ⇨ Map Network Drive and enter the path to the computer and drive with the CD-ROM.

2. Move past the first few introduction screens until you get to the Setup Type screen. Choose the Compact option so that Max installs only the minimum number of files it needs to be able to render. You also need to choose a destination directory where you want Max to be installed. If possible, just accept the displayed default destination and click Next.

TIP Installing 3ds Max in the same directory on every computer can save you some maintenance headaches later on. Managing bitmap and plug-in directories is much easier if each machine has the same directory layout.

3. Continue with the rest of the installation as you would do for a normal installation of Max (although you can skip installing the online reference manuals if you want to save some disk space).

After the installation files get copied over, you'll probably have to reboot your computer for the changes to take effect.

Configuring shared directories

The last step in building your rendering farm is to tell Max where it can find the information it needs to render a scene. Max must be able to find textures and other information, and it must know where to put each frame that it renders.

Tutorial: Sharing directories

Instead of copying needed files to every machine in your rendering farm, you can share your directories across the network, which means that other computers on the network can use the files in that directory.

To make a directory shared, follow these steps:

1. Open Windows Explorer by selecting Start on the Windows taskbar and then choosing Computer.
2. Find the directory that you want to share, right-click it, and choose Share.
   The File Sharing dialog box opens for that directory.
3. In the File Sharing dialog box, select those machines that you want to share the file with. Under the Permission Level, you can choose each machine to be a Reader, Contributor, Co-owner, or Remove. For network rendering, choose the Co-owner option and click the Share button.

After sharing is enabled, a dialog box appears informing you that sharing has been set up, as shown in Figure 47.5.

FIGURE 47.5

Sharing a directory so that other computers on the network can use it

TIP Other computers will refer to the shared directory by its shared name instead of its actual name, so to keep things simple, accept the default of using the actual name for the shared name.

CAUTION Enabling the Allow network users to change my files option gives all network users full control access, letting everyone on the entire network read and write or erase the files in your shared directory. For now, leaving it this way until you're sure everything is configured properly is best. Later, however, restricting access to only those accounts that should have access would be a good idea.

4. Click Done in the File Sharing dialog box to close it, and you're back at Windows Explorer. If you press F5, Windows refreshes the display and your directory now has a little icon to show that the folder is shared. Figure 47.6 shows the "renderoutput" directory denoted as a shared directory.

Other computers can access your shared directory by specifying the full name of the directory's location. In the example, we've been using, the "renderoutput" directory is on a computer named "Bricker," so the full path to that directory is as follows:

```
\\bricker\renderoutput
```

You can test this by opening Windows Explorer on a different computer, choosing Tools ➪ Map Network Drive, and entering the full path to that directory. After you've mapped a drive to a directory, Windows treats that directory as if it were an actual drive on your machine. In Figure 47.7, the Z drive is mapped to point to the "renderoutput" directory on Bricker.

After you've mapped to a new drive, go back to Windows Explorer and press F5 to refresh the display again. You now have a new drive for that network directory.

FIGURE 47.6

Other computers can now access the shared "renderoutput" directory.

FIGURE 47.7

Mapping the Z drive to point to \\dungar\scenes\

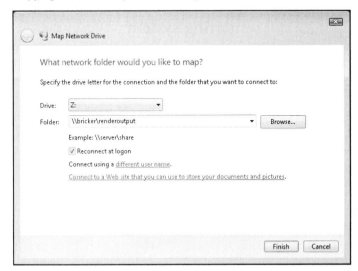

Tutorial: Choosing shared directories

Now you need to decide where to put the shared files and the output files. These directories are the place from which all machines in your rendering farm read files and images and to which they all write finished frames of your animation. The following procedure takes you through the steps for doing this using the directories I've set up on my own rendering farm.

To set up your shared directories, follow these steps:

1. First, decide which drives to use and then share them.

   On my network, Bricker has plenty of disk space, so I used the maps, images, scenes, and render-output directories that were already there from when I installed Max.

> **TIP** Use the maps, images, scenes, and renderoutput directories for all the scenes that you render via a network. In each directory, you can create other directories to organize files for your different scenes, but putting all needed files in the same place facilitates maintenance.

2. On each computer in your rendering farm, map a drive to your shared maps, images, scenes, and renderoutput directories as described in the previous section. If possible, choose the same drive letters on all machines. I used the letter Z for the renderoutput directory on each computer.

Congratulations! You've made it through the installation and setup of your network rendering system. And no matter how long it took you, it was time well spent. The ability to render via a network will easily save you more time than you invested in setting up your network.

Starting the Network Rendering System

You can finally put all your hard work into action. We're ready to start up your network rendering system.

Tutorial: Initializing the network rendering system

The very first time you start your rendering farm, you need to help Max do a little initialization.

To initialize the network rendering system, follow these steps:

1. Start the network manager on one machine in your rendering farm. This program, Manager.exe, is in the Backburner directory. You can start the manager by selecting it and pressing Enter in Windows Explorer. After it starts up, you first see the Backburner Manager General Properties dialog box. This dialog box appears only the first time you run the Manager.exe program or if you choose Edit ➪ General Settings. I cover its settings later in the chapter. After setting these properties, click the OK button, and the Manager window, shown in Figure 47.8, runs.

FIGURE 47.8

Starting the network manager

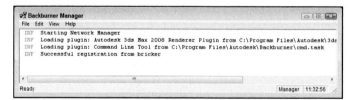

2. Now start a network server on each computer that you plan to use for rendering. To do this, find and start the Server.exe program just like you did with Manager.exe. When you start this program for the first time, the Backburner Server General Properties dialog box appears. This dialog box is covered later in the chapter. Click OK, and the Network Server window appears, as shown in Figure 47.9.

FIGURE 47.9

Starting a network server. Notice that the server is already looking for the manager.

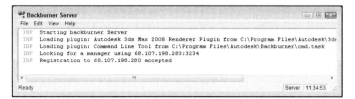

When the server finds the manager, it displays a message that the registration is accepted. The Network Manager window also shows a similar message.

If the server had trouble connecting to the manager, you need to follow these two additional steps:

1. If automatic detection of the manager fails, the server keeps trying until it times out. If it times out, or if you just get tired of waiting, choose Edit ➪ General Settings to open the Backburner Server General Properties dialog box, shown in Figure 47.10. In this dialog box, uncheck the Automatic Search box and type in the name or IP address of the computer that is running the network manager. In this case, the server tried but couldn't quite find the manager, so it had to be told that the manager was running on the computer whose IP address is 150.150.150.150.

FIGURE 47.10

Manually choosing the manager's IP address

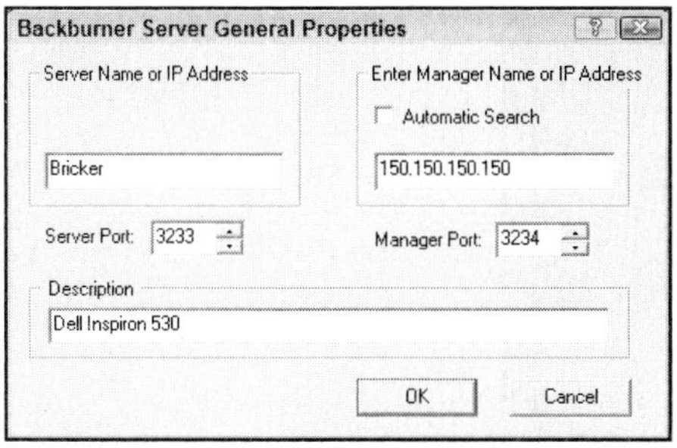

2. Click OK to close the Backburner Server General Properties dialog box, and then click Close to shut down the server (doing so forces the server to save the changes you've made). Restart the server the same way you did before, and now the server and manager are able to find each other.

NOTE The network manager does not need to have a computer all to itself, so you can also run a network server on the same computer and use it to participate in the rendering.

Tutorial: Completing your first network rendering job

Your rendering farm is up and running and just dying to render something, so let's put those machines to work.

To start a network rendering job, follow these steps:

1. Start Max, and create a simple animation scene.

   This should be as simple as possible because all we're doing here is verifying that the rendering farm is functional.

2. In Max, choose Rendering ➪ Render (F10) to bring up the Render Scene dialog box. In the Time Output section of this dialog box, be sure that Range is selected so that you really do render multiple frames instead of the default single frame.

3. In the Render Output section of the Render Scene dialog box, click Files to open the Render Output File dialog box. In the Save In section, choose the output drive that can be accessed over the network and directory that you created in the "Configuring shared directories" section.

4. In the File name section of the Render Output File dialog box, type the name of the first frame. Max automatically numbers each frame for you. Choose a bitmap format from the Save as type list (remember, an animation format will not work).

5. Click Save to close the Render Output File dialog box. (Some file formats might ask you for additional information for your files; if so, just click OK to accept the default options.) Back in the Render Scene dialog box, Max displays the full path to the output directory.

6. In the Render Output section of the Render Scene dialog box, check the Net Render option, as shown in Figure 47.11. Change any other settings you want, such as selecting a viewport, and then click Render.

FIGURE 47.11

The Net Render option must be enabled to start a network rendering job.

A Network Job Assignment dialog box opens, like the one shown in Figure 47.12.

FIGURE 47.12

Using the Network Job Assignment dialog box to locate the manager to handle the rendering job

7. In the Enter Subnet section of the Network Job Assignment dialog box, click Connect if the Automatic Search box is checked. If it isn't checked, or if your servers had trouble finding the manager in the "Initializing the network rendering system" tutorial earlier in this chapter, type the IP address of the machine that's running the manager and then click Connect.

8. Max then searches for any available rendering servers, connects with it, and adds its name to the list of available servers. Click the server name once, and click Submit.

TIP   If you try to submit the same job again (after either a failed or a successful attempt at rendering), Max complains because that job already exists in the job queue. You can remove the job using the Monitor, or you can click the + button on the Network Job Assignment dialog box, and Max adds a number to the job name to make it unique.

After you've submitted your job, notices appear on the manager and the servers (like the ones shown in Figures 46.13 and 46.14) that the job has been received. Soon Max starts up on each server, and you see a Rendering dialog box showing the progress of the rendering task. As you can see, this displays useful information such as what frame is being rendered and how long the job is taking. When the entire animation has been rendered, you can go to your output directory to get the bitmap files that Max generated. The render servers and the render manager keep running, ready for the next job request to come in.

Job assignment options

The Network Job Assignment dialog box, shown previously in Figure 47.12, has an important section that we didn't use for our first simple render job; it's called Options.

FIGURE 47.13

The network manager detects the new job.

FIGURE 47.14

One of the network servers receives the command to start a new job.

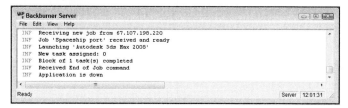

The Options section has the following settings:

- **Enabled Notifications:** Lets you tell Max when to notify you that certain events have occurred. If you check the Enable Notifications option, the Define button becomes active. The Define button opens a Notifications dialog box, shown in Figure 47.15.

FIGURE 47.15

The Notifications dialog box lets you specify which type of notifications to receive.

- **Split Scan Lines:** This option breaks a rendered image into strips that can be rendered separately. The Define button lets you specify the Strip Height, Number of Strips, and any Overlap.
- **Ignore Scene Path:** Use this option to force the servers to retrieve the scene file via TCP/IP. If disabled, the manager copies the scene file to the server.

■ **Rendered Frame Window:** Use this option if you want to be able to see the image on the server as it gets rendered.

■ **Include Maps:** Checking this box makes Max compress everything that it needs to render the scene (including the maps) into a single file and send it to each server. This option is useful if you're setting up a rendering farm over the Internet, although it takes more time and network bandwidth to send all that extra information.

■ **Initially Suspended:** This option pauses the rendering before it starts so that you can manually start it when the network is ready.

■ **Use Selected/Use Group/Use All Servers:** The Server Usage option makes the selected server, a group of servers, or all servers listed in the Server panel fair game for rendering.

■ **Use Alternate Path File:** This option lets you specify an alternate path for map and other files, which is entered in the text field below the check box.

Configuring the Network Manager and Servers

You can configure both the manager and servers using their respective General Properties dialog boxes. You open these dialog boxes by choosing Edit ⇨ General Settings.

The network manager settings

The rendering manager has some options that let you modify how it behaves. You specify these options in the Network Manager General Properties dialog box, shown in Figure 47.16. To open this dialog box, select Edit ⇨ General Settings in the Manager window.

FIGURE 47.16

The Backburner Manager General Properties dialog box

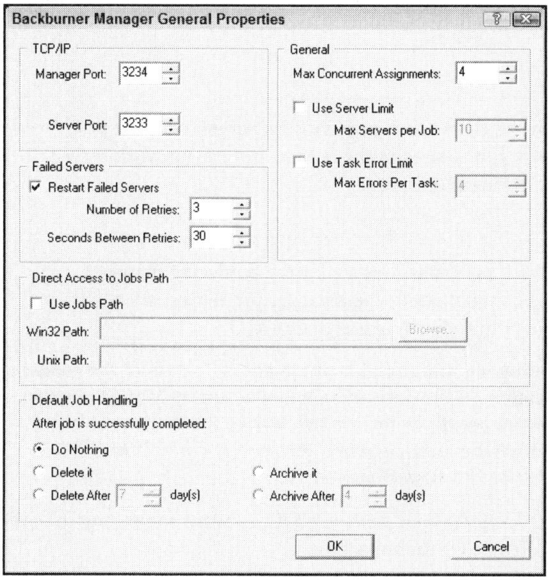

This dialog box includes the following sections:

- **TCP/IP:** Here you can change the communications ports used by the manager and the servers. In general, leaving these alone is a good idea. If some other program is using one of these ports, however, Max won't be able to render via the network, so you need to change them. If you change the Server Port number, be sure to change it to the same number on all your rendering servers. If you change the Manager Port number, you also need to change two files on your hard drive to match: queueman.ini (in your 3dsmax directory) and client.ini (in your 3dsmax\network directory). Both have lines for the Manager Port, and you can edit these files with any text editor or word processor.

- **General:** The Max Concurrent Assignments field is used to specify how many jobs the rendering manager sends out at a time. If you make this number too high, the manager might send out jobs faster than the servers can handle them. The default value here is fine for most cases.

> **NOTE** The network manager can automatically attempt to restart servers that failed, giving your rendering farm much more stability.

- **Failed Servers:** Usually, Max doesn't send more frames to a server that previously failed. If you check the Restarts Failed Servers box, Max tries to give the server another chance. The Number of Retries field tells Max how many times it should try to restart a server before giving up on the particular server for good, and the Minutes Between Retries field tells Max the number of minutes it should wait before trying to give the failing server another job.

> **NOTE** The rendering manager writes the configuration settings to a file on the disk that gets read when the manager loads. If you make changes to any of the settings, shutting down the manager and starting it up again to guarantee that the changes take effect is best.

- **Direct Access to Jobs Path:** This setting lets you specify a different path that exists anywhere on the network, regardless of where the manager is running. Separate fields are available for Win32 paths and Unix paths. If the Use Jobs Path option is selected, then the specified path is used.

- **Default Job Handling:** This section lets you tell the Manager what to do after the rendering job is finished. The options include Do Nothing, Delete or Archive, and Delete or Archive after a specified number of days. This option gives you a way to clean out your queue.

The network servers settings

As you may have guessed, the Properties button on the Network Server window serves a similar purpose as the one on the Network Manager window: It enables you to specify the behavior of the network server. Clicking this button displays the Backburner Server General Properties dialog box.

This dialog box has the following section:

- **TCP/IP:** The port numbers serve the same function as they do for the rendering manager, described in the previous section. If you change them in the manager properties, change them here. If you change them here, change them in the manager properties.

> **NOTE** The Manager Name or IP Address setting lets you override automatic detection of the rendering manager and specify its exact location on the network. Generally, letting Max attempt to find the manager itself is best; if it fails, override the automatic detection by clearing the Automatic check box. If you happen to be running multiple managers on the same network, the servers connect to the first one they find. In this case, you have to manually choose the correct server.

Keep in mind that the server properties aren't shared among your servers, so if you want something to change on all your servers, you have to make that change on each machine.

 As with the rendering manager settings, if you change anything in the Network Servers Properties dialog box, be sure to shut down the server and restart it.

Logging Errors

Both the Network Manager and Network Server windows have a Logging button that you can click to access the Logging Properties dialog box, where you can configure how log information gets handled. This dialog box, shown in Figure 47.17, looks the same for managers and servers. You can access this dialog box with the Edit ➪ Log Settings command.

FIGURE 47.17

The logging options for managers and servers let you tell Max where to report what.

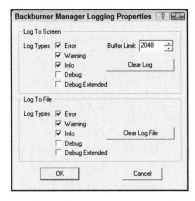

Max generates the following types of messages:

- **Error:** Anything that goes wrong and is serious enough to halt the rendering of a frame.
- **Warning:** A problem that Max can still work around. If a server fails, for example, a warning is generated, but Max continues the rendering job by using other servers.
- **Info:** A general information message, such as notification that a job has arrived or that a frame is complete.
- **Debug:** A lower-level message that provides information to help debug problems with the rendering farm.
- **Debug Extended:** The same as the Debug option with more details.

Max displays the type of message and the message itself in two locations: in the list window and in a log file (in your 3dsmax\network directory). The Logging Properties dialog box lets you choose whether each type of message gets reported to the screen, the log file, both places, or neither place. You can also use the Clear buttons to get rid of old messages.

Using the Monitor

The Monitor is a powerful utility that helps you manage your rendering farm and all the jobs in it. If you use network rendering frequently, then the Monitor quickly becomes your best friend. You start it the same way that you start a rendering server or manager: Go to the 3dsmax directory, find QueueManager.exe, and double-click it. Every computer that has Max installed on it also has a copy of the Monitor, so you can use it from any machine on your network. The main screen is shown in Figure 47.18.

The Monitor makes managing a rendering farm quick and easy.

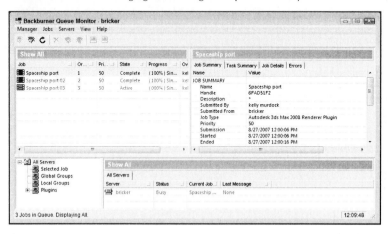

When the Monitor starts up, it automatically searches for the rendering manager and connects to it. (If you have more than one manager running, you have to choose which one to connect to.)

The main screen is divided into three panes. The top-left pane shows the job queue, and their Priority and Status, and the top-right pane shows information about whatever you have selected in the left pane. You can use the tabs at the top of this pane to select the information that you want to view. The information tabs include Job Summary, Frames Summary, Advanced (which shows the rendering parameters), Render Elements, and Log.

The bottom pane lists all the available servers. Next to each server in the left pane is an icon that reflects its current status. Green icons mean that the job or server is active and hard at work. Yellow means the server is idle. Red means that something has gone wrong, and gray means that a job has been inactivated or that a server is assigned to a job but is absent. When a job is complete, it can be deleted from the queue.

Jobs

If you choose a job in the top-left pane, the top-right pane displays information about the selected job. The panels in the top-right pane are as follows:

- **Job Summary:** Lists some of the rendering options you chose before you submitted the job. Among other things, the example in the figure shows that the job was rendered to 640 × 480 pixels.
- **Frames Summary:** Lists the details of rendering each frame in the animation, including the time required to render and the server used.
- **Advanced:** Lists advanced settings from the Render Scene dialog box and gives limited information about the scene itself.

- ■ **Render Elements:** Lists the details of each render element included as part of the job.
- ■ **Log:** Displays important messages from the job log. Whereas the log file on each server lists events for a particular server, this pane lets you see all the messages relating to a particular job.

When you point at a job in the top-left pane and right-click, a small pop-up menu appears. On this menu, you can delete a job from the queue or you can choose to activate or deactivate it. If you deactivate a job, all the servers working on that job save their work in progress to disk and then move on to the next job in the queue. This feature is very useful when you have a lower-priority job that you run when no other jobs are waiting; when something more important comes along, you deactivate the job so that you can later activate it when the servers are free again.

One last useful feature for jobs is that you can reorder them by dragging a job above or below other jobs. Jobs higher on the screen are rendered before lower ones, which enables you to "bump up" the priority of a particular job without having to deactivate other ones.

 A file with a Critical priority is rendered immediately.

Servers

If you right-click a server and select Properties from the pop-up menu, the Server Properties dialog box, shown in Figure 47.19, opens. This dialog box contains information about the selected server.

FIGURE 47.19

The Server Properties dialog box displays information about the server.

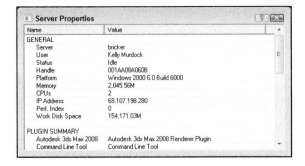

Many other features are available in the right-click pop-up menu. Using this pop-up menu, you can assign the server to a selected job, remove the server from its selected job, display specific server information, create a server group, or view the Week Schedule, as shown in Figure 47.20. Using the Week Schedule dialog box, you can set the active rendering period for a server.

The Week Schedule dialog box lets you decide when a particular machine is available for rendering. (For example, you can have your coworker's computer automatically become available for rendering after he or she goes home for the night.)

Click and drag with your mouse over different hours to select a group of times. Alternatively, you can click a day of the week to select the entire day or click a time to select that time for every day. In the example shown in Figure 47.18, the server is scheduled to render in the evenings and on the weekends.

FIGURE 47.20

The Week Schedule dialog box can set the time during the week when a server is available for rendering.

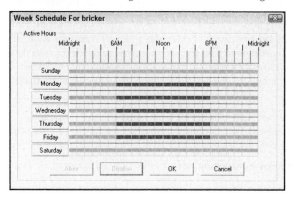

After you've selected a group of times, click Allow to make the server available for rendering during that time or click Disallow to prevent rendering. When you're finished, click OK to close the Server Properties dialog box and return to the Monitor dialog box.

If you have several jobs going at once but suddenly need to get one finished quickly, you can take servers off one job and put them on another. To remove a server, right-click its name in the left pane of the Monitor dialog box and choose Delete Server (Ctrl+Enter) from the pop-up menu. The icon next to the server turns black, indicating that it has been unassigned. To assign this server to another job, right-click the server name in the list of servers for the job you want to assign it to, and choose Assign to Selected Jobs.

Summary

If your goal is to spend more time modeling and less time waiting for rendering jobs to complete, then the network rendering services provided by 3ds Max can help you take a step in the right direction. After the initial complexities of setting up a rendering farm are out of the way, network rendering can be a great asset in helping you reach important deadlines, and it lets you enjoy your finished work sooner. Even if you can afford to add only one or two computers to your current setup, you'll see a tremendous increase in productivity—an increase that you can't truly appreciate until you've completed a job in a fraction of the time it used to take!

In this chapter, you accomplished the following:

- Used the Batch Render window to create a batch render queue
- Set up a network suitable for network rendering with Max
- Set up a 3ds Max rendering farm
- Used the rendering manager and servers to carry out rendering jobs
- Used the Monitor to control job priority
- Made Max notify you when problems occur or when jobs finish
- Performed batch rendering even if you don't have a network

In the next chapter, we look at the compositing options including Video Post and the various Render Elements that are available in Max.

Chapter 48

Compositing with Render Elements and the Video Post Interface

After you've completed your scene and rendered it, you're finished, right? Well, not exactly. You still have post-production to complete — that's where you work with the final rendered images to add some additional effects. This phase of production typically takes place in another package, such as Photoshop, Autodesk's Combustion, or Adobe's After Effects, and understanding how to interact with these packages can be a lifesaver when your client wants some last-minute changes (and they always do).

You can set Max to render any part in the rendering pipeline individually. These settings are called *render elements*. By rendering out just the Specular layer or just the shadow, you have more control over these elements in your compositor.

If you don't have access to a compositing package or even if you do, Max includes a simple interface that can be used to add some post-production effects. This interface is the Video Post interface.

You can use the Video Post window to composite the final rendered image with several other images and filters. These filters let you add lens effects like glows and flares, and other effects like blur and fade, to the final output. The Video Post window provides a post-processing environment within the Max interface.

> **NOTE** Many of the post-processing effects such as glows and blurs also are available as render effects, but the Video Post window is capable of much more. Render effects are covered in Chapter 45, "Using Atmospheric and Render Effects."

Using External Compositing Packages

Before delving into the Video Post interface, let's take a quick look at some of the available compositing packages. Several of these packages have direct links into Max that can be used to give you a jump on the post-production process.

Compositing with Photoshop

Perhaps the most common tool for compositing images is Photoshop. Photoshop can bring multiple images together in a single file and position them relative to one another. Working with layers makes applying simple filters and effects to the various element pieces easy.

Figure 48.1 shows Photoshop with several separate pieces, each on a different layer.

FIGURE 48.1

Photoshop is an important compositing tool for static images.

To composite images in Photoshop, you need to load all the separate images into Photoshop and then select the portions of the images that you want to combine. When saving image files in Max, be sure to include an alpha channel. You can see the alpha channel in the Rendered Frame window if you click the Display Alpha Channel button, as shown in Figure 48.2.

In Photoshop, you can see an image's alpha channel if you select the Channels panel in the Layers palette. Selecting the alpha channel and using the Magic Wand tool makes selecting the rendered object easy. After it's selected, you can copy and paste the rendered image onto your background image as a new layer.

NOTE Not all image file formats support an alpha channel. When rendering images to be composited, but sure to use an alpha channel format such as RLA, RPF, PNG, or TGA.

After all your images have been positioned on the background image, you can apply a Filter, such as a Gaussian Blur, to smooth the edges between the composite images.

FIGURE 48.2

The Rendered Frame window can display an image's alpha channel.

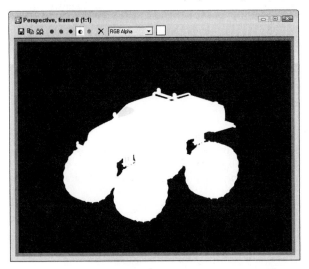

Video editing with Premiere

Photoshop works with still images, but if you work with animations, then Adobe has Premiere to help with your video editing needs. The editing that Premiere makes possible includes patching several animation clips together, adding sound, color-correcting the frames, and adding transitions between animation clips.

Within Premiere, various animation clips can be imported (or dragged directly from Windows Explorer) into the Project panel. From here, the clips can be dropped onto the Timeline in the desired order. The Monitor panel shows the current animation or individual animation clips.

Sound clips can be dropped in the Timeline in the Audio track. The Title menu also can be used to add text to the animation. Another common activity in Premiere is to add transition effects between clips. This is done by clicking the Effects tab in the Project panel, selecting a transition effect, dragging the effect to the Timeline, and dropping it between two animation clips.

When the entire sequence is completed, you can render it using the Sequence ➪ Render Work Area menu command. The completed animation file then can be saved using the File ➪ Export menu command.

Tutorial: Creating a montage of Space Warp animations

In this example, we combine several animations into a single animation sequence.

To create a montage of several animations using Premiere, follow these steps:

1. Open Premiere, and drag the Space Warp animations from the Chap 48 directory on the DVD to the Project panel.
2. Select all five animation clips, and drag them to the Video 1 row in the Timeline panel. Select Sequence ➪ Zoom In four times to space the animations out in the Timeline panel so they are visible.
3. If you want to change the order of the animation clips, just drag them to the desired position in the Timeline panel. Make sure that they run consecutively.

4. Click the Effects tab in the Project panel, and open the Video Transitions folder. Select one of the transition effects, and drag it from the Project panel to the Timeline panel. You can drop a different effect where each animation clip meets its neighbor.

5. Click the Play button in the Monitor panel to see the resulting animation sequence. If you're comfortable with it, select Sequence ➪ Render Work Area to render the final sequence.

6. When the rendering completes, save the animation using the File ➪ Export ➪ Movie menu command.

Figure 48.3 shows the Premiere interface with the animation clips loaded and positioned in the Timeline panel.

Video compositing with After Effects

If you need to add a little more to your animations than just transitions, you should look into Adobe's After Effects. After Effects lets you composite 2D and 3D clips into a single image or animation. You can paint directly on the animation frames, add lights and cameras, and create visual effects such as Distort, Shatter, and Warp.

After Effects includes a library of resources much like those found in Premiere. These resources can be positioned on a Composition pane. Effects applied to the loaded animation clip are listed in the Effects panel along with all the effects settings.

FIGURE 48.3

Premiere can be used to combine several animation sequences together.

After Effects includes many of the same tools used in Photoshop and Illustrator. These tools let you paint and select portions of the animation clip as if it were a still image, but the results can be added or removed over time.

Tutorial: Adding animation effects using After Effects

Some effects are much easier to add using a package like After Effects than to create in Max. A good example is adding a blurry look and the waves coming from a heat source to the melting snowman animation created in Chapter 21.

To add video effects using After Effects, follow these steps:

1. Open After Effects, and drag the Melting snowman.avi file from the Chap 48 directory to the Project panel.

2. Select Composition ⇨ New Composition, select the NTSC, 640 × 480 option from the Preset list, and click OK.

3. Drag the Melting snowman.avi file from the Project panel, and drop it on the Composition pane.

4. With the animation selected in the Composition pane, select Effect ⇨ Distort ⇨ Wave Warp. The Wave Warp effect appears in a panel. Set the Wave Height to **4**, the Wave Width to **30**, the Direction to Vertical, and the Wave Speed to **1**. This adds a heat wave effect to the entire animation.

5. Select Effect ⇨ Blur & Sharpen ⇨ Gaussian Blur, and set the Blurriness value to **3.0**.

6. In the Timeline panel, drag the Work Area End icon so that it coincides with the end of the animation.

7. Select Composition ⇨ Make Movie. In the Render Queue dialog box that opens, click the Render button to render the animation with its effects.

Figure 48.4 shows the After Effects interface with the animation clip loaded.

Introducing Combustion

Autodesk offers an end-to-end solution for production houses to complete their work; on the receiving end of Max is a product called Combustion. Combustion is a different animal from Max, but its array of weapons is just as deadly in a slightly different arena. The biggest difference between Combustion and Photoshop is that Combustion can handle animations and Photoshop can work only with static images.

Combustion enables motion graphics, compositing, and visual effects, which doesn't sound too different from what Max does, except for that funny word — compositing. If you think of the final rendered image produced using Max as just an image that needs to be combined with other elements such as text, logos, other images, or even a DVD menu, then you're starting to see what post-production teams know. Compositing is the process of combining several different elements into a finished product. Positioning these elements can even be done in 3D by placing images behind or in front of other images or in time by working with animations.

But wait, you say; this is a book about Max, not about Combustion. Yes, but Combustion is integrated with Max very nicely, and that is what I want to show. Several key integration points include Combustion maps and Render Elements.

Using Combustion maps

If you apply a Combustion type map to the Diffuse map channel of a material, then the Combustion Parameters rollout, shown in Figure 48.5, appears. Clicking the Edit button in the rollout actually opens Combustion and lets you create a new workspace.

FIGURE 48.4

After Effects can add special effects to an animation sequence.

FIGURE 48.5

Combustion maps work between Max and Combustion.

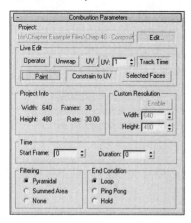

If you select a Paint type workspace, then you can paint right on the composite object in Combustion, and the painted map shows up in Max. Figure 48.6 shows a simple spiral shape painted in Combustion using its tools. Figure 48.7 shows a magnified sample slot in Max that has the same painted shape.

FIGURE 48.6

Combustion maps painted in Combustion show up in Max.

FIGURE 48.7

Shapes that are painted in Combustion show up in Max.

The Live Edit section of the Combustion Parameters rollout includes features that you can access from Combustion. The Operator button lets you select and update an operator from Combustion to apply to the texture map. The Unwrap button shows an unwrapped mesh in Combustion, allowing you to easily paint precisely. The Paint button lets you paint directly in the viewports using Combustion's Paint tools, and the Filtering options let you specify the type of anti-aliasing to use.

Using Render Elements with Combustion

At the bottom of the Render Elements rollout found in the Render Elements panel of the Render Scene dialog box is an option to Output to Combustion. If this option is Enabled, then you can specify a filename for the Combustion files that are generated, and the Render button actually creates the Render Elements and saves them in a Combustion Workspace (.CWS) file.

Using other compositing solutions

In addition to the packages mentioned here, several other compositing solutions are available. Another popular compositing package is Digital Fusion. Most of these products are similar enough, but look through the feature set before buying a solution to make sure that it meets your needs.

Using Render Elements

If your production group includes a strong post-processing team that does compositing, then there may be times when you just want to render certain elements of the scene, such as the alpha information or a specific atmospheric effect. Applying individual elements to a composite image gives you better control over the elements. For example, you can reposition or lighten a shadow without having to re-render the entire scene.

Using the Render Elements rollout of the Render Scene dialog box, shown in Figure 48.8, you can render a single effect and save it as an image.

You can select and render several render elements at the same time. The available render elements include Alpha, Atmosphere, Background, Blend, Diffuse, Hair and Fur, Illuminance HDR Data, Ink, Lighting, Luminance HDR Data, Material ID, Matte, Object ID, Paint, Reflection, Refraction, Self-Illumination, Shadow, Specular, Velocity, and Z Depth.

The Render Elements rollout can render several elements at once. The Add button opens the Render Elements dialog box, where you can select the elements to include. The Merge button lets you merge the elements from another Max scene, and the Delete button lets you delete elements from the list. To be included in the rendered image, the Elements Active option must be checked. The Display Elements option causes the results to be rendered separately and displayed in the Rendered Frame Window.

The Enable check box can turn off individual elements; Enable Filtering enables the anti-aliasing filtering as specified in the Max Default Scanline A-Buffer rollout. A separate Rendered Frame Window is opened for each render element that is enabled.

Clicking the Browse button opens a file dialog box where you can give the rendered element a name. Max automatically appends an underscore and the name of the element on the end of the filename. For example, if you name the file **myScene** and select to render the Alpha element, the filename for this element is **myScene_alpha**.

FIGURE 48.8

You can use the Render Elements rollout to render specific effects.

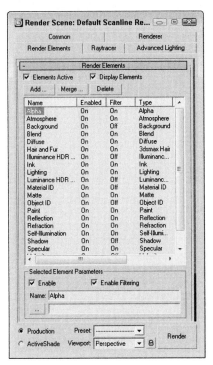

When you select the Blend and Z Depth render elements, an additional rollout of parameters appears. You can use the Blend render element to combine several separate elements together. The Blend Element Parameters rollout includes check boxes for each render element type. The Z Depth render element includes parameters for setting Min and Max depth values.

Figure 48.9 shows the resulting image in the Rendered Frame Window for the Alpha render element.

The Render Elements rollout can also output files that Autodesk's Combustion product can use. These files have the .CWS extension. Combustion is a compositing product that can work with individual elements to increase the highlights, change color hues, darken and blur shadows, and do many other things without having to re-render the scene.

FIGURE 48.9

The Alpha render element shown in the Rendered Frame Window

Completing Post-Production with the Video Post Interface

Post-production is the work that comes after the scene is rendered. It is the time when you add effects, such as glows and highlights, as well as add transitional effects to an animation. For example, if you want to include a logo in the lower-right corner of your animation, you can create and render the logo and composite several rendered images into one during post-production.

Video Post interface is the post-processing interface within Max that you can use to combine the current scene with different images, effects, and image processing filters. Compositing is the process of combining several different images into a single image. Each element of the composite is included as a separate event. These events are lined up in a queue and processed in the order in which they appear in the queue. The queue can also include looping events.

The Video Post interface, like the Render Scene dialog box (covered in Chapter 22, "Learning to Render a Scene"), provides another way to produce final output. You can think of the Video Post process as an artistic assembly line. As the image moves down the line, each item in the queue adds an image, drops a rendered image on the stack, or applies a filter effect. This process continues until the final output event is reached.

The Video Post interface, shown in Figure 48.10, includes a toolbar, a pane of events and ranges, and a status bar. You can open it by choosing Rendering ➪ Video Post.

In many ways, the Video Post interface is similar to the Track View interfaces. Each event is displayed as a track in the Queue pane to the left. To the right is the Range pane where the range for each track is displayed as lines with square boxes at each end. You can edit these ranges by dragging the squares on either end. The time bar, above the Range pane, displays the frames for the current sequence, and the status bar at the bottom of the interface includes information and view buttons.

FIGURE 48.10

The Video Post interface lets you composite images with your final rendering.

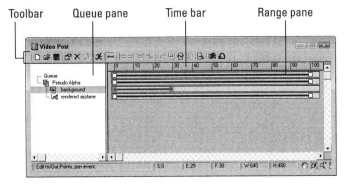

Toolbar   Queue pane   Time bar   Range pane

The Video Post toolbar

At the top of the Video Post interface is a toolbar with several buttons for managing the Video Post features. Table 48.1 shows and explains these buttons.

TABLE 48.1

Video Post Toolbar Buttons

Toolbar Button	Name	Description
	New Sequence	Creates a new sequence
	Open Sequence	Opens an existing sequence
	Save Sequence	Saves the current sequence
	Edit Current Event	Opens the Edit Current Event dialog box where you can edit events
	Delete Current Event	Removes the current event from the sequence
	Swap Events	Changes the position in the queue of two selected events
	Execute Sequence	Runs the current sequence
	Edit Range Bar	Enables you to edit the event ranges
	Align Selected Left	Aligns the left ranges of the selected events

continued

TABLE 48.1 *(continued)*

Toolbar Button	Name	Description
	Align Selected Right	Aligns the right ranges of the selected events
	Make Selected Same Size	Makes the ranges for the selected events the same size
	Abut Selected	Places event ranges end-to-end
	Add Scene Event	Adds a rendered scene to the queue
	Add Image Input Event	Adds an image to the queue
	Add Image Filter Event	Adds an image filter to the queue
	Add Image Layer Event	Adds a compositing plug-in to the queue when two events are selected
	Add Image Output Event	Sends the final composited image to a file or device
	Add External Event	Adds an external image-processing event to the queue
	Add Loop Event	Causes other events to loop

The Video Post Queue and Range panes

Below the toolbar are the Video Post Queue and Range panes. The Queue pane is on the left; it lists all the events to be included in the post-processing sequence in the order in which they are processed. You can rearrange the order of the events by dragging an event in the queue to its new location.

You can select multiple events by holding down the Ctrl key and clicking the event names, or you can select one event, hold down the Shift key, and click another event to select all events between the two.

Each event has a corresponding range that appears in the Range pane to the right. Each range is shown as a line with a square on each end. The left square marks the first frame of the event, and the right square marks the last frame of the event. You can expand or contract these ranges by dragging the square on either end of the range line.

If you click the line between two squares, you can drag the entire range. If you drag a range beyond the given number of frames, then additional frames are added.

The time bar is at the top of the Range pane. This bar shows the number of total frames included in the animation. You can also slide the time bar up or down to move it closer to a specific track by dragging it.

The Video Post status bar

The status bar includes a prompt line, several value fields, and some navigation buttons. The fields to the right of the prompt line include Start, End, Current Frames, and the Width and Height of the image. The navigation buttons include (in order from left to right) Pan, Zoom Extents, Zoom Time, and Zoom Region.

Working with Sequences

All the events that are added to the Queue pane make up a *sequence*. You can save these sequences and open them at a later time. The Execute Sequence button (Ctrl+R), found on the toolbar, starts the compositing process.

To save a sequence, click the Save button on the toolbar to open the Save Sequence dialog box, where you can save the queue sequence. Sequences are saved along with the Max file when the scene is saved, but they can also be saved independently of the scene. By default, these files are saved with the .VPX extension in the vpost directory.

 Saving a sequence as a VPX file maintains the elements of the queue, but it resets all parameter settings. Saving the file as a Max file maintains the queue order along with the parameter settings.

You can open saved sequences using the Open Sequence button on the toolbar. When a saved sequence is opened, all the current events are deleted. Clicking the New Sequence button also deletes any current events.

The Execute Sequence toolbar button opens the Execute Video Post interface, shown in Figure 48.11. The controls in this dialog box work exactly the way those in the Render Scene dialog box work.

 The time and resolution settings in the Execute Video Post dialog box are unique from those in the Render Scene dialog box.

FIGURE 48.11

The Execute Video Post interface includes the controls for producing the queue output.

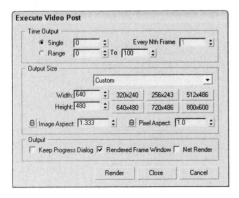

The Time Output section enables you to specify which frames to render, and the Output Size section lets you specify the size of the output. The Custom selection lets you enter Width and Height values, or you can use one of the presets in the drop-down list or one of the preset resolution buttons. This dialog box also includes controls for entering the Image Aspect and Pixel Aspect ratios.

The Output options let you select to keep the Progress dialog box open, to render to the Rendered Frame Window, and/or to use network rendering. When you're ready to render the queue, click the Render button.

Adding and Editing Events

The seven event types that you can add to the queue are Image Input, Scene, Image Filter, Image Layer, Loop, External, and Image Output. If no events are selected, then adding an event positions the event at the bottom of the list. If an event is selected, the added event becomes a sub-event under the selected event.

Every event dialog box, such as the Add Image Input Event dialog box shown in Figure 48.12, includes a Label field where you can name the event. This name shows up in the queue window and is used to identify the event.

FIGURE 48.12

The Add Image Input Event dialog box lets you load an image to add to the queue.

Each event dialog box includes a Video Post Parameters section. This section contains VP Start Time and VP End Time values for defining precisely the length of the Video Post range. It also includes an Enabled option for enabling or disabling an event. Disabled events are grayed out in the queue.

To edit an event, you simply need to double-click its name in the Queue pane (or press Ctrl+E) to open an Edit Event dialog box.

Adding an image input event

The Add Image Input Event dialog box lets you add a simple image to the queue. For example, you can add a background image using this dialog box rather than the Environment dialog box. To open the Add Image Input Event dialog box, click the Add Image Input Event button (Ctrl+I) on the toolbar.

 If you don't name the image event, then the filename appears in the Queue pane as the name for the event.

The Files button in this dialog box opens the Select Image File for Video Post Input dialog box where you can locate an image file to load from the hard disk or network. Supported image types include AVI, BMP, MPEG, Kodak Cineon, Combustion, FLC, GIF, IFL, JPEG, PIC, PNG, PSD, MOV, SGI Image, RLA, RPF, TGA, TIF, and YUV. The Devices button lets you access an external device such as a video recorder. The Options button becomes enabled when you load an image. The Cache option causes the image to be loaded into memory, which can speed up the Video Post process by not requiring the image to be loaded for every frame.

The Image Driver section of the Add Image Input Event dialog box lets you specify the settings for the image driver, such as the compression settings for an AVI file. Clicking the Setup button opens a dialog box of options available for the selected format, but note that the Setup button is not active for all formats.

The Image Input Options dialog box, shown in Figure 48.13, lets you set the alignment, size, and frames where the image appears. The Alignment section of the Image Input Options dialog box includes nine presets for aligning the image. Preset options include top-left corner, top centered, top-right corner, left centered, centered, right centered, bottom-left corner, bottom centered, and bottom-right corner. You can also use the Coordinates option to specify in pixels the image's upper-left corner.

FIGURE 48.13

The Image Input Options dialog box lets you align and set the size of the image.

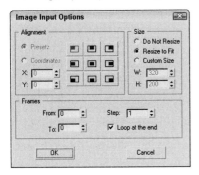

In the Size section of this dialog box, you can control the size of the image, using the Do Not Resize, Resize to Fit, or Custom Size options. The Custom Size option lets you enter Width and Height values.

The Frames section applies only to animation files. The From and To values define which frames of the animation to play. The Step value lets you play every nth frame as specified. The Loop at the End value causes the animation to loop back to the beginning when finished.

Adding scene events

A scene event is the rendered scene that you've built in Max. When you click the Add Scene Event button on the toolbar, the Add Scene Event dialog box shown in Figure 48.14 opens. This dialog box lets you specify the scene ranges and define the render options.

Below the Label field where you can name the event is a drop-down list that lets you select which viewport to use to render your scene. The active viewport is selected by default. The Render Options button opens the Render Scene panel, except the Render button has been replaced with OK and Cancel buttons because the rendering is initiated with the Execute Sequence button.

CROSS-REF For more information about the Render Scene panel, see Chapter 22, "Learning to Render a Scene."

The Scene Options section of the Add Scene Event dialog box also includes an option for enabling Scene Motion Blur. This motion blur type is different from the object motion blur that is set in the Object Properties dialog box. Scene motion blur is applied to the entire image and is useful for blurring objects that are moving fast. The Duration (frames) value sets how long the blur effect is computed per frame. The Duration Subdivisions value is how many computations are done for each duration. The Dither % value sets the amount of dithering to use for blurred sections.

FIGURE 48.14

The Add Scene Event dialog box lets you specify which viewport to use to render your scene.

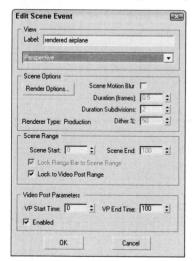

CROSS-REF You can find more information on object motion blur in Chapter 6, "Selecting Objects, Setting Object Properties, and Using Layers and Scene Explorer."

In the Scene Range section, the Scene Start and Scene End values let you define the range for the rendered scene. The Lock Range Bar to Scene Range option maintains the range length as defined in the Time Slider, though you can still reposition the start of the rendered scene. The Lock to Video Post Range option sets the range equal to the Video Post range.

Adding image filter events

The Add Image Filter Event button (Ctrl+F) on the toolbar opens the Add Image Filter Event dialog box, shown in Figure 48.15, where you can select from many filter types. The available filters are included in a drop-down list under the Label field.

Below the filter drop-down list are two buttons: About and Setup. The About button gives some details about the creator of the filter. The Setup button opens a separate dialog box that controls the filter. The dialog box that appears depends on the type of filter that you selected in the drop-down list.

Several filters require a mask such as the Image Alpha filter. To open a bitmap image to use as the mask, click the Files button in the Mask section and select the file in the Select Mask Image dialog box that opens. A drop-down list lets you select the channel to use. Possible channels include Red, Green, Blue, Alpha, Luminance, Z Buffer, Material Effects, and Object. The mask can be Enabled or Inverted. The Options button opens the Image Input Options dialog box for aligning and sizing the mask.

NOTE Several Lens Effects filters are also included in the drop-down list. These filters use an advanced dialog box with many options, which is covered in the "Working with Lens Effect Filters" section later in the chapter.

FIGURE 48.15

The Add Image Filter Event dialog box lets you select from many filter types.

Contrast filter

You use the Contrast filter to adjust the brightness and contrast. Selecting this filter and clicking the Setup button opens the Image Contrast Control dialog box. This simple dialog box includes values for Contrast and Brightness. Both values can be set from 0 to 1. The Absolute option computes the center gray value based on the highest color value. The Derived option uses an average value of the components of all three colors (red, green, and blue).

Fade filter

You can use the Fade filter to fade out the image over time. You can select it from the drop-down list. Clicking the Setup button opens the Fade Image Control dialog box where you select to fade either In or Out. The fade takes place over the length of the range set in the Range pane.

Image Alpha filter

The Image Alpha filter sets the alpha channel as specified by the mask. This filter doesn't have a setup dialog box.

Negative filter

The Negative filter inverts all the colors, as in the negative of a photograph. The Negative Filter dialog box includes a simple Blend value.

Pseudo Alpha filter

The Pseudo Alpha filter sets the alpha channel based on the pixel located in the upper-left corner of the image. This filter can make an unrendered background transparent. When this filter is selected, the Setup button is disabled because it doesn't have a setup dialog box.

Simple Wipe filter

The Simple Wipe filter removes the image by replacing it with a black background. The length of the wipe is determined by the event's time range. The Simple Wipe Control dialog box, shown in Figure 48.16, lets you wipe from the left to the right or from the right to the left. You can also set the mode to Push, which displays the image, or to Pop, which erases it.

FIGURE 48.16

The Simple Wipe Control dialog box lets you select which direction to wipe the image.

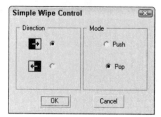

Starfield filter

The Starfield filter creates a starfield image. By using a camera, you can motion blur the stars. The Stars Control dialog box, shown in Figure 48.17, includes a Source Camera drop-down list that you can use to select a camera.

FIGURE 48.17

The Stars Control dialog box lets you load a custom database of stars.

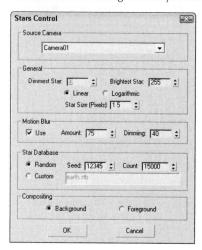

The General section sets the brightness and size of the stars. You can specify brightness values for the Dimmest Star and the Brightest Star. The Linear and Logarithmic options use two different algorithms to compute the brightness values of the stars as a function of distance. The Star Size value sets the size of the stars in pixels. Size values can range from 0.001 to 100.

The Motion Blur settings let you enable motion blurring, set the blur Amount, and specify a Dimming value.

The Star Database section includes settings for defining how the stars are to appear. The Random option displays stars based on the Count value, and the random Seed determines the randomness of the star's positions. The Custom option reads a star database specified in the Database field.

 Max includes a starfield database named earth.stb that includes the stars as seen from Earth.

You can also specify whether the stars are composited in the background or foreground.

Tutorial: Creating space backdrops

Space backgrounds are popular backdrops, and Max includes a special Video Post filter for creating starfield backgrounds. You would typically want to use the Video Post interface to render the starfield along with any animation that you've created, but in this tutorial, we render a starfield for a single planet that we've created and outfitted with a planet material.

To create a starfield background, follow these steps:

1. Open the Planet with starfield background.max file from the Chap 48 directory on the DVD.

   This file includes a simple space scene with a camera because the Starfield filter requires a camera.

2. Choose Rendering ⇨ Video Post to open the Video Post interface. A Scene Event must be added to the queue in order for the render job to be executed. Click the Add Scene Event button, type **planet scene** in the Label field, and click OK.

   This adds the event to the Queue pane.

3. Click the Add Image Filter Event button (or press Ctrl+F) to open the Add Image Filter Event dialog box, and in the Label field, type the name **starfield bg**. Select Starfield from the drop-down list, and click the Setup button to open the Stars Control dialog box. Select Camera01 as the Source Camera, set the Star Size to **3.0** and the Count to **150,000**, and click OK. Click OK again to exit the Add Image Filter Event dialog box and add this event to the Queue pane.

4. Click the Execute Sequence button (or press Ctrl+R), select the Single output time option and an Output Size, and click the Render button.

Figure 48.18 shows the resulting space scene.

Adding image layer events

In addition to the standard filters that can be applied to a single image, several more filters, called *layer events,* can be applied to two or more images or rendered scenes. The Add Layer Event button (Ctrl+L) is available on the toolbar only when two image events are selected in the Queue pane. The first image (which is the selected image highest in the queue) becomes the source image, and the second image is the compositor. Both image events become sub-events under the layer event.

 If the layer event is deleted, the two sub-event images remain.

The dialog box for the Add Image Layer Event is the same as the Add Image Filter Event dialog box shown earlier except that the drop-down list includes filters that work with two images.

FIGURE 48.18

A space scene with a background, compliments of the Video Post interface

Adobe Premiere Transition filter

When it comes to transitions, Adobe Premiere already has created so many cool transitions that it makes sense to just use theirs. In Max, you can access these filters through the Adobe Premiere Transition Filter Setup dialog box.

This dialog box includes an Add path button to tell Max where to look for filters. All available filters are displayed in the Filter Selection list. You can access the filter interface with the Custom Parameters button. The two preview windows to the right display the filter effects. You also have options to Swap Input (which switches the source image) and Use Stand-In (which lets you specify a sample image to preview the effect).

Simple Wipe compositor

The Simple Wipe compositor is similar to the Simple Wipe filter, except that it slides the image in or out instead of erasing it. Its setup dialog box looks just like that of the Simple Wipe Control dialog box.

Other layer filters

The remaining layer filters include simple methods for compositing images and some simple transitions. None of these other filters has a Setup dialog box.

You can use the Alpha compositor to composite two images, using the alpha channel of the foreground image. The Cross Fade Transition compositor fades one image out as it fades another image in. You can use the Pseudo Alpha compositor to combine two images if one doesn't have an alpha channel. This compositor uses the upper-left pixel to designate the transparent color for the image. The Simple Additive Compositor combines two images based on the intensity of the second image.

Adding external events

The Add External Event button on the toolbar lets you use an external image-processing program to edit the image. This button is available only when an image event is selected and the image event becomes a sub-event under the external event. The Add External Event dialog box, shown in Figure 48.19, includes a Browse button for locating the external program. It also includes a Command Line Options field for entering text commands for the external program. Many external programs use the clipboard to do their processing, so the Write image to clipboard and Read image from clipboard options make this possible.

FIGURE 48.19

The Add External Event dialog box lets you access an external program to edit images.

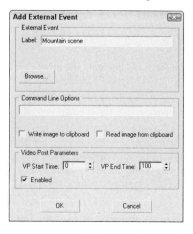

Using loop events

The Add Loop Event button is enabled on the Video Post toolbar when any single event is selected. This button enables an event to be repeated a specified number of times or throughout the Video Post range. The Add Loop Event dialog box, shown in Figure 48.20, includes a value field for the Number of Times to repeat the event, along with Loop and Ping Pong options. The Loop option repeats from beginning to end until the Number of Times value is reached. The Ping Pong option alternates playing the event forward and in reverse. You can name Loop events using the Label field.

Adding an image output event

If you've added all the events you need and configured them correctly, and you click the Execute Sequence button and nothing happens, then chances are good that you've forgotten to add an Image Output event. This event adds the surface that all the events use to output to and should appear last in the queue.

The Add Image Output Event dialog box (Ctrl+O) looks the same as the Add Image Input Event dialog box shown earlier. The output can be saved to a file or to a device using any of the standard file types.

FIGURE 48.20

The Add Loop Event dialog box lets you play an event numerous times.

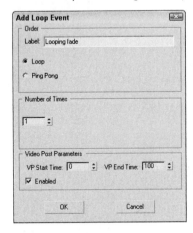

 If you don't give the output event a name, the filename automatically becomes the event name.

Working with Ranges

The Range pane in the Video Post interface is found to the right of the Queue pane. It displays the ranges for each event. These turn red when selected. The beginning and end points of the range are marked with squares. You can move these points by dragging the squares. This moves the beginning and end points for all selected events.

 Before you can move the ranges or drag the end points of a range, you need to select the Edit Range Bar button from the toolbar. The button is highlighted yellow when active.

When two or more events are selected, several additional buttons on the toolbar become enabled, including Swap Events, Align Selected Left, Align Selected Right, Make Selected Same Size, and Abut Selected. (These buttons were shown earlier in Table 48.1.)

The Swap Events button is enabled only if two events are selected. When clicked, it changes the position of the two events. Because the order of the events is important, this can alter the final output.

The Align Selected Left and Align Selected Right buttons move the beginning or end points of every selected track until they line up with the first or last points of the top selected event.

The Make Selected Same Size button resizes any bottom events to be the same size as the top selected event. The Abut Selected button moves each selected event under the top event until its first point lines up with the last point of the selected event above it.

Figure 48.21 shows four image events that have been placed end-to-end using the Abut Selected button. Notice that the queue range spans the entire distance.

You can use the Abut Selected button to position several events end-to-end.

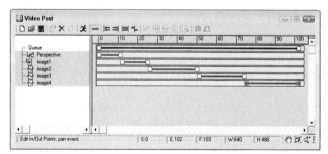

Working with Lens Effects Filters

The Add Image Filter Event dialog box's drop-down list has several Lens Effects filters. These filters include Lens Effects Flare, Focus, Glow, and Highlight. Each of these filters is displayed and discussed in the sections that follow, but several parameters are common to all of them.

Many lens effects parameters in the various Lens Effects setup dialog boxes can be animated such as Size, Hue, Angle, and Intensity. These are identified in the dialog boxes by green arrow buttons to the right of the parameter fields. These buttons work the way the Animate button in the main interface works. To animate a parameter, just click the corresponding arrow button, move the Time Slider to a new frame, and change the parameter. Figure 48.22 shows how these buttons look in the Lens Effects Flare dialog box.

Green arrow buttons in the Lens Effects Flare dialog box identify the parameters that can be animated for this effect.

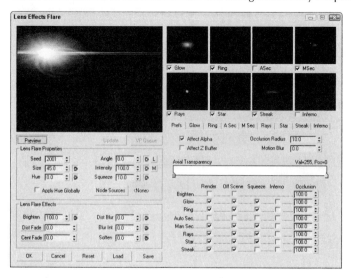

Each Lens Effects dialog box also includes a preview pane in the upper-left corner with three buttons underneath. Clicking the Preview button renders all enabled lens effects in the preview pane. The VP Queue button renders the current Video Post queue. Using the preview pane, you can get an idea of how the final output should look. With the Preview button enabled, any parameter changes in the dialog box are automatically updated in the preview pane. The Update button enables you to manually update the preview. You can right-click the Preview pane to change its resolution for faster updates at lower resolutions.

TIP   If the VP Queue button is enabled, then a default Lens Effects image is displayed. Using this image, you can play around with the various settings while the Preview mode is enabled to gain an idea of what the various settings do.

You can save the settings in each Lens Effect dialog box as a separate file that can be recalled at any time. These saved files have an .LZF extension and can be saved and loaded with the Save and Load buttons at the bottom left of the dialog box.

Adding flares

The Lens Effects Flare dialog box includes controls for adding flares of various types to an image. This dialog box includes a main preview pane and several smaller preview panes for each individual effect. The check boxes below these smaller preview panes let you enable or disable these smaller panes.

Under the main preview pane are several global commands, and to their right is a series of tabbed panels that contain the settings for each individual effect type. The first panel is labeled Prefs and sets which effects are rendered (on and off scene), which are squeezed, which have the Inferno noise filter applied, and which have an Occlusion setting.

The settings for the individual flare types are included in the subsequent tabbed panels. They include Glow, Ring, A Sec, M Sec, Rays, Star, Streak, and Inferno. These tabbed panels include gradient color bars for defining the Radial Color, Radial Transparency, Circular Color, Circular Transparency, and Radial Size. Each of these tabbed panels has different settings, but Figure 48.23 shows the tabbed panels for the Glow and Ring effects.

FIGURE 48.23

The Glow and Ring tabbed panels are representative of all the different lens effect settings.

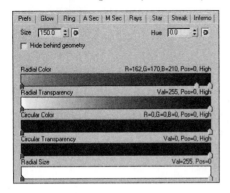
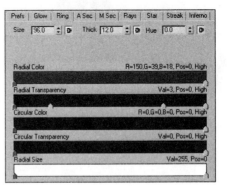

The gradient colors found in these tabbed panels are controlled by flags that appear under the gradient band. Double-clicking a flag opens a Color Selector dialog box where you can select a new color. Dragging these flags moves the gradient color. You can add a new flag to the band by clicking under the gradient away from the existing flags. The active flag is colored green. To delete flags, select them and press the Delete key. By right-clicking the gradient band, you can access a pop-up menu of options that let you access several options for the selected gradient color. You can even load and save gradients. Gradients are saved as files with the .DGR extension.

The rightmost tabbed panel, shown in Figure 48.24, is labeled Inferno and provides a way to add noise to any of the effects. The Prefs tabbed panel includes a check box for enabling the Inferno settings for each effect. Inferno noise can be set to three different states: Gaseous, Fiery, and Electric. If your effect is looking too perfect, you can add some randomness to it with the Inferno option.

FIGURE 48.24

The Inferno tabbed panel includes options for enabling noise for the various flare effects.

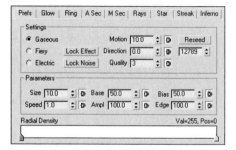

Adding focus

The Lens Effects Focus dialog box, shown in Figure 48.25, includes options for adding Scene Blur, Radial Blur, and Focal Node effects. If you click the Select button, the Select Focal Object dialog box opens and lets you choose an object to act as the focal point for the scene.

You can also set values for the Horizontal Focal Loss and Vertical Focal Loss or enable the Lock button to lock these two parameters together. The Focal Range and Focal Limit values determine the distance from the focal point where the blurring begins or reaches full strength. You can also set the blurring to affect the Alpha channel.

Adding glow

The Lens Effects Glow dialog box, shown in Figure 48.26, enables you to apply glows to the entire scene or to specific objects based on the Object ID or Effects ID. Other Source options include Unclamped, Surf Norm (Surface Normals), Mask, Alpha, Z High, and Z Lo. This dialog box also enables you to filter the glow using options such as Edge, Perimeter Alpha, Perimeter, Bright, and Hue.

Additional tabbed panels under the preview pane let you control the Preferences, Gradients, and Inferno settings. In the Preferences tabbed panel, you can set the color of the glow to be based on the Gradient tabbed panel–defined gradients, based on Pixel or a User-defined color. You can also set the Intensity in the Preference tabbed panel.

FIGURE 48.25

You can use the Lens Effects Focus dialog box to blur an image.

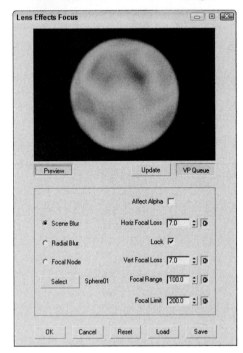

Adding highlights

The Lens Effects Highlight dialog box, shown in Figure 48.27, includes the same Properties, Preferences, and Gradient tabbed panels as the Glow dialog box, except that the effects it produces are highlights instead of glows. The Geometry tabbed panel includes options for setting the Size and Angle of the highlights and how they rotate away from the highlighted object.

Tutorial: Making a halo shine

When it comes to glowing objects, I think of radioactive materials, celestial objects like comets and meteors, and heavenly objects like angels. In this tutorial, I'm leaning toward heaven in an attempt to create some glory. But because I couldn't locate an angel, we use a simple halo.

To add highlights to a halo using the Video Post interface, follow these steps:

1. Open the Glowing halo.max file from the Chap 48 directory on the DVD.

    This file contains a head model and a halo. The halo object has been set to the G-Buffer Object Channel of 1 in its Object Properties dialog box.

2. Choose Rendering ➪ Video Post to open the Video Post interface. Click the Add Scene Event button on the toolbar.

    The Add Scene Event dialog box appears.

FIGURE 48.26

Use the Lens Effects Glow dialog box to make objects and scenes glow.

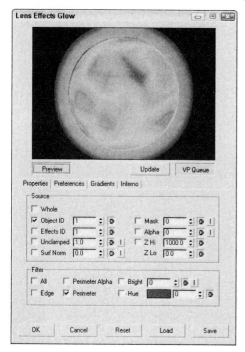

3. Type a name for the event in the Label text field, and click OK.

   The event is added to the Queue pane.

4. Select the halo object in the viewport and click the Add Image Filter Event button on the toolbar (or press Ctrl+F) to open the associated dialog box. Select Lens Effects Highlight from the drop-down list, and click the Setup button.

   The Lens Effects Highlight dialog box appears.

5. Click the VP Queue button followed by the Preview button to see the rendered scene. In the Properties tabbed panel, select the Object ID option and set the Object ID to 1 to match the G-Buffer channel for the halo object. In the Filter section, enable the All option. In the Preferences tabbed panel, set the Size to **3.0**, Points to **4**, the Color option to Pixel, and Intensity to **100**. Then click OK.

6. Click the Execute Sequence button on the toolbar (or press Ctrl+R), and then click Render in the Execute Video Post dialog box.

Figure 48.28 shows the completed halo in all its shining glory.

FIGURE 48.27

Use the Lens Effects Highlight dialog box to add highlights to scene objects.

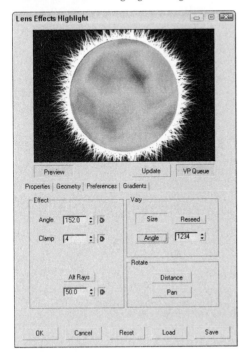

FIGURE 48.28

Using the Lens Effects Highlight dialog box, you can add shining highlights to objects like this halo.

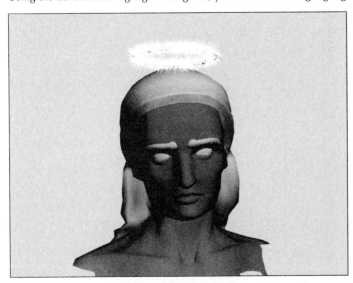

Adding backgrounds and filters using Video Post

As an example of the Video Post interface in action, we composite a background image of a waterfall with a rendered scene of an airplane model created by Viewpoint Datalabs. We then add some filter effects.

To composite an image with the Video Post interface, follow these steps:

1. Open the Airplane over waterfall.max file from the Chap 48 directory on the DVD.

   This file includes an airplane model. The directory also includes an image called waterfall.tif that is used later.

2. Open the Video Post interface by choosing Rendering ➪ Video Post.

3. Add a background image to the queue by clicking the Add Image Input Event button (or press Ctrl+I). Click the Files button. Locate the waterfall.tif image from the Chap 48 directory on the DVD, and click OK. Then click OK again to exit the Add Image Input Event dialog box.

4. Next add the rendered image by clicking the Add Scene Event button and selecting the Perspective view. Name the event **rendered airplane**. Click the Render Options button to open the Render Scene panel and select the Renderer panel. Disable the Anti-Aliasing option in the MAX Default Scanline Renderer rollout in the Renderer panel, and click OK. Click OK again to exit the Edit Scene Event dialog box.

5. Select both the background (waterfall.tif) and rendered airplane (Perspective) events, and click the Add Image Layer Event button (or press Ctrl+L). Select the Alpha Compositor option, and click OK.

   This composites the background image and the rendered image together by removing all the green background from the rendered scene.

6. To run the processing, click the Execute Sequence button on the toolbar (or press Ctrl+R) to open the Execute Video Post interface, select the Single output range option, click the 640 × 480 size button, and click Render.

Figure 48.29 shows the final composited image.

FIGURE 48.29

The airplane in this image is rendered, and the background is composited.

Summary

Post-production is an important, often overlooked, part of the production pipeline. Using compositing packages, as simple as Photoshop and Premiere or as advanced as Combustion and After Effects, enables you to make necessary edits after rendering.

Max's render elements enable you to pick apart the rendering details of your scene. Rendering using render elements allows you to have more control over individual scene elements in the compositing tool.

Using the Video Post interface, you can composite several images, filters, and effects together. All these compositing elements are listed as events in a queue. The Video Post interface provides, along with the Render Scene dialog box, another way to create output. In this chapter, you learned about the following:

- The post-production process
- How Photoshop can be used to composite images
- How Premiere and After Effects can be used to composite animations
- The Combustion interface
- How to use render elements
- The Video Post interface
- How to work with sequences
- The various filter types
- How to add and edit events and manipulate their ranges
- The Lens Effects filters

This concludes the Advanced Lighting and Rendering part of the book. The next part, "MAXScript and Plug-Ins," presents ways to extend the functionality of Max using MAXScript and plug-ins. You'll have the means to extend the software even further so the party never ends.

Part XII

MAXScript and Plug-Ins

Chapter 49

Automating with MAXScript

The Max designers went to great lengths to make sure that you are limited only by your imagination in terms of what you can do in Max. They've packed in so many different features and so many different ways to use those features that you could use Max for years and still learn new ways of doing things.

Despite Max's wide range of capabilities, there may come a time when you wish for a new Max feature. With MAXScript, you can actually extend Max to meet your needs, customize it to work the way you want, and even have it do some of the more monotonous tasks for you.

What Is MAXScript?

In this chapter, we look at MAXScript — what it's for and why in the world you would ever want to use it. But before we get into the nitty-gritty details, let's start with a brief overview.

Simply put, MAXScript is a tool that you can use to expand the functionality of Max. You can use it to add new features or to customize how Max behaves, so that it's tailored to your needs and style. You can also use MAXScript as a sort of VCR; it can record your actions so you can play them back later, eliminating repetitive tasks.

You can use MAXScript to "talk" to Max about a scene and tell it what you want to happen, either by having Max watch what you do or by typing in a list of instructions that you want Max to execute.

The beauty of MAXScript lies in its flexibility and simplicity: It is easy to use and was designed from the ground up to be an integral part of Max. But don't let its simplicity fool you; MAXScript as a language is rich enough to let you control just about anything.

In fact, you have already used MAXScript without even knowing it. Some of the buttons and rollouts use bits of MAXScript to carry out your commands. And after you've created a new feature with MAXScript, you can integrate it into Max transparently and use it just as easily as any other Max feature.

MAXScript is a fully functional and very powerful computer language, but you don't have to be a computer programmer or even have any previous programming experience to benefit from MAXScript. In the next few sections, we look at some simple ways to use MAXScript. For now, just think of a script in Max as you would a script in a movie or play — it tells what's going to happen, who's going to do what, and when it's going to happen. With your scene acting as the stage, a script directs Max to put on a performance for you.

One final note before we dive in: MAXScript is so powerful that an entire book could be written about it and every last feature it supports, but that is not the purpose here. This chapter is organized to give you an introduction to the world of MAXScript and to teach you the basic skills you need to get some mileage out of it. What is given here is a foundation that you can build upon according to your own interests and needs.

MAXScript Tools

MAXScript is pervasive and can be found in many different places. This section looks at the MAXScript tools and how different scripts are created and used.

Let's look at some of the tools used in working with MAXScript. Max has several tools that make creating and using scripts as simple as possible.

The MAXScript menu

The MAXScript menu includes commands that you can use to create a new script, open and run scripts, open the MAXScript Listener window (keyboard shortcut, F11) or the MAXScript Editor window, enable the Macro Recorder, open the Visual MAXScript Editor, or access the Debugger dialog box.

The New Script command opens a MAXScript Editor window, a text editor in which you write your MAXScript. See the "MAXScript Editor windows" section later in this chapter for more on this editor window. The Open Script command opens a file dialog box that you can use to locate a MAXScript file. When opened, the script file is opened in a MAXScript Editor window, as shown in Figure 49.1. MAXScript files have an .MS or .MCR extension. The Run Script command also opens a file dialog box where you can select a script to be executed.

 **When you use Run Script, some scripts do something right away, whereas others install themselves as new tools.**

The MAXScript Listener command opens the MAXScript Listener window. You also can open this window by pressing the F11 keyboard shortcut. The Macro Recorder command starts recording a MAXScript macro. The MAXScript Listener and recording macros are covered later in this chapter.

The MAXScript Utility rollout

You access the MAXScript Utility rollout, shown in Figure 49.2, by opening the Utilities panel in the Command Panel and clicking the MAXScript button. This opens a rollout where you can do many of the same commands as the MAXScript menu.

The MAXScript rollout also includes a Utilities drop-down list, which holds any installed scripted utilities. Each scripted utility acts as a new feature for you to use. The parameters for these utilities are displayed in a new rollout that appears below the MAXScript rollout.

FIGURE 49.1

MAXScript is written using standard syntax in a simple text editor window.

```
C:\Temp1\Authoring\3ds max 10 Bible\Chapter Example Files\Chap 49 - Automati...
File  Edit  Search  View  Tools  Options  Language  Windows  Help
1 SphereArray.ms
1     utility sphereArray "Sphere Array"
2   (
3     spinner objCount "Object count:" range:[1,100,20] type:#integer
4     spinner radius "Radius:" range:[1,1000,50]
5
6     button go "Go!"
7
8     on go pressed do
9     (
10      a = selection[1]
11      if a != undefined do
12      (
13        c = objCount.value
14        r = radius.value
15        for i = 1 to c do
16        (
17          someObj = copy a
18          someObj.position.x = someObj.position.x + r
19          about selection rotate someObj (random 0 359) x_axis
20          about selection rotate someObj (random 0 359) y_axis
21          about selection rotate someObj (random 0 359) z_axis
22        )
23      )
24    )
25  )
li=1 co=1 offset=0 INS (CR+LF) R
```

FIGURE 49.2

The MAXScript rollout on the Utilities panel is a great place to start working with MAXScript.

Tutorial: Using the SphereArray script

Here's a chance for you to play around a little and get some experience with MAXScript in the process. In the Chap 49 directory of the DVD is a simple script called SphereArray.ms. It's similar to the Array command found in the Tools menu, except that SphereArray creates copies of an object and randomly positions them in a spherical pattern.

To load and use the SphereArray script, follow these steps:

1. Select Create ➪ Standard Primitives ➪ Box, and drag in the Top viewport to create a Box object that has a Length of 10 and Width and Height values of 1.0.

2. Select the box object, open the Utilities panel in the Command Panel (the icon is a hammer), and click the MAXScript button.

   The MAXScript rollout appears.

1147

3. Click the Run Script button in the MAXScript rollout to open the Choose Editor file dialog box, locate the SphereArray.ms file from the Chap 49 directory on the DVD, and click Open.

   The SphereArray utility installs and appears in the Utilities drop-down list. (Because SphereArray is a scripted utility, running it only installs it.)

4. Choose SphereArray from the Utilities drop-down list. Make sure that the box object is selected.

5. In the Sphere Array rollout, enter **50** in the Object Count field and **2.0** for the Radius field. Now click the Go! button to run the script.

   The script adds 50 copies of your box to the scene and randomly positions them two units away from the box's position.

Figure 49.3 shows the results of the SphereArray MAXScript utility. Notice that the SphereArray script looks much like any other function or tool in Max.

FIGURE 49.3

The results of the SphereArray MAXScript utility

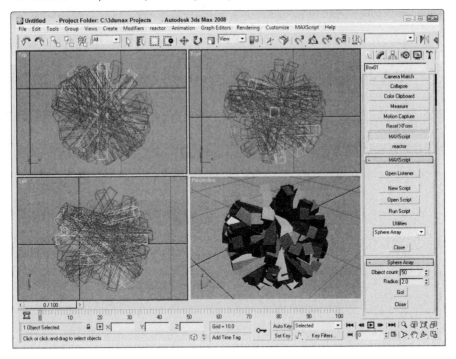

The MAXScript Listener window

Figure 49.4 shows the MAXScript Listener window (keyboard shortcut, F11), which lets you work interactively with the part of Max that interprets MAXScript commands. The top pane of the Listener window (the pink area) lets you enter MAXScript commands; the results are reported in the bottom pane (the white area) of the Listener window. You can also type MAXScript commands in the bottom pane, but typing them in the top pane keeps the commands separated from the results. If you drag the spacer between the two panes, you can resize both panes as needed.

FIGURE 49.4

The MAXScript Listener window interprets your commands.

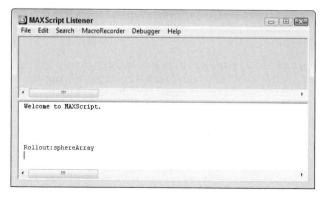

When you type commands into either pane and press Enter, the MAXScript interpreter evaluates the command and responds with the results. For example, if you type a simple mathematical expression such as **2+2** and press Enter, then the result of 4 is displayed in blue on the next line. Most results appear in blue, but the results display in red for any errors that occur. For example, if you enter the command **hello there**, then a Type error result appears in red because the MAXScript interpreter doesn't understand the command.

CAUTION The MAXScript interpreter is very fickle. A misspelling generates an error, but MAXScript is *case-insensitive*, which means that uppercase and lowercase letters are the same as far as Max is concerned. Thus, you can type **sphere**, **Sphere**, or **SPHERE**, and Max sees no difference.

The Listener window has these menus:

- **File:** You can use this menu to close the window (Ctrl+W), save your work (Ctrl+S), run scripts (Ctrl+R), open a script for editing (Ctrl+O), or create a new script from scratch (Ctrl+N).
- **Edit:** This menu is where you access all the common editing functions you need, such as cutting, pasting, and undoing.
- **Search:** You use this menu for searching through the window to find specific text (Ctrl+F), find the next instance (Ctrl+G), or replace text (Ctrl+H).
- **MacroRecorder:** This menu lets you set various options for the MAXScript Macro Recorder.
- **Debugger:** This menu provides a way to open the Debugger dialog box.
- **Help:** This menu provides access to the MAXScript Reference (F1).

Tutorial: Talking to the MAXScript interpreter

This tutorial gives you a little experience in working with the MAXScript Listener window and a chance to try some basic MAXScript commands.

To start using MAXScript, follow these steps:

1. Choose File ⇨ Reset to reset Max.
2. Choose MAXScript ⇨ MAXScript Listener (or press F11) to open the MAXScript Listener window.

3. Click anywhere in the bottom pane of the Listener window, type the following, and press Enter:

   ```
   sphere()
   ```

   A sphere object with default parameters is created.

4. Next enter the following in the lower pane, and press the Enter key:

   ```
   torus radius1:50 radius2:5
   ```

   Max creates a torus and adds it to your scene. As you specified in your MAXScript, the outer radius (radius1) is 50, and the radius of the torus itself (radius2) is 5. The output tells you that Max created a new torus at the origin of the coordinate system and gave that torus a name: Torus01.

5. Now use MAXScript to move the torus. In the Listener window, type the following:

   ```
   $Torus01.position.x = 20
   ```

   After you press Enter, you see the torus move along the positive X-axis. Each object in Max has certain properties or attributes that describe it, and what you've done is access one of these properties programmatically instead of by using the rollout or the mouse. In this case, you're telling Max, "Torus01 has a position property. Set the X-coordinate of that position to 20."

> **NOTE** The $ symbol identifies a named object. You can use it to refer to any named object.

6. To see a list of some of the properties specific to a torus, type the following:

   ```
   Showproperties $Torus01
   ```

   A list of the Torus01 properties appears in the window.

Figure 49.5 shows the MAXScript Listener window with all the associated commands and results.

FIGURE 49.5

Use the MAXScript Listener window to query Max about an object's properties.

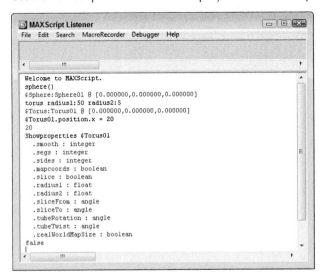

An important thing to understand from this tutorial is that you can do almost anything with MAXScript. Any property of any object that you can access via a rollout is also available via MAXScript. You could go so far as to create entire scenes using just MAXScript, although the real power comes from using MAXScript to do things for you automatically.

> **TIP** Max remembers the value of the last MAXScript command that it executed, and you can access that value through a special variable: ? (question mark). For example, if you type 5 + 5 in the Listener window, Max displays the result, 10. You can then use that result in your next MAXScript command by using the question mark variable. For example, you could type **$Torus01.radius2 = ?**, and Max would internally substitute the question mark with the number 10.

At the left end of the status bar, you can access the MAXScript Mini Listener control by dragging the left edge of the status bar to the right. By right-clicking in this control, you can open a Listener window and view all the current commands recorded by the Listener. Figure 49.6 shows this control with another command along with the objects from the last example.

FIGURE 49.6

The resulting objects created via the MAXScript Listener window

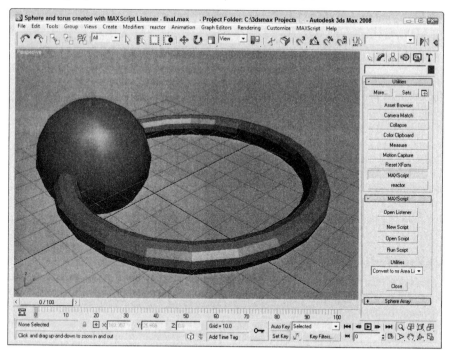

MAXScript Editor windows

The MAXScript Editor window enables you to open and edit any type of text file, although its most common use is for editing MAXScript files. Although you can have only one Listener window open, you can open as many editor windows as you want. Each opened script appears in a separate tab at the top of the Editor window.

NEW FEATURE **The MAXScript Editor has been entirely redesigned for 3ds Max 2008.**

To open a new MAXScript Editor window, you can choose MAXScript ➪ New Script, choose File ➪ New from the MAXScript Listener window, or click the New Script button in the MAXScript rollout in the Utility panel. You can also use MAXScript Editor windows to edit existing scripts.

To create a new script, opening both an Editor window and the Listener window is usually best. Then you can try out things in the Listener window, and when the pieces of the MAXScript work, you can cut and paste them into the main Editor window. Then you can return to the Listener window, work on the next new thing, and continue creating, cutting, and pasting until the script is done.

TIP **You can also send text back to the Listener window for Max to evaluate. Just select some text with the cursor or mouse, and press Shift+Enter (or just Enter on the numeric keypad). Max copies the selected text to the Listener window and evaluates it for you.**

The File menu includes several commands for working with script files including New, Open, Save, Save As, and Revert. Another command exports the opened script to HTML, RTF, PDF, LaTeX, or XML. The Editor also integrates with a Source Control repository. Finally, the Editor's File menu includes the ability to print out the opened script.

The Edit menu includes commands for undoing, redoing, cutting, copying, and pasting script sections between different scripts and to and from the Listener window. The Match Brace and Select to Brace commands let you easily create and edit scripts, the Block Comment command allows you to quickly comment out certain areas of script, and the Make Selection Uppercase lets you quickly make variables identifiable.

The Search menu includes Find and Replace features. Another feature finds text in a directory of files. You also can set bookmarks that allow you to quickly move to a specific point in the code. The Views menu includes options for making the Editor appear full screen. You also can expand and contract bracketed sections of the script and display editor elements including a toolbar, status bar, line numbers, and indentation guide.

The Tools menu includes the Evaluate All command. This command is a fast way of having Max evaluate your entire script. The result is the same as if you had manually selected the entire text, copied it to the Listener window, and pressed Enter. An Evaluate Selection option also is available. The Tools menu also includes access to the Visual MAXScript window with the New Rollout and Edit Rollout menu commands. You also have access to the various options and properties files including the User and Global Options, the Abbreviations file, and the MAXScript Properties file, as shown in Figure 49.7.

The Macro Recorder

The MAXScript Macro Recorder is a tool that records your actions and creates a MAXScript that can be recalled to duplicate those actions. Using the Macro Recorder is not only a quick and easy way to write entire scripts, but it is also a great way to make a working version of a script that you can then refine. After the Macro Recorder has created a MAXScript from your recorded actions, you can edit the script using a MAXScript Editor window to make any changes you want.

You can turn the Macro Recorder on and off either by choosing MAXScript ➪ Macro Recorder or by choosing Macro Recorder ➪ Enable in the MAXScript Listener window. The check mark next to Macro Recorder command on the MAXScript menu indicates that the Macro Recorder is turned on.

When the Macro Recorder is on, every action is converted to MAXScript and sent to the MAXScript Listener window's top pane. You can then take the MAXScript output and save it to a file or copy it to a MAXScript Editor window for additional editing. The Macro Recorder continues to monitor your actions until you turn it off, which is done in the same way as turning it on.

FIGURE 49.7

The MAXScript Editor can open several script files at once.

The MacroRecorder menu in the MAXScript Listener window includes several options for customizing the macro recorder, including

- **Enable:** This option turns the Macro Recorder on or off.

- **Explicit scene object names:** With this option, the Macro Recorder writes the MAXScript using the names of the objects you modify so that the script always modifies those exact same objects, regardless of what object you have selected when you run the script again. For example, if the Macro Recorder watches you move a pyramid named $Pyramid01 in your scene, then the resulting MAXScript will always and only operate on the scene object named $Pyramid01.

- **Selection-relative scene object names:** With this option, the Macro Recorder writes MAXScript that operates on whatever object is currently selected. So if (when you recorded your script) you moved the pyramid named $Pyramid01, you could later select a different object and run your script, and the new object would move instead.

NOTE To decide which of these options to use, ask yourself, "Do I want the script to always manipulate this particular object, or do I want the script to manipulate whatever I have selected?"

- **Absolute transform assignments:** This tells the Macro Recorder that any transformations you make are not relative to an object's current position or orientation. For example, if you move a sphere from (0,0,0) to (10,0,0), the Macro Recorder writes MAXScript that says, "Move the object to (10,0,0)."

- **Relative transforms operations:** Use this option to have the Macro Recorder apply transformations relative to an object's current state. For example, if you move a sphere from (0,0,0) to (10,0,0), the Macro Recorder says, "Move the object +10 units in the X-direction from its current location."

- **Explicit subobject sets:** If you choose this option and then record a script that manipulates a set of subobjects, running the script again always manipulates those same subobjects, even if you have other subobjects selected when you run the script again.

- **Selection-relative subobject sets:** This tells the Macro Recorder that you want the script to oper-ate on whatever subobjects are selected when you run the script.
- **Show command panel switchings:** This option tells the Macro Recorder whether or not to write MAXScript for actions that take place on the Command Panel.
- **Show tool selections:** If this option is selected, the Macro Recorder records MAXScript to change to different tools.
- **Show menu item selections:** This option tells the Macro Recorder whether or not you want it to generate MAXScript for menu items you select while recording your script.

Tutorial: Recording a simple script

In this tutorial, we create a simple script that squashes whatever object you have selected and turns it purple.

To create a script using the Macro Recorder, follow these steps:

1. Open the Purple pyramid.max file from the Chap 49 directory on the DVD.

   This file includes a simple pyramid object.

2. With the pyramid object selected, choose MAXScript ⇨ MAXScript Listener (or press F11) to open the MAXScript Listener window.

3. In the Listener window, open the MacroRecorder menu and make sure that all the options are set to the relative and not the absolute object settings, thereby telling the script to work on any selected object instead of always modifying the same object.

4. Returning to the MacroRecorder menu, select Enable. The Macro Recorder is now on and ready to start writing MAXScript. Minimize the Macro Recorder window (or at least move it out of the way so you can see the other viewports).

5. Dock the MAXScript Listener window to the Left viewport by right-clicking the viewport name and choosing Views ⇨ Extended ⇨ MAXScript Listener.

   Now you can keep things out of the way while you work.

6. With the object selected, choose Modifiers ⇨ Parametric Deformers ⇨ XForm to add an XForm modifier to the object.

7. Select the non-uniform scale tool and restrict it to the Y-axis. Right-click anywhere in the Front viewport to make it active (if it's not already), and then drag the Y-axis gizmo downward to squash the pyramid.

8. In the Modify panel, click the color swatch next to the object name field to open the Object Color dialog box. Pick one of the purple colors, and click OK.

9. The script is done, so in the MAXScript Listener window, choose MacroRecorder ⇨ Enable to turn off the Macro Recorder.

10. Now it's time to try out your first MAXScript effort. Add a sphere to your scene. Make sure that it's selected before moving to the next step.

11. In the top pane of the MAXScript Listener window, select all the text (an easy way to do so is by pressing Ctrl+A), and then hold down the Shift key and press the Enter key to tell Max to execute the MAXScript.

In Figure 49.8, you can see the script and the sphere that has been squashed and has changed color.

FIGURE 49.8

Running the new squash-and-turn-purple script

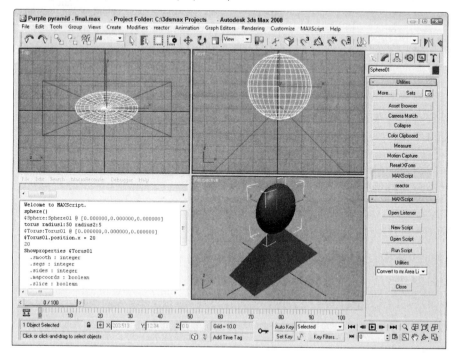

The MAXScript Debugger

The MAXScript Debugger, shown in Figure 49.9, is a separate window that allows you to stop the execution of a script using breaks and look at the variable's values as the script is being run. This information provides valuable information that can help to identify bugs with your script.

FIGURE 49.9

The MAXScript Debugger lets you check the values of variables as the script runs.

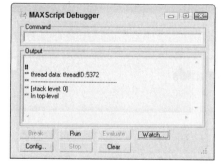

The MAXScript Debugger dialog box is opened using the Debugger menu command in the various MAXScript tool windows or using the MAXScript ⇨ Debugger Dialog menu command on the main interface. The Command field at the top of the Debugger window lets you input commands directly to the debugger. The Output area displays the results. Several buttons at the bottom of the Debugger window let you control how the debugger works:

- **Break:** Causes the current script to break out of its execution
- **Run:** Starts the execution of the current script
- **Evaluate:** Executes the command entered into the Command field
- **Watch:** Opens the Watch Manager window where you can specify distinct variables to watch
- **Config:** Opens the MAXScript Debugger Parameters dialog box where you can configure the debugger
- **Stop:** Halts the execution of the current script
- **Clear:** Clears all the text in the Output field

Watching variables

The Watch button opens the Watch Manager, shown in Figure 49.10. Clicking the Variable column lets you type in a new variable to watch. The Value column displays the value of the listed variables as the script is executed.

FIGURE 49.10

The Watch Manager lets you watch the value of specific variables.

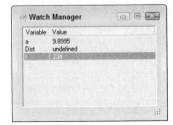

Using debugger commands

Once the execution of a script has been halted by clicking on the Break button, you can enter specific commands in the Command field at the top of the debugger and click the Evaluate button to execute them. Table 49.1 lists the available debugger commands.

TABLE 49.1

MAXScript Debugger Commands

Command	What It Does
threads	Displays a list of all current threads.
setThread (thread no.)	Makes the specified thread number the active thread.

Command	What It Does
stack	Dumps the stack for the active thread.
setFrame (frame no.)	Makes the specified frame number the active frame.
locals (variable)	Dumps the value for the specified variable for the active thread and frame. If no variable is listed, then all variable values are dumped.
getVar (variable)	Gets the value of the specified variable.
setVar (variable)	Sets the value of the specified variable.
eval (expression)	Evaluates the specified expression.
?	Displays a list of debugger commands.

Configuring the debugger

The Config button opens the MAXScript Debugger Parameters dialog box, shown in Figure 49.11. This dialog box includes several options for deciding when to break out of the script execution. It also lets you define the time for each break.

FIGURE 49.11

The MAXScript Debugger Parameters let you set the break cycle time, among other settings.

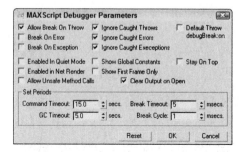

Setting MAXScript Preferences

The Preference Settings dialog box, opened with the Customize ⇨ Preference Settings menu command, includes a panel of MAXScript settings, shown in Figure 49.12. Using these settings, you can set which scripts load automatically, the default settings for the Macro Recorder, and even what font is displayed in the Script Editor window. The Use Fast Node Name Lookup option causes all indexed MAXScript names to be saved in a cache buffer to speed the execution of the script.

Max includes two directories in its default installation that can be used to automatically load scripts when Max starts. These directories are scripts and scripts\startup, but you can change these directories using the Configure Paths dialog box. The Load Startup Scripts option causes any scripts in these directories to be loaded automatically when Max starts.

FIGURE 49.12

The MAXScript panel in the Preference Settings dialog box includes options for controlling MAXScript.

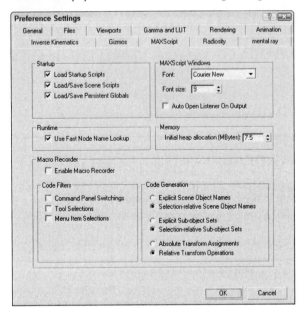

Types of Scripts

All scripts are not created equal, and Max categorizes different scripts based on how they work. For more information, the MAXScript online help provides exhaustive information on their various options.

The main thing to consider when deciding what type of script to create is the user interface. Ask yourself what the most logical user interface would be for the type of tool you're creating, and this gives you a hint as to which type of script is well suited for the task.

Macro scripts

Macro scripts are scripts created with the Macro Recorder. Any script associated with a toolbar button is considered a Macro script. Max organizes Macro scripts by their category, which you can change by editing the script file. To call a Macro script from another script, you can use the macros command. For example,

```
macros.run "objects" "sphere"
```

runs the "sphere" script in the "objects" category.

Macro scripts generally require no other user input; you just click a button, and the script works its magic.

Scripted utilities

A *scripted utility* is a MAXScript that has its own custom rollout in the Utilities panel, like the SphereArray example. This type of script is particularly useful when your script has parameters that the user needs to enter, such as the radius in the SphereArray script. Scripted utilities are easy to build using the Visual MAXScript Editor.

Scripted right-click menus

When you right-click an object in your scene, Max opens a pop-up menu of options for you to choose from, much like a quadmenu. Scripted right-click menus let you append your own menu items to the right-click menu. If you create a script that modifies some property of an object, making the script available through the right-click menu makes it easily accessible.

Scripted mouse tools

You can use scripted mouse tools to create scripts that handle mouse input in the viewports. These scripts listen for commands from the mouse, such as clicking the mouse buttons and clicking and dragging the cursor. For example, you would use this type of MAXScript if you were making a new primitive object type so that users could create the new objects just like they would a sphere or a box.

Scripted plug-ins

Scripted plug-ins are by far the most complex type of MAXScript available. They mirror the functionality of non-MAXScript plug-ins (which are written in other programming languages such as C++). You can create scripted plug-ins that make new geometry, create new shapes, control lights, act as modifiers, control texture maps and materials, and even produce special rendering effects.

Writing Your Own MAXScripts

This section presents the basics of the MAXScript language and shows you how to use the various parts of MAXScript in your own scripts. You can test any of these scripting commands using the MAXScript Listener window.

CROSS-REF Much of the discussion that follows will sound familiar if you've already read the material on expressions found in Chapter 33, "Animating with the Expression Controller and Wiring Parameters." Expressions use many of the same constructs as MAXScript.

Variables and data types

A *variable* in MAXScript is sort of like a variable in algebra. It represents some other value, and when you mention a variable in an equation, you're actually talking about the value that the variable holds. You can think of variables in MAXScript as containers that you can put stuff into and take it out of later. Unlike variables in algebra, however, variables in MAXScript can "hold" other things besides numbers, as we'll soon see.

To put a value into a variable, you use the equal sign. For example, if you type

    X = 5 * 3

in the MAXScript Listener window, Max evaluates the expression on the right side of the equal sign and stores the result in the variable named X. In this case, Max would multiply 5 and 3 and would store the result (15) in X. You can then see what is in X by just typing **X** in the Listener window and pressing Enter. Max then displays the value stored in X, or 15.

You can name your variables whatever you want, and naming them something that helps you remember what the variable is for is a good idea. For example, if you want a variable that keeps track of how many objects you're going to manipulate, the name "objCount" would be better than something like "Z."

NOTE Variable names can be just about anything you want, but you must start a variable name with a letter. Also, the variable name can't have any special characters in it, like spaces, commas, or quotation marks. You can, however, use the underscore character and any normal alphabetic characters.

Variables can also hold *strings,* which are groups of characters. For example,

```
badDay = "Monday"
```

stores the word "Monday" in the variable badDay. You can attach two strings together using the plus sign, like this:

```
grouchy = "My least favorite day is" + badDay
```

Now the variable grouchy holds the value "My least favorite day is Monday."

Try this:

```
wontWork = 5 + "cheese"
```

Max prints out an error because it's confused: You're asking it to add a number to a string. The problem is that 5 and "cheese" are two different data types. *Data types* are different classes of values that you can store in variables. You can almost always mix values of the same data type, but values of different types usually don't make sense together.

 To see the data type of a variable, use the classof command. Using the previous example, you could type **classof grouchy**, and Max would in turn print out String.

Another very common data type is Point3, which represents a three-dimensional point. Following are a few examples of using points, with explanatory comments:

```
Pos = [5,3,2]          -- Marks a point at (5,3,2)
Pos.x = 7              -- Change the x coordinate to 7
                       -- Now the point is at (7,3,2)
Pos = Pos + (1,2,5)    -- Take the old value for Pos,
                       -- move it by (1,2,5) to (8,5,7)
                       -- and store the new value in Pos
```

In addition to these basic data types, each object in your scene has its own data type. For example, if you use classof on a sphere object, Max prints out Sphere. Data types for scene objects are actually complex data types or structures, which means that they are groups of other data types in a single unit. The pieces of data inside a larger object are called *members* or *properties.* Most scene objects have a member called Name, which is of type String. The Name member tells the specific name of that object. Another common property is Position, a Point3 variable that tells the object's position.

Max has a special built-in variable that represents whatever object is currently selected. This variable is $ (the dollar sign), which is used in the following tutorial.

Tutorial: Using variables

In this tutorial, you learn more about variables in MAXScript by using them to manipulate an object in your scene.

To use variables to manipulate scene objects, follow these steps:

1. Open the Teapot.max file from the Chap 49 directory on the DVD.

    This file has a simple teapot object.

2. Right-click on the title for the Left viewport, and choose Views ⇨ Extended ⇨ MAXScript Listener to open the MAXScript Listener window in the Left viewport.

3. Select the teapot object, type $, and press Enter.

   Max displays information about the teapot. (Your numbers will probably be different depending on where you placed your teapot.)

4. Type the following lines one at a time in the top pane to see the property values stored as part of the teapot object:

   ```
   $.position
   $.wirecolor
   $.radius
   $.name
   $.lid
   ```

5. Now type these lines, one at a time, to set the property values of the teapot object:

   ```
   $.lid = false
   $.position.x = -20
   $.segs = 20
   ```

Figure 49.13 shows the commands, their results in the MAXScript Listener window, and the resulting teapot object.

FIGURE 49.13

The script commands entered in the MAXScript Listener affect the objects in the viewports.

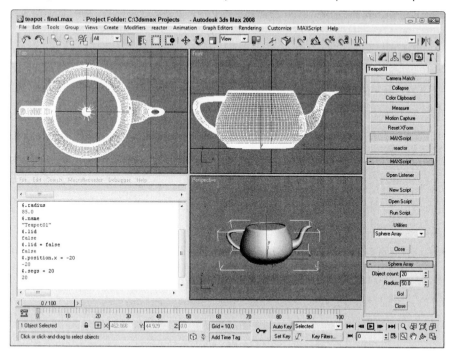

Program flow and comments

In general, when Max begins executing a script, it starts with the first line of the script, processes it, and then moves on to the next line. Execution of the script continues until no more lines are in the script file. (Later, we look at some MAXScript keywords that let you change the flow of script execution.)

Max lets you embed comments or notes in your script file to help explain what is happening. To insert a comment, precede it with two hyphens (--). When Max encounters the double hyphen, it skips the comment and everything else on that line and moves to the next line of the script. For example, in this line of MAXScript

```
$Torus01.pos = [0,0,0]   -- Move it back to the origin
```

Max processes the first part of the line (and moves the object to the origin) and then moves on to the next line after it reaches the comment.

Using comments in your MAXScript files is very important because as your scripts start to become complex, figuring out what is happening can get difficult. Also, when you come back a few months later to improve your script, comments will refresh your memory and help keep you from repeating the same mistakes you made the first time around.

NOTE Because Max ignores anything after the double hyphen, you can use comments to temporarily remove MAXScript lines from your script. If something isn't working right, you can *comment out* the lines that you want Max to skip. Later, when you want to add them back in, you don't have to retype them. You can just remove the comment marks, and your script is back to normal.

Expressions

An *expression* is what Max uses to make decisions. An expression compares two things and draws a simple conclusion based on that comparison.

CROSS-REF These same expressions can be used within the Expression controller. You can find details on this controller in Chapter 33, "Animating with the Expression Controller and Wiring Parameters."

Simple expressions

The expression

```
1 < 2
```

is a simple expression that asks the question, "Is 1 less than 2?" Expressions always ask yes/no type questions. When you type an expression in the MAXScript Listener window (or inside of a script), Max evaluates the expression and prints true if the expression is valid (like the preceding example) and false if it isn't. Try the following expressions in the Listener window, and Max will print the results as shown in Figure 49.14 (you don't have to type in the comments):

```
1 < 2           -- 1 IS less than 2, so expression is true
1 > 2           -- 1 is NOT greater than 2, so false
2 + 2 == 4      -- '==' means "is equal to". 2 + 2 is
                -- equal to 4, so true
2 + 2 == 5      -- 4 is NOT equal to 5, so false
3 * 3 == 5 + 4  -- 9 IS equal to 9, so true

3 * 3 != 5 + 4  -- '!=' means 'not equal to'. '9 is not
```

```
                           -- equal to 9' is a false statement, so
                           -- the expression is false

     a = 23                -- store 23 in variable a
     b = 14 + 9            -- store 23 in variable b
     a == b                -- 23 IS equal to 23, so true
```

FIGURE 49.14

Using the MAXScript Listener to evaluate expressions

Play around with simple expressions until you're familiar with what they mean and have an intuitive feel for whether or not an expression is going to evaluate to true or false.

Complex expressions

Sometimes you need an expression to decide on more than just two pieces of data. MAXScript has the and, or, and not operators to help you do this.

The and operator combines two expressions and asks the question, "Are both expressions true?" If both are true, then the entire expression evaluates to true. But if either is false, or if they are both false, then the entire expression is false. You can use parentheses to group expressions, so an expression with the and operator might look something like this:

```
     (1 < 2) and (1 < 3)     -- true because (1 < 2) is true AND
                             -- (1 < 3) is true
```

The or operator is similar to and, except that an expression with or is true if either of the expressions is true or if both are true. Here are some examples:

```
     (2 > 3) or (2 > 1)      -- even though (2 > 3) is false, the
                             -- entire expression is true because
                             -- (2 > 1) is true
```

```
(2 > 3) and (2 > 1)      -- false because both expressions are
                         -- not true
```

Try some of these complex expressions to make sure that you understand how they work:

```
a = 3
b = 2
(a == b) or (a > b)      -- true because a IS greater than b
(a == b) and (b == 2)    -- false because both expressions are
                         -- not true
(a > b) or (a < b)       -- true because at least one IS true
(a != b) and (b == 3)    -- false because b is NOT equal to 3
```

The not operator negates or flips the value of an expression from true to false, or vice versa. For example:

```
(1 == 2)                 -- false because 1 is NOT equal to 2
not (1 == 2)             -- true. 'not' flips the false to true
```

Conditions

Conditions are one way in which you can control program flow in a script. Normally, Max processes each line, no matter what, and then quits; but with *conditions,* Max executes certain lines only if an expression is true.

For example, suppose you have a script with the following lines:

```
a = 4
If (a == 5) then
(
  b = 2
)
```

Max would not execute the line b = 2 because the expression (a == 5) evaluates to false. Conditional statements, or "if" statements, basically say, "If this expression evaluates to true, then do the stuff inside the block of parentheses. If the expression evaluates to false, skip those lines of script."

Conditional statements follow this form:

```
If <expr> then <stuff>
```

where <expr> is an expression to evaluate and <stuff> is some MAXScript to execute if the expression evaluates to true. You can also use the keyword else to specify what happens if the expression evaluates to false, as shown in the following example:

```
a = 4
if (a == 5) then
(
  b = 2
)
else
(
  b = 3
)
```

After this block of MAXScript, the variable b would have the value of 3 because the expression (a == 5) evaluated to false. Consequently, Max executed the MAXScript in the else section of the statement.

Collections and arrays

MAXScript has some very useful features to help you manipulate groups of objects. A group of objects is called a *collection*. You can think of a collection as a bag that holds a bunch of objects or variables. The things in the bag are in no particular order; they're just grouped together.

You can use collections to work with groups of a particular type of object. For example, the MAXScript

```
a = $pokey*
a.wirecolor = red
```

creates a collection that contains every object in your scene whose name starts with "Pokey" and makes every object in that collection turn red.

MAXScript has several built-in collections that you might find useful, such as cameras and lights, containing all the cameras and lights in your scene. So

```
delete lights
```

removes all the light objects from your scene (which may or may not be a good idea).

An *array* is a type of collection in which all the objects are in a fixed order, and you can access each member of the array by an index. For example

```
a = #()        -- creates an empty array to use
a[1] = 5
a[2] = 10
a[5] = 12
a
```

After the last line, Max prints out the current value for the array:

```
#(5, 10, undefined, undefined, 12)
```

Notice that Max makes the array big enough to hold however many elements we want to put in it, and that if we don't put anything in one of the positions, Max automatically puts in `undefined`, which simply means that array location has no value at all.

One last useful trick is that Max lets you use the `as` keyword to convert from a collection to an array:

```
LightArray = (lights as array)
```

Max takes the built-in collection of lights, converts it to an array, and names the array `LightArray`.

The members of an array or a collection don't all have to have the same data type, so it's completely valid to have an array with numbers, strings, and objects, like this:

```
A = #(5,"Mr. Nutty",box radius:5)
```

> **NOTE** You can use the `as` MAXScript keyword to convert between data types. For example, (5 as string) converts the number 5 to the string "5," and (5 as float) converts the whole number 5 to the floating-point number 5.0.

Loops

A *loop* is a MAXScript construct that lets you override the normal flow of execution. Instead of processing each line in your script once and then quitting, Max can use loops to do something several times.

For example,

```
j = 0
for i = 1 to 5 do
(
  j = j + i
)
```

This MAXScript uses two variables — i and j — but you can use any variables you want in your loops. The script sets the variable j to 0 and then uses the variable i to count from 1 to 5. Max repeats the code between the parentheses five times, and each time the variable i is incremented by 1. Inside the loop, Max adds the current value of i to j. Can you figure out what the value of j is at the end of the script? If you guessed 15, you're right. To see why, look at the value of each variable as the script is running:

```
When                      j     i
--------------------------------
First line                0     0
Start of loop             0     1
After first loop          1     1
Start of second loop      1     2
After second loop         3     2
Start of third loop       3     3
After third loop          6     3
Start of fourth loop      6     4
After fourth loop         10    4
Start of fifth loop       10    5
After fifth loop          15    5
```

A loop is also useful for processing each member of an array or collection. The following MAXScript shows one way to turn every teapot in a scene blue:

```
teapots = $teapot*              -- get the collection of teapots
for singleTeapot in teapots do
(
 singleTeapot.wirecolor = blue
)
```

You can use a for loop to create a bunch of objects for you. Try this MAXScript:

```
for I = 1 to 10 collect
 (
 sphere radius:15
 )
```

The collect keyword tells Max to create a collection with the results of the MAXScript in the block of code inside the parentheses. The line

```
sphere radius:15
```

tells Max to create a sphere with radius of 15, so the entire script created 10 spheres and added them to your scene. Unfortunately, Max puts them all in the same spot, so let's move them around a bit so we can see them:

```
i = -50
For s in spheres do
```

```
(
  s.position = [i,i,i]
  i = i + 10
)
```

Study this script to make sure that you understand what's going on. We use a for loop to process each sphere in our collection of spheres. For each one, we set its position to [i,i,i], and then we change the value of i so that the next sphere is at a different location.

Functions

The last feature of basic MAXScript that we look at is the *function*. Functions are small chunks of MAXScript that act like program building blocks. For example, suppose that you need to compute the average of a collection of numbers many times during a script you're writing. The MAXScript to do this might be:

```
Total = 0
Count = 0
For n in numbers do
(
 total = total + n
 count = count + 1
)
average = total / (count as float)
```

Given a collection of numbers called numbers, this MAXScript computes the average. Unfortunately, every time you need to compute the average, you have to type all that MAXScript again. Or you might be smart and just cut and paste it in each time you need it. Still, your script is quickly becoming large and ugly, and you always have to change the script to match the name of your collection you're averaging.

A function solves your problem. At the beginning of your script, you can define an average function like this:

```
Function average numbers =
( -- Function to average the numbers in a collection
 local Total = 0
 local Count = 0
 For n in numbers do
 (
 total = total + n
 count = count + 1
 )
 total / (count as float)
)
```

Now any time you need to average any collection of numbers in your script, you could just use this to take all the numbers in the collection called num and store their average in a variable called Ave:

```
Ave = average num       -- assuming num is a collection
```

Not only does this make your script much shorter if you need to average numbers often, but it makes it much more readable, too. It's very clear to the casual reader that you're going to average some numbers. Also, if you later realize that you wrote the average function incorrectly, you can just fix it at the top of the script. If you weren't using functions, you would have to go through your script and find every case where you averaged numbers and then fix the problem. (What a headache!)

Let's take another look at the function definition. The first line

```
Function average numbers =
```

tells Max that you're creating a new function called `average`. It also tells Max that to use this function, you have to pass in one piece of data, and that inside the function you refer to that data using a variable called `numbers`. It doesn't matter what the name of the actual variable was when the function was called; inside the function, you can simply refer to it as `numbers`.

Creating functions that use multiple pieces of data is also easy. For example,

```
Function multEm a b c = (a * b * c)
```

creates a function that multiplies three numbers together. To use this function to multiply three numbers and store the result in a variable called `B`, you would simply enter

```
B = multEm 2 3 4
```

The next two lines

```
local Total = 0
local Count = 0
```

create two variables and set them both to 0. The `local` keyword tells Max that the variable belongs to this function. No part of the script outside of the function can see this variable, and if there is a variable outside the function with the same name, changing the variable inside this function won't affect that variable outside the function. That way, you never have to worry about what other variables are in use when someone calls average; even if variables are in use that are named `Total` or `Count`, they won't be affected.

The last line

```
total / (count as float)
```

uses the `Total` and `Count` values to compute the average. How does that value get sent back to whoever called the function? Max evaluates all the MAXScript inside the function and returns the result. Because the last line is the last thing to be evaluated, Max uses the result of that calculation as the result of the entire function.

Tutorial: Creating a school of fish

Let's look at an example that puts into practice some of the things you've learned in this chapter. In this multipart tutorial, we use MAXScript to create a small school of fish that follows the dummy object around a path.

Part 1: Making the fish follow a path

In this part of the tutorial, we use MAXScript to move one of the fish along a path in the scene. To do this, follow these steps:

1. Open the Fish scene.max file from the Chap 49 directory on the DVD.

   This scene consists of two fish and a dummy object that follows a path. What we need to do is use MAXScript to create a small school of fish that follows the dummy object around the path.

2. Press F11 to open the MAXScript Listener window. In the window, choose File ⇨ New Script to open the MAXScript Editor window, and type the following script:

```
pathObj = $Dummy01
fishObj = $Fish1/FishBody
```

```
relPos = [0,-150,-50]    -- How close the fish is to the path

animate on
(
 for t = 1 to 100 do at time t
 (
 fishObj.position = pathObj.position + relPos
 )
)
```

3. Select the Camera01 viewport. Choose File ⇨ Evaluate All (or press Ctrl+E) to evaluate all the MAXScript in the Editor window, right-click the Camera01 viewport to activate it, and click the Play Animation button.

   The fish rigidly follows the dummy object's path. Figure 49.15 shows one frame of this animation.

First attempt at making the fish follow a path

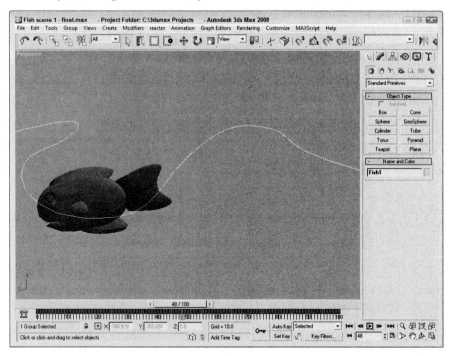

Now let's explain the MAXScript entered in the previous tutorial. The first few lines create some variables that the rest of the script uses. `pathObj` tells the name of the object that the fish will follow, and `fishObj` is the name of the fish's body. (Notice that we can reference parts of the group hierarchy by using the object name, a forward slash, and then a child part.) Why bother creating a variable for the fish object? After we get this first fish working, we want to apply the same script to another fish. All we have to do is rename `Fish1` as `Fish2`, re-execute the script, and we're finished!

The script also creates a variable called `relPos`, which we use to refer to the relative position of the fish with respect to the dummy object. If we have several fish in the scene, we don't want them all in the exact same spot, so this is an easy way to position each one.

The next block of MAXScript is new: We're using the `animate on` construct. This tells Max to generate keyframes for our animation. It's the same as if we had pressed Max's Animation button, run our script, and then shut Animation off. So any MAXScript inside the `animate on` parentheses creates animation keyframes. These parentheses define a section of the script we call a block.

Inside the animation block, we have a loop that counts from 1 to 100 (corresponding to each frame of our animation). On the end of the loop line, we have at `time t`, which tells Max that for each time through the loop, we want all the variables to have whatever values they'll have at that time. For example, if we want the fish to follow the dummy object, we have to know the position of the object at each point in time instead of just at the beginning; so each time through the loop, Max figures out for us where the dummy object will be.

Inside the loop, we set the fish's object to be that of the dummy object (at that point in time) and then adjust the fish's position by `relPos`.

Part 2: Adding body rotation and tail animation

Let's make that fish look a little more lifelike by animating its tail and having it rotate its body to actually follow the path. Also, we add a little unpredictability to its motion so that when we add other fish, they aren't exact copies of each other.

To improve the fish's animation, follow these steps:

1. Type the revised version of the script (the new lines are in bold):

```
pathObj = $Dummy01
fishObj = $Fish1/FishBody
fishTail = $Fish1/FishBody/FishTail
relPos = [0,-150,-50]   -- How close the fish is to the path

fishTail.bend.axis = 0 -- 0 is the x-axis
zadd = 4                      -- vertical movement at each step
tailFlapOffset = (random 0 100)
tailFlapRate = 25 + (random 0 25)
animate on
(
  for t = 0 to 100 do at time t
  (
    fishObj.position = pathObj.position + relPos
    fishObj.position.z = relPos.z
    relPos.z += zadd

    -- let's say that there's a 10% chance that the fish will
    -- change directions vertically
    if ((random 1 100) > 90) then
    (
      zadd = -zadd
    )

    fishTail.bend.angle = 50 * sin (t * tailFlapRate +
    tailFlapOffset)

    oldRt = fishObj.rotation.z_rotation
```

```
newRt = (in coordsys pathObj pathObj.rotation.z_rotation)

if ((random 1 100) > 85) then
(
  fishObj.rotation.z_rotation += (newRt - oldRt) *
  (random 0.5 1.5)
  )
 )
)
```

2. Save your script (File ➪ Save), and then press Ctrl+E to evaluate the script again. This script is saved in the Chap 49 directory as FishPath2.ms. Make the Camera01 viewport active, and click Play Animation. Figure 49.16 shows another frame of the animation. As you can see, the fish is heading in the right direction this time, and the tail is flapping wildly.

FIGURE 49.16

A tail-flapping fish that faces the right direction as it follows the path

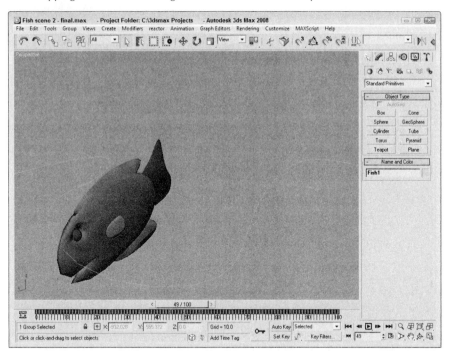

Okay, let's look at what changed. First, we added a variable to refer to the fish's tail, so that it is easy to change when we add another fish. Also, we accessed the bend modifier of the tail and set its axis to 0, which corresponds to the X-axis. (You can try other values to see that it really does change the axis parameter in the rollout.)

Next, we created some more variables. We use zadd to tell Max how much to move the fish in the Z-direction at each step (we don't want our fish to always swim at the same level). tailFlapOffset and tailFlapRate are two variables used to control the tail flapping (I explain this when we get to the part of the script that uses them).

Inside the `for` loop, notice that we've overridden the fish's Z-position and replaced it with just the relative Z-position, so that each fish swims at its own depth and not the dummy object's depth. Then, at each step, we add `zadd` to the Z-position so that the fish changes depth slowly. We have to be careful, or our fish will continue to climb out of the scene or run into the ground, so at each step we also choose a random number between 1 and 100 with the function `(random 1 100)`. If the random number that Max picks is greater than 90, we flip the sign of `zadd` so that the fish starts moving in the other direction. This is a fancy way of saying, "There's a 90 percent chance that the fish will continue moving in the same direction and a 10 percent chance that it will switch directions."

In the next part, we again access the tail's `bend` modifier, this time to set the bend angle. To get a nice back-and-forth motion for the tail, we use the `sin` function. In case you've forgotten all that math from when you were in school, a sine wave oscillates from 1 to –1 to 1 over and over again. By multiplying the function by 50, we get values that oscillate between 50 and –50 (pretty good values to use for our bend angle). We use `tailFlapOffset` to shift the sine wave so that the tail flapping of additional fish is out of synch slightly with this one (remember, we're trying to get at least a little realism here) and `tailFlapRate` to make each fish flap its tail at a slightly different speed.

The only thing left for us to do is to make the fish "follow" the path; that is, rotate its body so that it's facing the direction it's moving. The simplest way to do this is to use the following MAXScript (split into two lines to make it easier to read):

```
newRt = (in coordsys pathObj pathObj.rotation.z_rotation)
fishObj.rotation.z_rotation = newRt
```

The `in coordsys` construct tells Max to give us a value from the point of view of a particular coordinate system. Instead of `pathObj`, we could have asked for the Z-rotation in the world, local, screen, or parent coordinate system, too. In this case, we want to rotate the fish in the same coordinate system as the dummy object. To randomize the direction of the fish a little, we've made the rotation a little more complex:

```
oldRt = fishObj.rotation.z_rotation
newRt = (in coordsys pathObj pathObj.rotation.z_rotation)

if ((random 1 100) > 85) then
(
  fishObj.rotation.z_rotation += (newRt - oldRt) *
                                 (random 0.5 1.5)
)
```

First, we save the old Z-rotation in `oldRt`, and then we put the new rotation in `newRt`. Again, we pick a random number to decide whether we'll do something; in this case we're saying, "There's an 85 percent chance we won't change directions at all." If our random number does fall in that other 15 percent, however, we adjust the fish's rotation a little. We take the difference between the new rotation and the old rotation and multiply it by a random number between 0.5 and 1.5, which means we adjust the rotation by anywhere from 50 percent to 150 percent of the difference between the two rotations. So any fish will basically follow the same path, but with a little variation here and there.

 Max lets you use shorthand when adjusting the values of variables. Instead of saying `a = a + b`, you can just say `a += b`. Both have the same effect.

Part 3: Animating the second fish

This scene actually has two fish in it (the other one has been sitting patiently off to the side), so for the final part of this tutorial, we get both fish involved in the animation. To animate the second fish alongside the first one, follow these steps:

1. At the top of the script, change these three lines (changes are in bold):

```
pathObj = $Dummy01
fishObj = $Fish2/FishBody
fishTail = $Fish2/FishBody/FishTail
relPos = [50,75,0]    -- How close the fish is to the path
```

2. Choose File ⇨ Evaluate All (or press Ctrl+E) to run the script again, and then animate it. Figure 49.17 shows both fish swimming merrily.

This script generates keyframes for the second fish because we changed the `fishObj` and `fishTail` variables to refer to the second fish. We've also moved the second fish's relative position so that the two don't run into each other.

FIGURE 49.17

Both fish swimming together

Learning the Visual MAXScript Editor Interface

Building scripts can be complicated, and piecing together a rollout for a scripted utility can be especially time-consuming and frustrating when done by hand. To help create such custom rollouts, Max includes the Visual MAXScript Editor. Using this editor, you can drag and drop rollout elements and automatically create a code skeleton for certain events.

Working with textual commands can be time-consuming. In order for the script to work, you need to enter the commands exactly. This can be especially tricky when you're trying to lay out the controls for a rollout. Max includes a tool called the Visual MAXScript Editor that speeds up the creation of rollouts.

To access the Visual MAXScript window, shown in Figure 49.18, select it from the MAXScript menu. Another way to access this window is to select Edit ➪ New Rollout or Edit Rollout (F2) in the MAXScript Editor window.

FIGURE 49.18

The Visual MAXScript window makes building rollouts easy.

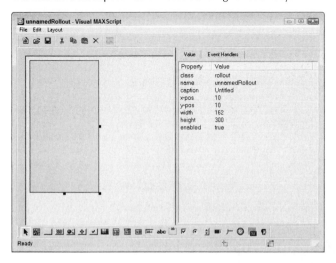

Layouts for a rollout created in the Visual MAXScript window can be saved as files with the .VMS extension using the File menu. If you access the window from a MAXScript Editor window, then the Save menu automatically updates the editor window.

The Editor interface

The window includes two major panes. The left pane is where the various rollout elements are assembled, and the right pane holds the Value and Event Handlers tabbed panels. The Value panel lists all the properties and their associated values for the selected element. You can change the property values by clicking on them and entering a new value. For example, if you select a Button element in the left panel, then the properties for that control are presented in the Value panel. If you click the Caption Property, its value becomes highlighted; you can type a new caption, and the new caption appears on the button.

The Event Handlers panel lists all the available events that can be associated with the selected element. Clicking the check box to the left of these events can enable the events. For a button element, you can enable the pressed event. With this event enabled, the code includes a function where you can define what happens when this event is fired.

The menus and the main toolbar

At the top of the interface are some menu options and a main toolbar. The File menu also lets you create a new layout (Ctrl+N), save layouts to a file (Ctrl+S), and open saved layouts (Ctrl+O). The Edit menu allows you to cut (Ctrl+X), copy (Ctrl+C), and paste (Ctrl+V) form elements. You can find these same features as buttons on the top toolbar.

The Layout menu includes options for aligning elements left (Ctrl+left arrow), right (Ctrl+right arrow), top (Ctrl+up arrow), bottom (Ctrl+down arrow), vertical center (F9), and horizontal center (Shift+F9); to space elements evenly across (Alt+right arrow) or down (Alt+up arrow); make elements the same size by width, height, or both; center vertically (Ctrl+F9) or horizontally (Ctrl+Shift+F9) in the dialog box; and flip. You can use the Layout ⇨ Guide Settings menu command to specify grid snapping and spacing. Grids are enabled using the Toggle Grid/Snap button on the right end of the main toolbar.

You can also access these commands using a right-click pop-up menu when clicking on the left pane.

Toolbar elements

The toolbar along the bottom of the window contains the form elements that you can drop on the form. These buttons and elements include those shown in Table 49.2.

TABLE 49.2

Visual MAXScript Form Elements

Button	Element	What It Does
	Bitmap	Lets you add bitmap images to a rollout
	Button	Adds a simple button
	Map Button	Adds a mapping button that opens the Material/Map Browser
	Material Button	Adds a material button that also opens the Material/Map Browser
	Pick Button	Adds a button that lets you pick an object in a viewport
	Check Button	Adds a button that can be toggled on and off
	Color Picker	Adds a color swatch that opens the Color Picker dialog box when clicked
	Combo Box	Adds a list with several items
	Drop Down List	Adds a list with one item displayed
	List Box	Adds a list with several items displayed
	Edit Box	Adds a text field that can be modified
	Label	Adds a text label

continued

1175

TABLE 49.2 *(continued)*

Button	Element	What It Does
	Group Box	Adds a grouping outline to surround several controls
	Check Box	Adds a check box control that can be toggled on or off
	Radio Buttons	Adds a set of buttons where only one can be selected
	Spinner	Adds an up and down set of arrows that can modify a value field
	Progress Bar	Adds a bar that highlights from left to right as a function is completed
	Slider	Adds a slider control that can move from a minimum to a maximum value
	Timer	Adds a timer that counts time intervals
	ActiveX Control	Adds a generic ActiveX control created by a separate vendor
	Custom	Adds a custom control that can be defined as needed

At the bottom right of the window are two text fields that display the coordinates of the current mouse cursor position and the size of the rollout. The default size of the rollout is 162 × 300, which is the size needed to fit perfectly in the Command Panel.

Laying Out a Rollout

The rollout space, which appears gray in the left pane, can be selected and resized by dragging the black square handles at the edges of the form. As you change its size, its dimensions are displayed in the lower-right corner of the interface. With the rollout space correctly sized, you are ready to add elements to the space.

To add one of these elements to the form, click the element button on the toolbar and drag on the form. The element appears and is selected. The selected element is easy to identify by the black handles that surround it. Dragging on these handles resizes the element, and clicking and dragging on the center of the element repositions it within the rollout space.

The Value and Events panels are automatically updated to show the values and events for the selected element. Values such as width and x-pos are automatically updated if you drag an element or drag its handles to resize it.

Aligning and spacing elements

Although only one element at a time can be surrounded by black handles, you can actually drag an outline in the rollout space to select multiple elements at once. With several elements selected, you can align them all to the left (Ctlr+left arrow), horizontally centered (Shift+F9), right (Ctrl+right arrow), top (Ctrl+up arrow), vertically centered (F9), or bottom (Ctrl+down arrow).

Multiple elements can also be spaced across (Alt+right arrow) or down (Alt+up arrow). To make several elements the same width, height, or both, use the Layout ➪ Make Same Size menu command. The Center in Dialog menu aligns elements to the center of the dialog box either vertically (Ctrl+F9) or horizontally (Ctrl+Shift+F9). The Flip command reverses the position of the selected elements.

Figure 49.19 shows a form with several aligned elements added to it.

FIGURE 49.19

You can add control elements to the form in the Visual MAXScript window.

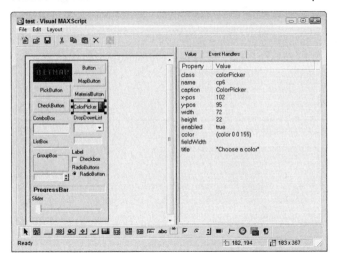

Tutorial: Building a custom rollout with the Visual MAXScript Editor

Now you need some practice using this powerful tool. In this example, you use the Visual MAXScript window to lay out a rollout and code the script to make it work.

To create a custom rollout using the Visual MAXScript Editor, follow these steps:

1. Open the BuildCube.max file from the Chap 49 directory on the DVD.

   This file includes a simple sphere object.

2. Choose MAXScript ➪ New Script to open the MAXScript Editor window. In the editor window, enter the following:

   ```
   utility buildCube "Build Cube" ( )
   ```

1177

This line creates a utility named buildCube. The rollout name is Build Cube. Make sure to include a space in between the parentheses.

3. Choose Tools ⇨ New Rollout from the window menu (or press the F2 key). The Visual MAXScript window opens. The properties for this rollout are displayed in the Properties panel. Drag the lower-right black square handle to resize the rollout form.

4. Click the spinner button on the bottom toolbar, and drag in the rollout form to create a spinner element. In the Properties panel, set the name to **SideNum**, set the caption value to **No. of Side Objects**, select the #integer for the type, and set the range to [**1,100,5**]. The range values set the lower, upper, and default values for the spinner. Then drag the element handles to resize the element to fit in the form.

5. Click the spinner button again, and drag in the rollout form to create another spinner element. In the Properties panel, set the name to **length**, set the caption value to **Side Length**, select the #integer for the type, and set the range to [**1,1000,50**]. Then drag the element handles to resize the element to fit in the form.

6. Click the button icon on the bottom toolbar, and drag in the rollout form to create a button below the spinners. In the Properties panel, set the name to **createCube** and the caption value to **Create Cube**. Then drag the element handles to resize the button so the text fits on the button. Open the Event Handlers panel, and select the Pressed check box.

7. Drag over the top of both the spinners to select them both, and choose Layout ⇨ Align ⇨ Right (or press Ctrl+right arrow) to align the spinners. Figure 49.20 shows how the rollout layout looks.

FIGURE 49.20

The rollout laid out in the Visual MAXScript window

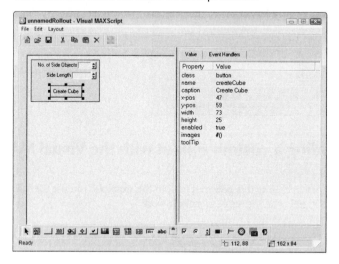

8. With the layout complete, choose File ⇨ Save (or press Ctrl+S) to save the layout, and then close the Visual MAXScript window.

   The script code associated with the layout is automatically placed in the editor window.

9. Complete the script by entering the script commands immediately after the open parenthesis that appears on the line following the on createCube pressed do event, as shown in Figure 49.21. Then, copy and paste the code from the BuildCube.ms file from the Chap 49 directory on the DVD.

10. Open the Utilities panel, and click the MAXScript button. Then click the Run Script button, and select the BuildCube.ms file from the Chap 49 directory on the DVD.

    The utility installs and appears in the Utility drop-down list in the MAXScript rollout.

11. Select the BuildCube utility from the drop-down list in the MAXScript rollout, and scroll down the Command Panel to see the Build Cube rollout. Select the sphere object, and click the Create Cube button.

    The script executes, and a cube of spheres is created.

FIGURE 49.21

The MAXScript Editor window is updated with the code from the Visual MAXScript window.

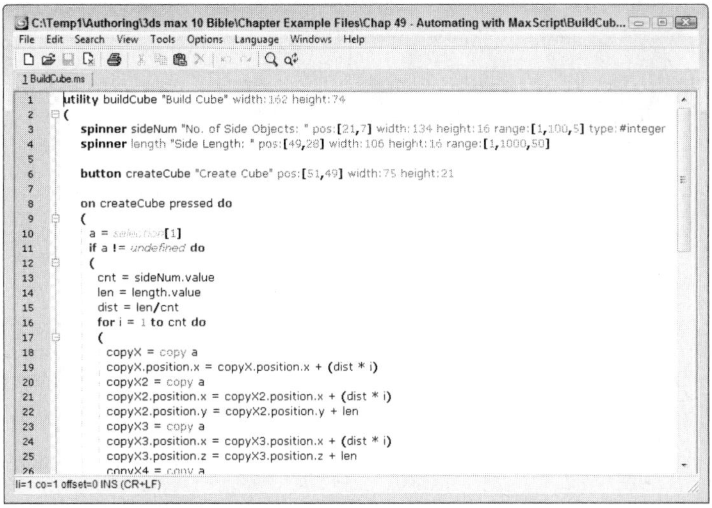

Figure 49.22 shows the results of the BuildCube.ms script. You can use this script with any selected object.

FIGURE 49.22

The results of the BuildCube.ms script

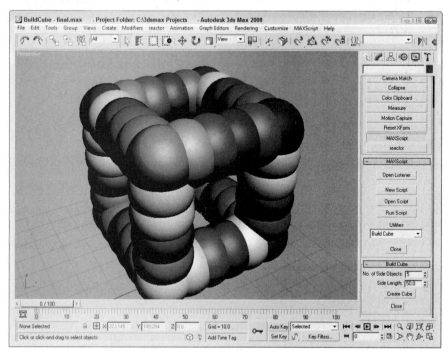

Summary

This chapter gave you a brief introduction to MAXScript, 3ds Max's powerful, built-in scripting language. Besides describing the different types of scripts you can create, the chapter covered the following topics:

- The basics of MAXScript
- Using the MAXScript tools such as the MAXScript Editor and Listener windows
- Using the Macro Recorder to create scripts
- Using the MAXScript Debugger
- The different script types
- The basics of writing your own scripts
- The Visual MAXScript Editor interface
- The features of each rollout element
- How to create scripted utilities with custom rollouts

Now that you're feeling more comfortable with scripts, we look at the pinnacle of added functionality — plug-ins.

Chapter 50

Expanding Max with Third-Party Plug-Ins

A plug-in is an external program that integrates seamlessly with the Max interface to provide additional functionality. Autodesk has adopted an architecture for Max that is open and enables all aspects of the program to be enhanced. Max ships with a Software Developer's Kit (SDK) that enables users to generate their own plug-ins. Many companies currently produce plug-ins, and other users create and distribute freeware and shareware plug-ins.

The purpose of this chapter isn't to cover all the available plug-ins or to teach you how to create plug-ins, but simply to show you how to install and access plug-ins. At the end of the chapter is a list of Web links you can use to locate plug-ins for Max. The entire architecture of Max is built around plug-ins, and many of the core components of Max are implemented as plug-ins. Max ships with a robust SDK that includes all the information you need to create your own plug-ins.

A key feature that allowed Max to become and remain so popular is that users can download and install plug-ins that extend Max's power and functionality. Plug-ins allow Max to adapt to the needs of each user as well as keep up with new ideas.

One plug-in that is worth closer inspection ships with Max and is installed by default. The Turbo Squid Tentacles plug-in provides access to a Web site of content that you can buy, download, and use. This content includes models, textures, and even plug-ins.

IN THIS CHAPTER
Using Turbo Squid Tentacles
Understanding plug-ins
Locating plug-ins
Installing, viewing, and managing plug-ins
Looking at plug-in examples

Using Turbo Squid Tentacles

If you need a frog for the background of your scene and you don't have the time or the inclination to create one (maybe you're worried about getting warts), then another option is to buy a model that is already made.

Turbo Squid Tentacles is a separate installation, but it is included by default when Max is installed. In fact, you need to specifically select it not to be installed if you don't want it.

Once installed, it shows up as a menu option to the right of all other menus. The menu options include Search Marketplace for browsing content online, Open My Files for retrieving any downloaded content that you've purchased, and Save to Tentacles for uploading content to the Turbo Squid marketplace.

When you choose the Search Marketplace menu command, a Web browser opens with thumbnails showing the available content, as shown in Figure 50.1. The browser lets you sort by product, file format, and price. Most items are rated and each item's price and creator are listed.

FIGURE 50.1

Turbo Squid Tentacles is an online marketplace of content available for purchase.

> **NOTE**   The Turbo Squid marketplace can be browsed without registering, but if you plan to download or purchase any content, you need to create an account.

The product categories include 3D Models, Materials & Shaders, Texture Maps, Motion Capture, and Scripts. Many free items are available for downloading.

When you've selected and purchased an item, a download link appears and the file is downloaded to a local folder or saved in an online folder called My Files. You can access your online My Files folder using the Tentacles ➪ Open My Files command.

The Tentacles ➪ Save to Tentacles menu lets you upload your current scene to your My Files space where you can make it available for others to download.

Working with Plug-Ins

After you've located a plug-in that you would like to add to your system, you need to install the plug-in. Most commercial plug-ins come with an executable setup program that automates this for you, but others need to be installed manually, which isn't difficult.

 Plug-ins typically don't work from one version of Max to another. If the plug-in is commercial, then the developers usually release an updated version of the plug-in for the new Max version.

As you begin to add plug-ins to Max, you may eventually want to see which plug-ins are installed and even disable certain plug-ins. Max includes tools to view installed plug-ins and to manage your current plug-ins.

Installing plug-ins

For commercial plug-ins that include an installation program, the installation process asks where the Max root directory is located. From this root directory, the plug-in program files are typically installed in the "plugins" directory, help files for the plug-ins are installed in the "help" directory, and example scenes are installed in the "scenes" directory.

Plug-in program files typically have a .DLC, .DLR, .DLO, .DLU, .DLV, or .DLM extension, depending on the type of plug-in. When Max loads, it searches the /plugins directory for these files and loads them along with the program files. You can manually install freeware plug-ins simply by copying the plug-in file into the plugins directory and restarting Max.

You can also place plug-ins in a different directory and load them from this directory. The Configure System Paths dialog box includes a panel titled 3rd Party Plug-Ins where you can specify additional plug-in paths.

CROSS-REF Find out more about the Configure System Paths dialog box in Chapter 4, "Customizing the Max Interface and Setting Preferences."

Most commercial plug-ins require that the plug-in be authorized after installation. You must do this before you can use the plug-in, and you can usually do it via telephone, fax, or e-mail.

To remove a plug-in, use the uninstall feature that is part of the setup process, or delete the associated program files from the plugins directory.

Plug-ins can also create a help file that explains how to work with the plug-in. These help files are installed in the /help directory where Max is installed. To view these help files, open the Additional Help dialog box by choosing Help ⇨ Additional Help.

Viewing installed plug-ins

To see all the currently installed plug-ins, choose File ⇨ Summary Info to open the Summary Info dialog box and click the Plug-In Info button. This opens the Plug-In Info dialog box that lists all installed plug-ins with their details, as shown in Figure 50.2. As you can see, many plug-ins created by Autodesk (or Discreet) are installed with just the default installation.

 Even if you haven't installed any plug-ins, this dialog box lists many plug-ins. These are core functions in Max that are implemented as plug-ins.

Managing plug-ins

You can manage which installed plug-ins are available using the Plug-in Manager dialog box, shown in Figure 50.3. Open this dialog box by choosing Customize ⇨ Plug-in Manager.

FIGURE 50.2

The Plug-In Info dialog box includes a list of all the currently loaded plug-ins, both internal and external.

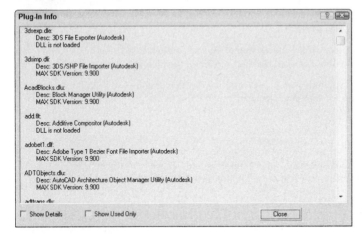

FIGURE 50.3

Use the Plug-in Manager dialog box to disable plug-ins.

Each column in the Plug-in Manager dialog box includes information about the plug-ins. The columns include Tag, Name, Description, Status, Size, and Full Path. You can sort the list of plug-ins alphabetically by column if you click on the column name. An asterisk appears to the right of the column title that is used to sort.

Each unique directory that is specified within the Configure System Paths dialog box appears in the bottom pane of the Plug-in Manager. Use the check boxes to remove all plug-ins in that directory from the list.

 **If you install all your plug-ins into a custom directory, you can use the bottom pane to filter only the plug-ins you've installed.**

In the list of plug-ins, you select a specific plug-in by clicking it. You can select multiple plug-ins in the list using the Ctrl and Shift keys. A right-click pop-up menu of options lets you control the selected plug-ins. You can also tag (or mark) certain plug-ins using the Tag Selected option in the right-click pop-up menu. For tagged plug-ins, a white check mark appears in the left column.

You can also choose to load or defer selected or checked plug-ins using the right-click pop-up menu. Plug-ins with a status of loaded are currently loaded in memory and available; these plug-ins are identified with a green circle in the Status column. The deferred plug-ins are waiting in the wings and load when needed; these plug-ins are identified with a yellow circle in the Status column. Plug-ins that are marked Unloaded (with a red circle) are not in memory.

Using the right-click pop-up menu, you can also select Load New Plug-in, which opens the Choose Plug-in File dialog box where you can select a plug-in file. The file is then accessed from this directory and loaded into the Plug-in Manager list.

Tutorial: Installing and using the AfterBurn Plug-in Demo

If you'd like to try out some plug-ins before purchasing them, check out the Partners and Samples section on the 3ds Max install disc or visit the developers' Web sites to download a demo copy of the plug-in.

CAUTION These demos are full-featured, but most of them are save-disabled, which prevents you from saving the file that includes the plug-in's features. Look at the readme file as the plug-in is installed to see what has been disabled.

To install a demo plug-in from the Max install disc, follow these steps:

1. Insert the 3ds Max installation disc into your CD-ROM drive. When a menu of options appears, click the Partners and Samples link and then click the Autodesk Certified Animation Plug-Ins link.

   A page of certified plug-in demos appears, including AfterBurn, Absolute Character Tools, DreamScape, and others.

2. Click AfterBurn to select it, and click the Install button to launch the installation wizard. Follow the Installation Wizard's instructions, and press Next to complete each step. Click the Finish button when the installation is complete.

3. You need to restart Max before the plug-ins features become available, so select Start ⇨ Program Files ⇨ Autodesk ⇨ Autodesk 3ds Max 2008 ⇨ 3ds Max 2008 to restart Max.

4. You can learn to use the AfterBurn plug-in using the help files that were installed; select Help ⇨ Additional Help, and double-click the AfterBurn reference in the list that appears to open the Help files for the plug-in.

5. After reviewing the help files, select Create ⇨ Helpers ⇨ Atmospherics ⇨ Sphere Gizmo and drag in the Top viewport to create a gizmo.

6. Most of the AfterBurn plug-in features are found in the Environment & Effects dialog box. Select Rendering ⇨ Environment (keyboard shortcut, 8), and click the Add button in the Atmosphere rollout. In the Add Atmospheric Effect list, double-click on the AfterBurn Combustion Demo effect. This adds the AfterBurn Combustion effect along with the AfterBurn Renderer to the Effects list and makes several new rollouts appear.

7. In AfterBurn Combustion Parameters rollout, click the Pick Gizmos button and select the Sphere Gizmo icon in the Top viewport.

8. Select Rendering ⇨ Render (F10) to open the Render Scene dialog box. Make sure that the Atmospherics option is enabled, and render the Perspective viewport to see the resulting AfterBurn flame effect.

Figure 50.4 shows the resulting fireball created using the AfterBurn demo plug-in.

FIGURE 50.4

This simple fireball was created using the AfterBurn plug-in.

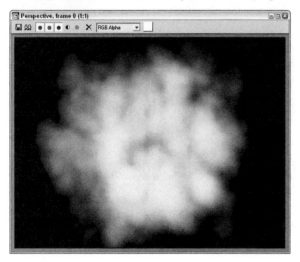

Locating Plug-Ins

Before you can take advantage of plug-ins, you need to locate, acquire, and install them. You can find plug-ins from a variety of sources: commercial, shareware, or freeware.

The first place to look for commercial plug-ins is Digimation. It is not only a plug-in developer, but it resells many plug-ins for other companies. Another good site to check out is the list at Autodesk. Autodesk evaluates plug-ins as part of the Certified Plug-Ins program to ensure compatibility with Max.

In addition to the commercially developed plug-ins, many plug-ins are available as freeware or shareware. You can find many of these plug-ins and download them via the Web.

If you're looking for plug-ins, both commercial and shareware, you should visit these sites:

- **Digimation:** www.digimation.com/
- **BoboLand:** www.scriptspot.com/bobo/
- **Max Plugins.De:** www.maxplugins.de/
- **Pluginz.com:** http://www.pluginz.com/3ds+Max
- **Autodesk:** http://usa.autodesk.com/adsk/servlet/index?id= 5659455&siteID=123112
- **Turbo Squid:** www.turbosquid.com/

CAUTION Plug-ins typically are not compatible between different versions of Max. For example, a plug-in written for version 2.5 does not work on versions 8, 9, or 2008, and vice versa. When downloading and purchasing plug-ins, be sure to get a version that matches your current version of Max.

NEW FEATURE Although plug-ins aren't compatible between versions, plug-ins created for 3ds Max 9 work in 3ds Max 2008 without being recompiled. However, plug-ins compiled for 3ds Max 2008 do not work in 3ds Max 9.

Summary

By adding plug-ins, you can increase the functionality of Max far beyond its default setup. In this chapter, we've covered the following topics:

- Using Turbo Squid Tentacles
- What plug-ins are and how they can extend Max
- How to install, view, and manage plug-ins
- Where to find plug-ins

Well, you did it. You reached the end of the book. Congratulations. Before diving head-first into Max, you may want to check out the appendixes, but keep this book handy because it is useful as a reference.

Appendix A

What's New with 3ds Max 2008

IN THIS APPENDIX

Finding the new features in Max

Enjoying the minor enhancements that Max has to offer

With each revision of Max, I'm always amazed at the new features that are included. Max is a large and complex piece of software, and just about the time that I think it can't hold anything more, a new revision with a host of new features appears. Max 2008 is no different, starting with a new name that breaks the mold from other versions by following the year instead of a version number.

You can find the real coverage of the new features in the various chapters, but this appendix provides a quick overview of these new features along with references on where to learn more about them. Throughout the book, the New Feature icon identifies the features that are new to 3ds Max 2008.

NOTE If Max needs some improvements that haven't made it into the latest release, you can join Autodesk's Customer Involvement Program using the Help ▷ Customer Involvement Program menu command. This program lets you provide feedback and suggestions to the Max team.

Major Improvements

3ds Max 2008 includes lots of new improvements. Some are considered major because they likely will affect every user's workflow, and others are minor because they are smaller in scale. However, an improvement listed as minor may be the one you've been waiting for.

NOTE Within the Introduction section of the Max User Reference is a What's New in 3ds Max 2008 page. At the top of this page are links to several videos that show these new features.

Vista and Direct X 10 enabled

3ds Max 2008 is officially compatible with Microsoft Vista 32-bit and 64-bit. It also is compatible with DirectX 10.

Updated viewport display

The viewport display has been overhauled to include a new mode that displays interactive light and shadow previews directly in the viewport. This mode also can display Max's Sun & Sky system as well as Architectural and Design materials applied to objects in the scene using the new Show Hardware Map in Viewport option.

The viewports also have a new Adaptive Degradation System that can be configured to simplify the display in order to maintain a designated frame rate. The topics of customizing the viewports and using these new display modes are covered in Chapter 2, "Controlling and Configuring the Viewports."

Scene Explorer

The Scene Explorer interface provides a quick view of all the object properties in the whole scene in a convenient table interface that can be sorted, filtered, and customized to show exactly what you need to see. The Scene Explorer interface lets you easily make global changes to multiple objects without having to navigate the viewports. You can learn more about this interface in Chapter 6, "Selecting Objects, Setting Object Properties, and Using Layers and the Scene Explorer."

MAXScript ProEditor

If you've spent any time building MAXScripts, then you'll appreciate the new MAXScript ProEditor. This new editor is much easier to use than Windows Notepad for building scripts. It has multiple levels of undo, search and replace features, line numbers, and the ability to color code the script syntax. More on the MAXScript ProEditor is presented in Chapter 49, "Automating with MAXScript."

Working Pivot

The new Working Pivot lets you place and enable a temporary pivot that is used to rotate and scale objects without affecting the current object pivot. This Working Pivot is handy when you need to rotate objects about the center of another object without altering the object's base pivot. The Working Pivot is covered in Chapter 7, "Transforming Objects, Pivoting, Aligning, and Snapping."

Sky Portal

The new mental ray Sky Portal light type lets you focus all the light streaming through a window from a Daylight system so that the projected rays are localized to the designated window boundaries. This results in a much better lighting solution that is computed faster requiring fewer Final Gather rays. More on this new lighting type is found in Chapter 46, "Raytracing and mental ray."

Biped Improvements

Biped keeps getting updated with each new edition, and this edition is no different. The new improvements to Biped allow new custom defined joints called Xtras to be added to the base Biped. These new custom joints can have up to 25 links and can be copied to the opposite side of the Biped. Another improvement is that the head can move independent of the body. Biped files now can be divided and saved into layers. These and other Biped features are covered in Chapter 42, "Creating and Animating Bipeds and Crowds."

Apply Unwrap UVs to multiple objects

The Unwrap UVs interface can now open and work with multiple objects at once. This allows you to easily apply a single texture map seamlessly across multiple objects. This new feature is covered in Chapter 30, "Unwrapping UVs and Using Pelt Mapping."

Editable Poly improvements

Editable Poly modeling is the preferred modeling method in Max, and it is still being improved. The new improvements include a subobject mode that lets you see and select multiple vertices, edges, and faces without having to switch modes. A new Normal constraint lets you constrain the movement of objects along the surface normal. Also, snapping works in Polygon Create mode, and the subobject selection color can be customized. The new press-and-release keyboard shortcuts let you work more quickly without having to spend time selecting different modes. These new modeling features are covered in Chapter 12, "Modeling with Polygons."

Improved performance

Although performance issues aren't really covered throughout the text, they are important concerns for Max users, and Autodesk has responded with multiple performance improvements that make the software faster in performing certain tasks, especially when working with a large number of objects. The following is a short list of the performance improvements found in 3ds Max 2008:

- Max now treats multiple meshes as if they were one large mesh, resulting in faster viewport display.
- Selecting objects when multiple objects are in the scene is now much faster.
- Assigning materials to multiple objects is now up to 10 times faster than before.
- Moving, scaling, or rotating a large number of objects is much faster in 3ds Max 2008 and is even faster when the Track bar is hidden.
- Converting multiple objects to a different object type is faster when the Modify panel is selected.
- Cloning, grouping, linking, and duplicating objects also is faster in the new version.

Minor Improvements

In addition to the major improvements are many minor improvements that make working with objects, materials, and other facets of Max easier. Minor improvements found in version 2008 include the following:

- **Motion Mixer Selection Sets:** A set of animation clips can be designated as a selection set, making them easy to choose.
- **Default zero frame preference:** A new preference in the Animation pane allows you to set the default beginning frame of an animation to something besides zero.
- **Assigning a Controller to multiple objects:** Controllers used to require that each object be assigned separately, but now multiple objects can be assigned to a Controller at once.
- **Curling hierarchies:** Each object linked in a hierarchical chain can be rotated about its local pivot to create a curling effect.
- **Cloth Compress attributes:** To allow better definition of cloth objects, the new U Compress and V Compress attributes are included to define how the cloth acts when forces push it into itself.
- **Improved DWG format support:** The DWG format has been improved again to support mapping types and UVs imported from AutoCAD 2008. The improvements also include support for Daylight systems.
- **Select colors from any open window:** The Color Selector includes an Eyedropper tool that can select colors from any open window.

- **Render to Texture presets:** The Render to Texture feature can save and load presets in the Objects to Bake rollout.
- **Self-Illumination in the Architectural and Design materials:** The Architecture and Design materials now include a new Self-Illumination property that can be used to create lights from materials.
- **Photographic Exposure Control:** The new Photographic Exposure Control includes settings that mimic camera settings including aperture and shutter speed. This control lets you do tone mapping for images.
- **mental ray 3.6:** 3ds Max 2008 includes the latest version of mental ray, version 3.6, which includes new shaders such as the Lume Glare shader.
- **Backwards compatible plug-ins:** All plug-ins that were compiled for the 3ds Max 9 SDK work in 3ds Max 2008.

Appendix B

Installing and Configuring 3ds Max 2008

Before you can enjoy all the great features in 3ds Max, you have to install the software and get your system configured properly. This appendix helps you do just that. After you're finished here, you're ready to go.

Choosing an Operating System

If you're purchasing a new computer to run 3ds Max and have the luxury of customizing your system, you can do several things to make life easier. One of your first decisions is what operating system to use to run Max. 3ds Max 2008 can run on both Windows XP and Windows Vista.

If you choose to run 3ds Max on Windows XP Professional, make sure that you have installed the latest Service Pack (which you can download for free from Microsoft's Web page at www.microsoft.com). Both operating systems enable you to run multiple copies of 3ds Max at the same time on a single machine. If you're running the 64-bit version of Max, then you need to be running a 64-bit operating system.

> **NOTE** You also can run Max on Windows XP Home without any trouble.

Also note that Windows 2000, NT, Windows 98, and Windows ME are not supported.

Hardware Requirements

To get good performance from 3ds Max, you need a fairly meaty machine. A good default system to use is a Pentium-IV or an AMD Athlon-based computer with 1GB or more of RAM (and 2GB of swap space) and a decent-sized hard drive and monitor. If need be, you can get by with as little as 512MB of RAM

IN THIS APPENDIX

Choosing an operating system

Understanding hardware requirements

Installing 3ds Max 2008

Authorizing the software

Setting the display driver

(with 500MB swap space), but you may spend lots of time watching your computer churn furiously to keep up. A dual Intel Xeon, a dual AMD Athlon, or a 32-bit Opteron system is recommended.

 **Max under Windows 2000 or XP can take advantage of multiprocessor machines.**

3ds Max has been compiled to run on both 32-bit and 64-bit computers. If you select to use a 64-bit system, Max will be able to deal with dramatically larger data sets. For the 64-bit version of Max, you need a minimum of 1GB of memory with 4GB recommended.

One element of your system that will probably have the greatest impact on the performance of 3ds Max is the graphics card. Any good graphics card has specialized hardware that will take much of the workload off your computer's CPU, freeing it up to do other tasks. 3ds Max is very graphics-intensive, and a little extra money in the graphics card department will go a long way toward boosting your performance.

The good news is that hardware accelerated graphics cards are becoming cheaper: You can get great cards for $200–300. When searching for a graphics card, make sure that it can support a resolution of at least 1024 × 768 at 16-bit color with 3D graphics acceleration including support for OpenGL and/or DirectX 9.0c and 10. You'll also want a minimum of 64MB on the graphics card, but look for cards with at least 256MB or more for 3D graphics acceleration. You can use some of the graphics boards built to run computer games; however, be aware that some boards claim to support OpenGL but actually support only a subset of it. Before going out to make your purchase, visit the Autodesk Web site (`www.autodesk.com/3dsmax`) to see performance metrics for various popular graphics cards.

TIP **A video card is only as good as the available drivers. Max relies heavily on these drivers. If the driver has trouble, then your display flickers, has speed problems, or just plain doesn't work. Both nVidia and ATI video cards have excellent drivers with broad support.**

For the complete installation, you need 650MB of hard drive space. You can get by with less if you choose the Compact installation option. Another handy piece of hardware to have is a scrollable mouse. A scrollable mouse makes moving through menus and the Command Panel easier, and it gives you a third button, which can be used to navigate the viewports. Max also ships on DVD-ROM, so you need a DVD-ROM drive to install the software. Max also supports graphics tablets.

TIP **If you can install Max on a separate physical drive from the drive that Windows runs on, then you'll see an increase in speed because Max doesn't need to compete with Windows for access to the hard drive.**

Installing 3ds Max 2008

Installing Max is straightforward. Here's what you need to do:

1. Insert the Max Installation DVD into the DVD drive. The setup program starts up automatically. If you don't have Windows Autorun enabled, or if the setup program doesn't start, run the Setup.exe program on the DVD.

2. When the setup program starts, the 3ds Max 2008 Installation window, shown in Figure B.1, displays a menu of three options: Install Products, Create Deployments, and Install Tools and Utilities. The Create Deployments link begins a wizard for installing a network version of Max, and the Install Tools and Utilities link gives you access to install the supporting tools including the Max SDK. Click the Install Products link to continue.

> **NOTE** The Install Tools and Utilities link includes links to install Autodesk Design Review 2008, 3ds Max 2008 SDK and SDK Help for Visual Studio 2005, Network License Manager and Activation Utility, Autodesk CAD Manager Tools 4.0, SAMreport-Lite (which requires a license), RPC Plug-in, EASYnat 2.5 trial, and Okino plug-in demos. You also find info links for learning more about each of these tools and utilities along with links to download a trial of Autodesk Combustion, Java, QuickTime 7, and the Adobe Flash Player 9.

FIGURE B.1

The first page of the installation wizard divides the products into three choices.

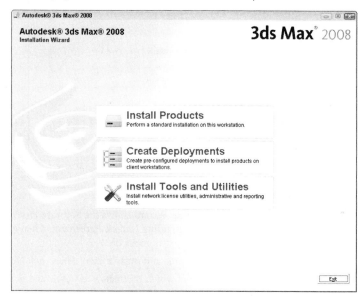

3. The next couple of screens show some legal wording and links to view the Readme file and some Tutorial files. The Readme file and the Tutorials can be accessed later. Continue clicking the Next button to move through these screens until you get to a screen where the various products are listed, as shown in Figure B.2.

> **TIP** Unlike many Readme files, Max's Readme file includes detailed information about a huge list of features, including clearer descriptions about the features' idiosyncrasies and a troubleshooting section. If you're having trouble with a specific feature, see the Readme file.

4. After reviewing the product list, click the checkbox for either the 32-bit or 64-bit versions of Max along with any additional products that you want to install at the same time. Be sure to select the version that matches your operating system.

> **TIP** Many of the features of 3ds Max are listed as separate installations on the Products screen including the Help files, additional maps and materials, the Architectural materials, videos, Vault, and Turbo Squid Tentacles. If you don't select some of these options, you can save some disk space, but the feature is not installed. You can install them later if you need them.

FIGURE B.2

The Products to Install screen splits the products into several different installations.

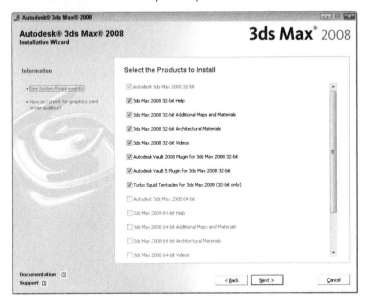

5. In the next screen, the 3ds Max 2008 Setup Wizard shows the Software License Agreement. Choose your country, and read the corresponding License Agreement. After you've read the agreement, click the "I Accept" option. Click Next to move on.

6. The next screen asks you to input your name and organization. Then click Next.

7. The next screen shows a summary page of which products you've selected to install, as shown in Figure B.3.

8. If you click the Configure button, you can cycle through several pages of configuration options, including the choice to install Max as a standalone version or as a network version. If the Network License option is selected, you need to enter the name of the server that is running the Network License Server. The next configuration option is to install a Typical or a Custom installation. If you choose a Custom installation, you can choose which sub-components to install. You also can select the location where Max will be installed. The final option is to enable a port number for mental ray to use Backburner, the network rendering engine. After Max is configured, you can click on the Backburner panel to walk through the configuration for Backburner. Click on the Configuration Complete button to continue with the installation. When all products are configured, click the Install link. Each of the various selected options is then installed and the wizard, shown in Figure B.4, shows the progress.

9. When the installation is complete, a screen appears informing you that the installation is complete.

NOTE When Max installation is complete, it does not require Windows to be rebooted.

In the lower-left corner of the installation window are links for Documentation, and Support. Information links to the left provide additional information such as the hardware requirements.

FIGURE B.3

The wizard shows a summary page before beginning the installation.

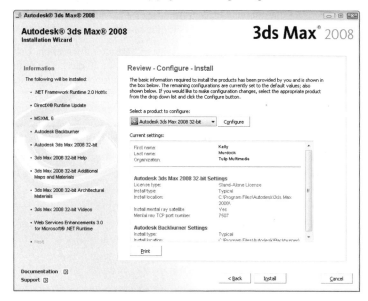

FIGURE B.4

The summary page lets you configure the various products before they are installed.

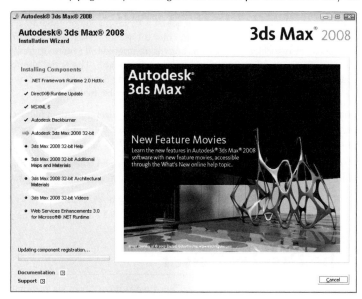

Registering and Activating the Software

After Max is installed, you can start Max using the desktop shortcut or the Start menu, but Max requires that you register and activate the software through Autodesk for permanent use. The software continues to run for 30 days without activation, but after 30 days it quits working.

Figure B.5 shows the screen that first appears when you start Max after installation. Using this screen, you can launch the Activation Wizard or run the software unactivated for 30 days. The Registration Wizard automatically appears when you select the Activate the product option and click the Next button.

The first screen to appear after first running Max lets you activate your software or run it without activation.

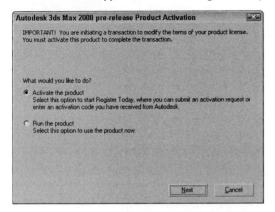

The first screen of the Registration Wizard lets you get an activation code or enter an activation code if you have one. To obtain an activation code, you need to enter information such as your name, address, and company name. You can also specify whether this copy is an upgrade. If you're upgrading your Max version, you need to include the serial number for your previous version. The Serial Number and Request Code are automatically filled in using the numbers entered during the installation. You can authorize the software using a direct connection to the Web, fax, e-mail, or regular mail.

If you receive an activation code via fax, e-mail, or mail, you can select the "Already have an activation code" option on the first screen that appears when you run Max and click Next. A screen opens where you can enter the activation code. The wizard registers this number with Max and completes the registration process.

 The activation code is specific to a specific computer and works only for that computer. If you want to install the software on a separate computer, you need to obtain another activation code.

Within Max, the Help ⇨ Activate 3ds Max menu command lets you enter an activation number to activate the software.

Setting the Display Driver

When Max is first run, a Welcome Screen appears. This screen shows seven short movies that explain the basic features of Max and are worth previewing. As part of the Max default installation, Direct X drivers are installed. Because Max knows these drivers are available, it uses them to run the software in Direct 3D mode by default. The current display driver is identified on the title bar at the top of the Max window. Even though Direct 3D is used by default, you can change the display driver to OpenGL if you want.

If Max is running, you can change the display driver in Max by choosing Customize ➪ Preferences and clicking the Choose Driver button in the Viewports panel. This opens the Direct3D Driver Setup dialog box. If you click the Revert from Direct3D button, then the Graphics Driver Setup dialog box, shown in Figure B.6 opens. If you change the graphics driver, you need to restart Max before the new driver is used.

 Most recent graphics cards include support for both OpenGL and DirectX built in, so you may want to try OpenGL or Direct3D to see if they work.

FIGURE B.6

This dialog box lets you choose the display driver to use.

You can choose one of three different drivers to use in Max: Software, OpenGL, or Direct3D. You also have the option of selecting a custom driver.

 If you want to change a display driver when starting Max, select the Start ➪ All Programs ➪ Autodesk ➪ Autodesk 3ds Max 2008 ➪ Change Graphics Mode program.

Software

The software display driver option is Max's own built-in software graphics driver. Because the software driver does not take advantage of any special graphics hardware that your graphics card supports, your computer's CPU does all the work. The nice thing about this option is that it works on any computer, even if you don't have a good graphics card.

If you're having display problems, try starting up Max using software drivers to make sure that everything has installed correctly. Next, try the different graphics drivers to see whether you can move up to something faster.

OpenGL

If your graphics card supports OpenGL in hardware, this is a great driver to use. OpenGL works under all Windows operating systems and is typically present on high-end graphics cards. In order for Max to use OpenGL, the drivers must support OpenGL 1.1 or later. One of the features enabled with the OpenGL drivers is Virtual Viewports.

Direct3D

Direct3D uses the graphics card's hardware capabilities and simulates anything else it needs in software. You must have DirectX 8.1 or higher installed for these drivers to work, but it is installed by default automatically, so you should be good to go. Simulating different features makes Direct3D run on a wide range of computers, but it can be much slower. If your graphics card's drivers support all of Direct3D in hardware, then using this driver might give you good performance. If it switches to software mode, however, it will be much slower.

Custom

Max also can use custom drivers created by a graphics card manufacturer. You need to add the driver file to the \Drivers directory where Max is installed.

Updating Max

Max includes a feature for checking for and automatically installing updates. From within Max, you can select Help ⇨ 3ds Max on the Web ⇨ Updates. This menu command opens a Web page where the updates are posted.

You also can schedule Max to look for updates automatically using the Communication Center button at the bottom of the interface. This button provides access to a dialog box where you can set Max to look for updates Daily, Weekly, Monthly, or On Demand.

Moving Max to Another Computer

A stand-alone license of Max can exist on only one computer at a time. If you reinstall Max on a different computer, you need to export the license to the new computer. Exporting a license is accomplished using the Portable License Utility, shown in Figure B.7. This utility can be found in the Start ⇨ All Programs ⇨ Autodesk ⇨ Autodesk 3ds Max 2008 folder.

NOTE If you are running Max from a network, an alternative to exporting a license is borrowing one using the Help ⇨ License Borrowing ⇨ Borrow License. The Help ⇨ License Borrowing ⇨ Return License menu command returns the borrowed license when you're finished.

FIGURE B.7

Use the Portable License Utility to move a Max license to another computer.

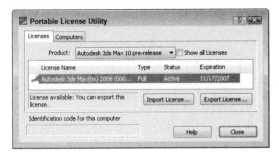

The Portable License Utility displays all licenses on the current computer and the identification code for the computer (which has been blanked out for this figure). Select the license to export, and click the Export License button. This saves the license to a file that you can import using the same utility on the new computer. After you export your license, it continues to work on the original computer for a 24-hour grace period.

Appendix C

3ds Max 2008 Keyboard Shortcuts

The key to working efficiently with Max is learning the keyboard shortcuts. If you know the keyboard shortcuts, you don't need to spend time moving the mouse cursor all around the interface; you can simply press the keyboard shortcut and get instant access to commands and tools.

Using Keyboard Shortcuts

Most of the major dialog boxes such as the Material Editor and the Track View have their own set of keyboard shortcuts. When the Keyboard Shortcut Override toggle button on the main toolbar is enabled, keyboard shortcuts work for both the main interface and the separate dialog boxes. If there is a conflict, the dialog box's shortcut takes precedence.

For example, in the main Max window, the A key toggles the Angle Snap feature on and off, but in the Track View–Curve Editor window, the A key enables Add Keys mode. If the Curve Editor is open and the Keyboard Shortcut Override toggle is enabled, then the Add Keys mode is enabled. If the Keyboard Shortcut Override toggle is off, then the Angle Snap is activated.

If you want to change any of the keyboard shortcuts, the Customize User Interface dialog box includes a Keyboard panel for making changes. You can open this dialog box using the Customize ➪ Customize User Interface command.

CROSS-REF Chapter 4, "Customizing the Max Interface and Setting Preferences," offers more details on creating custom keyboard shortcuts.

IN THIS APPENDIX

Overriding the keyboard shortcuts

Using the Hotkey Map

Main interface shortcuts

Dialog box shortcuts

Character Studio shortcuts

Miscellaneous shortcuts

Using the Hotkey Map

In the Help menu, you can find the Hotkey Map menu command that opens an interactive window, shown in Figure C.1, that displays all the current keyboard shortcuts for the main interface.

 The Hotkey Map window is a Flash-enabled application that runs within a Web browser.

Moving the mouse cursor over the keyboard displayed in the lower-right corner of the Hotkey Map window highlights the respective section of the keyboard and displays all keyboard shortcuts associated with those keys. The icon in the upper-right corner refreshes the interface, and the triangle in the lower-right corner cycles through all the keys.

FIGURE C.1

The Hotkey Map window displays keyboard shortcuts interactively.

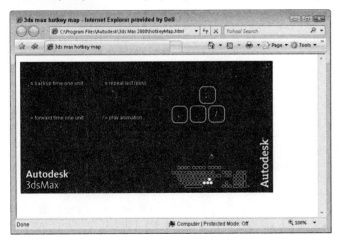

Main Interface Shortcuts

Tables C.1 through C.17 present the shortcut keys for the main interface.

TABLE C.1

Menus

Command	Shortcut	Command	Shortcut
File ➪ New Scene	Ctrl+N	Views ➪ Match Camera To View	Ctrl+C
File ➪ Open File	Ctrl+O	Views ➪ Redraw All Views	`
File ➪ Save File	Ctrl+S	Views ➪ Adaptive Degradation Toggle	O
File ➪ Asset Tracking	Shift+T	Views ➪ Expert Mode Toggle	Ctrl+X

Command	Shortcut	Command	Shortcut
Edit ⇨ Undo Scene Operation	Ctrl+Z	Animation ⇨ Parameter Editor	Alt+1
Edit ⇨ Redo Scene Operation	Ctrl+Y	Animation ⇨ Parameter Collector	Alt+2
Edit ⇨ Hold	Alt+Ctrl+H	Animation ⇨ Wire Parameters	Ctrl+5
Edit ⇨ Fetch	Alt+Ctrl+F	Animation ⇨ Parameter Wire Dialog	Alt+5
Edit ⇨ Delete Objects	Delete	Graph Editors ⇨ Particle View	6
Edit ⇨ Clone	Ctrl+V	Rendering ⇨ Render Scene	F10
Edit ⇨ Move	W	Rendering ⇨ Environment	8
Edit ⇨ Rotate	E	Rendering ⇨ Advanced Lighting	9
Tool ⇨ Transform Type-In	F12	Rendering ⇨ Render to Texture	0 (zero)
Edit ⇨ Select All	Ctrl+A	Rendering ⇨ Material Editor	M
Edit ⇨ Select None	Ctrl+D	Customize ⇨ Show/Hide Main Toolbar	Alt+6
Edit ⇨ Select Invert	Ctrl+I	Customize ⇨ Lock User Interface	Alt+0 (zero)
Edit ⇨ Select Similar	Ctrl+Q	MAXScript ⇨ MAXScript Listener	F11
Edit ⇨ Select by Name	H	File Menu	Alt+F
Tool ⇨ Align	Alt+A	Edit Menu	Alt+E
Tool ⇨ Quick Align	Shift+A	Tools Menu	Alt+T
Tool ⇨ Spacing Tool	Shift+I	Group Menu	Alt+G
Tool ⇨ Normal Align	Alt+N	Views Menu	Alt+V
Tool ⇨ Place Highlight	Ctrl+H	Create Menu	Alt+C
Tool ⇨ Isolate Selection	Alt+Q	Rendering Menu	Alt+R
Views ⇨ Undo View Change	Shift+Z	Customize Menu	Alt+U
Views ⇨ Redo View Change	Shift+Y	MAXScript Menu	Alt+M
Views ⇨ Viewport Background	Alt+B	Help Menu	Alt+H
Views ⇨ Update Background Image	Alt+Shift+Ctrl+B		

TABLE C.2

Main and Floating Toolbars

Command	Shortcut	Command	Shortcut
Undo	Ctrl+Z	Snap to Edge/Segment Toggle	Alt+F10
Redo	Ctrl+Y	Snap to Face Toggle	Alt+F11
Select Object	Q	Snap to Frozen Objects Toggle	Alt+F2
Select by Name	H	Snaps Use Axis Constraints Toggle	Alt+D, Alt+F3
Rectangle, Circle, Fence, Lasso Selection Cycle	Ctrl+F, Q	Snap Type Cycle	Alt+S

continued

TABLE C.2 *(continued)*

Command	Shortcut	Command	Shortcut
Select and Move	W	Snap Hit Cycle	Alt+Shift+S
Select and Rotate	E	Align	Alt+A
Select and Scale	R	Normal Align	Alt+N
Scale Cycle	R, Ctrl+E	Place Highlight	Ctrl+H
Snap Toggle	S	Material Editor	M
Angle Snap Toggle	A	Render Scene	F10
Snap Percent	Shift+Ctrl+P	Quick Render	Shift+Q
Snap to Grid Point Toggle	Alt+F5	Restrict to X	F5
Snap to Pivot Toggle	Alt+F6	Restrict to Y	F6
Snap to Vertex Toggle	Alt+F7	Restrict to Z	F7
Snap to Endpoint Toggle	Alt+F8	Restrict Plane Cycle	F8
Snap to Midpoint Toggle	Alt+F9		

TABLE C.3

Viewports

Command	Shortcut	Command	Shortcut
Front View	F	View Edged Faces	F4
Top View	T	Polygon Counter	7
Bottom View	B	Sound Toggle	\
Left View	L	Show Safeframes	Shift+F
Perspective View	P	Default Lighting	Ctrl+L
Isometric User View	U	See-Through Display	Alt+X
Camera View	C	Redraw All Views	`
Light View	Shift+4 ($)	Offset Snap	Alt+Ctrl+ Spacebar
Disable Viewport	D	Show/Hide Cameras	Shift+C
Viewports Pop-up Menu	V	Show/Hide Geometry	Shift+G
Background Lock Toggle	Alt+Ctrl+B	Show/Hide Grids	G
Dynamic Resizing	Drag viewport borders	Show/Hide Helpers	Shift+H
Transform Gizmo Toggle	X	Show/Hide Lights	Shift+L
Transform Gizmo Size Down	-	Show/Hide Particle Systems	Shift+P
Transform Gizmo Size Up	=	Show/Hide Shapes	Shift+S
Shade Selected Subobject Faces	F2	Show/Hide Space Warps	Shift+W
Wireframe/Smooth+Highlights Toggle	F3	Show/Hide Floating dialog boxes	Ctrl+`

TABLE C.4

Key and Time Controls

Command	Shortcut	Command	Shortcut
Selection Lock Toggle	Spacebar	Backup Time One Unit	, (comma)
Auto Key Mode	N	Forward Time One Unit	. (period)
Set Key Mode	'	Go to Start Frame	Home
Set Keys	K	Go to End Frame	End
Play / Stop Animation	/		

TABLE C.5

Viewport Navigation Controls

Command	Shortcut	Command	Shortcut
Zoom Mode	Alt+Z	Zoom Viewport In	[or scroll wheel forward
Zoom Extents	Alt+Ctrl+Z	Zoom Viewport Out	] or scroll wheel backward
Zoom Extents All	Shift+Ctrl+Z	Pan View	Ctrl+P or drag with middle button
Zoom Extents Selected All	Z	Interactive Pan	I (held down)
Zoom In 2X	Alt+Shift+Ctrl+Z	Walk Through mode	Up arrow
Zoom Out 2X	Alt+Shift+Z	Arc Rotate	Ctrl+R, Alt+drag with middle button
Zoom Region Mode	Ctrl+W	Min/Max Toggle	Alt+W

TABLE C.6

Walk Through Mode

Command	Shortcut	Command	Shortcut
Forward	W, Up Arrow	Decelerate	Z
Back	S, Down Arrow	Increase Step Size	]
Left	A, Left Arrow	Decrease Step Size	[
Right	D, Right Arrow	Reset Step Size	Alt+[
Up	E, Shift+Up Arrow	Level	Shift+Spacebar
Down	C, Shift+Down Arrow	Lock Vertical Rotation	Spacebar
Accelerate	Q		

TABLE C.7

Quadmenus

Command	Shortcut	Command	Shortcut
Animation Quadmenu	Alt+right mouse click	Viewports Quadmenu	V
Lighting/Rendering Quadmenu	Ctrl+Alt+right mouse click	reactor Quadmenu	Shift+Alt+right mouse click
Modeling Quadmenu	Ctrl+right mouse click	Custom 2 Quadmenu	Shift+Ctrl+Alt+right mouse click
Snap Quadmenu	Shift+right mouse click	Custom 3 Quadmenu	Shift+Ctrl+right mouse click

TABLE C.8

Virtual Viewport

Command	Shortcut	Command	Shortcut
Virtual Viewport Toggle	/ (numeric keypad)	Virtual Viewport Pan Left	4 (numeric keypad)
Virtual Viewport Zoom In	+ (numeric keypad)	Virtual Viewport Pan Right	6 (numeric keypad)
Virtual Viewport Zoom Out	- (numeric keypad)	Virtual Viewport Pan Up	8 (numeric keypad)
Virtual Viewport Pan Down	2 (numeric keypad)		

 NOTE The Virtual Viewport option is available only when the OpenGL display driver is used.

TABLE C.9

Subobjects

Command	Shortcut	Command	Shortcut
Subobject mode toggle	Ctrl+B	Subobject Level 4	4
Subobject Level Cycle	Insert	Subobject Level 5	5
Subobject Level 1	1	Delete Subobject	Delete
Subobject Level 2	2	Local Select Subobject by Name	Ctrl+H
Subobject Level 3	3		

TABLE C.10

Hierarchies

Command	Shortcut	Command	Shortcut
Select Ancestor	Page Up	Select Children	Ctrl+Page Down
Select Child	Page Down	Select Entire Hierarchy	Double-click parent

TABLE C.11

Editable Mesh

Command	Shortcut	Command	Shortcut
Vertex Subobject Mode	1	Bevel Mode	Ctrl+V, Ctrl+B
Edge Subobject Mode	2	Chamfer Mode	Ctrl+C
Face Subobject Mode	3	Extrude Mode	Ctrl+E
Polygon Subobject Mode	4	Edge Invisible	Ctrl+I
Element Subobject Mode	5	Edge Turn	Ctrl+T
Detach	Ctrl+D	Weld Selected	Ctrl+W
Cut Mode	Alt+C	Weld Target Mode	Alt+W

All commands in Table C.12 that are listed in bold can be used as press-and-release keyboard shortcuts. These enable you to access a different command by pressing and holding the keyboard shortcut; when you release the keyboard shortcut, Max returns to the previous mode. Press-and-release commands are activated only if the Overrides Active option in the Keyboard panel of the Customize User Interface dialog box is enabled.

NEW FEATURE   Press-and-release keyboard shortcuts are new to 3ds Max 2008.

The following commands can be accessed using press-and-release keyboard shortcuts if you define a keyboard shortcut for them: Bridge, Constrain to None, Constrain to Normal, Paint Deform Push, Pull, Relax, Paint Soft Selection, and Turn.

NOTE   Don't confuse the keyboard shortcuts that work with the Edit Poly modifier with those for the Editable Poly object. Some of the same keyboard shortcuts work for both, but most don't work for the Editable Poly object.

TABLE C.12

Edit Poly Modifier

Command	Shortcut	Command	Shortcut
Vertex Subobject Mode	1	**Bevel Mode**	**Shift+Ctrl+B**
Edge Subobject Mode	2	Bevel Settings	Ctrl+B
Border Subobject Mode	3	**Chamfer Mode**	**Shift+Ctrl+C**
Face Subobject Mode	4	Chamfer Settings	Alt+Ctrl+C
Element Subobject Mode	5	**Inset Mode**	**I**
Object Level (disable sub object mode)	**6**	Inset Settings	Ctrl+I
Select by Vertex	Alt+V	**Outline Mode**	**O**

continued

TABLE C.12 *(continued)*

Command	Shortcut	Command	Shortcut
Soft Selection Affect Backfacing	Ctrl+F	Outline Settings	Ctrl+O
Ignore Backfacing in Selections	Shift+Ctrl+I	**Extrude Mode**	**E**
Shaded Face Toggle	Alt+F	Extrude Settings	Ctrl+E
Grow Selection	Ctrl+Page Up	Extrude Poly Face	Alt+E
Shrink Selection	Ctrl+Page Down	Extrude Along Spline Mode	Alt+E
Select Edge Loop	Alt+L	**Hinge from Edge Mode**	**L**
Select Edge Ring	Alt+R	Hinge from Edge Settings	Ctrl+L
Use Soft Selection	Ctrl+S	Auto Smooth	A
Repeat Last Operation	;	MeshSmooth	M
Constrain to Faces	**X**	MeshSmooth Settings	Ctrl+M
Constrain to Edges	**Shift+X**	Retriangulate	Shift+Ctrl+T
Create	**C**	**Edit Triangulation Mode**	**Shift+T**
Collapse Poly Object	Shift+L	Tessellate	T
Attach	Shift+A	Tessellate Settings	Ctrl+T
Attach List	Shift+Ctrl+A	Flip Normals	F
Detach	Ctrl+D	Hide	H
Break	Shift+B	Hide Unselected	Alt+I
Create Shape From Edge	Shift+M	Unhide All	Alt+U
Insert Vertex Mode	**Shift+I**	**Target Weld Mode**	**Shift+Ctrl+W**
Connect	Shift+Ctrl+E	Weld Settings	Ctrl+W
Connect Edge Settings	Ctrl+N	Make Planar	P
Cut	**Alt+C**	Remove	Shift+R
Quickslice Mode	**Shift+Ctrl+Q**	Remove Isolated Vertices	Shift+Ctrl+R
Slice	Shift+S	Remove Unused Map Vertices	Alf+Shift+Ctrl+R
Slice Plane Mode	S	Align to Grid	G
Reset Slice Plane	Alt+S	Align to View	V
Split Edges	Shift+P	Cap Poly Object	Alt+P

You can use press-and-release keyboard shortcuts, highlighted in bold in Table C.13, with Editable Poly objects.

TABLE C.13

Editable Poly

Command	Shortcut	Command	Shortcut
Vertex Subobject Mode	1	Constrain to Edges	Shift+X
Edge Subobject Mode	2	**Quickslice Mode**	**Shift+Ctrl+Q**
Border Subobject Mode	3	**Bevel Mode**	**Shift+Ctrl+B**
Face Subobject Mode	4	**Chamfer Mode**	**Shift+Ctrl+C**
Element Subobject Mode	5	**Extrude Mode**	**Shift+E**
Object Level (disable subobject mode)	**6**	Extrude Poly Face	Alt+E
Repeat Last Operation	;	MeshSmooth	Ctrl+M
Grow Selection	Ctrl+Page Up	Hide	Alt+H
Shrink Selection	Ctrl+Page Down	Hide Unselected	Alt+I
Select Edge Loop	Alt+L	Unhide All	Alt+U
Select Edge Ring	Alt+R	**Target Weld Mode**	**Shift+Ctrl+W**
Connect	Shift+Ctrl+E	Cap Poly Object	Alt+P
Constrain to Edges	**Shift+X**	Collapse Poly Object	Alt+Ctrl+C
Cut	**Alt+C**		

TABLE C.14

NURBS

Command	Shortcut	Command	Shortcut
Lock 2D Selection	Spacebar	Select Next in V	Ctrl+Up Arrow
CV Constrained Normal Move	Alt+N	Select Previous in V	Ctrl+Down Arrow
CV Constrained U Move	Alt+U	Tessellation Preset 1	Ctrl+1
CV Constrained V Move	Alt+V	Tessellation Preset 2	Ctrl+2
Display Curves	Shift+Ctrl+C	Tessellation Preset 3	Ctrl+3
Display Surfaces	Shift+Ctrl+S	Switch to Point Level	Alt+Shift+P
Display Lattices	Ctrl+L	Switch to Curve Level	Alt+Shift+C
Display Shaded Lattice	Alt+L	Switch to Curve CV Level	Alt+Shift+Z
Display Dependents	Ctrl+D	Switch to Surface Level	Alt+Shift+S
Display Toolbox	Ctrl+T	Switch to Surface CV Level	Alt+Shift+V
Display Trims	Shift+Ctrl+T	Switch to Imports Level	Alt+Shift+I
Select Next in U	Ctrl+Right Arrow	Switch to Top Level	Alt+Shift+T
Select Previous in U	Ctrl+Left Arrow	Transform Degrade	Ctrl+X

TABLE C.15

Free-Form Deformations

Command	Shortcut	Command	Shortcut
Switch to Control Point Level	Alt+Shift+C	Switch to Set Volume Level	Alt+Shift+S
Switch to Lattice Level	Alt+Shift+L	Switch to Top Level	Alt+Shift+T

TABLE C.16

Edit Normals Modifier

Command	Shortcut	Command	Shortcut
Object Level	Ctrl+0	Paste Normal	Ctrl+V
Normal Level	Ctrl+1	Reset Normals	R
Vertex Level	Ctrl+2	Specify Normals	S
Edge Level	Ctrl+3	Unify Normals	U
Face Level	Ctrl+4	Make Explicit	E
Copy Normal	Ctrl+C	Break Normals	B

TABLE C.17

Hair Styling

Command	Shortcut	Command	Shortcut
Select Hair by Ends	Ctrl+1	Puff Roots Transformation	Ctrl+P or Shift+Ctrl+3
Select Whole Guide	Ctrl+2	Clump Transformation	Ctrl+M or Shift+Ctrl+4
Select Guide Vertices	Ctrl+3	Rotate Transformation	Ctrl+R or Shift+Ctrl+5
Select Hair by Roots	Ctrl+4	Scale Transformation	Ctrl+E or Shift+Ctrl+6
Invert Selection	Shift+Ctrl+N	Attenuate Hair	Shift+Ctrl+A
Rotate Selection	Shift+Ctrl+R	Pop Selected	Shift+Ctrl+P
Expand Selection	Shift+Ctrl+E	Pop Zero-sized	Shift+Ctrl+Z
Hide Selected Guides	Shift+Ctrl+H	Recomb Hair	Shift+Ctrl+M
Show Hidden Guides	Shift+Ctrl+W	Replace Rest	Shift+Ctrl+T
Hair Brush	Ctrl+B	Toggle Collisions	Shift+Ctrl+C
Hair Cut	Ctrl+C	Toggle Hairs	Shift+Ctrl+I
Select Hair	Ctrl+S	Lock Guides	Shift+Ctrl+L
Distance Fade	Shift+Ctrl+F	Unlock Guides	Shift+Ctrl+U
Ignore Back Hairs	Shift+Ctrl+B	Undo Styling	Ctrl+Z

Command	Shortcut	Command	Shortcut
Translate Transformation	Ctrl+T or Shift+Ctrl+1	Split Selected Hair Groups	Shift+Ctrl+-
Stand Transformation	Ctrl+N or Shift+Ctrl+2	Merge Selected Hair Groups	Shift+Ctrl+=

Dialog Box Shortcuts

Tables C.18 through C.25 show shortcut keys that work with the various dialog boxes. The dialog box must be selected for these shortcuts to work. It is possible for modeless dialog boxes to have the dialog box visible but not selected.

TABLE C.18

Material Editor

Command	Shortcut	Command	Shortcut
Background	B	Move to Sibling	Left Arrow and Right Arrow
Backlight	L	Go to Parent	Up Arrow
Cycle No. of Sample Slots	X	Make Preview	P
Get Material	G	Material Editor Options	O

TABLE C.19

Track View

Command	Shortcut	Command	Shortcut
Filters	Q	Lock Tangents	L
Assign Controller	C	Nudge Keys Left	Left Arrow
Copy Controller	Ctrl+C	Nudge Keys Right	Right Arrow
Paste Controller	Ctrl+V	Move Highlight Down	Down Arrow
Make Unique	U	Move Highlight Up	Up Arrow
Add Keys	A	Backup Time One Unit	, (comma)
Move Keys	M	Forward Time One Unit	. (period)
Snap Frames	S	Scroll Down	Ctrl+Down Arrow
Apply Ease Curve	Ctrl+E	Scroll Up	Ctrl+Up Arrow
Apply Multiplier Curve	Ctrl+M	Undo Scene Operation	Ctrl+Z
Add Parameters	Ctrl+1	Redo Scene Operation	Ctrl+A
Collect Parameters	Alt+4	Zoom	Z
Expand Track	T, Enter	Zoom Horizontal Extents All	Alt+X
Lock Selection	Spacebar	Pan	P

TABLE C.20

Schematic View

Command	Shortcut	Command	Shortcut
Connect Tool	C	Free All	Alt+F
Select Tool	S	Shrink Toggle	Ctrl+S
Select All Nodes	Ctrl+A	Move Children	Alt+C
Select None	Ctrl+D	Preferences	P
Select Inverted	Ctrl+I	Add Bookmark	B
Select Children	Ctrl+C	Next Bookmark	Left Arrow
Zoom Selected Extents	Z	Previous Bookmark	Right Arrow
Show Grid Toggle	G	Rename Object	R
Display Floater	D	Collect Parameters	Alt+3
Free Selected	Alt+S		

TABLE C.21

Video Post

Command	Shortcut	Command	Shortcut
New Sequence	Ctrl+N	Add Image Layer Event	Ctrl+L
Add New Event	Ctrl+A	Add Image Output Event	Ctrl+O
Add Scene Event	Ctrl+S	Edit Current Event	Ctrl+E
Add Image Input Event	Ctrl+I	Execute Sequence	Ctrl+R
Add Image Filter Event	Ctrl+F	Undo Scene Operation	Ctrl+Z

TABLE C.22

Unwrap UVW

Command	Shortcut	Command	Shortcut
Load UVW	Alt+Shift+Ctrl+L	Mirror Vertical	Alt+Shift+Ctrl+M
Edit UVWs	Ctrl+E	Move Horizontal	Alt+Shift+Ctrl+J
Unwrap Options	Ctrl+O	Move Vertical	Alt+Shift+Ctrl+K
Update Map	Ctrl+U	Texture Vertex Contract Selection	-
Break Selected Vertices	Ctrl+B	Texture Vertex Expand Selection	+
Lock Selected Vertices	Spacebar	Texture Vertex Move Mode	Q
Filter Selected Faces	Alt+F	Texture Vertex Rotate Mode	Ctrl+R

Command	Shortcut	Command	Shortcut
Get Face Selection From Stack	Alt+Shift+Ctrl+F	Texture Vertex Weld Selected	Ctrl+W
Get Selection From Viewport	Alt+Shift+Ctrl+P	Texture Vertex Target Weld	Ctrl+T
Detach Edge Vertices	D, Ctrl+D	Pan	Ctrl+P
Planar Map Faces/Patches	Enter	Zoom	Z
Show Seams in Viewports	Alt+E	Zoom Extents	X
Hide Selected	Ctrl+H	Zoom Extents Selected	Alt+Ctrl+Z
Freeze Selected	Ctrl+F	Zoom Region	Ctrl+X
Snap	Ctrl+S	Zoom Selected Elements	Alt+Shift+Ctrl+Z
Mirror Horizontal	Alt+Shift+Ctrl+N	Zoom to Gizmo	Shift+Spacebar

TABLE C.23

ActiveShade

Command	Shortcut	Command	Shortcut
Close	Q	Select Object	S
Draw Region	D	Toolbar Toggle	Spacebar
Render	R		

TABLE C.24

Particle Flow

Command	Shortcut	Command	Shortcut
Particle View window	6	Select All	Ctrl+A
Particle Emission Toggle	;	Copy Selected	Ctrl+C
Selected Particle Emission Toggle	Shift+;	Paste Selected	Ctrl+V

TABLE C.25

MAXScript Editor

Command	Shortcut	Command	Shortcut
File ⇨ New	Ctrl+N	Edit ⇨ Box Comment	Ctrl+Shift+C
File ⇨ Open	Ctrl+O	Edit ⇨ Stream Comment	Ctrl+Shift+Q
File ⇨ Open Selected File	Ctrl+Shift+O	Edit ⇨ Make Selection Uppercase	Ctrl+Shift+U
File ⇨ Close	Ctrl+W	Edit ⇨ Make Selection Lowercase	Ctrl+U

continued

TABLE C.25 *(continued)*

Command	Shortcut	Command	Shortcut
File ⇨ Save	Ctrl+S	Search ⇨ Find	Ctrl+F
File ⇨ Save As	Ctrl+Shift+S	Search ⇨ Find Next	F3
File ⇨ Save a Copy	Ctrl+Shift+P	Search ⇨ Find Previous	Shift+F3
File ⇨ Revert	Ctrl+R	Search ⇨ Replace	Ctrl+H
File ⇨ Source Control ⇨ Add File	Ctrl+F5	Search ⇨ Find in Files	Ctrl+Shift+F
File ⇨ Source Control ⇨ Remove File	Ctrl+Shift+F5	Search ⇨ Go to	Ctrl+G
File ⇨ Source Control ⇨ Check In	Shift+F5	Search ⇨ Next Bookmark	F2
File ⇨ Source Control ⇨ Check Out	F5	Search ⇨ Previous Bookmark	Shift+F2
File ⇨ Print	Ctrl+P	Search ⇨ Toggle Bookmark	Ctrl+F2
Edit ⇨ Undo	Ctrl+Z	View ⇨ Full Screen	F11
Edit ⇨ Redo	Ctrl+Y	View ⇨ Whitespace	Ctrl+Shift+8
Edit ⇨ Cut	Ctrl+X	View ⇨ End of Line	Ctrl+Shift+9
Edit ⇨ Copy	Ctrl+C	Tools ⇨ Evaluate All	Ctrl+E
Edit ⇨ Paste	Ctrl+V	Tools ⇨ Evaluate Line/Selection	Shift+Enter
Edit ⇨ Select All	Ctrl+A	Tools ⇨ Next Message	F4
Edit ⇨ Duplicate	Ctrl+Shift+D	Tools ⇨ Previous Message	Shift+F4
Edit ⇨ Delete	Delete	Tools ⇨ Clear Output	Shift+F5
Tool ⇨ Delete All	Ctrl+Alt+D	Tools ⇨ Switch Pane	Ctrl+F6
Edit ⇨ Match Brace	Ctrl+B	Options ⇨ Change Indentation Settings	Ctrl+Shift+I
Edit ⇨ Select to Brace	Ctrl+Shift+B	Options ⇨ Use Monospaced Font	Ctrl+F11
Edit ⇨ Complete Word	Ctrl+Enter	Language ⇨ Text	Shift+F11
Edit ⇨ Expand Abbreviation	Ctrl+Shift+A	Windows ⇨ Previous	Shift+F6
Edit ⇨ Insert Abbreviation	Ctrl+Shift+R	Windows ⇨ Next	F6
Edit ⇨ Block Comment or Uncomment	Ctrl+Q	Help ⇨ Help	F1

Character Studio Shortcuts

Tables C.26 through C.27 show shortcut keys that work with the Character Studio modules.

TABLE C.26

Biped

Command	Shortcut	Command	Shortcut
Change Leg State	Alt+Ctrl+S	Play Biped	V
Reset All Limbs	Alt+K	Lock Selected Keys	Alt+Ctrl+L

Command	Shortcut	Command	Shortcut
Set Range	Alt+R	Set Key	0 (zero)
Copy Posture	Alt+C	Scale In Transform	Alt+Ctrl+E
Paste Posture	Alt+V	Toggle Biped Keys in Trackbar	Alt+T
Paste Posture Opposite	Alt+B	Select End of Footsteps in Track View	Alt+D
Collapse Move All	Alt+M	Select Entire Footstep in Track View	Alt+S
Fix Graphs	Alt+Ctrl+F	Select Start of Footsteps in Track View	Alt+A

TABLE C.27

Physique

Command	Shortcut	Command	Shortcut
Solve	S	Next Selection Level	I
Copy Envelope	Ctrl+C	Previous Selection Level	Shift+I
Paste Envelope	Ctrl+V	Next	Page Down
Reset Envelope	Ctrl+E	Previous	Page Up
Delete	Ctrl+D		

Miscellaneous Shortcuts

In addition to specific shortcuts for the main interface and the dialog boxes, Max provides several general shortcuts that can be used in many different places, as listed in Table C.28.

TABLE C.28

General Shortcuts

Command	Shortcut	Command	Shortcut
Numeric Expression Evaluator	Ctrl+N when a spinner field is selected	Highlight any text field	Double-click current value
Cut value	Ctrl+X	Nudge selection	Arrow keys
Copy value	Ctrl+C	Make viewport active	Right-click in an inactive viewport
Paste value	Ctrl+V	Display quadmenus	Right-click in an active viewport
Apply settings	Enter	Display First Tab	Alt+1
Highlight next text field	Tab	Help	F1
Highlight previous text field	Shift+Tab		

Appendix D

What's on the DVD

Throughout this book, you'll find many tutorials that help you to understand the principles being discussed. All the example files used to create these tutorials are included on the DVD that comes with this book. In addition to these files, you'll find sample 3D models and an electronic version of the book.

This appendix provides you with information on the contents of the DVD. For the latest and greatest information, please refer to the ReadMe file located at the root of the DVD.

IN THIS APPENDIX

System requirements

Using the DVD with Windows

What's on the DVD

Troubleshooting

System Requirements

Make sure that your computer meets the minimum system requirements listed in this section. If your computer doesn't match up to most of these requirements, you may have a problem using the contents of the DVD.

For Windows Vista, Windows XP Professional SP2 (recommended), Windows XP Home Edition SP2, or Windows 2000 SP4:

- Intel® Pentium® III or AMD® processor, 500 MHz or higher (dual Intel)
- Xeon® or dual AMD Athlon® or Opteron® 32-bit system recommended)
- 512MB RAM (1GB recommended)
- 500MB swap space (2GB recommended)
- Graphics card supporting 1024 × 768 × 16-bit color with 64MB RAM (OpenGL® and Direct3D® hardware acceleration supported; 3D graphics accelerator 1280 × 1024 × 32-bit color with 256MB RAM recommended)

- Microsoft® Windows®–compliant pointing device (optimized for Microsoft IntelliMouse®)
- Microsoft Internet Explorer 6
- A DVD drive

Using the DVD with Windows

To install the items from the DVD to your hard drive, follow these steps:

1. Insert the DVD into your computer's DVD drive. The license agreement appears.

NOTE The interface won't launch if you have autorun disabled. In that case, click Start ↪ Run. In the dialog box that appears, type D:\start.exe. (Replace D with the proper letter if your DVD drive uses a different letter. If you don't know the letter, see how your DVD drive is listed under My Computer.) Click OK.

2. Read through the license agreement, and then click the Accept button if you want to use the DVD. After you click Accept, the License Agreement window won't appear again.

   The DVD interface appears. The interface allows you to install the programs and run the demos with just a click of a button (or two).

What's on the DVD

The following sections provide a summary of the software and other materials you'll find on the DVD.

Author-created materials

The example files used in the tutorials throughout the book are included in the "Chapter Example Files" directory. Within this directory are separate subdirectories for each chapter. Supplemental files such as models and images are also included in these directories. Animated scenes include a rendered AVI file of the animation. For each tutorial, the resulting example after all steps are completed has the word "final" in the filename. Using these final examples, you can compare the results to your own work.

Applications

The following applications are on the DVD:

- Adobe Reader
- Autodesk 3ds Max Trial

  Create stunning 3D in less time with Autodesk® 3ds Max® 2008 software. This release dramatically improves your productivity by streamlining workflows involving complex scenes. It also delivers Review — for interactive previewing of shadows and sophisticated mental ray® material settings.

  A new MAXscript ProEditor and improved support for DWG[(tm)]-based pipelines round out this productivity-enhancing offering.[1]

- Poser 7 demo

---

[1]Autodesk, DWG, and 3ds Max are registered trademarks or trademarks of Autodesk, Inc., in the USA and/or other countries. mental ray is a registered trademark of mental images GmbH licensed for use by Autodesk, Inc. All other brand names, product names, or trademarks belong to their respective holders.

Shareware programs are fully functional, free, trial versions of copyrighted programs. If you like particular programs, register with their authors for a nominal fee and receive licenses, enhanced versions, and technical support.

Freeware programs are free, copyrighted games, applications, and utilities. You can copy them to as many PCs as you like — for free — but they offer no technical support.

GNU software is governed by its own license, which is included inside the folder of the GNU software. There are no restrictions on distribution of GNU software. See the GNU license at the root of the DVD for more details.

Trial, demo, or *evaluation* versions of software are usually limited either in terms of the time you can use them or the functionality they offer (such as not letting you save a project after you create it).

3D models

Viewpoint Datalabs and Zygote Media have provided sample 3D models. Many of these models were used in the tutorials, and you can find the complete set of models in the "3D Models" directory.

eBook version of *3ds Max 2008 Bible*

All the text for the book is included on the DVD in PDF format along with Adobe Reader. Using the electronic version of the book, you can search the text. You'll also be able to see the book's figures in color.

Troubleshooting

If you have difficulty installing or using any of the materials on the companion DVD, try the following solutions:

- **Turn off any anti-virus software that you may have running.** Installers sometimes mimic virus activity and can make your computer incorrectly believe that it is being infected by a virus. (Be sure to turn the anti-virus software back on later.)
- **Close all running programs.** The more programs you're running, the less memory is available to other programs. Installers also typically update files and programs; if you keep other programs running, installation may not work properly.
- **See the ReadMe file.** Please refer to the ReadMe file located at the root of the DVD for the latest product information at the time of publication.

Customer Care

If you still have trouble with the DVD, please call the Wiley Product Technical Support telephone number: (800) 762-2974. Outside the United States, call 1 (317) 572-3994. You can also contact Wiley Product Technical Support at `http://support.wiley.com`. John Wiley & Sons will provide technical support only for installation and other general quality control items. For technical support on the applications themselves, consult the program's vendor or author.

To place additional orders or to request information about other Wiley products, please call (800) 225-5945.

Index

Symbols and Numerics

Wiley Publishing, Inc.
End-User License Agreement

READ THIS. You should carefully read these terms and conditions before opening the software packet(s) included with this book "Book". This is a license agreement "Agreement" between you and Wiley Publishing, Inc. "WPI". By opening the accompanying software packet(s), you acknowledge that you have read and accept the following terms and conditions. If you do not agree and do not want to be bound by such terms and conditions, promptly return the Book and the unopened software packet(s) to the place you obtained them for a full refund.

1. **License Grant.** WPI grants to you (either an individual or entity) a nonexclusive license to use one copy of the enclosed software program(s) (collectively, the "Software" solely for your own personal or business purposes on a single computer (whether a standard computer or a workstation component of a multi-user network). The Software is in use on a computer when it is loaded into temporary memory (RAM) or installed into permanent memory (hard disk, CD-ROM, or other storage device). WPI reserves all rights not expressly granted herein.

2. **Ownership.** WPI is the owner of all right, title, and interest, including copyright, in and to the compilation of the Software recorded on the disk(s) or CD-ROM "Software Media". Copyright to the individual programs recorded on the Software Media is owned by the author or other authorized copyright owner of each program. Ownership of the Software and all proprietary rights relating thereto remain with WPI and its licensers.

3. **Restrictions On Use and Transfer.**

   (a) You may only (i) make one copy of the Software for backup or archival purposes, or (ii) transfer the Software to a single hard disk, provided that you keep the original for backup or archival purposes. You may not (i) rent or lease the Software, (ii) copy or reproduce the Software through a LAN or other network system or through any computer subscriber system or bulletin-board system, or (iii) modify, adapt, or create derivative works based on the Software.

   (b) You may not reverse engineer, decompile, or disassemble the Software. You may transfer the Software and user documentation on a permanent basis, provided that the transferee agrees to accept the terms and conditions of this Agreement and you retain no copies. If the Software is an update or has been updated, any transfer must include the most recent update and all prior versions.

4. **Restrictions on Use of Individual Programs.** You must follow the individual requirements and restrictions detailed for each individual program in the "What's on the DVD" appendix of this Book. These limitations are also contained in the individual license agreements recorded on the Software Media. These limitations may include a requirement that after using the program for a specified period of time, the user must pay a registration fee or discontinue use. By opening the Software packet(s), you will be agreeing to abide by the licenses and restrictions for these individual programs that are detailed in the "What's on the DVD" appendix and on the Software Media. None of the material on this Software Media or listed in this Book may ever be redistributed, in original or modified form, for commercial purposes.

5. **Limited Warranty.**

(a) WPI warrants that the Software and Software Media are free from defects in materials and workmanship under normal use for a period of sixty (60) days from the date of purchase of this Book. If WPI receives notification within the warranty period of defects in materials or workmanship, WPI will replace the defective Software Media.

(b) WPI AND THE AUTHOR OF THE BOOK DISCLAIM ALL OTHER WARRANTIES, EXPRESS OR IMPLIED, INCLUDING WITHOUT LIMITATION IMPLIED WARRANTIES OF MERCHANTABILITY AND FITNESS FOR A PARTICULAR PURPOSE, WITH RESPECT TO THE SOFTWARE, THE PROGRAMS, THE SOURCE CODE CONTAINED THEREIN, AND/OR THE TECHNIQUES DESCRIBED IN THIS BOOK. WPI DOES NOT WARRANT THAT THE FUNCTIONS CONTAINED IN THE SOFTWARE WILL MEET YOUR REQUIREMENTS OR THAT THE OPERATION OF THE SOFTWARE WILL BE ERROR FREE.

(c) This limited warranty gives you specific legal rights, and you may have other rights that vary from jurisdiction to jurisdiction.

6. **Remedies.**

(a) WPI's entire liability and your exclusive remedy for defects in materials and workmanship shall be limited to replacement of the Software Media, which may be returned to WPI with a copy of your receipt at the following address: Software Media Fulfillment Department, Attn.: *3ds Max 2008 Bible*, Wiley Publishing, Inc., 10475 Crosspoint Blvd., Indianapolis, IN 46256, or call 1-800-762-2974. Please allow four to six weeks for delivery. This Limited Warranty is void if failure of the Software Media has resulted from accident, abuse, or misapplication. Any replacement Software Media will be warranted for the remainder of the original warranty period or thirty (30) days, whichever is longer.

(b) In no event shall WPI or the author be liable for any damages whatsoever (including without limitation damages for loss of business profits, business interruption, loss of business information, or any other pecuniary loss) arising from the use of or inability to use the Book or the Software, even if WPI has been advised of the possibility of such damages.

(c) Because some jurisdictions do not allow the exclusion or limitation of liability for consequential or incidental damages, the above limitation or exclusion may not apply to you.

7. **U.S. Government Restricted Rights.** Use, duplication, or disclosure of the Software for or on behalf of the United States of America, its agencies and/or instrumentalities "U.S. Government" is subject to restrictions as stated in paragraph (c)(1)(ii) of the Rights in Technical Data and Computer Software clause of DFARS 252.227-7013, or subparagraphs (c) (1) and (2) of the Commercial Computer Software - Restricted Rights clause at FAR 52.227-19, and in similar clauses in the NASA FAR supplement, as applicable.

8. **General.** This Agreement constitutes the entire understanding of the parties and revokes and supersedes all prior agreements, oral or written, between them and may not be modified or amended except in a writing signed by both parties hereto that specifically refers to this Agreement. This Agreement shall take precedence over any other documents that may be in conflict herewith. If any one or more provisions contained in this Agreement are held by any court or tribunal to be invalid, illegal, or otherwise unenforceable, each and every other provision shall remain in full force and effect.